October 6–10, 2014
Foster City, Silicon Valley,
California, USA

Association for
Computing Machinery

Advancing Computing as a Science & Profession

RecSys'14

Proceedings of the 8th ACM Conference on Recommender Systems

Sponsored by:

ACM SIGCHI

In cooperation with:

ACM SIGIR, ACM SIGKDD, ACM SIGWEB, & ACM SIGecom

Association for
Computing Machinery

Advancing Computing as a Science & Profession

The Association for Computing Machinery
2 Penn Plaza, Suite 701
New York, New York 10121-0701

ISBN: 978-1-4503-2668-1 (Digital)

ISBN: 978-1-4503-3372-6 (Print)

Additional copies may be ordered prepaid from:

ACM Order Department
PO Box 30777
New York, NY 10087-0777, USA

Phone: 1-800-342-6626 (USA and Canada)
+1-212-626-0500 (Global)
Fax: +1-212-944-1318
E-mail: acmhelp@acm.org
Hours of Operation: 8:30 am – 4:30 pm ET

Printed in the USA

Chairs' Welcome

It is our great pleasure to welcome you to the *8th ACM Conference on Recommender Systems* (RecSys 2014) held between October 6th and 10th in Foster City, Silicon Valley, U.S.A. The annual RecSys conference is the premier international forum that brings together researchers and practitioners from academia and industry to share their challenges, research results, and experiences in the broad field of recommender systems. RecSys 2014 features keynote talks, research paper presentations, industry sessions, poster sessions, workshops, tutorials, demonstrations, a doctoral symposium, and the RecSys Challenge.

The success of a conference largely depends on the quality of the submitted works. We would like to take this opportunity to thank all the authors for submitting their original research to Recsys 2014. The RecSys conference has seen remarkable growth since its inception as "Recommenders 06 Summer School on the Present and Future of Recommender Systems". It has evolved into a full-fledged, top research conference since 2007, underscoring the increasing role and significant challenges related to recommender systems. This year we received a record number of 234 submissions and accepted 35 long papers for oral presentation (acceptance rate 23%) and 20 short papers for poster presentation (acceptance rate 24%).

The RecSys conference is driven by real-world challenges. The key topics covered in this year's research program include ranking and top-n recommendations (7.5% of papers), matrix factorization (5.6%), cold start (5.6%), implicit feedback (4.3%), context awareness (3.6%), metrics and evaluation (3.5%), novel applications (2.9%), and more.

The quality of a conference program also depends on the competence and hard work of its devoted volunteers. To select the 55 accepted papers out of the initial 234 submissions, this year, we implemented a two-tier review process, where each paper received detailed reviews from three program committee members, followed by a meta-review by a senior program committee member. Our entire committee involved 20 senior and 102 regular Program Committee members. We are extremely grateful to all the PC members for volunteering their time to generate more than 900 detailed and insightful reviews and discussions.

In addition to the technical paper program, the program provides a diverse array of exciting venues for our attendees to interact with top experts from academia and industry on topics related to recommender systems. We are very fortunate to have three world-class keynote speakers this year spanning industry and academia, providing inspirational talks on cutting-edge challenges and directions in the field. We also feature an industry program capitalizing on being located in Silicon Valley's backyard. The invited industry speakers include renowned executives from top Silicon Valley companies, and representatives of new age companies using Recommender Systems in unique and disruptive ways. In addition, this year's program will host an industry panel discussing the topic of using smart systems monitoring and guiding our socio-digital experience. Our poster and demonstration event showcases numerous posters and nine live system demonstrations. Before and after the main conference, four tutorials and nine workshops will be held, including the RecSys Challenge. In addition, nine students were selected and invited to participate in the doctoral symposium of the conference.

Last, but not least, we thank all sponsors, who form a very important part of the conference, and our colleagues who volunteered their time during the past year to make this conference a success.

This conference would not happen without the hard work and devotion from the members of our organizing committee. We would like to extend our special thanks to all of them.

Please join us at RecSys 2014 to see, experience, and share exciting new research results, state-of-the-art practices, and high impact applications in recommender systems. We hope that you will find our program exciting and thought-provoking, and that this conference will provide you with the valuable opportunity to meet and interact with leading researchers and practitioners from institutions around the world.

Alfred Kobsa and Michelle Zhou
RecSys'14 General Chairs

Martin Ester and Yehuda Koren
RecSys'14 Program Chairs

Table of Contents

Session 5: Diversity, Novelty and Serendipity

Session 6: Recommendation Methods and Theory

Session 7: Ranking and Top-N Recommendation

Session 8: Matrix Factorization

Short Papers

Demonstrations

Workshops

Tutorials

Doctoral Consortium

RecSys 2014 Conference Organization

General Co-Chairs: Alfred Kobsa *(University of California, Irvine)*
Michelle Zhou *(IBM)*

Program Co-Chairs: Martin Ester *(Simon Fraser University)*
Yehuda Koren *(Google)*

Workshop Co-Chairs: Lior Rokach *(Ben Gurion University)*
Badrul Sarwar *(eBay)*

Tutorial Co-Chairs: Alexander Felfernig *(Technical University of Graz)*
Bee-Chung Chen *(LinkedIn)*

Doctoral Symposium Co-Chairs: Yi Zhang *(University of California, Santa Cruz)*
Shlomo Berkovsky *(NICTA)*

Poster and Demo Co-Chairs: Li Chen *(Hong Kong Baptist University)*
Jalal Mahmud *(IBM Research)*

Proceedings Chair: Bart Knijnenburg *(University of California, Irvine)*

Publicity Co-Chairs: Alan Said *(CWI)*
Tim Hussein *(University of Duisburg-Essen)*

Industry Co-Chairs: Anmol Bhasin *(LindedIn)*
Joaquin Quiñonero Candela *(Facebook)*

Treasurer: Susan Crow *(IBM)*

Local Arrangements & Student Volunteer Co-Chairs: Jian Wang *(LinkedIn)*
Susan Crow *(IBM)*

Senior Program Committee: Shlomo Berkovsky *(CSIRO)*
Robin D. Burke *(DePaul University)*
Pablo Castells *(Universidad Autónoma de Madrid)*
Boi Faltings *(EPFL)*
Li Chen *(Hong Kong Baptist University)*
Alexander Felfernig *(Graz University of Technology)*
Jill Freyne *(CSIRO)*
Dietmar Jannach *(TU Dortmund)*
George Karypis *(University of Minnesota)*
Joseph A. Konstan *(University of Minnesota)*
Ronny Lempel *(Yahoo Labs)*

Senior Program Committee (continued):

Pasquale Lops *(University of Bari Aldo Moro)*
Wolfgang Nejdl *(L3S and University of Hannover)*
Pearl Pu *(EPFL)*
Francesco Ricci *(Free University of Bozen-Bolzano)*
Lior Rokach *(Ben Gurion University)*
Lars Schmidt-Thieme *(University of Hildesheim)*
Harald Steck *(Netflix)*
Domonkos Tikk *(Gravity)*
Alexander Tuzhilin *(NYU)*

Program Committee:

Jussara Almeida *(Universidade Federal de Minas Gerais)*
Sarabjot Anand *(University of Warwick)*
Linas Baltrunas *(Telefonica Research)*
Alejandro Bellogin *(Universidad Autónoma de Madrid)*
Derek Bridge *(University College Cork)*
Ivan Cantador *(Universidad Autónoma de Madrid)*
Licia Capra *(University College of London)*
Enhong Chen *(University of Science and Technology of China)*
Jilin Chen *(IBM)*
Paolo Cremonesi *(Politecnico di Milano)*
Elizabeth Daly *(IBM)*
Marco de Gemmis *(University of Bari)*
Ernesto William De Luca *(University of Applied Sciences Potsdam)*
Toon De Pessemier *(iMinds-WiCa-Ghent University)*
Tommaso Di Noia *(Technical University of Bari)*
Ernesto Diaz-Aviles *(IBM Research – Dublin)*
Simon Dooms *(Ghent University)*
Hendrik Drachsler *(Open Universiteit Nederland)*
Casey Dugan *(IBM T.J. Watson Research)*
Michael Ekstrand *(University of Minnesota)*
Zeno Gantner *(HERE Maps Search)*
Florent Garcin *(EPFL)*
Franca Garzotto *(Politecnico di Milano)*
Yong Ge *(University of North Carolina at Charlotte)*
Fatih Gedikli *(Dortmund University of Applied Sciences and Arts)*
Werner Geyer *(IBM T.J. Watson Research Lab in Cambridge)*
Aristides Gionis *(Aalto University)*
Marcos Goncalves *(Universidade Federal de Minas Gerais)*
Derek Greene *(University College Dublin)*
Ido Guy *(IBM Haifa Research Lab)*
Frank Hopfgartner *(Technische Universität Berlin)*
Rong Hu *(EPFL)*
Neil Hurley *(University College Dublin)*
Alejandro Jaimes *(Yahoo! Research)*
Mohsen Jamali *(Walmart Labs)*

Program Committee (continued):

Guy Shani *(Ben Gurion University)*
Bracha Shapira *(Ben-Gurion University of the Negev)*
Yue Shi *(Delft University of Technology)*
Fabrizio Silvestri *(Yahoo Labs)*
Neel Sundaresan *(eBay Research Labs)*
Panagiotis Symeonidis *(Aristotle University of Thessaloniki)*
Nava Tintarev *(University of Aberdeen)*
Mitul Tiwari *(LinkedIn)*
Nicolas Usunier *(Heudiasyc)*
Paolo Viappiani *(Université Pierre et Marie Curie)*
Jian Wang *(LinkedIn)*
Martijn Willemsen *(Eindhoven University of Technology)*
David Wilson *(University of North Carolina at Charlotte)*
Evan Xiang *(Baidu)*
Qiang Yang *(Hong Kong University of Science and Technology)*
Quan Yuan *(Taobao)*
Markus Zanker *(University Klagenfurt)*
Jie Zhang *(Nanyang Technological University)*
Tingshao Zhu *(Graduate University of Chinese Academy of Sciences)*
Nivio Ziviani *(Federal University of Minas Gerais)*

External Reviewers:

Liang Tang *(Florida International University)*
Yexi Jiang *(Florida International University)*
Guibing Guo *(Nanyang Technological University)*
Yang Bao *(Nanyang Technological University)*
Anirban Basu *(KDDI R&D Laboratories)*
Chao Shen *(Florida International University)*
Houssem Jerbi *(University College Dublin)*
Youngki Park *(Seoul National University)*
Yeonchan Ahn *(Seoul National University)*
Sungchan Park *(Seoul National University)*
Franco Maria Nardini *(ISTI - CNR)*
Michele Trevisiol *(UPF, Barcelona)*
James Schaffer *(University of California, Santa Barbara)*
Byungkyu Kang *(University of California, Santa Barbara)*
Tristan Ratchford *(IBM Research Cambridge)*
Annalina Caputo *(University of Bari Aldo Moro)*
Benjamin Kille *(TU Berlin)*
Fred Morstatter *(Arizona State University)*
Isaac Jones *(Arizona State University)*
Tahora H. Nazer *(Arizona State University)*
Suhang Wang *(Arizona State University)*
Ashwin Rajadesingan *(Arizona State University)*
Reza Zafarani *(Arizona State University)*
Hu (Ben) Xia *(Arizona State University)*
Umberto Panniello *(Technical University of Bari)*

RecSys 2014 Sponsor & Supporters

Sponsor:	SIGCHI	
In cooperation with:	SIGIR Special Interest Group on Information Retrieval	acm SIGecom
	sig web	acm KDD.org
Diamond Supporters:	NETFLIX	LinkedIn
Platinum Supporters:	Google™	YAHOO! LABS
	Baidu 百度	
Gold Supporters:	IBM Research	
	facebook	comcast®
Supporter:	NSF	

LinkedIn Skills: Large-Scale Topic Extraction and Inference

Mathieu Bastian
LinkedIn Corporation
2029 Stierlin Ct.
Mountain View, CA 94043
mbastian@linkedin.com

Matthew Hayes
LinkedIn Corporation
2029 Stierlin Ct.
Mountain View, CA 94043
mhayes@linkedin.com

William Vaughan
LinkedIn Corporation
2029 Stierlin Ct.
Mountain View, CA 94043
wvaughan@linkedin.com

Sam Shah
LinkedIn Corporation
2029 Stierlin Ct.
Mountain View, CA 94043
samshah@linkedin.com

Peter Skomoroch
LinkedIn Corporation
2029 Stierlin Ct.
Mountain View, CA 94043
pskomoro@linkedin.com

Hyungjin Kim
LinkedIn Corporation
2029 Stierlin Ct.
Mountain View, CA 94043
ekim@linkedin.com

ABSTRACT

"Skills and Expertise" is a data-driven feature on LinkedIn, the world's largest professional online social network, which allows members to tag themselves with topics representing their areas of expertise. In this work, we present our experiences developing this large-scale topic extraction pipeline, which includes constructing a folksonomy of skills and expertise and implementing an inference and recommender system for skills. We also discuss a consequent set of applications, such as Endorsements, which allows members to tag themselves with topics representing their areas of expertise and for their connections to provide social proof, via an "endorse" action, of that member's competence in that topic.

Categories and Subject Descriptors

H.4 [**Information Systems Applications**]: Miscellaneous

Keywords

inferring attributes; social networks; recommender system; folksonomy

1. INTRODUCTION

LinkedIn, the world's largest professional online social network, consists of a collection of profiles that represent a member's professional identity. A profile contains a member's current and past work history, education, and projects, among other pieces of his identity. For many members an important part of that identity is the set of skills and talents for which they are known. The "Skills and Expertise" section is a part of the profile that allows the member to display this information, as shown in Figure 1. We refer to

RecSys'14, October 6–10, 2014, Foster City, Silicon Valley, CA, USA.

ACM 978-1-4503-2668-1/14/10 ...$15.00.
http://dx.doi.org/10.1145/2645710.2645729.

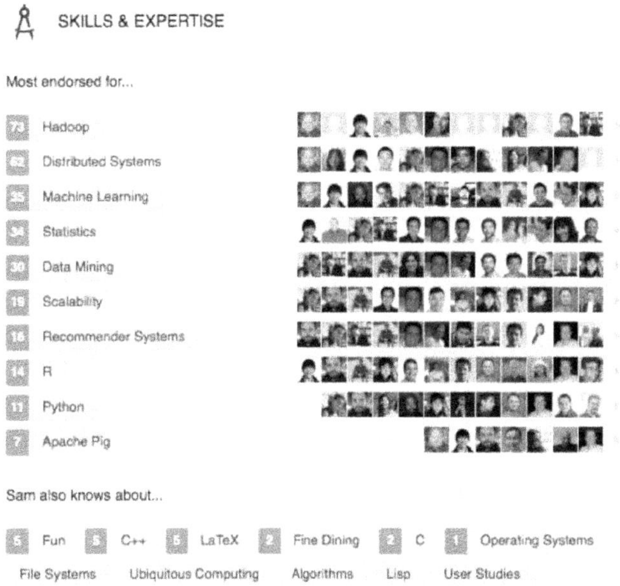

Figure 1: Example skills and expertise section with endorsements

this section as "Skills and Expertise" rather than just "Skills" because it can also include domains of expertise, which are not strictly skills. For instance, "Natural Gas" is a domain of expertise an energy professional might want to be known for. The member may add skills to his/her profile either by manually entering them, in which case a type-ahead prompt is provided, or by accepting recommendations of inferred skills.

There is an important value in helping members enter their skills and expertise in the system in a standardized fashion and the goal of the skills feature on LinkedIn is to facilitate that. Standardized entities help members be better found by increasing the coverage in search engines. It also helps job matching algorithms, as the definition of a member's competencies is crisper and less noisy.

Prior to the introduction of the skills and expertise section on profiles, we chose to create a folksonomy of skills that represented the full breadth and diversity of members' skills on LinkedIn so an exhaustive type-ahead could be provided. We evaluated several publicly available skill listings, but none were sufficiently comprehensive or detailed. LinkedIn contains hundreds of millions of member profiles representing professional interests as diverse as ballet, machine learning, air traffic control, and scuba diving. Manually creating this taxonomy was an infeasible task due to the size and diversity of these profiles.

We decided that the best way to create this taxonomy was to derive it from the data of member's profiles directly, thus opting for a folksonomy. Creating a data-driven solution was feasible, but still challenging. The hundreds of millions of profiles contained millions of keywords that might or might not be skills. Additionally, many of these potential skills are duplicates. For example, "Java programming" and "Java development" are both equivalent to the skill "Java". Also, many of these phrases have different meanings depending on context. The phrase "Organ" on a musician's profile probably means a musical instrument while the same phrase on a physician's profile likely refers to a part of the body.

To create this folksonomy from the data we broke the problem down into three phases: discovery, identification of the potential candidate skill phrases; disambiguation, where we attached the appropriate context to each meaning of each phrase; and deduplication, where we merged phrases that were semantically identical into a single skill. Our implementation of this approach uses a mixture of established and novel approaches in machine learning techniques and crowdsourcing.

Once the folksonomy was in place and the initial skills and expertise section had launched, we recognized a need to provide recommendations to allow members to more easily enter their skills and expertise. The intuition was that it would be more effective to ask members to confirm that they have a set of skills rather than asking which skill they have and provide a blank form. We implemented an inference system that calculates the likelihood of each member having each skill and presented these inferences as recommendations. The lack of initial skills data created a cold-start problem but we designed a solution leveraging the rich set of other profile attributes. The introduction of this recommender system significantly increased the number of members adding skills.

The main contribution of this work is a description of a large-scale folksonomy generation of skills and expertise and the system to infer and recommend them to members. We describe the challenges around discovery, disambiguation, and deduplication to create the folksonomy and discuss our approach to build a collaborative filtering (CF) skills recommender system based on profile attribute data. We also discuss implementations of a diverse set of applications of this folksonomy and inference algorithm.

2. SKILLS AND EXPERTISE

The purpose of the skills feature on LinkedIn is to provide a definitive section on a member's profile to list that member's skills and expertise. Prior to the creation of this section, information about a member's skills was spread among a number of sections and embedded in free text. To assist the member in standardizing this information in the skills section we first created a folksonomy of skills to provide a type-ahead. After observing a lower than desired interaction with the type-ahead, we then created a recommender system to allow members to more easily add skills and expertise to their profile.

2.1 Folksonomy creation

Our goal was to create a large enough list of skills and expertise that members might choose from to add on their profile. This list should contain skills and expertise that everyone might expect in a professional context such as "Management" or "Public Speaking" but also rare competencies such as "Atmospheric Physics" or "Economics Education". To accomplish this goal, we first considered using an existing taxonomy. We evaluated a number of available lists, but found none that were sufficiently broad in scope. Instead of attempting to find a sufficient number of experts to construct such a list, we decided to discover the list from the data available in the members' profiles and created a folksonomy [9].

Folksonomies are often used within Internet communities to categorize content [12] and are directly edited through users' contributions. In our case, we already had skill information across all sections of a profile but it wasn't structured or organized so a list can be extracted. Identifying domain-specific terms from free text in order to create a folksonomy has been studied in [3] [18] [11]. In our case, we observed that in a particular profile section, the specialties section, a large number of members provided free text matching a simple pattern, a comma-separated list, and that the entries in this list were very frequently skills. The specialty section was a common section on LinkedIn profiles at the time of the initial extraction process, appearing on over 12 million profiles. We decided to use this observation to extract a list of candidate topic *phrases*. In this section, we prefer to use "phrase" instead of "keyword" as the entities we're looking for can have multiple words. The number of words was limited to six for display purposes.

2.1.1 Discovery: Entity extraction

The first step in identifying entities that would become skills was to extract phrases from profile specialty sections containing comma-separated lists of topics. The profile section was a free text field, which could contain complete sentences, lists of topics delimited by commas, bullet points, or other characters. We first aimed to recognize that the section was actually a comma-separated list and used a simple technique based on the punctuation frequency. We define Cf as the comma frequency in the text section and filtered out texts based on CT, a minimum threshold.

$$Cf = \frac{number\ of\ commas}{number\ of\ characters} > CT$$

Heuristically, we found that CT = 0.02 is a good trade-off to obtain a relatively consistent dataset for the case of specialties on LinkedIn profiles. By looking at the results, we found that a lower threshold allows too many sections which enumerate lengthy accomplishments rather than skill keywords. We also found that a higher threshold penalizes sections with multiple compound words such as "Supply Chain Optimization".

All sections with a sufficient Cf frequency were then tokenized to obtain phrases. A stop-word list was finally applied to remove phrases that are common parts of speech. This stop-list was augmented with a domain specific stop list which removed commonly observed entity prefixes and suffixes. The remaining phrases of up to six words were preserved.

This phrase list contained the candidate skills along with other entities. The next step was to remove phrases, which represented other known types of entities, such as companies, degrees, and titles. Fortunately, these entities could be extracted from member profiles as well, but in a structured format. However, simply filtering out every phrase that matched with a known entity would have been too aggressive because some skills overlapped with other known entities. For instance, "Oracle" is both a domain of expertise and a company name and "Computer Science" could be both a degree and a skill. To address this issue we compared the phrase frequency of occurrences in the specialty section with the frequency of occurrences in other sections of the profile to create a ratio. We then introduced a threshold for which entities were placed in the stop list if their frequency in the specialties section wasn't sufficient. The threshold was chosen heuristically by comparing the results at different values.

Finally, we counted the number of profiles in which each phrase occurred and removed all candidates that were below a minimum frequency threshold of twenty. This threshold was chosen to be low enough to allow rare skills to go through but high enough to remove much of the long tail noise. This filtering produced a rich dataset of about 150,000 skill phrases. As expected, the number of occurrences is long-tail distributed with a few thousand common phrases and a majority of rare ones. In fact, only 6% of skill phrases represented approximately 80% of occurrences.

2.1.2 *Disambiguation: Clustering to provide context*

After finding an initial set of skill phrases, we had to disambiguate those phrases that had multiple meanings dependent on their context. For example, the phrase "organ" has a separate meaning in the contexts of music and anatomy and is a valid expertise in both cases. The first step of the disambiguation process was to generate a set of related phrases for each candidate skill phrase. Related phrases are those skill phrases that appear often with another skill phrase on profiles. The intuition is that an ambiguous phrase would have distinctly different sets of related phrases in each context. In other words, a relationship between two phrases was induced by the neighborhood of these phrases. For instance with "organ", the term "piano" appears frequently in the musical meaning and rarely co-occurs in the medical meaning, where phrases such as "surgery" are common. An example of such a rare co-occurrence might be a physician's profile where piano is also listed as a skill. This technique is more formally described in the query expansion chapter of [2]. Finally, clustering was applied to distinguish the distinct senses for each phrase.

More formally, let p_i be a skill phrase, d_k a member profile, $P = \{p_1, p_2, ..., p_t\}$ be the set of all skill phrases and $D = \{d_1, d_2, ..., d_{t'}\}$ be the set of all member profiles. Let $f_{i,k}$ be the occurrence of the phrase p_i in a section of a member profile d_k, such as the previously mentioned specialties section. The occurrence count F_i of phrase p_i in D is defined as

$$F_i = \sum_{k=1}^{t' \in D} f_{i,k}$$

In addition, let $f_{i,j,k}$ be the co-occurrence of the phrases p_i and p_j on the a same section of a profile d_k. The co-occurrence count between two phrases i, j is then defined as

$$F_{i,j} = \sum_{k=1}^{t' \in D} f_{i,j,k}$$

The Jaccard similarity $S_{i,j}$ between two phrases is then calculated as

$$S_{i,j} = \frac{F_{i,j}}{F_i + F_j - F_{i,j}}$$

For each phrase p_i, the top-n most related phrases are kept based on the highest Jaccard similarity with n being set in advance and we define $R_{i,n}$ as the vector of size n of related phrases $r_{i,j}$ for p_i with $j \in P$. Other standard similarity metrics were tried but Jaccard was heuristically chosen as it seemed to yield the best results and remained simple to implement. R_i is then transformed into a matrix M_i by using R_j as a column for each element $r_{i,j}$ of the vector. The $S_{i,j}$ similarity is inserted for each $r_{i,j}$ cell of the resulting M_i matrix.

$$M_i = \begin{bmatrix} S_{1,1} & S_{1,2} & \dots & S_{1,n} \\ S_{2,1} & S_{2,2} & \dots & S_{2,n} \\ \vdots & \vdots & \ddots & \vdots \\ S_{n,1} & S_{n,2} & \dots & S_{n,n} \end{bmatrix}$$

This matrix M_i is next transformed by calculating the cosine-similarity $T_{i,j}$ [15] for each cell using the R_i and R_j vectors. Each cell of the resulting matrix N_i is now the cosine-similarity score between the related phrases of p_i and p_j.

$$N_i = \begin{bmatrix} T_{1,1} & T_{1,2} & \dots & T_{1,n} \\ T_{2,1} & T_{2,2} & \dots & T_{2,n} \\ \vdots & \vdots & \ddots & \vdots \\ T_{n,1} & T_{n,2} & \dots & T_{n,n} \end{bmatrix}$$

Clustering was then applied on the N_i matrix to distinguish multiple senses associated with the $p_i \in P$ phrase. We used the SVD technique to find the top components for each phrase by dimensionality reduction. Heuristically, we found that the first six or seven components yielded the best results. Finally, we ran a KMeans algorithm to identify clusters of phrases. The best K was chosen dynamically based on the inter-cluster distance and a penalty to avoid having too many clusters. We observed that most phrases would only have one dominant cluster but ambiguous terms would often have two or three groups.

To aid in interpretability of the clusters, an industry label was attached to each of them. Each member profile possesses an industry attribute entered by the member at registration. To determine the cluster industry label we simply took the most frequent industry among the member profiles from which the phrase was found. For instance, the phrase "organ" appears in clusters in the industries "music" and "medicine".

2.1.3 *Deduplication: crowdsourcing*

In the previous sections we described the generation of candidate skill phrases and the disambiguation of these phrases to multiple senses. But many of these phrases were semantic duplicates of each other. This duplication results from members entering synonyms in phrases such as "java development" and "java programming", making typos such as "government liaison" and "goverment liason", abbreviating words or referring to acronyms, such as "B2B" and "Business to Business", and a number of other possible scenarios.

Duplicate skills hinder the user experience. For example, a user may be unsure whether "Java programming", "Java development", or simply "Java" is the preferred way to list a skill. However, manual identification of all duplicates across the large number of phrases would be extremely difficult. To address this problem we investigated a crowdsourcing solution to handle the deduplication.

During a small-scale experiment, we found that more than two thirds of the skill phrases we considered could be matched to a Wikipedia page describing the topic using a simple Web search. We also found that in some instances many phrases were related to the same page and that, in those cases, those phrases referred to the same skill. Based on these findings, we decided to use relationship to the same Wikipedia page as a criterion for deduplication.

In order to do this mapping at scale, we built a crowdsourcing task using Amazon's Mechanical Turk [1] platform. Each task asked the worker to identify the best Wikipedia page for a given phrase. Additional information like the industry cluster and the related phrases were provided to give the worker sufficient context to make an informed decision. Figure 2 shows an example for the "organ" phrase.

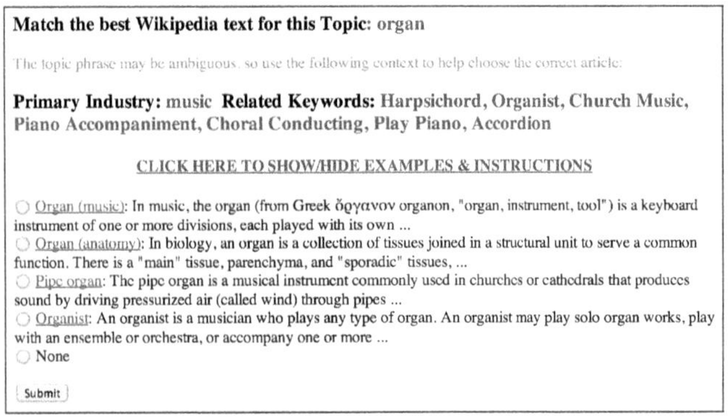

Figure 2: Crowdsourcing task for the "organ" phrase

Once this task was complete, phrases which matched to the same Wikipedia page were combined into a single *skill*. This skill was given the label of its most frequent phrase. This process resulted in a mapping of the 150,000 skill phrases to approximately 50,000 skill topics. Finally, this list of skills was curated to remove obvious errors and then served as a type-ahead to members editing their profile.

2.2 Skills Inference and Recommendation

In the previous sections, we described how we built the folksonomy of standardized skills. This list was used by members to edit their profile and was an improvement over no standardization at all but didn't meet the desired profile completeness growth objective. Therefore, we decided to create a skill inference algorithm and directly suggest additional skills to members through a recommender system [13]. A system of this kind should be personalized and aims to only suggest the skills members have. When presented with

[1]https://www.mturk.com

Type	Coverage	Example
Title (Headline)	89%	Product Manager
Function	70%	Engineering
Industry	100%	Healthcare
Title (Employment Position)	53%	Product Manager
Company	46%	LinkedIn
Group membership	29%	Healthcare Professionals
Field of Study	24%	Computer Science

Table 1: Profile attributes dataset with coverage

skills recommendations, we assume members would only add the skills they possess and reject the ones that were unknown or not relevant. This problem is often encountered in discovering latent attributes in social network profiles [7] [10] [1]. These techniques use a variety of explicit and implicit profile attributes and often leverage the homophily characteristic of social networks.

Unlike common recommender systems, which recommend a large set of items such as movies or products, the number of skills relevant to a member is relatively limited. In fact, the maximum number of skills a member can add to his LinkedIn profile is fifty. In this regard, this problem is quite similar to recommending tags for content such as photos or articles, which is discussed in [4] [16] [8]. In our case, the content would be the member's profile and the tag the skill. These systems often try to find the best trade-off between popularity and personalization, and the same is true in our case. On one hand, the most popular skills are a small fraction of the approximately 50,000 distinct skills in the folksonomy, but a large proportion of members list them. On the other hand, rare and more specific skills might be more descriptive and appealing to members as they more accurately describe their competencies.

We investigated different approaches to solve this problem and ultimately developed a collaborative filtering (CB) solution. There was limited information available about the skills themselves so content-based are difficult to apply directly. However, a member's profile normally includes explicit data such as employment history, education information or group affiliations and we noticed that members who share these profile attributes were likely to have similar skills and expertise. For instance, if a member is an *Apple* employee, it is likely that he/she has the skill "Mac OS" because other employees at Apple have this skill. Similarly, most members of an interest group such as "Healthcare Professionals" should have many skills in common. Therefore, we started building a training dataset by collecting standardized profile attributes that are likely to be shared by members with similar skills along with the skills these profile list.

At the time of this extraction, the number of members with skills was too limited and we experimented adding the skills extracted from the free text specialty section to complete the training set. Although this introduced some noise it helped create a larger training set to start with. A description of this dataset is in Table 1 with an indicative coverage metric, which represents the number of members who have a particular attribute in the dataset.

We first considered using a Logistic Regression model to estimate the likelihood that a member has a particular skill. Since training a model per skill was impractical given the size of the folksonomy and unsuitable for ranking applications, we looked into an alternative approach - creating a unique regression model based on collaborative filtering. This approach would require transforming the profile attributes and creating a user-similarity based metric in order to associate skills with members. Given the diversity of the attributes we planned to use, this approach seemed to create a quite difficult undertaking. Instead, we looked into using a simpler naive Bayes classifier model which is suitable for both large vocabularies and large number of classes. Although our profile features are not truly independent, naive Bayes often compares with more sophisticated classifiers [14] in terms of performance.

2.2.1 Naive Bayes Classifier

We identified standardized profile attributes such as the company, title, industry, field of study or group membership to be useful in inferring skills or areas of expertise. Given a profile that contains a set of these uniquely identified attributes $a_1 ... a_n$, we define the likelihood to have a skill as $P(s|a_1...a_n)$ where $s \in S$ and $S = \{s_1, s_2, .., s_n\}$ the folksonomy of skills. Let $n(a_i, s)$ be the number of co-occurence of the attribute a_i and the skill s on member profiles in our training dataset and $n(s)$ the total number of member profile with that skill. Using the naive Bayes formula, we define

$$P(s|a_1, \ldots, a_n) = \frac{1}{Z} P(s) \prod_{i=1}^{n} P(a_i|s)$$

where $Z = P(a_1, \ldots, a_n)$, $P(s)$ is the prior probability of a skill $s \in S$ and $P(a_i|s)$ is the probability of a_i given s. We define

$$P(a_i|s) = \frac{n(a_i, s)}{n(s)}$$

When calculating the most likely skill a member has, it gives

$$\underset{s \in S}{\text{argmax}}\ P(s) \prod_{i=1}^{n} P(a_i|s)$$

Because $n(a_i, s)$ might be missing for some feature and skill, we're using Laplacian smoothing to avoid zero predictions. We then have

$$P(a_i|s) = \frac{1 + n(a_i, s)}{|W_i| + n(s)}$$

where $|W_i|$ is the vocabulary size for attribute i. Our implementation used log probabilities to avoid underflow.

Using a naive Bayes classifier to infer skills required strong prior associations between members' skills and the profile attributes used in the training phase. While the set of members with each attribute type varies, most members' profiles contain at least a couple of distinct attributes. For instance, most of them have an industry, which has about 150 distinct categories, as it's asked at registration time. Therefore, this approach allowed producing an inferred skills ranking for almost every member on LinkedIn. That said, the ranking quality varied from simply the most frequent skills in your industry to a more accurate prediction as the number of attributes used as feature increased.

2.2.2 Feature selection

Using this naive Bayes model, we found that the number of features could easily become unmanageable. Because profile attributes include entities like interest groups or companies, the number of distinct attributes can grow very large. For instance, there are more than 3 millions distinct companies on LinkedIn for which members can have worked. Not only does the expansion of these attributes become unwieldy to work with, but the large number of very rare or very common occurrences might also decrease the prediction accuracy, as presented in [5]. Therefore, we aimed to reduce the number of features using a feature selection technique. We compared two feature selection techniques with the objective of finding the best trade-off between accuracy and the size of the training data.

At first, we used a frequency filter to remove attribute and skill occurrences below a certain threshold but found that this technique overly penalize rare skills when set too aggressively.

We then opted to use a mutual information calculation, which is often used with naive Bayes to evaluate which feature to select. The mutual information between a skill s and an attribute a_i class measures how much the presence/absence of an attribute contributes to a correct classification of a skill. Formally:

$$\sum_{e_s \in \{1,0\}} \sum_{e_a \in \{1,0\}} P(U = e_s, C = e_a) log_2 \frac{P(U = e_s, C = e_a)}{P(U = e_s)P(C = e_a)}$$

where U is a random variable that takes values $e_s = 1$ (profile has skill) and $e_s = 0$ (profile doesn't have skill) and C is a random variable that takes values $e_a = 1$ (profile does have attribute) and $e_a = 0$ (profile doesn't have attribute). We calculated the mutual information between each skill s and attribute a_i and defined this result as our utility function to filter out (feature,skill) pairs with low information gain. We then used the utility score distribution to select a threshold. We tested multiple thresholds and compared the recall@50 on a sample of profiles and features for a threshold set at the 1st, 5th, 10th, 25th and 50th percentile. Figure 3 is showing the result of this comparison.

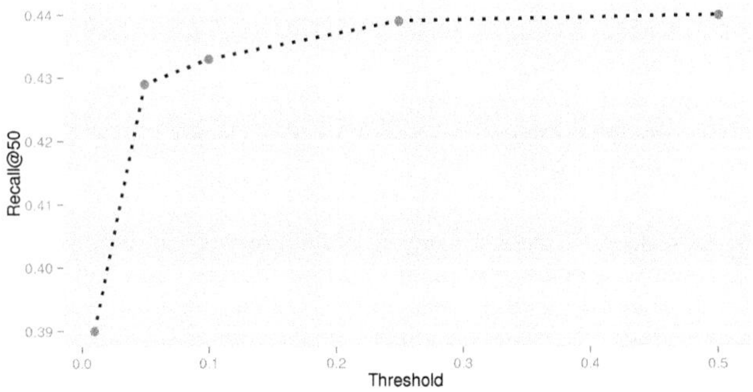

Figure 3: Mutual information threshold effect on classification performance

We observed that the classification performance is holding out well even with only a fraction of the complete training data. That said, the recall is calculated using members who already have skills so there was a bias in this dataset. We finally opted for a threshold at the 25th percentile as it maintained performance, did not penalize rare entities too much and reduced the training data to a manageable size.

2.2.3 Evaluation

We first evaluated the accuracy of the naive Bayes classifier by comparing predicted skills with actual occurrences using a holdout dataset. The classification result is a sorted list of inferred skills and this order is being used by the recommender system. We primarily cared about the quality of this ranking and designed our evaluation methodology around that. True positives were inferred skills members had in the skills section of their profile and our proxy for true negatives were inferred skills members do not have. Whether the skill phrase was present in the profile free text was not taken into account in the evaluation. We could use information retrieval metrics such as MAP [2] to directly evaluate ranking performance but also precision and recall at a particular k position. The area under the ROC curve is also a valid evaluation but can only be performed per skill, as scores are comparable. Although the classifier output is not a probability we could use a normalized score per skill to obtain an ROC curve. Figure 4 shows the ROC curve for the "Hadoop" skill in sample.

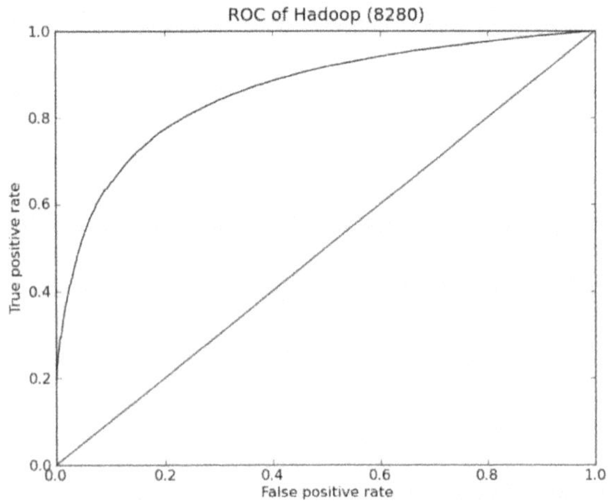

Figure 4: ROC curve for the "Hadoop" skill

The average AUC on ROC curves on all skills with a minimum occurrences of 100 members was 0.77. Figure 5 shows the distribution of these scores.

We observed that more specific skills obtain better AUC results. For instance, technical skills, such as "Hadoop", are well above the average but soft and vague skills such as "Ability to learn" obtain AUC scores around 0.5. This observation can be explained by studying how skills and attributes co-occur. Soft skills tend to co-occur with a much broader set of attributes whereas technical skills are often only co-occurring with a small set of companies, titles or groups. We also looked at the impact of different feature set on the classification performance. Table 2 shows the classifier recall for different combination of features as an illustrative example.

2.2.4 Results

We applied the skills inference algorithm to suggest to members skills to add to their profile and evaluated. This

[2]Mean Average Precision

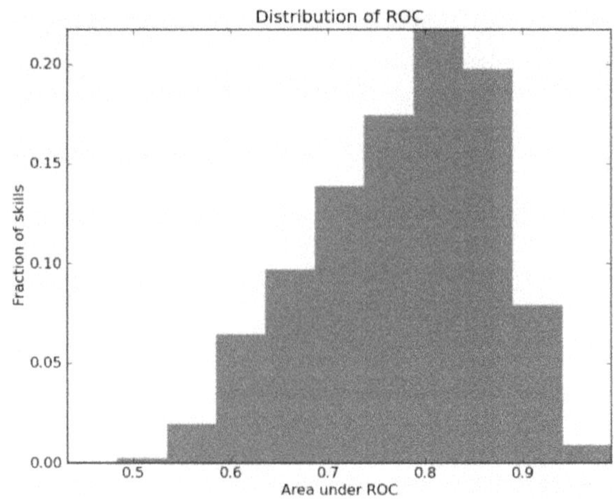

Figure 5: Distribution of ROC AUC across all skills

Feature Set	Recall@50
industry	0.45
industry+company+function	0.60
industry+company+function+title	0.66
industry+company+function+title+group	0.71

Table 2: Classification performance with different feature sets

suggested skills task was presented to a large set of members on LinkedIn in a system that invited them to complete their profile. Because a large majority of members have at least one standardized profile attribute, generally an industry - we could provide skills suggestions for >95% of LinkedIn members, even if their profile was not in English. We primarily looked at two metrics to evaluate the effectiveness of the system: conversion and acceptance rate. The conversion is defined by the ratio of members adding at least one skill over the members who saw the task. The acceptance rate is defined as the ratio of skills added over skills impressed.

One of the key results was that the recommender system led to far greater conversion of members adding skills to their profiles. Specifically, we compared two different user interfaces as shown on Figure 6. The user interface with suggestions led to a 49% conversion compared to 4% with a simple blank field with type-ahead.

We also performed experiments regarding the number of skills to suggest. We started with three skills and found that there wasn't a significant penalty in adding more skills to suggest up to ten. We monitored the conversion and acceptance rate but also the dismissal rate, which represented the percentage of suggestions members dismissed. We were concerned that too many suggestions would overload the member with information and halt the healthy "pick-n-choose" behavior we were observing. Indeed, we wanted members to continue to dismiss the suggestions they did not found relevant. Figure 7 compares the frequency of skills added during an A/B test, which shows either five or ten suggestions.

We observed that 57% of members added five skills when five were shown and 45% of members added ten skills when ten were shown. Therefore, we did not observe an increase in the frequency of members adding all the presented suggestions.

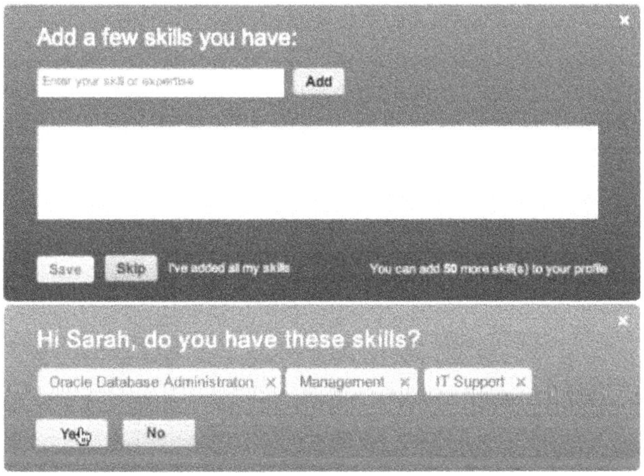

Figure 6: Add skills with just typeahead: 4% conversion. Add skills with recommendations: 49% conversion

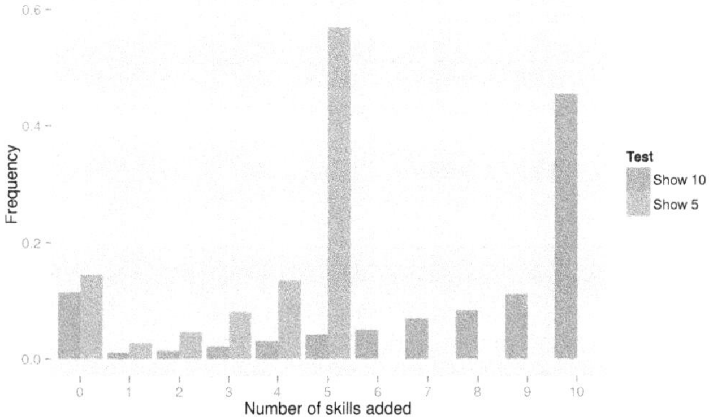

Figure 7: Skills added with 5 or 10 suggestions shown

3. IMPLEMENTATION

The skills data pipeline is running on Hadoop, an open source implementation of MapReduce, as part of LinkedIn's big data ecosystem [17]. MapReduce provides a framework for processing big datasets on a large number of commodity computers and further simplifies the process of writing parallel programs by providing the underlying infrastructure, failure handling, and simple interfaces for programmers.

Incoming query logs and other activity-based tracking data is aggregated from production services using Kafka [6], a publish-subscribe system for event collection and dissemination. This log data can be easily represented as a set of tuples, which is a natural fit for Hadoop's distributed computing paradigm.

The skills pipeline consists of a series of automated MapReduce jobs, separated in two workflows: one for the folksonony creation and one for the inference. In total, there are over 150 MapReduce jobs, from initially pre-processing the profiles to performing entity extraction, disambiguation, deduplication and inference.

In addition, an online classifier is running as part of our inference service, which is classifying members with skills upon each profile update. This data is available via an API or as a stream for data consumers.

4. APPLICATIONS

We present a set of key applications that directly leverages the skills folksonomy and the inference system.

4.1 Endorsements

In September 2012, LinkedIn released the Endorsements feature, which allows members to provide social proof of their connections' skill or expertise in a given topic via means of a new social gesture, an "one-click endorse." The endorsing member's endorsement is then displayed next to the respective skill of the endorsed member's skill section. An example skills and expertise section with endorsements is shown in Figure 1.

One of the goals of the Endorsements product was to encourage those people who had few skills on their profile to add more. When a member A endorses another member B for a skill that member B does not yet have, member B is notified of that endorsement and prompted to accept it and add that skill to his/her profile. Towards this goal, a recommender system was built to suggest (*connection*, *skill*) pairs which a member might want to endorse.

An important aspect of this recommender system is the fact that it can create endorsement recommendations for skills that the endorsement's target does not yet have. In this process the results of the inferred skill algorithm are a primary feature in the choice of skills to recommend. The ability for members to suggest skills to other members via an endorsement added a social component into the skills recommendation and has proven a very effective technique to increase the number of members adding skills.

4.2 Query Expansion

For search applications, query expansion can be an effective technique to improve the search quality, especially in situations were the number of results are low. The idea is to expand the query to include additional terms as alternatives that are related to those within the query. A typical example of this technique is including synonyms of search terms. For example, a query consisting of just "car" could be expanded to include "automobile" as well. As these two terms are closely related, it is reasonable to return results matching either of them, perhaps with the one from the original query weighted more heavily.

One common type of query a member may perform on LinkedIn is searching by skill. For example, a recruiter may be seeking members with particular skills that they would like to reach out to. Query expansion can make their skill-based searches more effective by automatically including other closely related skills.

The key ingredient in making a skills-based query expansion work is a measure of how closely related skills are to each other. Fortunately the collection of member profiles and job postings, with the skills identified in them, provide this. If we assume that closely related skills are more likely to co-occur on the same document (i.e. profile, job posting), then we can use the frequency of co-occurrence to derive similarity scores between all the skills in the folksonomy. These scores can then be used to expand the skills-based queries to include skills that fall above a certain similarity threshold.

4.3 Job Recommendations

Effectively recommending jobs to members is important for a professional networking site. An effective feature in such a recommender system could be the skill similarity between a job and a member. A member is likely to show interest in a job that has a skill profile similar to their own skill set. Some of the techniques from query expansion can be applied here.

We can begin by identifying skills within the text of member profiles and job recommendations. This produces a set of skills for each profile and job posting. This skill set can then be expanded with similar skills using the same query expansion technique described earlier. For each skill we can generate a score that indicates the relevance of that skill for the particular profile or job posting. Several factors may influence relevance. Skills that appear explicitly are more relevant than skills that are inferred due to query expansion. Skills that are closely related and co-occur in the same profile or job posting have a reinforcing effect that boosts relevancy of those skills. From the set of skills and their associated relevancy scores we can construct skill vectors that summarize how closely related each profile or job posting is to each known skill. Given these skill vectors we can compute similarity between the member and job posting using any number of metrics. This score can then be yet another important signal in a job recommender system.

5. CONCLUSION AND FUTURE WORK

In this paper we have presented the "Skills and Expertise" data driven feature that is part of LinkedIn. We have discussed the initial creation of the folksonomy, covering entity discovery, disambiguation, and deduplication. The combination of techniques presented has created a set of skills and expertise that covers a broad scope of domains with minimal need for editorial influence.

In addition, we have also presented the design of an inference and recommender system to suggest skills and expertise to members. This system allowed to rapidly expand the set of members with a qualified set of standardized skills on their profile. Subsequent applications have been able to leverage the work done in the extraction and inference of skills to provide additional value in multiple domains.

The folksonomy of members' skills and expertise is inherently dynamic. Continuing work is required to better understand how folksonomies such as this one evolve over time and how the knowledge encoded in them may be best utilized. Moreover, the expansion of this approach to non-English languages might be an interesting challenge. Better leveraging what we know about the skills from the Wikipedia link might also be a promising direction, especially regarding the disambiguation of the multiple meanings of a skill entity.

The inference system could also be expanded with more features and a more sophisticated approach. This approach was a good start with the data we had but with the recommender system being used we can collect real-world feedback data, which can be leveraged in a machine-learnt model. We also suspect that the skills members might want to add to their profile are slightly different from the skills we infer they might have - leading to a slightly different objective function. Additional features, which are not profile attributes could also be explored such as the frequency of the skill within the member's connections or bag-of-words.

6. ADDITIONAL AUTHORS

Additional authors: Sal Uryasev (LinkedIn Corporation, email: `suryasev@linkedin.com`) and Christopher Lloyd (LinkedIn Corporation, email: `clloyd@linkedin.com`).

7. REFERENCES

[1] F. Abel, Q. Gao, G.-J. Houben, and K. Tao. Analyzing user modeling on twitter for personalized news recommendations. In *User Modeling, Adaption and Personalization*, pages 1–12. Springer, 2011.

[2] R. Baeza-Yates, B. Ribeiro-Neto, et al. *Modern information retrieval*, volume 463. ACM press New York, 1999.

[3] F. Echarte, J. J. Astrain, A. Córdoba, and J. E. Villadangos. Ontology of folksonomy: A new modelling method. *SAAKM*, 289:36, 2007.

[4] R. Jäschke, L. Marinho, A. Hotho, L. Schmidt-Thieme, and G. Stumme. Tag recommendations in folksonomies. In *Knowledge Discovery in Databases: PKDD 2007*, pages 506–514. Springer, 2007.

[5] D. Koller and M. Sahami. Toward optimal feature selection. 1996.

[6] J. Kreps, N. Narkhede, and J. Rao. Kafka: A distributed messaging system for log processing. In *Proceedings of the NetDB*, 2011.

[7] J. Li, A. Ritter, and E. Hovy. Weakly supervised user profile extraction from twitter. ACL, 2014.

[8] M. Lipczak. Tag recommendation for folksonomies oriented towards individual users. *ECML PKDD discovery challenge*, 84, 2008.

[9] A. Mathes. Folksonomies-cooperative classification and communication through shared metadata. *Computer Mediated Communication*, 47(10):1–13, 2004.

[10] A. Mislove, B. Viswanath, K. P. Gummadi, and P. Druschel. You are who you know: Inferring user profiles in online social networks.

[11] R. Navigli and P. Velardi. Learning domain ontologies from document warehouses and dedicated web sites. *Computational Linguistics*, 30(2):151–179, 2004.

[12] I. Peters. *Folksonomies: Indexing and retrieval in Web 2.0*, volume 1. Walter de Gruyter, 2009.

[13] F. Ricci, L. Rokach, and B. Shapira. *Introduction to recommender systems handbook*. Springer, 2011.

[14] I. Rish. An empirical study of the naive bayes classifier. In *IJCAI 2001 workshop on empirical methods in artificial intelligence*, volume 3, pages 41–46, 2001.

[15] G. Salton and M. J. McGill. Introduction to modern information retrieval. 1986.

[16] B. Sigurbjörnsson and R. Van Zwol. Flickr tag recommendation based on collective knowledge. In *Proceedings of the 17th international conference on World Wide Web*, pages 327–336. ACM, 2008.

[17] R. Sumbaly, J. Kreps, and S. Shah. The "big data" ecosystem at LinkedIn. In *SIGMOD '13*, pages 1125–1134, New York, NY, USA, 2013.

[18] L. Zhang, X. Wu, and Y. Yu. Emergent semantics from folksonomies: A quantitative study. In *Journal on Data Semantics VI*, pages 168–186. Springer, 2006.

Automating Readers' Advisory to Make Book Recommendations for K-12 Readers

Maria Soledad Pera
Computer Science Department
Brigham Young University
Provo, Utah 84604, U.S.A.
mpera@cs.byu.edu

Yiu-Kai Ng
Computer Science Department
Brigham Young University
Provo, Utah 84604, U.S.A.
ng@compsci.byu.edu

ABSTRACT

The academic performance of students is affected by their reading ability, which explains why reading is one of the most important aspects of school curriculums. Promoting good reading habits among K-12 students is essential, given the enormous influence of reading on students' development as learners and members of society. In doing so, it is indispensable to provide readers with engaging and motivating reading selections. Unfortunately, existing book recommenders have failed to offer adequate choices for K-12 readers, since they either ignore the reading abilities of their users or cannot acquire the much-needed information to make recommendations due to privacy issues. To address these problems, we have developed Rabbit, a book recommender that emulates the readers' advisory service offered at school/public libraries. Rabbit considers the readability levels of its readers and determines the facets, i.e., appeal factors, of books that evoke subconscious, emotional reactions on a reader. The design of Rabbit is unique, since it adopts a multi-dimensional approach to capture the reading abilities, preferences, and interests of its readers, which goes beyond the traditional book content/topical analysis. Conducted empirical studies have shown that Rabbit outperforms a number of (readability-based) book recommenders.

Categories and Subject Descriptors

Information Systems [**Retrieval tasks and goals**]: [Recommender systems]

Keywords

Recommendation system; books; K-12; readers' advisory

1. INTRODUCTION

Besides watching TV, text messaging, and playing computer games, children and teenagers these days often spend spare time browsing through the Internet, looking for something fun to do. YouTube and Facebook are examples of popular sites among young audiences that offer free entertainment on demand anytime and anywhere. Recent statistics[1] have shown that children/teenagers spend an average of seven hours a day on (smart) devices. This is alarming, since a significant number of children/teenagers are underachieving at school, especially in *reading*. According to the 2013 National Assessment of Educational Progress,[2] only 32% of American 4th graders are proficient in reading. Kids should allocate some of their free time on reading to enhance their educational experience. To turn the tide, educators, parents, government agents, and private organizations must join force to encourage kids to read. Unfortunately, very few existing websites/(non-)government agents are equipped with the resources/technologies to cope with the problem.

To motivate K-12 readers, it is necessary to avoid presenting these readers with books that are either too easy/difficult to read or involve topics unappealing to them which could diminish their interest in reading. In fact, finding the right books for the right audience is not easy. Even though existing recommenders can assist readers in finding books, they rely either on large historical data, e.g., personal tags/ratings, (which might not be available) or readers' interactions on social sites (which may not be accessible involving K-12 readers due to privacy issues). Furthermore, these systems *ignore* the reading abilities of the respective readers in recommending books. To address the shortcomings of these design methodologies, we have developed Rabbit, a Readers' advisory-based book recommendation tool that makes personalized, appealing suggestions on books to K-12 readers.

Rabbit is unique, since it simulates readers' advisory (RA), a service offered at school/public libraries which are established to champion and encourage reading. RA involves knowledgeable professionals in finding reading materials of interest for their patrons [14]. During the search process, librarians identify the *topics*, *contents*, and *appeal factors*, i.e., literary elements, appealing to each reader and suggest books accordingly. By offering this service, which is in high demand even in the era of the Web 2.0, libraries provide "a vital link between library materials and readers" [14]. Unfortunately, (young) readers may not approach readers' advisors to ask for suggestions, feel their interest are *obscure* or *low-brow*, or not even visit libraries in person [5]. By automating the RA process, we replace RA in finding books appealing to K-12 readers, which eliminates the interaction with professionals and at the same time handles any num-

[1]nytimes.com/2010/01/20/education/20wired.html?_r=0
[2]http://goo.gl/Ad1VbE.

RecSys'14, October 6–10, 2014, Foster City, Silicon Valley, CA, USA.
Copyright 2014 ACM 978-1-4503-2668-1/14/10$15.00.
http://dx.doi.org/10.1145/2645710.2645721.

ber of readers simultaneously that cannot be achieved by traditional RA.

Rabbit is novel, since besides analyzing the reading ability of a reader R, it examines appeal factors to capture the reasons why a book Bk is appealing to R. Rabbit determines the facets of Bk that instigate a reaction to Bk, which in turn impacts the perception of R on Bk. Rabbit explores the literary elements of books that identify the *rate* in which the stories unfold (pace), their *overall structure* (storyline), the *feelings* that these stories evoke on a reader (tone), and subject *matters* that some readers might find unpleasant or offensive (special topics), in addition to the *qualities* of the *characters* (characterization) and the *language* and *level of details* (writing style) of the stories. Rabbit is neither affected by the cold-start problem nor requires feedback from its users, and its design surpasses the content or reading patterns explored by state-of-the-art recommenders.

While topics and content descriptions of books are freely and publicly available from reputable online sources, such as the Library of Congress,[3] appeal-factor/-term descriptions, which are fundamental for our recommendation strategy, are either determined by professionals on-the-fly or accessed through a paid subscription to RA databases. To automate the process of extracting appeal-term descriptions of books, we have developed ABET (Appeal-based extraction tool), a component of Rabbit, which relies on book reviews retrieved from book-related websites, such as Amazon(.com) and Powells.com. ABET is based on rules that examine typed dependencies and part-of-speech tags of words in reviews to identify appeal factors and their terms. ABET relies on reviews for extracting appeal-term descriptions on books, since they are readily available online and capture readers' varied opinions on the literary elements of a book.

2. RELATED WORK

Numerous approaches have been developed to identify and extract either features, (the polarity of) opinions, or feature-opinion pairs from reviews based on bootstrapping, natural language processing, machine learning, extraction rules, latent semantic analysis, statistical analysis, and information retrieval. (An in-depth review of state-of-the-art approaches adopted for opinion mining and extraction can be found in [11].) A product review describes the product's actual features, such as the "zoom" of a camera, which is unlike a book review that evaluates "organization and writing style, possible market appeal, and cultural, political, or literary significance" of a book [15]. A book review is a form of literary criticism in which the work is analyzed based on its content, style, and merit. We have observed that existing information extraction approaches on product reviews are ill-equipped for book reviews, since sentences expressed in book reviews tend to be more elaborated than the ones used to describe products. For this reason, ABET is not designed using any existing extraction approach. Instead, it relies on simple rules to perform linguistic and semantic analysis of the content and writing style of book reviews.

A number of book recommendation systems have been developed in the past. Amazon's recommender suggests books based on the purchase patterns of its users [8], whereas Yang et al. [17] analyze users' access logs to infer their preferences and apply the traditional collaborative-filtering (CF) strategy to make book recommendations. Givon and Lavrenko [4] combine CF and social tags to capture the content of books for recommendation. Sieg et al. [16] rely on the standard user-based CF framework and incorporate semantic knowledge in the form of a domain ontology to capture the topics of interest to a user. The hybrid-based recommenders in [4, 16, 17], in addition to Rabbit, overcome the cold-start problem. Unlike Rabbit, however, the others require (i) historical data on the users in the form of ratings, which may not always be available, or (ii) an ontology, which can be labor-intensive and time-consuming to construct.

Unlike Rabbit, PReF [12] examines users' connections as part of the recommendation process, which may not be accessible as they involve K-12 readers due to privacy imposed on children. BReK12 [12], which is the closest book recommender compared with Rabbit, is based on content and readability analysis. The former, however, relies on the availability of bookmarking information offered by social bookmarking site users to analyze reading patters of users. Furthermore, with the exception of BReK12, neither of the aforementioned recommenders considers the readability level of their users as part of their recommendation strategies. Although Rabbit is not a recommendation system for learning, its design goal is to enhance reading selections for K-12 users. (An in-depth description of existing recommenders in the educational domain can be found in [9].)

3. READERS' ADVISORY (RA)

Rabbit emulates the readers' advisory (RA) service available at public libraries since the late 1800's [3, 14]. RA offers (non-)fiction materials of potential interest with "the help of knowledgeable and non-judgmental library staff" [14]. While traditional RA involves face-to-face discussions between patrons and librarians, a number of public libraries, such as Williamsburg Regional,[4] take advantage of existing technologies and replace human interactions with online forms filled out by patrons to capture their interests [5].

Either through face-to-face conversations or filled-out online forms, a RA librarian's task is to identify the type of books preferred by readers based on the reasons behind their preferences. Besides analyzing the *topical areas* and *content descriptions* of books favored by a reader R, during the RA process, librarians examine the *appeal factors* of books that R is interested in [14]. Appeal factors, such as the pacing or description of characters in books, are "the elements of a book—whether definable or just understood—that make readers enjoy the book" [14]. These factors capture general traits of a book that attract the attention of a reader and are considered in answering one of the most important RA questions, "Why is the reader interested in a given book?" For example, some readers might enjoy the Harry Potter books (by J.K. Rowling) because of the established friendships among students and the boarding school setting, whereas others like the fantasy aspect of the story.

To the best of our knowledge, there is no consensus on the set of appeal factors that must be considered during the RA process. The most prominent appeal factors, as articulated in RA-related literature [3, 5, 14] include: (i) characterization, (ii) frame, (iii) pacing, (iv) storyline, (v) language and writing style, (vi) tone, and (vii) special topics. The first six appeal factors are well-known literary elements of

[3]catalog.loc.gov/

[4]wrl.org/books-and-reading/adults/looking-good-book

Table 1: Sample appeal terms associated with each of the appeal factors considered by Rabbit

Appeal Factors	Appeal Terms
Characterization	Believable, distant, dramatic
Frame	Bittersweet, contemporary, descriptive
Language and Writing Style	Candid, complex, conversational, extravagant, poetic, prosaic
Pacing	Easy, fast, slow
Special Topics	Addiction, bullying, violence
Storyline	Action-oriented, character-centered
Tone	Dark, happy, surreal

(non-)fiction books [2], whereas the latter identifies subjects addressed in a book that can cause emotional stress to some readers but tolerated/enjoyed by others [3]. Each appeal factor is associated with a vocabulary, which is a set of keywords, called *appeal terms*, employed to describe the factor, which we have defined based on well-known RA literature [3, 14]. The appeal factors considered by Rabbit and a sample of their respective appeal terms are shown in Table 1.

Based on the contents, topics, and appeal terms that describe the appeal factors of books *preferred* by a reader *R*, librarians suggest other books matching (to a certain degree) the interests/preferences of *R*. However, due to the amount of books being published on a regular basis these days, it is an impossible task for a librarian to be familiar with every existing book to determine if it could be a potential relevant recommendation for *R*. For this reason, librarians turn to RA databases, which are available at NoveList, Fiction Connection, Which Book, and Readers' Advisory Online, to conduct fact-based, appeal factor-oriented, and read-alike searches in locating books to suggest to a reader [3].

4. APPEAL-TERM DESCRIPTIONS

While Rabbit conducts topical and content analysis of books using data from book-related websites, appeal-term descriptions are only available through RA databases or determined by professionals. Unfortunately, accessing reputable RA databases, such as NoveList Plus, comes with a price tag, i.e., paid subscription, whereas professionals might not have read a particular book and thus it would not be possible for them to infer the corresponding appeal-term description on-the-fly. To address these constraints, we have developed ABET, a tool that automatically extracts appeal-term descriptions of books from reviews available at well-known book-related websites, such as Amazon, Bertrams, Bookfinder4u, Bookmooch, Dogobooks and Fishpond.As reading is a personal experience, it is anticipated that a book is (not) appealing to a reader for various reasons. By analyzing reviews, we extract diverse readers' opinions on a book based on appeal terms that describe the corresponding appeal factors of the book, which in turn facilitates the task of identifying why books are appealing to a reader based on their literary elements.

To generate the appeal-term description for a given book, ABET relies on the taxonomy defined in Section 3, which despite being comprehensive, cannot account for a given appeal factor/term being specified differently in readers' reviews. For example, a reviewer may refer to the "Storyline" of a book as "story" or "narrative", and (s)he may also use either "quick" or "fast" to describe its "Pace". For this reason, we extend the appeal factors/terms by including the (stemmed) synonyms of each term/factor, which are identified using WordNet.[5] (The complete list of appeal terms for each appeal factor can be found at goo.gl/BSwuPw.)

While the taxonomy can serve as an aid to identify potential appeal factors/terms in reviews, it is imperative to properly associate these appeal terms and appeal factors in the reviews so that appeal factor-appeal term pairs can be correctly extracted to generate an accurate appeal-term description for a given book. To accomplish this task, we have defined a number of extraction rules[6] (as given in Table 2) for ABET based on typed dependency relations between word pairs in sentences extracted from reviews. It is natural for ABET to turn to typed dependencies, since they capture the *semantic connection*, i.e., association, between words in sentences. (A detailed discussion on typed dependencies is available at http://goo.gl/31Puwm.)

Rules used by ABET are based on written patterns identified in book reviews and capture the semantic link between appeal factors and their corresponding terms. Consider sentence S_A, "The narrative of the book is dramatic", and sentence S_B, "He creates believable characters". In S_A the *subject* of the sentence, i.e., "narrative," is characterized as being "dramatic", whereas in S_B its *object*, i.e., "characters", is described as "believable". As illustrated by the aforementioned examples, if the subject/object of a sentence is an appeal factor, then a word in the sentence that is semantically directly linked to the mentioned object/subject is often an appeal term. ABET captures these connection patterns using Rules 1 and 2 as defined in Table 2.

In a sentence, an appeal terms can also be indirectly connected with an appeal factor. Consider sentence S_C, "The descriptions included are extravagant". "Extravagant" is *indirectly* related to the subject of S_C, i.e., "descriptions", through the word "included". Using Rule 3, ABET examines pairs of grammatical relations that involve indirect connections among words. Now consider sentence S_D, "The characters are not simple". Based on Rule 1, ABET would mistakenly connect "Characterization" with "simple". This example reveals the need to examine pairs of grammatical relations in the presence of negated terms. ABET applies Rule 4, which identifies a negated term as a modifier of an appeal term *t* and then extracts as the appeal term for the corresponding factor the antonym of *t* (if it is included in the vocabulary defined in ABET's taxonomy for the factor).

Rules 3 and 4 take precedence over Rules 1 and 2, since once a typed dependency in a sentence is used by either of the former rules, it cannot be considered by the latter ones.

While majority of other relations (beyond the ones captured by Rules 1 to 4) seldom appeared in reviews, we observed three *special cases* that facilitate the extraction of appeal terms for "Special Topics" and "Frame", respectively, which we defined in Rules 5 to 7. Consider S_E, "It is about violence at schools", S_F, "Bullying is depicted in the book", and S_G, "The action is set in a school", which include special written patterns pertaining to the "Frame" and "Special Topics" appeal factors that are based on prepositions, subjects, and objects identified in sentences in reviews. The preposition "about" in S_E captures an appeal term employed to describe the factor "Special Topics", i.e., "violence", whereas

[5] wordnet.princeton.edu

[6] ABET performs linguistic/semantic analysis on sentences in reviews using Stanford Parser (http://goo.gl/Pxj2QW).

Table 2: Rules considered by ABET to identify appeal factor-appeal term pairs in book reviews

Notations
$rel(A, B)$ is a *grammatical relation* between a *dominant*, i.e., *governor* or *head*, word (A) and a *subordinate*, i.e., *dependent* or *modifier*, word (B)
L_F, L_T, EL_F, and EL_T are the list of appeal factors, list of appeal terms, extended list of appeal factors, and extended list of appeal terms, respectively
w_f is an appeal factor in L_F, and w_t is an appeal term in L_T
$w \rightsquigarrow w_f$ ($w \rightsquigarrow w_t$, respectively) denotes that w is a synonym of w_f (w_t, respectively)
$POS(w)$ is the part-of-speech tag of w which is a verb (adverb, respectively) if $POS(w)$ = "VB" ("RB", respectively)
Abbreviation: adv(erbial)mod(ifier), a(djectival)mod(ifier), c(lausal)comp(lement), d(irect)obj(ect), neg(ation modifier), nn (noun compound modifier), n(ominal)subj(ect), nsubjpass (passive nominal subject), prep(_*) (Prepositional modifier)
ABET extracts a pair $< w_f, w_t >$ only if w_t is in the corresponding vocabulary defined for w_f

Rule	Objective	Conditions	Identified Factors/Terms
1	To capture the written patterns based on a keyword, i.e., appeal term, that immediately precedes/ follows the subject or object of a sentence S, i.e., appeal factor	$A \in EL_T, B \in EL_F, rel \in$ {nn, nsubj}, (If A is a synonym of a term that applies to "Characterization" or "Storyline", then $POS(A) \notin$ {"VB", "RB"})	$B \rightsquigarrow w_f$ $A \rightsquigarrow w_t$
2		$A \in EL_F, B \in EL_T, rel \in$ {advmod, amod, prep_in, prep_about}	$A \rightsquigarrow w_f$ $B \rightsquigarrow w_t$
3	To identify an appeal term that qualifies its indirectly-related appeal factor in S	$rel \in$ {nn, nsubj}, $B \in EL_F$, and $\exists rel_2(C, D) \in$ {amod, dep, ccomp}, $A = C, D \in EL_T$	$B \rightsquigarrow w_f$ $D \rightsquigarrow w_t$
4	To explicitly consider *negated* appeal terms in S	$B \in EL_F, rel \in$ {nn, nsubj}, $\exists neg(C, D)$, A $(= C)$ is an antonym of $\bar{A} \in EL_T$, D is a negation term	$B \rightsquigarrow w_f$ $\bar{A} \rightsquigarrow w_t$
5	To account for the multiple ways in which a reviewer can describe the setting of books or peeves/favored subject matters in books to handle special cases of "Special Topic" and "Frame" factors in S	$A \in EL_T, rel \in$ {prep_about}, A is a synonym of a term that describes "Special Topics"	w_f = "Special Topics" $A \rightsquigarrow w_t$
6		$B \in EL_T, rel \in$ {dobj, nsubj, nsubjpass}, $POS(A)$ = "VB", B is a synonym of an appeal term that describes "Special Topics"	w_f = "Special Topics" $B \rightsquigarrow w_t$
7		$A \rightsquigarrow$ "Frame" $\in EL_F$, B (a synonym of an appeal term that describes "Frame") $\in EL_T, rel \in$ {prep_in}	w_f = "Frame" $B \rightsquigarrow w_t$

Frame: gritty (9), political (1), small-town (8) ...
Tone: dark (10), eerie (8), happy (1), ...
Storyline: action-oriented (1), complex (3), ...
Special Topics: death (6), violent (7), war (3), ...
Characterization: believable (6), well-developed (11), ...
Language and Writing Style: candid (1), unusual (4), ...
Pacing: fast (8), slow (1), ...

Figure 1: ABET-generated appeal-term description for "The Hunger Games"

"in" in S_G is connected with an appeal term, i.e., "school", that describes the factor "Frame". Moreover, "bullying" in S_F, which is assigned a "VB" part-of-speech tag, is an appeal term describing the factor "Special Topics".

ABET creates the appeal-term description for a book Bk by applying rules defined in Table 2 on (up to) 500 distinct reviews of Bk, if they are available. In generating the appeal-term description of Bk, ABET considers not only the appeal terms extracted from reviews on Bk, but also their *frequency of occurrence*. The latter captures the relative *degree of significance* of an appeal term in describing its corresponding factor based on reviewers' varied opinions on appeal factors that apply to Bk. (A sample of the appeal term description generated using ABET for the book "The Hunger Games" by Suzanne Collins is shown in Figure 1.)

5. OUR PROPOSED RECOMMENDER

In making suggestions, Rabbit first analyzes the *profile* of a reader R, which consists of a set of N (≥ 1) books either given or bookmarked[7] by R on a social bookmarking site. Based on the profile, Rabbit identifies books that are compatible with the readability level of R, which are treated as *candidate books* to be considered for recommendation. These books are selected among those available at a book repository, including (i) *reputable websites*, such as OpenLibrary.org or WorldCat.org, which are two of the largest online library catalogs, (ii) *school/public libraries*, and (iii) book-related *bookmarking sites*, such as BiblioNasium.com, which is a website that encourages reading among children/teenagers. Rabbit computes a ranking score, which quantifies the *degree of relevance*, of each candidate book with respect to (books in) the profile of R using a regression model applied to the analytical results of the book using diverse publicly available information.

5.1 Candidate Books

It is imperative for Rabbit to locate books with grade levels adequate for each individual reader, since "reading for understanding cannot take place unless the words in the text are accurately and efficiently decoded" [10]. To accomplish this task, Rabbit first determines the readability level of a reader R by analyzing the grade levels of books in R's profile. The readability level of R is determined by averaging the grade level of each book P_B in R's profile, computed using TRoLL [12], a tool for regression analysis of literacy levels,

[7]Only books bookmarked by a user during the most recent academic year are examined to account for the fact that the users enhance their reading comprehension skills over time.

which captures the *central tendency* of the grade levels of books that have been read by R. Unlike popular prediction formulas/tools (such as Flesch-Kincaid, Lexile, and ATOS [1]), which rely on text of a book to compute its grade level (a severe constraint, since text is not always freely accessible due to copyright laws), TRoLL computes the grade level of any book using book metadata publicly accessible from reputable online sources, even in the absence of sample text.

Rabbit applies Equation 1 to determine the set of candidate books considered for recommendation.

$$SCB(R) = \{CB \mid CB \in Rep \wedge$$
$$TRoLL(CB) \in [\frac{\sum_{P_B \in P} TRoLL(P_B)}{|P|} \pm 0.25]\} \quad (1)$$

where CB is a candidate book available at a book repository Rep, $|P|$ denotes the number of books in R's profile, and $TRoLL(CB)$ ($TRoLL(P_B)$, respectively) is the grade level of CB (P_B, respectively) determined by TRoLL. By selecting books within *half a grade level* of the *mean* readability level of R, Rabbit considers books for recommendation within an appropriate level of (text) complexity for R based on the grade levels of books in R's profile.

5.2 Multiple-Evidence Analysis

Rabbit suggests books that not only readers can comprehend, but also they are interested in by analyzing diverse publicly accessible metadata as described below

5.2.1 Exploring Topical Information

Rabbit examines the *topical description* (i.e., topic) of a book defined by Library of Congress Subject Headings (LCSH) assigned to the book by professional cataloguers. LCSH, a de facto controlled vocabulary, constitute the largest general indexing vocabulary in the English language. Subject headings, which are *terms* or *phrases* that denote concepts, events, or names, are used by librarians to index books according to their themes. Examples of LCSH include "Juvenile Fiction," and "Archaeology–History–18th century".

Rabbit, which explores the topical resemblance between CB and books in R's profile P, examines the degree to which the distribution of topics in CB matches the distribution of topics of books in P. This *topical similarity* measure, which is defined using the vector space model (VSM) and computed in Equation 2, prioritizes candidate books that have been assigned LCSH which match the LCSH favored by R, i.e., most frequent LCSH assigned to books in P.

$$TSim(CB, P) = \frac{\vec{CB} \cdot \vec{P}}{||\vec{CB}|| \times ||\vec{P}||} \quad (2)$$

where CB and P are represented as n-dimensional vectors $\vec{CB} = < W_{CB_1}, \ldots, W_{CB_n} >$ and $\vec{P} = < W_{P_1}, \ldots, W_{P_n} >$, respectively, n is the number of distinct subject headings assigned to CB and books in P, W_{CB_i}, the weight of CB_i ($1 \leq i \leq n$) is "1" if CB_i is a subject heading of CB, and is "0" otherwise, and W_{P_i}, which is the weight of P_i ($1 \leq i \leq n$), is computed as a proportion between the number of books in P that have been assigned P_i and the total number of books in P, i.e., $|P|$.

In computing the *topical similarity* measure, in addition to other similarity measures presented below, we rely on VSM, since VSM handles frequency distributions, which is essential in comparing candidate books based on multiple perspectives with the profile of a reader. We have empirically verified that given the short length of the descriptions for each book based on its topics, content, and appeal factors (which include very few LCSHs, words, and terms, respectively), VSM is a more reliable distance measure compared with its probabilistic counterparts, such as KL-divergence.

5.2.2 The Book Content Analysis

Besides determining the topics that are of interest to a reader R, Rabbit also identifies written matters covered in books that are generally appealing to R by analyzing the content description of each book in P (and each candidate book CB), which is extracted from reputable book-related websites, such as Amazon and the Library of Congress.

Rabbit computes the *content similarity* of each CB with respect to P based on the "bag-of-words" representation of the *brief descriptions* of CB and (books in) P. Rabbit favors candidate books with contents compatible with the contents that are most commonly addressed in books belonged to R's profile. To compute $CSim(CB, P)$, the *content similarity* score defined in Equation 3, Rabbit employs an *enhanced* version of the cosine similarity measure based on word-correlation factors (WCF) [6], which relaxes the *exact matching* constraint imposed by the cosine measure by exploring words in the content description of CB that are analogous to, besides the same as, words in the content description of books in P. Rabbit relies on WCF, as opposed to other popular similarity metrics applied to WordNet, since we have empirically verified that word-similarity scores predicted by using WCF correlate with human assessments on word similarity. Using WordSim353,[8] which is a test collection for measuring word relatedness, and STS,[9] which provides human assessments on sentence similarity for 750 pairs of sentences, we compared the performance of WCF with FaITH[10] [13], which is a feature and information theoretic-based similarity measure. (Only FaITH was considered, since as reported in [13], it outperforms other well-known information-theoretic, ontology, and hybrid-based approaches that exploit word-related information available at WordNet to estimate the degree of similarity between pairs of words.) The results of the experiments verified that the performance of WCF is comparable to that of FaITH.

$$CSim(CB, P) = \frac{\vec{CB} \cdot \vec{P}}{||\vec{CB}|| \times ||\vec{P}||} \quad (3)$$

where the content of CB and P are represented as vectors $\vec{CB} = <W_{CB_1}, \ldots, W_{CB_n}>$ and $\vec{P} = <W_{P_1}, \ldots, W_{P_n}>$, respectively, n is the number of distinct non-stop, stemmed keywords in the brief descriptions of CB and each book in P, and W_{P_i} and W_{CB_i} are the *weights* of keywords P_i and CB_i, respectively, which are calculated using Equations 4 and 5 such that the frequency distributions of words in $\vec{CB}$ and $\vec{P}$ are determined based on the frequency distributions of non-stop, stemmed words among the brief descriptions of CB and all the books in P, respectively.

$$W_{CB_i} = \begin{cases} \frac{f_{CB_i, CB}}{max_{CB_j \in CB}(f_{CB_j, CB})} & \text{if } CB_i \in CB \\ \frac{\sum_{c \in HS_{P_{B_i}}} f_{c, CB}}{|HS_{P_{B_i}}|} & \text{otherwise} \end{cases} \quad (4)$$

[8] cs.technion.ac.il/~gabr/resources/data/wordsim353/
[9] goo.gl/KzMHgn
[10] Available at grid.deid.unical.it/similarity

$$W_{P_i} = \begin{cases} \frac{f_{P_i,P}}{max_{P_i \in P}(f_{P_i,P})} & \text{if } P_i \in P \\ \frac{\sum_{c \in HS_{CB_i}} f_{c,P}}{|HS_{CB_i}|} & \text{otherwise} \end{cases} \quad (5)$$

where $|HS_w|$ is the size of HS_w, $f_{w,D}$ is the *frequency of occurrence* of w in D, and HS_w is the set of words that are *highly similar* to, but not the same as, a given word w in the brief description D of either CB or P. (A word is highly similar if it is included in a reduced WCF matrix [12].)

5.2.3 Examining Appeal-Term Descriptions

Rabbit also examines the appeal elements of books preferred by R and captures the *overall degree of resemblance* between the appeal-term description of CB and (each book in) the profile P of R, which are generated using ABET. In calculating $ATSim(CB, P)$, the *appeal-term similarity* score of CB with respect to P, Rabbit adopts the cosine measure as defined in Equation 6.

$$ATSim(CB, P) = \frac{\sum_{f \in F} \frac{\vec{CB_f} \cdot \vec{P_f}}{||\vec{CB_f}|| \times ||\vec{P_f}||}}{|F|} \quad (6)$$

where F is the set of appeal factors in the appeal-term descriptions for CB and P, $|F|$ is the size of F, $\vec{CB_f}$ and $\vec{P_f}$ are the n-dimensional vector representations of the appeal-term distribution of an appeal factor f for CB and P, respectively, n is the number of distinct appeal terms in the distributions of the corresponding appeal factor for CB and P, $W_{CB_{f_i}} = \frac{freq_{i,CB_f}}{\max_{i \in CB_f} freq_{i,CB_f}}$ is the *weight* of the ith $(1 \leq i \leq n)$ term in $\vec{CB_f}$, and $W_{P_{f_i}} = \frac{\sum_{P_B \in P} freq_{i,P_{B_f}}}{\max_{i \in P_f} \sum_{P_B \in P} freq_{i,P_{B_f}}}$ is the *weight* of the ith term in P_f.

5.3 Ranking Candidate Books

To predict the ranking score of CB, Rabbit employs multiple linear regression, which is a statistical technique for building estimation models that accounts for the influence of multiple contributing factors, i.e., the topical, content, and appeal-term descriptions of CB in our case. The top-10 ranked books are recommended to R.

$$Y = \beta_0 + \beta_1 X_1 + \beta_2 X_2 + \ldots + \beta_n X_n \quad (7)$$

where Y is the dependent variable, i.e., ranking score of CB, β_0 is the intercept parameter, $\beta_1, \ldots, \beta_n$ are the coefficients of regression, $X_1, \ldots X_n$ are the independent variables (predictors), i.e., the scores defined in Section 5.2 for CB, and n is the number of predictors in the regression analysis.

In Equation 7, the intercept and coefficients of regression are estimated through a one-time training process using the Ordinary Least Squares method and the $Tset$ dataset (introduced in Section 6.2.1). $Tset$ consists of 1,663 instances, each of which is a book B that is either a relevant or non-relevant recommendation for a given reader R. Each instance is represented as a vector of the form $< B_1, B_2, B_3, rel_R >$, where B_i is the (value of the) i^{th} $(1 \leq i \leq 3)$ predictor computed for B, and rel_R is the target, which is "1" if B is a relevant recommendation for R, and is "0" otherwise.

6. EXPERIMENTAL RESULTS

In this section, we present the results of the empirical studies conducted to assess the performance of ABET and Rabbit. To perform these studies, we relied on a number of sample sets of books, i.e., SB_1 and SB_2. (Due to space constraints, we posted the sample sets under goo.gl/PWE9u2)

6.1 Assessing the Performance of ABET

Due to the lack of existing benchmark datasets for validating the performance of tools that automatically extract appeal factor-appeal term pairs, we have assessed the performance of ABET by (i) computing the precision and recall of appeal factor-appeal term pairs extracted from book reviews, (ii) analyzing the correctness of appeal-term descriptions created by ABET, and (iii) comparing appeal-term descriptions generated by ABET with respect to the ones extracted from NoveList on the same set of books.

We randomly selected a set of 100 books written for K-12 readers, and for each book we randomly examined a review. We *manually annotated* the appeal factor-appeal term pairs in each of the 100 examined reviews and compared the annotated pairs in each review with the ones extracted by ABET. The precision, recall, and F-measure achieved by ABET, which are 0.85, 0.82, and 0.83, respectively, verify the high accuracy of the rules defined for ABET in identifying appeal factors and their corresponding appeal terms in reviews. We have observed that majority of the pairs excluded by ABET were due to keywords used by reviewers to describe a given factor which are not included in the pre-constructed vocabulary of the corresponding factor defined for ABET (as described in Section 4). We have also observed that poor phrasing in reviews, which in turn yields nonsensical grammatical relations between pairs of words, and improper anaphora resolution in ABET have caused the majority of the extraction errors.

To further evaluate the appeal-term descriptions created by ABET, we relied on SB_1, a sample set of *eight books*, and conducted two surveys on Amazon Mechanical Turk.

In both surveys, we asked appraisers to select the keywords, i.e., appeal terms, that best describe each appeal factor for one of the books in SB_1. While the first survey includes the appeal terms considered by ABET for each appeal factor as the corresponding possible keyword choices, the second survey contains appeal terms defined by either ABET or NoveList. In the two surveys, we treated the appeal terms selected for each factor by appraisers as the "gold standard" for the factor and computed the accuracy of ABET (NoveList, respectively) based on the proportion of terms in the gold standard of a given factor defined by appraisers which match its counterpart identified by ABET (NoveList, respectively) for the factor. We relied on Mechanical Turk, since it is a "marketplace for work that requires human intelligence" that allows individuals/businesses to programmatically access thousands of diverse workers and has been used in the past to collect user feedback for information retrieval tasks [7]. Furthermore, we considered NoveList for the comparison purpose, since NoveList is a premier database for RA [3] and, to the best of our knowledge, is the only RA database that includes appeal-term descriptions for books.

As shown in Figure 2, based on the 200 responses collected in September 2013, ABET achieves an overall 94% accuracy in identifying appeal terms (in reviews) that describe a book. More importantly, the accuracy on the identified appeal terms for each appeal factor considered by ABET is in the upper eighty percentile or higher. Figure 3, on the other hand, shows the accuracy ratios of ABET and Nov-

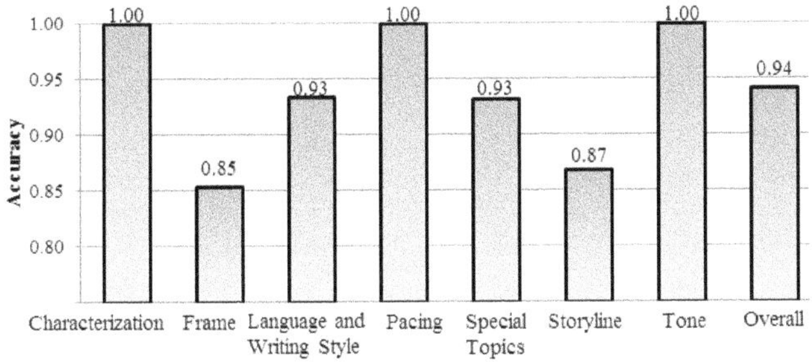

Figure 2: Performance evaluation of ABET conducted using Amazon Mechanical Turk

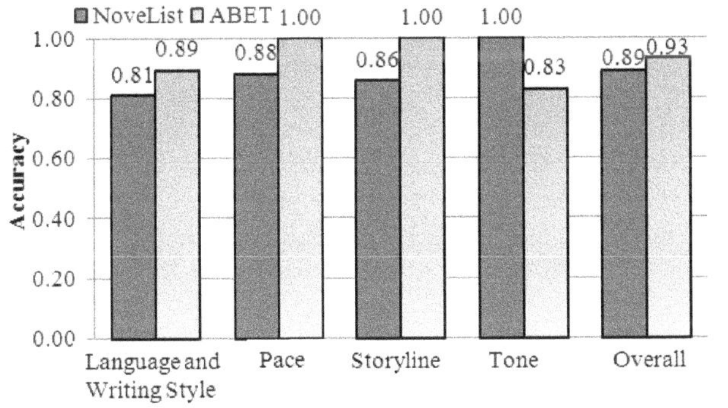

Figure 3: Performance evaluation of ABET and NoveList using Amazon Mechanical Turk

eList calculated using the 200 responses provided by Mechanical Turk appraisers for the second survey. NoveList describes books using only four appeal factors, as opposed to the seven considered by ABET. For this reason, we have compared the performance of ABET and NoveList based on their common appeal factors (as shown in Figure 3). Based on the appraisers' assessments, we claim that appeal-term descriptions provided by ABET are favoured over the ones defined by professionals who maintain the RA database at NoveList. Note that the improvement in overall accuracy ratio achieved by ABET over NoveList, in addition to the improvement on "Language and Writing Style", "Pacing" and "Storyline" factors, are statistically significant ($p < 0.01$).

6.2 Assessing the Performance of Rabbit

In this section, we discuss the empirical studies conducted to assess the design and performance of Rabbit.

6.2.1 Dataset and Evaluation Strategy

Even though BookCrossing[11] has been employed to evaluate book recommenders tailored to a general audience, it is not specifically designed for assessing the performance of recommenders for K-12 readers. We used data provided by BiblioNasium, which is a secure social networking site on books that targets children and teenagers, to evaluate Rabbit instead. The dataset consists of books that have been bookmarked by each one of the 5,580 BiblioNasium users who joined the site within the first four months of its establishment. A portion of the dataset, called *Tset*, which consists of 10% of the 5,580 users and their profiles, was employed for training Rabbit's regression model, whereas the remaining users and their profiles, called *Eset*, were used for evaluation purposes. The design methodology of Rabbit relies on *topical*, *brief content*, and *appeal-term* descriptions, in addition to the predicted grade levels of books. Thus, we retrieved the brief book descriptions and LCSH from reputable book-related websites, the appeal-term descriptions from book reviews using ABET, and the book readability levels using TRoLL.

We adopt the popular 5-fold cross validation strategy to evaluate recommenders. Since only withheld books are considered relevant, it is not possible to account for potentially relevant books a user has not bookmarked, a well-known limitation of this evaluation protocol. As the limitation applies to all the recommenders evaluated in the empirical studies, the results are consistent for the comparison purpose.

[11]Informatik.unifreiburg.de/~cziegler/BX

6.2.2 The Performance Evaluation of Rabbit

We assessed the performance of Rabbit using *Eset* in terms of *Normalized Discounted Cumulative Gain* (nDCG), which determines the overall (ranking) performance of a recommender and penalizes relevant recommendation positioned lower in the recommendation list. We observed that ranking candidate books solely based on *appeal factors* or *topical information* yields the lowest nDCG scores, i.e., 0.19 and 0.18, respectively This is anticipated, since LCSH and appeal-term descriptions mainly identify the types of books preferred by a reader R from a general perspective. Even though the content-based approach yields a relatively high nDCG score (i.e., 0.24), the experimental results show that the multi-dimensional strategy of Rabbit, of which content-based analysis is a component, locates more relevant books, which is justified by the statistically significant improvement in nDCG (i.e., 0.32) generated by the latter ($p < 0.001$).

Linearly combining different similarity scores considered by Rabbit yields a lower nDCG value (i.e., 0.27) than the one obtained by using the regression model, which is statistically significant ($p < 0.001$). The results validate the necessity of accounting for the impact, i.e., weight, of each individual similarity score. Furthermore, we have verified that bypassing the candidate selection step would have a *negative* impact on the overall performance of Rabbit, since recommending books that only match the interests or general traits of books preferred by a reader R, without considering R's readability level, increases the number of non-relevant suggestions (as demonstrated by the 0.19 nDCG achieved by Rabbit if no candidate selection step is applied.)

6.2.3 Rabbit versus BReK12

We also compared the performance of Rabbit with BReK12 (as introduced in Section 2). We perform the comparison, since to the best of our knowledge BReK12 is the only available recommender that explicitly considers the readability level of its users in making personalized book recommendations. Furthermore, other state-of-the-art approaches for (book) recommendations are excluded for the comparison purpose using *Eset*, since they require either *personal ratings* on books provided by individual users or *social connections* established by social bookmarking site users, neither are available on social websites for K-12 readers nor in the *Eset* dataset. Rabbit achieves a statistically significant improvement ($p < 0.001$) over BReK12 in terms of nDCG, which are 0.32 and 0.18, respectively.

6.2.4 Rabbit versus Other Recommendation Modules

To further validate the performance of Rabbit, we conducted a survey using Mechanical Turk on 10 sample books in another test set SB_2, which evaluated the degree to which books recommended by Rabbit are preferred over those suggested by recommendation modules at well-known book-related websites. We have selected recommenders that adopt diverse strategies in making suggestions: (i) Amazon, which considers purchasing patterns of its users [8], GoodReads,[12] which combines multiple proprietary algorithms to "analyze 20 billion data points," and (iii) NoveList,[13] which examines book-related information, including title, publication date, and appeal factors for recommending books.

Each survey included the top-2 (for which some of them can be identical) recommendations made by the aforementioned recommenders for a given sample book Bk. Appraisers were asked to select, to the best of their knowledge, the top-two books most closely related to Bk, which were treated as the *gold standard* for Bk. Based on the 500 responses collected during November 2013, we computed the accuracy of the top-2 recommendations made by Amazon, GoodReads, NoveList, and Rabbit, which are 0.50, 0.18, 0.24, and 0.44, respectively. Recommendations made by Rabbit and Amazon are preferred over the suggestions made by GoodReads and NoveList. Furthermore, the improvement, in terms of accuracy ratios, achieved by Rabbit over GoodReads and NoveList is statistically significant ($p < 0.001$). In terms of the overall accuracy, Amazon outperforms Rabbit. However, their differences in nDCG are not statistically significant ($p < 0.001$).

Rabbit can make suggestions regardless of the number of books of interest to R. It differs from the recommendation modules employed at Amazon and NoveList, since the latter can only examine books of interest to a user one at the time. Rabbit is also different from GoodReads, since GoodReads processes either a given book or the entire profile of a user. Furthermore, Rabbit can treat a book as a candidate suggestion immediately after the book is published, whereas Amazon requires the existence of a number of purchasing transactions involving the new book in order to suggest it to a user. In addition, in making recommendations for children and teenagers, Rabbit considers books provided directly by K-12 readers to generate personalized suggestions. Recommendations generated by Amazon that target children and teenagers, on the other hand, are the result of extensive analysis of the purchasing patterns of adults.

7. CONCLUSIONS

We have introduced Rabbit, a recommender which makes personalized suggestions on books that match the *interests* and *reading abilities* of its K-12 users. Rabbit emulates the readers' advisory process offered at public/school libraries to recommend books that are similar in *contents*, *topics*, and *literary elements* of other books appealing to a reader, with the latter based on extracted appeal-term descriptions.

Rabbit can be a stand-alone tool used by readers (educators/parents, respectively) or adopted by (K-12) social bookmarking sites for providing suitable reading selections. Even though we have developed Rabbit with K-12 readers in mind, the readers' advisory-based methodology of Rabbit can also be used to suggest books for adults (with reading levels below/above the 12th grade level) as well.

The results of the conducted experiments have (i) validated the correctness of the design methodology of Rabbit and (ii) demonstrated the superiority of Rabbit over other recommenders that either explicitly consider or ignore the reading ability of its users by using data from BiblioNasium and Mechanical Turk appraisers.

[12]goo.gl/99me5f

[13]support.epnet.com/knowledge_base/detail.php?id=4772

8. REFERENCES

[1] R. Benjamin. Reconstructing Readability: Recent Developments and Recommendations in the Analysis of Text Difficulty. *Ed. Psych. Review*, 24:63–88, 2012.

[2] C. Coulter and M. Smith. The Construction Zone: Literary Elements in Narrative Research. *Educational Researcher*, 38(8):577–590, 2009.

[3] A. Cox and K. Horne. Fast-Paced, Romantic, Set in Savannah: A Comparison of Results from Readers' Advisory Databases in the Public Library. *Public Library Quarterly*, 31(4):285–302, 2012.

[4] S. Givon and V. Lavrenko. Predicting Social-Tags for Cold Start Book Recommendations. In *ACM RecSys*, pages 333–336, 2009.

[5] N. Hollands. Improving the Model for Interactive Readers' Advisory Service. *Reference & User Services Quarterly*, 45(3):205–212, 2006.

[6] J. Koberstein and Y.-K. Ng. Using Word Clusters to Detect Similar Web Documents. In *KSEM*, pages 215–228, 2006.

[7] M. Koolen, J. Kamps, and G. Kazai. Social Book Search: Comparing Topical Relevance Judgments and Book Suggestions for Evaluation. In *ACM CIKM*, pages 185–194, 2012.

[8] G. Linden, B. Smith, and J. York. Amazon.com Recommendations: Item-to-Item Collaborative Filtering. *IEEE Internet Computing*, 7(1):76–80, 2003.

[9] N. Manouselis, H. Drachsler, K. Verbert, and E. Duval. *Recommender Systems for Learning.* Springer Briefs in Electr. and Comp. Eng., 2013.

[10] J. Oakhill and K. Cain. The Precursors of Reading Ability in Young Readers: Evidence From a Four-Year Longitudinal Study. *SSR*, 16(2):91–121, 2012.

[11] B. Pang and L. Lee. Opinion Mining and Sentiment Analysis. *FTIR*, 2(1-2):1–135, 2008.

[12] M. Pera. *Using Online Data Sources to Make Recommendations on Reading Materials for K-12 and Advanced Readers.* PhD thesis, BYU, April 2014.

[13] G. Pirro and J. Euzenat. A Feature and Information Theoretic Framework for Semantic Similarity and Relatedness. In *ISWC*, pages 615–630, 2010.

[14] J. Saricks. *Readers' Advisory Service in the Public Library*, 3rd *Ed.* ALA Store, 2005.

[15] R. Shaban. A Guide to Writing Book Reviews. *JEPHC*, 4(3):Article 11, 2006.

[16] A. Sieg, B. Mobasher, and R. Burke. Improving the Effectiveness of Collaborative Recommendation with Ontology-based User Profiles. In *ACM HetRec*, pages 39–46, 2010.

[17] C. Yang, B. Wei, J. Wu, Y. Zhang, and L. Zhang. CARES: a Ranking-oriented CADAL Recommender System. In *ACM/IEEE JCDL*, pages 203–212, 2009.

Exploiting Sentiment Homophily for Link Prediction

Guangchao Yuan Pradeep K. Murukannaiah Zhe Zhang Munindar P. Singh
North Carolina State University, Raleigh, NC, USA
{gyuan,pmuruka,zzhang13,singh}@ncsu.edu

ABSTRACT

Link prediction on social media is an important problem for recommendation systems. Understanding the interplay of users' sentiments and social relationships can be potentially valuable. Specifically, we study how to exploit sentiment homophily for link prediction. We evaluate our approach on a dataset gathered from Twitter that consists of tweets sent in one month during U.S. 2012 political campaign along with the "follows" relationship between users. Our first contribution is defining a set of sentiment-based features that help predict the likelihood of two users becoming "friends" (i.e., mutually mentioning or following each other) based on their sentiments toward topics of mutual interest. Our evaluation in a supervised learning framework demonstrates the benefits of sentiment-based features in link prediction. We find that Adamic-Adar and Euclidean distance measures are the best predictors. Our second contribution is proposing a factor graph model that incorporates a sentiment-based variant of cognitive balance theory. Our evaluation shows that, when tie strength is not too weak, our model is more effective in link prediction than traditional machine learning techniques.

Categories and Subject Descriptors

H.2.8 [**Information Systems**]: Database Applications—*Data mining*; J.4 [**Computer Applications**]: Social and Behavioral Sciences—*Sociology*

General Terms

Algorithms, Experimentation

Keywords

Social media; Social networks; Link prediction; Sentiment analysis; Topic affiliation

RecSys'14, October 6–10, 2014, Foster City, Silicon Valley, CA, USA.

http://dx.doi.org/10.1145/2645710.2645734.

1. INTRODUCTION

Link prediction refers to inferring potential relationships from a snapshot of a social network. A common intuition behind link prediction approaches is the presence of *homophily* in networks—similarity breeds connections [25]. Existing works derive similarities among users from network topology [21] (structural similarity), and users' interests [30] and geography [29] (semantic similarity).

However, structurally or semantically similar users may express different sentiments toward a common characteristic. Thelwall [33] found some evidence of both positive and negative sentiment homophily among MySpace friends. We posit that there exists a *sentiment homophily* in networks—similarity in users' sentiments breeds connection. Sentiment can be an important trait for link prediction because of its application in different domains such as political election prediction [9], location recommendation [37], and event detection [34].

Romero et al. [28] found that topics of interest to users can predict social relationships. For example, two users interested in the topic "Obama for President" are likely to be friends. However, the two users may exhibit the same (both support or oppose Obama) or contradictory sentiments (one supports and the other opposes Obama) toward the topic. Motivated by sentiment homophily, we imagine that the two users are more likely to become friends in the former case than in the latter. Based on the above intuition, we ask two questions:

- How may we exploit sentiments for link prediction?
- Can sentiment homophily help in link prediction?

Two challenges arise when answering the first question. First, how can we design sentiment-based features between two users in order to quantify sentiment homophily? Unlike features such as number of common friends, age, number of common places, designing sentiment features is much more complex because interpreting the sentiment of a tweet depends upon its domain and topic.

Second, employing traditional machine learning techniques (e.g., logistic regression) for link prediction assumes independence among pairs of nodes in a network, i.e., whether A–B is connected is independent of other connected pairs. However, such a case seldom exists in the real world. Heider [16] proposed cognitive balance theory in social psychology suggesting that if strong ties A–B and A–C exist, the likelihood of B–C becoming a tie (whether weak or strong) increases because of the "psychological strain": C will want to maintain his or her own feelings to agree with A and A's friend, B. Granovetter claimed that the B–C tie is always present in this case. The strength of a tie can be "a combination of the amount of time, the emotional intensity, the intimacy, and the reciprocal services" [11]. Therefore, we hypothesize that it is nontrivial to capture dependence between pairs of nodes (e.g., A–B and A–C ties predicting the B–C tie) via a machine learning technique. If sentiment homophily exists, can we leverage such homophily to quantify the strength of a tie? Will the sentiment-based cognitive balance theory help in link prediction? How to build such a model and how to define the strength of a tie through sentiments are our second challenge.

We employ a dataset of political tweets (and associated users) to address the second question. We extract users' sentiments toward different topics from their tweets, where sentiments are modeled as numeric scores and categorical values. Further, we design several sentiment-based features, and evaluate the effect of sentiment homophily in a supervised setting on two social networks: the mutual-follow graph and the graph formed by users referring to each other using "@" mentions (Section 4). We find that sentiment-based features improve the performance of link prediction in terms of the F_1 score on both networks. We also investigate each sentiment-based feature and find that sentiment features based on the Adamic-Adar and Euclidean distance measures are the best predictors (Section 6.1).

We further propose a factor graph model based on Dong et al. [10], incorporating Heider's cognitive balance theory, where the strength of ties is defined based on sentiment-based features (Section 5). Our model outperforms the other two well-known classifiers (logistic regression and random forest) in the mutual-follow graph and in mention graphs where the strength of ties is not too weak (number of mentions exceeds three) (Section 6.2).

Although our analyses focus on Twitter, we conjecture that our approach can extend to a broad setting involving online information sharing, e.g., for restaurant or movie recommendations.

Contributions

Sentiment-based features. We define features that quantify the likelihood of two users becoming friends based on their sentiments toward topics of mutual interest. We evaluate the potential benefits of each feature.

Graphical model. We propose a model that incorporates the sentiment-based cognitive balance theory for link prediction. Our evaluation suggests that our model yields improved the performance (F_1 score) of link prediction when compared to traditional machine learning models.

2. DATA AND OBSERVATIONS

To obtain a dataset involving strong sentiments, we crawled Twitter during U.S. 2012 political campaign (from March 23 to April 23 in 2012) using the keywords "Obama" and "Romney." We preprocessed the dataset by first removing tweets that contain more than 10 hashtags. Because Twitter limits 140 characters in one tweet, a tweet containing too many hashtags is likely to be spam [18]. In addition, we treat users with less than five tweets as "inactive" and exclude them. The resulting dataset contains $3,970,974$ tweets from $123,073$ distinct user accounts.

Topics. A Twitter hashtag [35] is a string beginning with "#", which is viewed as a topic marker in the tweet. Typically, users adopt the same hashtag to discuss a particular topic. Thus, we use hashtags to represent different topics.

Graphs. We investigate two kinds of undirected graphs: the mention graph and the mutual-follow graph. The mention graph is based on "@" mentions: whether a retweet, a reply, or direct reference to a user. If two users mention each other more often than a certain threshold, we create an edge in their mention graph (we experiment with multiple thresholds). In the mutual-follow graph, we create an edge between two users if they follow each other.

2.1 Sentiment Extraction

We use an established sentiment lexicon, SentiWordNet [3], to obtain the sentiment scores of all tweets. SentiWordNet contains three real-valued scores for each word in its lexicon indicating *positivity*, *negativity*, and *objectivity*; the sum of the three scores is one. In addition, we extract emoticons from tweets and estimate the three sentiment scores of each emoticon. Agarwal et al. [2] provide a list of emoticons and categorize them into five categories: *extremely positive*, *positive*, *neutral*, *negative*, and *extremely negative*. We assign the sentiment scores to each category as triples of positivity, objectivity, and negativity scores, respectively, $\langle 1,0,0\rangle$, $\langle 3/4,0,0\rangle$, $\langle 0,1,0\rangle$, $\langle 0,0,3/4\rangle$, and $\langle 0,0,1\rangle$.

We adapt the major methods described by Bakliwal [5] to compute the sentiment score of a tweet. First, we choose only the adjectives in the lexicon and extract their stems [27] to build a pairwise stem-score mapping dictionary. We consider only adjectives because adjectives are strong indicators of sentiment [15] and can improve sentiment prediction accuracy [5]. Second, we use the Twitter part-of-speech tagger to extract the adjectives and emoticons in a tweet. Third, we handle the negation pattern through the Stanford parser [8], which contains a dependency schema (*neg*) to indicate negation. We reverse the sentiment polarity for each word marked in a *neg* schema. Finally, we obtain the positivity and negativity scores of a tweet by averaging the two scores for each adjective and emoticon; The objectivity score of the tweet is one minus the two polar scores.

2.2 Observations on the Data

As a sanity check on our intuition about sentiment homophily in the graphs we consider, we first determine the probability of two users sharing a same sentiment toward a topic of mutual interest, conditioned on whether they are connected.

We construct a mention graph choosing the threshold of mentions as three. That is, two users are connected if they mention each other at least three times. From the mutual-follow graph, we randomly choose a subgraph with 175 users and their friends. A pair of users is connected if there is an edge between them. For each graph, we construct pairs of unconnected users, whose number is identical to the number of connected pairs in the same graph. We choose the six most frequent topics (hashtags) in our dataset, and we want to compare the probability of two connected users sharing a sentiment with that of two unconnected users.

As Figure 1 shows, the probability of sharing a sentiment is 6% higher, on average, for connected users than unconnected users in the mention graph. In the mutual-follow graph (Figure 2), the mean difference in probability between connected and unconnected users is 4%, but the difference varies across topics. The probability difference is

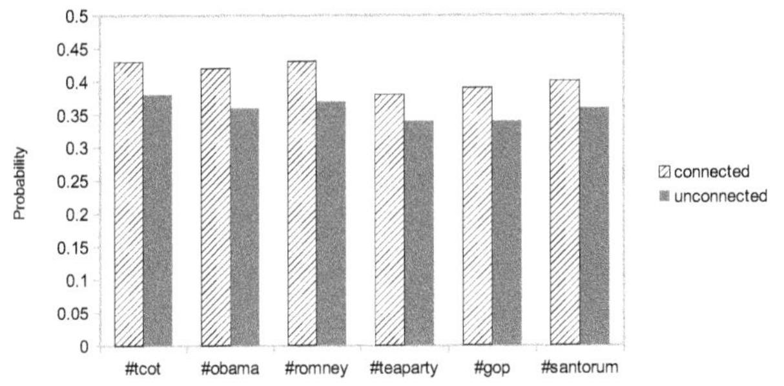

Figure 1: Probability of two users in the mention graph sharing a sentiment toward the six most frequent topics.

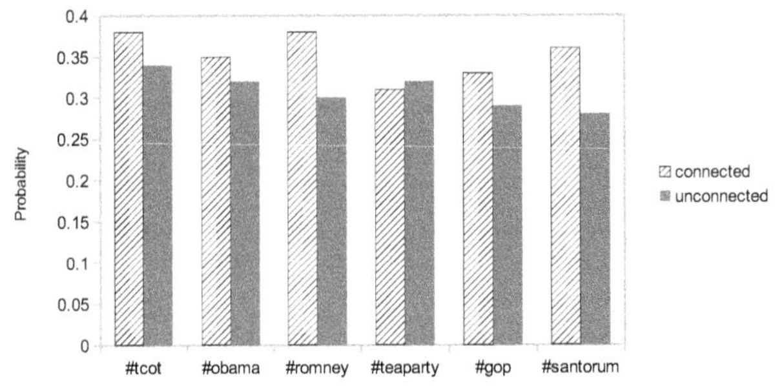

Figure 2: Probability of two users in the mutual-follow graph sharing a sentiment toward the six most frequent topics.

pronounced for "#romney" and "#santorum" (8%), whereas the difference is −1% for "#teaparty". These observations support our intuition that sentiments and connections are correlated.

3. PROBLEM DEFINITION

Let $G(V, E)$ be a social network, where V is the set of users and E is the social relationship between the users. For a given node v_s and a candidate set $C = \{v_1, v_2, \ldots, v_{|C|}\}$, our goal is to predict whether there is a link between v_s and v_i ($v_i \in C$). Specifically, the task is to find a predictive function for v_s such that: $Y = f(G, v_s, C)$, where $Y = \{y_{si}|v_i \in C\}$ is a vector of inferred results; i.e., $y_{si} = p(1|G, v_s, C)$ represents the probability that v_s will create a link with v_i.

To do so, we take two steps. First we generate a candidate set for a source node v_s as described next. Second, we learn a predictive function by defining prediction features (Section 4) and applying a factor graph model incorporating cognitive balance theory (Section 5).

3.1 Candidate Generation

For each source node v_s, we choose its two-hop neighborhood as its candidate set: friends and friends of friends. We choose the two-hop neighborhood as the candidate set because (1) the number of candidates increases exponentially with the number of hops [22]; (2) the number formed friendships decays exponentially with the number of hops [20].

We model our problem as a classification problem, where friends are positive instances and friends of friends are negative instances. We assign half of the source nodes into a training set and half into a test set. We measure F_1 scores to validate our recommendations with respect to the existing friends of v_s in the test set.

We can derive the potential friends of v_s from its friends of friends and then make recommendations based on ranked probabilities of links between v_s and its friends of friends. However, measuring the validity of such recommendations requires that we train a model from candidates at one time instance and test for candidates at a future time instance. Since our dataset does not have information about when the links were formed, such an evaluation is out of our scope.

4. PREDICTION FEATURES

With the development of online information sharing, the coevolution of social and affiliation networks is gaining attention, e.g., [38]. We consider a user as *affiliating* with a topic if the user evinces interest in it, and we call the affiliation *topical affiliation*. On Twitter, topical affiliation happens when a user includes a hashtag in his or her tweet.

Combining sentiment analysis of users' messages and topical affiliation, we call such an affiliation the *topic-sentiment affiliation*. That is, a user affiliates with a set of topics, and associates a sentiment with each topic. We now describe how a user's topic-sentiment affiliation can help link prediction by describing our prediction features.

We consider three kinds of features: sentiment, structural, and topical. Sentiment features are extracted from topic-sentiment affiliation; structural features are based on the graph-based similarity between two users; topical features are based on the topical affiliation of two users, measuring the similarity in their usage of topics. The sentiment features are our contribution whereas the other two categories serve as baseline predictors.

4.1 Topic-Sentiment Affiliation Construction

We compute each tweet's positivity, negativity, and objectivity scores using the methods of Section 2.1. If a user mentions a hashtag in one of his or her tweets, we affiliate him with the topic-sentiment pair; if a user mentions the same hashtag in several tweets, we take the mean of the three scores of these tweets. We further adopt the *sentiment-volume-objectivity* (SVO) function [13] to measure the aggregate effect of a user's level of interest and his or her sentiment scores toward a topic. The SVO score is a real value between 0 and 1 that incorporates three elements: polar sentiment (positivity or negativity), number of times a user mentions a topic, and objectivity. Therefore, the sentiment in the affiliation system consists of four numeric scores: positivity, negativity, objectivity, and the SVO score. In this way, we obtain a topic-sentiment affiliation for each user from his or her tweets.

4.2 Sentiment Features

We use the difference between the positivity and negativity scores to decide a user's categorical sentiment toward a hashtag. The opinion is positive (negative) if the difference is greater (less) than zero; otherwise, the opinion is objective. In addition, the *size* of a hashtag is the number of users who have adopted it. We adopt the following notation:

- Let v_1, v_2, ..., v_N be N users.
- Let h_1, h_2, ..., h_M be M hashtags.

- Let P_i, N_i, O_i be user v_i's adopted hashtags set with positive, negative, objective sentiments, respectively.
- Let $\overline{P_j}$, $\overline{N_j}$, $\overline{O_j}$ be the set of users who expressed positive, negative, objective sentiments in a hashtag h_j, respectively.
- Let $H_i = P_i \cup N_i \cup O_i$
- Let $U(h_j) = \overline{P_j} \cup \overline{N_j} \cup \overline{O_j}$
- Let $s_i(h_j)$ be user v_i's SVO score toward hashtag h_j.

Given two users v_s and v_t, we divide sentiment features into the following seven categories:

1. **The number of hashtags for which they have the same sentiments.**
   - SENTIMENT-AGREEMENT: $|P_s \cap P_t| + |N_s \cap N_t| + |O_s \cap O_t|$
2. **Sentiment alignment coefficient**: among the common hashtags, the number that involve the same or opposite polar sentiments.
   - SENTIMENT-ALIGNED: $(|P_s \cap P_t| + |N_s \cap N_t|)/|H_s \cap H_t|$
   - SENTIMENT-MISALIGNED: $(|P_s \cap N_t| + |N_s \cap P_t|)/|H_s \cap H_t|$
3. **Size of the rarest common hashtags**: among the hashtags for which the users share polar sentiments, the one that is the least adopted by all of them.
   - SENTIMENT-RAREST: $\min(\min_{h_j \in P_s \cap P_t} |\overline{P_j}|, \min_{h_j \in N_s \cap N_t} |\overline{N_j}|)$
4. **Adamic-Adar**: sum of the Adamic-Adar distances for each hashtag set affiliated with the three opinions.
   - SENTIMENT-AA: $\sum_{h_j \in P_s \cap P_t} 1/\log|\overline{P_j}| + \sum_{h_j \in N_s \cap N_t} 1/\log|\overline{N_j}| + \sum_{h_j \in O_s \cap O_t} 1/\log|\overline{O_j}|$
5. **Sum of inverse size.**
   - SENTIMENT-INVERSE: $\sum_{h_j \in P_s \cap P_t} 1/|\overline{P_j}| + \sum_{h_j \in N_s \cap N_t} 1/|\overline{N_j}| + \sum_{h_j \in O_s \cap O_t} 1/|\overline{O_j}|$
6. **Mean size of common hashtags for which they share the same sentiment.**
   - SENTIMENT-MEAN: $\frac{1}{\text{SENTIMENT-AGREEMENT}} \times (\sum_{h_j \in P_s \cap P_t} |\overline{P_j}| + \sum_{h_j \in N_s \cap N_t} |\overline{N_j}| + \sum_{h_j \in O_s \cap O_t} |\overline{O_j}|)$
7. **Topic-SVO distance.**
   - EUCLIDEAN: $\sqrt{\sum_{h_j \in H_s \cap H_t} (s_s(h_j) - s_t(h_j))^2}$
   - COSINE: $d_s d_t / \|d_s\| \|d_t\|$, where d_s and d_t are the SVO score vectors for common hashtags

4.3 Structural Features

These features are based on graph structure without considering semantic information. We choose four predictors introduced by Liben-Nowell et al. [21].

1. Number of common neighbors (CN) between two users.
2. Jaccard's coefficient (JC): CN divided by the total number of neighbors.
3. Adamic-Adar (STRUCTURAL-AA) [1]: weighting the importance of a common neighbor by the degree of the neighbor.
4. Preferential attachment (PA): the product of two users' degrees.

4.4 Topical Features

These features, introduced by Romero et al. [28], are baseline predictors in our study.

1. The number of common hashtags (COMMON): $|H_s \cap H_t|$
2. Size of the smallest common hashtag (SMALLEST): $\min_{h_j \in H_s \cap H_t} |U(h_j)|$
3. Adamic-Adar distance (TOPICAL-AA): $\sum_{h_j \in H_s \cap H_t} 1/\log|U(h_j)|$
4. Sum of inverse sizes (INVERSE): $\sum_{h_j \in H_s \cap H_t} 1/|U(h_j)|$
5. Mean size of common hashtags (MEAN): $\frac{1}{|H_s \cap H_t|} \sum_{h_j \in H_s \cap H_t} |U(h_j)|$

5. PROPOSED MODEL: TSAM

To investigate how to better exploit sentiments for link prediction, we propose a topic-sentiment affiliation based graphical model (TSAM). The motivation underlying TSAM arises from cognitive balance theory: if A–B and A–C are strong ties, then these two links are not independent because B–C is likely to be present. We seek (1) a way of building such relationships where the strength of a tie incorporates sentiment and (2) to study whether this sentiment-based cognitive balance theory could improve link prediction.

A TSAM model is an undirected graph $\mathcal{G}(\mathcal{V}, \mathcal{E})$, where $\mathcal{V}$ represents the set of variables and $\mathcal{E}$ is the set of edges in the graphical model. Below, *variables* and *edges* refer to entities in TSAM, and *nodes* and *links* refer to entities in the social network.

We now describe how we build a TSAM model $\mathcal{G}(\mathcal{V}, \mathcal{E})$ by representing links and their relationships in a social network $G(V, E)$. Given the social network $G(V, E)$, a source node v_s and its candidate set $C = \{v_1, v_2, \ldots, v_{|C|}\}$, link prediction seeks to infer the probability y_{si} that v_s will create a link with v_i. Thus, we treat y_{si} as a variable (hidden) and the relationships between such variables as edges $\mathcal{E}$ in the TSAM model.

There is an edge between any two hidden variables if they contain the same source node v_s. Thus, for each source node, there is a clique in the TSAM model. For each hidden variable, an observed variable is connected with it, representing a vector of features associated with the hidden variable.

For example, suppose v_s has five candidates: $\{v_1, v_2\}$, its one-hop friends, and $\{v_3, v_4, v_5\}$, its friends of friends. The resulting TSAM model of Figure 3 has five hidden variables $\{y_{s1}, \cdots, y_{s5}\}$ and five observed variables $\{x_{s1}, \cdots, x_{s5}\}$.

Even though the figure only shows the factor graph for one source node, our model captures a scenario with multiple source nodes. Correspondingly, a TSAM model with multiple source nodes is composed of multiple disconnected components, where all the hidden variables in one component form a clique.

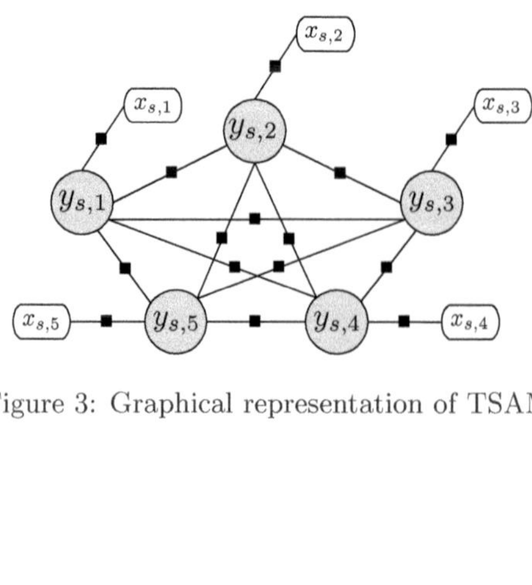

Figure 3: Graphical representation of TSAM.

Let T represent the set of indices for any link between a source node and one of its candidates. Then $Y = \{y_t | t \in T\}$ and $X = \{x_t | t \in T\}$ denote the set of hidden and observed variables in the TSAM model, respectively.

The graph can be modeled as a conditional random field [19] that defines a distribution over the graph:

$$P(Y|X) = \frac{1}{Z} \prod_{t \in T} \varphi(y_t, x_t) \prod_{(y_t, y_{t'}) \in \mathcal{E}} \psi(y_t, y_{t'})$$

where Z is a constant that ensures $\sum_Y P(Y|X) = 1$.

The model incorporates two factor functions, which we instantiate by the Hammersley-Clifford theorem [14]. We follow the presentation of Dong et al. [10]: the **attribute factor** models the influence of different features on the hidden variable (link).

$$\varphi(y_t, x_t) = \exp\{\sum_{m=1}^{d} \alpha_m f_m(y_t, x_{t_m})\} \tag{1}$$

where α_m is a weight constant and d is the number of features associated with y_t. We include all the features in Section 4 to build the attribute factor. Second, the **edge factor** encodes the relationships between connected hidden variables.

$$\psi(y_t, y_{t'}) = \exp\{\sum_{n=1}^{k} \beta_n g_n(y_t, y_{t'})\} \tag{2}$$

where β_n is a weight constant and k is the number of features associated with the edge $(y_t, y_{t'})$ in the TSAM model.

We define $g_n(y_t, y_{t'})$ as a binary function. For any two hidden variables y_t and $y_{t'}$, a triad is potentially involved because y_t and $y_{t'}$ contain the same source node. The triad would be cognitively balanced if both y_t and $y_{t'}$ are strong ties. We can use any sentiment feature that satisfies the axioms of Gupte and Eliassi-Rad [12] to define tie strength. Let's take the feature SENTIMENT-AA as an example. Following Hopcroft et al.'s [17] definition of the importance of an user, we select the top 1% edges in the social network $G(V, E)$ in terms of SENTIMENT-AA features as strong ties. Therefore, $g_n(y_t, y_{t'})$ is one when both y_t and $y_{t'}$ are strong ties; otherwise, it is zero.

Accordingly, the log-likelihood objective function is

$$\mathcal{O}(\theta, Y|X) = \log P(Y|X) = \sum_{i \in T} \sum_{m=1}^{d} \alpha_m f_m(y_i, x_{i_m}) +$$

$$\sum_{(i,j) \in \mathcal{E}} \sum_{n=1}^{k} \beta_n g_n(y_i, y_j) - \log Z$$

Here $\theta = (\alpha, \beta)$ is the model (parameter configuration) that we seek to learn to maximize the log-likelihood objective function: $\theta^\star = \arg\max_\theta \mathcal{O}(\theta, Y|X)$.

We adapt the methods in [32] to learn the model except that we conduct experiments in a supervised setting; we use gradient descent to optimize the objective function, where the gradient is approximated by loopy belief propagation [26]. With the estimated model $\theta^\star$, the goal of link prediction is to determine the probabilities of hidden variables that maximize the joint probability $P(Y|X, \theta^\star)$:

$$Y^\star = \arg\max_Y P(Y|X, \theta^\star) \tag{3}$$

6. EXPERIMENTAL EVALUATION

We seek to answer two questions:

- Do sentiment features help in link prediction?
- Does our proposed graphical model incorporating the sentiment-based cognitive balance theory benefit link prediction?

6.1 Sentiment Features Evaluation

Evaluation Strategy. We conduct our experiments using the mention and mutual-follow graphs. For the mention graphs, the number of "@" references between users can be viewed as the strength of a tie. We therefore define several mention graphs by setting different strengths of ties. Table 1 shows the statistics of mention graphs with different thresholds and of the mutual-follow graph.

Table 1: Graph statistics.

Graph	Nodes	Edges	Mean degree
$@ \geq 1$	23,915	53,009	4.43
$@ \geq 2$	8,936	12,978	2.90
$@ \geq 3$	4,770	5,933	2.49
$@ \geq 5$	2,106	2,134	2.03
$@ \geq 7$	1,201	1,100	1.83
$@ \geq 9$	762	639	1.68
Follow	11,239,979	48,572,793	8.64

For each mention graph, we choose all users whose degree is less than 50 as v_s. For the mutual-follow graph, we select users who adopt at least 50 hashtags; additionally, we only select "active" users, with the degree falling within range $[50, 100]$. Then we generate the two-hop candidate set for each source node. A pair is constructed between each source node and any one of its candidates. Doing so leads to the class imbalance being extremely high, a common problem in link prediction [22]. Because we first want to investigate the effect of sentiment features in link prediction, we undersample the negative instances to obtain a balanced dataset. Table 2 shows the number of instances of all the learning datasets after preprocessing.

Table 2: Learning dataset statistics.

Graph	Overall	Positive	Negative
$@ \geq 1$	183,359	78,301	105,058
$@ \geq 2$	46,357	22,087	24,270
$@ \geq 3$	21,816	10,763	11,053
$@ \geq 5$	7,429	3,981	3,448
$@ \geq 7$	3,653	2,094	1,559
$@ \geq 9$	2,064	1,232	832
Follow	11,153	5,193	5,960

We normalize all the features to $[0, 1]$. We apply logistic regression and random forest models from the WEKA framework, and we conduct a 10-fold cross-validation with default parameters. The F_1 score and the Area under the Receiver-Operating-Characteristic Curve (AUC) are two widely used metrics in evaluating performance of classifiers [7]. In our setting, we are more interested in the *true positive* than the *true negative* metric for two reasons. First, positive instances (links between source nodes and their existing friends) are ground truth, and ensuring high *recall* of positive instances is nontrivial. Second, *false positive* with zero, indicating no new friends to recommend, is not necessarily desirable. Because AUC incorporates both positive and negative instances equally whereas F_1 ignores the true negative metric, we adopt F_1 as our performance metric.

Results. Table 3 shows F_1 scores on different combinations of features for logistic regression and random forest classifiers. In general, sentiment features yield better performance in terms of F_1 scores, no matter whether they are combined with structural features to build the model. To investigate whether sentiment features indeed help improve the F_1 score, we conduct a paired t-test: each value in sample one is the F_1 score with sentiment or sentiment plus structural features; each value in sample two is the F_1 score with topical or topical plus structural features. The p-value is 0.0012, indicating the difference is statistically significant. In addition, structural features perform much better than both sentiment and topical features, but adding sentiment features can generally improve performance. Thus, sentiment features can indeed help in link prediction, but as adjuncts to the structural features.

Individual Feature Evaluation. We show the performance of each sentiment feature for random forest since it outperforms logistic regression in Table 3. Table 4 shows the F_1 score for individual sentiment feature. We highlight the top three ranked features in each graph. We find that in the mention graphs, the features EUCLIDEAN, SENTIMENT-MEAN, and SENTIMENT-AA perform best. We find that in the mutual-follow graph, the feature SENTIMENT-AGREEMENT performs best, but EUCLIDEAN and SENTIMENT-AA are good indicators. And, SENTIMENT-RAREST is not as informative as SMALLEST (topical features). In addition, SENTIMENT-ALIGNED outperforms SENTIMENT-MISALIGNED in general in all graphs, indicating the existence of sentiment homophily. Therefore, our evaluation suggests that sentiment homophily exists and can benefit link prediction.

6.2 TSAM Model Evaluation

Following the preprocessing strategy proposed by Backstrom and Leskovec, we choose "active" source nodes in all graphs. That is, active nodes are those whose degree is within the range [lower, upper]. After constructing pairs consisting of each source node and each of its candidates, we remove those whose number of common friends is less than a threshold, because users with only a few common friends are unlikely to form friendships. Table 5 shows the criteria we used. The criteria differ for graphs with differing statistics. As the ties become stronger, the mention graph becomes smaller. Thus an overfitting problem may arise if the dataset is too small. We therefore limit our evaluation to graphs with more than 100 source nodes left after preprocessing.

Table 5: Preprocessing parameters for evaluating TSAM.

Graph	Lower	Upper	Threshold
$@ \geq 1$	10	50	4
$@ \geq 2$	10	50	4
$@ \geq 3$	5	50	4
$@ \geq 5$	3	50	2
$@ \geq 7$	3	50	2
$@ \geq 9$	3	50	2
Follow	50	100	4

Because the feature SENTIMENT-AA ranks in the top three features for each graph in Table 4, we choose it to define the strength of a tie in the edge-factor function. For each graph, we assign half of the source nodes into a training and half into a test set. In the training phase, we set the learning rate $\lambda = 0.001$ and the number of iterations as 500. We split each graph five times and report the mean precision, recall, and F_1 scores of the TSAM model as well as for logistic regression and random forest, and identify the best performing model in terms of F_1. TSAM outperforms the other two models in the mutual-follow graph. In the mention graphs, TSAM performs best when the ties are strong ($@ \geq 3$ and $@ \geq 5$), but not for weak ties ($@ \geq 1$ and $@ \geq 2$). This suggests that when the ties are weak, sentiment-based cognitive balance theory does not help because the links between users are somewhat random; hence, a balanced cognitive structure does not necessarily mean any relationship between two pairs.

Overall, our results indicate that performance of link prediction could be improved when we incorporate sentiment-based cognitive balance theory, especially on graphs where the strength of relationship is not too weak (mutual-follow graph or mention graphs where the number of mentions exceeds three).

7. RELATED WORK

Link Prediction. Existing work on link prediction can be classified into two categories. For the unsupervised methods, Liben-Nowell and Kleinberg evaluated different "proximity" features extracted from network topology. They found that the Adamic-Adar metric performs best in predicting links. Most recent works are based on supervised methods. Lichtenwalter et al. [22] provided a detailed analysis of challenges, such as class imbalance, of using supervised methods in link prediction. Dong et al. [10] proposed a probabilistic graphical model to predict links. Backstrom and Leskovec [4] developed a supervised random walk algorithm for friend recommendation on Facebook. Scellato et al. [29] exploited place features in predicting links on location-based social networks. Whereas we adopt a supervised approach, we additionally consider sentiment features and investigate how they improve link prediction.

Collaborative Tagging Systems. These are based on a tripartite structure: users, tags, and resources, enabling users to share their tags for particular resources. Combined with social structure, collaborative tagging systems provide new modalities of link prediction. Marlow et al. [24] found that users tend to have a larger similarity of tag vocabularies with their friends compared with random users. Markines et al. [23] built a foundation for the folksonomy-based similarity measures, such as matching, overlap, Jaccard, and cosine similarity. Romero et al. [28] studied the relationship between topical affiliations and social network on Twitter. They found that the adoption of hashtags can predict users' social relationships. We design sentiment features based on Romero et al.'s findings. Further, we propose a graphical model based on sentiment features.

Sentiment Analysis. With the popularity of social media, sentiment analysis brings us deeper understanding of social network analysis. Twitter enables researchers to access huge amounts of data to discover collective sentiments [6, 34], predict political elections [9, 36], and so on. In other applications, Yang et al. [37] extracted sentiments from users'

Table 3: F_1 scores on the positive instances for different classifiers on different combination of features.

Classifier	Set of features	$@ \geq 1$	$@ \geq 2$	$@ \geq 3$	$@ \geq 5$	$@ \geq 7$	$@ \geq 9$	Follow
Logistic Regression	Topical	0.295	0.489	0.530	0.650	0.720	0.735	0.479
	Sentiment	0.312	0.500	0.550	0.650	0.712	0.739	0.499
	Structural	0.736	0.740	0.759	0.792	0.812	0.846	0.666
	Topical+Structural	0.689	0.777	0.792	0.818	0.846	0.880	0.678
	Sentiment+Structural	0.717	0.789	0.800	0.834	0.861	0.877	0.679
	All	0.705	0.778	0.795	0.838	0.858	0.880	0.682
Random Forest	Topical	0.628	0.765	0.804	0.839	0.853	0.880	0.516
	Sentiment	0.723	0.818	0.845	0.859	0.876	0.883	0.517
	Structural	0.875	0.908	0.913	0.939	0.946	0.957	0.667
	Topical+Structural	0.914	0.946	0.956	0.971	0.972	0.972	0.680
	Sentiment+Structural	0.916	0.949	0.959	0.972	0.975	0.979	0.685
	All	0.916	0.949	0.958	0.972	0.970	0.979	0.684

Table 4: F_1 scores on individual sentiment feature with Random Forest classifier.

Feature	$@ \geq 1$	$@ \geq 2$	$@ \geq 3$	$@ \geq 5$	$@ \geq 7$	$@ \geq 9$	Follow
SENTIMENT-AGREEMENT	0.166	0.430	0.498	0.636	0.696	0.711	**0.488**
SENTIMENT-ALIGNED	0.192	0.291	0.555	0.650	0.700	0.735	0.452
SENTIMENT-MISALIGNED	0.122	0.509	0.526	0.640	0.689	0.710	0.390
SENTIMENT-RAREST	0.122	0.307	0.360	0.691	0.721	0.742	0.295
SENTIMENT-AA	**0.430**	**0.589**	**0.706**	**0.753**	**0.789**	**0.822**	**0.466**
SENTIMENT-INVERSE	0.349	0.501	0.648	0.741	0.785	0.812	0.452
SENTIMENT-MEAN	**0.455**	**0.593**	**0.706**	**0.757**	**0.791**	**0.825**	0.454
EUCLIDEAN	**0.589**	**0.721**	**0.751**	**0.788**	**0.825**	**0.832**	**0.467**
COSINE	0.247	0.480	0.525	0.625	0.692	0.748	0.456

Table 6: Evaluation results for the TSAM.

Feature	Logistic Regression			Random Forest			TSAM		
	Precision	Recall	F_1	Precision	Recall	F_1	Precision	Recall	F_1
$@ \geq 1$	0.350	0.443	**0.391**	0.445	0.196	0.272	0.193	0.890	0.317
$@ \geq 2$	0.456	0.780	**0.576**	0.616	0.535	0.573	0.602	0.539	0.569
$@ \geq 3$	0.727	0.596	0.655	0.667	0.628	0.647	0.712	0.620	**0.663**
$@ \geq 5$	0.752	0.701	0.726	0.863	0.806	0.834	0.859	0.863	**0.861**
Follow	0.794	0.636	0.705	0.759	0.664	0.708	0.677	0.801	**0.734**

reviews on venues to improve location recommendation services; Tan et al. [31] used the social relationship to improve user-level sentiment prediction. We conduct our work with a different purpose: using sentiment homophily to predict links.

8. CONCLUSIONS

We study how to exploit sentiments for link prediction, and evaluate the extent to which sentiment homophily can help improve link prediction. By extracting users' sentiments from their tweets on different topics, we describe a set of sentiment features to quantify the likelihood of two users becoming friends. The evaluation results suggest that sentiment features improve the performance of link prediction in terms of F_1 in both mutual-follow and mention graphs. Upon investigating the predictive power of each sentiment feature, we find that Adamic-Adar and Euclidean distance based measures perform best. We propose a factor graph model considering the sentiment-based cognitive balance theory. The results show that our model outperforms the other two well-known classifiers (logistic regression and random forest) in the mutual-follow graph and mention graphs where the strength of ties is not too weak ($@ \geq 3$). In future work, we plan to evaluate our work in a friend recommendation framework by exploiting temporal information regarding how links form.

Acknowledgments

We thank the Laboratory for Analytic Sciences at NC State University, the National Science Foundation (grant 0910868), and IBM (for a Ph.D. fellowship to Zhang) for support. We also thank Tong Sun for sharing her dataset.

9. REFERENCES

[1] L. A. Adamic and E. Adar. Friends and neighbors on the web. *Social Networks*, 25:211–230, 2001.

[2] A. Agarwal, B. Xie, I. Vovsha, O. Rambow, and R. Passonneau. Sentiment analysis of Twitter data. In *Proc. LSM*, pages 30–38. 2011.

[3] S. Baccianella, A. Esuli, and F. Sebastiani. SentiWordNet 3.0: An enhanced lexical resource for sentiment analysis and opinion mining. In *Proc. LREC*. May 2010.

[4] L. Backstrom and J. Leskovec. Supervised random walks: Predicting and recommending links in social networks. In *Proc. WSDM*, pages 635–644. 2011.

[5] A. Bakliwal, J. Foster, J. van der Puil, R. O'Brien, L. Tounsi, and M. Hughes. Sentiment analysis of political tweets: Towards an accurate classifier. In *Proc. LASM*, pages 49–58. June 2013.

[6] J. Bollen, H. Mao, and A. Pepe. Modeling public mood and emotion: Twitter sentiment and socio-economic phenomena. In *Proc. ICWSM*, 2011.

[7] S. Daskalaki, I. Kopanas, and N. Avouris. Evaluation of classifiers for an uneven class distribution problem. *Applied Artificial Intelligence*, 20:381–417, Sept. 2006.

[8] M.-C. de Marneffe, B. MacCartney, and C. D. Manning. Generating typed dependency parses from phrase structure parses. In *Proc. LREC*, pages 449–454, 2006.

[9] N. A. Diakopoulos and D. A. Shamma. Characterizing debate performance via aggregated Twitter sentiment. In *Proc. CHI*, pages 1195–1198. 2010.

[10] Y. Dong, J. Tang, S. Wu, J. Tian, N. V. Chawla, J. Rao, and H. Cao. Link prediction and recommendation across heterogeneous social networks. In *Proc. ICDM*, pages 181–190. 2012.

[11] M. S. Granovetter. The strength of weak ties. *American J. Sociology*, 78(6):1360–1380, May 1973.

[12] M. Gupte and T. Eliassi-Rad. Measuring tie strength in implicit social networks. In *Proc. WebSci*, pages 109–118. 2012.

[13] D. F. Gurini, F. Gasparetti, A. Micarelli, and G. Sansonetti. A sentiment-based approach to Twitter user recommendation. In *Proc. RsWeb*. 2013.

[14] J. M. Hammersley and P. E. Clifford. Markov random fields on finite graphs and lattices. Unpublished manuscript, 1971.

[15] V. Hatzivassiloglou and J. M. Wiebe. Effects of adjective orientation and gradability on sentence subjectivity. In *Proc. COLING*, pages 299–305. 2000.

[16] F. Heider. *The Psychology of Interpersonal Relations*. Wiley, 1958.

[17] J. Hopcroft, T. Lou, and J. Tang. Who will follow you back?: Reciprocal relationship prediction. In *Proc. CIKM*, pages 1137–1146. 2011.

[18] H. Kwak, C. Lee, H. Park, and S. Moon. What is Twitter, a social network or a news media? In *Proc. WWW*, pages 591–600. 2010.

[19] J. D. Lafferty, A. McCallum, and F. C. N. Pereira. Conditional random fields: Probabilistic models for segmenting and labeling sequence data. In *Proc. ICML*, pages 282–289. 2001.

[20] J. Leskovec, L. Backstrom, R. Kumar, and A. Tomkins. Microscopic evolution of social networks. In *Proc. KDD*, pages 462–470. 2008.

[21] D. Liben-Nowell and J. Kleinberg. The link prediction problem for social networks. In *Proc. CIKM*, pages 556–559. 2003.

[22] R. N. Lichtenwalter, J. T. Lussier, and N. V. Chawla. New perspectives and methods in link prediction. In *Proc. KDD*, pages 243–252. 2010.

[23] B. Markines, C. Cattuto, F. Menczer, D. Benz, A. Hotho, and G. Stumme. Evaluating similarity measures for emergent semantics of social tagging. In *Proc. WWW*, pages 641–650. 2009.

[24] C. Marlow, M. Naaman, D. Boyd, and M. Davis. HT06, tagging paper, taxonomy, Flickr, academic article, to read. In *Proc. HYPERTEXT*, pages 31–40. 2006.

[25] M. McPherson, L. Smith-Lovin, and J. M. Cook. Birds of a feather: Homophily in social networks. *Annual Review of Sociology*, 27(1):415–444, Aug. 2001.

[26] K. P. Murphy, Y. Weiss, and M. I. Jordan. Loopy belief propagation for approximate inference: An empirical study. In *Proc. UAI*, pages 467–475. 1999.

[27] M. F. Porter. An algorithm for suffix stripping. *Program: electronic library and information systems*, 14(3):130–137, July 1980.

[28] D. M. Romero, C. Tan, and J. Ugander. On the interplay between social and topical structure. In *Proc. ICWSM*, 2013.

[29] S. Scellato, A. Noulas, and C. Mascolo. Exploiting place features in link prediction on location-based social networks. In *Proc. KDD*, pages 1046–1054. 2011.

[30] P. Singla and M. Richardson. Yes, there is a correlation: From social networks to personal behavior on the Web. In *Proc. WWW*, pages 655–664. 2008.

[31] C. Tan, L. Lee, J. Tang, L. Jiang, M. Zhou, and P. Li. User-level sentiment analysis incorporating social networks. In *Proc. KDD*, pages 1397–1405. 2011.

[32] W. Tang, H. Zhuang, and J. Tang. Learning to infer social ties in large networks. In *Proc. ECML PKDD*, pages 381–397. 2011.

[33] M. Thelwall. Emotion homophily in social network site messages. *First Monday*, 15(4), 2010.

[34] M. Thelwall, K. Buckley, and G. Paltoglou. Sentiment in Twitter events. *J. Amer. Soc. Info. Sci. Tech.*, 62(2):406–418, Feb. 2011.

[35] O. Tsur and A. Rappoport. What's in a hashtag?: Content based prediction of the spread of ideas in microblogging communities. In *Proc. WSDM*, pages 643–652. 2012.

[36] A. Tumasjan, T. O. Sprenger, P. G. Sandner, and I. M. Welpe. Predicting elections with Twitter: What 140 characters reveal about political sentiment. In *Proc. ICWSM*, pages 178–185, 2010.

[37] D. Yang, D. Zhang, Z. Yu, and Z. Wang. A sentiment-enhanced personalized location recommendation system. In *Proc. HYPERTEXT*, pages 119–128. 2013.

[38] E. Zheleva, H. Sharara, and L. Getoor. Co-evolution of social and affiliation networks. In *Proc. KDD*, pages 1007–1016. 2009.

A Robust Model for Paper-Reviewer Assignment

Xiang Liu
New York University
Brooklyn, NY
xl493@nyu.edu

Torsten Suel
New York University
Brooklyn, NY
suel@poly.edu

Nasir Memon
New York University
Brooklyn, NY
memon@poly.edu

ABSTRACT

Automatic expert assignment is a common problem encountered in both industry and academia. For example, for conference program chairs and journal editors, in order to collect "good" judgments for a paper, it is necessary for them to assign the paper to the most appropriate reviewers. Choosing appropriate reviewers of course includes a number of considerations such as expertise and authority, but also diversity and avoiding conflicts. In this paper, we explore the expert retrieval problem and implement an automatic paper-reviewer recommendation system that considers aspects of expertise, authority, and diversity. In particular, a graph is first constructed on the possible reviewers and the query paper, incorporating expertise and authority information. Then a Random Walk with Restart (RWR) [1] model is employed on the graph with a sparsity constraint, incorporating diversity information. Extensive experiments on two reviewer recommendation benchmark datasets show that the proposed method obtains performance gains over state-of-the-art reviewer recommendation systems in terms of expertise, authority, diversity, and, most importantly, relevance as judged by human experts.

Categories and Subject Descriptors

H.3.3 [**Information Search and Retrieval**]: Retrieval models; H.3.3 [**Information Search and Retrieval**]: Relevance Feedback

General Terms

Algorithms, Measurement, Performance, Experimentation

Keywords

Review Assignment; Expert Retrieval; Information Propagation; Topic Model; Random Walk; Diversity; Ranking

RecSys '14, October 06 - 10 2014, San Jose or vicinity, CA, USA

http://dx.doi.org/10.1145/2645710.2645749

1. INTRODUCTION

The task of expert recommendation and assignment is a common problem in both industry and academia. Consider a job recruiting process where, in order to decide whether an applicant should receive an on-site interview, HR has to make an evaluation of an applicant's educational record, previous work experience, personal skills, and fit with job requirements. For the task of planning a workshop and deciding who should be invited, expertise, communication skills, and diverse background might be preferred. In general, for each expert recommendation task, several aspects are usually jointly considered to make the final decision. Accordingly, an automatic expert recommendation system should take into account multiple criteria for a specific task.

In this paper, we focus on the problem of paper-reviewer recommendation, which has been widely studied [2, 8, 3, 4]. For conference program chairs and journal editors, a good review assignment should satisfy several criteria, e.g., reviewers' authority, expertise, diversity, availability, conflict, etc. However, most existing methods often focus on one aspect, expertise (topic coverage), in the design of their approach, and attempt to maximize their definitions of expertise. In this work, we take three criteria as the main design objectives, including authority, whether the reviewer has a good recognition in the larger scientific community; expertise, whether the reviewer is a specialist in the specific domain related to the paper; and diversity, whether the selected reviewers have diverse research interests and background. The final goal of our work is to assign papers to reviewers that are considered highly qualified to perform the review. To achieve that goal, we are first targeting two intermediate goals: expertise, and authority. While expertise can be approximated by a variety of methods, e.g., text similarity, topic similarity, etc., authority can be explored by graph-based propagation. We will show that by maximizing expertise and authority, we can in fact achieve a better assignment as judged by human experts. Finally, we show how to also achieve the third objective, diversity, without significant decreases in expertise, authority, or quality as viewed by human experts.

Given a query paper and a candidate reviewer pool with N reviewers (shown in Figure 1), we first construct a graph with $N + 1$ nodes representing the candidate reviewers and the query paper. A standard topic model is then applied to the query paper and the published papers of the candidate reviewers, so that the link between a candidate reviewer and the query paper can be built and measured by the topic model-based similarity. Thus it ensures a strong connection between the query paper and a reviewer if he or she has strong background knowledge in the specific area (e.g., has published

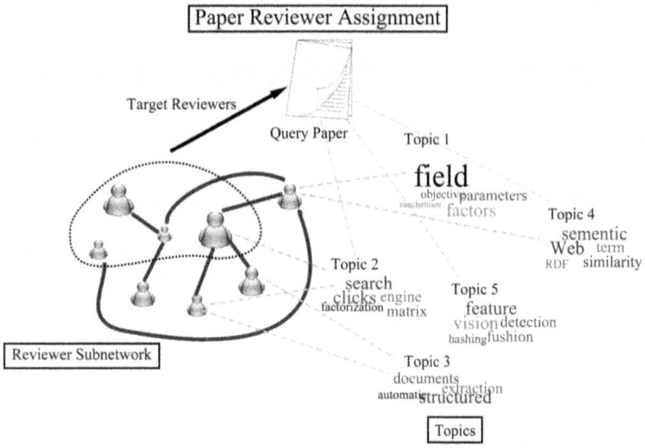

Figure 1: The proposed graph contains the query paper, candidate reviewers, and topics. Given a query paper, the recommendation algorithm selects the nodes with most expertise and propagates the query to the other nodes in the graph. After the propagation process, each node is assigned with a utility score, which is used to measure both the relevance between the node, and the query, and the authority of the node in the graph. Finally, a set of nodes with highest scores are selected as target reviewers.

a lot of papers on the same topic as the query paper). To achieve the authority objective, academic co-authorship is considered as the social link representation among the N reviewers (the Reviewer Subnetwork in Figure 1), so that by using graph propagation, the authority information can be incorporated. To better integrate the expertise and authority scores for each candidate reviewer, we propose a Random Walk with Restart (RWR) model. With such a model, there is some probability to jump back to the start node at each step. The hope is that the RWR will achieve a better balance between expertise and authority in the propagation process.

To achieve the diversity objective, the N candidate reviewers are first clustered into groups based on their research topic distributions. We then select only a small set of individual nodes from each cluster so that an unbiased selection is achieved from diverse research areas. We call such strategy a sparsity constraint for each cluster. Finally, together with the sparsity constraint, an RWR process employed on the $N+1$ nodes will provide us a stable probability of each node. In our recommender system, this probability is considered as the ranking score for a reviewer under the criteria of expertise, authority and diversity.

We formulate the RWR and the group sparsity as a uniformed optimization framework. An efficient gradient descent-based method is proposed to solve the minimization objective. Extensive experiments confirm the effectiveness of the proposed method as compared to the state-of-the-arts.

The rest of this paper is organized as follows. In Section 2 we discuss related work. We explain our graph construction in Section 3. Then we describe our problem formulation and optimization approach for paper-reviewer assignment in detail in Section 4. In Section 5, we present our experimental results. Finally, we provide concluding remarks in Section 6.

2. RELATED WORK

There has been a lot of research on both reviewer assignment and graph propagation. In this section, we summarize the related work on these two topics.

2.1 Paper-Reviewer Assignment

Some recent work has focused on utilizing information retrieval and machine learning techniques to solve the problem of paper-reviewer assignment. For example, the widely used Toronto recommender system [5] addressed the assignment as a minimum cost network flow using some novel metrics. It also considered reviewers' bids, which expressed their interests or disinterests in specific papers, as available feedbacks. Hettich *et al.* [7] used TF-IDF to exploit the suitability between manuscripts and reviewers. Mimno and McCallum [8] applied a topic model to measure a reviewer's expertise. Charlin *et al.* [5] utilized LDA model, linear regression and collaborative filtering to determine reviewer assignments. Tang *et al.* [4] assumed that every reviewer had an expertise level, which was already known. Then they defined some specific matching criteria to optimize the reviewer arrangement procedure. Rodriguez *et al.* [9] built a co-authorship graph with the references of a submitted paper as starting points to suggest reviewers. Conry *et al.* [6] first studied the preference of reviewers for specific papers as available feedbacks. A linear programming-based optimization formulation was then used to solve the reviewer assignment problem.

Most existing papers have focused on improving the relevance between the query and experts. Expertise was often considered as the main criterion in these methods while diversity and authority were often ignored. Moreover, some of the previous work needed a labeling of the research interests and expertise levels of candidate reviewers as prior knowledge for better assignment. In comparison, our work incorporates three criteria at the same time, while no label information is needed. By collecting human judgments on relevance between candidate reviewers and the query paper, and evaluating our results on this ground truth data, we show the effectiveness of our model.

2.2 Graph Propagation

In network science, many algorithms have been proposed to determine the importance of the nodes in a network. Such well-known query-dependent ranking algorithms include HITS [11], Topic-Sensitive PageRank [12], and personalized PageRank [13].

Most of these models were based on random walks on the network structure. Random walk algorithms, which follow the trajectory of a random walker that takes successive random steps, have received a lot of attention. In this paper, we use a modified random walk model, RWR [1, 10], into which we can easily integrate both the expertise matching score between a candidate reviewer and the query paper, and the authority of the candidate reviewer together to make better recommendation. Different from the RWR model, we formulate our problem as an optimization framework that integrates RWR and a sparsity constraint together to obtain a stable probability for each node. That represents a balance of expertise, authority, and diversity.

3. GRAPH CONSTRUCTION

In this section, we introduce the procedure to construct a graph among the query paper and the reviewers, and explain how to measure the relations among the graph nodes.

For each query paper and all candidate reviewers, a graph can be constructed as follows: Let $\mathcal{R} = \{r_1, ..., r_N\}$ denote the candidate reviewers, and let $\mathcal{Q} = \{q_1, ..., q_m\}$ denote the query paper to be assigned reviewers. Here we consider the reviewers and the query paper as nodes in the graph, and then establish the edges and assign the associated weights.

3.1 Reviewer-Reviewer Connection

For reviewer r_i and reviewer r_j, we first search their previous publication and co-author lists using Microsoft Academic Search system[15]. An edge is established if and only if the two reviewers have co-authored at least one paper. The edge weight is set as the number of papers they have co-authored. The intuition behind this is that if a reviewer is well connected, e.g., has many co-authorship connections with others, he or she would be considered as having higher authority. As a result, during the process of connection construction between reviewer and reviewer, we incorporate the first type of criteria, the authority.

3.2 Reviewer-Query Connection

In order to establish edges between reviewers and the query paper, for each candidate reviewer we first crawl all of her previously published papers using Microsoft Academic Search. Suppose the list of published papers associated with reviewer r_i is denoted by $p_i = \{p_i^1, ..., p_i^j, ..., p_i^{m_{p_i}}\}$, where m_{p_i} is the number of publications and p_i^j is the jth paper of reviewer r_i. Then the edge weight between query paper q and reviewer r_i can be estimated by the similarity between q and the set of papers p_i published by reviewer r_i.

Since topic models such as LDA [16, 17] have been successfully applied in document analysis, we directly utilize LDA for the paper-to-paper similarity measurement. First, all of the published papers from all candidate reviewers and the query papers are collected and used as the input corpus of the LDA model. Each paper is considered as one document in the corpus. Suppose the total number of topics is T. After LDA topic model analysis, the published paper p_i^j associated with reviewer r_i will have a topic distribution denoted by $\theta_{p_i^j} \in \mathbb{R}^T$, and the query paper q will have a topic distribution denoted by $\theta_q \in \mathbb{R}^T$ [4]. Then cosine similarity is calculated between paper p_i^j and paper q in terms of the topic distribution representation. Finally, the edge weight between reviewer r_i and the query paper node q is estimated by max pooling [14] among all the similarities between reviewer r_i's published papers p_i and the query paper q.

Now we explain the rationale behind this construction. The basic assumption is that if one reviewer has published a paper in the same topic as the query paper, she should be considered as an expert candidate to review that paper. By involving the LDA model, we construct the connection between reviewers and query paper in terms of topic distribution representation. Accordingly the expertise criterion is taken into account during this graph construction process.

4. PROPAGATION OVER THE GRAPH

In this section, we present our proposed propagation method over the constructed graph. We first introduce the formulation based on RWR with a certain sparsity constraint, and then introduce an efficient gradient descent-based method to solve the objective.

4.1 Problem Formulation

4.1.1 Notation and Definition

Let $G = (V, E)$ denote a graph. The nodes set is $V = \{r_1, ..., r_N, q\}$ where r_i denotes a reviewer and q denotes the query paper. The edge set is $E = \{e_{ij} | 0 < i, j \leq N\}$ where e_{ij} denotes the edge between node v_i and v_j. Given the initial query paper node q, our goal is to propagate the initial query information through the entire graph and predict the query-reviewer relevance score for each node. Let $\mathbf{f} = [f_1, ..., f_{N+1}]^T$ denote the predicted score vector for all the nodes. Let $\mathbf{y} = [y_1, ..., y_{N+1}]^T$ denote the initial query vector where $y_i = 1$ if $v_i = q$ and $y_i = 0$ otherwise.

4.1.2 Modeling Expertise and Authority

In this work, we directly apply a Markov random walk process [21] on the graph. We use Q'_{ij} to denote the transition probability from node v_i to node v_j, which can be calculated in the following way:

$$Q'_{ij} = \begin{cases} \frac{exp(e_{ij})}{\sum_j exp(e_{ij})}, & \text{if } V_i = q \\ & V_j \neq q \\ \frac{exp(e_{ij})}{\sum_j exp(e_{ij})}, & \text{if } V_i \neq q \\ & V_j \neq q \\ 0, & otherwise \end{cases} \tag{1}$$

where the edge weight of e_{ij} is as defined in Section 3.

For a query, we would like to assign higher weight to nodes that are both well connected and relevant to the query. Thus we use an RWR process. Specifically, starting at a reviewer node, the random walker has two choices at each step: either moving to a neighbor, or jumping back to the origin node (query node) with probability η. Then the transition matrix $\mathbf{Q}$ is further revised as:

$$Q_{ij} = \begin{cases} (1-\eta)Q'_{ij}, & \text{if } V_i \neq q \; and \; V_j \neq q \\ \eta, & \text{if } Vi \neq q \\ & V_j = q \end{cases} \tag{2}$$

According to the Markov random walk process, in order to obtain the stationary distribution vector $\mathbf{f}$ we need to solve the following eigenvector equation:

$$\mathbf{f} = \mathbf{Q}^T \mathbf{f} \tag{3}$$

We solve this by minimizing $||\mathbf{f} - \mathbf{Q}^T\mathbf{f}||_2^2$, such that two nodes connected by strong edges will have similar scores after propagation. Note that expertise and authority have already been incorporated during the construction process of the transition matrix $\mathbf{Q}$. Using the random walk process, the initial scores are propagated to the entire graph. After obtaining the stationary distribution of the random walk process, the probability score of each reviewer node provides us with a reviewer ranking that considers both expertise and authority.

4.1.3 Modeling Diversity

To achieve the diversity criterion, we first cluster candidate reviewers into groups according to their publication topic distributions, to make sure that each cluster of reviewers has similar research interests. Then an ℓ_1-norm is applied within each group so that only a small set of individual nodes will get non-zero utility scores and thus be selected from each cluster by minimizing the ℓ_1-norm. The accumulation of the ℓ_1-norm across all the groups can be defined as follows:

$$\sum_{g=1}^{G} ||\mathbf{f}_g||_1 \tag{4}$$

where G denotes the number of groups, and $\mathbf{f}_g$ denotes the predicted score vector for all the nodes in group g. This sparsity constraint within each group is intuitive since we are trying to balance the group utility scores by not selecting all reviewers from the same research area. It is easy to see that the summation of $\mathbf{f}_g$ across all groups is equivalent to applying the ℓ_1-norm on $\mathbf{f}$.

4.1.4 *RWR with Sparsity over the Graph*

Finally, another term $||\mathbf{f} - \mathbf{y}||_2^2$ is added into the fomula, where the minimization on it will enforce the RWR process not go too far from the initial query.

Now we introduce our formulation which considers expertise, authority, and diversity at the same time as follows:

$$F(\mathbf{f}) \;=\; \frac{1}{2}||\mathbf{f} - \mathbf{Q}^T\mathbf{f}||_2^2 + \frac{\lambda}{2}||\mathbf{f} - \mathbf{y}||_2^2 + \gamma||\mathbf{f}||_1 \tag{5}$$

where $\lambda, \gamma > 0$ are two trade-off parameters, which can be tuned trough cross-validation.

By minimizing the objective function, we can obtain the ranking scores for all candidate reviewers as:

$$\begin{aligned} \min_{\mathbf{f}} \quad & F(\mathbf{f}), \\ \text{s.t.} \quad & \mathbf{f} \geq 0. \end{aligned} \tag{6}$$

We will show how to solve this based on a gradient descent method in the next section.

4.2 Optimization Procedure

The gradient of $\mathbf{f}$ in Equation (6) cannot be calculated due to the non-smoothness of the ℓ_1-norm regularizer. In this subsection, we show that by using the dual norm, the ℓ_1-norm term can be approached by a smoothing approximation. When the gradient of $\mathbf{f}$ is tractable, we will employ a gradient descent-based method for the optimization.

4.2.1 *Smoothing Approximation*

Note that the dual of the ℓ_1-norm is the ℓ_∞-norm. Similar to [21], based on Nesterov's smoothing approximation method [22], the $||\mathbf{f}||_1$ can be approximated by a smooth function as follows:

$$l_\mu(\mathbf{f}) = \max_{||\mathbf{u}||_\infty \leq 1} < \mathbf{u}, \mathbf{f} > -\frac{\mu}{2}||\mathbf{u}||_2^2 \tag{7}$$

where $<\cdot,\cdot>$ denotes the inner product operator and the optimal auxiliary variable $\mathbf{u}(\mathbf{f})$ can be defined as:

$$\mathbf{u}(\mathbf{f}) = S_\infty(\frac{\mathbf{f}}{\mu}) \tag{8}$$

where S_∞ is the projection operator which projects a value to the ℓ_∞-ball:

$$S_\infty(x) = \begin{cases} x, -1 \leq x \leq 1, \\ 1, x > 1, \\ -1, x < -1. \end{cases} \tag{9}$$

From the above approximation, the original formulation can be rewritten as the following smoothed objective function:

$$F_\mu(\mathbf{f}) \;=\; \frac{1}{2}||\mathbf{f} - \mathbf{Q}^T\mathbf{f}||_2^2 + \frac{\lambda}{2}||\mathbf{f} - \mathbf{y}||_2^2 + \gamma l_\mu(\mathbf{f}) \tag{10}$$

where the sparsity term in Equation (6) can be replaced by $l_0(\mathbf{f})$ with $\mu = 0$.

4.2.2 *Optimization with Gradient Descent*

The smooth objective function $F_\mu(\mathbf{f})$ is differentiable w.r.t. f_i as follows:

$$\begin{aligned} \partial_{f_i} F_\mu = (f_i - \sum_k f_k Q_{ki}) + \sum_{j \in \mathcal{N}_i} (f_j - \sum_k f_k Q_{kj})(-Q_{ij}) \\ + \lambda(f_i - y_i) + \gamma \nabla l_\mu(f_i) \end{aligned} \tag{11}$$

where $\mathcal{N}_i$ is the set of neighbors of node v_i. We summarize our optimization procedure in Algorithm 1.

Algorithm 1 Solving the Problem in Equation (6) by Gradient Descent Optimization

```
1: Input: y ∈ {0,1}^{N+1}, f^0 ∈ R^n, λ, γ
2: Initialize: Set t = 0, initialize f^t = 1.
3: repeat
4:    Employ Polack-Ribière conjugate gradient algorithm
      to estimate f^{t+1} based on ∂_{f_i} F_μ.
5:    Force the negative entries in f^{t+1} to 0.
6:    t = t + 1.
7: until Convergence
8: Output: The optimized f*
```

In our experiments, we use the SLEP toolbox [23] to solve the objective function.

5. EXPERIMENTS

We have demonstrated the ability of our algorithms to incorporate expertise, authority, and diversity of candidate reviewers. In this section, we describe our experiments for evaluating the performance of the proposed method against the state-of-the-art methods. We first begin with a brief description of the two reviewer recommendation benchmark datasets and the evaluation metrics, and then introduce the baseline methods, followed by discussion of our experimental results.

5.1 Datasets

5.1.1 *Multi-Aspect Review Assignment Dataset*

The multi-aspect review assignment evaluation dataset is a benchmark dataset from UIUC [2]. It contains 73 papers accepted by SIGIR 2007, and 189 prospective reviewers who had published more than three papers from 1971 to 2006 in the main information retrieval conferences such as SIGIR, CIKM, and WWW. There is no label information between the 73 papers and the 189 reviewers. The dataset provides an extra expertise profile for each reviewer and each paper to generate the pseudo-label between papers and reviewers. Specifically, 25 major topics based on the topic areas in the CFPs of ACM SIGIR in recent years were pre-defined by an information retrieval expert. For each paper in the set of 73 test papers, the expert provided a 25-dimensional label on that paper based on the defined topics. This could be considered as the expertise representation of that test paper. For the 189 reviewers, all of their publications were crawled, and through the same labeling procedure, each paper published by the reviewers also had a 25-dimensional expertise representation. By average pooling, it is then easy to achieve a similar expertise representation for each reviewer. Then the expertise matching score between each test paper and each reviewer could be measured by the distance of their pseudo-labels (e.g., cosine similarity based on the 25-dimensional expertise representation). The details are described in 5.2.2.

Besides the profile information available in the dataset, we have further constructed the co-authorship graph of the 189 prospective reviewers. Since this dataset was published in CIKM 2008, we call it the CIKM dataset for short.

5.1.2 NIPS Dataset

The second dataset was collected by Mimno and McCallum [8], who approximated the task of assigning reviewers to submitted papers by gathering expertise relevance judgments from humans experts. The dataset contains 148 papers accepted by NIPS 2006, and 364 reviewers. Several prominent researchers from the NIPS community were asked to provide a ground truth relevance judgment of a query paper and a proposed reviewer. The ground truth consists of 650 reviewer-paper relevance judgments from nine annotators using a four-level relevance scheme as follows: Very Relevant (score = 3), Relevant (score = 2), Slightly Relevant (score = 1) and Irrelevant (score = 0).

Since they labeled the ground truth according to the top 10 retrieved reviewers for their baselines, it is difficult to compare the performance of our proposed method with this based on the partial relevance judgments. We have further collected 766 more reviewer-paper labels from researchers in Machine Learning, following the same four-level relevance scheme. Moreover, we have crawled the publication lists of all 85537 co-authors of the 364 prospective reviewers and constructed the co-authorship graph.

5.2 Evaluation Metrics

In order to test the paper reviewer assignment performance, we define the following metrics to quantitatively evaluate the results.

5.2.1 Precision at Position k

Intuitively, for a given paper, it is desirable to retrieve the n reviewers with the highest relevance judgment scores. For the NIPS dataset with the ground truth, we apply precision at position k to measure the relevance of the top n results retrieved by a given query. Specifically, we measure the mean precision across all queries in terms of P@1, P@2, ..., P@10.

5.2.2 Expertise Matching Score

Unlike in the NIPS dataset, there is no ground truth in the CIKM dataset. Instead of using P@k to measure the assignment quality, we use the provided expertise profiles and apply the expertise matching score at position k as follows:

$$Expertise@k = \frac{\sum_{q=1}^{Q} \frac{\sum_{n=1}^{k} cosine(t_n, t_q)}{k}}{Q} \quad (12)$$

Here, $cosine(t_n, t_q)$ measures the expertise similarity between the n-th ranked reviewer R_n and the query paper q, while t_n and t_q represent the topic distribution of R_n and q, and Q represents the total number of query papers.

5.2.3 Authority

In addition to maximizing the paper reviewer relevance score, we also want to maximize the top n reviewers' authority. We use the h-index to measure the authority of each prospective reviewer.

$$Authority@k = \frac{\sum_{q=1}^{Q} \frac{\sum_{n=1}^{k} h\text{-}index(n,q)}{k}}{Q} \quad (13)$$

Here $h\text{-}index(n, q)$, the h-index of the n-th ranked reviewer of query paper q, represents the assignment quality in terms of authority, while Q represents the total number of query papers.

5.2.4 Diversity

We adopt two natural definitions of diversity. First, we use the Kullback Leibler (KL) divergence $KL(p||q)$, which represents the difference between two probability distributions p and q [24], to measure the dissimilarity between each pair of candidate reviewers based on their publication topic distributions, as mentioned in Section 3. The KL divergence is given by:

$$KL(p||q) = \sum_i p(i) log \frac{p(i)}{q(i)} \quad (14)$$

Similarly, we have the topic divergence measurement:

$$d_{topic} = \frac{\sum_{q=1}^{Q} \sum_{i,j \in N_q} KL(i|j)}{Q} = \frac{\sum_{q=1}^{Q} \sum_{i,j \in N_q} \sum_t i(t) log \frac{i(t)}{j(t)}}{Q} \quad (15)$$

Here N_q represents the retrieved reviewers of query q, $i(t)$ and $j(t)$ are the topic distribution of reviewers i and j over topic t, and Q is the total number of query papers.

We also evaluate the diversity among retrieved reviewers by leveraging the notion of density from network science. The density of a graph is defined as the number of edges existing in the graph, divided by the maximal possible number of edges in the graph, as follows [18]:

$$d_{graph} = \frac{\sum_{u \in V} \sum_{v \in V, u \neq v} I[w(u, v) > 0]}{|V| \times (|V| - 1)} \quad (16)$$

where $|V|$ is the number of nodes in graph G, $w(u, v)$ is the weight between node u and node v, and I is an indicator function. Given the top-n ranked reviewers of query paper q, we can construct a graph G_n with each node denoting one reviewer in N_q and each edge weight $w(u, v)$ defined as in Section 3.1. Then we use d_{graph} as an inverse measurement of diversity among the top-n reviewers.

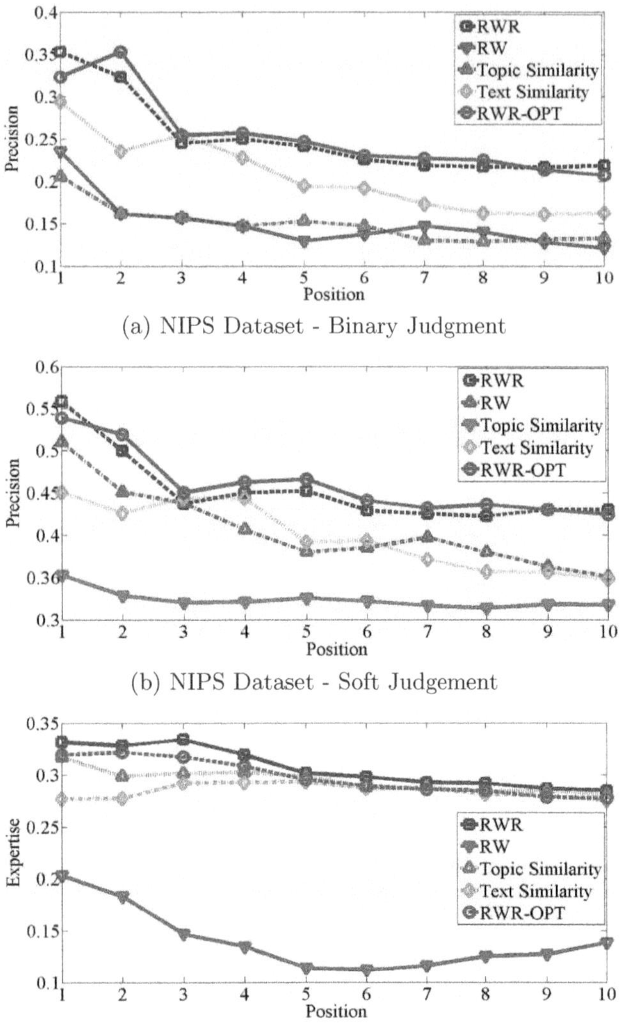

(a) NIPS Dataset - Binary Judgment

(b) NIPS Dataset - Soft Judgement

(c) CIKM Dataset

Figure 2: The relevance performance for the NIPS dataset and the expertise matching performance for the CIKM dataset.

5.3 Experimental Results

In this section, we compare our proposed RWR method and RWR with sparsity constraint (RWR-OPT) with several baselines as follows: (1) Text Similarity: we first crawl all the published papers for a reviewer, and then use bag-of-words cosine similarity between the query paper and the reviewer's published papers to measure the relevance score between the query paper and the reviewer. (2) Topic Similarity: we first crawl all the published papers of a reviewer, and then use topic cosine similarity between the topic distribution of the query paper and the topic distribution of the reviewer's publication to measure the relevance score between the query paper and the reviewer. Both (1) and (2) are estimated by max pooling as introduced in Section 3.2. (3) Random Walk (RW): We only apply a random walk process on the graph instead of RWR. (4) State-of-art APT model as introduced in [8]. Since only $p@5$, $p@10$, ... , $p@45$ are provided in [8], we can only compare our results with theirs on $p@5$ and $p@10$.

5.3.1 *Precision Evaluation Results on NIPS Dataset*

Our first experiment shows the assignment performance of different models on the NIPS dataset. We evaluate each algorithm under two relevance settings. The first one is a binary relevance judgment, similar to [8], that only uses Very Relevant (score = 3) as relevant (label = 1); otherwise, label = 0. For the second setting, instead of binary judgment, we use a soft judgment as follows: Very Relevant (score = 3) as label = 1, Relevant (score = 2) as label = 0.67, Slightly Relevant (score = 1) as label = 0.33, and Irrelevant (score = 0) as label = 0.

The results for precision at position k for both relevance settings are shown in Tables 1 and 2, showing the performance (mean precision at position k) for all the methods. In Tables 1 and 2, the best result in each column is highlighted in bold. When a relevance value reaches the 5% level of test significance, it is denoted by one star, and when it reaches the 1% level, it is denoted by two stars. We see that our RWR method consistently achieves the best performance, with high significance level at several positions. Note that since there is less data at top positions, it is more difficult to get high-confidence numbers in these cases.

We further compare our proposed RWR-OPT method with the others and plot the performance comparisons in Figure 2 (a) and (b). The proposed RWR consistently beats all the other baselines (RW, text-similarity, and topic-similarity), which demonstrates its effectiveness in terms of relevance. In fact, RWR-OPT performs slightly better than the basic RWR algorithm in several cases. Thus, even with the added sparsity constraint, there is no reduction in relevance.

5.3.2 *Expertise Evaluation on the CIKM Dataset*

Since there is no human evaluation data in the CIKM dataset, we use the expertise matching scores described in Section 5.2.2 to evaluate the expertise performance of each model, shown in Figure 2 (c). From the experimental results, we see that the RWR and RWR-OPT models achieve the best performance.

Table 1: The mean precision performance for binary judgment on the NIPS dataset. The best result in each column is highlighted in bold. Star-annotated values indicate a significance level of 0.95, and two stars indicate a significance level of 0.99.

Method	P@1	P@2	P@3	P@4	P@5
RWR	**0.353**	**0.324**	0.245	**0.25**	**0.241***
RW	0.235	0.162	0.157	0.147	0.129
Topic-Sim	0.206	0.162	0.157	0.147	0.153
Text-Sim	0.294	0.235	**0.255**	0.228	0.194
APT200	-	-	-	-	0.2059
Method	P@6	P@7	P@8	P@9	P@10
RWR	**0.225**	**0.218**	**0.217***	**0.216****	**0.218****
RW	0.137	0.147	0.140	0.128	0.121
Topic-Sim	0.147	0.130	0.129	0.131	0.133
Text-Sim	0.192	0.173	0.162	0.161	0.162
APT200	-	-	-	-	0.1412

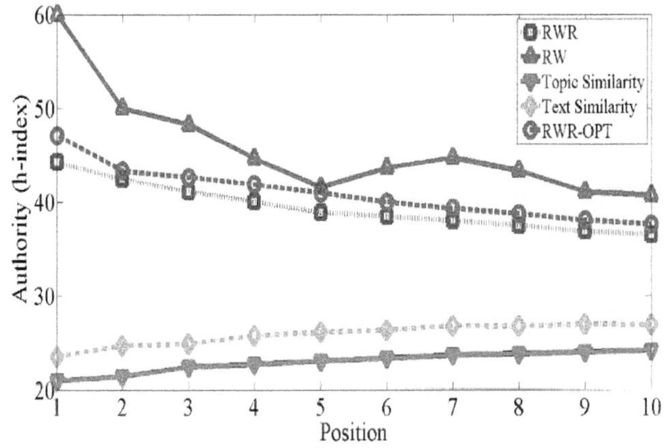

(a) NIPS Dataset

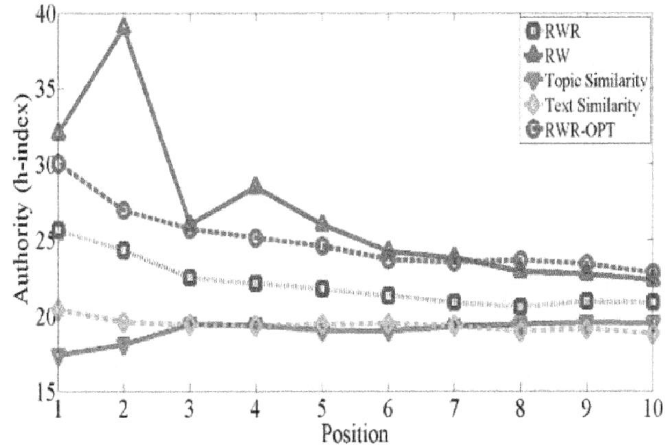

(b) CIKM Dataset

Figure 3: Average authority of top k reviewers retrieved, for NIPS and CIKM datasets.

Table 2: The mean precision performance for soft judgment on the NIPS dataset. The best result in each column is highlighted in bold.

Method	P@1	P@2	P@3	P@4	P@5
RWR	**0.559**	**0.500**	0.438	**0.450**	**0.453**
RW	0.510	0.451	0.438	0.407	0.380
Topic-Sim	0.352	0.328	0.320	0.321	0.325
Text-Sim	0.451	0.426	**0.444**	0.443	0.392
Method	P@6	P@7	P@8	P@9	P@10
RWR	**0.429**	**0.425**	**0.423**	**0.430***	**0.430***
RW	0.385	0.398	0.380	0.363	0.351
Topic-Sim	0.322	0.316	0.314	0.318	0.318
Text-Sim	0.394	0.371	0.357	0.356	0.348

5.3.3 *Authority Evaluation*

Besides expertise, authority is another intermediate goal for us to achieve better reviewers as evaluated by humans. In this experiment, we evaluate the mean authority performance at position k. The authority performance of each model on the two benchmark datasets is shown in Figure 3. From the results, we can conclude that the RW method consistently beats all the other methods, which is to be expected since random walk processes are usually used for graph-based prestige measurement. We also find that the proposed RWR-OPT and RWR models perform better than the other expertise matching baselines (i.e., text similarity and topic similarity).

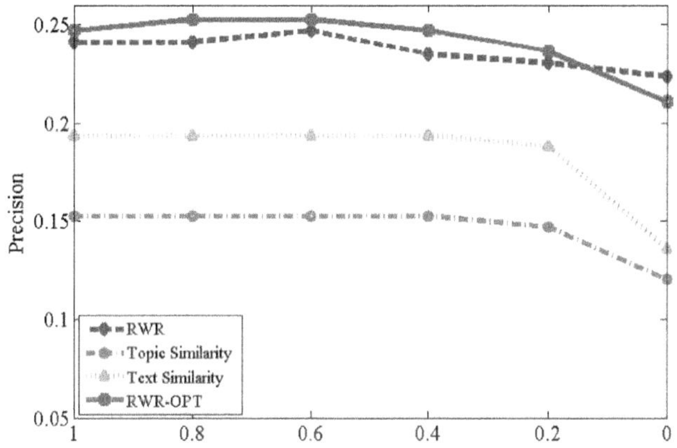

(a) Graph Density d_{graph}

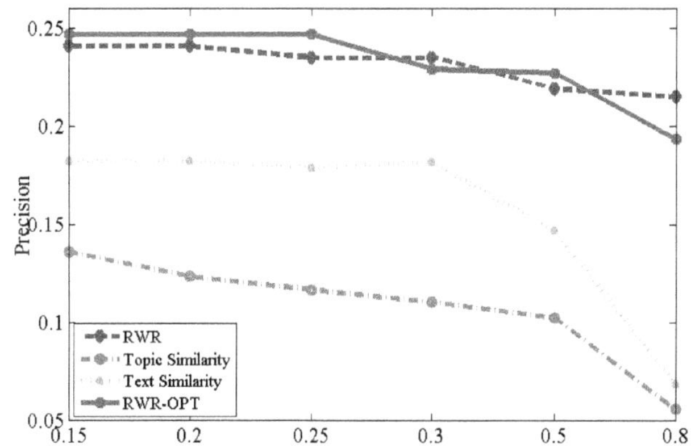

(b) Topic Divergence d_{topic}

Figure 4: The trade-off between relevance and diversity of a group of k (k=5) reviewers for NIPS dataset.

5.3.4 *Diversity Evaluation*

In this experiment, we measure how the average relevance for a group of k reviewers changes as the required diversify score for the same group increases. To explore the trade-off between relevance and diversity, we first define a set of diversity threshold scores T_i, and utilize a post-processing process to choose a group of k reviewers that has the highest accumulated ranking score while having at least diversity score T_i. Then the average relevance score for all the reviewers in the group is considered as the relevance score for the group. As T_i increases, more diversity is required.

We use two definitions of diversity introduced in Section 5.2.4 to evaluate the trade-off between relevance and diversity, as shown in Figure 4. We see that from both (a) and (b) that each model has a relevance drop as the diversity increases. However, both the text-similarity and topic-similarity see a significant decrease when the diversity threshold is approaching the maximum diversity possible, while both RWR and RWR-OPT drop only slightly. Also we find that with the same precision score, RWR-OPT achieves higher diversity than RWR, which proves the effectiveness of the sparsity constraint in our optimization formula.

6. CONCLUSION

As an expert retrieval problem, paper reviewer assignment is a labor-intensive task. To reduce the time required to manually assign submitted papers to suitable reviewers, many automatic review assignment systems have been introduced. The major disadvantage for existing work is that they are trying to conduct the matching according to expertise while omitting the other criteria. In this paper, we study how to rank candidate reviewers while balancing three objectives: authority, expertise and diversity. We propose a graph constructed on candidate reviewers and the query paper, and then an optimization framework with sparsity principle is introduced. We tested all the methods on two benchmark datasets. Experiment results show that the RWR outperforms text similarity and topic similarity baselines in both expertise and authority measurements, and the selected reviewers obtain higher diversity scores when we enforce group sparsity on the grouped reviewers.

7. REFERENCES

[1] H. Tong, C. Faloutsos, and J.-Y. Pan. Fast random walk with restart and its applications. In IEEE International Conference on Data Mining (ICDM) 2006, pages 613-622.

[2] M. Karimzadehgan and C. Zhai. Constrained multi-aspect expertise matching for committee review assignment. In ACM International Conference on Information and Knowledge Management (CIKM) 2009, pages 1697-1700.

[3] F. Wang, B. Chen, and Z. Miao. A survey on reviewer assignment problem. In International Conference on Industrial, Engineering and Other Applications of Applied Intelligent Systems (IEA/AIE) 2008, pages 718-727.

[4] W. Tang, J. Tang, and C. Tan. Expertise Matching via Constraint-Based Optimization. In IEEE/WIC/ACM International Conference on Web Intelligence (WI) and Intelligent Agent Technology (IAT) 2010, pages 34-41.

[5] L. Charlin, R. S. Zemel. The Toronto paper matching system: an automated paper-reviewer assignment system. In International Conference on Machine Learning (ICML) 2013, Workshop on Peer Reviewing and Publishing Models.

[6] D. Conry, Y. Koren, N. Ramakrishnan. Recommender Systems for the Conference Paper Assignment Problem. In ACM Recommender System Conference (RecSys) 2009, pages 357-360.

[7] S. Hettich, M. J. Pazzani. Mining for Proposal Reviewers: Lessons Learned at the National Science Foundation. In ACM SIGMOD Conference on Knowledge Discovery and Data Mining (KDD) 2006, pages 862-871.

[8] D. M. Mimno, A. McCallum. Expertise modeling for matching papers with reviewers. In ACM SIGMOD Conference on Knowledge Discovery and Data Mining (KDD) 2007, pages 500-509.

[9] M. A. Rodriguez, J. Bollen. An algorithm to determine peer-reviewers. In ACM International Conference on Information and Knowledge Management (CIKM) 2008, pages 319-328.

[10] Y. Fujiwara, M. Nakatsuji, M. Onizuka, and M. Kitsuregawa. Fast and Exact Top-k Search for Random Walk with Restart. In The Proceedings of the VLDB Endowment (PVLDB), 5(5):442-453, 2012.

[11] J. M. Kleinberg, Authoritative Sources In A Hyper-linked Environment. Journal of the ACM, 46(5):604-632, 1999.

[12] T. Haveliwala, Topic-sensitive PageRank. In International World Wide Web Conference (WWW) 2002, pages 517-526.

[13] P. Berkhin. A Survey on PageRank Computing. Internet Math. 2(1), 73-120, 2005.

[14] J. Yang, K. Yu, Y. Gong, T. Huang. Linear Spatial Pyramid Matching Using Sparse Coding for Image Classification. In Conference on Computer Vision and Pattern Recognition (CVPR), 2009.

[15] Microsoft Academic Search. `http://academic.research.microsoft.com/`

[16] D. Blei, A. Ng, and M. Jordan. Latent Dirichlet allocation. Journal of Machine Learning Research 2003, 3:993-1022.

[17] L. Li and N. Memon. Mining Groups of Common Interest: Discovering Topical Communities with Network Flows. In International Conference on Machine Learning and Data Mining (MLDM) 2013, pages 405-420.

[18] Q. Mei, J. Guo, and D. Radev. Divrank: the interplay of prestige and diversity in information networks. ACM SIGMOD Conference on Knowledge Discovery and Data Mining (KDD) 2010, pages 1009-1018.

[19] B. Wilson. The Machine Learning Dictionary. `http://www.cse.unsw.edu.au/~billw/mldict.html`

[20] T. Griffiths, M. Steyvers. Finding Scientific Topics. In Proceedings of the National Academy of Sciences, 2004, 101 (suppl. 1), 5228-5235.

[21] D. Liu, G. Ye, C. Chen, S. Yan, S. Chang. Hybrid Social Media Network. In ACM Multimedia, 2012.

[22] Y. Nesterov. Smooth minimization of non-smooth functions. Mathematical Programming, 2005.

[23] J. Liu, S. Ji, J. Ye. SLEP: Sparse learning with efficient projections. Software Tool. Arizona State University, 2009. `www.public.asu.edu/~jye02/Software/SLEP`

[24] L. AlSumait, D. Barbará, C. Domeniconi. On-Line LDA: Adaptive Topic Models for Mining Text Streams with Applications to Topic Detection and Tracking. In IEEE International Conference on Data Mining (ICDM), 2008.

[25] L. Page, S. Brin, R. Motwani, and T. Winograd. The pagerank citation ranking: Bringing order to the web. Technical report, Stanford Digital Library Technologies Project, 1998.

[26] M.R. Morris, J. Teevan, and K. Panovich. A comparison of information seeking using search engines and social networks. In International Conference on Weblogs and Social Media (ICWSM) 2010, pages 291-294.

[27] D. Horowitz, S. D. Kamvar. Anatomy of a large-scale social search engine. In International World Wide Web Conference (WWW) 2010.

Factored MDPs for Detecting Topics of User Sessions

Maryam Tavakol[†]
[†]Technische Universität Darmstadt
Department of Computer Science
Darmstadt, Germany
tavakol@kma.informatik.tu-darmstadt.de

Ulf Brefeld[†‡]
[‡]German Institute for Educational Research
Information Center for Education
Frankfurt, Germany
brefeld@kma.informatik.tu-darmstadt.de

ABSTRACT

Recommender systems aim to capture interests of users to provide tailored recommendations. User interests are however often unique and depend on many unobservable factors including a user's mood and the local weather. We take a contextual session-based approach and propose a sequential framework using factored Markov decision processes (fMDPs) to detect the user's goal (the topic) of a session. We show that an independence assumption on the attributes of items leads to a set of independent models that can be optimised efficiently. Our approach results in interpretable topics that can be effectively turned into recommendations. Empirical results on a real world click log from a large e-commerce company exhibit highly accurate topic prediction rates of about 90%. Translating our approach into a topic-driven recommender system outperforms several baseline competitors.

Categories and Subject Descriptors

H.3 [**Information Storage and Retrieval**]: Information Search and Retrieval

Keywords

MDP; recommender systems; session-based; user intent

1. INTRODUCTION

Recommender systems are designed to satisfy user's information and tangible needs. Guessing the intention of users is not only fundamental for the overall user experience but directly linked to revenue. User intent however is driven by unobservable internal (e.g., mood, spontaneous inspiration) as well as external (e.g., weather, location) processes [15]. Capturing user intent is therefore one of the most challenging problems in many retrieval and recommendation tasks.

The context of a user is often seen as a proxy for the unobserved processes [34]. Context may be provided by previously visited pages [8], viewed items [28], or user profiles [11], and is often studied together with personalisation [20]. There is a broad range of applications using contextual variables of users including query refinement [27], re-ranking for web search [12], market segmentation [14], and latent variable models for spoken language understanding [9]. An alternative approach to capturing the intent of users are topic models. Topic models [5] can be seen as a generative probabilistic semantics that have been proposed for retrieval [31] as well as recommender systems [23, 10]. Topic models for temporal data however often require stationary data distributions [4, 1], an assumption too restrictive for highly dynamic scenarios such as e-commerce.

In this paper, we focus on recommender systems where user feedback is recorded implicitly, for instance through clicks on result pages of search engines or on lists of recommended items. The implicit feedback can be used to train autonomous recommender systems as the noisy and incomplete batch of user responses provides a partial labelling of the data. Note that these partial labels do not suffice for purely supervised approaches as the outcome of recommending alternative items is undefined. On the other hand, the task neither fits a purely unsupervised setting as the valuable (partial) ground-truth would be discarded. The abstract problem setting matches that of reinforcement learning-style approaches where uncertainty about the value of actions (e.g., recommending an item) is minimised by trading off exploration and exploitation [28, 18]. Reinforcement learning-based approaches are naturally sequential models with intrinsic Markov assumptions that allow for capturing the context of a user by explicitly representing sequences of previously clicked items [28, 35].

We study factored Markov decision processes (fMDPs) [6] to detect topics of user sessions. We take a sequential approach and leverage ideas from [35] and [28] to characterise sessions in terms of the history of viewed items. However, straight forwardly solving the resulting fMDPs is infeasible due to exponentially increasing state spaces. Moreover, the structure of the value function does not necessarily retain the structure of the process after factorisation [17]. Hence, many approaches to approximate value functions have been proposed (e.g., [13, 7]).

Commencing with a standard fMDP on the history of viewed items, our main contributions are as follows. We show that an independence assumption on the attributes of items allows to equivalently represent the fMDP by an ensemble of independent fMDPs. Compared to the initial fMDP, the resulting state space is orders of magnitude smaller and the ensemble can be optimised efficiently. In addition, we propose a robust approximation following ideas from Shani et al. [28] to improve the predictive accuracy in the presence of data sparsity and large-scale applications. We show that the learned Q-values can be easily turned into interpretable topics and recommendations.

In extensive experiments on real world data at enterprise-level scales provided by Zalando, we observe highly accurate topic de-

RecSys'14, October 6–10, 2014, Foster City, Silicon Valley, CA, USA.

ACM 978-1-4503-2668-1/14/10 ...$15.00.
http://dx.doi.org/10.1145/2645710.2645739.

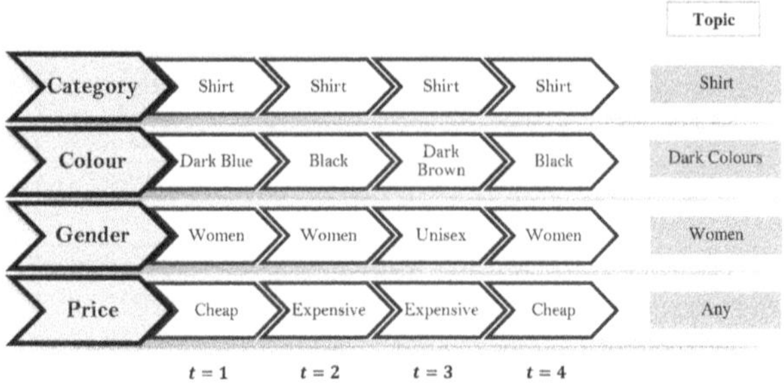

Figure 1: An exemplarily user session of an e-commerce platform. The session is viewed as a (possibly independent) sequences of item attributes. The right hand side shows the topic of the session.

tection rates of about 90%. We show that these topics can effectively be utilised to recommend items of interest with high accuracy. Translating our approach into a topic-driven recommender system outperforms collaborative baseline methods in terms of average rank.

The remainder of our paper is structured as follows. Section 2 motivates the problem setting and presents a running example that we will use throughout the paper. We introduce our technical contribution in Section 3 and present empirical results in Section 4. Section 5 briefly reviews related work on topic detection for sequential prediction problems including recommender systems and Section 6 concludes.

2. PRELIMINARIES

Traditional recommender systems and personalisation approaches are designed to capture long-term preferences of users. Prominent examples are movie [3] and job recommendations [21], conference paper assignments [25], or e-commerce application scenarios [19]. Short-term interests of users provide valuable additional information to improve the quality of recommendations. Short-term interests may rise from unexpected events (got an MP3 player, need headphones) spontaneous moods and ideas (split-up with partner, need action movie for distraction), or external sources (its freezing outside, need winter coat).

Figure 1 visualises the scenario using an e-commerce example. The figure shows an exemplary user session where a user views a series of garments. The first item is a *cheap dark blue shirt* followed by an *expensive black shirt* and so on. Instead of addressing the items and their attributes jointly, we treat their features as independent. We thus focus on sequences *shirt, shirt, shirt, shirt* for the attribute *category* or *dark blue, black, dark brown, black* for *colour*, respectively. Every such sequence gives us an expectation about the value of the next item. For instance, the former (constant) sequence is likely extended by another *shirt* while the latter gives rise to a dark coloured item. The attribute *price* in Figure 1 constitutes a special case as the sequence does not allow to confine the possible values. Hence, *any* of the attribute values is possible or, in other words, the attribute *price* is not important for the user session.

Given the session in Figure 1, the user's goal is to find *dark coloured shirts for women of any price level.* We call the corresponding distribution of attribute values the *topic* of the session. For the attribute *colour*, we expect dark colours to be very likely while light colours are associated with small probabilities close to zero. Formally, a topic is defined as follows.

DEFINITION 1. *Let s be a (possibly ongoing) user session and $\{\mathcal{X}_1, \ldots, \mathcal{X}_n\}$ be a set of random variables encoding attributes of items. The topic of a session s is defined as the distribution of attributes of the next item given by $P(\mathcal{X}_1 = x_1, \ldots, \mathcal{X}_n = x_n|s)$.*

Once the topic of a session has been detected, a recommender system could leverage the estimate to recommend items that lie in the very topic of the session. Note that the topic of a session is independent of other sessions of that user and its lifetime therefore well suited to adapt to short-term interests of users.

In this paper, we aim to accurately identify the topic of user sessions. We propose factored Markov decision processes (fMDPs) and define user sessions as sequences of viewed (clicked) items. The detection of topics is consequentially addressed as a sequential Markov decision problem. In the next section, we deploy reinforcement learning agents to detect the topic and to translate the estimate into topic-driven recommendations.

3. MDP-BASED TOPIC DETECTION

3.1 A Standard Approach

We are given a set of items $\mathcal{I}$ described by a set of n random variables $\mathcal{I} = (\mathcal{X}_1, \ldots, \mathcal{X}_n)$, where each $\mathcal{X}_j$ encodes an attribute (e.g., colour, category) and takes on values in a discrete and finite set $dom(\mathcal{X}_j)$. Every item $i \in \mathcal{I}$ is therefore defined by a set of n attributes $i = (x_1^i, \ldots, x_n^i)$ with $x_j \in dom(\mathcal{X}_j)$ for $1 \leq j \leq n$. Items are completely characterised by their attributes, that is, the existence/probability of an item is equivalent to the existence/probability of its combination of attributes. Assuming for instance that item i has attributes $i = (x_1^i, \ldots, x_n^i)$ it holds

$$\Pr(\mathcal{I} = i) = \Pr(\mathcal{X}_1 = x_1^i, \ldots, \mathcal{X}_n = x_n^i). \quad (1)$$

To avoid cluttering the notation unnecessarily, we omit the superscript i in the remainder.

An MDP is a four-tuple $(\mathcal{S}, \mathcal{A}, R, P)$ consisting of the set of states $\mathcal{S}$, the set of actions $\mathcal{A}$, a reward function $R : \mathcal{S} \times \mathcal{A} \to \mathbb{R}$, and a transition function $P : \mathcal{S} \times \mathcal{A} \times \mathcal{S} \to [0, 1]$ representing the dynamics of the environment. The goal of MDP is to find the optimal value function $V : \mathcal{S} \to \mathbb{R}$ for the state space [29].

In a straight forward sequential MDP for contextual item recommendation, the set of states $\mathcal{S}$ is defined as the Kleene closure of the set of items, that is $\mathcal{S} = \mathcal{I}^*$. The set $\mathcal{S}$ thus contains all possible sequences of items and every element $s \in \mathcal{S}$ can be identified with a (possibly unfinished) user session in terms of the viewed items. An action $a \in \mathcal{A}$ corresponds to recommending a particular item from $\mathcal{I}$, so that we may identify $\mathcal{A} = \mathcal{I}$ and consequentially for every $i \in \mathcal{I}$ there exists an $a \in \mathcal{A}$ such that $i = a$ and vice versa.

The described MDP is trivially infeasible due to the infinite number of states $\mathcal{S}$. Though in practice not all possible sequences will actually be observed and an additionally incorporated Markov assumption may further reduce the state space, the model remains intractable even for small and medium-sized ranges of items.

3.2 Factorisation

We therefore take a different approach and define the MDP over the set of attributes $\mathcal{X}_1, \ldots, \mathcal{X}_n$ instead of the items $\mathcal{I}$. Due to Equation (1), we obtain an equivalent factored MDP (fMDP) where the set of states is given by the Kleene closure $\mathcal{S} = (\mathcal{X}_1, \ldots, \mathcal{X}_n)^*$. An element $s \in \mathcal{S}_j$ corresponds to a sequence of realisations of the j-th attribute. Consequentially, the factorisation also impacts the set of actions which is now given by $\mathcal{A} = \mathcal{A}_1 \times \ldots \times \mathcal{A}_n$ with $\mathcal{A}_j = dom(\mathcal{X}_j)$ for all j. We use $a_j \in \mathcal{A}_j$ and $x_j \in \mathcal{X}_j$ interchangeably in the remainder for convenience.

The reward after taking action a (i.e., recommending the corresponding item i) in state s is given by the reward function $R(s, a)$.

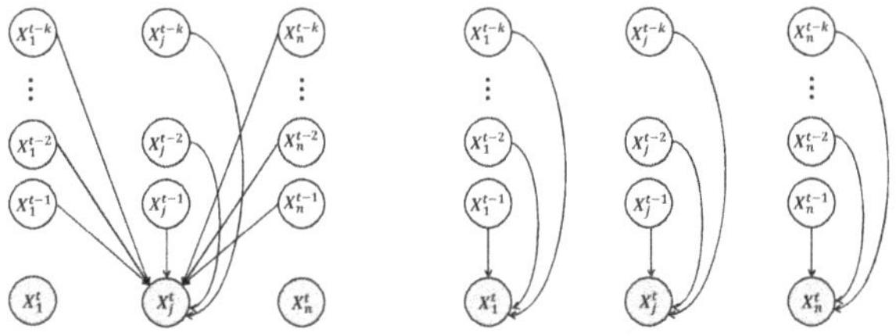

Figure 2: Left: Transition model of a joint factored MDP. Every attribute value depends on the complete history of all previously viewed items and their attributes which leads to an infeasible model. Right: Sequences of attributes form independent components. There are no dependencies between attributes.

Positive rewards indicate a click on a recommended item in which case the recommendation was successful and has been accepted by the user. The transition function $P(s'|s,a)$ estimates the probability of entering state s' after recommending a in state s. Note that s serves as a prefix of s' which is given by $s' = s \circ i'$, where i' is the clicked item by the user and $\circ$ the operator that appends two sequences, e.g., $q \circ p = pq$.

The length of the actual state s is continuously increased by appending clicked items, exactly one at a time. Thus, instead of addressing the complex $P(s'|s,a)$, transition probabilities $P(i'|s,a)$ are often used as an equivalent proxy due to their simpler structure. The quantity $P(i'|s,a)$ is the transition probability of clicking on item i' when in state s and recommending item a. The transition probabilities can be represented as a two-layer acyclic graph that connects the attributes of the previously viewed items in s with the attributes of the item to be clicked denoted by i'. Theoretically, the joint transition probability can be efficiently computed by factorising conditional probabilities, e.g.,

$$\Pr(\mathcal{X}_1', ..., \mathcal{X}_n'|s,a) = \prod_{j=1}^{n} \Pr(\mathcal{X}_j'|parents(\mathcal{X}_j'), a),$$

where $parents(\mathcal{X}_j')$ denotes the parents of the node $\mathcal{X}_j'$ in the underlying graphical model. However, the state space of the fMDP grows exponentially and renders practical application infeasible as the exact estimation of the optimal policy is not feasible due to the curse of dimensionality [13]. Thus, we haven't won anything yet in terms of feasibility but successfully rephrased the model over attribute sequences of the viewed items (Figure 2 left).

3.3 Exploiting Independence

Directly addressing the joint $\Pr(\mathcal{X}_1, \ldots, \mathcal{X}_n|s,a)$ requires a state space that is intractable even for small and medium-sized warehouses. We therefore treat the attributes of the items as independent and approximate the intractable joint by a product of independent decisions,

$$\Pr(\mathcal{X}_1, \ldots, \mathcal{X}_n|s,a) \approx \prod_{j=1}^{n} \Pr(\mathcal{X}_j|s_j, a_j).$$

The idea is to split the fMDP into an ensemble of n disjoint and independent fMDPs, one for each attribute. The j-th fMDP focuses on only the j-th attribute and recommends a realisation a_j of $\mathcal{X}_j$ based on the sequence of attributes s_j of the previously viewed items. In Figure 1 for instance, guessing that the next item will be another *shirt* can trivially be done in the absence of all other attributes. A similar argument holds for expecting a *dark colour* or a garment for *women*.

The following theorem shows that an fMDP with independent chains of random variables admits an equivalent representation as an ensemble of n independent fMDPs. In order to propagate single receiving reward through all fMDPs, we consequentially assume additive factorised rewards $R(x,a) = \sum_{j=1}^{n} R_j(x_j, a_j)$.

THEOREM 1. *A factored MDP with a set of n independent components $\mathcal{X} = \{\mathcal{X}_1, \ldots, \mathcal{X}_n\}$ allows an equivalent representation as an ensemble of n independent fMDPs, one for each component $\mathcal{X}_j$ where $1 \leq j \leq n$. Let $V^*(x)$ be the optimal value for state $\mathcal{X} = x$ in the joint fMDP and $V^*(x_j)$ be the optimal value for attribute $\mathcal{X}_j = x_j$ in the j-th fMDP, for all $1 \leq j \leq n$. It holds*

$$V^*(x) = \sum_{j=1}^{n} V^*(x_j).$$

PROOF. The standard update rule of value iteration is given by

$$V^{N+1}(x) = \max_a [R(x,a) + \gamma \textstyle\sum_{x'} P(x'|x,a) V^N(x')] [29].$$

Replacing the maximum operator by a softmax gives

$$V^{N+1}(x) = \frac{1}{\rho} \log \sum_a \exp[\rho R(x,a) + \gamma\rho \sum_{x'} P(x'|x,a) V^N(x')],$$

where ρ controls the degree of the approximation and the exact maximum is recovered for $\rho \to \infty$. We show the claim by induction for value iteration. For $N = 1$, we have

$$V^1(x_j) = \frac{1}{\rho} \log \sum_{a_j} \exp[\rho R_j(x_j, a_j)]$$

for the j-th fMDP of the ensemble and the joint is obtained by

$$\begin{aligned} V^1(x) &= \frac{1}{\rho} \log \sum_a \exp[\rho R(x,a)] \\ &= \frac{1}{\rho} \log \sum_{a_1} [\sum_{a_2} \cdots [\sum_{a_n} \prod_j \exp\{\rho R_j(x_j, a_j)\}]] \end{aligned}$$

The innermost summation can be rewritten as

$$\begin{aligned} &\sum_{a_n} \Big[\exp\{\rho R_1(x_1,a_1)\} \times \cdots \times \exp\{\rho R_n(x_n,a_n)\}\Big] \\ &= \exp\{\rho R_1(x_1,a_1)\} \times \cdots \times \exp\{\rho R_{n-1}(x_{n-1},a_{n-1})\} \\ &\quad \times \sum_{a_n} \exp\{\rho R_n(x_n,a_n)\} \end{aligned}$$

by drawing unrelated terms out of the sum. Continuing for the other summations gives

$$\begin{aligned} V^1(x) &= \frac{1}{\rho} \log \Big[\prod_j \sum_{a_j} \exp\{\rho R_j(x_j,a_j)\}\Big] \\ &= \frac{1}{\rho} \sum_j \log \sum_{a_j} \exp[\rho R_j(x_j,a_j)] = \sum_j V^1(x_j), \end{aligned}$$

which shows the claim for $N = 1$. Now assume that $V^N(x) = \sum_{j=1}^{n} V^N(x_j)$ holds for all x. For the joint fMDP, the second summand in the exponent is simplified by

$$\begin{aligned} &\sum_{x'} P(x'|x,a) V^N(x') = \sum_{x'} P(x_1'|x_1,a_1) \cdots P(x_n'|x_n,a_n) V^N(x') \\ &= \sum_{x'} P(x_1'|x_1,a_1) \cdots P(x_n'|x_n,a_n) [V^N(x_1') + \cdots + V^N(x_n')], \end{aligned}$$

where the latter gives rise to the telescope sum

$$\sum_{x_1'} P(x_1'|x_1,a_1)\Big[\sum_{x_2'} P(x_2'|x_2,a_2)\Big[\times\cdots$$

$$\cdots\times\Big[\sum_{x_n'} P(x_n'|x_n,a_n)\Big[V^N(x_1')+...+V^N(x_n')\Big]\Big]\Big]\Big].$$

The innermost summation over the new state x_n' yields

$$V^N(x_1')\sum_{x_n'} P(x_n'|x_n,a_n)+\cdots+\sum_{x_n'} P(x_n'|x_n,a_n)V^N(x_n')$$

and since $\sum_{x_n'} P(x_n'|x_n,a_n)=1$ we obtain

$$V^N(x_1')+...+V^N(x_{n-1}')+\sum\nolimits_{x_n'} P(x_n'|x_n,a_n)V^N(x_n').$$

Drawing out the remaining terms from unrelated summations and putting things together gives

$$V^{N+1}(x)=\frac{1}{\rho}\log\sum_{a_1}\Big[\cdots\Big[\sum_{a_n}\prod_j \exp[\rho\{R_j(x_j,a_j)$$
$$+\gamma\sum_{x_j'} P(x_j'|x_j,a_j)V^N(x_j')\}]\Big]\Big].$$

Reordering terms shows the claim. □

Theorem 1 shows that any high dimensional fMDP with independent attributes can be equivalently expressed by several independent fMDPs. Exploiting the independence between the attributes, the resulting ensemble consists of an fMDP for every component. The resulting state spaces are independent sequences over a single attribute given by the Kleene closure $\mathcal{S}_j=(dom(\mathcal{X}_j))^*$ for all components j. Note that a result by [17] shows that the value function of fMDPs does in general not retain the structure of the process. Our theorem proves that a structured value function is generally obtainable for fMDPs with independent components.

Still, a major drawback of the model is the dependence on the whole session, that is, every viewed item impacts all subsequent actions. We therefore take a k-th order Markov assumption to represent only the k most recently viewed items explicitly. The set of states of the j-th fMDP is effectively reduced to $\mathcal{S}_j=(dom(\mathcal{X}_j))^k$. The Markov assumption discards long-range dependencies and lead, together with the previous independence assumption, to an efficient and compact representation of the ensemble as shown in Figure 2 (right).

3.4 Optimisation

The resulting independent fMDPs can be optimised independently and in parallel using standard reinforcement learning techniques such as value iteration. Value iteration learns the state-value function, $V(s)$, using the model of the environment; the reward and transition functions $R(s,a)$ and $P(s'|s,a)$, and converges to the optimal solution in a discounted finite MDP [29].

The set of states in the j-th fMDP is described by a k-sequence of realisations of the j-th attribute $\mathcal{X}_j$ given by $s_j=(x_j^{t-k},\ldots,x_j^t)$. The task of the agent is to predict the value of action $a_j\in dom(\mathcal{X}_j)$ in the actual state s_j. The transition function P encodes the probability of observing the subsequent state $s_j'=(x_j^{t-k+1},\ldots,x_j^{t+1})$ and the reward function R_j provides feedback for recommending a_j in s_j. Value iteration uses the following update rule for value determination,

$$V^{N+1}(s_j)=\max_{a_j}\Big[R_j(x_j,a_j)+\gamma\sum\nolimits_{s_j'} P(s_j'|s_j,a_j)V^N(s_j')\Big].$$

When the value function converges to the optimal V^*, state-action values $Q(s_j,a_j)$ can be derived

$$Q(s_j,a_j)=R(s_j,a_j)+\gamma\sum\nolimits_{s_j'} P(s_j'|s_j,a_j)V^*(s_j'),$$

where $Q(s_j,a_j)$ measures the quality of recommending a_j in state s_j. Realisations with high Q-values are likely to be observed in the next page view while small Q-values indicate very unlikely observations. We use the terms $Q(s_j,a_j)$ and $Q(s_j,x_j)$ interchangeably in the remainder.

Reinforcement learning techniques often perform poorly in large scale problems due to slow convergence rates. Adapting the model to data is therefore performed in two steps; offline and online. First, an initial model is learned by value iteration where transition and reward functions are adapted to historic data by maximum likelihood. The trained model is then deployed in an online scenario where it is gradually updated according to the user feedback to improve estimations. In practice, value iteration can be repeated periodically (e.g., once in a week) to keep the system up to date.

3.5 Approximation

In practical applications, the available data is often too sparse to allow for an accurate estimation of the transition probabilities. In addition, applications on large-scales render keeping the whole set of transition probabilities infeasible due to memory requirements. We thus propose an efficient approximation of our model based on the ideas of Shani et al. [28].

The main idea is to focus on estimating the probability $\Pr(i'|s)$ of item i' to be clicked next, irrespectively of the action. The transition $\Pr(i'|s,a)$ can be approximatively reconstructed from $\Pr(i'|s)$ as follows. Recall that action a is identical to an item $i\in\mathcal{I}$. There are three possible outcomes of taking action $i=x$ when in state s: (i) The user accepts the recommendation i with probability $P(i|s,i)$, (ii) she rejects i and clicks instead on item i' with probability $P(i'|s,i)$, or (iii) the session terminates with probability $P(\emptyset|s,i)$. Consider the former two events. The task is to estimate $P(i|s,i)$ and $P(i'|s,i)$ as a surrogate for the entire transition function. Note that in the latter, a click on i' is independent of the recommended item i.

The assumption is that the probability of clicking on a recommended item is larger than the probability of choosing the item in the absence of a recommendation, that is $P(i|s,i)\geq P(i|s)$ [28]. Analogously, the probability of clicking on item i in the absence of any recommendation is higher than for clicking on i when the recommended item is actually $i'\neq i$, that is $P(i|s,i')\leq P(i|s)$. By choosing appropriate constants $\alpha>1$ and $0<\beta<1$, the desired quantities are approximated by $[P(i|s,i)\approx\alpha P(i|s)$ and $P(i|s,i')\approx\beta P(i|s)$, subject to $P(i|s,i)+\sum_{i'\neq i}P(i'|s,i)+P(\emptyset|s,i)=1$, which is obtained by normalisation.

3.6 Topic Extraction

Once approximate or exact Q-values $Q(s_j,x_j)$ are computed, they can be used to extract the topic of the session as follows. The value $Q(s_j,x_j)$ is proportional to the probability that the user clicks on an item with attribute x_j given the sequence of realisations s_j. In other words, realisations with high Q-values are likely observed next and thus constitute a part of the topic of s_j. For uniformly distributed Q-values, e.g., $Q(s_j,x_j)\approx Q(s_j,x_j')$ for all x_j,x_j', the topic contains the whole domain $dom(\mathcal{X}_j)$, indicating that the j-th attribute does not contribute to the topic. As a consequence, any realisation of that attribute may be observed next. Intermediate Q-values are ranked according to their difference to the maximum Q-value, such that the expected realisations of attribute

j are computed by the min-max normalisation

$$q(\mathcal{X}_j = x_j|s_j) = \frac{Q(s_j, x_j) - \min_{x'_j}[Q(s_j, x'_j)]}{\max_{x'_j}[Q(s_j, x'_j)] - \min_{x'_j}[Q(s_j, x'_j)]}, \quad (2)$$

for all $1 \leq j \leq n$. The independent results are then multiplicatively combined to approximate the desired probabilities

$$P(x_1, \ldots, x_n|s) \propto \prod_{j=1}^{n} q(x_j|s_j).$$

3.7 Recommendation

Our approach can also be turned into a recommender system. In contrast to the topic extraction, we use a softmax instead of the min-max normalisation to translate Q-values into probabilities,

$$\Pr(\mathcal{X}_j = x_j|s_j) = \frac{\exp\{Q(s_j, x_j)\}}{\sum_{x'_j} \exp\{Q(s_j, x'_j\}}. \quad (3)$$

The softmax gives us a probability distribution over the state space of every attribute. The use of the exponential function penalises even small differences and thus acts like a probabilistic winner-takes-all. Note that in practice, recommendations have to be computed very efficiently under rigid time constraints. Having a clear set of winners helps to speed-up the computation by continuously filtering out items at early stages that cannot make it into the top-m to save time for more promising candidates.

Given the estimates in Equation (3), the score for item i with attribute combination $x_1, \ldots, x_n$ is simply given by the product of the corresponding probabilities, or alternatively, by the sum of the corresponding log-probabilities, that is,

$$score(i; s) = \prod_{j=1}^{n} P(\mathcal{X}_j = x_j|s_j) \propto \sum_{j=1}^{n} \log P(\mathcal{X}_j = x_j|s_j).$$

The scores impose a ranking on the items and the top-scoring products can be recommended.

4. EMPIRICAL EVALUATION

In this section, we evaluate our approach on an anonymised click log from Zalando[1], a large European online fashion retailer. The data distribution is modified so that no conclusions on customer data or business figures of the company can be drawn. There are $1,721,483$ user sessions consisting of $24,353,852$ clicks in total. Sessions are split after 25 minutes idle time and the average session consists of 14 clicks. Every click is associated with a timestamp, the attributes of the viewed item, user ID, and the recommended items. We focus on attributes colour, gender, category, and price. There are 62 different colours, 16 genders (including types of accessories), 61 categories, and 16 discrete levels of price in the log.

4.1 Small-scale Topic Detection

Measuring the performance of topic detection methods using real world data is difficult as topics are not observed variables but contained only implicitly in the data. We therefore test the topic prediction against the attribute values of the next clicked item. We translate the distribution in Equation (2) into a discrete set of attribute values. A simple thresholding approach discards unlikely realisations and returns a set T_j for every attribute $1 \leq j \leq n$ given a session $s = (s_1, \ldots, s_n)$,

$$T_j(s_j) = \{x_j | x_j \in dom(\mathcal{X}_j) \wedge q(\mathcal{X}_j = x_j|s_j) > c\}$$

[1] www.zalando.com

where c is a user defined constant. Large values of c thin out the topic and focus on highly probable attribute values. On the other hand, small values of c weaken the interpretability and usability of the resulting topics unnecessarily that may contain many unlikely realisations. In the first set of experiments, we use $c = \frac{1}{2}$ and study variations of the parameter afterwards. The joint topic $T(s)$ is then given as the union over all attributes by $T(s) = \bigcup_{j=1}^{n} T_j(s_j)$.

We evaluate the accuracy of the extracted topics for every attribute as well as for the joint topic using indicator functions $[[z]]$ yielding one if the argument z is true and 0 otherwise. Let $T_j(s_j)$ be the topic of an ongoing session and x'_j the corresponding realisation of the next clicked item. The topic prediction is correct if $[[x'_j \in T_j(s_j)]]$. The joint topic is then evaluated by concatenating the individual results with an and-operator,

$$acc(T, s, i') = \bigwedge_{j=1}^{n} [[x'_j \in T_j(s_j)]].$$

Note that high accuracies in individual attributes do not necessarily indicate a good joint performance as the all attribute values need to be contained in the topic.

We compare the ensemble approach of Section 3.4 (M1) with its approximation in Section 3.5 (M2). As a baseline, we deploy a simple Markov process (MP) that uses estimates $P(i'|s)$ directly instead of $Q(s, i')$ for the computation of the topic. Thus, its probabilities are proportional to the number of times that item i' has been clicked in state s estimated by maximum likelihood. Additionally, we include LDA [5] as another baseline. To this end, every session is treated a document where the attributes of the viewed items are considered the words of the document. The set of words is thus defined by $\bigcup_{j=1}^{n} dom(\mathcal{X}_j)$ and contains 155 distinct words. We apply the method by [5] for both estimation and inference of topic proportions as well as word distribution per topic. At testing time, LDA determines the topic mixture of the ongoing session based and computes the probability distribution of attributes according to the mixture. Thresholding is identical for all methods.

For the first set of experiments, we only use a subset of the data for evaluation as the exact variant cannot be evaluated on all available data due to memory issues. In the corresponding subset, there are $34,343$ user sessions consisting of $722,179$ clicks in total with the average of 21 clicks per session. We split 70% of the resulting sessions for training, 20% as holdout, and 10% as test sessions according to the temporal nature of the data. Optimal parameters for M2 and LDA are found by model selection and are given by $\alpha = 2$, $\beta = 0.001$ for M2 and $\alpha_{LDA} = 0.1$ and 100 topics for LDA, respectively. Rewards are positive for clicks on recommended items as well as adding to cart, and sale actions. Removing items from the cart is penalised with negative rewards, all other actions realise a reward of zero.

Table 1 shows average accuracies of the best models for Markov assumptions of order $k \in \{1, 2, 3, 4\}$ and LDA. The exact ensemble M1 performs poorly for short histories but improves significantly for larger k. We credit this finding to the necessity of taking chains of consecutive clicks into account. Although the individual predictions on attribute levels are promising, the joint topic is not well captured. Further, the high sparsity of small data sample leads to the predictive accuracy of below 70%. By contrast, the approximate M2 performs much better for short histories and detects the correct topic in 94% of the cases for $k = 1$. The performance decreases for longer chains. The observed effect originates from the approximation itself. The data sample is not sufficiently large for reliably approximating longer histories. We will address this issue in the next experiment again.

Table 1: Accuracies for the topic detection on a subset.

	k	joint	colour	gender	category	price
MP	4	33.69	49.78	92.24	78.52	63.96
	3	37.70	52.98	92.31	79.50	65.06
	2	37.65	52.15	92.22	79.68	64.24
	1	28.06	44.31	91.85	79.01	56.28
M1	4	67.53	85.61	95.00	90.70	78.68
	3	69.56	93.94	95.21	93.36	72.01
	2	40.62	45.96	95.30	94.90	78.39
	1	16.47	28.37	95.31	95.28	46.55
M2	4	75.33	81.92	94.65	90.05	92.38
	3	89.52	92.95	94.83	92.81	94.48
	2	93.69	95.12	94.97	94.45	95.00
	1	94.14	95.25	94.98	94.82	94.97
LDA	-	1.65	11.76	85.89	52.8	21.14

LDA characterises the next click by dominant attributes of the ongoing session. The results show that users tend to click on items with so far unseen attribute values, particularly for price and colour. However, apart from M2, the joint topics are mostly inaccurate and do not reflect the performance for individual attributes. The outcomes of MP show that simply counting frequencies of subsequent events is not sufficient for achieving state-of-the-art performances.

4.2 Large-scale Topic Detection

In this section, we focus on the approximate ensemble (M2) and repeat the previous experiment on the whole click log. We split all available data into consecutive training (70%), holdout (20%), and test (10%) sets to preserve the temporal nature of the data. Table 2 shows the results for MP and the approximate M2 for histories of size $k \in \{1, 2, 3, 4\}$ as well as LDA. All three methods exploit the abundance of data and improve their performance. However, the overall joint performance of LDA is still far from a real-world deployment and even for MP still stays constantly below 40%. The approximate M2 clearly outperforms the baselines and yields impressive joint accuracies of about 90% for all k. The additional data trades-off the approximation issues observed in the previous experiment for larger k at the expense of smaller k.

4.3 Analysing the Topics

In this experiment, we study the variation of the detected topics in the course of the sessions using the experimental setup of Section 4.2. We measure the difference of subsequent topics $T(s)$ and $T(s')$ by their Jaccard distance. A large distance indicates rapid changes in neighbouring topics and either refers to a badly adapted model or to undetermined users who are just browsing instead of following a specific goal. By contrast, small distances indicate that users are very predictable and only search for very particular items without digressing.

Figure 3 (left) depicts the session on the x-axis and the variation of neighbouring topics in terms of their Jaccard distance on the y-axis averaged over all sessions. Unsurprisingly, for all histories $1 \leq k \leq 4$, the variation decreases rapidly after a few clicks. The more clicks a user performs, the more feedback is provided to the system and can be exploited by the model. Except for histories of length $k = 4$, all models converge quickly to only a few variations. That is, only very few attribute values are replaced between time steps. For longer histories $k = 4$, we observe more variations which is also reflected by lower overall accuracies in Table 2.

Figure 3 (center) shows the impact of the topic threshold c on the average size of the topics for the attribute *category*. Increasing the threshold effectively thins-out the topics on average. However, changing the topic threshold c also impacts the accuracy. Figure 3 (right) shows that tighter topics may fail to capture the user's intent and we observe decreasing accuracies for larger values of c. The actual value of c trades-off the specificity of topics and the accuracy of the topic prediction.

Table 2: Accuracies for the topic detection using all data.

	k	joint	colour	gender	category	price
MP	4	39,56	53,50	89,70	77,93	71,25
	3	39,53	52,83	89,70	78,09	71,04
	2	38,37	50,78	89,57	77,94	71,09
	1	30,82	42,37	89,15	77,29	70,02
M2	4	88,3	91,09	92,61	90,88	92,19
	3	91,13	92,73	92,45	92,04	92,56
	2	91,48	92,82	92,46	92,37	92,49
	1	91,53	92,85	92,4	92,39	92,55
LDA	-	2.84	12.31	81.18	51.22	41.71

4.4 Topic-driven Recommendations

We now demonstrate the effectiveness of the topic detection by translating the detected topics into recommendations according to Section 3.7. We use again the experimental setup from Section 4.2 and compare the approximate ensemble M2 with a collaborative filtering using matrix factorisation (CF) and a combination of topic models and collaborative filtering presented in [31] (TM). Both CF and TM are the same methods as described in [31], however we set $\alpha_{LDA} = 0.1$, number of topics $= 100$, and the number of factors in matrix factorisation = 200 by model selection. To evaluate these two baselines, items are ranked according to the previous clicks of the actual user as given by the user-item matrix. Note the conceptual difference of our fMDP and the collaborative filtering approaches. While the former takes a session-based approach and thus aims at short-term interests, the latter two are user-specific and could be considered global models for long-term user interests. Additionally, we incorporate three simple baselines: ranking items randomly (Rnd), ranking items according to their similarity to the previously viewed item so that items with the same attributes are ranked on top (Prev), and ranking items according to their popularity (Pop).

We also wanted to include a sequential MDP-based approach [28] as another competitor. However, a standard MDP approach as described in Section 3.1 is defined in terms of the items and turns out infeasible even for the small sample that we used in Section 4.1. There are more than 80,000 items in the small sample, leading to a minimum memory requirement of about 52GB for maintaining two tables of size $80,000 \times 80,000$, one for transitions and the other for the Q-values (for $k = 1$) using only four byte representations. The data set we are experimenting with in this section contains more than 240,000 items. We therefore leave this comparison for future work.

Figure 4 shows average ranks of the recommendations in the course of the sessions. Note that the average rank is a variant of Average Relative Position (ARP) [22]. As the baselines are static recommender systems that do not exploit the sequential nature of the data, their performance is more or less constant in the length of the session; small fluctuations disappear in the figure due to the log-scaled y-axis. The sequential M2 exploits the temporal nature of the data and adapts quickly to the topic of the session. The best method realises a second-order Markov assumption. The figure could be extended to the right to include longer sessions but the information gain is rather small as the performance of all methods does not change significantly.

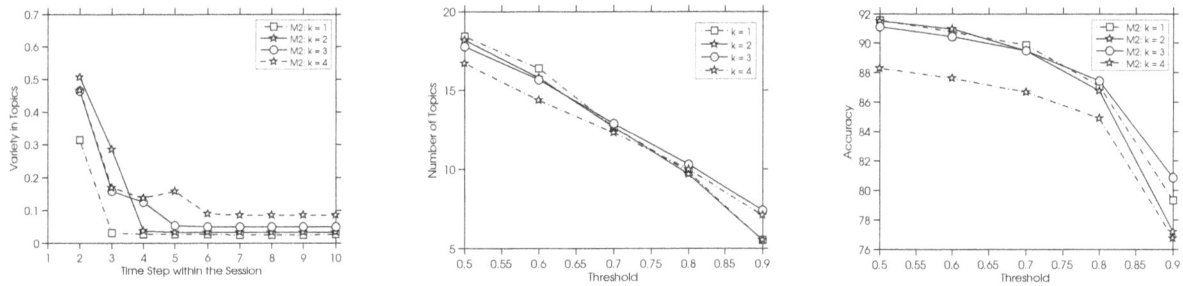

Figure 3: Left: Variance of topics. Center: Size of topics for attribute *category*. Right: Impact of topic threshold.

Table 3 shows aggregated results by averaging the performances over the length of the session. The baselines perform worse than M2, and among them, Prev and Pop outperform Collaborative based methods. The best method for histories of length two realises average ranks of about 15,000. Although the absolute number appears quite high, recall that there are more than 240,000 items in the data set. On average, clicked items are among the top 7% of the ranking for $k = 2$.

Table 3: Aggregated Average Ranks (in hundreds)

M2, $k =$								
1	2	3	4	TM	CF	prev	pop	rnd
174	158	209	270	723	749	272	295	1213

4.5 Discussion

Tables 1 and 2 exhibit differences in the predictability of the attributes. Unsurprisingly, *gender* is always predicted with high accuracy as it is unlikely that users switch often between genders within a session. The same is held for the attribute *category*. In contrast to *gender* and *category*, attributes *colour* and *price* prove more difficult. Apparently, users are somewhat flexible about prices and colours. Nevertheless, we observe highly accurate predictions for these attributes for the approximate ensemble M2.

Note that the choice of k depends on the application at hand. Our results show that the performance of the exact M1 increases with larger k (Tables 1). However, the larger the history, the longer it may take to adapt to a change in the topic; for instance because the user has not found what she was searching for or is distracted by a completely different item that is also displayed on the page. In practice, the fMDPs could be reset after cart or purchase operations by the user. The approximate fMDPs however perform better for short histories although the effect becomes smaller for larger training sets. We credit this finding to difficulties in the approximation caused by sparsity in the data distribution.

Since the internal representation of the factored MDPs is a graphical model, it is straight forward to augment additional variables to capture the context of the user. A promising candidate seems to be the time the user spends on the page before clicking. Very short stays could be an indicator for dissatisfaction, possibly followed by a change in topic while longer stays may give rise to a careful examination of the item at hand and a possible cart operation.

Finally, recall the conceptual differences of the fMDP-based recommender and the collaborative filtering baselines. While the former takes a session-based approach (short-term interests), the latter is user-centric and implements the notion of personalisation (long-term interests). Thus, the two strategies can be considered orthogonal. An interesting open questions is therefore whether it is possible to combine session-based with personalised strategies to obtain the best of the two worlds.

5. RELATED WORK

Topic detection is a broad field in machine learning, particularly for processing text. Topics of static data collections such as text corpora are traditionally identified using Latent Dirichlet Allocation (LDA) [5] and variations thereof. The evolution of topics in data streams is for instance detected by modelling time [33] or by introducing additional dependencies [2]. Other approaches, such as dynamic topic models [4] and online LDA [1], study segmented data streams. The idea is to turn topics of previous segments into priors for the actual time slice. A drawback of these approaches is that the topics remain constant across segments; effectively the same topics are re-identified and there is no mechanism to discard outdated topics or to introduce new ones.

Barbieri et al. [2] extend LDA to a first-order Markov model that determines topics of interest for collaborative recommendations. They propose a personalised recommender system based on user click histories where topics are identified for every user in the system. Wang and Blei [31] study LDA with collaborative filtering and matrix factorisation. They deploy topic models to assess content similarities in the reduced space of topics. Similarly, Chatzis [10] proposes to combine collaborative filtering with indian buffet processes for movie recommendations. The three approaches therefore aim at capturing long-term interests of users and an application to short-term goals of a session is not straight forward. By contrast, Wang and Zhang [32] propose a session aware recommender system that aims to capture the general intention of users in terms of three predefined and abstract categories: repurchase, variety-seeking, and buying new products. Note that the topics in [2, 31, 10, 32] are computed prior to the recommendation and can thus be considered static.

Markov decision processes (MDPs) [29, 24] are frequently used for sequential decision-making under uncertainty. Shani et al. [28] introduce sequential MDPs for recommender systems. Prior to their work, Zimdars et al. [35] propose a sequential recommender system where item recommendations are computed by random forests. Rendle et al. [26] study first-order Markov chains with matrix factorisation for basket recommendations. A reinforcement learning approach to recommender systems based on Q-learning has been presented in [30]. Moreover, Karatzoglou [16] combines temporal and collaborative aspects by minimising regularised loss functions. We design our approach based on fMDPs to take advantages of both, MDPs and factorisations. Factored MDPs are introduced by Boutilier [6].

6. CONCLUSIONS

We presented a sequential session-based approach for detecting the intention of user sessions on the Web. We phrased the problem as a topic detection task in terms of item attributes and proposed to solve the task via factored MDPs. We argued that a straight forward application is infeasible and devised an efficient formulation

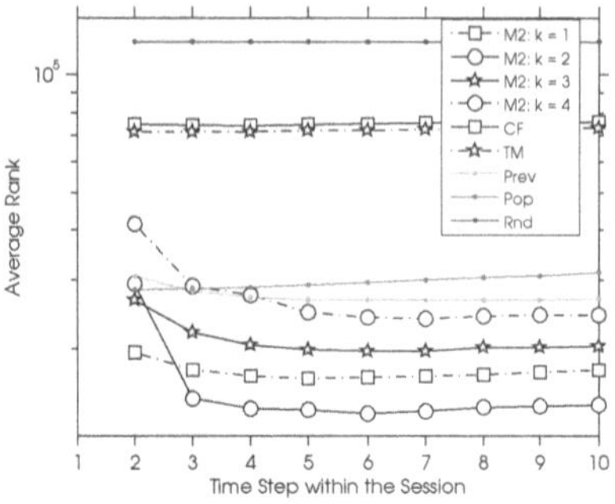

Figure 4: Average ranks for the recommendation task.

by assuming independence of attributes. We showed that factored MDPs with independent components admit an equivalent representation as an ensemble of independent fMDPs with structured value functions. Additionally, we presented an approximation of the ensemble and evaluated both methods on a large click log. Our empirical results showed that our methods were able to accurately detect topics of sessions. Translating our approach into a topic-driven recommender system outperformed collaborative baseline methods simple straw men.

Acknowledgements

We would like to thank Chong Wang and David M. Blei for sharing their code with us on short notice. We are grateful to Zalando for sharing data and actively supporting our work. Maryam Tavakol is supported by a Zalando scholarship.

7. REFERENCES

[1] L. AlSumait, D. Barbará, and C. Domeniconi. Online LDA: adaptive topic models for mining text streams with applications to topic detection and tracking. In *ICDM*, 2008.

[2] N. Barbieri, G. Manco, E. Ritacco, M. Carnuccio, and A. Bevacqua. Probabilistic topic models for sequence data. *MLJ*, 93:5–29, 2013.

[3] R. Bell and Y. Koren. Scalable collaborative filtering with jointly derived neighborhood interpolation weights. In *ICDM*, 2007.

[4] D. M. Blei and J. D. Lafferty. Dynamic topic models. In *ICML*, 2006.

[5] D. M. Blei, A. Y. Ng, and M. I. Jordan. Latent dirichlet allocation. *JMLR*, 3:993–1022, 2003.

[6] C. Boutilier, T. Dean, and S. Hanks. Decision-theoretic planning: Structural assumptions and computational leverage. *JAIR*, 11:1–94, 1999.

[7] C. Boutilier, R. Dearden, and M. Goldszmidt. Stochastic dynamic programming with factored representations. *Artificial Intelligence*, 121(1):49–107, 2000.

[8] H. Cao, D. H. Hu, D. Shen, D. Jiang, J.-T. Sun, E. Chen, and Q. Yang. Context-aware query classification. In *Conf. on Res. and Dev. in IR*, 2009.

[9] A. Celikyilmaz, D. Hakkani-Tür, and G. Tür. Leveraging web query logs to learn user intent via bayesian discrete latent variable model. In *ICML*, 2011.

[10] S. P. Chatzis. A coupled indian buffet process model for collaborative filtering. In *ACML*, 2012.

[11] M. Daoud, L. Tamine-Lechani, M. Boughanem, and B. Chebaro. A session based personalized search using an ontological user profile. In *Proceedings of the 2009 ACM Symposium on Applied Computing*, 2009.

[12] G. Giannopoulos, U. Brefeld, T. Dalamagas, and T. Sellis. Learning to rank user intent. In *CIKM*, 2011.

[13] C. Guestrin, D. Koller, R. Parr, and S. Venkataraman. Efficient solution algorithms for factored MDPs. *JAIR*, 19:399–468, 2003.

[14] P. Haider, L. Chiarandini, and U. Brefeld. Discriminative clustering for market segmentation. In *KDD*, 2012.

[15] A. Hassan, R. Jones, and K. Klinkner. Beyond DCG: user behavior as a predictor of a successful search. In *WSDM*, 2010.

[16] A. Karatzoglou. Collaborative temporal order modeling. In *RecSys*, 2011.

[17] D. Koller and R. Parr. Computing factored value functions for policies in structured MDPs. In *IJCAI*, volume 99, pages 1332–1339, 1999.

[18] L. Li, W. Chu, J. Langford, and R. E. Schapire. A contextual-bandit approach to personalized news article recommendation. In *WWW*, 2010.

[19] G. Linden, B. Smith, and J. York. Amazon.com recommendations: item-to-item collaborative filtering. *IEEE Internet Computing*, 7(1):76–80, 2003.

[20] Z. Ma, G. Pant, and O. R. L. Sheng. Interest-based personalized search. *ACM Trans. Inf. Syst.*, 25(1), 2007.

[21] I. K. Paparrizos, B. B. Cambazoglu, and A. Gionis. Machine learned job recommendation. In *RecSys*, 2011.

[22] I. Pilászy, D. Zibriczky, and D. Tikk. Fast ALS-based matrix factorization for explicit and implicit feedback datasets. In *Proceedings of the fourth ACM conference on Recommender systems*, pages 71–78. ACM, 2010.

[23] S. Purushotham, Y. Liu, and C.-C. J. Kuo. Collaborative topic regression with social matrix factorization for recommendation systems. In *ICML*, 2012.

[24] M. Puterman. *Markov Decision Processes*. Wiley, New York, 1994.

[25] N. Ramakrishnan, D. Conry, and Y. Koren. Recommender systems for the conference paper assignment problem. In *RecSys*, 2009.

[26] S. Rendle, C. Freudenthaler, and L. Schmidt-Thieme. Factorizing personalized Markov chains for next-basket recommendation. In *WWW*, 2010.

[27] E. Sadikov, J. Madhavan, L. Wang, and A. Halevy. Clustering query refinements by user intent. In *WWW*, 2010.

[28] G. Shani, D. Heckerman, and R. I. Brafman. An MDP-based recommender system. *JMLR*, 6:1265–1295, 2005.

[29] R. Sutton and A. Barto. *Reinforcement learning: An introduction*. MIT Press, Cambridge, MA, 1998.

[30] N. Taghipour, A. Kardan, and S. S. Ghidary. Usage-based web recommendations: A reinforcement learning approach. In *RecSys*, 2007.

[31] C. Wang and D. M. Blei. Collaborative topic modeling for recommending scientific articles. In *KDD*, 2011.

[32] J. Wang and Y. Zhang. Opportunity model for e-commerce recommendation: right product; right time. In *Conf. on Res. and Dev. in IR*, 2013.

[33] X. Wang and A. McCallum. Topics over time: a non-Markov continuous-time model of topical trends. In *CKDM*, 2006.

[34] R. W. White, P. N. Bennett, and S. T. Dumais. Predicting short-term interests using activity-based search context. In *CIKM*, 2010.

[35] A. Zimdars, D. Chickering, and C. Meek. Using temporal data for making recommendations. In *UAI*, 2001.

Context Adaptation in Interactive Recommender Systems

Negar Hariri
DePaul University
Chicago, IL 60604, USA
nhariri@cs.depaul.edu

Bamshad Mobasher
DePaul University
Chicago, IL 60604, USA
mobasher@cs.depaul.edu

Robin Burke
DePaul University
Chicago, IL 60604, USA
rburke@cs.depaul.edu

1. ABSTRACT

Contextual factors can greatly influence the utility of recommendations for users. In many recommendation and personalization applications, particularly in domains where user context changes dynamically, it is difficult to represent and model contextual factors directly, but it is often possible to observe their impact on user preferences during the course of users' interactions with the system. In this paper, we introduce an interactive recommender system that can detect and adapt to changes in context based on the user's ongoing behavior. The system, then, dynamically tailors its recommendations to match the user's most recent preferences. We formulate this problem as a multi-armed bandit problem and use Thompson sampling heuristic to learn a model for the user. Following the Thompson sampling approach, the user model is updated after each interaction as the system observes the corresponding *rewards* for the recommendations provided during that interaction. To generate contextual recommendations, the user's preference model is monitored for changes at each step of interaction with the user and is updated incrementally. We will introduce a mechanism for detecting significant changes in the user's preferences and will describe how it can be used to improve the performance of the recommender system.

Keywords

Context-aware recommendation; Collaborative filtering; Multi-armed bandit problem; Thompson sampling

2. INTRODUCTION

Context-aware recommender systems have been the focus of various research studies in the past few years. The main motivation for designing these systems is that the contextual factors can influence users' preferences. Therefore, the *utility* or usefulness of each recommended item does not remain static and changes over time based the current context of the user.

RecSys'14, October 6–10, 2014, Foster City, Silicon Valley, CA, USA.

http://dx.doi.org/10.1145/2645710.2645753 .

The system may not always have complete knowledge of the contextual factors and their values at all times. Based on the classification presented in [1], knowledge of a recommender system about context can be of three types: fully observable, partially observable, and unobservable. The contextual information is fully observable if all the relevant contextual factors, their structure and values are explicitly known. On the other hand, if only part of this knowledge is available, then it is partially observable to the system. For example, if a restaurant recommender system knows that location, and time are the only important contextual factors and the values of these factors are explicitly given to the system, the contextual knowledge is fully observable in the system. But often part of this information might be missing or unknown at design time making context only partially observable. In the case of unobservable knowledge, no explicit information is available about the contextual factors.

If the system has full knowledge of the contextual factors, a representational approach to modeling context [6] can be used where context is defined and represented as a specific set of attributes of the environment within which the user's interaction with the system takes place. On the other hand, if context is unobservable or only partially observable, a recommender designed based on the representational view will not be able to adapt to unforeseen contextual situations that arise dynamically. However, the activity that arises from the context can be observed in terms of changes in user preferences and behavior. Therefore, in such situations, an interactional view to modeling context [6] may be the more appropriate.

Although representational context has been extensively investigated [11][3][9], there has been less focus on interactional systems in context-aware recommendation research. This is partly due to the fact that it is more difficult to capture the contextual information when it is not known to the system at design time.

In this paper, we investigate this problem using an interactive recommender system framework that can dynamically adapt to changes in context. At each step of the interaction, the system presents a list of recommendations and the user provides feedbacks for the recommended items. The feedbacks can be explicit, such as item ratings, or it can be implicitly inferred from user's actions such as a click-through, lingering on a Web page, or purchasing a product. The user's feedback is an indication of the recommendation's utility and is used by the recommender to update the user's preference model after each interaction.

The main objective of the proposed recommendation approach is to identify the recommendation list at each step such that the average obtained utility is maximized over the interaction session with the user. Choosing the best recommendation list at each step requires a strategy in which the best trade-off between *exploitation* and *exploration* is achieved. During an exploitation phase, the recommender system generates the recommendation list maximizes the immediate utility for the current step. During exploration, the system may recommend items that do not optimize the immediate utility, but reduce the uncertainty in modeling a user's preferences and eventually help maximize the utility over the whole session.

This problem can be formulated as a *multi-armed bandit problem (MAB)* which has been studied in various systems and applications [5][10]. However, considering users' changes in context when designing bandit strategies has received very little attention despite the fact that changes in users' preferences can greatly impact the performance of interactive recommender systems. For example, consider an online radio application that receives users' feedback for each song played in a playlist. Assume that a user starts the session while reading but later changes her context to exercising. This change in context can greatly affect the type of feedback the user provides for the recommendations. If the recommender does not distinguish the feedbacks before and after the context transition, it may take many interactional steps to adapt the recommendations to the new contextual state of the user.

In this paper, we introduce an interactive context-aware recommendation algorithm that takes into account the user's interactional context. Our algorithm tracks changes in a user's feedback behavior and detects any sudden significant changes in the user's preferences. It will then adapt the recommendations to match the user's most current preferences. In our experiments, we evaluate the precision of our method in detecting contextual changes and investigate the extent to which our context-aware recommendation approach can provide improvements over non-contextual baselines.

3. RELATED WORK

Several researchers have previously investigated the use of contextual information in various recommendation applications [13, 1]. Many of these studies assume a representational view to modeling context [11, 3, 9]. In [11], a context-aware playlist recommendation system is proposed which provides users the opportunity to browse their music by mood. The system described in [3], focuses on social context and proposes Poolcasting as a method to customize musical sequences for groups of listeners. The music recommender introduced in [9], recommends music suited for places of interest. The contextual recommender described in [8] assumes that context is explicitly given as a query to the system. Our approach is different from [11], [3], [9], and [8] as the contextual factors are not pre-specified in our system.

In [7], a context-aware music recommender is introduced which infers contextual information based on the most recent sequence of songs liked by the user and their associated top frequent tags mined from social tagging Web sites. The system introduced in this paper is different from [7] in various aspects: the recommender presented in this paper does not rely on the item meta-data such as tags (which may not always be available). Instead, contextual changes are inferred just based on users' feedbacks on items. Also, the presented recommender in this paper optimizes the utility over the whole user session rather than individual interactions.

Bandit algorithms have been widely used for the application of producing personalized recommendations [5, 10]. The news recommender introduced in [10] adapts to the temporal changes of existing content. In the proposed system, both users and items are represented as sets of features. Features of a user can include demographic attributes as well as features extracted from the user's historical activities such as clicking or viewing items while item features may contain descriptive information and categories. They formulate this problem as a bandit problem with linear payoff and introduced an upper confidence bound bandit strategy which is shared among all the users. Similarly, the system in [5] uses a bandit algorithm based on Thompson sampling for the task of news recommendation and display advertisement. Similar to [10], several features are used to represent the user and the items and the recommender learns a single bandit strategy for all users while representing each user as a fixed set of features. Our approach is different from [10] and [5] as we are learning a bandit strategy for each user. While these two methods focus on adapting to the changes in content (or items), we are interested in capturing and adapting to the changes in users' interests. Representing each user as a fixed set of features, as in [10] and [5] would prevent us from detecting changes in the users' preferences and capturing interactional context. However, our approach enables us to monitor changes in the users' behaviors.

[4] uses a multi-armed bandit approach for mobile contextual recommendation.The main difference of our approach with [4] is that we are not taking a representational view towards context, instead we are interested in capturing change of behavior which can be induced by contextual changes.

4. INTERACTIVE CONTEXT-AWARE RECOMMENDATION

Interactive recommenders have been extensively used in a variety of application domains. These systems usually rely on an online learning algorithm that gradually learns users' preferences. At each step of the interaction, the system generates a list of recommendations and observes the user's feedback on the recommended items indicating the utility of the recommendations. The goal of such a system is to maximize the total utility obtained over the whole interaction session.

4.1 Multi-Arm Bandit Approach to Online Recommendation

Choosing the best strategy to select the recommendation list at each step can be formulated as a *multi-armed bandit problem (MAB)*. Consider a gambler who can choose from a row of slot machines known as one-armed bandits. The gambler receives a reward from playing each of these arms. To maximize his or her benefit, the gambler should decide on which slot machines to play, the order of playing them and the number of times that each slot machine is played. A similar type of decision problem occurs in many real-world applications including interactive recommender systems. For an interactive recommender, the set of arms corresponds to a collection of items that can be recommended at each step, and the rewards correspond to the user's feedback, such as ratings or a clickthrough on a recommended item.

An important consideration in a bandit algorithm is the trade-off between *exploration* and *exploitation*. Exploitation is referred to the phase where the available information gathered during the previous steps is used to choose the most profitable item. During exploration, the most profitable alternative may not necessarily be picked but the algorithm may choose other items in order to acquire more information about the preferences of the user which would help to gain more rewards in future interactions.

Several techniques have been proposed for solving the multi-armed bandit problem. Optimal solutions for multi-armed bandit problems are generally difficult to obtain computationally. However, various heuristics and techniques have been proposed to compute sub-optimal solutions effectively. The *ϵ-greedy* approach is one of the most famous and widely used techniques for solving the bandit problems. At each round t, the algorithm selects the arm with the highest expected reward with probability $1 - \epsilon$, and selects a random arm with probability ϵ. The *Upper Confidence Bounds (UCB)* class of algorithms, on the other hand, attempt to guarantee an upper bound on the total regret (difference of the total reward from that of an optimal strategy).

Thompson Sampling is another heuristic that plays each arm in proportion to its probability of being optimal. As we are using this heuristic in our system, we briefly describe it in more details. In the next section, we will discuss how this heuristic is used in our system to generate the recommendation list at each interaction step.

The reward (or utility) distribution for each item can depend on various factors including characteristics of the item, general preferences of the user, and the current context of the user. Let $p(r|a, \theta)$ represent the utility distribution for item a, and θ indicate the unknown parameter characterizing the distribution. Also, let $E_r(r|a, \theta)$ represent the expected reward for the item a for the given θ.

At the first step of an interaction, the set of observations, denoted by D, is empty and $p(\theta|D)$ is initialized with a prior distribution for θ. As more rewards are observed at each step, Bayesian updating is performed to update the θ distribution based on the observed rewards.

Algorithm 1 describes the Thompson sampling procedure [5, 15]. At each step, θ is drawn as a sample from $p(\theta|D)$. The expected reward for each of the items is then computed and the arm having maximum expected reward is played and the reward for that arm is observed. The selected arm and the observed reward is then added to the observations set.

Algorithm 1 Thompson Sampling

```
D=∅
for t = 1 to T do
    Draw θ^t ~ P(θ|D)
    Select a_t = argmax E_r(r|a, θ^t)
    Observe reward r_t
    D = D ∪(a_t, r_t)
end for
```

4.2 Context-Aware Recommendation Using Thompson Sampling

We adapt Thompson sampling heuristic as the bandit strategy for generating a recommendation list at each step of interaction with a user. In this setting, θ which characterizes the utility distribution for each item, represents a user's preference model. It is a k-dimensional random vector drawn from an unknown multivariate distribution. The user model is updated after each interaction.

Linearly parameterized bandits[14] are a special type of bandits where the expected reward of each item is a linear function of θ. It has been shown that Thompson sampling with linear rewards can achieve theoretical regret bounds that are close to the best lower bounds [2]. In our approach we also assume that the rewards follow a linear Gaussian distribution.

Given d observations, let $r \in R^d$ be the observed rewards for the recommended items and let F represent a $d \times k$ constant matrix containing the *features* of the recommended items. For example, given two observations (a_1, r_1) and (a_2, r_2), $r = [r_1, r_2]$ has two elements r_1 and r_2 and $F = [f_{a_1}, f_{a_2}]$ where f_{a_i} represents the k-dimensional feature vector for item a_i. The item features can be obtained in various ways. They can be extracted based on the available content data for the items or can be extracted from the users' feedback using different techniques such as matrix factorization. Given a training data set represented as a matrix of users' preferences on items, we apply Principal Component Analysis to represent each item in a k-dimensional space (where $k \ll$ the number of users in the training data).

Assuming a linear Gaussian distribution, we have the following prior and likelihood distributions:

$$p(\theta) = \mathcal{N}(\theta; \mu_\theta, \Sigma_\theta) \quad (1)$$

$$p(r|\theta) = \mathcal{N}(r; F\theta, \Sigma_r) \quad (2)$$

Also, we assume Σ_θ and Σ_r are diagonal matrices with diagonal values of σ_θ, and σ_r respectively.

Given a linear Gaussian system, the posterior $p(\theta|r)$ can be computed as follows (see [12] for a proof):

$$p(\theta|r) = \mathcal{N}(\mu_{\theta|r}, \Sigma_{\theta|r}) \quad (3)$$

$$\Sigma_{\theta|r}^{-1} = \Sigma_\theta^{-1} + F^T\Sigma_r^{-1}F \quad (4)$$

$$\mu_{\theta|r} = \Sigma_{\theta|r}[F^T\Sigma_r^{-1}(r) + \Sigma_\theta^{-1}\mu_\theta] \quad (5)$$

At each step t, θ^t is drawn as a sample from the posterior distribution. The expected reward for each item x is then estimated as $r_x = f_x \cdot \theta$, where f_x represents the extracted features for the item x. The items are then ranked based on the estimated expected reward values. The item with the highest reward is recommended to the user.

4.3 Adaptation to Contextual Changes

This section describes our approach for adapting the recommendations to contextual changes. Our method has two main steps. The first step, is to detect context transitions and the second step is to adapt the recommendations based on the detected transitions.

Our system includes a change detection module that tracks users' interactions and detects any sudden and significant changes in the users' behaviors. At each step t of interaction with a given user u, the change detection module models the user's interactions in interval $I_t = (t-N, t]$ as well as the interactions in the interval $I_{(t-N)} = (t-2N, t-N]$, where N is a fixed pre-specified parameter representing the length of the interval. These two windows are modeled by computing the following posterior distributions:

$$W_{I_t} = p(\theta|I_t) = \mathcal{N}(\mu_t, \Sigma_t) \quad (6)$$

$$W_{I_{(t-N)}} = p(\theta|I_{(t-N)}) = \mathcal{N}(\mu_{t-N}, \Sigma_{t-N}) \quad (7)$$

The above two distributions can each be computed according to equation 3 where r, and F are substituted with the rewards and the item features of the recommendations in the corresponding window.

The distance between W_{I_t} and $W_{I_{(t-N)}}$ is used as a measure of dissimilarity between these two windows. Various measures such as KL-divergence can be used to compute the distance between the two windows. In our experiments, we used *Mahalanobis distance* which is computed as follows:

$$\Sigma = \frac{\Sigma_t + \Sigma_{t-N}}{2} \quad (8)$$

$$distance = (\mu_t - \mu_{t-N})^T \Sigma^{-1} (\mu_t - \mu_{t-N})$$

If the user feedback behavior is significantly different between the two windows, then the models for W_{I_t} and $W_{I_{(t-N)}}$ would be different. Therefore, the change detection module in our system is based on the heuristic that sudden changes in the users' feedback behavior would result in sudden changes of the distance measure computed in 8. Based on this heuristic, we compute the distance measure at each step t, and exploit a change point analysis approach to detect sudden changes in a user's feedback behavior.

In our system, we utilize the technique described in [16] for change point analysis. This procedure involves iteratively applying a combination of cumulative sum charts (CUSUM) and bootstrapping to detect the changes. For each of the detected changes, a confidence level is provided which represents the confidence of the predicted change point. Given a pre-specified threshold, only those change points that have confidence level above that threshold are accepted. Also, in our adaptation of this approach, we have incorporated a *look ahead (LA)* parameter to improve the accuracy. Our change detection module accepts a change point only if there are at least LA observations after the predicted change point.

In our system, we assume a user's interactions after the change point reflect his or her most recent preferences and the interactions before the change point reflect the user's preferences in a different context. The strategy to aggregate the preferences from different contextual states depends on the specific application in which the recommender is being used. In some applications, a user's preferences in a different context may still contain some useful information about the *general* preferences of that user. In this case, a good strategy for the recommender would be to consider all the user's preferences while giving more weight to the feedbacks in the current context. In other applications, a user's preferences in different contexts are almost independent. For example, the user may follow different independent tasks at different contextual states. In this situation, a good strategy would be to provide recommendations just based on the preferences corresponding to the current context of the user, or in other words, discarding the interactions before the change of context. The recommender presented in this paper, discards users' interactions before the last detected change point and produces the recommendations only based on the interactions in the current context.

Depending on the type of utility (binary, rating), the change point detection may falsely detect change points at earlier interactions where it starts to learn the users' preferences. To avoid this situation, we have incorporated another parameter in our model to avoid splitting the user profile if there are fewer interactions in the user's profile than the pre-specified *splitting threshold.*

In our future work, we plan to investigate adapting a bandit strategy that considers all of user's preferences. This would include, defining a utility function that while giving more weight to the preferences in the current context, also considers the interactions before the change point.

5. EVALUATIONS

Evaluation of contextual recommenders can be very challenging if contextual factors are unobservable. In this case, as explained in section 2, context cannot be represented as a set of known attributes. Instead, change of context is inferred from the change in users' activities and interactions with the system. There are various datasets based on representational view to context. However, there are very few publicly available datasets that explicitly contain users' change of preferences that could be used as the ground truth for evaluation if contextual factors are not known. In our evaluations, we designed two different experiments for simulating users' change of behaviors. In our first experiment, we used Yahoo user-artist ratings dataset where ratings are in the range of 0 to 100. To simulate sudden changes in a user's rating behavior, we built test hybrid profiles by merging two random user profiles. Treating the two selected user profiles as the rating behavior of a single hybrid user in two different contextual states, we evaluated our method in correctly predicting the change of context and producing context-aware recommendations.

In the second experiment, we used a Web navigational dataset containing users' browsing sessions. Assuming that a user's change of context is more likely to happen between sessions rather than within sessions, we evaluated our algorithm ability in correct detection of the transition between two sessions. We then compared our recommender with various non-contextual baselines.

5.1 Experiment I

The dataset used in our first experiment was the Yahoo! Music ratings of musical artists version 1.0. This dataset represents a snapshot of the Yahoo! Music community's preferences for various musical artists. It contains over ten million ratings of musical artists given by Yahoo! Music users over the course of a one month period sometime prior to March 2004. It contains ratings in the range of 0 to 100 given by 1948882 users to 98213 artists.

This experiment evaluated our algorithm in adapting to changes in users' rating behaviors that could be a result of contextual changes. For example, members of a household may use a single account to rate movies on a movie streaming application. Each member can rate movies differently and as a result, the *household hybrid* user may show significant differences in rating behavior. The purpose of this experiment was two-fold: first, we evaluated the accu-

Table 1: Method parameters in experiment I

Method	Parameters
Bandit recommender	Number of features = 5, $\mu_\theta = 0$, $\sigma_\theta = 0.5$, $\sigma_r = 0.5$
Contextual Recommender (proposed method)	Number of features = 5, $\mu_\theta = 0$, $\sigma_\theta = 0.5$, $\sigma_r = 0.5$, Change detection window size = 5, Change detection confidence = 0.95, Chage detection look ahead = 3, splitting threshold = 10
User-based kNN	Number of neighbors = 10

racy of our change detection approach in real-time detection of changes. Secondly, we examined the performance of our recommender compared with non-contextual methods. The evaluation was performed in the framework of an interactive recommender that interacts with the user in a number of consecutive rounds. In each round, the recommender presents a recommendation and observes the user's feedback (utility) for the recommended item. The recommenders were evaluated based on the average utility gained over the session of interaction.

We followed a five-fold cross validation approach for evaluation. In each round, one of the folds was used for testing, one was used for tuning the parameters and the remaining folds were used for training the model. To simulate the changes in a user's rating behavior, we randomly selected two users u_1 and u_2 from our test data and combined them to create a hybrid user u_h. We treated each of these two users as the rating behavior of a single hybrid user in two different contextual states.

To simulate an interactive recommendation process, at each step of interaction, the recommender used the ratings in the hybrid test user profile to recommend a new item that has not been presented to the user before. We randomly chose an item rating from the u_1 profile and used it as the initial profile of the hybrid user. For the first $T = 30$ rounds of interaction, the observed utility for each recommended item x, was assumed to be the rating assigned to x by the user u_1. We assumed that the contextual change occurs after T steps of interactions. Therefore, for the next $T = 30$ steps, the same process was repeated with the difference that the observed utility for a recommended item was set to the rating for that item in the profile of u_2. For this evaluation, we filtered the test users so that each user had at least T ratings in the user's profile.

If the user has not rated a recommended item, one option would to ignore the recommendation and discard it from the evaluation results. However, this would create a bias in the experiment. If the user rates none of the recommendations, then the recommender should be negatively scored (in comparison to a recommender that recommends items that at least are rated by the user). Setting the utility to zero for the non-rated items would also be too strict, as the user may not necessarily dislike the items that she hasn't rated yet. Another possibility would be to set the utility to average rating of all the users for that item. This also creates a bias as item popularities are not uniform. For example, if an algorithm suggests very rare items with high average ratings, it will gain a high utility score in the evaluation. A similar bias occurs if the average rating of the user is used as the utility for non-rated items. In our evaluation, if a recommended item had not been rated in the user's profile, the observed utility was set to the average rating of all items in the dataset.

The set of parameters used in this experiment for each of the algorithms are specified in table 1.

User-based kNN was used as one of our baselines for this experiment. Cosine similarity metric was used to compute the similarity of users. In each round of interaction, the kNN algorithm computed the item scores and recommended a new item that has the highest score.

The *optimal recommender* was chosen as another baseline to compare our method with an ideal algorithm. This recommender has full knowledge of users' preferences and the contextual changes. For the first $T = 30$ iterations, it followed a greedy strategy and recommended new items that had the highest rating in the u_1 profile. After change of context at $T = 30$, in each round it recommended a new item that had the highest rating in the u_2 profile. The standard bandit algorithm with Thompson sampling heuristic (as describe in section 4.2) was used as another baseline in our experiment and was trained with the parameters specified in table 1. In the remaining of the paper, we refer to this baseline as the standard bandit recommender.

Table 2 illustrates an example interaction session generated based on the standard bandit recommender for this experiment.

The recommendations that are not rated in the user's profile are marked as '-'. For each recommended artist, a few of most similar artists that have previously been presented to the user are also shown. The artist similarities are determined based on the Last.FM data. For any given artist, the Last.FM API can be used to find the most similar artists as well as the degree of similarity between the artists. In table 2, the similarity levels are abbreviated as M(medium), H(high), VH(very high), and SH(super high). As can be

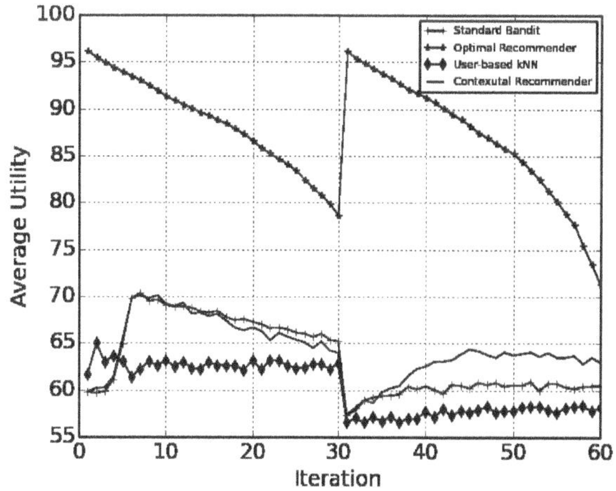

Figure 1: Experiment I-Average utility at each iteration

seen, most of the first few (5) recommendations are not rated by u_1. After iteration 6, the recommender starts generating better recommendations as most of them have high ratings in the u_1 profile. After the simulated change of context occurs at iteration 31, the user (u_2) has not rated most of the

Table 2: An example interaction session generated using the standard bandit recommender

Step	Artist Name	Utility	Similar artists	Step	Artist Name	Utility	Similar artists
1	Chingy	-		31	Foo Fighters	-	Nirvana(SH), Red Hot Chili Peppers(SH)
2	Disturbed	90		32	Hoobastank	-	Trapt(SH), 3 Doors Down(SH)
3	Led Zeppelin	-		33	System Of A Down	-	Korn(H), Disturbed(H)
4	Faith Hill	-		34	No Doubt	70	
5	Eminem	-		35	U2	-	Red Hot Chili Peppers(L)
6	Linkin Park	100	Disturbed(M), Eminem(M)	36	Alien Ant Farm	-	Incubus(SH),Puddle Of Mudd(SH)
7	Staind	100	Disturbed(H)	37	Creed	-	Staind(VH), 3 Doors Down(H)
8	Good Charlotte	-		38	Smile Empty Soul	-	Trapt(SH), Staind(VH)
9	Metallica	90	Led Zeppelin(H), Disturbed(H)	39	Slipknot	-	Korn(VH), System of a Down(VH)
10	Green Day	90	Good Charlotte(M), Linkin Park(L)	40	Michelle Branch	-	-
11	Red Hot Chili Peppers	90	Metallica(M)	41	The Ataris	-	Jimmy Eat World(VH)
12	The Offspring	-	Metallica(VH), Green Day(VH)	42	The White Stripes	-	Nirvana(M)
13	Korn	-	Disturbed(H), Metallica(H)	43	Avril Lavigne	-	
14	Evanescence	100	Disturbed(H), Linkin Park(H)	44	Dashboard Confessional	-	Jimmy Eat World(SH)
15	Blink 182	90	Good Charlotte(H), Green Day(H)	45	Matchbox Twenty	-	-
16	Limp Bizkit	50	Korn(SH), Disturbed(H)	46	New Found Glory	-	blink-182(SH)
17	Nickelback	100	Linkin Park(VH), Staind(VH)	47	Chevelle	-	Staind(VH), Trapt(H)
18	Trapt	90	Staind(VH), Disturbed(M)	48	Brand New	-	Jimmy Eat World(H)
19	Simple Plan	-	Green Day(VH), Blink 182(H)	49	Nine Inch Nails	-	-
20	Papa Roach	90	Nickelback(VH), Linkin Park(VH)	50	Switchfoot	-	
21	Nirvana	90	Metallica(H)	51	Goo Goo Dolls	-	3 Doors Down(H), Trapt(H)
22	Godsmack	100	Disturbed(SH), Staind(H)	52	Rob Zombie	-	Korn(M)
23	P.O.D.	100	Papa Roach(VH), Staind(VH)	53	Audioslave	-	Foo Fighters(SH), Incubus(VH)
24	All-American Rejects	90	Good Charlotte(SH), Blink 182(VH)	54	Sugarcult	-	Good Charlotte(VH)
25	Puddle Of Mudd	100	Staind(SH), Trapt(VH)	55	Deftones	-	Korn(VH), Limp Bizkit(H)
26	Sum 41	-	Blink 182(SH), Green Day(SH)	56	The Used	-	Blink-182(H), Papa Roach(H)
27	3 Doors Down	100	Nickelback(SH), Trapt(SH)	57	Lifehouse	-	3 Doors Down(SH)
28	Incubus	100	Staind(H)	58	Static-X	-	Korn(VH), Disturbed(VH)
29	A.F.I.	90	Good Charlotte(L)	59	Fountains Of Wayne	-	
30	Jimmy Eat World	90	Blink 182(VH), A.F.I(H)	60	Taking Back Sunday	-	Jimmy Eat World(VH)

recommendations, showing the dramatic degradation of the recommender performance. Note that many of the recommendations are artists similar to those rated highly by u_1. For example, Foo fighters recommended at iteration 31, is highly similar to Nirvana recommended at iteration 21 or Hoobastank, recommended at iteration 32, has super high similarity to 3 Doors Down, which has received utility of 100 at iteration 27. This example shows that a traditional bandit approach cannot adapt to the changes in the users' preferences.

Figure 1 presents the average utility at each iteration computed over the set of test users. The optimal recommender achieves the highest utility of 96 at the first step and its utility decreases as more iterations pass. This can be explained by the fact that in the first T iterations items are recommended in the decreasing order of their ratings in the u_1 profile, therefore the average utility gradually decreases. After iteration 30, the optimal baseline recommends items based on their ratings in the u_2 profile and so a jump in utility can be observed at iteration 31. Both the standard bandit recommender and the contextual recommender need 5-6 iterations to learn users' preferences and show a dramatic improvement in the utility. As indicated in table 1, the number of factors is set to 5 for these two methods. We repeat this experiment for different number of factors. The experiments revealed that by lowering the number of factors, it takes less iteration for the algorithm to reach its best performance. However, the highest achieved utility would be smaller as well.

Figure 2 illustrates the average distance computed as in equation 8 in each round of interaction. As can be seen in the figure, at iterations 33 to 35, distance has the maximum value. As the window size for change detection is set to 5, it takes at least 3 rounds until W_{I_t} mostly contains the interactions after the change of context and $W_{I_{t-N}}$ only has the interactions before the change of context and therefore, the distance metric become maximized.

Figure 3 presents the average number of change points detected at each iteration. As evident in the figure, the average frequency of change points reaches the maximum value of 0.5 at iteration 6 where $W_{I_{t-N}}$ has one interaction and W_{I_t} window contains 5 (window size) interactions. Setting

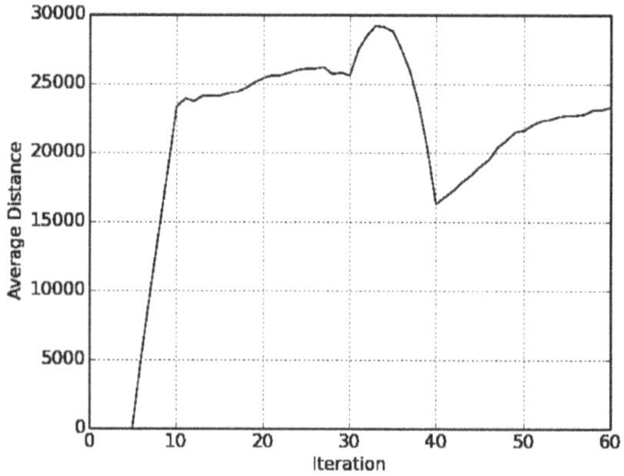

Figure 2: Expriment I-Average distance at each iteration

the splitting threshold to 10 ensures that the user profile is not split for the detected change points before round 10. Also, at iteration 38 there's another local maximum point where average frequency of change points reaches 0.4. This peak corresponds to the change of context in the hybrid user profile.

5.2 Experiment II

The data set used in our second experiment is the "CTI data", which is generated based on the server log data from the host Computer Science department. The site contains various online applications, including admissions application, online advising, online registration, and faculty-specific Intranet applications. The dataset contains 20950 sessions. We pre-processed the data to remove pages with frequency of one in the whole dataset and also the top 30 most frequent pages. After pre-processing the data, we identified 5319 users, and 2453 distinct pageviews. Following a 10-fold cross-validation approach, the data was randomly split into ten folds. In each run, one of the folds was used for testing, one was used for tuning the parameters and the remaining folds were used for training the model. For evaluation, we further filtered the test cases to include only those

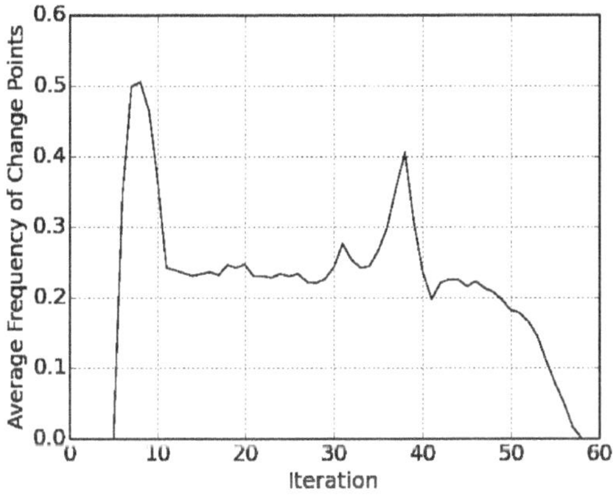

Figure 3: Experiment I-Average frequency of change points at each iteration

users that have at least two sessions in their profiles each containing at least L pageviews where L is the rounded up average session size and equals to seven in our dataset. For each test user, we randomly chose two sessions s_1 and s_2 (with the minimum length of L) and discarded the remaining sessions. We chose the first pageview in s_1 and used it as the initial profile (or entry page) of the user. To simulate an interactive recommendation process, for the first $T = 10$ iterations, the recommender used the current pageviews in the user's profile to recommend an item that she had not yet viewed. If s_1 contained the recommended page, then it was counted as a *hit*, and otherwise, it was counted as a *miss*. The recommended item and the corresponding binary feedback (miss or hit) were then added to the user's profile. After $T = 10$ iterations, we assumed the user starts a new session, s_2. For the new session, the same interactive recommendation process was repeated for another T iterations with the difference that if the recommended page was included in s_2, it was counted as a hit, and otherwise a miss. Note that the user profile in iterations between T and $2T$ contains the recommended items from both sessions s_1 and s_2.

The recommendation approaches were evaluated based on average Click Through Rate (CTR) obtained in each iteration across all the test users. CTR at iteration t equals to the total number of hits at step t divided by the total number of recommendations at that step.

We used *First Order Markov Model* as one of our baselines. This approach models each page as a state and the state transition probabilities are estimated from the navigational training data. It generates recommendations based on the state transition probability of the last page in the active user session.

The standard bandit recommender with Thompson sampling heuristic was used as another baseline in our approach. The set of parameters used for each of evaluated algorithms are specified in table 3. Figure 4 indicates the average CTR over the set of all the test users at different interaction steps for each of the recommendation algorithms. The CTR value for both the standard bandit and the contextual recommenders almost increases at each step for the first 7 iterations. The CTR reaches its maximum at the seventh iteration and has value of 0.31, and 0.32 for the contextual recommender and the standard bandit recommender respectively. Similar to experiment I, the number of iterations it

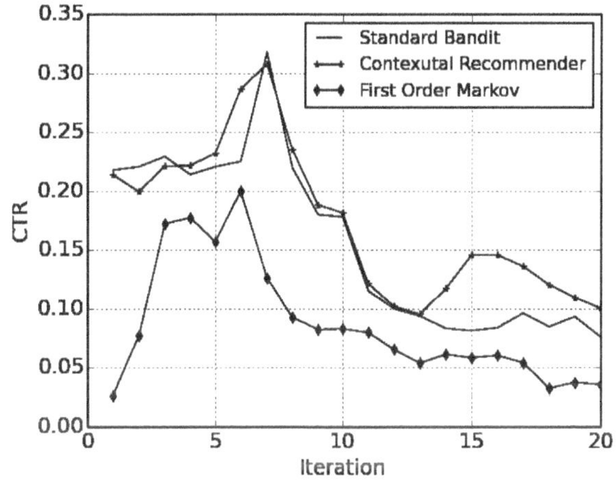

Figure 4: Experiment II-Click through rate at different iterations

takes for the algorithm to reach the maximum utility peak almost equals to the number of features. In our experiments, we tuned the parameters to maximize the average CTR.

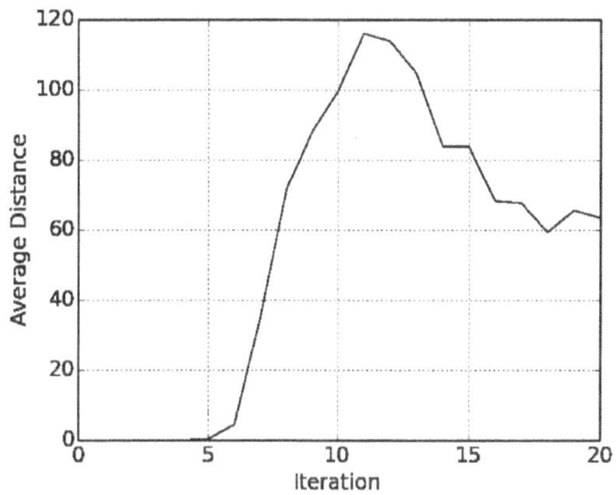

Figure 5: Experiment II-Average distance at each iteration

Note that the popularity of the pages is not uniform in our dataset. Some of the pages are more popular and have higher prior of being visited by the users. As the recommender recommends only new pages, the CTR gradually starts decreasing as the popular pages are recommended.

The contextual recommender and the standard bandit recommender both show very similar CTR values for the first 10 iterations with the contextual recommender having a slightly better performance after the third iteration. Also, after change of context at iteration 11, the CTR decreases with a higher rate (in comparison to the iteration 10). After change of context, the difference between the CTR achieved by these two algorithms starts increasing. At iteration 15, the CTR for contextual recommender is close to 0.15 while it is only 0.08 for the standard bandit recommender.

In comparison to both the bandit and contextual recommenders, Markov model has much smaller CTR at all the iterations. For Markov Model recommender, CTR mostly increases in the first 6 iterations and reaches to its maximum peak of 0.2 at the sixth iteration. The CTR then decreases till the last iteration.

Table 3: Method parameters in experiment II

Method	Parameters
Bandit recommender	Number of features = 6, $\mu_\theta = 0$, $\sigma_\theta = 1$, $\sigma_r = 0.001$
Contextual Recommender	Number of features = 6, $\mu_\theta = 0$, $\sigma_\theta = 1$, $\sigma_r = 0.001$, Change detection window size = 3, Change detection confidence = 0.99, Change detection look ahead = 0, splitting threshold = 3

Figure 5 indicates the average distance measure at each iteration, computed by the change detection module. Note that the average distance has its peak value right after change of context (at iteration 11). Figure 6 indicates the average frequency of change points at each iteration. For this dataset, choosing a high confidence threshold value helps to avoid false detection of change points at the earlier iterations. The average detected change points have its maximum at iteration 13 corresponding to the change of context.

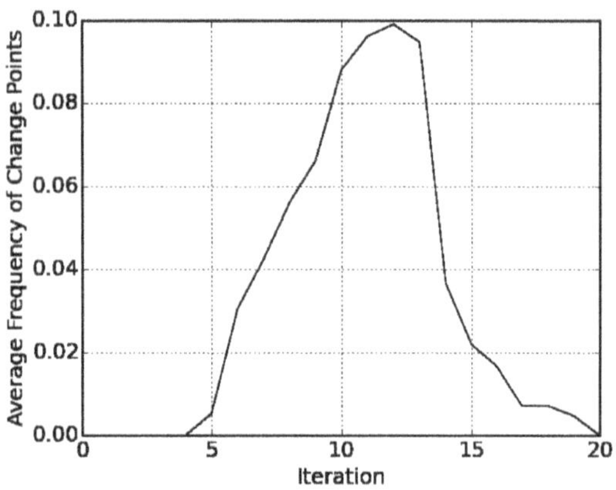

Figure 6: Experiment II-Average frequency of change points at each iteration

6. CONCLUSIONS

In this paper we have presented a novel approach for adaptation to contextual changes in interactive recommender systems. In an online recommendation scenario, at each step the system provides the user with a list of recommendations and receives feedback from the user on the recommended items. Various multi-armed bandit algorithms can be used as recommendation strategies to maximize the average utility over each user's session. Our approach extends the existing bandit algorithms by considering the sudden variations in the user's feedback behavior as a result of contextual changes. Our system contains a change detection component that determines any significant changes in the users' preferences. If a change is detected, the bandit algorithm based on Thompson sampling, prioritizes the observed feedback after the detected change point reflecting the preferences of the user in the current context. The proposed recommender, discards users' interactions before the last detected change point and produces the recommendations just based on the interactions in the current context. In our future work, we plan to investigate various approaches to take into account the impact of users' interactions in prior contexts on the current user behavior. One approach might involve defining a utility function that while giving more priority to the interactions in the current context, would also take into account user's feedback before the change point.

7. REFERENCES

[1] G. Adomavicius, B. Mobasher, F. Ricci, and A. Tuzhilin. Context-aware recommender systems. *AI Magazine*, 32(3):67–80, 2011.

[2] S. Agrawal and N. Goyal. Thompson sampling for contextual bandits with linear payoffs. volume 28 of *JMLR Proceedings*, pages 127–135, 2013.

[3] C. Baccigalupo. *Poolcasting: an intelligent technique to customise music programmes for their audience.* PhD thesis, Universitat Autonoma de Barcelona, 2009.

[4] D. Bouneffouf, A. Bouzeghoub, and A. L. GanÃğarski. A contextual-bandit algorithm for mobile context-aware recommender system. In *ICONIP (3)*, volume 7665 of *Lecture Notes in Computer Science*, pages 324–331. Springer, 2012.

[5] O. Chapelle and L. Li. An empirical evaluation of thompson sampling. In *NIPS*, pages 2249–2257, 2011.

[6] P. Dourish. What do we talk about when we talk about context. *Personal and Ubiquitous Computing*, 8(1):19–30, 2004.

[7] N. Hariri, B. Mobasher, and R. D. Burke. Context-aware music recommendation based on latenttopic sequential patterns. In *RecSys*, pages 131–138. ACM, 2012.

[8] N. Hariri, B. Mobasher, and R. D. Burke. Query-driven context aware recommendation. In *RecSys*, pages 9–16. ACM, 2013.

[9] M. Kaminskas, F. Ricci, and M. Schedl. Location-aware music recommendation using auto-tagging and hybrid matching. In *RecSys*, pages 17–24. ACM, 2013.

[10] L. Li, W. Chu, J. Langford, and R. E. Schapire. A contextual-bandit approach to personalized news article recommendation. In *WWW*, pages 661–670. ACM, 2010.

[11] O. Meyers. A mood-based music classification and exploration system. Master's thesis, Massachusetts Institute of Technology, 2007.

[12] K. P. Murphy. *Machine Learning: A Probabilistic Perspective (Adaptive Computation and Machine Learning series)*. The MIT Press, 2012.

[13] F. Ricci, L. Rokach, B. Shapira, and P. B. Kantor, editors. *Recommender Systems Handbook*. Springer, 2011.

[14] P. Rusmevichientong and J. N. Tsitsiklis. Linearly parameterized bandits. *Math. Oper. Res.*, 35(2):395–411, 2010.

[15] S. L. Scott. A modern bayesian look at the multi-armed bandit. *Appl. Stochastic Models Bus. Ind.*, 26(6):639–658, Nov. 2010.

[16] T. Wayne. Change-point analysis: a powerful new tool for detecting changes. 2000.

Question Recommendation with Constraints for Massive Open Online Courses

Diyi Yang
Language Technologies Institute
Carnegie Mellon University
Pittsburgh, PA, 15213
diyiy@cs.cmu.edu

David Adamson
Language Technologies Institute
Carnegie Mellon University
Pittsburgh, PA, 15213
dadamson@cs.cmu.edu

Carolyn Penstein Rosé
Language Technologies Institute
Carnegie Mellon University
Pittsburgh, PA, 15213
cprose@cs.cmu.edu

ABSTRACT

Massive Open Online Courses (MOOCs) have experienced a recent boom in interest. Problems students struggle with in the discussion forums, such as difficultly in finding interesting discussion opportunities or attracting helpers to address posted problems, provide new opportunities for recommender systems. In contrast to traditional product recommendation, question recommendation in discussion forums should simultaneously consider constraints on both students and questions. These considerations include (1) *Load Balancing* - students should not be over-burdened with too many requests; and (2) *Expertise Matching* - students should not be requested to address problems they are not capable of addressing. In this work, we formulate a novel constrained question recommendation problem to address the above considerations. We design a context-aware matrix factorization model to predict students' preferences over questions, then build a max cost flow model to manage the constraints. Experimental results conducted on three MOOC datasets demonstrate that our method significantly outperforms baseline methods in optimizing overall forum welfare, and in predicting which specific questions students might be interested in.

Categories and Subject Descriptors

H.3.3 [**Information Systems**]: Information Search and Retrieval—*Information Filtering*

Keywords

Constrained Question Recommendation; Massive Open Online Courses; Load Balance; Expertise Matching

1. INTRODUCTION

Massive Open Online Courses (MOOCs) have drawn a great deal of attention recently. MOOC platforms, such as Coursera[1] and EdX[2], have demonstrated extremely high student registration rates, with equally dramatic rates of attrition. MOOC discussion forums, where course instructors and students ask questions, discuss ideas, provide help to or even socialize with other students, face a similar problem, in that the number of questions asked in a forum increases rapidly, while around half of the posted questions are never resolved. Discussion that is productive for learning must be accessible and engaging to the students involved [4]. With thousands of questions for thousands of students to sift through, the challenge is in directing students to accessible, interesting topics, while simultaneously possibly helping unanswered questions get answered. Recommender systems, which have proven to be powerful in addressing similar problems [10], can be utilized to suggest to each student a short list of questions that they might be interested in. Students will be able to find questions that match their interests, and more otherwise unanswered questions will be addressed by students capable of answering them.

Traditional product recommendation [12] focuses on the extent to which a product will be desirable to users. Additionally, there have been some explorations of question recommendation in general discussion forums [22]. However, in contrast to existing work, question recommendation for MOOC discussion forums must address reciprocal constraints representing the needs of both the students who post questions and the needs of the students who might be able to offer some help or support in response.

In particular, the related constraints include(1) *Load Balancing*, respecting that students have limited time for participating in the discussion; (2) *Expertise Matching*, students have differing levels of expertise, and some questions will therefore be too difficult, whereas some are so simple that they do not make use of the students' particular skills and abilities. These facets of question recommendation have not been fully addressed in existing work. Thus we propose this *Constrained Question Recommendation* (CQR) task to take into account load balancing and expertise matching constraints. The focus of our work is on the solution formalism, which can be tailored to alternative operationalizations of skills, abilities, and difficulty levels. To the best of our knowledge, this is the first work describing a question recommendation problem with constraints. Our main contributions in this work are as follows:

- We propose a question recommendation task in the MOOC discussion forums, and formulate a constrained question recommendation problem, which considers constraints on both students and questions.

[1]https://www.coursera.org/
[2]https://www.edx.org/

RecSys'14, October 6–10, 2014, Foster City, Silicon Valley, CA, USA.

http://dx.doi.org/10.1145/2645710.2645748.

- We design a context-aware matrix factorization combined with rich contextual information to predict students' interests over questions in the MOOC discussion forum, then build a max cost flow model to fit the constraints and optimize the overall welfare of the forum community.
- Experiments conducted on three different MOOC datasets demonstrate the effectiveness of our model over several baselines.

This paper is organized as follows. In Section 2, we present related work. Section 3 focuses on the problem's motivation and definitions. Section 4.1 gives the context-aware relevance prediction model. Section 4.2 discusses constraint satisfaction, where we adopt a max cost flow model to satisfy constraints. Experimental setup and discussion of results are presented in Section 5. We conclude our work and point out the implications in Section 6.

2. RELATED WORK

The field of recommendation can be categorized into two kinds of work. The first is recommendation of products [10], a one-way recommendation where the focus is how desirable an item will be to users. This includes recommending books [12], music [23], Tweets [5], and movies. For instance, Koren et al. [9] proposes a combination of latent modeling and similarity based matching between users and movies to suggest movies that fit users' needs. The second is social recommendation [21, 11] which requires the match should be attractive in both directions, such as friend recommendation in social media like Facebook and online dating services [3]. For example, Pizzato et al. [15] propose a reciprocal recommender system for online dating where profile messages are utilized to learn users' interests and consider also preferences of the recommendation recipients.

Traditional question recommender systems [16], such as those that recommend questions to potential answerers in Yahoo! Answers, are mostly focused on approximating the affinity between users and questions [22]. Hu et al. [6] introduces a user modeling method that estimates the interests and professional areas of each user in order to generate a suitable user set to answer a given question. Similarly, Kabutoya et al. [8] uses the question and answer histories of each user, combining collaborative filtering schemas and content based filtering schemas to recommend questions. Most existing question recommenders can be categorized into the product recommendation field because they do not address the issue of reciprocity, or the potential for constraints associated with users and questions. Especially for question recommendation in the context of MOOC forums, recommendations should be based not only on what would be attractive to the recipient [19], but also on how their expertise and question-answering capacity can be balanced against the load of available questions [20].

In this work, we seek to develop a recommender algorithm to suggest questions to users, respecting both their level of expertise and capacity for taking on work (e.g., load balancing). There are many effective recommendation techniques, including content based filtering [13] and collaborative filtering, etc. Collaborative filtering can be categorized as model based [10] or neighborhood based methods [9]. Matrix factorization models [10], are one of the most successful model-based approaches to predict the affinity between users and items. Rendle et al. [17] proposes a context-aware factorization machine. Such matrix factorization models enable us to integrate rich contextual information, such as implicit feedback [9, 23] and user attribute information [1, 5] for predicting matches. However, these approaches do not address our concerns with respect to load balancing.

3. OVERVIEW

In this section, we present our motivation for conducting the constrained question recommendation task and define related terms that will be used in later sections.

3.1 Motivation

Engagement in course-related discussions can have a positive influence on learning [4]. In the MOOC context, where the interaction or guidance of instructors is limited and dropout is very high, it is critical to increase the participation and engagement of students in the course [7]. Guiding students to topics that suit their interests among a large set of questions is challenging. This problem is even more pronounced for students who post questions seeking help as well as the would-be helpers who are unable find the questions they're most able to respond to [18]. Suggesting appropriate questions to students is not simply determined by matching their interests, but is also subject to constraints on the students' time and the questions' difficulty.

Traditional question recommendation approaches mostly focus on figuring out the best matches of topic-interest between student question pairs, ignoring practical constraints like load balancing and expertise matching. In fact, ignoring constraints is likely to cause a long tail problem [14] - for example, a large number of students may be directed to just a few popular questions, and too many questions may be recommended to a small set of high-expertise students. However, there are limits on how many questions any one student can answer, and such imbalanced recommendations may leave other students idle. Further, popular questions might not need such a large number of students to offer help. These imbalances will not only lead to a waste of valuable human resources, but also leave many un-popular questions deserted, and their askers at a loss for help.

In this work, we focus on how to recommend a list of questions to students on the given set of constraints on both students and questions (here expressed as load balancing and expertise matching). Our constrained question recommendation framework guides appropriate students to questions in a discussion forum such that (1) students will benefit from their interaction with questions that are interesting to them, (2) questions are discussed by students with sufficient expertise, and (3) students are not over-burdened with too many requests. By taking such constraints into account, we produce a set of recommendations that is mutually beneficial to both the community of question-askers and potential question-answerers. To the best of our knowledge, this is the first work to address question recommendation with constraints on both students and questions.

3.2 Definitions

Existing recommender systems usually produce "relevance" scores to rank the pool of available questions for a given user, and offer the highest-ranked ones as recommendations. Here, we make a similar choice (although

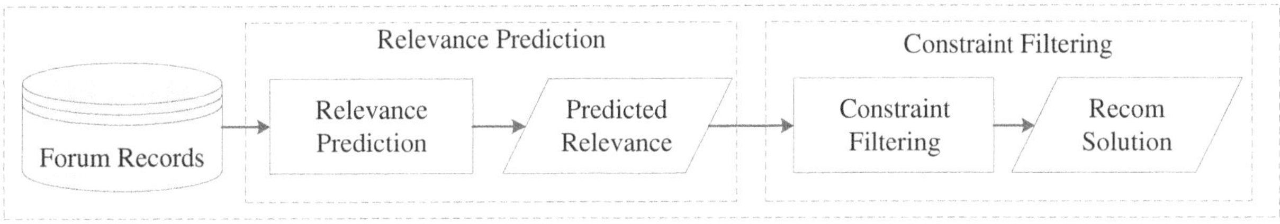

Figure 1: The Framework of Constrained Question Recommendation

subject to constraints) and denote the "relevance" score of question q to student u as $r_{u,q} \in [0, 1]$. For a specific student u, the larger $r_{u,q}$, the more relevant the question is. In what follows, we introduce our Constrained Question Recommendation (CQR) problem. To model load balancing and expertise matching, we first define several values associated with students and questions, including student capacity, student capability, and question hardness.

DEFINITION 1. ***Capacity*** *of student u is a load balance range $[L_u, R_u]$, i.e. the number of questions that would be comfortable for a student u should be no less than L_u and no more than R_u.*

DEFINITION 2. ***Capability*** *B_u is the capability/expertise of student u to solve problems.*

DEFINITION 3. ***Hardness*** *H_q stands for how difficult the question q is, or how much expertise it requires.*

The *Load Balancing* constraint requires that the number of questions recommended to students be in the range of the students' Capacity, and that the number of students we guide to a given question should not be too few or too many; while *Expertise Matching* means that among students we guide to a specific question, there should be at least one student whose Capability is equal to or larger than the Hardness of that question. Those constraints enable us to give the formal definition of CQR. CQR is a general question recommendation framework that recommends a list of questions to students, subject to load balancing and expertise matching. It is worth mentioning that existing question recommender systems are a special case of CQR that ignores all constraints.

4. FRAMEWORK

Figure 1 presents the overview of our constrained question recommendation framework. To address this constrained question recommendation problem, in the first step, we design a context-aware matrix factorization model to predict students' preferences over questions (relevance prediction); in what follows, we build a max cost flow network using the predicted relevance scores to meet the constraints (constraint filtering) and show how to solve this model to provide the final recommendation list.

4.1 Context-Aware Relevance Prediction

In this section, we briefly present our context-aware relevance prediction model, which can be fit into a class of popular matrix factorization models [17]. The predicted relevance scores are the basis of the subsequent constraint filtering phase. The relevance matrix between students and questions is denoted as R with entry $r_{u,q}$ representing the relevance between student u and question q. The relevance score $r_{u,q}$ is 1 if and only if student u has joined the discussion of question q. 0 entries are obtained by negative sampling as described below where we specify our experimental settings. This context-aware relevance prediction model mainly exploits three aspects of contextual information as follows, i.e. *Student Features*, *Question Features*, and finally *Implicit Feedback*.

Student Features include statistical features related to individual students, such as their posting and replying activities in the discussion forum. Here, **Question Count**, denoted as ϕ_u, represents how many unique questions the student has participated in prior to the current week and could indicate that student's typical participation level, which could then be used as a long term activity level expectation. **Previous Count** θ_u, is calculated to indicate how many posts the student has made in the last week, and can be regarded as a short term or local activity level. **Cohort** γ, representing the week in which this student registered for the course, could be treated as a proxy for the level of motivation (i.e. early course registration is typically associated with above average commitment to the course) [25]. This can be formally described as:

$$\hat{r}_{u,q} = bias + (P_u + \phi_u \Phi + \theta_u \Theta + \Gamma_\gamma)^T Q_q$$

Here, $\hat{r}_{u,q}$ is the predicted score of u on q; $bias$ represents various biases related to student and question, and P_u and Q_q are latent vectors associated with u and q. Φ, Θ are each one-dimensional feature vectors and $\Gamma_{(\cdot)}$ is a feature vector with dimension of different cohort numbers.

Question Features are those statistical features related to questions [24]. **Reply Number** δ_q is utilized to evaluate how many replies and comments a question q has garnered until now. Similarly, **Question Length** l_q is designed to estimate how much effort and expertise is required to answer the current question, which is computed as the total number of words appearing in that question, including all its replies and comments. We formulate this as:

$$\hat{r}_{u,q} = bias + P_u^T (Q_q + \delta_q \Delta + l_q L)$$

where, Δ and L are two one-dimensional features associated with Reply Number and Question Length respectively.

Implicit Feedback [10] represents whether students express their implicit preferences over questions through their participation in other discussions(or not). Denote $U(q)$ as the set of students participating in question q and $\varphi_{(v)}$ as the predicted preference v of u, then we have:

$$\hat{r}_{u,q} = bias + P_u^T (Q_q + \frac{1}{\sqrt{|U(q)|}} \sum_{v \in U(q)} \varphi_v)$$

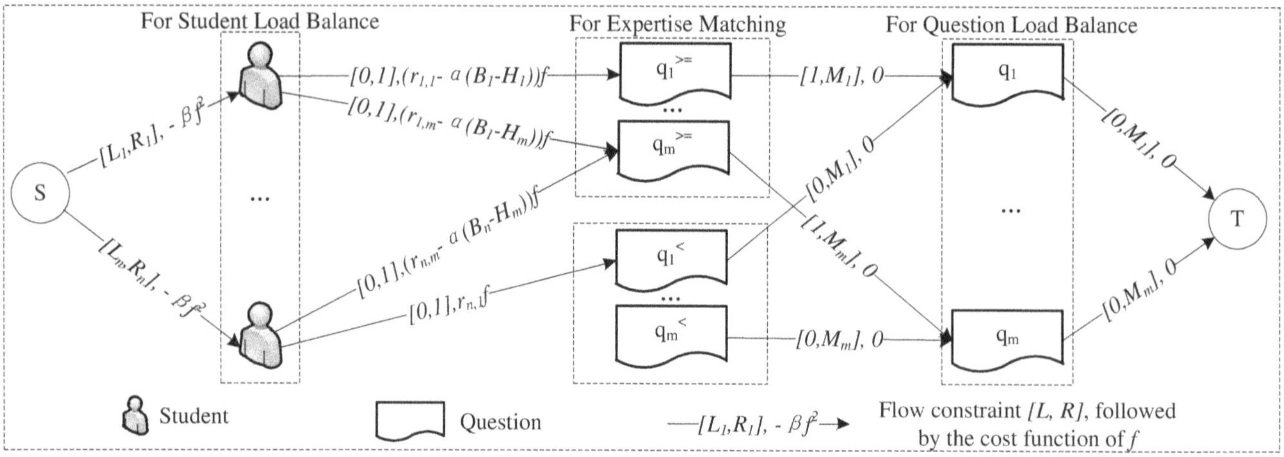

Figure 2: The Max Cost Flow Network Model

Taking those three feature sets into account, we formulate our context-aware relevance prediction model as below:

$$\hat{r}_{u,q} = bias + (P_u + \phi_u \Phi + \theta_u \Theta + \Gamma_\gamma)^T \left(Q_q + \delta_q \Delta + l_q L + \frac{1}{\sqrt{|U(q)|}} \sum_{v \in U(q)} \varphi_v\right) \quad (1)$$

The relevance score should be in the range $[0, 1]$ and the observed matrix is binary, thus it is common to use a sigmoid function to ensure the final prediction in the range and logistic loss as the loss function:

$$f(\hat{r}_{u,q}) = \frac{e^{\hat{r}_{u,q}}}{e^{\hat{r}_{u,q}} + 1} \quad (2)$$

$$l(\hat{r}_{u,q}, r_{u,q}) = r_{u,q} \ln(1+e^{-\hat{r}_{u,q}}) + (1-r_{u,q}) \ln(1+e^{\hat{r}_{u,q}}) \quad (3)$$

To decrease the risk of overfitting, the l_2-norm is chosen as the regularization term and λ is the learning rate. The parameters of this model can be learned by the feature based matrix factorization framework [17], which is a class of state-of-the-art methods that can utilize contextual information and implicit feedback [9].

$$L = \sum_{u,q} l(\hat{r}_{u,q}, r_{u,q}) + \frac{1}{2}\lambda(\|P\|^2 + \|Q\|^2 + bias^2) \quad (4)$$

4.2 Max Cost Flow Constraint Filtering

In this section, we firstly formalize the CQR task as an integer linear programming problem, which is equivalent to a max cost flow model and then we describe how we solve this max cost flow model.

4.2.1 Integer Linear Programming Form of CQR

Before giving a detailed description of the max cost flow model, we start with an introduction to our notation. Here, we denote $f_{u,q} \in \{0, 1\}$ as an indicator of whether the question q is recommended to the student u. Recall the definitions in Section 3.2, $r_{u,q} \in [0, 1]$ is the relevance score between the question q and the student u. We formulate the constraints by using $f_{u,q}$ in Section 3.2, and we obtain the rephrased representation as below:

- **Load Balancing**: For each student u, $L_u \leq \sum_q f_{u,q} \leq R_u$ must be satisfied - we can only recommend a proper amount of questions to a student; Additionally, the load $\sum_q f_{u,q}$ of student u should be minimized. Each question q should satisfy $0 \leq \sum_u f_{u,q} \leq M_q$. Here, M_q means that each question has a limit on the number of students who can be invited to participate. If there is no constraint, M_q can be $+\infty$.

- **Expertise Matching**: For each question q, the constraint $\exists u, B_u \cdot f_{u,q} \geq H_q$ must be satisfied - at least one student u that we guide to question q should have an expertise no less than that which q requires[3]. Besides, term $\sum_u \sum_q \mathbb{I}(B_u \cdot f_{u,q} > H_q)(B_u - H_q)$ should be minimized, which enables us to avoid wasting human resources by assigning overly-qualified students to answer questions. The intuition is that we should guide students to proper questions, and avoid assigning tasks that are not challenging.

Taking those constraints into consideration, we then can give a mathematical formulation of our CQR problem. Here, U and Q are student and question sets respectively. $\mathbb{I}(\cdot)$ is an indicator function. $r_{u,q}$ is generated by context-aware matrix factorization model. α, β are parameters used to balance the importance of different components.

$$\begin{aligned} \max & \sum_{u,q} f_{u,q} \cdot r_{u,q} - \beta \cdot \sum_u (\sum_q f_{u,q})^2 \\ & - \alpha \cdot \sum_q (\sum_u (\mathbb{I}(B_u \cdot f_{u,q} > H_q)(B_u - H_q))) \\ \text{subject to } & \forall u \in U,\ q \in Q, f_{u,q} \in \{0, 1\} \\ & L_u \leq \sum_q f_{u,q} \leq R_u, 0 \leq \sum_u f_{u,q} \leq M_q \\ & \forall q \in Q, \exists v \in U, B_v \cdot f_{v,q} \geq H_q \end{aligned} \quad (5)$$

[3]Here, we want to help each question get response/feedback and do not allow some questions to be left with no reply.

4.2.2 *Max Cost Flow Model and Algorithm*

To maximize the objective function in Equation 5, we construct a concave cost network illustrated in the graphical representation in Figure 2. Conducting max cost flow on this network gives an optimal solution for the integer linear programming problem in Equation 5.

THEOREM 1. *The cost network constructed in Figure 2 is equivalent to the problem defined in Equation 5.*

PROOF. First, the maximum concave cost flow (MCCF) problem can be formulated as the following optimization problem:

$$\max \sum_{(a\to b)\in E(G)} Cost_{a\to b}(Flow_{a\to b})$$

subject to

$$\forall a(\neq S,T)\in V(G), \sum_b Flow_{a\to b} = \sum_b Flow_{b\to a}$$
$$L_{a\to b} \leq Flow_{a\to b} \leq R_{a\to b} \tag{6}$$

Here, the $Flow_{a\to b}$ is the flow from node a to b, $Cost_{a\to b}$ is the concave cost function on the edge. In our network, there are only (negative) square functions, linear functions, and constant functions. Then, if we set $f_{u,q}$ by the flows in the network as below:

$$f_{u,q} = \begin{cases} flow_{u\to q^{\geq}}, & if B_u \geq H_q \\ flow_{u\to q^{<}}, & if B_u < H_q \end{cases}$$

Then, the objective in MCCF is equal to Equation 5. After that, we consider the remaining constraints one by one.

- The **Load Balance** of students is bounded by the capacity constraints $[L_u, R_u]$ between the source node S and the student nodes u with penalty cost $-\beta\cdot f^2$; the question constraints are limited by the flow constraints M_q between question nodes q and the sink node T.

- The lower bound of the flow constraints between nodes $q^{\geq}$ and question nodes q guarantees **Expertise Matching** constraint, i.e. there is at least one high expertise student guided to question q.

In summary, all constraints in CQR problem are satisfied in the network flow model and these constraints are the only limits in the network. Thus the MCCF problem defined here is equivalent to the CQR problem. Then we can formally build the network as shown in Figure 2, solve the MCCF problem by computing the maximum cost flow of network [2], and get the final recommendation plan by examining flows between u and the corresponding $q^{\geq}$ or $q^{<}$. □

5. EXPERIMENT

In this section, we present a set of experiments, and a discussion of their results. We start with an introduction to the three MOOC datasets, followed by experiments in our framework and a comparison of their performance against several baselines. We also explore some practical tradeoffs by investigating how the number of relevant edges used in the optimization of the objective function affects the overall recommendation performance.

Dataset	Student	Question	Candidate Pairs
Accountable	1,148	511	582,945
Fantasy	770	603	460,448
Python	3,633	3,079	11,172,604

Table 1: Statistics on Datasets

5.1 Dataset

Our experiments are conducted on the discussion forums from three different types of courses from the Coursera MOOC platform [4], (1) 'Accountable Talk: Conversation that works', hereafter shortened to 'Accountable', is a professional development course for teachers; (2) 'Fantasy and Science Fiction: the human mind, our modern world', shortened to 'Fantasy', is a course about literature writing and discussion; (3) 'Learn to Program: The Fundamentals', shortened to 'Python', teaches Python programming skills. Summary statistics are presented in Table 1. For our purposes, a question is defined as a thread starter post asking a question or requesting help. In our datasets, most posts (around 82%) are about proposing and resolving problems - since the Coursera discussion forums mainly focus on Lectures, Exercises, Assignments and Exams. Thus, these datasets are quite appropriate for evaluating our CQR problem.

5.2 Relevance Prediction Discussion

In this part, we firstly explain our experimental settings and evaluation metrics. Then we describe and discuss the comparison performance of our model with baselines.

5.2.1 *Settings and Metrics*

To evaluate the performance of relevance prediction, we randomly divide the observed records into train and test sets, with 70% and 30% of records respectively. The ground truth only contains student participation history, namely whether the students participated in a question discussion($r_{u,q} = 1$), denoted as positive samples. To simulate a realistic scenario, we randomly generate negative examples ($r_{u,q} = 0$ entries) for each positive instance by selecting threads the user did not participate in. Specifically, for each $r_{u,q} = 1$, we sample 5 different questions p such that $r_{u,p}$ is not observed, and set $r_{u,p} = 0$. In the context of question recommendation, the relevance score is binary and we use Mean Average Precision (MAP) [5] (with 95% confidence interval) as the evaluation metric. MAP@K focuses on the first top K questions in the recommended list and we use MAP@1, MAP@3, and MAP@5 for the comparison.

5.2.2 *Recommendation Performance*

We proposed two baselines to compare the performance with the context-aware matrix factorization **CAMF**, in order to validate that we can provide accurate relevance score for constraint filtering modeling. Baseline **Popularity** is a simple method in which only the popularity of questions is considered. Baseline **BasicMF** is the plain matrix factorization model without incorporation of contextual features. The comparison results are summarized in Figure 3 From this figure, we can observe that, 1) BasicMF works

[4]Permission to conduct research on Coursera datasets was provided by Coursera.

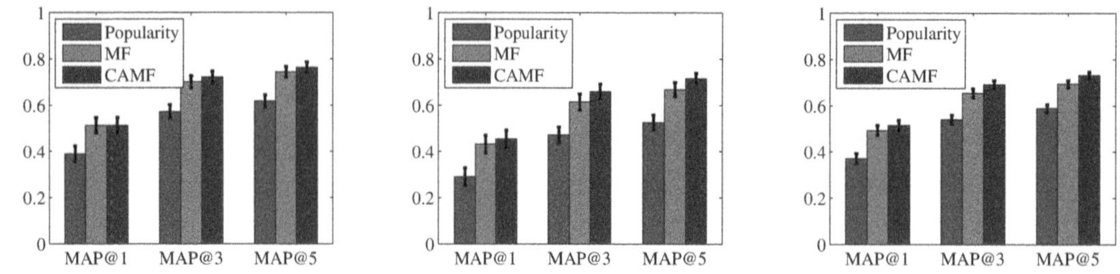

(a) on Accountable Course (b) on Fantasy Course (c) on Python Course

Figure 3: MAP Performance Comparison on Three MOOC Forums

better than Popularity, because it identifies the latent match between student preferences and question properties; 2) CAMF archives the best performance among three models due to consideration of MOOC specific contextual features; 3) The performance of MAP@1 achieves 0.513 on the Accountable Course, 0.455 on the Fantasy Course, and 0.516 on the Python Course, which guarantees quite accurate input for constraint filtering.

5.3 Constraint Filtering Discussion

We begin the introduction to this part with metrics and baselines of constraint filtering. In what follows, we present the performances of our CQR framework applied to predicted scores from the earlier relevance prediction part; Further exploration on how filtering relevant edges affects the overall community benefit is also discussed.

5.3.1 Metrics and Baselines

There is no widely used standard metric to evaluate our CQR problem. For possible comparison, we design three evaluation metrics. Two types of coverage: Student Coverage (SC) and Question Coverage (QC) i.e. how many questions/students are recommended to a student/question on average, respectively. These are used to reflect the load balance statistics of students and questions.

$$QC = \frac{1}{|Q|}\sum_{u}\sum_{q} f_{u,q}, SC = \frac{1}{|U|}\sum_{q}\sum_{u} f_{u,q}$$

Overall Community Benefit (OB) stands for the objective function value defined in Equation 5, representing the sum of relevance scores we achieve excluding the loss caused by violation of recommendation constraints. Higher OB means better performance and is our most important evaluation metric. Nevertheless, it is important to consider the three metrics together in order to evaluate model performance, i.e. the community spends SC effort and generates QC activity on thread in order to achieve OB welfare. The student question pairs we use here are all unobserved pairs with relevance scores predicted by CAMF in the first phase. To compare the effectiveness of our CQR framework (with max concave cost flow method denoted as **MCCF**), we propose three baselines as below:

- **Student-Question**[5]: First, select top R_u relevant questions for each student u. Then among those selected student-question pairs, choose the top M_q students for each question.
- **Question-Student**: Similar to Student-Question, instead we first select the top M_q relevant students for each question. Then among those selected pairs, choose the top R_u questions for each student u.
- **Greedy**: Based on the decreasing order of relevance score, first traverse this order and add one high expertise student to each question; in a second pass, guarantee the lower bound of each student in terms of question assignment; in the third pass, for each student consider the tentatively assigned pairs ordered by decreasing relevance, and retain the pairs that meet the constraints.

[5]For the first two baselines, we ignore the Expertise Matching constraint and the lower bound of Load Balance

Method	SC	QC	OB
Question-Student	2.986	1.329	1342
Student-Question	4.810	2.141	1715
Greedy	9.977	4.441	2534
MCCF	8.697	3.871	**2897**

Table 2: Community Benefit on Accountable Course

Method	SC	TC	OB
Question-Student	2.419	1.683	1120
Student-Question	3.668	2.873	1376
Greedy	7.745	6.065	2324
MCCF	6.715	5.258	**2652**

Table 3: Community Benefit on Fantasy Course

5.3.2 Constraint Approximation

The approach we propose in this paper does not make specific assumptions about the constraints on specific students' capabilities or capacity, or specific question difficulty. Rather, we present a parameterized approach that can be used with any desired method for estimating these specific constraints. The metadata about student and question constraints are not explicitly expressed in the forum data we have access to. For the experiments presented, we approximated the implicit capability and capacity of students and the hardness of questions based on available forum data, just as an example of one way these might be forumulated. In particular, the hardness H_q of a question q is defined here as the length of that question in terms of number of words. The underlying assumption is that longer questions are more complex, and thus require higher expertise in order to offer effective help. However, we acknowledge the limitations of such an operationalization and do not make any formal claims about its adequecy. The

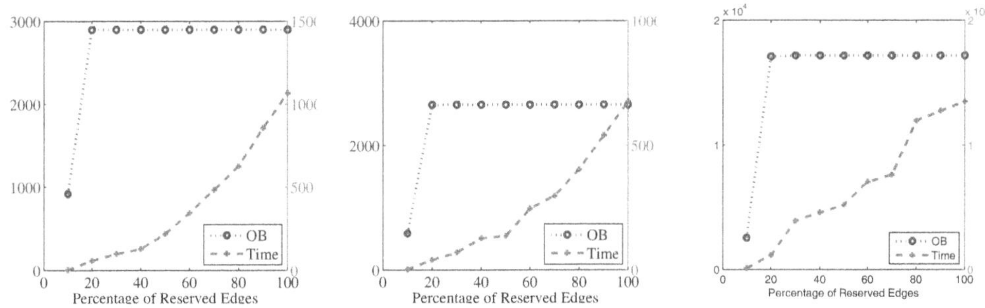

(a) on Accountable Course (b) on Fantasy Course (c) on Python Course

Figure 4: Overall Benefit and Running Time Changes over Edge Ratio

Method	SC	QC	OB
Question-Student	1.657	1.405	5017
Student-Question	2.201	1.865	6089
Greedy	6.950	5.890	13712
MCCF	6.134	5.189	**17185**

Table 4: Community Benefit on Python Course

upper bound R_u of capacity of u is defined as how many questions this student has participated so far in the forum; we set the lower bound L_u as 1, since every student needs at least one question to be actively involved. To capture the capability B_u of student u, we formulate it as $B_u = \max\{H_q | q \in T(u)\}$, i.e. the expertise B_u of student u is the maximum hardness of all questions he/she participated in at earlier time points. Here, $T(u)$ is the question set that student u has participated in. Various approximation strategies can be adopted in our framework to function within realistic scenarios. We leave this operationalization and validation work to subsequent research.

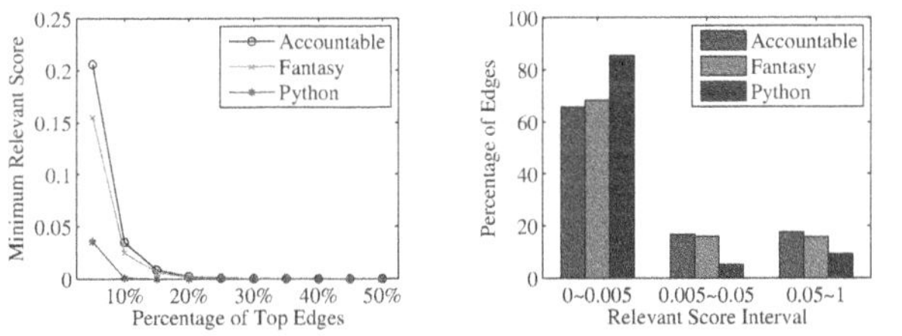

(a) Score Statistics (b) Percentage Statistics

Figure 5: Why top $\sim$ 20% edges are enough for OB

5.3.3 *Overall Community Benefit Comparison*

In this section, we compare our max cost flow model with three baselines. Results on three datasets are listed in the Table 2, Table 4, Table 3. Empirically, we set α as 0.005 and β as 0.001. From the three tables, we can observe that the Student-Question and Question-Student baselines have consistently lower SC, QC and OB compared to the two others. This is because in the first step in both baselines, traditional top-k selection is applied such that many students are directed to a small set of popular questions and a lot of popular questions attract almost all attention of students. Therefore, the coverage is low, which leads to the low overall benefit. That is why we consider constraints here: traditional top-k question recommendation results in considerable waste of resources in its assignment. MCCF achieves an OB value of 2652 on the Fantasy course, 327 higher than the OB of Greedy; the SC and QC of MCCF are lower than Greedy, which indicates that our MCCF achieves a significantly higher overall benefit to the community with less work on average per participant, and less extraneous activity on threads. This conclusion is consistent across three datasets.

5.3.4 *Edge Ratio Exploration*

As shown above, the max cost flow model achieves better performance in optimizing OB under the constraints of students and questions. To explore how many edges we should reserve in the constraint filtering phase, we vary the percentage of top relevant edges in the network per each student and measure the OB obtained. That is, we use the top x% most relevant questions for each student to run CQR model. The machine we used is and Intel(R) Core i7-4700MQ with CPU @2.40GHz. Each subfigure in Figure 4 illustrates two curves; the upper curve represents how OB changes as the edge ratio varies. The lower curve shows how the running time of the corresponding model changes as the edge ratio varies. Based on this we conclude that the top 20% of relevant edges are sufficient to gain a relatively satisfying OB. For example in Figure 4(a), the OB is 2897 if we use the top 100% edges; but if we only keep the top 20% edges, we achieve an OB of 2894. The two OB metrics has no big difference but the later model only needs 57 seconds, which is only 5% of original running time. The reason why OB is quite low when we use top 10% edges is because there is no feasible solution to the CQR problem under this number of edges.

We also conduct statistics to analyze why around 20% edges are enough to get a satisfying OB. Figure 5(a) presents minimum relevance scores of different top x, and Figure 5(b) gives the statistics of the percentage of edges falling in different relevance score bins. The minimum relevance scores after top 20% edges are almost zero, and relevance scores in the range $[0, 0.005]$ accounts for around 80% of all records. Edges with lower relevance scores contribute less to OB. Based on Figure 4, we conclude that using around top 20% edges for our model can achieve high OB and need fair time cost. Thus, this top edge ratio and the minimum relevance score exploration can help speed up our model.

6. CONCLUSION

In this paper, we have formulated the constrained question recommendation (CQR) problem that simultaneously considers potential load balancing and expertise matching constraints. Our framework employs a novel combination of (1) a context-aware matrix factorization model to predict students' preferences over questions; (2) and a max cost flow model to optimize community benefit under multiple constraints. Experimental results show that our method is significantly better than proposed baselines. It is worthwhile to mention that we could adopt any state-of-the-art strategies to predict the relevance scores and conduct constraint approximation using them. However, since metadata about constraints including student capability, student capacity and question difficulty are not explicitly expressed, how to accurately approximate such constraints remains a challenge for future work. In the future, we plan to conduct online deployment studies in MOOC platforms by using our constrained question recommendation framework to test its effect in practice. In addition, we will also consider how to generalize this recomemndation with constraints problem to other contexts and address scalability issues with the constraint satisfaction.

ACKNOWLEDGEMENT

This research was supported by NSF Grant IIS-1320064. The authors want to thank Tianqi Chen, Weinan Zhang, Jingbo Shang, Miaomiao Wen for their helpful discussions and the anonymous reviewers for their valuable comments.

7. REFERENCES

[1] D. Agarwal and B.-C. Chen. Regression-based latent factor models. In *Proceedings of the 15th ACM SIGKDD international conference on Knowledge discovery and data mining*, KDD '09, pages 19–28, New York, NY, USA, 2009. ACM.

[2] R. K. Ahuja, T. L. Magnanti, and J. B. Orlin. *Network flows: theory, algorithms, and applications.* Prentice hall, 1993.

[3] M. S. Amin, B. Yan, S. Sriram, A. Bhasin, and C. Posse. Social referral: Leveraging network connections to deliver recommendations. In *Proceedings of the Sixth ACM Conference on Recommender Systems*, RecSys '12, pages 273–276, New York, NY, USA, 2012. ACM.

[4] R. M. Carini, G. D. Kuh, and S. P. Klein. Student engagement and student learning: Testing the linkages*. *Research in Higher Education*, 47(1):1–32, 2006.

[5] K. Chen, T. Chen, G. Zheng, O. Jin, E. Yao, and Y. Yu. Collaborative personalized tweet recommendation. In *Proceedings of the 35th international ACM SIGIR conference on Research and development in information retrieval*, SIGIR '12, pages 661–670, New York, NY, USA, 2012. ACM.

[6] D. Hu, S. GU, S. Wang, L. Wenyin, and E. Chen. Question recommendation for user-interactive question answering systems. In *Proceedings of the 2Nd International Conference on Ubiquitous Information Management and Communication*, ICUIMC '08, pages 39–44, New York, NY, USA, 2008. ACM.

[7] R. Junco. The relationship between frequency of facebook use, participation in facebook activities, and student engagement. *ComputersEducation*, 58(1):162–171, 2012.

[8] Y. Kabutoya, T. Iwata, H. Shiohara, and K. Fujimura. Effective question recommendation based on multiple features for question answering communities. In *ICWSM*, 2010.

[9] Y. Koren. Factorization meets the neighborhood: A multifaceted collaborative filtering model. In *Proceedings of the 14th ACM SIGKDD International Conference on Knowledge Discovery and Data Mining*, KDD '08, pages 426–434, New York, NY, USA, 2008. ACM.

[10] Y. Koren, R. Bell, and C. Volinsky. Matrix factorization techniques for recommender systems. *Computer*, 42(8):30–37, Aug. 2009.

[11] J. Kunegis, G. Gröner, and T. Gottron. Online dating recommender systems: The split-complex number approach. In *Proceedings of the 4th ACM RecSys workshop on Recommender systems and the social web*, pages 37–44. ACM, 2012.

[12] D.-R. Liu and Y.-Y. Shih. Hybrid approaches to product recommendation based on customer lifetime value and purchase preferences. *Journal of Systems and Software*, 77(2):181–191, 2005.

[13] P. Lops, M. de Gemmis, and G. Semeraro. Content-based recommender systems: State of the art and trends. In *Recommender Systems Handbook*, pages 73–105. Springer, 2011.

[14] Y.-J. Park and A. Tuzhilin. The long tail of recommender systems and how to leverage it. In *Proceedings of the 2008 ACM conference on Recommender systems*, pages 11–18. ACM, 2008.

[15] L. Pizzato, T. Rej, T. Chung, I. Koprinska, K. Yacef, and J. Kay. Reciprocal recommender system for online dating. In *Proceedings of the Fourth ACM Conference on Recommender Systems*, RecSys '10, pages 353–354, New York, NY, USA, 2010. ACM.

[16] M. Qu, G. Qiu, X. He, C. Zhang, H. Wu, J. Bu, and C. Chen. Probabilistic question recommendation for question answering communities. In *Proceedings of the 18th international conference on World wide web*, pages 1229–1230. ACM, 2009.

[17] S. Rendle. Factorization machines. In *Data Mining (ICDM), 2010 IEEE 10th International Conference on*, pages 995–1000. IEEE, 2010.

[18] I. Roll, V. Aleven, B. M. McLaren, and K. R. Koedinger. Improving students help-seeking skills using metacognitive feedback in an intelligent tutoring system. *Learning and Instruction*, 21(2):267–280, 2011.

[19] Y. Shi, D. Ye, A. Goder, and S. Narayanan. A large scale machine learning system for recommending heterogeneous content in social networks. In *Proceedings of the 34th international ACM SIGIR conference on Research and development in Information Retrieval*, pages 1337–1338. ACM, 2011.

[20] W. Tang, J. Tang, T. Lei, C. Tan, B. Gao, and T. Li. On optimization of expertise matching with various constraints. *Neurocomputing*, 76(1):71–83, 2012.

[21] L. Terveen and D. W. McDonald. Social matching: A framework and research agenda. *ACM Trans. Comput.-Hum. Interact.*, 12(3):401–434, Sept. 2005.

[22] F. Xu, Z. Ji, and B. Wang. Dual role model for question recommendation in community question answering. In *Proceedings of the 35th International ACM SIGIR Conference on Research and Development in Information Retrieval*, SIGIR '12, pages 771–780, New York, NY, USA, 2012. ACM.

[23] D. Yang, T. Chen, W. Zhang, Q. Lu, and Y. Yu. Local implicit feedback mining for music recommendation. In *Proceedings of the Sixth ACM Conference on Recommender Systems*, RecSys '12, pages 91–98, New York, NY, USA, 2012. ACM.

[24] D. Yang, M. Piergallini, I. Howley, and C. Rose. Forum thread recommendation for massive open online courses. In *Proceedings of 7th International Conference on Educational Data Mining*, 2014.

[25] D. Yang, T. Sinha, D. Adamson, and C. P. Rose. Turn on, tune in, drop out: Anticipating student dropouts in massive open online courses. In *Workshop on Data Driven Education, Advances in Neural Information Processing Systems 2013*, 2013.

Attacking Item-Based Recommender Systems with Power Items

Carlos E. Seminario and David C. Wilson
Software and Information Systems Department
College of Computing and Informatics
University of North Carolina at Charlotte
Charlotte, NC 28223 USA
cseminar@uncc.edu davils@uncc.edu

ABSTRACT

Recommender Systems (RS) are vulnerable to attack by malicious users who intend to bias the recommendations for their own benefit. Research in this area has developed attack models, detection methods, and mitigation schemes to understand and protect against such attacks. For Collaborative Filtering RSs, model-based approaches such as item-based and matrix-factorization were found to be more robust to many types of attack. Advice in designing for system robustness has thus been to employ model-based approaches. Our recent work with the Power User Attack (PUA), however, determined that attackers disguised as *influential users* can successfully attack (from the attacker's viewpoint) SVD-based recommenders, as well as user-based. But item-based systems remained robust to the PUA. In this paper we investigate a new, complementary attack model, the Power Item Attack (PIA), that uses *influential items* to successfully attack RSs. We show that the PIA is able to impact not only user-based and SVD-based recommenders but also the heretofore highly robust item-based approach, using a novel multi-target attack vector.

Categories and Subject Descriptors

H.3.3 [**Information Storage and Retrieval**]: Information Search and Retrieval–*Information filtering*

Keywords

Recommender Systems; Power Item; Attacks; Evaluation

1. INTRODUCTION

Recommender systems help users decide which products and services to buy by making use of preference information provided by the community of system users. Unfortunately, these systems are subject to attack by malicious self-interested users who enter fake information to either promote their own products ("push"), disparage their competition ("nuke"), or to create havoc in the recommender [13, 8, 11]. Commercial system operators do not tend to disclose detailed information about attacks on their systems. But we know that real attacks on recommender systems are not uncommon, and they take on a variety of forms, the most popular of which is providing fake reviews known as opinion spam.[1] The problem with attacks on ratings-based Collaborative Filtering (CF) Recommender Systems (RS) is that predictions and recommendations can become biased in accordance with the type of attack perpetrated. In turn, attacks can potentially corrupt the system dataset and cause users to distrust the information and results provided by the system. In the absence of live attack data from service providers, research on RS attacks has focused primarily on similarity-based statistical models of user ratings, such as random and average hypothetical users [13, 8, 11]. Additionally, attack detection techniques have been developed based on these models of rating behavior, e.g., [11, 9, 18, 7]. Overall, model-based approaches such as item-based and matrix-factorization strategies were found to be more robust to many types of attack. The conventional advice in designing for system robustness has thus been to employ model-based approaches [12]. Because attackers continue to develop new approaches for biasing RS results, it is critically important for researchers, system designers and operators to keep pace in analyzing and understanding robustness characteristics and potential attack vectors.

We have previously studied a novel category of RS attacks based explicitly on measures of influence, in particular the potential impact of high-influence, or *power users* [19]. Power users in the RS context are those that are able to influence the largest group of RS users; influence is indicated by the ability of power user i to change (positively or negatively) the RS prediction for another user j, or for power user i's target item to appear in user j's top-N list. *To be clear, the power user attack in our research is not about having many actual power users collude to mount an attack, rather, it is about being able to generate a set of synthetic power user profiles that, when entered into a RS database, can effectively bias the recommendations.* We found that Power User Attacks (PUAs) are able to successfully impact SVD-based and user-based recommenders [16, 19, 20]; we also confirmed previous research [8, 11, 20] that item-based systems are fairly robust to attack.

In order to successfully attack (from the attacker's viewpoint) the item-based algorithm, we turned our attention to the complementary notion of influential *power items*. Selected in the same manner as power users, we conjectured whether power items would exhibit the same type of influence found with power users. Therefore, the overall question for this research is, **Can a Power Item Attack successfully impact item-based recommenders as measured with Hit Ratio, Prediction Shift, and Rank robustness metrics?** [2]

[1] For example see, http://www.reuters.com/article/2013/09/23/us-fake-reviewers-idUSBRE98M0YU20130923

[2] See § 6 for description of robustness metrics.

RecSys'14, October 6–10, 2014, Foster City, Silicon Valley, CA, USA.

ACM 978-1-4503-2668-1/14/10 ...$15.00.
http://dx.doi.org/10.1145/2645710.2645722.

This paper presents our definition of power items and the power item attack model, as well as a series of experiments conducted to determine how well the Power Item Attack (PIA) is able to impact the traditional item-based algorithm [15].

2. RELATED WORK

Attacking RSs by entering false ratings has been termed a *profile injection attack* [11] or *shilling attack* [8]. Burke et al provide a summary overview of RS attack models, attack detection, and algorithm robustness [2]. Most of the attack research has targeted the use of similarity-focused attack models that generate synthetic attack user profiles using random or average item ratings or a variant of these two approaches [8, 11]. Average attacks focus on attack coverage by broad similarity to all users or to a segment of RS users, and were shown to be more effective than Random attacks. Using these similarity-focused attack models, user-based systems were shown to be vulnerable to attack while item-based systems were more robust to this type of attack [8, 11]. Previous work on RS attacks has also indicated that recommenders using matrix factorization/SVD-based algorithms are robust to attack [9, 10]. However, this is only the case when attackers have been detected and removed from the recommendation process. None of these models used explicit measures of influence for coverage.

Our research has investigated using explicit measures of influence to create attack models based on the notion of *power users* [19]. We used well-known concepts from Social Network Analysis, i.e., Degree Centrality [17], and applied them to recommender systems. Furthermore, research showed that collaborative relationships in recommender systems can be represented as a social network [14]. In earlier work, we defined the *Power User Attack* model as a set of power user profiles with biased ratings that influence the results presented to other users [19]. The PUA consists of one or more user profiles containing item ratings (called attack user profiles) that push or nuke a specific item. The PUA demonstrated that influential users can impact recommendations for user-based and SVD-based systems; to a much lesser extent, item-based systems can also be impacted [19, 16, 20]. These attacks were successful because power users are able to correlate with many non-power users to impact the target item ratings.

Based on successful results with power users, we turn our attention to the complementary notion of *power items*, wherein attackers methodically select certain items to include in their attack user profiles that can be used to effectively influence other users and items in the RS. Power item identification has not been widely examined in the context of RS attacks, so our initial effort will use the same influence-based methods we used to select power users (see § 3). Certain attack models, such as the Bandwagon, Segment, and Average over Popular (AOP) attacks [1, 11, 7], specified the use of popular items (those with many ratings) in the attack user profiles to correlate with selected groups of users. While these attacks were successful (from the attacker's viewpoint) against user-based algorithms, only the Segment attack was found to be effective against a small subset of users using an item-based recommender. However, none of these attack models were successful against the full complement of users in the dataset. The item-based algorithm has proven to be robust against these attacks and this remains an open challenge in RS robustness research that we explore in this study.

3. SELECTING POWER ITEMS

To select *power items* our initial study employs the same methods we used previously for power user selection [20]. We believe this is sound for similarity-based methods because the similarity calculations between items are symmetric to those between users. The methods are as follows:

InDegree or ID: Our approach is based on in-degree centrality [17], where power items participate in the highest number of similarity neighborhoods. For each item i compute similarity with every item j applying significance weighting $n_{cij}/50$, where n_{cij} is the number of users that have rated the same items i and j, then discard all but the top-N neighbors for each item i.[3] Count the number of similarity scores for each item j (# neighborhoods item j is in), and select the top-N item j's.

Aggregated Similarity (AggSim or AS): Analogous to the user-based Most Central heuristic from [4]. The top-N items with the highest aggregate similarity scores become the selected set of power items. This method requires at least 5 users who have rated the same item i and item j; this method does not use significance weighting.[4]

Number of Ratings (NumRatings or NR): Power users were defined in [6] as users with the highest number of item ratings, thus the analog for power items would be those items with the highest number of user ratings. Therefore, we select the top-N items based on the total number of user ratings they have in their profile. Items selected by this method are also referred to as popular items in the context of Bandwagon, Segment, and AOP attacks [1, 11, 7].

When evaluating power item selection methods, there are attack dimensions such as cost and knowledge required that should be considered [8, 2]. The cost to mount an attack is controllable by the attacker and relates to the effort required to yield the desired outcome; the objective is to keep the cost low. The more knowledge an attacker has about the dataset's users, items, and ratings, the more effective the attack; however, that knowledge is difficult, albeit not impossible, to obtain. We note here that the knowledge required for the NumRatings method can be considerably lower than InDegree or AggSim because popular items are usually well known and are publicly-available information; this may give NumRatings an edge over the other selection methods, costs being equal.

Although PIA detection is beyond the scope of this paper, we should note that detailing the Power Item Model (§ 4) and the methods for selecting power items (§ 3) provides the basic information required for detection analysis.

4. POWER ITEM MODEL

We have developed a Power Item Model (PIM) that can be used to generate synthetic power item profiles (SPIP) for attack purposes. Unlike classic attack models (e.g., random, average, bandwagon) that employ straightforward statistical templates (e.g., average item rating, popularity, and likability) to generate synthetic attack profile filler items [11], very little is known about the characteristics of power items. And without this knowledge, it is difficult to build attack user profiles. So, for the PIA, our initial work uses influence-based methods to select power items (§ 3) and we set other attack user profile elements in the SPIP according to more traditional attack models.

To describe the PIM, we use the specification framework from [11]. The attack user profile elements consist of the following:

Selected items (I_S) have particular characteristics determined by the attacker. For the PIM, these are the power items and they are items that are likely to correlate with many user profiles in the system. The selected item size, or the number of items in each profile, is an experimental design parameter and is usually expressed as a percentage of the total number of items in the dataset. A larger size

[3]We used a divisor of 50 users as an analog to work done with co-rated items in user neighborhoods by [5] to optimize RS accuracy.
[4]Based on personal communication with the authors.

may have more impact, however, it is also more easily detectable. Previous work [11] has shown that a 5-10% profile size should be sufficient to have an impact on recommendation robustness. I_S selection is based on the methods described in § 3. The I_S rating value for each of these items in the profile is selected randomly from a normal distribution around the mean and standard deviation of the item's rating in the dataset. Our intent was for SPIP's to have a rating profile that was strong rather than just randomly assigning rating values. We used a normal distribution because this has been typical in RS attack research. [8, 11].
Filler items (I_F) are usually set randomly according a normal distribution and are used to establish correlations with other users in the dataset. For the PIM, this set is empty because we wanted a strong correlation between the selected items I_S and the target item I_T; we believe that having filler items would tend to confound or dilute this relationship.
Unrated items (I_U) are the items exclusive of the I_S, I_F, and I_T and have null values in the PIM.
Target item (I_T) is usually a single item that is typically set to the maximum r_{max} or minimum r_{min} rating depending on the attack intent (push or nuke). Our initial experiment in this study consisted of a *single target item* attack (PIA-ST) in keeping with traditional attack models; our subsequent experiments (2 and 3) used the novel *multiple target item* attack (PIA-MT) on the item-based algorithm. The selection of the target item is also a key part of the attack model. We experiment with "new" items (those with only one rating) because this is a typical scenario in which power users are asked to provide ratings and because items with few ratings are more vulnerable to attack; we also use a mix of "new and established" items for subsequent experiments.

Other factors in building effective RS attacks include [8, 11]:
Attack size, the number of attack user profiles to be injected. A larger attack size may be more effective, however, it is more easily detectable. The attack size or number of profiles is an experimental design parameter and is usually expressed as a percentage of the total number of user profiles in the dataset. Previous work [11] has shown that a 5-10% attack size should be sufficient to have an impact on recommendation robustness. We vary the attack size for our experiments to understand the scope of impact.
Attack intent, for a typical 1-5 rating scale, 5 is used for push attacks and 1 for nuke attacks. In this study, we focus on push attacks, leaving nuke attacks for future work.

Therefore, to generate a set of SPIP's for a given PIA, we specify the following elements:

- Dataset with (user, item, rating) triples
- Power Item selection methods: similarity-based, influence-based, etc.
- Attack size or number of attackers: Expressed as a percentage of number of users in the dataset
- Selected Item (I_S) size or number of power items: Expressed as a percentage of number of items in the dataset
- Target Item (I_T): New items, Established items
- Target Item size or number of target items: Expressed as a percentage of number of items in the dataset
- Attack intent: Push

The push version of the PIA-ST is similar to the Bandwagon, Segment, and AOP attacks, when the power item selection method is based on the Number of Ratings method, as described in § 3. However, these attack models differ primarily in the contents of I_F and I_S as shown in Table 1. Furthermore, the PIA-MT differs radically from previously studied attacks using popular items, not only in the profile contents shown in Table 1 but also in that the

Table 1: Attack Model Profile Content Differences

Attack Model	I_S	I_F
Bandwagon	Popular items, ratings set to r_{max}	Random items, ratings set with normal dist around *system* mean
Segment	Segment items, ratings set to r_{max}	Random items, ratings set to r_{min}
Average Over Popular	Empty	x-% Popular Items, ratings set with normal dist around *item* mean
Power Item	Power items, ratings set with normal dist around *item* mean	Empty

PIA-MT uses multiple targets simultaneously rather than a single target item in order to mount the attack.

The PIM approach goes beyond prior research primarily in two areas: first, we utilize influence-based methods (§ 3) to select the power items for the attack user profile, and second, we utilize multiple rather than just single target items. We believe that this combination can yield powerful attacks, especially against the item-based algorithm that has been resistant to attack in the past [8, 11].

5. ANALYZING POWER ITEM ATTACKS

We conducted a series of three experiments to address our main research question — whether the PIA could have a substantial impact on item-based recommenders. First, to see whether the PIA had traction as an attack vector overall, which it did. Second, to see whether a multiple-target variant would have a greater impact on item-based approaches, which it did. And third, to see whether the multiple-target PIA could have an impact on both new and established items, which it can. The line of experimentation was to find a PIA approach that was more successful in attacking item-based recommenders than previous research [11] had indicated.
Experiment 1: Consists of the PIA with a number of "new" (low # ratings) item targets pushed one at a time and averaged over all target items. We call this the PIA Single Target (PIA-ST) attack because we are, in effect, attacking the recommender with a single target item. The objective of this experiment is to determine the effectiveness of the PIA against various recommender algorithms and to compare with the results we obtained with the PUA against similar recommenders.
Experiment 2: Although it is easy to envision an attacker with an intent to promote a single item, e.g., a book they just published, it is also possible for an attacker to have several items to attack at once in order to promote (or disparage) a group of products as opposed to only one product. This experiment consists of the PIA with multiple "new item" targets all pushed at the same time and is called the PIA Multiple Target (PIA-MT). The objective of this experiment is to test how well the power item approach can significantly impact item-based systems, above and beyond previously-observed results by further exploiting item-item similarities in the SPIP's.
Experiment 3: A question that also needs to be answered is whether the PIA can still be effective when using a mix of new and established target items rather than just new items. This experiment consists of the PIA with multiple "new and established item" targets all pushed at the same time and is another variation of the PIA-MT. The objective of this experiment is to determine how well the PIA-MT is able to impact recommendations for a mix of new and established items.

Based on our research question, we note two hypotheses:

H1: *A PIA with relatively small number of SPIP's (<=5% of all users) can have significant effects on RS predictions and top-N lists of recommendations, measured with robustness metrics.* For Experiments 1 and 2 that use new items as targets, we expect Hit Ratio to be > 50% and Rank < 20 to qualify as significant impacts. For Hit Ratio, a majority of users (> 50%) should have target items in their top-N lists. In our experiments we use a top-N value of 40 for Hit Ratio calculations based on the analysis in [8] that the median recommendation search ends within the first 40 items displayed. Therefore, a Rank of 20 would be well within the median search. Since there is no precedent for measuring a PIA that uses new and established items as targets, for Experiment 3 we used values based on the "all-users" Hit Ratio and Prediction Shift results for the Segment attack against the item-based systems [1, 11], i.e, Hit Ratio > 11% and Prediction Shift > 0.1.
H2: *SPIP's identified using the InDegree power user selection method will have a higher level of impact, compared to SPIP's identified using NumRatings or AggSim, on RS predictions and top-N recommendation lists as measured with Hit Ratio and Rank.* This hypothesis is based on the findings from Social Network Analysis [17] that high InDegree centrality is indicative of nodes (users) that have strong influence over other users.

6. EXPERIMENTAL DESIGN

Evaluation Metrics: Evaluations were performed before and after the attacks using the Apache Mahout 0.8 platform[5]. For robustness metrics [11, 2], we use Hit Ratio (HR), Average HR ($\overline{HR}$), Prediction Shift (PS), Average PS ($\overline{PS}$), Rank (R), and Average R ($\overline{R}$). For example, a high Hit Ratio and a low Rank indicates that the attack was successful (from the attacker's standpoint). Since we are using multiple targets simultaneously in Experiments 2 and 3, the interpretation of Hit Ratio is changed from its traditional meaning, i.e., HR is now the percentage of users that have at least one of the multiple target items in their top-N list. We also defined a new metric, Number of Targets per User (NTPU), associated with Hit Ratio that provides the average number of target items present in a user's top-N list of recommendations. This metric provides a measure of the effectiveness of a multiple-item attack, a higher NTPU meaning higher attack effectiveness, and is averaged over all users with hits (target items in their top-N lists). For a test run T, let U_T be the set of users, UH_T the set of users with hits, and IT_T the set of target items; and let R_u be the set of top-N recommendations for user u. If the target item appears in R_u for user u, the scoring function H_{ui} has value 1; otherwise it is zero. NTPU for a user u is given by $NTPU_u = \sum_{i \epsilon IT_T} H_{ui}$, and then averaged over all users with hits to yield $NTPU = \frac{\sum_{i \epsilon U_T} NTPU_u}{|UH_T|}$. To compare the NTPU metrics within and between experiments, a normalized NTPU or NNTPU is calculated using average Hit Ratio as the normalizing factor. So, for a given test run T, $NNTPU_T = \overline{HR_T} * NTPU_T$. Since the PIA's being evaluated for Experiments 1 and 2 are for "new" items, i.e., items with one rating, the Prediction Shift is expected to be close to r_{max} of 5.
Datasets and Algorithms: We used MovieLens[6] ML100K[7], ML1M[8], and ML10M[9] datasets. The RS algorithms used were provided in Apache Mahout and customized for this study. The CF user-based weighted algorithm (UBW) [3] uses Pearson similarity with a threshold of 0.0 (positive correlation), neighborhood size of 50, and significance weighting of n/50 where n is the number of co-rated items [5]. The item-based weighted algorithm (IBW) [15] uses Adjusted Cosine similarity with a threshold of 0.0 and significance weighting of n/50. For the SVD-based algorithm (SVD), we used RatingStochasticGradientDescent (RSGD); run-time parameter settings were number of features (=100) and number of training steps or iterations (=50) and were determined empirically to optimize recommender accuracy.
Attack User Profiles: To mount the Power Item Attack, attack user profiles were generated as described in § 4 and converted to attack profiles by setting target items to the Attack Intent.
Power Item Selection: Methods used for power item selection are described in § 3.
Target Item Selection: For Experiments 1 and 2, we used 'new' items, i.e., target items with only one rating were selected randomly from the corresponding dataset. Experiment 3 used "new and established" items, i.e., target items were selected randomly and had the following average number of ratings, average rating, and average rating entropy, respectively: ML100K (73.78, 3.13, 1.77), ML1M (253.40, 3.26, 1.81), Ml10M (675.76, 3.15, 1.71).
Attack Parameter Selection: The Attack Intent is Push, i.e., target item rating is set to max (= 5). The Attack Size or number of power users in each attack was varied for these experiments; the I_S size (number of power items) and the number of target items used were also varied as shown in Table 2. The Attack profiles were generated as described in § 4 and the target item rating was injected at run time.
Test Variations: For all three experiments, we used all three power item selection methods (§ 3). For Experiment 1 we used UBW, IBW, and SVD algorithms, ML100K and ML1M datasets, and single new target items. For Experiments 2 and 3 we focused on the IBW algorithm and used all three datasets. Experiment 2 used new multiple target items and Experiment 3 used new and established multiple target items.

Table 2: Attack Parameters by Dataset

	Attackers	Power Items	Target Items
MovieLens 100K:			
% of Dataset	1, 5	1, 5, 10	1, 5
# Attackers, Items	10, 50	17, 83, 166	10, 50
MovieLens 1M:			
% of Dataset	0.1, 1	0.1, 1, 10	0.5, 1, 3
# Attackers, Items	6, 60	4, 37, 368	18, 37, 110
MovieLens 10M:			
% of Dataset	0.1, 1	0.1, 1, 10	0.5, 1
# Attackers, Items	70, 699	11,107,1068	50, 100

7. EXPERIMENTS AND RESULTS

7.1 E1: PIA-ST with "New" Item Targets

Single target item attacks have been used in the past [11, 2] to eliminate confounds between the selected/filler items (that are used to correlate with other users) and the target item. This is especially important for user-based recommenders because user-user similarities with multiple target items would form neighborhoods of users that have similar tastes not only with selected/filler items but also

[5]http://mahout.apache.org
[6]http://www.grouplens.org
[7]nominal 100,000 ratings, 1,682 movies, and 943 users.
[8]nominal 1,000,209 ratings, 3,883 movies, 6,040 users.
[9]nominal 10,000,054 ratings, 10,676 movies, 69,878 users.

with the multiple target items, effectively reducing the focus of the attack. To successfully attack item-based systems, prior research showed that item-item similarities can be manipulated; e.g., this was demonstrated in the Bandwagon and Segment attacks [1, 11].

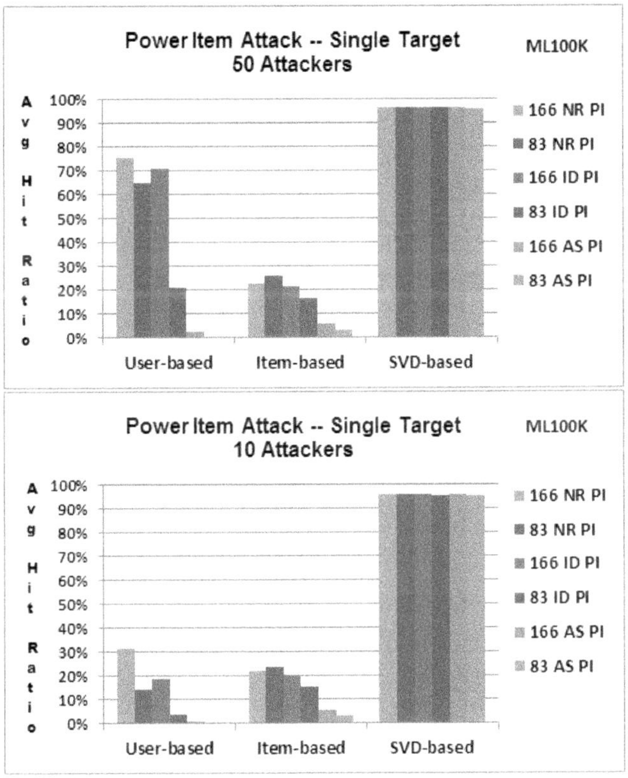

Figure 1: ML100K – Experiment 1 Hit Ratio Results

For this experiment we select 50 target items from the ML100K dataset that only have one rating, with the intent of attacking a "new" item. We calculate impacts on robustness metrics (see § 6) for each target item individually and then average the results over all 50 targets. We repeat this calculation for three levels of power items (17, 83, and 166) and two levels of SPIP's (10 and 50) for each of the three power item selection methods (InDegree, NumRatings, and AggSim) and using each of the three recommender algorithms (UBW, IBW, SVD). The Hit Ratio results for ML100K are shown in Figure 1. For the case with 50 attackers or 5% of user base (top of Figure 1), both InDegree and NumRatings show strong $\overline{HR}$ results using 166 power items for UBW and SVD (70% to 75% for UBW and 96% for SVD) and significantly weaker results for IBW (21% to 22%). AggSim shows strong results for SVD (96%) and very weak results for UBW and IBW (< 5%). Results for $\overline{R}$ (not shown) indicate little variation across the power item selection methods and average as follows: 3.0 for UBW, 14.6 for IBW, and 2.0 for SVD. And results for $\overline{PS}$ (not shown) also indicate little variation across the power item selection methods and are at a higher level (> 4) because of the "new" item targets. For the case with 10 attackers or 1% of user base (bottom of Figure 1), we observe similar results against IBW and SVD as well as a significantly weaker attack against UBW.

To see whether these results would scale, we repeated a similar experiment using the ML1M dataset for two levels of power items (37 and 368) and two levels of SPIP's (6 and 60) for each of the three power item selection methods (InDegree, NumRatings, and AggSim) and using each of the three recommender algorithms (UBW, IBW, SVD). Results for this ML1M attack (not shown) using 60 attackers (1% of user base) and each with 368 power items (10% of all items), are similar to those obtained for ML100K with 10 attackers (also 1% of user base), i.e., a weak attack for UBW (high of 21% to 36% $\overline{HR}$) and IBW (13% to 19% $\overline{HR}$), and a strong attack for SVD (81% to 98% $\overline{HR}$). This would indicate that more attackers are required for a stronger attack. Results for $\overline{R}$ average as follows over all power item selection methods: 6.7 for UBW, 15.4 for IBW, and 5.5 for SVD.

Overall, these results indicate that under a specific set of conditions (e.g., using 50 attackers and 166 power items for ML100K), the PIA is effective (high $\overline{HR}$, low $\overline{R}$) against the UBW and SVD algorithms. We also found that the PIA is not very effective against the IBW, regardless of the test conditions. While we had hoped to see a larger impact on IBW using the PIA, our results are consistent with previous findings (including our PUA) [8, 11, 19], showing that the item-based algorithm is resistant or robust to attack. Hypothesis H1 is accepted for both UBW and SVD recommenders, meaning that a relatively small number of power users (5% or less of the user base on a given dataset) can have significant effects on RS predictions and top-N lists of recommendations regardless of power user selection method. IBW is partially accepted because $\overline{R}$ < 20, however, $\overline{HR}$ does not meet the 50% requirement. Hypothesis H2 is rejected for all three algorithms. Although the InDegree and NumRatings perform well at a high level, NumRatings is a slightly better method for selecting power items, i.e., simply inserting popular items into SPIP's creates very effective attacks against some recommender systems (UBW and SVD in our experiment).

7.2 E2: PIA-MT with "New" Item Targets

The motivation for Experiment 2 was to develop a PIA model that had higher impacts on IBW than had been previously observed. Intuitively, we expect for carefully configured single-item attacks such as Average, Bandwagon, and Segment attacks [8, 11, 2] to be effective against user-based algorithms because of the similarity correlations established between the selected and filler items of the attacker profiles and the corresponding items in the profiles of non-attackers in the dataset. Once that strong correlation is made (by the algorithm), then the correlation between the selected/filler items and the target item allows the algorithm to calculate a higher prediction value for the target item which is then recommended to the non-attacker. Previous results indicate that larger attack and filler sizes create stronger attacks and research has shown that these attack models consistently impact user-based systems with impunity [8, 11, 2]. The item-based algorithm, however, establishes similarity correlations between the selected/filler items and the target item of the attacker profiles that are then used to calculate recommendations for non-attackers. The Segment attack [11, 1] was successful against the item-based algorithm to the extent that it impacted users who belonged to a particular segment of the user base (e.g., the "Horror" movie crowd), however, this attack did not have a high impact over the entire user base. We believe that to mount a stronger attack against item-based systems, two elements are required in the attack user profile. First, the set of selected items must correlate with a broad cross-section of the user base and second, multiple target items must be used to establish strong correlations with the selected items. Experiment 2 takes on this challenge.

We recognize that because of multiple target items, there can be impacts to the robustness metrics, i.e., the $\overline{HR}$ for a single target item will be different due to confounding when a target item is grouped with multiple other target items during the similarity and prediction calculation process. An analysis of this situation was performed and we found that a metric such as Hit Ratio decreases slightly for any given target item as the number of multiple target items in the SPIP increase. For example, for a set of attacks using ML100K and IBW, we found that the HR for a single target item across all users decreased from 0.225 to 0.208 to 0.184 going from 1 to 10 to 50 targets, respectively. However, at the same time, the $\overline{HR}$ across all target items and users increased from 22% to 70%, so the confounding effect for IBW does not present a major issue for the PIA.

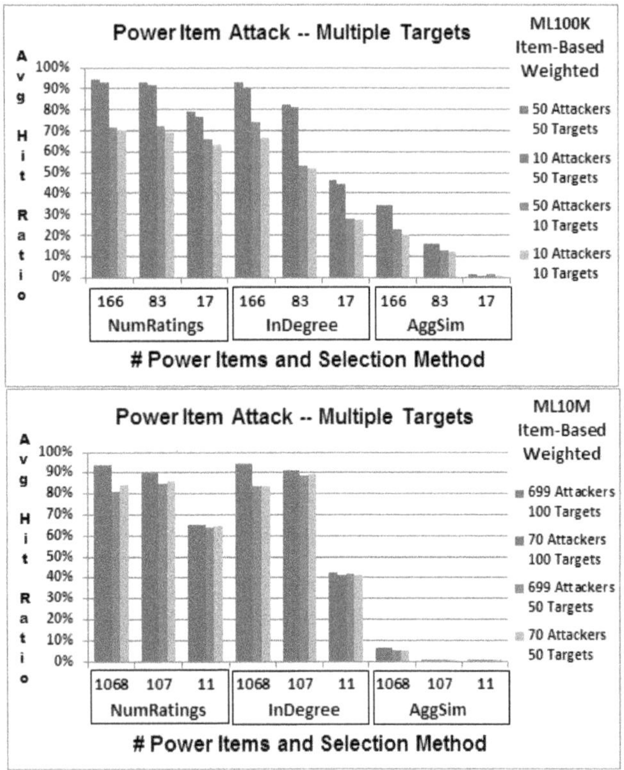

Figure 2: ML100K / ML10M – Experiment 2 Hit Ratio Results

The effectiveness of Experiment 2 was measured using robustness metrics (see § 6). For each dataset used in this experiment, we select a specified number of target items that only had one rating with the intent of attacking "new" items. Those target items are injected into the dataset at one time and then $\overline{HR}$, $\overline{R}$, and $\overline{PS}$ impacts over all targets are calculated. This process is repeated for three levels of power items, up to three levels of SPIP's for each of the three power item selection methods (InDegree, NumRatings, and AggSim), and using only the IBW recommender algorithm. See Table 2 for parameter settings. The ML100K $\overline{HR}$ results shown in the upper chart of Figure 2 indicate some interesting characteristics for this type of attack. InDegree and NumRatings show strong $\overline{HR}$ values (80% to 90%) when attack profiles used 166 and 83 power items and 50 target items, while AggSim impacts were weaker (15% to 34%) for the same number of power items and target items. Average Hit Ratio is sensitive to the number of power items and target items, and somewhat insensitive to number of attackers; *i.e., the PIA can be effective with a small number of attack user profiles*. NumRatings shows the least amount of this sensitivity across the number of power items and target items, i.e., 10 attackers, each with 17 power items and 10 target items (a total of 270 ratings) impacts over 60% of the user base with 100,000 ratings.

To see if these results scaled, we also ran this experiment on ML1M and ML10M. For the ML1M dataset (not shown), we observed a similar set of characteristics in the results. InDegree and NumRatings continue to show strong $\overline{HR}$ results while AggSim results are much weaker. And a NumRatings attack with 6 attackers, each with 4 power items and 37 target items (a total of 888 ratings) impacts 40% of the user base with a million ratings. For the ML10M dataset, results are shown in the lower chart of Figure 2. InDegree and NumRatings continue to show strong $\overline{HR}$ results while AggSim results are much weaker. And a NumRatings attack with 70 attackers, each with 11 power items and 50 target items (a total of 38,500 ratings or 0.4% of the total number of ratings) impacts 64% of the user base with ten million ratings. Average Rank for each of these cases was also calculated: for ML100K, $\overline{R}$ varied from 9 to 19 (mean 15.9); for ML1M, $\overline{R}$ varied from 14 to 19 (mean 16); and for ML10M, $\overline{R}$ varied from 10 to 20 (mean 16). To compare the attack effectiveness within and between datasets in the experiment, the NNTPU metric is shown in Figure 3. The highest number of targets per user occurs with the SPIP's containing 11 power items and 100 target items generated using the NumRatings method for ML10M; a close second would be SPIP's containing 107 power items generated using the InDegree method. For all three datasets, the results for $\overline{PS}$ (not shown) indicate little variation across the power item selection methods and are at a higher level (> 4) because of the "new" item targets. To further confirm our results, we also ran a complete set of baseline PIAs across all datasets, attack sizes, and power item levels for IBW *without any target items*. The robustness metrics were all zero, meaning that injecting SPIP's without any target item ratings had no effect on the RS recommendations.

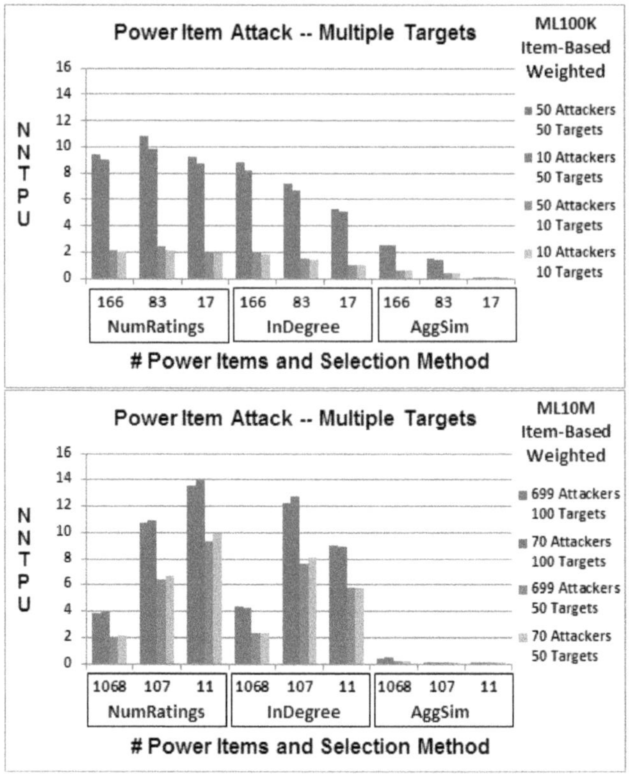

Figure 3: ML100K / ML10M – Experiment 2 Normalized Number of Targets Per User (NNTPU) Results

Most notable is that the $\overline{HR}$ results exceed Hit Ratio measurements reported previously for attacks against item-based recommenders, including the Segment attack. We conclude that the use of power items and multiple (new) target items in the SPIPs has resulted in a powerful attack against the item-based algorithm. Hypothesis H1 is accepted for the higher levels of attack size and number of targets for all power item selection methods and all three datasets. Hypothesis H2 is partially accepted for the IBW algorithm. Although the InDegree and NumRatings both perform well at a high level, NumRatings is a slightly better method for selecting power items, especially at lower levels of power items; both methods are superior to AggSim.

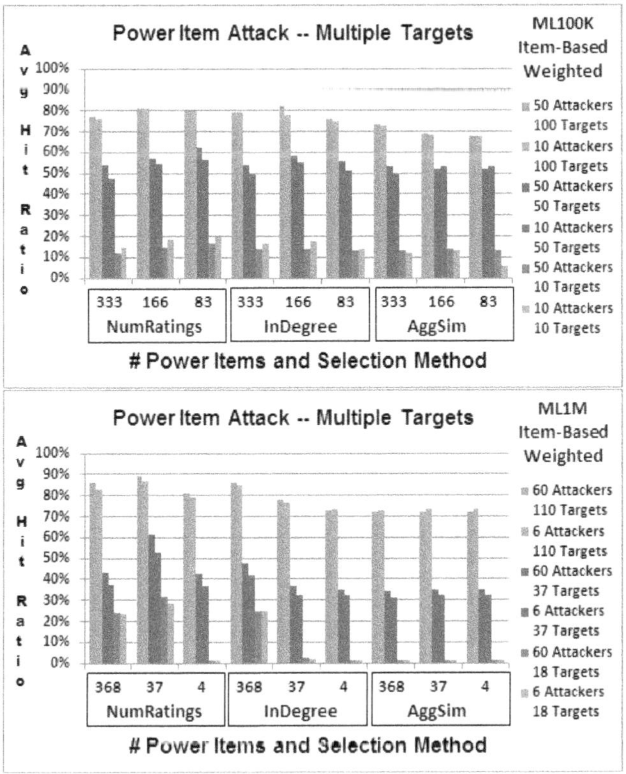

Figure 4: ML100K / ML1M – Experiment 3 Hit Ratio Results

7.3 E3: PIA-MT with "New and Established" Item Targets

In general, the robustness results for this experiment were lower than Experiment 2; this was expected since new items are more vulnerable to attack than established items. For each dataset used in this experiment, we select a specified number of target items to obtain a mix of items with a range of "age" based on number of ratings. The attack and calculation processes described for Experiment 2 are used again here. See Table 2 for parameter settings. For the ML100K dataset, we added a third level of SPIP's with 100 target items (10% of the total number of items) to compare with the three levels of target items in ML1M and to observe the impacts resulting from adding more target items to the SPIP's. The $\overline{HR}$ results shown in the upper chart of Figure 4 indicate sensitivity to the number of target items and insensitivity to number of attackers and power items. A similar pattern can be observed for the ML1M dataset shown in the lower chart of Figure 4; this is also the case for ML10M (not shown) except for the sensitivity to the number of power items for NumRatings and InDegree. For higher numbers of target items, ML100K and ML1M show strong $\overline{HR}$ results across all power item selection methods; for ML10M, NumRatings and InDegree still have a slight edge (40% to 50%) over AggSim (31%)

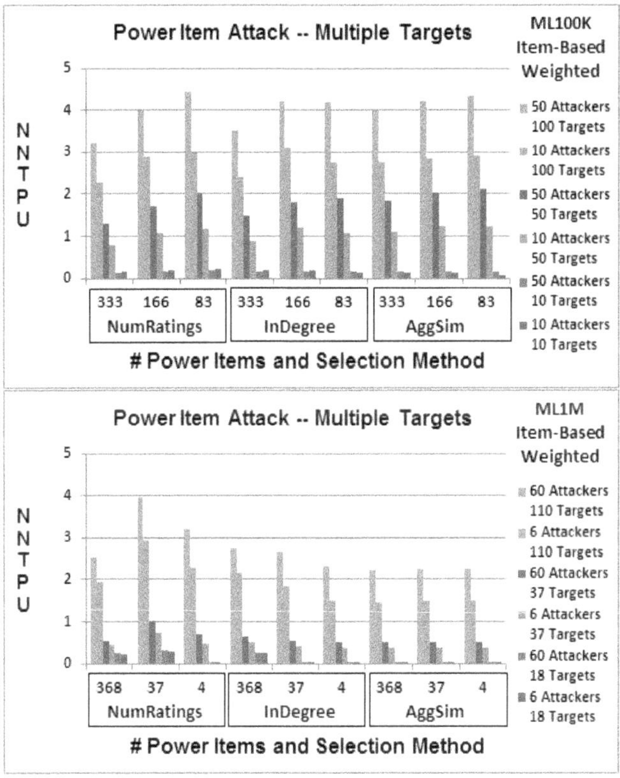

Figure 5: ML100K and ML1M – Experiment 3 Normalized Number of Targets Per User (NNTPU) Results

although not quite as substantial as in Experiments 1 and 2. Average Rank for each of these cases was also calculated: for ML100K, $\overline{R}$ varied from 17 to 21 (mean 19.6); for ML1M, 18 to 23 (mean 20.6); and for ML10M, 19 to 21 (mean 20.3).

To compare the attack effectiveness between Experiments 2 and 3, we used the NNTPU metric shown in Figure 5 for ML100K and ML1M. The results confirm that attacks in Experiment 2 had more impact than those in Experiment 3. For example, for ML100K and 50 target items, Experiment 2 had NNTPU values between 4.5 and 11 for NumRatings and InDegree, AggSim had values between 0 and 2. Experiment 3 had NNTPU values between 1.3 and 2.1 for all three selection methods. An interesting result for ML100K is that NNTPU displays a phenomenon similar to one reported in previous work, i.e., as the number of power items increases, the attack effectiveness decreases (see upper chart in Figure 5); this occurs consistently for all three power item selection methods. Reported in [11], as the number of filler items increases, PS decreases; the explanation for this was that attack user profiles need to achieve a balance between "coverage" (including enough item ratings to correlate with other users) and "generality" (including too many item ratings that could make the profile dissimilar to a given user). We also observed this for NumRatings and InDegree for ML10M in this experiment (not shown) and in Experiment 2 (see Figure 3).

Regarding Prediction Shift results, for ML100K we observed $\overline{PS}$ values in the range of 0.2 to 0.4 and for ML1M they ranged from 0.03 to 0.19. By comparison, [1, 11] reported PS values of 0.1 and 0.15 for the Segment and Bandwagon attacks, respectively, against the item-based algorithm for all users in ML100K with an attack size of 1%. Our $\overline{HR}$ and $\overline{PS}$ results for ML100K were significantly improved over previously reported results. Given time constraints, full re-implementation, testing, and execution of Segment / Bandwagon attacks for more direct comparison was beyond the scope of the experiment. It is a limitation of the study to be addressed in future work.

To further determine the quality of our results, we computed $\overline{PS}$ for attack datasets that included the power items but not the target items and compared results statistically. For ML100K and 100 target items, differences in $\overline{PS}$ with and without the target items were significant (p <0.005) for NumRatings, InDegree, and AggSim across all three levels of power items. For ML1M, differences were significant (p <0.05) for NumRatings and InDegree (368 power items only). As in Experiment 2, we ran a set of PIA's across all datasets, attack sizes, and power item levels for IBW *without any target items* as a baseline. In this case, the robustness metrics were all $>$ zero. The interpretation is that, because Experiment 3 uses "new and established" items as target items, it is possible (and expected) that some of them will show up in top-N recommendation lists as confirmed by our findings. However, we found significant differences in key metrics for cases with and without targets. For example, averaged over all the cases run with ML1M, NNTPU was 2.29 (with targets) and 1.38 (without targets) and $\overline{PS}$ was 0.09 and 0.01, respectively; this indicates that the attack had impacts above and beyond the baseline.

Hypothesis H1 is accepted for the highest levels of attack size and number of targets across all power item selection methods for ML100K and ML1M, given the threshold rates of 11% $\overline{HR}$ and 0.1 $\overline{PS}$. H1 is partially accepted for ML10M for $\overline{HR}$. Hypothesis H2 is partially accepted for the IBW algorithm. We find that the InDegree and NumRatings methods, on average, perform the same at all levels of power items and both methods are superior to AggSim.

8. CONCLUSION

In this study we have developed a power item model that is able to generate synthetic power item profiles that can be used to mount effective power item attacks against user-based and SVD-based recommenders measured by traditional Hit Ratio, Rank, and Prediction Shift robustness metrics. In addition, we showed how the power item attack using a novel multi-target approach can generate effective attacks against the typically robust item-based algorithm using new, as well as established, dataset items. We have also compared power item selection methods used to generate synthetic power item profiles and shown that, because of its low-cost and low-knowledge requirements, the NumRatings method is the more effective, by a small margin, in attacking recommenders than the influence-based InDegree method. We have shown that a relatively small number of NumRatings and InDegree synthetic power item profiles can have significant effects on RS predictions and top-N recommendation lists. And, in order to compare attack effectiveness results within and between our experiments, we developed a metric that measures the number of target items per user resulting from the multi-target approach. Future work includes evaluation in other domains / datasets and developing PIA detection methods.

9. REFERENCES

[1] R. Burke, B. Mobasher, R. Bhaumik, and C. Williams. Segment-based injection attacks against collaborative filtering recommender systems. In *Proceedings of the International Conference on Data Mining*, 2005.

[2] R. Burke, M. P. O'Mahony, and N. J. Hurley. Robust collaborative recommendation. In F. Ricci et al., editors, *Recommender Systems Handbook*. Springer, 2011.

[3] C. Desrosiers and G. Karypis. A comprehensive survey of neighborhood-based recommendations methods. In F. Ricci, L. Rokach, B. Shapira, and P. B. Kantor, editors, *Recommender Systems Handbook*. Springer, 2011.

[4] A. Goyal and L. V. S. Lakshmanan. Recmax: Exploiting recommender systems for fun and profit. In *Proceedings KDD*, 2012.

[5] J. L. Herlocker, J. A. Konstan, A. Borchers, and J. Riedl. An algorithmic framework for performing collaborative filtering. In *Proc of the ACM SIGIR Conf*, 1999.

[6] J. L. Herlocker, J. A. Konstan, L. G. Terveen, and J. Riedl. Evaluating collaborative filtering recommender systems. *ACM Transactions on Information Systems*, 2004.

[7] N. Hurley, Z. Cheng, and M. Zhang. Statistical attack detection. In *Proceedings of the third ACM conference on Recommender systems*, 2009.

[8] S. K. Lam and J. Riedl. Shilling recommender systems for fun and profit. In *Proceedings of the 13th international conference on World Wide Web*. ACM, 2004.

[9] B. Mehta and W. Nejdl. Attack resistant collaborative filtering. In *SIGIR '08: Proceedings of the 31st annual international ACM SIGIR conference on Research and development in information retrieval*. ACM, 2008.

[10] B. Mehta and W. Nejdl. Unsupervised strategies for shilling detection and robust collaborative filtering. *User Modeling and User-Adapted Interaction*, 19(1-2), 2009.

[11] B. Mobasher, R. Burke, R. Bhaumik, and C. Williams. Toward trustworthy recommender systems: An analysis of attack models and algorithm robustness. *ACM Trans. Internet Technol.*, 2007.

[12] B. Mobasher, R. Burke, and J. Sandvig. Model-based collaborative filtering as a defense against profile injection attacks. In *Proceedings of the 21st National Conference on Artificial Intelligence (AAAI'06)*, July 2006.

[13] M. P. O'Mahony, N. Hurley, and G. C. M. Silvestre. Promoting recommendations: An attack on collaborative filtering. In *Proceedings of DEXA'02*, 2002.

[14] J. Palau, M. Montaner, B. Lopez, and J. L. D. L. Rosa. Collaboration analysis in recommender systems using social networks. In *Cooperative Information Agents VIII: 8th International Workshop, CIA 2004*, 2004.

[15] B. Sarwar, G. Karypis, J. Konstan, and J. Riedl. Item-based collaborative filtering recommendation algorithms. In *Proceedings of the World Wide Web Conference*, 2001.

[16] C. E. Seminario and D. C. Wilson. Assessing impacts of a power user attack on a matrix factorization collaborative recommender system. In *Proceedings of the 27th Florida Artificial Intelligence Research Society Conf.*, 2014.

[17] S. Wasserman and K. Faust. *Social Network Analysis: Methods and Applications*. Cambridge University Press, New York, NY, 1994.

[18] C. Williams, B. Mobasher, and R. D. Burke. Defending recommender systems: detection of profile injection attacks. *Service Oriented Computing and Applications*, 2007.

[19] D. C. Wilson and C. E. Seminario. When power users attack: assessing impacts in collaborative recommender systems. In *Proceedings of the 7th ACM conference on Recommender Systems*, RecSys '13. ACM, 2013.

[20] D. C. Wilson and C. E. Seminario. Evil twins: Modeling power users in attacks on recommender systems. In *Proceedings of the 22nd Conference on User Modelling, Adaptation and Personalization*, 2014.

Recommending with an Agenda: Active Learning of Private Attributes using Matrix Factorization

Smriti Bhagat, Udi Weinsberg, Stratis Ioannidis, Nina Taft
Technicolor, Los Altos, CA
smriti.bhagat, udi.weinsberg, stratis.ioannidis, nina.taft}@technicolor.com

ABSTRACT

Recommender systems leverage user demographic information, such as age, gender, etc., to personalize recommendations and better place their targeted ads. Oftentimes, users do not volunteer this information due to privacy concerns, or due to a lack of initiative in filling out their online profiles. We illustrate a new threat in which a recommender learns private attributes of users who do not voluntarily disclose them. We design both passive and active attacks that solicit ratings for strategically selected items, and could thus be used by a recommender system to pursue this hidden agenda. Our methods are based on a novel usage of Bayesian matrix factorization in an active learning setting. Evaluations on multiple datasets illustrate that such attacks are indeed feasible and use significantly fewer rated items than static inference methods. Importantly, they succeed without sacrificing the quality of recommendations to users.

Categories and Subject Descriptors: H.2.8 Database Applications: Data Mining
Keywords: Recommendations, Privacy, Active Learning.

1. INTRODUCTION

Recommender systems rely on knowing their users – not just their preferences (i.e., ratings on items), but also their social and demographic information, e.g., age, gender, political affiliation, and ethnicity [14, 19]. A rich user profile allows a recommender system to better personalize its services, and at the same time enables additional monetization opportunities, such as targeted advertising.

Users of a recommender system know they are disclosing their preferences (or ratings) for movies, books, or other items (we use movies as our running example). A recommender may obtain additional social and demographic information about its users by explicitly soliciting it [14, 19]. While some users may willingly disclose such information, others may be more privacy-sensitive and elect to only reveal their ratings. Privacy research has shown that some users are uncomfortable revealing their demographic data to personalization systems [1, 15]. Even when such services provide transparency about their data collection and use practices [1], some users are unwilling to disclose personal data despite the allure of personalized services. In [14] the authors conduct a small scale user study on Amazon Turk that examines how to motivate users to disclose their demographic data.

For users who wish to withhold some demographic information, a recommender can still undermine their attempt at privacy. In previous work [30], we show that users' movie ratings can be used to predict their gender with 80% accuracy. Other studies also show the potential to infer demographics from a range of online user activities [2, 4, 18, 20]. In this work, we consider a recommender system that offers a legitimate service, yet is simultaneously malicious: it purposefully attempts to extract certain attributes from users who choose to withhold them. Unlike previous work that studies static attacks on the complete data, we consider an *active learning* setting, in which the recommender system aims to efficiently (quickly and accurately) infer a user's private attribute via interactive questioning. Recommender systems routinely ask users to rate a few items, as a means to address a "cold start" setting, or to improve the quality of recommendations. We leverage these instances of interactions with the user, alongside with the observation that item selection is at the recommender's discretion, to propose a new attack. We hypothesize that if the sequence of questions (items to rate) is carefully selected, the recommender system can quickly (so as not to be detected by the user) determine a user's private attribute with high confidence, thereby violating her privacy. A key idea in the design of this attack is to leverage matrix factorization (MF) as the basis for inference. Most recommender systems use matrix factorization (MF) models as a building block for providing recommendations [17]. While MF is well understood for rating prediction, it has generally not been applied for inference. To the best of our knowledge, this paper is the first to leverage MF as the basis for building both (a) an inference method of private attributes using item ratings and (b) an active learning method that selects items in a way that maximizes inference confidence in the smallest number of questions.

Our contributions are as follows:

- First, we propose a novel classification method for determining a user's binary private attribute – her *type* – based upon ratings alone. In particular, we use matrix factorization to learn item profiles and type-dependent biases, and show how to incorporate this information into a clas-

RecSys'14, October 6–10, 2014, Foster City, Silicon Valley, CA, USA.

http://dx.doi.org/10.1145/2645710.2645747.

sification algorithm. This classification is consistent with Bayesian matrix factorization.

- Second, we demonstrate that the resulting classification method is well suited for learning of a user's type. A simple *passive* approach, ordering items based on a set of weights computed off-line, works quite well in many cases. Beyond this, we design an *active learning* algorithm for selecting the next item to ask a user to rate: each selection maximizes the expected confidence of the private attribute's inference. Equivalently, the selections of the active learning algorithm minimize the expected risk of misclassifying the user's private attribute.
- Third, we show that our active learning method is very efficient, as item selection can reuse computations made during previous selections. We show that this reduces the naïve solution that is cubic in the number of ratings, to one that is quadratic in the number of ratings.
- Fourth, we extensively evaluate the above classifier and selection methods on three real-world datasets: Movielens, Flixster and Politics-and-TV. We show that our methods consistently outperform other baselines; with only 10 questions, we achieve between 3-20% higher classification accuracy on different datasets. Importantly, such an attack can be carried out without any sacrifice to the recommendations made to the user.

2. RELATED WORK

A number of studies have shown that user demographics can be inferred from various types of online user activity. For example, Bhagat *et al.* [2] show that it is possible to learn age and gender information from blogs. Mislove *et al.* [20] study data from online social networks and illustrate that even when only a fraction of users provide profile attributes (such as location, interests, etc.), it is possible to infer these attributes among users who do not disclose them. Bi *et al.* [4] show how demographics can be inferred from search queries, and Kosinski *et al.* [18] show that several personality traits, including political views, sexual orientation, and drug use can be accurately predicted from Facebook "likes".

Recommender systems were shown to be exploitable by several works utilizing off-line attacks [5, 22, 30]. Closest to our setting, Weinsberg et al. [30] empirically studied how to infer a user's gender from her movie ratings using a variety of different classifiers, showing that logistic regression and SVMs succeed with an accuracy close to 80%. We depart from [30] in multiple ways. First, we introduce a novel factor-based classifier, that relies on the Bayesian assumptions behind MF. Second, we study a recommender system in an adversarial setting that actively adapts item selection to quickly learn the private attributes. Finally, we establish that our classifier is very well suited for this task.

The Bayesian model underlying MF (discussed in detail in Section 3.2) was recently employed by Silva and Carin [28] to actively learn the actual factors (*i.e.*, the user and item profiles) in MF. More specifically, the authors consider a recommender system that adaptively selects which items to ask its users to rate in order to diminish the entropy of its user and item profiles as quickly as possible. The entropy estimation is based on the Gaussian noise and prior assumptions underlying MF, which we also employ in our work. A variety of active learing objective were also studied by Sutherland et al. [29], including minimizing the prediction error on unrated items, reducing the profile uncertainty, and identifying highly rated items. We depart from the above works as the goal of our learning task is to discover a user's demographic information, captured by a categorical type, rather the above objectives motivated by rating prediction.

In the classic active learning setting [8,9], a learner wishes to disambiguate among a set of several possible hypotheses, each represented as a function over a set of inputs. Only one of the hypotheses is valid; to discover it, the learner has access to an oracle that returns the evaluation of the valid hypothesis on a given input. In the case of a *noiseless* oracle, that always returns the correct evaluation on a query, Generalized Binary Search (GBS) discovers the valid hypothesis in a number of queries within a polylogarithmic factor from the optimal [8, 9]. Our setup can be cast into the above framework in the context of a *noisy* oracle, whose evaluations may not necessarily be exact. GBS is known to yield arbitrarily suboptimal results in the presence of noise [10]. Though algorithms for restricted noise models exist (see, e.g., [23] and [10]), no algorithm with provable performance guarantees is known in the presence of an oracle with arbitrary noise. Unfortunately, none of the existing models apply to the noisy setting we encounter here.

3. SYSTEM DESCRIPTION

3.1 Problem Statement

We consider a recommender system that provides a legitimate item recommendation service, but at the same time maliciously seeks to infer a private user attribute. The system has access to a dataset, provided by non-privacy-sensitive users, that contains item ratings as well as a categorical variable, which we refer to as the user *type*. The type is a private attribute such as gender, age, political affiliation, etc. A new user, who is privacy sensitive (i.e., her type is unknown) interacts with the system. The recommender system actively presents items for the user to rate, masquerading it as a way to improve recommendations in the cold-start setting. In this context, our goal is twofold:

1. We wish to design a *type classifier* that discovers the type of the user based on her ratings. We seek to leverage the latent factor model prevalent in matrix-factorization, a technique successfully used for rating prediction by recommender systems.
2. We wish to address the problem of *actively learning* a user's type. We aim to design an item selection method, that determines the order in which items are shown to a user for her to rate. The best order finds the user's type as quickly as possible.

For the attack to be considered successful, the recommender system needs to obtain high confidence in the value of the inferred type, with a minimum number of questions posed to the user. As our classifier and item selection methods rely heavily on matrix factorization, we review this as well as the latent factor model that underlies it below.

3.2 Data Model & Matrix Factorization

We use the following notation to describe the training dataset of the recommender. The dataset comprises of ratings to m items in set $\mathcal{M} \equiv \{1, \dots, m\}$ given by n users in set $\mathcal{N} \equiv \{1, \dots, n\}$. We denote by r_{ij} the rating of user $i \in \mathcal{N}$ to item $j \in \mathcal{M}$, and by $\mathcal{E} \subset \mathcal{N} \times \mathcal{M}$ the set of user-item pairs (i, j), for which a rating r_{ij} is present in the dataset.

Each user is characterized by a categorical type, which captures demographic information such as gender, occupation, income category, *etc.* Focusing on binary types, we denote by $t_i \in \mathcal{T} \equiv \{+1, -1\}$ the type of user $i \in \mathcal{M}$.

We assume that the ratings are generated from the standard generative model used in matrix factorization, augmented with type-dependent biases. More specifically, there exist latent factors $u_i \in \mathbb{R}^d$, $i \in \mathcal{N}$, and $v_j \in \mathbb{R}^d$, $j \in \mathcal{M}$ (the *user* and *item profiles*, resp.) such that ratings are:

$$r_{ij} = u_i^T v_j + z_{jt_i} + \epsilon_{ij}, \quad (i,j) \in \mathcal{E} \tag{1}$$

where $\epsilon_{ij} \sim N(0, \sigma_0^2)$ are independent Gaussian noise variables and z_{jt} is a *type bias*, capturing the effect of a type on the item rating. Our model is thus parametrized by $U = [u_i^T]_{i\in\mathcal{N}} \in \mathbb{R}^{n\times d}$, $V = [v_j^T]_{j\in\mathcal{M}} \in \mathbb{R}^{m\times d}$, and $Z = [z_{j,t}]_{j\in\mathcal{M},t\in\mathcal{T}} \in \mathbb{R}^{m\times|\mathcal{T}|}$. We further assume a *prior* on user and item profiles: for all $i \in \mathcal{N}$, $j \in \mathcal{M}$,

$$u_i \sim N(\mathbf{0}, \sigma_u^2 I), \text{ and } v_j \sim N(\mathbf{0}, \sigma_v^2 I), \tag{2}$$

i.e., profiles are sampled from independent zero-mean multivariate Gaussian priors.

The Gaussian priors (2) are used in many works on so-called Bayesian matrix factorization (see, *e.g.*, [21, 25, 28]). Under (1) and (2), the maximum likelihood estimation of the model parameters reduces to the standard [16, 17] minimization of the (non-convex) regularized error:[1]

$$\min_{U,V,Z} \sum_{(i,j)\in\mathcal{E}} (r_{ij} - u_i^T v_j - z_{jt_i})^2 + \lambda \sum_{i\in\mathcal{N}} \|u_i\|_2^2 + \mu \sum_{i\in\mathcal{M}} \|v_j\|_2^2 \tag{3}$$

with $\lambda = \frac{\sigma_0^2}{\sigma_u^2}$ and $\mu = \frac{\sigma_0^2}{\sigma_v^2}$. Given a dataset of ratings r_{ij}, $(i,j) \in \mathcal{E}$ and types t_i, $i \in \mathcal{N}$, the parameters U, V, Z can be computed as local minima to (3) through standard methods [17], such as gradient descent or alternating minimization, while λ and μ are computed through cross-validation.

4. A FACTOR-BASED CLASSIFIER

We now turn our attention to the following classification problem. Suppose that the recommender system, with access to the dataset of ratings and types, has computed a set of item profiles V as well as a set of biases Z, *e.g.*, by minimizing (3) through gradient descent. A new user arrives in the system and submits ratings for items in some set $A \subseteq \mathcal{M}$, *but does not submit her type.* In order to bypass the user's attempt at privacy, we need to construct a classifier to infer the type of this new user.

In this section, we present a classifier that uses the item profiles and biases (*i.e.*, the latent factors obtained through matrix factorization) to accomplish this task. We refer to this classifier as a *Factor-Based Classifier* (FBC). Crucially, FBC is consistent with the Bayesian model of matrix factorization presented in the previous section. In particular, it amounts to the maximum a-posteriori estimation of the type under the bi-linear noise model (1) and the priors (2).

4.1 Type Posterior

For $A \subset \mathcal{M}$ the set of items for which the user submits ratings, we introduce the following notation. We denote by $r_A \equiv [r_j]_{j\in A} \in \mathbb{R}^{|A|}$ the vector of ratings provided by the user, by $V_A \equiv [v_j^T]_{j\in A} \in \mathbb{R}^{|A|\times d}$ the matrix of profiles for items rated, and by $z_{At} \equiv [z_{jt}]_{j\in A} \in \mathbb{R}^{|A|}$ the vector of type-t biases for items rated.

As in the previous section, we assume the new user has an unknown profile $u \in \mathbb{R}^d$ and a type $t \in \{-1, +1\}$, such that the ratings she submits follow (1), *i.e.*,

$$r_j = u^T v_j + z_{jt} + \epsilon_j, \quad j \in A, \tag{4}$$

where $\epsilon_j \sim N(0, \sigma_0^2)$. That is, conditioned on u and t, the ratings $r_A = [r_j]_{j\in A} \in \mathbb{R}^{|A|}$ given to items in $A \subset [M]$ are distributed as follows:

$$\Pr(r_A \mid u, t) = e^{-\|r_A - V_A u - z_{At}\|_2^2/2\sigma_0^2} / (\sigma_0\sqrt{2\pi})^{|A|} \tag{5}$$

where σ_0^2 is the noise variance.

Moreover, we assume as in the previous section that profile u follows a zero-mean Gaussian prior with covariance $\sigma_u^2 I$, and that the type follows a uniform prior (*i.e.*, each of the two types is equally likely), i.e.:

$$\Pr(u, t) = 0.5 e^{-\|u\|_2^2/2\sigma_u^2} / (\sigma_u\sqrt{2\pi})^d \tag{6}$$

4.2 Classification

Under the above assumptions, it is natural to classify the incoming user using maximum a posteriori estimation of the type t. In particular, FBC amounts to

$$\hat{t}(r_A) = \arg\max_{t\in\mathcal{T}} \Pr(t \mid r_A). \tag{7}$$

Under this notation, FBC can be determined as follows:

THEOREM 1. *Under noise model* (5) *and prior* (6), *the* FBC *classifier is given by*

$$\hat{t}(r_A) = \text{sgn}(\delta_A^T M_A \bar{r}_A) \tag{8}$$

where $\bar{r}_A \equiv r_A - \frac{z_{A+} + z_{A-}}{2}$, $\delta_A \equiv \frac{z_{A+} - z_{A-}}{2}$, $M_A \equiv I - V_A \Sigma_A^{-1} V_A^T$, *and* $\Sigma_A \equiv \lambda I + V_A^T V_A$, *for* $\lambda = \frac{\sigma_0^2}{\sigma_u^2}$.

The proof can be found in the extended version of our paper [3]. There are several important observations to be made regarding FBC, as defined by Theorem 1.

Set of Classifiers. We first note that FBC in fact defines a *set* of classifiers, each parametrized by set $A \subseteq \mathcal{M}$: each such classifier $\hat{t} : \mathbb{R}^{|A|} \to \{-1, +1\}$ takes as input any possible set of ratings $r_A \in \mathbb{R}^{|A|}$ as input. Note however that all classifiers are trained *jointly* from the ratings dataset: this "training" amounts to determining the item profiles V and the item biases Z through matrix factorization. With V and Z learned, when presented with ratings r_A, the classifier can compute the vectors $\bar{r}_A$, δ_A and the matrix M_A needed to determine the type. Indeed, the fact that training the classifier amounts to computing the latent factors/item profiles is consistent with the observation that FBC shares the same underlying Bayesian assumptions as matrix factorization.

5. LEARNING STRATEGIES

The second task in designing this threat is to find a user's type *quickly*. In what follows, we present two strategies for addressing this problem. The first is a *passive* strategy: the recommender presents items to the user in a predetermined order, computed off-line. The second is an *active* strategy: the recommender selects which item to present to the user next based on the answers she has given so far. Both strategies are extensively evaluated in Section 6.

[1] Note that, as is common practice, to ensure that the profiles U, V obtained by (3) are invariant to a translation (shift) of the ratings, we do not regularize the category biases (or, equivalently, we assume no prior on Z).

Algorithm 1 FBC-SELECTION

```
Input: Item profiles V, item biases Z, confidence τ
A ← ∅
r_A ← ∅
repeat
    for all j ∈ M \ A do
        Compute L_j through (9)
    j* ← argmin_{j ∈ M\A} L_j
    Query user to obtain r_{j*}
    A ← A ∪ {j*}, r_A ← r_A ∪ r_{j*}
until Pr(t̂(r_A) | r_A) > τ
```

5.1 MAXGAP: A Passive Strategy

A simple, passive method for presenting items to the user is to (a) sort items $j \in \mathcal{M}$ with respect to $|\delta_j|$, the absolute value of the gap between the type biases, and (b) present items to the user in decreasing order. We call this strategy MAXGAP: intuitively, this method identifies the most discriminative items in the dataset, and solicits responses to these items first. Clearly, MAXGAP does not take into account (or adapt to) how the user rates the items presented so far. Despite this limitation, as we will see in Section 6, this simple strategy actually performs surprisingly well in many cases, especially when there exist many highly discriminative items. When this is not the case, however, an active strategy is needed, motivating our second method.

5.2 FBC-SELECTION: An Active Strategy

Our active method, FBC-SELECTION, is summarized in Algorithm 1. Let $\hat{t}$ be the FBC classifier defined by (8). Given observed ratings $r_A \equiv [r_j]_{j \in A} \in \mathbb{R}^{|A|}$, for some $A \subset \mathcal{M}$, we define the *risk* $L(\hat{t}(r_A))$ of the classifier to be 0 if the prediction is correct, and 1 otherwise. Conditioned on r_A, the expected risk is $\mathbb{E}[L(\hat{t}(r_A)) \mid r_A] = 1 - \Pr(\hat{t}(r_A) \mid r_A)$, *i.e.*, it equals the 1 minus the *confidence* of the classifier, the posterior probability of the predicted type, conditioned on the observed ratings. Since, by (7), FBC selects the type that has the maximum posterior probability, the expected risk is at most (and the confidence at least) 0.5.

FBC-SELECTION proceeds greedily, showing the item that minimizes the classifier's expected risk at each step. More specifically, let A be the set of items whose ratings have been observed so far. To select the next item to present to the user, the algorithm computes for each item $j \in \mathcal{M} \setminus A$, the expected risk $\mathbb{E}[L(\hat{t}(r_A \cup r_j)) \mid r_A]$ if rating r_j is revealed:

$$\int_{r_j \in \mathbb{R}} (1 - \Pr(\hat{t}(r_A \cup r_j)) \mid r_A \cup r_j) \Pr(r_A \cup r_j \mid r_A) dr_j.$$

This expected risk depends on the *distribution* of the unseen rating r_j *conditioned* on the ratings observed so far.

Under noise model (5) and prior (6), the expected risk for each item j can be computed in a closed form. In particular, let M_A, $\bar{r}_A$, δ_A be as defined in Theorem 1. Then, the expected risk when revealing the rating of item j is proportional to the following quantity, derived in [3]:

$$L_j = \int_{r_j} e^{-\frac{\bar{r}_{A_j}^T M_{A_j} \bar{r}_{A_j} + 2|\delta_{A_j}^T M_{A_j} \bar{r}_{A_j}| + \delta_{A_j}^T M_{A_j} \delta_{A_j}}{2\sigma_0^2}} dr_j / \sqrt{\det \Sigma_{A_j}} \quad (9)$$

where $A_j = A \cup \{j\}$. The integration above is w.r.t. r_j, *i.e.*, the predicted rating for item j. The outcome of the above integration can be computed in closed form in terms of the error function erf (i.e., *no numerical integration is necessary*). The formula can be found in [3]. Each iteration amounts to computing the "scores" L_j for each item j not selected so far, and picking the item with the lowest score (corresponding to minimum expected risk). Once the item is presented to the user, the user rates it, adding one more rating to the set of observed ratings. The process is repeated until the confidence of the classifier (or, equivalently, the expected risk) reaches a satisfactory level.

5.3 INCFBC: An Efficient Implementation

FBC-SELECTION requires the computation of the scores L_j after each interaction with the user. Each such calculation involves computing the determinant $\det(\Sigma_{A_j})$, as well as the matrix $M_{Aj} = (I - V_{A_j} \Sigma_{A_j}^{-1} V_{A_j}^T)$, both of which appear in (9). Though having a closed form formula for (9) avoids the need for integration, computing each of these matrices directly from their definition involves a considerable computational cost. In particular, the cost of computing $\Sigma_A = \lambda I + V_A^T V_A$ is $O(d^2|A|)$. Computing Σ_A^{-1} and $\det(\Sigma_{A_j})$ have a cost $O(d^3)$ multiplications using, *e.g.*, LU-decomposition, which can be dropped to $O(d^{2.807})$ using Strassen's algorithm for multiplication [7]. Finally, the computation of M_A requires $O(|A| \times d^2 + |A|^2 \times d)$ multiplications. As a result, the overall complexity of computing L_j directly is $O(|A| \times d^2 + |A|^2 \times d + d^{2.807})$. However, the performance of these computations can be significantly reduced by constructing these matrices incrementally: M_{A_j}, $\Sigma_{A_j}^{-1}$ and $\det(\Sigma_{A_j})$ can be computed efficiently from M_A, Σ_A^{-1}, and $\det(\Sigma_A)$, exploiting the fact that $\Sigma_{A_j} = \Sigma_A + v_j v_j^T$, *i.e.*, it results from Σ_i through a *rank-one* update. We discuss this below.

Incremental computation of $\det(\Sigma_{A_j})$**.** The determinant can be computed incrementally using only $O(d^2)$ multiplications through the Matrix Determinant Lemma [11], namely:

$$\det(\Sigma_{A_j}) = (1 + v_j^T \Sigma_A v_j) \det(\Sigma_A). \quad (10)$$

Incremental computation of $\Sigma_{A_j}^{-1}$**.** The inverse of a rank-one update of a matrix can be computed through the Sherman-Morisson formula [27], which gives:

$$\Sigma_{A_j}^{-1} = \Sigma_A^{-1} - \Sigma_A^{-1} v_j v_j^T \Sigma_A^{-1} / (1 + v_j^T \Sigma_A^{-1} v_j), \quad (11)$$

and again reduces the number of multiplications to $O(d^2)$.

Incremental computation of M_{A_j}**.** Finally, using (11), we can also reduce the cost of computing M_{A_j}, as:

$$M_{A_j} = \begin{bmatrix} M_A + \frac{\phi\phi^T}{1 + v_j^T \Sigma_A^{-1} v_j} & -\xi \\ -\xi^T & 1 - v_j^T \xi \end{bmatrix} \quad (12)$$

where $\xi = V_A(\Sigma_{A_j}^{-1} v_j)$ and $\phi = V_A(\Sigma_A^{-1} v_j)$, which reduces the computation cost to $O(|A|^2 + d^2)$ multiplications.

In conclusion, using the above adaptive operations reduces the cost of computing L_j by one order of magnitude to $O(|A|^2 + d^2)$, which is optimal (as M_A is an $|A| \times |A|$ matrix, and Σ_A is $d \times d$). The rank-one adaptations yield such performance without sophisticated matrix inversion or multiplication algorithms, such as Strassen's algorithm. The we refer to resulting algorithm as INCFBC; we empirically compare the two implementations in Section 6.

Algorithm 2 POINTEST ACTIVE LEARNING

Input: Item profiles V, item biases Z, classifier C, confidence τ

$A \leftarrow \emptyset$, $r_A \leftarrow \emptyset$
repeat
  $\hat{t} \leftarrow \arg\max_{t \in \mathcal{T}} \Pr_C(t \mid r_A)$
  $\hat{u} \leftarrow (\lambda I + V_A^T V_A)^{-1} V_A^T (r_A - z_{A\hat{t}})$
  for all $j \in \mathcal{M} \setminus A$ **do**
    $\hat{r}_j \leftarrow \hat{u}^T v_j + z_{j\hat{t}}$
    $L_j \leftarrow \min_{t \in \mathcal{T}} \Pr_C(t \mid r_A \cup \hat{r}_j)$
  $j^* \leftarrow \arg\min_j L_j$
  Query user to obtain r_{j*}
  $A \leftarrow A \cup \{j^*\}$, $r_A \leftarrow r_A \cup r_{j*}$
until $1 - L_{j*} > \tau$

5.4 Selection Through Point Estimation

An alternative method for selection can be constructed by replacing the exact estimation of the expected risk with a "point estimate" (see also [28]). In fact, such a selection method can be easily combined with an arbitrary classifier that operates on user-provided ratings as input. This makes such an approach especially useful when the expected risk is hard to estimate in a closed form. We therefore outline this method below, noting however that several problems arise when the risk is computed through such a point estimation.

We describe the method for a general classifier C, also summarized in Algorithm 2. Given a set of ratings r_A over a set $A \subseteq \mathcal{M}$, the classifier C returns a probability $\Pr_C(t \mid r_A)$, for each type $t \in \mathcal{T}$. This is the probability that the user's type is t, conditioned on the observed ratings r_A. Given a set of observed ratings r_A, we can estimate the type of the user using the classifier C though maximum likelihood a-posteriori estimation, as $\hat{t}(r_A) = \arg\max_{t \in \mathcal{T}} \Pr_C(t \mid r_A)$. Using this estimate, we can further estimate the most likely profile $\hat{u} \in \mathbb{R}^d$ through ridge regression [12] over the observed ratings r_A and the corresponding profiles V_A (see Algorithm 2 for details). Using the estimated profile $\hat{u}$ and the estimated type $\hat{t}$, we can predict the rating of every item $j \in \mathcal{M} \setminus A$ as $\hat{r}_j = \hat{u}^T v_j + z_{j\hat{t}}$, and subsequently estimate the expected risk if the rating for item j is revealed as $\min_{t \in \mathcal{T}} \Pr_C(t \mid r_A \cup \hat{r}_j)$. We refer to this as a "point estimate", as it replaces the integration that the expected risk corresponds to with the value at a single point, namely, the predicted rating $\hat{r}_j$.

Using such estimates, selection can proceed as follows. Given the set of observed ratings A, we can estimate the risk of the classifier C for every item j in $\mathcal{M} \setminus A$ through the above estimation process, and pick the item with the minimum estimated risk. The rating of this item is subsequently revealed, and new estimates $\hat{t}$ and $\hat{u}$ can thusly be obtained, repeating the process until a desired confidence is reached.

Clearly, point estimation avoids computing the expected risk exactly, which can be advantageous when the corresponding expectation under a given classifier C can only be computed by numerical integration. This is not the case for FBC, as we have seen, but this can be the only tractable option for an arbitrary classifier. Unfortunately, this estimation can be quite inaccurate in practice, consequently leading to poor performance in selections; we observe such a performance degradation in our evaluations (Section 6). Put differently, a point estimate of the risk takes into account what the predicted rating of an item j is in *expectation*, and how this rating can potentially affect the risk; however, it does not account for how *variable* this prediction is. A highly variable prediction might have a very different expected risk; the exact computation of the expectation does take this into account whereas point estimation does not.

Dataset	Type	Users	Items	Ratings
Movielens	All	6K	3K	1M
	Gender (Female:Male)	1:2.5	-	1:3
	Age (Young:Adult)	1:1.3	-	1:1.6
PTV	All	992	50	29.9K
	Gender (Female:Male)	1.8:1	-	1.6:1
	Political Views (R:D)	1:1.6	-	1:2.1
Flixster	All	26K	9921	5.6M
	Gender (Female:Male)	1.7:1	-	1.5:1

Table 1: Dataset statistics.

6. EVALUATION

In this section we evaluate the performance of our methods using real datasets. We begin by describing the datasets and experiments, then perform a comparative analysis of both passive and active methods.

6.1 Experimental Setup

Datasets. We evaluate our method using three datasets: Movielens, Flixster [13], and Politics-and-TV (PTV) [26]. The Movielens dataset includes users' ratings for movies alongside with the users' gender and age. For simplicity, we categorize the age group of users as *young adults* (ages 18–35), or *adults* (ages 36–65). Flixster is a similar movie ratings dataset, and contains user gender information. PTV includes ratings by US users on 50 different TV-shows, along with each user's gender and political affiliation (Democrat or Republican). We preprocessed Movielens and Flixster to consider only users with at least 20 ratings, and items that were rated by at least 20 users. Since PTV includes only 50 TV-shows, we preprocessed the data to ensure that each user has at least 10 ratings. Table 1 summarizes the datasets used for evaluation. For each user type, the table shows the ratio between the number of users of one type versus the other type (as labeled in the table). Further details on the datasets can be found in [3].

Evaluation Method. In our setting, the recommender system infers user attributes from a set of strategically selected items. To understand the effectiveness of FBC compared to other classification methods in an adversarial setting, we perform the following evaluation. We first split the dataset into a training set (e.g., users that are willing to disclose the private attribute) and evaluation set (e.g., users that are privacy-sensitive), and train different classifiers on the training set – e.g., in the case of FBC we learn the item profiles and biases. Then, for each user in the evaluation set, we incrementally select items for the user to rate. In the passive methods, the selection of next item does not depend on the previous ratings provided by the user, whereas in the active methods it does.

After the user rates an item, we use the classifier to infer the private type. For any user, since we only have the rating information for the set of movies that she has rated, we limit the selection process to this set. Users may have rated different number of movies, for instance, roughly 50% of the users of Movielens have rated less than 100 movies out of 3000 (see [3]). Therefore, we limit the number of questions asked to 100 for Movielens and Flixster and all 50 for PTV. Unless specified, all evaluations of FBC were done using the efficient incremental implementation INCFBC.

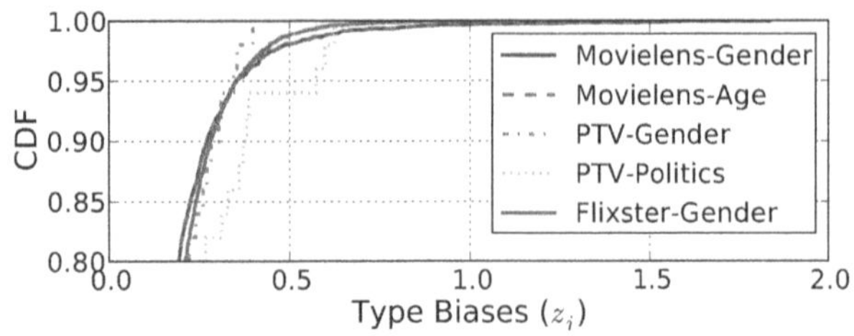

Figure 1: Cumulative distributions of the type bias ($|z_j|$) for the different datasets, zoomed to the top 20% of items.

Evaluation Metrics. We evaluate classification performance through the area under the curve (AUC) metric, and prediction performance through the root mean squared error (RMSE). If a recommender system uses our method to maliciously learn user features, it is important that such a mechanism for strategic solicitation of ratings has a minimal impact on the quality of recommendations, otherwise the user may detect its hidden agenda. We measure the quality of recommendations by holding out an evaluation set of 10 items for each user. After every 10 questions (solicited ratings) we predict the ratings on the evaluation set by applying ridge regression using the provided ratings and item profiles to learn a user profile. We predict the ratings on the evaluation set and compute the RMSE over all users.

Parameter settings. We split each dataset into training and testing and perform MF with 10-fold cross validation. We learn the item latent factors required by FBC using the training set, with type biases for age, gender and political affiliation as applicable to the three datasets. For MF, we use 20 iterations of stochastic gradient descent [17] to minimize (3), using the same regularization parameter for users and movies. Through 10-fold cross validation we determined the optimal dimension to be $d = 20$, and the optimal regularization parameter to be 0.1, for each of the biases. We also compute the optimal λ used in the classifier (8) through 10-fold cross validation to maximize the AUC, resulting in $\lambda = 100$ for gender and $\lambda = 200$ for age for the Movielens dataset, $\lambda = 10$ for gender and political views for the PTV dataset, and $\lambda = 200$ for gender for the Flixster dataset.

6.2 Passive Learning

Figure 2 shows the AUC and RMSE obtained using MaxGap, and two other passive methods – Random and Entropy. For reference, we also show the performance of our active method IncFBC. Random selection is a natural baseline as users may rate items in any arbitrary order. The second method, Entropy, presents items to the user in descending order of their rating entropy, i.e., start with items that have polarized ratings. This method was shown to be efficient in a cold-start setting in [24] as it can quickly build user profiles in a matrix factorization based recommender system.

AUC. Figure 2a shows that MaxGap performs significantly better than the other passive methods on both Movielens and PTV datasets. For the first 10 questions, which are critical when considering the need for quick inference, it is the best passive method on all datasets. Interestingly, on Movielens-Gender and PTV-Politics, MaxGap performs very similar to the adaptive, more complex IncFBC. As a result of the greedy nature of MaxGap, we expect it to perform well on datasets that have items with large biases. To better understand MaxGap's performance, Figure 1 shows the top 20% of the cumulative distributions of the type biases over the set of items in the different datasets. The plot clearly shows that the items in PTV-Gender have the lowest biases, resulting in the poorest performance of MaxGap. Conversely, in Movielens-Gender, the biases are the largest, thus MaxGap performs well, in par with the adaptive IncFBC. In PTV-Politics the biases are not overly high, but since most users rate all items, a few discriminating items are sufficient to enable MaxGap to perform well. This observation is supported by the findings of [6] that identified 5 TV-shows that immediately reveal a user's political views.

RMSE. Figure 2b plots the RMSE over increasing number of rated items, for MaxGap, Random, and Entropy, along with IncFBC. Even though IncFBC and MaxGap are designed to explore a specific attribute of the user's profile, they perform very well. Their RMSE is very close to that of Random and Entropy, with the MaxGap visibly worse only in one case, the PTV-Gender dataset. Since IncFBC and MaxBias focus on quickly learning a singe attribute of the user's profile, it is expected that they perform worse than the other methods, that aim to explore attributes more broadly. However, the figures show that IncFBC and MaxGap are almost identical to the other methods, and MaxGap only perform worse in the PTV-Gender dataset. Moreover, in all datasets, IncFBC performs close to a random selection, indicating that IncFBC does not incur significant impact on the RMSE relative to an arbitrary order in which a user may rate items. Finally, IncFBC has an RMSE similar to the entropy method, which is designed to improve the RMSE in a cold-start setting.

These results show that a malicious recommender system that uses IncFBC to infer a private attribute of its users can also use the solicited ratings to provide recommendations, making it difficult for users to detect the hidden agenda.

6.3 Active Learning

We compare our selection method to the logistic and multinomial classifiers by adapting them to an active learning setting. These classifiers were the top performing among those studied in previous work [30] for gender prediction. Following [30], we train both of these classifiers over rating vectors padded with zeros: an item not rated by a user is marked with a rating value of 0. In order to use logistic and multinomial classifiers in an active learning setting we use the point-estimate (PointEst) method as described in Section 5.4 (see Algorithm 2). For the remainder of this section we refer to PointEst with a logistic and multinomial classifiers as *Logistic* and *Multinomial*, respectively.

AUC. Figure 3a plots the AUC of classification for a given number of question using PointEst and IncFBC selection, for all datasets. PointEst selector enables us to compare FBC with the other classifiers for which we do not have a closed-form solution for selection. In all datasets, the plots show that IncFBC significantly outperforms both logistic and multinomial within a few questions, and reaches an improvement in AUC of 10–30% in the Movielens and Flixster datasets. PointEst with the other classifiers is unable to achieve a good classification accuracy.

To put this in perspective, Table 2 shows the performance of these classifiers, and that of a non-linear classifier SVM with RBF kernel, using all user ratings. Note that this table

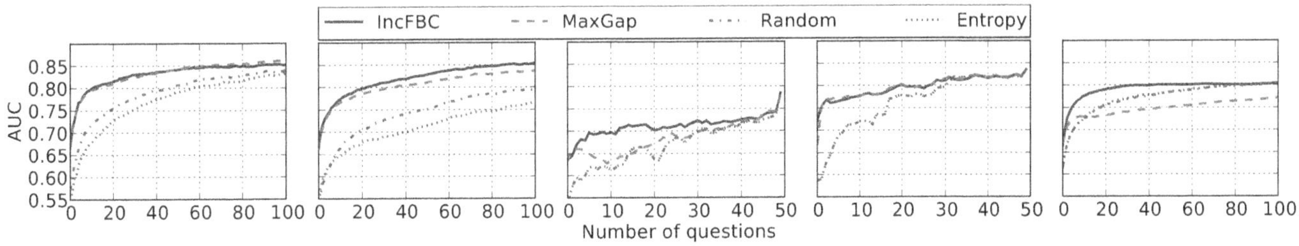

(a) AUC with passive learning

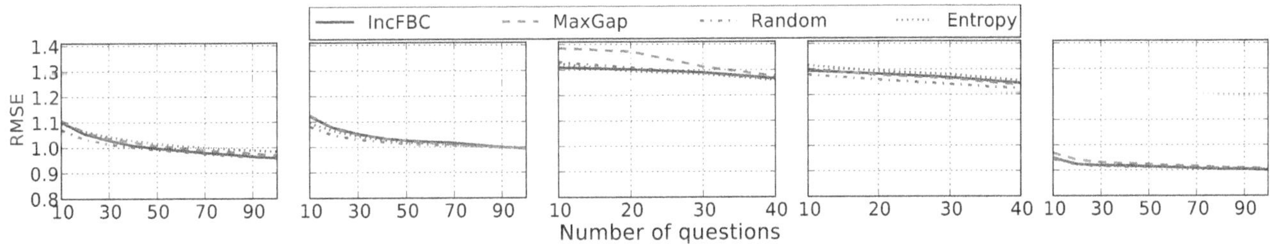

(b) RMSE with passive learning

Figure 2: Average AUC and RMSE of the FBC classifier with increasing questions for different passive selection strategies, and IncFBC for comparison. Datasets (left to right) – Movielens-Gender, Movielens-Age, PTV-Gender, PTV-Political Views, Flixster-Gender.

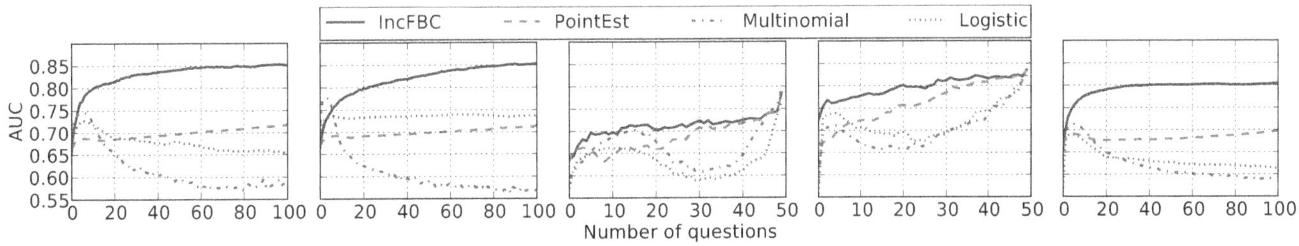

(a) AUC with active learning

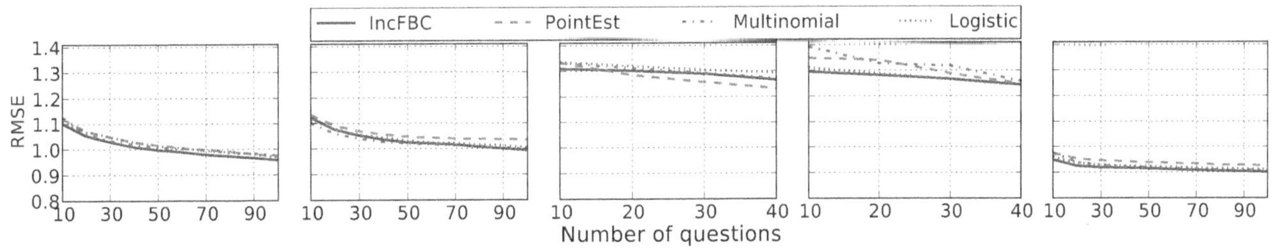

(b) RMSE with active learning

Figure 3: Average AUC and RMSE per number of questions for the three classifiers: IncFBC, multinomial (using PointEst selector) and logistic (using PointEst selector). Datasets from left to right – Movielens-Gender, Movielens-Age, PTV-Gender, PTV-Political Views, Flixster-Gender.

considers *all* ratings performed by *all* users in each dataset, whereas the plots in Figure 3a show the average AUC computed over the users that have rated the indicated number of questions. Logistic and in some cases multinomial classifiers perform significantly better than FBC, when classifying over the entire dataset. This shows that although any of these classifiers could be used for a static attack [30], FBC is better suited to adaptive attacks with fewer available ratings. For instance, using IncFBC with just 20 movies per user we obtain a classification accuracy that is reasonably close to that obtained by static inference techniques which use the complete dataset.

	Movielens		PTV		Flixster
	Gender	Age	Gender	Politics	Gender
FBC	0.827	0.825	0.683	0.748	0.650
Logistic	0.865	0.906	0.756	0.778	0.861
Multinomial	0.810	0.817	0.753	0.758	0.747
SVM (RBF)	0.838	0.893	0.613	0.737	NA

Table 2: AUC of classification with full user history.

RMSE. For completeness, Figure 3b provides the RMSE using the different active methods, showing that IncFBC has a lower RMSE on almost all datasets.

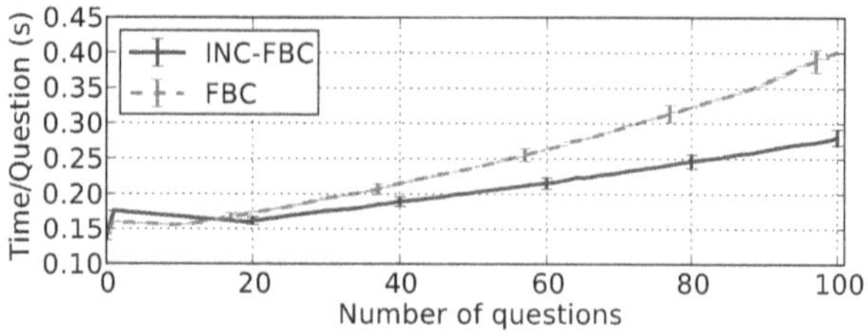

Figure 4: Running time improvement of IncFBC over FBC.

Running Time. Finally, we seek to quantify the improvement in execution time obtained by the incremental computations of IncFBC. We ran both FBC and IncFBC on a commodity server with a RAM size of 128GB and a CPU speed of 2.6GHz. Figure 4 shows the average time per movie selection for both FBC and IncFBC for increasing number of questions (movies presented to the user). The error bars depict the 95% confidence interval surrounding the mean. The plot shows that when the number of questions is small the time per question is relatively constant, and increases with the number of questions. As discussed in Section 5.3, when the number of questions is smaller than the dimension of the factor vectors (in our case $d = 20$), the complexity of the efficient algorithm is dominated by d. In the first few questions FBC is slightly faster than IncFBC as a result of the efficient implementation of inversion for small matrices. However, as the matrix becomes larger, the size of the matrix dominates the complexity and the incremental computations performed in IncFBC are significantly faster than FBC, reaching a speedup of 30%.

7. CONCLUSION AND FUTURE WORK

We presented a new attack that a recommender system could use to pursue a hidden agenda of inferring private attributes for users that do not voluntarily disclose them. Our solution, that includes a mechanism to select which question to ask a user, as well as a classifier, is efficient both in terms of the number of questions asked, and the runtime to generate each question. Moving beyond binary attributes to multi-category attributes is an interesting open question. Exploring the attack from the user's perspective, to better advise users on ways to identify and potentially mitigate such attacks is also an important future direction.

8. REFERENCES

[1] N. Awad and M. Krishnan. The personalization privacy paradox: An empirical evaluation of information transparency and the willingness to be profiled online for personalization. In *MIS Quarterly*, March 2006.

[2] S. Bhagat, I. Rozenbaum, and G. Cormode. Applying link-based classification to label blogs. In *WebKDD*, 2007.

[3] S. Bhagat, U. Weinsberg, S. Ioannidis, and N. Taft. Recommending with an agenda: Active learning of private attributes using matrix factorization, 2013. `http://arxiv.org/abs/1311.6802`.

[4] B. Bi, M. Shokouhi, M. Kosinski, and T. Graepel. Inferring the demographics of search users. WWW, 2013.

[5] J. A. Calandrino, A. Kilzer, A. Narayanan, E. W. Felten, and V. Shmatikov. "You Might Also Like:" Privacy Risks of Collaborative Filtering. IEEE SSP, 2011.

[6] F. Calmon and N. Fawaz. Privacy against statistical inference. In *Allerton*, 2012.

[7] T. H. Cormen, C. E. Leiserson, R. L. Rivest, and C. Stein. *Introduction to algorithms*. MIT press, 2001.

[8] S. Dasgupta. Analysis of a greedy active learning strategy. In *NIPS*, 2005.

[9] D. Golovin and A. Krause. Adaptive submodularity: A new approach to active learning and stochastic optimization. In *COLT*, 2010.

[10] D. Golovin, A. Krause, and D. Ray. Near-optimal Bayesian active learning with noisy observations. In *NIPS*, 2010.

[11] D. A. Harville. *Matrix Algebra From a Statistician's Perspective*. Springer-Verlag, 1997.

[12] T. Hastie, R. Tibshirani, and J. H. Friedman. *The elements of statistical learning*. Springer-Verlag, 2001.

[13] M. Jamali and M. Ester. A matrix factorization technique with trust propagation for recommendation in social networks. In *RecSys*, 2010.

[14] B. Knijnenburg and A. Kobsa. Making decisions about privacy: Information disclosure in context-aware recommender systems. *ACM Trans on Intelligent Interactive Systems*, 2013.

[15] A. Kobsa, B. Knijnenburg, and B. Livshits. Let's do it at my place instead? attitudinal and behavioral study of privacy in client-side personalization. In *CHI*, 2014.

[16] Y. Koren. Factorization meets the neighborhood: a multifaceted collaborative filtering model. In *KDD*, 2008.

[17] Y. Koren, R. Bell, and C. Volinsky. Matrix factorization techniques for recommender systems. *Computer*, 2009.

[18] M. Kosinski, D. Stillwell, and T. Graepel. Private traits and attributes are predictable from digital records of human behavior. *PNAS*, 2013.

[19] A. Levi, O. Mokryn, C. Diot, and N. Taft. Finding a needle in a haystack of reviews: Cold-start context-based recommender system. In *ACM RecSys*, 2012.

[20] A. Mislove, B. Viswanath, K. P. Gummadi, and P. Druschel. You are who you know: Inferring user profiles in Online Social Networks. In *WSDM*, 2010.

[21] S. Nakajima and M. Sugiyama. Implicit regularization in variational bayesian matrix factorization. ICML, 2010.

[22] A. Narayanan and V. Shmatikov. Robust de-anonymization of large sparse datasets. IEEE SSP, 2008.

[23] R. Nowak. The geometry of generalized binary search. *Transactions on Information Theory*, 2012.

[24] A. M. Rashid, I. Albert, D. Cosley, S. K. Lam, S. M. Mcnee, J. A. Konstan, and J. Riedl. Getting to know you: Learning new user preferences in recommender systems. In *IUI*, 2002.

[25] R. Salakhutdinov and A. Mnih. Probabilistic matrix factorization. In *NIPS*, 2008.

[26] S. Salamatian, A. Zhang, F. du Pin Calmon, S. Bhamidipati, N. Fawaz, B. Kveton, P. Oliveira, and N. Taft. How to hide the elephant-or the donkey-in the room: Practical privacy against statistical inference for large data. In *GlobalSIP*, 2013.

[27] J. Sherman and W. J. Morrison. Adjustment of an inverse matrix corresponding to changes in the elements of a given column or a given row of the original matrix. *Annals of Mathematical Statistics*, 20:621, 1949.

[28] J. Silva and L. Carin. Active learning for online bayesian matrix factorization. KDD, 2012.

[29] D. J. Sutherland, B. Póczos, and J. Schneider. Active learning and search on low-rank matrices. In *KDD*, 2013.

[30] U. Weinsberg, S. Bhagat, S. Ioannidis, and N. Taft. Blurme: Inferring and obfuscating user gender based on ratings. In *ACM RecSys*, 2012.

Ensemble Contextual Bandits for Personalized Recommendation

Liang Tang Yexi Jiang Lei Li Tao Li
School of Computing and Information Sciences
Florida International University
11200 S.W. 8th Street, Miami, FL 33199
{ltang002,yjian004,lli003,taoli}@cs.fiu.edu

ABSTRACT

The cold-start problem has attracted extensive attention among various online services that provide personalized recommendation. Many online vendors employ contextual bandit strategies to tackle the so-called *exploration/exploitation* dilemma rooted from the cold-start problem. However, due to high-dimensional user/item features and the underlying characteristics of bandit policies, it is often difficult for service providers to obtain and deploy an appropriate algorithm to achieve acceptable and robust economic profit.

In this paper, we explore ensemble strategies of contextual bandit algorithms to obtain robust predicted click-through rate (CTR) of web objects. The ensemble is acquired by aggregating different pulling policies of bandit algorithms, rather than forcing the agreement of prediction results or learning a unified predictive model. To this end, we employ a meta-bandit paradigm that places a hyper bandit over the base bandits, to explicitly explore/exploit the relative importance of base bandits based on user feedbacks. Extensive empirical experiments on two real-world data sets (news recommendation and online advertising) demonstrate the effectiveness of our proposed approach in terms of CTR.

Categories and Subject Descriptors:
H.3.3 [Information Search and Retrieval]: Information Filtering; H.3.5 [Information Systems]: On-line Information Services; I.2.6 [Computing Methodologies]: Learning

Keywords: Personalized Recommendation; Ensemble Recommendation; Contextual Bandit; CTR Prediction; Meta Learning

1. INTRODUCTION

Personalized recommendation services aim to identify popular items and tailor the content according to users' preferences. In practice, a large number of users or items might be completely new to the system, which is referred to as the *cold-start* problem [21]. This issue is often recognized as an exploration/exploitation problem, in which we have to find a trade-off between two competing goals: maximizing users' satisfaction in a long run, while exploring uncertainties of user interests [1]. For example, a news recommender should provide breaking news to users while maintaining user preferences based on aging news stories.

The aforementioned issue is often modeled as a contextual bandit problem [29]. A contextual bandit problem is a series of trials with a fixed number of arms. In each trial, the algorithm selects an arm to pull based on the given context. By pulling an arm, it can obtain a reward, drawn from some unknown distribution determined by the pulled arm and the context. The objective of bandit algorithms is to maximize the total obtained reward. In the cold-start situation, a recommender system does not have enough training data to build the predictive model. In such a case, people often use a bandit algorithm to solve the recommendation problem, where each trial can be treated as a user visit, and each arm is an item (e.g., a news article or advertisement). Pulling an arm is recommending that item, where the context is a set of user features. The reward is the user response (e.g., a click), which is also determined by the recommended item and user features. The objective of recommender systems is to maximize the total user response, which is equivalent to maximizing the total reward in bandit algorithms [13].

Recently, a series of algorithms have been reported to tackle the multi-armed bandit problem, including unguided exploration (e.g., ϵ-greedy [28], and epoch-greedy [12]), guided exploration (e.g., LinUCB [13], EXP4 [2], and Thompson sampling [6]). These existing algorithms can achieve promising performance under specific settings. The performances of different policies vary significantly in many recommendation applications. A common practice of picking the appropriate policy is to first evaluate these policies and then select the best one to deploy. However, in the cold-start situation, it is often difficult to conduct an unbiased offline evaluation due to the deficiency of the historical data. For online evaluation, e.g., A/B test, the user visit traffic has to be split to multiple buckets for different policies, and therefore the number of testing policies running in parallel is restricted in order to obtain acceptable daily income.

In our work, we explore the possibility of utilizing ensemble strategies to obtain a robust policy that can achieve acceptable CTR in various recommender systems. As the predictive result of each contextual bandit algorithm is the pulled arm (item), it is not appropriate to adopt the majority voting or consensus prediction as the ensemble. We hence resort to meta learning to build a hyper policy that adaptively allocates the pulling chances to different base policies

RecSys'14, October 6–10, 2014, Foster City, Silicon Valley, CA, USA.
Copyright 2014 ACM 978-1-4503-2668-1/14/10 ...$15.00.
http://dx.doi.org/10.1145/2645710.2645732.

based on the estimation of their performance. The proposed ensemble bandit algorithms may not produce the optimal CTR of base policies, but it can always approach to the best one, which gives a robust mechanism for online personalized recommendation in the cold-start situations. In summary, the contribution of our work is three-fold:

- We explore the possibility of stabilizing the CTR estimation of recommender systems by integrating the advantages of different bandit policies.
- We propose two ensemble strategies to address the cold-start problem in personalized recommender systems, which employ a meta-bandit learning paradigm to achieve the robustness of the CTR.
- We conduct extensive experiments on real-world data sets to demonstrate the efficacy of the proposed method compared with other baseline algorithms. The results show that our method is robust in terms of CTR.

The rest of this paper is organized as follows. In Section 2, we describe a brief summary of prior work relevant to contextual bandit problems, ensemble recommendation and meta learning. We then formulate the problem in Section 3, and present the detailed algorithmic description in Section 4. Extensive empirical evaluation results are reported in Section 5. Finally, Section 6 concludes the paper.

2. RELATED WORK

In our work, we employ ensemble strategies combined with a meta learning paradigm to stabilize the output of contextual bandit algorithms. In the following, we highlight the previous research that are most relevant to our work.

Contextual Bandits: When predicting the CTR of web data, the *cold-start* problem is often modeled as a contextual bandit problem with exploration/exploitation trade-off, where user features are regarded as contextual information. Typical solutions of this problem involve unguided exploration (e.g., ϵ-greedy [28], epoch-greedy [12]), guided exploration (e.g., LinUCB [13], EXP4 [2]) and probability matching (e.g., Thompson sampling [6, 22]). Most existing methods require either a parameter to control the importance of exploration or prior information of Bayesian learning models; however in practice, it is difficult to determine the optimal value for the input due to the insufficiency of user feedbacks. Hence, the prediction performance of these algorithms is not stable along both exploration and exploitation phases, unless the selection policy/model converges.

Ensemble Recommendation: Ensemble based algorithms have been well explored to improve the performance of prediction [20, 27], and are often preferred in recommendation competitions, such as the Netflix Prize contest [11, 24] and KDD Cups [17, 30]. Typically, an ensemble method combines the prediction of different algorithms to obtain a final prediction [18], which is often referred to as "blending" [10]. The most basic blending strategy is to acquire the final prediction based on the mean over all the prediction results or the majority vote. Learning based approaches have also been proposed to unify different recommendation algorithms [31]. In our work, to obtain a robust policy, we resort to ensemble strategies that assimilate the advantages of different contextual bandit algorithms.

Meta Learning: In machine learning community, the goal of meta learning is to accumulate experience on the performance of multiple learning algorithms [8]. Meta learning has been widely used in algorithm selection [16, 19]. Due to the uncertainty of learning algorithms, i.e., we do not know in advance the predictive performance, a lot of work has modeled algorithm selection as a multi-armed bandit problem [7, 25] and tries to balance the trade-off between exploring algorithm capabilities and exploiting the predictive power of algorithms. In addition, some recent research efforts [15, 23] focus on meta learning of exploration/exploitation strategies, where the base learners are bandit algorithms.

3. PROBLEM FORMULATION

In this section, we formulate the problem studied in this paper. Let $\mathcal{A}$ denote the set of items (or bandit arms), $\mathcal{A} = \{a_1, ..., a_k\}$, and $\Pi = \{\pi_1,...,\pi_m\}$ be a given set of recommenders (or policies), where each recommender is a contextual bandit algorithm with a specific parameter setting. $\pi_i(\mathbf{x}) = a$ indicates that the policy π_i pulls a with respect to $\mathbf{x}$, where $a \in \mathcal{A}$ and $\mathbf{x}$ is a context feature vector. Let $\mathcal{D}$ be the space of $\mathbf{x}$ and $p(\mathbf{x})$ denote the probability density of $\mathbf{x}$. After the pulling, π_i receives a reward r, where r is a value drawn from the conditional distribution $p(\cdot|\mathbf{x}, a)$. In our work, we only consider $r \in \{0, 1\}$, i.e., a non-click/click on a specific item. Thus, $p(\cdot|\mathbf{x}, a)$ is a Bernoulli distribution.

Each policy $\pi_i \in \Pi$ aims to maximize the expected received reward denoted by $\mathrm{E}[r_{\pi_i}]$, where

$$\begin{aligned} \mathrm{E}[r_{\pi_i}] &= \int_{\mathcal{D}} \sum_{a\in\mathcal{A}} \sum_{r\in\{0,1\}} r \cdot p(r|\mathbf{x}, a) \cdot p(a = \pi_i(\mathbf{x})|\mathbf{x}) \cdot p(\mathbf{x})\, \mathrm{d}\mathbf{x} \\ &= \int_{\mathcal{D}} \sum_{\pi_i(\mathbf{x})\in\mathcal{A}} \sum_{r\in\{0,1\}} r \cdot p(r, \pi_i(\mathbf{x}), \mathbf{x})\, \mathrm{d}\mathbf{x}. \end{aligned}$$

The expected reward $\mathrm{E}[r_{\pi_i}]$ is known as the CTR of the policy π_i, which is often used as the performance metric.

Existing studies propose different contextual bandit algorithms and show their empirical performances on various real-world data sets [5, 6, 13]. It is known that a bandit algorithm with different parameter settings can have different performance [22]. The choice of parameters depends on the distribution of the real data, which is often unknown in the *cold-start* situation. Therefore, given a set of policies Π, individual polices in Π can have very different performance for a particular recommender system. Let π^* denote the best policy in terms of the performance, i.e.,

$$\pi^* = \arg\max_{\pi_i\in\Pi} \mathrm{E}[r_{\pi_i}].$$

For different recommendation problems, π^* is different and not known in advance. The goal of this paper is to develop an ensemble contextual bandit policy such that its performance can be close to the performance of π^*.

4. ALGORITHM

This section presents two ensemble bandit algorithms, `HyperTS` and `HyperTSFB`, for solving the contextual recommendation problem in the cold-start situation. The idea of these two algorithms is to distribute the trials to the base bandit policies. Given a set of policies $\Pi = \{\pi_1, ..., \pi_m\}$ and a context $\mathbf{x}$, both algorithms make two decisions to deicide which arm to pull:

- Decision 1. Select a policy from Π, denoted by π_i;
- Decision 2. Select the arm $a = \pi_i(\mathbf{x})$ to pull.

For Decision 1, if we know which base policy is the best one, i.e., π^*, we can always select it. However, the performance of each policy is unknown at the beginning. To estimate their expected rewards, we need to select them and observe the received rewards. Same as Decision 2, the exploration-exploitation dilemma also exists in Decision 1. In this paper, we focus on Decision 1.

To address the policy selection problem in Decision 1, both of the proposed algorithms leverage non-contextual Thompson sampling [6, 26]. Generally, in each trial, the algorithms randomly select a policy $\pi_i \in \Pi$, where the probability of selecting π_i is equal to the probability of π_i being π^*, i.e., $p(\hat{\mathrm{E}}[r_{\pi_i}] = \max_{\pi_j \in \Pi} \hat{\mathrm{E}}[r_{\pi_j}])$, where $\hat{\mathrm{E}}[r_{\pi_i}]$ is the estimated expected reward of the policy π_i. It is difficult to directly compute this probability [22]. Thus, in each trial, we randomly draw a value, denoted by $\tilde{r}_{\pi_i}$, from the distribution of $\hat{\mathrm{E}}[r_{\pi_i}]$ for each $\pi_i \in \Pi$, and then select the policy that has the maximum value of $\tilde{r}_{\pi_i}$. In the following, we present two approaches to estimate $\mathrm{E}[r_{\pi_i}]$.

4.1 HyperTS Algorithm

HyperTS estimates the expected reward $\mathrm{E}[r_{\pi_i}]$ of each policy $\pi_i \in \Pi$ using Monte Carlo method. Concretely, let $\mathbf{x}_1,...,\mathbf{x}_n$ be the contexts of n trials in which π_i is selected. $\mathbf{x}_1,...,\mathbf{x}_n$ are samples drawn from $p(\mathbf{x})$. For an input context $\mathbf{x}_j$, π_i pulls the arm a_j and receives the reward r_j, where a_j is seen as a sample from $p(a = \pi_i(\mathbf{x}_j)|\mathbf{x}_j)$, r_j is seen as a sample drawn from $p(r|\mathbf{x}_j, a_j)$. Thus, $(\mathbf{x}_j, a_j, r_j)$ is a sample drawn from the joint distribution $p(\mathbf{x}, a, r)$, $j = 1, ..., n$. The Monte Carlo estimate is $\hat{\mathrm{E}}[r_{\pi_i}] = \frac{1}{n}\sum_{j=1}^{n} r_j$. The rewards $r_1, ..., r_n \in \{0, 1\}$ are the sample drawn from the Bernoulli distribution $p(r)$, which is a marginal distribution of $p(\mathbf{x}, a, r)$. Therefore, $\hat{\mathrm{E}}[r_{\pi_i}]$ follows the Beta distribution:

$$\hat{\mathrm{E}}[r_{\pi_i}] \sim \mathrm{Beta}(1 + \alpha_{\pi_i}, 1 + \beta_{\pi_i}),$$

where $\alpha_{\pi_i} = \sum_{j=1}^{n} r_j$ and $\beta_{\pi_i} = n - \alpha_{\pi_i}$. For the prior, Beta(1, 1) is used. Algorithm 1 shows the pseudo-code of `HyperTS`. In each trial, r_i is a sample of $\hat{\mathrm{E}}[r_{\pi_i}]$, drawn from a Beta distribution. The selected policy is the one having the maximum r_i.

Algorithm 1 `HyperTS`(Π)

Input: Π : the set of base bandit policies.
for $i = 1, ..., m$ **do**
  $\alpha_{\pi_i} \leftarrow 0$, $\beta_{\pi_i} \leftarrow 0$
end for
for $t = 1, 2, ...$ **do**
  for $i = 1, ..., m$ **do**
    Draw r_i from $\mathrm{Beta}(1 + \alpha_{\pi_i}, 1 + \beta_{\pi_i})$.
  end for
  Pull the arm $a = \pi_j(\mathbf{x}_t)$, where $j = \arg\max_{i=1,...,m} r_i$.
  Receive the reward $r_{\mathbf{x}_t,a}$ and feed π_j with $r_{\mathbf{x}_t,a}$.
  if $r_{\mathbf{x}_t,a} = 1$ **then**
    $\alpha_{\pi_j} \leftarrow \alpha_{\pi_j} + 1$
  else
    $\beta_{\pi_j} \leftarrow \beta_{\pi_j} + 1$
  end if
end for

4.2 HyperTSFB Algorithm

In `HyperTS`, the expected reward of each base policy is estimated only from the feedback when that policy is selected. The feedback of the decision made by other policies is not utilized. If the number of policies in Π is large, the total number of trials needed for exploring the performance of base policies will be large and the total reward will be smaller. To improve the estimation efficiency, we propose `HyperTSFB` (`HyperTS` with shared feedback), an algorithm that fully utilizes every received feedback for expected reward estimation.

Given the context $\mathbf{x}$, `HyperTSFB` requires each base policy $\pi_i \in \Pi$ provide the probability of π_i pulling the arm a, i.e., $p(a = \pi_i(\mathbf{x})|\mathbf{x})$. Then, even though the policy π_i is not selected in the trial, `HyperTSFB` can still utilizes the feedback for $\mathbf{x}$ to estimate the expected reward of π_i. For some policy, $p(a = \pi_i(\mathbf{x})|\mathbf{x})$ can be computed directly. For instance, if π_i denotes `random` policy, then $p(a = \pi_i(\mathbf{x})|\mathbf{x}) = 1/k$, $k = |\mathcal{A}|$; if π_i is ϵ-`greedy`, then

$$p(a = \pi_i(\mathbf{x})|\mathbf{x}) = \begin{cases} \epsilon/k + (1-\epsilon) & \text{if } a = a^* \\ \epsilon/k & \text{if } a \neq a^*, \end{cases}$$

where a^* is the arm that has the maximum predicted reward by the input $\mathbf{x}$. For some policy, $p(a = \pi_i(\mathbf{x})|\mathbf{x})$ can be difficult to compute, e.g. contextual Thompson sampling. We can invoke $\pi_i(\mathbf{x})$ multiple times to estimate this probability according to the frequency of a being output.

Once we compute $p(a = \pi_i(\mathbf{x})|\mathbf{x})$, $\mathrm{E}[r_{\pi_i}]$ can be rewritten as Eq.(1) and importance sampling [32] can be leveraged for estimation.

$$\begin{aligned}
\mathrm{E}[r_{\pi_i}] &= \sum_{a\in\mathcal{A}} \int_{\mathcal{D}} \sum_{r\in\{0,1\}} r \cdot p(r|\mathbf{x}, a) p(a = \pi_i(\mathbf{x})|\mathbf{x}) p(\mathbf{x})\, d\mathbf{x} \\
&= \sum_{a\in\mathcal{A}} \int_{\mathcal{D}} \sum_{r\in\{0,1\}} r \frac{p(a = \pi_i(\mathbf{x})|\mathbf{x})}{p(a|\mathbf{x})} p(r|\mathbf{x}, a) p(a|\mathbf{x}) p(\mathbf{x})\, d\mathbf{x} \\
&= \sum_{a\in\mathcal{A}} \int_{\mathcal{D}} \sum_{r\in\{0,1\}} (r \cdot w_{a,\mathbf{x}}^{\pi_i}) \cdot p(r|\mathbf{x}, a) p(a|\mathbf{x}) p(\mathbf{x})\, d\mathbf{x} \\
&= \sum_{a\in\mathcal{A}} p(a) \int_{\mathcal{D}} \sum_{r\in\{0,1\}} (r \cdot w_{a,\mathbf{x}}^{\pi_i}) \cdot p(r, \mathbf{x}|a)\, d\mathbf{x} \\
&= \sum_{a\in\mathcal{A}} p(a)\, \mathrm{E}_{r,\mathbf{x}}[r \cdot w_{a,\mathbf{x}}^{\pi_i} | a]. \qquad (1)
\end{aligned}$$

In Eq.(1), $w_{a,\mathbf{x}}^{\pi_i} = \frac{p(a=\pi_i(\mathbf{x})|\mathbf{x})}{p(a|\mathbf{x})}$ is the importance weight, and $\mathrm{E}_{r,\mathbf{x}}[r \cdot w_{a,\mathbf{x}}^{\pi_i} | a]$ is the expected reward of π_i by pulling a. Eq.(1) states that the expected reward estimation can be separated into multiple estimations for different arms. In the importance weight, $p(a|\mathbf{x})$ is the probability of the arm a being pulled given the context $\mathbf{x}$,

$$p(a|\mathbf{x}) = \sum_{\pi_i \in \Pi} p(a = \pi_i(\mathbf{x})|\mathbf{x}) p(\pi_i = \arg\max_{\pi_j \in \Pi} \hat{\mathrm{E}}[r_{\pi_j}]).$$

In the implementation, we use a sampling-based method to obtain the value of $p(a|\mathbf{x})$. For each given context $\mathbf{x}$, we invoke `HyperTSFB` multiple times and then estimate $p(a|x)$ according to the frequency of a being selected. $p(a)$ is the marginal probability of a being selected, which is simply approximated by the ratio of a being pulled in all previous trials done by `HyperTSFB`.

In Eq.(1), the expected reward of π_i by pulling a is

$$\begin{aligned}
\mathrm{E}_{r,\mathbf{x}}[r \cdot w_{a,\mathbf{x}}^{\pi_i}|a] &= \int_{-\infty}^{+\infty} y \cdot p(r \cdot w_{a,\mathbf{x}}^{\pi_i} = y|a)\,\mathrm{d}y \\
&= \int_{-\infty}^{+\infty} y \cdot p(r = 1, w_{a,\mathbf{x}}^{\pi_i} = y|a)\,\mathrm{d}y \\
&= \int_{-\infty}^{+\infty} y \cdot p(w_{a,\mathbf{x}}^{\pi_i} = y|r = 1, a)p(r = 1|a)\,\mathrm{d}y \\
&= p(r = 1|a) \cdot \int_{-\infty}^{+\infty} y \cdot p(w_{a,\mathbf{x}}^{\pi_i} = y|r = 1, a)\,\mathrm{d}y \\
&= \mathrm{E}_{r,\mathbf{x}}[r|a] \cdot \mathrm{E}_{\mathbf{x}}[w_{a,\mathbf{x}}^{\pi_i}|r = 1, a]. \qquad (2)
\end{aligned}$$

In Eq.(2), $\mathrm{E}_{r,\mathbf{x}}[r|a]$ is the expected reward of pulling arm a, which is also the overall CTR of a and determined by the popularity of a. The importance weight $w_{a,\mathbf{x}}^{\pi_i}$ is proportional to the probability of π_i pulling a given $\mathbf{x}$. $\mathrm{E}_{\mathbf{x}}[w_{a,\mathbf{x}}^{\pi_i}|r = 1, a]$ reflects how likely will π_i pulls a if the reward of a is 1. Intuitively, Eq.(2) states that the expected reward of π_i by pulling a is determined by the popularity of a and the likelihood of π_i pulling a if the reward of a is 1. Since $r \in \{0, 1\}$, we use a Beta distribution to model $\hat{\mathrm{E}}_{r,\mathbf{x}}[r|a]$, i.e.

$$\hat{\mathrm{E}}_{r,\mathbf{x}}[r|a] \sim \mathrm{Beta}(1 + \alpha_a, 1 + \beta_a),$$

where α_a is the number of trials that the received reward is 1 by pulling a, β_a is the number of trials that the received reward is 0 by pulling a. For the prior, uniform distribution $\mathrm{Beta}(1, 1)$ is used. $\mathrm{E}_{\mathbf{x}}[w_{a,\mathbf{x}}^{\pi_i}|r = 1, a]$ is estimated by the mean of importance weights in previous trials in which a is pulled and the reward is 1. Assuming for one policy and one arm those importance weights will converge in one distribution, based on Central Limit Theory, the sample mean follows a normal distribution when the sample size is sufficient large, i.e.

$$\hat{\mathrm{E}}_{\mathbf{x}}[w_{a,\mathbf{x}}^{\pi_i}|r = 1, a] \sim \mathcal{N}(\mu_{a,i}, \sigma_{a,i}^2/n_{a,i}),$$

where $\mu_{a,i}$ and $\sigma_{a,i}^2$ are the mean and variance of the distribution of the importance weights, $n_{a,i}$ is the sample size to calculate the the mean and variance. If the sample size $n_{a,i}$ is not sufficient large (less than 30 [9]), we draw $\hat{\mathrm{E}}_{\mathbf{x}}[w_{a,\mathbf{x}}^{\pi_i}|r = 1, a]$ from uniform distribution $\mathcal{U}(0, 1)$.

Algorithm 2 shows the pseudo-code of `HyperTSFB`. For trial $t = 1, 2, ...$, given the context $\mathbf{x}_t$, the sampled expected reward of π_i is r_{π_i}, which is calculated based on two other sampled values from each arm (Line 8 to 21). As for the received reward, $r_{\mathbf{x}_t,a}$, the estimated parameters of every base policy and arm a are updated (Line 24 to 34).

Algorithm 2 `HyperTSFB`(Π)

Input: Π : the set of base bandit policies.
1: **for** $j = 1, ..., k$ **do**
2: $\quad\alpha_{a_j} \leftarrow 0$, $\beta_{a_j} \leftarrow 0$, $n_{a_j} \leftarrow 0$
3: $\quad$**for** $i = 1, ..., m$ **do**
4: $\quad\quad n_{a_j,i} \leftarrow 0$
5: $\quad$**end for**
6: **end for**
7: **for** $t = 1, 2, ...$ **do**
8: $\quad$**for** $j = 1, ..., k$ **do**
9: $\quad\quad$Draw r_{a_j} from $\mathrm{Beta}(1 + \alpha_{a_j}, 1 + \beta_{a_j})$
10: $\quad$**end for**
11: $\quad$**for** $i = 1, ..., m$ **do**
12: $\quad\quad r_{\pi_i} \leftarrow 0$
13: $\quad\quad$**for** $j = 1, ..., k$ **do**
14: $\quad\quad\quad$**if** $n_{a_j,i} < 30$ **then**
15: $\quad\quad\quad\quad$Draw $w_{a_j}^{\pi_i}$ from $\mathcal{U}(0, 1)$
16: $\quad\quad\quad$**else**
17: $\quad\quad\quad\quad$Draw $w_{a_j}^{\pi_i}$ from $\mathcal{N}(\mu_{a_j,i}, \sigma_{a_j,i}^2/n_{a_j,i})$
18: $\quad\quad\quad$**end if**
19: $\quad\quad\quad r_{\pi_i} \leftarrow r_{\pi_i} + n_{a_j}/t \cdot r_{a_j} \cdot w_{a_j}^{\pi_i}$
20: $\quad\quad$**end for**
21: $\quad$**end for**
22: $\quad$Pull the arm $a = \pi_{s^*}(\mathbf{x}_t)$, where $s^* = \arg\max_{i=1,...,m} r_{\pi_i}$.
23: $\quad$Receive the reward $r_{\mathbf{x}_t,a}$, feed each $\pi_i \in \Pi$ with $r_{\mathbf{x}_t,a}$
24: $\quad n_{a_j} \leftarrow n_{a_j} + 1$
25: $\quad$**if** $r_{\mathbf{x}_t,a} = 1$ **then**
26: $\quad\quad$**for** $i = 1, ..., m$ **do**
27: $\quad\quad\quad w_t \leftarrow \frac{p(a=\pi_i(\mathbf{x}_t)|\mathbf{x}_t)}{p(a|\mathbf{x}_t)}$
28: $\quad\quad\quad$Update $\mu_{a,i}$ and $\sigma_{a,i}^2$ by w_t
29: $\quad\quad\quad n_{a,i} \leftarrow n_{a,i} + 1$
30: $\quad\quad$**end for**
31: $\quad\quad \alpha_a \leftarrow \alpha_a + 1$
32: $\quad$**else**
33: $\quad\quad \beta_a \leftarrow \beta_a + 1$
34: $\quad$**end if**
35: **end for**

5. EVALUATION

5.1 Data Collections

We verify our approaches on two real-world data sets, including news recommendation data (*Yahoo! Today News*) and online advertising data (*KDD Cup* 2012, Track 2).

Yahoo! Today News data set is collected by Yahoo! Today module[1]. News articles were randomly displayed on the *Yahoo! Front Page* from October 2nd, 2011 to October 16th, 2011. The data set contains 28,041,015 user visit events to the *Yahoo! Today Module*. Each visit event is associated with the user's information, e.g., age, gender, behavior targeting features, etc., represented by a binary feature vector of dimension 136. This data set has been used for evaluating contextual bandit algorithms in other literatures [6, 13, 14]. 10 million user visit events are used in this evaluation.

KDD Cup Online Advertising data set is published by *KDD Cup 2012*[2]. Each record of this data set is an ad impression, containing user profile, queries, ad information and click counts. In our work, the context is represented as a binary feature vector, each entry of which denotes whether a query token is contained in the search query. User profiles, e.g., gender and age, are also appended to the context vector using the binary format. The dimension of the context features for this data set is 1,070,866. One issue of this data set is that the click information is extremely sparse due to the large pool of the ads. To alleviate this problem, we only select the top 50 ads with the most impressions. The generated data set contains 9 million user visit events.

5.2 Evaluation Methods

The experiments on *Yahoo! Today News* data set is evaluated by the *Replayer* method [14], which provides an unbiased offline evaluation by utilizing the historical log. It has been shown that the CTR estimated by this *Replayer* approaches the real CTR of the deployed online system if

[1]http://webscope.sandbox.yahoo.com/catalog.php.

[2]http://www.kddcup2012.org/c/kddcup2012-track2.

the items in historical user visits are randomly and uniformly recommended [14]. However, for *KDD Cup* data set, the search ads in historical logs are not uniformly recommended. We hence evaluate this data set using a simulation method [6]. In the simulation method, we first train a logistic regression model for each ad using the entire data offline. Then, for each impression with context $\mathbf{x}$, the click of an ad is generated with a probability $(1+\exp(-\mathbf{w}^T\mathbf{x}))^{-1}$. Although the evaluated CTR is not the real CTR, it provides a methodology for comparing different policies in such high dimensional data.

5.3 Experimental Setup

For evaluation purpose, we use the averaged reward as the metric, which is the total reward divided by the total number of trials, i.e., $\frac{1}{n}\sum_{t=1}^{n} r_t$, where n is the number of trials. The higher the CTR, the better the performance. In the experiments, to avoid the leakage of business-sensitive information, we report the relative CTR, which is the overall CTR of an algorithm divided by the overall CTR of random selection. The base policies used for the ensemble contain multiple types of algorithms, including:

- `Random`: it randomly selects an arm to pull.
- ϵ`-greedy` (ϵ): it randomly selects an arm with probability ϵ and selects the arm of the largest predicted reward with probability $1-\epsilon$.
- `LinUCB` (α) [13]: In each trial, it pulls the arm of the largest score, which is a linear combination of the mean and standard deviation of the predicted reward. Given a context $\mathbf{x}$, the score is $\hat{\boldsymbol{\mu}}^T\mathbf{x} + \alpha\sqrt{\mathbf{x}^T\hat{\boldsymbol{\Sigma}}^{-1}\mathbf{x}}$, where $\hat{\boldsymbol{\mu}}$ and $\hat{\boldsymbol{\Sigma}}$ are the estimated mean and covariance of the posterior distribution, and α is a predefined parameter for controlling the balance of exploration and exploitation.
- `Softmax` (τ) [3]: it randomly selects an arm a_i with probability $\frac{\exp(r_{a_i}/\tau)}{\sum_{a_j\in\mathcal{A}}\exp(r_{a_j}/\tau)}$, where r_{a_i} is the predicted reward for the arm a_i.
- `Epoch-greedy` [12]: it defines an epoch with length L, in which a one-step exploration is first performed, and the rest trials in the epoch are used for exploitation.
- `TS` (q_0) [6]: thompson sampling with logistic regression, which randomly draws the coefficients from the posterior distribution, and selects the arm of the largest predicted reward. The priori distribution is $\mathcal{N}(\mathbf{0}, q_0^{-1}\mathbf{I})$.
- `TSNR` (q_0): it is similar to `TS`(q_0), but in the stochastic gradient ascent, there is no regularization by the prior. The priori distribution $\mathcal{N}(\mathbf{0}, q_0^{-1}\mathbf{I})$ is only used in the calculation of the posterior distribution for the parameter sampling, but not in the learning algorithm.

In the experiments, the reward in a single recommendation activity is the user click, which is a binary value. Therefore, *logistic regression* is applied as the learning model in all policies (except for `Random`). Since the contextual bandit algorithms are online algorithms, *stochastic gradient ascent* is used as the learning algorithm [4]. Notice that the algorithms digest the data in an online manner, hence all the user visits in the data sets are used for the testing purpose.

In our problem setting, we utilize ensemble strategies to obtain a unified policy. To evaluate the effectiveness of the ensemble, we empirically compare the following ensemble algorithms:

- `HyperRandom`: it randomly selects a policy from the policy pool, and then performs the recommendation based on the selected policy.
- `HyperTS`: The one proposed in Section 4.1.
- `HyperTSFB`: The one proposed in Section 4.2.

5.4 Result Analysis

For each policy, we test its performance on the entire data to obtain the overall CTR. To emphasize the robustness of our proposed ensemble strategy, we also split the data into multiple time buckets, and evaluate how the policies perform on each individual time bucket.

5.4.1 On Overall CTR

For base policies, most of them are randomized except for `LinUCB`. For each trial, we randomly shuffle the pool of items to be recommended. Thus, the performance of `LinUCB` may vary in different runs. We run each policy 10 times, and calculate the mean, standard deviation, minimum and maximum of the overall CTR. Table 1 reports the results. The mean values of the top 5 base policies are highlighted in **bold**, and the comparable mean values of ensemble strategies are emphasized by **bold***.

As depicted in the table, the performance of the base policies varies significantly with different parameter values. Except for `Random` (pure exploration) and ϵ-greedy(0.0) (pure exploitation), all the base policies take into account both exploration and exploitation. If the parameter that controls the relative importance of exploration and exploitation is perfectly set, then the performance approaches to the optimal; otherwise, the performance is relatively poor. However in practice, it is often difficult to determine the optimal value for the input parameter of each policy, primarily due to the online learning process of the algorithms as well as the unknown data distribution for learning models.

Our proposed ensemble strategies can achieve comparable performance with the top ranked policies in terms of the overall CTR, by virtue of the bandit property of the hyper model. It is worthy to note that the two ensemble strategies have no parameter to choose. Intuitively, with more trials, the base policies with the bandit property can produce better results as there are more data used for learning. By employing the ensemble strategies that select base policies based on their corresponding overall CTR, we can certainly obtain a unified policy with acceptable CTR. From Table 1, we observe that: (1) The `HyperRandom` policy performs pure exploration on the base policies. This may work well at the beginning of the learning process; however, after a long run, it cannot obtain acceptable performance due to the randomness of the policy selection. (2) The bandit-based ensemble strategies, i.e., `HyperTS` and `HyperTSFB`, are able to achieve comparable performance with the top ranked base policies.

The advantages of the meta-bandit policies involve two aspects: (1) by exploring/exploiting multiple base policies that have different parameter settings, the meta-bandit policies are able to absorb the merits of good policies, and hence produce robust results in terms of the overall CTR; and (2) there is no parameter setting required for meta-bandit policies. `HyperTS` does not have the mechanism of sharing feedbacks among different policies, then for each base policy, the digested click traffic may not be sufficient to produce a high-quality learning model and an accurate CTR estimate. Without enough click traffic, the base policies

Table 1: Relative CTR on the experimental data.

Algorithm	Yahoo! Dataset				KDD Dataset			
	mean	std	min	max	mean	std	min	max
Random	1.0000	0.0120	0.9706	1.0149	1.0000	0.0018	0.9972	1.0029
ϵ-greedy(0.0)	2.0404	0.0509	1.9527	2.1101	2.3761	0.1398	2.1687	2.6573
ϵ-greedy(0.01)	**2.0546**	0.0685	1.9267	2.1776	**2.6204**	0.0266	2.5572	2.6477
ϵ-greedy(0.1)	**2.0668**	0.0404	1.9811	2.1114	**2.5282**	0.0107	2.5136	2.5429
ϵ-greedy(0.3)	1.8001	0.0303	1.7454	1.8507	2.1974	0.0047	2.1892	2.2041
ϵ-greedy(0.5)	1.5265	0.0234	1.4866	1.5550	1.8511	0.0029	1.8470	1.8555
LinUCB(0.01)	1.8897	0.0561	1.7832	1.9645	2.3696	0.0885	2.1814	2.4318
LinUCB(0.1)	1.3450	0.0169	1.3215	1.3643	2.2158	0.0036	2.2109	2.2227
LinUCB(0.3)	1.1961	0.0076	1.1877	1.2118	1.9469	0.0046	1.9404	1.9560
Softmax(0.01)	1.9572	0.0572	1.8877	2.0578	**2.5435**	0.0102	2.5196	2.5586
Softmax(0.1)	1.1138	0.0133	1.0905	1.1308	1.1946	0.0025	1.1881	1.1971
Softmax(1.0)	1.0063	0.0119	0.9809	1.0199	1.0147	0.0012	1.0125	1.0166
Epoch-greedy(5)	1.9512	0.0378	1.8750	2.0237	2.3627	0.0064	2.3490	2.3721
Epoch-greedy(10)	**2.0517**	0.0841	1.8673	2.1752	**2.5278**	0.0075	2.5141	2.5378
Epoch-greedy(100)	**2.0473**	0.0742	1.9198	2.1616	**2.5794**	0.0645	2.4374	2.6379
Epoch-greedy(500)	**2.0473**	0.0325	1.9751	2.1022	2.5209	0.0853	2.3721	2.6176
TS(0.01)	1.2100	0.0121	1.1909	1.2238	2.0258	0.0021	2.0228	2.0296
TS(0.1)	1.1654	0.0074	1.1540	1.1801	1.9715	0.0039	1.9652	1.9794
TS(1.0)	1.1401	0.0112	1.1249	1.1603	1.6673	0.0024	1.6625	1.6707
TS(10.0)	0.8779	0.0990	0.6907	1.0322	1.2194	0.5090	0.4646	1.8784
TSNR(0.01)	1.2728	0.0184	1.2486	1.3060	2.0039	0.0025	2.0003	2.0072
TSNR(0.1)	1.2823	0.0108	1.2570	1.2956	2.0589	0.0025	2.0545	2.0621
TSNR(1.0)	1.3471	0.0152	1.3208	1.3741	2.2051	0.0019	2.2024	2.2089
TSNR(10.0)	1.8847	0.0389	1.8013	1.9270	2.4945	0.0031	2.4882	2.4993
HyperRandom	1.1856	0.0099	1.1702	1.2041	1.7379	0.0158	1.7115	1.7597
HyperTS	2.0095	0.0708	1.8719	2.1187	2.5175	0.1279	2.2364	2.6587
HyperTSFB	**2.1183***	0.0572	2.0115	2.1842	**2.6536***	0.0101	2.6390	2.6709

that exhibit relatively poor performance at the beginning of the trails may have very limited opportunities to be explored/exploited in the subsequent trials, even though they are good policies if running solely. This is the primary reason that the performance of the **HyperTS** policy is inferior to the one of the **HyperTSFB** policy, as indicated in Table 1.

5.4.2 On CTR of Time Buckets

Besides the overall CTR of each policy, we also evaluate the CTR on individual time bucket. The CTR on each bucket is calculated by the clicks collected in that bucket. The entire *Yahoo! Today News* data is split into 100 time buckets, where each bucket has 100,000 impressions on news articles. The *KDD Cup* data set is split into 90 time buckets, with 100,000 impression for each bucket. All the user visit events are order by the time.

For the purpose of illustration, we compare the ensemble strategies, i.e., **HyperTS** and **HyperTSFB**, with each type of contextual bandit policies, including **ϵ-greedy**, **LinUCB**, **Softmax**, **Epoch-greedy**, **TS** and **TSNR**. At each time bucket, these policies are executed independently, and the relative CTR for each policy is calculated. The results for *Yahoo! Today News* data set and *KDD Cup* data set are reported in Figure 1 and 2, respectively. We can observe that the policy of **HyperTSFB** achieves consistent performance on both data sets. Although in some time buckets the relative CTR of **HyperTSFB** is slightly lower than the one of some specific base policies, its overall performance is quite robust compared with other baselines.

From Figure 1 we observe that the CTR curves of different policies have wide fluctuations. This is because the CTR estimated in *Yahoo! news* data is close to the real CTR in each bucket. The real CTR of an online recommender system usually varies over the time. For instance, popular news articles may become unpopular since the news is aging. User interests may change from daytime to nighttime. In contrast, the CTR curves for *KDD Cup* data, as described in Figure 2, are quite flat except the first few time buckets, and the reason is straightforward. The click of *KDD Cup* data is simulated by a group of logistic regression models. The time factor is not included in those models. Despite different characteristics of the two data sets, our proposed meta-bandit policy performs in a very robust way. This further demonstrates the generalization capability of our proposed method in dealing with different recommendation problems.

Another interesting phenomenon is that the CTR lift of **HyperTSFB** is significantly higher than the one of **HyperTS** at the first few time buckets on both *Yahoo! Today News* data and *KDD Cup* data. The reason here is straightforward: by sharing feedbacks among different policies, the data used for exploring/exploiting the policies become rich, and hence there are more data used for training the underlying learning model and estimating the performance of base policies. Therefore, at the initial time buckets, **HyperTSFB** outperforms **HyperTS** in terms of CTR.

To further demonstrate the robustness of our proposed methods, we consider to rank all the policies based on their CTR lift, and then examine if the result of **HyperTSFB** is in the top ranked list. Specifically in each time bucket, we rank the base and ensemble policies based on the CTR lift, and then count the number of times that a policy appears in the top@k ranked list. Next, we calculate the ratio of this count with the total number of buckets for each policy. Finally, we rank the policies based on their ranking ratios. For this evaluation, 4 best performed policies of *Yahoo! Today News* data and *KDD Cup* data are reported in Table 2 and 3, respectively, in which we consider the top@1, top@3 and top@5 results.

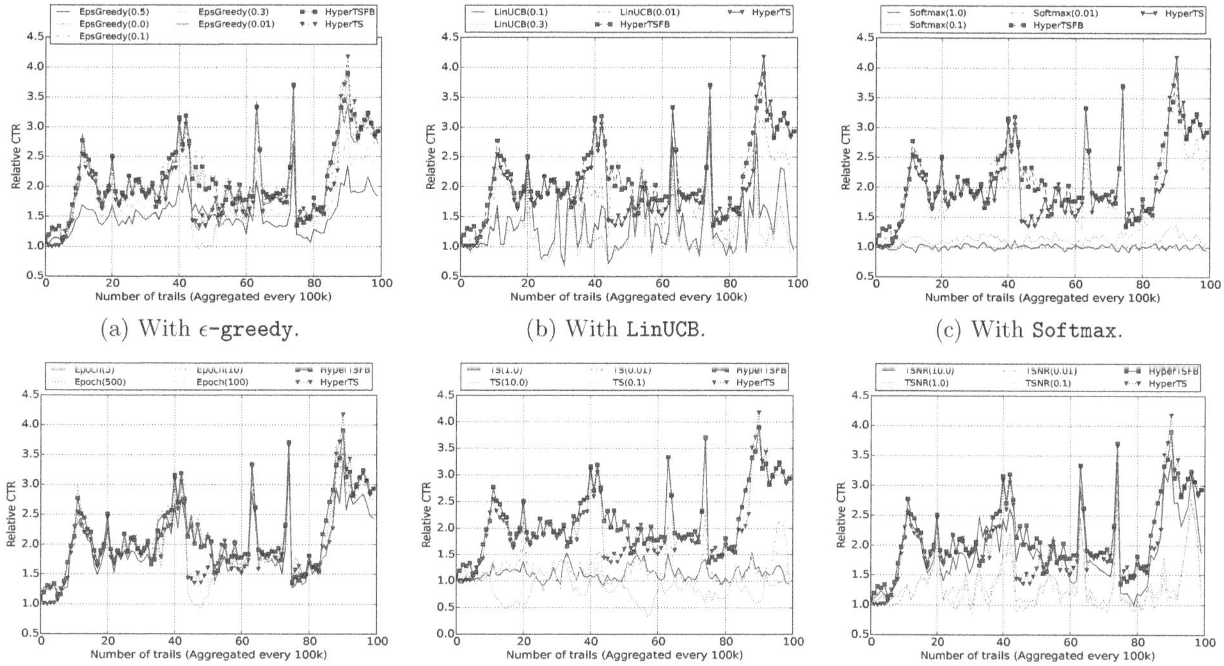

(a) With ϵ-greedy. (b) With LinUCB. (c) With Softmax.

(d) With Epoch-greedy. (e) With TS. (f) With TSNR.

Figure 1: Comparison on Yahoo! News Data.

Table 2: CTR ranking on buckets for Yahoo! data.

top@1		top@3		top@5	
Policies	Ratio	Policies	Ratio	Policies	Ratio
HyperTSFB	88.89%	HyperTSFB	100.00%	HyperTSFB	100.00%
ϵ(0.01)	11.11%	ϵ(0.01)	97.78%	ϵ(0.01)	100.00%
-	-	Epoch(100)	78.89%	Epoch(100)	80.00%
-	-	Softmax(0.01)	16.67%	Softmax(0.01)	80.00%

As observed in Table 2, our proposed policy HyperTSFB on *Yahoo! Today News* data always achieves the 1st place in the top@1, top@3 and top@5 results. Also in Table 3, HyperTSFB reaches the 2nd place of top@1, 3rd place of top@3, and 1st place of top@5. The results indicate that HyperTSFB is able to achieve promising performance in most time buckets. Such an observation further confirms the robust capability of our proposed policy in handling different online recommendation problems.

Table 3: CTR ranking on buckets for KDD data.

top@1		top@3		top@5	
Policies	Ratio	Policies	Ratio	Policies	Ratio
ϵ(0.0)	18.00%	ϵ(0.0)	43.00%	HyperTSFB	72.00%
HyperTSFB	12.00%	Epoch(500)	43.00%	Epoch(500)	68.00%
Epoch(500)	12.00%	HyperTSFB	39.00%	ϵ(0.0)	61.00%
LinUCB(0.01)	11.00%	Epoch(100)	34.00%	Epoch(100)	57.00%

In addition, the performance of base policies with different parameter settings may vary significantly over different experimental data. From Table 2, we observe that ϵ-greedy(0.01) and Epoch(100) perform very well on *Yahoo! Today News* data, indicating that for this data set, the bandit policies can have achieve striking performance with a limited exploration. Comparatively in Table 3, ϵ-greedy(0.0) and Epoch(500) are able to produce promising results, meaning that higher CTR can be achieved on *KDD Cup* data based on the policies with much less exploration.

6. CONCLUDING REMARKS

In personalized recommender systems, the dilemma of exploration/exploitation in the cold-start situation remains a challenging issue due to the uncertainty of user preferences. A lot of contextual bandit policies have been proposed to tackle this dilemma; however, the prerequisite of the input parameters limits the predictive power of the policies. In real-world applications, these policies cannot be easily evaluated under different parameters as they may require too much web traffic and affect the profit of service providers.

In this work, we explore ensemble strategies of multiple contextual bandit policies to obtain robust predicted CTR. Specifically, we employ a meta-bandit paradigm that places a hyper bandit over the base bandits, to explicitly explore/exploit the relative importance of base bandits based on user feedbacks. The proposed approach does not have the restriction on the number of policies being involved, and can always obtain an acceptable CTR close the the optimal. Extensive empirical evaluation on two data sets demonstrates the efficacy of our proposed approach in terms of CTR.

Acknowledgment

The work was supported in part by the National Science Foundation under grants DBI-0850203, HRD-0833093, CNS-1126619, and IIS-1213026, the U.S. Department of Homeland Security under grant number 2010-ST-06200039, Army Research Office under grants W911NF-10-1-0366 and W911NF-12-1-0431, and an FIU Dissertation Year Fellowship.

7. REFERENCES

[1] D. Agarwal et al. Online models for content optimization. In *NIPS*, pages 17–24, 2008.

[2] P. Auer, N. Cesa-Bianchi, Y. Freund, and R. E. Schapire. The nonstochastic multiarmed bandit problem. *SIAM Journal on Computing*, 32(1):48–77, 2002.

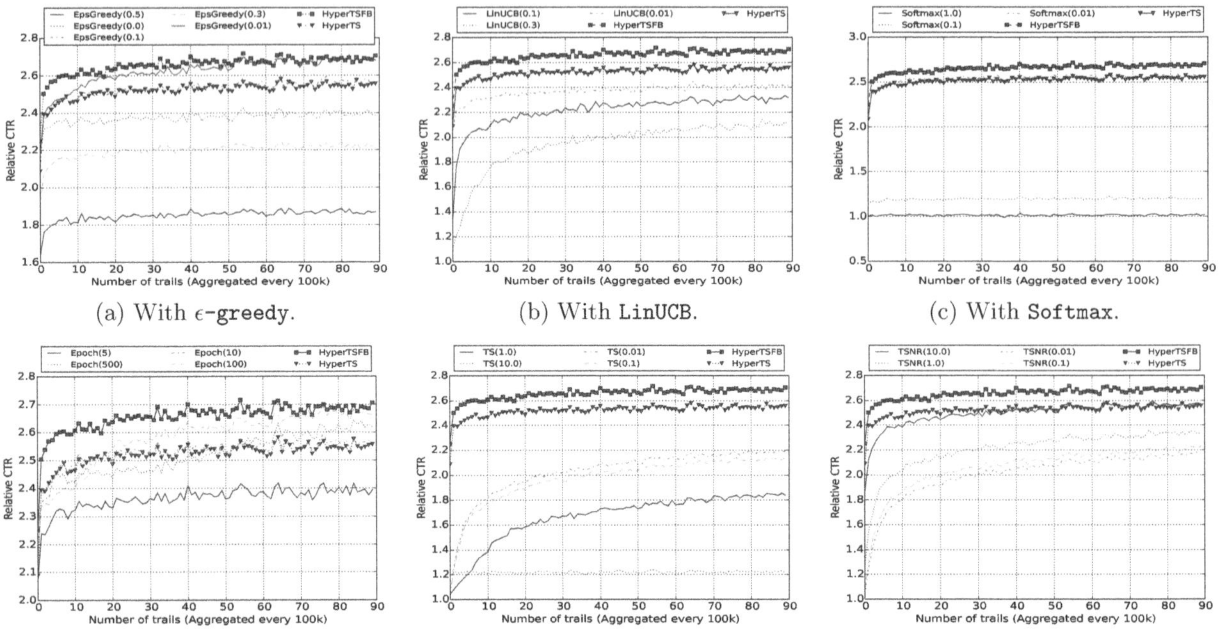

(a) With ϵ-greedy. (b) With LinUCB. (c) With Softmax.

(d) With Epoch-greedy. (e) With TS. (f) With TSNR.

Figure 2: Comparison on KDDCup Data.

[3] A. G. Barto. *Reinforcement learning: An introduction.* MIT press, 1998.

[4] C. M. Bishop et al. *Pattern recognition and machine learning*, volume 1. Springer, 2006.

[5] D. Bouneffouf, A. Bouzeghoub, and A. L. Gançarski. A contextual-bandit algorithm for mobile context-aware recommender system. In *NIPS*, pages 324–331, 2012.

[6] O. Chapelle and L. Li. An empirical evaluation of thompson sampling. In *NIPS*, pages 2249–2257, 2011.

[7] M. Gagliolo and J. Schmidhuber. *Algorithm selection as a bandit problem with unbounded losses.* Springer, 2010.

[8] C. Giraud-Carrier. Metalearning-a tutorial. In *ICMLA*, 2008.

[9] R. V. Hogg and E. A. Tanis. *Probability and Statistical Inference.* Prentice Hall, 1996.

[10] M. Jahrer, A. Töscher, and R. Legenstein. Combining predictions for accurate recommender systems. In *SIGKDD*, pages 693–702. ACM, 2010.

[11] Y. Koren. The bellkor solution to the netflix grand prize. *Netflix prize documentation*, 2009.

[12] J. Langford and T. Zhang. The epoch-greedy algorithm for contextual multi-armed bandits. *NIPS*, pages 817–824, 2007.

[13] L. Li, W. Chu, J. Langford, and R. E. Schapire. A contextual-bandit approach to personalized news article recommendation. In *WWW*, pages 661–670. ACM, 2010.

[14] L. Li, W. Chu, J. Langford, and X. Wang. Unbiased offline evaluation of contextual-bandit-based news article recommendation algorithms. In *WSDM*, pages 297–306. ACM, 2011.

[15] F. Maes, L. Wehenkel, and D. Ernst. *Meta-learning of exploration/exploitation strategies: The multi-armed bandit case.* Springer, 2013.

[16] A. Maurer. Algorithmic stability and meta-learning. In *JMLR*, pages 967–994, 2005.

[17] T. G. McKenzie et al. Novel models and ensemble techniques to discriminate favorite items from unrated ones for personalized music recommendation. In *KDDCUP*, 2011.

[18] R. Polikar. Ensemble based systems in decision making. *Circuits and Systems Magazine, IEEE*, 6(3):21–45, 2006.

[19] A. Prodromidis, P. Chan, and S. Stolfo. Meta-learning in distributed data mining systems: Issues and approaches. *Advances in distributed and parallel knowledge discovery*, 3, 2000.

[20] J. B. Schafer, J. A. Konstan, and J. Riedl. Meta-recommendation systems: user-controlled integration of diverse recommendations. In *CIKM*, pages 43–51. ACM, 2002.

[21] A. I. Schein, A. Popescul, L. H. Ungar, and D. M. Pennock. Methods and metrics for cold-start recommendations. In *SIGIR*, pages 253–260. ACM, 2002.

[22] S. L. Scott. A modern bayesian look at the multi-armed bandit. *Applied Stochastic Models in Business and Industry*, 26(6):639–658, 2010.

[23] J. Seiler. *Meta learning in recommendation systems.* Master Thesis, Technical University of Berlin, 2013.

[24] J. Sill, G. Takács, L. Mackey, and D. Lin. Feature-weighted linear stacking. *arXiv preprint arXiv:0911.0460*, 2009.

[25] C. Tekin and M. van der Schaar. Decentralized online big data classification-a bandit framework. *arXiv preprint arXiv:1308.4565*, 2013.

[26] W. R. Thompson. On the likelihood that one unknown probability exceeds another in view of the evidence of two samples. *Biometrika*, pages 285–294, 1933.

[27] M. Tiemann and S. Pauws. Towards ensemble learning for hybrid music recommendation. In *RecSys*, pages 177–178. ACM, 2007.

[28] M. Tokic. Adaptive ε-greedy exploration in reinforcement learning based on value differences. In *KI*, pages 203–210, 2010.

[29] J. Vermorel and M. Mohri. Multi-armed bandit algorithms and empirical evaluation. In *ECML*, pages 437–448, 2005.

[30] M. Wu. Collaborative filtering via ensembles of matrix factorizations. In *KDDCUP*, 2007.

[31] K. Yu, A. Schwaighofer, and V. Tresp. Collaborative ensemble learning: Combining collaborative and content-based information filtering via hierarchical bayes. In *UAI*, pages 616–623, 2002.

[32] B. Zadrozny. Learning and evaluating classifiers under sample selection bias. In *ICML*, pages 114–121. ACM, 2004.

Cold-start News Recommendation with Domain-dependent Browse Graph

Michele Trevisiol [2,1] Luca Maria Aiello[1] Rossano Schifanella[3,*] Alejandro Jaimes[1]

[1]Yahoo Labs, Barcelona, Spain {laiello,ajaimes}@yahoo-inc.com
[2]Web Research Group, Universitat Pompeu Fabra, Barcelona, Spain trevisiol@acm.org
[3]Università degli Studi di Torino, Torino, Italy schifane@di.unito.it

ABSTRACT

Online social networks and mash-up services create opportunities to connect different web services otherwise isolated. Specifically in the case of news, users are very much exposed to news articles while performing other activities, such as social networking or web searching. Browsing behavior aimed at the consumption of news, especially in relation to the visits coming from other domains, has been mainly overlooked in previous work. To address that, we build a *BrowseGraph* out of the collective browsing traces extracted from a large viewlog of Yahoo News (0.5B entries) and we define the *ReferrerGraph* as its subgraph induced by the sessions with the same referrer domain. The structural and temporal properties of the graph show that browsing behavior in news is highly dependent on the referrer URL of the session, in terms of type of content consumed and time of consumption. We build on this observation and propose a news recommender that addresses the *cold-start* problem: given a user landing on a page of the site for the first time, we aim to predict the page she will visit next. We compare 24 flavors of recommenders belonging to the families of content-based, popularity-based, and browsing-based models. We show that the browsing-based recommender that takes into account the referrer URL is the best performing, achieving a prediction accuracy of 48% in conditions of heavy data sparsity.

Categories and Subject Descriptors

H.4 [**Information Systems Applications**]: Miscellaneous

Keywords

BrowseGraph; cold-start; news recommendation; browsing behavior; sessions

*This work has been performed when the author was a Visiting Scientist at Yahoo Labs, Barcelona, within the framework of the FREP grant.

RecSys'14, October 6–10, 2014, Foster City, Silicon Valley, CA, USA.

http://dx.doi.org/10.1145/2645710.2645726.

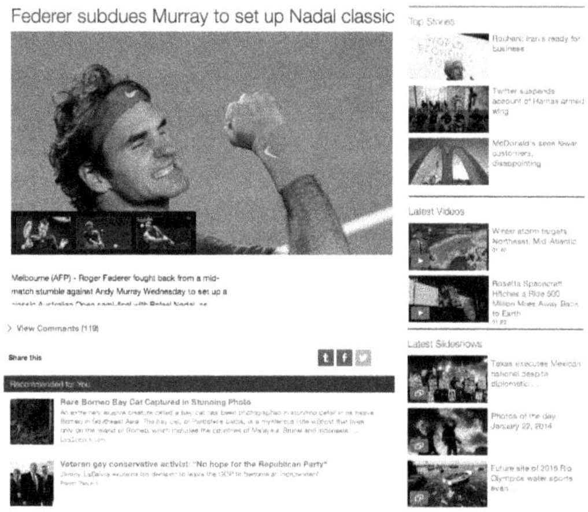

Figure 1: An article page from Yahoo News (compacted layout). Right rail boxes and the infinite-scroll section at the bottom allow the user to browse to other articles.

1. INTRODUCTION

In recent years the consumption of online news has increased rapidly, in contrast with the decline of traditional newspapers[1]. Between 2009 and 2012 the percentage of users visiting news portals raised steadily up to the point to represent the major portion of overall Web traffic[2], comparable to the volume of visits to top domains like Google search[3]. For its importance, richness of content, and abundant user participation, the field of online news has become a crowded arena for research in several areas including retrieval, ranking, recommendation, and personalization [6, 2, 30]. Despite the vast amount of work in the field, there are two aspects of news consumption that are still largely unexplored. First, modern online news providers have turned into more globally connected systems able to attract a wider audience than their core of regular users. News articles are very often shared on different external websites and social media platforms, thus providing a growing number of browsing shortcuts to news portals. To mention two examples, modern search engines serve queries relevant to news stories by directly featuring news articles from major providers, and social media are increasingly used as daily

[1] http://bit.ly/1mwLHg3
[2] http://bit.ly/1iWzvRK
[3] http://bit.ly/1mwLEkc

tools for journalists and casual news readers[4] to spread and consume news provided by external parties [2, 17, 28]. Despite such increasing level of integration and mashup, news portals have been studied mostly in isolation. The latter aspect that has drawn very little attention is user *browsing behavior*. Although recent literature is rich in studies about browsing patterns in several online platforms [18, 9, 25], little has been done with respect to the news domain. One reason for this is that the browsing sessions in online news outlets have been found to be short, aimed in most cases to quick catch ups on news [9].

In this work we address these two aspects in combination and exploit them in a task of news recommendation in a *cold-start* scenario. We study the way users browse news content in relation to the *type* of online domain they were browsing *before* landing on the news page, also known as *referrer* domain. Our contribution begins with finding that browsing is a meaningful phenomenon to study also for online news, as the browsing graphs have a coherent and well-formed structure also in this domain. We find that the referrer partly determines the type of news consumed and the time when it is consumed. In the wake of previous studies about the impact of the referrer domains on user browsing behavior [4], we use the browsing graph induced by the referrer of the browsing sessions to predict the next article a newcomer will visit right after she lands on a page of the site. Using a very large sample of viewlogs from Yahoo News (~500M entries), we compare 24 flavors of recommenders for next-article consumption, including popularity-, item-, and browsing-based models. We find that browsing-based recommendations achieves the best overall precision@1 among all the methods: up to 48% in conditions of heavy volatility of news articles and of high data sparsity arising from the large amount of candidate articles to recommend.

We summarize our main contributions as follows:

- We introduce the *BrowseGraph* in the context of news and we define the notion of domain-dependent *BrowseGraph* (*ReferrerGraph*), namely a graph composed by the browsing sessions of users coming from the same referrer domain, *e.g.*, *facebook.com*. (§3).
- We study the *BrowseGraph* built from a large sample of browsing activity from Yahoo News. We explore it with respect to time and topic, providing insights on relations between the domain of origin, the type of news consumed and the temporal patterns of consumption (§4).
- We provide a method to recommend the next article to read in a cold-start scenario using the information from the *ReferrerGraphs*. Our recommender outperforms a number of item-, popularity-, and browsing-based baselines (§5).

Our work differs from the state-of-the-art in the fact that we consider previous users navigational patterns and the referrer domain to recommend the news article that users are likely to visit next; we are not aware of any other work that use the *BrowseGraph* for news recommendation. Moreover, we introduce and study for the first time the *ReferrerGraph*, and show how its information helps to improve the accuracy of the recommendation.

[4]http://bit.ly/1bQG1uL

2. RELATED WORK

Cold-Start Recommendation. Cold-start problem recommendation refers either to new items or to new users, and we consider the latter case. Some solutions to the problem require an initial, even though small, set of preferences about the newcomer user [22, 21, 1](*warm-start* scenario). The user profile can be populated by asking to the users to rate a set of items first or importing their preferences from external systems [19]. When a minimal user profile is available, a common approach is to apply association rules in order to expand the user profile. Sobhanam *et al.* [22] used clustering algorithms to find the most similar known items and then they extended the profile of the users with item related to their tastes. Shaw *et al.* [21] used also non-redundant rule sets showing how they can improve the results. Yang *et al.* [31] presented a Bayesian-inference based recommendation system that exploit the social network structure of the user in order to perform personalized recommendation. In this paper, the only information we have is the external referrer URL from which the user is coming from, and the news article the user is currently watching. While no one has considered the first information in the field of recommender system, the latter one could be integrated in a content-based approach, that is one of the baseline we implemented (§5.2).

News Recommendation. Despite the progress of recommender systems in general, news recommendation is still a very active area [5]. The majority of news recommender systems are based on user information collected over time [12, 5, 10, 11], relying on logged-in users only and combining collaborative filtering and content-based approaches. However, when reading news website the user is most often not logged-in, making impossible (or at least very difficult) the creation of a reliable user profile. There are approaches based on models of similarity among news articles [16, 10, 20] considering different key factors like textual similarity, recency, coherence, novelty and popularity. Tsagkias and Blanco [26] proposed a language intent model that extracts a query from the user browsing session. In this way they model the user interest using the queries of the users. There are also approaches looking for the most authoritative news sources as a proxy for quality [6, 24]. However, most of previous work relies on the user historical profiles. Our work is different since it is based on the *BrowseGraph*, using previous collected behavior of users grouped based on the external domain where they come from.

BrowseGraph and Referrer URL. In recent years there have been numerous studies on user traffic in term of navigation/browsing of web pages. Browsing sessions have been leveraged for different tasks such as recommending photos and photostreams [3], predicting the users demographic [8], or optimizing the web crawler [13]. Liu *et al.* [14] introduced the *BrowseGraph*, a graph built by the users navigation patterns where the nodes are webpages and the edges are transitions made by users. They compared different centrality metrics computed on the standard hyperlink graph model, on the *BrowseGraph*, and on their combination, finding that the *BrowseGraph* rank has higher quality. The *BrowseGraph* has been used to rank items like photos in Flickr [25], where the external referrer domain (*i.e.* the last domain vi-

[5]http://recsys.acm.org/recsys13/nrs/

sited by the user before entering in Flickr), was considered to attribute more importance to the images with highest external visibility. The referrer domain has been proved to be useful for studying the popularity of media items (such as YouTube videos [7]), and to characterize the type of session the user is likely to perform [4]. However, we are not aware about studies that exploit this important information in the context of news or that use the *ReferrerGraphs* for new recommendation purposes as we do.

3. BROWSEGRAPH IN THE NEWS DOMAIN

To investigate the activity of news consumption and browsing we analyze the Yahoo News viewlog, also considering the browsing activity of users coming from different (*families* of) domains. In this section, we describe the raw data we use and its preprocessing (§3.1) and how we leverage it to generate the *BrowseGraphs* (§3.2).

3.1 News site viewlogs

Each article page in Yahoo News contains a nearly inexhaustible variety of options to transition to other article pages. As shown in Figure 1, the typical news page contains a right rail with several boxes of recommended news (*e.g.*, recent articles) and an infinite-scroll list of personalized news at the bottom. To capture the user's browsing activity we consider a sample of the site's *viewlog*[6], where each pageview is recorded by the following fields:

$$\langle BCookie, Time, ReferrerURL, CurrentURL, UserAgent\rangle$$

BCookie is an anonymized user identifier computed from the browser cookie. *CurrentURL* and *ReferrerURL* represent, respectively, the URL of the page the user is currently visiting and the URL of the page from which she transitioned to the current one, possibly including external domains. Last, the *User-Agent* identifies the browser in use, and the *Time* indicates when the page was visited. By preserving only the traffic from well-known browser identifiers (to remove spider-generated requests), we are left with approximately 0.5 billion pageviews.

To model browsing transitions we group pageviews in *sessions*, consisting of a sequence of pageviews made by the same user in a *continuous* time frame. As is standard practice [23], we split sessions by timeout (inactivity between two pageviews is longer than 25 minutes) but also when the user leaves the site for another domain, disregarding the timeout. In addition to the browsing transitions, we gather also the information about the *topic* of each article page (assigned by editors), the article headline and its body. There are 22 article topics in total, some of which are listed in Table 3.

3.2 Domain-dependent BrowseGraph

We aggregate the session data over all users to generate a *BrowseGraph* [14], namely a graph where the nodes are pages and the directed links connect pages that have been visited in sequence during a browsing session. The edges of the graph therefore have the following structure:

$$\langle Pageview_{source}, Pageview_{destination}, weight\rangle ,$$

where *weight* is the total volume of transitions, aggregated over all sessions. Because the *BrowseGraph* captures patterns of user flow, it has been leveraged in several applications, ranging from estimation of page importance [14] to multimedia ranking [3, 25]. In the news domain, the *BrowseGraph* is particularly valuable as the links between articles may vary depending on time (*e.g.*, turnover of the "top stories" during the day) or even on the user, as the set of links shown may vary in a personalized fashion. In addition, we go beyond the study of the general browsing patterns by comparing the browsing behavior of users who land on the news website from *different domains*. We aim to verify empirically the idea that users coming from different types of external web services are interested (or exposed) to different types of content and therefore behave differently.

To decompose the overall *BrowseGraph* G into subgraphs G_d that account for the sessions originated from a specific domain d, we use only the sessions whose first referrer URL matches the domain d. For instance, a user who accesses a news page from a tweet will start a new session that will be part of the Twitter *ReferrerGraph*. We refer to the subgraph G_d as the *ReferrerGraph* for the domain d. In particular, we consider 9 source domains. Three search engines: *Bing*, *Google*, and *Yahoo*; three social networks: *Facebook*, *Reddit*, and *Twitter*; and the *homepage* of the news portal, a special case of referrer URL that represents a significant entry point for Yahoo News users. In addition, we also consider two aggregated *ReferrerGraphs* created by the union of the graphs in the *search engines* and *social networks* respectively (we call them *Search* and *Social*), as some of the characteristics of the *ReferrerGraphs* of domains belonging to the same family are quite similar (see §4). Last, since the consumption of news items is strictly dependent on time, we define a *temporal BrowseGraph* G^t as the *BrowseGraph* originated by the browsing sessions occurring in an hourly time slot t. We partition the *BrowseGraphs* on hourly intervals, ending up with $1,440$ temporal graphs for each domain, for a total of $12,960$ graphs.

4. ANALYSIS

In this section we report the structural properties of the full BrowseGraph and of the *ReferrerGraphs* induced by the different domains of origin (§4.1) and a study of their evolution in time (§4.2).

4.1 Domain-dependent news consumption

We find the distribution of the number of hops per session to be broadly distributed (not shown) but with very low average values (Table 1), in agreement with previous work that found the user interaction with news portals being short and time-constrained [9]. Despite that, the BrowseGraph built from the full set of user sessions is connected, with a greatest weakly connected component that spans up to 95% of all the pages and whose nodes are ~5 hops away on average (statistics are summarized in Table 2). This means that although the individual browsing interactions with the news portal are short, the collective browsing behavior weaves an implicit network of associations between articles whose points are on average 5 hops away. The connectivity of the BrowseGraph appears to be scale-invariant, as very similar connectivity values are found for the *ReferrerGraphs*, the most disconnected one being Twitter, with 87% of nodes in its giant component. The average in-degree can be considerably high due to the large number of possible connections that an article page has with others (as illustrated in §3), and it is by far the largest in the *homepage* graph, which dominates in terms of traffic volume. Although the degree

[6]The processing was performed in aggregate on anonymized data

Full	Homepage	Google	Yahoo
1.94021	3.10963	1.81442	1.96733
Bing	**Facebook**	**Twitter**	**Reddit**
1.79329	1.34167	1.24211	1.12242

Table 1: Average number of hops during browsing sessions with different referrer domains.

Graph	#Nodes	#Edges	Density	%GCC	$\langle k_{in} \rangle$	$\langle d \rangle$
full	745,720	10,017,826	$1.8 \cdot 10^{-5}$	0.95	2551	5.14
homepage	257,465	3,516,661	$5.3 \cdot 10^{-5}$	0.99	1830	4.15
google	163,411	928,364	$3.5 \cdot 10^{-5}$	0.93	400	3.98
yahoo	116,403	490,239	$3.6 \cdot 10^{-5}$	0.95	229	2.91
bing	70,665	308,824	$6.2 \cdot 10^{-5}$	0.91	224	3.34
facebook	24,058	84,837	$1.6 \cdot 10^{-4}$	0.95	141	3.31
twitter	5,065	8,922	$3.5 \cdot 10^{-4}$	0.87	39	3.17
reddit	2,840	5,851	$7.3 \cdot 10^{-4}$	0.95	81	3.67

Table 2: Structural statistics of the *ReferrerGraphs* ($\langle d \rangle$ indicates the average shortest path length and GCC indicates the Giant Connected Component).

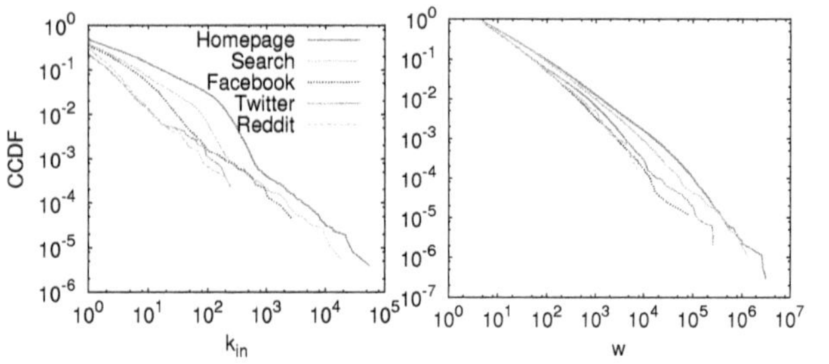

Figure 2: Distributions of indegree (k_{in}) and edge weight (w) in some *ReferrerGraphs*. Search graphs are collapsed in one curve due to their similar distributions.

distributions vary considerably (Figure 2), the edge weight distributions are closer to each other, the vast majority of edges having very low weights.

A natural question is whether the graphs are different just in terms of structural properties or also with respect to the *type* of their nodes. To measure the overlap between graphs we compute the Jaccard similarity between the set of their nodes (Figure 3a). As one might expect, similarity is lower between the two major families: search and social. Surprisingly though, there are conspicuous differences also within each group. For instance, Twitter and Reddit have only ~20% of the overall amount of their nodes being covered by both. This means that the users coming from Twitter are visiting only a small portion of the news articles visited by users coming from Reddit. In other words, the users interest is strongly dependent by the type of website they are coming from. We spot also significant differences in the type of news content consumed in the different networks. To measure that, we count the frequency of articles belonging to each of the news topics (see §3.1), and we rank topics by their frequency in each network (Table 3). Naturally, the most popular type of news content in all the cases is related to general-type news. But except for the top position, the rankings show substantial differences, with celebrity-related news being the main interest for users coming from search engines, while blogs, sports, and entertainment are the most popular topics in Facebook, Twitter and Reddit respectively.

The differences in terms of graph structure, their size and

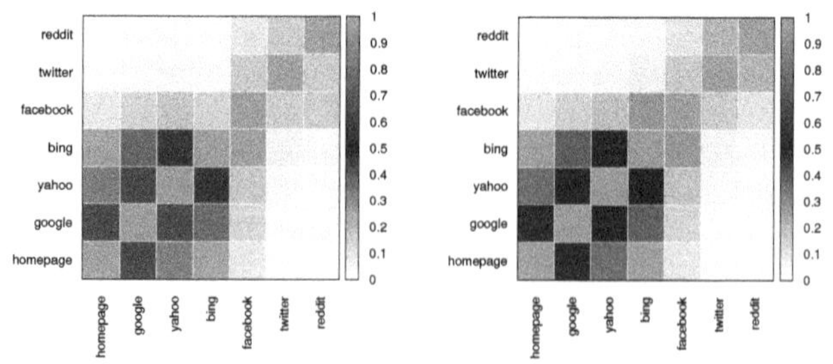

(a) *Jaccard similarity of node sets* (b) *Kendall τ between news pageranks*

Figure 3: Node overlap between graphs and article ranking comparison.

type of nodes impact directly the type of articles that are consumed the most or that are perceived as most interesting by the users. To gauge that, we consider two metrics of news importance, namely the *pageview count* and the *PageRank centrality* computed on the weighted graphs. We apply each metric separately to the *ReferrerGraphs* and we compute pairwise the Kendall's τ similarity between the ranks. Figure 3b displays the values for PageRank, similar results are found for the viewrank (not shown for brevity). To discount for the different dimensionality, τ is measured only on the elements contained in the intersection of the two sets. To account for the noise that can be potentially introduced by the permutations on the latest positions on the rank (i.e., articles with very similar scores in the long-tail of the popularity curve), we repeat the same measure on the top 100 and 1000 articles, obtaining very similar results. Rankings tend to be more similar within domain families ($\tau \in [0.50, 0.68]$ for search and $\tau \in [0.20, 0.27]$ for social) rather across families ($\tau \in [0.14, 0.4]$).

4.2 News consumption in time

4.2.1 *Time and domain*

Time plays a central role in news content consumption as news articles tend by their nature to become rapidly stale. In Figure 4 (left) we plot the distribution of the relative volume of views that articles receive in time (hours). In Figure 4 (right) we show the same measure but on a normalized time axis that starts from the article publishing time ($t = 0$) up to the last visit received ($t = 1$). We refer to this normalized timeline as the article *lifespan*. Consistently with previous work, we find that 80% of visits are received within the first 30 hours after the article publication and before the first 20% of the overall article lifespan.

One question, however, is whether the temporal aspect of news consumption depends on the type of network the user is coming from. To investigate this aspect, we repeat the previous measures separately on the three *ReferrerGraphs homepage*, *search*, and *social* in separation. For each of them, we measure the distribution of the total volume of visits at each point of the article normalized lifespan (Figure 5). A phenomenon of rapid decay emerges in all the three cases, however the curves exhibit major differences in skew. While news consumption through the homepage tends to happen in earlier stages of the lifespan, accesses through social networks and search engines are shifted towards later stages. In particular, for the *social* domain we observe evident pea-

Full	Homepage	Search	Facebook	Twitter	Reddit
News	News	News	News	News	News
Celeb.	Video	Celeb.	Entertain.	Sports	Blogs
Finance	Celeb.	Finance	Celeb.	Finance	Politics
Video	Finance	Video	Video	Video	Sports
Sports	Sports	Sports	Finance	Entertain.	Technology
Politics	Politics	Movie	Blogs	Lifestyle	Finance
Movie	Movie	Politics	Sports	Movie	Movie
Lifestyle	Lifestyle	Blogs	Photos	Photos	Video
Blogs	Blogs	Music	Lifestyle	Celeb.	Lifestyle
Music	Music	Entertain.	Movie	Music	Celeb.
Entertain.	Entertain.	Lifestyle	Politics	Politics	Health

Table 3: Most popular news topics for different browse graphs. We grouped *Google*, *Bing*, and *Yahoo* into the same network (*search*) since their ranks are nearly identical.

ks of accesses during late stages of the article life. Even if these peaks account for rather small percentage of the whole traffic (up to 2%), they still represent a non-negligible number of accesses. Examples of news that largely contribute to the visit volume inside the peaks belong to the "trivia" type of stories that are most commonly seen on social networks[7].

4.2.2 Time and topic

The referrer domain is just one variable that might impact the temporal patterns of content consumption for news, and the type (or topic) of the article can also have a role on that. In Figure 6 we show the aggregated volume of views in time for news articles belonging to six different categories. The relative positions of the accesses from homepage, social sites, and search engines change depending on the topic. The baseline consumption behavior is given by the general type of news, for which the view volume from the homepage is consistently higher than the volume from search engines, which is in turn higher than the one from social networks. For blogs instead, the view volume is more similar across the three macro-networks and the curves intersect more often, with two clear phases. First, the number of visits from social networks goes above search for a short time, likely explained by the fact that blog posts in important news sites are usually written by bloggers who are heavily involved in the activity of online social networking. Last, the accesses from homepage and search become comparable in volume. Similar observations hold for other categories: sports, movies, and celebrities get a higher volume of accesses in later stages of the article life. In the case of celebrities in particular, we observe that accesses from social exceed even the ones from the homepage, after a certain point. This may happen when news about specific events (*e.g.*, academy awards) cause an outburst in the social media discourse. Last, an interesting case emerges from visual news such as photo-galleries related to news events. In this case, the accesses from social and search are comparable in the early life of the news, while the volume from search and homepage are comparable in the later stages. This delineates a scenario in which images lend themselves to spread easily in social media.

4.2.3 Rank variation

Besides studying the attention received in time by the overall set of articles, it is interesting to check how the attention received by an article changes in relation to others. In other words, if we rank articles by viewcount, we can explore how the rank changes in time and across *ReferrerGraphs*. To quantify that, we consider *Homepage*, *Search*, and *Social ReferrerGraphs* separately and for each of them we compute an hourly view rank R_t for all the articles they contain. Then, for each set of articles published in the hourly time slot t_i, we compute the Kendall's τ between their view rank at t_i and the view ranks in subsequent hours, more formally $\tau(R_{ti}, R_{ti+j}), \forall j \geq 1$. Then, we shift each measurement back in time by i hours, so that all sets of articles start from time 0, and we average all the measurements, with resulting curves in Figure 7. The lower the value of τ, the farther the ranking at time t is from the ranking of at the original publication time. In all the cases we observe the values decrease rapidly in the first 5 hours and a steady-state occurs within the first 24 hours. This finding is consistent with the volume of views dropping of several orders of magnitude in few hours. The τ value after 2 days is, on average, not higher than 0.55, meaning that the final ranking changes considerably from the initial one. Although the trend of the three curves is analogous, they have different offsets. Articles accessed via search change their relative position less and the ranking stabilize slightly quicker, while on the other extreme accesses from social networks impact the view rank more.

[7]See, for instance: http://abcn.ws/1fPcOzu and http://abcn.ws/1iX4nHD

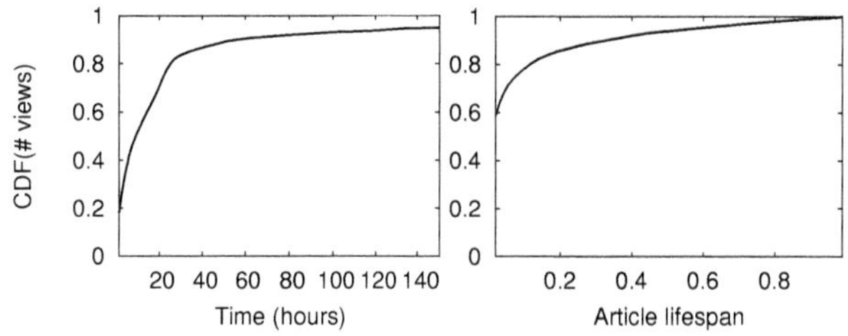

Figure 4: Cumulative number of page views in time

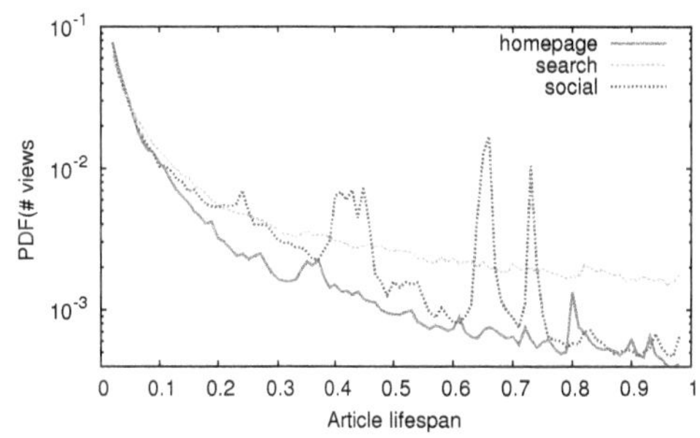

Figure 5: PDF of the number of views received in each of three *ReferrerGraphs* over the normalized lifespan of the news, from the publication ($x = 0$) to the last visit ($x = 1$).

5. COLD-START PREDICTION OF NEXT VIEW

Item recommendation is a crucial task in news sites as they have to deal with a rapidly changing pool of thousands of fresh articles and millions of users, each one with a specific range of interests. In such a scenario, profiling users with their explicit (*e.g.*, comments, article saved, printed, shared) and implicit (*e.g.*, views, time spent) activities on-site is an effective way to recommend new content that matches the user interest. However, personalization is not possible in cases of *cold-start*, when a user who is a newcomer or is not logged-in lands on the site. In this context, the information of the *BrowseGraph* can help, as the activity of

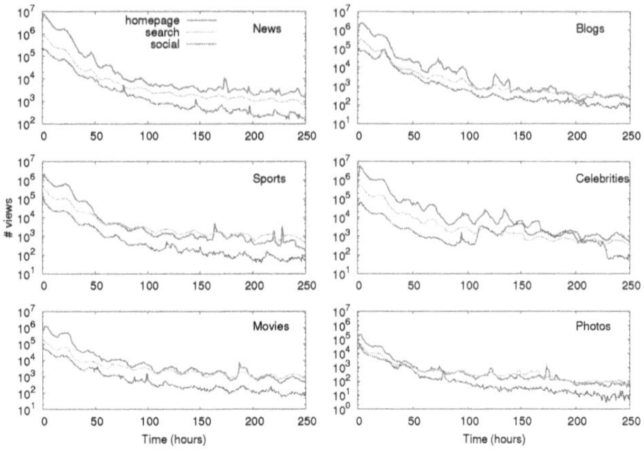

Figure 6: Number of views in each *ReferrerGraph* in time, breakdown by news topic.

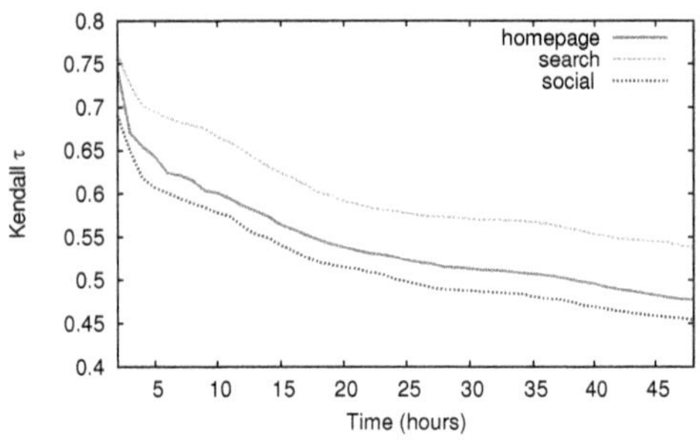

Figure 7: Kendall's τ calculated between the view rank at time t and the view rank at time 0.

previous users provide a collective trace of previous browsing patterns that can be recommended also to the new user. In particular, we show that the *ReferrerGraphs* are particularly effective to this end. Next, we formally define the recommendation problem (§5.1), describe a number of methods to address it (§5.2), compare them on a large scale dataset (§5.3), and discuss the results.

5.1 Problem definition

The prediction problem we address is defined as follows. A newcomer user $u \in U$ is given, who begins a new session at time t on page $p_{start} \in P$, with referrer domain $d \in D$. The task consists in predicting a page p_{next} that u will visit right after p_{start}, given that we restrict the problem to users whose sessions will include at least two pageviews, *i.e.*, an additional pageview after p_{start}. We consider, for simplicity, a time line quantized in discrete 1-hour slots and we assume to know the information about the browsing sessions generated by other users in the previous time slot t-1. To be able to draw a comparison also with recommendation methods based on textual content or item popularity, we consider an additional set of metadata for every page $p \in P$, specifically, v_p^{t-1}: cumulative number of pageviews at time $t-1$; cat_p: the page's topical category; h_p: the page textual headline; b_p: the textual body of the page.

5.2 Prediction methods

All the prediction algorithms we consider are determined by the combination of three components we describe next.

5.2.1 *Selection of candidate pages*

Full neighbors set (full). After the initial visit of p_{start}, the target user could transition, in principle, to any other page in P. However, we measure that in the 95% of the cases, p_{next} is included among the set $\Gamma_G^{t-1}(p_{start}) = \{p_i | (p_{start}, p_i) \in E(G^{t-1})\}$, namely the out-neighbors of p_{start} in the *BrowseGraph*created from the browsing sessions occurring during the timeslot t-1. This happens because, even though the cardinality of $\Gamma_G^{t-1}(p_{start})$ can be very big (recall the degree distribution in Figure 2), most of the browsing links between p_{start} and its neighbors are created shortly after the news are published. For this reason, an effective strategy would be to consider only the set $\Gamma_G^{t-1}(p_{start})$ as output range for the prediction. We call this selection strategy **"full"**, after the full *BrowseGraph*we use to perform the selection.
Referrer neighbors set (ref). In §4 we observed that the type of referrer URL determines to a certain extent the type of news consumed. One might argue that adapting the candidate page selection based on the user domain of origin d, could potentially improve the prediction accuracy. We could therefore restrict the output range to the neighbors of p_{start} in the domain-dependent graph G_d^{t-1}. Using G_d^{t-1} instead of the full graph G^{t-1} implies a drop in the chance of finding p_{next} in the set $\Gamma_G^{t-1}(p_{start})$ from 95% to a minimum of 48% for the Yahoo graph and a maximum of 72% for Homepage. However, based on our previous analysis, the subset of remaining pages could have a higher likelihood of being good candidates for prediction. Similarly to the previous case, we name this selection strategy **"ref"**.
Mixed neighbors set (mix). A natural extension is to combine the **ref** and **full** approaches in cascade. By definition, G_d^{t-1} has a subset of the nodes in G^t. Therefore, it may happen that the node p_{start} is not present in the subgraph or does not have any out-neighbor. So, we adopt the following strategy: if $p_{start} \in N(G_d^{t-1}) \wedge k_{out}(p_{start}) > 0$, then use the **ref** strategy, otherwise rollback to **full**. In the following, we refer to this strategy as **"mix"**.

In the following, we call C the set of candidate nodes, disregarding the strategy used to obtain it.

5.2.2 *Topical filtering*

As we report in Table 4, the probability of transitioning from a page with a topical category cat_p to another page with the same category, computed over all the sessions, varies depending on the domain of origin for that session. In the cases of *Twitter* and *Facebook*, there is a slight tendency to stick to the same topic, whereas for the other domains two consecutive pages in the session tend to belong to different categories. We leverage this information to enrich the initial candidate selection strategy keep only those articles in C that belong to the same topic as p_{start} for *Twitter* and *Facebook*, or to a different topic for the other domains.

5.2.3 *Prediction of next page*

All the methods use the *BrowseGraph* information to select an initial set of candidate pages C, according to one of the strategies defined above. After that, a criterion for the selection of the predicted next page among the ones in the set is needed. Next, we describe four algorithms, with their shortnames in parenthesis.
Random (rand). A simple baseline that selects at random a node in C.
Content-based (cb). A standard approach to recommend

Total	Facebook	Twitter	Reddit	Google	Bing	Homepage
0.34	0.59	0.64	0.48	0.44	0.44	0.33

Table 4: Probability that a user navigates between pageviews of the same category.

items at cold-start is to select the most similar article to the one the user is currently consuming, according to text-based metrics. When the body of the article is available (35% **of articles in our dataset**) the similarity is computed between the bodies, otherwise their headline (always available) is used. We compute the cosine similarity of the vector representation weighted with TD-IDF of p_{start} with the ones of every $p_i \in C$. Text is preprocessed with stopword removal and stemming [29].

Most Popular (pop). Another typical cold-start recommendation approach is to select the most popular item. We recommend the node in C with the highest view count, considering the views until time $t-1$.

Edge-based (edge). Consider the weight on the edges that encode the likelihood of transition between nodes according to the browsing traces recorded at time $t-1$. Hence, we predict p_{next} to be the node in $\Gamma_G^{t-1}(p_{start})$ with highest weight on the incoming edge from p_{start}. Depending on the initial candidate selection strategy (§5.2.1), the edges considered (and their weights) will be either the ones in the *BrowseGraph* (for the **full** selection) or the ones in the *ReferrerGraph* (for the **ref** selection).

5.3 Experimental results

We apply our prediction strategies to the sessions of 1,438 hourly timeslots, for an average of $350K$ users per timeslot. We evaluate the goodness of the prediction by measuring its overall **Precision@1**: a true positive occurs when the predicted page is equal to p_{next}, a false positive when that condition does not hold. Additionally, since all the methods we presented lend themselves to produce ranking of pages (based on popularity, similarity, *etc.*), we also measure their Mean Reciprocal Ranking for the top 3 news articles (**MRR@3**). As noticed earlier, there is always a chance that the correct article cannot be possibly predicted because p_{next} might be not included in the set of candidates $\Gamma_G^{t-1}(p_{start})$ (for example because the article is published at time t and does not exists yet at time $t-1$). We adopt a conservative approach and we count also these cases as false positives. Figure 8 summarizes the prediction results. To have a more detailed picture of the cases in which the different approaches work best, we report separate evaluation results for the sessions with different referrer domains. Twelve bars for each group represent the precision and MRR scores for the combinations of the three selection strategies (**full**, **ref**, **mix**) with the next-node selection methods (**random**, **cb**, **pop**, **edge**). The maximum precision achieved for the different domains partially depends on the dimensionality of the session volume for that domain. This is mainly because the smaller the $\Gamma_G^t(p_{start})$ set, the higher the probability of giving in output a correct prediction just by chance. The most interesting experimental findings, lie instead in the offsets between different methods' results within each referrer domain. First, the random baseline achieves always the worst performance, followed by the content, popularity and edge strategies in order. About the low performance of **cb**, our hypothesis is that the selection of next article is not driven by patterns of content similarity. In other words, after having read an article on a topic the user is likely not motivated to keep reading about the same (or similar) topic right after. The **pop** approach works only slightly better, as it relies on aggregate information about the amount of page visits, but disregarding where such visits came from. The best method by far is **edge**, meaning that previous transitions from p_{start} and p_{next} constitute the stronger signal for the prediction of future transitions. For the social referrer domains it is able to reach up to 48% and 54% in P@1 and MRR@3. For the search domains instead, it reaches up to 27% and 34%. Regarding the node selection strategies, **ref** outperforms **full** in all the three social domains (except for the **ref-edge** combination in Facebook). The fact that a more specific type of recommendation works better suggests that people coming from social networks tend to retrace the same browsing paths other people from the same referrer domain have already explored, with limited serendipitous discovery. The opposite occurs for the search domains, where **full** beats **ref**. This may happen because query-driven systems provide a wider range of entry points to the news site than the links posted on social networks, thus making the prediction task harder. The same happens for the homepage, where the variability of content displayed is very wide and dynamic. However, for both families, **mix** is the most effective strategy that is able to significantly boost even more the precision for social networks and to fill the performance gap with **full** for the search domain. Homepage, which is the domain originating the highest number of sessions, is the only one in which **full** has top precision. In this case, the behavior of users is so varied that restricting the options to a subgraph turns out to be detrimental for the prediction quality. Last, when the topical filtering is applied (§5.2.2), the precision experiences a drop in performance loosing from 10.6% up to 69.5% (not shown in plots). This happens because discarding too many nodes introduces the high risk of ruling out very good candidates (*e.g.*, a node connected to p_{start} with a high-weight edge). In our case, as shown in Table 4, the probability of transitioning to the same topic (or to a different one) is not far from 0.5 in all cases, therefore the topical information is not discriminative enough to filter out nodes without losing the most likely next pages.

The experiments highlight how the referrer URL of a browsing session can help to understand the user behavior, predicting the navigation pattern and improving the next-hop recommendation in news browsing. A recommender that uses the weights of the *BrowseGraph* edges appears to be an effective way to anticipate user needs and keep them longer on site, especially for people coming from social media. This is particularly important, as it as been shown [2, 17, 28] that social media platforms are playing an increasingly important role on the news propagation[8] and they are becoming event more critical connections with the news world.

6. CONCLUSION

We present an analysis of the browsing traces extracted from a very large viewlog from Yahoo News, introducing the definition of a special case of the *BrowseGraph* model, namely the *ReferrerGraph*, that consists of a subgraph built from the browsing sessions with homogeneous referrer URL. We find that the browsing graphs of news sites are well-connected despite the tendency to rapid staleness of con-

[8] http://bit.ly/1bQG1uL

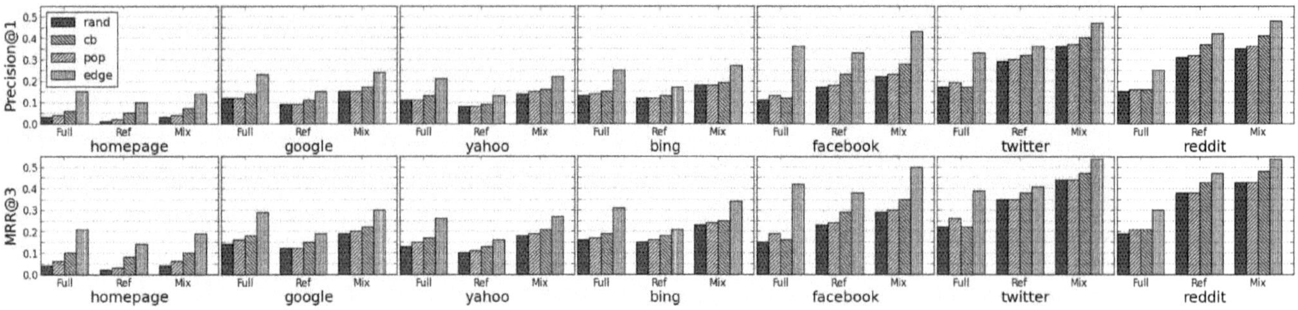

Figure 8: Prediction accuracy for the 9 recommendation strategies, computed for the sessions in each *ReferrerGraph* separately.

tent and to the typically short user sessions. *ReferrerGraphs* built considering 9 major domains appear to be quite non-overlapping, to cover articles of different topics, and to lead to the emergence of different sets of most popular articles. Traffic traces coming from different families of referrer domains have different time consumption patterns: for example, the sessions originating from search engines and social networks tend to consume content slightly after the visits coming from the news site homepage, and with some bursty consumption peaks for social networks caused by occasional spread of viral stories. Last, we build on our analytical findings by showing that the *ReferrerGraph* can be applied to effective article recommendation in a cold-start scenario. In terms of modeling our prediction setup could be extended using continuous-time models, and a comparison between *BrowseGraphs* built at multiple time scales is also a natural extension. Our experiments mainly prove the point that the referrer domain has a big predictive potential that should be considered when building any browsing user model. As our goal is limited to the prediction of the *next page* visited, more general content-based techniques for cold-start [1, 27] are not directly comparable with our approach, although a more extensive comparison would be valuable to gain a broader view on the problem. At any rate, we hope the findings highlighted in this paper lead to a greater consideration of the referrer domain with particular focus on cold-start problems.

Acknowledgments

This research is partially supported by the Ministry of Science and Innovation of Spain.

7. REFERENCES

[1] D. Agarwal and B.-C. Chen. flda: Matrix factorization through latent dirichlet allocation. In *WSDM*. ACM, 2010.

[2] C. Castillo, M. El-Haddad, J. Pfeffer, and M. Stempeck. Characterizing the life cycle of online news stories using social media reactions. In *CSCW*. ACM, 2014.

[3] L. Chiarandini, P. Grabowicz, M. Trevisiol, and A. Jaimes. Leveraging browsing patterns for topic discovery and photostream recommendation. In *ICWSM*. AAAI, 2013.

[4] L. Chiarandini, M. Trevisiol, and A. Jaimes. Discovering Social Photo Navigation Patterns. In *ICME*. ACM, 2012.

[5] A. S. Das, M. Datar, A. Garg, and S. Rajaram. Google news personalization. In *WWW*. ACM, 2007.

[6] G. M. Del Corso, A. Gullí, and F. Romani. Ranking a stream of news. In *WWW*. ACM, 2005.

[7] F. Figueiredo, F. Benevenuto, and J. Almeida. The Tube over Time : Characterizing Popularity Growth of YouTube Videos. In *WSDM*, 2011.

[8] J. Hu, H.-J. Zeng, H. Li, C. Niu, and Z. Chen. Demographic prediction based on user's browsing behavior. In *WWW*, 2007.

[9] R. Kumar and A. Tomkins. A characterization of online browsing behavior. In *WWW*. ACM, 2010.

[10] L. Li, D. Wang, T. Li, D. Knox, and B. Padmanabhan. SCENE: a scalable two-stage personalized news recommendation system. In *SIGIR*. ACM, 2011.

[11] C. Lin, R. Xie, L. Li, Z. Huang, and T. Li. Premise: personalized news recommendation via implicit social experts. In X. wen Chen, G. Lebanon, H. Wang, and M. J. Zaki, editors, *CIKM*, pages 1607–1611. ACM, 2012.

[12] J. Liu, P. Dolan, and E. R. Pedersen. Personalized news recommendation based on click behavior. In *IUI*. ACM, 2010.

[13] M. Liu, R. Cai, M. Zhang, and L. Zhang. User browsing behavior-driven web crawling. In *CIKM*. ACM, 2011.

[14] Y. Liu, B. Gao, T.-Y. Liu, Y. Zhang, Z. Ma, S. He, and H. Li. BrowseRank: letting web users vote for page importance. *SIGIR*, 2008.

[15] Y. Liu, M. Zhang, S. Ma, and L. Ru. User Browsing Graph : Structure , Evolution and Application. In *WSDM*, 2009.

[16] Y. Lv, T. Moon, P. Kolari, Z. Zheng, X. Wang, and Y. Chang. Learning to model relatedness for news recommendation. In *WWW*. ACM, 2011.

[17] R. M. C. McCreadie, C. Macdonald, and I. Ounis. News article ranking: leveraging the wisdom of bloggers. In *RIAO*, 2010.

[18] A. L. Montgomery, S. Li, K. Srinivasan, and J. C. Liechty. Modeling online browsing and path analysis using clickstream data. *Marketing Science*, 23(4):579–595, 2004.

[19] A. M. Rashid, G. Karypis, and J. Riedl. Learning Preferences of New Users in Recommender Systems : An Information Theoretic Approach. In *ACM SIGKDD Explorations Newsletter*, volume 10, page 90, Dec. 2008.

[20] A. Said and A. Bellogín. News Recommendation in the Wild : Recommendation Algorithms in the NRS Challenge. 2013.

[21] G. Shaw, Y. Xu, and S. Geva. Using Association Rules to Solve the Cold-Start Problem in Recommender Systems. In *Advances in Knowledge Discovery and Data ...*, pages 21–24, 2010.

[22] H. Sobhanam and a. K. Mariappan. Addressing cold start problem in recommender systems using association rules and clustering technique. In *ICCCI*, pages 1–5. Ieee, Jan. 2013.

[23] A. Spink, M. Park, B. J. Jansen, and J. Pedersen. Multitasking during web search sessions. *Inf. Process. Manage.*, 42(1):264–275, 2006.

[24] I. Trajkovski. Pagerank-Like Algorithm for Ranking News Stories and News Portals. *ICT Innovations*, 231:87–96, 2013.

[25] M. Trevisiol, L. Chiarandini, L. M. Aiello, and A. Jaimes. In *SIGIR*. ACM, 2012.

[26] M. Tsagkias and R. Blanco. Language intent models for inferring user browsing behavior. In *SIGIR*, page 335, New York, New York, USA, 2012. ACM Press.

[27] M. Tsagkias and R. Blanco. Language intent models for inferring user browsing behavior. In *SIGIR*. ACM, 2012.

[28] M. Tsagkias, M. de Rijke, and W. Weerkamp. Linking online news and social media. In *WSDM*. ACM, 2011.

[29] W. Wagner. Steven bird, ewan klein and edward loper: Natural language processing with python, analyzing text with natural language toolkit. *Lang.Resour.Eval.*, 44(4):421–424, 2010.

[30] C. Wang, M. Zhang, L. Ru, and S. Ma. Automatic online news topic ranking using media focus and user attention based on aging theory. In *CIKM*. ACM, 2008.

[31] X. Yang, Y. Guo, and Y. Liu. Bayesian-inference based recommendation in online social networks. In *IEEE INFOCOM*, pages 551–555. Ieee, Apr. 2011.

Item Cold-Start Recommendations: Learning Local Collective Embeddings

Martin Saveski*
Yahoo Labs, Barcelona
msaveski@yahoo-inc.com

Amin Mantrach
Yahoo Labs, Barcelona
amantrac@yahoo-inc.com

ABSTRACT

Recommender systems suggest to users items that they might like (e.g., news articles, songs, movies) and, in doing so, they help users deal with information overload and enjoy a personalized experience. One of the main problems of these systems is the item cold-start, i.e., when a new item is introduced in the system and no past information is available, then no effective recommendations can be produced. The item cold-start is a very common problem in practice: modern online platforms have hundreds of new items published every day. To address this problem, we propose to learn *Local Collective Embeddings*: a matrix factorization that exploits items' properties and past user preferences while enforcing the manifold structure exhibited by the collective embeddings. We present a learning algorithm based on multiplicative update rules that are efficient and easy to implement. The experimental results on two item cold-start use cases: news recommendation and email recipient recommendation, demonstrate the effectiveness of this approach and show that it significantly outperforms six state-of-the-art methods for item cold-start.

1. INTRODUCTION

Recommender systems are aimed to help users of online platforms to deal with the large volumes of information and to provide them a personalized experience. This is achieved by suggesting items of interest to the users based on their explicit and implicit preferences. Recommender systems use a number of different technologies, but may be broadly classified into two groups: content-based and collaborative filtering systems. Content-based systems examine the properties of the items and recommend items which are similar to the ones the user preferred in the past. They model the taste of a user by building a user profile based on the properties of the items the user liked, and use the profile to compute the similarity with new items. Items which are most similar to the user's profile are recommended. Collaborative filtering systems, on the other hand, ignore the properties of the items and base their recommendations on community preferences. They recommend items that users with similar tastes and preferences liked in the past. Two users are considered similar if they have many items in common.

One of the main problems for recommender systems is the cold-start problem, i.e., when a new item or user is introduced in the system. In this study we focus on the problem of producing effective recommendations for new items: the item cold-start. Collaborative filtering systems suffer from this problem as they rely on the previous ratings of the users. Content based approaches, on the other hand, may still produce recommendations using the description of the items and are the default solution to the item cold-start. However, they tend to achieve lower accuracy and, in practice, they are seldom the only choice.

The problem of item cold-start is of great practical importance because of two main reasons. First, modern online platforms publish hundreds of new items everyday and effectively recommending them is essential for keeping the users continuously engaged. Second, collaborative filtering methods are at the core of most recommendation engines, as they tend to achieve the state-of-the-art accuracy [1]. However, to produce recommendations at the expected accuracy they require that items are rated by a sufficient number of users. Therefore, it is crucial for every collaborative recommender to reach this state as soon as possible. Having methods that produce accurate recommendations for new items will allow enough feedback to be collected in a short amount of time, making effective collaborative recommendations possible.

Recently, matrix factorization techniques have been extensively used in the recommendation systems and topic modelling literature. Many collaborative filtering systems approximate the collaborative matrix by applying techniques such as Singular Value Decomposition (SVD) or UV decomposition [20]. Similar matrix factorization techniques have been used to discover topics in document collections by decomposing the content, i.e., document-term matrix. Non-negative Matrix Factorization (NMF) is one such approach that factorizes the document-term matrix in two non-negative, low-rank matrices, where one matrix corresponds to the topics in the collection and the other represents the extent to which documents belong to these topics. Due to the non-negativity constraints, NMF produces a so-called "additive parts-based" representation of the data that increases the sparsity and interpretability of the hidden factors [22].

In this paper, we propose a new hybrid recommendation approach that exploits both the properties of the items and

* This work was done while the author was an intern at Yahoo.

RecSys'14, October 6–10, 2014, Foster City, Silicon Valley, CA, USA.

http://dx.doi.org/10.1145/2645710.2645751.

the similarity of the user preferences. We introduce *Local Collective Embeddings* (LCE), a collective matrix factorization technique that collectively decomposes the content and the collaborative matrices in a common low-dimensional space while preserving the local geometrical structure of the data.

Given the description of a new item (e.g., the content of a news article), we may project it on the common low-dimensional space and infer the users that are most likely to be interested in it. By doing so, we are able to overcome the item cold-start problem. Moreover, LCE provides a natural way of explaining the recommendations – in terms of user's affinity to topics. Finally, we perform an extensive experimental evaluation of the models on two item cold-start use cases: email recipient recommendation (based on explicit feedback) and news recommendation (based on implicit feedback). We show that the proposed models outperform six state-of-the-art baseline approaches.

Our contributions in this paper can be summarized as follows:

- We introduce a new method for recommendation, LCE, that combines the content and collaborative information in a unified matrix factorization framework while exploiting the local geometrical structure of the data;
- We propose a simple and efficient learning algorithm, based on multiplicative update rules and prove its convergence;
- We conduct an extensive experimental study and we show that the proposed methods outperform six state-of-the-art methods for item-cold start recommendation.

2. RELATED WORK

In this section, we briefly describe several hybrid recommender systems that can handle the item cold-start scenario.

Soboroff [28] proposed a technique based on Latent Semantic Indexing (LSI) for combining the collaborative filtering input and the document content for recommendation of textual items. The method builds a content profile for each user, as a linear combination of the preferred documents, and applies LSI to discover topics in the collection and implicitly learn commonalities among the user profiles. Incoming documents are projected on the LSI space and compared to the user profiles. The documents are recommended to the users with the most similar profiles. The author argues that applying LSI on the user profiles instead of the documents allows one to take into account the collaborative input and consequently improves the recommendation performance. However, the system is not evaluated in the cold-start scenario. In section 5, we compare this technique against the method we propose.

Schein *et al.* [25] propose a probabilistic model for cold-start recommendations that is very similar to the one proposed by Soboroff. Their approach extends the work of Hoffman and Puzicha [18] which models the joint distribution of users and items through an aspect model that clusters users and items in a latent space. In order to deal with new items, instead of modelling the joint distribution of users and items, the authors propose to model the joint distribution of users and content features. At query time a "folding-in"' technique [17] is used to embed new items into the latent space so that items can be recommended. After careful analysis one may notice that the technique essentially boils down to building user profiles and applying pLSA to discover latent factors. Taking into account that previous studies have shown the correspondence between pLSA and NMF [16], one may clearly distinguish between this approach and our proposal. Instead of explicitly building user profiles and finding latent features, we discover a latent space common to both the content and collaborative information that allows us to link one to the other.

Singh and Gordon [27] propose the idea of collective matrix factorization, a general framework for multi-relational factorization models. They subsume models on any number of relations as long as their loss function is a twice differentiable decomposable loss. In their work, they address both rating prediction and item recommendation. The matrix factorization approach proposed in this work is based on a similar idea of collective factorization. However, we enforce non-negativity constraints on the factorization to obtain sparse and interpretable factors, and we consider the specific scenario of cold-start recommendations.

Shmueli *et al.* [26] consider a similar scenario of news recommendation (Section 5.3), i.e., predicting the articles a user is most likely to comment on. They combine content-based and collaborative filtering approach using a latent factor model. The odds that a user will comment an article are estimated as the inner product of the user and article factors, where the article factors are represented as the sum of the latent factors associated with the textual content (tags–named entities) and the commenters. A modification of the model for real-time scenarios is presented in [4]. The authors show that the recommendation accuracy grows as the number of commenters grows. However, in an item cold-start scenario articles are not yet associated with commenters, thus an article can only be represented with the latent factors of the textual tags.

Exploiting the local geometric structure of the data to discover better low-dimensional representations has been investigated by Cai *et al.* [11]. Inspired by the success of using the nearest neighbor graph for label propagation in semi-supervised learning, they propose a clustering technique. The algorithm favours factorizations for which similar instances have similar low-dimensional representations. The authors show that, by imposing this constraint, they outperform classical clustering and factorization techniques. In this work, we impose such geometrical constraints but for collective factorization for which we can handle multiple data sources, i.e., the content and collaborative data matrices.

Finally, it is worth noting the 2011 ECML-PKDD Discovery Challenge which focused on cold-start recommendations of video lectures [5].

3. LOCAL COLLECTIVE EMBEDDINGS

In this section we formally define the item cold-start problem, we explain the intuition behind learning local collective embeddings, and finally we show how such embeddings can be learnt and used for prediction.

3.1 Problem Statement

The scenario we consider is the item cold-start recommendation, where we would like to suggest new items – for which no interests has been expressed so far – to potentially interested users. Given a new item, its corresponding description and the patterns of past activities of the users, we want to retrieve the users who are most likely to manifest interest in this item. More formally, we can define the problem as follows. At training time, we are given a collection of n items described by: (1) a set of m properties stored in a matrix $\mathbf{X_s} \in \mathbb{R}^{n \times m}$, where a row corresponds to an item and a column to an item property; and (2) a set of u users stored in a matrix $\mathbf{X_u} \in \mathbb{R}^{n \times u}$, where a cell (i, j) indicates if the user j has shown interest in item i. At test time, we are given a new item $\mathbf{q}$ with description $\mathbf{q}_s \in \mathbb{R}^{1 \times m}$, and our goal is to predict $\mathbf{q}_u \in \mathbb{R}^{1 \times u}$, i.e., to score how likely is a user to show interest in the new item.

3.2 Intuition Behind Collective Factorization

Given the problem defined, items are associated with a description and a set of users who consumed them. In the case of news, each news article is described by the set of words it contains and by all the users that commented on it. This information is then represented with two matrices, a document-term matrix $\mathbf{X_s} \in \mathbb{R}^{n \times v}$, and a document-user matrix $\mathbf{X_u} \in \mathbb{R}^{n \times u}$, where n is the number of documents, v is the vocabulary size and u is the number of users. The document-term matrix ($\mathbf{X_s}$) may be a boolean matrix or may represent the TF-IDF scores of the words in the document. On the other hand, the entries of the document-user matrix ($\mathbf{X_u}$) reflect whether a given user commented on a given article. If we factorize $\mathbf{X_s}$ in two lower-dimensional matrices, we will discover the topics that appear in the documents and the extent to which each document belongs to these topics. Similarly, factorizing $\mathbf{X_u}$ leads to the discovery of user communities and the extent to which each document triggers interest within the communities. However, if factorized independently each factorization will represent a different latent space and there will be no correspondence between the topics and the communities. The idea of LCE is that both, documents and users, should be represented in a common latent space. In other words, each factor can be described by a set of words (i.e., a topic) but also by a set of users (i.e., a community). To achieve this, we collectively factorize $\mathbf{X_s}$ and $\mathbf{X_u}$ and enforce a low-dimensional representation in a common space. Additionally, to achieve an additive effect we impose non-negativity constraints that lead to interpretable and sparse latent representations.

More formally, given the matrices $\mathbf{X_s}$ and $\mathbf{X_u}$, we define the following optimization problem:

$$\min : J = \frac{1}{2}[\alpha||\mathbf{X_s} - \mathbf{W}\mathbf{H_s}||_{\mathrm{F}}^2 + (1-\alpha)||\mathbf{X_u} - \mathbf{W}\mathbf{H_u}||_{\mathrm{F}}^2 + \\ + \lambda(||\mathbf{W}||_{\mathrm{F}}^2 + ||\mathbf{H_s}||_{\mathrm{F}}^2 + ||\mathbf{H_u}||_{\mathrm{F}}^2)] \quad (1)$$

$$s.t. \quad \mathbf{W} \geq \mathbf{0}, \mathbf{H_s} \geq \mathbf{0}, \mathbf{H_u} \geq \mathbf{0}$$

The first two terms correspond to the factorization of the matrices $\mathbf{X_s}$ and $\mathbf{X_u}$. The common latent space representation is achieved by using the same matrix $\mathbf{W}$ in the decompositions of both $\mathbf{X_s}$ and $\mathbf{X_u}$. $\alpha \in [0, 1]$ is a hyper-parameter that controls the importance of each factorization. Setting $\alpha = 0.5$ gives equal importance to both factorizations, while values of $\alpha > 0.5$ (or $\alpha < 0.5$) give more importance to the factorization of $\mathbf{X_s}$ (or $\mathbf{X_u}$). The remaining terms are Tikhonov (Frobenius norm) regularization of $\mathbf{W}$, $\mathbf{H_u}$, and $\mathbf{H_s}$, controlled by the hyper-parameter $\lambda \geq 0$. It is used to enforce smoothness of the solution and avoid overfitting.

3.3 Exploiting Locality

When performing collective factorization, as in Eq. (1), we attempt to find a common low-dimensional space that is optimized for the linear approximation of the data from both views. We make an implicit assumption that the data from both views is drawn from a common distribution. One may hope that additional knowledge of this distribution can be exploited to discover a better low-dimensional space. A natural assumption could be that: if two data points x_i and x_j, in any view, are close in the intrinsic geometry of the distribution, then their representations in the low-dimensional space should also be close to each other. This assumption is commonly referred to as the *manifold assumption* and plays an essential role in algorithms for dimensionality reduction [8] and semi-supervised learning [9].

In reality the geometric structure of the distribution is not known and cannot be directly used. However, recent studies on spectral graph theory [12] and manifold learning [7] have shown that the local geometric structure can be effectively modeled through a nearest neighbor graph on a scatter of data points. Consider a graph with n nodes where each node represents a data point. For each point we find the p nearest neighbors and we connect the corresponding nodes in the graph. The edges may be binary (1 if one of the nearest neighbors, 0 otherwise) or may be weighted (e.g., cosine similarity). This results in a matrix $\mathbf{A}$ which can later be used to measure the local closeness of two points x_i and x_j.

Recall that the collective factorization maps each data point x_i into a low-dimensional representation w_i (a row of the matrix $\mathbf{W}$). A natural way to measure the distance between two low dimensional representations, given the choice of a loss function, is to compute the Euclidean distance: $||w_i - w_j||^2$. Using the above defined weight matrix $\mathbf{A}$ we may measure the local smoothness of the low dimensional representation as:

$$\begin{aligned} S &= \frac{1}{2}\sum_{i,j=1}^{n} ||w_i - w_j||^2 \mathbf{A}_{ij} \\ &= \sum_{i=1}^{n}(w_i^T w_i)\mathbf{D}_{ii} - \sum_{i,j=1}^{n}(w_i^T w_j)\mathbf{A}_{ij} \\ &= \mathrm{Tr}(\mathbf{W}^{\mathrm{T}}\mathbf{D}\mathbf{W}) - \mathrm{Tr}(\mathbf{W}^{\mathrm{T}}\mathbf{A}\mathbf{W}) = \mathrm{Tr}(\mathbf{W}^{\mathrm{T}}\mathbf{L}\mathbf{W}), \end{aligned}$$

where $\mathbf{D}$ is a diagonal matrix whose entries are the row sums of $\mathbf{A}$ (or column, as $\mathbf{A}$ is symmetric), i.e., $\mathbf{D}_{ii} = \sum_i \mathbf{A}_{ij}$; $\mathbf{L} = \mathbf{D} - \mathbf{A}$ is called the Laplacian matrix of the graph [12] and $\mathrm{Tr}(\bullet)$ is the trace operator.

3.4 LCE Optimization Problem

Given the above, we modify the formulation of in Eq. (1) as to enforce locality when discovering the factors. This leads to the following optimization problem:

$$\min : J = \frac{1}{2}[\alpha||\mathbf{X_s} - \mathbf{W}\mathbf{H_s}||_{\mathrm{F}}^2 + (1-\alpha)||\mathbf{X_u} - \mathbf{W}\mathbf{H_u}||_{\mathrm{F}}^2 + \\ + \beta\mathrm{Tr}(\mathbf{W}^{\mathrm{T}}\mathbf{L}\mathbf{W}) + \lambda(||\mathbf{W}||_{\mathrm{F}}^2 + ||\mathbf{H_s}||_{\mathrm{F}}^2 + ||\mathbf{H_u}||_{\mathrm{F}}^2)]$$

$$s.t. \quad \mathbf{W} \geq \mathbf{0}, \mathbf{H_s} \geq \mathbf{0}, \mathbf{H_u} \geq \mathbf{0}, \quad (2)$$

where $\mathbf{L}$ is the Laplacian matrix of the graph, and β is a hyper-parameter which controls the extent to which locality is enforced. The hyper-parameters α and λ have the same semantics as in Eq. (1).

3.5 Learning Algorithm

The optimization problem defined above is non-convex in terms of all parameters ($\mathbf{W}$, $\mathbf{H_s}$, $\mathbf{H_u}$) together. Thus, it is unrealistic to expect an algorithm to find the global minimum. In what follows, we derive an iterative algorithm based on multiplicative update rules which can achieve a stationary point.

The partial derivatives of J w.r.t. $\mathbf{W}$, $\mathbf{H_s}$, and $\mathbf{H_u}$ are:

$$\nabla_{\mathbf{W}} J = \alpha \mathbf{W}\mathbf{H_s}\mathbf{H_s}^{\mathrm{T}} - \alpha \mathbf{X_s}\mathbf{H_s}^{\mathrm{T}} + (1-\alpha)\mathbf{W}\mathbf{H_u}\mathbf{H_u}^{\mathrm{T}} - (1-\alpha)\mathbf{X_u}\mathbf{H_u}^{\mathrm{T}} + \beta \mathbf{L}\mathbf{W} + \lambda \mathbf{W}, \quad (3)$$

$$\nabla_{\mathbf{H_s}} J = \alpha \mathbf{W}^{\mathrm{T}}\mathbf{W}\mathbf{H_s} - \alpha \mathbf{W}^{\mathrm{T}}\mathbf{X_s} + \lambda \mathbf{H_s} \quad (4)$$

$$\nabla_{\mathbf{H_u}} J = (1-\alpha)\mathbf{W}^{\mathrm{T}}\mathbf{W}\mathbf{H_u} - (1-\alpha)\mathbf{W}^{\mathrm{T}}\mathbf{X_u} + \lambda \mathbf{H_u} \quad (5)$$

Applying the Karush-Kuhn-Tucker (KKT) first-order optimality conditions to J [13], we derive:

$$\mathbf{W} \geq \mathbf{0}, \quad \mathbf{Hs} \geq \mathbf{0}, \quad \mathbf{Hu} \geq \mathbf{0}, \quad (6)$$

$$\nabla_{\mathbf{W}} J \geq \mathbf{0}, \quad \nabla_{\mathbf{H_s}} J \geq \mathbf{0}, \quad \nabla_{\mathbf{H_u}} J \geq \mathbf{0}, \quad (7)$$

$$\mathbf{W} \odot \nabla_{\mathbf{W}} J = \mathbf{0}, \quad \mathbf{Hs} \odot \nabla_{\mathbf{H_s}} J = \mathbf{0}, \quad \mathbf{Hu} \odot \nabla_{\mathbf{H_u}} J = \mathbf{0}, \quad (8)$$

where $\odot$ corresponds to the element-wise matrix multiplication operator.

Substituting the derivatives of J from Equations (3), (4) and (5) in Equation (8) leads to the following update rules:

$$\mathbf{W} \leftarrow \mathbf{W} \odot \frac{[\alpha \mathbf{X_s}\mathbf{H_s}^{\mathrm{T}} + (1-\alpha)\mathbf{X_u}\mathbf{H_u}^{\mathrm{T}} + \beta \mathbf{A}\mathbf{W}]}{[\alpha \mathbf{W}\mathbf{H_s}\mathbf{H_s}^{\mathrm{T}} + (1-\alpha)\mathbf{W}\mathbf{H_u}\mathbf{H_u}^{\mathrm{T}} + \beta \mathbf{D}\mathbf{W} + \lambda \mathbf{W}]}, \quad (9)$$

$$\mathbf{H_s} \leftarrow \mathbf{H_s} \odot \frac{[\alpha \mathbf{W}^{\mathrm{T}}\mathbf{X_s}]}{[\alpha \mathbf{W}^{\mathrm{T}}\mathbf{W}\mathbf{H_s} + \lambda \mathbf{H_s}]}, \quad (10)$$

$$\mathbf{H_u} \leftarrow \mathbf{H_u} \odot \frac{[(1-\alpha)\mathbf{W}^{\mathrm{T}}\mathbf{X_u}]}{[(1-\alpha)\mathbf{W}^{\mathrm{T}}\mathbf{W}\mathbf{H_u} + \lambda \mathbf{H_u}]}, \quad (11)$$

where $\div$ denotes the element-wise matrix division operator. We define the following theorem:

THEOREM 1. *The objective function J in Equation* (2) *is nonincreasing under the update rules in Equations* (9), (10), *and* (11). *The objective function J is invariant under these updates if and only if $\mathbf{H_u}$, $\mathbf{H_s}$ and $\mathbf{W}$ are at a stationary point of the function.*

A detailed proof of the above theorem is provided as supplement material[1].

3.6 Inference

Once the model has been trained to learn $\mathbf{W}$, $\mathbf{H_s}$ and $\mathbf{H_u}$, we can use these factors for prediction. For instance, given the bag-of-words vector of a new news article $\mathbf{q}_s$, we can predict the users that are most likely to post a comment, i.e., $\mathbf{q}_u$. To do so, we project the document vector $\mathbf{q}_s$ to the common latent space by solving the overdetermined system $\mathbf{q}_s = \mathbf{w}\mathbf{H_s}$ using the least squares method (with a projection to 0 of the negative values, see [10]). The vector $\mathbf{w}$, computed online, captures the factors – in the common latent space – that explain the observed news article $\mathbf{q}_s$. Then, by using this low dimensional vector $\mathbf{w}$ we may infer the missing part of the query: $\mathbf{q}_u \leftarrow \mathbf{w}\mathbf{H_u}$. Each element of $\mathbf{q}_u$ represents a score of how likely it is that the user will comment the new article. Then, given these scores, we may rank the users.

[1] `https://github.com/msaveski/LCE/blob/master/Th1Proof.pdf`

4. EXPLAINING RECOMMENDATIONS

Good recommendations are not only accurate but also transparent, i.e., supported with explanations. This allows the end users to understand the reasoning behind the recommendations and helps them build trust towards the system.

LCE provides a natural way of explaining recommendations in terms of users' affinity to topics. To obtain the topical interest profile for a user i we can construct a vector $\mathbf{x_u} \in \mathbb{R}^{1\times u}$ (u is the number of users), where all elements are equal to zero except $[\mathbf{x_u}]_i = 1$, and solve for $\mathbf{w}$ in $\mathbf{x_u} = \mathbf{w}\mathbf{H_u}$; every element of $\mathbf{w}$ quantifies the user's affinity to a specific topic. Topics may be presented using the top-k terms or by automatic annotation (e.g., [21]). Furthermore, by computing $\mathbf{x_s} \leftarrow \mathbf{w}\mathbf{H_s}$ ($\mathbf{x_s} \in \mathbb{R}^{1\times m}$), we obtain the association between the user and every word in the vocabulary; we may present this information to the user, e.g., using a word cloud.

To debug and track down the source of unexpected behaviour of the system one may examine the link between topics and communities (e.g., by looking at the top words and users). This link may also be exploited in other applications, such as advertising, where advertisers can easily identify target users based on their topical interests.

5. EXPERIMENTAL EVALUATION

In this section we present a series of experiments to evaluate the performance of LCE in the item cold-start scenario. We first describe the baselines and then we compare them with LCE in two item cold-start use cases: email recipient recommendation and news recommendation. Finally, we analyse the parameter settings and the running times.

5.1 Baselines for Comparison

We compare LCE to six other approaches: pure content-based recommender, content-topic-based recommender, LSI applied on the author profiles, author topic-model, learning attribute-to-feature mappings, and fLDA.

Content-based Recommender (CB). We build a profile for each user based on the properties of the items preferred in the past. Experimentally we find that weighting each item inversely proportional to the number of users that interacted with the item leads to an improved performance. Thus, in the user profile, very popular items are given less importance, while less popular items are given more importance. More formally, a user profile U is defined as: $U = \sum_{i\in I}(\vec{v_i}/freq_i)$, where I is the set of items the user interacted with in the past, $\vec{v_i}$ is the description of item i and $freq_i$ is the number of users that interacted with i. At test time, we rank the items by computing the cosine similarity between the new items and the user profiles.

Content-topic-based Recommender (CTB). We extract topics from the content of the items by applying NMF and we describe each item as a mixture of the topics extracted. We then build a topical profile for each user based on the topics of the items the user interacted with in the past. At test time, we infer the topics of the new items and we rank the items based on the cosine similarity between the item's topics and the users' topical profiles. The CTB recommender allows us to investigate the importance of performing joint factorization of both the content and collaborative matrix, instead of factorizing only the content matrix.

LSI on the User Profiles (UP-LSI). We apply the hybrid recommendation system proposed in [28] (see Section 2). The approach combines the content and collaborative information by building user profiles and applying Latent Semantic Indexing (LSI) to discover latent factors. At test time, the new items are projected in the latent space and compared to the user profiles. Finally, the items are recommended to the users with the most similar profiles.

Author-topic Model (ATM). The author-topic model [23] is a generative probabilistic model which extends LDA to include authorship information. It associates each author with a multinomial distribution over topics, and each topic with multinomial distribution over words. As the authors point out, the model may not only be used to find the topics associated with the authors, but also to predict the authors of unobserved documents. In the email recipient recommendation experiment we model the recipients as authors, while in the news recommendation scenario we model the users as authors. As recommended, we set the parameters as: $\alpha = 50/k$, where k is the number of topics, $\beta = 0.01$, and we perform 500 iterations of the Gibbs Sampler.

Learning Attribute-to-Feature Mappings (BPR-kNN). This method [15] handles the cold-start in two steps: (1) factorizing the collaborative matrix to learn latent factor representation of the users and items, (2) learning a mapping between the user/item attributes and the corresponding latent factors. When a new user/item arrives in the system, the mapping from (2) is used to infer the factors from the attributes, and then the factors are used to make predictions. As proposed by the authors, we used Bayesian Personalized Ranking (BPR) to factorize the collaborative matrix. To learn the mappings we used the K-Nearest-Neighbor and BPR optimization; however, the kNN mapping was superior in all cases and thus we report the results for only for kNN mapping. This is consistent with their experimental results. We test with different number of latent factors $k \in \{100, 200, 300, 400, 500, 600, 700, 800, 900, 1000\}$.

fLDA. Is a latent factor model proposed in [3] and it is an extension of the Regression Based Latent Factor model [2] for applications where "bag-of-words" representation of items is natural. The main idea is regularizing the user and item factors simultaneously through the user features and the words associated with the items. The user ratings are modelled as user's affinity to the item's topics, where the user's affinity to topics and topic assignments to items are learned jointly in supervised fashion. In our experiments we only use the item feature as user features are not available. As recommended by the authors, we run 20 EM iterations with 100 samples, drawn after 10 burn-in samples. In the email recommendation experiment, we test for $k \in \{10, 25, 50\}$ factors, while for the news recommendation experiment we test only $k = 10$ due to the long running times.

5.2 Email Recipient Recommendation

When people write emails they do not necessarily start by filling in the recipient address (i.e., the "to" field), but may start by writing the body of the message. Given the content of the message and the messaging habits of the user, i.e., with whom the user exchanged messages with similar content in past, we would like to predict the most likely recipients of the new message. In this experiment, we test

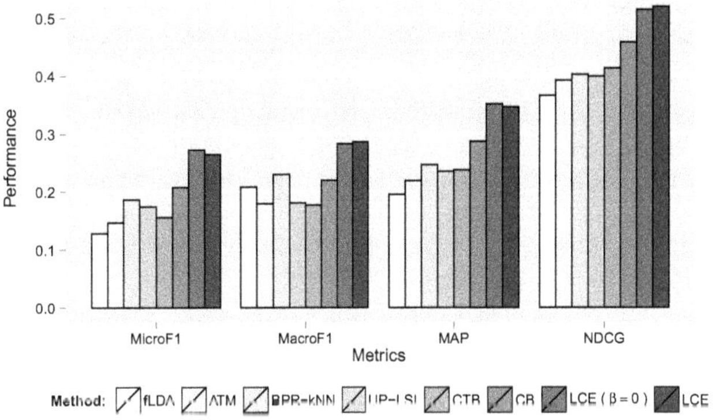

Figure 1: Comparison of the different methods on the Enron dataset.

the accuracy of the recipient recommendations produced by LCE against the six baseline techniques.

Dataset. The data is composed of email messages released during investigation of the Federal Energy Regulatory Commission against the Enron Corporation. We consider the 10 largest mailboxes and within each mailbox the emails sent by the owner. There are 36,010 emails sent to 4,984 recipients. The size of the vocabularies for each mailbox ranges from 12,375 to 56,193 unique tokens. The messages have been preprocessed by removing the headers (from/to/cc fields), converting all tokens to lower case and removing numbers, stop-words and infrequent tokens (appearing < 5 times).

Evaluation Metrics. The output of the algorithms is a ranking of the past recipients of how likely they are to be recipients of the new email. The feedback from the users is explicit, i.e., we have ground truth of who are the recipients of the mail as specified by the user. To evaluate the ranking produced by each algorithm we use the state-of-the-art metrics from Information Retrieval: Micro and Macro F1, Mean Average Precision (MAP), and Normalized Discounted Cumulative Gain (NDCG) [6].

Evaluation Protocol. As the data is intrinsically influenced by time we sort the 10 mailboxes chronologically. We divide the messages in 80% training and 20% testing, resulting in 10 independent train/test subsets. Only the recipients that appear in the training period are considered as potential receivers. We tune the hyper-parameters of the methods on independent validation set, 10% of the training set. Finally, we evaluate the statistical significance of the differences in performance by using a Wilcoxon signed rank test [14].

Results. Figure 1 shows the average performance of each method across the 10 mailboxes. LCE performs better than the other methods in all measures with differences ranging from 5%-15%. All differences are statistically significant (Wilcoxon signed rank test, $p < 0.05$). Imposing locality leads to small performance improvements in some measures, however the differences are not statistically significant. This indicates that nearest neighbor graph does not bring additional information in the case of emails. One explanation may be that emails are user generated content and as such contain a lot of noise, such as misspellings or informal expressions, that leads to inaccurate nearest neighbor graphs.

5.3 News Recommendation

To improve the user experience, online news platforms allow users to engage with articles by posting comments. Moreover, to encourage user engagement on the platform the users are recommended articles that they may be interested in. We consider the item cold-start scenario, i.e., when a new article is published and none of the users have commented on it yet. Thus, given the content of the new articles and the past commenting patterns we would like to recommend to the users the articles that they are most likely to comment.

Dataset. We consider a random sample of news articles and the corresponding comments posted on the Yahoo! News website in a period of 40 days. The dataset contains ~41K articles, ~3.5M comments posted by ~650K users. The size of the vocabulary is ~60K (i.e., unique tokens in all articles) and ~9M tokens in total. The content of the articles is preprocessed such that all tokens are converted to lower case, and stop-words, digits, punctuation, short (< 3 characters) and infrequent (appearing < 3 times) tokens are removed.

Evaluation Metrics. Similar to the previous experiment, the output of each algorithm is a ranking. In this experiment, however, we do not have an explicit feedback of which news articles were undesired by the users. While, commenting an article is an evidence of the user's interest in it, the absence of a comment is not an indication that the article was undesired, as not commenting may stem from multiple different reasons. Therefore, we adopt the average percentile ranking, a measure proposed in [19] and widely used to evaluate ranking based on implicit feedback (e.g., [24]). We define $rank_{u,i}$ as the percentile ranking of article i in the ranked list of articles for the user u; if $rank_{u,i} = 0\%$, then the article i is predicted to be the most interesting for u, while $rank_{u,i} = 100\%$ implies that the article is predicted to be the least interesting. Our quality measure is then the total average percentile ranking of an article:

$$\overline{rank} = \frac{\sum_{u,i} comment_{u,i} \cdot rank_{u,i}}{\sum_{u,i} comment_{u,i}},$$

where $comment_{u,i}$ is an indicator function that equals to: 1 if the user u commented on article i; and 0 otherwise. The lower $\overline{rank}$, the better the quality of the ranking. For random predictions, the expected value of $\overline{rank}$ is 50%. Thus, if $\overline{rank} < 50\%$, then the algorithm is better than random. To ease illustration, we convert the percentile ranking into *ranking accuracy* (RA). That is 1 (best/ideal predictions), if the percentile ranking is 0%; and it is 0 (random predictions), if the percentile ranking is 50%:

$$Ranking\ Accuracy = \frac{50\% - \overline{rank}}{50\%}.$$

We evaluate the Ranking Accuracy (RA) at different positions: 3, 5, 7 and 10.

Evaluation Protocol. We sort the data chronologically and we produce train/test subsets by shifting a time window. We train using the past 30 days and we predict the comments on the next day, shifting for one day at a time, resulting in 10 independent folds. We also restrict our test set to those users who have commented at least once in the training period. We tune the hyper-parameters of each method on an independent validation set, 10% of the training set, and we evaluate the statistical significance of the differences in performance by using Wilcoxon signed rank test [14].

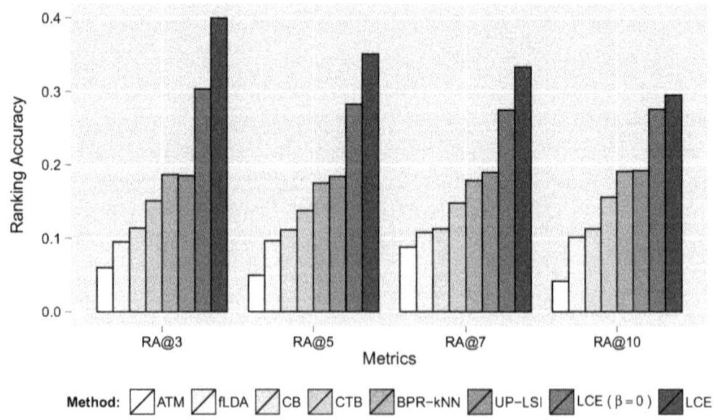

Figure 2: Comparison of the different methods on the Yahoo! News dataset.

Results. We evaluate the different methods in each of the 10 testing days and we compute the average performance (Figure 2). All algorithms perform better then random, i.e., RA > 0%. LCE outperforms all other methods with statistically significant differences (Wilcoxon signed rank test, $p < 0.05$). Imposing locality leads to better ranking accuracy in all positions, however, the effect diminishes as we consider larger lists. The difference is statistically significant only for RA@3 and RA@5 (Wilcoxon signed rank test, $p < 0.05$). This indicates that exploiting the manifold structure of the data allows the algorithm to push the relevant items towards the top of the list. As users are usually presented a short list of recommendations, making accurate recommendations on the top of the list is crucial for improving the satisfaction of the users.

5.4 Parameter Analysis

The LCE model has three essential parameters: k, number of latent variables, i.e., topics/communities; α, weight of the content versus the collaborative information; and λ, controlling the smoothness of the solution. Figure 3 shows a typical behaviour of the algorithm for different values of the parameters. The results are averaged over 10 runs of all algorithms on one mailbox from the Enron dataset.

The parameter k controls the complexity of the model. Small values of k, i.e., simple models under-fit whereas large values of k over-fit the data and lead to poor performance (Figure 3, left). Thus, one has to find a balance between the two that fits best the problem at hand. Furthermore, balancing the importance of the content versus the collaborative information, i.e., $\alpha \approx 0.5$ tends to achieve the best performance. Figure 3 (middle) suggests that giving slightly more importance to the collaborative information (e.g., $\alpha \in [0.2, 0.5]$) may be helpful. Finally, adding the Tikhonov regularization helps; however, large values of λ, oversimplify the model and decrease performance. Setting $\lambda \in (0, 1)$ leads to stable and high performance (Figure 3, right).

The nearest neighbor graph (**A**) in LCE may be constructed using the content or the collaborative information. The weights associated with the neighbors may be binary or the cosine similarity between the documents. We find that

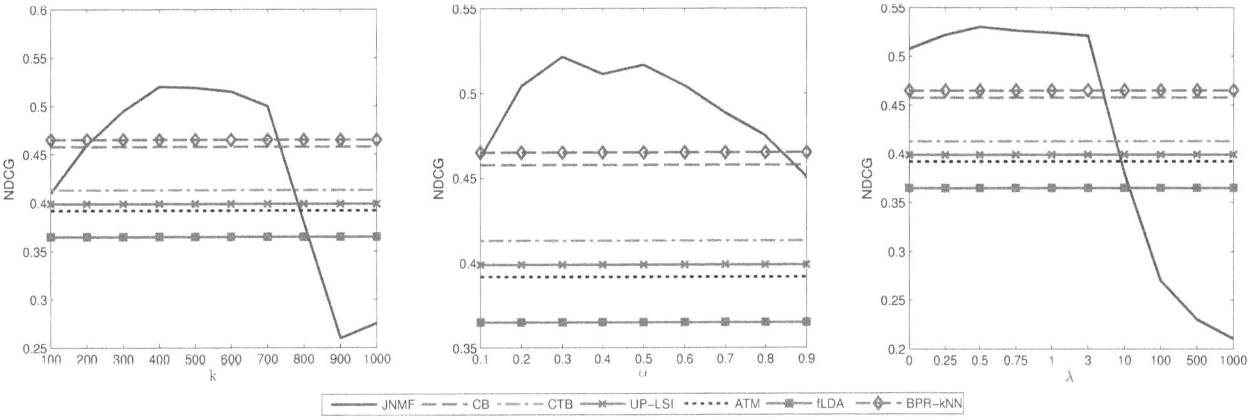

Figure 3: Behaviour of the LCE hyper-parameters ($\beta = 0.25$). Left: k, number of topics; Middle: α, weight of the content versus the collaborative information; and λ, the smoothness of the solution. The results are averaged over 10 runs of the methods on Tana Jones' mailbox from the Enron data set.

imposing the graph regularization based on the collaborative information leads to better performance (Figure 4). The binary weighting scheme is more sensitive to the number of nearest neighbors (p) and works better for small p, while the cosine weighting scheme, as expected, is less sensitive to the choice of p.

The parameter β behaves similarly to λ and setting $\beta = 0.25$ leads to higher performance (for brevity we do not report results for different values of β).

5.5 Running Time Analysis

In this section, we measure the CPU time required by the methods under different settings of the model complexity. All models are comparably fast at inference time, as they require only simple operations such as projections in the latent space or computing similarities. Hence, we only report the running times needed to train the models.

For this experiment, we consider one mailbox from the Enron dataset (4K messages, 500 recipients, 18K unique terms) on which we perform 10 runs of each method under different values of the hyper-parameter k. The averaged CPU times are reported in Figure 5. Due to the long computation time required, we test the author-topic model up to $k = 500$ and fLDA up for $k \in \{10, 25, 50\}$. In the case of UP-LSI k is bounded by 500 due to the rank of the matrix.

The content-based recommender (CB) takes least time for training as it only requires building the user profiles. Little time is also required by the UP-LSI method relying on a fast sparse SVD implementation. ATM and fLDA are computationally most expensive; ATM requires between 3 and 35 hours to train, and fLDA requires between 5 and 46 hours to train even for small values of k. The LCE (with $\beta = 0$, i.e., without building kNN graph) and BPR-kNN have similar running times. The LCE with $\beta = 0.25$, on the other hand, is slightly slower than other methods, except for ATM and fLDA. LCE is reasonably fast and requires 25 minutes to train for the highest values of k, suggesting that frequent updates of the model are possible.

5.6 Reproducibility of the Experiments

The Matlab implementations of the LCE are made publicly available at: `https://github.com/msaveski/LCE`. As

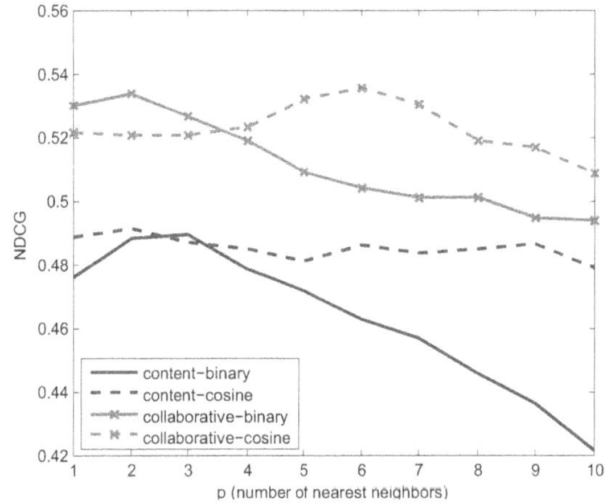

Figure 4: Different ways of constructing the nearest neighbor graph in LCE. The results are averaged over 10 runs on Tana Jones' mailbox.

discussed in Section 5.4, the parameters may be set as: $\alpha = 0.5$, $\beta = 0.25$, and $\lambda = 0.5$, while the parameter k depends on the data and needs to be tuned. A Matlab implementation of the Author-topic Model is publicly available as part of the Matlab Topic Modeling Toolbox at: `http://psiexp.ss.uci.edu/research/programs_data/toolbox.htm`. An R and C/C++ implementation of fLDA is available at: `https://github.com/beechung/Latent-Factor-Models`. An implementation of BPR-kNN is available at: `https://github.com/zenogantner/MyMediaLite`. Finally, the Enron dataset is available at: `https://www.cs.cmu.edu/~enron/`. In the experiments, we consider the 10 largest mailboxes owned by: Steven Kean, Vince Kaminski, Jeff Dasovich, Sally Beck, Tana Jones, Mark Haedicke, Sara Shackleton, Mark Taylor, John Lavorato, and Louise Kitchen.

6. CONCLUSIONS AND FUTURE WORK

To overcome the item cold-start, in this work we have proposed LCE, a recommender system that combines content and collaborative information in a unified matrix factoriza-

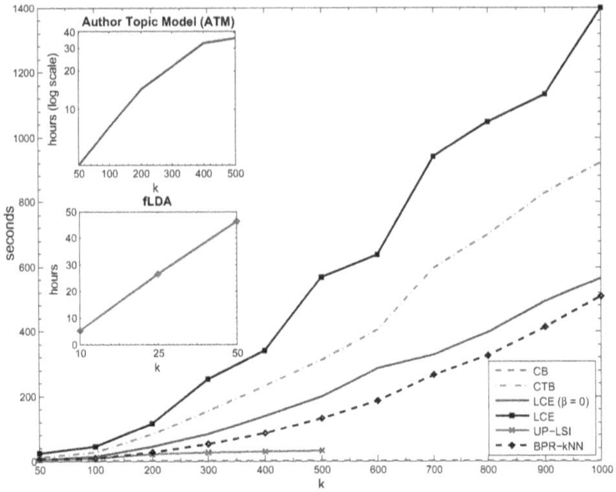

Figure 5: CPU times required to train each method, averaged over 10 runs on Tana Jones' mailbox.

tion framework. Our proposed algorithm outperforms existing item-cold start recommenders. Interestingly, in case of rich content (e.g., news articles) imposing locality to exploit the manifold structure of the data improves the ranking accuracy in the top positions of the rankings which is crucial for improving the user satisfaction on news platforms.

Towards Online Adaptive Models. In some scenarios it is desired that the models are updated as new data arrive. In such context, time plays an important role in modeling user preferences. In this line of research, recently, Vaca *et al.* [29] introduced a temporal regularization for learning evolving representations in an NMF framework. To our knowledge none of the existing "time-aware" approaches have been applied to item cold-start recommendations. As a future work we consider extending our models to close this gap.

7. REFERENCES

[1] G. Adomavicius and A. Tuzhilin. Toward the next generation of recommender systems: A survey of the state-of-the-art and possible extensions. *IEEE Transactions on Knowledge and Data Engineering*, 17(6):734–749, 2005.

[2] D. Agarwal and B.-C. Chen. Regression-based latent factor models. In *International Conference on Knowledge Discovery and Data Mining*, pages 19–28, 2009.

[3] D. Agarwal and C. Chen. flda: Matrix factorization through latent dirichlet allocation. In *International Conference on Web Search and Data Mining*, pages 91–100, 2010.

[4] M. Aharon, A. Kagian, R. Lempel, and Y. Koren. Dynamic personalized recommendation of comment-eliciting stories. In *ACM conference on Recommender Systems*, pages 209–212, 2012.

[5] N. Antulov-Fantulin, M. Bošnjak, M. Znidaršic, M. Grcar, M. Morzy, and T. Šmuc. Ecml-pkdd 2011 discovery challenge overview. *Discovery Challenge*, pages 7–20, 2011.

[6] R. Baeza-Yates and B. Ribeiro-Neto. *Modern information retrieval.* ACM press New York, 1999.

[7] M. Belkin. *Problems of learning on manifolds.* PhD thesis, The University of Chicago, 2003.

[8] M. Belkin and P. Niyogi. Laplacian eigenmaps and spectral techniques for embedding and clustering. In *Advances in Neural Information Processing Systems*, volume 14, pages 585–591, 2001.

[9] M. Belkin, P. Niyogi, and V. Sindhwani. Manifold regularization: A geometric framework for learning from labeled and unlabeled examples. *Journal of Machine Learning Research*, 7(2006):2399–2434, 2006.

[10] M. Berry, M. Browne, A. Langville, P. Pauca, and R. Plemmons. Algorithms and applications for approximate nonnegative matrix factorization. *Computational Statistics & Data Analysis*, 52(1):155–173, 2007.

[11] D. Cai, X. He, X. Wu, and J. Han. Non-negative matrix factorization on manifold. In *International Conference on Data Mining*, pages 63–72, 2008.

[12] F. Chung. *Spectral Graph Teory.* AMS, 1997.

[13] A. Cichocki, R. Zdunek, A. H. Phan, and S.-i. Amari. *Nonnegative matrix and tensor factorizations: applications to exploratory multi-way data analysis and blind source separation.* Wiley, 2009.

[14] J. Demsar. Statistical Comparison of Classifiers over Multiple Data Sets. *Journal of Machine Learning Research*, 7:1–30, 2006.

[15] Z. Gantner, L. Drumond, C. Freudenthaler, S. Rendle, and L. Schmidt-Thieme. Learning attribute-to-feature mappings for cold-start recommendations. In *International Conference on Data Mining*, pages 176–185, 2010.

[16] E. Gaussier and C. Goutte. Relation between plsa and nmf and implications. In *Special Interest Group on Information Retrieval*, pages 601–602, 2005.

[17] T. Hofmann. Probabilistic latent semantic indexing. In *Special Interest Group on Information Retrieval*, pages 50–57, 1999.

[18] T. Hofmann and J. Puzicha. Latent Class Models for Collaborative Filtering. *Machine Learning*, 16:688–693, 1999.

[19] Y. Hu, Y. Koren, and C. Volinsky. Collaborative filtering for implicit feedback datasets. In *International Conference on Data Mining*, pages 263–272, 2008.

[20] Y. Koren, R. Bell, and C. Volinsky. Matrix factorization techniques for recommender systems. *Computer*, 42:30–37, 2009.

[21] H. Lau, K. Grieser, D. Newman, and T. Baldwin. Automatic labelling of topic models. In *Annual Meeting of the Association for Computational Linguistics*, pages 1536–1545, 2011.

[22] D. Lee and S. Seung. Learning the parts of objects by non-negative matrix factorization. *Nature*, 401:788–791, 1999.

[23] M. Rosen-Zvi, T. Griffiths, M. Steyvers, and P. Smyth. The author-topic model for authors and documents. In *Uncertainty in Artificial Intelligence*, pages 487–494, 2004.

[24] D. Saez-Trumper, D. Quercia, and J. Crowcroft. Ads and the city: considering geographic distance goes a long way. In *ACM Conference on Recommender Systems*, pages 187–194, 2012.

[25] A. I. Schein, A. Popescul, L. H. Ungar, and D. M. Pennock. Methods and metrics for cold-start recommendations. In *SIGIR Conference on Research and Development in Information Retrieval*, volume 46, pages 253–260, 2002.

[26] E. Shmueli, A. Kagian, Y. Koren, and R. Lempel. Care to comment?: recommendations for commenting on news stories. In *International World Wide Web Conference*, pages 429–438. ACM, 2012.

[27] A. Singh and G. Gordon. Relational learning via collective matrix factorization. In *International Conference on Knowledge Discovery and Data Mining*, pages 650–658, 2008.

[28] I. Soboroff and C. Nicholas. Combining content and collaboration in text filtering. In *International Joint Conferences on Artificial Intelligence*, volume 99, pages 86–91, 1999.

[29] C. Vaca, A. Mantrach, A. James, and M. Saerens. A time-based collective factorization for topic discovery and monitoring in news. In *International World Wide Web Conference*, pages 527–538, 2014.

Improving The Discriminative Power Of Inferred Content Information Using Segmented Virtual Profile

Haishan Liu
LinkedIn Corporation
2029 Stierlin Court
Mountain View, CA, 94043
haliu@linkedin.com

Anuj Goyal
LinkedIn Corporation
2029 Stierlin Court
Mountain View, CA, 94043
agoyal@linkedin.com

Trevor Walker
LinkedIn Corporation
2029 Stierlin Court
Mountain View, CA, 94043
twalker@linkedin.com

Anmol Bhasin
LinkedIn Corporation
2029 Stierlin Court
Mountain View, CA, 94043
abhasin@linkedin.com

ABSTRACT

We present a novel component of a hybrid recommender system at LinkedIn, where item features are augmented by a *virtual profile* based on observed user-item interactions. A virtual profile is generated by representing an item in the user feature space and leveraging the overrepresented user features from users who interacted with the item. It is a way to think about Collaborative Filtering with content features. The core principle is that if the feature occurs with high probability for the users who interacted with an item (henceforth termed as relevant users) versus those who did not (henceforth termed as non-relevant users), then that feature is a good candidate to be included in the virtual profile of the item in question. However, this scheme suffers from the data imbalance problem because observed relevant users are usually an extremely small minority group compared to the whole user base. Feature selection in this skewed setting is prone to noise from the overwhelming non-relevant examples that belong to the majority group. To alleviate the problem, we propose a method to select the most relevant non-relevant examples from the majority group by segmenting users on certain intelligently selected feature dimensions. The resulting virtual profile from the method is called the *segmented virtual profile*. Empirical evaluation on a real-world large scale recommender system at LinkedIn shows that our strategies for segmentation yield significantly better results.

Categories and Subject Descriptors

H.2.8 [**Database Management**]: Data Mining

RecSys'14, October 06–10, 2014, Foster City, Silicon Valley, CA, USA.
Copyright 2014 ACM 978-1-4503-2668-1/14/10 ... $15.00.
http://dx.doi.org/10.1145/2645710.2645738.

1. INTRODUCTION

As of today LinkedIn has more than 300 million users. As the largest and most popular professional networking site, LinkedIn presents some unique opportunities and challenges for content discovery and recommendation. It is imperative that users are given an effective and efficient tool to navigate the data deluge. Large scale recommender systems have emerged as a solution to this challenge. Rather than hoping for serendipitous encounters, we have created a hybrid recommender system that incorporates information from a myriad of sources, which presents a smaller pool of relevant items to users from a massive set of candidates.

Since there is no dearth of information about either users or items at LinkedIn, the foundation of the recommender system is a content-based filtering approach. A significant challenge to address while pursuing a content filtering approach is vocabulary dissonance, i.e., the user and item features are not always represented in the same vocabulary. Thus, a feature augmentation method was developed to abstract optimal item features for recommendation in the system, which matches user features in a content filtering setting. Specifically, when several users have interacted with an item that has been deemed relevant for their information need, a "profile" is automatically learned for the item. This allows it to be easily matched (recommended) to other likeminded and potentially interested users. To distinguish from other content features inherently contained within the item, we call such inferred information, derived from user-item interactions, the *virtual profile*.

The creation of the virtual profile can be viewed as a feature selection problem with underpinnings in Information Theory. We have described a method to retrieve relevant terms for the virtual profile by a filter-based feature selection method from labeled examples [10], i.e., the users who are relevant to the item because of positive interaction, and non-relevant users. The learned virtual profile is then added to the vector space representation of the item's original content features, and matched against new users in the system. If a new user matches the augmented item profile adequately, then the item is assumed to be of potential interest to the user and is recommended to the user. The degree to which our approach improves the pure content-based filtering, then, is largely dependent upon the quality of the generated item virtual profile.

More specifically, to create a virtual profile, the algorithm selects a set of features (terms appearing in user profiles) whose presence or absence indicates potential relevance or non-relevance for a user. We use mutual information as the selection criteria. The mutual information values of the selected terms are assigned as weights, indicating the relative importance of the features in predicting relevance of a user. The central idea of this scheme is that if a term occurs with a high probability in the relevant users but with a low probability in the non-relevant users, then it is a good indicator of relevance and should be assigned a high weight in the virtual profile. Other feature selection methods (based on some variation of the probability of occurrence, such as Chi-square [23], Correlation coefficient [14], Odds ratio [13], etc.) can be used, as well.

An item is inferred to fulfill a certain user information-need by its observed interactions with users. However, when the number of users who have interactions with the item is small and the non-relevant users who have no interaction with the item is large, feature selection can become prone to noise. This phenomenon of imbalanced data is a known problem in the study of feature selection commonly encountered in text categorization tasks (see a motivating example on job recommendations in Section 3).

To tackle this problem, we propose a method to obtain more balanced relevant and non-relevant examples by segmenting users on intelligently selected feature dimensions. Specifically, define an item's user segment as the set of users that have some similarity to the item according to some measure. In this study, we show that using a selected set of non-relevant users that belongs to an item's user segment to learn the virtual profile yields better results than using the entire non-relevant user base. Results show that our strategies to select non-relevant users for learning the virtual profile yield significantly better performance. The resulting virtual profile generated by such strategy is called the segmented virtual profile.

The rest of the paper is organized as follows. In Section 2 we briefly review related work and provide necessary background. In Section 3 we describe details of the segmented virtual profile generation process. In Section 4 we present experiment results from both online and offline evaluations. Finally, we conclude the paper in Section 5 and discuss possible future directions.

2. BACKGROUND AND RELATED WORK

This section surveys previous work in recommender systems and feature selection as well as providing necessary background information related to virtual profiles.

2.1 Recommender Systems

The recommender system approaches can be mainly classified into four categories: Collaborative filtering [8, 19], Content-based filtering [6, 17], Knowledge-based [3, 4] and Hybrid algorithms [2].

A fundamental assumption in collaborative filtering (CF) is that if user x and y rate n items similarly, they will rate other items similarly too. The CF techniques are known to suffer from data sparsity and cold start problems [18]. Content-based filtering (CBF) methods are based on a description of the item and a profile of the user's preference and can be treated as a information retrieval or machine learning problem. CBF techniques are sometimes prone to deliver skewed recommendations [17]. Knowledge-based approach attempts to suggest objects based on inferences on user's needs and preferences. The main challenge for these systems is difficulties of knowledge acquisition and knowledge engineering. To avoid certain limitations of content and collaborative filtering systems, hybrid approaches are proposed to combine CF and CBF based techniques. In [2] authors propose to use a taxonomy of recommender systems, where multiple recommenders are arranged to allow execution in a parallel or cascaded topology. The system described in [1] combined the output of multiple collaborative filtering approaches by using a linear combination of weights learned via linear regressions. In [16], the author proposes a hybrid approach where the content based user profiles are used to group similar users which is subsequently used to predict user preferences.

In this paper, we experiment our recommender system in a job recommendation application. There has been good amount of research in the domain of matching job candidates (resumes) with job postings. Simple Jobs recommendation algorithm [11] are based on the boolean filtering techniques that cannot sufficiently capture the complexity of a person-job fit. In [12], authors propose to consider unary attributes such as individual skills, mental abilities and personality that control the fit between the individual and the task to be accomplished, as well as the relational attributes that determine the fit between the individual and the team members. A decision support tool named PROSPECT proposed in [20] mines resumes to extract features of candidate profiles such as skills, education, and experience. It then uses information retrieval techniques to rank applicants for a given job position. In [15], authors exploit all past job transitions as well as the data associated with employees and institutions to predict an employee's next job transition.

2.2 Feature Selection

The creation of virtual profiles is closely related to the study of feature selection. A feature selection algorithm can be seen as the combination of a search technique for proposing new feature subsets, along with an evaluation measure which scores the different feature subsets. The choice of evaluation distinguishes between the three main categories of feature selection algorithms: wrappers, filters and embedded methods [7]. Wrapper methods use a predictive model to score feature subsets. Embedded methods perform feature selection as part of the model construction process. Filter methods produce a feature set which is not tuned to a specific type of predictive model. Filter methods use a proxy measure instead of the error rate to score a feature subset. Common measures include mutual information [7], Chi-square [23], Correlation coefficient [14], Odds ratio [13], inter/intra class distance, and the scores of significance tests for each class/feature combinations [24].

Recent studies have explored the topic of feature selection on imbalanced data. Imbalanced datasets are commonly encountered in text categorization problems. There are often overwhelming numbers of non-relevant training documents especially when analyzing a large collection of categories assigned to small numbers of documents. To overcome this problem, *query zone* [21] has been introduced to select a subset of the most relevant non-relevant documents as the non-relevant training data. The user segment proposed in this paper aims at achieving the same objective by segmenting the user base on intelligently selected feature dimensions. These techniques try to obtain a more balanced relevant and non-relevant training data by under-sampling negative examples. Zheng et al. [25] consider the imbalanced data problem from a different perspective. Instead of balancing the training data, the authors propose a way to find the optimal way to combine positive and negative features according to the imbalanced data.

2.3 Virtual Profile

The creation of a virtual profile can be viewed as a feature selection process [10]. From a total of n user-item interaction features, it aims at selecting a subset with $k(<= n)$ features that gives the maximum information about the item. From a text categorization point of view, the item that we generate a virtual profile for represents a class label for a set of documents (user profiles). We can use mutual information to evaluate the information content of each individual feature with regard to the class label. In accordance with Shannon's information theory, the uncertainty of a document class C as a random variable can be measured as:

$$H(C) = -\sum_{c \in C} P(c) \log P(c) ,$$

In this case, a document class is a virtual profile of a target item, while documents are profiles of users who have interacted with the target item. After knowing the occurrence of a feature F, the conditional entropy $H(C|F)$ measures the remaining uncertainty about C:

$$H(C|F) = -\sum_{f \in F} P(f) \sum_{c \in C} P(c|f) \log P(c|f) .$$

The mutual information, i.e., the amount of decreased class uncertainty is defined as:

$$I(C;F) = H(C) - H(C|F) = \sum_{c,f} P(c,f) \log \frac{P(c,f)}{P(c)P(f)} . \quad (1)$$

To generate virtual profiles, the goal is to find the optimal feature subset, $S \subseteq F$, such that $I(C;S)$ is maximized. We employ a straightforward best individual features strategy (BIF [9]) by making a first-order class dependence assumption (each feature independently influences the class variable). The BIF method evaluates all features individually, sort them and select the best k features based on the mutual information score.

3. METHOD

In this section, we describe details of the segmented virtual profile. We first give a motivating example to illustrate the data imbalance problem that causes the suboptimal quality of features selected in the virtual profile.

3.1 Motivation

Consider a content-based filtering system that recommends jobs to users. Content features from both jobs and users can be abstracted from their textual description into predefined standardized fields, such as location, industry, function, skill, etc., which constitutes their primary profiles. Additionally, a virtual profile can be created for each job based on the observed behavior of users applying the job. Virtual profile aims at selecting indicative features from users that correlate well with the application of the job. In other words, features selected for the virtual profile should be able to distinguish job applicants (relevant users) from non-applicants (non-relevant users). However, since features from job applicants are evaluated against a vast amount of non-applicants, most of whom are completely irrelevant to the job, the resulting virtual profile may not include the real indicative features.

Take a job posting about *professor of economics* for example. If we regard all applicants to this job as the set of relevant users, and all non-applicants as the set of non-relevant users, the term *teaching* from its applicants' skills will score a high mutual information value with regard to the job. It is because the frequency of the term is low for non-relevant users and high for relevant users. Therefore according to such choice of relevant/non-relevant users, *teaching* would appear as a very strong indicator of relevance. However, in reality, this term will not be very good at separating this job from other academic jobs, such as a *professor of history*. In this case, the use of all non-applicants as non-relevant users has boosted the importance of a term that is possibly not very important. Therefore we need a way to constrain the set of non-relevant users to include only those that have some reasonable similarity to the item. For example, if we consider only users from the higher education field, the term teaching would lose its significance but terms such as *economics* and *history* would be able to surface. Following this idea, we define user segments in the next section as a solution for this purpose.

3.2 User Segments

A user segment for a target item is a set of users that have some reasonable similarity to the item. It provides a small set of negative, or non-relevant users for the purpose of selecting more indicative terms in the virtual profile generation process. In practice, a user segment can be simulated by performing "slice and dice" in the vector space model, which is to filter both the item vector and the user vector space on one or multiple dimensions simultaneously. Take job postings as an example. A user segment for one job posting can be users from the same industry to the job. The aim therefore, is to select a set of non-relevant users that relate well to the target item, from the whole corpus of labeled example set, to be used in the virtual profile generation process.

To answer the question of how to select the feature dimension to generate the user segment, we propose the following steps:

1. Construct a labeled pilot dataset with observed positive user-item interactions from a time period as positive examples, and randomly sampled non-interactive user-item pairs as negative examples.

2. Construct features in the above dataset so that each feature represents a similarity between a pair of corresponding values from a user-item pair on the same dimension of their vector space model. For instance, in the job application example, the feature in the dataset can be the similarity between the user industry and the job industry, the similarity between user skills and job skills, user location and job location, and so forth.

3. Select top features based on this dataset, then use the corresponding dimensions from the original user/item-

feature	MI
geo_region	0.034
skill	0.0075
seniority	0.0055
function	0.0055
industry	0.0014

Table 1: Top features selected from the pilot dataset using mutual information. Each row represents an interaction feature between a user and a job.

feature vector space as the candidates to generate user segments.

An example of the pilot dataset constructed from job application data within a two-week period is shown in Table 1, together with the top five features selected from the dataset using mutual information. It is worth pointing out that domain knowledge is a valuable source in deciding the dimension to segment on. For instance, we only use *function* and *industry* features in our experiments reported in Section 4, because the *geo_region* and *skill* features are sparse (too many categories, some of which contains very few users), while the *seniority* feature is coarse (only nine categories in total).

3.3 Mutual Information in User Segments

The class membership C and feature F in Equation 1 are both binary-valued (indicating whether a user-item interaction exists and whether a feature is present). Therefore Equation 1 for calculating the mutual information $I(C;F)$ can be written in the following form:

$$I(C;F) = \sum_{e_f \in \{1,0\}} \sum_{e_c \in \{1,0\}} P_{CF}(e_c, e_f) \log \frac{P_{CF}(e_c, e_f)}{P_C(e_c) P_F(e_f)}, \tag{2}$$

where f is a random variable that takes values $e_f = 1$ (the feature f appeared in a user) and $e_f = 0$ (the feature f does not appear in a user), and c is a random variable that takes values $e_c = 1$ (the user positively interacted with c) and $e_c = 0$ (the user did not positively interact with c). Equation 2 can be solved by the contingency table shown in Table 2, in which the joint probabilities are approximated by maximum likelihood estimation from the data.

	$F(e_f = 1)$	$F(e_f = 0)$
$C(e_c = 1)$	N_{fc}	$N_c - N_{fc}$
$C(e_c = 0)$	$N_f - N_{fc}$	$N - N_c - (N_f - N_{fc})$

Table 2: The contingency table to calculate the regular mutual information between a term and a job.

As a concrete example, the counts in Table 2 have the following meaning if we instantiate each item as a job, and a user-item interaction as a job application.

- N_c: number of people who applied the job
- N_{fc}: number of people who have the feature and applied the job
- N: total number of people who have applied any job
- N_f: number of people who have the feature

To calculate the mutual information with a specific user segment, we can use the contingency table shown in Table 3, which has a slight modification in the calculation of joint probabilities when non-relevant users are involved ($e_c = 0$).

	$F(e_f = 1)$	$F(e_f = 0)$
$C(e_c = 1)$	N_{fc}	$N_c - N_{fc}$
$C(e_c = 0)$	$N_{fs} - N_{fc}$	$N_s - N_c - (N_{fs} - N_{fc})$

Table 3: The contingency table to calculate the mutual information between a term and a job, with negatives chosen from a specific user segment.

The counts in Table 3 have the following meaning in the job application setting.

- N_c: number of people who applied the job
- N_{fc}: number of people who have the feature and applied the job
- N_s: total number of people who are from a specific user segment
- N_{fs}: number of people who are from the specific user segment and have the feature.

3.3.1 Frequency Threshold

The mutual information score should be interpreted with care when data is sparse. It is known to attribute high scores to low frequency terms. For instance, in the job posting example, suppose some terms only appear in a small number of applicants to a job but not in the general public. Those terms will have high scores since as far as mutual information is concerned, they correlate well with the event of users applying to the specific job. Therefore we impose two thresholds on term frequency to prevent terms being selected simply because of rarity. They are, namely, the *global frequency threshold* θ_g (i.e., the minimum frequency of a feature in the global feature space across all users), and the *per-item frequency threshold* θ_i (i.e., the minimum frequency of a feature in users who interacted with the specific item). These two thresholds are the parameters of the virtual profile generation process and should be tuned as per application requirement. When the feature or item space is large, aggressive thresholding can be an effective way to provide additional scalability.

4. EXPERIMENTS

Our main goal in the experiment design is to estimate the impact of segmented virtual profile on recommendation performance. In addition, we want to do a comparative performance analysis between segmented and non-segmented virtual profile. Furthermore, since segmented virtual profile can be generated in different ways depending on the dimension it is segmented on, we also want to compare the performances of these different segmented virtual profiles.

4.1 Experiment Design

LinkedIn has a wide variety of recommendation products available on its website. In this study, we experiment with LinkedIn's renowned jobs recommendation engine named as

Table 4: Performance of baseline and non-segmented virtual profile models

Model	Precision			Recall			F1		
	P@1	P@5	P@10	R@1	R@5	R@10	F1@1	F1@5	F1@10
Baseline	.829	.307	.160	.589	.928	.963	.659	.442	.268
Non-segmented Virtual Profile	.833	.309	.161	.590	.931	.965	.661	.445	.269

Table 5: NDCG and MAP of baseline and non-segmented virtual profile models

Model	NDCG			MAP
	NDCG@1	NDCG@5	NDCG@10	
Baseline	.829	.876	.890	.854
Non-segmented Virtual Profile	.833	.879	.893	.858

Jobs You May Be Interested In (JYMBII). JYMBII plays a crucial role in helping LinkedIn members explore relevant jobs. JYMBII leverages the user's profile content as well as the user's activity to recommend relevant jobs. Apart from JYMBII provided recommendations, users can also use the job search functionality to find relevant jobs. We record various kinds of members-jobs interactions in both the JYMBII and Search system.

We extract two kinds of features from entities (users and jobs) in this application domain:

1. **Content Features (Primary Profile):** standardized features extracted from the textual content of the job's posting and the user's profile (e.g., skills, degrees, specialties, industry, function, location, etc.).

2. **Virtual Profile:** A set of features extracted from a job's applicants. These features are in the same vector space as user features, and are intended to be a maximally informative features about a job given its observed interaction with users.

We model the job recommendation problem as a classification problem where the classifier outputs score is $p(j|u)$, which can be ideally interpreted as the probability that a job j is relevant to the given user u. We train a model by using $L2$-regularized logistic regression classifier with different user-job interaction features as input features. The model's output score is used to rank the relevant jobs for a user.

In our experiments, we train two types of models: baseline and virtual profile. The baseline model is trained by using the content features while the virtual profile model is trained by using both content and virtual profile features. The best model (best regularization parameters) under each configuration is selected by optimizing the area under the ROC curve (AUC-ROC).

The training set consists of all the applications (from any of the source, i.e., JYMBII or search) a job has received in a month. Training data is required for two purposes: 1) extracting virtual profiles, and 2) training a classifier. Since the same training data is used to generate the virtual profile feature as well as to train the model, extra care is required in the way we use the training data. If we use the same user-job pair in generating the virtual profile as well as in training the model, the learned model will be highly biased towards the virtual profile features. This is mainly due to the fact that information from a user-job pairs are used twice, in generating features as well as in training the model. To overcome this bias, we partitioned the application data into two equal sized random parts. The first part is used to generate the virtual profile features and the other is used to train the model. As discussed in section 3 and based on our domain knowledge and pilot studies, we use *global frequency threshold* θ_g equals to 2000 and *per-item frequency threshold* θ_i equals to 2 to generate the virtual profile.

Based on the domain knowledge and the approach discussed in section 3, we generate virtual profile segmented on function feature and industry feature. Function features are pre-defined job functions based on the user's current job position for example Engineering, Finance, Sales, and Administrative etc. Industry features are pre-defined industries based on user's current employer for example Banking, Farming, Food Production, Higher Education etc.

Performances of different models are evaluated in both offline and online settings. The next section discusses the results of these evaluations.

4.2 Results

4.2.1 Offline evaluation

In these experiments, we adopt an offline evaluation method similar to the one described in [22]. The job applications data set is split into training set R and test set T. In order to measure different information retrieval measures, we first train the model by using the training set R. Then, for each job i applied by user u in T:

1. We randomly select 1000 additional jobs not applied by the user. We assume that these random jobs are likely to be irrelevant to the user.

2. We calculate the relevance score for the job i and for the additional 1000 drawn jobs.

3. We build a ranked list by ordering all the 1001 items according to their relevance score. Let p denote the rank of the test job i within the list. The best model corresponds to the case where the applied job i precedes all the random items (i.e., $p = 1$).

To compute different information retrieval metrics, we form a top-K recommendation list by picking the top K ranked items from the list. The metrics we calculate include *Precision@K, Recall@K, F1@K, NDCG(Normalized Discounted Cumulative Gain)@K* and *Mean Average Precision (MAP)* measures. We calculated these for $K = \{1, 5, 10\}$.

We conduct two experiments, one to compare the baseline with the non-segmented virtual profile and the other to

Table 6: Performance of baseline and segmented virtual profile models

Model	Precision			Recall			F1		
	P@1	P@5	P@10	R@1	R@5	R@10	F1@1	F1@5	F1@10
Baseline	.848	.435	.234	.400	.879	.936	.520	.560	.365
Industry Segmented Virtual Profile	.878	.447	.238	.415	.902	.951	.539	.575	.370
Function Segmented Virtual Profile	.860	.440	.236	.405	.889	.942	.527	.567	.367

Table 7: NDCG and MAP of baseline and segmented virtual profile models

Model	NDCG			MAP
	NDCG@1	NDCG@5	NDCG@10	
Baseline	.848	.850	.876	.833
Industry Segmented Virtual Profile	.878	.877	.899	.860
Function Segmented Virtual Profile	.860	.861	.886	.844

compare with the proposed segmented virtual profile. Since these experiments were conducted on the data collected from different time periods, the baseline model has different numbers in these two experiments.

Table 4 and Table 5 compare the performance between the baseline and the non-segmented virtual profile models. Table 6 and Table 7 compare the performance between the baseline and the segmented virtual profile models.

As can be seen in the tables, the non-segmented virtual profile model performs better than the baseline. Segmented models outperform the baseline by an even bigger margin across all metrics. Between the segmented models, the industry segmented model outperforms the function one. It is worth noting that these gains are considered significant because the baseline we used in the experiments is a sophisticated model currently deployed in the production. The model has gone through numerous rounds of fine tuning, resulting in the use of a comprehensive list of features, including interaction content features, user behavior features, and interest/preference features.

4.2.2 *Online evaluation*

Once we picked the best performing models from the offline evaluation, we deployed them to serve real time online JYMBII recommendation traffic and compare performances through a bucket (A/B) test. We assign a distinct bucket of 5% randomly selected users to each model from the whole user base.

Since industry segmented virtual profile perform better than the function segmented virtual profile in the offline setting, we deployed only industry segmented virtual profile in the online setting. To compare segmented with non-segmented virtual profile, we also deployed the non-segmented virtual profile.

We collected the data from the A/B test for 11 days. From the collected data, we calculate two metrics:

1. **Unique User-Job view pairs:** Total number of (u, j) pairs where user u has viewed the job j recommended to her at least once during the online test.
2. **Unique User-Job application pairs:** Total number of (u, j) pairs where user u has applied to the job j recommended to her at least once within the duration of the online test.

Figure 1 presents results of the test by showing the percentage change in the unique user-job view pairs for the

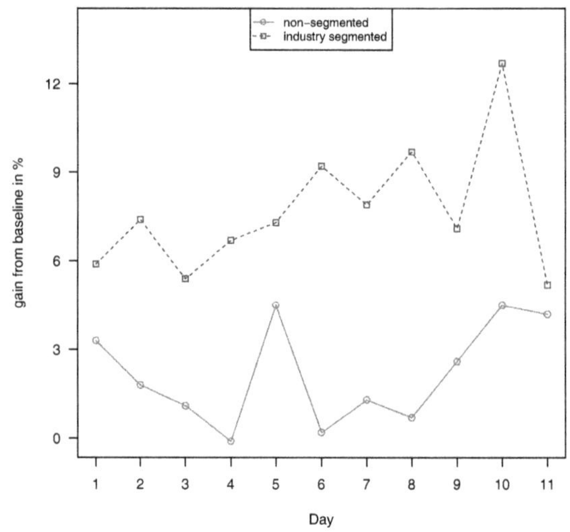

Figure 1: Online Job Views Performance improvement over baseline for virtual profile models

virtual profile models relative to the baseline, on each individual day of the test. Figure 2 presents the percentage change in the unique user-job application pairs for virtual profile models relative to the baseline. As expected, both segmented and non-segmented virtual profile models beat the baseline in the performance. More importantly, the proposed segmented virtual profile model performs better than the non-segmented virtual profile model in both job views and applications.

Overall, the industry segmented virtual profile model outperforms the baseline by 10.4% in applications and 6.5% in views (p value $< .0008$). The non-segmented virtual profile model outperformed the baseline by 4.3% in applications and 2% in views (p value $< .003$). Our experiment's main goal is to study the impact of segmented virtual profile on recommendation performance. From these results we can say that segmented virtual profile improves the quality of the job recommender system at LinkedIn.

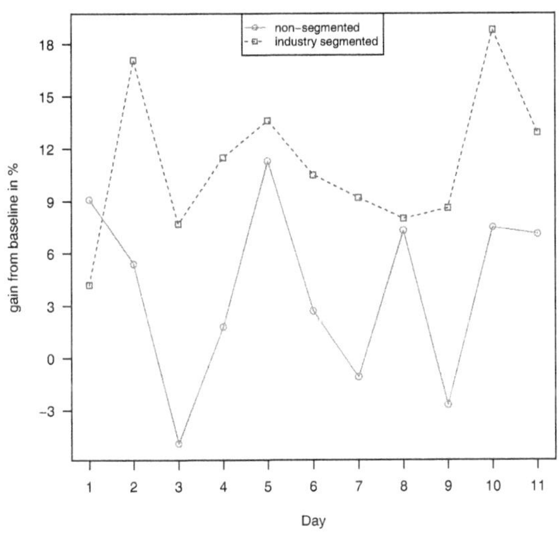

Figure 2: Online Job Application Performance improvement over baseline for virtual profile models

4.3 Analysis

In this section, we conduct a series of in-depth investigation to study the reasons behind the improvements achieved through the segmented virtual profile model, as well as if there is any possible side effect incurred by the model.

As we discuss in the previous section, the segmented virtual profile model performs better in terms of both the metrics in the offline setting, and the volume of job views and applications in the online settings. Virtual profile's better performance may attribute to the following two reasons:

1. Users apply to more jobs when served by the virtual profile model, and/or
2. More users engage in applying to jobs when served by virtual profile model.

The first point can be concluded from the online performance shown in Figure 1 and 2. To verify the second point, we analyze the collected data from the online evaluation. We collect activities of all members in the bucket served with the baseline model and the bucket served with the virtual profile model.

We conduct a paired t-test between the distribution of users who applied to n number of jobs from the two buckets. The paired t-test shows that more users apply for a job in the virtual profile bucket (p value = .005). This is indicating that virtual profile model helps jump start users in the application process. In other words, the virtual profile improves the whole job application ecosystem by getting more users to start interacting with the job recommender system.

We further analyze the results to verify if the virtual profile may cause any side effect on the overall job recommendation ecosystem. One possible side effect could be that virtual profile based models give higher preference to jobs having virtual profiles than jobs that do not have virtual profiles. This problem can be seen as a cold start problem. Let us call jobs without virtual profiles (jobs without applicants) as *cold jobs* and jobs with virtual profiles (jobs with applicants) as *warm jobs*. The cold start problem occurs when warm jobs are shown to more users than cold jobs due to the fact that cold jobs has missing virtual profile features.

To verify this we partitioned the jobs into two subgroups, jobs with virtual profiles (warm jobs) and jobs without virtual profiles (cold jobs), and analyze the impact on the impressions (i.e., the showing of the job) and applications separately from the data collected in the virtual profile model bucket.

Results show that, for warm jobs, number of impressions increase by 1.63%, while number of applications increase by 1%. However, for cold jobs, impressions decrease by 7.8%, but applications increase by 6.4%. The increase in applications for cold jobs is seemingly larger than the warm jobs, which can be explained by the fact that the base number of applications for cold jobs is low. However, the increase in number of applications for cold jobs can be attributed to the following two reasons.

1. It is mostly irrelevant non-virtual profile jobs that are getting replaced by the jobs having virtual profiles. A very relevant job is still getting impressed to the user even though it does not yet have the virtual profile.
2. Since virtual profile based model is improving the overall quality of the recommendations, it may result in higher user interactions, which may even help the jobs not having virtual profile.

In other words, although virtual profiles are generated only for warm jobs, both warm jobs and cold jobs are benefited from them. Low-quality cold jobs have a fewer chance to surface in the recommendation because of being replaced by warm jobs with higher feature coverage due to virtual profiles. And overall, users get more engaged after interacting with high-quality jobs. Therefore, in general, the adoption of segmented virtual profile resulted in a more healthy job ecosystem.

5. CONCLUSION AND FUTURE WORK

We presented an improved content feature extension method called segmented virtual profiles. The goal of virtual profiles is to provide a means to tap into rich-content information from one type of entity and propagate features extracted therein to other related entities that may suffer from relative data scarcity. The segmented virtual profile addresses the data imbalance problem in the feature selection process. Totally irrelevant examples in the majority class decrease the signal-to-noise ratio in the feature selection process. The proposed strategies for user segmentation provide a warranty against the data imbalance by constraining the non-relevant example space to a smaller set that only contains the most likely good quality examples. Evaluation on real-world recommender system shows that the segmented virtual profile performs significantly better than baselines.

One possible future direction is to investigate ways to improve label quality within a user segment. Since only observed positive user-item interactions are deemed to be positive examples in feature selection, negative interactions are increasingly vulnerable to mislabeling. This is due to the fact that the user segment consists of users who are *a priori* likely to positively interact with the item in the first place (a user may not have positively interacted with the item simply because she had not seen it yet). Previous research showed that noise in the labeled data can cause serious degradation in feature selection performance [5]. Therefore, one important future direction is to look at how implicit user feedback can be utilized to generate better quality negative labeling within the user segment. Another direction is to generate virtual profiles for new jobs with few applicants. One possible way is to backfill the virtual profiles of a job using those of similar jobs.

6. REFERENCES

[1] R. M. Bell, Y. Koren, and C. Volinsky. The BellKor solution to the Netflix Prize.

[2] R. Burke. Hybrid recommender systems: Survey and experiments. *User Modeling and User-Adapted Interaction*, 12(4):331–370, Nov. 2002.

[3] A. Felfernig. Koba4ms: selling complex products and services using knowledge-based recommender technologies. In *CEC 2005. Seventh IEEE International Conference on E-Commerce Technology*, pages 92–100, July 2005.

[4] A. Felfernig, M. Schubert, M. Mandl, F. Ricci, and W. Maalej. Recommendation and decision technologies for requirements engineering. In *Proceedings of the 2Nd International Workshop on Recommendation Systems for Software Engineering*, RSSE '10, pages 11–15, New York, NY, USA, 2010.

[5] B. Frénay, G. Doquire, and M. Verleysen. Estimating mutual information for feature selection in the presence of label noise. *Computational Statistics & Data Analysis*, 71:832–848, 2014.

[6] K. Goldberg, T. Roeder, D. Gupta, and C. Perkins. Eigentaste: A constant time collaborative filtering algorithm. *Information Retrieval*, 4(2):133–151, July 2001.

[7] I. Guyon and A. Elisseeff. An introduction to variable and feature selection. *J. Mach. Learn. Res.*, 3:1157–1182, Mar. 2003.

[8] J. L. Herlocker, J. A. Konstan, and J. Riedl. Explaining collaborative filtering recommendations. In *Proceedings of the 2000 ACM conference on Computer supported cooperative work*, CSCW '00, pages 241–250, New York, NY, USA, 2000.

[9] A. K. Jain, R. P. W. Duin, and J. Mao. Statistical pattern recognition: A review. *IEEE Transactions on Pattern Analysis and Machine Intelligence*.

[10] H. Liu, M. Amin, B. Yan, and A. Bhasin. Generating supplemental content information using virtual profiles. In *Proceedings of the 7th ACM Conference on Recommender Systems*, RecSys '13, pages 295–302, New York, NY, USA, 2013.

[11] J. Malinowski, T. Keim, O. Wendt, and T. Weitzel. Matching people and jobs: A bilateral recommendation approach. In *System Sciences, 2006. HICSS '06. Proceedings of the 39th Annual Hawaii International Conference on*, volume 6, pages 137c–137c, Jan 2006.

[12] J. Malinowski, T. Weitzel, and T. Keim. Decision support for team staffing: An automated relational recommendation approach. *Decision Support Systems*, 45(3):429–447, June 2008.

[13] D. Mladenic. *Machine learning on non-homogeneous, distributed text data*. PhD thesis, University of Ljubljana, Faculty of Computer and Information Science, 1998.

[14] H. T. Ng, W. B. Goh, and K. L. Low. Feature selection, perceptron learning, and a usability case study for text categorization. In *Proceedings of the 20th Annual International ACM SIGIR Conference on Research and Development in Information Retrieval*, SIGIR '97, pages 67–73, New York, NY, USA, 1997.

[15] I. Paparrizos, B. B. Cambazoglu, and A. Gionis. Machine learned job recommendation. In *Proceedings of the Fifth ACM Conference on Recommender Systems*, RecSys '11, pages 325–328, New York, NY, USA, 2011.

[16] M. J. Pazzani. A framework for collaborative, content-based and demographic filtering. *Artificial Intelligence Review*, 13(5-6):393–408, Dec. 1999.

[17] M. J. Pazzani and D. Billsus. The adaptive web. chapter Content-based recommendation systems, pages 325–341. Springer-Verlag, Berlin, Heidelberg, 2007.

[18] P. Resnick, N. Iacovou, M. Suchak, P. Bergstrom, and J. Riedl. Grouplens: an open architecture for collaborative filtering of netnews. In *Proceedings of the 1994 ACM conference on Computer supported cooperative work*, CSCW '94, pages 175–186, New York, NY, USA, 1994.

[19] B. Sarwar, G. Karypis, J. Konstan, and J. Riedl. Item-based collaborative filtering recommendation algorithms. In *Proceedings of the 10th international conference on World Wide Web*, WWW '01, pages 285–295, 2001.

[20] A. Singh, C. Rose, K. Visweswariah, V. Chenthamarakshan, and N. Kambhatla. Prospect: A system for screening candidates for recruitment. In *Proceedings of the 19th ACM International Conference on Information and Knowledge Management*, CIKM '10, pages 659–668, New York, NY, USA, 2010.

[21] A. Singhal, M. Mitra, and C. Buckley. Learning routing queries in a query zone. In *Proceedings of the 20th Annual International ACM SIGIR Conference on Research and Development in Information Retrieval*, SIGIR '97, pages 25–32, New York, NY, USA, 1997. ACM.

[22] J. Wang, Y. Zhang, C. Posse, and A. Bhasin. Is it time for a career switch? In *Proceedings of the 22Nd International Conference on World Wide Web*, WWW '13, pages 1377–1388, Republic and Canton of Geneva, Switzerland, 2013.

[23] Y. Yang. An evaluation of statistical approaches to text categorization. *Information Retrieval*, 1(1-2):69–90, May 1999.

[24] Y. Yang and J. O. Pedersen. A comparative study on feature selection in text categorization. In *Proceedings of the Fourteenth International Conference on Machine Learning*, ICML '97, pages 412–420, San Francisco, CA, USA, 1997. Morgan Kaufmann Publishers Inc.

[25] Z. Zheng, X. Wu, and R. Srihari. Feature selection for text categorization on imbalanced data. *SIGKDD Explor. Newsl.*, 6(1):80–89, June 2004.

Ratings Meet Reviews, a Combined Approach to Recommend

Guang Ling[1,2], Michael R. Lyu[1,2] and Irwin King[1,2]
[1]Shenzhen Key Laboratory of Rich Media Big Data Analytics and Applications
Shenzhen Research Institute, The Chinese University of Hong Kong, Shenzhen, China
[2]Department of Computer Science and Engineering
The Chinese University of Hong Kong, Shatin, N.T., Hong Kong
gling@cse.cuhk.edu.hk, lyu@cse.cuhk.edu.hk, king@cse.cuhk.edu.hk

ABSTRACT

Most existing recommender systems focus on modeling the ratings while ignoring the abundant information embedded in the review text. In this paper, we propose a unified model that combines content-based filtering with collaborative filtering, harnessing the information of both ratings and reviews. We apply topic modeling techniques on the review text and align the topics with rating dimensions to improve prediction accuracy. With the information embedded in the review text, we can alleviate the cold-start problem. Furthermore, our model is able to learn latent topics that are interpretable. With these interpretable topics, we can explore the prior knowledge on items or users and recommend completely "cold" items. Empirical study on 27 classes of real-life datasets show that our proposed model lead to significant improvement compared with strong baseline methods, especially for datasets which are extremely sparse where rating-only methods cannot make accurate predictions.

Categories and Subject Descriptors

H.3.3 [**Information Storage and Retrieval**]: Information filtering; I.2.6 [**Artificial Intelligence**]: Learning-parameter learning

Keywords

Collaborative Filtering; Content-based Filtering; Cold-start Problem

1. INTRODUCTION

With the ever growing number of choices available online, recommender systems are becoming more and more indispensable. We rely on them to select favorite songs from millions of collections in music streaming services like Spotify and iTunes Radio. We depend upon them to suggest interesting movies in movie rating website such as IMDb and video streaming providers such as Netflix. Amazon uses recommender systems to suggest products to potential users. Now the company even takes it to another level by shipping the products to the warehouse near the customer based on speculated order produced by recommender systems[1].

RecSys'14, October 6–10, 2014, Foster City, Silicon Valley, CA, USA.
Copyright 2014 ACM 978-1-4503-2668-1/14/10 $15.00.
http://dx.doi.org/10.1145/2645710.2645728.

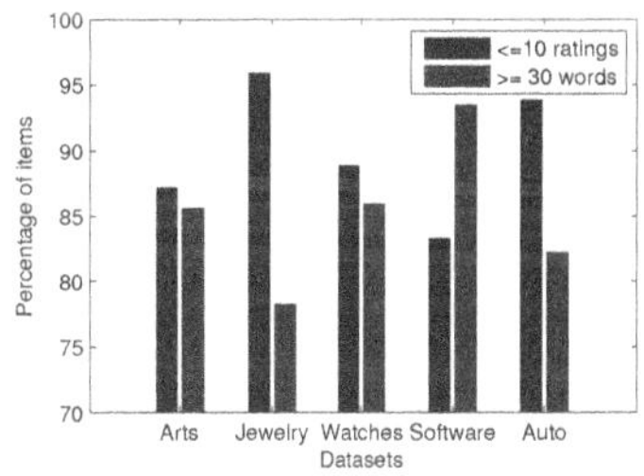

Figure 1: Percentage of items having less than 10 ratings and more than 30 words in various Amazon datasets

Although recommender systems employed in industry seem to perform well in practice, there are some deficiencies with existing approaches. The first problem confronted with most recommender system is their inability to deal with so called *cold-start* problem [28]. When a new user joins a recommender system, there is little data available for the system to learn the preferences of the user accurately. Without an accurate representation of the user, the system cannot make recommendations confidently. Similarly, the systems defer the recommendations for newly included items as well. The cold-start problem leads to poor experience for new users and also when recommending new items. In real-life recommender systems, the cold-start problem is a severe problem. Shown in Figure 1 are the statistics of 5 categories in Amazon datasets [16]. Across the 5 listed datasets, over 80% of items have few ratings (less than 10). While at the same time, over 70% of items have review text at length (over 30 words). The ratings alone are inadequate to learn the preferences accurately. Review comments complement the ratings by providing rich knowledge of the items and preferences of the users. Harnessing the information embedded in the review text is the key to successful recommendation in such scenarios.

Another drawback of existing recommender systems is their poor interpretability, making further understanding of users' preference as well as items' properties impossible. For example in matrix-factorization [25] based methods, we learn two latent feature matrices corresponding to users' latent features and items' latent features. The dot product between a user's and an item's feature vector is used to predict the rating that the user would assign to the item. It is challenging to associate these real valued features with con-

[1]http://on.rt.com/c8v82n

ceivable physical meanings. We know that a user might like an item due to a particular latent feature since they both have a large positive (or negative) value on that feature. But we have no clue of the feature's physical meaning. Does it mean that the user is fond of Sci-Fi and the movie belongs to Sci-Fi genre? Or is it that the user loves the leading actor of the movie? We do not know. In fact, it is possible that each feature corresponds to a combination of the human interpretable features, rendering the feature interpretation problem more difficult.

Both of the above problems can be solved or at least alleviated by combining *content-based filtering* and *collaborative filtering*. In collaborative filtering, we make predictions on a user's preferences over items based on all users' past ratings. Collaborative filtering rooted in the keen observation that users who shared similar preferences in the past tend to rate similarly in the future. A collaborative filtering model uses only the past rating information and does not take the contents of the items into consideration. On the other hand, content-based filtering approaches the recommendation problem by analyzing the content of the items and matches it with the preference of a user.

In a recommender system, apart from an integer score, users are often allowed to write text reviews about the item to complement the rating. The review text contains a source of rich information *explaining* the reason why the user assigns such a rating to the item. These reviews provide text contents of the items, which can be leveraged to alleviate cold-start problem when the ratings are sparse. This is because the information embedded in the text review is much richer that an integer rating. When we have few ratings, it is nearly impossible to learn an accurate feature of the concerned user/item. However, the text review might allow us to better estimate the features. To solve the interpretation problem, we align latent topic spaces with the rating spaces. Each latent dimension is tagged with a word cloud, explaining the physical meaning of the dimension. For example, when we see that a user and a movie have large positive value on the third feature, which has text label "thriller, sci-fi, nolan", we know that this user likes the science fiction thriller movie directed by Christopher Nolan.

Interpretability and the cold-start problem are not two isolated problems. Learning an interpretable model could help alleviate the cold-start problem [1, 13]. We can leverage prior knowledge of items and suggest completely "cold" items with confidence. For example, if we know that a user assigns high scores for the topic tagged with "fantasy, adventure, peter, jackson", a recommender system can confidently recommend "The Hobbit: There and Back Again" (a fantasy adventure movie directed by Peter Jackson) to the user even if this movie is not being shown yet.

The contribution of this paper is three-fold. First, we propose a novel method to combine content-based filtering seamlessly with collaborative filtering, modeling the reviews and ratings simultaneously. Secondly, we derive an efficient collapsed Gibbs sampling method to learn the model. Thirdly, we demonstrate our model's advantage in prediction accuracy compared with previous work, especially under the cold-start setting, on large real-life datasets with millions of users and items. We also show the interpretability of the model using a few examples.

2. RELATED WORK

Recommender systems can broadly be classified into two types: *content-based filtering* [21] and *collaborative filtering*. Content-based filtering recommends an item to a user by matching up the features of the item with the preferences of the user, both of which are learnt by analyzing the contents and profiles. Collaborative filtering (CF), on the other hand, approaches the recommendation problem by analyzing the co-occurrence patterns of user-item pair, which is often attached with an integer rating. There are extensive investigations on collaborative filtering, from neighborhood-based methods [27, 11] to model-based methods [9, 26]. Recently, some methods concentrated on ranking [10, 24] the items better. Other approaches leveraged social [14, 15] and side information [32] to improve the performance.

Due to the advantage of taking the review text into consideration, there are a few efforts [2, 4, 16, 17] explored the combination of content-based filtering and collaborative filtering. In the early work [17], the authors cast the content-based filtering as a classification problem, using which they filled out some of the unobserved user item rating matrix and apply collaborative filtering methods on this denser matrix. The authors of [2] cast the recommendation problem as an ordinal regression problem and applied a combination of kernels to handle the side information. In [4], the authors found that there were a few aspects that affect how users rate items. They harnessed the information embedded in the review text to learn how a user weights these aspects and how an item distributes on these aspects. However, their method required human annotators with expert domain knowledge to pre-define these aspects rather than learning them automatically from the reviews.

In the recent work [16], the authors proposed the Hidden Factors and Hidden Topics (HFT) model, which learnt a Latent Dirichlet Allocation (LDA) [3] model for items using the review text and a matrix factorization model to fit the ratings. To bridge the gap between the stochastic vector obtained from LDA and the real-valued vector in MF model, the authors proposed a transformation to link the two. Their method demonstrated significant improvement over baseline methods that use ratings or reviews alone. However, the transformation function they employ, the exponential function, fixed the relationship between latent vector in MF and the topic distribution. Although a parameter is employed to maintain a more flexible relationship, it is still difficult to ensure that this transformation is correctly scaled.

In [8, 29, 30], the authors also considered the interpretable aspects to make better predictions. However, their approaches differ from ours in that either they had *explicit* ratings per aspect (i.e., multiple ratings on prescribed aspects per user item pair), or these aspects were inferred from other context than review text. In another line of research called sentiment analysis [6, 12], a positive or negative label rather than an integer score is learnt for a short text. Our work also differs from [18], which recommends personalized reviews. In [31], the authors proposed Collaborative Topic Regression (CTR) to suggest scientific articles to potential readers. Later work [22] extended it to take the social network among users into consideration. As pointed out in [16], the latent dimensions they discovered were not necessarily correlated with ratings.

3. RATINGS MEET REVIEWS

Our model, titled "Ratings Meet Reviews" (RMR), is a probabilistic generative model that combines a topic model seamlessly with a rating model. We describe it as follows.

3.1 Model and Notations

Suppose there are N users $\mathcal{U} = \{u_1, u_2, \cdots, u_N\}$, M items $\mathcal{V} = \{v_1, v_2, \cdots, v_M\}$, a set of observed indices $Q = \{i, j\}$, where $\{u_i, v_j\} \in \mathcal{U} \times \mathcal{V}$ defines the observed ratings $\mathcal{X} = \{x_{i,j}\}$, each of which is optionally associated with a review $r_{i,j} = \{w | w \subset V\}$ of length $L_{i,j}$, where V is the set of vocabulary used in the review text. Alternatively, let $\mathcal{U}_j$ denote the indices of users who have rated item v_j. Let K denote the number of topics.

RMR operates on items[2], which has an intrinsic distribution θ on topics. This distribution describes the proportion that the item belongs to each topic.

We present the generative process below:

1. For each user $u \in \mathcal{U}$:

   (a) For each latent topic dimension $k \in [1, K]$:

      i. Draw $\mu_{u,k} \sim \text{Gaussian}(\mu_0, \sigma_0^2)$

2. For each latent topic dimension $k \in [1, K]$:

   (a) Draw $\psi_k \sim \text{Dirichlet}(\beta)$

3. For each item $v \in \mathcal{V}$:

   (a) Draw topic mixture proportion $\theta_v \sim \text{Dirichlet}(\alpha)$

   (b) For each description word $w_{v,n}$:

      i. Draw topic assignment $z_{v,n} \sim \text{Multinomial}(\theta_v)$

      ii. Draw word $w_{v,n} \sim \text{Multinomial}(\psi_{z_{v,n}})$

   (c) For each observed rating assigned by u to v:

      i. Draw topic assignment $f_{v,u} \sim \text{Multinomial}(\theta_v)$

      ii. Draw the rating $x_{v,u} \sim \text{Gaussian}(\mu_{u,f_{v,u}}, \sigma^2)$.

From the generative process, we can identify that the text reviews are generated similarly as the LDA model. We use a mixture of Gaussian rather than matrix factorization based methods [16, 31] to model the ratings. These user-topic specific Gaussian distributions have clear interpretations. They describe how a user values the aspects denoted by each latent topic. The item is modeled as a distribution of topics, which together with the user-topic specific Gaussian distributions determine how a user would rate the item. The ratings and review text are connected by the same item topic distribution θ. The more a user talks about certain aspects concerning an item, the higher the distribution will be on these topics, which in turn affects the rating that the user would assign to the item.

We choose to model ratings using mixture of Gaussians for two reasons. First, we can avoid the difficult choice of the transformation function employed in [16]. As discussed above, the transformation function is restrictive and the scaling parameter is nontrivial to select. Secondly, we can retain the interpretability of the topics with no compromise. The interpretability of the latent dimensions is an important factor to solve the cold start problem. Take book recommendation for example, when a user showed strong interest in dimension with high probability on words "da vinci code dan brown". We can confidently recommend Dan Brown's new book "Inferno". We are able to associate the latent dimensions with the *prior* knowledge (for example, Meta data) that is available *without* ratings or reviews.

Given the generative process, the probability of observing the review text and the ratings given the model parameters $\Theta = \{\theta, \psi, \mu\}$ is

$$P(\mathbf{w}, \mathbf{x}|\Theta; \alpha, \beta, \mu_0, \sigma_0^2, \sigma^2) = \prod_{j=1}^{M} P(\theta_j|\alpha) \prod_{i\in\mathcal{U}_j} \left(\sum_{f=1}^{K} P(f|\theta_j)P(x_{i,j}|\mu_{i,f}, \sigma^2)\right) \left(\prod_{l=1}^{L_{i,j}} \sum_{z=1}^{K} P(z|\theta_j)P(w_l|\psi_z)\right) \left(\prod_{i=1}^{N}\prod_{k=1}^{K} P(\mu_{i,k}|\mu_0, \sigma_0^2)\right) \left(\prod_{k=1}^{K} P(\psi_k|\beta)\right). \quad (1)$$

If we take the log of Eq. (1), we get the log-likelihood of model parameters. However, because of the summation inside the log, direct optimization is not feasible. We subsequently develop an efficient collapsed Gibbs sampling method to learn the model parameters in Section 3.3. We now take a deeper look at RMR and compare it with HFT and CTR.

3.2 Comparison with HFT and CTR

Shown in Figure 2 are the graphical models of RMR and several related work. As is clear from the figure, the left parts of CTR, HFT and RMR resemble LDA, which was originally proposed by David Blei et al. to learn the latent topics in a corpus of documents (items in our setting) in an unsupervised manner. The LDA algorithm assumes there are K latent topics in the corpus, which are K multinomial distributions over the vocabulary. Each document in the corpus is a mixture of these topics. A document specific topic distribution over the K latent topics, θ_j with Dirichlet prior α, governs how much weight each topic takes in document j. This θ_j is a length-K stochastic vector with non-negative entries which sums up to 1.

Both HFT and CTR adopt the matrix factorization method to model the ratings. Arrange users' ratings on items in a partially observed matrix $X \in \mathbb{R}^{N\times M}$. The matrix factorization model assumes that X has a low rank structure and thus can be decomposed in to the product of two matrices $U^T V$, where both U and V are of rank $K \ll \min(M, N)$. The columns of U and V can be interpreted as the latent features of users and items respectively. The dot product between a user's feature vector and an item's feature vector approximates the rating that the user would assign to the item. To regularize the value that the latent features can assume, often zero-mean isotropic Gaussian priors are placed on both the user and item latent features. The objective function of a matrix factorization model can be formulated as follows,

$$\mathcal{L} = \sum_{i,j\in Q} (U_i^T V_j - X_{i,j})^2 + \lambda_U \|U\|_F + \lambda_V \|V\|_F, \quad (2)$$

in which the first term is the difference between observed and prediction and the rest are regularization terms.

Clearly, there is a discrepancy between the item topic distribution θ_j in LDA and the item feature vector V_j in MF model. The former is a distribution which is all positive and sums up to 1 while the later can assume any real value. Both HFT and CTR try to align the item features with the item topic distribution and hence the rich text review can be exploited to better model the item features. The main difference between HFT and CTR model lies in the way they align the topic distribution θ_j and the item feature V_j. In CTR, the item feature V_j is assumed to be a Gaussian random variable with mean θ_j and precision c. In other words, the θ_j is taken as the *default* value of V_j, but the later can adapt to match the ratings. If an item receives a lot of ratings, it is possible that V_j differs from θ_j significantly. The interpretation of the latent topics in such case

[2]RMR is symmetrical in that the topic distribution θ can also be user specific. We found, however, that item specific θ performs better in practice.

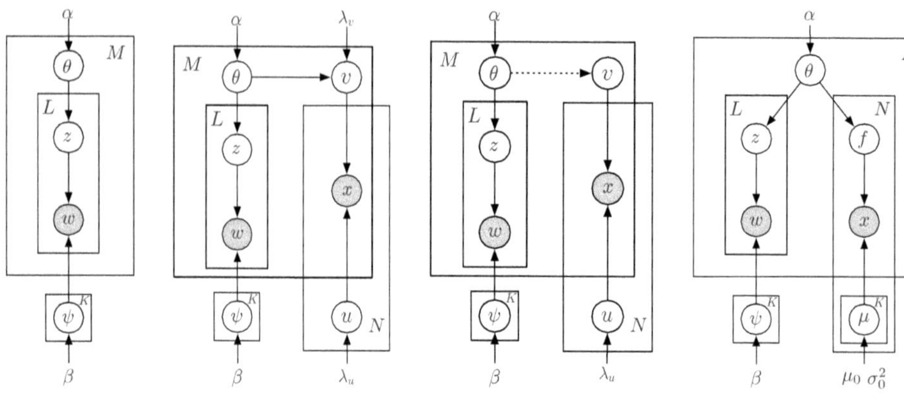

Figure 2: Graphical Models

might be distorted. CTR model was proposed to recommend scientific articles to potential readers, which is a one-class collaborative filtering task [7, 20]. It adopt the strategy to set different c for observed ratings ($X_{i,j} = 1$) and unobserved ratings ($X_{i,j} = 0$). In our setting, we try to match only the observed ratings with the given rating scales (for example, 1 to 5). On the other hand, HFT adopts a fixed transformation function to map one-to-one between θ_j and V_j. In Figure 2(c), we use a dashed line to represent this relationship. The HFT model is effectively a matrix factorization model with the item feature regularization replaced by the corpus likelihood. This fixed transformation function is difficult to select and restrictive in modeling capability.

RMR adopt a mixture of Gaussian to model the ratings. The mixture proportion is assumed to have the same distribution as the topic distribution. Thus when there are few ratings for an item, the text review can still allow us to learn the topic distribution θ accurately. We avoid the difficult choice of the transformation function in HFT and retain the interpretability of the latent topics.

3.3 Collapsed Gibbs Sampler

To develop a Gibbs sampler for RMR, we need to specify the conditional probability of the hidden variables z and f, which are the hidden topics associated with the observed words w and observed ratings x, $P(\mathbf{z}, \mathbf{f}|\mathbf{w}, \mathbf{x})$. This conditional probability does not have a closed form and is difficult to sample directly. The collapsed Gibbs sampler runs a Markov chain that uses the full conditional in order to simulate it. In our case, we need to specify the following two conditional probabilities

$$P(z_i = j|\mathbf{z}_{\neg\mathbf{i}}, \mathbf{w}, \mathbf{f}, \mathbf{x}), \quad P(f_i = j|\mathbf{z}, \mathbf{w}, \mathbf{f}_{\neg\mathbf{i}}, \mathbf{x}). \tag{3}$$

We will briefly derive the expression for the second probability in Eq. (3). Using Bayes' theorem and the conditional independence, we obtain

$$\begin{aligned} &P(f_i = j|\mathbf{z}, \mathbf{w}, \mathbf{f}_{\neg\mathbf{i}}, \mathbf{x}) \\ &\propto P(x_i|f_i = j, \mathbf{f}_{\neg\mathbf{i}}, \mathbf{x}_{\neg\mathbf{i}})P(f_i = j|\mathbf{f}_{\neg\mathbf{i}}, \mathbf{z}) \end{aligned} \tag{4}$$

Now we will derive the expression for the two terms in Eq. (4). Let the index i denote the rating assigned by user u to item v.

$$\begin{aligned} &P(x_i|f_i = j, \mathbf{f}_{\neg\mathbf{i}}, \mathbf{x}_{\neg\mathbf{i}}) \\ &= \int_{\mu_{u,j}} P(x_i, |\mu_{u,j}, f_i = j)P(\mu_{u,j}|\mathbf{f}_{\neg\mathbf{i}}, \mathbf{x}_{\neg\mathbf{i}})\mathrm{d}\mu_{u,j} \end{aligned} \tag{5}$$

The second term in Eq. (5) is a Gaussian distribution, because

$$P(\mu_{u,j}|\mathbf{f}_{\neg\mathbf{i}}, \mathbf{x}_{\neg\mathbf{i}}) \propto P(\mathbf{x}_{\neg\mathbf{i}}|\mu_{u,j}, \mathbf{f}_{\neg\mathbf{i}})P(\mu_{u,j}). \tag{6}$$

Since $P(\mu_{u,j})$ is Gaussian $\mathcal{N}(\mu_0, \sigma_0^2)$ and conjugate to $P(\mathbf{x}_{\neg\mathbf{i}}|\mu_{u,j}, \mathbf{f}_{\neg\mathbf{i}})$, the posterior distribution $P(\mu_{u,j}|\mathbf{f}_{\neg\mathbf{i}}, \mathbf{x}_{\neg\mathbf{i}})$ will be Gaussian $\mathcal{N}(\mu_i, \sigma_i^2)$, where

$$\sigma_i^2 = \frac{1}{\sigma_0^2} + \frac{|x_{u,(\cdot)}^j|}{\sigma^2}, \tag{7}$$

$$\mu_i = (\sigma_i^2)^{-1}\left(\frac{\mu_0}{\sigma_0^2} + \frac{\sum_m x_{u,m}^j}{\sigma^2}\right). \tag{8}$$

The predictive posterior in Eq. (5) is Gaussian $\mathcal{N}(\mu_i, \sigma_i^2 + \sigma_0^2)$ [19]. Similarly, the expression for the second term in Eq. (4) is

$$P(f_i = j|\mathbf{f}_{\neg\mathbf{i}}, \mathbf{z}) \propto \int_{\theta_v} P(f_i = j|\theta_v)P(\theta_v|\mathbf{f}_{\neg\mathbf{i}}, \mathbf{z})\mathrm{d}\theta_v, \tag{9}$$

of which the second term is

$$P(\theta_v|\mathbf{f}_{\neg\mathbf{i}}, \mathbf{z}) \propto P(\mathbf{f}_{\neg\mathbf{i}}|\theta_v)P(\mathbf{z}|\theta_v)P(\theta_v). \tag{10}$$

Again, since $P(\theta_v)$ is Dirichlet(α) and conjugate to $P(\mathbf{f}_{\neg\mathbf{i}}|\theta_v)$ and $P(\mathbf{z}|\theta_v)$, the posterior is also a Dirichlet distribution and the posterior predictive of Eq. (9) is

$$P(f_i = j|\mathbf{z}, \mathbf{f}_{\neg\mathbf{i}}) = \frac{n_{f,\neg i,j}^v + n_{z,j}^v + \alpha}{n_{f,\neg i,(\cdot)}^v + n_{z,(\cdot)}^v + K\alpha}. \tag{11}$$

Combine the result in Eq. (5) and Eq. (9), we get the expression for the full conditional for the first probability in Eq. (3)

$$\begin{aligned} &P(f_i = j|\mathbf{z}, \mathbf{w}, \mathbf{f}_{\neg\mathbf{i}}, \mathbf{x}) \\ &\propto \mathcal{N}(x_i|\mu_i, \sigma_i^2 + \sigma_0^2)\frac{n_{f,\neg i,j}^v + n_{z,j}^v + \alpha}{n_{f,\neg i,(\cdot)}^v + n_{z,(\cdot)}^v + K\alpha}, \end{aligned} \tag{12}$$

and by employing a similar procedure, we get the expression for the first probability in Eq. (3)

$$\begin{aligned} &P(z_i = j|\mathbf{z}_{\neg\mathbf{i}}, \mathbf{w}, \mathbf{f}, \mathbf{x}) \\ &\propto \frac{n_{\neg i,j}^{w_i} + \beta}{n_{\neg i,j}^{(\cdot)} + |V|\beta} \frac{n_{z,\neg i,j}^v + n_{f,j}^v + \alpha}{n_{z,\neg i,(\cdot)}^v + n_{f,(\cdot)}^v + K\alpha}. \end{aligned} \tag{13}$$

We summarize the notations used in the derivation process in Table 1. Note that we omit the $\neg i$ subscription in some of the notations to save space. With this notation, it means that when counting

Symbol	Description
$\|x^j_{u,(\cdot)}\|$	# of ratings assigned by u with topic j
$x^j_{u,m}$	value of rating assigned by u to m with topic j
$n^v_{z,j}$	# of z of item v assigned to topic j
$n^v_{z,(\cdot)}$	total # of review words v received
$n^v_{f,j}$	# of f of item v assigned to topic j
$n^v_{f,(\cdot)}$	total # of ratings item v received
$n^{w_i}_j$	# of word w_i assigned to topic j
$n^{(\cdot)}_j$	total # of words assigned to topic j

Table 1: Notations

the respective values, we exclude current word w_i or current rating x_i.

3.3.1 Readout Parameters

Once the sampling process is finished, we can readily readout the model parameters

$$\theta_{v,j} = \frac{n^v_{z,j} + n^v_{f,j} + \alpha}{n^v_{z,(\cdot)} + n^v_{z,(\cdot)} + K\alpha}, \psi_{j,w_i} = \frac{n^{w_i}_j + \beta}{n^{(\cdot)}_j + |V|\beta}, \tag{14}$$

and

$$\mu_{u,j} = \left(\frac{1}{\sigma_0^2} + \frac{|x^j_{u,(\cdot)}|}{\sigma^2}\right)^{-1} \left(\frac{\mu_0}{\sigma_0^2} + \frac{\sum_m x^j_{u,m}}{\sigma^2}\right). \tag{15}$$

The notations denote the same meaning as is in Table 1, except that the counters now count all effective samples.

3.3.2 Time and Space Complexity of the Sampler

Our collapsed Gibbs sampler mainly use the following counters to keep track of current states: counter $n^v_{z,j}$ of size $M \times K$, counter $n^v_{f,j}$ of size $M \times K$, counter $n^w_{\neg i,j}$ of size $V \times K$, counter $\sum_m x^j_{n,m}$ of size $N \times K$ and counter $|x^j_{n,(\cdot)}|$ of size $N \times K$. Other than the above listed counters, there are summation counters that are one order smaller than the above counters and thus negligible. So the total Space complexity is $O((M + N + V) \times K)$.

To sample z or f conditioned on everything else, we only need to calculate the conditional probabilities in Eq. (3). This operation requires $O(K)$ operations. Given a fixed K, our sampler scales *linearly* with the length of the observed review text and the number received ratings. Usually the number of latent topics K is small, making our sampler scales up well. Note that training a RMR model is faster than training a HFT model [16]. This is because the later one requires an additional step to learn the feature vectors for all the users.

3.4 Prediction

In order to make a prediction that user u assigns to item v, we compute the expected value

$$x_{u,v} = \sum_k \theta_{v,k}\mu_{v,k}. \tag{16}$$

In practice, we compute the empirical global mean g, user bias b_u and item bias b_v for all users and all items from the training set. We feed the $x'_{u,v} = x_{u,v} - g - b_u - b_v$ to the sampler and when making predictions, add g, b_u, and b_v back.

4. EXPERIMENTS

We conduct an empirical study of RMR and various baseline models to show the following facts:

1. Our model leads to significant improvement on prediction accuracy across various categories of items over several strong baseline models.

2. Our model learns latent topic dimensions that are clearly interpretable.

3. Our model performs better in datasets which are extremely sparse, which resembles the cold-start settings.

4.1 Dataset

We use the Amazon Review dataset collected by [16]. This dataset is a collection of 27 datasets corresponding to various types of items that are available on Amazon[3]. This is the largest rating dataset with text reviews publicly available, to the best of our knowledge. We show the statistics of the datasets in Table 2. Refer to Table 2; there are two facts that are evident immediately. First, the datasets are extremely sparse. The sparseness would clearly deteriorate the performance of most existing recommender systems which only model the ratings. Secondly, a review contains 116.87 words on average across all categories. As will be apparent in the results shown later, these review texts are key to model the ratings accurately.

4.2 Baseline Methods

We compare our model with four baseline models MF, LDAMF, CTR and HFT.

- **MF** This is the standard matrix factorization model as is described in [25]. We ignore the review texts completely and model the ratings only. This is typically a very strong baseline model in collaborative filtering [10, 23].

- **LDAMF** This baseline model is proposed in [16]. This baseline model tries to harness the information in the review text by fitting an LDA model on the review text and then treat the learnt topic distribution on items (or users) as the latent factors in matrix factorization models. By holding the latent factors for items (or users) fixed, the latent factors for users (or items) are learnt by gradient descent methods.

- **CTR** This is the state-of-the-art method that recommends scientific articles to potential interested readers [31]. The CTR model solves the one-class collaborative filtering problem by using different precision parameter c. In our setting, we use it to match the observed integer ratings using the same precision c. We employ LDA-C [3] to pre-train the model. Note that CTR utilizes both ratings and reviews information.

- **HFT** This is the state-of-the-art method that combines reviews with ratings [16]. HFT models the ratings using a matrix factorization model with an exponential transformation function to link the stochastic topic distribution in modeling the review text and the latent vector in modeling the ratings. The topic distribution can be modeled on either users or items. On most datasets, the item specific topic distribution produces more accurate predictions. We report the results whichever are more accurate.

[3]The statistics of category Baby we calculated differs from the description provided on the webpage and we exclude it from consideration.

Dataset	#users	#items	#review	#words	words/review	reviews/item
Arts	24,071	4,211	27,980	2,006,874	71.73	6.64
Jewelry	40,594	18,794	58,621	3,100,948	52.90	3.12
Industrial Scientific	29,590	22,622	13,7042	6,920,151	50.50	6.06
Watches	62,041	10,318	68,356	5,436,671	79.53	6.62
Cell Phones and Accessories	68,041	7,438	78,930	7,567,961	95.88	10.61
Musical Instruments	67,007	14,182	85,405	7,442,294	87.14	6.02
Software	68,464	11,234	95,084	11,012,882	115.82	8.46
Gourmet Foods	112,544	23,476	154,635	10,542,984	68.18	6.59
Office Products	110,472	14,224	138,084	11,206,338	81.16	9.71
Automotive	133,256	47,577	188,728	13,249,641	70.21	3.97
Patio	166,832	19,531	206,250	17,290,881	83.83	10.56
Pet Supplies	160,496	17,523	217,170	18,684,153	86.03	12.39
Beauty	167,725	29,004	252,056	17,889,577	70.97	8.69
Shoes	73,590	48,410	389,877	23,604,059	60.54	8.05
Kindle Store	116,191	4,372	160,793	21,533,201	133.92	36.78
Clothing and Accessories	128,794	66,370	581,933	34,267,151	58.89	8.77
Health	311,636	39,539	428,781	33,277,423	77.61	10.84
Toys and Games	290,713	53,600	435,996	35,034,001	80.35	8.13
Tools and Home Improvement	283,514	51,004	409,499	34,591,409	84.47	8.03
Sports and Outdoors	329,232	68,293	510,991	38,898,738	76.12	7.48
Video Games	228,570	21,025	463,669	55,532,148	119.77	22.05
Home and Kitchen	644,509	79,006	991,794	81,923,017	82.60	12.55
Amazon Instant Video	312,930	22,204	717,651	88,958,349	123.96	32.32
Electronics	811,034	82,067	1,241,778	124,064,510	99.91	15.13
Music	1,134,684	556,814	6,396,350	774,791,468	121.13	11.49
Movies and TV	1,224,267	212,836	7,850,072	997,261,969	127.04	36.88
Books	2,588,991	929,264	12,886,488	1,613,603,531	125.22	13.87
All categories	6,643,669	2,441,053	34,686,880	4,053,795,667	116.87	14.21

Table 2: Statistics of the datasets

4.3 Evaluation

We use Mean Squared Error (MSE) to evaluate various models. For each of the dataset, we randomly select 80% as training set up to 2 million reviews. The remaining reviews are split evenly into validation set and testing set. The initial latent variables z and f are uniformly randomly assigned. We run 2500 iterations with a thinning of 50 iterations to get samples and MSE readout. We report the MSE of the testing set which has the lowest MSE on the validation set. The training of the baseline methods MF, LDAMF, CTR and HFT follow the same routine described in [16]. We use $K = 5$ for all models. We set hyperparameters[4] $\alpha = 0.1$, $\beta = 0.02$, $\mu_0 = 0$, $\sigma_0^2 = 1$ and we use the empirical variance of x as σ^2. In practice, the time required to train the RMR model is about half the time spend on training the HFT model on the same machine.

4.4 Rating Prediction

Shown in Table 3 are the MSE results. The best MSE of each dataset is in bold. We listed the performance of various models on the datasets and the average improvement. The standard deviations of MSE results are shown in parenthesis. Out of the 27 datasets, RMR performs the best on 19 datasets among all considered methods.

Compared with matrix factorization (MF column in Table 3), RMR performs better on 26 out of the 27 datasets with an average improvement on MSE of nearly 8%. Matrix factorization method usually performs well in practice [10, 23] and is a strong baseline method. However, as is shown in our case, in datasets which are extremely sparse, MF is unable to learn an accurate representation of users/items and thus under-performs other methods which take the review text into consideration. However, in the datasets such as Music, Movies and TV and Books, which are relatively denser compared with other datasets; the MF method still performs very well.

The baseline method LDAMF, which was proposed as a baseline method in [16], is probably the simplest model that combines review text and ratings. This baseline method takes the item topic distribution produced by LDA as the feature vectors for the items and then learns the user feature vectors by fitting the observed ratings with item features fixed. The feature vectors of items are learnt using *only* the reviews, which might be sub-optimal to fit the rating data. The expressiveness is thus restricted and we think this restriction caused the nearly 8% improvement produced by RMR.

Compared with CTR, which take the full advantage of the combined information of both the reviews and ratings, our proposed model still leads to an average improvement of 3.28% and performs better on 25 out of the 27 datasets. Similar to LDAMF, CTR takes the item topic distribution produced by LDA as the initial item features. However unlike LDAMF, during the training period, CTR alters both the user features and item features to fit the ratings. The regularization parameter λ_V controls how much the item features can deviate from the item topic distribution vectors. It performs better due to the more flexible modeling capability. However, the CTR does not perform as well as RMR in the extremely sparse datasets such as Arts and Jewelry. We observe that during the experiment, CTR can learn a model that fits the data with a small training error. But the generalization of the learnt model to the unobserved rating is not as good. Note that we report the performance of CTR on the test set by setting λ_V and λ_U to the value which gives best performance on validation set. So the issue of under-regularization is minimized. The performance of CTR on the relatively dense datasets is very competitive.

Compared with HFT, another recommendation method that takes review text into consideration, RMR is still able to improve the performance by 1.22% on average and performs better or equally well in 21 out of 27 datasets. As discussed in previous sections, we think

[4]We searched through the parameters linearly and reported hyperparameters which performed the best.

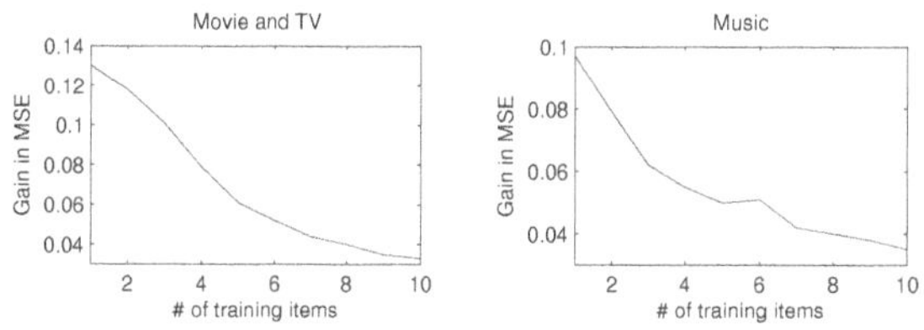

Figure 3: Gain in MSE for user with limited training data

the fixed one-to-one mapping between the item topic distribution and item feature vector impose restrictions of the expressiveness of HFT and allow RMR to out-perform it. Due to large size of the datasets, the improvements reported are significant at 1% level.

We consider the improvements of RMR over CTR (3.28%) and HFT (1.22%) significant because both of these two baselines are full-fledged models that take both the ratings and reviews into consideration. Also, these improvements are verified on 27 real-life datasets. In a real system where recommendation plays a central role, e.g. Amazon, Netflix, these improvements could lead to better revenue and profit.

4.5 Cold-start Setting

An interesting phenomenon we found in the results is that the improvement of RMR over the traditional collaborative filtering methods (matrix factorization) is more significant for datasets that are sparse. For classes such as Arts, Industrial Scientific, RMR show substantial improvement. In such cases, the number of ratings is too scarce to model the items and users adequately. The text in the review associated with the ratings come as rescue, which allow our model to learn a more accurate topic distribution. Whereas for classes such as Music, Movies and Books, which are the largest 3 datasets with larger reviews per user and reviews per item, the traditional methods tend to produce accurate predictions. We further verify this finding by comparing the performance of RMR with MF on users with limited training data. Shown in Figure 3 is the gain of RMR compared with MF for users with limited training items. We show the result on two datasets due to space limit and the phenomenon repeats across all the datasets. As we can see, our model gains the most when the user has few training items. The performance gain starts to decrease with the number of training items available for each user. This further demonstrates that RMR is valuable for the cold-start settings.

4.6 Interpretability of Topics

Apart from being more accurate at prediction, another advantage of RMR is that it learns interpretable latent topics. We show two examples of the top words in each topic learnt in RMR in Table 4 and Table 5. Table 4 shows the top words for topics learnt with *software* dataset. Note that Roxio is software for burning DVDs and Quicken is personal financial software. Leopard and Tiger are the code name of Mac OS X and Parallels is a popular virtual machine on OS X. The fourth topic is about the company Microsoft and its products and the last topic is related to Linux. Table 5 shows the top words for topics learnt with Movie and TV dataset. The first topic is dedicated to workout related videos. The second topic contains commonly used words to describe TV series. Batman, Matrix trilogy, Alien and Harry Potter are either science fiction, adventure or fantasy movies. Godzilla is a disaster thriller and Hitchcock is

roxio	quicken	leopard	office	suse
contacted	son	os	excel	accounts
perfect	pick	parallels	2007	2004
burning	given	apple	student	nav
dvds	spanish	turbo	activation	federal
care	starting	tiger	microsoft	symantec

Table 4: Top words for topics in Software

workout	season	batman	disney	godzilla
yoga	match	effects	christmas	hitchcock
workouts	episodes	alien	animation	kidman
videos	seasons	harry	kids	murder
exercises	vs	matrix	shrek	densel
cardio	episode	edition	animated	nicole

Table 5: Top words for topics in Movie and TV

a famous director of psychological thrillers. Nicole Kidman is the leading actress of the classic thriller "Eyes Wide Shut".

Clearly these interpretable topics would help us understand items and users better. For items, the top topic words can be employed as extended tags attached to the item and may improve the prediction accuracy in a tag-aware recommender system [5]. We may also gain better understanding of items by analyzing the topic distribution similarities. For users, once obtaining the topic preferences, we can recommend "cold" items which have few or no ratings to the users with confidence. For example, if we know that a user tends to rate high for topic three and five in Table 5, we can confidently recommend the movie "Interstellar" (a Sci-Fi Thriller movie) even if this movie is not being shown yet. Our prior knowledge of items therefore can help alleviate the cold-start problem.

5. CONCLUSION

In this paper, we propose a model that combines content-based filtering with collaborative filtering seamlessly. By exploiting the information in both ratings and reviews, we are able to improve the prediction accuracy significantly across various classes of datasets over existing strong baseline methods, especially under the cold-start settings where the data are extremely sparse. We develop an efficient collapsed Gibbs sampler for learning the model parameters. Our model also learns topics that are interpretable, enabling us to exploit prior knowledge to alleviate the cold start problem. We plan to explore RMR's ability in discovering user communities and new genres in future work.

Acknowledgement

The work described in this paper was fully supported by the National Grand Fundamental Research 973 Program of China (No. 2014CB340401 and No. 2014CB340405), the Research Grants Council of the Hong Kong Special Administrative Region, China (Project No. CUHK 413212 and CUHK 415113), and Microsoft Research Asia Regional Seed Fund in Big Data Research (Grant No. FY13-RES-SPONSOR-036).

6. REFERENCES

[1] D. Agarwal and B.-C. Chen. flda: matrix factorization through latent dirichlet allocation. In *WSDM*, pages 91–100, 2010.

[2] J. Basilico and T. Hofmann. Unifying collaborative and content-based filtering. In *ICML*, 2004.

Dataset	a MF	b LDAMF	c CTR	d HFT	e RMR	Improvement of RMR versus min(a,b)	c	d
Arts	1.565 (0.04)	1.575 (0.04)	1.471 (0.04)	1.390 (0.04)	**1.371 (0.04)**	14.15%	7.29%	1.39%
Jewelry	1.257 (0.03)	1.279 (0.03)	1.206 (0.03)	1.177 (0.02)	**1.160 (0.02)**	8.36%	3.97%	1.47%
Industrial Scientific	0.461 (0.02)	0.462 (0.02)	0.382 (0.02)	**0.359 (0.02)**	0.362 (0.02)	27.35%	5.52%	-0.83%
Watches	1.535 (0.03)	1.518 (0.03)	1.491 (0.03)	1.488 (0.03)	**1.458 (0.02)**	4.12%	2.26%	2.06%
Cell Phones and Accessories	2.230 (0.04)	2.308 (0.04)	2.177 (0.04)	2.135 (0.03)	**2.085 (0.03)**	6.95%	4.41%	2.40%
Musical Instruments	1.506 (0.02)	1.520 (0.02)	1.422 (0.02)	1.395 (0.02)	**1.374 (0.02)**	9.61%	3.49%	1.53%
Software	2.409 (0.02)	2.214 (0.02)	2.254 (0.02)	2.219 (0.02)	**2.173 (0.02)**	1.89%	3.73%	2.12%
Gourmet Foods	1.515 (0.01)	1.491 (0.01)	1.482 (0.01)	**1.457 (0.01)**	1.465 (0.01)	1.77%	1.16%	-0.55%
Office Products	1.814 (0.01)	1.796 (0.01)	1.733 (0.01)	1.669 (0.01)	**1.638 (0.01)**	9.65%	5.80%	1.89%
Automotive	1.570 (0.01)	1.585 (0.01)	1.492 (0.01)	1.432 (0.01)	**1.403 (0.01)**	11.90%	6.34%	2.07%
Patio	1.771 (0.01)	1.793 (0.01)	1.720 (0.01)	1.698 (0.01)	**1.669 (0.01)**	6.11%	3.06%	1.74%
Pet Supplies	1.700 (0.01)	1.700 (0.01)	1.613 (0.01)	1.583 (0.01)	**1.562 (0.01)**	8.83%	3.27%	1.34%
Beauty	1.399 (0.01)	1.414 (0.01)	1.361 (0.01)	1.358 (0.01)	**1.334 (0.01)**	4.87%	2.02%	1.80%
Shoes	0.305 (0.00)	0.335 (0.00)	0.271 (0.00)	**0.247 (0.00)**	0.251 (0.00)	21.51%	7.97%	-1.59%
Kindle Store	1.553 (0.01)	1.561 (0.01)	1.457 (0.01)	1.437 (0.01)	**1.412 (0.01)**	9.99%	3.19%	1.77%
Clothing and Accessories	0.393 (0.00)	0.406 (0.00)	0.355 (0.00)	0.349 (0.00)	**0.336 (0.00)**	16.96%	5.65%	3.87%
Health	1.615 (0.01)	1.608 (0.01)	1.552 (0.01)	1.538 (0.01)	**1.512 (0.01)**	6.35%	2.65%	1.72%
Toys and Games	1.467 (0.01)	1.395 (0.01)	1.389 (0.01)	**1.370 (0.01)**	1.372 (0.01)	1.68%	1.24%	-0.15%
Tools and Home Improvement	1.600 (0.01)	1.610 (0.01)	1.513 (0.01)	1.510 (0.01)	**1.491 (0.01)**	7.31%	1.48%	1.27%
Sports and Outdoors	1.219 (0.01)	1.223 (0.01)	1.150 (0.01)	1.138 (0.01)	**1.129 (0.01)**	7.97%	1.86%	0.80%
Video Games	1.610 (0.01)	1.608 (0.01)	1.572 (0.01)	1.528 (0.01)	**1.510 (0.01)**	6.49%	4.11%	1.19%
Home and Kitchen	1.628 (0.05)	1.610 (0.05)	1.577 (0.05)	1.531 (0.04)	**1.501 (0.04)**	7.26%	5.06%	2.00%
Amazon Instant Video	1.330 (0.01)	1.328 (0.01)	1.291 (0.01)	**1.260 (0.01)**	1.270 (0.01)	4.57%	1.65%	-0.79%
Electronics	1.828 (0.00)	1.823 (0.00)	1.764 (0.00)	**1.722 (0.00)**	**1.722 (0.00)**	5.87%	2.44%	0.00%
Music	**0.956 (0.00)**	0.958 (0.00)	0.959 (0.00)	0.980 (0.00)	0.959 (0.00)	-0.31%	0.00%	2.19%
Movies and TV	1.119 (0.00)	1.117 (0.00)	**1.114 (0.00)**	1.119 (0.00)	1.120 (0.00)	-0.27%	-0.54%	-0.09%
Books	1.107 (0.00)	1.109 (0.00)	**1.106 (0.00)**	1.138 (0.00)	1.113 (0.00)	-0.54%	-0.63%	2.25%
Average on all datasets						7.79%	3.28%	1.22%

Table 3: MSE results of various models

[3] D. M. Blei, A. Y. Ng, and M. I. Jordan. Latent dirichlet allocation. *Journal of Machine Learning Research*, 3:993–1022, 2003.

[4] G. Ganu, N. Elhadad, and A. Marian. Beyond the stars: Improving rating predictions using review text content. In *WebDB*, 2009.

[5] I. Guy, N. Zwerdling, I. Ronen, D. Carmel, and E. Uziel. Social media recommendation based on people and tags. In *SIGIR*, pages 194–201, 2010.

[6] X. Hu, J. Tang, H. Gao, and H. Liu. Unsupervised sentiment analysis with emotional signals. In *WWW*, pages 607–618, 2013.

[7] Y. Hu, Y. Koren, and C. Volinsky. Collaborative filtering for implicit feedback datasets. In *ICDM*, pages 263–272, 2008.

[8] Y. Jo and A. H. Oh. Aspect and sentiment unification model for online review analysis. In *WSDM*, pages 815–824, 2011.

[9] Y. Koren. Collaborative filtering with temporal dynamics. In *KDD*, pages 447–456, 2009.

[10] Y. Koren and J. Sill. Ordrec: an ordinal model for predicting personalized item rating distributions. In *RecSys*, pages 117–124, 2011.

[11] G. Linden, B. Smith, and J. York. Amazon.com recommendations: Item-to-item collaborative filtering. *IEEE Internet Computing*, 7:76–80, January 2003.

[12] B. Liu and L. Zhang. A survey of opinion mining and sentiment analysis. In *Mining Text Data*, pages 415–463. 2012.

[13] N. N. Liu, X. Meng, C. Liu, and Q. Yang. Wisdom of the better few: cold start recommendation via representative based rating elicitation. In *RecSys*, pages 37–44, 2011.

[14] H. Ma, I. King, and M. R. Lyu. Mining web graphs for recommendations. *IEEE Trans. Knowl. Data Eng.*, 24(6):1051–1064, 2012.

[15] H. Ma, D. Zhou, C. Liu, M. R. Lyu, and I. King. Recommender systems with social regularization. In *WSDM*, pages 287–296, 2011.

[16] J. J. McAuley and J. Leskovec. Hidden factors and hidden topics: understanding rating dimensions with review text. In *RecSys*, pages 165–172, 2013.

[17] P. Melville, R. J. Mooney, and R. Nagarajan. Content-boosted collaborative filtering for improved recommendations. In *AAAI/IAAI*, pages 187–192, 2002.

[18] S. Moghaddam and M. Ester. Aspect-based opinion mining from product reviews. In *SIGIR*, page 1184, 2012.

[19] K. P. Murphy. Conjugate bayesian analysis of the gaussian distribution. Technical report, University of British Columbia, 2007.

[20] R. Pan, Y. Zhou, B. Cao, N. N. Liu, R. M. Lukose, M. Scholz, and Q. Yang. One-class collaborative filtering. In *ICDM*, pages 502–511, 2008.

[21] M. J. Pazzani and D. Billsus. Content-based recommendation systems. In *The Adaptive Web*, pages 325–341, 2007.

[22] S. Purushotham and Y. Liu. Collaborative topic regression with social matrix factorization for recommendation systems. In *ICML*, 2012.

[23] S. Rendle. Factorization machines with libfm. *ACM TIST*, 3(3):57, 2012.

[24] S. Rendle, C. Freudenthaler, Z. Gantner, and L. Schmidt-Thieme. Bpr: Bayesian personalized ranking from implicit feedback. *CoRR*, abs/1205.2618, 2012.

[25] R. Salakhutdinov and A. Mnih. Probabilistic matrix factorization. In *NIPS*, 2007.

[26] R. Salakhutdinov and A. Mnih. Bayesian probabilistic matrix factorization using markov chain monte carlo. In *ICML*, pages 880–887, 2008.

[27] B. M. Sarwar, G. Karypis, J. A. Konstan, and J. Riedl. Item-based collaborative filtering recommendation algorithms. In *WWW*, pages 285–295, 2001.

[28] A. I. Schein, A. Popescul, L. H. Ungar, and D. M. Pennock. Methods and metrics for cold-start recommendations. In *SIGIR*, pages 253–260, 2002.

[29] A. Sharma and D. Cosley. Do social explanations work?: studying and modeling the effects of social explanations in recommender systems. In *WWW*, pages 1133–1144, 2013.

[30] I. Titov and R. T. McDonald. A joint model of text and aspect ratings for sentiment summarization. In *ACL*, pages 308–316, 2008.

[31] C. Wang and D. M. Blei. Collaborative topic modeling for recommending scientific articles. In *KDD*, pages 448–456, 2011.

[32] L. Zhang, D. Agarwal, and B.-C. Chen. Generalizing matrix factorization through flexible regression priors. In *RecSys*, pages 13–20, 2011.

Beyond Clicks: Dwell Time for Personalization

Xing Yi Liangjie Hong Erheng Zhong Nathan Nan Liu Suju Rajan
{xingyi, liangjie, erheng, nanliu, suju}@yahoo-inc.com
Personalization Sciences, Yahoo Labs, Sunnyvale, CA 94089, USA

ABSTRACT

Many internet companies, such as Yahoo, Facebook, Google and Twitter, rely on content recommendation systems to deliver the most relevant content items to individual users through personalization. Delivering such personalized user experiences is believed to increase the long term engagement of users. While there has been a lot of progress in designing effective personalized recommender systems, by exploiting user interests and historical interaction data through implicit (item click) or explicit (item rating) feedback, directly optimizing for users' satisfaction with the system remains challenging. In this paper, we explore the idea of using item-level dwell time as a proxy to quantify how likely a content item is relevant to a particular user. We describe a novel method to compute accurate dwell time based on client-side and server-side logging and demonstrate how to normalize dwell time across different devices and contexts. In addition, we describe our experiments in incorporating dwell time into state-of-the-art learning to rank techniques and collaborative filtering models that obtain competitive performances in both offline and online settings.

Categories and Subject Descriptors: H.3.5 [Information Storage and Retrieval]: Online Information Services

General Terms: Theory;Experimentation

Keywords: Content Recommendation;Personalization;Dwell Time;Learning to Rank;Collaborative Filtering

1. INTRODUCTION

Content recommendation systems play a central role in today's Web ecosystems. Companies like Yahoo, Google, Facebook and Twitter are striving to deliver the most relevant content items to individual users. For example, visitors to these sites are presented with a stream of articles, slideshows and videos that they may be interested in viewing. With a personalized recommendation system, these companies aim to better predict and rank content of interest to users by using historical user interactions on the respective sites. The underlying belief is that personalization increases long term user engagement and as a side-benefit, also drives up other aspects of the services, for instance, revenue. Therefore, there has been a

RecSys'14, October 6–10, 2014, Foster City, Silicon Valley, CA, USA.

http://dx.doi.org/10.1145/2645710.2645724.

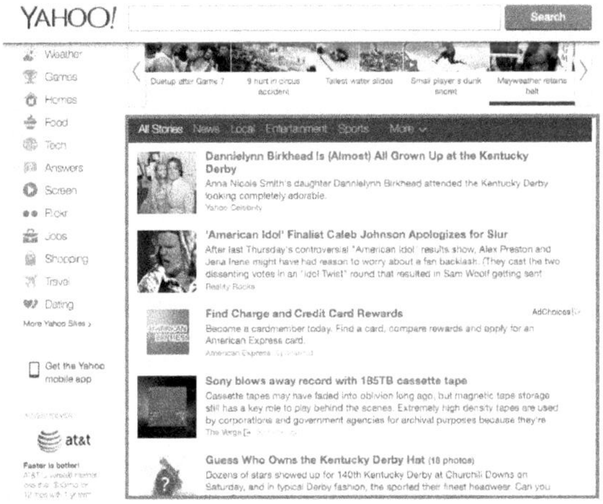

Figure 1: A snapshot of Yahoo's homepage in U.S. where the content stream is highlighted in red.

lot of work in designing and improving personalized recommender systems.

Traditionally, simplistic user feedback signals, such as click through rate (CTR) on items or user-item ratings, have been used to quantify users' interest and satisfaction. Based on these readily available signals, most content recommendation systems essentially optimize for CTR or attempt to fill in a sparse user-item rating matrix with missing ratings. Specifically for the latter case, with the success of the Netflix Prize competition, matrix-completion based methods have dominated the field of recommender systems. However, in many content recommendation tasks users rarely provide explicit ratings or direct feedback (such as 'like' or 'dislike') when consuming frequently updated online content. Thus, explicit user ratings are too sparse to be usable as input for matrix factorization approaches. On the other hand, item CTR as implicit user interest signal does not capture any post-click user engagement. For example, users may have clicked on an item by mistake or because of link bait, but are truly not engaged with the content being presented. Thus, it is arguable that leveraging the noisy click-based user engagement signal for recommendation can achieve the best long term user experience. In fact, a recommender system needs to have different strategies to optimize short term metrics like CTR and long term metrics like how many visits a user would pay in several months. Thus, it becomes critical to identify signals and metrics that truly capture user satisfaction and optimize these accordingly.

We argue that the amount of time that users spend on content items, the dwell time, is an important metric to measure user engagement on content and should be used as a proxy to user satisfaction for recommended content, complementing and/or replacing click based signals. However, utilizing dwell time in a personalized recommender system introduces a number of new research and engineering challenges. For instance, a fundamental question would be how to measure dwell time effectively. Furthermore, different users exhibit different content consumption behaviors even for the same piece of content on the same device. In addition, for the same user, depending on the nature of the content item and the context, the user's content consumption behavior can be significantly different. Therefore, it would be beneficial to normalize dwell time across different devices and contexts. Also, recommender systems usually employ machine learning-to-rank (MLR) techniques and collaborative filtering (CF) models, with a wide range of features, to obtain state-of-the-art performance. Using dwell time in these frameworks is not straight-forward.

In this paper, we use the problem of recommending items for the content feed or stream on the Yahoo's homepage, shown in Figure 1, as a running example to demonstrate how dwell time can be embedded into a personalized recommendation system. We have designed several approaches for accurately computing item-level user content consumption time from large-scale web browsing log data. We first use the log data to determine when each item page gains or loses the user attention. Capturing the user's attention on an item page enables us to compute per-user item-level dwell time. In addition, we leverage content consumption dwell time distributions of different content types for normalizing users' engagement signals, so that we can use this engagement signal for recommending multiple content type items to the user in the content stream. We then incorporate dwell time into machine learning-to-rank (MLR) techniques and collaborative filtering (CF) models. For MLR, we propose to use per-user item-level dwell time as the learning target, which can be easily considered in all existing MLR models, and demonstrate that it can result in better performances. For CF, we use dwell time as a form of implicit feedback from users and demonstrate that a state-of-the-art matrix factorization model to incorporate this information can yield competitive and even better performances than the click-optimized counterpart. To be more specific, we have made the following contributions in this paper:

- A novel method to compute fine-grained item-level user content consumption time for better understanding users' interests is proposed.
- A novel solution to normalize dwell time for multiple content-type items across different devices is proposed and presented.
- An empirical study of dwell time in the context of content recommendation system is presented in this paper.
- A MLR framework to utilize dwell time is proposed and its effectiveness in real-world settings is demonstrated.
- A CF framework to utilize dwell time is proposed and its effectiveness against non-trivial baselines is presented.

The paper is organized as follows. In §2, we review three related research directions. In §3, we demonstrate how dwell time can be measured and present some of its interesting characteristics. In the following sections, we show two important use cases for dwell time. In §4, we show how dwell time can be used in MLR to obtain superior performance than the models that optimize CTR. In §5, we plug dwell time into the state-of-the-art CF models and demonstrate that we can obtain competitive performance. We conclude the paper in §6.

2. RELATED WORK

In this section, we review three related research directions. First, we examine how dwell time is studied and used in web search or IR domains. We will carefully analyze which of the existing practices and experiences, on dwell time computation, can be utilized in the context of personalization. We then list several pointers for MLR as it has been extensively studied in the past decade, followed by a brief discussion on CF, paying special attention to how implicit user feedback is used in CF.

Dwell Time in Other Domains: A significant amount of previous research on web search has investigated using post-click dwell time of each search result as an indicator of its relevance for web queries and how it can be applied for different web search tasks. All such previous research focused on examining the dwell time's utility for improving search results. For instance, White and Kelly [15] demonstrated that using dwell time can potentially help improve the performance of implicit relevance feedback. Kim et al. [8] and Xu et al. [17, 18] showed that using webpage-level dwell time can help personalize the ranking of the web search results. Liu et al. [11] investigated the necessity of using different thresholds of dwell time, in order to derive meaningful document relevance information from the dwell time for helping different web search tasks. To the best of our knowledge, we are the first to use dwell time for personalized content recommendation. Furthermore, we consider different types of content (news articles, slideshows and videos), present several approaches to accurately measure content consumption time, and use the dwell time for understanding users' daily habit and interests. Most recently, Youtube has started to use users' video time spent instead of the click event [1] to better measure the users' engagement with video content. In contrast, we focus on

Learning To Rank in Web Search: The field of MLR has significantly matured in the past decade, mainly due to the popularity of search engines. Liu [12] and Li [10] provide an in-depth survey on this topic. Here, we point out that a fundamental issue with all existing MLR models is that they all optimize for *relevance*, an abstract yet important concept in IR. In the standard setting, the "relevance" between a particular query and a list of documents is objective and the same for all users. For IR, "relevance" is judged by human experts through a manual process and is difficult to scale to millions of real queries. In order to personalize IR, a natural alternative to "relevance" is to optimize CTR. In this paper, we explore the possibility of optimizing for dwell time under the existing framework of gradient boosted decision trees [6]. However, other MLR models can also be used such as pair-wise models (e.g., RankBoost [5] and AdaRank [16]) and list-wise models (e.g., RankNet [3] and ListNet [4]). Note that, we do not seek to propose new MLR models, but instead show the advantage of utilizing dwell time in existing models.

Collaborative Filtering: In CF systems, users' satisfaction with the items is usually not considered. Almost all previous work in CF (e.g., [9, 1]) take only explicit feedback such as ratings, or "implicit" click-based feedback into account. Hu et al. [7] considered implicit feedback signal, such as whether a user clicks or reviews an item, and incorporated it into the matrix factorization framework. Rendle et al. [13] proposed a learning algorithm for binary implicit feedback datasets, which is essentially similar to AUC optimization. None of them went beyond binary implicit feedback to investigate the interactions between users and items. The approach of Yin et al. [19] is the closest to our work. In that paper, the authors used

[1]http://youtubecreator.blogspot.com/2012/08/youtube-now-why-we-focus-on-watch-time.html

Table 1: Client-side Logging Example

User Behaviors	Client-side Events
A user opens a news article page.	$\{$`DOM-ready`$, t_1\}$
He reads the article for several seconds.	$\{$`Focus`$, t_2\}$
He switches to another browser tab or a window to read other articles.	$\{$`Blur`$, t_3\}$
He goes back to the article page and comments on it.	$\{$`Focus`$, t_4\}$
He closes the article page, or clicks the back button to go to another page.	$\{$`BeforeUnload`$, t_5\}$

a graphical model on the explicit feedback signals and dwell time data to predict the user's score. Our work is different in that our model does not require the presence of explicit user feedback.

3. MEASURING ITEM DWELL TIME

In this section, we describe how dwell time can be measured from web logs and show its basic characteristics.

3.1 Dwell Time Computation

Accurately computing item-level dwell time from web-scale user browsing activity data is a challenging problem. As an example, most modern browsers have a multi-tabbed interface in which users can open multiple stories simultaneously and switch between them. In the multi-tabbed setting, figuring out the tab that captured the user's attention is non-trivial. In this paper we describe two complementary methods to derive dwell time, one via client-side logging and the other via server-side logging. We have also conducted a simple study comparing these two approaches. Although client-side logging can capture fine-grained user behavior and has the potential of being highly useful, there is a lot of dependency on browser implementation and potential for large amounts of data loss. Therefore, when the client-side data is not available, we resort to reasonable approximation methods through server-side logging. Thus, we can reliably compute dwell time in a real world setting.

Client-Side Dwell Time: Client-side logging utilizes Javascript/DOM events [2] to record how users interact with the content story pages. Let us imagine the scenario demonstrated in Table 1 where the left column is a sequence of user interactions with a news article and the right column contains the corresponding client-side events, in the form of $\{\text{event name}, \text{time stamp}\}$ tuples. In these events, `DOM-ready` indicates the ready-time of the body of the page, which can be considered as the start of the dwell time. `Focus` indicates that the user's focus was back on the body of the news article. `Blur` means that the article body lost the user attention. `BeforeUnload` is the time point immediately prior to the page being unloaded. Based on these events, we can compute dwell time on the client-side by simply accumulating time differences between `Focus` event and `Blur` events. From the above example, we have the dwell time as: $(t_3 - t_2) + (t_5 - t_4)$. We can clearly see that client-side approach can accurately capture users' actual attention even in multi-tabbed modern browsers. The major drawback of client-side logging is that it relies on the correctness of Javascript execution and on

[2]http://en.wikipedia.org/wiki/DOM_events

Table 2: Comparison of dwell time measurement. The first two columns are for `LE`, the middle two columns are for `FB` and the last two columns are for client-side logs. Each row contains data from a day.

#	DT. (LE)	#	DT. (FB)	#	DT. (C)
3,322	86.5	3,197	134.4	3,410	130.3
5,711	85.4	5,392	132.6	5,829	124.0

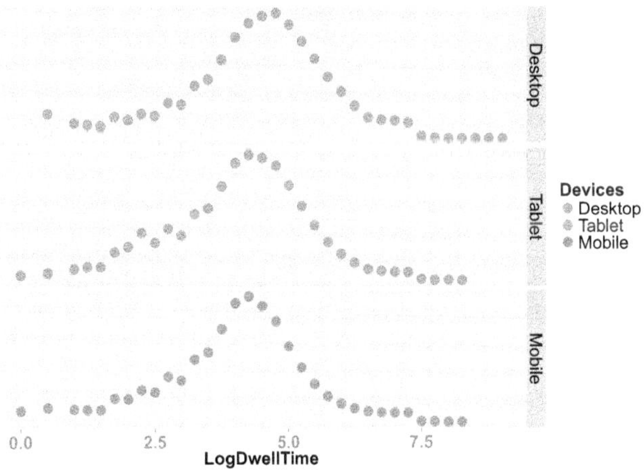

Figure 2: The (un)normalized distribution of log of dwell time for articles across different devices. The X-axis is the log of dwell time and the Y-axis is the counts (removed for proprietary reasons).

servers successfully receiving and logging client-sent data. Data loss in this client-server interaction can be very high, for example, because of loss in internet connection. In addition, users may also disable Javascript in their browsers.

Server-Side Dwell Time: When client-side logs are not available, we resort to server-side logging to infer users' attention on item pages. The computation of dwell time on server-side are built on a number of heuristics. One approach is to simulate client-side user attention events by identifying pseudo `Focus` and `Blur` events from server logs. Consider the following sequence of logging events:

$$\{i, \texttt{Click}, t_1\} \rightarrow \{j, \texttt{Click}, t_2\} \rightarrow \{k, \texttt{Click}, t_3\}$$

where each event is a tuple of an item id, a event type and a timestamp. The dwell time for i and j can be computed as $t_2 - t_1$ and $t_3 - t_2$ respectively. A more complicated example is:

$$\{i, \texttt{Click}, t_1\} \rightarrow \{j, \texttt{Click}, t_2\} \rightarrow \{k, \texttt{Click}, t_3\} \rightarrow$$
$$\{i, \texttt{Comment}, t_4\} \rightarrow \{n, \texttt{Click}, t_5\}$$

where the dwell time for page i can be computed as $(t_2 - t_1) + (t_5 - t_4)$. We denote this as `FB` (Focus/Blur) method. Another simpler heuristic is called `LE` (Last Event) method, which is to take the last event of the page as the *end-page* event and compute the interval of the first-event timestamp and the last one. From the example above, the dwell time of page i by `LE` would be $t_4 - t_1$. Both approximation methods have their own weaknesses: 1) The `FB` approach can *over-estimate* the dwell time because servers do not know the exact time the target story page loses its user attention. For the above example, if the last click happens on some other page, $(t_5 - t_4)$ interval could includes some user time spent outside the target page. The `FB` approach might also *under-estimate*

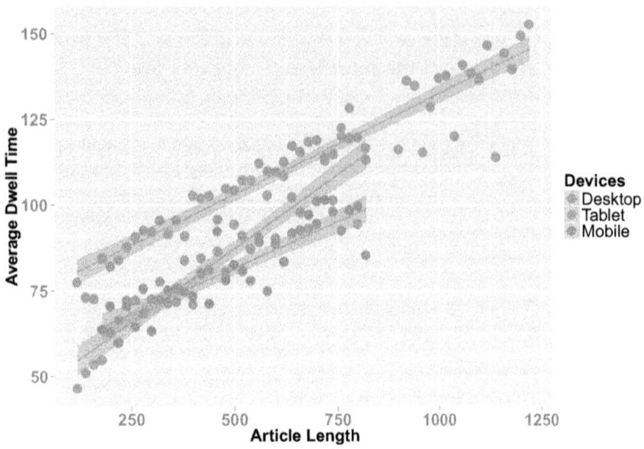

Figure 3: The relationship between the average dwell time and the article length where X-axis is the binned article length and the Y-axis is binned average dwell time.

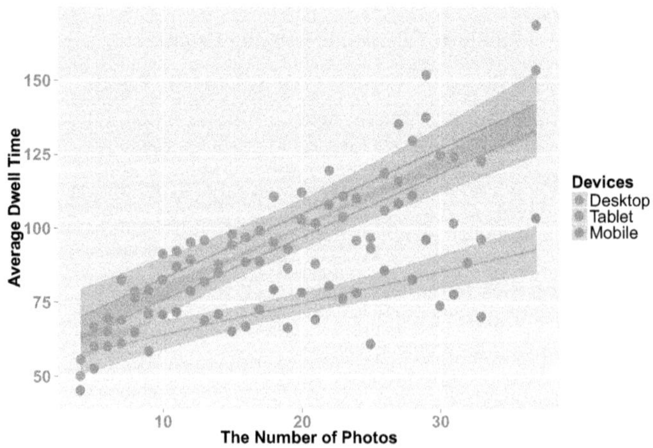

Figure 4: The relationship between the average dwell time and the number of photos on a slideshow where X-axis is the binned number of photos and the Y-axis is binned average dwell time.

the dwell time because servers also do not accurately know the time the target page gains user attention. For the above example, if users have returned to the target page and read it for some additional time before commenting at t_4, the dwell time computation will not include the additional time. 2) The `LE` approach does not consider the scenario in which the users' reading focus could switch among multiple browser page tabs, thus over-estimating the dwell time. On the other hand, because the LE approach conservatively uses the last event on the target page to compute dwell time and servers do not know when the user abandons or closes the page (without the client-side *unload* event), it can also under-estimate the dwell time.

Because both approaches could over-estimate or under-estimate the item-level dwell time, we conducted a simple comparison study among `FB`, `LE` and the client-side logging. The results are shown in Table 2. The purpose of this study is to explore which server-side approach can be used to better approximate the client-side logging. We use two days' server-side logging events and client-side logging events for article pages, and compute the **average** dwell time by each method. Note that even for the same time period, different approaches use different sets of events to compute dwell time (see above example) and client-side events can be lost. Thus, the total number of articles considered varies (the first, the third and the fifth column). From the table, we can see that the average dwell time computed by the `FB` approach is very close to the client-side logging.Meantime, the `LE` approach greatly under-estimates the dwell time, compared with the client-side events. This result shows: through simulating users' reading attention switch events from server-side, the `FB` approach better handles item-level dwell time computation in multi-tabbed modern browser setting. Therefore, we now use `FB` as a relative reliable fall-back proxy to measure the item-level dwell time from server-side logging events when client-side logging is not available.

3.2 Dwell Time Analysis

In order to understand the nature of it, we analyze per-item per-user dwell time from a large real-world data collection from Yahoo. We plot the unnormalized distribution of log of dwell time in Figure 2. The data used for this figure is from one month's Yahoo homepage sample traffic. It is obvious that the log of dwell time follows a bell-curve. Many would guess the distribution of log of dwell time is a Gaussian distribution. However, Q-Q plot and also Shapiro–Wilk test [14] reject such an assertion. A further study of its formal distribution is in future work. Regardless of its normality, we observe that the bell-curve pattern holds for different time periods and different types of devices (see Figure 5 and 6, which we will discuss later).

Since dwell time approximates the time users spend on an item, it is natural to assume that given the same content quality, a longer news article would attract longer average dwell time across all users. In order to demonstrate this behavior, we investigate this issue on text heavy news article [3], and plot a scatter-plot of average dwell time per article versus article length in Figure 3 where X-axis is the length of article and the Y-axis is the average dwell time of that particular article from all users. In order to show things clearly, the dwell times and article lengths are binned into smaller buckets where each point represents a bucket. We show the scatter-plot of the dwell time against the length of the article on different devices, namely desktop, tablet and mobile devices. The black line is a fitted linear line for a particular device type with the 0.95 confidence interval in the grey area. From the figure, it is very clear that the length of the article has good linear correlation with the average dwell time across devices. Also, matching our intuition, the average dwell time on desktop is longer for long articles and the reading behavior on tablet and mobile devices are similar. Furthermore, the correlation becomes weaker when articles are very long: for desktop when the article is longer than 1,000 words, the plot has big variance; this indicates that users may have run out of their time-budget to consume the complete long story. Although the high correlation between the length of articles and average dwell time naturally leads to using the length of articles as a feature to predict average dwell time, we point out based on the observed data: (1) per-user dwell time (rather than binned average dwell time over all users) has little correlation with the article length; and (2) long dwell time may not necessarily reflect that users are really interested in the article. In other words, content length alone can hardly explain the per-user per-item dwell time, and we need to be careful of the bias of dwell time based user engagement measurements

[3]For other content types such as slideshow and video, the content length could be the number of slides in the slideshow and the video clip's raw duration, respectively.

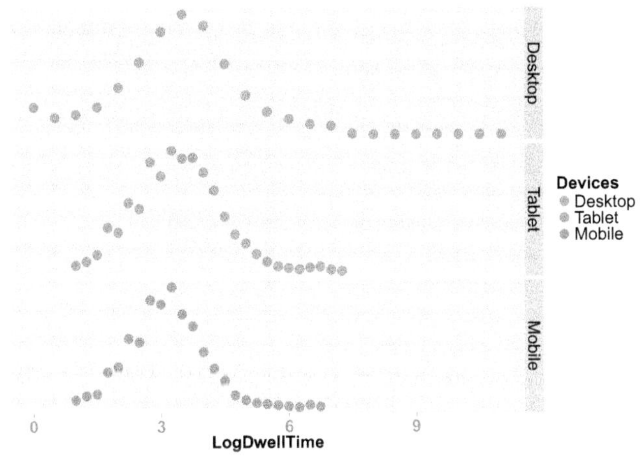

Figure 5: The (un)normalized distribution of log of dwell time for slideshows across different devices. The X-axis is the log of dwell time and the Y-axis is the counts (removed for proprietary reasons).

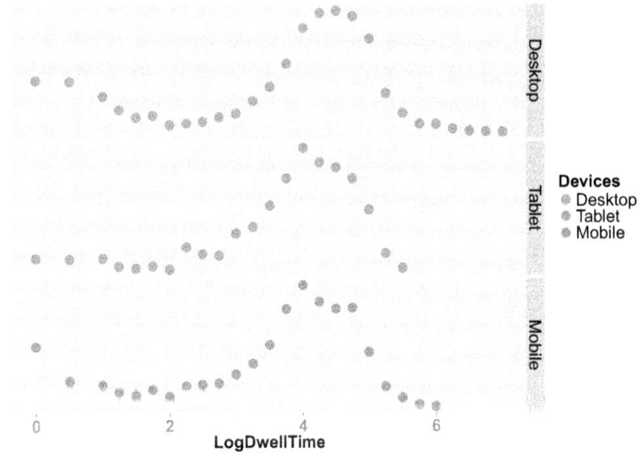

Figure 6: The (un)normalized distribution of log of dwell time for videos across different devices. The X-axis is the log of dwell time and the Y-axis is the counts.

towards long length content stories. (We will revisit this issue in §3.4.)

For slideshows, a natural assumption would be that the larger the number of photos/slides, the longer the average dwell time these items would receive over all users. We demonstrate the relationships between the number of photos and the average dwell time on slideshows in Figure 4. Again, we binned the number of photos and the average dwell time. It is clear that the correlation is not as strong as the length of articles. For videos, we also observe the similar weak correlations between the duration of a video clips' and it's average dwell time.

3.3 Normalized Dwell Time

As may be obvious, users' consumption of content items varies by context. For example, in historical data, we found that users have on average less dwell time per article on mobile or tablet devices than on desktops. Also, users on average spend less time per slideshow than per article. Indeed, different content types, by their nature, would result in different browsing behaviors; thus we would expect different dwell times among these content types. In order to extract comparable user engagement signals, we introduce the normalized user dwell time to handle users' different content consumption behaviors on different devices for personalization. The technique discussed here can also be used to blend multiple content sources (e.g., slide-shows and articles) into a unified stream.

Although the distributions of users' per-item dwell time (from all users) for each content type is different, we found that each content type's distribution remains similar over a long time period. To demonstrate this observation, we further plot the log of dwell time of two important types of content: slideshows and videos in Figure 5 and Figure 6, respectively. Similar to the article case, we do not report the absolute values for both types. However, the patterns are again obvious. In all these cases, the log of dwell time has Gaussian-like distributions. Indeed, most of the dwell time distributions for each different content-type on different device platforms all surprisingly share the similar pattern. The same conclusion holds for different lengths of the time period. Also, we can easily see that the peak of log of dwell time is highest for videos, followed by articles and slideshows, which matches our intuitive understanding of these three types of content items.

Thus, the basic idea is, for each consumed item, we would like to extract its dwell time based user engagement level such that it is comparable across different context (e.g. content types, devices, instrumentations, etc.). We do this by normalizing out the variance of the dwell time due to differences in context. In particular, we adopt the following procedure to normalize dwell time into a comparable space:

1. For each content consumption context C, collect the historical per-item time spent data and compute the mean μ_C and standard deviation σ_C, both in log space.
2. Given a new content item i's time spent t_I in its context C_i, compute the z-value in log space: $z_i = \frac{\log(t_i)-\mu_{C_i}}{\sigma_{C_i}}$.
3. Compute the normalized dwell time of item i in the article space: $t_{i,\text{article}} = \exp(\mu_{\text{article}} + \sigma_{\text{article}} \times z_i)$.

In other words, all other types of items are now "comparable" after this transformation, and the normalized user engagement signals are then used for training recommendation models to handle different content types and can be deployed in different contexts.

3.4 Predicting Dwell Time

The average dwell time of a content item can be viewed as one of the item's inherent characteristic, which provides important average user engagement information on how much time the user will spend on this item. Predicting average dwell time for each content item can help labeling items when their dwell time are not available/missing. For example, content items that have never been shown to users (such as new items) will not have available dwell time. As another example, a user's dwell time on her clicked story may not be always be computed because there may be no subsequent server-side events from the same user. Therefore, leveraging predicted average dwell time can greatly improve the "coverage" (or alleviate the missing data issue). Not handling these situations, could degrade the effectiveness of applying dwell time in personalization applications. In this sub-section, we present a machine learning method to predict dwell time of article stories using simple features.

The features we consider are topical category of the article and the context in which the article would be shown (e.g., desktop, tablet or mobile). We use Support Vector Regression (SVR)[4] models to predict dwell time. The model is trained from a sample of

[4]http://www.csie.ntu.edu.tw/~cjlin/liblinear/

Table 3: Features and corresponding weights for predicted dwell time. The features are shown in the order of magnitude of weights. The left column shows positive weights and the right negative weights.

Name	Weight	Name	Weight
Desktop	1.280	Apparel	-0.001
Mobile	1.033	Hobbies	-0.010
Tablet	0.946	Travel & Tourism	-0.039
Content Length	0.218	Technology	-0.040
Transportation	0.136	Environment	-0.065
Politics	0.130	Beauty	-0.094
Science	0.111	Finance	-0.151
Culture	0.100	Food	-0.173
Real Estate	0.088	Entertainment	-0.191

user-article interaction data. We show the features and their corresponding weights in Table 3. Most features are categorical and we use log(Dwell Time) as the model response. We can loosely interpret the weights of these features as how much that feature contributes to the article's average dwell time prediction. The feature weights match our **current** expectation for average users' article reading behavior: longer articles can lead to higher predicted average dwell time; people spend a longer time reading articles on desktop devices than mobile devices; more serious topics can lead users to dwell longer. Potentially, the predicted average dwell time could be leveraged to normalize the dwell time-based user engagement signal (as discussed in §3.3); however, this is non-trivial as the interplay between the dwell time features and users' experience is not obvious. For example, will recommending more serious topics that have long average dwell lead to better or worse user experience? We will leave answering this question for future work.

4. USE CASE I: LEARNING TO RANK

In this section, we investigate how to leverage item-level dwell time to train machine-learned ranking (MLR) models for content recommendation.

The Basic MLR Setting: In traditional MLR, a query q is represented as a feature vector $\boldsymbol{q}$ while a document d is represented as a feature vector $\boldsymbol{d}$. A function g takes these two feature vectors and outputs a feature vector $\boldsymbol{x}_{q,d} = g(\boldsymbol{q}, \boldsymbol{d})$ for this query-document pair (q, d). Note that g could be as simple as a concatenation. Each query-document pair has a response $y_{q,d}$, in traditional IR, which is usually the relevance judgment. Typically this judgment is common to all users, that is, there is no user-specific personalization. Depending on the particular paradigm (e.g., point-wise, pair-wise or list-wise), a machine learned model imposes a loss function l which takes one or all documents belonging to a query q as the input, approximating the individual relevance judgment, pair-wise relevance preferences or the whole list ordering. In the context of content recommendation, we can simply borrow the idea of MLR by treating user interests as queries and articles (or other types of items) as documents. Although this formulation looks promising, there are two challenges. One is how to construct a feature vector for queries (users) and the second is how to utilize user activities to infer relevancy between users and documents. The discussion of the first question is out of this paper's scope. Here, we focus on the second question. While the definition of relevance judgments might be unambiguous in IR, it is not straightforward in the context of content personalization. One cheap and easy approach is to use users' click-through data as relevance judgments. Essentially, in such case, we use $y_{d,u} = \{0, 1\}$, a binary variable, to indicate whether an article d (the "document" in IR setting) is clicked by the user u (the "query" in IR setting). Under this formalism, a MLR model indeed optimizes (CTR).

In this paper, we use the Gradient Boosted Decision Tree (GBDT) algorithm [6] to learn the ranking functions. GBDT is an additive regression algorithm consisting of an ensemble of trees, fitted to current residuals, gradients of the loss function, in a forward step-wise manner. It iteratively fits an additive model as:

$$f_t(x) = T_t(x;\Theta) + \lambda \sum_{t=1}^{T} \beta_t T_t(x;\Theta_t) \tag{1}$$

such that a certain loss function $L(y_i, f_T(x_i))$ (e.g., square loss, logistic loss) is minimized, where $T_t(x;\Theta_t)$ is a tree at iteration t, weighted by a parameter β_t, with a finite number of parameters Θ_t, and λ is the learning rate. At iteration t, tree $T_t(x;\beta)$ is induced to fit the negative gradient by least squares. That is:

$$\hat{\Theta} = \arg\min_{\beta} \sum_{i}^{N} w_i(-G_{it} - \beta_t T_t(x_i);\Theta)^2 \tag{2}$$

where w_i is the weight for data instance i, which is usually set to 1, and G_{it} is the gradient over the current prediction function: $G_{it} = \left[\frac{\partial L(y_i, f(x_i))}{\partial f(x_i)}\right]_{f=f_{t-1}}$. The optimal weights of tree β_t are determined by $\beta_t = \arg\min_\beta \sum_i^N L(y_i, f_{t-1}(x_i) + \beta T(x_i, \theta))$. More details about GBDT, please refer to [20]. As mentioned above, if we use click/non-click as responses, we simply treat $x_i = \boldsymbol{x}_{q,d}$ and $y_i = y_{d,u}$. In fact, all previous research on MLR-based content recommendation system has been focusing on using click-based information for training and evaluation. For example, Bian et al. [2] and Agarwal et al. [1] have used users' click/view data in Today module in Yahoo for optimizing CTR for content recommendation.

Dwell Time for MLR: There are two intuitive ways to incorporate dwell time into MLR frameworks. Let γ_d be the average dwell time for article d. Taking the GBDT algorithm mentioned above, we could have: 1) Use the per-article dwell time as the response, treating $y_i = h(\gamma_d)$ and 2) Use the per-article dwell time as the weight for sample instances, treating $w_i = h(\gamma_d)$ where the function h is a transformation of the dwell time. In both cases, we promote articles that have high average dwell time and try to learn models that can optimize for user engagements. In all our experiments, we found that $h = \log(x)$ yields the best performance.

We show the effectiveness of MLR model firstly from an offline experiment. We use data from a bucket of traffic of a Yahoo property and split it uniformly at random into training and test sets, using a 70-30 split. We repeat this sampling multiple times and the average results across all train-test splits are shown in Table 4. The first observation is that either method of using dwell time as learning target or instance weight can improve three major ranking metrics. The second observation is that, dwell time as an instance weight leads to the best performance. We further validate these findings in online buckets, shown in Figure 7. Without disclosing the absolute numbers, we show the same three buckets with respect to two types of performance metrics: 1) CTR (shown on the top) and 2) a user engagement metric(shown on the bottom). The user engagement metric is a proprietary one, which can be explained as the quality of users' engagement with Yahoo homepage's content stream. Each data point represents the metric on a particular day. We report the bucket metrics for a three month period between June 2013 and August 2013. Initially, the three buckets were running the same linear model and we can see from the first three data points

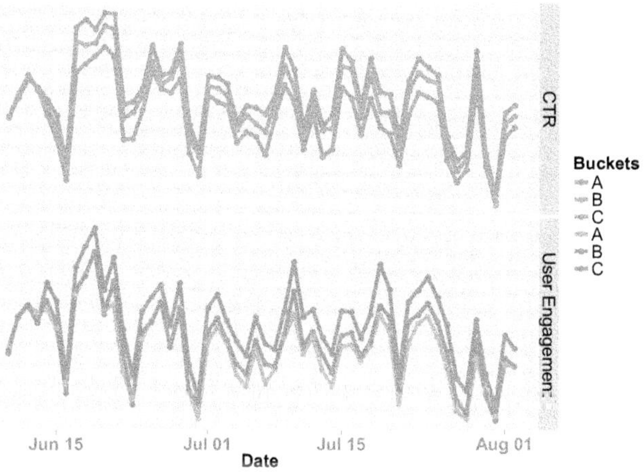

Figure 7: The relative performance comparison between three buckets. The top figure shows the relative CTR difference and the bottom figure shows the relative user engagement difference.

Table 4: Offline Performance for Learning to Rank

Signal	MAP	NDCG	NDCG@10
Click as Target	0.4111	0.6125	0.5680
Dwell Time as Target	0.4210	0.6201	0.5793
Dwell Time as Weight	0.4232	0.6226	0.5820

(three-day data), both CTR and the user engagement metric are similar. Then, we update the models as follows: 1) A: a linear model optimizes click/non-click, 2) B: a GBDT model optimizes click and 3) C: a GBDT model optimizes dwell time $h(\gamma_d)$. It is interesting that after updating models, we observe a divergence of the performances. Bucket A becomes the worst performing bucket in both metrics while bucket C outperforms other buckets consistently for almost two months time until all buckets were ended. Therefore, from our empirical experiences, optimizing dwell time not only achieves better user engagement metrics but also improves CTR as well. One plausible cause is when optimizing towards dwell-based engaging signals rather than high CTR, users may better like the content recommended, come back to the site and click more. We leave the thorough analysis of this finding as future work.

5. USE CASE II: COLLABORATIVE FILTERING

In the previous section, we elaborated how dwell time can be used in the context of MLR, requiring enough per-item interaction activities from a user to build usable interest profile. Thus, it is very challenging for the previous approach to recommend content to users who are not very active (e.g. new users), or to recommend new content that has no overlap with the users' historically read items. CF techniques utilize user engagement signals on particular stories to discover users who have similar reading interest from a broad audience and target them with the same or similar content. In this section, we validate how dwell time can be used in CF frameworks to better improve the performance.

We formalize the problem into the classic matrix factorization framework where latent features of items and user latent features are jointly learnt from a user-item interaction matrix. Matrix factorization models [9] have provided state-of-the-art performance in many CF problems. In prior work, MF models were developed to operate on discrete user ratings (e.g., movie ratings) as labels, thus making it difficult to directly apply these models in settings where explicit ratings are usually missing or hard to collect. For instance, users come to Yahoo's homepage to consume news items such as articles, videos and slideshows by only browsing and clicking on particular items that they are interested in without providing any explicit rating feedback, even though the user interface allows users to "like" or "dislike" the item. Therefore, users' feedback under this context is implicit.

In this paper, we propose to use dwell time of users rather than asking them to give ratings or using click information as implicit rating feedback. User feedback is represented as a $M \times N$ sparse matrix I, where M is the number of users, and N is the number of items, and each entry in the matrix is one user feedback, which is denoted as $r_{i,j}$. For dwell time, $r_{i,j} \in R$ or $[0, 6]$ for normalized dwell time; for click/view, $r_{i,j} \in [0, 1]$. Formally, we aim to predict the unobserved entries in the matrix based on the observed data. Rank-based matrix factorization is used. We decompose the sparse matrix I as U and V, to minimize the following objective function:

$$\arg\min_{U,V} \sum_{i=1}^{M} \sum_{r_{i,j}<r_{i,k}} U_i(V_j - V_k)^T + \lambda(|U|_2 + |V|_2) \quad (3)$$

where $r_{i,j}$ refers to positive examples, $r_{i,k}$ refers to negative examples. The difference between the training process of dwell time and click is the bootstrap process of negative examples. For click, no-click feedbacks are treated as negative data. For dwell time, for each click with dwell time, we randomly sample another click feedback with less dwell time or non-click feedback.

Dataset: The data used in this experiment is collected from a bucket (a small sample traffic) of a Yahoo property, spanning a three month period. We perform training on the first three months and prediction on last month. We further remove the users and items with less than 10 clicks. In this dataset, we have $147,069$ distinct users and $11,535$ distinct items, yielding $4,358,066$ events in the training set and $199,420$ events in the test set.

Evaluation Method and Metrics: We group users by time periods and construct sessions of all items a user consumed in a particular time period (e.g., months, day, hour and etc.). Instead of evaluating how well we can predict clicks/non-clicks, we evaluate the proposed methods in terms of ranking metrics. We use Mean Average Precision (MAP) and Normalized Discounted Cumulative Gain (NDCG) as main evaluation metrics. We start the definition of metrics by focusing on a particular user. Let Precision@k for a particular user in one session as: $\texttt{Prec@k} = \frac{1}{k}\sum_{j=1}^{k} r_j$ where k denotes the truncation position and r_j is whether the ranked document at the j position is relevant or not. Average Precision, the measure using two levels of relevance judgement, is depended on the basis of Precision $\texttt{AP} = \frac{1}{|D^+|}\sum_j r_j \times \texttt{Prec@j}$ where $|D^+|$ denotes the number of relevant items with respect to the user in this session. Given a ranked list for a session, we can compute an AP for this session. Then MAP is defined as the mean of AP over all sessions for all users. NDCG@k is a measure for evaluating top k positions of a ranked list using multiple levels (labels) of relevance judgement. It is defined as $\texttt{NDCG@k} = N_k^{-1}\sum_{j=1}^{k} \frac{2^{r_j}-1}{\log_2(1+j)}$ where NDCG is just for all positions.

Experimental Results: There are two different strategies for evaluation. The first experiment takes the data from first three months as training data while the last one as test data. The second one is to use sliding window to perform daily or weekly prediction. The overall performance is shown in Table 5 where the

Table 5: Performance for Collaborative Filtering

Performance for Monthly Prediction			
Signal	**MAP**	**NDCG**	**NDCG@10**
Click as Target	0.3773	0.7439	0.7434
Dwell Time as Target	0.3779	0.7457	0.7451
Performance for Weekly Prediction			
Signal	**MAP**	**NDCG**	**NDCG@10**
Click as Target	0.6275	0.5820	0.5813
Dwell Time as Target	0.6287	0.5832	0.5826
Performance for Daily Prediction			
Signal	**MAP**	**NDCG**	**NDCG@10**
Click as Target	0.6275	0.5578	0.5570
Dwell Time as Target	0.6648	0.5596	0.5589

table is split into three parts, the first part about monthly prediction, the middle part about weekly prediction and the bottom part about daily prediction. For weekly prediction and daily prediction, the metrics are averaged numbers across multiple weeks or days. We also vary the latent dimension K for both click version and the dwell time version and only report the best performance across different K values. We can observe that in all evaluation methods and all metrics, the model to optimize dwell time has a comparable performance as the one to optimize clicks. In addition, the performance of dwell time based models are consistently better than the click based ones. One plausible reason, for the small overall improvement, is that content features or user-side information may be needed for better predicting dwell time based rating. Deeper analysis and experimentation on the benefit of dwell time based CF models is future work.

6. DISCUSSION AND CONCLUSIONS

In this paper, we demonstrated how dwell time is computed from a large scale web log and how it can be incorporated into a personalized recommendation system. Several approaches are proposed for accurately computing item-level user content consumption time from both client side and server side logging data. In addition, we exploited the dwell time distributions of different content types for normalizing users' engagement signals into the same space. For MLR, we proposed using per-user per-item dwell time as the learning target and demonstrated that it can result in better performances. For CF, we used dwell time as a form of implicit feedback from users and demonstrated how it can be incorporated into a state-of-the-art matrix factorization model, yielding competitive and even better performances than the click-optimized counterpart. For future work, we would like to design dwell time based user engagement metrics and explore how to optimize these metrics directly. We would also like to investigate better ways to normalize dwell time. This will enable us to extract better user engagement signals for training recommendation systems thereby optimizing for long term user satisfaction.

7. REFERENCES

[1] D. Agarwal, B.-C. Chen, P. Elango, and R. Ramakrishnan. Content recommendation on web portals. *Communications of the ACM*, 56(6):92–101, June 2013.

[2] J. Bian, A. Dong, X. He, S. Reddy, and Y. Chang. User action interpretation for online content optimization. *IEEE TKDE*, 25(9):2161–2174, Sept 2013.

[3] C. Burges, T. Shaked, E. Renshaw, A. Lazier, M. Deeds, N. Hamilton, and G. Hullender. Learning to rank using gradient descent. In *Proceedings of ICML*, pages 89–96, 2005.

[4] Z. Cao, T. Qin, T.-Y. Liu, M.-F. Tsai, and H. Li. Learning to rank: From pairwise approach to listwise approach. In *Proceedings of ICML*, pages 129–136, 2007.

[5] Y. Freund, R. Iyer, R. E. Schapire, and Y. Singer. An efficient boosting algorithm for combining preferences. *The Journal of Machine Learning Research*, 4:933–969, Dec. 2003.

[6] J. H. Friedman. Stochastic gradient boosting. *Computational Statistics & Data Analysis - Nonlinear methods and data mining*, 38(4):367–378, Feb. 2002.

[7] Y. Hu, Y. Koren, and C. Volinsky. Collaborative filtering for implicit feedback datasets. In *Proceedings of ICDM*, pages 263–272, 2008.

[8] Y. Kim, A. Hassan, R. W. White, and I. Zitouni. Modeling dwell time to predict click-level satisfaction. In *Proceedings of WSDM*, pages 193–202, 2014.

[9] Y. Koren, R. Bell, and C. Volinsky. Matrix factorization techniques for recommender systems. *Computer*, 42(8):30–37, Aug. 2009.

[10] H. Li. Learning to rank for information retrieval and natural language processing. *Synthesis Lectures on Human Language Technologies*, 4(1):1–113, 2011.

[11] C. Liu, J. Liu, N. Belkin, M. Cole, and J. Gwizdka. Using dwell time as an implicit measure of usefulness in different task types. *Proceedings of the American Society for Information Science and Technology*, 48(1):1–4, 2011.

[12] T.-Y. Liu. Learning to rank for information retrieval. *Foundations and Trends in Information Retrieval*, 3(3):225–331, 2009.

[13] S. Rendle, C. Freudenthaler, Z. Gantner, and L. Schmidt-Thieme. BPR: Bayesian personalized ranking from implicit feedback. In *Proceedings of UAI*, pages 452–461, 2009.

[14] S. S. Shapiro and M. B. Wilk. An analysis of variance test for normality (complete samples). *Biometrika 52 (3-4)*, pages 591–611, 1965.

[15] R. W. White and D. Kelly. A study on the effects of personalization and task information on implicit feedback performance. In *Proceedings of CIKM*, pages 297–306, 2006.

[16] J. Xu and H. Li. Adarank: A boosting algorithm for information retrieval. In *Proceedings of SIGIR*, pages 391–398, 2007.

[17] S. Xu, H. Jiang, and F. C. M. Lau. Mining user dwell time for personalized web search re-ranking. In *Proceedings of IJCAI*, pages 2367–2372, 2011.

[18] S. Xu, Y. Zhu, H. Jiang, and F. C. M. Lau. A user-oriented webpage ranking algorithm based on user attention time. In *Proceedings of the 23rd National Conference on Artificial Intelligence - Volume 2*, pages 1255–1260, 2008.

[19] P. Yin, P. Luo, W.-C. Lee, and M. Wang. Silence is also evidence: Interpreting dwell time for recommendation from psychological perspective. In *Proceedings of SIGKDD*, pages 989–997, New York, NY, USA, 2013. ACM.

[20] Z. Zheng, K. Chen, G. Sun, and H. Zha. A regression framework for learning ranking functions using relative relevance judgments. In *Proceedings of SIGIR*, pages 287–294, 2007.

Evaluating Recommender Behavior For New Users

Daniel Kluver
GroupLens Research
Department of Computer Science and Engineering
University of Minnesota
Minneapolis, MN 55455 USA
kluver@cs.umn.edu

Joseph A. Konstan
GroupLens Research
Department of Computer Science and Engineering
University of Minnesota
Minneapolis, MN 55455 USA
konstan@cs.umn.edu

ABSTRACT

The new user experience is one of the important problems in recommender systems. Past work on recommending for new users has focused on the process of gathering information from the user. Our work focuses on how different algorithms behave for new users. We describe a methodology that we use to compare representatives of three common families of algorithms along eleven different metrics. We find that for the first few ratings a baseline algorithm performs better than three common collaborative filtering algorithms. Once we have a few ratings, we find that Funk's SVD algorithm has the best overall performance. We also find that ItemItem, a very commonly deployed algorithm, performs very poorly for new users. Our results can inform the design of interfaces and algorithms for new users.

Categories and Subject Descriptors

H.3.3 [**Information Search and Retrieval**]: Information filtering

General Terms

Algorithms, Measurement

Keywords

Recommender Systems, Evaluation, Profile Size, New User Experience, New User Problem, User Cold Start

1. INTRODUCTION

One of the important problems in recommender systems is the new user experience. If the system cannot provide a good user experience, then new users are likely to leave and not return. Even if the system can make accurate recommendations, accuracy alone is not enough to make a good first impression. If the system only recommends items the user has seen, then the user may see no value in the system and leave. Alternatively, if the system only recommends obscure items, then the user will have no way to know if the recommendations are worth taking. This problem is made more complex by how little information we have about new users.

Past work on new user experience in recommender systems has tended to focus on the 'cold start problem'. Cold start refers to the problem that no algorithm can make highly personal recommendations with very limited amounts of information. Unfortunately this means that regardless of the algorithm, no recommender system can make high quality recommendations for users who are still joining the system.

The most studied strategy for gathering more information for new users is to include a new user rating survey. Systems that utilize this practice do not allow their users to receive recommendations until some fixed number of ratings have been entered. The idea is that after enough ratings have been entered, the predictions will be 'good enough'. This idea has been explored by many authors; most consider a system in which the user is presented with a list of items and asked to rate items until they have enough ratings. For a good discussion of prior work in this direction see [8].

While past work has carefully covered the new user rating survey, it has not carefully evaluated which algorithm is best at recommending to new users. The new user survey work sidesteps this issue by assuming that the user will receive no personalization until the survey is complete. Even for systems with a new user survey, carefully choosing algorithms for new users may be very important. Users fresh out of the new user survey will still have far fewer ratings than the average user of the recommender system. Different algorithms may provide very different experiences for these users, even if they give very similar results for the average user.

The ideal way to study this issue would be a live study conducted on people who are new to a recommender system. Users could be randomly assigned an algorithm and then surveyed after a random number of ratings to establish what they thought of the new user experience. Unfortunately, there are many algorithms and new users are a scarce resource.

Fortunately, there has been a growing trend in recommender system research to perform multiple metric offline evaluations of recommender systems. This work comes out of a pushback against early recommender evaluations which only evaluated recommenders in terms of their predictive accuracy [13]. The response of this pushback has been the generation of many different metrics which allow us to more carefully understand the separate aspects of a recommender's output [11, 3, 18]. This strategy allows us to dig much deeper into the differences between algorithms, looking past simple measures of accuracy to more meaningful dimensions such

RecSys'14, October 6–10, 2014, Foster City, Silicon Valley, CA, USA.

ACM 978-1-4503-2668-1/14/10 ...$15.00.
http://dx.doi.org/10.1145/2645710.2645742 .

as how novel the recommendations are, or how frequently the recommendations change for any user. This allows us to capture the qualitative tradeoffs between algorithms which are otherwise quite similar, which helps us choose algorithms that are better suited for a particular domain.

In this work we combine these two streams of research: new user experience research and multiple metric algorithm evaluation. Our goal is to understand the differences between algorithms for new users, especially how these algorithms respond to different amounts of information. By using multiple metrics we can understand not just what algorithm is best in terms of absolute performance, but also gain a more nuanced understanding of the qualities of different algorithms' recommendations.

We structure our work around the following research question:

- RQ1: How do algorithms behave for users with few ratings?

Algorithm behavior is a very broad subject. We will look at three distinct sub-questions to help capture algorithm behavior.

- RQ1.a: How well can different algorithms predict the future ratings of new users?
- RQ1.b: How well can different algorithms rank and recommend good items to new users?
- RQ1.c: How do algorithms behave as measured by other metrics, such as popularity and diversity, for new users?

We will answer these questions by developing an evaluation framework that can be used to understand how algorithms perform for new users. This framework will compare algorithms on eleven different metrics to allow a more complete understanding of the differences between algorithms. We will then use this framework to study how three common algorithms behave for new users. Finally, we will draw conclusions from our evaluation and outline directions for future work.

2. METHODOLOGY

Ideally we would measure new user experience with a live survey on users who are just joining a recommender service. Because new users are a scarce resource we opt to first explore the new user experience in an offline setting. This allows us to test many more profile sizes and algorithms than an online study. We will adapt the standard train and test methodology so that test users have only a specified number of training ratings. By running this approach for various profile sizes we can generate plots of performance against profile size. This lets us understand both how the algorithms compare on these metrics, and how the algorithm performance changes with the number of ratings provided.

This, or a similar technique, has been used by previous authors to make plots of metric values over profile size [4, 2, 9, 11]. Past work used these plots to establish that more ratings lead to better results. We take this technique farther and develop a much more nuanced understanding of the different algorithms, and how they compare for different profile sizes.

Our approach is related to the temporal evaluation methodology, in which a recommender is repeatedly trained on all ratings up to a point in time, and then tested using the next ratings to be made for each user. Temporal evaluations have been used in the past to evaluate how the list of recommended items change as users enter more ratings into the system [11]. While the output of a temporal evaluation can be very similar to our own, the methodologies have some key differences. Where a temporal evaluation is designed specifically to consider the order in which users make ratings, our methodology is designed to try to eliminate this ordering effect from our consideration of the algorithm's behavior.

As mentioned earlier, many recommender systems use a new user survey to collect the first user ratings. These ratings are different than normal user ratings. As we explain shortly, our methodology uses randomization in key places to remove this ordering effect. This allows us to better capture the underlying algorithm performance on "normal" user data. While this makes our methodology unsuited for applying temporal metrics, it allows us to separate an algorithm's behavior from how ratings are collected for new users. We feel that this is better given the limitations of our dataset, and our focus on the algorithm, rather than how ratings are collected.

Algorithms

We seek to develop an understanding of how a range of different standard algorithms perform for new users. Rather than picking advanced algorithms that are tuned for new user performance, we decided to first understand how representatives of three common types of algorithms perform. Therefore we will compare UserUser[14], ItemItem[15], and Simon Funk's SVD[7] against two simple baseline algorithms.

Due to the low profile sizes involved in our evaluation, not every algorithm was able to make predictions for every user-item pair. In these cases, we use the UserItemBaseline prediction as a fallback. This ensured that our prediction based metrics were always evaluated over the same number of items. We found this unnecessary for recommendations as each algorithm was able to make a complete recommendation with only one rating. Therefore we form recommendations as the top 20 items with predictions from the algorithm which were not in the training set. More information about these algorithms can be found in table 1. Code for our evaluation, using the Lenskit evaluation framework [6] is available at `https://bitbucket.org/kluver/coldstartrecommendation`.

ItemBaseline	Item's average rating, with mild bayesian damping towards the global mean [7].
UserItem-Baseline	ItemBaseline adjusted by the user's average offset from the ItemBaseline. Mild bayesian damping is applied [7].
UserUser	User based nearest neighbor collaborative filtering [14] with a neighborhood size of 30 and ratings normalized by subtracting the UserItemBaseline score.
ItemItem	Item based nearest neighbor collaborative filtering [15] with a neighborhood size of 30 and ratings normalized by subtracting the ItemBaseline score.
SVD	Simon Funk's SVD based collaborative filtering approach [7] with 30 features and 150 training iterations per feature.

Table 1: Summary of algorithms.

Metric	Description	Range	Preferred direction
Accuracy and Ranking Metrics			
RMSE	Standard prediction accuracy metric [16].	0 to 5 stars	Smaller is better.
nDCG	Standard ranking quality metric [16].	0 to 1	Larger is better.
Monotonic Recommendation Metrics			
Precision@20	Count of recommended items in the test set and rated 4.0 or higher[1] [16].	0 to 1	Larger is better.
MAP@20	Average of precision at each rank one through twenty [12].	0 to 1	Larger is better.
Fallout@20	Count of recommended items in the test set and rated 2.0 or lower[1] [2].	0 to 1	Smaller is better.
MeanRating@20	Average rating of recommended items that are in the test set.	0 to 5 stars	Larger is better.
RMSE@20	RMSE computed only over those items that were recommended.	0 to 5 stars	Smaller is better.
Non-monotonic Recommender Metrics			
SeenItems@20	Count of recommended items in the test set.	0 to 20 items	Moderate values are better.
Average-Popularity@20	The average number of users in the training set that have seen recommended items [18].	1 to 6000 users	Moderate values are better.
AILS@20	The average pairwise similarity between recommended items [18].	-1 to 1	Moderate values are better.
Spread@20	The Shannon's entropy of the distribution of recommended items for users in the test set.	0 to 12 bits	Moderate values are better.

Table 2: Summary of metrics

Each algorithm was tuned based off of Ekstrand's 2012 evaluation [5]. Since this evaluation is on a different dataset (MovieLens 10M vs. MovieLens 1M), we performed minor tuning using Ekstrand's values as a starting point. We tuned based on RMSE performance. While tuning, we found that the previous damping parameter used for the baselines to be too large. We found that a value of 5 gave much better results for new user recommendation. Our key results are not sensitive to minor changes of algorithm parameters.

Metrics

We present results from eleven metrics. As has been seen in previous studies [10] we find that some of are metrics are redundant. Future work should be able to use a smaller list of metrics. The metrics are described in table 2. We split our metrics into three groups roughly along our three sub research questions.

Accuracy and Ranking Metrics.

RMSE and **nDCG** evaluate the recommender based on its prediction for each item. These evaluate the accuracy of the predictions and the ability of the recommender to rank the list of all items. We find that these two metrics perform quite similarly in our evaluation.

Monotonic Recommendation Metrics.

These metrics evaluate the top 20 recommendations produced by the recommender. The choice of 20 items for the evaluations was arbitrary, testing with other values showed similar results, except on one metric. This issue will be addressed later in the results section. We refer to these as monotonic metrics as there is a clear good direction for the metric.

[1]We also tried 5.0 and 1.0 as cutoffs respectively, and found no meaningful difference.

Precision@20, **MAP@20**, and **Fallout@20** are standard information retrieval metrics which measure the quality of the recommendations. As we show later, these metrics were not useful for our evaluation. Therefore, to help understand the quality of our recommendations, we also include MeanRating@20, and RMSE@20.

MeanRating@20 tries to establish how much users like their recommendations by measuring users average satisfaction with recommended items based on withheld ratings. **RMSE@20** accompanies this metric and lets us know if the recommended items are likely to be incorrectly predicted. This can help us understand why an algorithm scores well on MeanRatings@20.

Non-monotonic Recommendation Metrics.

SeenItems@20, **AveragePopularity@20**, **AILS@20**, and **Spread@20** are all non-monotonic measures of the user's recommendations. These metrics are harder to apply than the monotonic measures of recommendation quality. Unlike the previous metrics, we expect that users will be most satisfied by moderate values of these metrics, and that both extremes can lead to a negative user experience.

We use these metrics as they can help us understand important properties of how users perceive their recommendations. As mentioned in the introduction the number of recommended items that the user has seen (estimated by **SeenItems@20**) can have a major impact on how much users trust the recommendations. If an algorithm recommends too few items that the user has seen then we expect the user will have trouble evaluating if the recommendations are trustworthy. Too many, and the user may feel that the recommendations are not interesting or useful. Unfortunately, the optimal value for these metrics will vary by domain, user, and context. That said, we feel it is useful to understand how these metrics vary across algorithms for new users, as this knowledge can help inform default algorithm selection within a particular domain and context.

AveragePopularity@20 is a crude metric of how novel the recommendations are to the user [18]. Broadly speaking, we expect users will prefer recommendation lists containing more novel (less popular) items. However, if the recommended items are too novel the user is unlikely to have heard of the items and will have no point of reference in understanding their recommendations.

Past work has shown that users like their recommendations to be more diverse [18, 17]. The belief is that by providing more diverse lists we are giving the user a larger range of items to choose from. This can make choosing an item easier as the user is less likely to have to compare very similar options. It has also been shown, however, that too much diversity can lead to less user satisfaction [18]. This is probably due to a tradeoff between how diverse a list is and how well it captures a user's tastes. At some point, a list cannot become more diverse without including items that do not interest the user. We will measure diversity with the **AILS@20** metric.

The **AILS@20** metric is based on the Intra-List Similarity (ILS) metric introduced by Ziegler et al. [18]. AILS@N is simply a rescaling of ILS to be scale free with regards to N, this was done to make the metric easier to interpret, by putting it on the same scale as similarity values. We used the same item similarity metric for AILS@20 as we used in the ItemItem recommender.

The **Spread@20** metric is designed to measure how well the recommender spreads its attention across many items. We expect that algorithms with a good understanding of its users will be able to recommend different items to different users. Like diversity, however, we expect that it is not possible to reach complete spread (recommending each item an equal number of times) without making avoidably bad recommendations. When Spread is large we know that the recommender is recommending many items with a relatively even distribution. When Spread is small, the recommender is focusing on a small set of items which it recommends to every user. In this way spread is similar to an item coverage metric, but provides a more nuanced measure of item coverage as it considers how often each item is recommended.

Spread is computed by computing recommendations for each test user. Let $C(I)$ be the count of how many times item I showed up in the recommendations. Let $P(I) = C(I)/\sum_I C(I)$ be the probability that a random recommendation is for item I. We define spread as the Shannon's entropy of $P(I)$, $Spread = -\sum_I P(I)\log(P(I))$.

Expectations about algorithm performance.

We expect that the ItemBaseline algorithm will have approximately constant performance on all metrics. Since the ItemBaseline is such a simple algorithm we expect that any reasonable algorithm should be able to do better than it. That said, we expect the improvement over the ItemBaseline to be gradual, with larger improvements only happening with more data.

The UserItemBaseline should only differ from the ItemBaseline for metrics that use the prediction value. For all other metrics these two provide the same responses, and we will only report results for the ItemBaseline. As the UserItemBaseline is still quite a simple baseline, we expect that the non-baseline algorithm will beat this baseline as well given enough ratings.

We expect that the baseline algorithms will provide the most popular recommendations, with the least diversity, and the least spread. Any personalized algorithm should be able to make more nuanced recommendations than simply recommending the best rated items, which should translate as gains on these metrics. Furthermore, we expect that as an algorithm learns more about the user it should decrease in popularity, and increase in diversity, and spread, as it becomes able to make more personal and nuanced recommendations.

Dataset

For this evaluation we will use the MovieLens 1M dataset[2]. This dataset contains 1 million ratings from 6000 users on 4000 movies.

These ratings were collected from the MovieLens system, which requires 15 ratings in a new user survey before users can enter the system. To the best of our knowledge, at the time this data was collected the new user survey preferred items that were very popular. We will randomize the order of the ratings to try to avoid measuring the effect of these initial ratings, and instead focus on the algorithm's performance on normal ratings.

Each user in the dataset has at least 20 ratings. Therefore we will evaluate user profiles with up to 19 ratings. This will allow us to ensure that each user in the dataset has at least one test rating.

Evaluation Procedure

The natural way to perform this evaluation is with a modified user crossfold strategy. The normal five-fold cross validation strategy splits the users into five groups. In each of five folds all ratings from four of the groups will be kept in the training set, and then some subset of the ratings from each user in the fifth group will be set aside for the test set. The selection of a test set can be random to avoid any possible ordering effects in the data due to a new user rating strategy. To understand how metrics change with a different number of users we can simply generate separate random crossfolds for each simulated profile size. At each crossfold we include only a constant number of training ratings for each test user, ensuring that all test users have the specified profiles size.

Unfortunately, we found that this strategy causes biases in our evaluation. In particular, this strategy led to the size of the test sets changing as a function of the simulated profile size. As we kept more ratings for the training set, we would have fewer ratings in the test set. This biased our results; some metrics such as nDCG proved to be sensitive to the size of the test set. As we compared different profile sizes we would see trends that were solely a property of the changing test set size.

Our solution to this bias is to subsample from an existing crossfold. To generate training and test sets for different number of ratings from 1 to 19, we first generate a set of test and training splits so that test users have 19 training items using the crossfold strategy outlined above. Then, to generate any other number of ratings, we randomly downsample the 19 item training set. This allows us to generate training sets with a given number of ratings for test users, such that each profile size is evaluated with the same test set.

[2] `http://grouplens.org/datasets/movielens/`

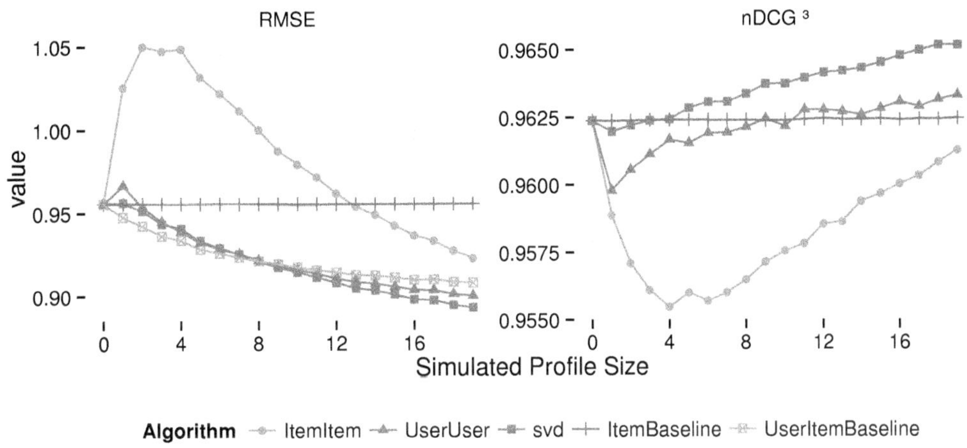

Figure 1: Accuracy and Ranking Algorithms

3. RESULTS

Using the methodology described in section 2 we generate plots for each metric showing how the five algorithms perform versus simulated profile size.

Accuracy and Ranking Metrics

RMSE.

Figure 1 shows how accurate our algorithms are as measured by RMSE. UserUser, and SVD both behaved essentially as expected. SVD shows no improvement with only one rating, and UserUser actually gets worse with the first rating. Other than that, these algorithms outperform ItemBaseline. Interestingly, UserItemBaseline outperforms both algorithms until around 8 ratings, at which point both algorithms start to perform better. Given the size of the differences between UserItemBaseline, UserUser, and SVD we conclude that all three are equally accurate for new users. That such a simple algorithm can outperform more complicated algorithms for small profile sizes suggests that recommending for users with very few ratings is a hard problem.

ItemItem performs quite poorly for new users. Until we have 13 ratings, ItemItem is less accurate than the ItemBaseline. In fact, for the first two ratings ItemItem appears to perform *worse* as more ratings are added. This trend is a result of the limited coverage of the ItemItem algorithm. Considering the accuracy of RMSE on only those items where it makes a personalized prediction, it shows a monotonic increase in accuracy similar to the other algorithms. However, for small rating counts ItemItem can only predict for some percent of the items (around 60% for users with two ratings, and around 75% for users with four ratings). Because of this, many of the predictions come from the better performing UserItemBaseline. As we get our first few ratings, the predictions become less likely to be from the UserItemBaseline, leading to an artificial upward trend in RMSE.

nDCG.

Figure 1 shows the algorithms performance on the nDCG metric. The results for nDCG are very similar to the RMSE results. Both UserUser and SVD take an initial hit to accuracy at the first rating. This time UserUser takes much longer to recover and only beats the baseline after around 12 ratings. Again ItemItem performs quite poorly. This leaves SVD performing the best, passing the baseline after about 3 ratings. Again we find that our best algorithm for the first few ratings is our baseline.

[3]We do not plot UserItemBaseline here as it is equivalent to ItemBaseline on this metric.

Monotonic Recommendation Quality Metrics

MAP@20, Precision@20, Fallout@20.

Figure 2 shows MAP@20, Precision@20, and Fallout@20. All three metrics show essentially the same trend, UserUser gets the lowest score, the baseline gets the highest score. On both MAP@20 and Precision@20, SVD gets a higher score than ItemItem throughout, performing almost as well as the baseline. On Fallout@20 ItemItem and SVD perform about as well as each other, with SVD showing a very slight lead. We also tested recall and mean reciprocal rank metrics, but found them to exhibit the same trend, so they were not explored further.

This result is rather strange as MAP and Precision are metrics where larger scores imply better performance, whereas Fallout is a metric where larger scores imply poor performance. Therefore we would not expect to see rank equivalent behavior from these metrics. Unfortunately this means that these metrics contradict each other. One possible reason for this is that these topN metrics are known to be biased toward algorithms that recommend more popular items [1]. Looking forward to the average popularity (figure 4) of recommended items, we see that the average popularity of the recommendations closely replicates the previous three plots. As a result of this, we discard these metrics, and consider less biased metrics to help us analyze the quality of the recommendations.

SeenItems@20.

We address this non-monotonic metric out of turn here as it provides important context for the next two metrics. The first graph in figure 3 shows the average number of items in the top 20 recommendations for each algorithm that were also in the test set. The average number of test set items in recommendations shows a similar trend to the MAP and precision metrics, with UserUser getting by far the fewest seen items, and the baseline getting the most. As UserUser gets less than one seen item on average we found that UserUser

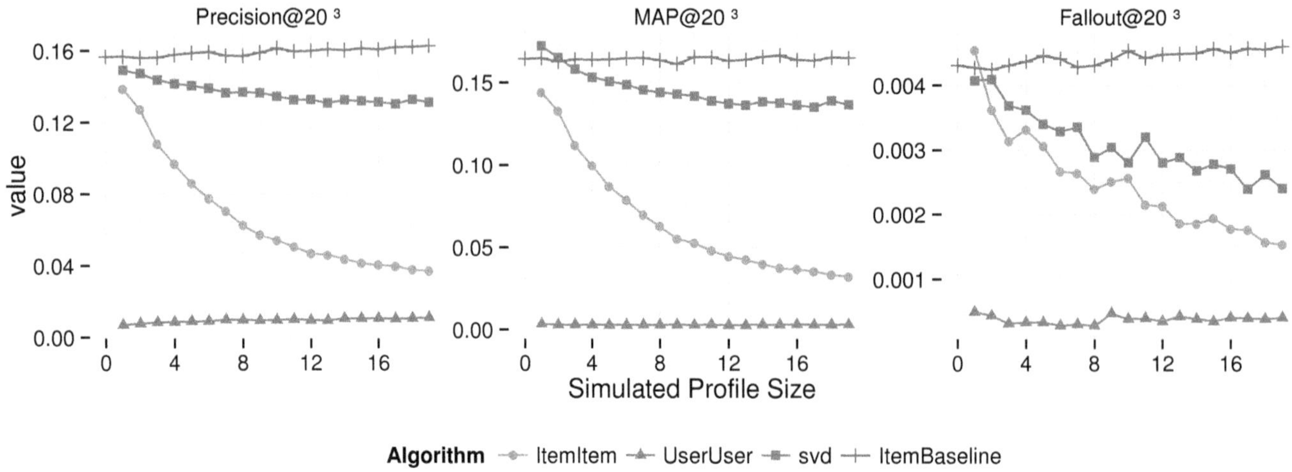

Figure 2: Information Retrieval Recommendation Quality Metrics

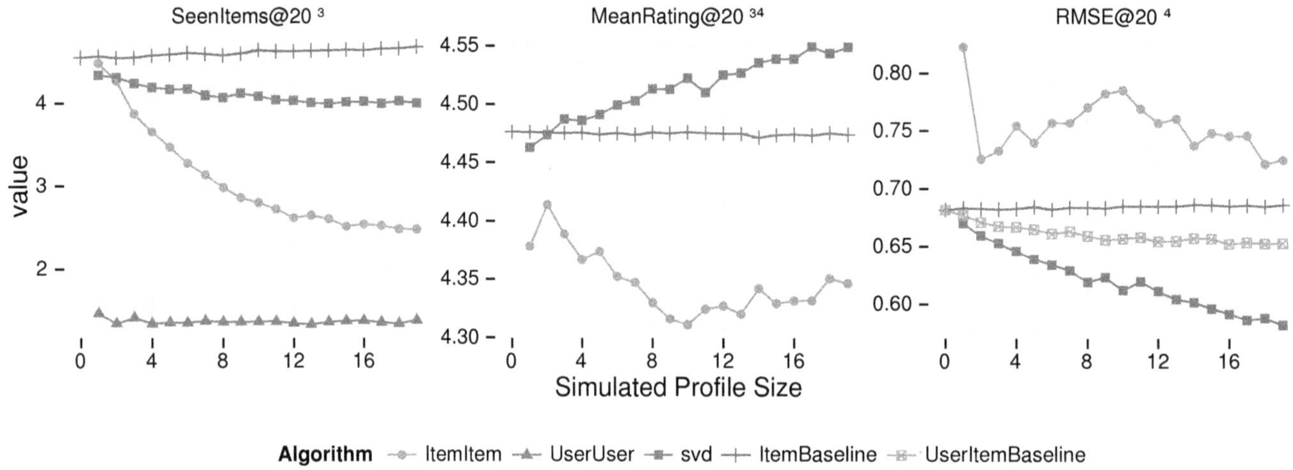

Figure 3: Recommendation Quality Metrics

was not appropriate for the MeanRating@20 and RMSE@20 metrics. In particular, we found that the UserUser results for these metrics are highly sensitive to recommendation list size. Because of this issue we will not include UserUser in our next two metrics and consider the next two metrics inconclusive for UserUser. That said, we consider the small number of seen items to be a bad result for UserUser. Put simply, if we cannot reliably estimate if the recommendations are reasonable, how can we expect a user to do so?

MeanRating@20.

The second graph in figure 3 shows the average rating for those items in the top 20 recommendations for each algorithm. The first thing to note about this graph is that all of these algorithms are doing a reasonable job of recommending items the user might like to watch, with all algorithms averaging above 4 stars (implying that the recommended items are, at least on average, enjoyable). SVD performs as expected, starting around the baseline for a few ratings, and then steadily improving to be the best algorithm after 3 ratings. Again, we find that ItemItem performs poorly until quite a few ratings are added, and does worse than baseline throughout.

RMSE@20.

The third graph in figure 3 shows the accuracy of our algorithms on items in the top 20 recommendations. Not surprisingly, this figure shows the same trends as the last one, meaning that the algorithms whose recommendations were (on average) most likable, were those whose recommendations were most accurate. Again, SVD performs quite well, easily beating the UserItemBaseline after only 1 rating.

Non-monotonic Recommender Quality Metrics

AveragePopularity@20.

The first graph in figure 4 shows the average popularity of items recommended by each algorithm. As expected the baseline algorithms makes the most popular recommenda-

[4]We do not plot UserUser here as it cannot be reliably measured for this metric.

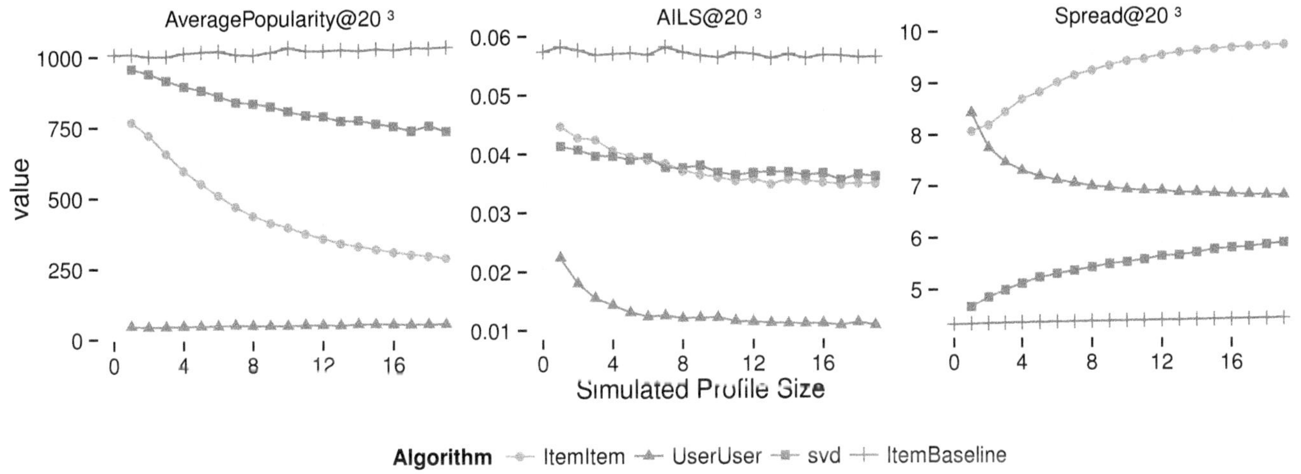

Figure 4: Non-monotonic Recommendation Quality Metrics

tions, followed by SVD, ItemItem, and then UserUser in a distant last. As stated earlier, We expect that users will feel the baseline's popularity (around 1000) is too high. We also expect that users will perceive UserUser's popularity (around 50) as too low. SVD and ItemItem both seem to perform well, with SVD generating more popular recommendations than Item-Item. SVD and ItemItem both show a trend of decreasing popularity as more ratings are entered, suggesting that these algorithms will make more nuanced, less popular recommendations for users they know more about.

AILS@20.
The second graph in 4 shows a similar trend to the popularity trend. Again, we expect that the baseline, which provides the least diverse recommendations, would be perceived as not very diverse by users. Quite possibly due to the preference for obscure movies, UserUser seems to produce the most diverse lists of any algorithm. We expect that the UserUser recommendation lists might be too diverse. Unlike popularity, SVD and ItemItem seem to perform equivalently in terms of diversity. We also see that all three collaborative filtering algorithms show a trend of increasing diversity (decreasing inter-list similarity) as more ratings are entered.

Spread@20.
The third graph in figure 4 shows the spread of the recommendations from each algorithm. As expected the baseline performs worst on spread, as it recommends essentially the same items to each user. SVD performs mildly better than the baseline, and shows definite improvement as more ratings are added. UserUser and ItemItem start at around the same value as each other, however, after only two ratings they have crossed, as ItemItem quickly increases to have the highest spread of all the algorithms, and UserUser quickly decreases into second place. Interestingly, only UserUser shows a trend to have less spread as it learns more about the user, ItemItem and SVD both show the expected trend of increasing Spread as they learn more. This could be some form of a regression towards the mean, where as it learns more about users its recommendations become less personalized to the users individual quirks. More research will be needed to understand this trend.

4. DISCUSSION

Algorithm	Prediction accuracy	Recommendation quality	Other properties
ItemItem	Poor	Poor	Good
UserUser	Good	Inconclusive	Poor
SVD	Good	Good	Good

Table 3: Summary of algorithm behavior for new users

The high level results of our evaluation are summarized in table 3. Overall we see that SVD seems to be the best performing algorithm for cold start use. SVD was the only algorithm that consistently outperformed the baseline algorithms on prediction and recommendation tasks. ItemItem had arguably better results on the average popularity and spread metrics, indicating that it was able to find more novel items, and make a larger range of recommendations to users. Unfortunately, ItemItem also performed quite poorly at both prediction and recommendation, which makes it less suitable for new users.

UserUser performed quite well at prediction, but tended to favor unpopular items in its recommendations. While some novelty is good, we believe that UserUser goes too far with obscure movies in its recommendations, and therefore does not make good recommendations. Therefore we conclude that UserUser alone is not well suited for new users. It is possible that careful tuning or hybridizing with another algorithm may help UserUser perform well for new users. Exploring this issue further is left as future work.

Interestingly, we repeatedly see that for very small numbers of ratings the UserItemBaseline is our strongest algorithm, both in terms of accuracy, and recommendation quality. This suggests a switching strategy for live systems, in which the UserItemBaseline is deployed until a user has enough ratings, after which they are switched to a better recommender. The switching point between algorithms can be determined with our methodology. The only downside of this approach is that the baseline performed poorly on our non-monotonic metrics, which may effect users as they first join the system.

One possible reason that the SVD algorithm performs as well as it does is the regularization built into the algorithm. UserUser and ItemItem algorithms have no built in method for damping their predictions towards the mean when they do not have much data. The regularization in the cost function of the SVD model makes it so its predictions will gradually shift away from the baseline predictions as more relevant ratings are added. The downside of this, however, could be the higher popularity and lower spread seen by the SVD algorithm. The same regularization that helps avoid making mistakes due to too little data may also prevent the algorithm from taking occasional risks on more obscure movies.

One of the limitations of our work is that we only evaluated on one dataset. Future work should replicate our experiment on other datasets from different domains, or where ratings are collected in different ways. This will establish which of our results are true properties of the algorithms, and which results are specific to our dataset.

One important issue that our methodology cannot address is that we can only compare users who have made some minimum number of ratings (20 for our dataset) Unfortunately, this means that we do not know if there are differences between users who do and do not survive in the system. This is an unfortunate side effect of insisting on a constant test set throughout the evaluation. More work needs to be done to understand users who only make one or two ratings to understand how they are different and discover why they leave the system.

Nonetheless, we feel that our methodology will allow offline comparisons of many different cold start experiences. Our work has only scratched the surface of recommender algorithms. Future work can be done comparing these standard algorithms against newer algorithms such as those designed for cold start, or those designed to leverage extra non-rating information. More work should be done to understand how extra information about a user can effect cold start ratings. Our methodology can be used to measure this effect, and even establish a tradeoff between the extra information or extra initial ratings.

5. CONCLUSION

We find that recommending for new users is hard and none of our algorithms can reliably beat a simple baseline for users with very few ratings. Once the user has a small number of ratings we find that the SVD algorithm performs best. This result can be useful both in designing new recommender systems, and in designing novel recommendation algorithms for new users. We also present a methodology and list of metrics for understanding recommender behavior that can be used to extend our results to other algorithms and datasets.

6. ACKNOWLEDGEMENTS

The authors would like to express their gratitude towards our colleagues at GroupLens research for their feedback and support while developing this work. We would like to specially thank Michael Ekstrand for his important work on the Lenskit recommendation framework. This research was supported by the National Science foundation under grants IIS 08-08692 and IIS 10-17697,

7. REFERENCES

[1] A. Bellogín. *Performance prediction and evaluation in Recommender Systems: an Information Retrieval perspective.* PhD thesis, Universidad Autónoma de Madrid, Madrid, Spain, Oct. 2012.

[2] P. Cremonesi, F. Garzottto, and R. Turrin. User effort vs. accuracy in rating-based elicitation. In *RecSys '12*. ACM, 2012.

[3] P. Cremonesi, Y. Koren, and R. Turrin. Performance of recommender algorithms on top-n recommendation tasks. In *RecSys '10*. ACM, 2010.

[4] S. Drenner, S. Sen, and L. Terveen. Crafting the initial user experience to achieve community goals. In *RecSys '08*. ACM, 2008.

[5] M. Ekstrand and J. Riedl. When recommenders fail: predicting recommender failure for algorithm selection and combination. In *RecSys '12*. ACM, 2012.

[6] M. D. Ekstrand, M. Ludwig, J. A. Konstan, and J. T. Riedl. Rethinking the recommender research ecosystem: Reproducibility, openness, and lenskit. In *RecSys '11*. ACM, 2011.

[7] S. Funk. Netflix update: Try this at home. http://sifter.org/~simon/journal/20061211.html, Dec. 2006.

[8] N. Golbandi, Y. Koren, and R. Lempel. Adaptive bootstrapping of recommender systems using decision trees. In *WSDM '11*. ACM, 2011.

[9] N. Golbandi, Y. Koren, and R. Lempel. Adaptive bootstrapping of recommender systems using decision trees. In *WSDM '11*. ACM, 2011.

[10] J. L. Herlocker, J. A. Konstan, L. G. Terveen, and J. T. Riedl. Evaluating collaborative filtering recommender systems. *ACM Trans. Inf. Syst.*, 22(1):5–53, Jan. 2004.

[11] N. Lathia, S. Hailes, L. Capra, and X. Amatriain. Temporal diversity in recommender systems. In *SIGIR '10*. ACM, 2010.

[12] C. D. Manning, P. Raghavan, and H. Schütze. *Introduction to information retrieval*, volume 1. Cambridge university press Cambridge, 2008.

[13] S. M. McNee, J. Riedl, and J. A. Konstan. Being accurate is not enough: How accuracy metrics have hurt recommender systems. In *CHI EA '06*. ACM, 2006.

[14] P. Resnick, N. Iacovou, M. Suchak, P. Bergstrom, and J. Riedl. Grouplens: an open architecture for collaborative filtering of netnews. In *CSCW '94*. ACM, 1994.

[15] B. Sarwar, G. Karypis, J. Konstan, and J. Riedl. Item-based collaborative filtering recommendation algorithms. In *WWW '01*. ACM, 2001.

[16] G. Shani and A. Gunawardana. Evaluating recommendation systems. In F. Ricci, L. Rokach, B. Shapira, and P. B. Kantor, editors, *Recommender Systems Handbook*, pages 257–297. Springer US, 2011.

[17] M. C. Willemsen, B. P. Knijnenburg, M. P. Graus, L. C. Velter-Bremmers, and K. Fu. Using latent features diversification to reduce choice difficulty in recommendation lists. *RecSys '11*, 2011.

[18] C.-N. Ziegler, S. M. McNee, J. A. Konstan, and G. Lausen. Improving recommendation lists through topic diversification. In *WWW '05*. ACM, 2005.

Comparative Recommender System Evaluation: Benchmarking Recommendation Frameworks

Alan Said*
TU-Delft
The Netherlands
alansaid@acm.org

Alejandro Bellogín*
Universidad Autónoma de Madrid
Spain
alejandro.bellogin@uam.es

ABSTRACT

Recommender systems research is often based on comparisons of predictive accuracy: the better the evaluation scores, the better the recommender. However, it is difficult to compare results from different recommender systems due to the many options in design and implementation of an evaluation strategy. Additionally, algorithmic implementations can diverge from the standard formulation due to manual tuning and modifications that work better in some situations.

In this work we compare common recommendation algorithms as implemented in three popular recommendation frameworks. To provide a fair comparison, we have complete control of the evaluation dimensions being benchmarked: dataset, data splitting, evaluation strategies, and metrics. We also include results using the internal evaluation mechanisms of these frameworks. Our analysis points to large differences in recommendation accuracy across frameworks and strategies, i.e. the same baselines may perform orders of magnitude better or worse across frameworks. Our results show the necessity of clear guidelines when reporting evaluation of recommender systems to ensure reproducibility and comparison of results.

Categories and Subject Descriptors: H.5.1 [Multimedia Information Systems]: Evaluation/methodology

General Terms: Experimentation, Documentation, Performance

1. INTRODUCTION

Recommender systems are a popular means of assisting users in online services, whether for music (Spotify, Last.fm), movies and videos (Netflix, YouTube) or other items (Amazon, eBay, etc.). In recent years, the recommender system-related research field has grown exponentially, and today most top-tier research venues feature tracks on recommendation (or closely related). There has been a parallel development in the industry and many of the positions in data science list knowledge of recommendation techniques as a top priority. This gain in popularity has led to an overwhelming amount of research literature over the last few years. With this in mind, it becomes increasingly important to be able to measure recommendation models *against each other* in order to objectively estimate their qualities. In today's recommender systems-related literature, a majority of papers state what datasets, algorithms, baselines and other potential settings are used in order to ensure replication, some manuscripts additionally present running times, hardware and software infrastructure, etc. In light of the vast variety of existing methods to implement and evaluate a recommender system, this is a very positive aspect. It should however be critically analyzed in order to ensure improvement in the field. It is known from Information Retrieval, that even when standard datasets are used and a well-established set of baselines are known, no overall improvement over the years is guaranteed [2].

Looking back on the accumulated amount of work in the research community, there have emerged three popular recommendation frameworks: *Apache Mahout* (Mahout) [24], *LensKit* [11] and *MyMediaLite* [13]. The latter two have been developed by researchers in academia, whereas Mahout is an Apache Software Foundation project. Even though the frameworks provide basically the same recommendation algorithms, they have differences in their implementations, data management, and evaluation methods. The frameworks provide basic evaluation packages able to calculate some of the most common evaluation metrics (e.g. precision, recall, root-mean-square error, etc.). However, due to the difference in implementation between the same algorithm across frameworks, even when using the same dataset, it becomes uncertain whether a comparison of results from different frameworks is possible.

To analyze if such a comparison between recommendation frameworks is indeed possible, we performed a standalone evaluation of recommendation results, allowing fine-grained control of a wide variety of parameters within the evaluation methodology. In this way, we aim to ensure an objective comparison of the recommendation accuracy under some common dimensions, such as the dataset used, the algorithms evaluated, the evaluation metrics analyzed and so on. Our work provides a cross-system and cross-dataset benchmark of some of the most common recommendation and rating prediction algorithms. It also highlights the differences in recommendation accuracy between implementations of the same algorithms on different frameworks, distinct levels of accuracy in different datasets, and variations of evaluation results on the same dataset and in the same framework when employing various evaluation strategies.

2. BACKGROUND

It lies in the nature of recommender systems that progress is measured by evaluating a system and benchmarking it towards other state of the art systems or algorithms. This is generally true for many machine learning-related approaches.

Recommender systems have experienced a steep evolution in the last decade, evaluation methods have seen a similar, although not as diverse development. Seminal works on recommender systems evaluation include Herlocker et al.'s survey [16] and Shani and Gunawardana's book chapter [30].

*Authors contributed equally to this work.

RecSys'14, October 6–10, 2014, Foster City, Silicon Valley, CA, USA.

ACM 978-1-4503-2668-1/14/10 ...$15.00.
http://dx.doi.org/10.1145/2645710.2645746 .

Currently, recommender systems-related research literature commonly include evaluation sections. However, it still often remains unclear how the proposed recommendations perform compared to others. Given the fact that many recommendation approaches are researched, developed and deployed for specific purposes, it is imperative that the evaluation should deliver a clear and convincing overview of the systems' recommendation qualities, i.e. show in detail how the system was evaluated in order to make a comparison to other systems feasible. As an experiment, we studied all full-length (8 page, non-industry) research papers from the two, at the time of writing, most recent ACM RecSys conferences (i.e. after the release of MyMediaLite [13] and LensKit [11]) and analyzed how *reproducible* the results were, 56 papers in total. Reproducibility refers to the description of the experimental setup, the dataset used, the recommendation framework used, etc., in order to allow replication and validation of the results by a third party. Our analysis focused on four aspects of the contributions:

- **Dataset** - if the dataset used is publicly available. Excluding proprietary datasets or ones collected specifically for the paper from public sources (unless made available for download).
- **Recommendation framework** - if the recommendations were generated by openly available frameworks or if the source code was made available. Excluding software not available publicly or where nothing was mentioned.
- **Data details** - if a feasible reproduction of training/test splits is possible (irrespective of dataset) or whether not enough details were given for a successful replication.
- **Algorithmic details** - if algorithms were described in sufficient detail, e.g., neighborhood sizes for nearest neighbor (kNN) or number of factors for matrix factorization approaches.

We see these aspects related to the two issues identified by Konstan and Adomavicius [18] as being critical for making research *cumulative* and allowing *rapid progress*, i.e. ensuring reproducibility and replication by (*i*) thoroughly documenting the research and using open data, and (*ii*) following standards and using best-practice methods for coding, algorithms, data, etc.

In our study we found that only about half of the papers (30) used open datasets, a similar amount (35) presented information on training/test splits, making similar splits possible, even though a direct replication often remained unfeasible. It stands to reason that some organizations cannot share their data openly, making a detailed description of how the data is used even more important. In total, from 56 papers, only one used a combination of an open dataset, an open framework and provided all necessary details for replication of experiments and results. Even though a majority presented an evaluation and comparison towards a baseline, in most cases the information provided was not sufficient for accurate replication, i.e. only providing the algorithm type without additional details (e.g. kNN without neighborhood size, similarity metrics, etc), stating that the data were split into 80%-20% training/test sets but not providing the splitting strategy (per-user, per-item, random, etc.), or what actually constituted an accurate recommendation. Algorithmic details were fully disclosed in only 18 papers, which could perhaps be motivated by the fact that certain algorithmic aspects should be learned on the data (or withheld as part of an organization's intellectual property); there is however no clear reason for withholding data splitting details. We believe this can be due to lack of space and/or the perceived lower importance of specific details concerning the deployment and evaluation.

3. EVALUATION & RECOMMENDATION

This section presents the evaluation methodology and recommendation frameworks used in this paper.

3.1 Evaluation

To provide a fair comparison, we believe complete control over the evaluation protocol needs to be retained. Because of this, we have identified four stages that will be benchmarked using different alternatives available in the literature: *data splitting*, *item recommendation*, *candidate item generation*, and *performance measurement*.

3.1.1 Data splitting

One aspect of the evaluation setting is the dataset partition strategy. Different training and test partitions may have considerable impact on the recommendation performance. Although an exhaustive analysis of data partitioning is out of the scope of our work, we briefly discuss some common methods.

Time-based approaches [6, 15] consider the timeline of events, i.e. the timestamps of when user-item interactions were performed. A basic approach is to select a point in time to separate training data (all interaction records prior to that point) and test data (after the split time point). The split point can be set so as to, e.g. have a desired training/test ratio which can be global, with a single common split point for all users, or user-specific, to ensure the same ratio per user. None of the recommenders evaluated in the scope of this work take time into consideration, hence this is left as future work, where a wider set of recommenders will be tested.

If we ignore time, there are at least three strategies to withhold items: *a*) sample a fixed (different) number for each user; *b*) sample a fixed (same for all) number for each user, also known as *given n* or *all but n* protocols; *c*) sample a percentage of all interactions using *cross validation*, where non-overlapping subsets are generated, i.e. every (user, item, rating) tuple is evaluated once. Protocol *c*, appears to be the most popular [14, 29], although *all but n* (*b*) is also common [5]. We will use cross validation (cv) and test two variations: global splitting into (non-overlapping) folds (global cv), and each user's ratings list divided into the given number of folds and assigned to its corresponding split (per-user cv). We also try other strategies using a fixed number of sampled items, selected as a percentage of the total ratings (global ratio) or as a percentage of a user's ratings, partitioning on a user basis (per-user ratio).

Independent of the partition, the goals of an evaluation may be different in each situation, thus, a different setting (and partition) should be employed [15, 16]. If this is not the case, the results obtained in one setting could be invalid, i.e. evaluating something not sought for. As a result, the partition protocol in use needs to be clearly specified, and assessed if it is appropriate in the context. In this work we benchmark different instantiations of some of these protocols to provide a comparison. In practice the protocol should be selected such that it aligns with the evaluated approach and research goals – not necessarily the protocol obtaining best results.

3.1.2 Recommendation

Once the training and test splits are available, we produce recommendations using three common state-of-the-art methods from the recommender systems literature: user-based collaborative filtering (CF), item-based CF and matrix factorization. One reason behind this choice is the availability of the methods in the compared frameworks, which is not the case for less standard algorithms.

Item-based recommenders look at each item rated by the target user, and find items *similar* to that item [29, 31]. Item similarity is defined in terms of rating correlations between users, although cosine-based or probability-based similarities have also been proposed [9]. Adjusted cosine has been shown to perform better than other similarity methods [29]. The rating prediction computed by item-based strategies is generally estimated as follows [29]:

$$\tilde{r}(u,i) = C \sum_{j \in S_i} \text{sim}(i,j) r(u,j) \quad (1)$$

where S_i is the set of items similar to i [9]. We should note that S_i is generally replaced by I_u – all items rated by user u – since unrated items are assumed to be rated with a zero.

The user-based CF algorithm can be found in the literature under two different formulations; in the first one, rating deviations from the user's and neighbor's rating means are considered [25] (Eq. 2), whereas in the second one raw scores given by each neighbor are used [31] instead (Eq. (3)):

$$r(u,i) = \bar{r}(u) + C \sum_{v \in N_k(u)} \text{sim}(u,v) \left(r(v,i) - \bar{r}(v) \right) \quad (2)$$

$$\tilde{r}(u,i) = C \sum_{v \in N_k(u)} \text{sim}(u,v) r(v,i) \quad (3)$$

where $N_k(u)$ is a neighborhood of (typically) the k most similar users to u [10]; $\bar{r}(u)$ is the user's average rating. Note that both variations are referred to using the same name, making it difficult to *a priori* know which version is used.

The user similarity $\text{sim}(u,v)$ is often computed using the Pearson correlation coefficient or the cosine similarity between the user preference vectors [1]. We include here a shrunk version of these similarities, as proposed in [19]:

$$\text{sim}_s(a,b) = \frac{n_{a,b}}{n_{a,b} + \lambda_s} \text{sim}(a,b) \quad (4)$$

where $n_{a,b}$ is the number of users who rated both items (or items rated by both users), and λ_s is the shrinking parameter.

Matrix factorization recommenders use dimensionality reduction in order to uncover latent factors between users and items, e.g. by Singular Value Decomposition (SVD), probabilistic Latent Semantic Analysis or Latent Dirichlet Allocation. Generally, these systems minimize the regularized squared error on the set of known ratings to learn the factor vectors p_u and q_i [21]:

$$\min_{q^*,p^*} \sum_{(u,i)} \left(r(u,i) - q_i^T p_u \right)^2 + \lambda \left(\|q_i\|^2 + \|p_u\|^2 \right) \quad (5)$$

Since a closed formulation for these models also depends on how the parameters are learned for Eq. (5) we selected the same learning approach in each framework (when possible).

Table 1 shows the classes in each framework corresponding to user-, item- and matrix factorization-based recommenders together with their parameters. Note that FunkSVD [12] is not available in MyMediaLite, instead SVDPlusPlus [19] is used as it performs similarly to the other methods, although it requires a longer training time – due to the algorithm, not the implementation.

3.1.3 *Candidate items generation*

Once recommendations have been generated, the next step is to measure recommendation performance based on predictive accuracy (the error with respect to the predicted rating) and/or ranking-based precision. Both types have their limitations: the former needs the recommender to output a score meaningful as a rating, the latter is sensitive to the number of unknown items in the generated ranking, and how they are selected [4]. Regarding this aspect, the following candidate generation strategies, where L_u is for the set of target items the recommender ranks (candidate items), have been proposed:

UserTest This strategy takes the same target item sets as standard error-based evaluation: for each user u, the list L_u consists of items rated by u in the test set. The smallest set of target items for each user is selected, including no unrated items. A relevance threshold is used to indicate which of the items in the user's test are considered relevant. Threshold variations can be static for all users [17], or per-user [3].

TrainItems Every rated item in the system is selected – except those rated by the target user. This strategy is useful when simulating a real system where no test is available, i.e. no need to look into the test set to generate the rankings.

RelPlusN For each user, a set of highly relevant items is selected from the test set. Then, a set of non-relevant items is created by randomly selecting N additional items. In [7], N is set to $1,000$ stating that the non-relevant items are selected from items in the test set not rated by u. Finally, for each highly relevant item i, the recommender produces a ranking of the union between this item and the non-relevant items. Metrics for each user are calculated by averaging the values obtained for the rankings associated to each user over every highly relevant item. The final performance values are averaged over the values obtained for each user.

3.1.4 *Performance measurement*

The final stage in the proposed evaluation protocol is to measure the performance of the produced scores. The last step (candidate items generation) is not required for error-based metrics, e.g. mean absolute error (MAE) and root-mean-square error (RMSE) as these only consider predictions on items in the test set, whereas the recommendation step generates predictions for all items in the dataset. Nevertheless, it is crucial to report the coverage of the methods – in terms of user coverage (fraction of users that receive at least one recommendation) and catalog coverage (fraction of items that can be recommended) [30]. This is due to the fact that, in principle, no *backup* recommender is used as fallback, i.e. if we expect to receive 10 recommendations for a user but only get 8, we measure the performance based on those 8 items. This is a well-known problem [16] and the suggested solution is to report both accuracy and coverage.

Error-based metrics are useful under the assumption that a system that provides more accurate predictions is preferred by the user [30]. Although this has been studied and refuted by several authors [8,22], it still is one of the *de facto* evaluation techniques used.

Ranking-based metrics like precision, recall, nDCG, and mean reciprocal rank (MRR) aim to capture the quality of a particular ranking, taking into account that the user has expressed a preference towards some items, typically those in the test set rated above a certain threshold. The candidate item generation strategy will change the value computed with these metrics since a different ranking is evaluated, although the order of the recommenders does not have to change. Bellogín et al. [4] observed that one difference in the results is the range of the evaluation metrics. This becomes clear when using the RelPlusN strategy with different values of N, the larger the N, the smaller the value of the metric, as more items are considered in the ranking. In our experiments, after the stages described above, we used *trec_eval*[1] to produce ranking-based metrics.

3.2 Recommendation Frameworks

Our analysis is based on three open source recommendation frameworks popular in the recommender systems community; Mahout, MyMediaLite, and LensKit. Even though the frameworks have been developed with a similar goal in mind (an easy way to deploy recommender systems in research and/or production environments) and share some basic concepts, there are certain differences. These vary from how data is interacted with to differences in implementation across algorithms, similarity metrics, etc.

[1] Available at `http://trec.nist.gov/trec_eval/`

Framework	Class	Similarity	
Item-based			
LensKit	ItemItemScorer	CosineVectorSimilarity, PearsonCorrelation	
Mahout	GenericItemBasedRecommender	PearsonCorrelationSimilarity	
MyMediaLite	ItemKNN	Cosine, Pearson	
User-based			**Parameters**
LensKit	UserUserItemScorer	CosineVectorSimilarity, PearsonCorrelation	SimpleNeighborhoodFinder, NeighborhoodSize
Mahout	GenericUserBasedRecommender	PearsonCorrelationSimilarity	NearestNUserNeighborhood, neighborhood size
MyMediaLite	UserKNN	Cosine, Pearson	neighborhood size
Matrix factorization			
LensKit	FunkSVDItemScorer	IterationCountStoppingCondition, factors, iterations	
Mahout	SVDRecommender	FunkSVDFactorizer, factors, iterations	
MyMediaLite	SVDPlusPlus	factors, iterations	

Table 1: Details for the item-based, user-based and matrix factorization-based recommenders benchmarked in each framework. Namespace identifiers have been omitted due to space constraints.

This section highlights some of the features of the frameworks and gives an overview of differences and similarities between them, specifically what the frameworks provide in terms of evaluation and data management (test and training splitting), but also how certain algorithms are implemented.

3.2.1 LensKit

LensKit is a Java framework and provides a set of basic CF algorithms. The current version at the time of writing was 2.0.5.

To demonstrate some of the implementational aspects of LensKit, we look at a common similarity method, the Pearson Correlation. In LensKit, it is based on Koren and Bell's description [20] (stated in the source code), having the possibility to set the shrinkage parameter λ_s mentioned in Eq. (4). Additionally, LensKit contains an evaluator class which can perform cross validation and report evaluation results using a set of metrics. Available metrics include RMSE, nDCG, etc. (although it lacks precision and recall metrics).

3.2.2 Mahout

Mahout, also written in Java, had reached version 0.8 at the time of writing. It provides a large number of recommendation algorithms, both non distributed as well as distributed (MapReduce); in this work we focus solely on the former for the sake of comparison.

Mahout's Pearson Correlation calculates the similarity of two vectors, with the possibility to infer missing preferences in either. λ_s is not used, instead a weighting parameter suits a similar purpose.

There are several evaluator classes, we focus on the Information Retrieval evaluator (GenericRecommenderIRStatsEvaluator) which calculates e.g. precision, recall, nDCG, etc. Generally, the evaluators lack cross validation settings, instead, a percentage can be passed to the evaluator and only the specified percentage of (randomly selected) users will be evaluated. Additionally, the evaluator trains the recommendation models separately for each user. Furthermore, while preparing individual training and test splits, the evaluator requires a threshold to be given, i.e. the lowest rating to be considered when selecting items into the test set. This can either be a static value or calculated for each user based on the user's rating average and standard deviation. Finally, users are excluded from the evaluation if they have less than $2 * N$ preferences (where N is the level of recall).

3.2.3 MyMediaLite

MyMediaLite had, at the time of writing, reached version 3.10. It is implemented in C# and offers multi-platform support via Mono.

One key difference between MyMediaLite and the other two frameworks is that MyMediaLite addresses rating and item prediction as separate problems. However, it provides a rating-based recommendation setting similar to the other frameworks.

Dataset	Users	Items	Ratings	Density	Time
Movielens 100k	943	1,682	100,000	6.30%	'97-'98
Movielens 1M	6,040	3,706	1,000,000	4.47%	'00-'03
Yelp2013	45,981	11,537	229,907	0.04%	'05-'13

Table 2: Statistics of the three datasets used in this paper.

MyMediaLite's Pearson correlation class cites [20] as the basis for the implementation. Similar to LensKit, the shrinkage parameter λ_s can be used through a constructor. It is not used by default.

4. EXPERIMENTS & EVALUATION

In order to provide a comparison, we performed an analysis of results obtained using a protocol using the four steps from Section 3.1, and using the internal evaluation methods of each framework. All experiments were run on computers with Fedora Linux (v.18), 8Gb RAM and Intel Core2 Quad Q6600 2.40GHz CPUs. For Mahout and LensKit, Java (1.7.0_25-b15) was allowed to use 3Gb of RAM. MyMediaLite was run on Mono 3.2.7.

4.1 Datasets

We use three datasets, two from the movie domain (Movielens 100k & 1M[2]) and one with user reviews of business venues (Yelp[3]). All datasets contain users' ratings on items (1-5 stars). The selection of datasets was based on the fact that not all evaluated frameworks support implicit or log-based data. The first dataset, Movielens 100k (ML100k), contains 100,000 ratings from 943 users on 1,682 movies. The second dataset, Movielens 1M (ML1M), with 1 million ratings from 6,040 users on 3,706 items. The Yelp 2013 dataset contains 229,907 ratings by 45,981 users on 11,537 businesses. The datasets additionally contain item meta data, e.g. movie titles, business descriptions, these were not used in this work. A summary of data statistics is shown in Table 2.

4.2 Controlled evaluation protocol

We used the Movielens 100k dataset to benchmark the four stages of the proposed controlled evaluation. More specifically, we tested the data splitting configuration experimenting with cross validation (5 folds) vs. random partition (80%-20% ratio), for both user and global splits (see Section 3.1.1) [27]. The recommendations were produced using the algorithms presented in Section 3.1.2, i.e., matrix factorization (SVD), user-based CF (UB) and item-based CF (IB) nearest neighbor. Then, error-based metrics were computed using the corresponding test splits and our own code (available in [27]), whereas the ranking-based metrics were calculated after running the different strategies to generate candidate items using the *trec_eval* tool; in this case, we considered an item relevant if it had been rated with a 5, similar to Cremonesi et al. [7]. For the RelPlusN strategy, N was set to 100, a lower value than the typical one (i.e., 1,000)

[2] `http://grouplens.org/datasets/movielens/`
[3] `http://www.kaggle.com/c/yelp-recsys-2013`

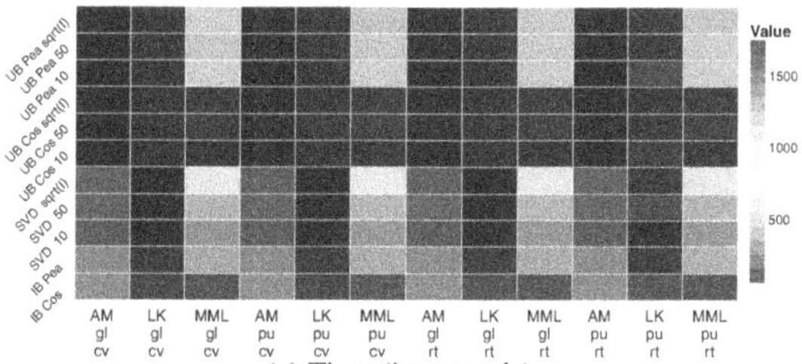

(a) Time (in seconds)

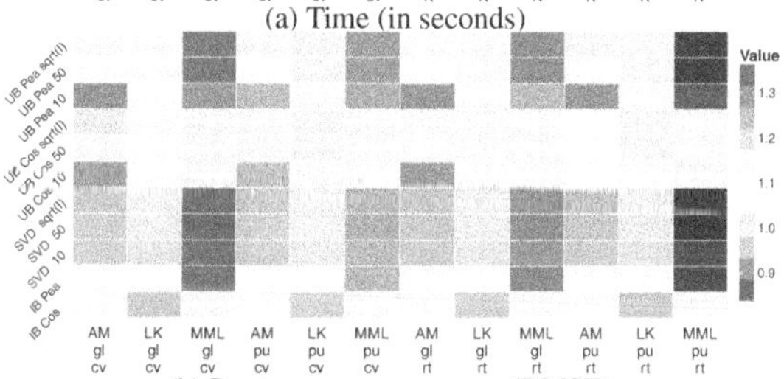

(b) Root-mean-square error (RMSE)

Figure 1: Time and RMSE for the controlled evaluation protocol. IB and UB refer to item- and user-based respectively; Pea and Cos to Pearson and Cosine; gl and pu to global and per user; AM, LK, MML to the frameworks; and cv, rt to cross validation and ratio. (NB: To be viewed in color.)

but it allows us to perform more exhaustive experiments, while keeping the comparison fair (since this parameter applies evenly to all evaluated recommenders). After that, we further extended our experiments with the other datasets, for a subset of the configurations used in the experiments with Movielens 100k.

4.3 Framework-dependent protocols

In addition to the controlled evaluation, we used each framework's internal evaluation methods. This was performed for Movielens 100k[4], default evaluation settings were used, e.g. the frameworks created the training/test splits based on default configurations. LensKit and MyMediaLite performed 5-fold cross validation, in Mahout, the recommender generates training/test splits individually for each user. Since there is no common evaluation metric calculated in these frameworks, we present nDCG values for LensKit and Mahout, and RMSE values for LensKit and MyMediaLite. The algorithms used were according to Table 1. In Mahout's case, the evaluator needs the level of recall (N) prior to recommendation and evaluation (see Section 3.2.2), thus we set $N = 50$ for Mahout. In the case of MyMediaLite, where it distinguishes between rating prediction and item recommendation, we used the rating prediction setting to generate predictions and recommendations.

5. RESULTS

Note that due to space constraints we do not present the results from all runs. Instead focus is on presenting a full coverage of the main benchmarking dataset, Movielens 100k, with additional results from the other datasets for completeness.

5.1 Controlled evaluation protocol

Figs. 1 and 2 show a subset of the most important metrics computed using the controlled evaluation protocol. The figures show a wide combination of strategies for data splitting, recommendation, and candidate items generation, along with prediction accuracy (RMSE Fig. 1b), ranking quality (nDCG@10 Fig. 2c), coverage (Figs. 2a and 2b), and running times of the different recommenders (Fig. 1a). Although the same gradient is used in all the figures, we have to note that for coverage and nDCG higher values (red) are better, whereas for time and RMSE lower values (blue) are better.

[4]Attempts to use the Yelp2013 dataset were also made. The running time and memory usage of the frameworks made it unfeasible.

In terms of running time, we see in Fig. 1a that the most expensive algorithm is MyMediaLite's item-based method (using Pearson correlation), regardless of splitting strategy. MyMediaLite's factorization algorithm needs more time than SVD in other frameworks, this is due to the base factorizer method being more accurate but also more computationally expensive (see Section 3.1.2). In general, we observe that LensKit has the shortest running time no matter the recommendation method or data splitting strategy. Note that for datasets with other characteristics this can differ.

Looking at the RMSE values, we notice (Fig. 1b) a gap in the MyMediaLite recommenders. This is due to MyMediaLite distinguishing between rating prediction and item recommendation tasks (Section 3.2.3). In combination with the similarity method used (cosine), this means the scores are not valid ratings. Moreover, MyMediaLite's recommenders outperform the rest. There is also difference between using a cross validation strategy or a ratio partition, along with global or per user conditions. Specifically, better values are obtained for the combination of global cross validation, and best RMSE values are found for the per user ratio partition. These results can be attributed to the amount of data available in each of these combinations: whereas global splits may leave users out of the evaluation (the training or test split), cross validation ensures that they will always appear in the test set. Performance differences across algorithms are negligible, although SVD tends to outperform others within each framework.

Finally, the ranking-based evaluation results should be carefully analyzed. We notice that, except for the UserTest candidate items strategy, MyMediaLite outperforms Mahout and LensKit in terms of nDCG@10. This high precision comes at the expense of lower coverage, specifically of the catalog (item) coverage. As a consequence, MyMediaLite seems to be able to recommend at least one item per user, but far from the complete set of items, in particular compared to the other frameworks. This is specifically noticeable in rating-based recommenders (as we recalled above, all except the UB and IB with cosine similarity), whereas the ranking-based approach obtains coverage similar to other combinations. In terms of nDCG@10, the best results are obtained with the UserTest strategy, with noticeable differences between recommender types, i.e. IB performs poorly, SVD performs well, UB in between, in accordance with e.g. [20]. The splitting strategy has little effect on the results in this setting.

Tables 3b and 3c show results for the Movielens 1M and Yelp2013 datasets respectively, where only a global cross validation splitting strategy is presented as we have shown that the rest of strategies do not have a strong impact on the final performance. We also include in Table 3a the corresponding results from Figs. 1 and 2 for comparison. In the tables we observe that most of the conclusions shown in Figs. 1 and 2 hold in Movielens 1M, likely due to both datasets having a similar nature (movies from Movielens, similar sparsity), even though the ratio of user vs. items and the number of ratings is different (see Table 2). For instance, the running time of IB is longest for Mahout; and Mahout and MyMediaLite have coverage problems when random items are considered in the evaluation (i.e., RPN item candidate strategy), in particular in the UB recommender. LensKit's performance is superior to Mahout's in most of the situations where a fair comparison is possible (i.e., when both frameworks have a similar coverage), while at the same time MyMediaLite outperforms LensKit in terms of nDCG@10 for the RPN strategy, although this situation is reversed for the UT strategy.

The majority of the results for the dataset based on Yelp reviews are consistent with those found for Movielens 1M. One exception is the IB recommender, where the LensKit implementation is slower and has a worse performance (in terms of RMSE and nDCG) than Mahout. This may be attributed to the very low density of this dataset, which increases the difficulty of the recommendation prob-

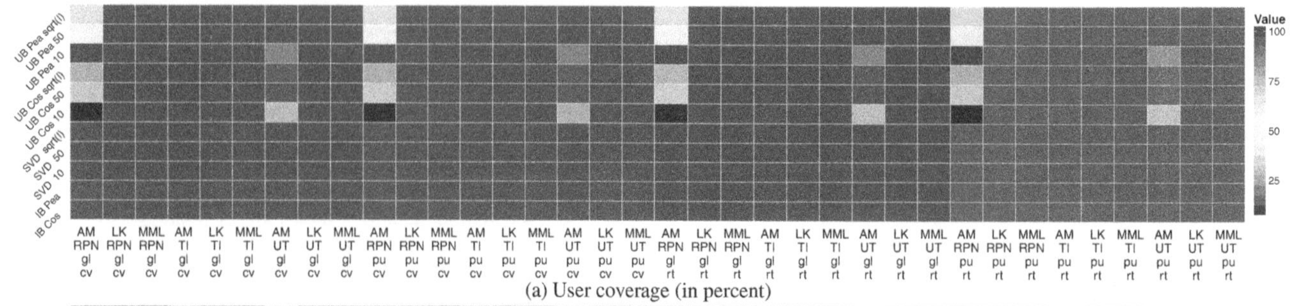

(a) User coverage (in percent)

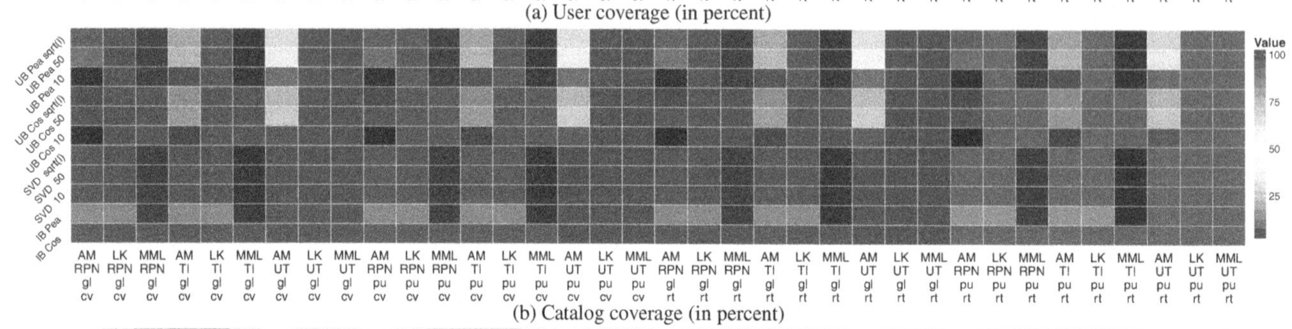

(b) Catalog coverage (in percent)

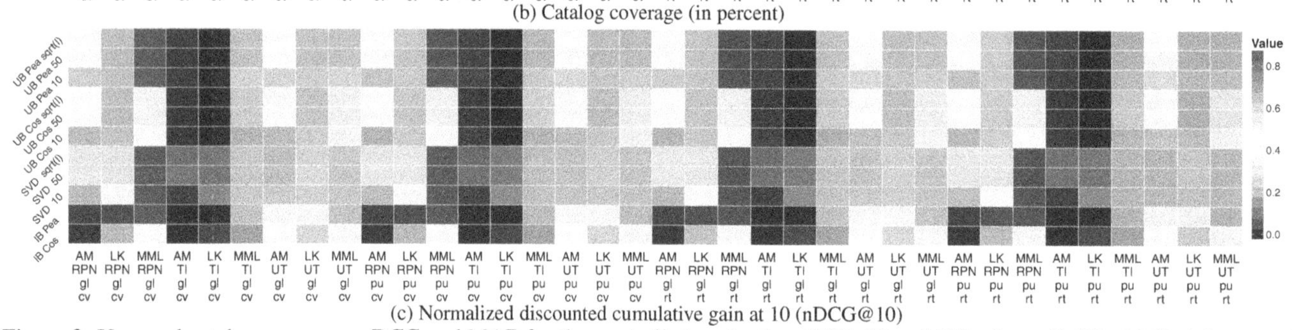

(c) Normalized discounted cumulative gain at 10 (nDCG@10)

Figure 2: User and catalog coverage, nDCG and MAP for the controlled evaluation. RPN, TI and UT refer to RelPlusN, TrainItems and UserTest strategies (other acronyms from Fig. 1). (NB: To be viewed in color.)

lem; nonetheless it should be noted that LensKit is able to achieve a much higher coverage for some recommenders – especially for the user-based – than Mahout. The performance of MyMediaLite is also affected in this dataset, where we were not able to obtain recommendations for three of the methods: two of them required too much memory, and the other required too much time to finish. For the recommenders that finished, the results are better for this framework, especially compared to LensKit, the other one with full coverage with the RPN strategy.

5.2 Framework-dependent protocols

The results of the framework-dependent evaluation are shown in Table 4. Table 4a shows evaluation results in terms of nDCG, generated by Mahout and LensKit, whereas Table 4b shows the RMSE values from LensKit and MyMediaLite. We start by studying the results presented in Table 4a, where it seems that LensKit outperforms Mahout at several orders of magnitude. The highest nDCG obtained by Mahout (0.2868) is less than one third of the lowest value obtained by LensKit (0.9422). This should be taken in the context of each framework's evaluator. Recall that Mahout's evaluator will only consider users with a certain minimum number of preferences (two times the level of recall). Our level of recall was set to 50, meaning only users with at least 100 preferences are evaluated (corresponding only to circa 33% of the users in this dataset).

Looking at the RMSE results obtained by LensKit and MyMediaLite in Table 4b, the difference between the frameworks is not as large as in the previous case. All RMSE results are between 7.5% (UBCos50) and 11.7% (UBCos10) of each other. In this case, both frameworks created five instances of training/tests splits with an 80%-20% ratio. The splits are randomly seeded, meaning that even though the frameworks only create five training/test datasets, they are not the same between the two frameworks.

A further observation to be made is how the framework's internal evaluation compares to our controlled evaluation. We see that the frameworks perform better in the controlled environment than in the internal ditto. This could be the effect of different ways of calculating the RMSE, i.e. how the average is computed (overall or per user), or what happens when the recommender cannot provide a rating.

In the case of nDCG (Table 4a), we see that Mahout's values fluctuate more in both versions of the controlled evaluation (RPN and UT) than in Mahout's own evaluation. The internal evaluation results consistently remain lower than the corresponding values in the controlled setting – although the RPN values are closer to Mahout's own results. The UT (UserTest) values obtained in the controlled evaluation are several orders of magnitude higher than in the internal setting, even though the setting resembles Mahout's own evaluation closer than the RPN setting. A link to the different results could potentially be the user and item coverage. Recall that Mahout's internal evaluation only evaluates users with more than $2 * N$ preferences, whereas the controlled setting evaluates the full set of users. LensKit's internal evaluation consistently shows better results than the controlled setting. We believe this could be an effect related to how the final averaged nDCG metric is calculated (similar to the mismatch in RMSE values mentioned above).

Given the widely differing results, it seems pertinent that in order to perform an inter-framework benchmarking, the evaluation process needs to be clearly defined and both recommendations and evaluations performed in a controlled and transparent environment.

(a) Movielens 100k

Alg.	F.W.	Time (sec.)	RMSE	nDCG@10		User cov.(%)		Cat. cov.(%)	
				RPN	UT	RPN	UT	RPN	UT
IBCos	AM	238	1.041	0.003	0.501	98.16	100	99.71	99.67
	LK	44	0.953	0.199	0.618	98.16	100	99.88	99.67
	MML	75	NA	0.488	0.521	98.16	100	100	99.67
IBPea	AM	237	1.073	0.022	0.527	97.88	100	86.66	99.31
	LK	31	1.093	0.033	0.527	97.86	100	86.68	99.31
	MML	1,346	0.857	0.882	0.654	98.16	100	2.87	99.83
SVD50	AM	132	0.950	0.286	0.657	98.12	100	99.88	99.67
	LK	7	1.004	0.280	0.621	98.16	100	100	99.67
	MML	1,324	0.848	0.882	0.648	98.18	100	2.87	99.83
UBCos50	AM	5	1.178	0.378	0.387	35.66	98.25	6.53	27.80
	LK	25	1.026	0.223	0.657	98.16	100	99.88	99.67
	MML	38	NA	0.519	0.551	98.16	100	100	99.67
UBPea50	AM	6	1.126	0.375	0.486	48.50	100	10.92	39.08
	LK	25	1.026	0.223	0.657	98.16	100	99.88	99.67
	MML	1,261	0.847	0.883	0.652	98.18	100	2.87	99.83

(b) Movielens 1M

Alg.	F.W.	Time (sec.)	RMSE	nDCG@10		User cov.(%)		Cat. cov.(%)	
				RPN	UT	RPN	UT	RPN	UT
IBCos	AM	23,027	1.028	0.002	0.534	100	100	99.88	99.99
	LK	1,571	0.906	0.225	0.627	100	100	100	100
	MML	1,350	NA	0.525	0.515	100	100	100	100
IBPea	AM	23,148	0.972	0.019	0.578	99.98	100	94.55	99.97
	LK	1,832	1.052	0.091	0.593	99.98	100	94.59	99.97
	MML	> 5 days	–	–	–	–	–	–	–
SVD50	AM	9,643	0.858	0.337	0.692	100	100	100	100
	LK	89	0.879	0.200	0.660	100	100	100	100
	MML	25,987	0.804	0.909	0.677	100	100	2.55	100
UBCos50	AM	118	1.123	0.544	0.421	31.36	99.43	3.04	20.37
	LK	2,445	0.957	0.293	0.676	100	100	100	100
	MML	1,046	NA	0.542	0.553	100	100	100	100
UBPea50	AM	149	1.077	0.513	0.504	38.88	99.98	5.05	25.96
	LK	2,408	0.957	0.293	0.676	100	100	100	100
	MML	181,542	0.807	0.906	0.660	100	100	2.55	100

(c) Yelp2013

Alg.	F.W.	Time (sec.)	RMSE	nDCG@10		User cov.(%)		Cat. cov.(%)	
				RPN	UT	RPN	UT	RPN	UT
IBCos	AM	737	1.146	0.109	0.761	85.32	80.60	70.05	90.01
	LK	5,955	1.231	0.065	0.824	100	100	100	100
	MML	30,718	0.229	0.668	100	100	100	100	
IBPea	AM	712	1.577	0.350	0.659	61.23	63.07	17.33	68.19
	LK	558	1.236	0.281	0.690	66.84	71.38	21.62	71.97
	MML	> 5 days	–	–	–	–	–	–	–
SVD50	AM	404	1.125	0.181	0.865	100	100	100	97.57
	LK	483	1.250	0.114	0.732	100	100	100	100
	MML	995	1.131	0.995	0.930	100	100	2.53	100
UBCos50	AM	967	1.204	0.569	0.662	43.81	76.57	5.85	32.38
	LK	4,298	1.149	0.090	0.863	100	100	99.99	97.57
	MML	ME	–	–	–	–	–	–	–
UBPea50	AM	774	1.307	0.643	0.531	29.95	46.31	3.06	29.67
	LK	4,311	1.149	0.090	0.863	100	100	99,99	97.57
	MML	ME	–	–	–	–	–	–	–

Table 3: Performance results in Movielens 100k, 1M and Yelp2013 with the controlled evaluation protocol with cross validation as splitting strategy for the frameworks (F.W) column.

6. DISCUSSION

In the light of the previous section, it stands clear that even though the evaluated frameworks implement the recommendation algorithms in a similar fashion, the results are not comparable, i.e. the performance of an algorithm implemented in one cannot be compared to the performance of the same algorithm in another. Not only do there exist differences in algorithmic implementations, but also in the evaluation methods themselves.

There are no *de facto* rules or standards on how to evaluate a recommendation algorithm. This also applies to how recommendation algorithms of a certain type should be realized (e.g., default parameter values, use of backup recommendation algorithms, and other *ad-hoc* implementations). However, this should perhaps not be seen as something negative *per se*. Yet, when it comes to performance comparison of recommendation algorithms, a standardized (or controlled) evaluation is crucial [18]. Without which, the relative performance of two or more algorithms evaluated under different conditions becomes essentially meaningless. In order to objectively

(a) nDCG for AM and LK

Alg.	F.W.	nDCG
IBCos	AM	0.000414780
	LK	0.942192050
IBPea	AM	0.005169231
	LK	0.924546132
SVD50	AM	0.105427298
	LK	0.943464094
UBCos50	AM	0.169295451
	LK	0.948413562
UBPea50	AM	0.169295451
	LK	0.948413562

(b) RMSE values for LK and MML.

Alg.	F.W.	RMSE
IBCos	LK	1.01390931
	MML	0.92476162
IBPea	LK	1.05018614
	MML	0.92933246
SVD50	LK	1.01209290
	MML	0.93074012
UBCos50	LK	1.02545490
	MML	0.95358984
UBPea50	LK	1.02545490
	MML	0.93419026

Table 4: Results using the internal evaluation methods of each framework.

and definitively characterize the performance of an algorithm, a controlled evaluation, with a defined evaluation protocol is a prerequisite.

To date, the most well-known recommender system-related event, the Netflix Prize[5], created a benchmarking environment where all participating algorithms were evaluated in the same controlled setting. It is debatable whether the research advances accomplished during the Prize's three-year run would have been matched if there had been no standardized and controlled evaluation and benchmarking environment. Having said this, we should also stress the importance of research conducted outside the scope of such actions. However, when it comes to recommender systems, given that much of the progress is measured in terms of higher precision or recall, lower RMSE, higher nDCG, etc., it seems intuitive that some form of controlled evaluation could lead to a broader understanding of recommender system algorithms' qualities in general.

As a note, we should mention that the Netflix Prize focused on improving Netflix' internal rating prediction algorithm by 10% in terms of RMSE. Even though this comparison is by no means fair (in the scope of the Netflix Prize at least), we have shown that RMSE values between the same algorithms implemented in different frameworks can often differ by more than 10%.

We have highlighted that there exist large discrepancies in recommender algorithm quality, not only for different algorithms, but specifically for the same algorithms implemented in different popular recommender system frameworks. Our analysis further shows that not only do the disparities exist in common metrics, but additionally in metrics which are perhaps more seldom used for recommender systems-related research purposes, e.g. user and catalog coverage as well as the time needed to train the algorithms. Given the recent investigation on how well common metrics actually correspond to users' taste, e.g. RMSE [23, 28], precision [22], etc. we believe that it is crucial to not only report the accuracy of recommender algorithms, but the evaluation methodology as well, in order to ensure reported progress is not only due to the specific implementation details of a particular framework. Especially, given the large amount of recommender systems-related research being conducted, and the variety of open source frameworks as well as individually implemented code, it is necessary to not only describe in detail the algorithms used, but also the complete evaluation process, including strategies for data splitting, specifics on the evaluation metrics and methods, etc.

For example, by working with the Yelp dataset we observed that not all the frameworks are able to deal equally with too sparse data; in particular this dataset is not too large (around 200k ratings, one fifth of the Movielens 1M dataset) but it contains a larger number of items and users than the other compared datasets. This condition made it impossible for us to run some of the algorithms implemented in the frameworks.

[5] http://www.netflixprize.com

7. CONCLUSION & FUTURE WORK

We have shown the disparity of evaluation results between three common recommendation frameworks. Even though the frameworks implement similar (if not the same) algorithms, there exist large differences in the reported recommendation quality, both in the frameworks internal evaluations as well as in the external evaluations performed in the scope of this work. Using three popular and publicly available datasets, we evaluated three types of recommendation algorithms (user-based and item-based nearest neighbor CF and SVD-based matrix factorization). We evaluated the results using each framework's internal evaluation modules as well as through a *controlled evaluation* – the latter case ensuring that no implementation-specific factors affected the results of the evaluation. Our analysis shows that, even in a controlled environment, the same algorithms evaluated on identical data show performance discrepancies. These discrepancies range from minor to quite significant, e.g. *catalog coverage* ranging between 3% and 100% for the same algorithm and setting in two different frameworks (Table 3a UBPea50, MML vs. LK), or a 33% difference in RMSE (Table 3b UBPea50, AM vs. MML). Similarly, our analysis of running times show large differences between the frameworks, e.g. a factor of 1,200 between AM and MML for user-based nearest-neighbor using Pearson (Table 3b). The differences in evaluation results using the internal evaluation methods provided by the frameworks show even larger discrepancies, e.g. IBCos AM vs. LK (Table 4), where nDCG differs a factor of 2,300 (0.00041 vs. 0.9422).

In light of the presented results, it stands clear that the evaluation and presentation of recommendation results should be given in ample detail in order to ensure a fair comparison to the baseline algorithms used. The presented work shows that inter-framework comparisons of recommendation quality can potentially point to incorrect results and conclusions, unless performed with great caution and in a controlled, framework independent environment.

We are currently performing further studies on evaluation discrepancies in recommender systems and attempting to limit the effects of this by developing an open source recommender systems evaluation toolkit[6] [27] (which was also used in this work). With this toolkit, our attempt is to formalize a set of standardized evaluation methodologies, independent of specific recommendation or evaluation strategy. In the future, we aim to extend our work to other evaluation dimensions (e.g., diversity, novelty), along with considering implicit feedback datasets and other contextual dimensions – like time and social networks – in the evaluation protocols.

8. ACKNOWLEDGMENTS

The authors thank Zeno Gantner and Michael Ekstrand for support during this work. This work was partly carried out during the tenure of an ERCIM "Alain Bensoussan" Fellowship Programme. The research leading to these results has received funding from the European Union Seventh Framework Programme (FP7/2007-2013) under grant agreements n°246016 and n°610594, and the Spanish Ministry of Science and Innovation (TIN2013-47090-C3-2).

9. REFERENCES

[1] G. Adomavicius and A. Tuzhilin. Toward the next generation of recommender systems: A survey of the state-of-the-art and possible extensions. *IEEE Trans. Knowl. Data Eng.*, 17(6):734–749, 2005.

[2] T. G. Armstrong, A. Moffat, W. Webber, and J. Zobel. Improvements that don't add up: ad-hoc retrieval results since 1998. In *CIKM*, 2009.

[3] C. Basu, H. Hirsh, and W. W. Cohen. Recommendation as classification: Using social and content-based information in recommendation. In J. Mostow and C. Rich, editors, *AAAI/IAAI*, pages 714–720. AAAI Press / MIT Press, 1998.

[4] A. Bellogín, P. Castells, and I. Cantador. Precision-oriented evaluation of recommender systems: an algorithmic comparison. In *RecSys*, 2011.

[5] J. S. Breese, D. Heckerman, and C. Kadie. Empirical analysis of predictive algorithms for collaborative filtering. In *UAI*, 1998.

[6] P. G. Campos, F. Díez, and I. Cantador. Time-aware recommender systems: a comprehensive survey and analysis of existing evaluation protocols. *User Model. User-Adapt. Interact.*, 24(1-2):67–119, 2014.

[7] P. Cremonesi, Y. Koren, and R. Turrin. Performance of recommender algorithms on top-n recommendation tasks. In *RecSys*, 2010.

[8] P. Cremonesi, A. Sansottera, and S. Gualandi. On the cooling-aware workload placement problem. In *AI for Data Center Management and Cloud Computing*, 2011.

[9] M. Deshpande and G. Karypis. Item-based top-n recommendation algorithms. *ACM Trans. Inf. Syst.*, 22(1):143–177, Jan. 2004.

[10] C. Desrosiers and G. Karypis. A comprehensive survey of neighborhood-based recommendation methods. In Ricci et al. [26], pages 107–144.

[11] M. D. Ekstrand, M. Ludwig, J. A. Konstan, and J. Riedl. Rethinking the recommender research ecosystem: reproducibility, openness, and lenskit. In *RecSys*, pages 133–140, 2011.

[12] S. Funk. Netflix update: Try this at home. http://sifter.org/˜simon/journal/20061211.html (retrieved Jan. 2014), Dec 2006.

[13] Z. Gantner, S. Rendle, C. Freudenthaler, and L. Schmidt-Thieme. Mymedialite: A free recommender system library. In *RecSys*, 2011.

[14] K. Goldberg, T. Roeder, D. Gupta, and C. Perkins. Eigentaste: A constant time collaborative filtering algorithm. *Inf. Retr.*, 4(2):133–151, July 2001.

[15] A. Gunawardana and G. Shani. A survey of accuracy evaluation metrics of recommendation tasks. *J. Mach. Learn. Res.*, 10:2935–2962, Dec. 2009.

[16] J. L. Herlocker, J. A. Konstan, L. G. Terveen, and J. T. Riedl. Evaluating collaborative filtering recommender systems. *ACM Trans. Inf. Syst.*, 22(1):5–53, Jan. 2004.

[17] T. Jambor and J. Wang. Optimizing multiple objectives in collaborative filtering. In *RecSys*, pages 55–62, New York, NY, USA, 2010. ACM.

[18] J. A. Konstan and G. Adomavicius. Toward identification and adoption of best practices in algorithmic recommender systems research. In *RepSys*, pages 23–28, New York, NY, USA, 2013. ACM.

[19] Y. Koren. Factorization meets the neighborhood: A multifaceted collaborative filtering model. In *KDD*. ACM, 2008.

[20] Y. Koren and R. Bell. Advances in collaborative filtering. In Ricci et al. [26], pages 145–186.

[21] Y. Koren, R. M. Bell, and C. Volinsky. Matrix factorization techniques for recommender systems. *IEEE Computer*, 42(8):30–37, 2009.

[22] S. M. McNee, J. Riedl, and J. A. Konstan. Being accurate is not enough: how accuracy metrics have hurt recommender systems. In *CHI Extended Abstracts*, pages 1097–1101, 2006.

[23] T. T. Nguyen, D. Kluver, T.-Y. Wang, P.-M. Hui, M. D. Ekstrand, M. C. Willemsen, and J. Riedl. Rating support interfaces to improve user experience and recommender accuracy. In *RecSys*. ACM, 2013.

[24] S. Owen, R. Anil, T. Dunning, and E. Friedman. *Mahout in Action*. Manning Publications Co., Greenwich, CT, USA, 2011.

[25] P. Resnick, N. Iacovou, M. Suchak, P. Bergstrom, and J. Riedl. Grouplens: An open architecture for collaborative filtering of netnews. In *CSCW*, pages 175–186, 1994.

[26] F. Ricci, L. Rokach, B. Shapira, and P. B. Kantor, editors. *Recommender Systems Handbook*. Springer, 2011.

[27] A. Said and A. Bellogín. Rival – a toolkit to foster reproducibility in recommender system evaluation. In *RecSys*, 2014.

[28] A. Said, B. J. Jain, S. Narr, and T. Plumbaum. Users and noise: The magic barrier of recommender systems. In *UMAP*. Springer, 2012.

[29] B. M. Sarwar, G. Karypis, J. A. Konstan, and J. Riedl. Item-based collaborative filtering recommendation algorithms. In *WWW*, 2001.

[30] G. Shani and A. Gunawardana. Evaluating recommendation systems. In Ricci et al. [26], pages 257–297.

[31] U. Shardanand and P. Maes. Social information filtering: Algorithms for automating "word of mouth". In *CHI*, pages 210–217, 1995.

[6] `http://rival.recommenders.net`

A Methodology for Learning, Analyzing, and Mitigating Social Influence Bias in Recommender Systems

Sanjay Krishnan, Jay Patel, Michael J. Franklin, Ken Goldberg
Department of Electrical Engineering and Computer Sciences, UC Berkeley
{sanjaykrishnan, patel.jay, franklin, goldberg}@berkeley.edu

ABSTRACT

The seminal 2003 paper by Cosley, Lab, Albert, Konstan, and Reidl, demonstrated the susceptibility of recommender systems to rating biases. To facilitate browsing and selection, almost all recommender systems display average ratings before accepting ratings from users which has been shown to bias ratings. This effect is called Social Influence Bias (SIB); the tendency to conform to the perceived "norm" in a community. We propose a methodology to 1) learn, 2) analyze, and 3) mitigate the effect of SIB in recommender systems. In the Learning phase, we build a baseline dataset by allowing users to rate twice: before and after seeing the average rating. In the Analysis phase, we apply a new non-parametric significance test based on the Wilcoxon statistic to test whether the data is consistent with SIB. If significant, we propose a Mitigation phase using polynomial regression and the Bayesian Information Criterion (BIC) to predict unbiased ratings. We evaluate our approach on a dataset of 9390 ratings from the California Report Card (CRC), a rating-based system designed to encourage political engagement. We found statistically significant evidence of SIB. Mitigating models were able to predict changed ratings with a normalized RMSE of 12.8% and reduce bias by 76.3%. The CRC, our data, and experimental code are available at: http://californiareportcard.org/data/

1. INTRODUCTION

In the 1950's, Solomon Asch performed a well-known series of experiments [4,5,9] where subjects were asked to choose which of a set of lines matched the length of a reference line. When working individually, 99% of the answers were correct. But when answering in the presence of a group of confederates who agreed on incorrect answers, 25% of participants conformed to the incorrect consensus. These results have been widely repeated to confirm what is now known as *social influence bias*: the tendency for participants to conform with the perceived community "norm" [15,27,36].

Susceptibility to influence has been studied in the context of recommender systems [12], and, in particular, Cosley et al. explored different rating scenarios and how system-generated rating predictions may influence participant ratings. They found that in a variety of scenarios including presenting manipulated predictions, presenting predictions on already rated items, and changing the rating scale had statistically significant influence on participants ratings. The key conclusion of Cosley et al. is that rating and recommender systems are easily biased and they argue that these biases can mask a user's true perception about a rated item.

RecSys'14, October 6–10, 2014, Foster City, Silicon Valley, CA, USA.

ACM ACM 978-1-4503-2668-1/14/10$15.00.

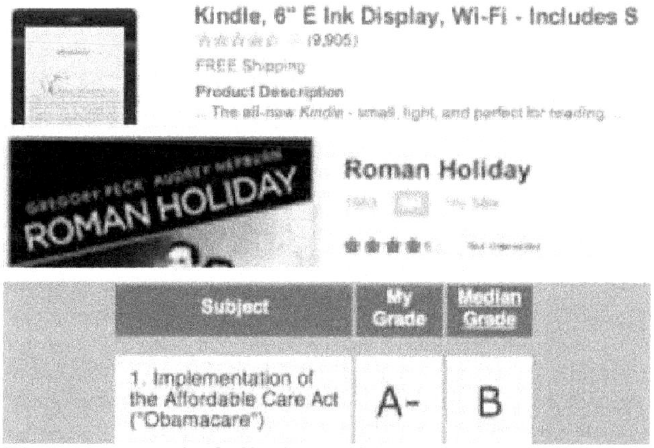

Figure 1: Typical displays of aggregate prior rating values (the mean or median) in Amazon, Netflix, and the California Report Card that has the potential to bias users.

In almost all recommender systems, participants see the community "norm" in the form of aggregate statistics (the average or median rating values) before entering a rating of their own; potentially introducing social influence bias into the rating data. This interface paradigm is, of course, reasonable to facilitate browsing and selection in a large lists of items. For example, online retailers such as Amazon display the average rating value for products and Netflix displays the average rating value of movies (Figure 1). Display of average ratings values can also be used as an incentive [23] to reveal information about peers after a participant enters his or her own grade. Display of statistics also increases the perceived transparency of open democracy platforms that encourage political engagement [1,30,31]. Social influence bias can yield ratings that are closer to the average, less diverse, and less representative of participants' true evaluations for items, which can in turn affect similarity measures between items and users and reduce the effectiveness of the recommendation system.

In this paper, we propose a methodology to learn, analyze, and mitigate the effects of social influence bias in recommender systems. As a case study, we evaluate our methodology on a new recommender system, the California

Report Card (CRC). In the CRC, participants assign ratings (letter grades A+ to F, a 13 point scale) to the State of California on six political issues. Then, the CRC uses the ratings to place participants in a open-ended political discussion with an initial set of comments from those who rated the state most similarly. Conformity ratings of the state can degrade the performance of the "recommendation", a set of comments from like-minded participants.

The CRC has novel interface that allows us to learn the effects of Social Influence Bias. The CRC interface reveals median grade values to participants *after* they enter their own rating and then allows participants to revise their rating. The key insight is that the combination of initial and revised ratings pairs allows us to determine if the social influence bias is statistically significant, and if so, can be used to build an inference model that can predict the biasing tendency; thus mitigate the bias in a dataset of already biased ratings.

Our methodology has three main components:

Learn To initialize with baseline data, an initial "learning" phase asks an initial set of participants to rate a set of items twice: before seeing the median rating, and again after the median is revealed. This collects triplets of ratings for each participant (initial rating, median rating, and final rating).

Analyze Given these triplets, we propose a new nonparametric significance test based on the Wilcoxon statistic to determine whether ratings that were changed are significantly closer to the median, i.e. the degree of social influence bias for each item.

Mitigate Using the Bayesian Information Criterion (BIC), we learn a polynomial function of optimal degree that estimates the initial rating from the final rating and the median. This can be used in a post-learning phase (when medians are always visible), or on historical ratings, to estimate what a participant's rating would be without social influence bias.

A key priority is a nonparametric approach to modeling social influence bias. Many earlier studies of social influence bias have focused on binary ratings (eg. up or down) [28,37]. However, recommender systems often have multi-valued rating scales (eg. 5 stars). Discrete multi-valued rating scales often exhibit multimodality and are not the optimal settings for parametric significance tests (eg. t-test and χ^2 test). In fact, it is known that Wilcoxon Rank statistical significance tests have far higher statistical power in these settings [24], and are further robust to outliers and long tails. We use these results and properties to derive a new significance test for Social Influence Bias.

Not only is our testing framework nonparametric, but we also show that we can relax assumptions about the structure of the social influence bias (eg. linear, conforming vs. contrarian). We use the Bayesian Information Criterion to jointly optimize over the model parameters and the complexity hyperparameter in polynomial regression. The result is a predictive model of social influence bias without having to make a strong assumption about the distribution of the data.

Results to date from the CRC suggest that given the opportunity, many participants will revise their grades/ratings: 862 out of 9390 ratings were changed after participants saw the median value. We found statistically significant effects of social influence bias, with ratings on average 19.3% closer to the median value than ratings that were not changed. We also conducted an independent reference survey using SurveyMonkey to ask a random sample of 611 participants from the company's paid pool of California participants to grade the same set of issues without displaying the median values. This data did not exhibit the same clustering around the median as the CRC, which comparably had ratings that were statistically significantly closer to the median (12.0%), suggesting that social influence bias is an important factor.

2. RELATED WORK

In their seminal 2003 work, Cosley, Lam, Albert, Konstan, and Reidl [12] studied the broad problem of biases in rating systems and tested the following relevant hypotheses: can manipulated "predicted" ratings influence a participant to change their rating, how consistent participants when re-rating an item, and how does rating scale (eg. stars, binary, unary) affect the average rating. The seminal result from Cosley et al. is that all of these hypotheses yielded significant influencing tendencies. In this paper, we formulate a predictive model for a specific type of bias, social influence bias, which is learned and isolated through the unique interface of the CRC. We also apply a nonparametric significance testing methodology.

The Asch model for conformity is the theoretical basis for what is sometimes called *social herding*, the tendency to conform [6,33], and this is a well-known choice model in economics [11,16,22]. Such models have also been studied in psychology and behavioral economics as "persuasion bias" [14,15,20,21]. In 2011, Lorenz et al. described how these biases can undermine the effectiveness of crowd intelligence in estimation tasks [25]. They argue that movement towards the group consensus causes a diminished diversity of opinion potentially leading to inefficiencies and inaccurate collective estimates. Danescu-Niculescu-Mizil et al. analyze helpfulness ratings on Amazon product reviews [13]. They found that the helpfulness ratings did not just depend on the content of the review but also its aggregate score and its relationship to other scores. In order to better distinguish social influence from other biases, Muchnik et. al designed a randomized experiment in which comments in an online forum were randomly up-treated or down-treated [28]. They concluded a statistically significant bias where a positive treatment increased the likelihood of positive ratings by 32%. In both Danescu-Niculescu-Mizil et al. and Muchnik et al., they looked at the problem of social influence bias in an a priori setting, where users see the aggregate statistic before giving their rating. Our work tests for a particular form of social influence where users are given the opportunity to change their opinions following the feedback.

Another line of relevant recommender systems research is the study of the consistency of repeat ratings [2,3]. It is an open problem, how to incorporate models of noisy ratings into our framework, however, as our non-parametric significance test is rank-based it statistically robust to small amounts of random noise. There has also been work on explaining recommendations [7,35], and one way to evaluate these explanation systems is to give users the option to change their ratings and evaluate how much (or how little) the explanation changes the users rating.

Zhu et al. conducted an experiment in which users evaluate an image on a subjective question with binary scale (eg. "Is this image cute?"), which was followed (either immediately or later) by a presentation of the crowd consensus opinion [37]. Users were given an opportunity to change their response, and they concluded that there was a significant tendency to change submissions. The tendency to change was the strongest when users were asked to make their second decision much later and not immediately after the first. Along these lines, Sipos et al. argue that context along with an aggregate rating plays a large role in the users' ratings. That is, users may attempt to "correct" the average, by voting in a more polarizing manner (more positively or negatively) [34]. We extend this prior work to measure and predict these changes when the input is more complex than a binary scale, and propose a non-parametric methodology that can be, in principle, extended to a variety of different input mechanisms. Our model can also account for a changing aggregate statistic such as a median rating changing as more data is collected.

3. LEARNING PHASE

In this section, we describe the learning phase of our technique where we collect the triplets (initial rating, final rating, and observed median) for building our model. We will explain in detail the system design of the California Report Card, how we record changed ratings, and define the notation that we will use in the following sections.

3.1 The California Report Card

The California Report Card (CRC) [1] is a prototype cross-platform web/mobile application designed to allow participants to advise California state leaders on timely policy issues. The CRC extends our earlier work with Opinion Space and Eigentaste [8,17–19,29]. In the CRC, participants assign letter grades (A+ to F) to the state of California on the following six issues: (1) Implementation of the Affordable Care Act ("Obamacare"), (2) Quality of K-12 public education, (3) Affordability of state colleges and universities, (4) Access to state services for undocumented immigrants, (5) Laws and regulations regarding recreational marijuana, and (6) Marriage rights for same-sex partners. Grades (Ratings) are assigned on a thirteen point scale (A+,A,A-,...,D-,F). These issues are posed in a fixed order each with the same input scale. Participants submit ratings using a click-and-drag slider interface as illustrated in Figure 2. On mobile devices, participants touch and drag to indicate the desired rating.

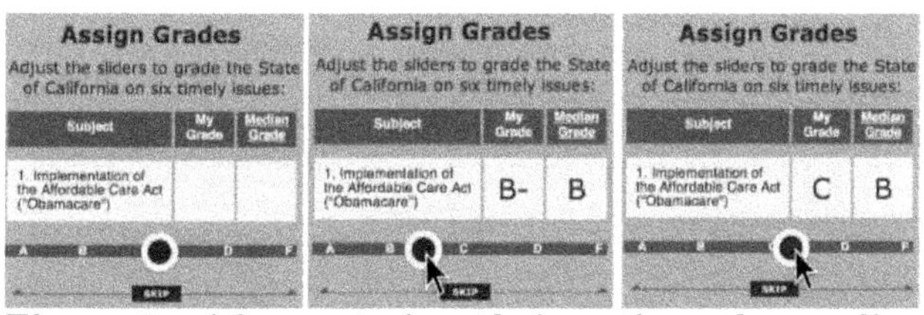

Figure 2: After entering their rating, the median rating over all participants is revealed. Participants have the option to change their rating after seeing the median.

Upon release of the slider, the CRC reveals the median for that issue over all prior participants. Even after the median is revealed the slider is still active and participants can change their ratings. However, it is important to note that participants were not explicitly told that they could change their rating. Another important observation is that participants who accessed the application at different times may have seen different medians as they were calculated based on the data up to that point. We recorded the initial rating, the median that the participant observed, and any subsequent changes along with timestamps for each of the events. Rating all of the six issues was not mandatory and participant had the option to skip any of the issues. To analyze this data, we mapped these 13 grade values linearly onto a scale from 0 to 1, with 1 being an A+ and 0 being an F.

3.2 Notation

Let P denote the set of all participants. For each participant $p_j \in P$, we associate a 3-tuple of ratings ($g_i[j]$, $m[j]$, $g_f[j]$) which represent the initial rating, median observed by the participant, and the final rating. For each issue, we divided the participants into three subsets of P: ones who did not change their ratings P_n, ones who changed P_c, and ones who skipped the question P_s. Our primary objective is to test the distributional properties of rating tuples from participants in P_n compared to those in P_c.

To ensure that all participants in the set P_c had an opportunity to see the median and then react, we filtered this group using the timestamps. The median appears in the interface with an animation whose completion time varied between devices, so we set a grace period of 3 seconds before we categorized the participant into set P_c.

For consistency, we use the same notation to describe participants in the reference survey. We denote the set of reference survey participants as set R, and each participant is associated with a 3-tuple ($g_i[j]$, $m[j]$, $g_f[j]$). However, since the reference survey does not reveal the median $g_i[j] = g_f[j]$ and $m[j]$ is the hypothetical median of the prior participants (which is not shown).

4. ANALYSIS PHASE

In the analysis phase, we determine whether social influence bias is statistically significant by analyzing spread of ratings around the median for the participants that changed their ratings. There are three principle challenges in testing this hypothesis. The first challenge is that parametric significance tests comparing two sample means such as the two sample t-test and z-test are known to perform poorly for multimodal and discrete distributions. Another significance test that is commonly applied to compare spreads of distributions is the F-test, which is also known to perform poorly for many non-normal distributions [26]. Furthermore, this test is usually used to test the spread of data around the mean, which only in very special conditions, such as normal distributions, aligns with the median which is the parameter of interest in the CRC. The discreteness of our data leads to multi-modal distributions which are not optimal for these testing methods.

The second challenge is that there is a natural tendency for ratings to concentrate around the median even without a bias. Consider the following participant behavioral model. Suppose that participants are not accustomed to a slider-based input. We can model the first rating that the participant leaves as uniformly randomly anywhere on the slider. As the participant begins to understand how to use the slider, their use becomes more accurate, ultimately settling on a rating from our observed distribution of final ratings. This model, the first rating is uniformly random and the second rating is a sample from the observed distribution, would result in a strong regression towards the median; even if there is no causal link with seeing the median.

Finally, the median m_i changes as ratings arrive and thus can be different for each participant. The median rating is calculated over all prior participants and thus is dependent on when the participant submitted their first rating.

[1]This study was approved by our Human Subjects committee as per IRB Protocol 2014-01-5918.

In practice, the median will eventually converge for a large number of participants, but it would be incorrect to measure concentration around a final median.

To address these three challenges, we propose a nonparametric model based on the Wilcoxon statistic to test the hypothesis that the group of participants that changed their ratings are more tightly centered around the median value that those participants observed. Our tests compare absolute deviations around the median for P_n, P_c, and R; which, as a relative comparison, controls for the natural tendency for ratings group around the median. Furthermore, it is more robust to the effects of alternate models such as the one described in our second challenge in comparison to a direct test of correlation (see Section 6.2.1).

4.1 Non-parametric Significance Test

Recall that P_n is the set of participants that did not change their ratings and P_c be the set of participants that changed their ratings. We define a set X_c, X_n of absolute deviations from the observed median of the final rating for each group:

$$X_c = \{|m[j] - g_f[j]|\} \; \forall j \in P_c \qquad (1)$$

$$X_n = \{|m[j] - g_f[j]|\} \; \forall j \in P_n \qquad (2)$$

For the purposes of hypothesis testing, we ignore the sign of the deviation. However, in Section 5, where we build a predictive model for the changes, we include the sign.

Now, for the set X_c, we calculate the Wilcoxon rank-sum statistic. We assign a rank to each of the absolute deviations in the union set $\mathbf{X} = X_c \cup X_n$ (ie. the largest change has rank 1 and the smallest has rank $|X_c \cup X_n|$. For X_c, we sum the ranks of the deviations within its set:

$$W_c = \sum_{j \in P_c} R_j \qquad (3)$$

The *Null Hypothesis* is that absolute deviations in X_c are the same size as X_n. Under this null hypothesis $median(X_n) = median(X_c)$, the ranks will be evenly distributed between each group. Therefore, the null expected value and variance of W is:

$$\mathbb{E}(W) = \frac{(|\mathbf{X}| + 1) \cdot |X_c|}{2} \qquad (4)$$

$$var(W) = \frac{(|\mathbf{X}| + 1) \cdot |X_c| \cdot |X_n|}{12} \qquad (5)$$

For the significance level α, we can test the probability that our calculated W_c comes from the null distribution. In other words, the test calculates the probability that a random subset of users (ignoring the categorization P_n and P_c) can have the observed difference in rank-sum values. A significant result means that for the participants that changed their ratings the changed changes are more tightly centered around the median they observed. For many distributions, the Wilcoxon statistic is more robust as it uses ranks rather than the actual values, making it more resilient to outliers. Even in the case where the data is normally distributed, the optimal condition for the t-test, the relative efficiency of the Wilcoxon rank-sum statistic compared to the typically used t-statistic is $\frac{3}{\pi} = 95.4\%$. We trade off a small amount of efficiency in the normally distributed case, for increased efficiency and robustness in many non-normal distributions (eg. exponential $3\times$ more efficient). Recommender system data is almost always collected from discrete inputs which are usually not normally distributed.

The same analysis can be used to test X_c against the absolute deviations in the reference survey X_r

$$X_r = \{|m[j] - g_i[j]|\} \; \forall j \in R \qquad (6)$$

or for initial vs. final ratings in the change group X'_c:

$$X'_c = \{|m[j] - g_i[j]|\} \; \forall j \in P_c \qquad (7)$$

4.2 Quantifying Concentration of Ratings

In addition to testing social influence bias, we can also estimate by how much the absolute deviations differ. The Wilcoxon statistic can be inverted to estimate a most likely *shift parameter* Δ, that is a shift Δ in the distribution of absolute deviations X_c that maximally aligns them with X_n. In other words, $X_c + \Delta$ is most supported by the null hypothesis (no social influence bias), or the distance from this hypothesis. An intuitive interpretation of Δ is that it measures how much our deviations have to be increased so that the no social influence bias hypothesis is the most likely conclusion. Since X_c is a set of absolute deviations, Δ tells us how much more concentrated X_c is than X_n around the observed medians. This parameter is relevant to the design of recommendation algorithms use similarity (eg. clustering or nearest neighbors), as it characterizes how much more on average are participants closer to the median.

We refer to [24] on the derivation of Δ and its confidence interval:

$$D = \{x_n[j] - x_c[i]\} \; \forall i, j \in X_n, X_c \qquad (8)$$

$$\Delta = median(D) \qquad (9)$$

5. BIAS MITIGATION

In our learning phase, we collect rating triplets ($g_i[j]$, $m[j]$, $g_f[j]$), and in our analysis phase, we determine whether the triplets exhibit statistically significant social influence bias. In the mitigation phase, we propose two models: a correction model (infers the initial rating given a final rating and the median), and a prediction model (predicts final ratings given an initial rating and the median). Once trained, the correction model can be applied to correct final grades collected without the triplet (either historical or post-learning). The prediction model can be used to analyze properties of the social influence bias eg. are ratings above the median affected the same way as ratings below the median.

Previous work, suggests that social influence is not a homogeneous bias, namely, positive influences are different from negative influences. In Muchnik et al. [28], they found that when they positively treated posts with higher up-vote counts it lead to a significant increase in the likelihood of additional up votes (32% more likely). On the other hand, they argue negative treatments inspired correction behavior; where some participants wanted to correct what they felt was an incorrect score. They found that this also increased the likelihood of up-voting (88% more likely); as opposed to the conforming response which would be increased down-votes.

These results suggest that the effects of viewing median ratings can be non-linear and are very context/question dependent. Similar to the previous section where we applied non-parametric tests that did not make a strong assumption about the distribution of the data, we propose a information theoretic polynomial function search that does not make strong assumptions about the nature of the relationship.

5.1 Correction Model

Recall that $g_f[j]$ is the final rating for participant j, and $m[j] - g_i[j]$ is the difference between the median and the initial rating. We want to find a polynomial function f such that:

$$f(g_f[j]) \approx m[j] - g_i[j] \qquad (10)$$

Let $f \in \mathcal{P}^k$ be a polynomial of degree k. The square loss of f, is the error in predicting $m[j] - g_i[j]$ from $f(g_f[j])$:

$$\mathcal{L}(X_c; f, k) = \sum_j ((m[j] - g_i[j]) - f(g_f[j]))^2 \quad (11)$$

For a given k, the best-fit polynomial minimizes this square-loss:

$$f_k^* = \arg\min_f \mathcal{L}(X_c; f, k) \quad (12)$$

For a given k, this problem can be solved with least squares. To search over the space of polynomial models, we apply a well-studied technique called the Bayesian Information Criterion (BIC) [10,32]. This technique converts the optimization problem into a penalized problem that jointly optimizes over the "complexity parameter" k. This penalty can be interpreted as bias towards lower degree models, in other words, an Occam's Razor prior belief. Cross-validation is an alternate method to empirically determine optimal model, and in practice, they give very similar results. BIC, however, is derived through maximum likelihood estimate and is not an empirical estimate so the learned model has a notion of optimality conditioned on the BIC prior belief.

Thus, we reformulate the optimization problem in the following way to incorporate the BIC penalty:

$$\arg\min_{f,k} |X_c| \log(\mathcal{L}(X_c; f, k)) + k \log(|X_c|) \quad (13)$$

The resulting optimal polynomial will tell how to correct a final rating to infer the initial one. Let q:

$$q(j) = m[j] - f(g_f[j]) \quad (14)$$

the predicted initial grade, and this value can be the input to our recommendation algorithm.

5.2 Applying the Corrections

There are two ways in which we can apply the correction model to existing recommender systems data. First, we can train our correction on all triplets, including ones that did not change, to get a correction that we can then apply to all ratings in the post-learning phase. The second way is to estimate the probability that a rating is changed, and if that probability is above a threshold α (eg. 50%) we can apply the correction. With the second way, the correction model is only trained on those triplets where the initial rating is different from the final one. To estimate this probability, we can apply a logistic regression model to predict whether or not a rating has been changed from all other ratings. Let $c(i, j)$ be 1 if participant j changed his or her rating for issue i and 0 if not. Our feature vector is the vector of all final ratings for that participant $v[j]_f = [g_f^1[j], ..., g_f^6[j]]$. Then, we can apply this logistic regression model to estimate the probability that $c(i, j) = 1$, using the logistic function:

$$P[c(i, j) = 1] = \frac{1}{e^{-\beta^T v[j]_f}} \quad (15)$$

We include results from both approaches in our experiments.

5.3 Prediction Model

For the prediction model, we make the dependent variable $m[j] - g_i[j]$ and the independent variable $g_f[j] - g_i[j]$. We apply the polynomial regression with the BIC optimization as before, and find an optimal function f such that

$$f(m[j] - g_i[j]) \approx g_f[j] - g_i[j] \quad (16)$$

f is a function of the difference between the initial rating and the median, that predicts the change in rating. This model allows us to reason about the nature of the social influence bias in the system. For example, if $|f(x)| > |f(-x)|$ for $x > 0$, we know that ratings above the median lead to a larger rating change. Additionally, $f'(x)$ tells us how the change varies as the observed difference with the median increases.

6. RESULTS

6.1 Dataset Description

The data for our case study was collected from the California Report Card between January 18th to April 20th. We also conducted an independent reference survey using SurveyMonkey's paid random panel system between March 8th and March 14th. As mentioned, ratings of six political issues were collected on a 13-point letter grade scale (A+,A,...,F) and for analysis we mapped these ratings linearly onto a scale from 0 to 1, with an F as 0 and A+ as 1. Participants also had the option to "skip" issues (not assign a grade). There were 1575 participants from the CRC and 611 participants from SurveyMonkey. Rating activity is summarized below.

Issue	No Change	Change	Skip	Median
CRC				
Obamacare	749	223	593	B (0.6667)
K12	849	172	544	C+ (0.5000)
College	923	139	503	C- (0.3333)
Immigration	693	105	767	C (0.4167)
Marijuana	881	118	566	C (0.4167)
Marriage Rights	929	105	531	B+ (0.7500)
Reference				
Obamacare	498	-	113	B (0.6667)
K12	561	-	50	C (0.4167)
College	573	-	38	C- (0.3333)
Immigration	375	-	236	C+ (0.5000)
Marijuana	498	-	113	C (0.4167)
Marriage Rights	554	-	57	B+ (0.7500)

For any given political issue, between 10% and 20% of those who assigned ratings registered a rating change. In all, 556 out of the 1575 CRC participants changed their rating at least once (Figure 3). We also found that the aggregate results of the reference survey matched the CRC nearly perfectly. On only two of the question (K12 and Immigration), we found a observed differences which were both less than a letter grade (+ or -).

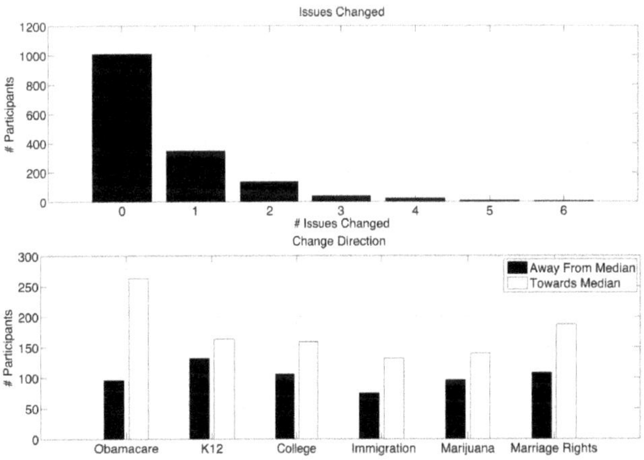

Figure 3: Among CRC participants, 65% changed none of their ratings, 22.0% changed one rating, 8.6% changed two, and 6.5% changed three or more. The lower figure omits those who didn't change and indicates that majority of rating changes were towards the median.

6.2 Analysis

6.2.1 *Correlation vs. Absolute Deviation*

In Section 4, we argued that using correlation as a test statistic can lead to erroneous conclusions of social influence bias, and proposed testing the absolute deviations around the median. We ran an experiment to illustrate the problems of using correlation instead of absolute deviation. In this experiment, we iterated through the initial ratings each of participants in the change group P_c. For each rating, we randomly sampled a final rating from group P_n, the ones that did not change. In this model, since we sample final ratings from the no change group, we know that the social influence bias hypothesis is not true, since in distribution those who changed their ratings and those who didn't are exactly the same. However, when we calculate the Pearson correlation coefficient between $g_f[j] - m[j]$ (the set of actual differences, not absolute deviations, between the final grade and the median) and $g_i[j] - m[j]$ (the set of actual differences, not absolute deviations, between the initial grade and the median), we find statistically significant correlations.

Issue	corr	p-val
Obamacare	0.709	5.2e-56
K12	0.659	4.73e-38
College	0.673	2.26e-36
Immigration	0.704	2.95e-32
Marijuana	0.689	1.42e-34
Marriage Rights	0.679	3.27e-41

There is a natural tendency for ratings to group around the median and the correlation coefficient does not account for this. However, if we measure the absolute deviation, we will find there is no statistically significant difference between the absolute deviations since they are the same in distribution.

6.2.2 *Significance in CRC*

Using the non-parametric test proposed in Section 4, we tested the hypothesis of whether rating changes led to significantly more concentration around the median. In our first experiment (Figure 4), we tested the absolute deviations of the CRC participants. We compared the group of participants that did not change their ratings to the group that changed their ratings. We found that while there were no statistically significant differences between the initial ratings of the two groups, the final ratings of the group that changed were statistically significantly more concentrated than both their own initial ratings and the ratings of the no change group. On average, the ratings were 19.3% closer to the median in the change group. The results of the hypothesis test for the set of participants who changed their ratings P_c and those who did not P_n are (we denote initial grades from P_c as i and final as f):

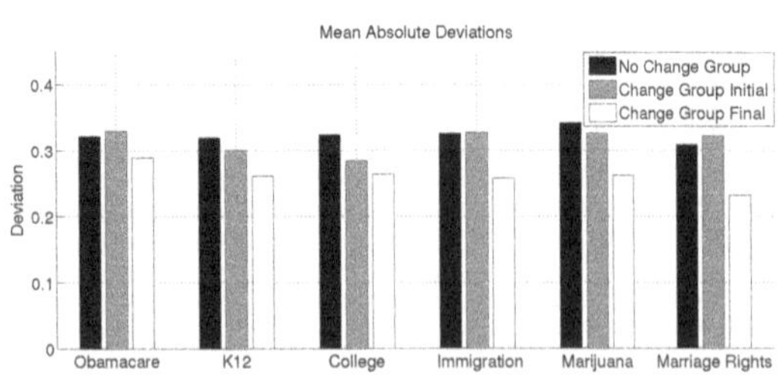

Figure 4: For those participants that changed their ratings, final ratings were significantly more concentrated around the median than their initial ratings.

Issue	p-val(P_c vs. P_n)	p-val(i vs. f)
Obamacare	0.0286	0.0161
K12	2.1314e-06	0.0086
College	1.3033e-04	0.0415
Immigration	7.3456e-07	4.4170e-05
Marijuana	2.7549e-10	4.2560e-05
Marriage Rights	3.5946e-06	2.4644e-10

These results are consistent with social influence bias. When participants change their ratings, they are more likely to concentrate around the median. It is however an encouraging and positive result that the two groups of participants P_n and P_c are very similar in terms of initial ratings, and the data suggests that a participant's susceptibility to social influence is not correlated with initial ratings.

6.2.3 *Comparison to Reference Survey*

In our second experiment (Figure 5), we apply the same testing procedure to compare the ratings from the CRC to to those in the reference survey. We compare absolute deviations of the group of participants who changed their ratings in the CRC against participants from the reference survey. The final ratings were 12.0% closer to the median in the CRC change group than in the reference survey. We also found that there was no statistically significant difference between the reference survey and initial ratings. The results of the hypothesis test for the set of participants who changed their ratings P_c and the reference group R are (we denote initial grades from P_c as i and final as f):

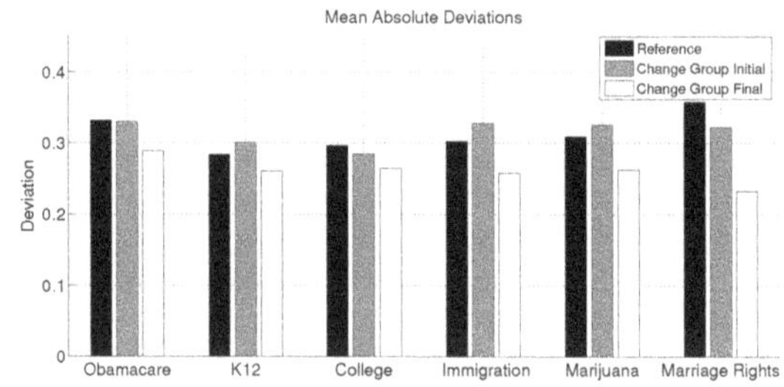

Figure 5: We found that final ratings were significantly more concentrated in the CRC compared to ratings in the reference survey, however the reference and the initial ratings did not differ significantly.

Issue	p-val(R vs. i)	p-val(R vs. f)
Obamacare	0.5386	0.0015
K12	0.8283	0.0097
College	0.1452	0.0091
Immigration	0.3765	1.1787e-04
Marijuana	0.7288	9.3111e-06
Marriage Rights	0.2478	0.0161

The results of our two experiments are consistent with social influence bias. We not only found that participants' changed ratings were statistically significantly more likely to concentrate around the median, they were also more likely in comparison to the reference survey.

6.3 Mitigation

6.3.1 *Classifying Final Grades As Changed*

In Section 5, we discussed how we could use logistic regression to estimate the probability that a rating has been changed. We applied logistic regression, as described in that section, and inferred which ratings were changed. In Figure 7, as is typically used to evaluate binary classifiers, we show the ROC plot of the logistic regression predictor. The prediction results were quite accurate with average AUC score

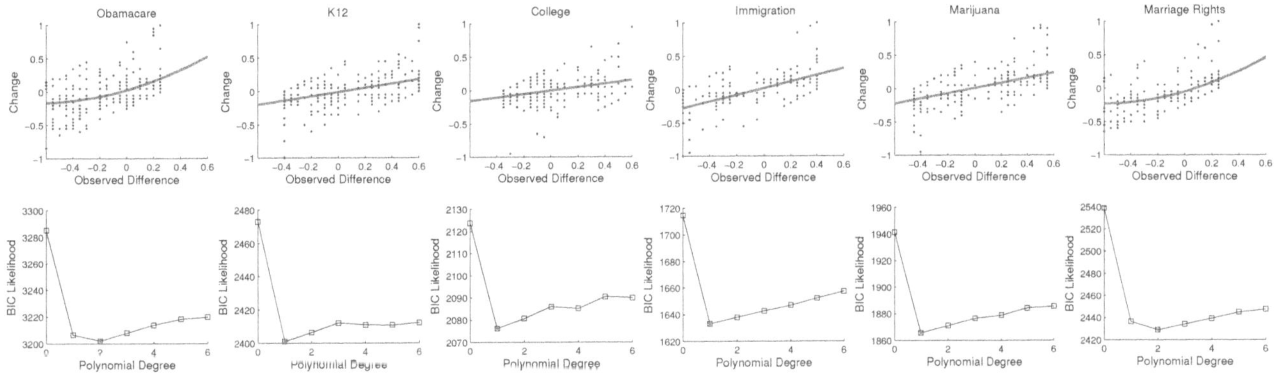

Figure 6: We plot the difference between ratings and the median (X-axis), and the change in rating (Y-axis). We overlay the optimal polynomial model to represent the relationship $f(x) = y$. Below each plot, is the BIC objective function showing how we picked an optimal degree of polynomial.

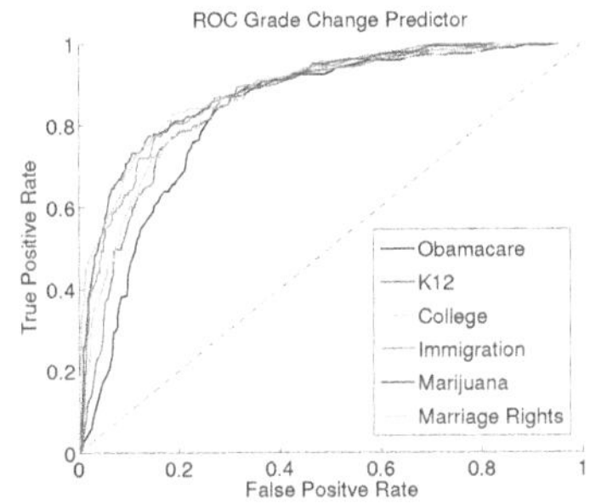

Figure 7: The true positive rate (correct classifications) as a function of the false positive rate. Substantially better than random (dashed line) with an average AUC score of 0.8670.

over all issues of 0.8670. At the .50 probability threshold (classified as changed if the estimated probability is greater than 0.5), we achieved an average precision of 84.7% and a recall of 70.0%.

6.3.2 Correction Model

In the first experiment, we train the polynomial/BIC correction model proposed in Section 5, and evaluated it in terms of RMSE (Figure 8). We look at model only for those changed their grades, and measure how accurate is the model in predicting the grade changes. We held out a random 20% of rating triplets and calculated the inference error in the correction model. We found that on average over all issues the RMSE was 0.1286 which corresponds to a little bit more than a + or - grade.

In the second experiment, we simulated a true post-learning setting. We used the logistic regression model to predict the probability that the participant changed their grade. Then, if this probability was above a threshold, we used 70% which was determined empirically, we then apply the polynomial correction model to infer the unbiased grade. Since the majority of participants did not change their grades, it would not be correct to simply measure RMSE error which would average predictions for those who changed and did not change. Thus, we invert the significance test proposed in Section 4, to calculate a parameter Δ which measures the distance from the null hypothesis. That is, how much would we have to shift the distribution of absolute deviations so the null hypothesis (of no social influence bias) is the most likely hypothesis. In Figure 8, we show a before and after for apply the correction model. We found that there was on average a 76.3% reduction in Δ for the entire pipeline predicting a change and then correcting for it.

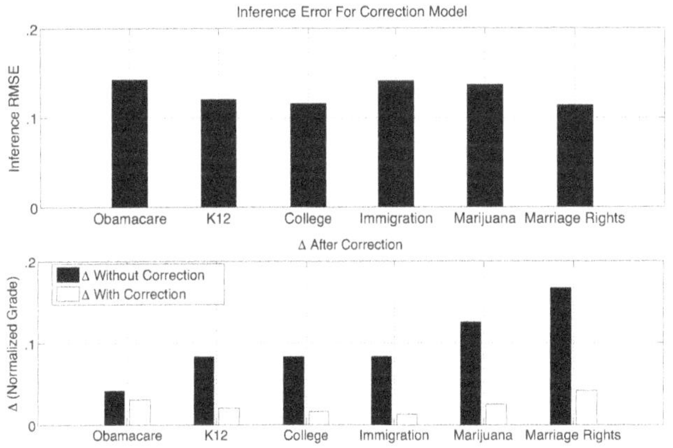

Figure 8: We found that we could predict changes in all of the issues with less than 2/3 of a letter grade RMSE error. In the lower figure, we applied this model to correct for the social influence bias and found that, on average, we could reduce the effects by 76.3%

6.3.3 Prediction Model

We applied the prediction from Section 5 and the results are shown in Figure 6. Our model search and optimization through the BIC discovered that for four out of the six issues, K12, College, Immigration, and Marijuana, the model was linear. This suggests homogeneity in positive and negative social influence effects for these issues. What this implies is that on average participants who rated above the median and below the median moved towards the median with the same magnitude. However, for Obamacare and Marriage Rights, we found that the relationship was quadratic. Interestingly enough, over the domain of changes, the learned quadratic function had steeper slope for ratings above the median. In other words, participants who initially rated the state higher than the median had a more significant tendency to change downwards, in comparison to the upward tendency of those who rated less than the median.

7. CONCLUSION AND FUTURE WORK

These results suggest that social influence bias can be significant in recommender systems and that this bias can be substantially reduced with machine learning. To apply this methodology to other recommender systems, a key question for future work is how is how to extend the approach to other recommender systems. We see an opportunity for this methodology in systems that combine their browsing and rating interfaces. For example, after selection, ie. users purchase a product, click on a movie, etc. the rating can be hidden. Once the user is ready to rate the item, which can be significant time after selection, we can reveal the average rating again after they have assigned a rating of their own. Then, we can apply our methodology to learn, analyze, and mitigate bias in the recommender systems.

An open question is how to extend this work to large item inventories and how much training data is required in such cases. One idea is to cluster/classify items into a small number of representative categories and train a model for each category. We believe that selecting an optimal set of items for training in this context may be posed as a submodular maximization problem. We are looking at applying this methodology to recommender systems in other domains (eg. movies) with alternative regression methods, such as Gaussian Process Regression and LOESS. We are also interested in performing more user studies where a false median is presented (as in the Asch experiments) and exploring methods to optimally classify participants as conformers and non-conformists. We would also like to study and quantify the role of social influence on textual data.

We like to thank Brandie Nonnecke, Allen Huang, Camille Crittenden, John Scott, Tanja Aitamurto, Daniel Catterson, Matti Nelimarkka, Henry Brady, and Lt. Governor Gavin Newsom for their work on the CRC project. This work is supported in part by NSF CISE Expeditions Award CCF-1139158, LBNL Award 7076018, and DARPA XData Award FA8750-12-2-0331, the Blum Center for Developing Economies and the Development Impact Lab (USAID Cooperative Agreement AID-OAA-A-12-00011), part of the USAID Higher Education Solutions Network, gifts from Amazon Web Services, Google, SAP, The Thomas and Stacey Siebel Foundation, Apple, Inc., C3Energy, Cisco, Cloudera, EMC, Ericsson, Facebook, GameOnTalis, Guavus, HP, Huawei, Intel, Microsoft, NetApp, Pivotal, Splunk, Virdata, VMware, WANdisco and Yahoo!.

8. REFERENCES

[1] J. Albors, J. C. Ramos, and J. L. Hervas. New learning network paradigms: Communities of objectives, crowdsourcing, wikis and open source. *International Journal of Information Management*, 28(3):194–202, 2008.

[2] X. Amatriain, J. M. Pujol, and N. Oliver. I like it... i like it not: Evaluating user ratings noise in recommender systems. In *User Modeling, Adaptation, and Personalization*, pages 247–258. Springer, 2009.

[3] X. Amatriain, J. M. Pujol, N. Tintarev, and N. Oliver. Rate it again: increasing recommendation accuracy by user re-rating. In *Proceedings of the third ACM conference on Recommender systems*, pages 173–180. ACM, 2009.

[4] S. E. Asch. Opinions and social pressure. *Readings about the social animal*, pages 17–26, 1955.

[5] S. E. Asch. *Studies of independence and conformity.* American Psychological Association, 1956.

[6] A. V. Banerjee. A simple model of herd behavior. *The Quarterly Journal of Economics*, 107(3):797–817, 1992.

[7] M. Bilgic and R. J. Mooney. Explaining recommendations: Satisfaction vs. promotion. In *Beyond Personalization Workshop, IUI*, volume 5, 2005.

[8] E. Bitton. A spatial model for collaborative filtering of comments in an online discussion forum. In *Proceedings of the third ACM conference on Recommender systems*, pages 393–396. ACM, 2009.

[9] R. Bond and P. B. Smith. Culture and conformity: A meta-analysis of studies using asch's (1952b, 1956) line judgment task. *Psychological bulletin*, 119(1):111, 1996.

[10] K. P. Burnham and D. R. Anderson. *Model selection and multimodel inference: a practical information-theoretic approach.* Springer, 2002.

[11] R. E. Burnkrant and A. Cousineau. Informational and normative social influence in buyer behavior. *Journal of Consumer research*, pages 206–215, 1975.

[12] D. Cosley, S. K. Lam, I. Albert, J. A. Konstan, and J. Riedl. Is seeing believing?: how recommender system interfaces affect users' opinions. In *Proceedings of the SIGCHI conference on Human factors in computing systems*, pages 585–592. ACM, 2003.

[13] C. Danescu-Niculescu-Mizil, G. Kossinets, J. Kleinberg, and L. Lee. How opinions are received by online communities: a case study on amazon. com helpfulness votes. In *Proceedings of the 18th international conference on World wide web*, pages 141–150. ACM, 2009.

[14] S. DellaVigna and M. Gentzkow. Persuasion: empirical evidence. Technical report, National Bureau of Economic Research, 2009.

[15] P. M. DeMarzo, D. Vayanos, and J. Zwiebel. Persuasion bias, social influence, and unidimensional opinions. *The Quarterly Journal of Economics*, 118(3):909–968, 2003.

[16] U. M. Dholakia, S. Basuroy, and K. Soltysinski. Auction or agent (or both)? a study of moderators of the herding bias in digital auctions. *International Journal of Research in Marketing*, 19(2):115–130, 2002.

[17] S. Faridani. Using canonical correlation analysis for generalized sentiment analysis, product recommendation and search. In *Proceedings of the fifth ACM conference on Recommender systems*, pages 355–358. ACM, 2011.

[18] S. Faridani, E. Bitton, K. Ryokai, and K. Goldberg. Opinion space: a scalable tool for browsing online comments. In *Proceedings of the SIGCHI Conference on Human Factors in Computing Systems*, pages 1175–1184. ACM, 2010.

[19] K. Goldberg, T. Roeder, D. Gupta, and C. Perkins. Eigentaste: A constant time collaborative filtering algorithm. *Information Retrieval*, 4(2):133–151, 2001.

[20] B. Golub and M. O. Jackson. Naive learning in social networks and the wisdom of crowds. *American Economic Journal: Microeconomics*, pages 112–149, 2010.

[21] H. Hong, J. D. Kubik, and J. C. Stein. Social interaction and stock-market participation. *The journal of finance*, 59(1):137–163, 2004.

[22] J.-H. Huang and Y.-F. Chen. Herding in online product choice. *Psychology & Marketing*, 23(5):413–428, 2006.

[23] L. Jian, J. MacKie-Mason, B. Chiao, A. Levchenko, A. Zellner, J. Kmenta, J. Dreze, and W. Oberhofer. Incentive-centered design for user-contributed content. *The Oxford Handbook of the Digital Economy, Oxford University Press Oxford*, pages 399–433, 2012.

[24] E. L. Lehmann and H. J. D'Abrera. *Nonparametrics: statistical methods based on ranks.* Springer New York, 2006.

[25] J. Lorenz, H. Rauhut, F. Schweitzer, and D. Helbing. How social influence can undermine the wisdom of crowd effect. *Proceedings of the National Academy of Sciences*, 108(22):9020–9025, 2011.

[26] C. A. Markowski and E. P. Markowski. Conditions for the effectiveness of a preliminary test of variance. *The American Statistician*, 44(4):322–326, 1990.

[27] S. Moscovici and C. Faucheux. Social influence, conformity bias, and the study of active minorities. *Advances in experimental social psychology*, 6:149–202, 1972.

[28] L. Muchnik, S. Aral, and S. J. Taylor. Social influence bias: A randomized experiment. *Science*, 341(6146):647–651, 2013.

[29] T. Nathanson, E. Bitton, and K. Goldberg. Eigentaste 5.0: constant-time adaptability in a recommender system using item clustering. In *Proceedings of the 2007 ACM conference on Recommender systems*, pages 149–152. ACM, 2007.

[30] B. S. Noveck. Wiki-government. *Democracy: A Journal of Ideas (7)*, 2008.

[31] K. O'Hara. Transparency, open data and trust in government: Shaping the infosphere. In *Proceedings of the 3rd Annual ACM Web Science Conference*, pages 223–232. ACM, 2012.

[32] G. Schwarz et al. Estimating the dimension of a model. *The annals of statistics*, 6(2):461–464, 1978.

[33] S. Sharma and S. Bikhchandani. *Herd behavior in financial markets-a review.* International Monetary Fund, 2000.

[34] R. Sipos, A. Ghosh, and T. Joachims. Was this review helpful to you?: it depends! context and voting patterns in online content. In *Proceedings of the 23rd international conference on World wide web*, pages 337–348. International World Wide Web Conferences Steering Committee, 2014.

[35] N. Tintarev and J. Masthoff. A survey of explanations in recommender systems. In *Data Engineering Workshop, 2007 IEEE 23rd International Conference on*, pages 801–810. IEEE, 2007.

[36] W. Wood. Attitude change: Persuasion and social influence. *Annual review of psychology*, 51(1):539–570, 2000.

[37] H. Zhu, B. Huberman, and Y. Luon. To switch or not to switch: understanding social influence in online choices. In *Proceedings of the SIGCHI Conference on Human Factors in Computing Systems*, pages 2257–2266. ACM, 2012.

Improving Sales Diversity by Recommending Users to Items

Saúl Vargas and Pablo Castells
Universidad Autónoma de Madrid, Spain
saul.vargas@uam.es, pablo.castells@uam.es

ABSTRACT

Sales diversity is considered a key feature of Recommender Systems from a business perspective. Sales diversity is also linked with the long-tail novelty of recommendations, a quality dimension from the user perspective. We explore the inversion of the recommendation task as a means to enhance sales diversity – and indirectly novelty – by selecting which users an item should be recommended to instead of the other way around. We address the inverted task by two approaches: a) inverting the rating matrix, and b) defining a probabilistic reformulation which isolates the popularity component of arbitrary recommendation algorithms. We find that the first approach gives rise to interesting reformulations of nearest-neighbor algorithms, which essentially introduce a new neighbor selection policy. The second approach, as well as the first, ultimately result in substantial sales diversity enhancements, and improved trade-offs with recommendation precision and novelty. Two experiments on movie and music recommendation datasets show the effectiveness of the resulting approach, even when compared to direct optimization approaches of the target metrics proposed in prior work.

Categories and subject descriptors: H3.3 [Information Search & Retrieval]: Information Filtering

Keywords: Recommender Systems; Sales Diversity; Novelty

1. INTRODUCTION

Sales diversity has been pointed out as a relevant quality of recommendation from the business point of view [7]. Sales diversity means that all or most products in the business catalog get purchased to some extent, rather than having sales concentrating around a few items. Sales diversity gets meaning in the context of recommendation in the sense that recommending a product exposes it to being sold. By linking recommendation to purchase in the analysis of diversity, "sales diversity" becomes a shorthand for "promoting sales diversity".

Sales diversity can be measured, for instance, by the total number or the ratio of items that are recommended in the top-N to at least one user [1]. Better yet, we can use the Gini coefficient as a finer measure of the concentration of top N recommendations around a few items [7]. Prior research has found there is an indirect connection between sales diversity and selling (recommending) in the long tail [1]: promoting long-tail (novel) items has a positive effect on sales diversity, even though sales diversity and long-tail novelty are not in themselves the same thing. Several approaches have been proposed in the literature to enhance recommendations over such metrics, most of which consist of re-sorting the top-K items ($K > N$) of an initial ranking produced by a baseline recommendation algorithm [1, 17]. Other authors have also researched the effect of different basic recommendation methods on sales concentration [7].

In the research presented here, we consider a different outlook on the problem of sales diversity. If we aim to procure a fair opportunity for most items to be recommended, one may consider selecting which users each item should be recommended to, instead of the other way around. This view entails a symmetric swap of the recommendation task, whereby users are recommended to items rather than the opposite. From this perspective, we address three main research questions: a) How can we define suitable and effective algorithms that recommend users to items? b) Does the inverted formulation actually enable any improvements in sales diversity? c) If so, what trade-offs if any are involved with respect to other qualities such as precision or recommendation novelty from the user point of view?

To address these questions we propose, firstly, to explore the application of state of the art collaborative filtering algorithms to the inverted recommendation task, that is, simply swapping the role of items and users in the algorithms. We find interesting derivations, equivalences, and new insights on the behavior of neighborhood-based algorithms in particular, where the inversion results in the emergence of new neighbor selection policies, with an impact on the potential connections to item popularity. We furthermore find that the inversion approach results in a significant increase of sales diversity while retaining a good trade-off on top-N item recommendation precision. In addition to this, we develop a probabilistic scheme which formulates user recommendation to items as a Bayesian layer which can be applied on top of any recommendation algorithm. The probabilistic scheme provides a principled means to isolate the item popularity component of the baseline algorithm; by means of simple smoothing techniques, the presence of this popularity component can be calibrated (i.e. kept unchanged or neutralized) to any desired degree. This parametrization is shown to enable an enhanced precision-diversity trade-off,

RecSys'14, October 6–10, 2014, Foster City, Silicon Valley, CA, USA.

ACM 978-1-4503-2668-1/14/10 ...$15.00.
http://dx.doi.org/10.1145/2645710.2645744 .

even above, somewhat surprisingly, direct optimization approaches targeting the precision vs. long-tail novelty trade-off. Furthermore, the resulting algorithmic scheme is competitive with respect to direct optimization even in terms of long-tail novelty.

The rest of the paper is structured as follows. In Section 2 we review the related work on assessment and enhancement of sales diversity and novelty. Section 3 discusses the popularity bias in collaborative filtering algorithms detected by several authors, and how this bias also influences the evaluation of Recommender Systems in ranking tasks. Section 4 introduces the inverted recommendation task of recommending users to items. Then, Section 5 describes our first proposal of using inverted neighborhoods to improve sales diversity. An analysis of the properties of standard and inverted neighborhoods and their differences is shown in Section 6. Section 7 presents our second proposal, a probabilistic reformulation layer that allows the calibration of the popularity bias in state-of-the-art collaborative filtering algorithms. Experiments with two different recommendation scenarios – movies and music – are described in Section 8. Finally, Section 9 offers the conclusions and future work.

2. SALES DIVERSITY AND NOVELTY

As Anderson [4] stated, some businesses or economic models present a *Long tail* effect, in which a few of the most popular items are extremely popular, while the rest – the long tail – is much less known. Promoting the recommendation of items in this long tail may offer benefits for both users and the business behind the recommender system. From the user side, offering not so popular items may help receive less obvious, unexpected recommendations, which correspond with the natural notion of a recommender system as a tool to help users discover new content. From the system side, avoiding the recommendation of short-head items may also contribute to make the most of the catalog.

Adomavicius et al. [1] proposed to measure sales diversity in terms of the aggregate diversity, i.e., how many different items of the catalog were recommended to the users. Given a recommender system S, they proposed a metric, denoted here as aggr-div, which return the total number of different items that have been recommended to at least one user:

$$\text{aggr-div}(S) = \left| \bigcup_{u \in \mathcal{U}} L_u^S \right| \quad (1)$$

where L_u^S is the recommendation list generated by the system S for the user u. This metric, while being simple and intuitive, may not be very robust, since the contribution to the metric of an item that has been recommended just once is equal to that of other item recommended a thousand times. Therefore, we think that using a metric to measure the imbalance in the number of times each item is recommended would be more adequate. Fleder and Hosanagar [7] proposed a better alternative by using the *Gini coefficient* to measure sales concentration:

$$\text{gini}(S) = 1 - \frac{1}{N-1} \sum_{k=1}^{N} (2k - N - 1) p(i_k \,|\, S) \quad (2)$$

where $p(i_k \,|\, S)$ is the probability of the k-th least recommended item being drawn from the recommendation lists generated by a system S:

$$p(i \,|\, S) = \frac{\sum_u \mathbf{1}_{i \in L_u^S}}{\sum_{u,j} \mathbf{1}_{j \in L_u^S}} \quad (3)$$

Note that in our definition we use the complement of the standard definition for the Gini coefficient so that higher values of our metric correspond to more balanced recommendations.

In previous work [17], we proposed the *expected popularity complement* metric to measure the long-tail novelty of the items in a recommendation list, which is defined as the average novelty of the recommended items:

$$\text{EPC}(L_u) = \frac{1}{|L_u|} \sum_{i \in L_u} nov(i) \quad (4)$$

where $nov(i)$ measures the *novelty* of an item as the probability of not to being known by a user:

$$nov(i) = 1 - \frac{\sum_u \mathbf{1}_{r_{u,i}>0}}{\sum_{u,j} \mathbf{1}_{r_{u,j}>0}} \quad (5)$$

Several proposals to promote sales diversity and novelty in recommender systems have been proposed [1, 11, 15, 17]. A simple approach, which we compare against our proposals, consist in a re-scoring of a previously generated recommendation baseline by using a normalized linear combination between the scores provided by the baseline and the novelty component described in 5:

$$s_{NR}(u,i) = (1-\lambda)\ norm_s\, s(u,i) + \lambda\ norm_{nov}\, nov(i) \quad (6)$$

where $norm_s$ and $norm_{nov}$ are normalizing functions that help making a balanced combination of both relevance and novelty components, such as the *standard score* $norm_X(x) = \frac{x-\mu_X}{\sigma_X}$.

3. THE POPULARITY BIAS IN RECOMMENDATIONS

In a ranking prediction task, the popularity-based recommendation is the obvious baseline to beat [3]. In terms of sales diversity and recommendation novelty, personalized algorithms easily improve over the popularity-based recommendation which, by definition, has the lowest scores in terms of the metrics described in the previous section. Improving the precision of popularity recommendation is less obvious than one might think but is also a feasible goal [6]. While it is clear that collaborative filtering algorithms outperform popularity-based recommendations in terms of accuracy and sales diversity, some authors have pointed out that they still suffer from a bias [18].

Collaborative filtering algorithms, in particular, are known to generally have a bias towards recommending popular items, commonly known as the "Harry Potter Effect"[1]. There is a natural reason for this trend to begin with: collaborative filtering thrives on the populated regions of the user-item interaction history matrix (rating matrix for short), and falls short in the sparser regions. Popular items live by definition in the more populated areas, since they carry more rating data that populates matrix cells, and collaborative algorithms are therefore more prone to end up recommending these items. The popularity bias of collaborative filtering algorithms has been pointed out by several authors and studied by some. For instance, Zhao et al. [18] show empirical evidence that popular items tend to be more recommended than not so popular ones, and proposes methods to alleviate his effect. Steck [15] examined this issue in further depth and justified this popularity bias by the selection bias towards popular items in the available data.

[1] `http://recsyswiki.com/wiki/Harry_Potter_effect`

Furthermore, common precision-based evaluation methodologies reward this behavior, since popular items have more test ratings and are more likely to be counted as hits for more users. This has motivated several evaluation protocols [5, 6, 15] that try to enable a less biased assessment of the personalized relevance of the recommendations, by removing the tip of the bias in the test data.

The popularity bias has a negative effect on the discovery-related added value and practical usefulness of collaborative filtering recommendations, as well as their effect on sales concentration [7]. The research and findings we report here provide means to better cope, directly and indirectly, with this bias, as we discuss in the next sections.

4. RECOMMENDING USERS TO ITEMS: PROBLEM STATEMENT

The recommendation task can be formulated as defining a scoring function $s : \mathcal{U} \times \mathcal{I} \to \mathbb{R}$ for pairs of users $u \in \mathcal{U}$ and items $i \in \mathcal{I}$ so that, for each user, a ranked list of items $L_u \subset \mathcal{I} \times \mathcal{I} \times \ldots$ is defined by sorting items by decreasing score order. The scoring function of a recommender algorithm is based on previous interactions between users and items recorded in a matrix $R = (r_{u,i})_{u,i} \in \mathbb{R}^{|\mathcal{U}|,|\mathcal{I}|}$ and, possibly, additional sources, as in the case of content or social-based recommenders. We shall focus here on collaborative filtering approaches, which use only the interaction matrix R.

Analogously to the original task of recommending items to users, the task of recommending users to items can be formulated as defining a scoring function

$$\tilde{s} : \mathcal{I} \times \mathcal{U} \to \mathbb{R} \tag{7}$$

which induces a ranking of users by their decreasing predicted relevance to item i. In a pure collaborative filtering setting, the input data for this task consists of the transposed rating matrix $\tilde{R} = R^t \in \mathbb{R}^{|\mathcal{I}|,|\mathcal{U}|}$.

Since collaborative filtering algorithms do not depend on the content or internal characteristics of both users and items, they can be adapted for this task without any modification apart from the change of roles between users and items. An initial observation is that, for many popular, state-of-the-art collaborative filtering algorithms, the scoring function $\tilde{s}$ is actually identical to that of the original problem s. That is the case, for instance, of many matrix factorization approaches, such as the implicit matrix factorization of Hu et al. [9]:

$$\tilde{s}_{iMF}(i,u) = q_i\, p_u^t = p_u\, q_i^t = s_{iMF}(u,i) \tag{8}$$

There are other collaborative filtering approaches that break this symmetry. That is the case of other matrix factorization approaches [13, 14, 16] which, even having the same scoring function as in Equation 8, have non-interchangeable roles for users and items in their model training, and thus provide new scoring functions between users and items. However, we focus on the case of nearest neighbors approaches, whose asymmetry offers an interesting, new alternative for generating diverse recommendations.

5. INVERTED NEAREST NEIGHBORS

A first application of the inverted recommendation task lies in the asymmetry of the nearest neighbor approaches when applied to the inverted recommendation task. Throughout this section we will focus on the user-based k-nearest neighbors (kNN) approach, since most of the observations, unless explicitly discussed, are straightforwardly translatable to the item-based alternative.

sim	u_1	u_2	u_3	u_4
u_1	-	0.1	0.3	0.4
u_2	0.1	-	0.5	0.0
u_3	0.3	0.5	-	0.6
u_4	0.4	0.0	0.6	-

u	$N_2(u)$	$N_2^{-1}(u)$
u_1	$\{u_3, u_4\}$	$\{u_2, u_4\}$
u_2	$\{u_1, u_3\}$	$\{u_3\}$
u_3	$\{u_2, u_4\}$	$\{u_1, u_2, u_4\}$
u_4	$\{u_1, u_3\}$	$\{u_1, u_3\}$

Table 1: Example of user neighborhoods of size 2.

The scoring functions of the user-based and item-based kNN recommenders[2, 6] can be formulated as follows :

$$s_{UB}(u,i) = \sum_{v \in \mathcal{U}} \mathbf{1}_{v \in N(u)}\, sim(u,v)\, r_{v,i} \tag{9}$$

$$s_{IB}(u,i) = \sum_{j \in \mathcal{I}_u} \mathbf{1}_{i \in N(j)}\, sim(i,j)\, r_{u,j} \tag{10}$$

where $sim(u,v)$ is a similarity function between two users and $N(u)$ is the neighborhood of user u, containing the topmost similar users to item u.

Reformulating these algorithms in the inverted recommendation task, the scoring functions become:

$$\tilde{s}_{UB}(i,u) = \sum_{j \in \mathcal{I}} \mathbf{1}_{j \in N(i)}\, sim(i,j)\, \tilde{r}_{j,u} \tag{11}$$

$$\tilde{s}_{IB}(i,u) = \sum_{v \in \mathcal{U}_i} \mathbf{1}_{u \in N(v)}\, sim(u,v)\, \tilde{r}_{i,v} \tag{12}$$

As previously commented, the symmetry of the nearest neighbors scoring functions with respect to the original problem is broken. In particular, the user-based approach s_{UB} in Equation 9 is notably different from the scoring function $\tilde{s}_{UB}$ in Equation 11. Interestingly, it is almost equivalent to the item-based approach $\tilde{s}_{IB}$ for the inverted recommendation in Equation 12, the difference lying on the neighborhood selection criterion, i.e., $\mathbf{1}_{u \in N(v)}$ against $\mathbf{1}_{v \in N(u)}$. Actually, one can re-formulate the scoring function $\tilde{s}_{IB}$ as a variant of the standard user-based approach s_{UB} in which the policy for neighbor selection is inverted, that is, by considering user *inverted neighborhoods* $N^{-1}(u)$ defined as

$$N^{-1}(u) = \{v \in \mathcal{U} \,:\, u \in N(v)\} \tag{13}$$

where $N(v)$ is the original neighborhood for a user v, so that $\mathbf{1}_{u \in N(v)} = \mathbf{1}_{v \in N^{-1}(u)}$. The concept of inverted neighborhoods originally appeared in [12], where it was proposed as an ad-hoc method to efficiently predict ratings for item-based approaches, without any relationship with the inverted recommendation tasks or the improvement of sales diversity.

Note what the resulting inverted neighborhood formation policy means: instead of selecting $N(u)$ as the top-K most similar users to the target user u, all the users v for which the target user is among the K most similar to v are selected as the neighbors $N^{-1}(u)$ of u. Table 1 shows an example of a community of users and their corresponding standard and inverted neighborhoods for $K = 2$. This has several consequences. In the first place, the resulting, inverted neighborhoods no longer have all the same size. The size of the inverted neighborhood of a user u is the number of users to whose neighborhood u belongs – in particular this means that some users might have an empty neighborhood at the cost of user coverage of the recommendation, but we have observed in our experiments that this situation does not happen in practice if the original neighborhoods are large enough. Having different neighborhood sizes is not necessarily a drawback, on the contrary, it may be favorable that users have as large a neighborhood as the reliability of the available data for each user enables.

	user	item
Netflix	209.25	5,654.50
MSD	43.03	127.88

Table 2: Average profile size

	user-based	item-based
S	$\text{avg}_u \text{avg}_{v \in N(u)} \lvert \mathcal{I}_v \rvert$	$\text{avg}_i \text{avg}_{j \in N(i)} \lvert \mathcal{U}_j \rvert$
G	$Gini(\lvert N^{-1}(u) \rvert)$	$Gini(\lvert N^{-1}(i) \rvert)$
C	$\rho(\lvert \mathcal{I}_u \rvert, \lvert N^{-1}(u) \rvert)$	$\rho(\lvert \mathcal{U}_i \rvert, \lvert N^{-1}(i) \rvert)$

Table 3: Definition of the neighborhood properties. N denotes in this case a generic user or item neighborhood, either standard or inverted.

The inverted neighborhoods approach implies, on the other hand, that all users will appear in exactly the same number $|N(u)|$ of inverted neighborhoods (except perhaps a few low activity users for which it was not possible to form a direct neighborhood of size K in the first place). This flattens the influence power of all users, so that all users' opinions "count" to the same extent overall in the produced recommendations. This may be expected to avoid a concentration of recommendations over the tastes of a reduced set of users, thereby indirectly enhancing a more even distribution of items across recommendations to the user population.

In the case of the item-based variant this effect is even more direct: if all items appear in the inverted neighborhood of the same number of items (neighbor items being the candidates for recommendation in the item-based kNN method), they will have more even chances of making it to the top-N of recommendations, whereby one may expect better distributed recommendations over the set of items (i.e. more diverse "sales"). Moreover, long-tail items, by getting a more equal opportunity to be recommended with respect to popular items, might make for a long-tail novelty enhancement of recommendations.

In order to have a preliminary understanding of these potential effects, we will analyze more closely in the next section the relation between user and item characteristics, namely profile size, and their distribution across neighborhoods for the direct and inverted selection policies. Our discussion of the potential effects on final recommendation diversity is so far speculative and needs to be tested empirically, as we report in Section 8.2.

6. NEIGHBORHOOD BIAS ANALYSIS

We test and illustrate the biases suggested in the previous section by taking some measurements on data from the Netflix Prize and the Million Song Dataset, for which we study the characteristics of user and item neighborhoods with different neighborhood sizes K.

We show in Table 4 the following measurements:

- Average profile size of the neighbors (**S**), in order to detect any possible bias towards neighbors with profile sizes significantly different from the average profile size (displayed in Table 2).
- Gini coefficient of the items distribution across neighborhoods (**G**), as an indicator to detect any imbalance in the distribution of the number $|N_K^{-1}(u)|$ of neighborhoods a user belongs to.
- Correlation between the profile size of a user and the number of neighborhoods she belongs to (**C**), to see if an existing imbalance is caused for a bias to users with big profiles in the neighbor selection process.

		S		G		C	
	K	N_K	N_K^{-1}	N_K	N_K^{-1}	N_K	N_K^{-1}
Netflix	10	286.39	137.91	0.18	1.00	0.07	-
	20	291.07	131.91	0.20	1.00	0.09	-
	50	298.20	124.68	0.22	1.00	0.11	0.00
	100	304.38	120.08	0.25	1.00	0.12	0.00
	200	311.24	116.46	0.27	1.00	0.15	0.00
	500	321.53	113.25	0.30	1.00	0.18	0.01
	1000	330.29	111.58	0.33	1.00	0.22	0.01
	2000	339.96	110.41	0.35	1.00	0.26	0.02
	5000	353.90	110.12	0.21	1.00	0.32	0.02
MSD	10	23.12	35.41	0.18	1.00	-0.11	0.00
	20	24.29	35.58	0.21	1.00	-0.11	0.00
	50	26.27	35.96	0.26	1.00	-0.12	0.00
	100	28.07	36.41	0.30	1.00	-0.12	0.00
	200	30.06	37.07	0.34	1.00	-0.12	0.01
	500	32.75	38.63	0.40	1.00	-0.11	0.01

Table 4: Properties of user neighborhoods with cosine similarity for the Netflix and Million Song datasets. Dashes mark undefined correlations since $|N^{-1}(u)|$ was constant for all the users. See Table 3 for the meaning of S, G and C.

		S		G		C	
	K	N_K	N_K^{-1}	N_K	N_K^{-1}	N_K	N_K^{-1}
Netflix	10	24,018.26	8,622.86	0.48	1.00	0.22	-
	20	25,484.00	7,888.98	0.49	1.00	0.28	-
	50	27,674.89	7,208.90	0.50	1.00	0.37	-
	100	29,497.64	6,824.87	0.50	1.00	0.44	-
	200	31,272.44	6,513.84	0.51	1.00	0.50	-
	500	32,565.92	6,525.21	0.51	1.00	0.56	-
	1000	30,964.19	7,301.09	0.54	1.00	0.57	-
	2000	26,208.78	9,150.45	0.62	1.00	0.53	0.01
	5000	17,001.67	12,839.88	0.80	1.00	0.26	0.01
MSD	10	146.76	120.09	0.60	1.00	0.02	0.00
	20	176.99	114.08	0.64	1.00	0.05	0.01
	50	248.41	108.56	0.67	0.99	0.12	0.02
	100	344.79	106.58	0.70	0.97	0.23	0.04
	200	497.18	116.77	0.70	0.94	0.42	0.05
	500	822.14	158.30	0.62	0.86	0.64	0.08
	1000	1,147.84	216.59	0.53	0.78	0.71	0.11
	2000	1,475.06	302.41	0.45	0.67	0.75	0.15
	5000	1,793.47	462.71	0.37	0.52	0.76	0.21

Table 5: Properties of item neighborhoods for the Netflix and Million Song datasets. Dashes mark undefined correlations since $|N^{-1}(i)|$ was constant for all the items. See Table 3 for the meaning of S, G and C.

A more formal definition of the above measurements is given in Table 3, where we denote by $N_K(u)$ the direct neighborhood formed by the K most similar users to a user u, and by $N_K^{-1}(u)$ the inverted neighborhood for u.

The results in Table 4 reveal, as hypothesized, biases and concentrations in the selection of user for standard neighborhoods. In the case of Netflix data, the standard neighborhood method is slightly biased towards selecting users with big profiles and shows a clear concentration on a small subset of users. In the case of the Million Song Dataset, there is an opposite bias towards small profiles, which also causes a concentration of neighbors. A possible explanation of why these methods differ in the direction of the bias may lie in the incomparable number of items between them and the different levels of sparsity in each dataset. In any case, the inverted selections strategy corrects this biases, that is, eliminates the correlation between profile size and the number of neighborhoods a user belongs to and, at the same time, creates a perfectly balanced distribution of this number.

Table 5 shows the equivalent measurements for item neighborhoods. Again, we can observe biases and concentration in the direct selection method that are partly solved by the inverted neighborhoods. The Netflix data shows a bias towards popular items that, ultimately, compose the majority of the neighborhoods. These issues are solved by the inverted item neighborhoods, which achieve a perfectly equitative distribution of the items in the neighborhoods, doing away with the bias towards popular items. In the Million Song dataset, a bias towards popular items is also observed for large neighborhood sizes, and an uneven distribution of the items in the distribution is observed for all neighborhood sizes. Again, inverted neighborhoods help solving these effects by significantly reducing the bias towards popular items and achieving more uniform distributions in the number of neighborhoods each item belongs to.

7. PROBABILISTIC REFORMULATION LAYER

The inverted recommendation task can also be addressed in probabilistic terms. Probabilistic formulations have been used extensively in the conventional item recommendation task as a means to develop collaborative filtering methods. For instance, Hofmann [8] proposed ranking items by the decreasing probability $p(i|u)$ that the target user would prefer each item over the others. This principle is developed by means of an adaptation of the probabilistic Latent semantic Indexing (pLSA) framework into an effective scoring procedure for producing ranked recommendations.

Turning the task around, recommending users for items would consist of estimating $p(u|i)$ for each user u given an item i. A straightforward way of linking any recommendation algorithm to a probabilistic formulation can be established by assuming that the recommender scoring function $s(u,i)$ is roughly proportional to $p(u,i)$. This assumption, coarse as it may be, provides a very direct means to bring the recommendation algorithm to a probabilistic interpretation as per:

$$p(u \mid i; s) \sim \frac{s(u,i)}{\sum_v s(v,i)} \tag{14}$$

We can therefore use this approach to obtain an inverted recommendation method out of any direct item recommendation algorithm. Note that the resulting formulation produces a totally equivalent output as its scoring function preserves the original ranking, i.e., $p(u \mid i; s) \propto s(u,i)$. The formulation is however useful as it enables a probability-based manipulation of the popularity bias in recommendation algorithms, as we see next.

First, the resulting output of the inverted recommendation should be reverted to a list of ranked items to be delivered to each user. A principled way to do this is by applying Bayesian inversion on $p(u|i)$, thereby obtaining an estimate for $p(i|u)$ as a suitable scoring function for ranking items for each user:

$$p(i \mid u; s) = \frac{p(u \mid i; s)\, p(i; s)}{\sum_j p(u \mid j; s)\, p(j; s)} \tag{15}$$

where the prior $p(i;s)$ represents how likely the item is to be the favorite of a random user.

	UB	IB	iMF
Netflix	0.99	0.73	0.95
MSD	0.92	0.78	

Table 6: Pearson correlation between prior $p(i;s,0)$ and item popularity.

Note that we could instead have derived an estimate of $p(i \mid u; s)$ by an equivalent symmetric version of equation 14. However, the advantage of equation 15 is that it explicitly reflects the popularity component carried by the item prior $p(i;s)$. Using the same assumption as before between the scoring function and probabilities, we have:

$$p(i; s) \sim \frac{\sum_u s(u,i)}{\sum_j \sum_u s(u,j)} \tag{16}$$

Now that the popularity component is isolated, we propose to smooth the prior estimate in a way that has it range from the literal estimate based on the recommender's scores, to a flat uniform background prior where all items are considered equally popular. We do so by an entropic regularization of the estimate – similar to the tempered expectation maximization algorithm in [8], which simply introduces an exponent in the expression:

$$p(i; s, \alpha) \sim \frac{\left(\sum_u s(u,i)\right)^{1-\alpha}}{\sum_j \left(\sum_u s(u,j)\right)^{1-\alpha}} \tag{17}$$

In the above expression, the $\alpha \in [0,1]$ smoothing parameter allows controlling how much of the algorithm popularity bias we wish to leave as is or remove.

Interestingly, by combining equations 15 and 17, the resulting probabilistic interpretation $p(i \mid u; s)$ can be simplified to a re-scoring procedure for a standard scoring function s as follows:

$$s_{BR}(u,i) = s(u,i) \left(\sum_v s(v,i) \right)^{-\alpha} \tag{18}$$

This last reformulation allows to see more clearly the role of the parameter α. On one hand, when $\alpha = 0$ we obtain the original recommendation list created with the scoring function. On the other hand, when $\alpha = 1$ the prior is uniform and thus the recommendations to users will be completely based on $p(u \mid i; \tilde{s})$, eliminating any possible popularity bias in the items. The use of intermediate values of α is a means to provide more varied recommendation lists while retaining an appropriate level of relevance, that is α is a parameter that controls the relevance/novelty trade-off, only that novelty is not applied as the opposite to popularity (as is the case in most novelty enhancement approaches [1, 17]), but rather as neutrality with respect to popularity.

To illustrate how we can control the popularity bias by the proposed approach, we show in Table 6 the Pearson correlation values between the priors $p(i;s,0)$ and the popularity of the items (understood as the number of users who know – i.e. have rated – the item) for some recommendations baselines – further detailed in Section 8.1 – for the Netflix and Million Song datasets. The values reveal a strong correlation between our score-based estimate of the item priors and the actual popularity of the items. This, on the other hand, empirically illustrates the popularity bias of these state of the art algorithms as discussed in Section 3, and shows how the prior component captures it, enabling its gradual adjustment by the α parameter.

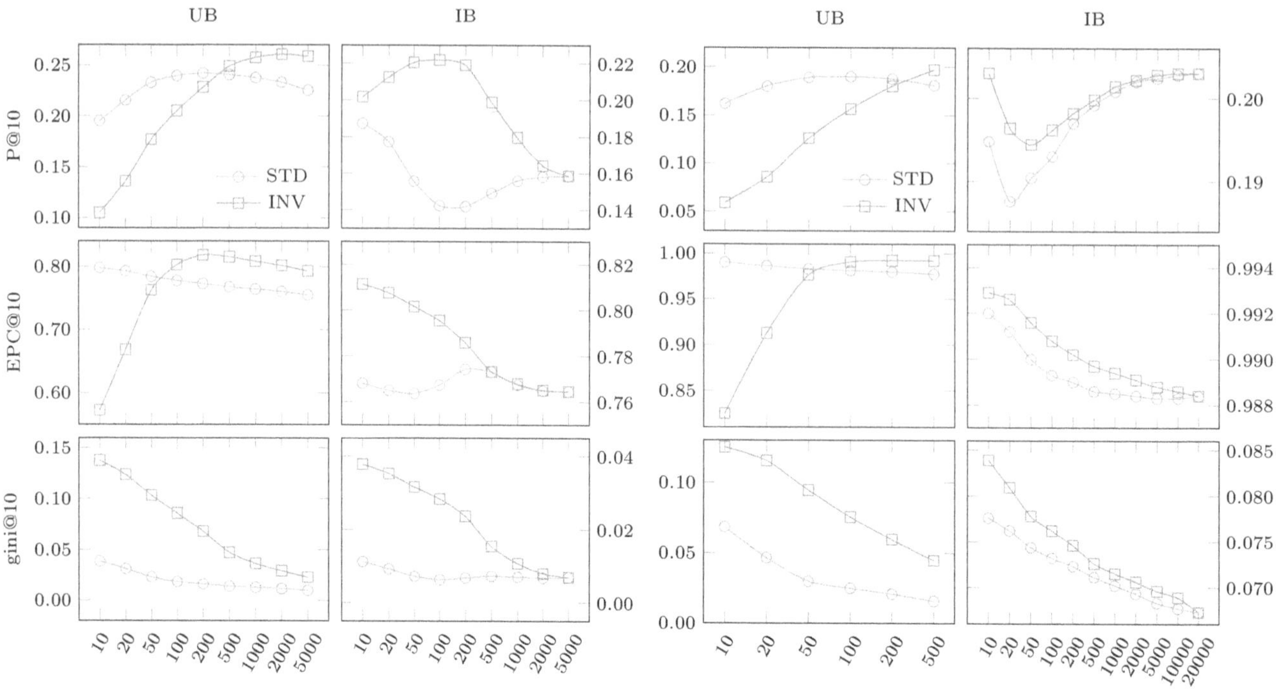

(a) Netflix Dataset

(b) Million Song Dataset

Figure 1: Experiments with Inverted Neighborhoods

	K	UB (N_K)	UB (N_K^{-1})	IB (N_K)	IB (N_K^{-1})
Netflix	**10**	0.9893	0.6602	0.9989	0.9989
	20	0.9961	0.7775	0.9989	0.9989
	50	0.9989	0.8995	0.9989	0.9989
	100	0.9989	0.9575	0.9989	0.9989
	200	0.9989	0.9871	0.9989	0.9989
	500	0.9989	0.9981	0.9989	0.9989
	≥1000	0.9989	0.9989	0.9989	0.9989
MSD	**10**	1.0000	0.8291	1.0000	1.0000
	20	1.0000	0.9178	1.0000	1.0000
	50	1.0000	0.9830	1.0000	1.0000
	100	1.0000	0.9980	1.0000	1.0000
	200	1.0000	0.9999	1.0000	1.0000
	≥500	1.0000	1.0000	1.0000	1.0000

Table 7: User coverage as the fraction of users in the test split which receive a recommendation in the Netflix and MSD data.

		P@10	EPC@10	gini@10	aggr-div@10
Netflix	**Random**	0.0022	0.9866	0.9683	1.0000
	Pop	0.1026	0.6920	0.0019	0.0100
	iMF	0.2084	0.8401	0.0507	0.3571
	UB (N_{100})	0.2396	0.7778	0.0183	0.2784
	UB (N_{100}^{-1})	0.2053	0.8028	0.0858	0.9591
	IB (N_{10})	0.1874	0.7681	0.0113	0.4691
	IB (N_{10}^{-1})	0.2018	0.8115	0.0378	0.6738
MSD	**Random**	0.0000	0.9999	0.6750	0.9424
	Pop	0.0306	0.9376	0.0000	0.0001
	UB (N_{100})	0.1899	0.9814	0.0249	0.1634
	UB (N_{100}^{-1})	0.1565	0.9908	0.0756	0.3119
	IB (N_{10})	0.1924	0.9920	0.0776	0.3341
	IB (N_{10}^{-1})	0.1965	0.9929	0.0839	0.3459

Table 8: Comparison of inverted neighborhood methods to other recommendation algorithms.

8. EXPERIMENTS

In order to test the effectiveness and analyze the properties of the proposed inverted nearest neighbor methods and the probabilistic popularity adjustment, we carry out two experiments on the Netflix Prize[2] and Million Song Dataset Challenge [10] datasets. The Netflix data contain 100M ratings (from one to five stars) by 480,000 users to 18,000 movies. And we used the Taste Profile Subset of the Million Song Dataset, containing 48M play count triplets by 1,100,000 users for 380,000 songs. As in the work of Aiolli [2], we take binarized play counts since, as warned by the challenge organizers, play counts are unreliable and not necessarily correlate with likings.

8.1 Setup

Each dataset is split for evaluation into training and test subsets. For Netflix, we do a 80-20% random split of the data, while in the Million Song dataset we take the partition provided with the data release. For every user with test data, we generate recommendation lists by ranking all the items with training data. We then measure rank-based precision, novelty and sales diversity for the top-10 items in the recommendation for each user. Precision is measured as the proportion of relevant test items of the user included in the recommendation he is delivered. Novelty is measured by EPC [17] and sales diversity by the Gini coefficient. For illustrative purposes, we also report results for aggregate diversity [1] normalized by the number of items.

For the inverted neighborhood approach, we compare the inverted kNN approaches described (Equations 11 and 12) to the corresponding standard user-based and item-based formulations (Equations 9 and 10). We used cosine as the similarity function between users and items, and explored a range of neighborhood sizes for both datasets.

[2]`http://www.netflixprize.com/`

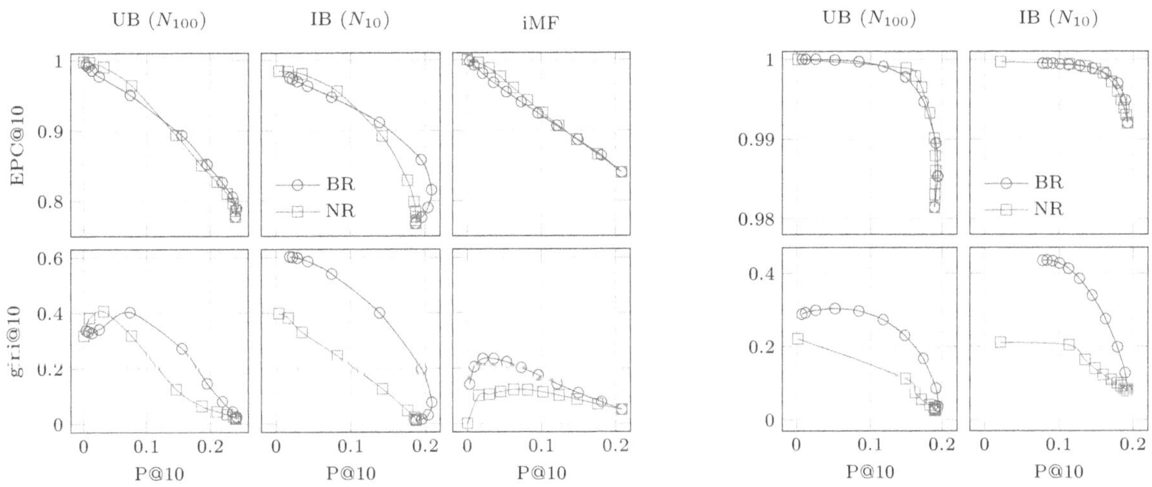

(a) Netflix Dataset (b) Million Song Dataset

Figure 2: Experiments with Bayes Rule

For the probabilistic reformulation, a comparison between our approach and the novelty-oriented re-scoring approach defined by Equation 6 in three different recommendation baselines, namely the standard user and item-based kNN recommenders (N_{100} and N_{10} respectively) and, for the case of the Netflix dataset, the implicit matrix factorization proposed by Hu et al. [9], by considering positive ratings as implicit data. As stated in [2], matrix factorization approaches are not effective in the Million Song dataset, as our attempts at it confirmed, whereby we omit results with this baseline in this dataset. The two compared approaches have a parameter that controls the trade-off between the original scoring function ($\alpha = 0.0$ and $\lambda = 0.0$) and a pure novelty component ($\alpha = 1.0$ and $\lambda = 1.0$). We explore these trade-offs by a grid search on the full interval by steps of 0.1.

8.2 Results for Inverted Nearest Neighbors

Figure 1 shows the comparison of the direct (i.e. standard) and inverted nearest-neighbor approaches in terms of the metrics of interest for different neighborhood sizes.

The results confirm a systematic increase in sales diversity (measured by the Gini coefficient), as hypothesized in Section 5. The improvement is consistent in the user-based and item-based versions for all neighborhood sizes on both datasets. Notably moreover, for the item-based approach, the inverted method offers better accuracy and novelty for every value of K. For inverted user-based kNN, accuracy and novelty are better than in direct kNN only for large enough neighborhoods ($K \geq 100$). This is caused by user coverage degradation that occurs with smaller K, that is, many users do not receive recommendations since their inverted neighborhoods are empty, resulting in a penalization in metrics such as precision and EPC (we sum zero precision and EPC when a user cannot be delivered a recommendation). The details about the user coverage degradation are shown in Table 7. In a real recommender system this would not be acceptable, and a fallback solution, such as using the standard neighborhood, should be resorted to in those cases. However, in this analysis we are interested in the properties of the pure algorithm, and we therefore report the results for a plain version of the approach.

In order to provide a wider perspective in the context of alternative recommendation algorithms, Table 8 shows the comparison of inverted kNN for $K = 100$ in user-based kNN and $K = 10$ in item-based kNN with random, popularity-based and matrix factorization recommendations. It can be seen that the inverted kNN approaches obtain the best results – after random recommendation of course – in sales diversity and novelty. Random recommendation, as expected, produces inaccurate but highly novel and diverse results in both datasets. Popularity-based recommendation also yields predictable outcomes, producing moderately accurate results – depending on the sparsity of each dataset – and the lowest possible novelty and sales diversity – which should be so by definition. Matrix factorization (only tested on Netflix for the aforementioned reasons) has good novelty and sales diversity, outperforming the standard nearest neighborhoods methods, but not the inverted variant.

8.3 Results for the Probabilistic Reformulation

The results of our experiments with the Probabilistic Layer approach are shown in Figure 2. For each dataset-baseline pair we display two scatter plots showing the trade-offs between precision vs. novelty and sales diversity for the novelty-oriented re-scoring technique (NR) and our probabilistic approach (BR). Curves for each approach start from $\alpha = \lambda = 0.0$ as the points with the lowest novelty and diversity and, as α and λ tend to 1.0, improve in terms of EPC and Gini while – generally – having lower precision values. Assuming that the interpolated lines are a good approximation to the continuous range of the trade-off parameters, we determine that a method is better that the other if its curve is generally above the other in each plot. Under this criterion, the results in Figure 2 show the validity of our probabilistic approach.

In the Netflix data, we can see how the compared approaches show practically identical trade-offs in terms on EPC and, in terms of Gini, our probabilistic method clearly outperforms the novelty-oriented re-ranking. Surprisingly, the probabilistic approach outperforms the original scoring function even in terms of precision and, among baselines, it is the one that achieves the highest sales diversity scores. On the other side, the improvements on the matrix factorization approach, although being perceptible, are more limited that those in the nearest neighbors recommenders.

In the Million Song dataset the results are analogous. Both re-ranking approaches present similar outcomes in terms of EPC, while the probabilistic approach clearly outperforms the novelty-oriented re-ranking. Again, item-based kNN is the baseline that enables a higher improvement in terms of sales diversity.

In conclusion, the proposed probabilistic approach provides a new method for improving trade-offs between accuracy, novelty and sales diversity. Compared to a simpler approach that optimizes directly the long-tail novelty of recommendations, our proposal obtains comparable results in terms of the novelty of recommendations, while it shows clearly better results in terms of sales diversity.

9. CONCLUSIONS AND FUTURE WORK

Starting from the aim of improving sales diversity by recommendation, we explore in this paper where the inversion of the recommendation task leads to. By ranking users for items, the recommendation approach focuses on the relevance of user-item pairs in a different way, and item popularity gets left aside as a result. Starting from this task inversion, we derive two approaches to improve the sales diversity of the original item recommendation task. The first one, inverted neighborhoods, results in a novel way of "democratizing" the weight of user opinions (in the user-based approach) and item opportunity (in the item-based variant), leading to substantial improvements in terms of sales diversity, competitive results in recommendation novelty and a good precision trade-off. The second approach, a probabilistic reformulation of the recommendation problem, allows isolating the popularity component of any recommendation baseline and calibrate it in order to increase the chances of less popular items to appear in recommendations lists. Experiments on two different datasets, namely Netflix for movie recommendation and the Million Song Dataset for music recommendation, confirm and illustrate the effectiveness of our proposals.

The symmetric inversion of the recommendation task entails more than a simple transposition of the rating matrix. It brings up a new view on the task where the system seeks the most appropriate users to whom an item can be recommended, even though the final action is still the delivery of a ranked list of items to each user. This problem statement can reflect real-world situations where a business is selecting targets for advertising a particular product.

As future work, we envisage deeper studies on the properties of neighborhoods we examined in Section 6 with additional metrics in order to uncover further potential biases in user and item neighborhoods. We also envision further improvements of the Bayesian reformulation. In particular, we intend to explore increasing the *exclusivity* of items, that is, recommending each item to only a limited selection of users. In our probabilistic scheme, this exclusivity could be carried out by re-defining the likelihood component $p(u \mid i; s)$ in Equation 14, for instance by creating a cut-off of the users with highest scores for item i or by means of parametrization similar to the one of the prior in Equation 17.

10. ACKNOWLEDGMENTS

This work was supported by the national Spanish project TIN2013-47090-C3-2.

11. REFERENCES

[1] G. Adomavicius and Y. Kwon. Improving aggregate recommendation diversity using ranking-based techniques. *IEEE Transactions on Knowledge and Data Engineering*, 24(5):896–911, 2012.

[2] F. Aiolli. Efficient top-n recommendation for very large scale binary rated datasets. In *Proceedings of the 7th ACM Conference on Recommender Systems*, RecSys '13, pages 273–280, New York, NY, USA, 2013. ACM.

[3] X. Amatriain. Mining large streams of user data for personalized recommendations. *SIGKDD Explor. Newsl.*, 14(2):37–48, Apr. 2013.

[4] C. Anderson. *The Long Tail: Why the Future of Business Is Selling Less of More*. Hyperion, 2006.

[5] A. Bellogín. *Performance prediction and evaluation in Recommender Systems: an Information Retrieval perspective*. PhD thesis, Escuela Politécnica Superior, Universidad Autónoma de Madrid, Spain, 2012.

[6] P. Cremonesi, Y. Koren, and R. Turrin. Performance of recommender algorithms on top-n recommendation tasks. In *Proceedings of the fourth ACM conference on Recommender systems*, RecSys '10, pages 39–46, New York, NY, USA, 2010. ACM.

[7] D. Fleder and K. Hosanagar. Blockbuster culture's next rise or fall: The impact of recommender systems on sales diversity. *Management Science*, 55(5):697–712, May 2009.

[8] T. Hofmann. Latent semantic models for collaborative filtering. *ACM Transactions on Information Systems*, 22(1):89–115, Jan. 2004.

[9] Y. Hu, Y. Koren, and C. Volinsky. Collaborative filtering for implicit feedback datasets. In *Proceedings of the 2008 Eighth IEEE International Conference on Data Mining*, ICDM '08, pages 263–272, Washington, DC, USA, 2008. IEEE Computer Society.

[10] B. McFee, T. Bertin-Mahieux, D. P. Ellis, and G. R. Lanckriet. The Million Song Dataset Challenge. In *Proceedings of the 21st International Conference Companion on World Wide Web*, WWW '12 Companion, pages 909–916, New York, NY, USA, 2012. ACM.

[11] A. Said, B. Fields, B. J. Jain, and S. Albayrak. User-centric evaluation of a k-furthest neighbor collaborative filtering recommender algorithm. In *Proceedings of the 2013 Conference on Computer Supported Cooperative Work*, CSCW '13, pages 1399–1408, New York, NY, USA, 2013. ACM.

[12] B. Sarwar, G. Karypis, J. Konstan, and J. Riedl. Item-based collaborative filtering recommendation algorithms. In *Proceedings of the 10th international conference on World Wide Web*, WWW '01, pages 285–295, New York, NY, USA, 2001. ACM.

[13] Y. Shi, A. Karatzoglou, L. Baltrunas, M. Larson, N. Oliver, and A. Hanjalic. CLiMF: learning to maximize reciprocal rank with collaborative less-is-more filtering. In *Proceedings of the sixth ACM conference on Recommender systems*, RecSys '12, pages 139–146, New York, NY, USA, 2012. ACM.

[14] Y. Shi, M. Larson, and A. Hanjalic. Unifying rating-oriented and ranking-oriented collaborative filtering for improved recommendation. *Inf. Sci.*, 229:29–39, Apr. 2013.

[15] H. Steck. Item popularity and recommendation accuracy. In *Proceedings of the Fifth ACM Conference on Recommender Systems*, RecSys '11, pages 125–132, New York, NY, USA, 2011. ACM.

[16] G. Takács and D. Tikk. Alternating least squares for personalized ranking. In *Proceedings of the Sixth ACM Conference on Recommender Systems*, RecSys '12, pages 83–90, New York, NY, USA, 2012. ACM.

[17] S. Vargas and P. Castells. Rank and relevance in novelty and diversity metrics for recommender systems. In *Proceedings of the fifth ACM conference on Recommender systems*, RecSys '11, pages 109–116, New York, NY, USA, 2011. ACM.

[18] X. Zhao, Z. Niu, and W. Chen. Opinion-based collaborative filtering to solve popularity bias in recommender systems. In H. Decker, L. Lhotská, S. Link, J. Basl, and A. Tjoa, editors, *Database and Expert Systems Applications*, volume 8056 of *Lecture Notes in Computer Science*, pages 426–433. Springer Berlin Heidelberg, 2013.

On Over-Specialization and Concentration Bias of Recommendations: Probabilistic Neighborhood Selection in Collaborative Filtering Systems

Panagiotis Adamopoulos
padamopo@stern.nyu.edu

Alexander Tuzhilin
atuzhili@stern.nyu.edu

Department of Information, Operations, and Management Sciences
Leonard N. Stern School of Business, New York University

ABSTRACT

Focusing on the problems of over-specialization and concentration bias, this paper presents a novel probabilistic method for recommending items in the neighborhood-based collaborative filtering framework. For the probabilistic neighborhood selection phase, we use an efficient method for weighted sampling of k neighbors that takes into consideration the similarity levels between the target user (or item) and the candidate neighbors. We conduct an empirical study showing that the proposed method increases the coverage, dispersion, and diversity reinforcement of recommendations by selecting diverse sets of representative neighbors. We also demonstrate that the proposed approach outperforms popular methods in terms of item prediction accuracy, utility-based ranking, and other popular measures, across various experimental settings. This performance improvement is in accordance with ensemble learning theory and the phenomenon of "hubness" in recommender systems.

Categories and Subject Descriptors

H.3.3 [**Information Storage and Retrieval**]: Information Search and Retrieval - Information filtering, Selection process; H.4.m [**Information Systems Applications**]: Miscellaneous

Keywords

Collaborative Filtering; Probabilistic Neighborhood Selection; k-PN; Concentration Bias; Over-Specialization; Diversity; Mobility; Popularity Reinforcement; Long Tail

1. INTRODUCTION

Even though the broad social and business acceptance of recommender systems (RSes) has been achieved, a key underexplored dimension for further improvement is admittedly the usefulness of recommendations. Common recommenders, such as collaborative filtering (CF) algorithms, recommend products based on prior sales and ratings. Hence, they tend not to recommend products with limited historical data, even if these items would be rated favorably by the users. Therefore, RSes can create a rich-get-richer effect for popular items while this *concentration bias* can prevent what may otherwise be better consumer-product matches [19]. At the same time, common RSes usually recommend items very similar to what the users have already purchased or liked in the past [1]. However, this *over-specialization* of recommendations is often inconsistent with sales goals and consumers' preferences.

Aiming at alleviating the important problems of over-specialization and concentration bias and enhancing the usefulness of collaborative filtering RSes, we propose to generate recommendation lists based on a probabilistic neighborhood selection approach. In particular, we aim at providing personalized recommendations from a wide range of items in order to escape the obvious and expected recommendations, while avoiding significant predictive accuracy loss.

In this paper, we present a significant improvement of the classical k-NN method in which the estimation of an unknown rating of a user for an item is based not on the weighted average of the ratings of the k most similar (nearest) neighbors but on k probabilistically selected neighbors. The key intuition for this *probabilistic nearest neighbors* (k-PN) collaborative filtering method and for selecting *diverse neighbors* is three-fold. First, using the neighborhood with the most similar users to estimate unknown ratings and recommend candidate items, the generated recommendation lists usually consist of known items with which the users are already familiar. Second, because of the multi-dimensionality of user preferences, there are many items that the target user may like and are unknown to her k most similar users. Third, selecting very similar neighbors might have a detrimental effect on the performance of a model since such neighbors tend to capture the same predictive signals and information. Thus, we propose the use of a probabilistic neighborhood selection approach in order to alleviate the aforementioned problems of over-specialization and concentration bias and move beyond the limited focus of rating prediction accuracy.

To empirically evaluate the proposed approach, we conduct an experimental study and show that our method indeed alleviates the common problems of concentration bias and over-specialization by selecting diverse sets of neighbors. It also outperforms popular approaches by a wide margin, in terms of item prediction accuracy measures, across various experimental settings. Besides, we demonstrate that this performance gain is combined with further enhancements of other popular performance measures.

RecSys'14, October 6–10, 2014, Foster City, Silicon Valley, CA, USA.

ACM 978-1-4503-2668-1/14/10 ...$15.00.
http://dx.doi.org/10.1145/2645710.2645752.

Finally, the performance improvement can be attributed to carefully selecting diverse sets of representative neighbors. This is not only captured in the works and ideas of ancient philosophers and essayists, such as Plutarch, but it can also be theoretically motivated by the phenomenon of "hubness" and the ensemble learning theory and, in particular, the reduction of covariance among the selected neighbors and the more equal distribution of the number of times each user (or item) is included in a neighborhood.

In summary, the main contributions of this paper are:

- We propose a probabilistic neighborhood-based method (k-PN) as an improvement of the k-NN approach.
- We formulate the classical neighborhood-based CF approach as an ensemble method showing the potential suboptimality of k-NN in terms of predictive accuracy.
- We empirically show that the proposed method outperforms, by a wide margin, the classical CF algorithm and practically illustrate the suboptimality of k-NN in addition to providing theoretical justification.
- We show that the proposed k-PN method alleviates the common problems of over-specialization and concentration bias of recommendations, in terms of various popular metrics and a new metric that measures diversity reinforcement (mobility of recommendations).
- We identify a particular implementation of the k-PN method that performs consistently well across various experimental settings.

2. RELATED WORK

Since the introduction of the first CF systems in the mid-'90s [21, 26], there have been many attempts to improve their performance focusing primarily on error metrics [15]. Even though the rating prediction perspective is the prevailing paradigm in RSes, there are other perspectives that have been gaining significant attention in the field and try to alleviate problems pertaining to the narrow rating prediction focus [2]. This narrow focus has been evident in laboratory studies and real-world online experiments, which indicated that higher predictive accuracy does not always correspond to higher levels of user-perceived quality or increased sales [14, 29]. Two of the most important problems related to this narrow focus of many RSes that have been identified in the literature and hinder the user satisfaction are the over-specialization and concentration bias of recommendations.

Focusing on these two problems, various streams of research identify and discuss the phenomenon, discover its implications, and suggest methods in order to alleviate it. Aiming at verifying and measuring over-specialization bias, [31] employs a longitudinal data set and finds that RSes indeed expose the users to narrowing sets of items over time. Similarly, regarding the concentration bias of recommendations, [25] compares different RS algorithms with respect to aggregate diversity and their tendency to focus on certain parts of the product spectrum and shows that many popular algorithms may lead to an undesired popularity boost of already popular items. However, [24, 27] maintain that whether over-specialization and concentration bias will be enhanced or alleviated depends on the applied personalization technology. Thus, appropriate technical solutions are still needed in order to alleviate these problems of RSes.

Discussing the business implication of over-specialization and concentration, [19] shows that these phenomena direct users towards a common experience, in contrast to the potential goals of RSes, and lead to a significant reduction in profits and sales diversity. Similar implications have also been observed in various other domains (e.g. [17]).

Finally, a stream of research in RSes attempts to alleviate these problems by proposing technical methods. Over-specialization is often practically addressed by injecting randomness in the recommendation procedure [10], filtering out items that are too similar to items the user has rated in the past [11], or increasing the individual diversity of recommendations [39]. Interestingly, [34, 35] present an inverted neighborhood model, k-furthest neighbors, to identify less ordinary neighborhoods for the purpose of creating more diverse recommendations by recommending items disliked by the least similar users. Finally, the concentration problem is typically addressed by re-ranking the list of candidate items taking into consideration their popularity [8] or using sophisticated graph-theoretic approaches [7].

3. MODEL

In this section, we present the proposed approach in the context of the classical user-based collaborative filtering (CF) method. However, the proposed approach is not specific to this algorithm and can be easily extended to any neighborhood-based CF method, including item-based approaches.

User-neighborhood based recommendation methods predict the rating $r_{u,i}$ of user u for item i using the ratings given to i by users most similar to u, called nearest neighbors and denoted by $\mathcal{N}_i(u)$. Taking into account the fact that the neighbors can have different levels of similarity, $w_{u,v}$, and considering the k users v with the highest similarity to u, the predicted rating is:

$$\hat{r}_{u,i} = \bar{r}_u + \frac{\sum\limits_{v \in \mathcal{N}_i(u)} w_{u,v} * (r_{v,i} - \bar{r}_v)}{\sum\limits_{v \in \mathcal{N}_i(u)} |w_{u,v}|}, \qquad (1)$$

where $\bar{r}_u$ is the average of the ratings given by user u. However, the ratings given by the nearest neighbors of user u can be combined into a single estimation using various combining (or aggregating) functions [9]. Examples of such functions include majority voting, distance-moderated voting, adjusted weighted average, and percentiles [5].

In the same way, the neighborhood used for estimating the unknown ratings and recommending items can be formed in different ways. Instead of using the k users with the highest similarity to the target user, any approach or procedure that selects k of the candidate neighbors can be used, in principle.

In this paper, we propose a novel k-NN CF method (k-PN) using a *probabilistic neighborhood selection technique that,* instead of the most similar neighbors, *systematically selects a set of diverse neighbors in order to alleviate the over-specialization and concentration problems.* The proposed approach uses a general algorithm for efficient sampling [38] that can also take into consideration the similarity levels between the target user and the n candidate neighbors.

3.1 Probabilistic Neighborhood Selection

For the probabilistic neighborhood selection phase of the proposed algorithm, we allow the neighbors to represent the whole spectrum of candidates, while focusing on specific areas of this spectrum. Selecting such diverse neighbors, the proposed method aims at alleviating the problems of over-specialization and concentration bias (see Section 3.2).

In a nutshell, for the neighborhood selection phase of the k-PN approach, an initial weight is assigned to each candidate neighbor and then the candidates are sampled, without replacement, proportionally to their assigned weights. These initial weights can be derived based on popular distance metrics (e.g. Cosine similarity, Pearson correlation, etc.), probability distributions, or other strategies and techniques. For instance, in order to use certain probability distributions aiming at specific areas of the spectrum of candidates, the initial weight w_i for each candidate i can be generated using some function of its distance from the target u or its ranking (based on the distance metric) and the corresponding probability density function (e.g. $w_i = \mathcal{P}(\text{rank}_i)$ or $w_i = \mathcal{P}(\text{sim}(u, i))$; for a complete example see Section 4.2). Based on the selection of the initial weights, the algorithm will select different neighborhoods and, thus, generate different recommendations. We should note here that including all the available candidates in a neighborhood, instead of a diverse set, does not alleviate the problems under study, as discussed in Section 3.2.

For implementing the proposed approach, we suggest an efficient method (based on [18, 38]) for weighted sampling of k neighbors without replacement that takes into consideration the similarity levels between the target user and the population of n candidate neighbors. In particular, the set of candidate neighbors at any time is described by values $\{w_1^{'}, w_2^{'}, \ldots, w_n^{'}\}$. In general, if user i is still a candidate for selection, then $w_i^{'} = w_i$ (where w_i is generated as previously described), whereas $w_i^{'} = 0$ if the user has been already selected in the neighborhood and, hence, removed from the set of candidates. Denote the sum of the weights of the first j candidates by $S_j = \sum_{i=1}^{j} w_i^{'}$, where $j = 1, \ldots, n$, and let $Q = S_n$ be the sum of the weights $\{w_i^{'}\}$ of all the candidates. In order to draw a neighbor, choose x with uniform probability from $[0, Q]$ and find l such that $S_{l-1} \leq x \leq S_l$. Then, add l to the neighborhood and remove it from the set of candidates while setting $w_l^{'} = 0$. After a candidate has been selected into the neighborhood, this neighbor is no longer available for later selection.

This method can be easily implemented using a binary search tree having all n candidate neighbors as leaves with values $\{w_1, w_2, \ldots, w_n\}$, whereas the value of each internal node of the tree is the sum of the values of the corresponding immediate descendant nodes. This sampling method requires $O(n)$ initialization operations, $O(k \log n)$ additions and comparisons, and $O(k)$ divisions and random number generations [38]. The suggested method can be used with any distance metric and valid probability distribution including the empirical distribution of users' similarity (see Section 4.2). Algorithm 1 summarizes the method for efficient weighted sampling without replacement [38].

Note that the same approach can also be used for item-based neighborhood methods by simply sampling diverse neighborhoods of items, instead of users.

3.2 Theoretical Motivation

In this section, we present the theoretical motivation for the proposed approach and the connections to the phenomenon of "hubness" as well as the ensemble learning theory. In particular, we discuss a major implication of selecting just the most similar candidates (or even all the candidates) as neighbors and we motivate how the proposed method can alleviate the over-specialization and concentration problems without significantly reducing, and even increasing, the predictive accuracy, demonstrating that *similar but diverse neighbors should be used in neighborhood-based methods.*

ALGORITHM 1: Weighted Sampling Without Replacement

Input: Initial weights $\{w_1, \ldots, w_n\}$ of candidates for neighborhood $\mathcal{N}_i(u)$
Output: Neighborhood of user u, $\mathcal{N}_i(u)$

k: Number of users in the neighborhood of user u, $\mathcal{N}_i(u)$
$L(v)$: The left-descendent of node v
$R(v)$: The right-descendent of node v
G_v: The sum of weights of the leaves in the left subtree from node v
Q: The sum of weights of the nodes in the binary tree

```
Build binary search tree with n leaves labeled 1, 2, ..., n;
Assign to leaves corresponding values w_1, w_2, ..., w_n;
Associate values G_v with internal nodes;
Set Q = Σ_{v=1}^{n} w_v;
Set N_i(u) = ∅;
for j ← 1 to k do
    Set C = 0;
    Set v = the root node;
    Set D = ∅;
    Select x uniformly from [0, Q];
    repeat
        if x ≤ G_v + C then
            Set D = D ⊎ {v};
            Move to node/leaf L(v);
        else
            Set C = C + G_v;
            Move to node/leaf R(v);
        end
    until a leaf is reached;
    Set N_i(u) = N_i(u) ⊎ {v};
    for each node d ∈ D do
        Set G_d = G_d − w_v;
    end
    Set Q = Q − w_v;
    Set w_v = 0;
end
```

It should be clear by now that selecting neighborhoods using underlying probability distributions can result in very different recommendations from those generated based on the standard neighborhood-based approaches. For the sake of brevity, we focus on the phenomenon of "hubness" and the effect of selecting diverse neighbors on the predictive accuracy of the proposed approach.

The phenomenon of "hubness" is related to a new aspect of the dimensionality curse and affects the distribution of k-occurrences: the number of times a point occurs among the k nearest neighbors of the other points in a data set, according to some distance measure [32]. This distribution becomes considerably skewed as dimensionality increases, causing the emergence of hubs, that is, points which appear in many more k-NN lists than other points, effectively making them "popular" nearest neighbors. This is an inherent property that depends on the intrinsic, rather than embedding, dimensionality of data and, thus, dimensionality reduction techniques, such as matrix factorization, do not alleviate the problem effectively. For the same reason "hubness" occurs even for small values of k and for all cosine-like measures, such as Pearson correlation, cosine similarity, and adjusted cosine. Besides, "hubness" is unrelated to other data properties like sparsity or skewness of the distribution of ratings [30]. Nevertheless, this phenomenon is part of the problem of concentration bias of recommendations. In particular, [36] shows that hubness reduces coverage and reachability, especially of long-tail items, in both content-based and CF systems. Thus, these problems can be alleviated by selecting *neighbors other than the most similar to the target.*

Moreover, in order to further theoretically motivate the proposed approach, we focus on ensemble learning theory; a more comprehensive discussion of neighborhood-based methods and ensembles can be found in [4]. According to ensemble learning theory, in addition to the bias and variance of the individual estimators, the generalization error of an ensemble also depends on the covariance between the individuals; an ensemble is controlled by a three-way trade-off. Hence, if two estimators f_i and f_j that are members of the ensemble are positively correlated, then the correlation increases the generalization error, whereas if they are negatively correlated, then the correlation contributes to a decrease in the generalization error. Thus, a diverse set of estimators is preferable for an ensemble.

In the context of neighborhood-based CF methods in RSes, we can conceptualize the ith most similar neighbor to the target user as corresponding to a single estimator f_i that simply predicts the rating of this specific neighbor; the different predictions can then be combined into a single estimation using a combining function. Hence, reducing the aggregated pairwise covariance of the neighbors (estimators) can decrease the generalization error of the model; at the same time, it may increase the bias or variance of the estimators and the generalization error. Therefore, one way to reduce the covariance is not to restrict the k estimators only to the k nearest (most similar) neighbors but to select a *diverse set of neighbors* (estimators).[1,2]

4. EXPERIMENTS

To empirically validate the k-PN method presented in Section 3 and evaluate the generated recommendations, we conduct a large number of experiments on "real-world" data sets and compare our results to different baselines. For an apples-to-apples comparison, the selected baselines include the user-based k-NN CF approach, which we promise to improve in this study. Compared to other popular algorithms, user-based k-NN generates recommendations that suffer less from concentration bias and over-specialization [15, 25] and has also been found to perform well in terms of other performance measures [12, 14, 3, 6]. Nevertheless, the proposed approach can be applied to any neighborhood-based method and it is not specific to the user-based approach, which has been selected for increased compatibility as well as interpretability of the results. Additionally, we also compare our results against furthest neighbors models (k-FN) [34, 35]. Finally, we also compare our experimental results against matrix factorization (MF) [20].

4.1 Data Sets

The data sets that we used are the MovieLens [22] and MovieTweetings [16] as well as a snapshot from Amazon [28]. The RecSys HetRec 2011 MovieLens (ML) data set [22] contains 855,598 ratings (on a 1-5 scale) from 2,113 users on 10,197 movies. Moreover, the MovieTweetings (MT) data set is described in [16] and consists of ratings included in well-structured tweets on Twitter. Owing to the extreme sparsity of the data set, we decided to condense the data set in order to obtain more meaningful results from collaborative filtering algorithms. In particular, we removed items and users with fewer than 10 ratings. The resulting data set contains 12,332 ratings (on a 0-10 scale) from 839 users on 836 movies. Finally, the Amazon (AMZ) data set is described in [28] and consists of reviews of fine foods during a period of more than 10 years. After removing items with fewer than 10 ratings and reviewers with fewer than 25 ratings each, the data set consists of 15,235 ratings (on a 1-5 scale) from 407 users on 4,316 items.

Table 1: Probability Distributions and Density Functions for Neighborhood Selection.

Label	Probability Distribution	Probability Density Function (weights)	Location and Shape Parameters	
k-NN	-	$\begin{cases} 1/k, \text{if } x \leq n-k \\ 0, \text{otherwise} \end{cases}$	-	
E	Empirical Similarity	$w_x / \sum_{i=1}^{n} w_i$	-	
U	Uniform	$1/n$	-	
N_1 N_2	Normal	$\frac{1}{\sqrt{2\pi\sigma^2}} e^{-\frac{(x-\mu)^2}{2\sigma^2}}$	$\mu = 0$ $\mu = (2.0/15.0)n$	$\sigma = (0.25/15.0)n$ $\sigma = (0.5/15.0)n$
Exp_1 Exp_2	Exponential	$\lambda e^{-\lambda x}$	$\lambda = 1/k$ $\lambda = 2/k$	
W_1 W_2	Weibull	$\frac{\mu}{\lambda} \left(\frac{x}{\lambda}\right)^{\mu-1} e^{-(x/\lambda)^{\mu}}$	$\mu = 0.25$ $\mu = 0.50$	$\lambda = n/20$ $\lambda = n/20$
FN_1 FN_2	Folded normal	$\frac{\sqrt{2}}{\sigma\sqrt{\pi}} e^{-\frac{\theta^2}{2}} e^{-\frac{x^2}{2\sigma^2}} \cosh\left(\frac{\theta x}{\sigma}\right)$	$\theta = 1$ $\theta = 1$	$\sigma = k$ $\sigma = k/2$
k-FN	-	$\begin{cases} 1/k, \text{if } x \geq n-k \\ 0, \text{otherwise} \end{cases}$	-	

4.2 Experimental Settings

Using the ML, MT, and AMZ data sets, we conducted a large number of experiments and compared the results against the standard user-based k-NN approach, different k-FN methods, and matrix factorization. In order to test the proposed approach of probabilistic neighborhood selection under various experimental settings, we used different sizes of neighborhoods ($k \in \{20, 30, \ldots, 80\}$) and different probability distributions ($\mathcal{P} \in$ {normal, exponential, Weibull, folded normal, uniform}), with various specifications (i.e. location and scale parameters), as well as the empirical distribution of user similarity, described in Table 1. The uniform distribution is used in order to compare the proposed method against randomly selecting neighbors. The specific distributions were selected because they focus on different areas of the spectrum of candidate neighbors and they constitute common but flexible examples that can be easily reproduced. Additionally, we used two k-FN models [34, 35]; the second furthest neighbor model (k-FN_2) employed in this study corresponds to recommending the least liked items of the furthest neighbors instead of the most liked ones (k-FN_1). We should note here that because of the strict deterministic nature of both k-NN and k-FN, it is not possible to interpolate between these two methods and select diverse neighbors that approximate the results of k-PN. In addition, we generated recommendation lists of different sizes ($l \in \{1, 3, 5, 10, 20, \ldots, 100\}$). In summary, we used 3 data sets, 7 different sizes of neighborhoods, 12 probability distributions, and 13 different lengths of recommendation lists, resulting in $3,276$ experiments in total.

For the probabilistic neighborhood selection, we used the method described in Section 3.1. In order to estimate the initial weights $\{w_i\}$ of the procedure, we used the probability density functions illustrated in Table 1. Without loss of gen-

[1] Let $r_{u,i}$ and $r_{u,j}$ be the correlation of target user u and candidate neighbors i and j respectively, then the correlation $r_{i,j}$ of neighbors i and j is bounded by the following expression: $r_{u,i}r_{u,j} - \sqrt{1-r_{u,i}^2}\sqrt{1-r_{u,j}^2} \leq r_{i,j} \leq r_{u,i}r_{u,j} + \sqrt{1-r_{u,i}^2}\sqrt{1-r_{u,j}^2}$.

[2] For a formal argument why the proposed probabilistic approach can result in very different recommendations from those generated based on the standard k-NN approach and how the item predictive accuracy can be affected, a 0/1 loss can be used in the context of classification ensemble learning. For a rigorous derivation of the generalization error in ensemble learning using the bias-variance-covariance decomposition and a 0/1 loss function see [33, 37].

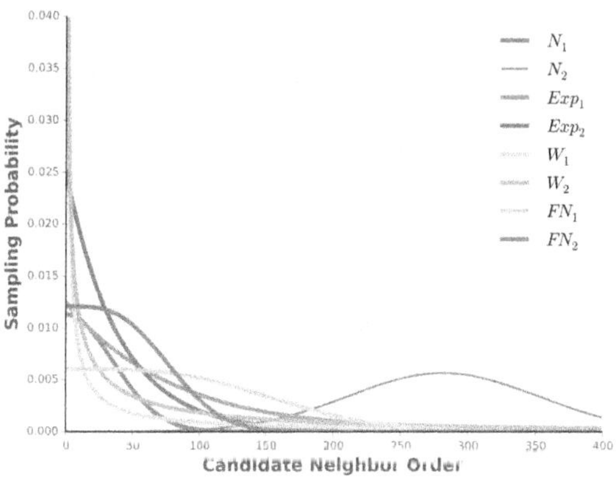

Figure 1: Sampling probability for the nearest candidate neighbors using different probability distributions for the ML data set.

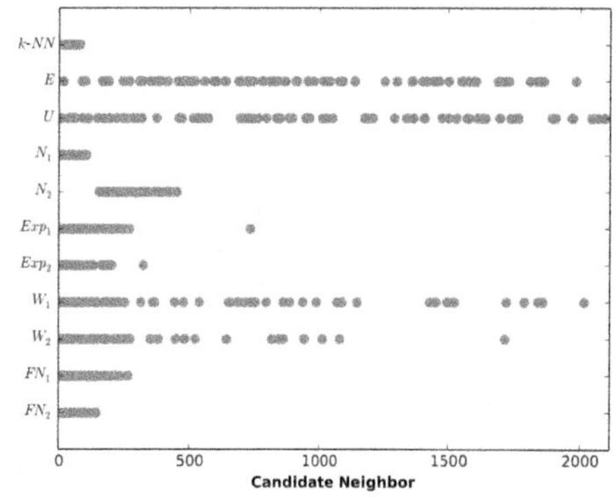

Figure 2: Sampled Neighborhoods using the different probability distributions for the MovieLens data set.

erality, in order to take into consideration the similarity levels of the candidate neighbors, the candidates can be ordered and re-labeled such that $s_{u,1} \geq s_{u,2} \geq \ldots \geq s_{u,n}$, where $s_{u,j}$ is the similarity level of target u and candidate j based on some distance metric. Then, the initial weight w_j for each candidate can be generated using its ranking and a probability density function. For instance, using the Weibull probability distribution (i.e. W_1 or W_2), the weight of the most similar candidate (i.e. $j = 1$) is $w_1 = \frac{\mu}{\lambda}\left(\frac{1}{\lambda}\right)^{\mu-1} e^{-(1/\lambda)^{\mu}}$, where μ and λ are the shape and scale parameters of the distribution and n is the total number of all the candidate neighbors.[3] In contrast to the deterministic k-NN and k-FN approaches, depending on the parameters of the employed probability density function, this candidate neighbor (i.e. the most similar to the target) may or may not have the highest weight w_j.[4] Figure 1 shows the likelihood of sampling each candidate neighbor using different probability distributions for the MovieLens data set and $k = 80$ and Figure 2 shows the sampled neighborhoods for a randomly selected target user using the different distributions; the candidate neighbors for each target user and item in the x axis are ordered based on their similarity to the target user with 0 corresponding to the nearest (i.e. most similar) candidate. As we can see, the selected distributions focus on different areas of the spectrum of candidate neighbors. We should note here that using the empirical distribution of user similarity resulted in *more diverse neighborhoods*.

In all the conducted experiments, in order to measure the similarity among the candidate neighbors, we used the Pearson correlation; similar results were also obtained using the cosine similarity. Also, we used significance weighting as in [23], in order to penalize for similarity based on few common ratings, and filtered any candidate neighbors with zero weight [15]. For the similarity estimation of the candidates in the k-furthest neighbor algorithm, we used the approach described in [34, 35]. Besides, we used the standard combining function as in Eq. (1). Similar results were also obtained using a combining function without a first-order bias approximation: $\hat{r}_{u,i} = \sum_{v \in \mathcal{N}_i(u)} w_{u,v} r_{v,i} / \sum_{v \in \mathcal{N}_i(u)} |w_{u,v}|$; any differences are explicitly discussed in the following section. In addition, we used a holdout validation scheme in all of our experiments with 80/20 splits of the rating tuples to the training/test parts in order to avoid overfitting. Finally, the evaluation of the various approaches in each experimental setting is based on users with more than k candidate neighbors, where k is the corresponding neighborhood size; if a user has k or fewer available candidate neighbors, then the same neighbors are always selected and the results for the specific user are in principle identical for all the examined approaches, apart from the inverse k-FN (k-FN$_2$) method. Similarly, the generated recommendation lists were also evaluated using a subset of the test set containing only highly rated items as well as only long-tail items [13].

[3] For continuous probability distributions, the cumulative distribution function can also be used such as $w_i = F(i + 0.5) - F(i - 0.5)$ or $w_i = F(i) - F(i - 1)$.

[4] For a probabilistic furthest neighbors model the candidates can be ordered in reverse similarity order such that $s_{u,1} \leq s_{u,2} \leq \ldots \leq s_{u,n}$. Initial experiments illustrated that such models underperform the proposed approach.

5. RESULTS

The aim of this study is to demonstrate that the proposed method indeed effectively generates recommendations that alleviate the over-specialization and concentration problems while performing well in terms of other important metrics of RSes. Therefore, we conduct a comparative analysis of our method and the standard baseline (k-NN), matrix factorization, and the k-furthest neighbor approaches, in different experimental settings.

Given the number and the diversity of experimental settings, the presentation of the results constitutes a challenging problem. A reasonable way to compare the results across the different settings is by computing the relative performance differences and discussing only the most interesting dimensions. Due to space limitations, detailed results, supplementary graphs and tables, and tests of statistical significance about all the conducted experiments as well as additional performance metrics measuring orthogonality of recommendations and predictive accuracy are included in [4].

Overall, *the proposed method generates recommendations that are very different from the classical CF approaches and alleviates the over-specialization and concentration problems*, based on metrics of coverage, dispersion, and diversity reinforcement (mobility of recommendations), while *avoiding any significant accuracy loss*. Fig. 3 illustrates the aforementioned findings. It shows an overview of the performance of all the methods on the ML data set across various metrics for recommendation lists of size $l = 10$.

5.1 Coverage and Diversity

In this section, we investigate the effect of the proposed method on coverage and aggregate diversity, two important metrics which in combination with other measures discussed in this study show whether the proposed approach alleviates

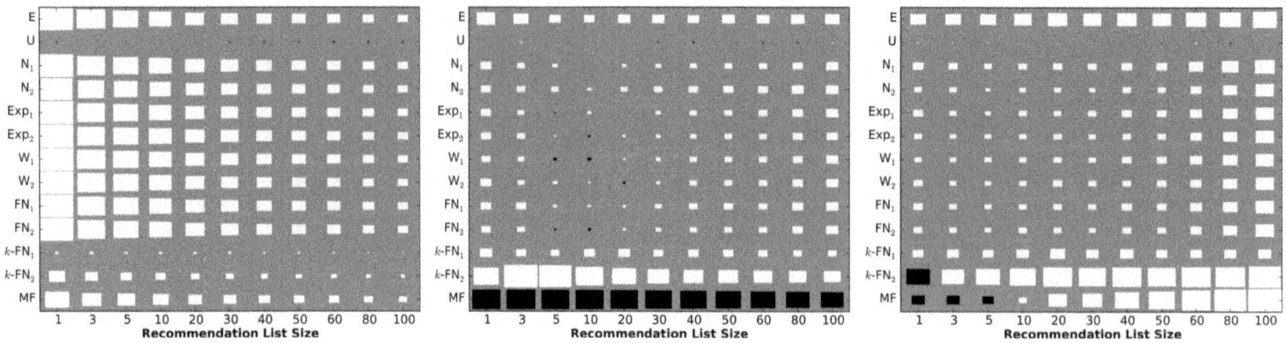

(a) MovieLens (ML) (b) MovieTweetings (MT) (c) Amazon (AMZ)

Figure 4: Increase in aggregate diversity performance for the different data sets and recommendation list sizes.

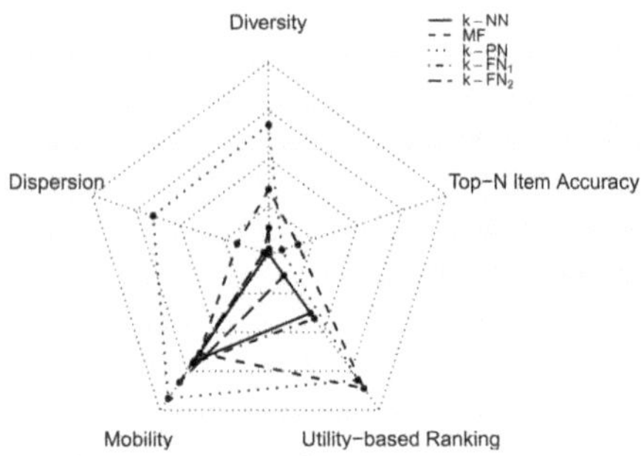

Figure 3: Summary of performance for the ML data set.

the over-specialization and concentration bias problems of common RSes. The results obtained using the *catalog coverage* metric are equivalent to those using the *diversity-in-top-N* metric for aggregate diversity; henceforth, only one set of results is presented. Fig. 4 presents the results obtained by applying our method to the ML, MT, and AMZ data sets. In particular, the Hinton diagram in Fig. 4 shows the percentage increase/decrease in performance compared to the k-NN baseline for each probability distribution and recommendation lists of size $l \in \{1, 3, 5, 10, 20, \ldots, 100\}$ over seven neighborhood sizes, $k \in \{20, 30, \ldots, 80\}$. Positive and negative values are represented by white and black squares, respectively, and the size of each square represents the magnitude of each value.

Fig. 4 demonstrates that *the proposed method in most cases performs better than the user-based k-NN, matrix factorization, and the k-FN methods.* The more diverse recommendations were achieved using the empirical distribution of user similarity and the inverse k-furthest neighbors approach (k-FN_2). In particular, the average aggregate diversity across all the probability distributions, neighborhoods, and recommendation list sizes was 22.10%, 46.09%, and 13.52% for the ML, MT, and AMZ data sets, respectively; the corresponding diversity using only the empirical distribution was 24.20%, 50.55%, and 17.04% for the different data sets. The corresponding performance of MF [20] was measured as 14.17%, 10.70%, and 14.39%, respectively.

Furthermore, the performance was increased both in the experiments where the k-NN method, because of the specifics of the particular data sets, resulted in low aggregate diversity (e.g. Amazon) and high diversity performance (e.g. MovieTweetings). In addition, the experiments conducted using the same probability distribution (e.g. Exp_1 and Exp_2) exhibit very similar performance. As one would expect, in most cases the aggregate diversity increased, whereas the magnitude of the difference in performance decreased, with increasing recommendation list size l. Without using the first-order bias approximation in the combining function, the standard k-NN method resulted in higher aggregate diversity and catalog coverage but the proposed approach still outperformed the classical algorithm in most of the cases by a narrower margin; using the inverse k-FN method (k-FN_2) without the first-order bias approximation resulted in decrease in performance for the Amazon data set. The performance of empirical distribution was 33.37%, 61.06%, and 41.50% for the different data sets. Nevertheless, *using all the candidates, instead of probabilistically selecting a diverse neighborhood, underperforms the proposed approach* since the overall contribution of neighbors other than the most similar is significantly discounted.

In terms of statistical significance, using the Friedman test and performing post hoc analysis, the differences among the employed baselines (i.e. k-NN, MF, k-FN_1, and k-FN_2) and all the proposed specifications are statistically significant ($p < 0.001$) for the ML data set. For the MT and AMZ data sets, all the proposed specifications (i.e. E, N_1, N_2, Exp_1, Exp_2, W_1, W_2, FN_1, and FN_2) significantly outperform the k-NN and matrix factorization algorithms; the empirical distribution significantly outperforms also the k-FN_1 method.

5.2 Dispersion and Diversity Reinforcement

In order to conclude whether the proposed approach alleviates the over-specialization and concentration bias, the generated recommendation lists should also be evaluated for the inequality across items using the Gini coefficient. Fig. 5 shows the percentage increase (white squares) or decrease (black squares) in dispersion of recommendations compared to the k-NN baseline. The Gini coefficient was on average improved by 6.81%, 3.67%, and 1.67% for the ML, MT, and AMZ data sets, respectively; the corresponding figures using only the empirical distribution were 7.48%, 6.73%, and 3.45% for the different data sets, which implies an improvement of 7.41%, 16.76%, and 1.54% over MF and 9.69%, 5.34%, and 2.84% over k-FN. The more uniformly distributed recommendation lists were achieved using the empirical distribution of user similarity and the inverse k-FN approach. Moreover, the larger the size of the recommendation lists, the larger the improvement in the Gini coefficient. Similarly, without using the first-order bias approximation in the rating combining function, the average dispersion was further improved by 6.48%, 6.83%, and 20.22% for the ML, MT, and AMZ data sets, respectively. This implies an improvement of 14.91%, 22.83%, and 21.19% against MF and 16.94%, 5.90%, and 2.38% against k-FN. As we can conclude, *in the*

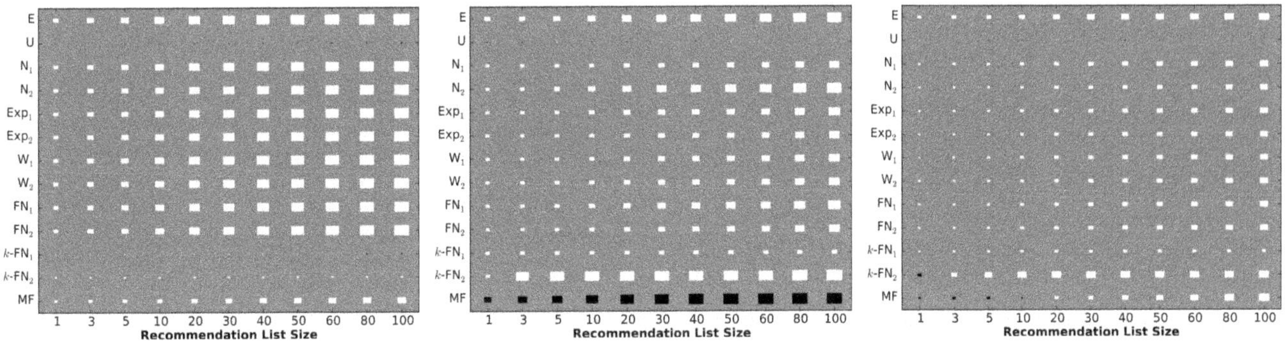

(a) MovieLens (ML) (b) MovieTweetings (MT) (c) Amazon (AMZ)

Figure 5: Increase in dispersion of recommendations for the different data sets and recommendation list sizes.

recommendation lists generated from the proposed method, the number of times an item is recommended is more equally distributed compared to other CF methods. In terms of statistical significance, all the proposed specifications (apart from the N_1, Exp_2, and FN_2 for the MT data set and the N_2, Exp_2 for the AMZ data set) significantly outperform the k-NN, matrix factorization, and k-FN$_1$ methods ($p < 0.001$). The empirical distribution also significantly outperforms the k-FN$_2$ method for the ML data set; the differences are not statistically significant for the other data sets.

However, simply evaluating the recommendation lists in terms of dispersion and inequality does not provide any information about the (popularity-based) diversity reinforcement and mobility of the recommendations (i.e. whether popular or long-tail items are more likely to be recommended) since these metrics do not consider the prior state of the system. Hence, we employ a *diversity reinforcement* measure M to assess whether the proposed recommender system approach follows or changes the prior popularity of items when recommendation lists are generated. Thus, we define M, which equals the proportion of items that are "mobile" (e.g. changed from popular in terms of number of ratings to "long tail" in terms of recommendation frequency), as follows:

$$M = 1 - \sum_{i=1}^{K} \pi_i \rho_{ii}$$

where the vector π denotes the initial distribution of each of the K (popularity) categories and ρ_{ii} the probability of staying in category i, given that i was the initial category.[5] A score of zero denotes no change (i.e. the number of times an item is recommended is proportional to the number of ratings it has received), whereas a score of one denotes that the RS recommends only the long-tail items (i.e. the number of times an item is recommended is proportional to the inverse of the number of ratings it has received).

In the conducted experiments, based on the 80-20 rule or Pareto principle, we use two categories, labeled as "head" and "tail", where the former category contains the top 20% of items (in terms of ratings or recommendations frequency) and the latter category the remaining 80%. The experimental results demonstrate that *the proposed method generates recommendation lists that exhibit in most cases higher diversity reinforcement compared to the k-NN, MF, and k-FN methods.* In particular, the performance was increased by 0.91%, 0.95%, and 0.19% for the ML, MT, and AMZ

[5]The proposed diversity reinforcement score can be easily adapted in order to differentiate the direction of change and the magnitude.

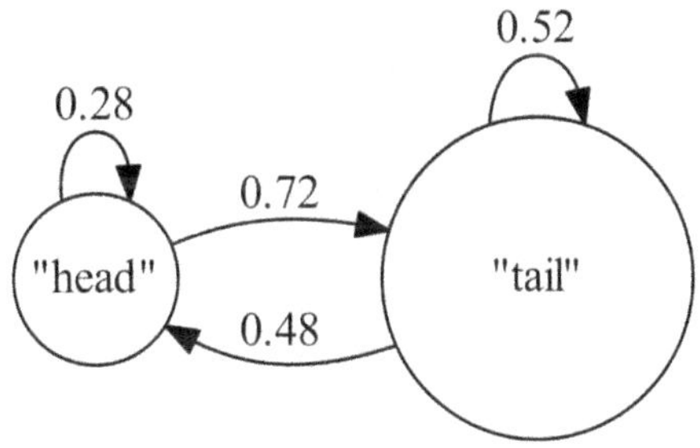

Figure 6: Diversity reinforcement for the MT data set.

data sets, respectively; the corresponding improvement using only the empirical distribution was 1.29%, 1.46%, and 0.45% for the different data sets, which implies an improvement of 1.52%, 1.12%, and 2.11% over MF and 1.01%, 1.31%, and 0.29% over k-FN. We also note that recommendation lists of larger size resulted on average in even larger improvements. Besides, considering a smaller number of items as popular also resulted in larger improvements. Similarly, without the first-order bias approximation the average diversity reinforcement was further increased by 0.69%, 0.53%, and 3.28% for the ML, MT, and AMZ data sets, respectively. This implies an improvement of 2.40%, 1.82%, and 1.65% against MF and 1.83%, 1.44%, and 1.82% against k-FN. Fig. 6 shows the transition probabilities of each category for recommendation lists of size $l = 100$ using the empirical distribution of similarity and the MovieTweetings data set. In terms of statistical significance, in most of the cases all the proposed specifications significantly outperform the baseline methods ($p < 0.005$) [4].

5.3 Utility-based Ranking and Accuracy

Further, in order to better assess the quality of the proposed approach, the recommendation lists should also be evaluated for the ranking of the items that are presented to the users, taking into account the rating scale of the selected data sets. Assuming that the utility of each recommendation is the rating of the recommended item discounted by a factor that depends on its position in the list of recommendations, we evaluate the generated recommendation lists based on the normalized Cumulative Discounted Gain (nDCG), where positions are discounted logarithmically; similar results were also obtained for item prediction accuracy.

The highest performance was again achieved using the empirical distribution of user similarity, the normal, or the Weibull distribution. In particular, the average increase of the nDCG score across all the examined probability distributions, neighborhoods, and recommendation list sizes was 100.06%, 20.05%, and 89.85% for the ML, MT, and AMZ data sets, respectively; the corresponding increase using only the empirical distribution was 117.65%, 23.01%, and 383.99% for the different data sets resulting on average in a 2-fold increase. The absolute performance of the empirical distribution for the different datasets was 73.54%, 74.62%, and 42.63%, respectively. Even though k-PN on average underperforms MF, it performs very well on both ML and MT, especially given the goals of this method. Without using the first-order bias approximation in the rating combining function, the proposed approach outperformed in most of the cases the classical k-NN algorithm and the k-FN methods by an even wider margin. The same wide margin was also observed focusing on long-tail items, except for MT. In terms of statistical significance, the differences among the employed baselines and all the proposed specifications (apart from the FN_1 for the MT data set and the N_1, Exp_2, W_2, and FN_2 for the AMZ data set) are statistically significant.

6. DISCUSSION AND CONCLUSIONS

In this paper, studying the problems of concentration bias and over-specialization, we present a novel *probabilistic neighborhood selection* method for generating recommendations in CF systems. We illustrate the practical implementation of the proposed approach in the context of memory-based systems adapting and improving the standard k-nearest neighbors (k-NN) method. In the proposed approach, the neighborhood is selected based on an underlying probability distribution, instead of just the k neighbors with the highest similarity level to the target. For the probabilistic neighborhood selection (k-PN) approach, we use an efficient method for weighted sampling of k neighbors that takes into consideration the similarity levels between the target and all the candidate neighbors. In addition, we conduct an empirical study showing that the proposed method, by selecting *diverse representative neighborhoods*, generates recommendations that are very different from the classical CF approaches and alleviates the over-specialization and concentration problems while outperforming k-NN, k-FN, and matrix factorization methods. We also demonstrate that using specific probability distributions the proposed method outperforms, by a wide margin in most cases, both the standard k-nearest neighbors and the k-furthest neighbors approaches in terms of both item prediction accuracy and utility-based ranking. The probabilistic nature of the proposed approach is a virtue since sampling different neighbors at each recommendation instance generates different recommendation lists that possess the same properties. The experimental results are also in accordance with the phenomenon of "hubness" and the ensemble learning theory that we employ in the neighborhood-based CF framework. Besides, we show that the performance improvement is not achieved at the expense of other popular performance measures.

7. REFERENCES

[1] Z. Abbassi, S. Amer-Yahia, et al. Getting recommender systems to think outside the box. In *RecSys '09*. ACM, 2009.

[2] P. Adamopoulos. On discovering non-obvious recommendations: Using unexpectedness and neighborhood selection methods in collaborative filtering systems. In *WSDM '14*. ACM, 2014.

[3] P. Adamopoulos and A. Tuzhilin. On Unexpectedness in Recommender Systems: Or How to Expect the Unexpected. In *DiveRS 2011 at RecSys '11*. ACM, 2011.

[4] P. Adamopoulos and A. Tuzhilin. Probabilistic neighborhood selection in collaborative filtering systems. *Working Paper: CBA-13-04, NYU*, 2013. http://hdl.handle.net/2451/31988.

[5] P. Adamopoulos and A. Tuzhilin. Recommendation opportunities: Improving item prediction using weighted percentile methods in collaborative filtering systems. In *RecSys '13*. ACM, 2013.

[6] P. Adamopoulos and A. Tuzhilin. On unexpectedness in recommender systems: Or how to better expect the unexpected. *ACM TIST*, 2015. http://tist.acm.org/papers/TIST-2012-09-0141.R2.pdf.

[7] G. Adomavicius and Y. Kwon. Maximizing Aggregate Recommendation Diversity: A Graph-Theoretic Approach. In *DiveRS at RecSys '11*. ACM, 2011.

[8] G. Adomavicius and Y. Kwon. Improving aggregate recommendation diversity using ranking-based techniques. *IEEE TKDE*, 24(5):896–911, 2012.

[9] G. Adomavicius and A. Tuzhilin. Toward the next generation of recommender systems: A survey of the state-of-the-art and possible extensions. *IEEE TKDE*, 17(6):734–749, 2005.

[10] M. Balabanović and Y. Shoham. Fab: content-based, collaborative recommendation. *CACM*, 40(3):66–72, 1997.

[11] D. Billsus and M. J. Pazzani. User modeling for adaptive news access. *UMUAI*, 10(2-3):147–180, 2000.

[12] R. Burke. Hybrid recommender systems: Survey and experiments. *UMUAI*, 12(4):331–370, 2002.

[13] P. Cremonesi et al. Performance of recommender algorithms on top-n recommendation tasks. In *RecSys '10*. ACM, 2010.

[14] P. Cremonesi, F. Garzotto, et al. Looking for "good" recommendations: A comparative evaluation of recommender systems. In *INTERACT '11*. 2011.

[15] C. Desrosiers and G. Karypis. A comprehensive survey of neighborhood-based recommendation methods. In *Recommender systems handbook*. Springer, 2011.

[16] S. Dooms et al. Movietweetings: a movie rating dataset collected from twitter. In *CrowdRec at RecSys '13*, 2013.

[17] J. A. Evans. Electronic publication and the narrowing of science and scholarship. *Science*, 321(5887):395–399, 2008.

[18] R. Fagin and T. G. Price. Efficient calculation of expected miss ratios in the independent reference model. *SICOMP*, 7(3), 1978.

[19] D. Fleder and K. Hosanagar. Blockbuster culture's next rise or fall: The impact of recommender systems on sales diversity. *Manage. Sci.*, 55(5):697–712, 2009.

[20] Z. Gantner, S. Rendle, et al. MyMediaLite: A free recommender system library. In *RecSys '11*. ACM, 2011.

[21] D. Goldberg, D. Nichols, et al. Using collaborative filtering to weave an information tapestry. *CACM*, 35(12):61–70, 1992.

[22] GroupLens research group, 2011. http://www.grouplens.org.

[23] J. L. Herlocker, J. A. Konstan, et al. An algorithmic framework for performing collaborative filtering. In *SIGIR*. ACM, 1999.

[24] O. Hinz, J. Eckert, et al. Drivers of the long tail phenomenon: an empirical analysis. *JMIS*, 27(4):43–70, 2011.

[25] D. Jannach, L. Lerche, et al. What recommenders recommend–an analysis of accuracy, popularity, and sales diversity effects. In *UMAP*. Springer, 2013.

[26] J. A. Konstan, B. N. Miller, et al. Grouplens: applying collaborative filtering to usenet news. *CACM*, 40(3), 1997.

[27] C. Matt, T. Hess, et al. The differences between recommender technologies in their impact on sales diversity. In *ICIS*, 2013.

[28] J. McAuley and J. Leskovec. Hidden factors and hidden topics: understanding rating dimensions with text. In *RecSys'13*, 2013.

[29] S. M. McNee, J. Riedl, et al. Being accurate is not enough: how accuracy metrics have hurt recommend. systems. In *CHI*, 2006.

[30] A. Nanopoulos et al. How does high dimensionality affect collaborative filtering? In *RecSys '09*. ACM, 2009.

[31] T. T. Nguyen, P.-M. Hui, et al. Exploring the filter bubble: the effect of using rec. sys. on content diversity. In *WWW*, 2014.

[32] M. Radovanović, A. Nanopoulos, et al. Hubs in space: Popular nearest neighbors in high-dimensional data. *JMLR*, 2010.

[33] F. Roli and G. Fumera. Analysis of linear and order statistics combiners for fusion of imbalanced classifiers. In *MCS*, 2002.

[34] A. Said, B. Fields, et al. User-centric evaluation of a k-furthest neighbor CF recommender algorithm. In *CSCW*. ACM, 2013.

[35] A. Said, B. J. Jain, et al. Increasing diversity through furthest neighbor-based recommendation. In *DDR at WSDM '12*, 2012.

[36] K. Seyerlehner, A. Flexer, et al. On the limitations of browsing top-n recommender systems. In *RecSys '09*. ACM, 2009.

[37] K. Tumer and J. Ghosh. Error correlation and error reduction in ensemble classifiers. *Connection science*, 8(3-4), 1996.

[38] C.-K. Wong and M. C. Easton. An efficient method for weighted sampling without replacement. *SICOMP*, 9(1):111–113, 1980.

[39] C.-N. Ziegler, S. M. McNee, et al. Improving recommendation lists through topic diversification. In *WWW '05*. ACM, 2005.

User Perception of Differences in Recommender Algorithms

Michael D. Ekstrand[1,2], F. Maxwell Harper[2], Martijn C. Willemsen[3], and Joseph A. Konstan[2]

[1]Dept. of Computer Science
Texas State University
San Marcos, TX, USA
ekstrand@txstate.edu

[2]GroupLens Research
Dept. of Comp. Sci. & Eng.
University of Minnesota
Minneapolis, MN, USA
{harper,konstan}@cs.umn.edu

[3]Human-Technology Interaction Group
School of Innovation Sciences
Eindhoven University of Technology
Eindhoven, The Netherlands
M.C.Willemsen@tue.nl

ABSTRACT

Recent developments in user evaluation of recommender systems have brought forth powerful new tools for understanding what makes recommendations effective and useful. We apply these methods to understand how users evaluate recommendation lists for the purpose of selecting an algorithm for finding movies. This paper reports on an experiment in which we asked users to compare lists produced by three common collaborative filtering algorithms on the dimensions of novelty, diversity, accuracy, satisfaction, and degree of personalization, and to select a recommender that they would like to use in the future. We find that satisfaction is negatively dependent on novelty and positively dependent on diversity in this setting, and that satisfaction predicts the user's final selection. We also compare users' subjective perceptions of recommendation properties with objective measures of those same characteristics. To our knowledge, this is the first study that applies modern survey design and analysis techniques to a within-subjects, direct comparison study of recommender algorithms.

Categories and Subject Descriptors

H.1.2 [**User/machine systems**]: Human factors; H.3.3 [**Information storage and retrieval**]: Retrieval models

Keywords

recommender systems; user study

1. INTRODUCTION

The ability of a recommender system to meet the needs of its users depends on many aspects of the recommender's behavior, the application domain, and the user's information needs. We want to understand the relevant properties of each of these entities (recommenders, domains, and needs) and how they interact to form a compelling recommendation experience in a robust and systematic fashion. This leads to a key question: how do users perceive the outputs from various recommender algorithms to be different, and how those differences affect their choice of algorithm?

The research community has long known that there are subjective differences in the output of recommender algorithms, even among algorithms with comparable accuracy [21, 12]. To map out some of those differences in the movie recommendation domain, we present a user study aimed at understanding the subjective differences users perceive between different collaborative filtering algorithms and how those differences affect their choice of recommender system.

We are taking advantage of a unique opportunity: we have a large base of experienced recommender system users (the MovieLens user community) and a software toolkit capable of supporting a wide array of recommender algorithms (LensKit [5]). Further, we are preparing the general release of a new version of the MovieLens platform, providing an opportunity to conduct an experiment in a context where the question of user preference among recommender algorithms has real meaning. Finally, new insights from user evaluation studies allow us to measure the subjective aspects that explain *why* particular recommender algorithms are preferred [11].

This paper is one installment in a series of work on understanding how recommenders can best meet users' information needs. It builds on extensive work on offline recommender evaluation and previous results identifying factors that influence user preference among recommendations and recommendation lists, such as diversity and novelty. Follow-up work will need to examine a greater range of algorithms, contexts of use, and properties that mediate a recommender's ability to satisfy its users needs. Critically, it will also need to look at users' long-term satisfaction with their recommender choices.

In the present work we seek to answer the following questions:

RQ1 How are users' overall preferences for recommendation lists predicted by the subjective properties of those lists?

RQ2 What differences do users perceive between the lists of recommendations produced by commonly-used collaborative filtering algorithms?

RQ3 How do objective algorithm performance metrics relate to users' subjective perception of recommender outputs?

To that end, we present the results of a user study we conducted users of the MovieLens recommender system, asking them to compare recommendation lists produced by popular recommender algorithms. We specifically explore item-item, user-user, and SVD algorithms, looking at user perceptions of accuracy, personalization, diversity, novelty, and overall satisfaction. Each user provided a first-impression preference between a pair of algorithms, subjective comparisons of the algorithms' output on our dimensions of interest, and selected an algorithm for future use. We build a model that predicts both the user's initial preference and their final choice of algorithm the subjective perceptions and objective measures of the recommender algorithms and their output.

RecSys'14, October 6–10, 2014, Foster City, Silicon Valley, CA, USA.
Copyright 2014 ACM 978-1-4503-2668-1/14/10 ...$15.00.
http://dx.doi.org/10.1145/2645710.2645737.

While this experiment focuses on one recommendation domain that is admittedly well-studied, it uncovers subjective characteristics of recommender behavior that explain users' selections in a manner that provides a good basis for generalization, replication, and further validation. We report specific relationships that can be tested for validity in additional contexts, providing much greater insight into what aspects of algorithm suitability for movie recommendation are task-specific and what are more general behaviors.

In addition to answering our immediate questions, the data collected in this survey should be a useful ground truth for calibrating new offline measures of recommender behavior to more accurately estimate how algorithms will be experienced by their users.

2. RELATED WORK

Many researchers have acknowledged the role of factors beyond accuracy — either predictive or retrieval accuracy — in evaluating recommender systems [13]. This has resulted in the development of offline evaluation protocols that incorporate metrics beyond accuracy [8, 20], user-based research on recommender perception [11, 16], and a number of workshops and tutorials on recommender system evaluation. Industrial applications often evaluate recommender approaches by measuring lift, click-through rates, and other observable user behaviors that affect the core business goals the recommender is intended to serve; these behaviors arise from the holistic impact of the recommender on the user's actions.

User studies are widely used to evaluate the usefulness of particular recommender applications [4] and to answer scientific questions about user interaction with recommender systems [1]. The design and execution of user studies has improved over time; historically, many studies involved relatively simple user questionaires (a practice that continues today), but recent years have seen increasing development and use of more sophisticated study designs and analysis techniques [11].

One such technique, structural equation modeling [10, 11], is a powerful tool for investigating the perceived factors that influence user satisfaction and choices. It allows us to not only measure what algorithms or items the user ultimately prefers, but also assess how specific aspects of the recommendations (such as novelty and diversity) influence their preferences and behavior. A user may prefer algorithm A over B because it is diverse and therefore more appropriate to meeting their needs, and SEM allows us to quantify and test these kinds of relationships.

The particular factors that we consider are motivated by a long line of work in human-recommender interaction and recommender user experience [14, 11, 16]. Novelty [25, 22] and diversity [27, 22, 26, 24] are both widely regarded as an important factor in recommender system perception and acceptance.

3. EXPERIMENT DESIGN

To assess the differences among various algorithms for recommending movies with explicit user ratings, we conducted an experiment in which users reviewed two lists of recommendations and took a survey comparing them. Figure 1 shows a screenshot of the experimental interface.

3.1 Users and Context

We conducted our experiment on users of MovieLens, a movie recommendation service. The survey was integrated into a beta launch of a new version of MovieLens; we invited active users to preview the beta with an on-site banner and required them to participate in the experiment prior to using MovieLens Beta. 1052 users attempted the survey, of which 582 completed it. Since we limited recruiting to active users, all users had at least 15 ratings (the median rating count was 473).

3.2 Algorithms

For this experiment, we tested three widely-used collaborative filtering algorithms as implemented in LensKit version 2.1-M2 [5]. To tune the algorithm parameters, we used the item-item CF configuration in the MovieLens production environment and values reported in the published literature [5, 6] as a starting point and refined the configurations with 5-fold cross-validation over the MovieLens database (using RMSE and prediction nDCG as our metrics to optimize) and manual inspection of recommender output. This resulted in the following algorithm configurations:

- Item-item CF [19] with 20 neighbors, model size of 4000, cosine similarity, item mean centering, neighbor threshold of 0.1, and requiring 2 neighbors to make a prediction.
- User-user CF [7] with 30 neighbors, cosine vector similarity between users, and normalizing user ratings by subtracting the personalized user-item mean, a neighbor threshold of 0.1, and requiring 2 neighbors to make a prediction; we additionally applied a small Bayesian damping of 5 to the user and item means for normalization.
- SVD with the FunkSVD [6, 15] training algorithm, using 50 features, 125 training epochs per feature, user-item mean baseline with damping of 5, and the LensKit default learning rate of 0.001 and regularization factor of 0.015.

For each user, we randomly selected two of the algorithms. For each algorithm, we computed a recommendation list containing the 10 movies with the highest predicted rating among those the user had not rated, sorted by predicted rating. We presented these lists as 'List A' and 'List B' (the ordering of algorithms was randomized).

In internal pre-testing, the user-user and SVD algorithms often recommended very obscure movies. This created a significant risk that users would be entirely unfamiliar with the recommendations of these algorithms. While we want to measure novelty, users are limited in their ability to judge completely unfamiliar lists. To test the algorithms in something close to their pure form, while increasing the likelihood that users would have at least heard of some of the movies and therefore be able to provide meaningful feedback, we limited each algorithm to recommending from the 2500 most-rated movies in MovieLens (about 10% of MovieLens's entire collection). This adjustment may limit effect sizes (e.g. decreasing perceived novelty of an algorithm's recommendations), but should allow each algorithm to still demonstrate its general behaviors relative to the others.

Not all algorithms could produce 10 recommendations for all users. If a user could not receive 10 recommendations from each algorithm, we exclude them from the analysis.

Most studies of recommender user experience employ a between-subjects design in which the users only see one condition (i.e. one algorithm at the time). Such between-subject designs are more realistic of real world experiences. However, in our present experiment we are primarily interested in detecting differences between algorithms, some of which may be quite subtle. If users evaluated each algorithm's output separately, their experience with that algorithm would not be related to another; this is problematic as evaluation is a naturally relative activity: absolute judgments are much more difficult than relative judgments and less sensitive to small differences [9]. Therefore we chose to evaluate these algorithms with a simultaneous within-subjects design in which our participants jointly evaluate two out of three algorithms side-by-side.

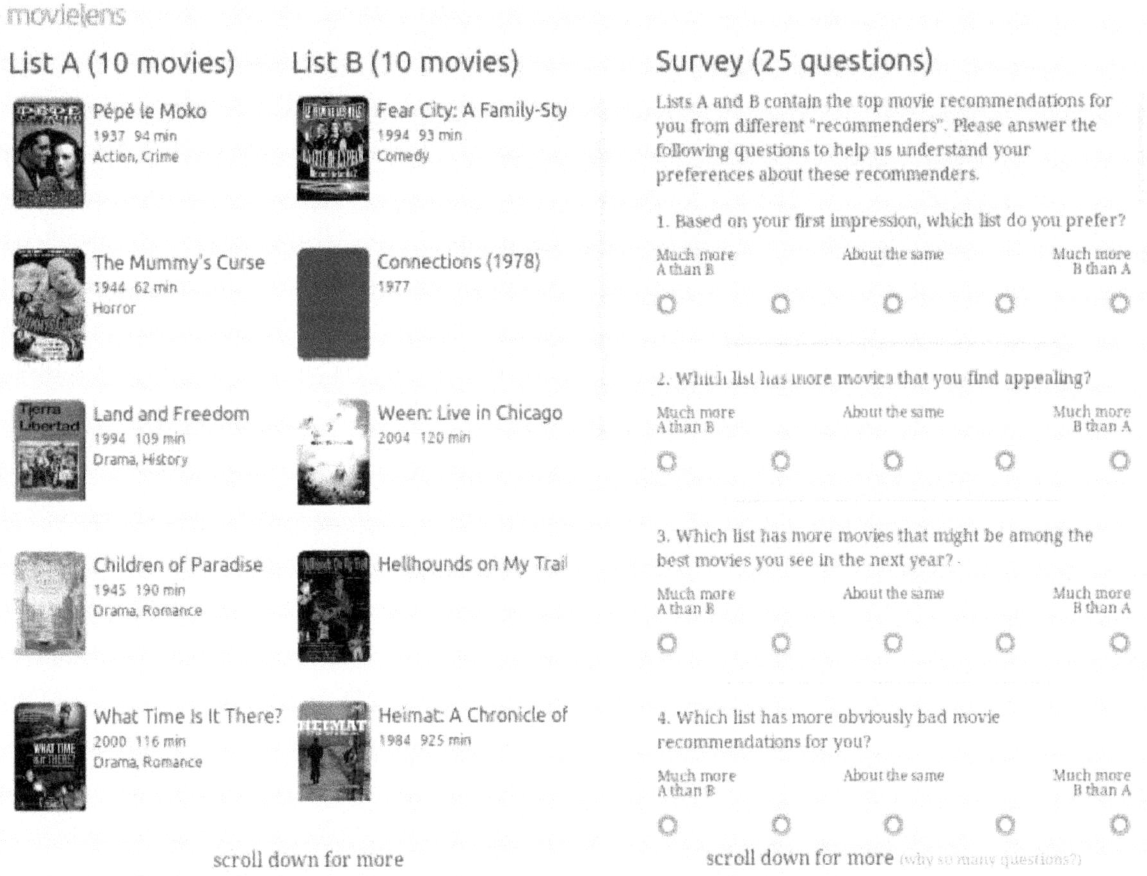

Figure 1: Screen shot of the experiment interface. Clicking on a movie in the list opens a pop-over with additional movie details.

3.3 Showing Predictions

Algorithms will not necessarily generate scores on the same portions of the rating scale. For example, one algorithm may tend to predict 4.5–5 stars, while another algorithm may be more conservative and predict 3.5–4.5 stars. While we want users to evaluate the recommendation lists, not the predictions, this could have a confounding affect if the predicted rating affects the user's perception of the movie lists. To control for this, we assigned each user randomly to one of the following prediction conditions:

- Show no predictions (just the list of recommended movies).
- Show a standard, unadjusted prediction.
- Show a normalized prediction. In this condition, we predicted the first 3 movies at 5 stars, the next 4 at 4.5, and the last 3 at 4 stars.

If predicted ratings do not affect the user's perception of the recommendation lists, then there should be no difference in response between these conditions and we can average across them in the final analysis.

3.4 User Survey

Our survey consists of four parts. The first question, visible in fig. 1, asks users which list of recommendations they prefer, based on their initial impression. 5 options are available, with the extremes labeled 'Much more A than B' and 'Much more B than A'.

Following initial preference are 22 questions about various aspects of the lists, designed to measure the user's perception of the recommendation lists across five factors:

Acc Accuracy — the recommender's ability to find 'good' movies.

Sat Satisfaction — the user's overall satisfaction with the recommender and their perception of its usefulness.

Und Perceived personalization ('Understands Me') — the user's perception that the recommender understands their tastes and can effectively adapt to them.

Nov Novelty — the propensity of the recommender to suggest items with which the user is unfamiliar.

Div Diversity — the diversity of the recommended items.

For this portion of the survey, we started with questions that have worked well in previous experiments [11], adapted them to be comparative instead of absolute, and wrote a small number of new questions. The full list of questions is in table 1a.

After the main body of questions, we ask users which algorithm they would like to use by default once MovieLens gains the ability to support multiple recommender algorithms in parallel (a feature we are planning to develop in the coming months). This question is forced-choice, requiring users to pick one of the two algorithms. It also carries some consequence for users: while they will be able to switch algorithms in their user settings page without much difficulty, the algorithm they select will be providing their default recommendations in the future.

3.5 Objective Metrics

In addition to soliciting users' subjective perceptions of the recommendations, we computed objective measures of the algorithms' behavior with respect to accuracy, novelty, and diversity.

We estimate the accuracy of each algorithm by computing the RMSE of using it to predict each user's last 5 ratings prior to taking the survey, averaging the errors per user. To estimate novelty, we take the simple approach of computing the mean popularity rank of the items recommended to the user (fig. 3b); this creates an 'obscurity' metric, where high values correspond to lists with more obscure items.

We compute diversity with intra-list similarity [27] using cosine between tag genome vectors [23] as the itemwise similarity function and normalizing the final metric so that a list of completely similar items has a score of 1; we exclude items for which tag genome data is not available (no list required us to exclude more than 2 items); fig. 3c shows these values.

To convert the metrics into comparative measures, we take the log ratio of the objective metric values for the two recommendation lists presented to a user[1]. This produces a single value for a pair of algorithms or recommendation lists that we can attempt to correlate with the users' subjective comparative judgements.

4. RESULTS

582 users completed the study over 81 days. Table 2 shows how many participated in each algorithm condition, along with their final choice of algorithm. Users generally selected both item-item and SVD over user-user ($p < 0.0001$), but there was no statistically significant difference in the proportion of users choosing between item-item vs. SVD. Table 1b summarizes the responses to each of our questions by algorithm condition, and fig. 3 shows the objective measures of each algorithm's output.

We observed no significant effect of either the ordering of algorithms or of the prediction condition[2], so we exclude those from the remainder of the analysis.

4.1 Response Model

To answer our more detailed research questions about the factors at play in users' choice of algorithms, we subjected the survey results to confirmatory factor analysis (CFA) and structure equation modeling (SEM). We used Lavaan [18] for R [17] to compute the CFA and SEM, treating all question responses as ordinal variables. Each question is mapped to the factor it was designed to target. Table 1c shows the question/factor loadings from both the initial CFA and a simplified SEM derived from it[3]. In the full CFA, there are several questions that have very low explanatory power (such as 'which recommender more represents mainstream tastes?' with $R^2 = 0.006$); in addition, the *Accuracy*, *Satisfaction*, and *Understands Me* factors are very highly correlated (corellation coefficents in excess of 0.9), so we cannot legitimately consider them to be measuring different constructs in this experiment. We simplify the model by removing the *Accuracy* and *Understands Me* factors (we retain *Satisfaction* because it has the highest explanatory power, as measured by the Average Variance Extracted, and all 5 of its questions load strongly), and removing poorly-loading questions from *Novelty*. We then expand the simplified CFA into an SEM, which we call the *Overall SEM*, by adding structural relationships between factors, regressing them against the experimental conditions and objective metrics, and regressing the user's first impression and final selection against the experimental factors.

Figure 2 and table 1c show the structure and question/factor loadings in this overall model. The overall SEM has good fit ($\chi^2_{139} = 229.5$, $p < 0.001$, CFI = 0.999, TLI = 0.998, RMSEA = 0.033). The model uses standardized factor scores, so a coefficient for the effect on or of a factor measures the effect in standard deviations of the factor. We use item-item vs. SVD as the baseline condition, encoding the item-item/user-user and SVD/user-user conditions with dummy condition variables.

4.2 RQ1: Predicting Preference

To address RQ1, we consider the impact of the factors (*Nov*, *Div*, and *Sat*) on the user's first impression of the recommendation lists and on their final choice of algorithm (see fig. 2). Most users who preferred one algorithm over the other at their first impression picked that algorithm in the final forced-choice question.

The only significant predictor (besides first impression) of the user's final choice of algorithm was their relative satisfaction with the two recommendation lists. Users tended to pick the algorithm with which they expressed more satisfaction.

Satisfaction in turn is influenced by the novelty (negatively) and diversity (positively) of the recommended items. Novelty also has a small positive impact on diversity, suggesting that there is an upside to novelty (as it correlating with more diverse lists, which correlates positively with satisfaction) but a strong downside (users don't like recommendation lists full of unfamiliar items).

In addition to its indirect effect through satisfaction, novelty had an additional negative influence on the user's first-impression preference. This means that novelty has a strong initial impact on user preference. However, after the user has made their first judgement, answered the more in-depth questions, and finally selected an algorithm, the direct impact of novelty went away and their final choice depended primarily on satisfaction. Novelty is still a significant negative influence, but it is mediated through satisfaction.

4.3 RQ2: Algorithm Performance

In RQ2, we want to understand how the algorithms themselves compare on relative satisfaction, diversity, novelty, and user preference as exhibited in their choice of algorithm. Table 2 summarizes the final choice performance of the three algorithms: as measured by users picking an algorithm for use, user-user clearly loses, and item-item and SVD are effectively tied.

Table 1b provides some insight into users' perception of the relative charateristics of the algorithms. Across most questions, item-item and SVD are indistinguishable (user responses are symmetrically distributed about the neutral response). Item-item shows slightly more diversity than SVD. The other algorithm pairings show more differences across the board, with the exception of item-item and user-user being indistinguishable on diversity.

Our overall SEM (fig. 2) and related factor analysis incorporate the experimental condition, but its impact is difficult to interpret due to the comparative nature of the experiment. To better understand each pair of algorithm's relative performance, we reinterpret our experiment as three pseudo-experiments. Each of these pseudo-experiments uses one of the algorithms as a baseline and compares the other two algorithms on their performance and behavior relative to the baseline in a between-subjects design; the experimental treat-

[1] We also experimented with computing raw differences, but generally found the log ratio to be a better predictor.

[2] There are at least 3 possible causes of this non-effect: recommenders all predicted in the same range, prediction had no effect on perception, or our questions successfully guided users to evaluate the lists independent of prediction. In any case, it did not confound our results.

[3] Full Lavaan output for the SEM is included in the thesis form of this work [3].

Factor / Question (*W. l.* = 'Which list', *W. r.* = 'Which recommender')	II v. SVD	II v. UU	SVD v. UU	Full CFA Coef.	R^2	SEM Coef.
First Impression						
Accuracy					**0.61**	
W. l. has more movies that you find appealing?				0.911	0.85	
W. l. has more movies that might be among the best movies you see in the next year?				0.786	0.64	
W. l. has more obviously bad movie recommendations for you?				−0.751	0.59	
W. r. does a better job of putting better movies at the top?				0.572	0.35	
Diversity					**0.64**	
W. l. has more movies that are similar to each other?				−0.772	0.61	−0.748
W. l. has amore varied selection of movies?				0.772	0.61	0.743
W. l. has movies that match a wider variety of moods?				0.838	0.71	0.806
W. l. would suit a broader set of tastes?				0.793	0.64	0.768
Understands Me					**0.63**	
W. r. better understands your taste in movies?				0.933	0.88	
W. r. would you trust more to provide you with recommendations?				0.943	0.90	
W. r. seems more personalized to your movie ratings?				0.842	0.73	
W. r. more represents mainstream tastes instead of your own?				−0.072	0.01	
Satisfaction					**0.82**	
W. r. would better help you find movies to watch?				0.923	0.86	0.737
W. r. would you be more likely to recommend to your friends?				0.846	0.73	0.678
W. l. of recommendations do you find more valuable?				0.884	0.79	0.717
W. r. would you rather have as an app on your mobile phone?				0.921	0.86	0.736
W. r. would better help to pick satisfactory movies?				0.928	0.87	0.745
Novelty					**0.43**	
W. l. has more movies you do not expect?				−0.770	0.64	0.750
W. l. has more movies that are familiar to you?				0.784	0.66	−0.762
W. l. has more pleasantly surprising movies?				0.454	0.24	
W. l. has more movies you would not have thought to consider?				−0.704	0.54	0.707
W. l. provides fewer new suggestions?				0.258	0.08	

(a) Questions

(b) Response distributions. Dark entries have significant bias (uncorrected Wilcox test, $p < 0.01$)

(c) CFA & SEM factor loadings.

Table 1: Overview of survey results. All SEM factor loadings are significant ($p < 0.01$); factor R^2 is AVE.

Condition (*A* v. *B*)	*N*	Pick *A*	Pick *B*	% Pick *B*	*p*
I-I v. U-U	201	144	57	28.4%	0.000
I-I v. SVD	198	101	97	49.0%	0.831
SVD v. U-U	183	136	47	25.7%	0.000

Table 2: Final algorithm selection by condition. *p*-values are for two-sided proportion tests, $H_0 : a/b = 0.5$.

ment is the choice of algorithm to compare against the baseline. We will refer to this algorithm as the *tested* algorithm.

Randomization ensures that the behavior characteristics of the baseline algorithm are likely to be evenly distributed between the two sets of users encountering that algorithm, so we can (with some limitations) interpret relative measurements of one algorithm's comparison with the baseline as absolute measurements of that algorithm's behavior for the purposes of comparing with measurements of another algorithm against the same baseline.

Table 3 shows the pseudo-experiments, their conditions, and user's selections under this interpretation. The first pair of rows describes one of the three pseudo-experiments. Examining all users assigned to one of the two conditions involving item-item CF, we use item-item as the baseline and ask how often users picked user-user or SVD over the baseline. We can apply this interpretation to all questions and factors, not just selection. This allows us to make cleaner inferences at the expense of some statistical power.

For each experiment, we re-analyzed the data using SEM and basic regressions to predict the user's relative preference and final choice. Each SEM reused the factor loadings from the overall SEM but re-learned the relationships between factors, choice, and condition. We also omitted the objective metrics from these SEMs in order to focus on the subjective differences between the algorithms. The model structure for each experiment is a simplification of fig. 2.

Baseline	Tested	% Tested > Baseline	*p*
ItemItem	SVD	48.99	0.0000
	UserUser	28.36	
SVD	ItemItem	51.01	0.0000
	UserUser	25.68	
UserUser	ItemItem	71.64	0.6353
	SVD	74.32	

Table 3: Split experiment summary. *p*-values are testing the null hypothesis that the user picked the tested algorithm over the baseline the same proportion of the time.

In addition to the condition, we also consider the number of ratings in the user's history prior to joining the experiment as a proxy for their level of experience. It is possible for algorithms to perform differently for different users, or for more experienced users to judge recommendation lists differently. We computed the median number of ratings for the users participating in the experiment and set a condition variable indicating whether a particular had 'many' or 'few' ratings relative to the median.

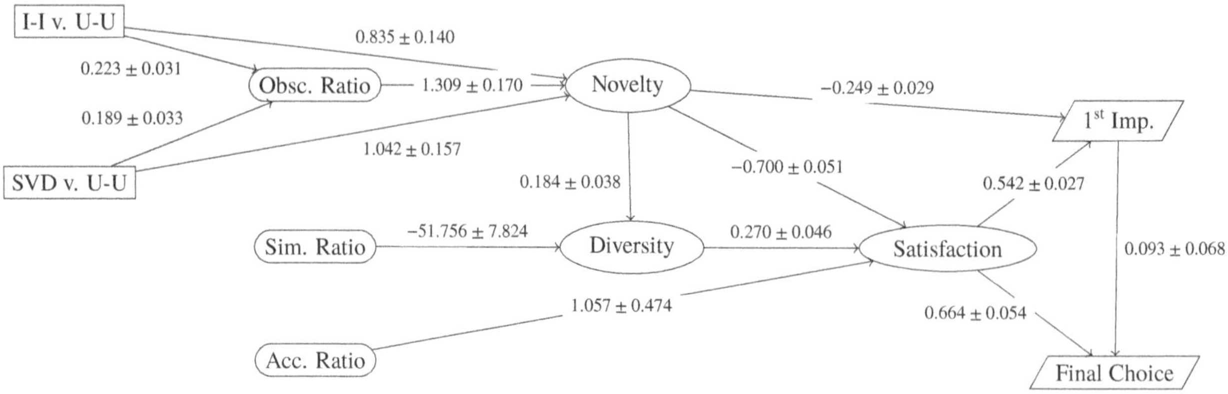

Figure 2: Overall SEM with bootstrapped standard errors. All displayed coefficients are significantly nonzero ($p < 0.01$). The baseline condition is I-I v. SVD; positive values & coefficients favor the right-hand algorithm (SVD or U-U).

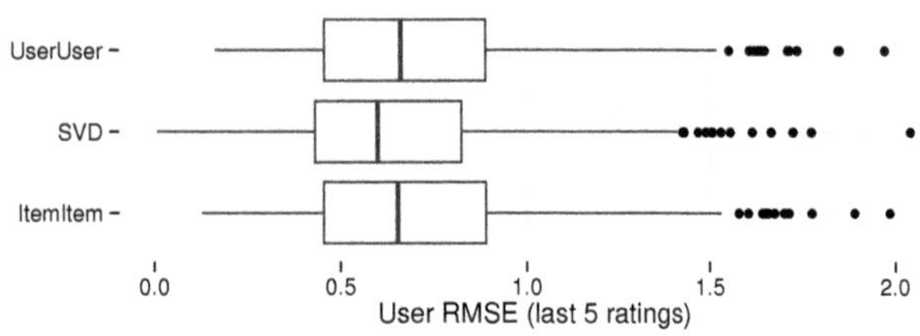

(a) Algorithm predictive accuracy.

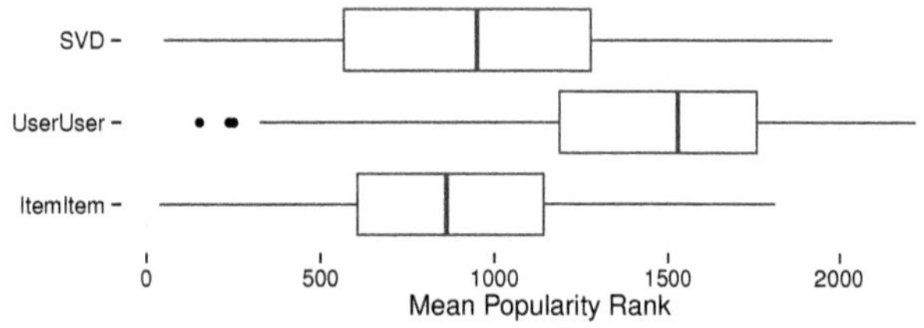

(b) Popularity rank of recommended items (lower is more popular).

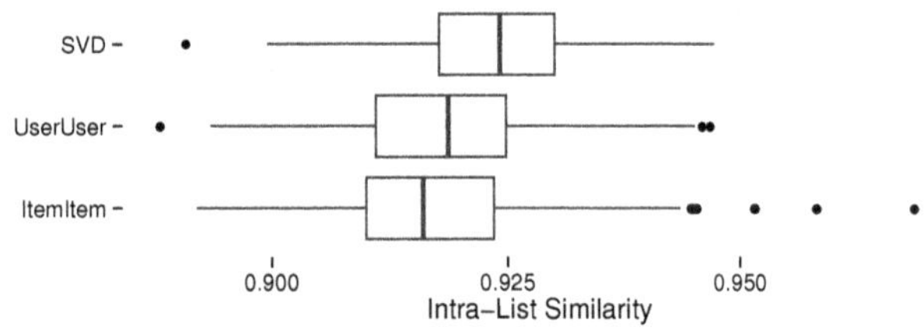

(c) List diversity (lower is more diverse).

Figure 3: Objective recommendation list properties.

4.3.1 SVD vs. User-User

Users perceived user-user's recommendations to be more novel than SVD's (coef. 0.953, $p < 0.001$). They also reported user-user to be producing more diverse recommendation lists (coef. 0.312, $p < 0.001$). The effect on novelty was substantially stronger; combined with novelty's strong negative influence on preference, impression, and choice, users generally found SVD's recommendations more satisfactory and desirable than user-users. The effect of novelty on diversity was not present in this model; novelty only affected satisfaction directly.

As explained above, these results are from comparative judgements between the output of the tested algorithm (SVD or user-user) and the baseline algorithm (item-item). However, due to randomization, we assume that there are no important differences in item-item's output between the users comparing it against SVD and those comparing it against user-user. Therefore, we can reasonably make inferences about the relative behavior of SVD and user-user. These results are consistent with the raw survey response data for direct comparisons between SVD and user-user (table 1b), providing further support for their validity. They are also consistent with the objective measures of obscurity and diversity (figs. 3b and 3c).

Users selected SVD significantly more often than user-user (table 3), consistent with the results from users directly comparing SVD and user-user (table 2).

4.3.2 Item-Item vs. User-User

We found no significant difference in diversity between item-item and user-user CF; this is consistent with the raw results of direct comparison of these two algorithms in table 1b.

User-user produced more novel recommendation lists than item-item (coef. −1.563, $p < 0.001$). This effect interacted with user experience (rating count); for high-rating users, user-user's recommendations were not as novel as they were for low-rating users. This moderating effect was small, however, and user-user was significantly more novel than item-item even for high-rating users. There was no significant difference in item-item's novelty performance between low- and high-rating users.

4.3.3 Item-Item vs. SVD

Item-item produced slightly more diverse recommendations than SVD (coef. −0.26, $p < 0.001$); this is consistent with the response distributions in table 1b as well as the difference in intra-list similarity (fig. 3c). However, diversity did not have a significant influence on satisfaction in this pseudo-experiment: the only significant predictor of satisfaction was novelty.

The number of ratings the user had in their history prior to the experiment had a significant effect on the algorithm: for high-rating users, both algorithms were more novel than user-user. Since item-item and SVD did not have significantly different perceived novelty, this effect is reflecting user-user's decreased novelty for high-rating users. Whether there is an additional increase the novelty of item-item and SVD for high-rating users, or just a decrease in user-user's novelty, is beyond this experiment's capability to measure.

4.4 RQ3: Objective Metrics

To address RQ3, we consider in more detail the relationships between the objective metrics and subjective factors. Figure 3 shows the distributions of all objective metrics we computed.

The raw distributions of novelty and diversity measurements are consistent with the user survey results. User-user produces lists with less popular (and therefore likely more novel) items than SVD or item-item. SVD tends to produce somewhat less diverse recommendation lists. All three algorithms had comparable retrospective accuracy, with SVD having a slight edge. Popularity/obscurity was the only objective metric that we found to significantly differ between conditions in the overall model.

Each objective metric was a statistically significant predictor of its corresponding subjective factor (fig. 2) and no other factor. Therefore, there is good correspondence between the subjective and objective measures of these three concepts, and the effect of the objective measures on final choice is completely mediated by their impact on the subjective measures. All indirect effects of objective measures on final choice are significant.

This means that predictive accuracy, for example, does affect the user's final choice, but only through the increased satisfaction that it produces. Further, the impact of novelty and diversity on satisfaction means that after controlling for predictive accuracy, diversity and novelty still have significant impacts on user satisfaction.

The direct effects of condition on novelty, in addition to the effect mediated through objective obscurity, suggest that user-user is producing lists that users perceive to be more novel beyond the sense of novelty that our objective metric can capture.

5. DISCUSSION

We set out to measure user perception of various interesting properties of the output of different recommender systems in a widely-studied domain. Our experiment uncovered mediation effects of novelty, diversity, satisfaction on users' choice of recommender algorithms. In this section, we highlight some of the key findings.

5.1 Effect of Novelty

One of the most striking things we found is that the novelty of recommended items has a signficiant negative impact on users' perception of a recommender's ability to satisfactorially meet their information needs. This effect was particularly strong in its impact on the user's first impression of an algorithm, and was present even though we restricted the depth of the long tail into which our algorithms could reach.

This suggests that recommender system designers should carefully watch the novelty of their system's recommendations, particularly for new users. Too many unfamiliar recommendations may give users a poor impression of a particular recommender, potentially driving them to use other systems instead. Increasing the novelty of recommendations as the user gains more experience with the system and has had more time to consider its ability to meet their needs may provide benefit, but our results cannot confirm or deny this. The users in our study are experienced with movie recommendation in general and MovieLens in particular (the median user has rated 473 movies), and their first impressions were still heavily influenced by novelty.

Our results complement the notion that that *trust-building* is an important goal of a recommender in the early stage of its relationship with its users [14]. They are also consistent with previous results finding that novelty is not necessarily positively correlated with user satisfaction or adoption of recommendations [2].

5.2 Diversity

We have also demonstrated that the diversity of recommendations has a positive influence on user choice of systems for general-purpose movie recommendation. Diversity is often framed as being in tension with accuracy, so that accuracy must be sacrificed in order to obtain diverse recommendation lists [27, 25, 26], and many diversification techniques do result in reduced accuracy by traditional objective measures. The strong correlation of perceived accuracy and satisfaction in our results provide evidence that there may not be such a tradeoff when considering user perception instead of traditional accuracy metrics.

The influence of novelty and diversity on satisfaction even after controlling for predictive accuracy provides direct, quantitative evidence for subjective but observable characteristics of recommendation lists affect user satisfaction and choice. Further, accuracy alone does not all aspects of satisfaction.

5.3 Algorithm Performance

When it comes to comparing the particular algorithms that we tested, item-item and SVD performed very similar, with users preferring them in roughly equal measure. We do not yet have insight into whether there are identifiable circumstances in which one is preferable over the other. It may be that one works better for some users than others; it may also be that their performance is roughly equivalent, and one does not work significantly better. The difference in the diversity of SVD and item-item, however, provides evidence for some kind of interesting difference between them.

User-user is the clear loser in our tests. Its prective accuracy was comparable to that of the other algorithms, but it had a significant propensity for novel recommendations that hurt both users' expressed satisfaction with its output and their interest in using it in the future. The lack of a significant independent effect of user-user condition on satisfaction or selection suggests that the increased novelty is the primary cause of user-user's poor subjective performance.

Finally, all three algorithms had similar predictive accuracy, but users still had strong preferences between some pairings. However, users selected item-item and SVD in almost equal numbers even though SVD had slightly higher predictive accuracy. This provides additional evidence that, at least beyond a certain point, offline metrics fail to capture much of what will impact the user's experience with a recommender system.

6. CONCLUSION AND FUTURE WORK

We have reported the results of a user study to compare the output of three common collaborative filtering algorithms and identify subjective, user perceptible differences between them. This work directly advances our understanding of the role of diversity and novelty in how users evaluate recommender systems for potential use. We hope that the collected data will also be useful for developing and refining additional measures of recommender behavior, allowing for high-throughput offline evaluation to more accurately estimate the user experience with recommendations.

In the future, we plan at least two direct extensions of this work. First, we will examine users' long-term use of the algorithm switching feature we are developing for MovieLens; in particular, we want to see if users' expressed preference in our study corresponds to their long-term stable choice of algorithm. Second, we want to see if there are aspects of a user's profile beyond their experience level that predict their algorithm preference. Even though user-user did poorly overall, about 25% of users preferred it: who are these users, and why does it work for them?

We also want to explore additional objective measures that may predict the subjective characteristics we describe here.

Our results are currently limited to a single domain and task, although they are consistent with results elsewhere [24]. They are also limited to single configurations of each of the tested algorithms; alternative tunings may result in very different performance. The structural model and mediating factors we have described, however, provide a valuable starting point for understanding exactly how our results do or do not generalize. Further experiments in other domains can examine the subjective characteristics we have studied to see whether their relationships hold across recommendation tasks.

Understanding how users perceive and interact with recommenders is critical to building better tools for meeting users' information needs. This work provides new insights into the factors at work in the usefulness of movie recommendations. We look forward to much more work, from ourselves and others, to build out a more systematic understanding of how to produce effective, useful, and even delightful recommendations in a broad range of applications.

Acknowledgements

We thank our colleagues in GroupLens Research for their support and assistance. This work has been funded by the National Science Foundation under grants IIS 08-08692 and 10-17697.

References

[1] D. Bollen, B. Knijnenburg, M. Willemsen, and M. Graus. Understanding Choice Overload in Recommender Systems. In *Proc. ACM RecSys 2010*. ACM, 2010, pp. 63–70. DOI: 10.1145/1864708.1864724.

[2] Ò. Celma and P. Herrera. A New Approach to Evaluating Novel Recommendations. In *Proc. ACM RecSys 2008*. ACM, 2008, pp. 179–186. DOI: 10.1145/1454008.1454038.

[3] M. D. Ekstrand. Towards Recommender Engineering: Tools and Experiments in Recommender Differences. PhD thesis. Minneapolis, MN: University of Minnesota, 2014. 263 pp.

[4] M. Ekstrand, P. Kannan, J. Stemper, J. Butler, J. A. Konstan, and J. Riedl. Automatically Building Research Reading Lists. In *Proc. ACM RecSys 2010*. ACM, 2010, pp. 159–166. DOI: 10.1145/1864708.1864740.

[5] M. Ekstrand, M. Ludwig, J. A. Konstan, and J. Riedl. Rethinking the Recommender Research Ecosystem: Reproducibility, Openness, and LensKit. In *Proc. ACM RecSys 2011*. ACM, 2011, pp. 133–140. DOI: 10.1145/2043932.2043958.

[6] S. Funk. Netflix Update: Try This at Home. The Evolution of Cybernetics. 2006. URL: http://sifter.org/~simon/journal/20061211.html (visited on 04/08/2010).

[7] J. Herlocker, J. A. Konstan, and J. Riedl. An Empirical Analysis of Design Choices in Neighborhood-Based Collaborative Filtering Algorithms. *Inf. Retr.* 5(4):287–310, 2002. DOI: 10.1023/A:1020443909834.

[8] J. Herlocker, J. A. Konstan, L. Terveen, and J. Riedl. Evaluating collaborative filtering recommender systems. *ACM Trans. Inf. Syst.* 22(1):5–53, 2004. DOI: 10.1145/963770.963772.

[9] C. K. Hsee and J. Zhang. General Evaluability Theory. *Persp. Psych. Sci.* 5(4):343–355, 2010. DOI: 10.1177/1745691610374586.

[10] R. B. Kline. *Principles and Practice of Structural Equation Modeling*. Guilford Press, New York, 1998. 354 pp.

[11] B. Knijnenburg, M. Willemsen, Z. Gantner, H. Soncu, and C. Newell. Explaining the User Experience of Recommender Systems. *UMUAI*, 22(4):441–504, 2012. DOI: 10.1007/s11257-011-9118-4.

[12] S. McNee, N. Kapoor, and J. A. Konstan. Don't Look Stupid: Avoiding Pitfalls When Recommending Research Papers. In *Proc. ACM CSCW 2006*. CSCW '06. ACM, Banff, Alberta, Canada, 2006, p. 171. DOI: 10.1145/1180875.1180903.

[13] S. McNee, J. Riedl, and J. A. Konstan. Being accurate is not enough: how accuracy metrics have hurt recommender systems. In *Ext. Abs. ACM CHI 2010*. ACM, Montréal, Québec, Canada, 2006, pp. 1097–1101. DOI: 10.1145/1125451.1125659.

[14] S. McNee, J. Riedl, and J. A. Konstan. Making recommendations better: an analytic model for human-recommender interaction. In *Ext. Abs. ACM CHI 2006*. ACM, 2006, pp. 1103–1108. DOI: 10.1145/1125451.1125660.

[15] A. Paterek. Improving regularized singular value decomposition for collaborative filtering. In *KDD Cup and Workshop 2007*, 2007.

[16] P. Pu, L. Chen, and R. Hu. A user-centric evaluation framework for recommender systems. In *Proc. ACM RecSys 2011*. In RecSys '11. ACM, 2011, pp. 157–164. DOI: 10.1145/2043932.2043962.

[17] R Core Team. *R: A Language and Environment for Statistical Computing*. R Foundation for Statistical Computing, Vienna, Austria, 2014.

[18] Y. Rosseel. lavaan: An R Package for Structural Equation Modeling. *J. Stat. Soft.* 48(2):1–36, 2012.

[19] B. Sarwar, G. Karypis, J. Konstan, and J. Reidl. Item-based collaborative filtering recommendation algorithms. In *Proc. ACM WWW '01*. ACM, 2001, pp. 285–295. DOI: 10.1145/371920.372071.

[20] G. Shani and A. Gunawardana. Evaluating Recommendation Systems. In F. Ricci, L. Rokach, B. Shapira, and P. B. Kantor, editors, *Recommender Systems Handbook*, pp. 257–297. Springer, 2010.

[21] R. Torres, S. McNee, M. Abel, J. A. Konstan, and J. Riedl. Enhancing Digital Libraries with TechLens+. In *Proc. ACM IEEE JCDL 2004*. ACM, 2004, pp. 228–236. DOI: 10.1145/996350.996402.

[22] S. Vargas and P. Castells. Rank and Relevance in Novelty and Diversity Metrics for Recommender Systems. In *Proc. ACM RecSys 2011*. ACM, 2011, pp. 109–116. DOI: 10.1145/2043932.2043955.

[23] J. Vig, S. Sen, and J. Riedl. The Tag Genome: Encoding Community Knowledge to Support Novel Interaction. *ACM Trans. Interact. Intell. Syst.* 2(3):13:1–13:44, 2012. DOI: 10.1145/2362394.2362395.

[24] M. C. Willemsen, M. P. Graus, and B. P. Knijnenburg. Understanding the Role of Latent Feature Diversification on Choice Difficulty and Satisfaction. *Under review*, 2014.

[25] M. Zhang and N. Hurley. Avoiding Monotony: Improving the Diversity of Recommendation Lists. In *Proc. ACM RecSys 2008*. ACM, 2008, pp. 123–130. DOI: 10.1145/1454008.1454030.

[26] T. Zhou, Z. Kuscsik, J.-G. Liu, M. Medo, J. R. Wakeling, and Y.-C. Zhang. Solving the apparent diversity-accuracy dilemma of recommender systems. *PNAS*, 107(10):4511–4515, 2010. DOI: 10.1073/pnas.1000488107.

[27] C.-N. Ziegler, S. McNee, J. A. Konstan, and G. Lausen. Improving recommendation lists through topic diversification. In *Proc. ACM WWW 2005*. ACM, 2005, pp. 22–32. DOI: 10.1145/1060745.1060754.

Offline and Online Evaluation of News Recommender Systems at swissinfo.ch

Florent Garcin
Artificial Intelligence Lab
Ecole Polytechnique Fédérale de Lausanne
Switzerland
firstname.lastname@epfl.ch

Boi Faltings
Artificial Intelligence Lab
Ecole Polytechnique Fédérale de Lausanne
Switzerland
firstname.lastname@epfl.ch

Olivier Donatsch
SWI swissinfo.ch
Swiss Broadcasting Corp.
Switzerland

Ayar Alazzawi
SWI swissinfo.ch
Swiss Broadcasting Corp.
Switzerland

Christophe Bruttin
SWI swissinfo.ch
Swiss Broadcasting Corp.
Switzerland

Amr Huber
SWI swissinfo.ch
Swiss Broadcasting Corp.
Switzerland

ABSTRACT

We report on the live evaluation of various news recommender systems conducted on the website *swissinfo.ch*. We demonstrate that there is a major difference between offline and online accuracy evaluations. In an offline setting, recommending most popular stories is the best strategy, while in a live environment this strategy is the poorest. For online setting, context-tree recommender systems which profile the users in real-time improve the click-through rate by up to 35%. The visit length also increases by a factor of 2.5. Our experience holds important lessons for the evaluation of recommender systems with offline data as well as for the use of the click-through rate as a performance indicator.

Categories and Subject Descriptors

H.3.3 [**Information Storage and Retrieval**]: Information Search and Retrieval—*Information filtering*

Keywords

recommender system; news; real-time; live; evaluation

1. INTRODUCTION

The proliferation of online news creates a need for filtering to focus on interesting articles. Compared to other products, however, recommending news has specific challenges [7, 22]: news preferences are subject to trends, users do not want to see multiple articles with similar content, and frequently we have insufficient information to profile the reader.

We addressed these challenges in our previous research by introducing a new class of news recommender systems based on Context Trees (CT) [7, 8]. This class of recommender systems adapts its model to current trends and reader preferences. The model evolves with the read articles such that it is always up to date and recommendations are generated in real-time.

Previously, we evaluated the context-tree recommender systems in an offline setting and showed that there exists a trade-off between accuracy and novelty of recommendations [7]. However, this trade-off can only be answered by performing a live evaluation. This led us to several open questions: Which recommender systems should be deployed in practice? Do CT recommender systems improve the click-through rate over baseline methods? Do recommender systems increase the time spent by the users on the news website? Is there a major difference between offline and online evaluation? Although we were able to find elements of answers in previous works [12, 15, 18, 20], they do not address the context-tree technique and so we performed our own live investigation on the news website *swissinfo.ch* operated by the Swiss Broadcasting Corporation.

In this paper, we report on the live evaluation of CT recommender systems. We show that CT systems significantly improve the click-through rate (CTR) on swissinfo.ch, and also increase the visit length. We also learn important lessons regarding the usefulness of offline evaluation: the relative performance predicted on offline data was in fact exactly the reverse order of what was actually observed on the live system. Furthermore, we show that the click-through rate is not always a good indicator of actual impact.

2. RELATED WORK

Although the first recommender systems were originally designed for news forums [17], the literature describing actual implementations and evaluations on live news websites is not common compared to the general literature on recommender systems [6, 12, 15, 18, 20].

Liu et al. [15] analyse the deployment of a hybrid recommender system on the news aggregator Google News. They compare their method against the existing collaborative filtering system implemented by Das et al. [6], and consider

RecSys'14, October 6–10, 2014, Foster City, Silicon Valley, CA, USA.
Copyright 2014 ACM 978-1-4503-2668-1/14/10 ...$15.00.
http://dx.doi.org/10.1145/2645710.2645745.

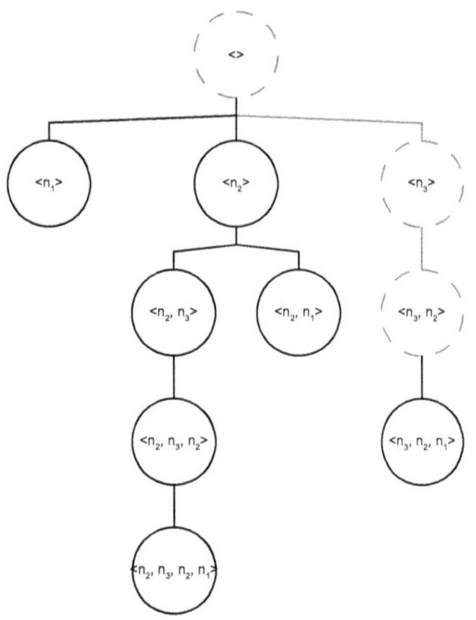

Figure 1: Context tree built with the sequence $\langle n_1, n_2, n_3, n_2 \rangle$. Nodes in red-dashed are contexts matching the new sequence $\langle n_2, n_3 \rangle$.

only logged-in users for the evaluation. They show a 30% improvement over the existing collaborative filtering system.

Kirchenbaum et al. [12] conduct an online evaluation with logged-in users of several recommender systems for news articles on Forbes.com. They report that a hybrid system performs the best, with a 37% improvement over popularity-based methods.

Said et al. [18, 20] study the weekly and hourly impressions and click-through rates in the Plista news recommender framework [11], which delivers recommendations to multiple news websites. They observe that live evaluation is sensitive to external factors not necessarily related to recommendations. They also identify trends in recommendations related to the type of news websites (traditional or topic-focused news sources). Readers of topic-focused websites are less likely to take recommendations than readers of traditional news websites [18]. Unfortunately, it is not clear which recommender algorithm is used in the Plista framework and their analysis.

Our evaluation is similar to the one of Kirchenbaum et al. [12], but differs in two crucial points. First, we consider anonymous users who are impossible to track across multiple visits. Second, the nature of the websites (Forbes.com and swissinfo.ch) is not the same, and thus readers' behaviours are different [18].

3. RECOMMENDER SYSTEMS

In our previous research [7], we have developed a new class of recommender systems based on Context Trees (CT). CT recommender systems create context-dependent recommendations by assigning a local prediction model to each context. We briefly recall how CT recommender systems work.

A context-tree recommender system builds a hierarchy of contexts, arranged in a tree such that a child node completely contains the context of its parents. A context can be the sequence of stories read by a user, the sequence of topics, or of topic distributions.

The root node corresponds to the most general context, i.e. when no information is available to profile the user. In that case, the recommendations are generated based on the most popular or most recent stories for instance. However, the more the user browses the stories, the more contexts we are able to extract, thus building a deeper context tree. This results in generating finer-grained recommendations, not only based on the most popular or most recent stories.

For instance, the sequence $\mathbf{s}_u = \langle n_1, n_2, n_3, n_2 \rangle$ is the ordered list of news stories $n_i \in \mathcal{N}$ read by a user u (her history). The corresponding context tree is depicted in Figure 1. A new user v with the browsing sequence $\mathbf{s}_v = \langle n_2, n_3 \rangle$ matches 3 contexts in that tree: the root context $\langle \rangle$ corresponding to an empty history, the context matching $\langle n_3 \rangle$ which corresponds to the latest read story by user v and the context matching $\langle n_3, n_2 \rangle$ corresponding to the complete history of user v.

Each context has a local prediction model. For instance, a particular model gives recommendations only for users who have read a particular sequence of stories, or users who have read an article that was sufficiently close to a particular topic distribution. We consider three possible models. The first model, called *std*, ignores the temporal dynamics. The second model, called *pop*, assumes that users are mainly looking at popular items, and the last model, called *fresh*, that they are interested in recent stories.

Recommendations are made by mixing the predictions of each local model for the given matching contexts. If a context is making poor recommendations, the CT recommender system decreases its influence by adjusting automatically the weight of the considered context.

A CT recommender system fits better the dynamic domain of news recommendations because it adapts its model to current trends and reader preferences. The model for recommendations changes along with the read articles, using a dynamically evolving context tree. In that way, the model is always up to date and recommendations are generated in real-time. In addition, CT recommender systems require only one tree and thus scales very well. They are not restricted to the history of logged-in users, but considers a one-time session for recommendation, where users do not log in.

Thanks to offline evaluations, we have shown that there is a trade-off between accuracy and novelty of recommendations, and CT recommender systems address it. In this work, we would like to explore how CT recommender systems perform on a live traffic website and how they compare to standard baselines. Thus, in addition to CT recommender systems, we consider the following baselines:

Most Popular recommends a set of stories with the highest number of clicks among the last read news items. This strategy is commonly implemented on most news websites. It does not recommend any new items, but only the ones that a reader would have already seen on the front page.

Random recommends a set of stories at random. This strategy has the advantage of recommending very diverse and potentially novel items.

There exist many news recommender systems [1, 2, 3, 10, 14], however we decided to select only these baselines for the following reasons. First, the most popular and random strategies are de-facto standards, very easy to implement and compare performance. Researchers can easily compare their results to ours relative to these baselines. Second, reproducing previous research takes time and correctly implementing an existing approach is tricky, even if it is well described. Third, most of these algorithms have not been tested on live traffic websites and thus there is no guarantee of scalability and real-time requirements. Last, we need to limit ourselves to compare simultaneously 3 to 4 algorithms. More algorithms would dilute the clicks and would not guarantee statistical significance of the evaluation.

4. EVALUATIONS

Since July 2013, we are evaluating CT-based recommender systems with live traffic on the news website *swissinfo.ch*. swissinfo.ch is a 10-language news website owned by the Swiss Broadcasting Corporation. Its content is produced specifically for an international audience with interests in Switzerland. swissinfo.ch gives priority to in-depth information on politics, society, business, culture and science & technology. It has about 3.9 million clicks per month. We have deployed recommendations only on the English version of the website.

All recommender systems are deployed with the PEN recsys framework [8], specifically designed to conduct multivariate online evaluation of news recommender systems.

With the online evaluation, we want to address the following questions:

QUESTION 1. *Do context-tree recommender systems bring an improvement in click-through rate over baseline methods?*

QUESTION 2. *Do recommendations in general, and recommendations made by context-tree systems in particular, increase the page views by the user on the news website?*

QUESTION 3. *Among all CT-based recommender systems, which version and set of parameters are optimal?*

The answers to these questions are not trivial, and are specific to each website. Similar to our study, the results and conclusion of the evaluation on Forbes.com [12] are unique to this website. In addition, the reasons behind each study are not the same.

Before conducting a live evaluation, we evaluated the behaviour of recommender systems on an offline dataset in order to forecast which methods would work the best and understand how the parameters influence the performance.

4.1 Offline

Only a small set of recommender systems can be evaluated on a live website, and it has to be carefully selected. An offline evaluation helps us to select the recommender systems and their parameters that are the most likely to bring good recommendations on swissinfo.ch. To do so, we had access to a 3-weeks "recommendations-free" clicks log from swissinfo.ch. During these 3 weeks, the swissinfo.ch website did not have any recommender systems deployed such as popularity-based methods ("top 10 popular items"). The log contains 227'831 clicks on 28'525 stories.

There has been a lot of discussion on the best way of evaluating recommender systems [9, 21]. For our offline evaluation, we use visit histories from the swissinfo.ch website, and

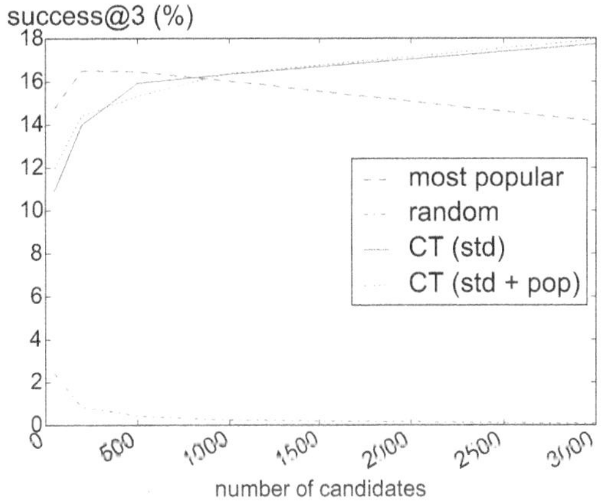

Figure 2: Offline *predicted* accuracy for different sizes of candidate set.

we can evaluate how well our recommendations match the news items that readers selected themselves. It is clear that this is a somewhat inaccurate measure: *a)* the user may not have liked all the items she visited; *b)* the user may have preferred one of the recommended items to the one she clicked, so the fact that a recommended item was not visited does not mean the recommendation is bad. However, it is common in recommender systems research to use the prediction of the visit history to *compare* the performance of different techniques, and select parameters for the live evaluation.

For a given recommender system and some fixed set of parameters, we imitated the online environment by sending clicks in the same sequence as saved in the log to the PEN recsys framework, and recorded the performance. Based on the articles last read by the user, the recommender system generates 3 recommendations. The recommendation is successful if one of these three recommendations is indeed the one that the user reads next, a measure we call *success@3*. While there are many different metrics to assess the performance of a recommender systems [5, 9], we focus on this metric because it can also be measured online and thus allows a comparison.

In addition to the baselines that recommend most popular and random items, we implemented a context-tree system with the *std* model, and one with a mixture of *std* and *pop* models. We were not able to add the *fresh* model because the log does not contain information about freshness.

Figure 2 illustrates the predicted accuracy for various sizes of the candidate set. When the number of candidates increases, the performance of the random strategy drops because interesting stories are diluted in the set. There is an optimal size for recommending the most popular items around 200 candidates. Increasing the number of candidates after this point does not improve the performance for the most popular strategy. However, CT recommender systems take advantage of more candidates to bring better recommendations. In the rest of the evaluations, we decided to pursue a conservative approach where we select parameters such that baselines are optimal, and we pick 200 as size of candidate set. This conservative choice of parameters is not in favour of CT recommenders but in that way, the performance of CT recommenders can only be improved. Note

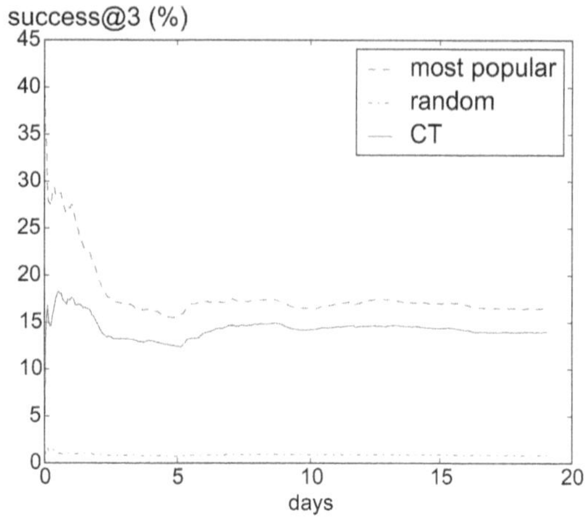

(a) Offline *predicted* accuracy

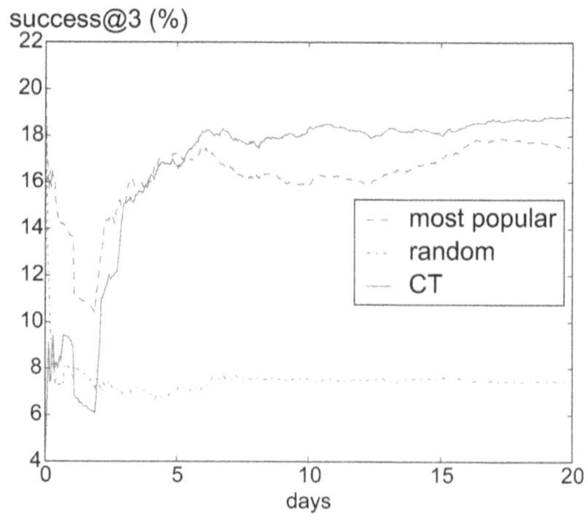

(b) Online *actual* accuracy

Figure 3: Accuracy of online (bootstrap + phase 1) and offline evaluations.

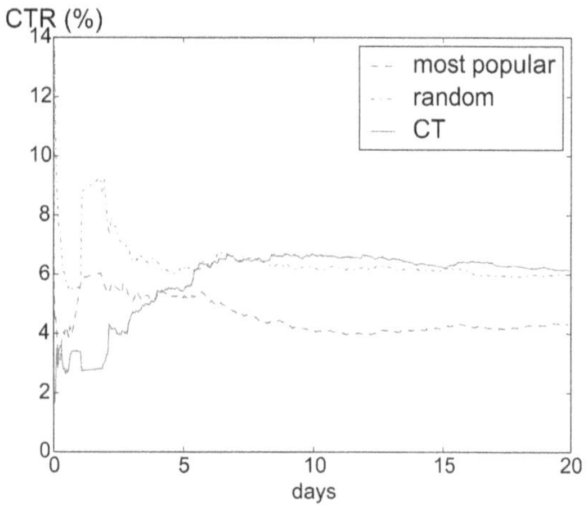

Figure 4: Online *actual* CTR (bootstrap + phase 1).

that although the websites are not the same, the behaviour of these recommender systems is similar than the one reported in our previous research [7].

Figure 3(a) shows the predicted accuracy over time. In this figure, we only implemented the *std* model in the CT recommender as it performs equally good as when we add the popular model. It takes about one week to stabilize the performance. As expected [7], recommending the most popular items outperforms other strategies. The random strategy is the poorest with an accuracy close to 1%.

4.2 Online

The online evaluation is split in two phases where we test different strategies against each other. The first phase consists of comparing a standard context-tree system against the baselines in terms of click-through rate (Question 1) and page views (Question 2). The second phase investigates different versions of CT recommender systems (Question 3). The recommenders together received 172'013 clicks on 10'653 stories in the first phase and 285'572 clicks on 10'830 stories in the second phase.

For each evaluation phase, we bootstrapped the recommender systems during one week, and evaluated them on the next two weeks. We estimated this time frame based on the previous offline evaluation, the expected traffic volume, and the time required to learn the model. It is crucial to run as many methods as possible in parallel to avoid biases in the evaluation due to trends and variations in the candidate set. However, we had to split the evaluation because we could not run more than 4 recommender systems in parallel in order to get statistical significant results.

The PEN recsys framework assigned randomly one recommender system to each visit, performing a multivariate evaluation. Note that visits are anonymous and we were not able to track a user across multiple visits. For all recommender systems, the candidate set was composed of the last 200 clicked items and 30 fresh items. We chose these conservative parameters based on our previous offline analysis. When a recommender system receives one click, it returns 3 recommendations.

4.2.1 Phase 1

For the first phase, we selected the context-tree recommender system with the standard model. For the baselines, we implemented the strategies that recommend the most popular stories and that recommend stories at random.

We evaluate the online performance by two different measures. Figure 3(b) shows the percentage of times that the 3 recommendations contain the article the user reads next, whether through a click on the recommendation or somewhere else. It is thus analogous to the success@3 metric used in the offline setting. Figure 4 shows the click-through rate, i.e. the percentage of times that the user clicked on a recommended article. The click-through rate is a widely used metric for evaluating success of recommendation, in particular in online advertising.

First consider the click-through rate (Figure 4). We can observe a reversal of the relative performance in comparison with the offline prediction. The strategy of recommending most popular articles performs the poorest by barely reaching a CTR of 4%. However, the CTR of the random strategy is now comparable to the one of the CT recommender, and it takes about 7 days for the CT recommender to reach the same CTR. Note that Figure 4 also illustrates nicely the time required (bootstrap phase) by the context-tree system to learn the behaviour of the users.

Now consider the success@3 measure (Figure 3(a) and Figure 3(b)). In contrast to the click-through rate, it measures the actual change that the recommender system brings to the user's behaviour, since it measures how recommendation influences the articles actually read. We observe that for the strategy of recommending the most popular items, the success rate increases by about 1% from 16.5 to 17.5%. Thus, about three quarters of the 4% clicks generated by the recommendation come at the expense of clicks that the user would have made elsewhere, and there is little use of having the recommender at all. This supports criticism by Zheng at al. [23] that the click-through rate for popular items is inflated by their popularity.

In contrast, for the CT recommender, readership of the recommended articles is increased by 5% from 14 to almost 19%. Here, about 5/6 of the 6% clicks on the recommendations actually increase readership of the recommended articles, and the recommender has more significant use. Even more remarkable is that recommending at random has an even bigger increase of the success rate from about 1% to over 7%, so here all of the 6% clicks actually go to increasing readership on the site.

The fact that random recommendations perform better than the recommender system is disturbing but actually explained by the fact that most users have a very short visit history (see Figure 5) and thus do not allow the recommender to make intelligent recommendations. Figure 6 shows the click-through rate per recommender system and over the length of the visit. Context-tree recommenders slightly outperform the baseline methods in general. When the visits are very short (exactly 2 articles), recommending random stories hardly increases the click-through rate (7.7%). However, for medium and long visits, the context-tree system greatly improves the CTR. For medium-length visits, the CT system has a 10.8% CTR while the random baseline is at 8.9%. For long visits, CT system is at 13.1% while the random baseline is at 9.7%. The strategy of recommending the most popular articles is definitely not the best solution: regardless of the visit length, the click-through rate stays below 7%. This is probably because users will have already read these stories elsewhere. Note that the click-through rate increases with visit length since the visitors with a longer history are also more interested users that click more in general.

When the visit length increases, CT recommenders outperform baseline methods because they take advantage of the personalized sequence of each user to create an accurate profile. No matter what the user's interest is, the baseline strategies will always perform the same. Overall, context-tree recommender system brings an 11% improvement over recommending random items, and more than a 20% improvement when considering medium to long visits (21% and 35% for medium and long visits respectively).

Another way of measuring the impact of a recommender system is to consider the influence on the average visit length as measured by the number of articles read by a user (Question 2). We break the visits into two groups: visits containing at least one click on a recommendation, and visits without any click on recommendations. Table 1 summarizes

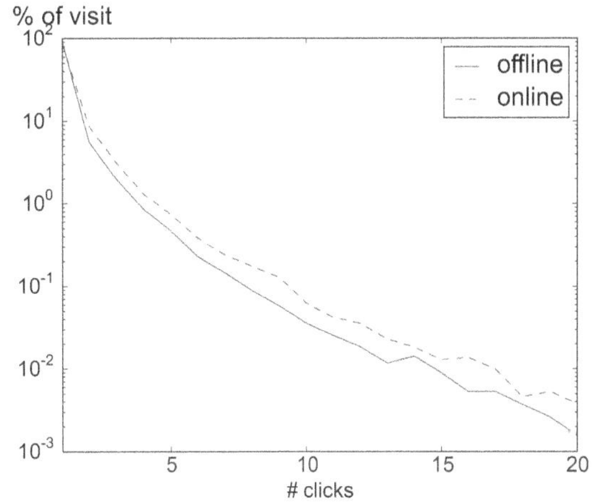

Figure 5: Distribution of visit length (in percent of the total number of visits) for online and offline evaluations.

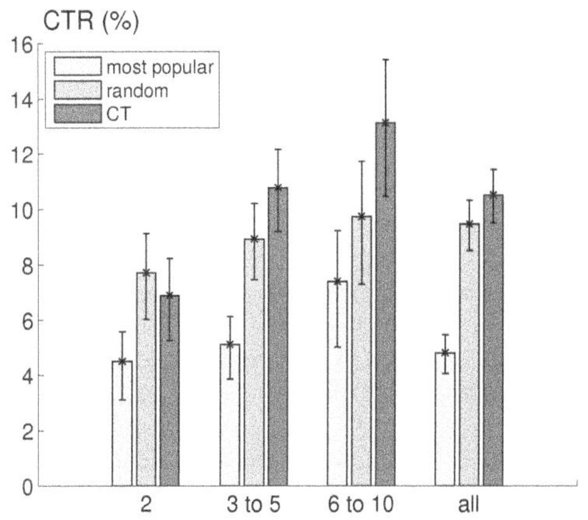

Figure 6: Online *actual* CTR over visit length, with confidence intervals at 95%.

our findings. The length of the visits without taking a recommendation averages 1.25 clicks, while visits with at least one click on a recommendations tripled, with an overall average at 3.75 clicks.

Most sessions are very short (Figure 5). Users reach the swissinfo.ch website through a search engine or a news aggregator, read one article, and leave. If we remove such behaviour by considering visits of length at least 3, the visit length increases by about 1 click, from 4.31 to 5.22 clicks. 90.4% of the visits have only one click, while with recommendations it drops to 85.0% of the visits. It is possible that users who click on recommendations are more likely to have longer visits. Since we are not tracking the users, but only their current session, it is difficult to answer this question. In Forbes.com for instance, this tendency has been observed [12].

4.2.2 *Phase 2*

In the second phase, where we compare different versions of CT recommenders (Question 3), the overall click-through rate of recommendations was slightly lower than during the

Table 1: average visit length with and without recommendations

Recommender system	w/o recommendations	w/ recommendations
Most Popular	1.25	3.36
Random	1.25	3.93
CT	1.25	**3.96**

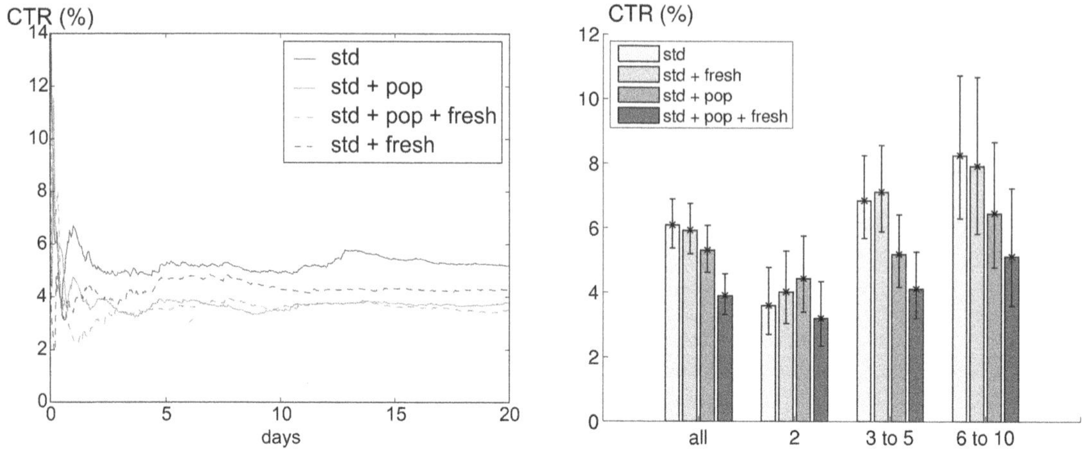

(a) bootstrap + phase 2

(b) Phase 2 only, with confidence intervals at 95%.

Figure 7: Online *actual* CTR of different mixtures of experts for phase 2.

first phase at 5.0%. Figure 7 illustrates the click-through rate with different mixtures of models. Again, we need a bootstrap phase of about one week until the model is correctly learnt. Incorporating the popularity model decreases the click-through rate, except when the visit is very short. This is not surprising since users with a very short visit are mostly interested in what is displayed on the main page of the website, thus reinforcing popular stories. However, when the length increases, users are no longer interested in popular stories. It is not clear whether the fresh model improves recommendations. However, this might be due to the fact that the number of fresh items considered here (30) is not optimal. We believe that tuning this parameter will improve the accuracy of recommenders with the fresh model.

5. DISCUSSION

In this section, we discuss the discrepancies between offline and online evaluation, and important factors that influence directly the recommendations.

5.1 Online vs Offline

We used the offline evaluation to select the recommender systems and their parameters that could most likely generate good recommendations in a live environment. However, the difference between online and offline evaluations is striking (Figure 3). In the offline setting, it is difficult to do better than recommending most popular articles because the recommendations do not directly influence the users. This method mimics the best the behaviour of the readers when no recommender systems are in place because items on the front page attract the most clicks. In the live evaluation, the popularity-based strategy is clearly not the most interesting because users do not want to read articles they have already seen on the front page.

Some recommender systems could have been ruled out of the live trial due to their poor performance during the offline evaluation. However, the conclusion would not have been the same in a live setting [19]. Almost all research in the recommender systems literature is based on offline evaluation with the assumption that it would at least reflect the relative performance of different techniques. However, at least in this case this turns out to be wrong.

The next step would be to study the relationship of recommendation performance to other criteria such as diversity and novelty. We define novelty as the fraction of recommended articles that are not among the most popular items. The CT recommender used here achieves a novelty of about 50% [7], whereas the random strategy is at almost 100% and the most popular strategy is at 0%. Thus, a combination of offline accuracy and novelty can predict the true relative performance of the different strategies from offline data. As the system runs longer, we plan to gather more data with different recommendation strategies to firm up what this relation may be.

5.2 Click-through Rate

Although there exist many metrics [9, 21] to assess the performance of a recommender system, the click-through rate is a de-facto standard in the industry because it is often correlated to the revenues generated by the news website. Indeed, these revenues come from either advertisements (ads) displayed on the website or paid articles (or sometimes both). In general for online advertisement, there are two revenue models: pay per impression or pay per click. With the former, the news website receives monetary compensation for displaying ads while with the latter every time a user clicks on the ad. In all cases, news websites are incentivized in increasing page views. So one way to justify the perfor-

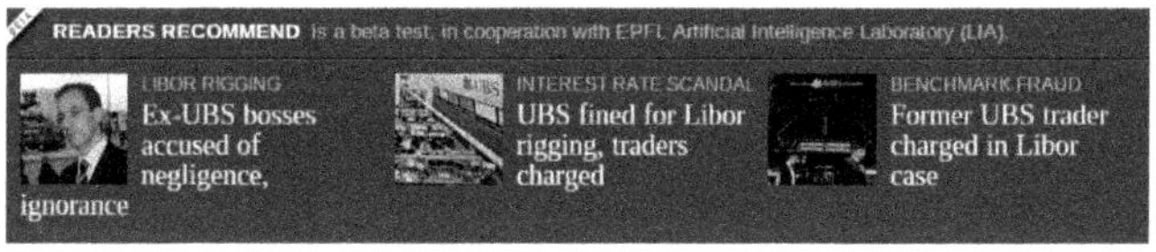

(a) bottom (stories and tickers)

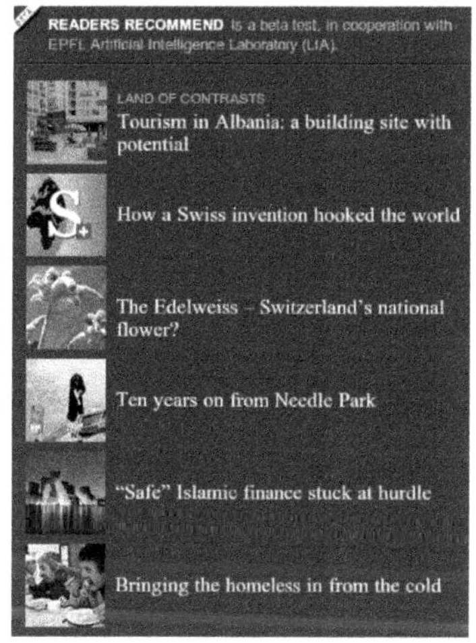

(b) top right (only tickers)

Figure 8: swissinfo.ch's dynamic recommendation boxes: bottom and top-right position. Note that the number of recommendations is not the same.

mance of a recommender system is through its generated revenue, or click-through rate.

Zheng et al. [23] suggest that CTR might not be the optimal metric for online evaluation, because some of the clicks are for popular items that people would have chosen anyway. We have observed the same phenomenon here: recommending popular items not only results in a lower than expected CTR, but an even lower increase in the number of reads.

We believe that rather than CTR, it would be better to measure the actual difference in success@k rates between offline and online evaluations. This measure would unequivocally indicate the net effect of using the recommender system on website performance, although it may be more complex to implement as a business model.

5.3 Page Layout

A recommender system is a small piece of a bigger and complex environment. In our case, we have little to no control over the other elements of the environment in particular the placement of the recommendations on the page and possible interference with manually-generated recommendations that were also shown on the same page in a more prominent position and may overlap with the ones generated by the recommender systems.

The layout of the page is extremely important [16, 4]. On swissinfo.ch, most of the news stories are long and do not fit on the displayed area of the screen. Thus, the placement of recommendations on the page plays an important role in drawing users' attention. When recommendations are placed at the bottom of the article, users need to scroll down the page to see the recommendation box (Figure 8), and we believe that users tend not to read articles down to the end.

We were able to conduct a simple A/B evaluation regarding the placement of the recommendations on one part of the swissinfo.ch website. We compared the performance with the same recommendations but placed in different positions on the page: top right and bottom. The top-right version allows us to display more recommendations (6 stories) than the bottom version (3 stories, see Figure 8). Figure 9 illustrates the difference in click-through rate between the two

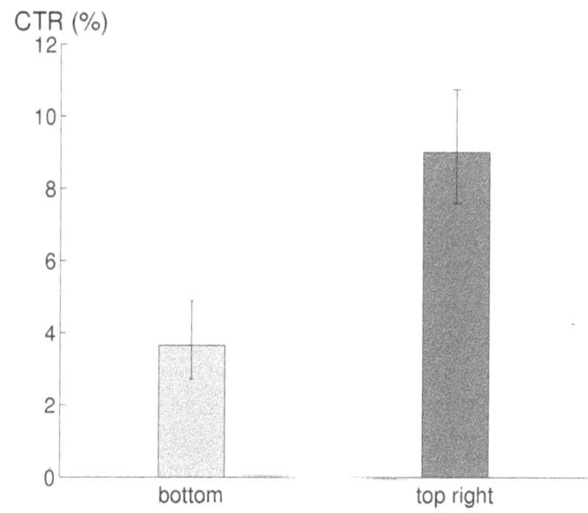

Figure 9: Online *actual* CTR on tickers for the two different placements, with confidence intervals at 95%.

placements. When the recommendations are at the top-right corner of the page, the CTR is more than double (2.25) the one at the bottom. Hence, displaying recommendations at the top-right is significantly (χ^2-test with $p < 0.01$) better than at the bottom. The placement might not be the only reason of this improvement. The width of the page limits the bottom recommendation box to only three items, while the top-right version contains 6 recommendations. So the larger choice available to the user might also play a role. An easy way to verify this claim would be to place the bottom version at the top of the page. Incorporating aspects of the page layout into the recommender algorithm could also improve the performance [13].

Another issue that has a major impact on performance are other recommendations generated by journalists and placed on the same page. They take into account only the current article, but not the history and preferences of the reader. For technical reasons, we have no access to these recommendations and they may thus overlap with the ones generated automatically. As they are placed in a more prominent position on the page, they would draw clicks away from our recommendations. Thus, our evaluation might underestimate the correct click-through rate because of this bias.

6. CONCLUSION

We implemented a novel recommendation technique based on context trees [7, 8] on the news website *swissinfo.ch*. In a live evaluation, we demonstrated that context-tree recommender systems significantly improved the click-through rate by up to 35% and the visit length by a factor of 2.5, with the best performance for users with long enough visits to reveal their preferences. The absolute performance is somewhat impaired by the poor placement of the recommendation and lack of coordination with manual recommendations on the same site, factors which we could not influence.

Besides the confirmation of the actual performance, an important message for recommender systems research is that offline evaluations of accuracy are not always meaningful for predicting the relative performance of different techniques. In our experience, the ranking of techniques in a live environment is the inverse of what it is in the offline evaluation. Thus, better models incorporating novelty are needed.

A second important lesson concerns the value of the CTR as a measure of performance. As in some earlier studies [23], we showed that the CTR overestimates the actual impact for popular items, and thus gives a skewed impression of the actual performance. Only comparing the actual article views can give a true picture of actual performance.

Finally, we observed that the placement of recommendations is important for the click-through rate and should be carefully selected when deploying recommendations on a live website. Placing the recommendations at the top of the page more than doubled the CTR than at the bottom.

With the live evaluation, we plan to refine the users' profile by tracing users across multiple visits, and enhance their profile with socio-demographic data. We believe that algorithms will benefit by incorporating information from the manual recommendations as well. By doing so, we would avoid duplicated recommendations in both manual and dynamic lists. We intend to blend the recommendations into the page design and change their positions to a more visible place. Finally, an interesting future direction would be to consider not only news articles, but also video and audio.

7. REFERENCES

[1] J. Ahn, P. Brusilovsky, J. Grady, and D. He. Open user profiles for adaptive news systems: help or harm? In *Conf. on WWW*, pages 11–20, 2007.

[2] D. Billsus and M. Pazzani. A hybrid user model for news story classification. In *Conf. on User Modeling*, pages 99–108, 1999.

[3] R. Burke. Hybrid recommender systems: Survey and experiments. *User Modeling and User-Adapted Interaction*, 12:331–370, November 2002.

[4] L. Chen and P. Pu. Eye-tracking study of user behavior in recommender interfaces. In *User Modeling, Adaptation, and Personalization*, pages 375–380, 2010.

[5] P. Cremonesi, Y. Koren, and R. Turrin. Performance of recommender algorithms on top-n recommendation tasks. In *Conf. on Rec. Systems*, pages 39–46, 2010.

[6] A. Das, M. Datar, A. Garg, and S. Rajaram. Google news personalization: scalable online collaborative filtering. In *Conf. on WWW*, pages 271–280, 2007.

[7] F. Garcin, C. Dimitrakakis, and B. Faltings. Personalized news recommendation with context trees. In *Conf. on Rec. Systems*, pages 105–112, 2013.

[8] F. Garcin and B. Faltings. Pen recsys: A personalized news recommender systems framework. In *Conf. on Rec. Systems*, pages 469–470, 2013.

[9] J. Herlocker, J. Konstan, L. Terveen, and J. Riedl. Evaluating collaborative filtering recommender systems. *Trans. on Info. Systems*, 22:5–53, 2004.

[10] W. IJntema, F. Goossen, F. Frasincar, and F. Hogenboom. Ontology-based news recommendation. In *Workshop on Data Semantics*, page 16, 2010.

[11] B. Kille, F. Hopfgartner, T. Brodt, and T. Heintz. The plista dataset. In *News Recommender Systems Workshop*, pages 16–23, 2013.

[12] E. Kirshenbaum, G. Forman, and M. Dugan. A live comparison of methods for personalized article recommendation at forbes.com. In *ECML - PKDD*, pages 51–66, 2012.

[13] K. Lerman and T. Hogg. Using a model of social dynamics to predict popularity of news. In *Conf. on WWW*, pages 621–630, 2010.

[14] L. Li, W. Chu, J. Langford, and R. Schapire. A contextual-bandit approach to personalized news article recommendation. In *Conf. on WWW*, pages 661–670, 2010.

[15] J. Liu, P. Dolan, and E. Pedersen. Personalized news recommendation based on click behavior. In *Proc. of IUI*, pages 31–40, 2010.

[16] P. Pu, L. Chen, and R. Hu. A user-centric evaluation framework for recommender systems. In *Conf. on Rec. Systems*, pages 157–164, 2011.

[17] P. Resnick, N. Iacovou, M. Suchak, P. Bergstrom, and J. Riedl. Grouplens: an open architecture for collaborative filtering of netnews. In *CSCW*, pages 175–186, 1994.

[18] A. Said, A. Bellogin, J. Lin, and A. de Vries. Do recommendations matter?: News recommendation in real life. In *CSCW*, pages 237–240, 2014.

[19] A. Said, B. Fields, B. Jain, and S. Albayrak. User-centric evaluation of a k-furthest neighbor collaborative filtering recommender algorithm. In *CSCW*, pages 1399–1408, 2013.

[20] A. Said, J. Lin, A. Bellogin, and A. de Vries. A month in the life of a production news recommender system. In *Workshop on Living Labs for Information Retrieval Evaluation*, pages 7–10, 2013.

[21] G. Shani and A. Gunawardana. Evaluating recommendation systems. In *Recommender Systems Handbook*, pages 257–297. Springer, 2011.

[22] M. Tavakolifard, J. Gulla, K. Almeroth, F. Hopfgartner, B. Kille, T. Plumbaum, A. Lommatzsch, T. Brodt, A. Bucko, and T. Heintz. Workshop and challenge on news recommender systems. In *Conf. on Rec. Systems*, pages 481–482, 2013.

[23] H. Zheng, D. Wang, Q. Zhang, H. Li, and T. Yang. Do clicks measure recommendation relevancy?: an empirical user study. In *Conf. on Rec. Systems*, pages 249–252, 2010.

Unifying Nearest Neighbors Collaborative Filtering

Koen Verstrepen
Bart Goethals
University of Antwerp
Antwerp, Belgium
{koen.verstrepen,bart.goethals}@uantwerp.be

ABSTRACT

We study collaborative filtering for applications in which there exists for every user a set of items about which the user has given binary, positive-only feedback (one-class collaborative filtering). Take for example an on-line store that knows all past purchases of every customer. An important class of algorithms for one-class collaborative filtering are the nearest neighbors algorithms, typically divided into user-based and item-based algorithms. We introduce a reformulation that unifies user- and item-based nearest neighbors algorithms and use this reformulation to propose a novel algorithm that incorporates the best of both worlds and outperforms state-of-the-art algorithms. Additionally, we propose a method for naturally explaining the recommendations made by our algorithm and show that this method is also applicable to existing user-based nearest neighbors methods.

Categories and Subject Descriptors: H.3.3 [Information Storage and Retrieval]: Information filtering

Keywords: One-class collaborative filtering, nearest neighbors, explaining recommendations, top-N recommendation, recommender systems.

1. INTRODUCTION

Typically, the training data for collaborative filtering is represented by a matrix in which the rows represent the users and the columns represent the items. A value in this matrix can be unknown or can reflect the preference of the respective user for the respective item. Here, we consider the specific setting of binary, positive-only preference feedback. Hence, every value in the preference matrix is 1 or 0, with 1 representing a known preference and 0 representing the unknown. Pan et al. [10] call this setting one-class collaborative filtering (OCCF). Applications that correspond to this version of the collaborative filtering problem are likes on social networking sites, tags for photo's, websites visited during a surfing session, articles bought by a customer etc.

RecSys'14, October 6–10, 2014, Foster City, Silicon Valley, CA, USA.
Copyright 2014 ACM 978-1-4503-2668-1/14/10 ...$15.00.
http://dx.doi.org/10.1145/2645710.2645731.

In this setting, identifying the best recommendations can be formalized as ranking all user-item-pairs (u, i) according to the probability that u prefers i.

One class of algorithms for solving OCCF are the nearest neighbors algorithms. Sarwar et al. [13] proposed the well known user-based algorithm that uses cosine similarity and Deshpande et al. [2] proposed several widely used item-based algorithms.

Another class of algorithms for solving OCCF are matrix factorization algorithms. The state-of-the-art algorithms in this class are Weighted Rating Matrix Factorization [7, 10], Bayesian Personalized Ranking Matrix Factorization [12] and Collaborative Less is More Filtering [14].

This work builds upon the different item-based algorithms by Deshpande et al. [2] and the user-based algorithm by Sarwar et al. [13] that uses cosine similarity. We introduce a reformulation of these algorithms that unifies their existing formulations. From this reformulation, it becomes clear that the existing user- and item-based algorithms unnecessarily discard important parts of the available information. Therefore, we propose a novel algorithm that combines both user- and item-based information. Hence, this algorithm is neither user-based nor item-based, but *nearest-neighbors-based*. Our experiments show that our algorithm not only outperforms the individual nearest neighbors algorithms but also state-of-the-art matrix factorization algorithms.

Furthermore, it is well accepted that every recommendation should come with a short explanation to why it is recommended [7, 6]. Good explanations help users to put the recommendations in the right perspective [17]. Typically, item-based nearest neighbors algorithms are considered to be superior for this task [3, 7].

Thanks to our reformulation however, we are able to challenge this belief and show that also other nearest neighbors algorithms have a natural explanation.

The main contributions of this work are:

- We propose a reformulation that unifies user-and item-based nearest neighbors algorithms for OCCF (Sec. 3) [13, 2].
- We propose KUNN, a novel algorithm for OCCF that is grounded in our unifying reformulation (Sec. 4).
- We extensively evaluate our algorithm on real life data and show that it outperforms state-of-the-art algorithms (Sec. 5).
- We propose a method that naturally explains the recommendations by our novel algorithm and user-based algorithms (Sec. 6)

2. PRELIMINARIES

Let $\mathcal{U}$ be a set of users and $\mathcal{I}$ a set of items. We are given a matrix with training data $\mathbf{R} \in \{0,1\}^{|\mathcal{U}|\times|\mathcal{I}|}$. $\mathbf{R}_{ui} = 1$ indicates that there is a known preference of user $u \in \mathcal{U}$ for item $i \in \mathcal{I}$. $\mathbf{R}_{ui} = 0$ indicates that there is no such information.

Furthermore, $c(x)$ gives the count of x, meaning

$$c(x) = \begin{cases} \sum_{i\in\mathcal{I}} R_{xi} & \text{if } x \in \mathcal{U} \\ \sum_{u\in\mathcal{U}} R_{ux} & \text{if } x \in \mathcal{I}. \end{cases}$$

The goal of OCCF is to rank all user-item-pairs (u, i) for which $\mathbf{R}_{ui} = 0$ according to the likelihood of u preferring i. The most well known algorithms perform this task by computing for every user-item-pair (u, i) a score $s(u, i)$, by which the user-item-pairs are then ranked.

A key element of nearest neighbors algorithms is their definition of the neighborhood of an object, or more specifically, the similarity measure $sim()$ used for computing it. A typical choice for $sim()$ is the cosine similarity. The cosine similarity between two users u and v is given by

$$cos(u, v) = \frac{\sum_{j\in\mathcal{I}} \mathbf{R}_{uj}\mathbf{R}_{vj}}{\sqrt{c(u)c(v)}}. \tag{1}$$

Analogously, the cosine similarity between two items i and j is given by

$$cos(i, j) = \frac{\sum_{v\in\mathcal{U}} \mathbf{R}_{vi}\mathbf{R}_{vj}}{\sqrt{c(i)c(j)}}. \tag{2}$$

We denote the $k_{\mathcal{U}}$ ($k_{\mathcal{I}}$) nearest neighbors of a user u (an item i) by $KNN(u)$ ($KNN(i)$).

3. UNIFYING NEAREST NEIGHBORS

In this section we propose a novel formulation of nearest neighbors collaborative filtering that unifies the known formulations of the user-based algorithm by Sarwar et al. [13] and the different item-based algorithms by Deshpande et al. [2]. This formulation is given by

$$s(u, i) = \sum_{v\in\mathcal{U}} \sum_{j\in\mathcal{I}} (\mathcal{L} \cdot \mathcal{N} \cdot \mathcal{G} \cdot \mathcal{S})\left((u, i), (v, j)\right). \tag{3}$$

The score $s(u, i)$, that represents the likelihood that a user u prefers an item i, is computed as a weighted sum over all possible user-item pairs (v, j). The weight of every (v, j)-pair with respect to the pair (u, i) is a multiplication of four functions: the local function $\mathcal{L}\left((u, i), (v, j)\right)$, the neighborhood function $\mathcal{N}\left((u, i), (v, j)\right)$, the global function $\mathcal{G}\left((u, i), (v, j)\right)$ and the rescaling function $\mathcal{S}\left((u, i), (v, j)\right)$.

Before giving a general definition of $\mathcal{L}, \mathcal{N}, \mathcal{G}$ and $\mathcal{S}$, we first discuss the reformulation of the user-based algorithm by Sarwar et al. [13] and the different item-based algorithms by Deshpande et al. [2].

3.1 Item-Based

Deshpande et al. [2] proposed the now widely used class of item-based nearest neighbors algorithms. We discuss the variation that uses cosine similarity without similarity normalization (*cosine, SNorm-*) because of its clean formulation. The analysis for the other variations is analogous.

This algorithm first finds the neighborhood $KNN(j)$ for every preferred item j ($\mathbf{R}_{uj} = 1$) by using the cosine similarity $cos(j, i)$. Next, every preferred item independently increases the score for its $k_{\mathcal{I}}$ most similar items $i \in KNN(j)$ with the similarity value $cos(j, i)$. Thus, the score of a candidate recommendation i for user u is given by [2]:

$$s(u, i) = \sum_{\substack{j\in\mathcal{I} \\ \mathbf{R}_{uj}=1}} cos(j, i) \cdot |KNN(j) \cap \{i\}|. \tag{4}$$

We reformulate this algorithm by substituting $cos(j, i)$ by its definition (Eq. 2) and regrouping the terms. This gives

$$s(u, i) = \sum_{v\in\mathcal{U}} \sum_{j\in\mathcal{I}} \mathbf{R}_{uj}\mathbf{R}_{vj}\mathbf{R}_{vi} \cdot |KNN(j) \cap \{i\}| \cdot \frac{1}{\sqrt{c(j)c(i)}}.$$

This particular formulation now nicely fits our Equation 3: a weighted sum over all possible user-item pairs (v, j) in which the weight of every (v, j)-pair with respect to the pair (u, i) is determined by the functions $\mathcal{L}, \mathcal{N}, \mathcal{G}$ and $\mathcal{S}$.

The local function $\mathcal{L}$ selects the pairs (v, j) based on their direct relation to the pair (u, i). For the item-based algorithm, it is given by

$$\mathcal{L}\left((u, i), (v, j)\right) = \mathbf{R}_{uj}\mathbf{R}_{vj}\mathbf{R}_{vi}.$$

It thus only selects those pairs (v, j) such that v and u share a preference for j and both i and j are preferred by v.

Next, the neighborhood function $\mathcal{N}$ further selects the pairs (v, j) based on their neighborhood relations to the pair (u, i). For the item-based algorithm, it is given by

$$\mathcal{N}\left((u, i), (v, j)\right) = |KNN(j) \cap \{i\}|.$$

Thus, only those pairs (v, j) for which i is in the neighborhood of j are selected. Notice that the selection of the pair (v, j) by $\mathcal{N}$ is independent of v. As such, the item-based algorithm ignores half of the neighborhood information about the pair (v, j).

Then, the global function $\mathcal{G}$ weighs the selected pairs (v, j) based on global statistics of the items i and j. For the item-based algorithm, it is given by

$$\mathcal{G}\left((u, i), (v, j)\right) = 1/\sqrt{c(i)c(j)}.$$

It thus gives lower weights to those pairs (v, j) for which j has a higher count. Intuitively, if j is more popular, the evidence related to the pair (v, j) is considered less informative. Similarly, if i is more popular, all evidence with respect to $s(u, i)$ is considered less informative. Notice that, in this case, also the weight of the pair (v, j), as determined by $\mathcal{G}$, is independent of v. As such, the item-based algorithm ignores $c(v)$ and $c(u)$, the global information about v and u. Notice furthermore that $\mathcal{G}$ is also used in the definition of the cosine similarity measure (Eq. 2), used to determine $KNN(j)$.

As in this case no rescaling is applied, $\mathcal{S}$ is given by

$$\mathcal{S}\left((u, i), (v, j)\right) = 1.$$

3.2 User-Based

For a given user u, the user-based nearest neighbors algorithm by Sarwar et al. [13] first finds the neighborhood $KNN(u)$ using the cosine similarity. Next, each neighboring user $v \in KNN(u)$ increases the score of a candidate recommendation i, if i is preferred by v. Thus, the score of a candidate recommendation i for user u is given by [13]:

$$s(u, i) = \frac{1}{|KNN(u)|} \sum_{v\in KNN(u)} \mathbf{R}_{vi}. \tag{5}$$

Multiplying the above equation with the constant $|\mathcal{I}| = \sum_{j \in \mathcal{I}} 1$ does not change the ordering of the pairs (u, i) and allows us to rewrite it as

$$s(u, i) = \sum_{v \in \mathcal{U}} \sum_{j \in \mathcal{I}} \mathbf{R}_{vi} \cdot |KNN(u) \cap \{v\}| \cdot \frac{1}{|KNN(u)|}.$$

Hence we have reformulated also the user-based algorithm as a weighted sum over all possible user-item pairs (v, j) in which the weight of a (v, j)-pair with respect to the pair (u, i) is determined by the functions $\mathcal{L}, \mathcal{N}, \mathcal{G}$ and $\mathcal{S}$ (Eq. 3).

The local function $\mathcal{L}$, which selects the pairs (v, j) based on their direct relation to the pair (u, i), is for the user-based algorithm given by

$$\mathcal{L}\big((u, i), (v, j)\big) = \mathbf{R}_{vi}.$$

It thus selects those pairs (v, j) such that v prefers i. Unlike the item-based algorithm, it does not consider the information $\mathbf{R}_{uj}$ and $\mathbf{R}_{vj}$ to discriminate between different (v, j)-pairs. Hence, the selection of the pair (v, j) by $\mathcal{L}$ is independent of j. As such, the user-based algorithm ignores local information related to j when weighing the pair (v, j).

Next, the neighborhood function $\mathcal{N}$ further selects the pairs (v, j) based on their neighborhood relations to the pair (u, i). For the user-based algorithm, it is given by

$$\mathcal{N}\big((u, i), (v, j)\big) = |KNN(u) \cap \{v\}|.$$

Thus, only those pairs (v, j) for which v is in the neighborhood of u are selected. Notice that the selection of the pair (v, j) by $\mathcal{N}$ is independent of j. As such, the user-based algorithm ignores half of the neighborhood information about the pair (v, j).

Furthermore, since this algorithm does not weight the pairs (v, j) with any global statistic of u, i, v or j, the global function for the user-based algorithm is given by

$$\mathcal{G}\big((u, i), (v, j)\big) = 1.$$

Finally, for the user-based algorithm, the rescaling function $\mathcal{S}$ rescales the weight of the pairs (v, j) with the size of the neighborhood of u and is therefore given by

$$\mathcal{S}\big((u, i), (v, j)\big) = |KNN(u)|.$$

3.3 Generalization

Now we generalize the definitions of the four functions $\mathcal{L}, \mathcal{N}, \mathcal{G}$ and $\mathcal{S}$ such that our formulation covers the most well known user- and item-based algorithms. Table 1 gives an overview of how these functions are defined for both the existing algorithms and our novel algorithm, which we will propose in the next section.

First, the local function $\mathcal{L}$ selects the pairs (v, j) depending on the direct relations $\mathbf{R}_{ui}$, $\mathbf{R}_{vj}$ and $\mathbf{R}_{vi}$ between (v, j) and (u, i). The user-based algorithm (Sec. 3.2) considers only $\mathbf{R}_{vi}$ and ignores the other information. The item-based algorithm (Sec. 3.1) on the other hand, combines all three pieces of direct information in the multiplication $\mathbf{R}_{ui}\mathbf{R}_{vj}\mathbf{R}_{vi}$, and thus selects those pairs (v, j) such that v and u share a preference for j and both i and j are preferred by v. Essentially, any combination of these direct relationships between u,i,v and j is possible.

Secondly, the neighborhood function $\mathcal{N}$ weighs the pairs (v, j) depending on the neighborhoods $KNN(u)$, $KNN(v)$, $KNN(i)$ and $KNN(j)$. Existing algorithms for OCCF consider only one of the four neighborhoods, as shown in Sections 3.2 and 3.1. Consequently, the weighing function $\mathcal{N}$ reduces to a selection function for these algorithms . However, any function of these four neighborhoods can be used. For example, in our novel algorithm KUNN, which we will propose in Section 4, we use

$$\mathcal{N}\big((u, i), (v, j)\big) = |KNN(u) \cap \{v\}| + |KNN(i) \cap \{j\}|.$$

Both the user- and the item-based algorithm discussed in the previous two sections used the cosine similarity measure to compute $KNN(x)$ of an object x. Our formulation however, covers a broader range of similarity measures. Let $p_u, p_i, p_v, p_j \in \mathbb{R}$. For users $u, v \in \mathcal{U}$, we define the similarity measure to compute $KNN(u)$ as

$$sim(u, v) = \sum_{r_{\mathcal{I}} \in \mathcal{I}} \mathbf{R}_{ur_{\mathcal{I}}} \mathbf{R}_{vr_{\mathcal{I}}} \cdot c(u)^{p_u} c(v)^{p_v} c(r_{\mathcal{I}})^{p_j}. \quad (6)$$

Similarly, for items $i, j \in \mathcal{I}$, we define the similarity measure to compute $KNN(i)$ as

$$sim(i, j) = \sum_{r_{\mathcal{U}} \in \mathcal{U}} \mathbf{R}_{r_{\mathcal{U}}i} \mathbf{R}_{r_{\mathcal{U}}j} \cdot c(i)^{p_i} c(r_{\mathcal{U}})^{p_v} c(j)^{p_j}. \quad (7)$$

Notice that, in our formulation, the similarity between users (Eq. 6) and the similarity between items (Eq. 7) share the parameters p_v and p_j. Thus, choosing the user similarity limits the possibilities for choosing the item similarity and vice versa.

Thirdly, the global function $\mathcal{G}$ uses the global statistics $c(u)$, $c(i)$, $c(v)$ and $c(j)$ to weigh the pairs (v, j) with respect to the pair (u, i). It is given by

$$\mathcal{G}\big((u, i), (v, j)\big) = \Big(c(u)^{p_u} c(i)^{p_i} c(v)^{p_v} c(j)^{p_j}\Big)^{p_g}, \quad (8)$$

with $p_g \in \{0, 1\}$ and p_u, p_i, p_v, p_j the same parameters as in Equations 6 and 7. Typically, these parameters are negative or zero. In that case, users u, v and items i, j with higher counts reduce the weight of the (v, j)-pairs with respect to (u, i). Intuitively, a more popular item is considered less informative for determining a taste, since this item is more likely preferred by diverse users. Similarly, a user that prefers many items is considered less informative for determining a taste, since this user's preferences are more likely to cover diverse items.

Notice that $\mathcal{G}$, $sim(u, v)$ and $sim(i, j)$ (Eq. 8, 7 and 6) share the factors $c(u)^{p_u}$, $c(i)^{p_i}$, $c(v)^{p_v}$ and $c(j)^{p_j}$. Therefore we introduce the notation

$$\mathcal{W}\big((u, i), (v, j)\big) = c(u)^{p_u} c(i)^{p_i} c(v)^{p_v} c(j)^{p_j},$$

which allows us to rewrite the global function (Eq. 8) as

$$\mathcal{G}\big((u, i), (v, j)\big) = \mathcal{W}\big((u, i), (v, j)\big)^{p_g}, \quad (9)$$

and the similarities (Eq. 6 and 7) as

$$sim(u, v) = \sum_{r_{\mathcal{I}} \in \mathcal{I}} \mathbf{R}_{ur_{\mathcal{I}}} \mathbf{R}_{vr_{\mathcal{I}}} \cdot \mathcal{W}\big((u, *), (v, r_{\mathcal{I}})\big),$$

$$sim(i, j) = \sum_{r_{\mathcal{U}} \in \mathcal{U}} \mathbf{R}_{r_{\mathcal{U}}i} \mathbf{R}_{r_{\mathcal{U}}j} \cdot \mathcal{W}\big((*, i), (r_{\mathcal{U}}, j)\big),$$

with $c(*) = 1$. This definition of $\mathcal{W}$ covers both the user-based algorithm by Sarwar et al. [13] and the different item-based algorithms by Deshpande et al. [2]. A more general

Table 1: Function definitions of the unifying formulation for selected algorithms. Our novel algorithm is bold faced and marked with a $\star$.

Algorithm	$\mathcal{L}((u,i),(v,j))$	$\mathcal{N}((u,i),(v,j))$	$\mathcal{S}((u,i),(v,j))$	$\mathcal{W}((u,i),(v,j))$	p_g	$k_{\mathcal{U}}$	$k_{\mathcal{I}}$
user-based, cosine [13]	$\mathbf{R}_{vi}$	$\lvert KNN(u) \cap \{v\}\rvert$	$\mathcal{S}_u(u)$	$\frac{1}{\sqrt{c(u)c(v)}}$	0	$\leq \lvert\mathcal{U}\rvert$	0
item-based, cosine, SNorm- [2]	$\mathbf{R}_{uj}\mathbf{R}_{vj}\mathbf{R}_{vi}$	$\lvert KNN(j) \cap \{i\}\rvert$	1	$\frac{1}{\sqrt{c(i)c(j)}}$	1	0	$\leq \lvert\mathcal{I}\rvert$
item-based, cosine, SNorm+ [2]	$\mathbf{R}_{uj}\mathbf{R}_{vj}\mathbf{R}_{vi}$	$\lvert KNN(j) \cap \{i\}\rvert$	$\mathcal{S}_j(j)$	$\frac{1}{\sqrt{c(i)c(j)}}$	1	0	$\leq \lvert\mathcal{I}\rvert$
$\star$ **KUNN**	$\mathbf{R}_{uj}\mathbf{R}_{vj}\mathbf{R}_{vi}$	$\lvert KNN(u) \cap \{v\}\rvert$ $+\lvert KNN(i) \cap \{j\}\rvert$	1	$\frac{1}{\sqrt{c(u)c(j)c(v)c(i)}}$	1	$\leq \lvert\mathcal{U}\rvert$	$\leq \lvert\mathcal{I}\rvert$

definition of $\mathcal{W}$ would cover a broader range of nearest neighbors algorithms. We choose this definition over a more general one to emphasize the strong similarity between the latter two algorithms.

Finally, some algorithms rescale the weights of the pairs (v,j) with the density of $KNN(u)$, $KNN(i)$, $KNN(v)$ or $KNN(j)$. A neighborhood $KNN(x)$ of x is denser if the total distance of x to its neighbors is smaller. In other words, if the sum of the similarities of x to its neighbors is higher. Depending on the choice for $KNN(u)$, $KNN(i)$, $KNN(v)$ or $KNN(j)$, the rescaling function is given by one of the four density functions

$$\mathcal{S}_u(u) = 1/\sum_{r_{\mathcal{U}} \in KNN(u)} sim(u, r_{\mathcal{U}})^{p_g},$$

$$\mathcal{S}_i(i) = 1/\sum_{r_{\mathcal{I}} \in KNN(i)} sim(i, r_{\mathcal{I}})^{p_g},$$

$$\mathcal{S}_v(v) = 1/\sum_{r_{\mathcal{U}} \in KNN(v)} sim(r_{\mathcal{U}}, v)^{p_g},$$

$$\mathcal{S}_j(j) = 1/\sum_{r_{\mathcal{I}} \in KNN(j)} sim(r_{\mathcal{I}}, j)^{p_g},$$

with p_g the same parameter as for the global function $\mathcal{G}$ (Eq. 9).

For an algorithm that does not apply rescaling,

$$\mathcal{S}((u,i),(v,j)) = 1$$

4. KUNN UNIFIED NEAREST NEIGHBORS

Looking at Table 1, we observe that the user-based algorithm by Sarwar et al. [13] ignores the information $\mathbf{R}_{uj}$, $\mathbf{R}_{vj}$, $c(i)$, $c(j)$, $KNN(i)$ and $KNN(j)$ for weighing the pairs (v,j) with respect to (u,i). Similarly, all item-based algorithms by Deshpande et al. [2] ignore the information $c(u)$, $c(v)$, $KNN(u)$ and $KNN(v)$ for weighing the pairs (v,j) with respect to (u,i). Thus, the existing algorithms ignore an important part of the available information. What is more, the information ignored by item-based algorithms is disjoint with the information ignored by the user-based algorithm. However, the fact that both user- and item-based algorithms generate acceptable results [13, 2], indicates that most likely both types of information are useful. Therefore, a novel algorithm that combines both types of information, KUNN[1], potentially leads to improved results. The experiments discussed in Section 5 confirm that this is indeed the case. It is not only possible to outperform the individual user- and item-based algorithms, but also to outperform state-of-the-art matrix factorization algorithms [12, 7, 10].

[1]KUNN is a recursive acronym for KUNN Unified Nearest Neighbors

The definitions of $\mathcal{L}$, $\mathcal{N}$, $\mathcal{G}$ and $\mathcal{S}$ corresponding to KUNN are given on the last row of Table 1.

For KUNN, the local function is given by

$$\mathcal{L}((u,i),(v,j)) = \mathbf{R}_{uj}\mathbf{R}_{vj}\mathbf{R}_{vi}$$

and thus selects those pairs (v,j) such that v and u share a preference for j and both i and j are preferred by v. As such, KUNN does not discard any information about the direct relation between (v,j) and (u,i).

Next, the neighborhood function for KUNN is given by

$$\mathcal{N}((u,i),(v,j)) = |KNN(u) \cap \{v\}| + |KNN(i) \cap \{j\}|.$$

It thus selects those pairs (v,j) such that v is in the neighborhood of u or j is in the neighborhood of i. If both conditions are fulfilled, the weight of the pair (v,j) with respect to $s(u,i)$ is doubled. As such, KUNN uses neighborhood information of both v and j to weight (v,j) with respect to (u,i).

Furthermore, for KUNN, $\mathcal{W}$ is given by

$$\mathcal{W}((u,i),(v,j)) = \frac{1}{\sqrt{c(u)c(i)c(v)c(j)}}.$$

Consequently, the user-similarity results in

$$sim(u,v) = \sum_{r_{\mathcal{I}} \in \mathcal{I}} \frac{\mathbf{R}_{ur_{\mathcal{I}}}\mathbf{R}_{vr_{\mathcal{I}}}}{\sqrt{c(u)c(v)c(r_{\mathcal{I}})}},$$

and the item-similarity:

$$sim(i,j) = \sum_{r_{\mathcal{U}} \in \mathcal{U}} \frac{\mathbf{R}_{r_{\mathcal{U}}i}\mathbf{R}_{r_{\mathcal{U}}j}}{\sqrt{c(i)c(r_{\mathcal{U}})c(j)}}.$$

Intuitively, if u and v share a preference for an item $r_{\mathcal{I}}$, it is only weak evidence of their similarity if $r_{\mathcal{I}}$ is popular and both u and v have many preferences. Similarly, if i and j are both preferred by $r_{\mathcal{U}}$, it is only weak evidence of their similarity if $r_{\mathcal{U}}$ has many preferences and both i and j are popular items.

In addition, the global function for KUNN is given by

$$\mathcal{G}((u,i),(v,j)) = \mathcal{W}((u,i),(v,j))^1 = \frac{1}{\sqrt{c(u)c(i)c(v)c(j)}}.$$

Intuitively, if the counts of u, i, v and j are higher, it is more likely that the direct relation between (v,j) and

$(u,i)(\mathcal{L}((u,i),(v,j)) = 1)$, exists by chance. Therefore, this direct relation is less informative.

Finally, we see no convincing arguments for making KUNN more complex by introducing a rescaling factor. Therefore we define

$$\mathcal{S}((u,i),(v,j)) = 1.$$

To enhance the intuitive understanding of KUNN, we rewrite Equation 3 as

$$s(u,i) = \frac{s_{\mathcal{U}}(u,i) + s_{\mathcal{I}}(u,i)}{\sqrt{c(u)c(i)}}, \tag{10}$$

with

$$s_{\mathcal{U}}(u,i) = \sum_{v \in KNN(u)} \mathbf{R}_{vi} \frac{1}{\sqrt{c(v)}} \sum_{\substack{j \in \mathcal{I} \\ \mathbf{R}_{uj}=1 \\ \mathbf{R}_{vj}=1}} \frac{1}{\sqrt{c(j)}}$$

and

$$s_{\mathcal{I}}(u,i) = \sum_{j \in KNN(i)} \mathbf{R}_{uj} \frac{1}{\sqrt{c(j)}} \sum_{\substack{v \in \mathcal{U} \\ \mathbf{R}_{vi}=1 \\ \mathbf{R}_{vj}=1}} \frac{1}{\sqrt{c(v)}}.$$

Thus, we can decompose $s(u,i)$ in a user-based part $s_{\mathcal{U}}(u,i)$ and an item-based part $s_{\mathcal{I}}(u,i)$. Notice that these two parts cannot be reduced to any existing user- or item-based algorithm.

The user-based part $s_{\mathcal{U}}(u,i)$ is a weighted sum over the neighbors of u in which the weight of a neighbor v is proportional to:

- $\mathbf{R}_{vi}$: v has a known preference for i,
- $1/\sqrt{c(v)}$: if v prefers many items, her known preference for i becomes less informative,
- $\sum_{j \in \mathcal{I}, \mathbf{R}_{uj}=1, \mathbf{R}_{vj}=1}$: every preference that v shares with u increases the weight of v for recommending items to u,
- $1/\sqrt{c(j)}$: if v and u share a preference for j, it is less informative if j is a more popular item.

A similar intuition holds for the item-based part $s_{\mathcal{I}}(u,i)$.

Finally, the denominator of Equation 10, reduces the strength of the evidence if u prefers many items and i is popular.

5. EXPERIMENTAL EVALUATION

We experimentally evaluate the accuracy of KUNN on three datasets: the *Movielens*, the *Yahoo!Music*^{user} and the *Yahoo!Music*^{random} datasets [19, 5]. These datasets contain ratings of users for movies and songs respectively. The ratings are on a 1 to 5 scale with 5 expressing the highest preference. We convert these datasets to binary, positive-only datasets. Following Pradel et al. [11], we convert the ratings 4 and 5 to preferences and the ratings 1 and 2 to dislikes. Furthermore, we ignore the ratings 3, effectively converting them to unknowns. As such, we obtain a buffer between preferences and dislikes. Since our setting presumes binary, positive-only data, both the unknowns and the dislikes are represented by zeros in the training data. For evaluating the recommendations however, we are allowed to distinguish between unknowns and dislikes.

In our evaluation we compare *KUNN* with five other algorithms. As a baseline, we select *pop*, the non-personalized algorithm that ranks all items according to their popularity, i.e. the number of users in the training set that prefer the item. Next, we select the *user-based* nearest neighbors algorithm with cosine similarity by Sarwar et al. [13] and the widely used *item-based* nearest neighbors algorithm with cosine similarity and similarity normalization (*SNorm+*) by Deshpande et al. [2]. We choose this item-based algorithm because it performed well in comparison to other item-based algorithms [2]. Furthermore, we also compare with *UB+IB*, a linear ensemble that computes a recommendation score as

$$s(u,i) = \lambda s_{UB}(u,i) + (1-\lambda) s_{IB}(u,i),$$

with $s_{UB}(u,i)$ the user-based score from the algorithm by Sarwar et al. and $s_{ID}(u,i)$ the item-based score from the algorithm by Deshpande et al. Finally, we compare with two state-of-the-art matrix factorization algorithms for OCCF: the *BPRMF* algorithm by Rendle et al. and the *WRMF* algorithm by Hu et al. [7]. For *WRMF* and *BPRMF* we used the MyMediaLite implementation [4]. For all other algorithms, we used our own implementation, which is available at `https://bitbucket.org/KVs/unncf_submit`.

To thoroughly evaluate the performance of KUNN, we use evaluation measures from multiple previous works [2, 12, 11, 13]. The experimental evaluation consists of two experimental setups. In the *user selected* setup (Sec. 5.1), the users selected which items they rated. In the *random selected* setup (Sec. 5.2), users were asked to rate randomly chosen items.

5.1 User Selected Setup

This experimental setup is applicable to the *Movielens* and the *Yahoo!Music*^{user} datasets. In both datasets, users chose themselves which items they rated. Following Deshpande et al. [2] and Rendle et al. [12], one preference of every user is randomly chosen to be the test preference for that user. If a user has only one preference, no test preference is chosen. The remaining preferences are represented as a 1 in the training matrix $\mathbf{R}$. All other entries of $\mathbf{R}$ are zero. We define the hit set $\mathcal{H}_u$ of a user u as the set containing all test preferences of that user. For this setup, this is a singleton, denoted as $\{h_u\}$, or the empty set if no test preference is chosen. Furthermore, we define $\mathcal{U}_t$ as the set of users with a test preference, i.e. $\mathcal{U}_t = \{u \in \mathcal{U} \mid |\mathcal{H}_u| > 0\}$. Table 2 summarizes some characteristics of the datasets.

For every user $u \in \mathcal{U}_t$, every algorithm ranks the items $\{i \in \mathcal{I} \mid \mathbf{R}_{ui} = 0\}$ based on $\mathbf{R}$. We denote the rank of the test preference h_u in such a ranking as $r(h_u)$.

Then, every set of rankings is evaluated using three measures. Following Deshpande et al. [2] we use hit rate at 10 and average reciprocal hit rate at 10. In general, 10 can be replaced by any natural number $N \leq |\mathcal{I}|$. We follow Deshpande et al. [2] and choose N=10.

Hit rate at 10 is given by

$$HR@10 = \frac{1}{|\mathcal{U}_t|} \sum_{u \in \mathcal{U}_t} |\mathcal{H}_u \cap top10(u)|,$$

with $top10(u)$ the 10 highest ranked items for user u. Hence, $HR@10$ gives the percentage of test users for which the test preference is in the top 10 recommendations.

Average reciprocal hit rate at 10 is given by

$$ARHR@10 = \frac{1}{|\mathcal{U}_t|} \sum_{u \in \mathcal{U}_t} |\mathcal{H}_u \cap top10(u)| \cdot \frac{1}{r(h_u)}.$$

Table 2: Dataset characteristics after transformation to binary, positive-only data.

				$c(u)$		$\|\mathcal{H}_u\|$		$\|\mathcal{M}_u\|$	
Dataset	$\|\mathcal{U}\|$	$\|\mathcal{U}_t\|$	$\|\mathcal{I}\|$	mean	std	mean	std	mean	std
Movielens	6040	6037	3706	94.3	105.0	1	0	NA	NA
Yahoo!Music^{user}	15400	13204	1000	7.70	11.57	1	0	NA	NA
Yahoo!Music^{random}	15400	2401	1000	8.70	11.57	1.89	1.23	6.17	2.09

Unlike hit rate, average reciprocal hit rate takes into account the rank of the test preference in the top 10 of a user.

Following Rendle et al. [12], we also use the AMAN version of area under the curve, which is for this experimental setup given by

$$AUC^{AMAN} = \frac{1}{|\mathcal{U}_t|} \sum_{u \in \mathcal{U}_t} \frac{|\mathcal{I}| - r(h_u)}{|\mathcal{I}| - 1}.$$

AMAN stands for All Missing As Negative, meaning that a missing preference is evaluated as a dislike. Like average reciprocal hit rate, the area under the curve takes into account the rank of the test preference in the recommendation list for a user. However, AUC^{AMAN} decreases slower than $ARHR@10$ when $r(h_u)$ increases.

We repeat all experiments five times, drawing a different random sample of test preferences every time.

5.2 Random Selected Setup

The *user selected* experimental setup introduces two biases in the evaluation. Firstly, popular items get more ratings. Secondly, the majority of the ratings is positive. These two biases can have strong influences on the results and are thoroughly discussed by Pradel et al. [11]. The *random selected* test setup avoids these biases.

Following Pradel et al. [11], the training dataset is constructed in the *user selected* way: users chose to rate a number of items they selected themselves. The test dataset however, is the result of a voluntary survey in which random items were presented to the users and a rating was asked. In this way, both the popularity and the positivity bias are avoided.

This experimental setup is applicable to the dataset *Yahoo!Music*^{random}. The training data, $\mathbf{R}$, of this dataset is identical to the full *Yahoo!Music*^{user} dataset. Additionally, this dataset includes a test dataset in which the rated items were randomly selected. For a given user u, the hit set $\mathcal{H}_u$ contains all preferences of this user which are present in the test dataset. The set of dislikes $\mathcal{M}_u$ contains all dislikes of this user which are present in the test dataset. We define $\mathcal{U}_t = \{u \in \mathcal{U} \mid |\mathcal{H}_u| > 0, |\mathcal{M}_u| > 0\}$, i.e. all users with both preferences and dislikes in the test dataset. Table 2 summarizes some characteristics of the dataset.

For every user $u \in \mathcal{U}_t$, every algorithm ranks the items in $\mathcal{H}_u \cup \mathcal{M}_u$ based on the training data $\mathbf{R}$. The rank of an item i in such a ranking is denoted $r(i)$.

Then, following Pradel et al. [11], we evaluate every set of rankings with the AMAU version of area under the curve, which is given by

$$AUC^{AMAU} = \frac{1}{|\mathcal{U}_t|} \sum_{u \in \mathcal{U}_t} AUC^{AMAU}(u),$$

with

$$AUC^{AMAU}(u) = \sum_{h \in \mathcal{H}_u} \frac{|\{m \in \mathcal{M}_u \mid r(m) > r(h)\}|}{|\mathcal{H}_u||\mathcal{M}_u|}.$$

AMAU stands for All Missing As Unknown, meaning that a missing preference does not influence the evaluation. Hence, $AUC^{AMAU}(u)$ measures, for a user u, the fraction of dislikes that is, on average, ranked behind the preferences. A big advantage of this measure is that it only relies on known preferences and known dislikes. Unlike the other measures, it does not make the bold assumption that items not preferred by u in the past are disliked by u.

Because of the natural split in a test and training dataset, repeating the experiment with different test preferences is not applicable.

5.3 Parameter Selection

Every personalization algorithm in the experimental evaluation has at least one parameter. For every experiment we try to find the best set of parameters using grid search. An experiment is defined by (1) the outer training dataset $\mathbf{R}$, (2) the outer hitset $\bigcup_{u \in \mathcal{U}_t} \mathcal{H}_u$, (3) the outer dislikes $\bigcup_{u \in \mathcal{U}_t} \mathcal{M}_u$, (4) the evaluation measure, and (5) the algorithm. Applying grid search, we first choose a finite number of parameter sets. Secondly, from the training data $\mathbf{R}$, we create five inner data splits, defined by $\mathbf{R}^k$, $\bigcup_{u \in \mathcal{U}_t} \mathcal{H}_u^k$, and $\bigcup_{u \in \mathcal{U}_t} \mathcal{M}_u$ for $k \in \{1,2,3,4,5\}$. Then, for every parameter set, we rerun the algorithm on all five inner training datasets $\mathbf{R}^k$ and evaluate them on the corresponding inner test datasets with the chosen evaluation measure. Finally, the parameter set with the best average score over the five inner data splits, is chosen to be the best parameter set for the outer training dataset $\mathbf{R}$ with respect to the chosen evaluation measure. Notice that, given an outer training dataset, the best parameters with respect to one evaluation measure, can differ from the best parameters with respect to another evaluation measure.

5.4 Results and Discussion

Table 3 shows the evaluation of the considered algorithms on different datasets, with different measures. The experiments belonging to the user selected setup were repeated 5 times, drawing a different random sample of test preferences every time. Therefore, we report both the mean and the standard deviation for these experiments. The experiments belonging to the random selected setup use a natural split between the test and training dataset. Therefore, randomizing the test set choice is not applicable and only one value is reported for every experiment. Scripts for automatically repeating all experiments are available at `https://bitbucket.org/KVs/unncf_submit`. The exact paramter

Table 3: Selected algorithms evaluated with multiple experiments. Our novel algorithm is marked with a ⋆

dataset	measure		⋆ KUNN	WRMF [7, 10]	BPRMF [12]	UB+IB	item-based, cosine, SNorm+ [2]	user-based, cosine [13]	pop
Movielens	$HR@10$	mean	**.217**	**.217**	.174	.209	.165	.209	.063
		std	.002	.001	.004	.002	.002	.002	.002
	$ARHR@10$	mean	**.093**	.091	.071	.090	.073	.090	.022
		std	.003	.002	.001	.002	.002	.002	.002
	AUC^{AMAN}	mean	.941	**.944**	.934	.927	.916	.927	.865
		std	.001	.001	.002	.001	.001	.001	.001
$Yahoo!Music^{user}$	$HR@10$	mean	**.378**	.338	.285	.365	.364	.316	.187
		std	.009	.007	.009	.003	.012	.012	.004
	$ARHR@10$	mean	**.163**	.145	.102	.160	.160	.127	.062
		std	.003	.007	.006	.006	.007	.003	.002
	AUC^{AMAN}	mean	**.926**	.910	.891	.910	.911	.910	.841
		std	.002	.002	.003	.003	.003	.003	.001
$Yahoo!Music^{random}$	AUC^{AMAU}		**.788**	.770	.755	.768	.768	.761	.670

combinations explored by the grid search procedure (Sec. 5.3) and other details can be inspected in these scripts.

From Table 3 we can make several observations. First of all, KUNN outperforms every other algorithm five out of seven times, shares one best performance with WRMF, and is one time outperformed by WRMF.

Secondly, the user-based algorithm clearly outperforms the item-based algorithm on the *Movielens* dataset. On the $Yahoo!Music^{user}$ dataset on the other hand, the item-based algorithm clearly outperforms the user-based algorithm. For UB+IB, the grid search procedure (Sec. 5.3) is successful in choosing λ such that the best of both algorithms in the ensemble gets the highest weight. However, UB+IB cannot outperform the best of both individual algorithms. KUNN, on the other hand, successfully combines the user- and item-based information and consistently outperforms both individual algorithms.

Thirdly, the rather disappointing performance of BPRMF stands out. A possible explanation lies in the choice of the parameters. Following Rendle et al. [12], we used grid search (Sec. 5.3) to choose the best out of 267 parameter combinations for BPRMF in every experiment. We can however not rule out that there exist parameter combinations outside our 267 possibilities, for which BPRMF performs better. Finding a good set of parameters is harder for BPRMF than for the other algorithms because BPRMF uses 7 parameters that can all take an infinite number of values. The parameters $k_{\mathcal{U}}$ and $k_{\mathcal{I}}$ of KUNN, on the other hand, are integers within the bounds $[0, |\mathcal{U}|]$ and $[0, |\mathcal{I}|]$ respectively. Therefore, we can find a good set of parameters among only 25 possibilities.

Finally, all personalized algorithms perform much better than the non personalized baseline *pop*.

6. EXPLAINABILITY

The consideration that explanations of item-based algorithms are superior comes from observing the formulas for computing the recommendation scores [3, 7]. For item-based algorithms on the one hand, this formula is given by Equation 4 in which every term can be attributed to one of the known preferences of the target user. Therefore the known preferences related to the biggest terms can naturally serve as an explanation for the recommendation. For user-based algorithms on the other hand, the formula is given by Equation 5 in which every term can be attributed to one of the collaborative users. This is much less useful because the most similar users give no intuitive explanation for the recommendation as they are probably strangers to the target user and the same for every recommendation. Furthermore, this kind of explanation would also be an invasion on the privacy of these collaborative users.

However, this difference is only artificial. Thanks to our reformulation, we can write both the user-based algorithm by Sarwar et al. [13] (Eq. 5) and KUNN as a sum over the known preferences of the target user.

We start with the user-based algorithm (Eq. 5). This algorithm can be rewritten as

$$s(u,i) = \frac{1}{|KNN(u)|} \sum_{v \in KNN(u)} \mathbf{R}_{vi} \left(\frac{\sum_{l_1 \in \mathcal{I}} \mathbf{R}_{ul_1} \mathbf{R}_{vl_1}}{\sum_{l_2 \in \mathcal{I}} \mathbf{R}_{ul_2} \mathbf{R}_{vl_2}} \right).$$

Notice that the last factor in the summation is simply 1, but allows us to rewrite the equation as

$$s(u,i) = \frac{1}{|KNN(u)|} \sum_{\substack{l_1 \in \mathcal{I} \\ \mathbf{R}_{ul_1}}} \left(\sum_{v \in KNN(u)} \frac{\mathbf{R}_{vl_1} \mathbf{R}_{vi}}{\sum_{l_2 \in \mathcal{I}} \mathbf{R}_{ul_2} \mathbf{R}_{vl_2}} \right),$$

In the above equation, we have written the user based score $s(u,i)$ as a weighted sum over the known preferences of u.

The known preferences l_1 with the biggest weights, serve as a natural explanation for recommending i to u. Hence, we have naturally explained the user-based recommendation of i for u.

Next, we consider KUNN, which can be rewritten as

$$s(u,i) = \frac{1}{\sqrt{c(u)c(i)}} \sum_{\substack{j \in \mathcal{I} \\ \mathbf{R}_{uj}=1}} \left(\frac{1}{\sqrt{c(j)}} \sum_{\substack{v \in \mathcal{U} \\ \mathbf{R}_{vi}=1 \\ \mathbf{R}_{vj}=1}} \frac{\mathcal{N}((u,i),(v,j))}{\sqrt{c(v)}} \right),$$

by regrouping Equation 3. Thus, also KUNN computes $s(u,i)$ as a weighted sum over the known preferences of u.

Again, the known preferences with the biggest weights serve as a natural explanation for recommending i to u. Hence, we have naturally explained recommendations made by KUNN.

7. RELATED WORK

The majority of the work on collaborative filtering presumes rating data. This setting is significantly different from our setting with binary, positive-only data. Therefore, the algorithms for rating based collaborative filtering differ on important aspects such as how they measure similarity, how their performance is measured and how they handle missing ratings, user- and item-biases.

Hence, specific algorithms have been proposed for OCCF. First, an analysis of user-based nearest neighbors algorithms for OCCF was given by Sarwar et al. [13]. We discussed their work in Section 3.2 and compared experimentally to it in Section 5.

Later, Deshpande et al. [2] introduced the item-based nearest neighbors approach for OCCF. We discussed their work in Section 3.1 and experimentally compared to it in Section 5. Afterwards, similar approaches were suggested [15, 1]. Recently, multiple authors proposed to minimize a global cost function for computing the item similarities [12, 9, 8].

Furthermore, Symeonidis et al. [16] recognized that combining user- and item-based approaches could be beneficial. Additionally, Wang et al. [18] proposed a unification of user- and item-based algorithms. However, their work presumes rating data.

Finally, there exist also matrix factorization algorithms for OCCF [7, 10, 12, 14]. In our experimental evaluation (Sec. 5), we compared with two state-of-the-art algorithms of this class: WRMF by Hu et al. [7] and BPRMF by Rendle et al. [12].

8. CONCLUSIONS AND FUTURE WORK

We proposed KUNN, a novel algorithm for one class collaborative filtering, a setting that covers many applications.

KUNN originates from a reformulation that unifies user- and item-based nearest neighbors algorithms. Thanks to this reformulation, it becomes clear that user- and item-based nearest neighbors algorithms discard important parts of the available information.

KUNN improves upon these existing nearest neighbors algorithms by actually using more of the available information. Our experimental evaluation shows that KUNN not only outperforms existing nearest neighbors algorithms, but also state-of-the-art matrix factorization algorithms.

Finally, we challenged the well accepted belief that item-based algorithms are superior for explaining the recommendations they produce. Thanks to our reformulation, we were able to show that also recommendations by KUNN and the traditional user-based algorithm come with a natural explanation.

We see research on novel definitions of the functions $\mathcal{L}$, $\mathcal{N}$, $\mathcal{G}$ and $\mathcal{S}$ as the most important direction for future work.

9. REFERENCES

[1] F. Aiolli. Efficient top-n recommendation for very large scale binary rated datasets. In *RecSys*, pages 273–280, 2013.

[2] M. Deshpande and G. Karypis. Item-based top-n recommendation algorithms. *TOIS*, 22(1):143–177, 2004.

[3] C. Desrosiers and G. Karypis. A comprehensive survey of neighborhood-based recommendation methods. In F. Ricci, L. Rokach, B. Shapira, and P. Kantor, editors, *Recommender Systems Handbook*. Springer, Boston, MA, 2011.

[4] Z. Gantner, S. Rendle, C. Freudenthaler, and L. Schmidt-Thieme. Mymedialite: A free recommender system library. In *RecSys*, pages 305–308, 2011.

[5] Grouplens. ml-1m.zip. http://grouplens.org/datasets/movielens/.

[6] J. Herlocker, J. Konstan, and J. Riedl. Explaining collaborative filtering recommendations. In *CSCW*, pages 241–250, 2000.

[7] Y. Hu, Y. Koren, and C. Volinsky. Collaborative filtering for implicit feedback datasets. In *ICDM*, pages 263–272, 2008.

[8] S. Kabbur, X. Ning, and G. Karypis. Fism: Factored item similarity models for top-n recommender systems. In *KDD*, pages 659–667, 2013.

[9] X. Ning and G. Karypis. Slim: Sparse linear methods for top-n recommender systems. In *ICDM*, pages 497–506, 2011.

[10] R. Pan, Y. Zhou, B. Cao, N. Liu, R. Lukose, M. Scholz, and Q. Yang. One-class collaborative filtering. In *ICDM*, pages 502–511, 2008.

[11] B. Pradel, N. Usunier, and P. Gallinari. Ranking with non-random missing ratings: Influence of popularity and positivity on evaluation metrics. In *RecSys*, pages 147–154, 2012.

[12] S. Rendle, C. Freudenthaler, Z. Gantner, and L. Schmidt-Thieme. Bpr: Bayesian personalized ranking from implicit feedback. In *UAI*, pages 452–461, 2009.

[13] B. Sarwar, G. Karypis, J. Kostan, and J. Riedl. Analysis of recommendation algorithms for e-commerce. In *EC*, pages 158–167, 2000.

[14] Y. Shi, A. Karatzoglou, L. Baltrunas, M. Larson, N. Oliver, and A. Hanjalic. Climf: learning to maximize reciprocal rank with collaborative less-is-more filtering. In *RecSys*, pages 139–146, 2012.

[15] B. Sigurbjornsson and R. van Zwol. Flickr tag recommendation based on collective knowledge. In *WWW*, pages 327–336, 2008.

[16] P. Symeonidis, A. Nanopoulos, A. Papadopoulos, and Y. Manolopoulos. Nearest-biclusters collaborative filtering based on constant and coherent values. *Inf. Retr.*, 11(1):51–75, 2008.

[17] N. Tintarev. Explanations of recommendations. In *RecSys*, pages 203–206, 2007.

[18] J. Wang, A. P. de Vries, and M. J. Reinders. Unifying user-based and item-based collaborative filtering approaches by similarity fusion. In *SIGIR*, pages 501–508, 2006.

[19] Yahoo!Research. Yahoo_webscope_r3.tgz. http://research.yahoo.com/Academic_Relations.

Recommending User Generated Item Lists

Yidan Liu
Dept. of Computer Science,
Univ. of British Columbia
yidanliu@cs.ubc.ca

Min Xie
Dept. of Computer Science,
Univ. of British Columbia
minxie@cs.ubc.ca

Laks V.S. Lakshmanan
Dept. of Computer Science,
Univ. of British Columbia
laks@cs.ubc.ca

ABSTRACT

Existing recommender systems mostly focus on recommending individual items which users may be interested in. User-generated item lists on the other hand have become a popular feature in many applications. E.g., Goodreads provides users with an interface for creating and sharing interesting book lists. These user-generated item lists complement the main functionality of the corresponding application, and intuitively become an alternative way for users to browse and discover interesting items to be consumed. Unfortunately, existing recommender systems are not designed for recommending user-generated item lists. In this work, we study properties of these user-generated item lists and propose a Bayesian ranking model, called LIRE for recommending them. The proposed model takes into consideration users' previous interactions with both item lists and with individual items. Furthermore, we propose in LIRE a novel way of weighting items within item lists based on both position of items, and personalized list consumption pattern. Through extensive experiments on a real item list dataset from Goodreads, we demonstrate the effectiveness of our proposed LIRE model.

Categories and Subject Descriptors

H.3.3 [**Information Storage and Retrieval**]: Information Search and Retrieval - Information Filtering

Keywords

List Recommendation; Collaborative Filtering

1. INTRODUCTION

Recommender systems have become extremely popular because of their wide application and success in domains such as E-commerce (Amazon), Music (iTunes), Movies (Netflix), and Apps (Apple App Store). E.g., back in 2006, Amazon already had 35% of purchases originating from recommended items [21].

RecSys'14, October 6–10, 2014, Foster City, Silicon Valley, CA, USA.
Copyright 2014 ACM 978-1-4503-2668-1/14/10 ...$15.00.
http://dx.doi.org/10.1145/2645710.2645750.

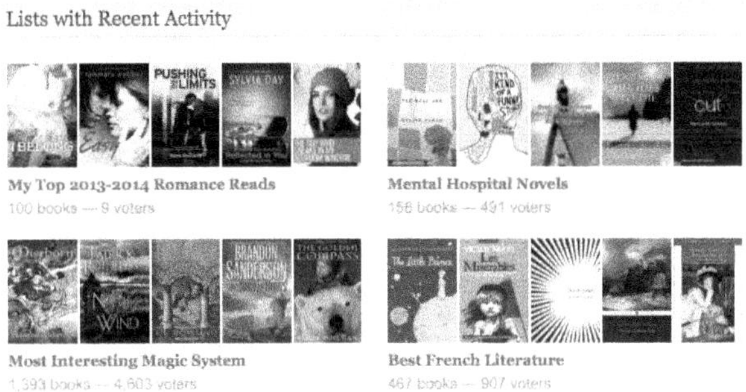

Figure 1: User-generated book lists on GoodReads.

Existing recommender systems usually help users find potentially interesting items by means of *collaborative filtering*. Initial works on collaborative filtering mainly focused on *neighborhood-based methods* [29, 22], which essentially leverage similarity between items or between users as measured by heuristic functions such as *cosine* or *Pearson correlation*. These similarities are calculated based on the ratings provided by (received by) users (resp., items) in the past. More recent works on collaborative filtering mostly focus on *latent factor models*, which have become widely known from their success at the *Netflix Competition* [12, 17, 19, 20].

Although existing collaborative filtering works are effective at recommending individual items to users, the proposed solutions usually lack flexibility in supporting more complex recommendation scenarios [4]. For example, existing recommendation algorithms are not optimized for recommending *user-generated item lists*, which are very popular among various applications such as lists of books created by readers on GoodReads [2], lists of twitter users created by users on Twitter [1], and lists of products created by shoppers on Amazon [3].

User-generated item lists are usually deployed as a way to help users organize and share items consumed in the corresponding application. These user-generated item lists are usually made public by default, so in addition to the main functionality provided by the service (e.g., recommending as well as shopping or consuming items), these lists serve as an alternative way to engage users of the service. For users, exploring user-generated item lists is often a very effective way for browsing and identifying interesting items, as each list contains only a small subset of all items, and items in each list are usually manually organized by other users around a specific theme. E.g., users can find from a book list on French Literature interesting and rare books on this topic, which may not be recognized by the item recommendation engine or through keyword search interface as these books may not explicitly contain the keywords "French Literature". An example of user-generated book lists on GoodReads is shown in Figure 1.

However, because of the sheer volume of user-generated item lists, and the complexity of each list (which typically contains tens or even hundreds of items), it is extremely challenging for a standard item presentation interface to help users discover lists which he/she might find interesting. Thus users usually have to resort to keyword search to find interesting lists, which again is extremely challenging because of the large number of items within each list, and also the huge number of lists which might match the query.

In this work, motivated by recent study on automatic recommendation of items based on user's previous interaction with the underlying system, we study the problem of how to generalize item recommendation to incorporate lists, and propose algorithms which can automatically find relevant *item lists* for each user based on her/his previous interactions with both lists and items in the corresponding service. Intuitively, these recommended item lists complements existing item recommender system and serve as a way for users to explore items around a small set of themes which might match users' interest.

We note that in the domain of music, playlists have a similar structure as the user-generated item lists studied in this work, and several existing works have been devoted to developing recommendation algorithms for playlists [7, 9, 8]. However, a huge difference between playlists and the item lists studied in this work is that there usually exists a strong correlation between neighboring songs in a playlist: in most cases songs in a playlist have to be consumed sequentially. This property has been explored extensively by existing works such as [9], [7]. However, it is clear that for the item lists under our consideration, such as book lists, twitter user lists, and shopping lists, items do not necessarily have to be consumed sequentially. In fact, a user might well be interested in only one or a few items in a list and may consume them in no particular order.

To address the limitations of previous approaches in modeling users' item list preference, we propose a new *List Recommendation Model* called LIRE in this work. In LIRE , we take a user's item preference into consideration when modeling the user's item list preference, where item preferences can be learned from user's previous interaction with individual items. We note that a simple way of aggregating item preferences into list preferences may not work very well. Indeed, one challenge in modeling a user's interest in user-generated item lists is that on websites such as Goodreads, because of the way user interface is presented and the huge number items contained in each list, users usually see just the top items in a list first, and they may often stop browsing an item list when enough items have been explored or consumed. To take these facts into consideration, we consider in our model, ingredients which can be leveraged to weight items which are ranked at different positions, and we also learn users' browsing patterns by fitting a parameter that indicates roughly how many items need to be consumed before a user stops browsing an item list.

We make the following contributions: First, we propose a Bayesian-based ranking model LIRE for recommending user-generated item lists, which, unlike playlists, need not be consumed sequentially; Second, in the LIRE model, we consider the problem of how preferences over individual items can be properly aggregated to model user's interest in an item list; Third, through extensive experiments on a real item list dataset obtained from Goodreads, we show that our LIRE model significantly outperforms various previously proposed recommendation algorithms on the task of recommending user-generated item lists.

In the rest of this paper, we first define the item list recommendation problem in Section 2.1. Then in Section 2.2, we present some intuitive baseline algorithms which can be applied to the item list dataset to generate list recommendations. In Section 3, we introduce our proposed list recommendation model. Experimental results comparing different algorithms on Goodreads dataset are presented in Section 4. Related work is discussed in Section 5. Finally, we conclude the paper and present possible future directions in Section 6.

2. PROBLEM STUDIED AND BASELINE ALGORITHMS

2.1 Item List Recommendation

To formulate the item list recommendation problem, consider a set of users $U = \{u_1, \dots, u_m\}$, a set of items $T = \{t_1, \dots, t_n\}$, and a set of item lists $L = \{l_1, \dots, l_q\}$, where each list $l_i \in L$ is composed of a subset of items from T.

Let the set of item lists which user u has shown interest in be denoted as L_u, $L_u \subseteq L$, where a list $l \in L_u$ can be a list which u has liked, voted, or commented on. Similar to many other recommendation problems such as those discussed in [12] and [27], typically user feedback on item lists is *implicit* as compared to explicit ratings which can be found on movie recommendation websites [20].

On most websites such as Goodreads which provide the functionality for creating and sharing item lists, each user u is also associated with a set of items T_u, namely the items which u has previously consumed/rated.

PROBLEM 1. **Item List Recommendation:** *Given T, U, L, for each user $u \in U$, based on u's previously consumed items T_u, and u's previously consumed item lists L_u, recommend to u the top-N item lists from $L \backslash L_u$ which u will be most interested in.*

2.2 Baseline Algorithms

2.2.1 Popularity-based Approach

For many a recommendation application be it item recommendations or item list recommendations, there is typically a long tail distribution w.r.t. the number of user ratings/interactions of each item. E.g., most of the items can observe only a few ratings, whereas only a few enjoy much attention from users. Thus this popularity bias becomes an important factor for explaining and understanding the underlying data, as was also observed in the Netflix competition [18].

One simple item list recommendation algorithm thus is to directly leverage the popularity bias and recommend item lists based on the popularity of each list. That is, we sort item lists w.r.t. the number of votes received, and recommend to every user the same set of top item lists which have received the highest number of votes. We note that this is very similar to how Goodreads website recommends item lists on every book detail page, i.e., every popular book is likely included in many book lists, and according to our observation, only two of the hottest book lists are shown on the detail page of every book.

We call above algorithm GLB (GLoBal), as the recommendation generated using the above approach is based on global statistics and is not personalized. We also consider the following two different personalized variants, among the baselines; these methods are in part motivated by the heuristic popularity-based approaches for generating playlists which have been demonstrated to have good performance [8].

The first alternative PPOP (Personalized POPularity) is based on the intuition that a user u may only be interested in item lists which contain items that u is familiar with. Thus instead of recommending the most popular item lists across all users, we recommend the most popular item lists which contain at least one item the user has interacted with before.

The second alternative PIF (Personalized Item Frequency) is based on the same intuition as PPOP that a user u is only interested in item lists which contain items that u is familiar with. But instead of ranking these candidate item lists by popularity, we rank these candidate item lists by how many items the list contains that the user has interacted before. The rationale for this heuristic is that the more books a list contains that the user is familiar with, the more interesting that list to the user. Ties in PIF are broken using popularity of the corresponding item list.

2.2.2 Collaborative Filtering for Implicit Data

Consider a matrix M^L of users' interest in each list, where each entry y_{ul} is 1 if u has voted list l before, and 0 otherwise. We could simply apply previously proposed collaborative filtering algorithms to this matrix M^L.

Typical collaborative filtering algorithms are based on latent factor models, which were made popular because of their success in the Netflix competition [20]. The nature of the datasets we consider is that user feedback is implicit, i.e., it tends to be in the form of votes. Thus, we adapt the recently proposed BPR method [27], demonstrated to be very effective on implicit feedback data, to item list recommendation.

In BPR [27], each user u is associated with a latent factor w_u, each item t_i is associated with a latent factor h_i, then similarly to other latent factor models, the rating $\hat{x}_{ui}$ of user u on item t_i can be predicted based on the dot product $w_u \cdot h_i$.

Because of the nature of the implicit dataset, similar to [27], we assume that items which have been voted by a user are preferred over other items. Thus, we let $t_i \succ_u t_j$ denote that user u prefers item t_i to item t_j. Following the notation introduced in [27], let D_S denote set of triples (u, t_i, t_j) such that $t_i \succ_u t_j$ holds. Then BPR formalizes a learning problem by maximizing the following log-posterior.

$$\begin{aligned}\ln P(\Theta \mid D_S) &\propto \ln P(D_S \mid \Theta) P(\Theta) \\ &= ln \prod_{(u,t_i,t_j)\in D_S} \sigma(\hat{x}_{ui} - \hat{x}_{uj}) p(\Theta) \\ &= \sum_{(u,t_i,t_j)\in D_S} \ln \sigma(\hat{x}_{ui} - \hat{x}_{uj}) + \ln p(\Theta) \\ &= \sum_{(u,t_i,t_j)\in D_S} \ln \sigma(\hat{x}_{ui} - \hat{x}_{uj}) - \lambda_\Theta \|\Theta\|^2 \quad (1)\end{aligned}$$

where $\sigma = \frac{1}{1+e^{-x}}$ is the logistic sigmoid function, Θ denotes all the parameters (latent factors of users and items), and each latent factor is assumed to be following a zero mean Gaussian prior. Finally, λ_Θ is a model specific regularization parameter.

As discussed in [27], the optimization criteria of BPR is closely related to *Area Under the ROC Curve* (AUC) [11]. And above posterior in Equation 1 can be optimized through *Stochastic Gradient Descent* (SGD) which has been demonstrated to be useful for learning various latent factor-based models [17].

2.2.3 Markov-based Recommendation

As we will discuss in Section 5, the item list recommendation problem resembles the playlist recommendation problem studied before [8, 9]. One important difference is that with playlists, there is an inherent assumption that items in the list are meant to be consumed sequentially, which may not be relevant for user-generated item lists such as book lists or product lists. We adapt algorithms proposed for playlist recommendation for the sake of comparison with the algorithms we develop.

In the literature, one very recent and representative model-based approach for playlist recommendation is LME or *Latent Markov Embedding* [9, 10]. In LME, similar to other latent factor models, each item t_i is associated with a latent vector h_i. Given a playlist l, let each item in l at position a be denoted as $l[a]$. In order to model the sequential property a playlist l, we consider the probability of each list being "generated" as a series of Markov transitions between consecutive songs.

$$P(l) = \prod_{a=1}^{|l|} P(l[a] \mid l[a-1]) \quad (2)$$

where the transition probability $P(l[a] \mid l[a-1])$ can be modeled as a function of the Euclidean distance $\Delta(h_{l[a]}, h_{l[a-1]})$ between the two songs under consideration. Let A denote the set of all songs which can following one specific song $l[a-1]$, we denote by $Z(l[a-1]) = \sum_{t\in A} e^{-\Delta(h_t, h_{l[a-1]})}$ the summation over transition probabilities w.r.t. all possible next song given $l[a-1]$. We can then use the following logistic model to estimate $P(l[a] \mid l[a-1])$.

$$P(l[a] \mid l[a-1]) = \frac{e^{-\Delta(h_{l[a]}, h_{l[a-1]})}}{Z(l[a-1])} \quad (3)$$

Similar to BPR, an SGD-like algorithm can be leveraged to learn the latent factor model in LME by maximizing the likelihood of generating the training playlists. We note that the original model in [9, 10] is not personalized.

3. LIST RECOMMENDATION MODEL

In this section, we propose a *List Recommendation Model* called LIRE for the item list recommendation problem. Similar to previous latent factor-based models, we map users, items, and lists into a joint latent factor space of dimensionality k. Accordingly, each user u is associated with a vector $w_u \in \mathbb{R}^k$, each item t_i with a vector $h_i \in \mathbb{R}^k$, and each list l_j with a vector $g_j \in \mathbb{R}^k$.

3.1 User Preference over Individual Item List

Intuitively, given a user u and an item list l_j, u's interest in l_j can be captured using two major factors: (i) the overall intrinsic quality of the list l itself, and (ii) the user's aggregate interest in the items in l_j. The first factor can be modeled simply as an inner product between w_u and g_j, while the second factor involves aggregating user's preferences over multiple items within l_j.

A simple idea to model the relationship between u and items in l_j is to assume that each item in l_j has an equal influence on user u. Thus we could model the preference of u on l_j using the following equation.

$$\hat{x}_{uj}^{L} = w_u g_j + \frac{1}{|l_j|} \sum_{t_i \in l_j} (w_u h_i) \quad (4)$$

where $|l|$ denotes the length of list l. In Equation (4), the first component $w_u g_j$ models user's intrinsic interest in the list as a whole, and the second component models the relationship between u and items in l_j. We call above model UNIFORM. Note that omitting the second component in Equation (4) amounts to directly factorizing the user list interaction matrix M^L into user latent vectors and item list latent vectors and using that solely as the model for recommendation.

As discussed in Section 4.1, usually different items in the list have different influence on a user. E.g., items which are shown at the top of a list, or items which are shown on the first page of the list if pagings are enabled, obviously have more significant influence on the user. This effect is usually due to the way different items of a ranking list are shown on the user interface, and how users consume items in a list. Similar effect can also be observed in information retrieval [13]. To capture this property, we adopt a function inspired by DCG (*Discounted Cumulative Gain*) [15], in order to weight down items which are ranked low in a displayed item list or are shown in later pages in case of a paging enabled interface. Without any ambiguity, let $t_i = l_j[i]$ denote the ith item in list l_j, $1 \leq i \leq |l_j|$, and let h_i be the corresponding latent factor associated with t_i.

$$\hat{x}_{uj}^{L} = w_u g_j + C(w_u h_1 + \sum_{i=2}^{|l_j|} \frac{w_u h_i}{\log_2 i}) \quad (5)$$

where $C = 1/(1 + \sum_{i=2}^{|l_j|} \frac{1}{\log_2 i})$ serves as a normalization constant. We call above model DCG.

Although DCG is able to weight down items with lower position in the displayed list, given the huge number of items which may exist in an item list, items which are ranked low down in a list usually will not be examined by the user. E.g., one list named "Best Book Cover Art" has 4,775 books and it's unlikely a user will dig deep down such lists. Thus, incorporating these lower ranked items in predicting a user's preference over an item list may introduce lots of noise. In this work, to address this issue, we make the reasonable assumption that users browse an item list top down, and stop browsing when enough items have been seen. Note that this threshold number of items which indicates the number of items users consume before stopping, may vary among different users, thus needs to be personalized. Even for a specific user, this number may change from list to list, which may motivate us to associate one random variable per user and per list. However, given the sparsity of the dataset, such fine granularity threshold modeling might easily lead to overfitting. Thus we consider in this work a trade-off approach by introducing a personalized granularity controlling browsing threshold τ_u.

We set $\tau_u = \beta \times \eta_u$. Here, $\eta_u \in \mathbb{Z}^+$ is a personalized discrete random variable with a positive integer as its value, β is a constant which is used to capture a coarse list browsing granularity. E.g., β can either be the number of items contained in a single page on the website, or can just be a constant such as 10 items, which captures a finer granularity. The value of β can be tuned according to the underlying data. In this work, using our Goodreads dataset, we set β to be 5 which leads to the best performance on our dataset.

Let $\mathbb{I}(i \leq \tau_u)$ be an indicator function which equals 1 if $i \leq \tau_u$ is true, and 0 otherwise. We could adapt DCG to the following model DCG-T.

$$\hat{x}_{uj}^{L} = w_u g_j + C(w_u h_1 + \sum_{i=2}^{|l_j|} \mathbb{I}(i \leq \tau_u) \frac{w_u h_i}{\log_2 i}) \quad (6)$$

where $C = 1/(1 + \sum_{i=2}^{|l_j|} \mathbb{I}(i \leq \tau_u) \frac{1}{\log_2 i})$ serves as a normalization constant. This model captures the idea that user u stops browsing beyond depth τ_u.

3.2 Modeling Observed Data

In general users' feedback data on item lists tends to be even more sparse than the feedback on items. This makes learning users' preference over item lists more challenging. Fortunately, for most applications in which users can create and share item lists, users also can and tend to interact with individual items. E.g., on Goodreads, users can vote for book lists which are generated by other users, and can also add books to their shelves, meaning they either have already read the books, or are interested in reading those books in the future. Thus in addition to the matrix M^L which captures interactions between users and lists, we also have the matrix M^T which captures interactions between users and items.

Motivated by recent effort on *Collective Matrix Factorization* [31], we consider that users share their preferences over items and lists. Thus we could potentially leverage information learnt from users' item preferences to help mitigate the sparsity issue when modeling users' list preferences. Considering the fact that the interactions between users and items or between users and item lists are often implicit, e.g., vote on Goodreads and subscription on Twitter, we adapt the framework of BPR [27] for deriving the optimization criteria for our item list recommendation problem. Let $\Theta = \{W, G, H, \tau\}$ be the set of parameters associated with the LIRE model. We assume Θ is associated with a zero-mean Gaussian prior. By assuming $\succ_u^L$ and $\succ_u^T$ are conditional independent given Θ, the log of the posterior of Θ given the observed user/item interactions and user/item list interactions can be calculated as follows.

$$\begin{aligned}
\mathcal{P}(\Theta) &= \ln p(\Theta \mid \succ_u^L, \succ_u^T) = \ln p(\succ_u^L, \succ_u^T \mid \Theta) p(\Theta) \\
&= \ln p(\succ_u^L \mid \Theta) p(\succ_u^T \mid \Theta) p(\Theta) \\
&= \ln p(\succ_u^L \mid \Theta) + \ln p(\succ_u^T \mid \Theta) - \lambda_\Theta \|\Theta\|^2 \\
&= \sum_{(u,l_i,l_j) \in D_s^L} \ln \sigma(\hat{x}_{uij}^L(\Theta)) + \sum_{(u,t_i,t_j) \in D_S^T} \ln \sigma(\hat{x}_{uij}^T(\Theta)) \\
&\quad - \lambda_\Theta \|\Theta\|^2 \qquad (7)
\end{aligned}$$

where D_S^L denotes the set of triples (u, l_i, l_j) for which $l_i \succ_u l_j$ holds, D_S^T denotes the set of triples (u, t_i, t_j) for which $t_i \succ_u t_j$ holds, And λ_Θ are the model specific regularization parameters. The relationship between user u, list l_i, and list l_j is captured by $\hat{x}^L_{uij}(\Theta)$, which can be estimated as $\hat{x}^L_{ui} - \hat{x}^L_{uj}$. Similarly, the relationship between user u, item t_i, and item t_j is captured by $\hat{x}^T_{uij}(\Theta)$, which can be modeled as $\hat{x}^T_{ui} - \hat{x}^T_{uj}$.

3.3 Model Learning

Given $\mathcal{P}(\Theta)$, we use *Maximum-a-Posteriori* (MAP) to perform a point estimation of the parameters of the LIRE model. Considering the fact that $\mathcal{P}(\Theta)$ is differentiable w.r.t. most parameters, one popular way to optimize $\mathcal{P}(\Theta)$ is through gradient-based algorithms. A naive approach to doing so would be to directly sample quadruples (l_i, l_j, t_i, t_j), where l_i, l_j are positive and negative item list instances for a user u, and t_i, t_j are positive and negative item instances. More precisely, user u prefers l_i to l_j and similarly t_i to t_j. However, this introduces a huge sampling space. Hence, we propose an alternating learning framework, where we first sample (u, t_i, t_j) from D^T_S, until convergence of $\mathcal{P}(\Theta)^T = \ln p(\Theta \mid \succ^T_u)$; then we sample (u, l_i, l_j) from D^L_S, until convergence of $\mathcal{P}(\Theta)^L = \ln p(\Theta \mid \succ^L_u)$. We iterate above process until the overall posterior converges. We note that the gradient of $\mathcal{P}(\Theta)^T$ w.r.t. Θ can be derived in a similar way as in [27], thus in the following, we focus on how a gradient-based algorithm can be applied to $\mathcal{P}(\Theta)^L$.

Recall from Section 3.1 that during the learning process to maximize $\mathcal{P}(\Theta)^L$, the threshold parameter τ_u for every user takes on positive integers as values, thus $\mathcal{P}(\Theta)^L$ is noncontinous w.r.t. Θ. To solve this issue, we further decompose the maximization of $\mathcal{P}(\Theta)^L$ into the following two steps: first, fix τ_u then optimize the remaining model parameters; then fix the remaining model parameters and optimize τ_u.

Given a fixed τ_u, the following is the gradient of $\mathcal{P}(\Theta)^L$ w.r.t. the model parameter Θ for DCG-T. Similar gradients can be derived for UNIFORM and DCG and we suppress the details. To simplify the notation, we omit mentioning Θ for $\hat{x}^T_{uij}(\Theta)$ and $\hat{x}^L_{uij}(\Theta)$ if there is no ambiguity.

$$\begin{aligned}\frac{\partial \mathcal{P}(\Theta)^L}{\partial \Theta} &= \sum_{(u,l_i,l_j)\in D^L_s} \frac{\partial \ln \sigma(\hat{x}^L_{uij})}{\partial \Theta} - \lambda_\Theta \frac{\partial \|\Theta\|^2}{\partial \Theta} \\ &= \sum_{(u,l_i,l_j)\in D^L_s} \frac{e^{-\hat{x}^L_{uij}}}{1+e^{-\hat{x}^L_{uij}}} \frac{\partial \hat{x}^L_{uij}}{\partial \Theta} - \lambda_\Theta \Theta \end{aligned} \quad (8)$$

Since $\partial \hat{x}^L_{uij}/\partial\Theta = \partial \hat{x}^L_{ui}/\partial\Theta - \partial \hat{x}^L_{uj}/\partial\Theta$, we list in the following equations how $\partial \hat{x}^L_{uj}/\partial\Theta$ can be derived for w, and g in DCG-T, where f indicates an index into the corresponding latent factor.

$$\frac{\partial \hat{x}^L_{uj}}{\partial \Theta} = \begin{cases} g_{jf} + C(h_{1f} + \sum_{i=2}^{|l_j|} \mathbb{I}(i \le \tau_u) \frac{h_{if}}{\log_2 i}) & \Theta = w_{uf} \\ w_{uf} & \Theta = g_{jf} \end{cases}$$

Given $\tau_u = \beta \times \eta_u$, η_u may have a small domain given the size $|l_j|$ of a list l_j. E.g., on Goodreads, when β is set to the number of items on a single web page, most lists have size less than 40 web pages. A simple idea thus is to enumerate all possible η_u and then find the optimal η^*_u which maximizes $\mathcal{P}(\Theta)^L$.

$$\eta^*_u = \underset{1 \le \eta_u \le \lceil |l_j|/\beta \rceil}{\arg\max}\ \mathcal{P}(\Theta)^L \quad (9)$$

However, when β is tuned to be at a finer granularity, the cost of above exhaustive search becomes prohibitive. Given the fact that $\mathcal{P}(\Theta)^L$ may not be monotone w.r.t. τ_u based on different possible values of the latent factors, we consider a local search algorithm LocalOpt (Algorithm 1) which finds a local maximum of τ_u.

Algorithm 1: LocalOpt(β,Θ,$|l|$)

$\eta^* \leftarrow$ A random integer between 1 and $\lceil |l|/\beta \rceil$;
$Q \leftarrow$ An empty candidate queue;
Q.add(($\max(\eta_u - 1, 1), left$));
Q.add(($\min(\eta_u + 1, \lceil |l|/\beta \rceil), right$));
while *Q is not empty* **do**
  (η, *direction*) $\leftarrow Q$.pop();
  if $\mathcal{P}_{\eta^*}(\Theta)^L < \mathcal{P}_\eta(\Theta)^L$ **then**
    $\eta^* \leftarrow \eta$;
    if *direction* $= left$ *and* $\eta > 1$ **then**
      Q.add(($\eta - 1, left$));
    if *direction* $= right$ *and* $\eta < \lceil |l|/\beta \rceil$ **then**
      Q.add(($\eta + 1, right$));
return η^*

The overall algorithm for learning LIRE is listed in Algorithm 2. In each iteration of the main loop, we first sample (u, t_i, t_j) from D^T_S and update model parameters W, H through *Stochastic Gradient Ascent* until convergence. Then we sample (u, l_i, l_j) from D^L_S, and update model parameters W, G through *Stochastic Gradient Ascent* until convergence. Finally, we find the optimal τ through Algorithm LocalOpt for every user. We repeat above three steps until the overall model has converged or the maximum number of iterations has been reached.

Algorithm 2: LIRE -Learn(Θ, D^L_S, D^T_S, β)

Random initialize Θ;
repeat
  repeat
    Draw (u, t_i, t_j) from D^T_S;
    Update W, H w.r.t. $\mathcal{P}(\Theta)^T$;
  until *convergence*;
  repeat
    Draw (u, l_i, l_j) from D^L_S;
    Update W. G w.r.t. $\mathcal{P}(\Theta)^L$;
  until *covergence*;
  foreach *User u* **do**
    $|l| \leftarrow$ Longest list size considered by u;
    $\tau_u \leftarrow \beta\times$ LocalOpt($\beta, \Theta, |l|$);
until *convergence or max-iter has been reached*;

4. EXPERIMENT RESULTS

4.1 Goodreads Data Setup

To evaluate our proposed model LIRE and compare it with existing models for item and playlist recommendation, we obtained during one month a 10% sample of all user-generated book lists on Goodreads. As can be found from the Goodreads website, there exist in total around 34,750 user-generated book lists, and our obtained sample includes 3,000 randomly selected book lists from the entire collection.

We filter book lists which have fewer than 5 voters, and the resulting dataset contains 1,998 book lists. For the set of voters obtained from these 1,998 book lists, we again filter

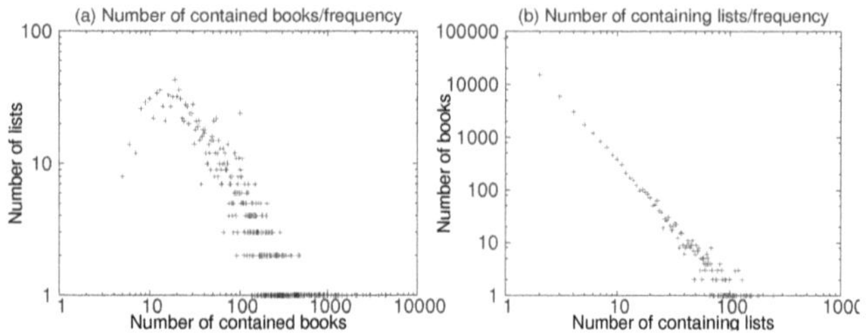

Figure 3: Statistics of Goodreads data w.r.t. lists and books

out those who have voted less than 5 times within the 1,998 book lists. The total number of unique users left at the end of this process is 3,425. To fit users' preference over individual items, we also obtained the set of books which have been added to these 3,425 users' book shelves. The total number of unique books is 105,030.

In Figure 3 (a), we group lists into different buckets based on how many books they contain, and plot the number of lists which belong to each bucket. It can be seen that the majority of the obtained book lists contain only a small number of books, but there does exist book list which contains 4,775 books. The average number of books per list is 109. Similarly, in Figure 3 (b), we group books into different buckets based on how many book lists they belong to, and plot the number of books belong to each bucket. Again, there is an obvious power law distribution between the number of lists a book belongs to and the number of books that belong to the same number of books.

Similar statistics of the Goodreads dataset can be observed between users and lists, and also between users and books, as shown in Figure 2. In a nutshell, the majority of users interact only with a few lists or books, while a few power users interact with a large number of lists or books.

From the obtained Goodreads dataset, we randomly sample 10% user/list interaction data as the test set, and the remaining data is treated as training set. To simplify the training process, we assume each parameter of the model is associated with the same regularization parameter λ. Learning rate γ in the Stochastic gradient descent step, and regularization parameter λ are selected based on grid search. In our experiments, we found that usually setting $\gamma = 0.1$ and $\lambda = 0.01$ leads to the best performance.

4.1.1 *Algorithms Compared*

We compare our proposed LIRE with the following 5 baseline algorithms as discussed in Section 2.2: 1. GLB; 2. PPOP; 3. PIF; 4. BPR; 5. LME. For BPR and LME, we also used grid search to find the best learning parameter settings. Finally, we consider two variations of LIRE – LIRE -UNIFORM with uniform item weighting, and LIRE -DCG-T with item position-based weighting and personalized browsing threshold.

4.1.2 *Performance Measure*

AUC is a commonly used metric for testing the quality of rank orderings. Following [27], we use the AUC metric described below to compare the proposed LIRE model with the baseline algorithms as it has been demonstrated to be a good metric for evaluating Top-N recommendation tasks [6]. Suppose the set of users, positive book list instance (book lists voted by the user in the test dataset), negative book list instance (book lists which have not been voted either in the training set or testing dataset) in the test dataset are denoted as D_S^{test}. Then, the formula to compute AUC is given by:

$$\frac{1}{|D_S^{test}|} \sum_{(u,l_i,l_j) \in D_S^{test}} \mathbb{I}(\hat{x}_{ui} > \hat{x}_{uj})$$

where $\mathbb{I}(\hat{x}_{ui} > \hat{x}_{uj})$ is an indicator function which returns 1 if $\hat{x}_{ui} > \hat{x}_{uj}$ is true, and 0 otherwise.

4.2 Granularity of Browsing

We first test how the granularity parameter β of the browsing threshold τ can affect the performance of the LIRE model. As discussed in Section 3, on one hand, when setting β to a small value, the predicted browsing threshold may lack flexibility in predicting user's browsing pattern across different lists. Whereas on the other hand, setting β to be a large value, we may incorporate unnecessary items into the prediction of user's interest in a specific list.

The above trade-off is confirmed by our results on Goodreads dataset as shown in Table 1. By fixing the dimensionality of D to be 10, the overall AUC on the test set increases when β is varied from 1 to 5, and AUC decreases when we further increase the value of β. We observed similar results for other D settings and suppress them for lack of space. This result indicates that β in practice can be tuned based on the actual dataset.

	β value				
	1	3	5	7	9
AUC	0.9778	0.9787	**0.9830**	0.9819	0.9800

Table 1: How β value affect the AUC.

4.3 Convergence of LIRE

In Figure 4, we demonstrate the convergence behavior of the LIRE model. As can be found in this figure, our model converges fairly quickly (around 5 iterations). We note that this convergence result also holds for other dimensionality setting of the latent factors.

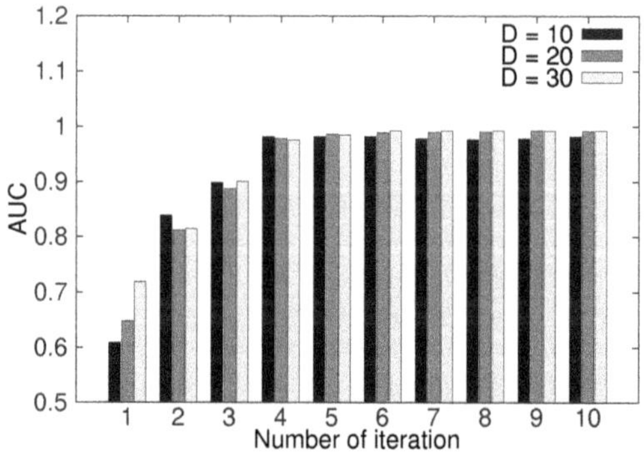

Figure 4: Convergence of LIRE when varying dimensionality of the latent factors.

4.4 Quality Comparison

Finally, we compare the performance of LIRE with other algorithms as presented in Section 2.2. From Figure 5, we can readily observe that the three baseline algorithms GLB, PPOP, PIF do not perform nearly as well as BPR and LIRE . We note that this is in contrast with the result on playlist dataset, where popularity-based methods, and especially personalized popularity-based methods excel [8]. Also the Markov-based approach LME does not perform as

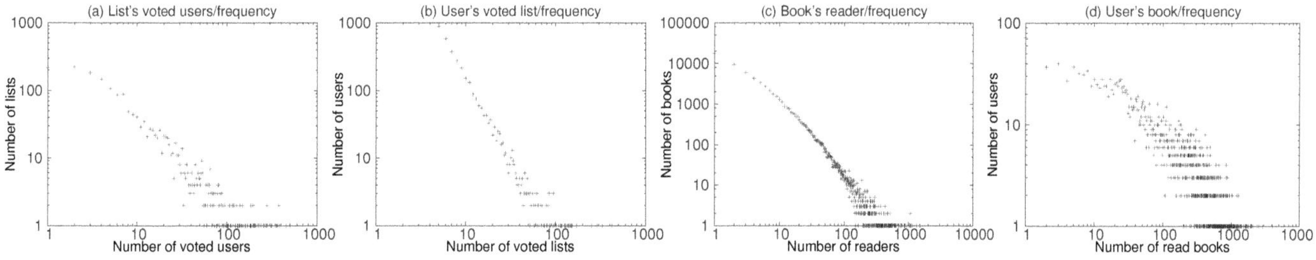

Figure 2: Statistics of Goodreads data w.r.t. lists and users, users and books

well as BPR and LIRE . We claim that the reason for this is that user-generated lists such as book lists on Goodreads do not have the sequential consumption property normally assumed by playlist modeling works.

For the two variations of LIRE , we can see from Figure 5, both of them perform better than the other algorithms. However, LIRE -DCG-T is better than LIRE -UNIFORM, for two reasons: (i) LIRE -UNIFORM may aggregate more than the necessary number of items' preference when modeling a user's interest in an item list, and (ii) it ignores the fact that preference over items positioned higher up in the list may have a larger impact on the user's preference for the list. In addition, because LIRE -UNIFORM needs to visit all items in an item list during training, training of LIRE -UNIFORM is much slower compared with LIRE -DCG-T.

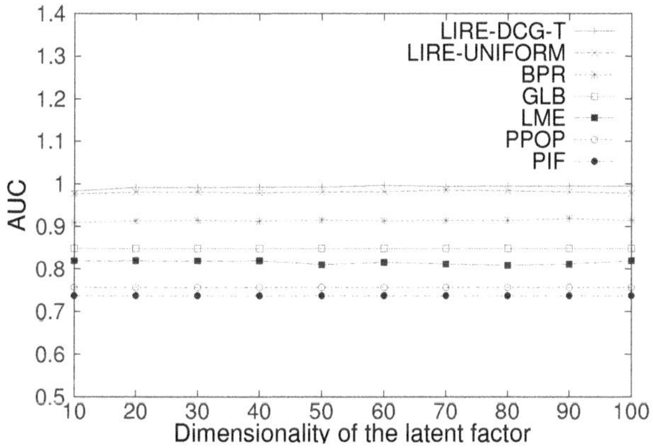

Figure 5: Quality comparison for various algorithms.

5. RELATED WORK

Latent factor models for recommendation have generated significant amount of attention due to their famous success at the Netflix competition [20]. In latent factor models, each observed rating in a recommender system can be explained as a dot product between two learned latent factors corresponding to the underlying user and item. Recently, latent factor models have been extended extensively to incorporate additional features such as time [19], context [16], and content features of items [5].

Many existing works on recommender system focus on explicit rating datasets in which ratings can take values from a small domain such as 1 to 5. However, for many recommendation scenarios, feedbacks from users take an implicit form, such as whether a user purchased a product, liked a feed, clicked on an item, etc. These implicit data settings create a huge challenging for existing latent factor models, and researchers have recently proposed various models for modeling implicit datasets. One notable work in this direction is BPR [27], in which the authors proposed to solve the implicit data problem through a general Bayesian ranking model, which can learn users' preferences over items by sampling positive and negative/missing entries from the user rating matrix. Another work which proposes to model implicit dataset through ranking is CLiMF [30], which instead of optimizing AUC as in BPR, considers *Mean Reciprocal Rank* as the optimization criterion. In [24], the authors argue that reasoning about preferences between individual items might be too fine a granularity, and propose to lift item preferences to preferences over sets of items. The focus of this work is still on item recommendation, and when aggregating item preferences, the proposed model does not consider the position of an item, and the defined item sets are hidden from users thus there is no need to model how users might view items within a set. Other works on implicit datasets include [12], in which the authors propose a different way of modeling implicit datasets by weighting the importance of each observed rating through heuristic functions. In [25], the authors propose a more complex model which models the relationship between the original implicit dataset (which can be considered as a bipartite graph between users and items) and random bipartite graphs which captures potential items which users have considered before actually consuming items in the original dataset.

User-generated item lists are similar to playlists as explored in previous works such as [9] and [7]. An important observation made by these works is that neighboring items in a playlist are usually correlated with each other and items in a playlist usually have to be consumed sequentially. E.g., in LME [9], the proposed model assumes that transitions between neighboring items in a playlist satisfy the Markovian property, i.e., next song in a playlist depend only on the current song which is playing. Similarly, in [7], the authors consider that each song in a playlist is closely related to other songs which are played within the same short time window. An interesting survey of algorithms for modeling playlists is presented in [8].

The proposed item list recommendation problem is also related to recent effort on package recommendation [26, 28, 32]. However, most of these works focus on handling hard constraints specified by users as opposed to learning user's preferences over item lists from previous feedback. In [23], the authors propose a *Probability Matrix Factorization*-based approach to model user's preferences over travel packages, where each package is composed of a set of places of interest. The focus of this work is on modeling the cost of a package, whereas in our work we focus on how item preferences can be aggregated to model user's preferences over item lists.

Finally, the way we model interactions between users and item lists, and also interactions between users and individual items is closely related to recent efforts on *collective matrix factorization* [31, 14], which has become a popular way of modeling scenarios with heterogeneous types of interactions through sharing latent factors.

6. CONCLUSION

In this paper, we motivated the problem of recommending user-generated item lists and proposed a novel model called LIRE for this purpose. Existing works in recommender system usually focus on item recommendation, thus do not consider how user's preference over item lists can be decomposed into preferences over individual items within the list. Though playlist recommendation considers item lists in a specific setting, the proposed model cannot be applied to other item list settings as studied in this work, due to the fact that items in these lists do not need to be consumed sequentially. In this work, we identify that there exist multiple challenges on how presentation of an item list in an application such as Goodreads might impact a user's preference over item lists. And based on our observations from Goodreads book list dataset, we propose to model users' preferences over item lists by aggregating users' preferences over individual items of a list, we capture how users perceive an item list by weighting items within a list based on position, and we also consider how many items a user might consume before deciding whether to like this list or not. Through extensive experiments we demonstrate that our proposed model has a better performance compared with many existing recommendation algorithms.

There exist multiple directions for future work: first, we can study how temporal information from the dataset can be leveraged to help better model a user's preference over item lists. E.g., we could check whether liking a list will result in a subsequent consumption of an item within the same list. Second, many applications which have user-generated item lists involve social network. This raises the question how social influence can be modeled in LIRE . Finally, it's interesting to ask how contents of lists and items can be incorporated into LIRE through methods such as [5].

7. ACKNOWLEDGEMENT

This work was supported in part by the Institute for Computing, Information and Cognitive Systems (ICICS) at UBC.

8. REFERENCES

[1] `https://support.twitter.com/articles/76460-using-twitter-lists`.

[2] `https://www.goodreads.com/list`.

[3] `http://www.amazon.ca/gp/help/customer/display.html?nodeId=1197914`.

[4] G. Adomavicius and A. Tuzhilin. Toward the next generation of recommender systems: A survey of the state-of-the-art and possible extensions. *IEEE Trans. Knowl. Data Eng.*, 17(6):734–749, 2005.

[5] D. Agarwal and B.-C. Chen. Regression-based latent factor models. In *KDD*, pages 19–28, 2009.

[6] A. Ahmed, B. Kanagal, S. Pandey, V. Josifovski, L. G. Pueyo, and J. Yuan. Latent factor models with additive and hierarchically-smoothed user preferences. In *WSDM*, pages 385–394, 2013.

[7] N. Aizenberg, Y. Koren, and O. Somekh. Build your own music recommender by modeling internet radio streams. In *WWW*, pages 1–10, 2012.

[8] G. Bonnin and D. Jannach. Evaluating the quality of generated playlists based on hand-crafted samples. In *ISMIR*, pages 263–268, 2013.

[9] S. Chen, J. L. Moore, D. Turnbull, and T. Joachims. Playlist prediction via metric embedding. In *KDD*, pages 714–722, 2012.

[10] S. Chen, J. Xu, and T. Joachims. Multi-space probabilistic sequence modeling. In *KDD*, pages 865–873, 2013.

[11] A. Herschtal and B. Raskutti. Optimising area under the roc curve using gradient descent. In *ICML*, 2004.

[12] Y. Hu, Y. Koren, and C. Volinsky. Collaborative filtering for implicit feedback datasets. In *ICDM*, pages 263–272, 2008.

[13] S. B. Huffman and M. Hochster. How well does result relevance predict session satisfaction? In *SIGIR*, pages 567–574, 2007.

[14] M. Jamali and L. Lakshmanan. Heteromf: recommendation in heterogeneous information networks using context dependent factor models. In *WWW*, pages 643–654, 2013.

[15] K. Järvelin and J. Kekäläinen. Cumulated gain-based evaluation of ir techniques. *ACM Trans. Inf. Syst.*, 20(4):422–446, 2002.

[16] A. Karatzoglou, X. Amatriain, L. Baltrunas, and N. Oliver. Multiverse recommendation: N-dimensional tensor factorization for context-aware collaborative filtering. In *RecSys*, pages 79–86, 2010.

[17] Y. Koren. Factorization meets the neighborhood: A multifaceted collaborative filtering model. In *KDD*, pages 426–434, 2008.

[18] Y. Koren. The bellkor solution to the netflix grand prize, 2009.

[19] Y. Koren. Collaborative filtering with temporal dynamics. In *KDD*, pages 447–456, 2009.

[20] Y. Koren, R. M. Bell, and C. Volinsky. Matrix factorization techniques for recommender systems. *IEEE Computer*, 42(8):30–37, 2009.

[21] P. Lamere and S. Green. Project aura: recommendation for the rest of us. In *Sun JavaOne Conference*, 2008.

[22] G. Linden, B. Smith, and J. York. Amazon.com recommendations: Item-to-item collaborative filtering. *IEEE Internet Computing*, 7(1):76–80, 2003.

[23] Q. Liu, Y. Ge, Z. Li, E. Chen, and H. Xiong. Personalized travel package recommendation. In *ICDM*, 2011.

[24] W. Pan and L. Chen. Cofiset: Collaborative filtering via learning pairwise preferences over item-sets. In *SDM*, pages 180–188, 2013.

[25] U. Paquet and N. Koenigstein. One-class collaborative filtering with random graphs. In *WWW*, pages 999–1008, 2013.

[26] A. G. Parameswaran and H. Garcia-Molina. Recommendations with prerequisites. In *RecSys*, pages 353–356, 2009.

[27] S. Rendle, C. Freudenthaler, Z. Gantner, and L. Schmidt-Thieme. Bpr: Bayesian personalized ranking from implicit feedback. In *UAI*, pages 452–461, 2009.

[28] S. B. Roy, S. Amer-Yahia, A. Chawla, G. Das, and C. Yu. Constructing and exploring composite items. In *SIGMOD*, pages 843–854, 2010.

[29] B. M. Sarwar, G. Karypis, J. A. Konstan, and J. Riedl. Item-based collaborative filtering recommendation algorithms. In *WWW*, pages 285–295, 2001.

[30] Y. Shi, A. Karatzoglou, L. Baltrunas, M. Larson, N. Oliver, and A. Hanjalic. Climf: learning to maximize reciprocal rank with collaborative less-is-more filtering. In *RecSys*, pages 139–146, 2012.

[31] A. P. Singh and G. J. Gordon. Relational learning via collective matrix factorization. In *KDD*, pages 650–658, 2008.

[32] M. Xie, L. V. Lakshmanan, and P. T. Wood. Breaking out of the box of recommendations: From items to packages. In *RecSys*, pages 151–158. ACM, 2010.

Question Recommendation for Collaborative Question Answering Systems with RankSLDA

Jose San Pedro
Telefonica Research
Barcelona, Spain
jspw@tid.es

Alexandros Karatzoglou
Telefonica Research
Barcelona, Spain
alexk@tid.es

ABSTRACT

Collaborative question answering (CQA) communities rely on user participation for their success. This paper presents a supervised Bayesian approach to model expertise in online CQA communities with application to question recommendation, aimed at reducing waiting times for responses and avoiding question starvation. We propose a novel algorithm called *RankSLDA* which extends the supervised Latent Dirichlet Allocation model by considering a learning-to-rank paradigm. This allows us to exploit the inherent collaborative effects that are present in CQA communities where users tend to answer questions in their topics of expertise. Users can thus be modeled on the basis of the topics in which they demonstrate expertise. In the supervised stage of the method we model the pairwise order of expertise of users on a given question. We compare *RankSLDA* against several alternative methods on data from the *Cross Validate* community, part of the Stack Exchange network. *RankSLDA* outperforms all alternative methods by a significant margin.

Categories and Subject Descriptors

H.4 [**Information Systems Applications**]: Miscellaneous

Keywords

Learning to Rank; Supervised Latent Dirichlet Allocation; Latent Topics Model; Question Recommendation; Community Question Answering; Expert Modeling

1. INTRODUCTION

Many users resort to the Internet for finding answers to their questions and solving their information needs [22]. Community Question Answering (CQA) websites, such as Yahoo! Answers or Stack Overflow, allow users to formulate questions to leverage the expertise of other members participating in the community. In the past years, CQA websites have rapidly grown in size and popularity. For instance, Yahoo! Answers includes over 300 million questions posted since it launched in 2005; only during 2012, it received an average of 7,000 questions and 21,000 answers per hour[1].

CQA websites are heavily dependent on community participation. While most provide passive question discovery tools, such as search or unanswered question lists, they still require significant effort from expert users to find the questions to which they can provide responses. This additional load on the community can potentially reduce participation and degrade the overall quality of the content.

A solution to this problem studied in previous work considers the task of automatically finding potential responders to questions [24, 10, 13, 18, 19, 11, 6, 20, 8]. These *question recommendation* systems aim at increasing participation by proactively warning users about the presence of questions suitable to their interests and expertise. The task of matching experts to questions given their previous answers to similar questions can be posed as a Recommendation problem. The expected result of implementing such a system is that less questions are left unanswered and the elapsed time for answers is significantly decreased. Note that such a system can be effectively used along with other participation encouragement tools, such as rewards, karma points, etc.

One common feature of most CQA systems is the presence of community feedback tools, which serve as a crowd-sourced and distributed curation mechanism. Users can easily vote, positively or negatively, for questions (if they consider them interesting for future reference) or answers (if they correctly solve the problem stated in the associated question). All votes casted for a post, and hence for the user that posted it, get aggregated into a single score, which serves as a proxy for question/answer quality. This rich source of information can be used for modeling user expertise.

State-of-the-art Recommender Systems are often based on factor models e.g. [9, 17, 12, 14]. Factor-based collaborative filtering methods represent both "items" and "users" with a vector of latent features. In our problem setting, the presence of text (questions and answers) allows us to use a more interpretable basis for modeling the experts and the questions, namely topic modeling [3]. The main idea behind the model we introduce is that users with expertise in similar topics are likely to answer similar questions, we use this fact both to recommend questions to experts but also to reinforce the learning of the corpus topics.

In this paper, we present *RankSLDA*, Rank Supervised Latent Dirichlet Allocation, a supervised probabilistic topic model with direct application to question recommendation. *RankSLDA* is based on a Bayesian inference framework that

RecSys'14, October 6–10, 2014, San Jose or vicinity, CA, USA.

ACM 978-1-4503-2668-1/14/10 ...$15.00.
http://dx.doi.org/10.1145/2645710.2645736 .

[1]Source: http://searchengineland.com

extends the LDA model to account for the authorship of questions and answers as well as for community feedback. The proposed model combines the semantic content modeling benefits of LDA with supervised ranking learning to model the observed community scores based on the latent topics assigned to each question.

The contribution of this paper is two-fold. First, we propose a novel learning-to-rank extension to supervised LDA, and provide the derivation of a Gibbs sampler to perform inference. Second, we apply this model to the question recommendation task and provide experimental results of its performance compared to several state-of-the art methods.

The paper is organized as follows. In Section 2 we review previous literature on related topics. In Section 3 we provide an in-depth description of the generative model proposed, and the procedure to train and tune its parameters. In Section 4 we describe the setup used to study the proposed method, and in Section 5 we present the results obtained. We conclude with Section 6.

2. RELATED WORK

A body of literature exists around expertise modeling in the CQA context. Two main approaches have been used to this end: network and content-based. Network-based methods are specifically targeted to CQA communities with a narrow topic focus. Networks built from the interaction of users in question threads are analyzed to infer their relative expertise order. Network centrality has been proven to be a good indicator of expertise on them [24]. Different network creation approaches have been proposed for comparing expertise between users to establish a global rank. For instance, competition-based expertise networks are formalized by establishing directed links between the best answerer and all the other contributors [10, 2].

Content-based methods consider an Information Retrieval centric vision, where users are profiled according to their contributions in the website, and are ranked with respect to an expertise query (e.g. a new question). Methods based on TF-IDF [13], pLSA [18], and probabilistic topic models [19] have been proposed using this general framework. A related line of work considers the use of a classification-based approach, where the user-question relationships are represented in a common feature space to find their reciprocal relevance [6]. Tensor factorization approaches, capturing known relationships between askers, question and answerers, have also been proposed to predict best answerers [20].

Several bayesian generative models have been used in this setting. Guo *et al.* introduced the User-Question-Answer model, which considers user profiles as topic mixtures, and uses question categories to improve the recommendation performance [8]. Ni *et al.* proposed the Topic-based User Interest model, which leverages community selected best answers to promote users that contribute high quality posts [11].

Beside *best answers*, which can be biased and unreliable [5], none of these works make explicit use of the rich community feedback available from most CQA communities. One previous work that uses aggregated voting scores is [21]. In it, observed votes are drawn as part of the generative process from a Gaussian Mixture Model. In contrast, we consider a generative model with a supervised stage, where observed votes are used for building optimized user profiles based on the latent topics of the questions and answers contributed. Also, the fLDA algorighm [1] predicts ratings of users for documents, expressed as topic mixtures, by using matrix factorization to model the affinity between users and topics. While it can be applied to question recommendation, the model is optimized for rating prediction instead of ranking.

3. METHODOLOGY

3.1 Problem Statement

In this section we provide the formalization of the question recommendation task that we use in the rest of the paper. The main element of this formalization is the question thread, which comprises the following components: one unique *question* (which originates the thread), one or more *answers* (that attempt to solve the problem stated in the question), *community feedback* (aggregated scores computed from the community votes to questions and answers), and *user information* (user identifier of each question and answer). For the sake of brevity, we will refer to the individual textual components of the thread, both questions and answers, as *posts*. In this scenario, each post has been authored by a single user and has an associated quality score given by the community. We can obtain an absolute ranking of experts for each question by sorting answers in decreasing order of aggregated voting scores. The question recommendation task is to predict this rank for new questions.

3.2 RankSLDA Model Description

RankSLDA builds on supervised latent Dirichlet allocation (sLDA [3]), an approach that combines LDA topic modeling, where document topic mixtures are drawn from a Dirichlet distribution, with a response variable associated to individual documents. The goal is to find the latent topics that best explain the observed responses. The key innovation of this paper is the extension of sLDA, originally restricted to a single response value per document, to a more flexible multitask scenario able to model the multiple pairwise preferential relationships observed for each document.

As noted, we pose question recommendation as a pairwise ranking problem. We denote as $s(d, u)$ the aggregated score for user u received for his/her contribution to question d. To optimize for the latent topics that best explain the observed preferential relationship of user pairs we consider r_d as the ordering for a given question thread d, so that user pairs $(u_i, u_j) \in r_d$ when $s(d, u_i) > s(d, u_j)$. The model observed responses are then defined by:

$$y_d^{(i,j)} = \begin{cases} 1, & (u_i, u_j) \in r_d \\ 0, & \text{otherwise} \end{cases}$$

Given $\Phi(d, u)$, a feature representation of the matching between a question thread d and a user u, the learning procedure finds the model $\boldsymbol{\gamma}$ that maximizes the number of pairs $(u_i, u_j) \in r_d$ where

$$\langle \boldsymbol{\gamma}, \Phi(d, u_i) \rangle > \langle \boldsymbol{\gamma}, \Phi(d, u_j) \rangle$$

A binary classification approach on pairwise differences of vectors $(\Phi(d, u_i) - \Phi(d, u_j))$ can be used to model this problem, which requires inverting some of the duplets (u_j, u_i) to balance the training dataset. The plate diagram of the *RankSLDA* model is shown in Figure 1.

3.3 Generative Model

Our model, depicted in Fig 1, can be expressed as a generative process that generates question threads and assigns

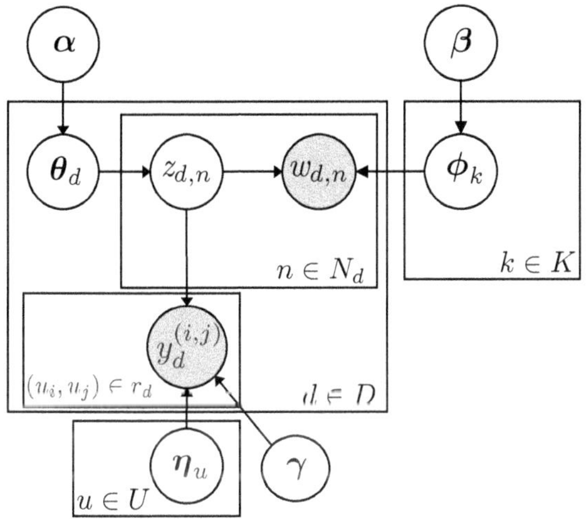

Figure 1: Graphic model representing *RankSLDA*. Shaded nodes represent observed variables and edges probabilistic dependencies.

pairwise preference scores, $y_d^{(i,j)}$. The observed scores, $y_d^{(i,j)}$, which encode the relative rank order between users, are assumed to come from a Bernouilli distribution parametrized by: 1) the ranking model (γ) and 2) the question-user features ($\Phi(d, u_i)$ and $\Phi(d, u_j)$):

$$y_d^{(i,j)} \sim \text{Bern}(p_d^{(i,j)} = \pi(\boldsymbol{\gamma}, \Phi(d, u_i), \Phi(d, u_j)))$$
$$\text{with } \pi(\boldsymbol{\gamma}, \boldsymbol{x}, \boldsymbol{y}) = \text{sigmoid}(\langle \boldsymbol{\gamma}, (\boldsymbol{x} - \boldsymbol{y}) \rangle)$$

Given the topic mixture of the current question, $\boldsymbol{\theta}_d$, and its matching to user profiles, $\Phi(d, u)$, the ranking model determines pairwise preference scores, where their sign determines the predicted ranking order. The sigmoid function maps these scores in the $[0, 1]$ interval, which serves as the parameter $p_d^{(i,j)}$ of the Bernouilli distribution from which the observed variable is drawn. Depending on the discrepancies of predicted and observed values, the model adapts both the ranking coefficients and the topic mixtures to maximize the likelihood of the observed data.

The influence of question topics and users' expertise on the observation is included in the feature vector $\Phi(d, u)$. As later described, we infer user's expertise during the supervised step using multitask regression over the actual observed scores, $s(d, u)$. The regression coefficients, $\boldsymbol{\eta}_u$, can be interpreted as the relevance of each topic for a given user u, effectively encoding their topical knowledge. With these user profiles, we can obtain the final feature vector as a function $\Phi(d, u) = f(\boldsymbol{\theta}_d, \boldsymbol{\eta}_u)$ (point-wise vector multiplication in our case). The generative model proceeds as follows:

1. Draw topic distributions $\boldsymbol{\phi}_k \sim Dir(\boldsymbol{\beta})$ with $i = 1 \dots K$.
2. For each question thread $d = 1 \dots D$:
   (a) Draw distribution over topics $\boldsymbol{\theta}_d \sim Dir(\boldsymbol{\alpha})$.
   (b) For each word in the document $n = 1 \dots N_d$, draw topic assignment $z_{d,n} \sim Mult(\boldsymbol{\theta}_d)$.
   (c) For each user pair $(u_i, u_j) \in r_d$, choose a response variable $y_d^{(i,j)} \sim \text{Bern}(\pi(\boldsymbol{\gamma}, f(\bar{\boldsymbol{z}}_d, \boldsymbol{\eta}_{u_i}), f(\bar{\boldsymbol{z}}_d, \boldsymbol{\eta}_{u_j})))$, with $\bar{\boldsymbol{z}}_d \equiv \frac{1}{N_d} \sum_{n=1}^{N_d} z_{d,n} = \hat{\boldsymbol{\theta}}_d$.

Note that we use the empirical topic distribution to define the documents' mixtures $\bar{\boldsymbol{z}}_d$. Statistical inference is then

Table 1: Notation used in the paper

Symbol	Description
d,u,k,n	index for documents, users, topics and words
U	Number of users in the community
D	Number of documents (i.e. question threads)
N_d	Number of words in document d
$z_{d,n}, w_{d,n}$	n-th topic assignment and term of document d
$y_d^{(i,j)}$	Response for user pair (u_i, u_j) and document d
r_d	Binary ordering between users for document d
$\boldsymbol{z}_d$	Topic mixture proportion of document d
$\boldsymbol{z}_d^{\neg n}$	Same as $\boldsymbol{z}_d$ excluding the n-th word of d
$\boldsymbol{\theta}_d$	Multinomial topic distribution of document d
$\boldsymbol{\phi}_k$	Multinomial word distribution of topic k
$\boldsymbol{\eta}_u$	User topical expertise model
$\boldsymbol{\gamma}$	Pair-wise ranking model

used to find the distribution over latent variables and the parameter values that best explain the observed data. We follow the approach described in [7] using stochastic EM, where the E-step is performed using collapsed Gibbs sampling to infer topic assignments for the terms in the documents. The process is started by randomly initializing the topics, and then alternates between sampling topics of words $z_{d,n}$ and optimizing the regression parameters $\boldsymbol{\eta}_u$ and ranking model $\boldsymbol{\gamma}$ for the given topic assignments and observations. Because there is a dependency between topic assignments and observed responses, the inferred topic distribution favors topic assignments that minimize the difference between the predicted and the observed responses.

In the remaining of the paper we used the notation summarized in Table 1 to refer to the variables and parameters of the model.

3.4 Gibbs Sampler

We use a collapsed Gibbs sampler to collect samples from the posterior distribution of the model. In this section, we derive the equations of the Gibbs sampler used, which presents interesting differences to LDA and sLDA due to its multitask nature. The collapsed Gibbs sampler needs to compute the probability distribution of $P(z_{d,n} = k)$ conditioned on the rest of the variables:

$$P(z_{d,n} | \boldsymbol{z}^{\neg n}, \boldsymbol{w}, \boldsymbol{y}; \boldsymbol{\alpha}, \boldsymbol{\beta}, \boldsymbol{\eta}, \boldsymbol{\gamma}) = \frac{P(z_{d,n}, \boldsymbol{z}^{\neg n}, \boldsymbol{w}, \boldsymbol{y}; \boldsymbol{\alpha}, \boldsymbol{\beta}, \boldsymbol{\eta}, \boldsymbol{\gamma})}{P(\boldsymbol{z}^{\neg n}, \boldsymbol{w}, \boldsymbol{y}; \boldsymbol{\alpha}, \boldsymbol{\beta}, \boldsymbol{\eta}, \boldsymbol{\gamma})}$$

For Gibbs sampling purposes, we can compute a proportional expression and then normalize:

$$P(z_{d,n} = k | \boldsymbol{z}^{\neg n}, \boldsymbol{w}, \boldsymbol{y}; \boldsymbol{\alpha}, \boldsymbol{\beta}, \boldsymbol{\eta}, \boldsymbol{\gamma})$$
$$\propto P(z_{d,n} = k, \boldsymbol{z}^{\neg n}, \boldsymbol{w}, \boldsymbol{y}; \boldsymbol{\alpha}, \boldsymbol{\beta}, \boldsymbol{\eta}, \boldsymbol{\gamma}) = P(\boldsymbol{z}, \boldsymbol{w}, \boldsymbol{y}; \boldsymbol{\alpha}, \boldsymbol{\beta}, \boldsymbol{\eta}, \boldsymbol{\gamma})$$
$$= \int P(\boldsymbol{\theta}|\boldsymbol{\alpha}) P(\boldsymbol{z}|\boldsymbol{\theta})\, \mathrm{d}\boldsymbol{\theta} \cdot \int P(\boldsymbol{w}|\boldsymbol{z}, \boldsymbol{\phi}) P(\boldsymbol{\phi}|\boldsymbol{\beta})\, \mathrm{d}\boldsymbol{\phi} \cdot P(\boldsymbol{y}|\boldsymbol{z}, \boldsymbol{\eta}, \boldsymbol{\gamma})$$

where the last equality is the joint probability distribution of the model. The first two terms of this expression are the standard factors of a collapsed LDA Gibbs sampler (expanded in equation 3). The term $P(\boldsymbol{y}|\boldsymbol{z}, \boldsymbol{\eta}, \boldsymbol{\gamma})$ of this conditional probability distribution includes information on the likelihood that new topic assignments $\boldsymbol{z}_d$ explain the observations, shifting the distribution towards topics that generate responses in consonance to their observed value $y_d^{(i,j)}$.

Note that the current topic assignment can only affect the predicted response for the current document d, hence:

$$P(\boldsymbol{y}|\boldsymbol{z}, \boldsymbol{\eta}, \boldsymbol{\gamma}) \propto P(\boldsymbol{y}_d | \boldsymbol{z}_d, \boldsymbol{\eta}, \boldsymbol{\gamma})$$

where proportionality is kept with respect to $z_{d,n}$. Given a set of topic assignments to document d, the probability of observing the response value for a given user pair (u_i, u_j) is

$$P(y_d^{(i,j)}|\boldsymbol{z}_d; \boldsymbol{\eta}_{u_i}, \boldsymbol{\eta}_{u_j}, \boldsymbol{\gamma}) \sim \text{Bern}(\pi(\boldsymbol{\gamma}, f(\boldsymbol{z}_d, \boldsymbol{\eta}_{u_i}), f(\boldsymbol{z}_d, \boldsymbol{\eta}_{u_j})))$$

Assuming independence, we can express the joint probability of observed user responses for a given document as

$$P(\boldsymbol{y}_d|\boldsymbol{z}_d; \boldsymbol{\eta}, \sigma) = \prod_{(u_i,u_j)\in r_d} P(y_d^{(i,j)}|\boldsymbol{z}_d; \boldsymbol{\eta}_{u_i}, \boldsymbol{\eta}_{u_j}, \boldsymbol{\gamma}) \quad (1)$$

Note that the expression considers only user pairs $(u_i, u_j) \in r_d$. The probability of topics assignments is therefore shifted towards those that maximize the correct number of ranking predictions from $\boldsymbol{\gamma}$. We can now completely specify the conditional distribution for our Gibbs sampler:

$$P(z_{d,n} = k|\boldsymbol{z}^{\neg n}, \boldsymbol{w}, \boldsymbol{y}; \boldsymbol{\alpha}, \boldsymbol{\beta}, \boldsymbol{\eta}, \sigma) \propto \quad (2)$$

$$(n_{d,k}^{\neg n} + \alpha_k) \frac{n_{w_{d,n},k} + \beta_{w_{d,n}}}{\sum_{j=1}^{W} n_{j,k} + \beta_j} \quad (3)$$

$$\prod_{(u_i,u_j)\in r_d} \frac{1}{1 + exp(\langle \boldsymbol{\gamma}, f(\boldsymbol{z}_d(\boldsymbol{\eta}_{u_i} - \boldsymbol{\eta}_{u_j}))\rangle)} \quad (4)$$

where $n_{w,k}$ refers to the number of times word w has been assigned to topic k, and $n_{d,k}$ refers to the frequency of topic k in document d. We use the standard notation $\neg n$ to refer to the counts where the term being sampled is excluded.

Computing pairwise preference scores of users on new questions is equivalent to marginalizing over $\boldsymbol{y}_d$ and sampling topics using eq. 3, as shown by [7].

3.5 Supervised Stage

After sampling topics for each document, we find new regression parameters for all users, $\boldsymbol{\eta}_u$, as well as the ranking model, $\boldsymbol{\gamma}$, that maximize the likelihood of the response variables conditioned on the current state of topic assignments.

The main issue for learning parameters $\boldsymbol{\eta}$ is that most users have relatively few documents (questions) so that finding an accurate representation might be difficult. To alleviate this issue we resort to multitask learning which allows us to jointly learn all the η_u vectors. Multitask learning [4] can be seen as a form of transfer learning in which similar learning "tasks" share information contained in their training signals. This is particularly well suited for our setting as each user can represent a task and we can easily assume that groups of users will be experts in a set of common topics thus allowing for transfer of information among them. Moreover, we use group lasso [23] to select the relevant topics for all the users. We thus optimize the following multitask lasso objective using an l_1/l_2 regularization norm:

$$\|\boldsymbol{s} - \boldsymbol{z}\boldsymbol{\eta}\|_F^2 + \lambda \sum_u \sqrt{\sum_k \eta_{u,k}^2}$$

where $\boldsymbol{s}$ the matrix of scores of all documents d and user u combinations, $\boldsymbol{z}$ is the matrix of document d topic k representations, $\boldsymbol{\eta}$ the matrix of all user u, topic k representations and λ the regularization parameter.

Regarding the ranking model $\boldsymbol{\gamma}$, the proposed framework is flexible enough to accomodate different binary classification methods. A metric notion of the decision function is required to properly assess the variation experienced by the predicted responses for different topic assignments, which gets transferred into the the Gibbs samping distribution (eq. 4). We experimented with two linear models, Logistic Regression and Linear SVM, because the linear formulation allows for several optimizations in the Gibbs sampling implementation. While both performed similarly in terms of accuracy, we chose logistic regression with l_2 regularization in our experimental setting as it empirically showed to be more stable w.r.t. the choice of hyperparameters.

3.6 Hyperparameter Tuning

The model counts with a number of hyperparameters that need to be properly tuned, in particular the Dirichlet priors α and β, the regression regularizer λ, and the classification regularizer C. These are treated as constants to be estimated instead of random variables of the model.

To describe our estimation strategy let us first define how the stochastic EM procedure is carried out. Firstly, we allow for a number burn-in iterations of the Gibbs sampler, which we set empirically to $M_b = 40$. During these iterations, we remove from the sampling distribution the factor corresponding to $P(\boldsymbol{y}|\boldsymbol{z}, \boldsymbol{\eta}, \boldsymbol{\gamma})$ as we have not yet enough information to initialize both $\boldsymbol{\eta}$ and $\boldsymbol{\gamma}$. From this point onwards, the procedure follows these steps:

1. Smooth topic assignments: we compute a smoothed version of the topic mixtures of documents, $\bar{z}_d$, by averaging the mixtures obtained on the previous M_s iterations. We fixed this value $M_s = 20$ empirically.
2. Build regression and ranking models: We find new values for $\boldsymbol{\eta}$ and $\boldsymbol{\gamma}$ using the current topic assignments $\bar{\boldsymbol{z}}_d$ and the observed training responses $\boldsymbol{y_d}$ following the procedure described in Section 3.5.
3. Draw topic assignments using CGS: We perform M_g iterations of the full Gibbs sampler to draw topics for all documents. We set $M_g = 40$ empirically.

This process is repeated until the total number of Gibbs sampling iterations reaches $M = 500$.

Regarding the estimation of the concentration parameters, α and β, we estimate them directly from data. Wallach *et al.* provided empirical evidence of the performance gains obtained by using asymmetric priors [16], which are unfeasible to set using grid-search approaches. In particular, we used the Digamma Recurrence Relation proposed by Wallach [15] to optimize both concentration parameters. This process is performed every 5 iterations of the Gibbs sampler. Regarding the regularization parameters λ and C, we chose them using grid-search with a 3-fold cross validation strategy.

4. EXPERIMENTAL SETUP

We consider the task of question recommendation, which comprises the prediction of the best experts for previously unseen questions. To this end, we consider a set of questions that has a known set of experts, generate a rank of possible experts using our model, and compare both. We use community feedback as ground truth for the quality of responses, so the the ideal rank to predict is obtained by sorting users for each question in decreasing order of score (i.e. aggregated number of votes).

4.1 Dataset

The study presented in this paper considers data from the *Cross Validate*[2] community of the Stack Exchange net-

[2]`http://stats.stackexchange.com`

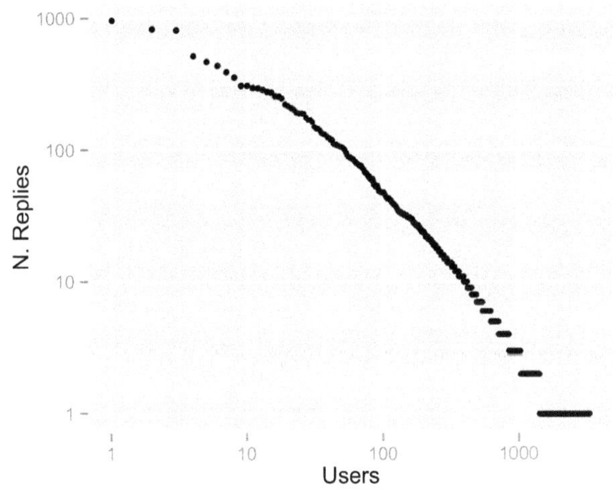

Figure 2: Number of replies for *Cross Validate* users, in decreasing order of participation (log-log scale)

work, focusing on Q&A about statistics and machine learning. Stack Exchange releases Creative Commons-licensed data dumps quarterly, which include the textual content of posts and other metadata (e.g. date, scores, authors).

Throughout the experiments of this paper, we used the Cross Validate data dump corresponding to June 2013, which comprises 3 years, $21,819$ questions, $28,429$ answers and $11,281$ unique users. Only $15,894$ of these questions have at least 1 answer, which represents 72.84% of the total. The median time to receive the first answer is 2.3 hours. Hence, there is room for improvement in terms of answer coverage and average waiting time.

Regarding participation, only $3,334$ users ($< 30\%$) answered at least 1 question. Low participation levels are organic to CQA communities, where most of the answers are generated by a minority of contributors. In this case, 80% of the answers have been contributed by the top 430 most active users. The median number of questions replied per user is 1, with a mean of 8.527. In Figure 2 we show this long-tail distribution of answering participation in our set.

In terms of community feedback, users make active use of the rating mechanisms. Both questions and answers can be voted as positive or negative; votes get aggregated into a score value, which we used as ground truth for the supervised stage of our model. In total, $23,986$ posts were voted by the community, representing almost 85% of all the posts.

4.2 Baseline Description

Section 5 evaluates the effectiveness of the presented model by comparing it to several other methods that we use as baselines. For every question in the test set we compare to:

- Popularity Ranking (**PR**): ranks users according to their answering frequency in decreasing order. This naive baseline approach does not entail profiling users from their history of previous contributions.
- TF-IDF (**BOW**): considers user profiles based on a *tf-idf* representation of the contributions of users to the system. In our setup, user profiles encompass all textual content (questions and answers) posted by the user and, additionally, the questions they have replied. Ranking is established in increasing order of cosine distance between the *tf-idf* representation of new questions with all user profiles.
- LSI (**LSI**): considers latent semantic indexing (LSI) for representing user profiles and questions. We consider question threads (including all contributed answers) as the documents for finding the latent topics of the corpus. User profiles are built by aggregating all their contributions as well as the questions they have provided answers to. These are then used as input documents to the learned LSI model to obtain users' topic mixtures. Ranking is established using the cosine distance between user profiles and questions.
- LDA+Ranking (**LDA-R**): considers a *RankSLDA* model where the supervised factor of the Gibbs sampler (eq. 4) is omitted. This corresponds to an unsupervised LDA model where topics are learned from the corpus and then used to train a pairwise ranking model using the observed responses $s(d,u)$ as ground truth. Similarly to *RankSLDA*, question threads act as the documents for finding the latent topics of the corpus $\boldsymbol{z}_d$, and user profiles $\boldsymbol{\eta}_u$ are learned from the observed responses via regression. These two pieces of information are used to build feature vectors $\Phi(d,u)$ as explained in section 3.2, which serve to train the pairwise ranking model. Comparing with this baseline enables us to observe the effect of including the observed scores as an integral part of the Bayesian inference process for the RandSLDA model.

4.3 Evaluation Metrics

We used ranking evaluation metrics to assess the precision of our method and the different baseline approaches considered. Note that our target rank to predict is obtained by sorting users for each question in decreasing order of community-provided score.

- **P@k:** Precision at cut-off k measures the number of users that provided a response in the top k positions of the predicted rank, normalized by the cut-off value. To binarize our ground truth we consider any user with an aggregated score over 0 as relevant. We evaluate precision at cut-off levels $K = \{1, 5, 10\}$.
- **nDCG@k:** Discounted Cumulative Gain (DCG) extends *P@k* to allow for multiple relevance values. It is defined by the expression:

$$\text{DCG@k} = \sum_{i=1}^{k} \frac{2^{s_i} - 1}{log_2(i+1)}$$

where s_i stands for the relevance score of the i-th author. The normalized DCG (nDCG) normalizes this score to allow comparison across different queries. The normalizing factor is obtained by computing the DCG@k for the ideal rank. We evaluate nDCG at cut-off levels $K = \{1, 5, 10\}$.

- **MAP:** Mean average precision for a set of queries is

$$\text{MAP} = \frac{\sum_{q=1}^{Q} AP(q)}{Q}$$

where $AP(q)$ denotes the average precision for query q, computed as

$$AP(q) = \frac{\sum_{k=1}^{U} P@k(q) \cdot \mathbb{I}(s_k > 0)}{\sum_{k=1}^{U} \mathbb{I}(s_k > 0)}$$

where $\mathbb{I}$(cond) is an indicator function with value 1 if *cond* is true, and 0 otherwise.

- **MRR:** Mean Reciprocal Rank is the average of the Reciprocal Rank for a set of queries. The reciprocal rank for a query q is defined as

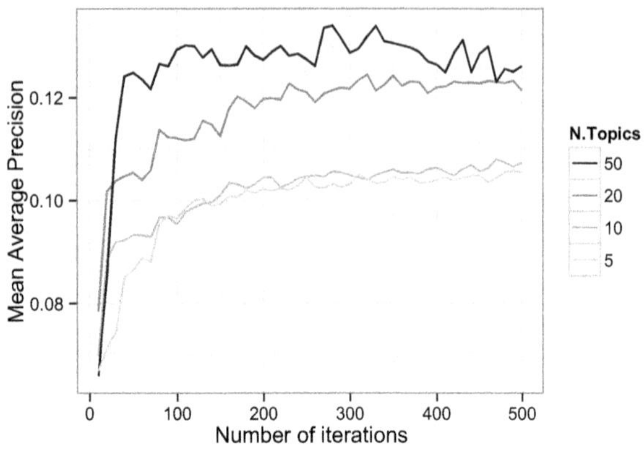

Figure 3: Evolution of MAP for *RankSLDA*

$$RR(q) = \frac{1}{r_q}$$

with r_q being the rank of the first relevant user for question q, using the same notion of relevance as for P@k.

5. RESULTS

In this section we present the results obtained from the application of the *RankSLDA* model, as well as the baseline methods, to the question recommendation scenario using the dataset introduced in Section 4. We split the original dataset into two partitions for training and test purposes following a strictly chronological criterion. Our training set comprises 75% of the question threads, from July 2010 to February 2013. The rest of the dataset, from February 2013 onwards, was used as the test collection.

The number of active users in the training set was 8,805, from which 2,930 contributed replies. We decided to set a minimum threshold of activity by discarding from the training set all users with 5 or less contributed replies, which led to a total of 967 users. Regarding the test set, we consider the same collection of 967 users as we do not have information to model new answerers. After applying this criterion for user selection, we removed the contributions of "inactive" users from the dataset. We then proceeded to eliminate question threads with less than two answers, leading to a total of 6,108 question threads for training and 2,092 for test. The dataset information is gathered in Table 2.

We show the overall results for all performance metrics in Table 3. We can observe that the *RankSLDA* method systematically outperforms the baselines for all metrics considered. The best performance is achieved by the *RankSLDA* method for $K = 50$ topics, as the higher number of topics enables the model to generate finer-grained models of user expertise, boosting the question-user matching accuracy.

Despite its simplicity, popularity ranking achieves comparable results to more sophisticated approaches (LSI with up to 500 topics) and not far from the *tf-idf* approach, especially if we factor in the high dimensionality of the latter, over 45,000 features in our corpus. The supervised approaches, LDA-R and *RankSLDA*, provide significant improvements over more simple baselines. Even with a low dimensionality, $K = 5$ topics, *RankSLDA* achieves a MAP of over 0.10, meaning that in average at least 1 of the top-10 users ranked is relevant for the question. None of the unsupervised methods was able to obtain this score.

Table 2: Characteristics of the test dataset

Collection	Type	N.Question threads	N.Users
Training	Unfiltered	16,893	2,930
	Filtered	6,108	967
Test	Unfiltered	4,926	811
	Filtered	2,092	967

The MAP evolution across iterations of the Gibbs sampler for different number of topics, K is depicted in Figure 3. After the initial burn-in period of the first 40 iterations, the full conditional sampling distribution starts being taken into account. This is followed by a steady increase in MAP, that is particularly noticeable for $K = \{5, 10, 20\}$.

For $K = 50$, we observe an initial growing trend that plateaus after the first 100 iterations. This evidences a tendency of the *RankSLDA* model to overfit the training data when increasing the number of topics. An early termination strategy could be used to avoid this artifact and get closer to the maximum test ranking performance, obtained in this case at iteration $i = 280$ with an MAP $= 0.1339$.

In Figure 4 we compare the evolution of MAP between *RankSLDA* and LDA-R across iterations of the Gibbs sampler for different number of topics. LDA-R shows a similar pattern in all cases, with a rapid increase in MAP after the burn-in period, and a plateau effect once the Gibbs sampler converges to the posterior distribution. *RankSLDA*, on the other hand, continuously improves MAP by alternating the EM steps described in Section 3. These plots show the impact of equation 4 in the assignment of document topics for the *RankSLDA* model, which effectively shifts topic assignments towards mixtures that better help explain the observed rankings during training.

Figures 5 and 6 show similar plots comparing *RankSLDA* and LDA-R for P@k and nDCG@k respectively. The results depict a similar scenario to the one described previously for Figure 4, with LDA-R plateauing after a small number of iterations, and *RankSLDA* improving in time thanks to the model capacity to adapt to observed scores when sampling topic assignments. We can observe the most notable difference between LDA-R and *RankSLDA* in the *P@1* case, which highlights the better ability of *RankSLDA* to choose a relevant user at the top of the rank.

6. CONCLUSIONS AND FUTURE WORK

In this paper, we have proposed *RankSLDA*, a Bayesian framework that combines supervised ranking with topic modeling. It can be applied to question recommendation, where both community feedback and text content topics are jointly modeled for ranking users according to their relevance for new questions. Our experiments using data from the Cross Validate community show empirical evidence of the ability of the model to influence topic assignments during training to better explain the observed community scores. CQA communities could benefit from question recommendation for decreasing the rate of unanswered questions and reducing the average waiting time for answers to new questions.

We plan to explore how this model could be used to encourage participation in the community by promoting the rank of less active users in the long-tail of participation. We are also interested in exploring alternative ranking models in this framework, e.g. list-wise ranking approaches.

Table 3: Performance evaluation of the question recommendation task for the different methods considered. The best score for each evaluation metric is highlighted in boldface.

#Topics	Method	MRR	MAP	P@1	P@5	P@10	nDCG@1	nDCG@5	nDCG@10
-	PR	0.0679	0.0597	0.0320	0.0269	0.0196	0.0304	0.0612	0.0757
-	BOW	0.0946	0.0908	0.0502	0.0316	0.0265	0.0433	0.0775	0.1030
100		0.0358	0.0350	0.0124	0.0123	0.0102	0.0106	0.0265	0.0359
500	LSI	0.0610	0.0598	0.0292	0.0202	0.0163	0.0292	0.0486	0.0629
1000		0.0713	0.0694	0.0382	0.0238	0.0197	0.0313	0.0572	0.0766
5	LDA-R	0.1060	0.0946	0.0654	0.0326	0.0249	0.0611	0.0912	0.1123
	RankSLDA	0.1176	0.1054	0.0831	0.0338	0.0237	0.0767	0.1016	0.1180
10	LDA-R	0.1085	0.0979	0.0530	0.0385	0.0283	0.0485	0.0976	0.1208
	RankSLDA	0.1205	0.1073	0.0697	0.0391	0.0300	0.0652	0.1063	0.1325
20	LDA-R	0.1249	0.1100	0.0745	0.0406	0.0294	0.0696	0.1102	0.1328
	RankSLDA	0.1375	0.1214	0.0874	0.0437	0.0325	0.0816	0.1222	0.1483
50	LDA-R	0.1359	0.1198	0.0869	0.0464	0.0316	0.0799	0.1251	0.1453
	RankSLDA	**0.1403**	**0.1261**	**0.0917**	**0.0481**	**0.0340**	**0.0832**	**0.1312**	**0.1559**

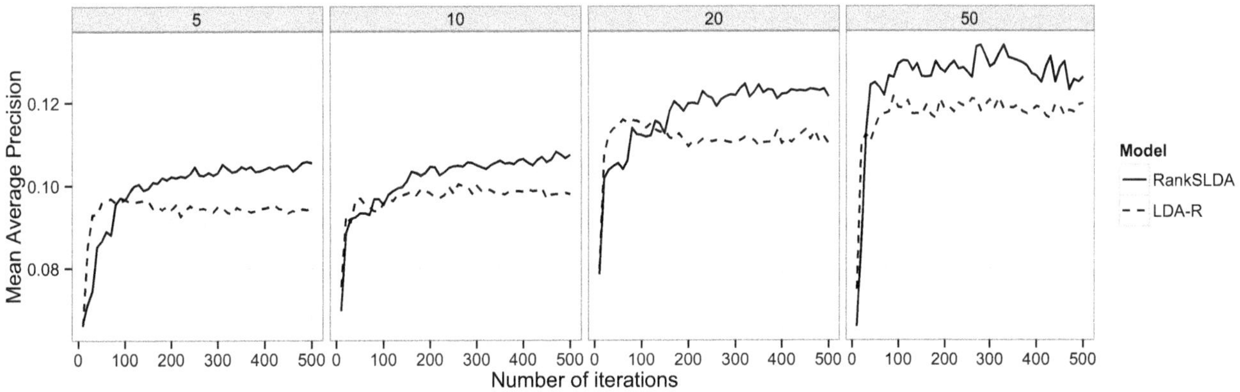

Figure 4: Evolution of MAP for *RankSLDA* vs LDA-R for different n. topics $K = \{5, 10, 20, 50\}$

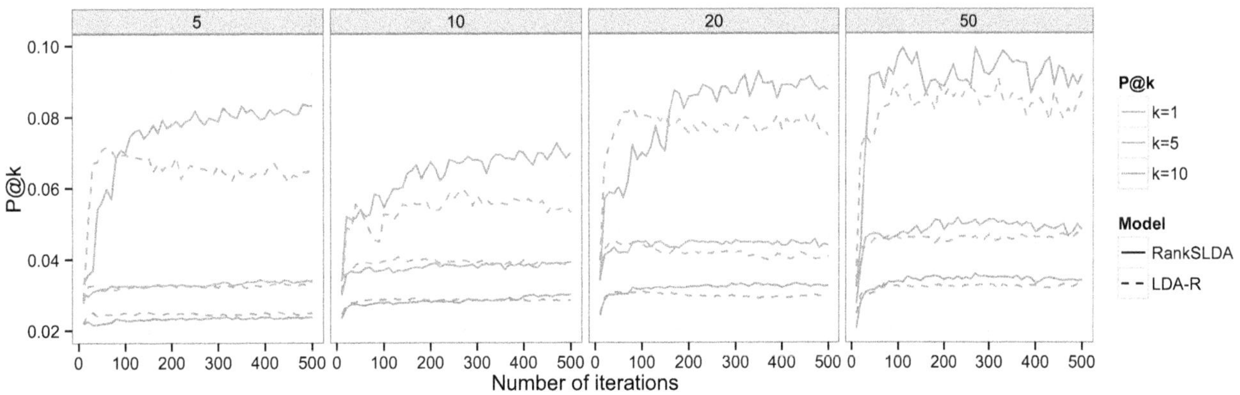

Figure 5: Evolution of P@k for *RankSLDA* vs LDA-R at levels for different n. topics $K = \{5, 10, 20, 50\}$

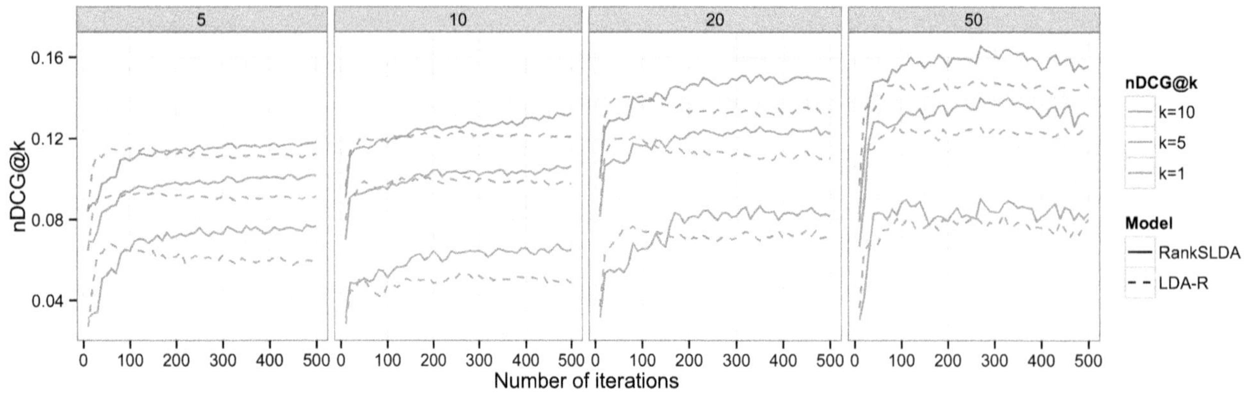

Figure 6: Evolution of nDCG@k for *RankSLDA* vs LDA-R at levels for different n. topics $K = \{5, 10, 20, 50\}$

7. ACKNOWLEDGEMENTS

The work leading to these results has received partial funding from the EU 7th Framework Programme (FP7/2007-2013) under grant agreement n° 610594 (CrowdRec).

8. REFERENCES

[1] D. Agarwal and B.-C. Chen. flda: Matrix factorization through latent dirichlet allocation. In *Proceedings of the Third ACM International Conference on Web Search and Data Mining*, WSDM '10, pages 91–100, 2010.

[2] c. Aslay, N. O'Hare, L. M. Aiello, and A. Jaimes. Competition-based Networks for Expert Finding. In *Proceedings of the 36th International ACM SIGIR Conference*, pages 1033–1036, 2013.

[3] D. M. Blei and J. D. McAuliffe. Supervised Topic Models, Mar. 2010.

[4] R. Caruana. Multitask learning. *Machine Learning*, 28(1):41–75, July 1997.

[5] B. C. Chen, A. Dasgupta, X. Wang, and J. Yang. Vote Calibration in Community Question-answering Systems. In *Proceedings of the 35th International ACM SIGIR Conference*, pages 781–790. ACM, 2012.

[6] G. Dror, Y. Koren, Y. Maarek, and I. Szpektor. I Want to Answer; Who Has a Question?: Yahoo! Answers Recommender System. In *Proceedings of the 17th ACM SIGKDD Conference*, pages 1109–1117. ACM, 2011.

[7] J. B. Graber and P. Resnik. Holistic sentiment analysis across languages: multilingual supervised latent Dirichlet allocation. In *Proceedings of the 2010 Conference on Empirical Methods in Natural Language Processing*, EMNLP '10, pages 45–55, Stroudsburg, PA, USA, 2010. Association for Computational Linguistics.

[8] J. Guo, S. Xu, S. Bao, and Y. Yu. Tapping on the Potential of Q&A Community by Recommending Answer Providers. In *Proceedings of the 17th ACM CIKM Conference*, pages 921–930, 2008.

[9] Y. Koren, R. Bell, and C. Volinsky. Matrix factorization techniques for recommender systems. *Computer*, 42(8):30–37, Aug. 2009.

[10] J. Liu, Y. I. Song, and C. Y. Lin. Competition-based user expertise score estimation. In *Proceedings of the 34th international ACM SIGIR conference*, SIGIR '11, pages 425–434, 2011.

[11] X. Ni, Y. Lu, X. Quan, L. Wenyin, and B. Hua. User interest modeling and its application for question recommendation in user-interactive question answering systems. *Information Processing & Management*, 48(2):218–233, Mar. 2012.

[12] S. Rendle, C. Freudenthaler, Z. Gantner, and L. Schmidt-Thieme. Bpr: Bayesian personalized ranking from implicit feedback. In *Proceedings of the 25th Conference on Uncertainty in Artificial Intelligence*, UAI '09, pages 452–461, 2009.

[13] F. Riahi, Z. Zolaktaf, M. Shafiei, and E. Milios. Finding expert users in community question answering. In *Proceedings of the 21st WWW conference*, pages 791–798. ACM, 2012.

[14] Y. Shi, A. Karatzoglou, L. Baltrunas, M. Larson, N. Oliver, and A. Hanjalic. Climf: Learning to maximize reciprocal rank with collaborative less-is-more filtering. In *Proceedings of the Sixth ACM Conference on Recommender Systems*, RecSys '12, pages 139–146, 2012.

[15] H. M. Wallach. *Structured Topic Models for Language.* PhD thesis, University of Cambridge, 2008.

[16] H. M. Wallach, D. M. Mimno, and A. Mccallum. Rethinking LDA: Why Priors Matter. In Y. Bengio, D. Schuurmans, J. Lafferty, C. Williams, and A. Culotta, editors, *Advances in Neural Information Processing Systems 22*, pages 1973–1981. 2009.

[17] M. Weimer, A. Karatzoglou, Q. V. Le, and A. Smola. Maximum margin matrix factorization for collaborative ranking. *Advances in Neural Information Processing Systems, NIPS*, 2007.

[18] H. Wu, Y. Wang, and X. Cheng. Incremental Probabilistic Latent Semantic Analysis for Automatic Question Recommendation. In *Proceedings of the 2008 ACM Conference on Recommender Systems*, RecSys '08, pages 99–106, New York, NY, USA, 2008. ACM.

[19] F. Xu, Z. Ji, and B. Wang. Dual role model for question recommendation in community question answering. In *Proceedings of the 35th international ACM SIGIR conference*, pages 771–780. ACM, 2012.

[20] Z. Yan and J. Zhou. A New Approach to Answerer Recommendation in Community Question Answering Services. In *34th European Conference on Advances in Information Retrieval*, pages 121–132, 2012.

[21] L. Yang, M. Qiu, S. Gottipati, F. Zhu, J. Jiang, H. Sun, and Z. Chen. CQArank: Jointly Model Topics and Expertise in Community Question Answering. In *Proceedings of the 22nd ACM International CIKM Conference*, pages 99–108. ACM, 2013.

[22] T. Yeh, B. White, J. San Pedro, B. Katz, and L. S. Davis. A case for query by image and text content: Searching computer help using screenshots and keywords. In *Proceedings of the 20th International Conference on World Wide Web*, WWW '11, pages 775–784. ACM, 2011.

[23] M. Yuan and Y. Lin. Model selection and estimation in regression with grouped variables. *Journal of the Royal Statistical Society: Series B (Statistical Methodology)*, 68(1):49–67, Feb. 2006.

[24] J. Zhang, M. S. Ackerman, and L. Adamic. Expertise networks in online communities: structure and algorithms. In *16th International Conference on WWW*. ACM, 2007.

Bayesian Binomial Mixture Model for Collaborative Prediction With Non-Random Missing Data

Yong-Deok Kim and Seungjin Choi
Department of Computer Science and Engineering
Pohang University of Science and Technology
77 Cheongam-ro, Nam-gu, Pohang 790-784, Korea
{karma13,seungjin}@postech.ac.kr

ABSTRACT

Collaborative prediction involves filling in missing entries of a user-item matrix to predict preferences of users based on their observed preferences. Most of existing models assume that the data is *missing at random* (MAR), which is often violated in recommender systems in practice. Incorrect assumption on missing data ignores the missing data mechanism, leading to biased inferences and prediction. In this paper we present a Bayesian binomial mixture model for collaborative prediction, where the generative process for data and missing data mechanism are jointly modeled to handle *non-random missing data*. Missing data mechanism is modeled by three factors, each of which is related to users, items, and rating values. Each factor is modeled by Bernoulli random variable, and the observation of rating value is determined by the Boolean OR operation of three binary variables. We develop computationally-efficient variational inference algorithms, where variational parameters have closed-form update rules and the computational complexity depends on the number of observed ratings, instead of the size of the rating data matrix. We also discuss implementation issues on hyperparameter tuning and estimation based on empirical Bayes. Experiments on Yahoo! Music and MovieLens datasets confirm the useful behavior of our model by demonstrating that: (1) it outperforms state-of-the-art methods in yielding higher predictive performance; (2) it finds meaningful solutions instead of undesirable boundary solutions; (3) it provides rating trend analysis on why ratings are observed.

Categories and Subject Descriptors

H.3.3 [**Information Search and Retrieval**]: Information filtering; I.2.6 [**Artificial Intelligence**]: Parameter learning

Keywords

Collaborative filtering; non-random missing data; probabilistic models; recommender systems; variational Bayesian inference

RecSys'14, October 6âĂŞ10, 2014, San Jose or vicinity, CA, USA

http://dx.doi.org/10.1145/2645710.2645754.

1. INTRODUCTION

Collaborative prediction is a popular technique used in recommender systems, the task of which is to fill in missing entries of a user-item matrix given a small set of observed entries, to predict preferences of users based on their observed preferences. Suppose that we are given a set of observed entries, $\boldsymbol{X}_\Omega = \{X_{ij} \,|\, (i,j) \in \Omega, 1 \leq i \leq I, 1 \leq j \leq J\}$, where $X_{ij} \in \{1,\ldots,V\}$ represents a value of rating by user i on item j, and Ω is the set of (i,j) pairs for which the corresponding X_{ij} is observed. Then, collaborative prediction involves inferring $\boldsymbol{X}_{\Omega^c}$ given $\boldsymbol{X}_\Omega$, where $\boldsymbol{X}_\Omega \cup \boldsymbol{X}_{\Omega^c} = \boldsymbol{X} \in \mathbb{R}^{I\times J}$.

The real-world collaborative prediction problem is challenging computationally as well as statistically, since the user-item matrix is extremely large and sparse. For example, in the Yahoo! Music dataset [2], there are 1000990 users and 624961 items, but only 262810175 observed ratings are available, which constitutes 0.0042 percent of $\boldsymbol{X}$. In addition to size and sparseness problems, the collaborative prediction is more than completing a matrix, because of *non-ignorable missing data mechanism*, which is a main concern of this paper.

It follows from the theory of missing data that the mechanism for missing data are divided into three cases: *missing completely at random* (MCAR), *missing at random* (MAR), and *missing not at random* (MNAR) [7]. MCAR is the most restrictive assumption, where the probability that X_{ij} is observed does not depend on the data in any way. Most of theories developed for matrix completion assume MCAR, where missing or non-missing is decided by coin-flips, regardless of index (i,j) and rating value [1]. However, the MCAR assumption is easily violated in collaborative prediction problems. For example, some users rate items more actively than others and some items are rated by many users while others are rarely rated. MAR is the case where missing or non-missing depends on the index (i,j) but does not depend on rating value X_{ij}. More precisely, in the MAR assumption, the probability that a data point is observed is related to particular variables but is not related to the values of those variables. Most of previous methods for collaborative prediction have been developed, assuming MAR. They include theory on weighted trace norm regularization for non-uniform sampling [18, 3], probabilistic models such as URP [8] and RBM [17], and Bayesian matrix factorization (BMF) [5, 15, 16, 21, 14, 4].

When the data is MAR, the missing data mechanism can be ignored and parameter estimation or inferences are unbiased. However there is a strong evidence that MAR is an incorrect assumption for collaborative prediction [11]. Intuitively, the MAR assumption is easily violated in recommendation system if, for instance: (1) users rate items they like more than ones they dislike; (2) users provides extreme ratings, that is, they only provide feedback particularly good or bad items. In these examples, dependencies between the missing data values and observation process exist, hence the data is not MAR. When the MAR assumption does not hold, inferences are biased, leading to the degraded prediction performance.

An approach to dealing with MNAR data is to learn jointly a *complete data model* that explain how the data is generated, and a *missing data model* that explains the observation process for the data [7]. In this paper, we choose a binomial mixture model as the complete data model for the ordinal rating data matrix and propose a novel missing data model that explains the reason of observation as the function of three factors, each of which related with users, items, and rating values. Each factor is modelled by Bernoulli random variable, and the observation of rating value is determined by the Boolean OR operation of three binary variables. Because of the property of OR operation, one of three factors can override others, hence it naturally models the 80-20 rule, which commonly arise in the recommendation systems.

The combination of binomial mixture model and our novel missing data model makes possible to develop computationally efficient variational inference algorithms, where variational parameters have closed-form update rules and the computational complexity depends on the number of observed ratings, instead the size of the rating data matrix. In fact for this reason, we select the binomial mixture model as the complete data model instead of widely used matrix factorization model. We also discuss implementation issues on hyperparameter tuning and estimation based on empirical Bayes.

Experiments on *Yahoo! Musing ratings for User Selected and Randomly Selected Songs* dataset show that our model outperforms the state-of-the-art method for MNAR data, which is a combination of multinomial mixture model and CPT-v+ missing data model [11, 9, 10]. Our model finds meaningful solution instead of undesirable boundary solution (see Figure 2-(d)), if hyperparameters are carefully estimated by empirical Bayes method. In addition to higher predictive performance on MNAR data, our model provides rating trend analysis on why ratings are observed. Preliminary experiments on Yahoo! Music and MovieLens datasets show that our model can capture the different rating trend between two domains: song and movie. Throughout the paper, we use notations described in Table 1.

2. RELATED WORK

We introduce a companion matrix of response indicator $\boldsymbol{R}$, where $R_{ij} = 1$ if X_{ij} is observed, and $R_{ij} = 0$ if X_{ij} is missing. Following the missing data theory [7], we formulate the non-ignorable missing data mechanism as a two-step procedure. First a complete data model with parameter Θ, $p(\boldsymbol{X}|\Theta)$, generates the complete data matrix $\boldsymbol{X} = \boldsymbol{X}_\Omega \cup \boldsymbol{X}_{\Omega^c}$. Then a missing data model with parameter Υ, $p(\boldsymbol{R}|\boldsymbol{X}, \Upsilon)$, determines which elements in $\boldsymbol{X}$ are observed. Hence, we can take a factorized joint distribution for $\boldsymbol{X}$ and $\boldsymbol{R}$ given Θ and Υ:

$$p(\boldsymbol{R}, \boldsymbol{X}|\Theta, \Upsilon) = p(\boldsymbol{R}|\boldsymbol{X}, \Upsilon)p(\boldsymbol{X}|\Theta). \quad (1)$$

Most prior researches on collaborative prediction focus on the estimation of the complete data model $p(\boldsymbol{X}|\Theta)$, and usually ignore the missing data model $p(\boldsymbol{R}|\boldsymbol{X}, \Upsilon)$. Important exceptions are Marlin's works, where the *multinomial mixture* (MM) model is combined with two different missing data models called *CPT-v* and *Logit-vd* [11, 9, 10]. The first, CPT-v is a simple missing data model where the probability of observing a rating depends only on the underlying rating value. This model can capture the intuition that a user's preference for a particular item can influence whether the user rates that item. The CPT-v missing data model is parameterized by using a conditional probability table consisting of V Bernoulli parameters $\boldsymbol{\gamma} = [\gamma_1 \cdots \gamma_V]$ (hence the name CPT-v). The parameter γ_v gives the probability that an item will be rated if its true rating value is v: $p(R_{ij} = 1|X_{ij} = v) = \gamma_v$.

Table 1: Notation

Notation	Description
Ω	Set of indices (i, j) for which X_{ij} is observed.
Ω_i	Set of indices j for which X_{ij} is observed.
Ω_j	Set of indices i for which X_{ij} is observed.
Ω_v	Set of indices (i, j) for which X_{ij} is v.
Ω^c	Complementary set of Ω.
$\boldsymbol{z}_i$	The ith column vector of $\boldsymbol{Z}$.
$\boldsymbol{X}_\Omega$	$\{X_{ij}\|(i, j) \in \Omega\}$.
$\boldsymbol{X}_{\Omega^c}$	$\{X_{ij}\|(i, j) \in \Omega^c\}$.
H	The number of observed ratings.
H_i	The number of ratings by user i.
H_j	The number of ratings for item j.
H_v	The number of ratings with value v.
$\mathbf{1}[s]$	Indicator function that takes 1 if s is true.
Bin$(x\|p, N)$	Binomial distribution, p : success probability, N : and the number of trial.
Dir$(\boldsymbol{\theta}\|\alpha, K)$	Symmetric Dirichlet distribution, α : concentration parameter, K : the number of category .
Beta$(x\|a, b)$	Beta distribution, a, b : shape parameters.
Bern$(x\|p)$	Bernoulli distribution, p : success probability.

The CPT-v model makes the very strong assumption that a single value-based selection effect is responsible for generating all missing data. The second, Logit-vd is more flexible missing data model because it allows the probability of observation to depend both on the underlying rating value and the identity of the item. The Logit-vd model specifies a logistic form for this relationship as:

$$p(R_{ij} = 1|X_{ij} = v) = \frac{1}{1 + \exp(-(\sigma_v + \omega_j))}, \quad (2)$$

where σ_v models a non-random missing data effect that depend on the underlying rating value, and w_j is a per-item bias. This parameterization is more suitable than simple factorizations, such as product of Bernoulli probabilities

$$p(R_{ij} = 1|X_{ij} = v) = \gamma_v \, \nu_j \leq \min(\gamma_v, \nu_j), \quad (3)$$

because (2) can model *80-20 rule* which commonly arises in the recommendation system. In practice, some items are rated by many users, while others are rarely rated. The Logit-vd model can account for this by setting to ω_j to a large value. The logistic combination rule (2) allows ω_j to override σ_v, and produces a high selection probability for these extremely popular items.

Compare to the widely used matrix factorization model, the MM model is less flexible as the complete data model. However this simplicity makes possible to develop computationally efficient learning algorithm based on the expectation maximization (EM), when it is combined with CPT-v or Logit-vd missing data model. In addition, experimental results on Yahoo! music dataset showed that the MM model with these missing data models significantly outperforms other collaborative prediction models based on MAR assumption.

Although Marlin's works opened the door for collaborative prediction with non-random missing data and showed promising results, several problems still remain unsolved. At first, when MM model and missing data model are jointly learned, the EM algorithm converges to undesirable boundary solution, where almost all of the missing rating data are predicted to the value 2, as shown in Fig. 2-(d). In fact the best performing model, referred to *MM/CPT-v+* in [9], was obtained by an unnatural way, where only parameters for the MM model is learned by EM algorithm, while parameters for the CPT-v model is fixed to optimal values

$$\hat{\gamma} = [0.014, 0.011, 0.027, 0.063, 0.225], \quad (4)$$

which is estimated by using a held-out dataset. Interestingly joint learning of complete data model and missing data model was converged to undesirable boundary solution even strong informative priors on γ were given by using $\hat{\gamma}$ [11, 9]. Secondly generalized EM algorithm for Logit-vd does not have close-form update rules, hence requires careful tuning of learning rate for gradient assent updates and a large number of iteration for convergence (more than 5000 iteration). In addition, although Logit-vd showed better predictive performance than CPT-v [10], it is still significantly worse than CPT-v+[9].

In this paper, we thoroughly try to solve the aforementioned problems. As a part of solution, we choose the binomial mixture model for modelling rating data because it takes account of the ordinal nature of rating values, which is ignored in the MM model. The idea of using the binomial distribution for modelling ordinal nature of rating values can also be found in binomial matrix factorization model [20], but it is based on the MAR assumption.

There are also several works which consider MNAR rating data in the widely used matrix factorization framework. Instead of explicitly modelling missing data model, AllRank model optimizes a ranking-based metric that is robust to MNAR data [19]. The resulting method can be applied to recommendation, but not to rating prediction task.

Response aware probabilistic matrix factorization model [6] combined probabilistic matrix factorization with missing data model which is similar to [11, 10]. Although this model is based on powerful matrix factorization, it has several weak points: (1) there is no closed form update rules; (2) careful tuning of learning rate and other meta parameters is required, hence reproducibility is bad; (3) the computational complexity is high, it depends on data matrix size instead of the number of observed ratings. In our empirical study, reported RMSE of this model on the randomly selected Yahoo! music dataset is significantly worse than MM/CPT-v+.

Another variation of probabilistic matrix factorization for MNAR rating data is specialized to implicit (a.k.a binary or one-class) feedback case [13], where Bayesian generative process for implicit rating data is proposed. It models the *like* probability by interpreting the missing signal as a two-stage process: firstly, by modelling the odds of a user considering an item, and secondly, by eliciting a probability that the item will be view or liked. In this paper we model the explicit MNAR rating data, and it is harder than implicit one because common users usually rate on the good item but sometimes will rate on the bad item to express their strong dissatisfaction.

3. BAYESIAN-BM/OR

We present our Bayesian binomial mixture model for collaborative prediction with non-random missing data, which is referred to as Bayesian-BM/OR in this paper. The graphical model for Bayesian-BM/OR is shown in Figure 1.

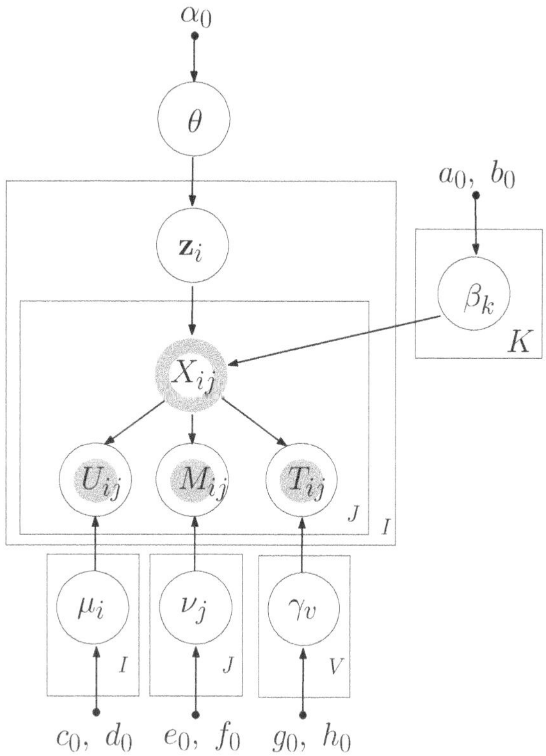

Figure 1: A graphical model for binomial mixture with our non-random missing data model. Blank and hollow circles denote unobserved and partially observed variables respectively. Note that if X_{ij} is observed, then U_{ij}, M_{ij}, T_{ij} are unobserved, and vice versa.

3.1 Model

The generative process of the rating data matrix and missing data mechanism are as follows.

1. Choose the number of clusters K.
2. Choose mixing proportions $\boldsymbol{\theta} \sim \text{Dir}(\boldsymbol{\theta}|\alpha_0, K)$,
3. Choose parameters for binomial distributions

$$\boldsymbol{\beta} \sim \prod_{k=1}^{K}\prod_{j=1}^{J} \text{Beta}(\beta_{kj}|a_0, b_0)$$

4. For each user $i \in \{1, \ldots, I\}$
   (a) Choose a cluster indicator
   $$\boldsymbol{z}_i|\boldsymbol{\theta} \sim \text{Mult}(\boldsymbol{z}_i|\boldsymbol{\theta}) = \textstyle\prod_{k=1}^{K} \theta_k{}^{Z_{ki}}.$$
   (b) For each item $j \in \{1, \ldots, J\}$
   Choose a rating
   $$X_{ij}|\boldsymbol{z}_i, \boldsymbol{\beta} \sim \textstyle\prod_{k=1}^{K} \text{Bin}(X_{ij} - 1|\beta_{kj}, V-1)^{Z_{ki}}.$$
5. Choose per-user, per-item, and per-value parameters for missing data model

$$\boldsymbol{\mu}, \boldsymbol{\nu}, \boldsymbol{\gamma} \sim \prod_{i=1}^{I} \text{Beta}(\mu_i|c_0, d_0) \prod_{j=1}^{J} \text{Beta}(\nu_j|e_0, f_0) \prod_{v=1}^{V} \text{Beta}(\gamma_v|g_0, h_0)$$

6. For each $(i, j) \in \{1, \ldots, I\} \times \{1, \ldots, J\}$
   (a) Choose $U_{ij}|X_{ij}, \boldsymbol{\mu} \sim \text{Bern}(U_{ij}|\mu_i)$

(b) Choose $M_{ij}|X_{ij}, \boldsymbol{\nu} \sim \text{Bern}(M_{ij}|\nu_j)$
(c) Choose $T_{ij}|X_{ij}, \boldsymbol{\gamma} \sim \text{Bern}(T_{ij}|\gamma_{X_{ij}})$
(d) $R_{ij} = 1 - (1 - U_{ij})(1 - M_{ij})(1 - T_{ij})$.
X_{ij} is observed if $R_{ij} = 1$, otherwise X_{ij} is missing.

We choose a binomial mixture model as the complete data model for the rating data matrix because (1) the mixture model can capture the simple intuition that users form clusters according to their preferences for items; (2) the binomial distribution is suitable for modelling discrete, finite, and ordered rating values; (3) combined with our missing data model, it allows the efficient learning algorithm, of which time and space complexity depend on the number of observed rating instead the data matrix size.

We consider following conditions for the missing data model: (1) user activity, item popularity, value-based selection effect should be modeled; (2) one of these factors can override other factors such that the 80-20 rule can be well modeled; (3) combined with binomial mixture model, the computationally efficient learning algorithm should be derived.

One possible solution will be a extending the Logit-vd model by simply adding a per-user bias τ_i:

$$p(R_{ij} = 1|X_{ij} = v) = \Lambda_{ijv} = \frac{1}{1 + \exp(-(\sigma_v + \tau_i + \omega_j))}. \quad (5)$$

However unlike CPT-v and Logit-vd, the parameterization (5) does not allow computationally efficient learning algorithm. For example, the complexity for computing a log-likelihood depends on the size of rating matrix IJ, not on the number of observed rating H:

$$\log p(\boldsymbol{R}, \boldsymbol{X}_\Omega) = \log p(\boldsymbol{R}_\Omega, \boldsymbol{X}_\Omega) + \log p(\boldsymbol{R}_{\Omega^c}), \quad (6)$$

$$\log p(\boldsymbol{R}_\Omega, \boldsymbol{X}_\Omega) = \sum_{(i,j)\in\Omega} \log(\sum_{k=1}^{K} \theta_k P_{kjX_{ij}} \Lambda_{ijX_{ij}}),$$

$$\log p(\boldsymbol{R}_{\Omega^c}) = \sum_{(i,j)\in\Omega^c} \log \left(\sum_{k=1}^{K} \theta_k \sum_{v=1}^{V} P_{kjv}(1 - \Lambda_{ijv}) \right),$$

where $P_{kjv} = p(X_{ij} = v|Z_{ki} = 1)$. Note that sum operations are involved with all entry $(i, j) \in \Omega \cup \Omega^c$.

Instead of the logistic combination rules, we present a novel missing data model which fulfils all above-mentioned conditions. We assume that for each entry (i, j), the observation of rating value X_{ij} is determined by the Boolean OR operation of three binary random variables U_{ij}, M_{ij}, and T_{ij}, each of which is related with users, items, and rating values:

$$R_{ij} = U_{ij} \vee M_{ij} \vee T_{ij} = 1 - (1 - U_{ij})(1 - M_{ij})(1 - T_{ij}).$$

In addition, we assume that these binary random variables follow the Bernoulli distribution conditioned on X_{ij}:

$$p(U_{ij}, M_{ij}, T_{ij}|X_{ij} = v, \boldsymbol{\mu}, \boldsymbol{\nu}, \boldsymbol{\gamma}) = \text{Bern}(U_{ij}|\mu_i)\text{Bern}(M_{ij}|\nu_j)\text{Bern}(T_{ij}|\gamma_v). \quad (7)$$

More precisely speaking, U_{ij}, M_{ij}, and T_{ij} are conditioned on the row index, column index, and value of X_{ij}. With our missing data model, the probability of observation is computed by

$$\begin{aligned} p(R_{ij} = 1|X_{ij} = v) &= 1 - p(R_{ij} = 0|X_{ij} = v) \\ &= 1 - p(U_{ij} = 0, M_{ij} = 0, T_{ij} = 0|X_{ij} = v) \\ &= 1 - (1 - \mu_i)(1 - \nu_j)(1 - \gamma_v). \quad (8) \end{aligned}$$

Our missing data model naturally allows that one of three factors can override the rest, because of following inequality:

$$1 - (1 - \mu_i)(1 - \nu_j)(1 - \gamma_v) \geq \max(\mu_i, \nu_j, \gamma_v). \quad (9)$$

Table 2: Examples of the probability of observation (8)

μ_i	ν_j	γ_v	$p(R_{ij} = 1\|X_{ij} = v)$
0.01	0.01	0.01	0.029
0.01	0.01	0.1	0.118
0.01	0.1	0.1	0.198
0.1	0.1	0.1	0.271
0.9	0.1	0.1	0.919
0.9	0.5	0.1	0.955

A behaviour of probability of observation under various combination of (μ_i, ν_j, γ_v) is illustrated in Table 2.

3.2 Variational Inference

Note that there is a interesting reverse observed/missing relationship between X_{ij} and (U_{ij}, V_{ij}, R_{ij}). If X_{ij} is observed (i.e. $R_{ij} = 1$), we only know that at least one of U_{ij}, M_{ij}, T_{ij} is one, hence they are latent variables. However if X_{ij} is missing (i.e. $R_{ij} = 0$), then $U_{ij} = M_{ij} = T_{ij} = 0$, consequently they are observed variables. Hence the set of of observed variables is defined by $\mathcal{D} = \{\boldsymbol{X}_\Omega, \boldsymbol{U}_{\Omega^c}, \boldsymbol{M}_{\Omega^c}, \boldsymbol{T}_{\Omega^c}\}$ and the set of latent variable is defined by $\mathcal{Z} = \{\boldsymbol{\theta}, \boldsymbol{\beta}, \boldsymbol{\mu}, \boldsymbol{\nu}, \boldsymbol{\gamma}, \boldsymbol{X}_{\Omega^c}, \boldsymbol{Z}, \boldsymbol{U}_\Omega, \boldsymbol{M}_\Omega, \boldsymbol{T}_\Omega\}$.

We approximately compute posterior distributions over latent variables by maximizing a lower-bound on the marginal log-likelihood. The marginal log-likelihood $\log p(\mathcal{D})$ is given by

$$\begin{aligned} \log p(\mathcal{D}) &= \log \int p(\mathcal{D}, \mathcal{Z}) d\mathcal{Z} \\ &\geq \int q(\mathcal{Z}) \log \frac{p(\mathcal{D}, \mathcal{Z})}{q(\mathcal{Z})} d\mathcal{Z} \equiv \mathcal{F}(q), \quad (10) \end{aligned}$$

where Jensen's inequality was used to obtain the *variational lower-bound* $\mathcal{F}(q)$ and $q(\mathcal{Z})$ is *variational distribution*. We assume that the variational distribution factorizes as

$$q(\mathcal{Z}) = q(\boldsymbol{\theta})q(\boldsymbol{\beta})q(\boldsymbol{\mu})q(\boldsymbol{\nu})q(\boldsymbol{\gamma})q(\boldsymbol{X}_{\Omega^c}, \boldsymbol{Z})q(\boldsymbol{U}_\Omega, \boldsymbol{M}_\Omega, \boldsymbol{T}_\Omega).$$

Due to the space limitation, we omit the detailed derivation of variational inference algorithms and only present the final results in Table 3. But we emphasize that auxiliary latent variables $\boldsymbol{U}, \boldsymbol{M}, \boldsymbol{T}$ play key role for deriving closed-form update rules. Without them, we have to compute following expectation of log-likelihood

$$\langle \log p(R_{ij} = 1|X_{ij} = v, \boldsymbol{\mu}, \boldsymbol{\nu}, \boldsymbol{\gamma}) \rangle = \langle \log(1 - \mu_i\nu_j\gamma_v) \rangle, \quad (11)$$

which is intractable because it is no more conjugate to Beta distribution. But the free-form optimization can be easily solved with auxiliary latent variables. For example, optimal $q(\mu_i)$ is given by

$$\begin{aligned} &\log q(\mu_i) \\ &\propto \log p(\mu_i) + \sum_{j\in\Omega_i} \langle \log p(U_{ij}|X_{ij}, \mu_i) \rangle_{q(U_{ij})} \\ &\quad + \sum_{j\in\Omega_i^c} \sum_{v=1}^{V} q(X_{ij} = v) \log p(U_{ij} = 0|X_{ij} = v, \mu_i), \\ &\propto (c0 - 1) \log \mu_i + (d0 - 1) \log(1 - \mu_i) \\ &\quad + \sum_{j\in\Omega_i} (\langle U_{ij} \rangle \log \mu_i + \langle 1 - U_{ij} \rangle \log(1 - \mu_i)) \\ &\quad + \sum_{j\in\Omega_i^c} \log(1 - \mu_i). \end{aligned}$$

Taking the exponential on both sizes, we recognize that $q(\mu_i)$ is $\text{Beta}(\mu_i|c_i, d_i)$, where c_i and d_i are defined in Table 3.

Table 3: Variational distributions and corresponding updating rules and sufficient statistics are summarized.

Variational distributions	Updating rules and sufficient statistics
$q(\boldsymbol{\theta}) = \text{Dir}(\boldsymbol{\theta}\|\boldsymbol{\alpha})$	$\alpha_k = \alpha_0 + \sum_{i=1}^{I}\langle Z_{ki}\rangle$, $\quad\langle\log\alpha_k\rangle = \psi(\alpha_k) - \psi(\sum_{k=1}^{K}\alpha_k)$.
$q(\boldsymbol{\beta}) = \prod_{k,j}\text{Beta}(\beta_{kj}\|a_{kj}, b_{kj})$	$\xi_{kj} = \sum_{i\in\Omega_j} X_{ij}\langle Z_{ik}\rangle + \sum_{i\in\Omega_j^c}\langle X_{ij}Z_{ik}\rangle$, $\quad\langle\beta_{kj}\rangle = a_{kj}/(a_{kj} + a_{kj})$, $a_{kj} = a_0 - \sum_{i=1}^{I}\langle Z_{ik}\rangle + \xi_{kj}$, $\quad\langle\log\beta_{kj}\rangle = \psi(a_{kj}) - \psi(a_{kj} + a_{kj})$, $b_{kj} = b_0 + V\sum_{i=1}^{I}\langle Z_{ik}\rangle - \xi_{kj}$, $\quad\langle\log(1-\beta_{kj})\rangle = \psi(b_{kj}) - \psi(a_{kj} + b_{kj})$.
$q(\boldsymbol{\mu}) = \prod_{i=1}^{I}\text{Beta}(\mu_i\|c_i, d_i)$	$\xi_i = \sum_{j\in\Omega_i}\langle U_{ij}\rangle$, $\quad\langle\mu_i\rangle = c_i/(c_i + d_i)$, $c_i = c_0 + \xi_i$, $\quad\langle\log\mu_i\rangle = \psi(c_i) - \psi(c_i + d_i)$, $d_i = d_0 + J - \xi_i$, $\quad\langle\log(1-\mu_i)\rangle = \psi(d_i) - \psi(c_i + d_i)$.
$q(\boldsymbol{\nu}) = \prod_{j=1}^{I}\text{Beta}(\nu_j\|e_j, f_j)$	$\xi_j = \sum_{i\in\Omega_j}\langle M_{ij}\rangle$, $\quad\langle\nu_j\rangle = e_j/(e_j + f_j)$, $e_j = e_0 + \xi_j$, $\quad\langle\log\nu_j\rangle = \psi(e_j) - \psi(e_j + f_j)$, $f_j = f_0 + I - \xi_j$, $\quad\langle\log(1-\nu_j)\rangle = \psi(f_j) - \psi(e_j + f_j)$.
$q(\boldsymbol{\gamma}) = \prod_{v=1}^{V}\text{Beta}(\gamma_v\|g_v, h_v)$	$\xi_v = \sum_{(i,j)\in\Omega_v}\langle T_{ij}\rangle$, $\quad\langle\gamma_v\rangle = g_v/(g_v + h_v)$, $g_v = g_0 + \xi_v$, $\quad\langle\log\gamma_v\rangle = \psi(g_v) - \psi(g_v + h_v)$. $h_v = h_0 + H_v + \sum_{(i,j)\in\Omega^c} q(X_{ij} = v) - \xi_v$, $\quad\langle\log(1-\gamma_v)\rangle = \psi(h_v) - \psi(g_v + h_v)$.
$q(\boldsymbol{X}_{\Omega^c}, \boldsymbol{Z})$ $= \prod_{i=1}^{I} q(X_{\Omega_i^c}\|\boldsymbol{z}_i)q(\boldsymbol{z}_i)$, $q(X_{\Omega_i^c}\|\boldsymbol{z}_i)$ $= \prod_{j\in\Omega_i^c} q(X_{ij}\|\boldsymbol{z}_i)$, $q(X_{ij} = v\|\boldsymbol{z}_i) = \prod_{k=1}^{K}(\lambda_{kjv})^{Z_{ki}}$, $q(\boldsymbol{z}_i) = \prod_{k=1}^{K}(\rho_{ki})^{Z_{ki}}$.	$\tilde{\lambda}_{kjv} = \langle\log(1-\gamma_v)\rangle + \log\binom{V-1}{v-1} + v\langle\log\beta_{kj}\rangle + (V-v)\langle\log(1-\beta_{kj})\rangle$, $\lambda_{kjv} = \exp(\tilde{\lambda}_{kjv})/\sum_{v'=1}^{V}\exp(\tilde{\lambda}_{kjv'})$, $\phi_{kj} = \sum_{v=1}^{V}(v-1)\,\lambda_{kjv}$, $\bar{\phi}_{kj} = \sum_{v=1}^{V}\langle\log(1-\gamma_v)\rangle\lambda_{kjv}$, $\hat{\phi}_{kj} = \sum_{v=1}^{V}\lambda_{kjv}\log\lambda_{kjv}$, $\tilde{\phi}_{kj} = \phi_{kj}\langle\log\beta_{kj}\rangle + (V-1-\phi_{kj})\langle\log(1-\beta_{kj})\rangle + \sum_{v=1}^{V}\lambda_{kjv}\log\binom{V-1}{v-1}$, $\tilde{\rho}_{ki} = \langle\log\theta_k\rangle + \sum_{j\in\Omega_i}[(X_{ij}\langle\log\beta_{kj}\rangle + (V-X_{ij})\langle\log(1-\beta_{kj})\rangle]$ $\quad + \sum_{j\in\Omega_i^c}(\tilde{\phi}_{kj} + \bar{\phi}_{kj} - \hat{\phi}_{kj})$, $\rho_{ki} = \exp(\tilde{\rho}_{ki})/\sum_{k'=1}^{K}\exp(\tilde{\rho}_{k'i})$, $\langle Z_{ki}\rangle = \rho_{ki}$, $\langle X_{ij}Z_{ki}\rangle = \sum_{v=1}^{V}(v-1)\,q(X_{ij} = v\|Z_{ki} = 1)q(Z_{ki} = 1) = \sum_{v=1}^{V}(v-1)\,\lambda_{kjv}\rho_{ki} = \phi_{kj}\rho_{ki}$, $q(X_{ij} = v) = \sum_{k=1}^{K} q(X_{ij} = v\|Z_{ki} = 1)q(Z_{ki} = 1) = \sum_{k=1}^{K}\lambda_{kjv}\rho_{ki}$.
$q(\boldsymbol{U}_\Omega, \boldsymbol{M}_\Omega, \boldsymbol{T}_\Omega)$ $= \prod_{(i,j)\in\Omega} q(U_{ij}, M_{ij}, T_{ij})$	For $(U_{ij}, M_{ij}, T_{ij}) \in \{0,1\}^3 - (0,0,0)$ $q(U_{ij}, M_{ij}, T_{ij}) = \frac{(\tilde{\mu}_i^1)^{U_{ij}}(\tilde{\mu}_i^0)^{1-U_{ij}}(\tilde{\nu}_j^1)^{M_{ij}}(\tilde{\nu}_j^0)^{1-M_{ij}}(\tilde{\gamma}_{X_{ij}}^1)^{T_{ij}}(\tilde{\gamma}_{X_{ij}}^0)^{1-T_{ij}}}{(\tilde{\mu}_i^1+\tilde{\mu}_i^0)(\tilde{\nu}_j^1+\tilde{\nu}_j^0)(\tilde{\gamma}_{X_{ij}}^1+\tilde{\gamma}_{X_{ij}}^0)-\tilde{\mu}_i^0\tilde{\gamma}_j^0\tilde{\gamma}_{X_{ij}}^0}$, where $\tilde{\mu}_i^1 = \exp(\langle\log\mu_i\rangle)$, $\quad\tilde{\mu}_i^0 = \exp(\langle\log(1-\mu_i)\rangle)$, $\tilde{\nu}_j^1 = \exp(\langle\log\nu_j\rangle)$, $\quad\tilde{\nu}_j^0 = \exp(\langle\log(1-\nu_j)\rangle)$, $\tilde{\gamma}_v^1 = \exp(\langle\log\gamma_v\rangle)$, $\quad\tilde{\gamma}_v^0 = \exp(\langle\log(1-\gamma_v)\rangle)$. $\langle U_{ij}\rangle = q(U_{ij} = 1) = \frac{\tilde{\mu}_i^1(\tilde{\nu}_j^1+\tilde{\nu}_j^0)(\tilde{\gamma}_{X_{ij}}^1+\tilde{\gamma}_{X_{ij}}^0)}{(\tilde{\mu}_i^1+\tilde{\mu}_i^0)(\tilde{\nu}_j^1+\tilde{\nu}_j^0)(\tilde{\gamma}_{X_{ij}}^1+\tilde{\gamma}_{X_{ij}}^0)-\tilde{\mu}_i^1\tilde{\gamma}_j^1\tilde{\gamma}_{X_{ij}}^1}$, $\langle M_{ij}\rangle = q(M_{ij} = 1) = \frac{(\tilde{\mu}_i^1+\tilde{\mu}_i^0)\tilde{\nu}_j^1(\tilde{\gamma}_{X_{ij}}^1+\tilde{\gamma}_{X_{ij}}^0)}{(\tilde{\mu}_i^1+\tilde{\mu}_i^0)(\tilde{\nu}_j^1+\tilde{\nu}_j^0)(\tilde{\gamma}_{X_{ij}}^1+\tilde{\gamma}_{X_{ij}}^0)-\tilde{\mu}_i^1\tilde{\gamma}_j^1\tilde{\gamma}_{X_{ij}}^1}$, $\langle T_{ij}\rangle = q(T_{ij} = 1) = \frac{(\tilde{\mu}_i^1+\tilde{\mu}_i^0)(\tilde{\nu}_j^1+\tilde{\nu}_j^0)\tilde{\gamma}_{X_{ij}}^1}{(\tilde{\mu}_i^1+\tilde{\mu}_i^0)(\tilde{\nu}_j^1+\tilde{\nu}_j^0)(\tilde{\gamma}_{X_{ij}}^1+\tilde{\gamma}_{X_{ij}}^0)-\tilde{\mu}_i^0\tilde{\gamma}_j^0\tilde{\gamma}_{X_{ij}}^0}$.

In Marlin's works, hyperparameters for the complete data model and missing data model are set to non-informative values and do not updated [11, 10]. However we empirically observed that hyperparameter estimation is crucial for finding meaningful solutions instead of undesirable boundary solutions. We estimate hyperparameters $\{a_0, b_0, c_0, d_0, e_0, f_0, g_0, h_0\}$ for Beta distributions and α_0 for symmetric Dirichlet distribution by empirical Bayes method, which maximizes the marginal log-likelihood of observed variables

$$\log p(\mathcal{D}|\alpha_0, a_0, b_0, c_0, d_0, e_0, f_0, g_0, h_0). \tag{12}$$

Since we can not compute the marginal log-likelihood exactly, an approximating approach is to maximize the variational lower bound (10). Unfortunately close-form updated rules can not be derived for these hyperparameters, hence numerical optimization methods are required. Empirically we observed that Newton-Raphson method do not work well for our problem since the resulting objective function is not well-approximated by a quadratic. Instead we apply the method in [12], which estimates the Dirchlet mean and precision separately. Note that Beta distribution is special case of Dirchlet distribution ($K = 2$).

3.3 Complexity Analysis

We analyse the time and space complexity of variational inference algorithms summarized in Table 3. We emphasize that pre-computing and caching intermediate factors are very important to implement computationally efficient learning algorithms. Table 4 summarizes the time and space complexity of our learning algorithms, of which complexity is depend on the number of observations, instead of the rating data matrix size.

In the perspective of the space complexity, main computational burdens are come from the saving $\langle X_{ij} Z_{ki}\rangle$ and $q(X_{ij} = v)$, for all $(i, j) \in \Omega^c$. A required memory for saving them is

$$O((IJ - H)(K + V))),$$

and it is depends on the the data matrix size ($\because H \ll IJ$). Instead of saving $\langle X_{ij} Z_{ki}\rangle$ and $q(X_{ij} = v)$, we save intermediate factors $\rho_{ki}, \phi_{kj}, \lambda_{kjv}$. This approach not only reduces the space complexity but also the time complexity. For example, in the update rule for $q(\gamma_v)$, a naive implementation requires $O(IJ - H)$ time complexity because of summing $q(X_{ij} = v)$ for all $(i, j) \in \Omega^c$. However it can be efficiently computed in $O(HK)$ by

$$\sum_{j=1}^{J}\sum_{i\in\Omega_i^c}\sum_{k=1}^{K}\lambda_{kjv}\rho_{ki} = \underbrace{\sum_{j=1}^{J}\sum_{k=1}^{K}\overbrace{\lambda_{kjv}\underbrace{\sum_{i\in\Omega_i}(\dot\rho_k - \rho_{ki})}_{O(H_i)}}^{O(H_iK)}}_{O(HK)}, \tag{13}$$

where $\dot\rho_k = \sum_{i=1}^{I}\rho_{ki}$ is pre-computed factor. Using the similar idea, other updating rules also can be efficiently implemented. [1]

4. NUMERICAL EXPERIMENTS

4.1 Dataset

We performed experiments on two datasets: *Yahoo! Musing ratings for User Selected and Randomly Selected Songs, version 1.0* (Yahoo! music dataset)[2] and MovieLens dataset [3].

[1]Source code: http://mlg.postech.ac.kr/~karma13

[2]http://webscope.sandbox.yahoo.com

[3]http://wwww.grouplens.org/datasets/movielens

Table 4: Complexity of variational inference algorithms

Variational distributions	Space	Time
$q(\boldsymbol{\theta})$	K	IK
$q(\boldsymbol{\beta})$	JK	HK
$q(\boldsymbol{\mu})$	I	H
$q(\boldsymbol{\nu})$	J	H
$q(\boldsymbol{\gamma})$	V	HKV
$q(\boldsymbol{X}_{\Omega^c}, \boldsymbol{Z})$	$(I + J + JV)K$	$(H + JV)K$
$q(\boldsymbol{U}_\Omega, \boldsymbol{M}_\Omega, \boldsymbol{T}_\Omega)$	H	H

Yahoo! Music dataset : This dataset provides a unique opportunity to test collaborative prediction methods that incorporate missing data models. The dataset consists of ratings collected during normal user interaction with Yahoo's LaunchCast internet radio service, as well as ratings for items collected using an online survey. The set of ratings collected through normal interaction with recommendation system are referred to as *ratings for user-selected items* and denoted by $\boldsymbol{X}^u$. There are 15400 users, 1000 songs, and 311704 ratings in $\boldsymbol{X}^u$. The set of ratings collected through survey are referred to as *ratings for randomly selected items* and denoted by $\boldsymbol{X}^r$. During a survey conducted by Yahoo! Research, exactly 10 songs are randomly selected and presented to each survey user. The survey users are enforced to rate on these randomly selected songs. In total 5400 users participated in this survey, hence $\boldsymbol{X}^r$ contains 54000 ratings.

Figure 2-(a) and 2-(b) show the marginal distribution of ratings for randomly selected items, $\boldsymbol{X}^r$, compared to the distribution of rating for user-selected items, $\boldsymbol{X}^u$. The two sets of ratings $\boldsymbol{X}^r$ and $\boldsymbol{X}^u$ exhibit significantly different marginal statistics. The most remarkable feature of the ratings in $\boldsymbol{X}^r$ is that they contain much fewer high ratings ($v = 5$) compared to the ratings for $\boldsymbol{X}^u$. This provides strong evidence on the violation of MAR condition in the Yahoo! ratings for user-selected items.

Our experimental protocol with the Yahoo! dataset is quite simple. We train the model on the ratings for user-selected items $\boldsymbol{X}^u$, and test on the ratings for randomly selected items $\boldsymbol{X}^r$. We used both root mean squared error (RMSE) and mean absolute error (MAE) to measure the predictive performance.

MovieLens dataset: We used MovieLens-1M dataset which consist of 1000209 ratings with 6040 users and 3706 movies. Although MovieLens dataset only consists of ratings for user-selected movies, it is well worth comparing two trained models from different domains (songs and movies), because the missing data mechanism for each domain can be different. The different behaviour of marginal statistics shown in Figure 2-(b) and 2-(c) support our assumption.

4.2 Results on Yahoo! Music Dataset

Firstly, we investigated on the benefit of binomial mixture model over multinomial mixture model. We combined binomial mixture model with CPT-v missing data model (referred to as BM/CPT-v). The number of cluster K is set to 10, and all hyperparameters for Beta distributions are set to 1 (i.e. uniform prior). Surprisingly BM/CPT-v model significantly outperformed the MM/CPT-v and it was comparable with MM/CPT-v+ as shown in Table 5.

However we observed that BM/CPT-v converge to a different kind of boundary solution. While MM/CPT-v found the boundary solution which predict almost all of the missing rating to the value 2 (see Figure 2-(d)), BM/CPT-v found the boundary solution which never predict value 5 for missing rating. The marginal statistics of

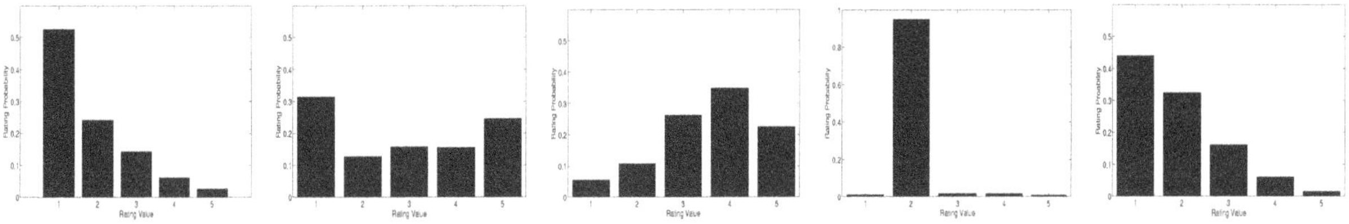

(a) Yahoo! Random (b) Yahoo! User (c) MovieLens (d) MM/CPT-v (e) Bayesian BM/OR

Figure 2: The sub-figure (a), (b), and (c) are distribution rating values for randomly selected Yahoo!, user-selected Yahoo!, and MovieLens dataset respectively. The sub-figure (d) and (e) are prediction results on the Yahoo! Random dataset by MM/CPT-V and Bayesian-BM/OR model respectively.

Table 5: RMSE, MAE, and trained parameters for missing data model (γ_v) of MM/CPT-v and BM/CPT-v on different hyper-parameter settings. Uniform denote uniform Beta prior ($g_0 = h_0 = 1$). In other case, $g_0/(g_0 + h_0)$ is fixed to 0.02, and scale of $(g_0 + h_0)$ is controlled from $H \times 10^{-3}$ to $H \times 10^{-1}$. RMSE and MAE of MM/CPT-v+ model are 0.989 and 0.727, respectively.

	MM/CPT-v			
	Uniform	$H \times 10^{-3}$	$H \times 10^{-2}$	$H \times 10^{-1}$
RMSE	1.1057	1.054	1.057	1.070
MAE	0.869	0.868	0.867	0.873
γ_1	0.437	0.365	0.247	0.098
γ_2	0.003	0.003	0.003	0.003
γ_3	0.191	0.174	0.143	0.070
γ_4	0.207	0.195	0.153	0.073
γ_5	0.493	0.423	0.261	0.109
	BM/CPT-v			
	Uniform	$H \times 10^{-3}$	$H \times 10^{-2}$	$H \times 10^{-1}$
RMSE	1.011	1.012	**0.997**	1.000
MAE	0.712	0.709	**0.704**	0.708
γ_1	0.011	0.011	0.011	0.017
γ_2	0.009	0.009	0.009	0.008
γ_3	0.034	0.035	0.030	0.018
γ_4	0.139	0.136	0.105	0.045
γ_5	0.999	0.943	0.640	0.186

predicted missing ratings was $[0.533, 0.3420.105, 0.002, 0.000]$. In addition we also observed that missing data model parameter γ_5 was also converged to boundary solution as shown in Table 5. This is quite undesirable result, because $\gamma_5 = 1$ implies that, all of the rating with the highest value 5 is already observed, consequently it implied that there is no more item with rating value 5.

We performed a second set of experiments where informative prior is given for missing data model parameter $\boldsymbol{\gamma}$ to suppress the over-estimated γ_5. Based on the observation that the sparsity of the rating data matrix is about 2 percent, hyperparameters of Beta prior are set to $g_0 = 0.02S$ and $h_0 = 0.98S$, such that mean of Beta prior is matched to 2 percent. S is the prior strength. We controlled the prior strength between $H \times 10^{-3}$ and $H \times 10^{-1}$. We observed that as the prior strength is increased, γ_5 is suppressed well. Especially in the case of $S = H \times 10^{-1}$, the prediction accuracy is good and trained missing data model parameters are similar to optimal ones used in CPT-v+ (4). We computed the variational lower bound for all trained models to check that we can select a meaningful model by empirical Bayes method. Against our expectations, the variational lower bound is maximized when uniform priors are set to missing data model parameters such that boundary solution is learned.

Finally we trained our Bayesian-BM/OR model, which considers not only the value-based selection effect but also user activity and item popularity. All hyperparameters for Dirichlet and Beta priors are initialized to 1, and variational parameters are initialized as

$$a_{kj} = 1 + \epsilon_{kj}, \quad b_{kj} = 4 + \epsilon_{kj},$$
$$c_i = H_i/J, \quad d_i = 1 - H_i/J,$$
$$e_j = H_j/I, \quad f_j = 1 - H_j/I,$$
$$g_v = H_v/H, \quad h_v = 1 - H_v/H,$$

where ϵ_{kj} are Gaussian random noise with standard deviation 0.01. Bayesian-BM/OR model showed best performing RMSE and MAE, which are 0.983 and 0.699 respectively. In addition the model did not converges to boundary solution. The marginal statistics of predicted missing ratings are shown in Figure 2-(e).

We observed that Bayesian-BM/OR model can also be converged to boundary solution if hyperparameters are not optimized. In this case, γ_2 was converged to zero. From these results, we concluded that both three factors are equally important to learn the meaningful model from the MNAR rating data:

- Modeling the ordered property of rating values.
- Modeling the activity of user, popularity of item, and value-based selection effect in the missing data model.
- Estimating hyper parameters via empirical Bayes method.

4.3 Rating Trend Analysis

In addition to outperforming predictive performance on MNAR data, Bayesin-BM/OR model has another advantage which other models do not have. For observed rating X_{ij}, by using variational posterior $q(U_{ij}, M_{ij}, T_{ij})$, our model can explain the reason of observation with user, item, and rating value factor. It can be used in analysis and comparison of rating trend between different recommendation systems.

Table 6 shows the our preliminary rating trend analysis on two datasets: Yahoo! music and MovieLens. Each value in the table is computed by summing and normalizing $q(U_{ij} = 1)$, $q(M_{ij} = 1)$, and $q(T_{ij} = 1)$ for $(i, j) \in \Omega_v$. For the ratings with value 5, the main reason of observation is rating value factor on both datasets, that means users rate on good items because they like them. However for the ratings with lower values 1 or 2, we can observe the difference between two datasets. In both datasets user and item factor are larger than rating value factor, that means some active users rate on bad items or popular items are rated even though their rating is low. However the rating value factor for lower ratings on in MovieLens (0.044, 0.075) is extremely smaller than that of Yahoo! music (0.213, 0.161). We guess the reason of this pattern following way: watching the movie require more money and time than

Table 6: Preliminary rating trend analysis on Yahoo! Music and MovienLens datasets.

Yahoo! music dataset				MovieLens dataset			
v	User	Item	Value	v	User	Item	Value
All	0.266	0.390	0.421	All	0.263	0.330	0.448
1	0.377	0.416	0.213	1	0.579	0.387	0.044
2	0.303	0.540	0.161	2	0.509	0.427	0.075
3	0.177	0.511	0.320	3	0.352	0.377	0.2943
4	0.084	0.424	0.506	4	0.178	0.291	0.580
5	0.035	0.180	0.832	5	0.098	0.274	0.701

listening the song in the internet radio, hence people may select the movie more conservative way than song.

5. CONCLUSIONS

We have presented a Bayesian binomial mixture model for collaborative prediction, where the generative process for the data and missing data mechanism are jointly modeled to handle non-random missing data. Missing data mechanism was modeled by three factors, each of which is related to users, items, and rating values. Each factor was modeled by Bernoulli random variable, and observation of rating value was determined by the Boolean OR operation. Computationally efficient variational inference algorithms were presented, where variational parameters have closed-form update rules and the computational complexity depend on the number of observed ratings, instead of the size of the rating data matrix. We also discussed implementation issues on hyperparameter tuning and estimation based on empirical Bayes. Finally, we presented experimental results demonstrating that (1) binomial mixture model is more suitable than multinomial mixture model for modellng discrete, finite, and ordered rating values; (2) our model finds meaningful solutions instead of undesirable boundary solutions, if hyperparameters are estimated by empirical Bayes; (3) our model can capture different rating trend between domain(e.g. songs and movies).

Acknowledgements

This work was supported by the IT R&D Program of MSIP/IITP (14-824-09-014, Machine Learning Center), National Research Foundation (NRF) of Korea (NRF-2013R1A2A2A01067464), and Samsung Electronics Co., Ltd.

6. REFERENCES

[1] E. Candès and T. Tao. The power of convex relaxation: Near-optimal matrix completion. *IEEE Transactions on Information Theory*, 56(5):2053–2080, 2009.

[2] G. Dror, N. Koenigstein, Y. Koren, and M. Weimer. The yahoo! music dataset and KDD-Cup'11. In *Proceedings of KDD Cup and Workshop*, 2011.

[3] Y.-D. Kim and S. Choi. Variational Bayesian view of weighted trace norm regularization for matrix factorization. *IEEE Signal Processing Letters*, 20(3):261–264, 2013.

[4] Y.-D. Kim and S. Choi. Scalable variational Bayesian matrix factorization with side information. In *Proceedings of the International Conference on Artificial Intelligence and Statistics (AISTATS)*, Reykjavik, Iceland, 2014.

[5] Y. J. Lim and Y. W. Teh. Variational Bayesian approach to movie rating prediction. In *Proceedings of KDD Cup and Workshop*, San Jose, CA, 2007.

[6] G. Ling, H. Yang, M. R. Lyu, and I. King. Response aware model-based collaborative filtering. In *Proceedings of the Annual Conference on Uncertainty in Artificial Intelligence (UAI)*, Catalina Island, California, USA, 2012.

[7] R. J. A. Little and D. B. Rubin. *Statistical Analysis with Missing Data.* John Willey & Sons, Inc., 1987.

[8] B. M. Marlin. Modeling user rating profiles for collaborative filtering. In *Advances in Neural Information Processing Systems (NIPS)*, volume 16, 2004.

[9] B. M. Marlin. *Missing Data Problems in Machine Learning.* PhD thesis, University of Toronto, 2008.

[10] B. M. Marlin and R. S. Zemel. Collaborative prediction and ranking with non-random missing data. In *Proceedings of the ACM International Conference on Recommender Systems (RecSys)*, New York, New York, USA, 2009.

[11] B. M. Marlin, R. S. Zemel, S. T. Roweis, and M. Slaney. Collaborative filtering and the missing at random assumption. In *Proceedings of the Annual Conference on Uncertainty in Artificial Intelligence (UAI)*, Vancouver, Canada, 2007.

[12] T. Minka. Estimating a Dirichlet distribution. Technical report, Microsoft Research, 2000.

[13] U. Paquet and N. Koenigstein. One-class collaborative filtering with random graphs. In *Proceedings of the International Conference on World Wide Web (WWW)*, Rio de Janeiro, Brazil, 2013.

[14] S. Park, Y.-D. Kim, and S. Choi. Hierarchical Bayesian matrix factorization with side information. In *Proceedings of the International Joint Conference on Artificial Intelligence (IJCAI)*, Beijing, China, 2013.

[15] T. Raiko, A. Ilin, and J. Karhunen. Principal component analysis for large scale problems with lots of missing values. In *Proceedings of the European Conference on Machine Learning (ECML)*, pages 691–698, Warsaw, Poland, 2007.

[16] R. Salakhutdinov and A. Mnih. Bayesian probablistic matrix factorization using MCMC. In *Proceedings of the International Conference on Machine Learning (ICML)*, Helsinki, Finland, 2008.

[17] R. Salakhutdinov, A. Mnih, and G. Hinton. Restricted Boltzmann machines for collaborative filtering. In *Proceedings of the International Conference on Machine Learning (ICML)*, Corvallis, OR, USA, 2007.

[18] R. Salakhutdinov and N.Srebro. Collaborative filtering in a non-uniform world: Learning with weighted trace norm. In *Advances in Neural Information Processing Systems (NIPS)*, volume 23. MIT Press, 2010.

[19] H. Steck. Training and testing of recommender systems on data missing not at random. In *Proceedings of the ACM SIGKDD Conference on Knowledge Discovery and Data Mining (KDD)*, Washington, DC, USA, 2010.

[20] J. Wu. Binomial matrix factorization for discrete collaborative filtering. In *Proceedings of the IEEE International Conference on Data Mining (ICDM)*, Miami, Florida, USA, 2009.

[21] J. Yoo and S. Choi. Bayesian matrix co-factorization: Variational algorithm and Cramér-Rao bound. In *Proceedings of the European Conference on Machine Learning and Principles and Practice of Knowledge Discovery in Databases (ECML-PKDD)*, Athens, Greece, 2011.

Coverage, Redundancy and Size-Awareness in Genre Diversity for Recommender Systems

Saúl Vargas[a]*, Linas Baltrunas[b], Alexandros Karatzoglou[b], Pablo Castells[a]
[a]Universidad Autónoma de Madrid, Spain
[b]Telefónica Research, Spain
saul.vargas@uam.es, linas@tid.es, alexk@tid.es, pablo.castells@uam.es

ABSTRACT

There is increasing awareness in the Recommender Systems field that diversity is a key property that enhances the usefulness of recommendations. Genre information can serve as a means to measure and enhance the diversity of recommendations and is readily available in domains such as movies, music or books. In this work we propose a new Binomial framework for defining genre diversity in recommender systems that takes into account three key properties: genre *coverage*, genre *redundancy* and recommendation list *size-awareness*. We show that methods previously proposed for measuring and enhancing recommendation diversity –including those adapted from search result diversification– fail to address adequately these three properties. We also propose an efficient greedy optimization technique to optimize Binomial diversity. Experiments with the Netflix dataset show the properties of our framework and comparison with state of the art methods.

Categories and subject descriptors: H3.3 [Information Search & Retrieval]: Information Filtering

Keywords: Recommender Systems; Diversity; Genres

1. INTRODUCTION

Recommender Systems [1] are intelligent personalized Information Retrieval tools where the information need of a user is fully or partially expressed by means of her profile or history rather than a query. The Recommender Systems literature has mostly focused on optimizing the accuracy of their results, either by predicting the preference for an item by a user (rating prediction task) or by selecting a list of items to present to the user (top-N recommendation task). Focusing solely on accuracy involves the risk of producing dull recommendations that do not capture all the facets of interest to the users. Additional properties such as diversity, novelty, explicability and context-awareness are key to expand the users' options and make recommendations more informative and useful. This paper tackles the diversity problem for recommendations.

Most users have quite diverse tastes even within the same domain such as movies or books. For example, in the movie domain the same user may like Action but also Drama movies. Standard recommender systems, especially content based algorithms [1], fail to address this diversity of tastes. Recommendation *list diversification* techniques can solve the user's need for more varied recommendations and help her discover new products (music, movies, apps). Diversity is a list-wise property that has been shown to enhance the user satisfaction with respect to the recommendations [14]. Several notions of diversity have been proposed in the field and, although they are closely related, they are not equivalent. In this paper we focus on the notion of intra-list diversity [22], i.e., providing a list of varied recommendations that covers the different interests of the user. We define the notion of diversity using genres, which are used in domains such as books, movies and music.

We analyze the properties of genres and their utility in providing diverse recommendations. We postulate three important properties that genre-based diverse recommendations should fulfill: 1) *genre coverage*, that is, each genre should be represented in a recommendation list according to both the interest of the user and its specificity; 2) *redundancy*: while it is important that all genres are represented it is equally important not to over-represent a particular genre – this is particularly important in domains where items can have more than one genre; and 3) recommendation *list size-awareness*, which focuses on the common screen space limitation to offer recommendations, and how it influences genre coverage and redundancy. Our analysis of state of the art diversification methods and metrics shows that they do not properly or fully address these three properties. We propose a new Binomial framework that takes into account all the aforementioned properties. The framework consists of a metric to assess the diversity of recommendations and a greedy re-ranking strategy to optimize the diversity of recommendations. We report experiments on a widely-known dataset for recommendation – Netflix[1] – showing the properties of our framework, and comparing it to state of the art methods.

2. RELATED WORK

We start by reviewing the related work and positioning our research with respect to the state-of-the-art. First, we present diversity as a key dimension of recommendation utility, and compare it to notions of diversity developed in the field of Information Retrieval. Second, we present the current state-of-the-art techniques for modeling recommendation diversity that our work compares to.

2.1 Diversity in Recommender Systems

Along with the progress targeting accuracy in Recommender Systems, researchers have realized that improving

*Work conducted during research stay at Telefónica Research.

RecSys'14, October 6–10, 2014, Foster City, Silicon Valley, CA, USA.

ACM 978-1-4503-2668-1/14/10 ...$15.00.
http://dx.doi.org/10.1145/2645710.2645743.

[1]http://www.netflixprize.com/

recommendations' usefulness and user satisfaction may require more than being accurate. In particular, Herlocker et al. [10] stated that accuracy alone may not give users of recommender systems an effective and satisfying experience. McNee et al. [13] further specified that there are properties other than accuracy that have an effect on user satisfaction, namely coverage, diversity, novelty or serendipity.

Diversity in Recommender Systems, that is, addressing the user's varied tastes and his/her need for diverse recommendations, has been shown to help improve the attractiveness and usefulness of recommendations [14]. In this paper we focus on the so-called intra-list distance as defined by Ziegler et al. [22], i.e., how different are the items in a recommendation list with respect to each other. In [22], Ziegler et al. propose taxonomies of products that are used to define a similarity metric between items, although other sources of diversity could be considered. For instance, in our previous work [19] we used movie genres as the source of diversity. On the other hand, Kabutoya et al. [12] and Shi et al. [17] extract latent topic models from the users' interactions with the system in order to create diverse recommendations.

The problem of intra-list diversity in Recommender Systems is related to search result diversification [7]. Users of general-purpose commercial search engines tend to submit short queries to represent their information needs. Such brevity in queries tends to lead to ambiguity – the query could have many possible interpretations – and underspecification, – the topic the query refers to may have different facets. A way to cope with this problem is the diversification of web search results i.e., presenting lists of documents that cover as many interpretations or facets as possible of the original query as early as possible in the ranking [15]. The term *subtopic* is a commonly used word in this area for referring to query interpretations or facets altogether.

2.2 Measuring and enhancing diversity

Different frameworks for measuring and enhancing the diversity of recommendation lists have been proposed in the Recommender Systems and Information Retrieval literature. We briefly recall here the most closely related and relevant research to the scope of our work. Based on different principles, most of them propose re-ranking an initial recommendation list so that diverse items can be shown early in the list. The most common approach is based on greedy selection, which tends to achieve a good and efficient approximation to an optimal re-ranking. Methods of this type fit in the algorithmic structure described in Algorithm 1. The algorithm depends on the specific definition of an objective function f_{obj} which defines the marginal utility of an item with respect to items ranked above it.

Algorithm 1 A greedy selection of the items in recommendation list R to produce a re-ranked list S.

```
S = ∅
while |R| > 0 do
    i* = arg max_{i∈R\S} f_obj(i; S)
    R = R \ {i*}
    S = S ∪ {i*}
end while
return S
```

One of the earliest and best-known proposals for diversity in Recommender Systems is the "topic list diversification" from Ziegler et al.[22], to which we will refer as **pair-wise framework** throughout this paper. This framework defines a diversity metric called intra-list similarity (ILS), as the sum of similarities between all pairs of items in the recommendation:

$$ILS = \sum_{i,j \in R} sim(i,j) \tag{1}$$

where *sim* is a similarity measure between items. In previous work [18], we defined an extension to this metric known as expected intra-list diversity (EILD), which allows to consider the relevance and position of the recommended items. Ziegler et al. also proposed a greedy re-ranking strategy to optimize ILS which is structurally equivalent to the maximal marginal relevance (MMR) by Carbonell and Goldstein [5]:

$$f_{MMR}(i;S) = (1-\lambda)\, rel(i) + \lambda \min_{j \in S} dist(i,j) \tag{2}$$

where λ is a trade-off parameter between the original ranking and the diversity component and $rel(i)$ is the relevance of the item i. Zhang and Hurley [21] also considered the problem of optimizing ILS as a quadratic optimization problem.

Another major line of work in measuring and enhancing diversity comes from search result diversification. In particular, the **intent-aware framework** [2] considers the sum of the weighted marginal relevance of each subtopic s of a query, as it is the case of the intent-aware version of the ERR metric [6]:

$$ERR-IA = \sum_s p(s) \sum_{k=1}^{|R|} \frac{1}{k} rel(i_k) \prod_{l=1}^{i-1} (1 - rel(i_l)) \tag{3}$$

where $p(s)$ is the probability of s being the intended subtopic behind the query. Santos et al. [15] proposed the *explicit query aspect diversification* (xQuAD), a re-ranking approach that optimizes intent-aware metrics by enhancing the coverage of the different subtopics while minimizing their redundancy:

$$f_{xQuAD}(i;S) = (1-\lambda)\, p(i) + \lambda \sum_s p(s)\, p(i|s) \prod_{j \in S} (1 - p(j|s)) \tag{4}$$

where $p(i|s)$ is the probability of choosing item i given the subtopic s. The IA-Select re-ranking approach of Agrawal et al. [2], with minor differences, can be considered as a subcase of xQuAD with $\lambda = 1.0$. This intent-aware framework was adapted to Recommender Systems in [19], by translating the concept of query subtopic to user aspects.

A third approach is the more recent **proportionality framework** by Dang and Croft [9] for search result diversification. They emphasize the need for covering each subtopic of the search query by offering a number of relevant documents proportional to the interest of the subtopic they cover. The basis for measuring this proportionality is the so-called disproportionality metric, defined as:

$$DP = \sum_s \mathbf{1}_{v_s \geq k_s^R} (v_s - k_s^R)^2 + \frac{1}{2} n_{NR}^2 \tag{5}$$

where v_s is the expected number of documents that cover the subtopic s, k_s^R the actual number of documents, and n_{NR} the number of non relevant documents. On top of DP, Dang and Croft propose a cumulative proportionality metric (CPR) that is the basis of their study. Analogously to the other proposals they define a greedy re-ranking approach, the proportionality method (PM), inspired on a seat assignment system for legislative elections in some countries:

$$f_{PM}(i;S) = \lambda \frac{v_{s^*}}{1 + 2\sum_{j \in S} \frac{p(j|s^*)}{\sum_{s'} p(j|s')}} p(i|s^*) + (1-\lambda) \sum_{s \neq s^*} \frac{v_s}{1 + 2\sum_{j \in S} \frac{p(j|s)}{\sum_{s'} p(j|s')}} p(i|s) \tag{6}$$

where s^* indicates the least-covered subtopic in S. Note that this proportionality framework admits a straightforward adaptation to recommendation similar to that of the intent-aware framework.

3. CHARACTERIZING GENRES

As defined in the Merriam-Webster dictionary[2], a genre is "a category of artistic, musical, or literary composition characterized by a particular style, form, or content". We argue that genres can be used as the source for defining diversity as they:

- explicitly define a conventional style of an item that has a common interpretation among users,
- have the potential of representing the different tastes of individual users,
- are well accepted for media categorization and are already available in most online media catalogs for movies, literature, music, etc.
- and it is safe to assume that the user will perceive the diversity of the recommendation list if the genres are diversified among the recommended items. Other alternatives such as using item-to-item distance based on consumption patterns may have an effect on the inherent diversity of the recommendation, although this may not directly translate to a user perception of diversity.

Genres, nonetheless, present some particularities that need to be addressed to be used effectively. First, genres can have different levels of generality: for example, in the movie domain "Drama" represents a very broad and vaguely defined style with many diverse movies belonging to this genre. On the other hand, "Western" is a quite specific movie type which is usually devoted to telling stories in the American Wild West. This generality is also reflected in the number of items for each genre. See Table 1 for the number of movies in each genre in the Netflix data set. We observe that the generality of each genre is also related to the perception of redundancy in a recommendation list. For example, three random westerns in a short recommendation list of five items feels more redundant than three random dramas. We will exploit this observation when defining our probabilistic model.

Genre	Count	Genre	Count	Genre	Count
Action	1,464	Fantasy	651	Romance	1,887
Adult	54	Film-Noir	70	Sci-Fi	819
Adventure	996	Game-Show	2	Short	237
Animation	381	History	317	Sport	284
Biography	384	Horror	900	Talk-Show	2
Comedy	3,025	Music	568	Thriller	1,989
Crime	1,319	Musical	418	War	422
Documentary	779	Mystery	709	Western	285
Drama	4,408	News	1		
Family	772	Reality-TV	15		

Table 1: Genre distribution in Netflix.

Second, genres do not usually define disjoint or isolated categories in their domains, and it is generally difficult to establish a precise hierarchy among them. For example, "The Lord of the Rings" by Tolkien can be classified as Adventure, Fiction, High fantasy and British literature all at once. Moreover, careless use of sub-genres can lead to lower perceived diversity. For example, heavy metal and white metal – two closely related sub-genres – share the same musical techniques, modes of dress and performance and could be perceived as similar by a listener.

In order to illustrate the aforementioned properties of genres, we present the case of movie recommendations of the Netflix dataset. This dataset contains one hundred million ratings (from 1 to 5 stars) from 480,000 to 17,770 different movies. Using IMDb[3], we found genre information for 9,320 movies in the dataset accounting for 83% of the ratings in the dataset.

[2]http://www.merriam-webster.com

[3]http://www.imdb.com/

As seen in Table 1 the number of movies for each genre varies greatly, from 4,408 movies in "Drama" to only 1 movie in "News". Genres do not form disjoint categories, as seen in Figure 1, which shows the overlap between the top 5 genres by a Venn diagram. One can see that, for instance, there are only 76 pure "Romance" movies, and the other 96% of movies in this genre overlap with at least one other genre. Other genres also have a high degree of overlap. In fact, there is no clear hierarchical structure between the genres. It also seems that overlaps between genres do not follow any particular distribution. Furthermore, pairwise overlaps between genres are not wide enough as to establish any clear sub-genre relationship between one another; even the narrowest and most specific genres (for example, Crime) have only partial overlaps (<60%) with more general genres such as Drama.

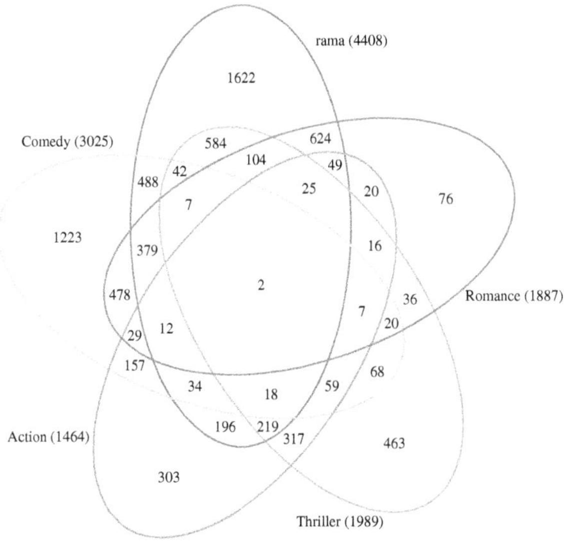

Figure 1: Venn diagram for the 5 most frequent genres in the Netflix dataset.

4. MEASURING GENRE DIVERSITY IN RECOMMENDATION LISTS

We all have an intuitive idea of what genre diversity means for a list of movies. Yet when it comes to translating the intuition to a mathematical expression that reflects degrees of diversity by a numeric value, one has to be more specific about what the value should reflect. In particular, drawing from the IR diversity literature [2, 5, 20], two different dimensions should be considered to this respect, namely genre coverage and redundancy. We take them as required properties that a genre-based recommendation diversity metric should capture. Furthermore, we argue that these dimensions should be captured in a way that takes into account the properties of genres discussed and exemplified in Section 3. Moreover, we add to these a third and new requirement, size-awareness, which has not been explicitly considered in prior work. We briefly discuss each of these three properties next.

Coverage is the simplest and most obvious property. Since most users enjoy items from a variety of genres, it is important that the recommendation list covers as many of them as possible. Moreover, this coverage should be proportional: even when a user is interested in several genres, the personalized importance of each genre is not equal. Therefore, the more a user is interested in a given genre, the more important it is that it is covered in the recommendation list.

Second, **redundancy** should also be considered. It is not enough to have a high coverage of genres in order to have a diverse recommendation list. We may put it this way: it is as important to present items that cover a certain genre as to present other items that do *not* cover it. This notion of redundancy should take into account the preferences for the user as well as how general each genre is. Consider the extreme example shown in Table 2 where three movies are recommended to a user. Even if these 3 movies cover a total of 6 genres, the diversity is not quite perceivable. This is because all three movies cover a very narrow Western genre which makes the recommendation list highly redundant.

Finally, **size-awareness**. Coverage and redundancy should depend on the length of the recommendation list. Since the rise of mobile devices, the issue of having limited screen real estate to show recommendations requires a careful selection of what to display in that list. We also improve over existing diversity enhancing techniques by specifically addressing the recommendation list size. For example, when generating a short recommendation list one should only recommend items from the most relevant genres. In a longer list we could have higher genre redundancy depending on the generality of the involved genres. To the best of our knowledge this kind of adaptation has not been explored in prior work on search or recommendation diversity.

The reviewed techniques in Section 2.2 do not satisfy all these properties, in particular:

- The intra-list similarity of Ziegler et al. [22] is defined as a pairwise property of elements in a list. A pair-wise property does not translate however as directly as we may expect to a list-wise property as we are stating. Further, it is not trivial to consider a similarity measure that takes into account by itself the generality of different genres and the user-specific importance of each of them. Essentially equivalent to the approach by Ziegler et al, the MMR scheme [5] displays the same limitations.
- The intent-aware framework (IA-metrics, IA-select and xQuAD) [2, 15] considers coverage and redundancy, but as to the latter, the scheme does not fully capture the view that it is equally important to present items that cover a certain genre as to present other items that do not cover it. Specifically, the redundancy component of ERR-IA and xQuAD reduces the contribution of items that cover redundant genres, rather than discounting them as negative from the list diversity value. Thus, items covering a redundant genre will contribute positively to the diversity even though the contribution diminishes with each additional occurrence of the genre. Furthermore, this redundancy does not detract at all from the contribution of additional genres the items can have in addition to the redundant one – that is, the genres are assumed to be totally independent from each other. The example in Table 2 illustrates this effect: it is fine (diversity-wise) in the context of this framework that all the movies in the recommendation list be westerns, as long as they cover also other genres. As a consequence, the diversifications are biased to retrieve items that cover many genres. We may reasonably question the implicit assumption in this scheme that multiple genres in the same item will procure the same diversity perception as multiple genres over different items.
- The work by Dang and Croft [9] does cover an idea of user-centric proportionality, but redundancy is not penalized and therefore, it may also suffer from the same problems as xQuAD for genre diversity.
- None of the prior search or recommendation diversification methods takes into account the size of the retrieved list that will be presented to (or browsed by) the user. The diversification schemes have therefore no means to consider this information to enhance diversity at a particular rank cutoff.

Movie	Genres
Wild Wild West	Action, Comedy, Sci-Fi, Western
Cowboys and Aliens	Action, Sci-Fi, Thriller, Western
The Good, the Bad and the Ugly	Adventure, Western

Table 2: Example of redundant recommendations

5. A BINOMIAL FRAMEWORK FOR GENRE DIVERSITY

A naïve approach for creating diverse recommendations consists in making a random selection of items. This approach offers highly diverse recommendations, but it tends to approximate the poorest possible output in terms of the relevance of recommendations for the user interests, which makes it an option of little practical use. Still, the nature of the selection of genres in a random recommendation provides a meaningful basis to build a revised notion of diversity upon it. In particular, we propose to use a binomial distribution to model how a personalized recommendation would match a random recommendation in terms of the diversity of genres, using the binomial distribution to model the likelihood that a given genre will appear by chance in a recommendation, and take this as a reference to assess the diversity value of a given genre distribution among recommended items. In essence, this approach means considering random item recommendation as the optimal approach in terms of pure genre diversity, and using a binomial distribution as the model for the genre distribution resulting from random item sampling.

5.1 The Binomial Diversity Metric

The binomial distribution is the discrete probability distribution of the number k of successes in a sequence of N independent Bernoulli trials with the same probability of success p. A random variable that follows this distribution, $X \sim B(N,p)$, has the following probability mass function:

$$P(X = k) = \binom{N}{k} p^k (1-p)^{N-k} \qquad (7)$$

We base our definition of a genre diversity metric on top of this as follows. For each genre, we measure its coverage and redundancy using binomial distributions. We consider the selection of an item covering each genre as a Bernoulli trial, whereby for each genre, a recommendation list can be viewed as a sequence of Bernoulli trials. It must be noticed that these trials are not independent: a recommendation list is actually a selection without replacement. However, given that the typical recommendation list size is usually much smaller than the set of movies covering each genre, we can treat these trials as if they were independent, and therefore use the binomial distribution to model how likely is a genre to appear in a recommendation list.

More formally, for an item i and a set of genres $G(i)$ covered by the item i, we consider the Bernoulli experiment of whether a randomly sampled genre g belongs to $G(i)$. Given a set of items S, we denote the number of items belonging to that genre – the number of successes – as $k_g^S = |\{i \in S \,:\, g \in G(i)\}|$. Given a recommendation list R of size N, we take the probability of a genre p_g as a measure of how "adequate" is the number k_g^R of items covering a genre g in that recommendation. As required in Section 4, this probability should take into account the generality of a genre and also the relevance of each genre for the user. We

	i_1	i_2		ILD	S-recall	ERR-IA	CPR	Coverage	NonRed	BinomDiv
				Yes	Yes	Not Always	Not Always	Yes	Yes	Yes
Better	b	a	Regardless of	1.0000	0.6666	**0.4000**	**0.7857**	0.8255	1.0000	0.8255
Worse	a	a	p(a), p(b)	0.0000	0.3333	**0.5000**	**0.8571**	0.6814	0.3333	0.2269
				No(=)	Yes	Yes	Yes	Yes	**No(=)**	Yes
Better	a c	b	Regardless of	**1.0000**	1.0000	0.7000	0.9643	1.0000	**1.0000**	1.0000
Worse	a	b	p(a), p(b), p(c)	**1.0000**	0.6666	0.5000	0.8929	0.8255	**1.0000**	0.8255
				Yes	**No(=)**	**No(<)**	**No(<)**	**No(=)**	Yes	Yes
Better	a	b	Regardless of	1.0000	**0.6666**	**0.5000**	**0.8929**	**0.8255**	1.0000	0.8255
Worse	a b	b	p(a), p(b)	0.5000	**0.6666**	**0.6500**	**0.9286**	**0.8255**	0.3780	0.3120
				No(=)	**No(=)**	Yes	Yes	Yes	Yes	Yes
Better	a	a	p(a) > p(b)	**0.0000**	**0.3333**	0.5000	0.8571	0.6814	0.3333	0.2271
Worse	b	b		**0.0000**	**0.3333**	0.2500	0.6429	0.5200	0.1429	0.0743

Table 3: Postulates of diversity. Each of the four postulates shows two rankings (displayed horizontally) with better or worse diversity. Each item in the ranking is represented by the genres (a, b, c) that it belongs to. We show in the table the diversity score that each of the metric assigns to the lists. In the computation of the metric values, we assume for simplicity there are only three genres in the dataset, with prior probabilities, as an example, p(a) = 0.5, p(b) = 0.25, p(c) = 0.25. For ERR-IA we use the same definition as in the TREC diversity task (as computed by the ndeval script), generalized to support non-uniform aspect distributions.

propose to combine global genre distribution statistics and personalized user preferences to estimate p_g as follows.

On one side, the relevance of a genre for the user u can be estimated by using historical data, i.e., considering the local proportion p''_g of the items the user has had some interaction with, denoted as $\mathcal{I}_u$. On the other side, the generality of the genre can be estimated by the global proportion p'_g of items in the user preferences covering it. To join both global and local probabilities, we propose a simple linear combination:

$$p''_g = \frac{k_g^{\mathcal{I}_u}}{|\mathcal{I}_u|} \quad p'_g = \frac{\sum_u k_g^{\mathcal{I}_u}}{\sum_u |\mathcal{I}_u|} \quad p_g = (1-\alpha)\, p'_g + \alpha\, p''_g \qquad (8)$$

With all the components of genre-based binomial distributions, we now define scores for the coverage and redundancy of a recommendation list R. We measure coverage as a property defined by the genres that are present in the recommendation list and those that are not. The maximum coverage would be achieved when all the genres of interest are covered in the recommendation list. However, this maximum is not always reachable, especially in small recommendation lists. Therefore, when some genres cannot be covered, the coverage should reflect the loss caused by their absence, which should be proportional to their importance. We thus define the coverage score as the product for the genres not represented in the recommendation list of their probabilities of not being randomly selected according to X_g, normalized by the $|G|$-th root:

$$Coverage(R) = \prod_{g \notin G(R)} P(X_g = 0)^{1/|G|} \qquad (9)$$

We define redundancy, in turn, only by the genres covered in the recommendation list. The moment one genre appears more than once in a recommendation list, it can be potentially redundant, although not all genres will be equally affected. We model the redundancy of a genre appearing k times in a recommendation list by a "remaining tolerance" score that reflects how probable it would be that the genre appeared at least k times in a random list:

$$P(X_g \geq k \mid X_g > 0) = 1 - \sum_{l=1}^{k-1} P(X_g = l \mid X_g > 0) \qquad (10)$$

Some examples of this "remaining tolerance" score are illustrated in Figure 2. The non-redundancy score is consequently defined as the product of the "remaining tolerance" scores for each covered genre, normalized by the $|G(R)|$-th root:

$$NonRed(R) = \prod_{g \in G(R)} P(X_g \geq k_g^R \mid X_g > 0)^{1/|G(R)|} \qquad (11)$$

Finally, the Binomial Diversity metric is defined as the product of both components:

$$BinomDiv(R) = Coverage(R) \cdot NonRed(R) \qquad (12)$$

The previous definition can be adapted to consider only the relevant recommended items by re-defining k_g^R as the number of relevant items covering the genre g and the number of trials N as the number of relevant recommended items.

Note that binomial relevance satisfies all the properties described in Section 4. It maximizes the coverage of the genres according to their p_g. It takes into account user preferences via p''_g. It penalizes over-represented genres by rapidly decreasing their redundancy score. Lastly, it is adapted to the recommendation length by parameter N.

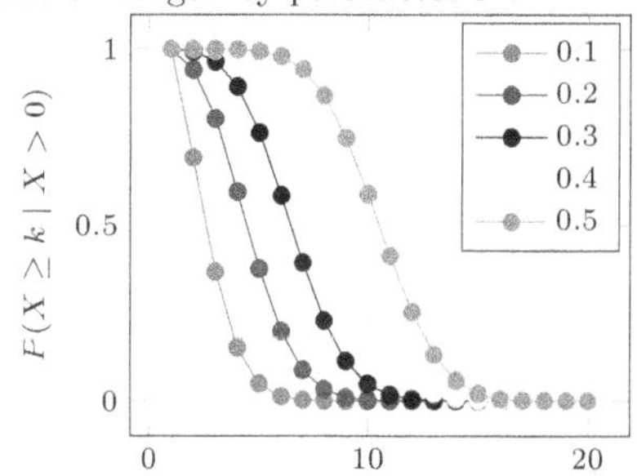

Figure 2: $P(X \geq k \mid X > 0)$ **for different values of** p **and** k **of binomial distributions with** $N = 20$ **(continuous lines are drawn just as a reference).**

5.2 A Binomial Re-ranking Algorithm

A greedy re-ranking approach to optimize binomial diversity can be straightforwardly derived from the proposed metric scheme by just defining an objective function that linearly combines relevance and binomial diversity as follows:

$$f_{BinomDiv}(i; S) = (1-\lambda)\, rel(i) + \lambda\, div(i; S) \qquad (13)$$

where the relevance component $rel(i)$ can be defined as the score that the baseline recommender system assigns to the items for the target user, and the diversity component is the difference in terms of the binomial diversity in Equation 12 after adding the candidate item to the re-ranked recommendation list:

$$div(i; S) = BinomDiv(S \cup \{i\}) - BinomDiv(S) \qquad (14)$$

Because we are combining variables with different ranges and distributions, in the practical implementation of the objective function we need to normalize both scores. In our experiments we do so by transforming them to z-scores, that is, we subtract their mean and divide by the standard deviation: $norm_X(x) = \frac{x-\mu_X}{\sigma_X}$.

5.3 Qualitative analysis

In addition to the empirical behavior of the proposed scheme, the Binomial Diversity metric fulfills qualitative properties that further specify the requirements stated earlier in Section 4. These properties can be formalized by four postulates shown in Table 3, which we propose as a basis on which diversification metrics can be analyzed and compared to each other, providing a clear way to show properties of each metric, identify and report the differences, in a similar perspective as proposed in [3]. Each postulate presents a rule, which expresses a simple idea on how we can reason about the genre-based diversity. We represent each of the postulates by providing two ranked lists of items (displayed horizontally in the table) with minimal differences. The ranked list denoted by "Better" should have strictly higher diversity that the one denoted by "Worse". For example, the first postulate expresses the idea that a ranked list of two items that cover two genres (a and b) is more diverse than a list of two items that cover only one genre (a). We mark a method with "Yes" only if the metric complies with the postulate, otherwise we indicate to what extent the metric fails to satisfy the postulated inequality (either the metric yields the opposite inequality, or is insensitive to the difference between the two lists). We can see that all of the state of the art methods fail at least one of the tests, and only our proposed Binomial Diversity that combines Coverage and NonRed properties complies with all the postulates. For illustration, we show in the same table the diversity score that each of the analyzed diversification metric assigns to the prototypical lists.

In order to further illustrate how the diversification metric works and to show the benefits of the genre-based approach, we may examine the working example shown in Table 4. The example shows the top 20 recommended movies by the item-based kNN method ($R_0 \cup R_1$) for a sample user from the Netflix dataset, and the re-ranking of this list by the binomial diversification ($R_0 \cup R_2$), shown by the movies that are removed (R_1) and added (R_2) as a result of the re-ranking. The first row of the table summarizes the user taste profile (p''_g), i.e. what fraction of movies of each genre he has rated. We see that the user is inclined towards Drama, Comedy and Action movies. We may also notice that the user seldom watched War movies. Both recommendation lists have an overlap of 11 movies (R_0) that are shown below the user profile information. If we compare the differences between both recommendation lists – the kNN baseline $R_0 \cup R_1$ and its diversification by the binomial scheme $R_0 \cup R_2$, we see that the baseline promotes Action and War movies that are over-represented in the final list of 20 movies, thus creating a highly redundant recommendation. The recommender under-represents other genres such as Comedy which plays a major part in the user profile. The binomial diversification, on the other hand, uses the p''_g and the list size as the reference for how many movies of each genre it should select to avoid redundancy. There are already 7 Action movies in the list and, therefore, it promotes several Comedies instead. Moreover, it includes new genres such as Animation, Children's and Mystery that help improve the coverage score. This leads to a significant increase of the diversification score for the diversified list.

6. EXPERIMENTS

In order to show the properties of the Binomial Diversity framework, we have carried out two experiments on two common datasets for movie recommendation: the MovieLens1M[4] collection and the data from the Netflix Prize. In the case of the Netflix Prize, no genre information was provided in the data, so we extracted that information from IMDb. Discarding the movies for which we could not find genres, the resulting dataset includes 83 million ratings (on a 1-5 scale) by 480,000 users for 9,320 movies classified into 28 different genres. Due to the similarities between the results for both datasets and the space limit, we only report and discuss the results for the Netflix dataset.

	Movie	Action	Adventure	Animation	Children's	Comedy	Crime	Drama	Mystery	Romance	Sci-Fi	Thriller	War	Western
	p''_g	0.25	0.20	0.04	0.08	0.39	0.13	0.42	0.07	0.19	0.15	0.25	0.06	0.02
Kept (R_0)	Braveheart	X						X					X	
	Jerry Maguire							X		X				
	Matrix, The	X									X	X		
	Negotiator, The	X										X		
	Patriot Games	X										X		
	Pulp Fiction						X	X						
	The Silence of the Lambs							X				X		
	Terminator 2	X									X	X		
	Titanic							X		X				
	Total Recall	X	X								X	X		
	True Lies	X	X			X				X				
Removed (R_1)	Air Force One	X										X		
	Enemy of the State	X										X		
	Get Shorty	X				X		X						
	Gladiator	X						X						
	Green Mile, The							X				X		
	Independence Day	X									X		X	
	Schindler's List							X					X	
	Star Wars: Episode V	X	X					X			X		X	
	Star Wars: Episode VI	X	X							X	X		X	
Added (R_2)	As Good As It Gets					X		X						
	Back to the Future III					X					X			X
	Elizabeth							X						
	Erin Brockovich							X						
	The Game								X			X		
	Leon: The Professional						X	X		X		X		
	South Park			X		X								
	There's Sth. About Mary					X								
	Toy Story			X	X	X								

Table 4: Binomial diversification in action.

6.1 Setup

We split the rating data into training and test in a 5-fold cross validation. We followed a common evaluation procedure [4, 8] in which for each target user the recommenders are required to rank a list which includes both relevant and non-relevant items. The relevant items include all those having a test rating for the target user, where the rating value is above a threshold. In the set of irrelevant items we include all movies with a test rating value below the threshold, plus a set of 1000 randomly sampled movies.

We take for our experiment two baseline collaborative filtering (CF) algorithms: an item-based nearest neighbors recommender [16] (Item-kNN) and the implicit Matrix Factorization algorithm (iMF) by Hu et al. [11]. We additionally include two non-personalized systems for further reference: recommendation by item popularity (PopRec) and random recommendation (Random). On each of the CF baselines, we applied the diversification approaches described in Section 2.2 (MMR, PM and xQuAD) and our Binomial diversification. The optimal value of the λ parameter in these diversifiers is set by a grid search in the $[0, 1]$ interval by steps of 0.1. We additionally report as a reference the effects of random re-ranking.

We evaluate the diversity of the recommendations with respect to genres by our proposed Binomial Diversity metric (BinomDiv), plus the diversity metrics presented in Section 2.2: EILD, ERR-IA and CPR. We report two addi-

[4]http://movielens.umn.edu/

	nDCG	BinomDiv			CPR			EILD	S-recall
		$\alpha = 0.0$	$\alpha = 0.5$	$\alpha = 1.0$	$\alpha = 0.0$	$\alpha = 0.5$	$\alpha = 1.0$		
Random	0.0172	**0.4391**	**0.4286**	0.2834	**0.7948**	0.7550	0.6857	**0.8147**	**0.6022**
PopRec	0.2988	0.2297	0.2886	0.2600	0.7905	0.7960	0.7632	0.7781	0.5087
Item-kNN	0.3762	0.2232	0.3035	0.2926	0.7847	**0.8154**	0.8006	0.7753	0.5125
iMF	**0.5221**	0.2091	0.3090	**0.3257**	0.7631	0.8121	**0.8131**	0.7488	0.5175

Table 5: Results for cut-off 20 of the recommendation baselines applied to the Netflix dataset. The results for the metrics BinomDiv, CPR, EILD and S-recall consider here the diversity provided by all recommended items. Results in bold indicate the best result for a given dataset and metric.

	nDCG	BinomDiv		CPR		EILD		ERR-IA	S-recall		SPI
		all	rel	all	rel	all	rel		all	rel	
iMF	**0.5221**	0.3090	0.2501	0.8121	0.5188	0.7488	0.2318	0.2176	0.5175	0.2933	2.7851
Random	0.1502	0.3683	0.1975	0.8235	0.2233	0.7740	0.2342	0.0724	0.5579	0.1758	2.7641
BinomDiv (0.7)	0.3740	**0.6890**	**0.3191**	**0.9398**	0.4367	0.8007	0.2465	0.1664	0.6817	0.2850	2.5899
PM (1.0)	0.4671	0.3035	0.2593	0.8863	0.5179	0.7423	0.2292	*0.2194*	0.5232	0.2889	2.9931
MMR (0.9)	0.3468	0.5996	0.3044	0.7278	0.3528	**0.8898**	**0.2716**	0.1866	**0.7387**	0.2618	2.3329
xQuAD (0.2)	0.5050	0.2837	0.2421	0.8504	**0.5252**	0.7446	0.2305	**0.2347**	0.5390	**0.3060**	**3.0295**

Table 6: Results for cut-off 20 and $\alpha = 0.5$ for different recommendation algorithms and their diversified re-rankings applied to the Netflix dataset. For diversifications, the parameter chosen (in parenthesis) is the one that achieves the best result with respect to its relevance-aware objective metric. Bold indicates the best result for a given baseline and metric. Italics indicate non statistically significant differences to the corresponding baseline (Wilcoxon $p < 0.05$).

tional simple diversity metrics: subtopic recall [20] (S-recall), which is the total number of returned genres (as a ratio on the total number of genres in the collection) in a recommendation; and the average number of subtopics (genres) per item (SPI), which will serve as a reference to study the bias discussed in Section 4 for the intent-aware framework. We consider two variants for the BinomDiv, EILD, CPR and S-recall metrics: one, denoted as *all*, where the genres of all recommended items are taken into account to measure the diversity of the list, and another, denoted as *rel*, in which only those items relevant to the user are taken into account. Complementarily to the diversity metrics, we report the normalized discount cumulative gain (nDCG) to check the relevance-based effectiveness (regardless of diversity) of all configurations.

6.2 Results for Baseline Diversity

Table 5 shows the results for all the recommender baselines without any diversification step. All the metrics are evaluated at a 20 ranking cut-off. The algorithms are sorted by their nDCG score. We omit in this table the *rel* variants since they strongly correlate with nDCG when comparing recommendation algorithms with very different levels of accuracy, and thus they are not informative. For the metrics BinomDiv and CPR we show three alternatives (see Equation 8): global or non-personalized ($\alpha = 0.0$), intermediate ($\alpha = 0.5$) and fully personalized ($\alpha = 1.0$).

As we can see, the random recommender, as expected, has a very low accuracy, but scores very high for all diversity metrics, especially the non-personalized ones (BinomDiv and CPR with $\alpha = 0.0$, EILD and S-recall). The popularity-based recommendation has a much higher accuracy than the random recommendations, but has generally lower scores for diversity metrics, specially in BinomDiv, where it is in general the worst alternative. The personalized recommenders, which have a higher accuracy than the non-personalized recommenders, tend to score low in terms of non-personalized diversity metrics (BinomDiv and CPR with $\alpha = 0.0$, EILD and S-recall), but clearly improve in BinomDiv and CPR when the user history is considered ($\alpha > 0.0$).

The results from Table 5 show consistent results, showing that random recommendations are diverse in nature, and personalized recommendations may benefit from a re-ranking diversification step.

6.3 Results for Diversified Results

We present in Table 6 the results of diversifying the iMF recommendation baseline. Diversifications of the other personalized recommendation (Item-kNN) were also carried out with similar outcomes, but we omit them because of the space limit. All the metrics are computed again at a 20 ranking cut-off. The α parameter in BinomDiv (metric and diversifier) and CPR is set to 0.5. As mentioned before, the λ parameter value (shown in parenthesis) for the binomial, PM, MMR and xQuAD diversifications is the one that maximizes the corresponding objective metric: BinomDiv-rel, CPR-rel, EILD-rel and ERR-IA, respectively.

A first overall trend we may observe is that, in terms of nDCG, all the diversifications involve a decrease in the accuracy of the recommendations, showing an also expectable trade-off between relevance and diversity. Second, each diversifier is always the best option with respect to its target metric, with the exception of PM, which is outperformed by BinomDiv in CPR-all and by xQuAD in CPR-rel. This can be explained because PM does not optimize directly the formulation of CPR (see Equations 5 and 7), while the rest of the diversifiers optimize directly their target metric. Third, for CPR-rel the improvements over the baseline are almost imperceptible, and restricted to xQuAD. This shows that a diversification algorithm (and the metric it is intended to target) devised for a search task may not get the expected results in a recommendation setting with a different subtopic-document (in our case, genre-item) distribution patterns, which is one of the motivations for our framework.

As to the intent-aware framework –the xQuAD diversifier and the ERR-IA metric– and the proportionality framework –the PM diversifier and the CPR metric–, the results evidence one of the problems pointed out in Section 4, namely the accumulation of genres without any penalization for redundancy. The SPI values show how the xQuAD and PM strategies notably increase the average number of genres per item in the diversified recommendations, which, as discussed in Section 4, does not necessarily fit well with an effective notion of diversity in recommendation. Regarding the metrics, ERR-IA and CPR-rel show a clear correlation with SPI, a bias that narrows the informativeness of this metric in a recommendation setting.

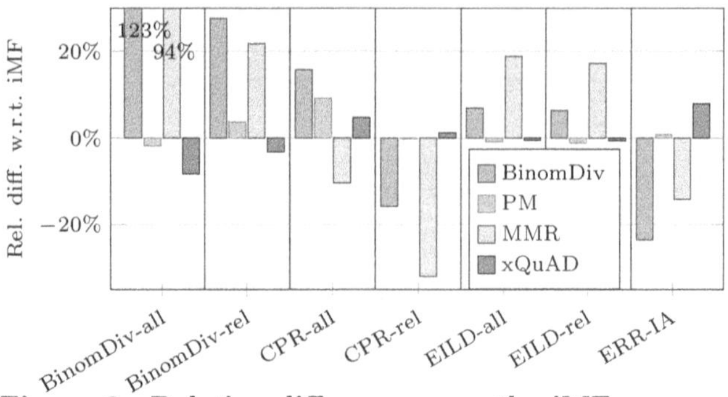

Figure 3: Relative difference over the iMF recommender baseline of the binomial, PM, MMR and xQuAD diversifiers on Netflix.

	all			rel		
	5	10	20	5	10	20
iMF	0.4282	0.3533	0.3090	0.4374	0.3429	0.2501
5	**0.9110**	0.5712	0.3984	**0.5692**	0.3753	0.2571
10	0.8535	**0.8906**	0.5523	0.5412	**0.4506**	0.2705
20	0.7811	0.8483	**0.8656**	0.5169	0.4229	**0.3191**

Table 7: Results at cutoffs N = 5, 10, 20 for the Binomial Diversity metric and diversifier ($\alpha = 0.5$) on Netflix. Bold indicates the best diversification cut-off for a each metric cut-off in each dataset.

Another key observation in the diversity-specific analysis concerns the relation between the frameworks. To facilitate the analysis of the results of Table 6, we show in Figure 3 the relative improvements over the baseline. The cross-wise relationships between diversifications and metrics from different frameworks show interesting findings. Overall, we can see in the figure that the binomial diversifier improves over the baseline when measured with BinomDiv, CPR-all and EILD, showing that the binomial framework is able to promote the proportionality of CPR-all and the dissimilarity of items of EILD by improving the coverage and non-redundancy of the recommendations. In turn, the proportionality of PM does not seem sufficient to promote the diversity when measured with BinomDiv, while the dissimilarity of MMR improves the coverage and non-redundancy of BinomDiv. The intent-aware framework shows some relation with the proportionality framework, most probably caused by the aforementioned accumulation of genres without penalization of redundancy, and does not offer improvements in the other frameworks. All these observations support our postulation that the binomial framework is able to capture and procure coverage while avoiding redundancy, uncovering a diversity angle beyond what the other frameworks can capture.

Finally, in order to evaluate the size-awareness of our Binomial framework, Table 7 shows the correspondence, using the iMF baseline, between the cut-off of the binomial diversification algorithm (the N in 13) and the cut-off of the binomial diversity metric. For each diversification cut-off, the results correspond to the best λ of the objective function. As expected, the best diversification cut-off always agrees with the cut-off of the diversity metric, in both *all* and *rel* variants. This shows that our approach is able to leverage knowledge of the desired result set size in order to bring an additional made-to-fit improvement at the targeted cut-off, a feature that is not supported in any prior framework.

7. CONCLUSIONS

We tackle in this paper the problem of diversity using genre information in Recommender Systems. An analysis of the properties of genres helps us define the requirements that a genre-based definition of diversity in recommendation should satisfy, namely coverage, non-redundancy and recommendation list size-awareness. We propose a binomial framework that satisfies these properties. A metric is defined upon this framework, and a greedy re-ranking algorithm that optimizes it. Experiments on two movie recommendation datasets validate the consistency of our framework, illustrate its properties, and show they comply with the stated requirements. As future work, we will extend our experiments to other datasets, such as music and books, and carry out user studies to further analyze and contrast the behavior and properties of the proposed framework.

8. ACKNOWLEDGMENTS

This work was supported by the national Spanish project TIN2013-47090-C3-2 and the European Union's Seventh Framework Programme (FP7/2007-2013) under grant agreement n° 610594 (CrowdRec).

9. REFERENCES

[1] G. Adomavicius and A. Tuzhilin. Toward the next generation of recommender systems: A survey of the state-of-the-art and possible extensions. *IEEE TKDE*, 17(6):734–749, June 2005.
[2] R. Agrawal, S. Gollapudi, A. Halverson, and S. Ieong. Diversifying search results. *WSDM* 2009, pp. 5–14.
[3] E. Amigó, J. Gonzalo, and F. Verdejo. A General Evaluation Measure for Document Organization Tasks. *SIGIR* 2013, pp. 643–652.
[4] A. Bellogín, P. Castells, and I. Cantador. Precision-oriented evaluation of recommender systems: an algorithmic comparison. *RecSys* 2011, pp. 333–336.
[5] J. Carbonell and J. Goldstein. The use of MMR, diversity-based reranking for reordering documents and producing summaries. *SIGIR* 1998, pp. 335–336.
[6] O. Chapelle, D. Metlzer, Y. Zhang, and P. Grinspan. Expected reciprocal rank for graded relevance. *CIKM* 2009, pp. 621–630.
[7] C. L. Clarke, M. Kolla, G. V. Cormack, O. Vechtomova, A. Ashkan, S. Büttcher, and I. MacKinnon. Novelty and diversity in information retrieval evaluation. *SIGIR* 2008, pp. 659–666.
[8] P. Cremonesi, Y. Koren, and R. Turrin. Performance of recommender algorithms on top-n recommendation tasks. *RecSys* 2010, pp. 39–46.
[9] V. Dang and W. B. Croft. Diversity by proportionality: an election-based approach to search result diversification. *SIGIR* 2012, pp. 65–74.
[10] J. L. Herlocker, J. A. Konstan, L. G. Terveen, and J. T. Riedl. Evaluating collaborative filtering recommender systems. *ACM ToIS*, 22(1):5–53, Jan. 2004.
[11] Y. Hu, Y. Koren, and C. Volinsky. Collaborative filtering for implicit feedback datasets. *ICDM* 2008, pp. 263–272.
[12] Y. Kabutoya, T. Iwata, H. Toda, and H. Kitagawa. A probabilistic model for diversifying recommendation lists. *WTA*, volume 7808 of *LNCS*, pp. 348–359, 2013.
[13] S. M. McNee, J. Riedl, and J. A. Konstan. Being accurate is not enough: how accuracy metrics have hurt recommender systems. *CHI* 2006, pp. 1097–1101.
[14] P. Pu, L. Chen, and R. Hu. A user-centric evaluation framework for recommender systems. *RecSys* 2011, pp. 157–164.
[15] R. L. Santos, C. Macdonald, and I. Ounis. Exploiting query reformulations for web search result diversification. *WWW* 2010, pp. 881–890.
[16] B. Sarwar, G. Karypis, J. Konstan, and J. Riedl. Item-based collaborative filtering recommendation algorithms. *WWW* 2001, pp. 285–295.
[17] Y. Shi, X. Zhao, J. Wang, M. Larson, and A. Hanjalic. Adaptive diversification of recommendation results via latent factor portfolio. *SIGIR* 2012, pp. 175–184.
[18] S. Vargas and P. Castells. Rank and relevance in novelty and diversity metrics for recommender systems. *RecSys* 2011, pp. 109–116.
[19] S. Vargas, P. Castells, and D. Vallet. Explicit relevance models in intent-oriented information retrieval diversification. *SIGIR* 2012, pp. 75–84.
[20] C. X. Zhai, W. W. Cohen, and J. Lafferty. Beyond independent relevance: methods and evaluation metrics for subtopic retrieval. *SIGIR* 2003, pp. 10–17.
[21] M. Zhang and N. Hurley. Avoiding monotony: improving the diversity of recommendation lists. *RecSys* 2008, pp. 123–130.
[22] C.-N. Ziegler, S. M. McNee, J. A. Konstan, and G. Lausen. Improving recommendation lists through topic diversification. *WWW* 2005, pp. 22–32.

Towards a Dynamic Top-N Recommendation Framework

Xin Liu
École Polytechnique Fédérale de Lausanne (EPFL)
Lausanne, Switzerland
x.liu@epfl.ch

Karl Aberer
École Polytechnique Fédérale de Lausanne (EPFL)
Lausanne, Switzerland
karl.aberer@epfl.ch

ABSTRACT

Real world large-scale recommender systems are always dynamic: new users and items continuously enter the system, and the status of old ones (e.g., users' preference and items' popularity) evolve over time. In order to handle such dynamics, we propose a recommendation framework consisting of an online component and an offline component, where the newly arrived items are processed by the online component such that users are able to get suggestions for fresh information, and the influence of longstanding items is captured by the offline component. Based on individual users' rating behavior, recommendations from the two components are combined to provide top-N recommendation. We formulate recommendation problem as a ranking problem where learning to rank is applied to extend upon matrix factorization to optimize item rankings by minimizing a pairwise loss function. Furthermore, to better model interactions between users and items, Latent Dirichlet Allocation is incorporated to fuse rating information and textual information. Real data based experiments demonstrate that our approach outperforms the state-of-the-art models by at least 61.21% and 50.27% in terms of mean average precision (MAP) and normalized discounted cumulative gain (NDCG) respectively.

Categories and Subject Descriptors

H.3.3 [**Information Search and Retrieval**]: Information filtering; H.4 [**Information Systems Applications**]: Miscellaneous

Keywords

top-N recommendation; learning to rank; matrix factorization; topic modeling

1. INTRODUCTION

Most large-scale recommender systems are highly dynamic, where new users and items continuously enter the system, and existing users' preference and items' popularity may vary over time. In order to handle such dynamics for personalized recommendation, a set of time-aware models have been proposed, which employed decay function to give more weight to recent observations [15], or considered only information in specific time-windows [14], or incorporated temporal effects into latent factor models [13, 25]. However, existing solutions either only focus on local information (e.g., recent data or data in certain time-windows) thus *deemphasizing* the influence of global information (e.g., the longstanding items) which might also reflect users' current preference (e.g., seasonal/periodic preference) [3], or suffer from the scalability issue, e.g., frequently re-training latent factor model over big data is computationally expensive.

In order to address the issues of existing time-aware recommendation models, we propose a flexible framework that takes into account both fresh information and longstanding information but processes them separately. The framework consists of an online component and an offline component, where the online component frequently updates the online recommendation model such that users are able to timely receive recommendations for continuously arrived items, and the offline component slowly updates the offline recommendation model to capture the influence of (typically huge volume) longstanding items[1]. When a recommendation query is issued, two recommendation lists from the two components are generated and combined to provide the final top-N recommendation to the user based on her past rating behavior (i.e., preference on the freshness of items).

For each component (online or offline), in contrast to the state-of-the-art solutions that focus on achieving high rating prediction accuracy, we model the recommendation problem as a ranking problem. Specifically, we apply learning to rank technique on the basis of matrix factorization to optimize recommendation ranking by minimizing a *pairwise* loss function. The rank of a pair of items is based on their relevance, where the relevance is determined by the users' preference on items, characterized by the corresponding user's and items' latent factors.

Furthermore, in addition to rating information, we consider textual contents which are pervasive in recommender systems (e.g., tags, descriptions of items) to more precisely model users' preference on items. In this setting, each item is represented by a "bag-of-words" and the words of all items

[1]In this work, we consider a generic recommendation scenario where every item is potentially a candidate for recommendation like movie and book recommendation. For the scenario where items have short lifespan (e.g., news recommendation), we can remove outdated items periodically *or* just use online component.

RecSys'14, October 06 - 10 2014, Foster City, Silicon Valley, CA, USA.
Copyright 2014 ACM 978-1-4503-2668-1/14/10...$15.00.
http://dx.doi.org/10.1145/2645710.2645720.

construct a text corpus. We apply latent dirichlet allocation (LDA) [4] to extract a set of topics from the corpus, and assign each topic a latent factor vector that shares the same space with that of users and items. A user's preference on an item is inferred by combining (1) the user's affinity to topics, derived by multiplying user-specific and topic-specific latent factors and (2) the correlation between topics and the item, i.e., the topic distribution of the item inferred by LDA. This is different from the state-of-the-art approaches [22, 17] that reconcile the number of topics and the dimensionality of latent factors (i.e., implicitly assume that textual content is the dominant factor that influences the distribution of latent factors[2]), thus is able to more flexibly incorporate textual contents into matrix factorization.

The contributions of this paper are summarized as follows: (1) We propose a recommendation framework consisting of an online component and an offline component to process the continuously arrived items and longstanding items separately. (2) We fuse learning to rank and latent factor model to provide top-N recommendation by optimizing a pairwise loss function. Additionally, we apply LDA to better model users' preference for item ranking. To the best of our knowledge, this is the first work that integrates topic modeling into learning to rank model to improve top-N recommendation. Note that such a recommendation model is used by both online an offline components. (3) We cluster each user's rated items based on their topic distribution such that the items in the same cluster can be more meaningfully compared for optimizing pairwise loss function. Moreover, such a clustering strategy removes the item pairs that are not meaningfully comparable, thus reducing the training data while keeping its informativeness. (4) We evaluate the performance of the proposed recommendation method over real datasets. Experimental results show that our approach significantly outperforms the state-of-the-art models.

2. RELATED WORK

Time-aware recommendation

Traditional neighborhood-based algorithms handle temporal effect by either giving more weight to recent information or focusing on observations in specific time windows. For instance, in [25], a decay function $f(x) = e^{-\alpha t}$ was utilized to reduce the effect of old ratings, where t is the time at which a rating was given and α is the decay rate. Liu. et al. [15] used the similar decay function for both similarity computation and rating prediction.

For latent factor models, Koren [13] tackled temporal effect by using time function to model user and item biases in matrix factorization. In [25], the authors split time in equal time intervals and added the time dimension to rating matrix to form a tensor. Alternating least square algorithm was applied to optimize the tensor model.

Recently, a series of solutions were proposed to particularly process the highly dynamic data stream for social media like Twitter. In [7], the authors proposed a collaborative ranking algorithm to recommend interesting tweets to users taking into account tweet topic level factors, user social relation factors, explicit features and the quality of tweets. In [9], tweet topic recommendation was studied, and a ranking algorithm called Stream Ranking Matrix Factorization was proposed where a pairwise ranking approach was applied to optimize the personalized ranking of topics. Agarwal et al. [2] proposed FOBFM model for fast online recommendation learning through effective model initialization using historical information.

Top-N recommendation

Recently, top-N recommendation that directly generates a list of items for users has attracted a lot of attention. In particular, learning to rank techniques have been applied to extend upon latent factor models for top-N recommendation. CofiRank [24] was the first solution in this trend, where NDCG was used as the loss function, and the model was trained by minimizing over a convex upper bound of the loss function. Kabbur et al. [12] proposed a factored item similarity based method, where a ranking loss function that optimizes the area under the curve (AUC) was used.

Shi et al. proposed a set of ranking-oriented algorithms by fusing learning to rank and latent factor models. TFMAP [20] directly maximized MAP to optimize a ranked list of items for individual users. Tensor factorization was applied to model implicit feedback data (e.g., click) under each type of context. Similar solutions include CLiMF [21] and xCLiMF [19], which focused on implicit binary relevance data and explicit rating respectively.

Topic modeling and collaborative filtering

By fusing topic models and latent factor models, hybrid filtering recommendation methods have been improved. The basic idea is to assign a latent topic to each word of an item, which is represented by a "bag-of-words", and then generate item latent factors by aggregating the topics of all words of this item (i.e., each latent factor is characterized by a topic). A missing rating is predicted by combining the target user's affinity to the topics and the correlation between the topics and the target item. A set of algorithms have been proposed to incorporate topics into user/item latent factors [1, 18, 17] to better model user-item interactions for rating prediction. For instance, collaborative topic regression [22] represented users' latent factors by topic interests and assumed that items' latent factors were generated by a topic model. In [17], a model called "Hidden Factors as Topics" (HFT) was proposed to combine ratings and reviews for product recommendation, where the topics were used as regularizers for the latent factors of users and products.

3. TOP-N RECOMMENDATION FRAMEWORK

In this section, we present our dynamic top-N recommendation framework. We start with framework architecture and notation definition in Section 3.1. A top-N recommendation model, which is built on learning to rank, matrix factorization and LDA, is elaborated in Section 3.2. We propose a heuristic algorithm to combine online and offline recommendations in Section 3.3. Related issues are discussed in Section 3.4.

3.1 Preliminaries

As illustrated in Fig. 1, the proposed recommendation framework consists of two main components: an online component that handles continuously arrived items and an offline component that processes longstanding items. Specif-

[2]This assumption is not always true in reality. For instance, users' preference on items may be influenced by other factors like contexts, e.g., users' emotion and social information [16].

ically, the online component stores the coming data in the online storage module (which is typically of small size, compared to the offline storage module) and updates the online recommendation model frequently such that the fresh information can be timely recommended to users. The update frequency depends on characteristics of the coming data (e.g., volume and velocity) as well as the capability of computing infrastructure. Periodically, the data in online storage module is merged to the offline storage module such that the online component only processes the most recent information timely. For instance, the online component only processes a window of 1000 recently entered items (for online recommendation); once the window is full, the 1000 items are moved to offline component and the online component starts processing new items. Due to the large volume of data in the offline storage module, the offline recommendation model is updated less frequently to capture users' preference on the longstanding items. When a recommendation query for a user is issued, both online and offline component provide a recommendation list respectively and the recommendation aggregator serves to combine the two lists based on the user's past rating behavior to provide final top-N recommendation.

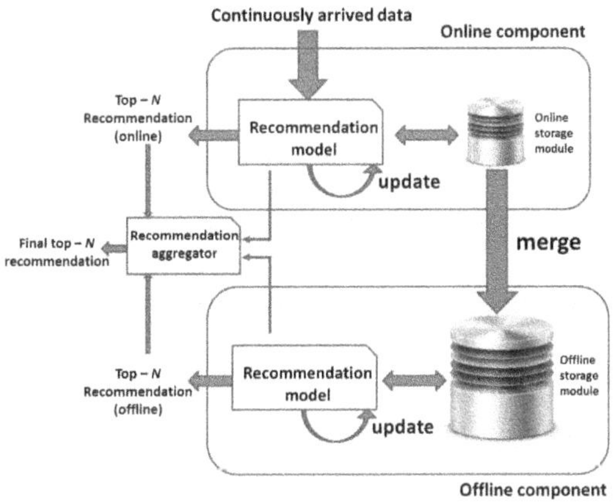

Figure 1: Top-N recommendation framework.

The notations used in this paper are introduced as follows. We denote the user set by $\mathcal{U} = \{u_1, u_2, ..., u_m\}$, and the item set by $\mathcal{V} = \{v_1, v_2, ..., v_n\}$. Any user can rate any item based on her preference. We assume that the value of a rating is a discrete variable in a range $\mathcal{L} = \{L_1, L_2, ..., L_l\}$, e.g., five-point likert scale used by Netflix. A rating provided by user u to item v is denoted by $R_{u,v}$. We assume each item v is associated with a "bag-of-words", denoted by T_v, which is constructed from relevant textual metadata such as the description and tags of the item[3]. The summation of such "bag-of-words" constructs a text corpus $\mathcal{T}$ for LDA.

3.2 Top-N recommendation model

3.2.1 Topic-boosted matrix factorization

Latent factor models, e.g., matrix factorization (MF) have become the state-of-the-art method for recommendation. The rating matrix $R \in \mathcal{R}^{m \times n}$ (m is the number of users and n is the number of items) is factorized into one user-specific matrix $U \in \mathcal{R}^{l \times m}$ and one item-specific matrix $V \in \mathcal{R}^{l \times n}$: $\hat{R} \approx U^T V$, where l is the dimensionality of a latent factor vector that characterizes a user or an item. For user u, the elements of U (i.e., U_u) measure u's affinity to the corresponding latent factors; for item v, the elements of V (i.e., V_v) measure the correlation between v and the corresponding latent factors. Accordingly, the resulting $U_u^T V_v$ captures the correlation between user u and item v, i.e., the predicted rating from u to v. In order to measure the accuracy of rating prediction, an objective function is defined as follows:

$$L = \min_{U,V} \frac{1}{2} \sum_{u=1}^{m} \sum_{v=1}^{n} I_{u,v} (R_{u,v} - U_u^T V_v)^2 + \frac{\lambda}{2} (\| U \|_F^2 + \| V \|_F^2), \tag{1}$$

where $I_{u,v}$ is 1 if user u has rated item v, and 0 otherwise. To avoid overfitting, regularization terms are added, where the parameter λ controls the extent of regularization. Equation 1 can be solved by stochastic gradient descent (SGD), which iteratively updates user-specific and item-specific latent factors to minimize the sum-of-squared-error.

Traditional approaches recommend items to users based on the predicted ratings. However, it is non-trivial to accurately interpret and infer a user's preference simply using ratings, in particular, when such rating information is sparse, which is common in most recommender systems. Recently, some effort has been made to integrate textual contents via topic modeling, e.g., LDA into MF to improve recommendation accuracy [22, 17]. However, in most existing solutions, the dimensionality of latent factors in MF is the same with the number of topics in LDA, and each latent factor is initialized or bounded by the corresponding topic distribution. This implicitly assumes that the latent factors of users and items are completely characterized by textual contents, which is not always true in reality. For instance, a user's preference may be affected by other factors like social relationships and users' emotions [16]. We therefore propose a novel model to fuse MF and LDA by relaxing the arguably strong coupling between topics and items' latent factors.

We apply LDA on the text corpus $\mathcal{T}$ to extract k topics $D = \{d_1, ..., d_k\}$ such that each word w has a probability $\phi_{w,d}$ of being assigned to topic d, and each item v is represented by a topic distribution θ_v. Different from previous methods [22, 17] that reconcile the number of topics and the dimensionality of user/item latent factor vector, in our approach, the topic number k is not necessarily equal to the factor latent vector dimensionality l, and each topic d is also associated with and characterized by a latent factor vector X_d that is sharing the same dimensional space with user/item latent factors.

Accordingly, the correlation between a user and an item, which was captured through the user specific and item specific latent factors, is reformulated by incorporating the effect of topics. Specifically, item specific latent factor matrix V is represented by the product of two matrices:

$$V = XY, \tag{2}$$

where $X \in \mathcal{R}^{l \times k}$ is a topic specific latent factor matrix where each column is a latent factor vector that characterizes the corresponding topic. $Y \in \mathcal{R}^{k \times n}$ is a matrix that stores correlations between items and topics, where the correlation between topic d and item v is measured by the corresponding topic distribution $\theta_{d,v}$ over this item. Therefore, when inferring user u's preference on item v, u's preferences on the k topics are firstly measured through user specific and topic

[3]This assumption holds in most online applications like e-commerce, review sites, social media, etc.

specific latent factors (i.e., dot product), and then the correlations between the k topics and item v are derived, finally the two aspects are fused to capture u's preference on item v. With topics, interactions between users and items can be more meaningfully modeled than traditional scenario where only rating information (less interpretable) is used. Furthermore, the dimensionality of latent factor vector is not bounded by the number of topics thus is more flexible to capture other latent effects besides texts. By incorporating topics the rating from user u to item v can be obtained by

$$\hat{R}_{u,v} \approx U_u^T X Y_v. \quad (3)$$

3.2.2 Learning to rank for recommendation

In contrast to the state-of-the-art approaches that focus on improving the accuracy of rating prediction, we aim to provide top-N recommendation which is more realistic in real-world recommendation scenarios. To this end, we apply learning to rank technique to directly optimize a ranking measure for recommendation. Among numerous loss functions employed by learning to rank algorithms, we choose the one used in RankNet [5], which is not only popular in academia, but is also used in a commercial search engine. Specifically, we employ a pairwise approach to learn top-N item ranking, where the ranking task is formulated as a pairwise classification task, i.e., to rank a pair of items. Note that besides pairwise approach, another two alternatives for learning to rank are pointwise and listwise approaches. Pointwise approach is actually equivalent to rating prediction. For listwise approach, when training the recommendation model, it is non-trial to meaningfully construct a list of ranked item (i.e., items are rated by a user individually thus cannot intuitively construct a list structure). We therefore choose a pairwise approach which can better structure each user's rated items for learning at a finer granularity.

To provide top-N recommendation, existing pairwise based learning to rank models are learned by comparing the relevance of *any* pair of rated items of each user [9]. However, this strategy fails to distinguish characteristics of items thus missing the semantic comparability among items. For instance, it is useful to learn that a user prefers rock music to lyric music, but meaningless to compare rock music and programming books. To solve this issue, we propose to cluster a user's ratings by leveraging LDA such that the rated items can be more meaningfully compared.

Recall that we extract k topics from corpus $\mathcal{T}$, and each item v is represented by a topic distribution θ_v. Based on such topic distributions, we divide user u's rated items into k groups by applying k-mean clustering algorithm[4]. Note that if the size of a group is smaller than a threshold (e.g., 2), this group is merged into the nearest one. *Within* each group, pairs of items, where in each pair the first item is assumed to be ranked higher than the second one (based on ratings), are obtained, and we denote $\Omega_u = \{(v_i, v_j) | v_i \in \mathcal{V}_u \bigwedge v_j \in \mathcal{V}_u \bigwedge v_i \rhd v_j\}$ as a set of item pais of user u across all groups. Aggregating all users' such item pairs constructs training data for pairwise learning to rank.

It is worth noting that a byproduct of such a topic based clustering strategy is that it removes the item pairs where the comparison of the two items is meaningless (instead of considering all possible item pairs, which is adopted by most existing approaches), thus reducing the volume of training data while keeping its informativeness.

Following its definition in RankNet [5], we apply a cross entropy cost function w.r.t. user u as follows:

$$l^u_{v_i,v_j} = -\bar{P^u_{i,j}} \cdot logP^u_{i,j} - (1 - \bar{P^u_{i,j}}) \cdot log(1 - logP^u_{i,j}), \quad (4)$$

where $P^u_{i,j}$ is the inferred posterior probability (by a logistic function) that item v_i is ranked higher than item v_j by user u:

$$P^u_{i,j} = \frac{e^{f(u,v_i) - f(u,v_j)}}{1 + e^{f(u,v_i) - f(u,v_j)}}, \quad (5)$$

where $f(u, v_i)$ returns item v_i's relevance score, which is the predicted rating from user u to item v_i, obtained by our topic-boosted approach (see Equation 3). $\bar{P^u_{i,j}}$ is the desired target value for the posterior probability (by a logistic function), which is derived using the *known* ratings $R_{u,i}$ and $R_{u,j}$ provided by user u to the pair of items v_i and v_j:

$$\bar{P^u_{i,j}} = \frac{e^{R_{u,i} - R_{u,j}}}{1 + e^{R_{u,i} - R_{u,j}}}. \quad (6)$$

By substituting $P^u_{i,j}$ and $\bar{P^u_{i,j}}$ with Eq. 5 and 6, the loss function Eq. 4 is reformulated as:

$$l^{u'}_{v_i,v_j} = -\frac{e^{R_{u,i} - R_{u,j}}}{1 + e^{R_{u,i} - R_{u,j}}} \cdot (f(u, v_i) - f(u, v_j)) + log(1 + e^{f(u,v_i) - f(u,v_j)}). \quad (7)$$

By considering all users' item pairs, we define the objective function that aims to minimize pairwise loss, taking into account the regularization for avoiding overfitting:

$$L' = \min_{U,X} \sum_{u=1}^{m} \sum_{(v_i,v_j) \in \Omega_u} -\frac{e^{R_{u,i} - R_{u,j}}}{1 + e^{R_{u,i} - R_{u,j}}} \cdot (f(u, v_i) - f(u, v_j)) + log(1 + e^{f(u,v_i) - f(u,v_j)}) + \frac{\lambda}{2}(\| U \|_F^2 + \| X \|_F^2), \quad (8)$$

To solve the objective function, which is non-convex, we apply Stochastic Gradient Descent (SGD) to try to find a local minima. We perform gradient descent with respect to user specific and topic specific latent factors respectively:

$$\frac{\partial L'}{U_u} = \sum_{(v_i,v_j) \in \Omega_u} -P^u_{i,j}(XY_i - XY_j) + \frac{e^{U_u XY_i - U_u XY_j}(XY_i - XY_j)}{1 + e^{U_u XY_i - U_u XY_j}} + \lambda U_u. \quad (9)$$

$$\frac{\partial L'}{X} = \sum_{u=1}^{m} \sum_{(v_i,v_j) \in \Omega_u} -P^u_{i,j}(U_u Y_i^T - U_u Y_j^T) + \frac{e^{U_u XY_i - U_u XY_j}(U_u Y_i^T - U_u Y_j^T)}{1 + e^{U_u XY_i - U_u XY_j}} + \lambda X. \quad (10)$$

The latent factors are updated iteratively:

$$U_u \leftarrow U_u - \gamma \frac{\partial L'}{U_u}, \quad X \leftarrow X - \gamma \frac{\partial L'}{X}, \quad (11)$$

[4]K-means clustering algorithm is applied due to its simplicity. More sophisticated clustering algorithms may be used, but the discussion on the tradeoff between the improved clustering quality and the increased computational complexity is beyond the scope of this work.

where γ is the learning rate. By sorting the predicted ratings (i.e., relevance scores) of items (in descending order) that user u has not rated, we generate top-N items for user u.

3.3 Combining online and offline recommendation

To produce final top-N recommendation by combining recommendations from online and offline components[5], we investigate a user's past rating behavior to assess her preference on the freshness of items. We denote the freshness of an item v when it was rated by ψ_v, which is a binary variable where 1 indicates that this item was fresh (i.e., processed by the online component) and 0 indicates that this item was longstanding (i.e., processed by the offline component).

For user u, we record the freshness of each item that u has rated: $\{\psi_1, \psi_2, ...\}$. These freshness indicators are modeled as observations of independent Bernoulli trials. In each trial, the success probability (i.e., the probability of rating a fresh item) is modeled by Beta distribution with parameters α and β (we start with $\alpha = \beta = 1$, which translates into complete uncertainty about the distribution of the parameter, modeled by uniform distribution: Beta(1, 1) = U(0, 1)). After observing s successes in n trials, the posterior density of the probability is Beta($\alpha = \alpha + s$, $\beta = \beta + n - s$). The expectation probability[6] of rating a fresh item is then obtained by $\Psi_u = \frac{\alpha}{\alpha+\beta}$. The higher the Ψ_u, the more likely user u will rate a fresh item.

Given the online recommendation list Ω^u_{on} and offline recommendation list Ω^u_{off} for user u, as well as u's preference on the freshness of items Ψ_u, the final top-N recommendation list Ω^u is generated iteratively: at each iteration, the top fresh item v' is picked from Ω^u_{on} with a probability of Ψ_u; otherwise, the top longstanding item v'' is picked from Ω^u_{off}. Once chosen, the item v' or v'' is appended to the end of Ω^u, and removed from Ω^u_{on} or Ω^u_{off}. This process continues until the size of Ω_u increases to N.

3.4 Discussion

To achieve personalized top-N recommendation, we proposed a recommendation framework by leveraging learning to rank, matrix factorization and LDA. Two important issues, scalability and cold-start, are discussed as follows.

The time complexity of the optimization procedure is $O(m \cdot \tilde{t}^2)$, where m is the number of users, and $\tilde{t}$ is the average number of items per user [5]. In practice, sampling methods might be applied to sample a subset of items for each users (i.e., decreasing the value of $\tilde{t}$), and hence reduce the computational complexity. Furthermore, for each user, we cluster the rated items based on their topic distribution to make the pairwise item relevance comparison more meaningful[7]. This greatly reduces the number of comparisons (i.e., $\tilde{t}^2$), thus simplifying the model training. Another way to cope with the complexity of the model is to parallelize the optimization procedure, e.g., distributed SGD [11] or downpour SGD [8], which makes our approach applicable to even larger data.

It is also worth noting that "cold-start" is still an open question in most recommender systems. For our approach, this issue is particularly important when fresh items are merged from online storage module to offline storage module (i.e., the input data for online recommendation model will be sparse). To address this issue, each user's most recently rated items are not only merged to the offline storage module but also kept in the online storage module as the buffer to bootstrap newly arrived items[8], e.g., by measuring the similarity between two items based on their topic distributions. Moreover, a user's recent ratings reflect her current preference, so the derived online recommendation is expected to be more accurate. Regarding the completely new users, existing solutions (e.g., [23]) can be applied on the basis of our recommendation approach, however, the detailed discussion about this issue is beyond the scope of this paper.

4. EVALUATION

4.1 Methodology

We use a dataset collected from Douban (www.douban.com), one of the largest Chinese based social platforms for sharing reviews and recommendations for books, movies and music. Users provide ratings in 5-star scale to indicate their preference on items. The dataset contains ratings submitted from 2007 to 2011. Table 1 summarizes the statistics of Douban dataset (shared by the first author of [26]).

Table 1: Statistics of Douban data

	# of ratings	# of users	# of items
Book	1,097,148	33,523	381,767
Movie	2,828,585	33,561	87,081
Music	1,387,216	29,287	257,288
All	5,312,949	36,673	726,136

Besides rating information, we crawled each item's textual metadata such as the summary and tags assigned by users for topic modeling. For our approach, we keep the items that enter the system before 2011 in offline storage module (see Fig. 1), and treat the items that enter the system in 2011 as continuously arrived data which will be handled by online component. The online recommendation model is updated when every 1000 new items enter the system and the offline recommendation model is updated when every 10,000 new items are merged from online storage module to offline storage module (i.e., the online model is updated 10 times more frequently than the offline model). Note that the ratings submitted in 2011 will be used as test data, and the ones submitted before 2011 will be used as training data. Since top-N recommendation is provided by combining online recommendation and offline recommendation, so the two components cannot be evaluated separately. Besides Douban data, we also use the Delicious bookmarks data [6]. In this dataset, 1,867 users bookmarked 69,226 URLs with 53,388 tags (for topic modeling). In the experiments, the purpose of a recommendation model is to recommend URLs that are likely to be bookmarked by users (i.e., binary rating is used). Note that due to space limitation, Delicious dataset is only used in comparison study in Section 4.2.2.

[5]Remind that online and offline components use the same recommendation model elaborated in Section 3.2.

[6]A straightforward extension is to add a decay factor to emphasize users' recent preference on items' freshness to improve prediction accuracy. We leave as a future work a more detailed discussion on such extensions.

[7]This may worsen the issue of data sparsity. In practice, we only apply clustering strategy to users who have rated sufficient number of items (e.g., at least 20)

[8]The number of users' most recently rated items that are kept in online component is a design parameter, which can be configured according to characteristics of the system or by cross validation. We set this number to 1 in our experiments.

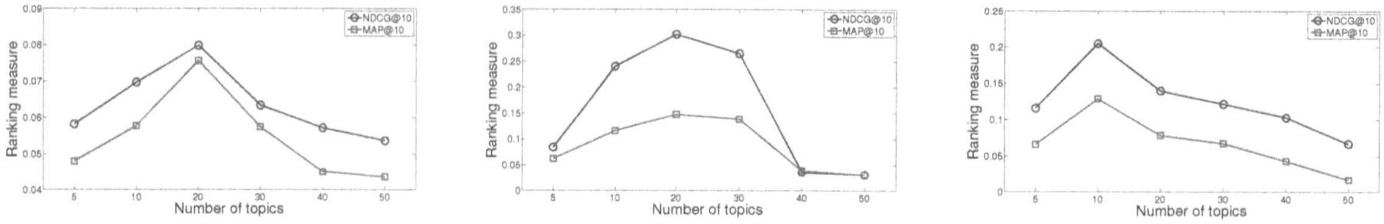

(a) Book data. (b) Movie data. (c) Music data.

Figure 2: Performance of our approach with varying topic number (top-10 recommendation, Douban data).

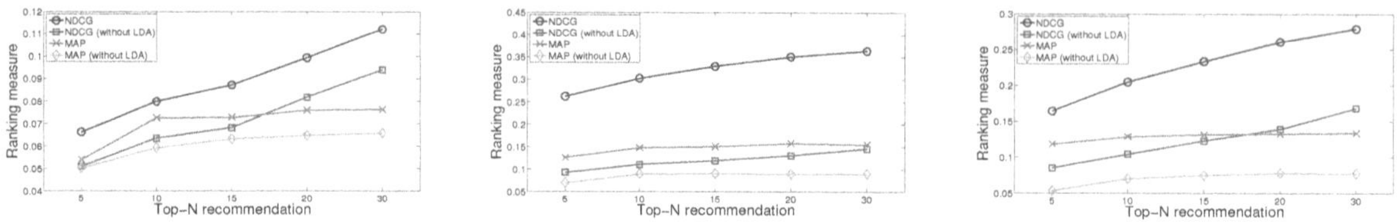

(a) Book data. (b) Movie data. (c) Music data.

Figure 3: Influence of textual content (Douban data).

We compare our approach with several representative baselines: (1) **BasicMF**. This is the basic matrix factorization model. Top-N recommendation is provided by sorting the candidate items in descending order of the predicted ratings. The dimensionality of factors, regularization parameter and learning rate are set to 10, 0.1 and 0.01 respectively (by cross validation). (2) **RMFX** [10]. This approach uses a (hinge loss based) pairwise approach with matrix factorization to optimize the ranking for social streams like Twitter. When processing continuously arrived items, it applies random sampling with a reservoir to sample user-item pairs for model update. The dimensionality of factors, regularization parameter, learning rate, and reservoir size are set to 10, 0.1, 0.1 and 100 respectively (by cross validation). (3) **CLiMF** [21]. This is a ranking-oriented algorithm that directly optimize a ranking measure Mean Reciprocal Rank (MRR). The dimensionality of factors, regularization parameter and learning rate are set to 10, 0.001 and 0.001 respectively (by cross validation). The implementation of this model is publicly available at http://dmirlab.tudelft.nl/users/yue-shi. (4) **timeSVD++**. This is a matrix factorization model incorporating temporal dynamics proposed in [13]. User bias, item bias and user latent factors are modeled as functions of time. For each of these approaches, we use the ratings submitted from 2007 to 2010 as the training data to train the model and validate its performance using ratings submitted in 2011. To obtain time-aware recommendation, we updated these models (except RMFX) when every 5000 new items enter the system. 5000 is chosen as the compromise of the online and offline components of our approach (see previous paragraph for the settings of our approach). For RMFX, the model is updated when every 1000 items enter the system. This is to compare with our approach's online component that is particularly designed to handle fresh items. Experiments are conducted 10 times and the averaged results are presented for each approach. Note that error bars are omitted in figures to avoid cluttering but in Tab. 2, we provide 95% confidence interval (all comparison results are statistically significant).

We measure the performance of recommendation models using Mean Average Precision (MAP) and Normalized Discounted Cumulative Gain (NDCG), two well-known metrics for measuring the performance of ranking algorithms.

4.2 Results

4.2.1 Influence of design parameters

As argued in Section 3.2.1, the number of topics in LDA should not be tied to the dimensionality of latent factors in matrix factorization such that textual contents can be more flexibly incorporated to model interactions between users and items. We thus first demonstrate the performance of our approach when different number of topics is set. Note that the dimensionality of latent factors, regularization parameter and learning rate are set to 5, 0.001 and 0.00001 which are optimized by cross validation. From Fig. 2 we observe the performance of our approach varies a lot with different number of topics. For every type of item (i.e., book, movie and music), the general trends are both NDCG and MAP first increase, when arriving at a certain point, they start decreasing with the increasing number of topics. Specifically, for book data and movie data, 20 topics achieve the highest NDCG and MAP, while for music data, the optimal number of topics is 10. This observation supports our claim that topic number should not be tied to the dimensionality of latent factors (i.e., 5 in this case), and a suitable topic number significantly improves the performance of our approach.

We next validate the effectiveness of combining LDA and matrix factorization for modeling users' preference on items for ranking. Fig. 3 shows the comparison results (with different recommendation list size) of our approach and a variant where textual contents are not considered. It is clear that when both textual contents and rating information are used, NDCG and MAP are significantly improved. This is because by deriving topic distribution for each item, users' preference can be more accurately modeled, especially when the target user and/or item's ratings are sparse (i.e., a single piece of textual content can reveal many of an item's characteristics thus is more informative than a single rating).

Recall that one contribution of our work is to cluster a user's rated items based on their topic distributions such that the training data (i.e., item pairs for optimizing pairwise loss function) is more compact and more meaningful. We next demonstrate the effectiveness of such item clustering. From Fig. 4 we notice that in all cases, considering topic based clustering evidently improves the performance of a variant of our approach where no clustering is conducted. This demonstrates that removing unnecessary item

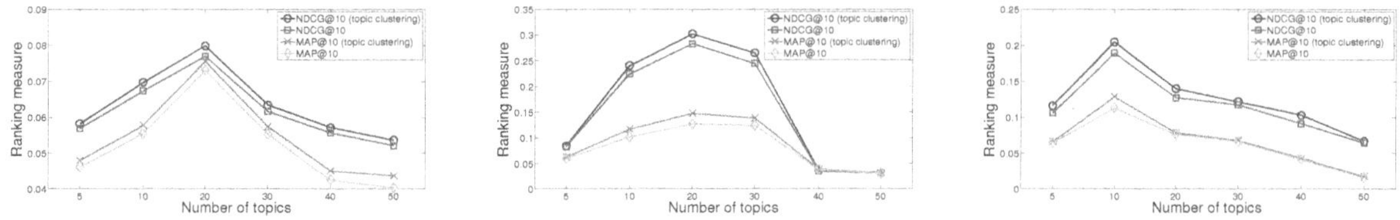

(a) Book data. (b) Movie data. (c) Music data.

Figure 4: Influence of topic clustering (top-10 recommendation, Douban data).

Table 2: Performance comparison (top-10 recommendation, 95% confidence interval, Douban dataset)

	Book		Movie		Music	
	NDCG@10 (95% C.I.)	MAP@10 (95% C.I.)	NDCG@10 (95% C.I.)	MAP@10 (95% C.I.)	NDCG@10 (95% C.I.)	MAP@10 (95% C.I.)
Our approach	**0.0799 (0.0785,0.0812)**	**0.0726 (0.0711,0.0740)**	**0.3021 (0.3001,0.3046)**	**0.1477 (0.1455,0.1498)**	**0.2048 (0.2014,0.2080)**	**0.1287 (0.1265,0.1306)**
BasicMF	0.0266 (0.0250,0.0281)	0.0255 (0.0238,0.0275)	0.0851 (0.0840,0.0863)	0.0754 (0.0741,0.0769)	0.0837 (0.0815,0.0861)	0.0416 (0.0399,0.0435)
RMFX	0.0525 (0.0504,0.0551)	0.0486 (0.0452,0.0509)	0.1923 (0.1895,0.1955)	0.0822 (0.0798,0.0842)	0.0985 (0.0960,0.0911)	0.0520 (0.0505,0.0538)
CLiMF	0.0585 (0.0565,0.0604)	0.0503 (0.0481,0.0525)	0.2152 (0.2111,0.2198)	0.0967 (0.0915,0.1008)	0.1180 (0.1150,0.1206)	0.0600 (0.0573,0.0631)
timeSVD++	0.0412 (0.0397,0.0431)	0.0395 (0.0371,0.0418)	0.1634 (0.1611,0.1660)	0.0951 (0.0921,0.0983)	0.1205 (0.1188,0.1224)	0.0614 (0.0588,0.0642)

pairs indeed refines the training data thus improving ranking measures. On average, such a clustering strategy improves the performance of our approach in terms of NDCG/MAP, by 2.99%/4.89%, 5.37%/9.02% and 7.99%/5.92% for book data, movie data and music data respectively.

4.2.2 *Comparison study*

We compare the performance of our approach with that of the state-of-the-art approaches (see Section 4.1). Note that

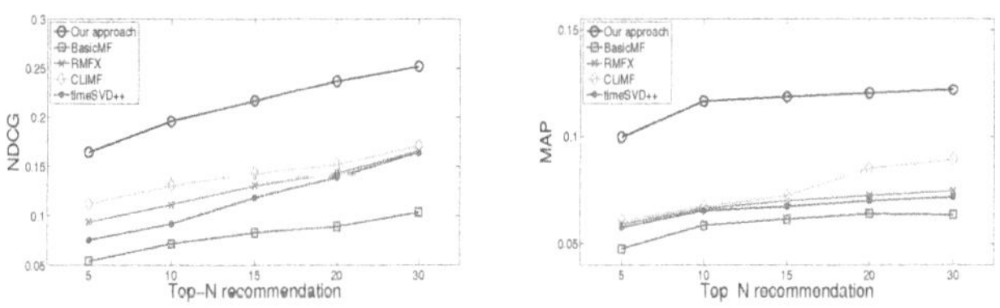

(a) NDCG. (b) MAP.

Figure 5: Performance comparison (Douban data).

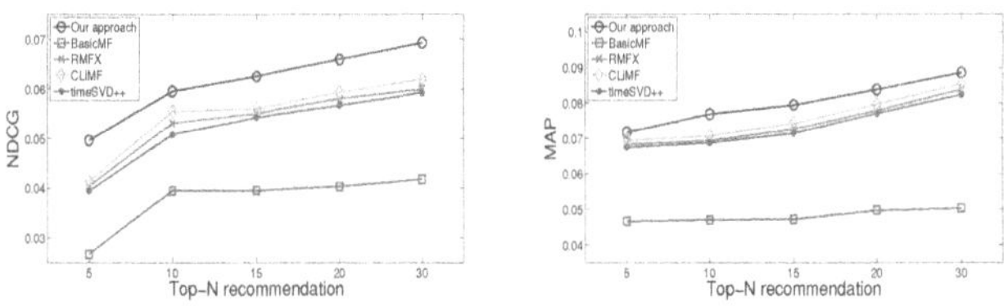

(a) NDCG. (b) MAP.

Figure 6: Performance comparison (Delicious data).

for our approach, optimal topic number is applied for different type of items. Table 2 summarizes NDCG and MAP for all recommendation approaches when top-10 recommendation is provided. Not surprisingly, BasicMF, which simply predicts a user's rating to an item for ranking, produces the lowest NDCG and MAP. This shows that optimizing rating prediction does not necessarily generates good recommendation ranking, in particular, when rating information is sparse. As a ranking-oriented recommendation approach, CLiMF significantly outperforms BasicMF. This proves the effectiveness of learning to rank for top-N recommendation. By optimizing a ranking measure, CLiMF directly generates a recommendation list instead of focusing on improving rating prediction accuracy. Similarly, RMFX, which applies pairwise learning to rank also outperforms BaseMF. However, to better handle scalability issue, RMFX applies sampling techniques to process the incoming items, which inevitably lose information (and hence, the accuracy). This makes RMFX slightly less accurate than CLiMF. timeSVD++, although is not particularly designed for ranking, by incorporating temporal effects into matrix factorization (via time-aware user/item bias and latent factors), still generates reasonable results: for music data, timeSVD++ is even better than CLiMF and RMFX. In all cases, our model consistently outperforms other methods due to four key designs: (1) learning to rank is applied to directly optimize item ranking instead of rating prediction; (2) textual contents are incorporated (by fusing LDA and matrix factorization) to better model users' preference; (3) topic distribution based item clustering refines the training data to more efficiently fit the model; (4) new items and longstanding items are modeled separately for providing personalized recommendation based on individual users' preference on the freshness of items.

We also compare the performance of all recommendation approaches when recommendation list size varies. Fig. 5(a) and 5(b) summarize NDCG and MAP for each recommendation approach when top-5, 10, 15, 20, 30 recommendations are provided. Note that we mix book data, movie data and music data to conduct comprehensive comparison study. Similar to previous comparison results, our approach generates the highest NDCG and MAP. In summary, by averaging performance when different recommendation list size is applied, our approach improves BasicMF, RMFX, CLiMF and timeSVD++ by 168.98%, 72.40%, 50.27% and 87.64% in terms of NDCG, 96.73%, 72.83%, 61.21% and 75.95% in terms of MAP. The comparison results using Delicious data (see Fig. 6) demonstrate the similar trends.

5. CONCLUSION

In this paper, we present a dynamic recommendation framework that consists of an online component that quickly processes the continuously arrived items and an offline component that captures the influence of longstanding items. We apply learning to rank to optimize a pairwise loss function. LDA is integrated to combine rating information and textual contents to better model users' preference on items. Furthermore, topic distribution based item clustering refines training data. A heuristic algorithm is proposed to combine online and offline recommendations based on users' preference on the freshness of items. Two real datasets based experiments demonstrate that our approach significantly outperforms the state-of-the-art models.

As for the future work, we intend to explore more sophisticated mechanisms to derive users' preference on the freshness of items for recommendation. Another direction is to investigate to further reduce computational complexity to better handle scalability issue (e.g., by sampling).

6. ACKNOWLEDGEMENTS

This work was partially supported by the grant Reconcile: Robust Online Credibility Evaluation of Web Content from Switzerland through the Swiss Contribution to the enlarged European Union.

7. REFERENCES

[1] D. Agarwal and B.-C. Chen. flda: matrix factorization through latent dirichlet allocation. In *Proceedings of the third ACM WSDM*, 2010.

[2] D. Agarwal, B.-C. Chen, and P. Elango. Fast online learning through offline initialization for time-sensitive recommendation. In *Proceedings of the 16th ACM SIGKDD*, 2010.

[3] M. Aly, S. Pandey, V. Josifovski, and K. Punera. Towards a robust modeling of temporal interest change patterns for behavioral targeting. In *Proceedings of the 22nd WWW*, 2013.

[4] D. M. Blei, A. Y. Ng, and M. I. Jordan. Latent dirichlet allocation. *J. Mach. Learn. Res.*, 3:993–1022, 2003.

[5] C. Burges, T. Shaked, E. Renshaw, A. Lazier, M. Deeds, N. Hamilton, and G. Hullender. Learning to rank using gradient descent. In *Proceedings of the 22nd ICML*, 2005.

[6] I. Cantador, P. Brusilovsky, and T. Kuflik. 2nd workshop on information heterogeneity and fusion in recommender systems (hetrec). In *Proceedings of the 5th ACM RecSys*, 2011.

[7] K. Chen, T. Chen, G. Zheng, O. Jin, E. Yao, and Y. Yu. Collaborative personalized tweet recommendation. In *Proceedings of the 35th ACM SIGIR*, 2012.

[8] J. Dean, G. Corrado, R. Monga, K. Chen, M. Devin, Q. V. Le, M. Z. Mao, M. Ranzato, A. W. Senior, P. A. Tucker, K. Yang, and A. Y. Ng. Large scale distributed deep networks. In *Proceedings of the 25th NIPS*, 2012.

[9] E. Diaz-Aviles, L. Drumond, L. Schmidt-Thieme, and W. Nejdl. Real-time top-n recommendation in social streams. In *Proceedings of the 6th ACM RecSys*, 2012.

[10] E. Diaz-Aviles, L. Drumond, L. Schmidt-Thieme, and W. Nejdl. Real-time top-n recommendation in social streams. In *Proceedings of the 6th ACM RecSys*, 2012.

[11] R. Gemulla, E. Nijkamp, P. J. Haas, and Y. Sismanis. Large-scale matrix factorization with distributed stochastic gradient descent. In *Proceedings of the 17th ACM SIGKDD*, 2011.

[12] S. Kabbur, X. Ning, and G. Karypis. Fism: factored item similarity models for top-n recommender systems. In *Proceedings of the 19th ACM SIGKDD*, 2013.

[13] Y. Koren. Collaborative filtering with temporal dynamics. In *Proceedings of the 15th ACM SIGKDD*, 2009.

[14] N. Lathia, S. Hailes, and L. Capra. Temporal collaborative filtering with adaptive neighbourhoods. In *Proceedings of the 32nd ACM SIGIR*, 2009.

[15] N. N. Liu, M. Zhao, E. Xiang, and Q. Yang. Online evolutionary collaborative filtering. In *Proceedings of the 4th ACM RecSys*, 2010.

[16] X. Liu and K. Aberer. Soco: a social network aided context-aware recommender system. In *Proceedings of the 22nd WWW*, 2013.

[17] J. McAuley and J. Leskovec. Hidden factors and hidden topics: Understanding rating dimensions with review text. In *Proceedings of the 7th ACM RecSys*, 2013.

[18] S. Purushotham and Y. Liu. Collaborative topic regression with social matrix factorization for recommendation systems. In *Proceedings of the 29th ICML*, 2012.

[19] Y. Shi, A. Karatzoglou, L. Baltrunas, M. Larson, and A. Hanjalic. xclimf: Optimizing expected reciprocal rank for data with multiple levels of relevance. In *Proceedings of the 7th ACM RecSys*, 2013.

[20] Y. Shi, A. Karatzoglou, L. Baltrunas, M. Larson, A. Hanjalic, and N. Oliver. Tfmap: optimizing map for top-n context-aware recommendation. In *Proceedings of the 35th ACM SIGIR*, 2012.

[21] Y. Shi, A. Karatzoglou, L. Baltrunas, M. Larson, N. Oliver, and A. Hanjalic. Climf: learning to maximize reciprocal rank with collaborative less-is-more filtering. In *Proceedings of the 6th ACM RecSys*, 2012.

[22] C. Wang and D. M. Blei. Collaborative topic modeling for recommending scientific articles. In *Proceedings of the 17th ACM SIGKDD*, 2011.

[23] F. Wang, W. Pan, and L. Chen. Recommendation for new users with partial preferences by integrating product reviews with static specifications. In *Proceedings of 21st UMAP*, 2011.

[24] M. Weimer, A. Karatzoglou, Q. Le, and A. Smola. Cofirank - maximum margin matrix factorization for collaborative ranking. In *Proceedings of the 21st NIPS*, 2007.

[25] L. Xiong, X. Chen, T.-K. Huang, J. Schneider, and J. G. Carbonell. Temporal collaborative filtering with bayesian probabilistic tensor factorization. In *Proceedings of SDM*, 2010.

[26] E. Zhong, W. Fan, J. Wang, L. Xiao, and Y. Li. Comsoc: adaptive transfer of user behaviors over composite social network. In *Proceedings of the 18th ACM SIGKDD*, 2012.

Explore-Exploit in Top-N Recommender Systems via Gaussian Processes

Hastagiri P Vanchinathan
ETH Zürich
hastagiri@inf.ethz.ch

Isidor Nikolic *
Microsoft, Zürich
inikolic@microsoft.com

Fabio De Bona
Google, Zürich
fdb@google.com

Andreas Krause
ETH Zürich
krausea@ethz.ch

ABSTRACT

We address the challenge of ranking recommendation lists based on click feedback by efficiently encoding similarities among users and among items. The key challenges are threefold: (1) combinatorial number of lists; (2) sparse feedback and (3) context dependent recommendations. We propose the CGPRANK algorithm, which exploits prior information specified in terms of a Gaussian process kernel function, which allows to share feedback in three ways: Between positions in a list, between items, and between contexts. Under our model, we provide strong performance guarantees and empirically evaluate our algorithm on data from two large scale recommendation tasks: Yahoo! news article recommendation, and Google books. In our experiments, CGPRANK significantly outperforms state-of-the-art multi-armed bandit and learning-to-rank methods, with an 18% increase in clicks.

Categories and Subject Descriptors

H.3.3 [**Information Search and Retrieval**]: Relevance feedback; H.3.5 [**Online Information Services**]: Web-based Services

Keywords

Recommender systems; CGPRANK; User feedback; Kernel methods; Exploration–exploitation tradeoffs

1. INTRODUCTION

Traditionally, recommender systems relied on supervised learning on a batch of data. Existing approaches like collaborative filtering, content based filtering or learning to rank techniques all try to learn a fixed optimal recommendation model given training data. These approaches fail to capture the dynamic nature of the user preferences and inventory. An ideal recommendation list for a given user/context has to take recent feedback into account.

Learning this optimal ordering leads to an "explore–exploit" tradeoff, where we need to gather information about the effectiveness of orderings, while at the same time maximizing conversions based on the estimated data. Standard multi-arm bandit algorithms which solve such tasks either use similarity information or cannot select lists of items. On a web scale, this is a daunting task, for mainly three reasons: (1) There is an exponential number of lists to choose from; (2) the number of items available for recommendation is often large, compared to the relatively sparse click feedback; (3) optimality of the ordering depends on the context which in itself could be from a large set (e.g., user to whom the item should be recommended).

In this work, we propose an algorithm – CGPRANK – for (re-) ranking recommendations from click feedback. In order to address above challenges, it uses a positive definite kernel function to encode prior assumptions about the similarity of items (and possible user features). This kernel is then used to share and exploit sparse feedback in multiple ways: across positions in the list (1), across items (2) and across users/contexts (3). CGPRANK navigates the exploration–exploitation tradeoff by predicting performance of as yet unexplored lists using nonparametric Gaussian process models, whose regularity is captured in the kernel function. Exploiting such regularity allows our algorithm to be statistically efficient, i.e., maximize the benefit drawn from sparse observations about the users' preferences.

We prove strong performance guarantees for our CGPRANK algorithm. In particular, we analyze its regret, i.e., the loss in conversions/clicks compared to using (hindsight) optimal orderings. We prove that under natural separability and regularity assumptions, the average regret vanishes. Further, we analyze the effect of increasing list sizes, and find a surprising theoretical result: Under some natural conditions, increasing the list size can parallelize exploration in a way to *accelerate* convergence, instead of an exponential slowdown. We extensively evaluate our approaches on two large datasets from real world recommendation tasks: Firstly, we consider news article recommendation, using data provided by Yahoo! [1]. Secondly, we evaluate CGPRANK on Google's infrastructure, using clickstream data from Google's ebooks store, demonstrating a significant improvement over existing multi-armed bandit and learning-to-rank techniques. In particular, our approach provides an 18% lift in total clicks compared to the existing approaches.

2. RELATED WORK

Our approach relates and builds on work in multiple areas.

Recommender systems, ranking and relevance: Popular techniques include collaborative filtering, matrix factorization and frequent item set mining [21], as well as learning to rank approaches [2]. These approaches usually estimate user's preferences ("ex-

*Work done while the author was a student at ETH, Zürich and working as an intern at Google, Zürich

[1] `http://webscope.sandbox.yahoo.com/`

RecSys'14, October 6–10, 2014, Foster City, Silicon Valley, CA, USA.
ACM 978-1-4503-2668-1/14/10 ...$15.00.
http://dx.doi.org/10.1145/2645710.2645733.

ploit") from a fixed training set collected a priori, and generally do not address how to dynamically collect data ("explore") for training in order to adapt to changing inventories and user bases. We empirically compare to learning to rank (LTR) approaches that learn from user interactions and demonstrate the benefit of our exploration strategy.

Multi-arm bandits (MAB): For single item recommendation, MAB is a classical formalism for studying the explore-exploit dilemma incurred when optimizing an unknown payoff function with noisy feedback limited only to the choices made. Early approaches such as ϵ-Greedy, UCB1 [3], do not exploit the similarity information between the choices, and thus fail when feedback is sparse. Modern research has addressed this challenge, under assumptions of linear [17] and Lipschitz [12] continuous payoff functions, as well as functions with regularity explained by a kernel [24, 15]. However, these approaches do not consider the challenges arising when selecting sets and lists.

Bandits for subset selection and ranking have been studied before in both ordered and unordered subset selection settings [14]. In particular, the best subset selection under 'bandit-feedback' setting has been studied [11]. In [26, 25], the authors study a similar problem under the setting that the feedback of a set is a submodular function of the concepts covered by the set, which allows to capture diversity, but no similarity among items. [23] considers choosing diverse rankings exploiting item similarity for the problem of ranked document retrieval. Our approach, while similar in principle to some of these works, is the first to systematically exploit sharing of feedback among items, contexts *and* positions.

Top-N recommendations are an important subclass of recommendation problems [21]. Researchers have long expressed the importance of explore–exploit schemes in dynamic top-N recommendation problems [16] and also found deficiencies in using RMSE optimisation techniques for online recommendations [7]. We develop efficient techniques for managing the explore-exploit tradeoff and use appropriate regret measures to show a marked improvement over RMSE based schemes.

3. PROBLEM STATEMENT

We have a set of items $\mathcal{S} = \{s_1, s_2, \ldots, s_n\}$ that we consider for recommendation (e.g., books, articles etc.). We model the recommendation task as a sequential decision problem over T rounds, where, in each round t, we are given a subset of items $\mathcal{S}_t \subseteq \mathcal{S}$ available for recommendation. To aid in the recommendation task, we are given a context $\mathbf{z} \in \mathcal{Z}$, which, e.g., models the key (anchor) item that the user is currently considering, or possibly also containing features describing the user. While such context could be presented as a feature vector, our algorithm does not require such vectorial representation. Our task is to select an ordered list $\mathcal{L}_t = [\mathbf{s}_t^{[1]}, \ldots, \mathbf{s}_t^{[b]}]$ of b items out of $\mathcal{S}_t$ that is recommended to the user. In response, we receive a stochastic vector of rewards, $\mathbf{y} = [y_t^{[1]}, \ldots, y_t^{[b]}]$, where $\mathbb{E}[y_t^{[i]}] = f(\mathbf{s}_t^{[i]}, \mathbf{z}_t, i)$. Hereby, we assume that there is some underlying *unknown* reward function $f : \mathcal{S} \times \mathcal{Z} \times \mathcal{P} \to \mathbb{R}$, such that the expected reward of recommending item $\mathbf{s}_t^{[i]}$ in context $\mathbf{z}_t$ at position $i \in \mathcal{P} = \{1, \ldots, b\}$ is given by $f(\mathbf{s}_t^{[i]}, \mathbf{z}_t, i)$. For concreteness, f may model the click-through rate (CTR), and the rewards $y_t^{[i]} \in [0, 1]$ model whether the user clicks on the item in position i. The total reward in round t is thus

$$y_t = \sum_{i=1}^{b} y_t^{[i]}, \tag{1}$$

and our goal is to maximize the expected cumulative reward $\mathbb{E}[\sum_t y_t]$. Note that, in this model, we assume that the items in the list do not influence the rewards (clicks) received by other items, i.e., we do not model side effects of other items in the list. In the experiments, we do study the effect of relaxing this assumption. We further assume that the expected reward

$$f(\mathbf{s}_t^{[i]}, \mathbf{z}_t, i) = r(\mathbf{s}_t^{[i]}, \mathbf{z}_t)p(i) \tag{2}$$

factorizes into a *relevance* term $r(\mathbf{s}_t^{[i]}, \mathbf{z}_t)$ (relevance measures the relatedness/interestingness of the item to the context which could be a query, user features or key item) and a position-dependent effect $p(i) \in [0, 1]$. Without loss of generality, we assume that $p(1) = 1$, and for all $i \leq j$, $p(i) \geq p(j) > 0$, i.e., showing an item in a later position in the list can only decrease the expected reward.

Under these assumptions, to maximize the reward (clicks), we need to position the items in decreasing order of their true relevance r. For a fixed position i and context $\mathbf{z}_t$, the expected number of clicks received by an item $\mathbf{s}_t^{[i]}$ will be proportional to its relevance to the context, i.e., $r(\mathbf{s}_t^{[i]}, \mathbf{z}_t)$.

The position dependence p can often be estimated effectively [6]. However, the true relevance r is a priori unknown, and must be estimated through experimentation. We face an exploration–exploitation dilemma, where we have to choose between exploiting the information we have about the best ordering, and exploring alternate orderings, which may or may not lead to higher rewards.

Instead of maximizing rewards, in the following we equivalently wish to minimize the *regret*. Hereby, the instantaneous regret r_t in round t is given by $r_t = \sum_{i=1}^{b}[f(\mathbf{s}_t^{[i]*}, \mathbf{z}_t, i) - f(\mathbf{s}_t^{[i]}, \mathbf{z}_t, i)]$, where $\mathcal{L}_t^* = [\mathbf{s}_t^{[1]*}, \ldots, \mathbf{s}_t^{[b]*}]$ is an optimal (in expectation) ordered list for context $\mathbf{z}_t$ observed at round t. Our goal is to minimize the cumulative regret, $R_T = \sum_{t=1}^{T} r_t$. In particular, we desire an algorithm such that the average regret vanishes, i.e., $R_T/T \to 0$ as $T \to \infty$. Note that this is quite a stringent performance requirement: Vanishing regret requires that the algorithm learns the optimal (in expectation) mapping from context to recommendations.

4. CGPRANK APPROACH AND ANALYSIS

Given the problem setup, we address the resulting challenges in this section. In Section 4.1, we show how we can share item feedback across positions. In Section 4.2, we discuss the use of statistical models for principled generalization of feedback to items/contexts that are not yet explored. Finally, the resulting exploration–exploitation dilemma is addressed in Section 4.3 leading up to the specification of the CGPRANK algorithm. Before we describe the algorithm in Section 4.4 and provide theoretical guarantees in Section 4.5, we first highlight the key technical challenges:

1. There is a combinatorial number of possible ordered lists. When n is large, these exponentially many choices are intractable even for small b. In Section 4.1, we show how we can share item feedback across positions in order to reduce this complexity.
2. In many applications, click feedback is sparse, potentially severely delaying convergence. In Section 4.2, we discuss the use of statistical models for generalizing the feedback to items that are not yet explored in a principled way.
3. Once we have settled on a statistical model for learning about reward, we face the exploration–exploitation dilemma of trading experimentation (for the purpose of parameter estimation) and exploitation (using the model's predictions to maximize reward). This dilemma is addressed in Section 4.3.

4.1 Sharing feedback across positions

Given a context (e.g., key-item), selecting an optimal ranked list of b recommendations is challenging due to the combinatorial number of choices. In general, we may need to estimate the reward associated with each of the exponentially many rankings. However, under our assumptions (1) and (2) that the reward of a list decomposes additively, and that the reward factors into a position-dependent effect independent of the item and a "relevance" effect that is position independent, the problem becomes statistically and computationally more tractable. If we know the position effects $p(i)$, $\forall i \in \{1, ..., b\}$, we can normalize the feedback received by an item across all positions that it has been shown at so far. That is, given context $\mathbf{z}_t$, if we observe $y_t^{[i]}$ for some item $\mathbf{s}$ shown in position i, $y_t^{[i]}/p(i)$ provides an unbiased estimate of $r(\mathbf{s}, \mathbf{z}_t)$. Consequently, an unbiased estimate for the reward obtained when showing $\mathbf{s}$ in position j instead is given by $y_t^{[i]}p(j)/p(i)$. This insight thus allows us to share feedback across positions.

4.2 Sharing across items/contexts via kernels

In order to generalize feedback across items/contexts, we need to incorporate prior information about their respective similarities. We assume that this prior information is presented in terms of an arbitrary positive definite *kernel function* $\kappa : (\mathcal{S} \times \mathcal{Z})^2 \to \mathbb{R}$. Hereby, for two item-context pairs $(\mathbf{s}, \mathbf{z})$ and $(\mathbf{s}', \mathbf{z}')$, the kernel $\kappa((\mathbf{s}, \mathbf{z}), (\mathbf{s}', \mathbf{z}'))$ represents our assumptions about how similar we expect the rewards of presenting item $\mathbf{s}$ in context $\mathbf{z}$, as opposed to presenting item $\mathbf{s}'$ in $\mathbf{z}'$ are. A multitude of kernel functions are available for accurately capturing similarity among various types of data [22]. We detail our specific choice in Section 6. What are the consequences of choosing any particular kernel? We effectively assume the reward function r can be represented as a linear combination

$$r(\mathbf{s}, \mathbf{z}) = \sum_j \alpha_j \kappa((\mathbf{s}, \mathbf{z}), (\mathbf{s}_j, \mathbf{z}_j)),$$

i.e., as a basis function expansion around a set of context–item pairs $((\mathbf{s}_j, \mathbf{z}_j))_j$. Such functions span the *Reproducing Kernel Hilbert Space* (RKHS) associated with kernel k, and the norm of r in that space,

$$||r||_\kappa = \sum_{i,j} \alpha_i \alpha_j \kappa((\mathbf{s}_i, \mathbf{z}_i), (\mathbf{s}_j, \mathbf{z}_j)),$$

measures the "complexity" (regularity) of function r. The performance of our algorithm, as analyzed in Theorem 1, will depend on this norm. Intuitively, if the kernel matches the regularity present in real data well, the norm will be small. Capturing similarity via kernels has important consequences: In particular, it allows interpreting the relevance function r as a sample from a *Gaussian Process (GP)* prior [20], with covariance (or kernel) function κ. Consequently, one interprets the relevance as a collection of normally distributed random variables, one for each item—context pair. They are jointly distributed in a dependent manner, such that their covariances are given by the kernel:

$$\mathrm{Cov}(r(\mathbf{s}, \mathbf{z}), r(\mathbf{s}_j, \mathbf{z}_j)) = \kappa((\mathbf{s}, \mathbf{z}), (\mathbf{s}_j, \mathbf{z}_j)).$$

This joint distribution then allows us to make predictions about unobserved item–context pairs via inference in the GP model. In particular, suppose we have already observed feedback for t recommendations, i.e., obtained data $\mathcal{D} = \{(\mathbf{s}_1, \mathbf{z}_1, y_1), \ldots, (\mathbf{s}_t, \mathbf{z}_t, y_t)\}$. Then, for a new item–context pair $(\mathbf{s}, \mathbf{z})$, its predictive distribution for $r(\mathbf{s}, \mathbf{z})$ is Gaussian, with mean and variance[2] given by

$$\mu_t(\mathbf{s}, \mathbf{z}) = \mathbf{k}_t(\mathbf{s}, \mathbf{z})^T (\mathbf{K}_t + \mathbb{I})^{-1} \bar{\mathbf{y}}_t, \tag{3}$$

$$\sigma_t^2(\mathbf{s}, \mathbf{z}) = \kappa((\mathbf{s}, \mathbf{z}), (\mathbf{s}, \mathbf{z})) - \mathbf{k}_t(\mathbf{s}, \mathbf{z})^T (\mathbf{K}_t + \mathbb{I})^{-1} \mathbf{k}_t(\mathbf{s}, \mathbf{z}), \tag{4}$$

where $\mathbf{k}_t(\mathbf{s}, \mathbf{z}) = [\kappa((\mathbf{s}_1, \mathbf{z}_1), (\mathbf{s}, \mathbf{z})), \ldots, \kappa((\mathbf{s}_t, \mathbf{z}_t), (\mathbf{s}, \mathbf{z}))]^T$ and $\mathbf{K}_t$ is the positive semi-definite kernel matrix such that $\mathbf{K}_{t,i,j} = [\kappa((\mathbf{s}_i, \mathbf{z}_i), (\mathbf{s}_j, \mathbf{z}_j))]$.

Choice of Kernels. Often, kernels over item–context pairs are naturally expressed as tensor products, where

$$\kappa((\mathbf{s}, \mathbf{z}), (\mathbf{s}', \mathbf{z}')) = \kappa_\mathcal{S}(\mathbf{s}, \mathbf{s}')) \cdot \kappa_\mathcal{Z}(\mathbf{z}, \mathbf{z}').$$

Hereby, $\kappa_\mathcal{S} : \mathcal{S}^2 \to \mathbb{R}$ is a kernel (similarity) among items, and $\kappa_\mathcal{Z} : \mathcal{Z}^2 \to \mathbb{R}$ is a kernel (similarity) among contexts. This choice of kernel expresses our prior assumption of how smoothly the CTR changes over the item-context space.

The choice of kernel $\kappa_\mathcal{S}$ depends on the particular recommendation problem. Often, similarity between items is given by a usually symmetric similarity function *sim* : $\mathcal{S}^2 \to R$. A valid kernel function however must additionally be positive definite (i.e., all resulting covariance matrices must be positive definite). Among various available candidates, we use diffusion kernels, a family of kernels first introduced in [13]. The first step is to consider the items $\mathcal{S}$ as nodes in a weighted, undirected graph G, so that the weight $w(i, j)$ of each edge (i, j) is given by the similarity function $\mathrm{sim}(i, j)$. The diffusion kernel is then given as matrix-exponential $\mathbf{K}_\mathcal{S} = \exp(\alpha \mathbf{L})$ of the graph Laplacian $\mathbf{L}$ of G. In the contextual setting, if the context is given as a key item, the same diffusion kernel can be used both for items and contexts. If the context is given in terms of user features, $\kappa_\mathcal{Z}$ can be chosen, e.g., as linear kernel $\kappa_\mathcal{Z}(\mathbf{z}, \mathbf{z}') = \mathbf{z}^T \mathbf{z}'$, or Gaussian kernel $\kappa_\mathcal{Z}(\mathbf{z}, \mathbf{z}') = \exp(||\mathbf{z} - \mathbf{z}'||_2^2/h^2)$. If no similarity information is known between contexts, the diagonal kernel $\kappa_\mathcal{Z}(\mathbf{z}, \mathbf{z}') = \mathbf{1}_{[\mathbf{z}=\mathbf{z}']}$ can be used. When features are explicitly available, we can use linear kernels, other kernels defined over Euclidean spaces or combinations thereof. In a special case of CGPRANK, we can recover the exact algorithms presented presented in [4] and [18] by choosing appropriate linear kernels. We employ CGPRANK with both diffusion and linear kernels and demonstrate their performance. However, in several real world applications, features are not easily available either for the contexts or the items and the nature of CGPRANK allows us to use any kind of kernel that can be computed from the similarity information that is available.

4.3 Explore-Exploit in List Selection

How should we use the predictive model (Equations (3) and (4)) to make recommendations? One approach could be to greedily maximize the expected reward according to our current model (i.e., rank items in order of their predictive mean (3)). However, this approach ignores the predictive uncertainty (4). If our goal were to conduct experiments to most effectively reduce uncertainty about the model, we may instead consider to pick items according to the predictive variance (4). Such an approach however would incur much regret, since it would equally explore high- and low value items. Therefore, in each step, we must trade off experimentation (showing items we have not explored yet) and exploitation (showing items with high expected reward). One way to achieve this is linearly trade off the relative importance of the predictive mean and the predictive variance to score each candidate item, i.e., select the item $\mathbf{s}$ that maximizes, for the current context $\mathbf{z}_t$ the surrogate objective $UCB_{\mathbf{s},\mathbf{z}_t}$, where

$$UCB_{\mathbf{s},\mathbf{z}_t} = \mu_{t-1}(\mathbf{s}, \mathbf{z}_t) + \beta_{t,\mathbf{s}}^{1/2} \sigma_{t-1}(\mathbf{s}, \mathbf{z}_t). \tag{5}$$

[2] using noise variance 1, according to our assumptions

For Gaussian predictive distributions, this criterion captures an upper confidence bound (UCB), i.e., an upper bound on the relevance function that holds with a certain probability that can be controlled via the tradeoff factor $\beta_{t,\mathbf{s}}$. I.e., the respective weighting of the mean and variance is handled by an item and time dependent variable, $\beta_{t,\mathbf{s}}$. We show how to pick $\beta_{t,\mathbf{s}}$ in Section 4.4 such that, with high probability, the UCB provides a valid upper bound on the true mean. At the same time, the choice is small enough so that the instantaneous regret provably decreases quickly over iterations.

In order to pick multiple items in each round, a first attempt would be to score every item $\mathbf{s}$ according to the selection rule (5), and select the b highest scoring items. However, given the regularity imposed by the kernel function, for a fixed context $\mathbf{z}$, the highest scoring items are likely very similar. Thus, the resulting list will explore sets of highly related items together, in a possibly redundant manner.

Instead, it may be desirable to encourage diversity when selecting lists to explore. One natural, and computationally efficient way is to *anticipate the reduction in uncertainty* achieved by the items already selected. Looking at the predictive mean and variance μ_t and σ_t in Equations (3) and (4), it can be observed that, while μ_t depends on the actual feedback $\bar{\mathbf{y}}_t$ observed so far, the predictive variance σ_t^2 does *not* depend on previous feedback. We can utilize this insight in the following way. Suppose, in round t, we receive context $\mathbf{z}_t$, and wish to recommend a list $\mathcal{L}_t = [\mathbf{s}_t^{[1]}, \ldots, \mathbf{s}_t^{[b]}]$. We select the first item $\mathbf{s}_t^{[1]}$ according to (5). Then, we update the predictive variance (4) *as if we had already observed* the feedback for the first item. The predictive mean is not updated (or equivalently, it is updated with its own prediction). Note that this will have the effect that the predictive variance – and hence the score (5) – for similar items is decreased. We now select the second item $\mathbf{s}_t^{[2]}$ according to the updated score, and proceed in this manner until the full list of b items has been selected.

After the ranked list has been selected, feedback $\mathbf{y}_t = [y_t^{[1]}, \ldots, y_t^{[b]}]$ is observed. According to our factorization assumption (2), each observation $y_t^{[i]}$ in position i provides a noisy observation of the underlying relevance score $\mathbb{E}[y_t^{[i]}] = p(i) \cdot r(\mathbf{s}_t^{[i]}, \mathbf{z}_t)$. Hence, we feed back $y_t^{[i]}/p(i)$ as unbiased estimate of $r(\mathbf{s}_t^{[i]}, \mathbf{z}_t)$.

4.4 Computing the Tradeoff Parameter

We now describe how to compute a value for $\beta_{t,\mathbf{s}}$ that allows us to prove rigorous bounds on the regret of CGPRANK. Note that in practice a more aggressive choice than this conservative prescription can lead to faster convergence. Our algorithm extends and generalizes the work of [24, 15, 8]. In these, the tradeoff parameter β_t ensures that, in each iteration, the true relevance function is contained within the constructed confidence bands ($\mu_t(\mathbf{s}) \pm \beta_t\sigma_t(\mathbf{s})$) with high probability. Similarly, for our problem, we compute $\beta_{t,\mathbf{s}}$ as

$$\beta_{t,\mathbf{s}} = C_b'\Big(2M^2 + 300\ln^3\Big(\frac{tb}{\delta}\Big)\Big)\Big(C_t + \frac{1}{2}\log(1+\sigma^{-2}\sigma_{t-1}^2(\mathbf{s},\mathbf{z}_t))\Big) \tag{6}$$

$$\text{where } C_b' = \frac{1}{p(b)^2} \max_{L \subseteq S \times \{\mathbf{z}_t\}; |L|=b} \frac{1}{2} \mid \mathbb{I} + \sigma^{-2}\mathbf{K}_{t-1}(L, L) \mid$$

$$C_t = \frac{1}{2}\sum_{\tau=1}^{t-1}\sum_{i=1}^{b} \log(1 + \sigma^{-2}\sigma_{\tau-1,i}^2(\mathbf{s}_\tau^{[i]}, \mathbf{z}_\tau)).$$

Hereby M is a bound on the RKHS norm of the reward function r, and $\sigma_{\tau-1,i-1}^2(\mathbf{s}_\tau^{[i]}, \mathbf{z}_\tau)$ is the predictive variance after having selected items 1 to $i-1$ in iteration τ. Note that C_t can be computed efficiently incrementally over the course of the algorithm. C_b' depends on the maximum determinant of any (posterior) kernel matrix $\mathbf{K}_{t-1}(L, L)$ that can be constructed using at most b items paired with the current context. While computing this quantity exactly requires solving a combinatorial optimization problem, it can be approximated efficiently and accurately during each iteration by running a simple greedy algorithm (uncertainty sampling) – see the longer version of the paper for details. For several commonly used kernel functions (linear, Gaussian and combinations thereof), $\beta_{t,\mathbf{s}}$ can be tightly bounded by the simple expression $\beta_t = C\log^{d'} t$ with suitable constants C, d'. It is this form that we use in the experiments.

Algorithm 1 presents pseudo-code for our CGPRANK algorithm. The procedure `GP-Inference(κ, D)` takes a kernel function κ and data set D, and returns the predictive mean and variance functions according to (3) and (4).

4.5 Regret Analysis of CGPRANK

Our analysis builds on and extends results of [15] for contextual GP bandit optimization (selecting individual items) and [8] for non-contextual GP bandit optimization with delayed feedback. We state our main result in the form of the following theorem and for reasons of space, reserve the details of the proof to a longer version of this paper.

THEOREM 1. *Let $\delta \in (0,1)$, $M > 0$, and κ be a kernel function, such that $||r||_\kappa \le M$. In each round, choosing $\beta_{t,\mathbf{s}}$ as specified in Equation 6 and running* CGPRANK *for T rounds, it holds that*

$$Pr\{R_T \le \frac{\sqrt{Tb\gamma_{Tb}(C_1 + C_2\gamma_{Tb}\ln^3(Tb/\delta))}}{p(b)} \forall T \ge 1\} \ge 1-\delta$$

where $C_1 = \frac{16\exp(2\gamma_b)M^2}{\log(1+\sigma^{-2})}$, $C_2 = 300$ *and*

$$\gamma_n = \max_{\mathcal{D} \subseteq \mathcal{S}\times\mathcal{Z}, |\mathcal{D}| \le n} \log|\mathbb{I} + \sigma^{-2}\mathbf{K}(\mathcal{D},\mathcal{D})|$$

The regret bound in Theorem 1 depends on the quantity γ_n, which quantifies the effective degrees of freedom of the kernel matrix $\mathbf{K}(\mathcal{D},\mathcal{D})$ that can be constructed from n context-item pairs. This quantity was analyzed in prior work [24], showing that for many common kernels (such as linear and Gaussian), γ_n only grows polylogarithmically in n. How can Theorem 1 be interpreted? It is instructive to consider the average regret per list slot, R_T/Tb. We can infer that, as long as γ_n grows only polylogarithmically in n (the common case),

$$\frac{R_T}{Tb} = O\Big(\frac{p(1)}{p(b)}\sqrt{\frac{\gamma_{Tb}M^2\exp(2\gamma_b)}{Tb}}\Big) = O^*\Big(\frac{M}{p(b)}\sqrt{\frac{\exp(2\gamma_b)}{Tb}}\Big),$$

where the O^* notation hides logarithmic factors in T and b. Thus, for fixed list size b, the average regret per slot decays to 0 at an essential rate of $O^*(\frac{1}{\sqrt{T}})$. It grows linearly with the complexity M of the reward function r, and inversely proportional to the decay of the position effect $p(b)$.

How does the regret scale with list size? Since $\exp(\gamma_b) = \Omega(b)$, as the list size b increases, straightforward application of the algorithm will incur average regret per slot that increases with b. However, in the non-contextual case (or the case of a finite set of contexts), it is possible to slightly modify the algorithm, such that, as long as $b = O(\log T)$, it can be ensured that γ_b remains bounded *irrespective* of b, at the cost of additional regret bounded by $O(\text{poly}\log(T))$. Thus, in this setting, one can achieve an average regret per slot of

$$\frac{R_T}{Tb} = O^*\Big(\frac{M}{p(b)}\sqrt{\frac{1}{Tb}}\Big). \tag{7}$$

Algorithm 1 The CGPRANK algorithm

Input: Kernel κ, selection batch size, b
Initialize data set of observations $D = \{\}$.
for $t = 1, 2, \ldots, T$ **do**
  Observe context $\mathbf{z}_t \in \mathcal{Z}$
  Receive set of available items $\mathcal{S}_t$
  Set $\hat{D} \leftarrow D$
  for $i = 1, 2, \ldots, b$ **do**
    $[\mu(\cdot), \sigma^2(\cdot)] \leftarrow$ GP-Inference$(\kappa, \hat{D})$
    $\mathbf{s}_t^{[i]} \leftarrow \text{argmax}_{\mathbf{s} \in \mathcal{S}_t} \mu(\mathbf{s}, \mathbf{z}_t) + \beta_{t,\mathbf{s}}^{1/2} \sigma(\mathbf{s}, \mathbf{z}_t)]$
    $\hat{D} \leftarrow \hat{D} \cup \{(\mathbf{s}_t^{[i]}, \mathbf{z}_t, \mu(\mathbf{s}_t^{[i]}, \mathbf{z}_t))\}$
  end for
  Recommend list $\mathcal{L}_t = [\mathbf{s}_t^{[1]}, \ldots, \mathbf{s}_t^{[b]}]$
  Observe feedback $\mathbf{y}_t = [y_t^{[1]}, \ldots, y_t^{[b]}]$
  $D \leftarrow D \cup \{(\mathbf{s}_t^{[1]}, \mathbf{z}_t, y_t^{[1]}/p(1)), \ldots, (\mathbf{s}_t^{[b]}, \mathbf{z}_t, y_t^{[b]}/p(b))\}$
end for

This result suggests that, perhaps surprisingly, as long as $p(b) \geq 1/\sqrt{b}$, increasing the list size can lead to *faster* convergence. This finding is further supported by our experimental results in Section 7.

5. SCALING CGPRANK TO WEB SCALE RECOMMENDATION TASKS

Naively implementing Algorithm 1 can be prohibitively slow for large data sets. For general kernels, the data set size $\mathcal{D}$ grows with the number of observations Tb, and performing exact Bayesian inference according to Equations (3) and (4) requires solving linear systems in Tb variables.

Scaling GP Inference. Fortunately, much work has been done scaling GP inference to massive data sets [20], also in online/streaming settings [10]. Since such inference is the essential subroutine in CGPRANK, it can immediately benefit from these techniques. Furthermore, in many practical applications (such as the recommendation tasks considered in our experiments), the kernel κ is of bounded rank d, in which case inference only requires solving a linear system in d dimensions. Often, approximate solution is acceptable for practical performance.

Speeding up selection. In order to speed up the selection rule (5), another computational trick can dramatically accelerate performance. Note that, in order to evaluate (5) naively, the mean $\mu_{t-1}(\mathbf{s}, \mathbf{z}_t)$ and variance $\sigma_{t-1}^2(\mathbf{s}, \mathbf{z}_t)$ has to be computed for each choice of $\mathbf{s} \in \mathcal{S}_t$. Inspecting Equations (3) and (4), it can be seen that computing (3) requires solving only one linear system, while computing (4) requires solving $|\mathcal{S}_t|$ linear systems. By exploiting the fact that, in GPs, predictive variance must monotonically decrease, i.e., $\sigma_t^2(\mathbf{s}, \mathbf{z}) \geq \sigma_{t+1}^2(\mathbf{s}, \mathbf{z})$, previous estimates can be used as upper bounds. This insight allows to use priority queues to dramatically reduce the number of linear systems that need to be solved. Similar ideas have been exploited in [8].

Delaying feedback. Instead of continuously performing updates, CGPRANK can be accelerated by reusing the same recommendation multiple times, accumulating feedback and performing delayed updates. However, delaying feedback for long periods of time can incur higher regret in the intermediate period where a fixed suboptimal ordering is chosen. Hence, careful choice of the frequency depending on the problem domain and taking into consideration speed of accumulation of feedback is an important aspect of scaling up CGPRANK.

For instance, exploiting some of these techniques, in our experiments with the Yahoo! dataset and using linear kernels, we were able to achieve an average selection time of 0.4 millisecond per slot including updating the model based on non-delayed feedback (timed on unoptimized C++ code compiled using gnu compiler and running on a single core of a Quad Core Intel Xeon E3, 3.5GHZ machine with 32GB RAM).

6. EXPERIMENTS

We extensively evaluate CGPRANK on two real-world recommendation tasks. The following questions guide our experimental study:

1. Can we exploit similarity to achieve accelerated convergence?
2. Can one parallelize exploration across lists to achieve faster convergence?
3. Can improved performance be achieved by incorporating context?

Benchmarks. In our experiments, we use the following approaches and compare the performance:

- CGPRANK-Lin, as described in Section 4. This builds on the LINUCB-HYBRID algorithm for single-item selection discussed in [17], which can be seen as a special case of CGPRANK.
- CGPRANK-G, is the version of CGPRANK with graph kernels on the items and clustering of contexts to model similarity. and can be used when we do not have access to user or item features. We use this version of CGPRANK for the experiments on Google books data.
- CGPRANK-b-Lin, which simply selects the top b items according to score (5)
- UCB1 of [3]. For list selection, we pick the top b items according to the UCB score. We also use a clustered version where we maintain an independent instance of the algorithm per cluster of contexts.
- Hierarchical versions of both UCB1 and CGPRANK (RANK-UCB and RANK-LINUCB), based on [26, 25].
- Learning to Rank Approaches: These are non-adaptive baselines that use a fraction of the data to train the model and then provide a ranking for every user request. In particular, we compare against two best performing algorithms from the RankLib module of the Lemur Toolkit software [3] (Coordinate Ascent (LTR-CA) [19] and Rank Boost (LTR-RB) [9])
- *Random* selection of lists.
- *Hindsight-Fixed* selection: Picking lists that are optimized in hindsight. This is an (unrealistic) upper bound benchmark.

6.1 Yahoo! news article recommendation

Data set. We first evaluate our algorithm on clickstream data made available by Yahoo! as part of the Yahoo! Webscope program [1]. Specifically, we use the R6A dataset containing a part of the user view/click log for articles displayed on the Today Module of Yahoo! during ten contiguous days. This data was collected in May 2009 and the displayed article was chosen uniformly at random from the list of available articles. This makes this dataset ideal for unbiased, offline evaluation of exploration–exploitation approaches. One can find detailed information on the dataset, the data collection methodology and an explanation of the unbiased offline evaluation in [1, 18, 5]. The dataset consists of more than 45 million lines of log. Each line consists of the following information:

- The timestamp of the user visit.

[3] `http://http://www.lemurproject.org/`

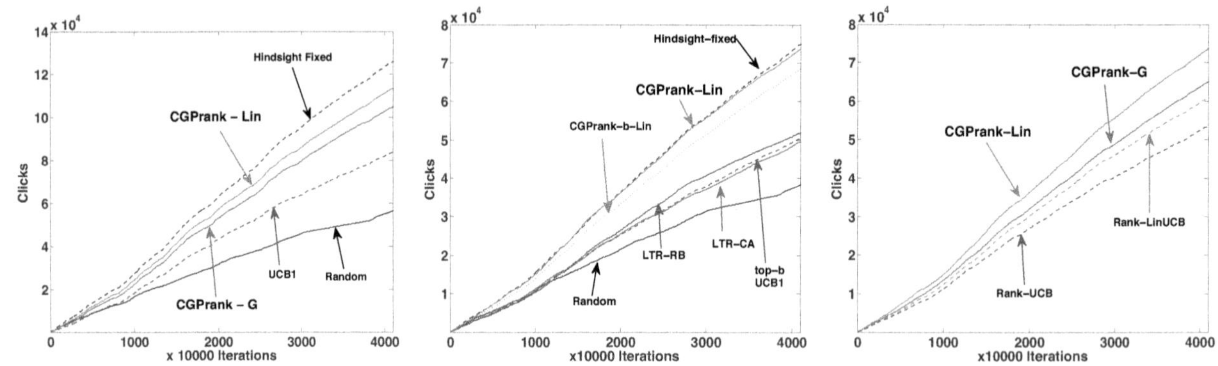

(a) *Article selection on Yahoo! News* (b) *Clicks over time, b=4* (c) *Clicks over time, b=4*

Figure 1: (a): Total clicks received by the algorithms when employed to select a single article per round, using unbiased estimates from log data. (b): Contextual list selection task with $b = 4$. These results are based on click feedback simulated according to the logs. (c): Similar to 1(b). Contextual list selection task with $b = 4$.

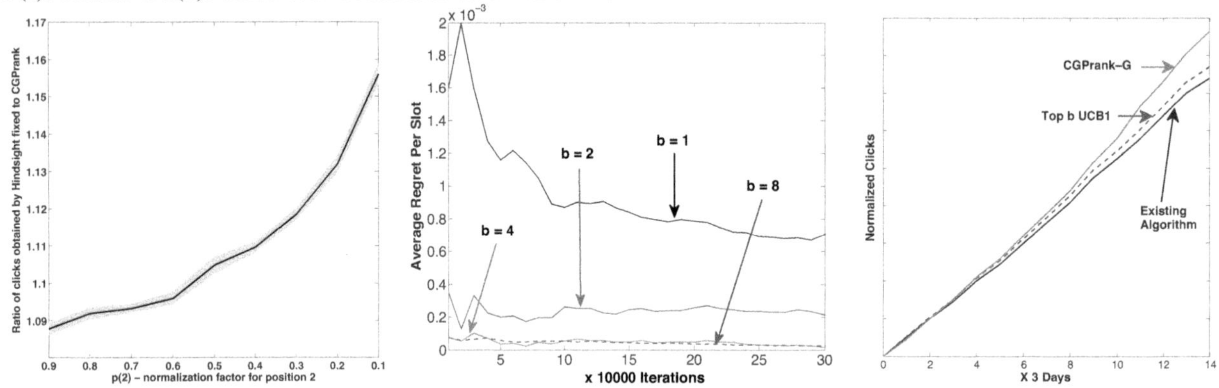

(a) *Position effects for b=2* (b) *Average regret per slot* (c) *Performance on Google logs*

Figure 2: (a) Effect of $p(b)$ on the total regret demonstrated for a $b = 2$ item selection task. The regret increases as $p(2)$ decreases, but not dramatically so. (b) demonstrates the power of parallelizing exploration within lists to achieve accelerated convergence. In terms of the per-slot average regret, it shows how the relative performance compared to *Ideal* – perhaps surprisingly – *increases* with b (also compare Section 4.5). (c): Results of using CGPRANK-G to rerank recommendations on a clickstream log from Google's ebooks store. For confidentiality, we only present normalized numbers. Note that CGPRANK-G offers a significant (∼18%) improvement over the existing non-adaptive method and also outperforms top-b UCB1.

- The article ID of the actual displayed article and whether a click was recorded or not.
- Anonymized user features denoting the context
- Article features for all the articles that were available in the pool for selection

Parameter choice. We initially chose the first 10% of the log entries as initialization data for optimizing parameters of the algorithms, training the learning-to-rank methods, and also to extract user features for clustering (see below). We used the results of this clustering for the contextual versions of CGPRANK-G and UCB1. We ignored this part of the data for all further evaluations the results reported are completely evaluated on the remaining 90% of the log entries.

The *hindsight-fixed* benchmark for these experiments used a weight vector obtained by solving to a linear regression problem for the click prediction task based on the entire log. The result is a single weight vector that maps any item-context pair $(\mathbf{s}, \mathbf{z})$ to an expected click probability.

The nature of the data set makes linear kernels the ideal choice for this task. With this choice, CGPRANK-Lin for single-item selection corresponds to the LINUCB-HYBRID algorithm as provided in [18]. In order to use CGPRANK-G on this dataset, we require a kernel function on the articles. We decided to model the articles as nodes in a graph. The weight on the edge connecting any two articles is simply the euclidean distance between their feature vectors. This choice allows us to compute a diffusion kernel on the articles. Note that computation of an appropriate diffusion kernel requires tuning of the heat parameter α. For our evaluations, we used the article features and their corresponding clickthrough rates to tune the parameter alpha α on the first 10% of the data.

For contextual versions of CGPRANK-G and UCB1, we used a simple technique of clustering the user features given in the logs, and maintaining one instance of all the evaluated algorithms per cluster (corresponding to a diagonal kernel κ_Z). We used k-means clustering on the user contexts extracted from the initialization bucket with $k = 10$, picking the best solution from multiple random restarts. During the actual evaluation, in each round t, the user context given in the log line was mapped to its nearest cluster center, and $\mathbf{z}_t$ was set to this cluster index.

We carry out experiments both in the contextual and non-contextual setting, and vary the size of the lists selected. For list size $b = 1$, we use the actual click feedback given by the log. For $b > 1$, we use simulated click feedback as described above. In order to maintain consistency over the amount of feedback available, we randomly sample portions of the actual log during our simulated feedback since the rejection sampling technique used for $b = 1$ provides feedback once in 20 iterations on an average.

Feedback. While the goal of our work was to choose the optimal ordered list for recommendation, this dataset only contains click stream data for the choice of a single item. Hence, for the purpose of evaluating the list selection procedures, we simulated list feedback. The feedback for an article at a given position depended on the base Clickthrough rate (CTR hereafter) of the article and the bias introduced by the position. Hence, given context $\mathbf{z}$, if an article $\mathbf{s}$ with base CTR $r(\mathbf{s}, \mathbf{z})$ was shown at position j with a bias of $p(j)$, then the stochastic feedback for this placement was simulated as a Bernoulli draw with click probability $r(\mathbf{s}, \mathbf{z})p(j)$. Estimating the positional effects $p(j)$ on CTR is a well studied problem. The base CTR $r(\mathbf{s}, \mathbf{z})$ used in the simulation was computed as the CTR predicted by the *hindsight-fixed* algorithm for the given $(\mathbf{s}, \mathbf{z})$ pair.

6.2 Google e-books recommendation

Data set. We carry out our second set of experiments on click-stream logs from the Google ebooks store. Here, the recommendation task is, given a key book (context) the user is currently exploring, recommend a set of related books that the user may also be interested in. At the time of this work, Google used metadata information about the books and also inputs from other sources to compute the ordering of the related list of books to any given key book. This is a good first approximation of true "relatedness" in the absence of any real click data. But, as we receive feedback in terms of clicks on the recommendations, we can modify the original ordering in order to reflect the tastes of the users and this new ordering represents the true "relatedness" of books in the presence of a large number of clicks. In this dataset, the only context available was the current item being viewed (key item).

We evaluated our algorithm on the clicklog data of Google's book store that was collected over 42 days in the beginning of 2012. Each event in the anonymized click log data consists of two components:

- The volume id, identifying the key book (anchor item);
- The position of the related book on which the user clicked in the related list.

We estimated the unbiased position effect on the CTR using standard techniques.

Parameter choice. For each key book $\mathbf{z}$, we created a graph structure capturing the initial ordering given by the metadata-similarity in terms of the edge weights. Because of computational considerations, we only consider the similarity between the key book $\mathbf{z}_t$ and all of its candidate books $\mathcal{S}_t$, but not the similarities between the candidate books themselves. This results in a star graph with the key book in the center. The weights on the edges are the similarity scores between the books as computed using the metadata of the books. Using the obtained related graph G, the diffusion kernel K can be computed using techniques presented in [13].

Feedback. Based on the data, we simulate feedback for each item when it was displayed in a specific related list. Note that the clicks are being aggregated over users and sessions such that we group feedback on a specific related list. Position independent base CTR models how much the users prefer seeing a related book $\mathbf{s}$ in the recommendation list of key item $\mathbf{z}$. We define this CTR as the number of position-normalized clicks that item $\mathbf{s}$ got while being shown in the related list for key book $\mathbf{z}$, divided by the position-normalized number of times $\mathbf{s}$ was shown as a related book for $\mathbf{z}$.

Based on these estimates, we use offline evaluation techniques to simulate feedback for any new ordering. Since we computed the position independent feedback for each of the items in the original list and we also have the position weight terms $p(j)$, given context $\mathbf{z}$, we simulate feedback for any item $\mathbf{s}$ with base CTR $r(\mathbf{s}, \mathbf{z})$ at position j with position weight $p(j)$ by sampling from a Bernoulli distribution with bias $r(\mathbf{s}, \mathbf{z})p(j)$.

7. RESULTS AND DISCUSSION

Performance comparison. The results on the Yahoo! webscope dataset presented in Figure 1(a) and the results from the Google books evaluation presented in Figure 2(c) show that all versions of CGPRANK offers a consistent performance improvement over approaches that do not take item similarity into account. The ability of CGPRANK to generalize feedback received from few items to a larger set of related items allows it to quickly estimate their relevance. Also, in a dynamic system where new items regularly become available for selection, this feature of CGPRANK allows it to reliably estimate relevance of new items faster. Thus, CGPRANK is well suited to handle the cold start problem in recommendations. For the Yahoo! Webscope dataset, CGPRANK produced an overall final CTR of 0.0496 for the context-free setting and 0.0603 for the contextual setting, which compares favorably with the Ideal policy (0.0559 and 0.064). In the case of the Google books dataset, CG-PRANK outperformed the then-existing algorithm by a margin of 18%. These findings substantiate our first hypothesis, that sharing feedback across similar items helps.

Performance without features. We decided to further test the performance of CGPRANK in settings where no explicit features are available. Instead, similarity information was provided in the form of a kernel function and the similarity between contexts was taken into account by clustering. The evaluation of this is also presented in Figures 1(a) and 1(c). While the overall performance of CGPRANK-G was outperformed by CGPRANK-Lin (CTR of 0.0574 compared to 0.0603 for single item selection), it still manages to perform well and is applicable even when explicit features are not present.

Figures 1(b) and 1(c) present the results of the list selection task with $b = 4$. From the plots, it can be inferred that adaptively learning the order is better than any fixed model learnt from training data. It can also be seen that even using context in an arguably naive manner (in terms of clustering users) provides a substantial improvement over not using context. For the single article selection case with actual click feedback, there was a 14% increase in the CTR while utilizing context information, further substantiating our hypothesis that exploiting context helps.

Relaxing the independence assumption. CGPRANK assumes that items do not influence the feedback of other items within a list. This simplifies the algorithm and its analysis, but is not necessarily true in practice. Hence, we relax this assumption by clustering the articles and model the user as diversity-preferring by ensuring that at most one article from a cluster is clicked on in a round. The recommended list might still contain multiple items from the same cluster. Although the total regret is $\sim 5\%$ more than in the independent case, CGPRANK still outperforms all other baselines and is better than the next best baseline by $\sim$10%.

Parallelizing exploration within lists. In our analysis in Section 4.5, we found that, perhaps surprisingly, increasing the list size can lead to accelerated convergence – at least under certain technical assumptions – as exploration is "parallelized" across list slots. We empirically assess this finding in Figure 2(b) which considers the per-slot average regret. In this experiment, we apply CGPRANK on the log data, using different batch sizes b. As b increases, faster convergence is obtained in relative terms compared to the *hindsight-fixed* predictions.

The experiments with multiple item selection corroborate our theoretical claims that having to select multiple items is beneficial if we consider the per slot regret as long as we gather enough feedback in the lower ranked slots. From the figures, it can be seen that while average regret per slot decreases as we move from single item selection to 2 and then 4 items, there is diminishing returns when we select 8 items. This is due to the low position CTR at positions higher than 4 and also the sparse nature of feedback in the problem. As long as $p(i)$ is high enough to garner enough feedback, the opportunity cost incurred by making mistakes down the order is less than that at the top of the list. This is because of the decreasing expected CTR $p(i)$ as position i increases. During the actual execution, it can be noticed that CGPRANK quickly settles on the top positions while continuing to experiment with different articles down the order.

To assess the quantitative dependence of the regret on the smallest CTR $p(b)$, we conduct an experiment varying $p(2)$ (for $b = 2$), shown in Figure 2(a). We note that the ratio of ideal clicks to clicks garnered by CGPRANK increases as $p(2)$ decreases. While our theoretical results suggests a much stronger dependence on $p(b)$, the effect is not as dramatic in the experiments. This is explained by the fact that our bounds are high probability bounds and in reality, the feedback is more benign.

8. CONCLUSION

We have developed a novel algorithm – CGPRANK– for efficiently reranking lists to reflect user preferences over the items displayed, taking context into account. It exploits assumptions on similarity of items and contexts as given by a positive definite kernel function, and separability assumptions on position dependence. In this way, CGPRANK is able to share sparse feedback across positions, items and contexts. We proved strong theoretical guarantees on its regret, indicating that, perhaps surprisingly, under natural assumptions, parallelization of exploration across lists can help accelerate convergence. Support for computational and statistical parallelism makes it a suitable candidate for adoption for large-scale online recommendation engines. We extensively evaluate CGPRANK on two real world recommendation tasks. On the Google ebooks recommendation task, CGPRANK achieves 18% click lift over the previous state of the art recommender system. We also showed significant improvements over state-of-the-art bandit and learning-to-rank approaches on the Yahoo! Webscope dataset. The experiments with the Yahoo! dataset demonstrates empirically our claim about being able to exploit similarity between items and context information and also shows that parallelizing exploration across the list leads to better performance compared to the single item selection problem. We believe our results present an important step towards addressing challenging, large-scale exploration–exploitation tradeoffs in practical recommender systems.

9. ACKNOWLEDGMENTS

This research was supported in part by SNSF grant 200021_137971, ERC StG 307036 and a Microsoft Research Faculty Fellowship.

References

[1] Yahoo! webscope program. `http://webscope.sandbox.yahoo.com`. Accessed: 20/02/2013.

[2] E. Agichtein, E. Brill, and S. Dumais. Improving web search ranking by incorporating user behavior information. In *ACM SIGIR*, 2006.

[3] P. Auer, N. C. Bianchi, and P. Fischer. Finite-time Analysis of the Multiarmed Bandit Problem. *Machine Learning*, 47(2-3):235–256, May 2002.

[4] W. Chu, L. Li, L. Reyzin, and R. E. Schapire. Contextual bandits with linear payoff functions. In *AISTATS*, 2011.

[5] W. Chu, S.-T. Park, T. Beaupre, N. Motgi, A. Phadke, S. Chakraborty, and J. Zachariah. A case study of behavior-driven conjoint analysis on yahoo!: front page today module. In *ACM SIGKDD*, 2009.

[6] N. Craswell, O. Zoeter, M. Taylor, and B. Ramsey. An experimental comparison of click position-bias models. In *WSDM*, 2008.

[7] P. Cremonesi, Y. Koren, and R. Turrin. Performance of recommender algorithms on top-n recommendation tasks. In *RecSys*, 2010.

[8] T. Desautels, A. Krause, and J. Burdick. Parallelizing exploration-exploitation tradeoffs with gaussian process bandit optimization. In *ICML*, 2012.

[9] Y. Freund, R. Iyer, R. E. Schapire, and Y. Singer. An efficient boosting algorithm for combining preferences. *J. Mach. Learn. Res.*, 4:933–969, Dec. 2003.

[10] R. Gomes and A. Krause. Budgeted nonparametric learning from data streams. In *ICML*, 2010.

[11] S. Kale, L. Reyzin, and R. E. Schapire. Non-stochastic bandit slate problems. In *NIPS*, 2010.

[12] R. Kleinberg, A. Slivkins, and E. Upfal. Multi-armed bandits in metric spaces. In *STOC*, 2008.

[13] R. I. Kondor and J. Lafferty. Diffusion kernels on graphs and other discrete structures. In *ICML*, 2002.

[14] W. M. Koolen, M. K. Warmuth, and J. Kivinen. Hedging structured concepts. In *COLT*, 2010.

[15] A. Krause and C. S. Ong. Contextual gaussian process bandit optimization. In *NIPS*, 2011.

[16] R. Lempel. Recommendation challenges in web media settings. In *RecSys*, 2012.

[17] L. Li, W. Chu, J. Langford, and R. E. Schapire. A contextual-bandit approach to personalized news article recommendation. In *WWW*, 2010.

[18] L. Li, W. Chu, J. Langford, and X. Wang. Unbiased offline evaluation of contextual-bandit-based news article recommendation algorithms. In *WSDM*, 2011.

[19] D. Metzler and W. Bruce Croft. Linear feature-based models for information retrieval. *Inf. Retr.*, 10(3):257–274, June 2007.

[20] C. E. Rasmussen and C. K. I. Williams. *Gaussian Processes for Machine Learning (Adaptive Computation and Machine Learning)*. The MIT Press, 2005.

[21] F. Ricci, L. Rokach, B. Shapira, and P. B. Kantor, editors. *Recommender Systems Handbook*. Springer, 2011.

[22] B. Scholkopf and A. J. Smola. *Learning with Kernels: Support Vector Machines, Regularization, Optimization, and Beyond*. MIT Press, Cambridge, MA, USA, 2001.

[23] A. Slivkins, F. Radlinski, and S. Gollapudi. Learning optimally diverse rankings over large document collections. In *ICML*, 2010.

[24] N. Srinivas, A. Krause, S. Kakade, and M. Seeger. Information-theoretic regret bounds for gaussian process optimization in the bandit setting. *IEEE Transactions on Information Theory*, 58(5):3250–3265, May 2012.

[25] M. Streeter, D. Golovin, and A. Krause. Online learning of assignments. In *NIPS*, 2009.

[26] Y. Yue and C. Guestrin. Linear submodular bandits and their application to diversified retrieval. In *NIPS*, 2011.

A Parameter-free Algorithm for an Optimized Tag Recommendation List Size

Modou Gueye
Université Cheikh Anta Diop
BP. 64432, Fann
Dakar, Sénégal
gmodou@ucad.sn
modou.gueye@enst.fr

Talel Abdessalem
Institut Telecom - Telecom ParisTech
46, rue Barrault 75013
Paris, France
talel.abdessalem@enst.fr

Hubert Naacke
LIP6 - UPMC Sorbonne Universités
4 place Jussieu 75005
Paris, France
hubert.naacke@lip6.fr

ABSTRACT

Tag recommendation is a major aspect of collaborative tagging systems. It aims to recommend suitable tags to a user for tagging an item. One of its main challenges is the effectiveness of its recommendations. Existing works focus on techniques for retrieving the most relevant tags to give beforehand, with a fixed number of tags in each recommended list. In this paper, we try to optimize the number of recommended tags in order to improve the efficiency of the recommendations. We propose a parameter-free algorithm for determining the optimal size of the recommended list. Thus we introduced some relevance measures to find the most relevant sublist from a given list of recommended tags. More precisely, we improve the quality of our recommendations by discarding some unsuitable tags and thus adjusting the list size.

Our solution is an add-on one, which can be implemented on top of many kinds of tag recommenders. The experiments we did on five datasets, using four categories of tag recommenders, demonstrate the efficiency of our technique. For instance, the algorithm we propose outperforms the results of the task 2 of the ECML PKDD Discovery Challenge 2009 [1]. By using the same tag recommender than the winners of the contest, we reach a F1 measure of 0.366 while the latter got 0.356. Thus, our solution yields significant improvements on the lists obtained from the tag recommenders.

Categories and Subject Descriptors

H.3.3 [**Information Search and Retrieval**]: Information Filtering

General Terms

Algorithms, Experimentation

1. http ://www.kde.cs.uni-kassel.de/ws/dc09/

RecSys'14, October 6–10, 2014, Foster City, Silicon Valley, CA, USA.
Copyright 2014 ACM 978-1-4503-2668-1/14/10 ...$15.00.
http://dx.doi.org/10.1145/2645710.2645727.

Keywords

Tag Recommender Systems, Quality of recommendations, Optimization

1. INTRODUCTION

Collaborative tagging is the practice of allowing users to annotate content. Users can organize, and search content with annotations so called tags. Nowadays the growth in popularity of social media sites has made the area of recommender systems for social tagging an active and growing topic of research [6].

Tag recommenders aim to suggest the most suitable tags to a user when tagging an item. They are a salient part of the web 2.0 where applications are user-centered. One of their main challenges is the effectiveness of their recommendations. People generally focus on techniques that enable retrieving the best suitable tags to give beforehand, with a fixed number of tags at each recommendation.

We follow another direction in order to improve tag recommendation accuracy. We aim to dynamically adjust the number of tags to recommend. In other words, consider $L_N = \{t_1, t_2, \ldots, t_N\}$ the list of N tags to be recommended to a user, the goal is to substitute L_N by one of its sublists that is more accurate, and provide a better quality of recommendation.

We consider all the sublists of L_N in increasing size (i.e., the prefixes : L_1, L_2, $\ldots L_{N-1}$ and L_N) so as to keep the tag order as illustrated below [2].

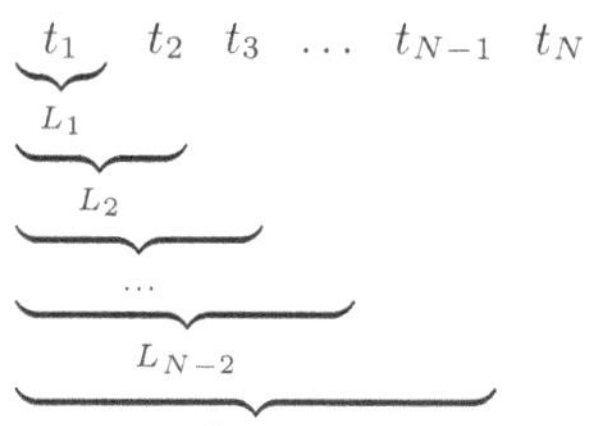

We introduce a relevance measure for the recommended lists $Rel(L_N|u,i)$, which estimates the probability that a user u will use all the recommended tags in L_N for the tagging of an item i. Based on this measure, we compute the best list (the one having the optimal size, *bls*) that will be finally recommended to the user. We define the optimal size as

2. $L_N = L_{N-1} \cup \{t_N\} = L_{N-2} \cup \{t_{N-1}, t_N\} \ldots$

follows :

$$bls = \max\left(s \mid s \in \mathcal{S}\right) \quad (1)$$

with

$$\mathcal{S} = \left\{ s \mid s \leq N \wedge \forall n \leq N,\ Rel(L_n|u,i) \leq Rel(L_s|u,i) \right\}$$

Existing approaches use linear combinations to compute the global average number of tags per post, the one related to a user and/or the one specific to an item [7, 8, 9]. These combinations are then used to infer a fixed list size. Such approaches need some calibrations which are generally difficult to set, and they lack of dynamicity which limits their accuracy.

The algorithm we propose here enables adjusting dynamically the size of the recommended list of tags, and then increases the accuracy of the recommendations. It is a parameter-free algorithm that adjusts the list of recommended tags by discarding those which are estimated irrelevant. Our method looks like an add-on filter on top of a tag recommender. It estimates the sublist which gives the best accuracy. We present in the paper two relevance measures and the algorithm that we use to retrieve the optimal sublist from a given tag recommendation list.

To evaluate the efficiency of our approach we implement it on top of four tag recommenders, from different approaches. One of our candidates is the pairwise interaction tensor factorization model (PITF) of Rendle and Schmidt-Thieme which won the task 2 of the ECML PKDD Discovery Challenge 2009 [9]. It is still considered in the literature as one of the best tag recommenders. We took also the well-known tripartite graph-based algorithm FolkRank [4] and the « Most Popular Tag » recommendation approach [6]. The last candidate is a network-based tag recommender we developed [3], and which computes the list of tags based on the opinions of the users' neighborhood and their tagging posts.

The experiments we did on five datasets demonstrate the efficiency of the optimization technique we propose in this paper.

The remainder of this paper is organized as follows. In Section 2 we present some preliminaries and describe briefly the four tag recommender candidates. Section 3 details the related work and presents our approach for finding the best size of a tag recommendation list to keep. In Section 4, we present our experiments and Section 5 concludes the paper.

2. PRELIMINARIES

A folksonomy is a system of classification that allows its users creating and managing tags to annotate and categorize content. It is related to the event of social tagging systems. A folksonomy $\mathbb{F}$ can be defined as a collection of a set of users U, a set of tags T, a set of items I, and a ternary relation between them $S \subseteq U \times I \times T$ as $\mathbb{F} := (U, I, T, S)$. A tagging triple $(u, i, t) \in S$ means that user u has tagged an item i with the tag t. A user can tag an item with one or more distinctive tags from T. We assume that a user can tag an item with a given tag at most once.

The interest of a tag t for a given user u to annotate an item i is generally estimated by a score $score(t|u,i)$. The purpose of a tag recommender is to compute the top-K highest scoring tags for a post (u, i) which represents its recommendations.

$$Top(u,i,K) = \underset{t \in T}{\overset{K}{argmax}}\ score(t|u,i) \quad (2)$$

For convenience, let us introduce some definitions and properties of a folksonomy :

$$\begin{aligned}
T(u) &\equiv \{t \in T \mid \exists i \in I : (u,i,t) \in S\} \\
T(i) &\equiv \{t \in T \mid \exists u \in U : (u,i,t) \in S\} \\
T(u,i) &\equiv \{t \in T \mid (u,i,t) \in S\} \\
I(u) &\equiv \{i \in I \mid \exists t \in T : (u,i,t) \in S\} \\
I(u,t) &\equiv \{i \in I \mid (u,i,t) \in S\} \\
U(i) &\equiv \{u \in U \mid \exists t \in T : (u,i,t) \in S\} \\
U(i,t) &\equiv \{u \in U \mid (u,i,t) \in S\}
\end{aligned}$$

In the following we describe how our four tag recommender candidates model the scores associated to the tags.

2.1 Factor Models for Tag Recommendation

Factorization models are known to be among the best performing models. They are a very successful class of models for recommender systems where they outperform the other approaches.

We chose the pairwise interaction tensor factorization model (PITF) of Rendle and Schmidt-Thieme in our experimentation due to its efficiency [9]. Indeed, it took the first place of the ECML PKDD Discovery Challenge 2009 for graph-based tag recommendation.

PITF proposes to infer pairwise ranking constraints from the set of tagging triples S. It captures the interactions between users and tags as well as between items and tags. Its model equation is given by :

$$score(t|u,i) = \sum_f \hat{U}_{u,f} \cdot \hat{T}^U_{t,f} + \sum_f \hat{I}_{i,f} \cdot \hat{T}^I_{t,f} \quad (3)$$

Where $\hat{U}$, $\hat{I}$, $\hat{T}^U$ and $\hat{T}^I$ are feature matrices which capture the latent interactions.

The main assumption of PITF is that within a post $T(u,i)$, a tag t can be preferred over another tag t' iff the tagging triple $(u,i,t) \in S$ (i.e., has been observed) and not (u,i,t'). PITF models these preferences in Equation 3 such as the score of a tag which is more preferred than another one is greater.

2.2 FolkRank - A Topic-Specific Ranking

FolkRank is a tripartite graph-based tag recommender designed in the spirit of PageRank [4, 5]. It assumes that a tag becomes important when it is used by important users or to tag important items. It also takes the same principle for users and items. Therefore FolkRank represents a folksonomy $\mathbb{F}$ as a graph where the vertices are mutually reinforcing each other by spreading their weights.

Let $G_{\mathbb{F}} = (V, E)$ be this graph. Its vertices are the users, items and tags (i.e. $V = U \cup I \cup T$) and the edges defined between them such as if a tagging triple $(u,i,t) \in S$ then $\big\{\{u,i\},\{u,t\},\{i,t\}\big\} \subset E$.

Let v_i a vertex of this graph, i.e. $v_i \in V$. We denote by $\mathcal{N}(v_i)$ the set of neighbors of v_i and by $w(v_i, v_j)$ the weight of the edge between the vertices v_i and v_j. The weight of an edge is equal to the number of times its two vertices appear together in the tagging triples in S. From that, the degree of a vertex v_i is defined as follows :

$$w(v_i) = \sum_{v_j \in \mathcal{N}(v_i)} w(v_i, v_j) \quad (4)$$

FolkRank ranks the vertices according to their importances that it computes as follows :

$$PR(v_i) = \lambda \sum_{v_j \in \mathcal{N}(v_i)} \frac{w(v_i, v_j)}{w(v_j)} \cdot PR(v_j) + (1-\lambda) \cdot p(v_i) \quad (5)$$

where $PR(v_i)$ is the PageRank value and $p(v_i)$ the preference value of the vertex v_i. Hence a straightforward idea for tag recommendation is to set a high preference to the considered user and item (item to be tagged by the user), and then compute ranking values using PageRank as in Equation 5. The parameter λ determines the influence of $p(v_i)$. Its value is between 0 and 1.

To recommend some tags for a user u and an item i, Fol kRank uses two random surfer models on the graph, $s^{(0)}$ and $s^{(1)}$, to infer the importance of each vertex of the graph. The first surfer, $s^{(0)}$, set the same preference value to all the vertices ($p(v) = 1, \forall v \in V$) while the second, $s^{(1)}$, set their preference values to 0 except for the user u and the item i for which $p(u) = 1$ and $p(i) = 1$.

After running the two surfers, the difference $s := s^{(1)} - s^{(0)}$ is computed. Then the tags are ranked according to their importance value s, and the first ones are recommended to user u.

2.3 Recommending the Most Popular Tags

The rational of Most Popular Tags' Recommenders (MPTR) is that when a tag t is popular (i.e., frequently used) for an item i and/or by a user u, that tag t may be a relevant recommendation for u aiming to tag i. Hence, MPTR model these popularities in their scoring models. A well-known MPTR model – also known as most popular ρ-mix – consists in adding the tag popularities (i.e. the ones of the user with those of the item) after normalizing and weighting them as follows :

$$score(t|u,i) = \rho \cdot \frac{|U(i,t)|}{|U(i)|} + (1-\rho) \cdot \frac{|I(u,t)|}{|I(u)|} \quad (6)$$

The parameter ρ in Equation 6 allows to tune the relative importance of the item or user-related tag popularity with respect to the second. When $\rho = 1$ we keep only the tags which are most specific to the item. On the other hand, when we set it to 0, we consider only the user's popular tags. By default we fix ρ to 0.5 in our experimentation. Thus, we consider the user tags as important as those associated to the item. The advantage of MPTR is that they are fast to compute, while giving good predictions [6].

2.4 Trust and popularity-based Recommender

One weakness of MPTR (which entirely relies on popularity measures) is that they are not able to decide between tags with close popularities. Furthermore, some particular users can have their own vocabulary (i.e., tags) and the popular tags of the item may not be relevant for them. Thus, having reliable opinions about the tags from some trusted neighbors, in addition to the popularities of tags, may be a great asset to make better recommendations.

FasTag [3] uses such an approach. It models the relevance score of a tag t for a user u and an item i (i.e. $score(t|u,i)$) as a popularity-dependent component, based a user's trust in his neighbors in the network. Let us denote by $score^{MPTR}(t|u,i)$ the scoring model of MPTR in Equation 6, the scoring one of FasTag is defined as

$$score(t|u,i) = score^{MPTR}(t|u,i) \cdot \Big(1 + \eta(t|u,i)\Big) \quad (7)$$

where $\eta(t|u,i)$ represents the opinion of the user's neighbors about tag t. It is a normalized sum of the user's trust values associated to his neighbors who already tagged this item with t. The rationale of this *score* function is to estimate a relative popularity of a tag depending on the trust neighbors of the user : i.e., the more a user trusts a neighbor, the more this neighbor's opinion contributes in the user recommendations. The sum $1 + \eta(t|u,i)$ enables taking into account the isolated users (when $\eta(t|u,i) = 0$).

We chose FasTag as a candidate for network-based tag recommenders, since it is fast and efficient as shown in [3]. Its scoring model is not only based on the trust associated to the direct neighbors of the user, it also considers trust propagation, following a natural interpretation that trust is, at some extent, transitive. See [10, 11] for more details on trust propagation models.

3. ADJUSTED RECOMMENDATION LIST SIZE

In this section, we present two ways to choose the best recommendation list size. The first one is based on existing works employing linear combination techniques, and the second one is our proposal to optimize dynamically the size of the recommended list.

3.1 Linear combination models

To choose the best list size (bls) of tags to recommend, usual approaches use some linear combinations of the global average number of tags per post, the one related to a user and/or the one specific to an item [9, 8, 7]. Therefore, we take as baseline the following general linear combination model

$$bls = \min\left(K, \lfloor \lambda + (\beta_G \cdot \mu_G) + (\beta_u \cdot \mu_u) + (\beta_i \cdot \mu_i) \rfloor\right) \quad (8)$$

where K stands for the maximum number of tags to recommend, i.e. the maximal list size ; μ_G the global average number of tags per post ; μ_u the average number of tags per user and per post, and μ_i the average number of tags per item and per post. The rest stands for parameters which allow us to make a lot of possible combinations. For instance, if we set the parameter β_u to 1 and all the other parameters to zero, we obtain as a list size the average number of tags per user and post. We denote in the following the linear combination method by *LC_bls*.

For our experiments, we apply a grid search in order to find optimal parameters to keep. We test $K \times 1,000$ combinations of these parameters each time a top-K query is asked (i.e., each time we look for a list of K tags maximum). For instance, we make 10,000 combinations for the top-10 query and 5,000 for the top-5 one. We vary the parameter λ from 0 to $K-1$, each time by a step of 1. And using nested loops, we vary each of the other parameters from 0 to 1 by a step of 0.1. Thus, we test enough combinations with different values of parameters. At the end, we keep the combination that gives the best result (in terms of reached F1-measure).

3.2 The blsC algorithm

blsC denotes the algorithm we propose to find the best list size. Let $Rel(t|u,i)$ be the relevance of a tag t, according to a user u, for the tagging of an item i. And $L_N =$

$\{t_1, t_2, \ldots, t_N\}$ is an ordered list of N tags. We define the relevance of the list L_N, for both a user u and an item i, as follows :

$$Rel(L_N|u,i) = \omega(L_N|u,i) \cdot \frac{\sum_{t \in L_N} Rel(t|u,i)}{N} \quad (9)$$

In this formula, $\omega(L_N|u,i)$ stands as a weight for the adjustment of the list relevance. It allows us to promote longer lists than the others. We will give its definition shortly in Subsection 3.2.2. $Rel(t|u,i)$ is the relevance of a tag t for a user u and an item i. Intuitively, it measures the probability that user u will tag the item i with the tag t.

Let Max be a maximal list size and $Rel(L_{Max}|u,i)$ the relevance of this list (L_{Max}). We look for the best list size starting from Max down to 1. At each step, we compute the relevance of the current list and update the best list size as shown in Algorithm 1. In case we obtain the same relevance for two different lists, we choose the longest one.

Algorithm 1: *blsC* : Best list size Computation

```
Input: L_Max      /* Initial recommended tags list*/
Output: bls       /* Suggested number of tags to keep */
bls ← Max                        /* bls : Best list size */
blR ← Rel(L_Max|u,i)             /* blR : Best list relevance */
for N = (Max − 1) to 1 do
    if Rel(L_N|u,i) > blR then
        bls ← N
        blR ← Rel(L_N|u,i)
    end
end
return bls
```

To compute the relevance of a tag, we propose two solutions. In the first one, we distinguish the known tags from the others and assign them different relevance values. In the second solution, we link the relevance values of the tags to some statistics we obtain from the available data (our training sets).

3.2.1 Simple relevance measure

Making a distinction between the known tags (those already used by the user and associated to the item) from the others may be useful to determine the relevance of a recommended list of tags. Our intuition is that the tags already linked to the user u and also to the item i are more relevant to recommend than the others.

Let $P_N = L_N \cap T(u) \cap T(i)$ be the sublist of L_N containing the known tags. We assign a unique high relevance value, Rel_{max}, to the tags in P_N and an unique low one, Rel_{min}, to the other tags. By fixing the weight of each list to one, we can rewrite the Equation 9 as follows :

$$Rel(L_N|u,i) = \frac{\sum\limits_{t_j \in P_N} Rel_{max} + \sum\limits_{t_j \in \{L_N \setminus P_N\}} Rel_{min}}{N} \quad (10)$$

After simplification it becomes :

$$Rel(L_N|u,i) = \frac{\left(|P_N| \cdot Rel_{max} + (N - |P_N|) \cdot Rel_{min}\right)}{N} \quad (11)$$

From Equation 11, one can see that the relevance of a recommendation list depends mainly on the ratio between $|P_N|$ and N. The relevance is an increasing function, having its inputs in the interval $[0, N]$. It reaches its maximum when $|P_N| = N$. Thus, we can simply consider the relevance of a recommendation list as follows :

$$Rel(L_N|u,i) = \frac{|P_N|}{N} \quad (12)$$

With this formula, we can easily adjust the list size in order to obtain the best relevance value. $Rel(L_N|u,i)$ can be seen as a density measure of known tags in the recommended list. Then, the *blsC* is just seeking for the best density.

3.2.2 Refining the relevance measure

Among the weaknesses of the relevance measure given in Equation 12 we can mention the fact that it fails to give a sublist when all the tags in the recommendation list are known (in P_N). We propose a relevance measure which faces the drawbacks of the previous one by taking into account the popularity of the tags for both the user and the item.

$$Rel(t|u,i) = \frac{|U(i,t)|}{|U(i)|} \times \frac{|I(u,t)|}{|I(u)|} \quad (13)$$

Naturally, we expect that the relevance of a tag decreases according to its rank in a recommended list (high relevance for the first tag and low relevances for the last ones). This intuition is confirmed by our experimentations, on all the datasets we used and for all the tag recommenders we tested, as shown in Figure 1. We limit our tests to the top-10 lists of recommended tags.

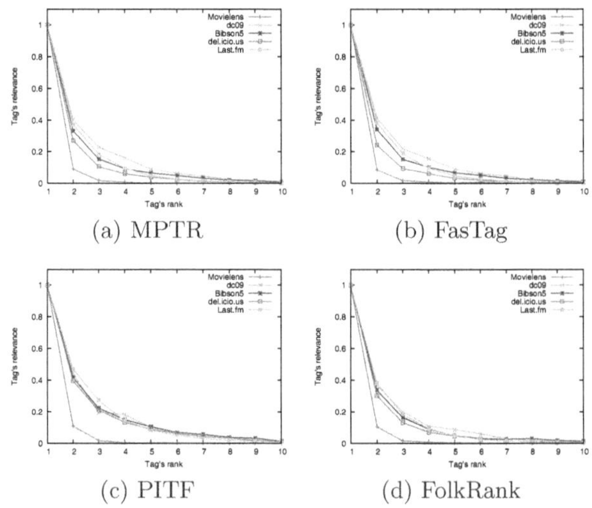

(a) MPTR (b) FasTag (c) PITF (d) FolkRank

Figure 1: Relative relevance of a tag according to its position in a recommended list and the relevance of the first tag

From these observation, we see the need to use weighted means when evaluating the relevance of recommended lists. Indeed, since a recommendation list is ordered, the first tag is generally more relevant than the others (the second one and so on). Thus, using the average of the relevances of the tags contained in a list may still lead to a singleton, i.e. L_1 as the best list.

To take into account this natural decrease of the relevances of tags according to their positions, we define the weight

$\omega(L_N|u,i)$ of a recommendation list L_N as follows :

$$\omega(L_N|u,i) = \frac{N}{\sqrt{\frac{1}{2}(N + Max)}} \quad (14)$$

This weight function estimates the importance of a list size compared to the maximal possible list size. It allows us to penalize short recommendation lists while promoting long lists. Therefore, from Equation 9 we derive a new list relevance measure :

$$Rel(L_N|u,i) = \frac{\sum_{t \in L_N} Rel(t|u,i)}{\sqrt{\frac{1}{2}(N + Max)}} \quad (15)$$

As one can see, we do not compute the mean of the relevance of tags but a relative list relevance according to the greatest possible list size. The comparison of the relevance of all the sublist is done as described in Algorithm 1. We just compute the most relevant list size from Max down to 1 by using this new relevance measure given in Equation 15. We denote this second proposal *blsC_v2*. The latter can overcome the weak points of *blsC*. Indeed, even if all the tags in a recommendation list are in P_N, *blsC_v2* does not rely on their presence but only on their relevance. Thus, it is able to decide when *blsC* fails.

4. EXPERIMENTATION

We demonstrate in this section the effectiveness of our proposals. We led a set of experiments with four tag recommender candidates on five publicly available datasets. In the next two subsections, we shortly describe these datasets and the evaluation measures and methodology we used. Then we present the results we obtained.

4.1 Datasets

We chose five datasets from four online systems : delicious [3], Movielens [4], Last.fm [5], and BibSonomy [6].

We took the ones of delicious, movielens, and last.fm from *HetRec 2011* [2] and the two other ones from Bibsonomy : a post-core at level 5 and a one at level 2 [1, 6]. We call them respectively *Bibson5* and *dc09*.

dc09 is the one of the task 2 of ECML PKDD Discovery Challenge 2009 [7]. This task was especially intended for methods relying on the graph structure of the training data only. The user, item, and tags of each post in the test data are all contained in the training data, a post-core at level 2. Let us remind that a post-core at level p is a subset of a folksonomy with the property that *each user, tag and item occur at least p times* in the tagging triples of S. Table 1 presents some details of these datasets.

4.2 Evaluation Measures and Methodology

To evaluate our solution, we used a variant of the leave-one-out hold-out estimation called LeavePostOut [6]. In all datasets except *dc09*, we picked randomly for each user u, one item i that he had tagged before. Thus, we created a test set and a training one. The task of our recommender was then to predict the tags the user assigned to the item.

3. http://www.delicious.com
4. http://www.grouplens.org
5. http://www.lastfm.com
6. http://www.bibsonomy.org
7. http://www.kde.cs.uni-kassel.de/ws/dc09/

Table 1: Characteristics of the datasets

dataset	$\|U\|$	$\|I\|$	$\|T\|$	$\|T(u,i)\|$
dc09	1,185	22,389	13,276	64,406
Last.fm	1,892	17,632	11,946	71,065
delicious	1,867	69,226	53,388	104,799
Movielens	2,113	10,197	13,222	27,713
Bibson5	116	361	412	2,526

Dataset	% of users with at most #tags per post				
	1	2	3	4	5
Bibson5	5.17	21.55	50.0	69.82	81.89
dc09	6.49	28.27	52.82	73.58	85.23
delicious	2.89	19.80	41.32	61.72	76.17
Last.fm	12.57	46.32	66.50	78.65	86.47
Movielens	**65.37**	**92.57**	**97.63**	**98.95**	**99.76**

Dataset	% of items with at most #tags per post				
	1	2	3	4	5
Bibson5	0.27	9.418	32.40	61.21	80.60
dc09	11.46	25.45	45.47	64.47	78.83
delicious	11.10	27.08	46.61	63.72	76.40
Last.fm	19.77	51.87	79.50	90.03	94.08
Movielens	**41.76**	**81.41**	**92.72**	**96.39**	**97.86**

On each dataset, we ran the choosed tag recommenders. We successively obtained from them a top-*1*, then a top-*2* and so on, up to a top-*10*. Then, we applied our algorithms *LC_bls*, *blsC* and *blsC_v2* on the tag recommendation lists in order to get better sublists. The performance evaluation was based on the the F1-measure.

Let us notice that for all the experiments, we fixed the parameter ρ of MPTR and FasTag to 0.5 (see Equation 6). Similarly, we set the parameter λ of FolkRank to 0.7 (see Equation 5) as in [5]. For PITF we used the software [8] and the parameters given by the winners of the task 2 of the ECML PKDD Discovery Challenge 2009, and we did not rely on assembling factor models as they did in [8]. We only computed one model with 64 factors as the dimensionality and a regularization value of $5 \cdot 10^{-5}$. We ran the learning phase for 2,000 iterations.

4.3 Results

We present in this part the results of our experimentation. We aim to point out that our proposal outstrips the methods based on linear combinations.

4.3.1 *Effectiveness of our proposals*

As we said, we show here the effectiveness of our proposals. We implemented them on top of the four tag recommenders. Figures 2 to 6 show the F1 quality of the original recommendation lists given by each tag recommender and the ones of each optimization method (i.e., *blsC*, *blsC_v2* and *LC_bls*). The x-axis of each of these figures gives the original number of tags to recommend before length optimization.

In almost all these figures, we see that the quality of the adjusted lists is increasing while the one of those with fixed sizes decreases when they exceed a certain size (specific to

8. http://bit.ly/1qL6NeF

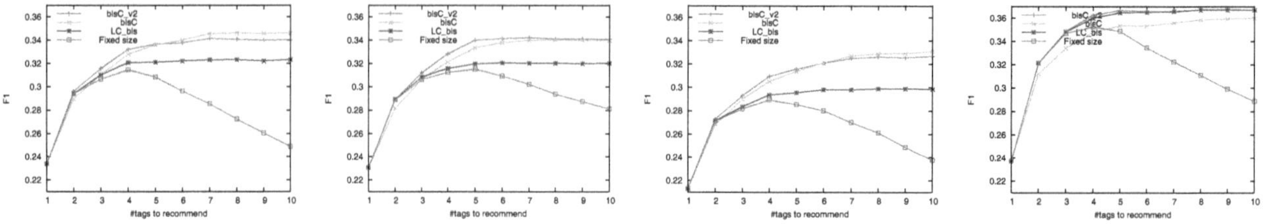

(a) MPTR (b) FasTag (c) FolkRank (d) PITF

Figure 2: Quality increases versus recommendation list sizes on *dc09*

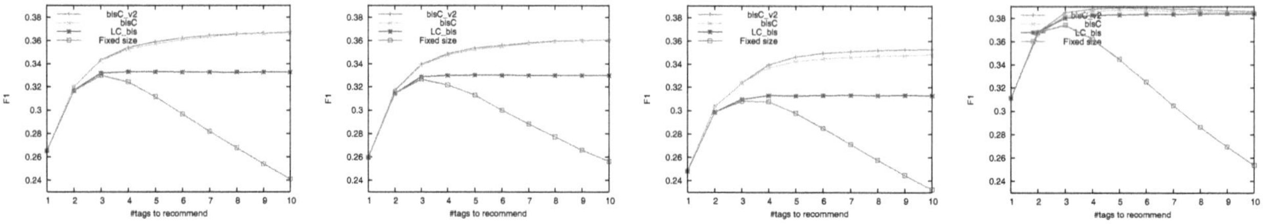

(a) MPTR (b) FasTag (c) FolkRank (d) PITF

Figure 3: Quality increases versus recommendation list sizes on *Last.fm*

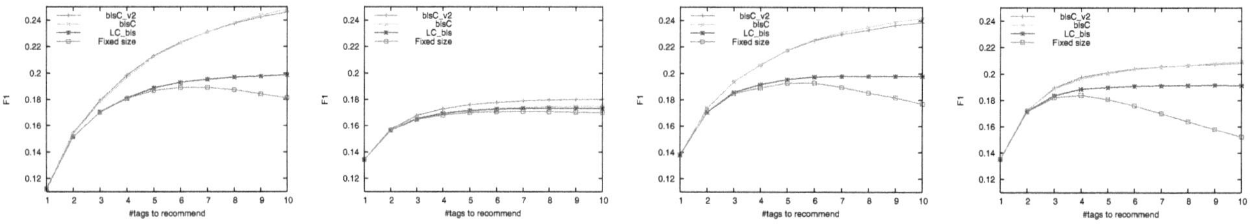

(a) MPTR (b) FasTag (c) FolkRank (d) PITF

Figure 4: Quality increases versus recommendation list sizes on *delicious*

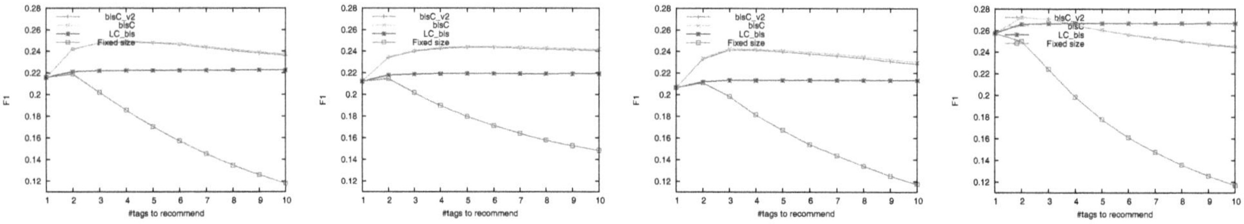

(a) MPTR (b) FasTag (c) FolkRank (d) PITF

Figure 5: Quality increases versus recommendation list sizes on *Movielens*

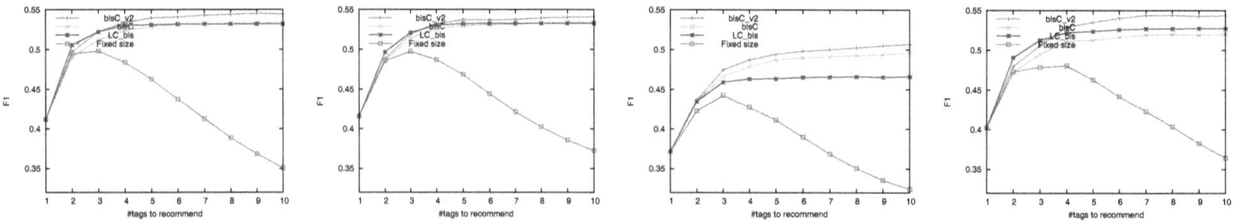

(a) MPTR (b) FasTag (c) FolkRank (d) PITF

Figure 6: Quality increases versus recommendation list sizes on *Bibson5*

each dataset). This demonstrates the importance of giving optimal recommendation list size.

Second, in the most cases *blsC_v2* outperforms *blsC* and linear combinations. For instance, it outstrips the results of the task 2 of the ECML PKDD Discovery Challenge 2009. With the same tag recommender than the winners, we reach an F1 measure of 0.366 while they got 0.356. They used a linear combination to adjust the size of the recommended lists (see [8]). *blsC_v2* yields 3% of improvement over their F1 score on the dataset of the challenge.

Tables 2 and 3 compare the percentage of cases where each of the optimization methods gives the best contribution. Linear combinations overpass our proposals in only 9.19% of cases (see 2). On all the rest, *blsC_v2* dominates with more than 60% of cases, and *blsC* follows with 30%. Linear combinations are mainly better on Movielens dataset, which was the worst dataset of our five ones. In this dataset around 65% of the users never used more than one tag in their posts, which is poor for accurate recommendations. Similarly 41.76% of the items have never been tagged with more that one tag (see Table 1). This explains why our methods which use the popularity of the tags fail to give better results than linear combinations.

Table 2: Comparison of the three methods

Method	% of cases with the best size
blsC_v2	**60.34**
blsC	30.45
LC_bls	9.19

Table 3: Comparison by pairs

Method	% of cases with the best size
blsC_v2	**90.85**
LC_bls	9.14

Method	% of cases with the best size
blsC	**76.96**
LC_bls	23.03

Method	% of cases with the best size
blsC_v2	**65.34**
blsC	34.09

4.3.2 Average optimal list size

Table 4 presents the average optimal list size given by the methods *LC_bls*, *blsC* and *blsC_v2*. In addition to the fact that *blsC_v2* leads to the best size for 90.85% of cases compared to *LC_bls* (see Table 3), we see it gives longer lists than the latter in 80% of cases.

5. CONCLUSION

We presented a new proposal that improves the accuracy of the obtained recommendations from a tag recommender system. Our solution optimizes the size of the recommended list in order to obtain a better recommendation quality. The experimentation we did shows the effectiveness of our approach. Furthermore, our approach suits well in the context of recommendation diversity. Since it shortens the number of relevant tags to recommend, it frees some space that can be used for the diversification purposes.

Table 4: Average optimal list length with 10 tags at maximum

Dataset	FasTag		
	LC_bls	*blsC*	*blsC_v2*
bibsonomy	3.28	3.73	**4.91**
movielens	1.96	6.51	**6.56**
delicious	**7.17**	2.92	3.08
lastfm	**5.94**	4.22	4.72
dc09	4.56	3.93	**4.86**

Dataset	MPTR		
	LC_bls	*blsC*	*blsC_v2*
bibsonomy	3.21	3.85	**5.00**
movielens	1.90	8.23	**8.28**
delicious	7.23	7.12	**7.35**
lastfm	**5.53**	4.81	5.34
dc09	4.56	4.57	**5.51**

Dataset	FolkRank		
	LC_bls	*blsC*	*blsC_v2*
bibsonomy	3.49	3.70	**4.94**
movielens	2.37	8.23	**8.29**
delicious	6.75	7.18	**7.51**
lastfm	**5.91**	4.76	5.28
dc09	4.41	4.44	**5.46**

Dataset	PITF		
	LC_bls	*blsC*	*blsC_v2*
bibsonomy	3.50	6.89	**7.70**
movielens	1.67	9.37	**9.41**
delicious	5.25	9.36	**9.47**
lastfm	6.08	7.51	**7.97**
dc09	4.53	6.35	**7.38**

6. REFERENCES

[1] D. Benz, A. Hotho, R. Jäschke, B. Krause, F. Mitzlaff, C. Schmitz, and G. Stumme. The social bookmark and publication management system BibSonomy. *The VLDB Journal*, 2010.

[2] I. Cantador, P. Brusilovsky, and T. Kuflik. 2nd workshop on information heterogeneity and fusion in recommender systems (hetrec 2011). In *Proceedings of the 5th ACM conference on Recommender systems*, 2011.

[3] M. Gueye, T. Abdessalem, and H. Naacke. An efficient trust- and popularity-based tag recommender. `http://www.infres.enst.fr/~mogueye/fastag.php`, 2013.

[4] A. Hotho, R. Jäschke, C. Schmitz, and G. Stumme. Folkrank : A ranking algorithm for folksonomies. In *Fachgruppe Information Retrieval (FGIR)*, 2006.

[5] R. Jäschke, L. Marinho, A. Hotho, L. Schmidt-Thieme, and G. Stumme. Tag recommendations in folksonomies. In *Proceedings of the 11th European conference on Principles and Practice of Knowledge Discovery in Databases*, 2007.

[6] R. Jäschke, L. Marinho, A. Hotho, L. Schmidt-Thieme, and G. Stumme. Tag recommendations in social bookmarking systems. *AI Commun.*, 2008.

[7] L. Marinho, C. Preisach, and L. Schmidt-Thieme. Relational classification for personalized tag recommendation. In *ECML PKDD Discovery Challenge*, 2009.

[8] S. Rendle and L. Schmidt-Thieme. Factor models for tag recommendation in bibsonomy. In *ECML PKDD Discovery Challenge*, Bled, Slovenia, 2009.

[9] S. Rendle and L. Schmidt-Thieme. Pairwise interaction tensor factorization for personalized tag recommendation. In *Int. Conf. on Web search and data mining (WSDM)*, 2010.

[10] M. Tahajod, A. Iranmehr, and N. Khozooyi. Trust management for semantic web. In *Computer and Electrical Engineering (ICCEE)*, 2009.

[11] C.-N. Ziegler and G. Lausen. Propagation models for trust and distrust in social networks. *Information Systems Frontiers*, 2005.

GASGD: Stochastic Gradient Descent for Distributed Asynchronous Matrix Completion via Graph Partitioning.*

Fabio Petroni
Department of Computer Control and Management Engineering Antonio Ruberti, Sapienza University of Rome
petroni@dis.uniroma1.it

Leonardo Querzoni
Department of Computer Control and Management Engineering Antonio Ruberti, Sapienza University of Rome
querzoni@dis.uniroma1.it

ABSTRACT

Matrix completion latent factors models are known to be an effective method to build recommender systems. Currently, stochastic gradient descent (SGD) is considered one of the best latent factor-based algorithm for matrix completion. In this paper we discuss GASGD, a distributed asynchronous variant of SGD for large-scale matrix completion, that (i) leverages data partitioning schemes based on graph partitioning techniques, (ii) exploits specific characteristics of the input data and (iii) introduces an explicit parameter to tune synchronization frequency among the computing nodes. We empirically show how, thanks to these features, GASGD achieves a fast convergence rate incurring in smaller communication cost with respect to current asynchronous distributed SGD implementations.

Categories and Subject Descriptors

G.4 [**Mathematics of Computing**]: Mathematical Software — *Parallel and vector implementations*

Keywords

Recommender system; Matrix completion; Stochastic gradient descent; Distributed computing; Graph partitioning

1. INTRODUCTION

Many of todays internet businesses strongly base their success in the ability to provide personalized user experiences. This trend, pioneered by e-commerce companies like Amazon [8], has spread to many different sectors. As of today, personalized user recommendations are commonly offered by internet radio services, social networks, media sharing platforms (e.g. YouTube) and movie rental services.

Building user recommendations can be abstracted as a *matrix completion problem*; given a set of users and a set of available items (e.g. songs, movies, tweets, etc.), these can be mapped to rows and columns of a *rating matrix* whose values represent preferences expressed by users on items. Building recommendations boils down to estimate, as precisely as possible, all missing values in this matrix.

Recent experiences in this field [4, 2] has promoted algorithms based on *latent factors* as the best approach to the matrix completion problem. These algorithms map users and items to a latent feature space and define their affinity as the product of their latent feature vectors. The basic idea is that latent features, albeit non clearly definable, contain useful information on user and item similarity and can thus be exploited to predict missing ratings. *Stochastic Gradient Descent* (SGD) [7, 12] is considered, as of today, the best latent factor based algorithm for matrix completion in all settings where the rating matrix is huge (e.g. millions of users with hundreds of thousands items and billions of available ratings). The SGD success stems from the availability of efficient parallel implementations [16, 9, 10] that make it possible to efficiently exploit modern multi-processor and multi-core computing architectures. However, as the problem size grows to massive scale the memory occupation of such algorithms become the limiting factor: the cost of computing infrastructures skyrockets, while the performance tend to grow non linearly due to more frequent contention on data shared among running processes. Thereby, the research trend is now focussed on *distributed SGD* implementations whose aim is to make the analysis of huge data sets feasible on possibly large clusters of cheap commodity machines. The shift toward distributed implementations is a key move to make recommendation algorithms a service easily and cheaply available through cloud platforms.

Recent proposals [13, 5] represent important steps in the right direction, but still suffer from some limitations that hinder their performance. Firstly, all these solutions divide the input dataset among the available SGD instances leveraging, at best, randomized partitioning approaches; partitioning is performed by subdividing the rating matrix in blocks of the same size; however, no attention is payed to the amount of data (user preferences) in each block, even if this value drives the real load of the SGD instance that will compute on that matrix block; as a consequence, this "blind" approach to partitioning, albeit easily applicable, can cause skewed load on the computing nodes. Furthermore, it is inefficient as it does not appropriately exploit some intrinsic characteristics of the input data. Secondly, all these solu-

*This work has been partially supported by the TENACE PRIN Project (n. 20103P34XC) funded by the Italian Ministry of Education, University and Research and by the academic project n. C26A133HZY funded by the University of Rome "La Sapienza"

RecSys'14, October 6–10, 2014, Foster City, Silicon Valley, CA, USA.

http://dx.doi.org/10.1145/2645710.2645725 .

tions employ a *bulk synchronous processing* approach where shared data values are concurrently updated on local copies and then periodically resynchronized. The synchronization frequency is a fundamental parameter for these solutions as it regulates a crucial tradeoff between the convergence rate of the algorithm toward the solution and the communication cost incurred during its functioning. To the best of our knowledge, none of the existing works in this field explored and leveraged this tradeoff.

Our proposal is to address the aforementioned problems with three distinct contributions. On one side we mitigate the load imbalance among SGD instances by proposing an input slicing solution based on graph partitioning algorithms (contribution 1). This approach looks at the input data as a graph where each node represents either a user or an item and each edge represents a rating expressed by the former on the latter. The graph is then greedily partitioned edge by edge thus providing a substantially more balanced load among the available computing nodes. A better balanced load has a positive impact on the overall efficiency of the system as less loaded processes will not wait idly while more loaded processes delay the bulk data synchronization phase (assuming homogeneous computing nodes).

On the other side we attack the efficiency problem with two distinct solutions:

1. By properly leveraging known characteristics of the input dataset, i.e. the fact that it is bipartite (users can only express ratings on items) and with skewed degree distributions (i.e. the user base is usually order of magnitude larger than the item base and the distribution of user ratings expressed on items follows a power-law) we show how to reduce the number of shared data values among SGD instances (contribution 2).

2. By tuning the frequency used by SGD instances to start the bulk synchronization phase during the computation we show how to leverage the tradeoff between communication cost and algorithm convergence rate to improve system performance without affecting the overall quality of the final result (contribution 3).

All our three contributions nicely integrate with the current state of the art as they don't require modifications to existing asynchronous distributed SGD algorithms, but rather complement them. In particular, contributions 1 and 2 are integrated in a *input partitioner* that must be used to preprocess input data before running the SGD algorithm, while contribution 3 is provided as an empirical evaluation on well known publicly-available data traces.

In the following we will first introduce the reader to the the matrix completion problem (Section 2) and then detail the SGD algorithm with its parallel and distributed variants (Section 3). Our novel input partitioner included in GASGD is then described in Section 4, followed by an experimental evaluation (Section 5) that backups our claims. Section 5 also contains a description of contribution 3. Finally, an analysis of the related work (Section 6), and some final remarks (Section 7) will conclude this paper.

2. THE MATRIX COMPLETION PROBLEM

We consider a system constituted by $U = (u_1, \cdots, u_n)$ users and $X = (x_1, \cdots, x_m)$ items. Items represent a general abstraction that can be case by case instantiated as news, tweets, shopping items, movies, songs, etc. Users can rate items with values from a predefined range. Without loss of generality, here we assume that ratings are represented with real numbers. By collecting user ratings it is possible to build a $n \times m$ rating matrix R that is usually a sparse matrix as each user rates a small subset of the available items. Denote by $O \subseteq \{1, ..., n\} \times \{1, ..., m\}$ the set of indices identifying observed entries in R; $(i, j) \in O$ implies that user u_i rated item x_j with vote r_{ij}. The *training set* is defined as $T = \{r_{ij} : (i, j) \in O\}$. The goal of a *matrix completion algorithm* is to predict missing entries $\widehat{r}_{ij}$ in R using ratings contained in the training set. As demonstrated by the Netflix competition [2] and the KDD-Cup 2011 [4], collaborative approaches (i.e., *collaborative filtering* techniques [11]) based on latent factors are today considered the best models for large-scale recommender systems.

Denote by $k \ll min(n, m)$ a rank parameter. These kind of solutions aim at finding an $n \times k$ row-factor matrix P^* (*user vectors matrix*) and an $k \times m$ column-factor matrix Q^* (*item vectors matrix*) such that $R \approx P^*Q^*$. The approximation is performed by minimizing an application dependent error function $L(P, Q)$, that measures the quality of the reconstruction. We call p_i, the i-th row of P, the k-dimensional vector of user u_i and q_j, the j-th column of Q, the k-dimensional vector of item x_j. Unobserved entries $\widehat{r}_{ij} \in R, (i, j) \notin O$ are predicted by multiplying the corresponding user and item vectors $p_i q_j$. There exists a wide range of objective functions for matrix completion and factorization. The most used error function is the regularized squared loss [7, 12, 13, 16]:

$$L(P, Q) = \sum_{(i,j) \in P} (r_{ij} - p_i q_j)^2 + \lambda(||P||_F^2 + ||Q||_F^2) \quad (1)$$

where $||\cdot||_F$ is the Frobenius norm and $\lambda \geq 0$ is a regularization coefficient used to avoid overfitting. In accordance with [13], we observe that Equation 1 is in *summation form* as it is expressed as a sum of *local losses* L_{ij} for each element in R:

$$L_{ij}(P, Q) = (r_{ij} - p_i q_j)^2 + \lambda \sum_{k=1}^{r} (P_{ik}^2 + Q_{kj}^2) \quad (2)$$

The most popular techniques to minimize the objective function are *Alternating Least Squares* (ALS) and *Stochastic Gradient Descent* (SGD). ALS [15] alternates between keeping P and Q fixed. The idea is that, although both these values are unknown, when the item vectors are fixed, the system can recompute the user vectors by solving a *least-squares* problem (that can be solved optimally), and vice versa. In this paper we will focus on SGD [7, 12], since it has been shown that it performs better on large-scale data [13]. SGD, in fact, was the approach chosen by the top three solutions of KDD-Cup 2011 [4].

3. STOCHASTIC GRADIENT DESCENT

SGD works by iteratively updating current estimations of P and Q with values proportional to the negative of the gradient of the error function. The term *stochastic* means that P and Q are updated, at each iteration, by a small step for each given training case toward the average gradient descent. For each observed entry $(i, j) \in O$, the objective function is expressed by Equation 2 and the variables are updated proportionally to the sub-gradient over p_i and q_j:

$$p_i \leftarrow p_i + \mu(\varepsilon_{ij} q_j - \lambda p_i) \tag{3}$$

$$q_j \leftarrow q_j + \mu(\varepsilon_{ij} p_i - \lambda q_j) \tag{4}$$

where $\varepsilon_{ij} = r_{ij} - p_i q_j$ is the error between the real and predicted ratings for the (i, j) entry, and μ is the learning rate. Therefore, in each SGD step only the involved user and item vectors are updated.

The algorithm proceeds performing several iterations through the available ratings until a convergence criterion is met. We refer to a single iteration over the data as an *epoch*.

The SGD algorithm is, by its nature, inherently sequential, however, sequential implementations are usually considered poorly scalable as the time to convergence for large-scale problems may quickly grow to significant amounts. Parallel versions of SGD have been designed to overcome this problem by sharing the computation among multiple processing cores working on shared memory. A straightforward approach [10] to manage concurrent updates of shared variables is to lock, before processing training point $(i, j) \in O$, both row p_i and column q_j. However, lock-based approaches are known to adversely affect concurrency and, in the end, limit the scalability of the algorithm. HogWild [9] proposed a lock-free version assuming an highly sparse rating matrix. Recently, Zhuang et al. [16] proposed FPSGD, a fast parallel SGD implementation for shared memory systems. They tackled similar problems to our: (i) how to reduce the cost that the algorithm faces when retrieving data and (ii) how to ensure that all the threads will process the same amount of data. The algorithm partitions the training data into several blocks (more than the available threads) and uses a task manager to distribute the load among the threads. Beside these recent improvements, parallel SGD algorithms are hardly applicable to large-scale datasets, since the time-to-convergence may be too slow or, simply, the input data may not fit into the main memory of a single computer. Storing training data on disk is inconvenient because the two-dimensional nature of the rating matrix R will force non-sequential I/O making disk-based SGD approaches unpractical and poorly performant, although technically feasible. These problems recently motivated several research efforts toward distributed versions of SGD.

Distributed SGD Algorithms.

This kind of algorithms [13, 3, 1] are designed for very large scale instances of the matrix completion problem.

DSGD [5] exploits the fact that some blocks of the rating matrix R are mutually independent (i.e., they share neither any row nor any column) so that the corresponding user and item vectors can be updated concurrently. For each epoch, several sequences of independent blocks of equal size (that constitute a *stratum*) are selected to cover the entire available data set. Then the algorithm proceeds by elaborating each stratum sequentially, assigning each block to a different computing node, until all the input data have been processed; at that point a new epoch starts. It is important to notice that with this solution a processing node must have complete knowledge of the rating matrix R in order to decompose it in blocks and strata, but this is unfeasible if the input data does not fit in the main memory of a single machine.

To cope with such massive scale, current solutions distribute the rating matrix R among the set of computing nodes C, so that each of them only owns a slice of the input data. A problem with such approach is that, in general, the input partitioner is forced to assign ratings expressed by a single user (resp. received by a single item) to different computing nodes, in order to maintain the load in the system balanced. Thereby, user and item vectors must be concurrently updated, during the SGD procedure, by multiple nodes. A common solution is to replicate vectors on all the nodes that will work on them, forcing synchronization among the replicas via message exchange.

The main challenge faced by distributed SGD algorithms is thus how to effectively partition the data across multiple processing node, in such a way that: (i) all the computing nodes are approximately fed with the same load and (ii) the communication between the computing nodes is minimized (iii) without compromising the quality of the result.

Given that each node has a local view of the vectors it works on, the algorithm needs to keep vector replicas on different nodes from diverging. This is achieved in two possible ways: either by maintaining replicas always in synch by leveraging a locking scheme (*synchronous* approach), or by letting nodes concurrently update their local copies and then periodically resynchronizing diverging vectors (*asynchronous* approach). Synchronous distributed SGD algorithms all employ some form of locking to maintain vector copies synchronized. This approach is however inefficient, because computing nodes spend most of their time in retrieving and delivering vector updates in the network, or waiting for lock to be released. The strictly sequential computation order imposed by this locking approach on shared vector updates negatively impacts the performance of such solutions.

Distributed Asynchronous SGD.

Differently from synchronous algorithms, in distributed asynchronous SGD (ASGD) algorithms computing nodes are allowed to concurrently work on shared user/item vectors, that can therefore deviate inconsistently during the computation. The system defines for each vector a unique *master copy* and $s \in [0, |C|)$ *working copies*. In the following we will refer to the node that store the master copy of a vector as *master node*. Each computing node updates only the local working copy of p_i and q_j[1] while processing training point $(i, j) \in O$. The synchronization between working copies and master is performed periodically according to the *Bulk Synchronous Processing* (BSP) model [13]. Initially all the vector copies are synchronized with their corresponding masters. The synchronization procedure is then repeated f times during each epoch. We refer to the parameter f as the *synchronization frequency* of the algorithm.

In this study we considered the following ASGD algorithm. At the beginning of an epoch, each node shuffles the subset data that it owns and divides it in f folds of equal size. Consequently, each epoch is divided in f steps. Each step y consists of: (i) a computation phase, where each node updates the local working copy of user and item vectors using data in the y-th fold; (ii) a global message transmission phase, where each node sends all the vector working copies that have been updated in the previous phase to the corresponding masters; (iii) a barrier synchronization, where each

[1] Also the vector master node updates a local working copy.

master node collects all the vector working copies, compute the new vector values, and sends back the result. New vector values, computed in phase (iii), are obtained by performing a weighted average of the received working copies. The weight is given by the number of training points in the y-th fold that lead to the update of the vector (i.e., the number of ratings in the y-th fold expressed by the user or received by the item). In [14] an exhaustive theoretical study of the convergence of ASGD is presented.

Current ASGD state-of-the-art implementations synchronize vector working copies either continuously during the epoch ($f = \frac{|T|}{|C|}$, each fold contains a single rating) or once after every epoch ($f = 1$) [13]. Obviously, the first approach ($f = \frac{|T|}{|C|}$) guarantees a *convergence rate*, defined as the speed at which the objective function approaches its lower limit with respect to the epochs passing, almost equal to the centralized version of SGD, since every update is from time to time notified to the entire system. This, however, comes at the cost of a huge number of messages that have to be exchanged in the system (i.e. large *communication cost*). Conversely, the second alternative ($f = 1$) incurs in the minimum communication cost, but its convergence rate can be quite slow. In Section 5 we will report on our empirical study of f that shows the tradeoff between convergence rate and communication cost, and how this can be leveraged to improve the efficiency of ASGD algorithms.

Another problem of current implementations is how to balance the load among the computing nodes. A known problem of the BSP approach, namely the *curse of the last reducer* [1], is that the slowest machine determines the runtime of each step. This shortcoming can be mitigated, assuming homogeneous computing resources, by perfectly balancing the load among the available nodes.

The problem is that, in general, the input ratings are not uniformly distributed in R. A common approach to input data partition is to grid the rating matrix R in $|C|$ blocks and then assign each block to a different computing node [13]. This partitioning approach clearly cannot guarantee a balanced number of ratings for each block, thus can possibly cause strong load imbalance among computing nodes. The authors of [13] proposed to mitigate this problem by applying some random permutations of columns and rows. While this approach improve the load balancing aspect, it still lead to non negligible skews in the rating distributions (See Section 5 for an empirical evaluation of this aspect). Furthermore, a second problem of the grid partitioning approach is that the communication cost between the computing nodes is not considered as a factor to be minimized. Matrix blocking, in fact, is performed without considering the relationships connecting users with items in R. As a consequence, the number of replicas for each user/item vector can possibly grow to the number C of available nodes.

In the next section we introduce a novel input splitter based on a graph partitioning approach that aims at solving both these problems.

4. INPUT PARTITIONER

Our partitioner treats input data as a graph, where users and items represent nodes and ratings represent edges. It works by assigning each edge in exactly one of C partitions (i.e. subgraphs of the input graph), each managed by a different computing node. As a baseline to our graph partitioning scheme we follow [6, 1]. In particular, we perform a balanced $|C|$-way vertex-cut partitioning of the graph, that aims both at minimizing the number of shared vertices and at balancing the load among the computing nodes.

The motivation behind the vertex-cut approach, with respect to the classical edge-cut one, is that SGD stores and exchanges data (i.e., user and item vectors) that are associated with vertices rather than edges. Moreover, one characteristic of real preference datasets is their skewed power-law degree distribution: most vertices have relatively few connections while a few have many. Figure 1 shows this characteristics from three popular datasets, namely MovieLens, Netflix and Yahoo! (see Section 5). It has been shown [6] that the vertex-cut approach performs better than edge-cut in these scenarios. Intuitively, by replicating the few very high degree vertices it is possible to quickly partition the graph, while maintaining a balanced load among the available computing nodes.

Given a weighted undirected graph $G = (V, E)$ that represents a rating matrix R, where $V = U \cup X$ and $e_{i,j} \in E$ iff $(i, j) \in O$, the input partitioner puts each edge $e_{i,j}$, together with the vertices v_i and v_j it connects, in one of the C available nodes. At the end of this operation, each edge will be stored exactly in one node, while some vertices will be replicated in more than one node. Note that, if a vertex resides in a single node (i.e. it has only one replica) no synchronization is needed for him in ASGD. However, in the general case, the storage overhead and the communication cost incurred by ASGD at runtime depend on the vertex replication factor, defined ad the average number of vertex replicas (i.e., $RF = \#replicas/\#vertices$). The goal of the input partitioner is thus twofold: (i) minimizing the *replication factor* (RF) and (ii) balance as much as possible the edge load among the available computing nodes. This objective is formalized by the *balanced Ω-way vertex-cut* problem [6], where Ω is the number of partitions (in our case $|C|$). Each edge $e_{i,j} \in E$ is assigned to a single node $A(e) \in C$. Each vertex v is then replicated on the set of nodes $A(v) \subseteq C$ that contain its adjacent edges. The balanced $|C|$-way vertex-cut objective function is defined as follows:

$$\min \frac{1}{|V|} \sum_{v \in V} |A(v)| \tag{5}$$

$$s.t. \quad \max_{c \in C} |\{e_{i,j} \in E | A(e) = c\}| < \sigma \frac{|E|}{|C|} \tag{6}$$

where $\sigma \geq 1$ is a small constant that defines the system tolerance to load imbalance.

For each vertex v with multiple replicas, one of the replicas is randomly selected as the one which maintains the master vector associated with the vertex. All remaining replicas of v maintain a working copy of the vector.

Greedy Vertex-Cut Streaming Algorithm.

Since we are here assuming that the input data doesn't fit in main memory, the algorithm used to partition it among the available nodes must work in a streaming fashion, requiring only a single pass over the input data. A limitation of this approach is that the assignment decision taken on an input element (i.e. an edge) can only be based on previously analyzed data and cannot be later changed.

A simple solution is given by the *hashing* algorithm that pseudo-randomly assigns each edge to a partition. This solu-

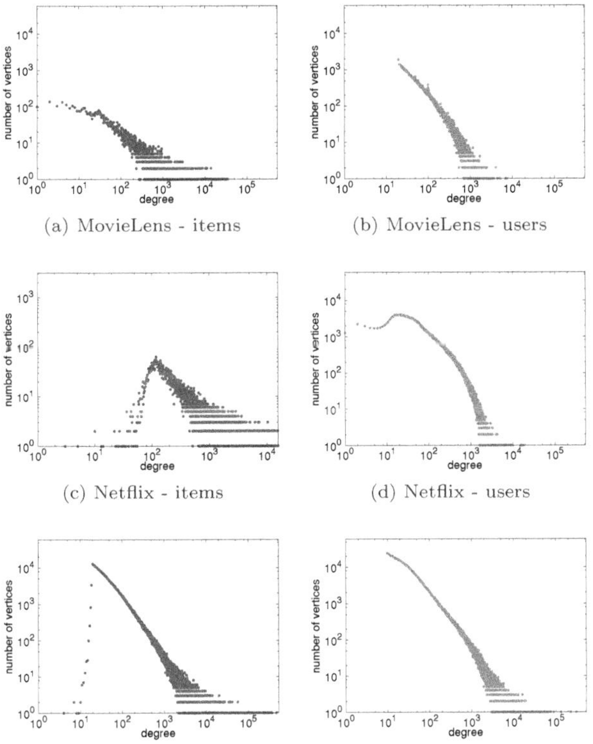

(a) MovieLens - items (b) MovieLens - users

(c) Netflix - items (d) Netflix - users

(e) Yahoo! - items (f) Yahoo! - users

Figure 1: The items and users degree distributions in the considered datasets (log-log scale).

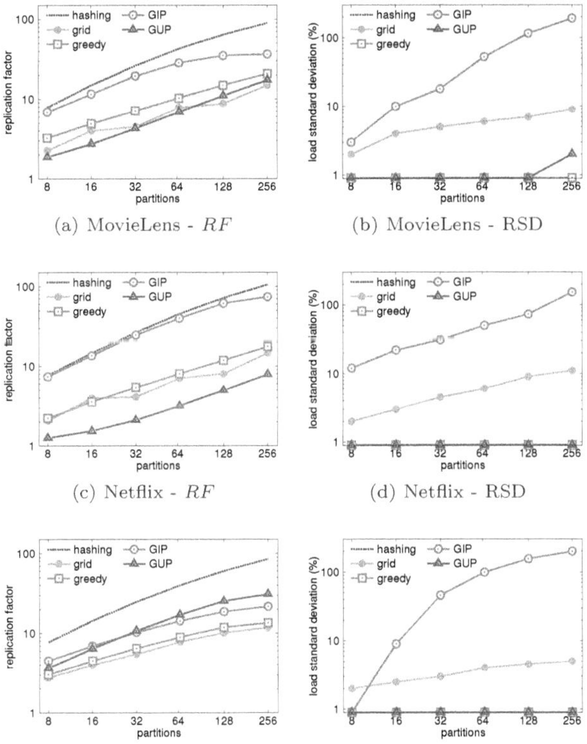

(a) MovieLens - RF (b) MovieLens - RSD

(c) Netflix - RF (d) Netflix - RSD

(e) Yahoo! - RF (f) Yahoo! - RSD

Figure 2: Replication factor and load RSD achieved by the various partitioning schemes (log-log scale).

tion achieves nearly perfect load balance on large graphs, but provides results with very high replication factors. A better solution is represented by a greedy approach [6, 1] that breaks the randomness of the hashing solution by maintaining some global status information. In particular, the system stores the set of computing nodes $A(v)$ to which each already observed vertex v has been assigned[2]. The algorithm, when processing edge $e_{i,j} \in E$ operates as follows:

Case 1 If neither u_i nor x_j have been assigned to a node, then $e_{i,j}$ is assigned to the least loaded node $c_l \in C$. c_l becomes the master node of u_i and x_j.

Case 2 If only one of the two vertices has been already assigned (without loss of generality assume that u_i is the assigned vertex) then $e_{i,j}$ is placed in the least loaded $c_l \in A(u_i)$. c_l becomes the master node of x_j.

Case 3 If $A(u_i) \cap A(x_j) \neq \emptyset$, then the edge $e_{i,j}$ is assigned to the least loaded node $c_l \in A(u_i) \cap A(x_j)$.

Case 4 If $A(u_i) \neq \emptyset$, $A(x_j) \neq \emptyset$ and $A(u_i) \cap A(x_j) = \emptyset$, then $e_{i,j}$ is assigned to the least loaded node $c_l \in A(u_i) \cup A(x_j)$. Without loss of generality assume $c_l \in A(u_i)$, then c_l becomes a working node for x_j.

We implemented the above procedure in a parallel fashion. In particular, the input data is randomly divided between the computing threads/nodes. All the threads/nodes have access to a shared key-value storage that maintains as key the id of the vertex v and as value $A(v)$. To manage concurrent access we define fine-grained locks, one for each entry.

The novelty of our solution lies on the idea to exploit the bipartite nature of the considered graph. A bipartite graph is a graph where the vertex set V can be split in two disjoint subsets $W1$ and $W2$ such that all edges connect vertices placed in distinct subsets: if $\{v, w\} \in E$, either $v \in W1$ and $w \in W2$ or $v \in W2$ and $w \in W1$. Such graphs are natural in the area of recommender systems, where vertices represent distinct classes of objects, e.g. users and items.

[2]The memory footprint needed to run such algorithm is orders of magnitude smaller than the input data.

Bipartite Aware Greedy Algorithm.

Our algorithm exploits the fact that in real word datasets the size of the two sets constituting the bipartite graph are often significantly skewed: one of the two sets is much bigger that the other. If this is the case, by perfectly splitting the bigger set it is possible to achieve an average replication factor smaller than the one obtained through the greedy approach (although we will show in Section 5 that this is not always enough to achieve a smaller communication cost).

It is therefore possible to identify two dual approaches:

- *item partitioned* strategy. Vectors for all items $x_j \in X$ always reside in a single node while vectors for users $u_i \in U$ are replicated as necessary.

- *user partitioned* strategy. Vectors for all users $u_i \in U$ always reside in a single node while vectors for items $x_j \in X$ are replicated as necessary.

Dataset	MovieLens	Netflix	Yahoo!
n	69878	480189	1000990
m	10677	17770	624961
$\lvert E\rvert$	10000054	100480507	252800275
k	50	50	50
λ	0.05	0.05	1
μ	0.015	0.015	0.0001

Table 1: Statistics and parameters for each dataset.

To achieve this result we modify *Case 4* of the greedy algorithm, that is the only case where replicas are generated. Assume without loss of generality a *user partitioned* strategy, so $|A(u_i)| = 1, \forall u_i \in U$.

Case 4 If $A(u_i) \notin A(x_j)$ then $e_{i,j}$ is assigned to $A(u_i)$, and the unique node in $A(u_i)$ creates a working copy for x_j.

5. EVALUATION

In this section we report the results of the experimental evaluation we conducted on a prototype implementation of GASGD. The goal of this evaluation was to show how the GASGD characteristics provide a solution able to reach high quality results in an efficient manner.

Experimental Settings and Test Datasets.

We used three datasets for the experiments: MovieLens 10M[3], Netflix [2] and Yahoo! [4]. Dataset statistics as well as simulation parameters are synthesized in Table 1. The reported learning rate μ only represents the starting value, as we adopted an adaptive mechanism called *bold driver* [13] to automatically vary the parameter during the computation. Furthermore, in our implementation each computing node shuffles the training points it analyzes before each epoch.

We implemented five different input partitioning scheme: *grid, hashing, greedy, greedy - item partitioned* (*GIP*), *greedy - user partitioner* (*GUP*). The *grid* partitioner, commonly used by DSGD (Section 3), simply shuffles rows and columns of the rating matrix R, and then divides it in $|C|$ identical blocks. The other four schemes are based on graph partitioning techniques (Section 4). As a baseline for comparison we used the solution obtained by running SGD on a single machine. For this centralized approach we employed the parallel-SGD algorithm (with locks) described in Section 3.

Partitioning quality.

We begin our experimental analysis by studying the quality of the various partitioning schemes, in terms of achieved replication factor (average number of copies for each vector) and load balancing (expressed as the *Relative Standard Deviation* (RSD) of the load among the nodes). Figure 2 reports the obtained results. As expected GUP achieves the smallest RF in those scenarios where the number of users is much bigger than the number of items (MovieLens and Netflix), sporting, moreover, a perfect load balance among the computing nodes. However, in the Yahoo! dataset users and items are comparable in number and the classical *greedy* solution outperforms its *user partitioned* variant. Interestingly, the *grid* solution always outperforms the *greedy* approach in RF, even if its load balancing performance are inferior. Intuitively, by shuffling rows and columns of R

[3]http://grouplens.org/datasets/movielens

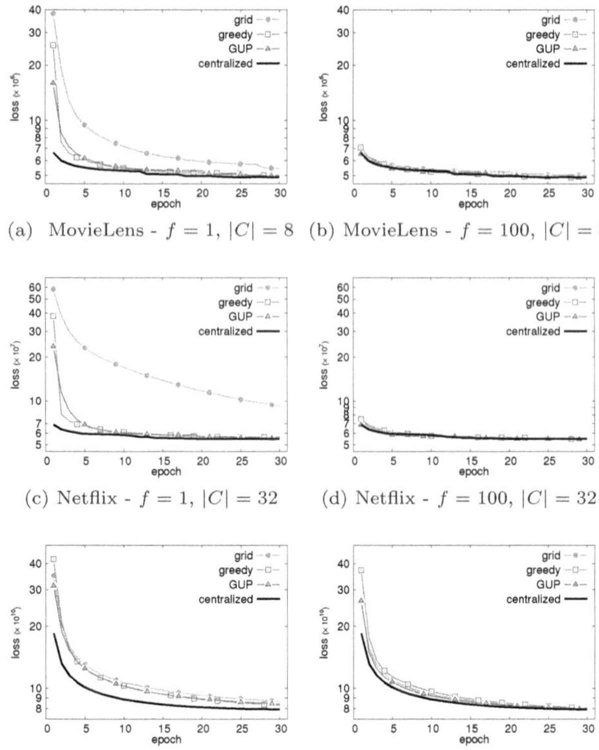

(a) MovieLens - $f = 1$, $|C| = 8$ (b) MovieLens - $f = 100$, $|C| = 8$

(c) Netflix - $f = 1$, $|C| = 32$ (d) Netflix - $f = 100$, $|C| = 32$

(e) Yahoo! - $f = 1$, $|C| = 4$ (f) Yahoo! - $f = 100$, $|C| = 4$

Figure 3: Algorithms convergence rate (loss vs epochs), with $f = 1$ and $f = 100$ (y-axis in log-scale).

and then grouping them in blocks, *grid* achieves the same objective of *greedy*, that is to replicate users or items with high degree, but does so in a more effective way, since it has complete knowledge of the rating matrix R while *greedy* processes the training set in a streaming fashion.

Overall SGD performance.

To assess the quality of the solution obtained from the asynchronous distributed SGD variants, we compare the convergence curves of the objective function expressed by Equation 1. Note that here our goal was not to assess the absolute solution quality achieved by the algorithm (i.e., RMSE), but rather to show how fast the solutions provided by the distributed solutions approach the centralized one. Figure 3 shows the loss curves for the various algorithms, applying two different synchronization frequencies: $f = 1$ and $f = 100$. In general, by increasing f the ASGD curves tend to reproduce the centralized SGD trend, while with $f = 1$ the distributed convergence rates are quite far from the centralized one. This was expected, since with $f = 1$ all the vector copies are free to diverge during the computation of an epoch while with $f = 100$ they are frequently synchronized, closely reproducing the behavior of a centralized implementation. The worst performance, with small synchronization frequencies, is provided by the *grid* solution: by shuffling R, in fact, *grid* uniformly distributes the ratings of an entity (i.e. user or item) among the available nodes, thereby favoring the divergence of vector copies.

To synthesize these results we used an aggregate value for the convergence curves difference: the *sum of squared*

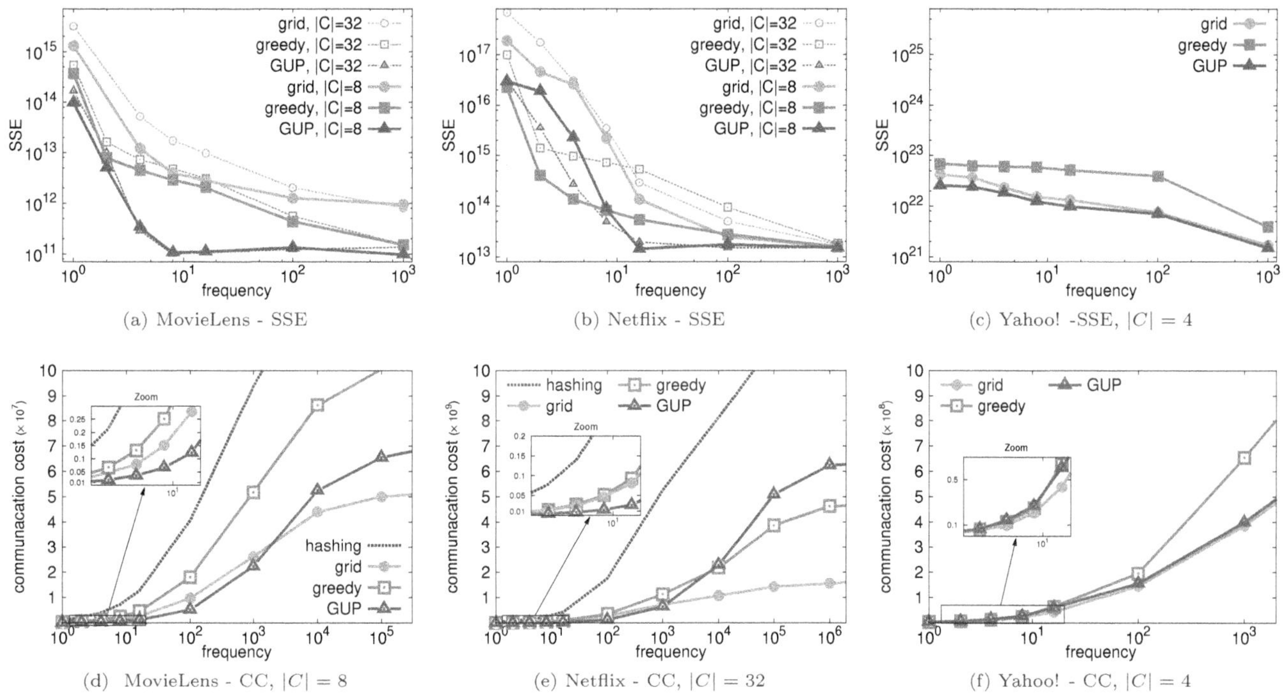

(a) MovieLens - SSE (b) Netflix - SSE (c) Yahoo! -SSE, $|C| = 4$

(d) MovieLens - CC, $|C| = 8$ (e) Netflix - CC, $|C| = 32$ (f) Yahoo! - CC, $|C| = 4$

Figure 4: SSE between ASGD variants and SGD convergence curves (log-log scale), in the top half. Communication cost varying synchronization frequency (x-axis in log scale), in the bottom part.

errors (SSE) between the ASGD curve points and the centralized ones (limited to the first 30 epochs). The top half of Figure 4 (Figures 4a, 4b and 4c) reports the obtained SSE values varying the synch frequency f. In datasets with significantly more users than items (MovieLens and Netflix) the *GUP* strategy convergence curve quickly approaches the centralized one (respectively with $f = 8$ and $f = 16$) while other solutions achieve the same result with larger frequencies. Furthermore, while increasing the number of nodes degrades the performance of both *greedy* and *grid* (dashed lines in the figures), the *GUP* solution is not affected by this problem; it actually sports a performance improvement to its convergence rate in the Netflix dataset (Figure 4b). Also in the Yahoo! dataset the *GUP* approach outperforms the other variants in convergence rate (Figure 4c).

Communication Cost.

The *GUP* loss curve is the one more quickly approaching the centralized SGD curve for the smallest value of f. Now we will show how, at that frequency f, the *GUP* solution is also the least expensive with respect to communication cost. We express the communication cost (CC) as the total number of messages that the system exchanges in an epoch. This cost depends on three factors: the number $|C|$ of processing nodes, the synchronization frequency f and the replication factor (RF). We remark that RF is a weighted average of the *replication factor* of item (RF_X) and user (RF_U) vectors.

More formally, each node $c \in C$ owns a slice T^c of the training set T, where $|T^c| = \frac{|T|}{|C|}$ assuming perfect load balance. At the beginning of each epoch all computing nodes shuffle the content of their slice T^c and cut it in f folds such that $T^c = \{K_1^c \cup ... \cup K_f^c\}$. Each fold K_y^c contains roughly $\frac{|T^c|}{f}$ ratings. We define $U_y^c = \{u_i \in U : \exists r_{ij} \in K_y^c\}$ (resp. $X_y^c = \{x_j \in X : \exists r_{ij} \in K_y^c\}$) the set of users (resp. items) with at least a rating in the fold. We denote with $U_y = \{U_y^1 \cup ... \cup U_y^{|C|}\}$ (resp. $X_y = \{X_y^1 \cup ... \cup X_y^{|C|}\}$) the set of users (resp. items) with at least one rating in the y-th fold on any computing node. The communication cost for an epoch is then defined as:

$$CC \approx \sum_{c \in C} \sum_{y=1}^{f} (|U_y^c| + |X_y^c|) + \sum_{y=1}^{f} \Big(\sum_{u \in U_y} |A(u)| + \sum_{x \in X_y} |A(x)| \Big) \quad (7)$$

The first part of Equation 7 considers messages that the working copies send to the master, while the second one considers messages that the vector master copies send to all the replicas after the update. For the sake of simplicity the equation does not consider the fact that working and master copies overlap on master nodes, and so they don't need a messages exchange.

The bottom half of Figure 4 (Figures 4d, 4e and 4f) shows the CC incurred by the various solutions varying f. To better understand the charts we show what happens to CC for the extreme values of f: $f = 1$, single synchronization at the end of each epoch, and $f = \frac{|T|}{|C|}$, vectors are synchronized after each observation.

$$f = 1 \rightarrow \quad CC \approx 2(|U|RF_U + |X|RF_X) = 2|V|RF \quad (8)$$

$$f = \frac{|T|}{|C|} \rightarrow \quad CC \approx |T|(2 + RF_U + RF_X) \quad (9)$$

By looking at (8), it is clear that, at low frequencies, the solution with the smallest RF achieves the lowest CC (i.e. *GUP* in MovieLens and Netflix, *grid* in Yahoo!). The situation changes by increasing f, since, for instance, in the

Netflix dataset (Figure 4e) the *GUP* solution gradually becomes the most expensive. This behavior is explained by Equation 9. At high frequencies, in fact, the *CC* basically depends on the sum of RF_U and RF_X. The *GUP* strategy, by partitioning the user set, is forced to highly replicate all items. This behavior has a small impact on RF, as the number of users is larger than the number of items; however, *GUP* sports large RF_X and thus incurs highly expensive synchronization phases for high sync frequencies.

The positive aspect highlighted by these tests is that it's not necessary to massively increase f in order to achieve a convergence rate similar to a centralized implementation. A dozen synchronizations per epoch, in fact, are enough for *GUP* to reach this goal in both the MovieLens and Netflix datasets (Figures 4a and 4b), and at such frequency it is the most efficient solution (Figures 4d and 4e). For the Yahoo! case, instead, a slightly higher frequency is required for *GUP* to reach the centralized convergence rate (Figure 4c). At that frequency, *GUP* is just a bit more expensive in CC than *grid* (Figure 4f), but with the advantage of (i) an almost perfect load balance and (ii) the streaming implementation, that makes it applicable to huge input data (i.e. exceeding the memory capacity of a single node).

6. RELATED WORK

The scalability of collaborative filtering algorithms is a research topic that was recently interested by a huge growth of contributions from the scientific community [13, 5, 16, 9, 10]; we already discussed most of them in Section 3 as they represent a cornerstone for the work proposed in this paper, so this section is devoted to a short description of a few further works that are connected to this paper.

The vertex-cut distributed graph placement problem is addressed by PowerGraph [6], a distributed graph-parallel computation paradigm, in which each vertex in parallel executes some software, respecting the Gather-Apply-Scatter (GAS) programming model. We already described their greedy partitioning algorithm in Section 4.

In the context of graph factorization, [1] proposes an asynchronous SGD version where the global explicit synchronization phase is eliminated. Vector copies, indeed, are synchronized continuously (a thread loops in local memory) in an asynchronous fashion and independently. We think that also in this case it's possible to tune the frequency of the synchronization, in a fine-grained fashion, and we leave this idea as part of our future work.

7. CONCLUSIONS

In this paper we described three distinct contributions aimed at improving the efficiency and scalability of Asynchronous distributed SGD algorithms. In particular, we proposed a novel input slicing solution based on graph partitioning approach that mitigates the load imbalance among SGD instances (i.e. better scalability), while, at the same time, providing lower communication costs during the algorithm execution (i.e. better efficiency) by exploiting specific characteristics of the training dataset. The paper also introduces a synchronization frequency parameter driving a tradeoff that can be accurately leveraged to further improve the algorithm efficiency.

8. REFERENCES

[1] A. Ahmed, N. Shervashidze, S. Narayanamurthy, V. Josifovski, and A. J. Smola. Distributed large-scale natural graph factorization. In *Proceedings of the 22nd international conference on World Wide Web*, 2013.

[2] J. Bennett and S. Lanning. The netflix prize. In *Proceedings of KDD cup and workshop*, 2007.

[3] J. Dean, G. Corrado, R. Monga, K. Chen, M. Devin, Q. V. Le, M. Z. Mao, M. Ranzato, A. W. Senior, P. A. Tucker, et al. Large scale distributed deep networks. In *Conference on Neural Information Processing Systems*, 2012.

[4] G. Dror, N. Koenigstein, Y. Koren, and M. Weimer. The yahoo! music dataset and kdd-cup'11. *Journal of Machine Learning Research-Proceedings Track*, 18:8–18, 2012.

[5] R. Gemulla, E. Nijkamp, P. J. Haas, and Y. Sismanis. Large-scale matrix factorization with distributed stochastic gradient descent. In *Proceedings of the 17th ACM SIGKDD international conference on Knowledge discovery and data mining*, 2011.

[6] J. E. Gonzalez, Y. Low, H. Gu, D. Bickson, and C. Guestrin. Powergraph: Distributed graph-parallel computation on natural graphs. In *Proceedings of the 10th USENIX Symposium on Operating Systems Design and Implementation (OSDI)*, 2012.

[7] Y. Koren, R. Bell, and C. Volinsky. Matrix factorization techniques for recommender systems. *Computer*, 42(8):30–37, 2009.

[8] J. Mangalindan. Amazon's recommendation secret. `http://tech.fortune.cnn.com/2012/07/30/amazon-5` CNN Money, 2012.

[9] F. Niu, B. Recht, C. Ré, and S. J. Wright. Hogwild!: A lock-free approach to parallelizing stochastic gradient descent. *Advances in Neural Information Processing Systems*, 24:693–701, 2011.

[10] B. Recht and C. Ré. Parallel stochastic gradient algorithms for large-scale matrix completion. *Mathematical Programming Computation*, 5(2):201–226, 2013.

[11] X. Su and T. M. Khoshgoftaar. A survey of collaborative filtering techniques. *Advances in Artificial Intelligence*, 2009:4, 2009.

[12] G. Takács, I. Pilászy, B. Németh, and D. Tikk. Scalable collaborative filtering approaches for large recommender systems. *The Journal of Machine Learning Research*, 10:623–656, 2009.

[13] C. Teflioudi, F. Makari, and R. Gemulla. Distributed matrix completion. In *International Conference on Data Mining*, 2012.

[14] J. N. Tsitsiklis, D. P. Bertsekas, M. Athans, et al. Distributed asynchronous deterministic and stochastic gradient optimization algorithms. *IEEE transactions on automatic control*, 31(9):803–812, 1986.

[15] Y. Zhou, D. Wilkinson, R. Schreiber, and R. Pan. Large-scale parallel collaborative filtering for the netflix prize. In *Algorithmic Aspects in Information and Management*, pages 337–348. Springer, 2008.

[16] Y. Zhuang, W.-S. Chin, Y.-C. Juan, and C.-J. Lin. A fast parallel sgd for matrix factorization in shared memory systems. In *Proceedings of the 7th ACM conference on Recommender systems*, 2013.

A Framework for Matrix Factorization Based on General Distributions

Josef Bauer
Katholische Universität Eichstätt-Ingolstadt
Auf der Schanz 49
85049 Ingolstadt, Germany
josef.bauer@ku.de

Alexandros Nanopoulos
Katholische Universität Eichstätt-Ingolstadt
Auf der Schanz 49
85049 Ingolstadt, Germany
alexandros.nanopoulos@ku.de

ABSTRACT

In this paper we extend the current state-of-the-art matrix factorization method for recommendations to general probability distributions. As shown in previous work, the standard method called "Probabilistic Matrix Factorization" is based on a normal distribution assumption. While there exists work in which this method is extended to other distributions, these extensions are restrictive and we experimentally show on the basis of a real data set that it is worthwhile considering more general distributions which have not been used in the literature. Our contribution lies in providing a flexible and easy-to-use framework for matrix factorization with almost no limitation on the form of the distribution used. Our approach is based on maximum likelihood estimation and a key ingredient of our proposed method is automatic differentiation. This allows for the automatic derivation of the corresponding optimization algorithm, without the need to derive it manually for each distributional assumption while simultaneously being computationally efficient. Thus, with our method it is very easy to use a wide range of even complicated distributions for any data set.

Categories and Subject Descriptors

H.3.3 [**Information Search and Retrieval**]: Information filtering

Keywords

Machine Learning; Matrix Factorization; Maximum Likelihood; Automatic Differentiation

1. INTRODUCTION

Matrix factorization (MF) is a model-based collaborative filtering method that has shown its ability to build accurate prediction models for recommender systems [7]. MF generates recommendations based on latent features of users and items that determine the preferences of users for given items. The only required information to apply MF is the past behavior of users. A state-of-the-art matrix factorization method is the Probabilistic Matrix Factorization (PMF) [13], which relies on a normal distribution assumption.

Our key innovation lies in providing a flexible framework that extends PMF to almost arbitrary probability distributions. Although there exist relevant extensions of PMF to other distributions in previous work, which we discuss in Section 2, these extensions are limited. As we show by using a real quantitative implicit feedback data set, the prediction accuracy can indeed be improved by considering more general distributions. While on the one hand we provide an algorithmic framework that enables the use of general distributions, we address on the other hand the applicability of this framework by automating it, thus overcoming the need to handle each distribution manually.

One important finding is that the estimation method for all the different models with various distributional assumptions take almost the same form, in which the partial derivatives of the particular density function are the only difference. A key advantage of our approach is automatic differentiation, with which it is possible that the corresponding optimization algorithm for every distribution is derived automatically. The way we use automatic differentiation, in particular forward-mode automatic differentiation, can be seen as a source code transformation. Hereby, the relevant functional expressions in symbolical form are parsed and known differentiation rules are applied inductively. These transformed expressions can then be used to automatically generate a function which depends on the same parameters as the original function and the output of this new function will be the same as the respective derivative of the original function. This function can then be called by the program. This way, no numerical approximation of the derivatives is needed and this has to be done only once for each distribution model, which makes it efficient. Particularly, the running time and memory requirements do not increase more strongly with the size of the data then manually coded analogues. More details on its theoretical background can be found, for example, in section 8.2 of [9].

The rest of this paper is organized as follows. First, we discuss related work in Section 2 and introduce standard PMF in Section 3.1. Then we present our problem formulation and modeling approach in Section 3.2. Afterwards, we present our parameter estimation approach based on the statistical method of maximum likelihood and the corresponding gradient-based optimization method in Sections 4.1 and 4.2, respectively. After addressing how predictions can be generated in Section 4.3 and outlining promis-

RecSys'14, October 6–10, 2014, Foster City, Silicon Valley, CA, USA.
Copyright 2014 ACM 978-1-4503-2668-1/14/10 ...$15.00.
http://dx.doi.org/10.1145/2645710.2645735.

ing applications in Section 4.4, we focus on the experiments in Section 5. Finally, we conclude with a summary and a discussion of future work in Section 6.

2. RELATED WORK

As we mentioned previously, our proposed method can be seen as an extension of the standard matrix factorization method PMF [13], which assumes a normal distribution, to almost arbitrary distributions. There are other approaches in the literature that extended PMF in several directions. Closely related to our method is the work of [15]. There it is shown that PMF can be extended to a more general MF framework which comprises many common models. The underlying distribution does not need to be normal in this case, but is allowed to be a member of the natural exponential family with a single variable parameter. The subsumed models in this setting can be described equivalently by a few modeling choices. Basically, this approach can be seen as a combination of MF and Generalized Linear Models (GLMs). Thereby, one can obtain a unified estimation method which corresponds to the minimization of a specific Bregman divergence that depends on the distribution. However, assuming that the distribution is from the natural exponential family is still restrictive. Our general approach does not make this assumption. For instance, in our experiments we investigate (among others) the log-normal and Pareto distributions. The log-normal distribution in particular achieves the best performance in our results. It belongs to the general exponential family, but is not a member of the natural exponential family, which corresponds to the definition of a regular exponential family in [15]. Thus, this distribution is not part of the framework provided in [15] like many other distributions, including power law distributions such as the Pareto distribution. Furthermore, in [15] only predictions of the mean are addressed (by using prediction link functions as in GLMs), while we focus on the whole distribution including quantiles such as the median, which is more appropriate when dealing with quantitative implicit feedback (e.g., number of downloads for a song or amount of items sold), because it is more robust. Also, this method is not as flexible while still being easily applicable as our general maximum likelihood approach, since it does not allow for basic transformations of the user-item interactions and the biases and does not make use of computational advantages like automatic differentiation. On the other hand, the framework in [15] provides ways to deal with multi-relational data as well as with constraints on the factor matrices. Future work includes extensions of our proposed method that are capable of these additional advantages as well.

Another related generalization concept of standard MF are Factorization Machines (FMs) [11, 12] and special cases of them like in [3]. The main difference to our proposed method is the fact that FMs are developed in terms of certain loss functions and particular losses are proposed for a given task. For instance, squared loss for all kinds of regression, which corresponds to a normal distribution assumption like in PMF, regardless of the actual distribution of the data. In contrast, our method relies on flexible probability distributions than can be chosen in accordance with the data and we show that it is indeed beneficial not to make such restrictive assumptions as FMs do in this respect. On the other hand, the strength of FMs lies in combining many previously proposed MF models into one customizable framework. By feature engineering, FMs are able to mimic attribute- and context-aware approaches or to include other side information like temporal information etc. In fact, due to these advantages it is promising for future work to extend our proposed method with the benefits provided by FMs.

Furthermore, there exists work related to our application in which we focus on implicit feedback in the form of count data. According to [6], one can deal with implicit feedback in the form of frequency data by thresholding. Here, one only distinguishes whether a count value is below a fixed threshold or not, which results in binary implicit feedback. Other approaches in the literature deal directly with count data. [4] considers an advertisement problem setting, [8] addresses web site recommendations and [5] deals with location-based social networks. All these approaches extend the standard PMF model by using a Poisson distribution assumption and more precisely a variant of the GaP-model, which was developed for document data in [2]. Again, the crucial difference to our approach is that these works are based on a single model with a fixed distributional assumption while we provide a flexible framework that allows the use of almost arbitrary distributions. In our experiments we show that this is indeed valuable, since a log-normal distribution is better than a Poisson distribution for our data set. Furthermore, their way of using the Poisson distribution is different from ours. While in [4, 8, 5] gamma priors are assumed, we use L^2-norm-based regularization of the rows of the factor matrices in our application, like it is done in the standard PMF method for a normal distribution. Additionally, we use customer and item biases in our model because in [7] it is shown that this results in improvements of the prediction accuracy for the standard PMF method assuming a normal distribution. Also, we demonstrate that it is worthwhile to use a shifted version of the Poisson distribution instead of the usual one. In contrast to previous work, such adaptions can be easily done within our framework.

3. MODELING APPROACH

3.1 Probabilistic Matrix Factorization Based on a Normal Distribution Assumption

Here, we provide a short summary on the Probabilistic Matrix Factorization method [13], which assumes a normal distribution. In fact, we present an enhancement of this based on [7], which takes biases into account, since these will also be an ingredient in our general framework. This method has proved to be very successful in applications with explicit ratings like the Netflix Million Dollar Prize Challenge. Let us assume we have n users, m items and a user-item matrix $X \in \mathbb{R}^{n \times m}$, in which we identify every user by the row index $i \in \{1, ..., n\}$ and every item by the column index $j \in \{1, ..., m\}$. Each entry X_{ij} of this matrix represents the rating of item j given by user i in case it is available, e.g., measured in 1–5 stars. The goal in this setting is to infer the missing entries given the observed ones. And the key idea in this model is that users and items can be characterized by "latent features". For instance, this could be the preference for a certain genre of music and the corresponding feature of the item (song) represents the extent it belongs to this genre. However, no apriori assumptions are needed on the type of the features, but they are learned by the algorithm. Now, suppose there exist $k \in \mathbb{N}$ latent features. We store these features for all users in a matrix $U \in \mathbb{R}^{n \times k}$ and for all items in a matrix $V \in \mathbb{R}^{m \times k}$. Hereby, the interaction between user i and item j is modeled by the dot product of the corresponding feature vectors, namely $U_{i.}V_{j.}^T = \sum_{l=1}^{k} U_{il}V_{jl}$, where $U_{i.}$ denotes the i-th row of U, $V_{j.}$ the j-th row of V and V^T is the transpose of matrix V. In this model, a higher value of $U_{i.}V_{j.}^T$ means a higher preference of user i for item j, which in turn suggests a higher value of the expected rating X_{ij}. In many cases, however, this expected rating will not only depend on such an interaction, but it can partly be explained by characteristics that depend only on the user or the item. Some users tend to rate items higher than others and some items are overall more popular than the remaining ones. Thus, biases are included to capture these effects, which are modeled as variables representing the deviations between the average rating of a particular user or item and the overall mean rating μ. Let us denote by $b_{U_{i.}} \in \mathbb{R}$ the bias of user i and by $b_{V_{j.}} \in \mathbb{R}$ the bias of item j. As shown in [13], the standard method can be derived by assuming a normal distribution of all ratings. In this model, missing ratings are not included in the optimization. If we denote by $\mathcal{O}$ the set of observed rating values, by this approach the maximization of the corresponding likelihood function is equivalent to the following optimization problem:

$$\underset{U,V,b_U,b_V}{\arg\min} \sum_{(i,j):\, X_{ij} \in \mathcal{O}} \Bigg(\left(X_{ij} - U_{i.}V_{j.}^T - \mu - b_{U_{i.}} - b_{V_{j.}} \right)^2 + \lambda \left(\sum_{l=1}^{k} \left((U_{il})^2 + (V_{jl})^2 \right) + (b_{U_{i.}})^2 + (b_{V_{j.}})^2 \right) \Bigg) \tag{1}$$

In (1), $\lambda > 0$ is a constant adjusting the influence of the regularization term in order to prevent overfitting. The model parameters that have to be estimated are given by the latent feature matrices U and V as well as the bias vectors b_U of the n user biases and b_V of the m item biases. A common method to solve this is stochastic gradient descent, which we describe below in a more general fashion.

3.2 Problem Statement and Modeling

Now, we focus on generalizing PMF to a framework that allows for the automatic use of general distributions. As mentioned in Section 2, previous work extended standard PMF to natural exponential family distributions with one real-valued parameter. However, this is still a major limitation on the possible distributions. In contrast, in our framework there is almost no restriction on the distribution. And in Section 4.2 we show that this generalization can be accomplished without additional costs by using automatic differentiation to derive the corresponding optimization algorithm. We keep the same notation as before and now treat each rating X_{ij} of item j by user i as a realization of a random variable whose distribution is determined by the corresponding probability density function $f(. \mid \theta_{ij}, \vartheta)$, with a hyperparameter ϑ and a user and item dependent parameter θ_{ij} which is specified below. The specific value θ_{ij} of the variable parameter θ determines the form of the distribution for the rating of item j by user i. In general, θ can represent a vector, so that we have in fact multiple user and item dependent parameters. This way, almost any distribution can be modeled. In our application with quantitative implicit feedback, we use for example the log-normal and the Pareto distribution, which are not from the natural exponential family. One promising example for future work with explicit feedback is the skew normal distribution, which is a generalization of the normal distribution that is able to deal with positive and negative skewness. For simplicity of presentation, in the following we focus on a real-valued parameter θ. For a vector-valued parameter θ, the same framework applies, whereby each component of this vector is treated the same way as described below. In this case, in each step of the algorithm the updates of the parameters corresponding to each component can be done successively while the remaining parameters are fixed. In our experiments, we have also used a real-valued parameter θ. Future work will investigate more complex distributions with θ being a parameter vector. While in classical PMF the ratings usually represent explicit ratings from a discrete set, we consider real-valued X_{ij} that can, for example, arise implicitly. In particular, in our experiments we focus on the case of quantitative implicit feedback data in the form counts, where $X_{ij} \in \mathbb{N}_0$. (For consistency with existing literature we still refer to such counts as ratings, also assuming that higher count values –e.g., number of downloads for a song– express higher preference.) We assume that all X_{ij} are independent and we require that $\theta \mapsto f(x \mid \theta, \vartheta)$ is differentiable for every fixed x, although some nondifferentiable points could be dealt with by subgradient methods. By differentiability, the existence of the corresponding partial derivatives in the gradient descent-based optimization method in Section 4.2 is ensured. This assumption is satisfied for most distributions in general and for all that are used in the present paper.

For the specification of each parameter θ_{ij}, we use the same building blocks as in the standard method, namely the user-item interaction $U_{i.}V_{j.}^T$ and the bias term $\mu + b_{U_{i.}} + b_{V_{j.}}$, where in our case the number μ can problem dependent represent an average (like the mean or median) or zero. However, we will not only focus on the sum of both parts, but rather consider a transformation of both ingredients. For this purpose, in the following let τ denote a transformation function which maps the bias term and the user-item interaction to a real number, i.e., $\tau : \mathrm{dom}(\tau) \subseteq \mathbb{R}^2 \to \mathbb{R}, (x, y) \mapsto \tau(x, y)$, and we require that τ is differentiable with respect to x and y. This transformation function can be used for reparameterization purposes, for instance to allow the convenient calculation of a target measure of interest. Appropriate choices of τ for different distributions and targets will become clear below in Section 4.3. Often, for example in case of a normal distribution, we can simply set $\tau(x, y) = x + y$, which leads to the same form as in standard PMF with biases. We then model every θ_{ij} by this transformation, therefore having

$$\theta_{ij} = \tau\left(U_{i.}V_{j.}^T, \mu + b_{U_{i.}} + b_{V_{j.}} \right). \tag{2}$$

4. MAXIMUM LIKELIHOOD ESTIMATION BASED ON AUTOMATIC DIFFERENTIATION AND GENERATION OF PREDICTIONS

In the following, we first derive our maximum likelihood-based objective function and afterwards we develop an efficient (stochastic) gradient-based learning algorithm which uses automatic differentiation as a key ingredient. Finally, we address the generation of predictions.

4.1 Maximum Likelihood-based Problem Formulation

Under the assumption that the X_{ij} are independent, the joint density factorizes into the product of all marginal densities. Thus, in this general fashion, this leads at first to the following maximum likelihood optimization problem:

$$\arg\max_{U,V,b_U,b_V} \left(\prod_{\substack{i\in\{1,..,n\},\\ j\in\{1,..,m\}}} f\left(X_{ij}\,|\theta_{ij},\vartheta\right) \right), \tag{3}$$

where θ_{ij} is given by (2) and we are initially assuming that all X_{ij} are observed and equally important. In (3), the X_{ij} denote observed values of the corresponding random variables, e.g., concrete explicit or implicit ratings. For the parameter estimation, we minimize the negative log-likelihood function, since this is equivalent to maximizing the likelihood function and the resulting sums are more convenient. Furthermore, we also use regularization in order to prevent overfitting. In a more general formulation, let $R_{ij} \in \mathbb{R}_0^+$ denote the regularization term for all parameters associated with X_{ij}, which are given by $U_{i.}$, $b_{U_{i.}}$, $V_{j.}$ and $b_{V_{j.}}$. Additionally, we use observation weights $W_{ij} \in \mathbb{R}_0^+$ for $i \in \{1,..,n\}$ and $j \in \{1,..,m\}$ in order to handle cases when certain observations are more important than others. By this approach, the negative log-likelihood minimization problem becomes:

$$\arg\min_{U,V,b_U,b_V} \left(- \sum_{(i,j):\,W_{ij}>0} \left(W_{ij} \log\left(f\left(X_{ij}\,|\theta_{ij},\vartheta\right)\right) - R_{ij}\right) \right) \tag{4}$$

Here, the summation is done over all user-item pairs (i, j) for which the corresponding observations X_{ij} have non-zero weights. In our experiments, where the X_{ij} are count data, we have used either $W_{ij} = 0$ (in case of missing values, noise and outliers) or $W_{ij} = 1$, meaning that we include the observation X_{ij} and treat all of the included observations equally. Furthermore, for simplicity we have used the common way of L^2-norm-based regularization given by

$$R_{ij} := \lambda \left(\sum_{l=1}^{k} \left((U_{il})^2 + (V_{jl})^2\right) + \left(b_{U_{i.}}\right)^2 + \left(b_{V_{j.}}\right)^2 \right), \tag{5}$$

with one regularization constant $\lambda > 0$.

4.2 Gradient-based Optimization Algorithm

First, we derive the gradients with respect to all parameters of our objective function in (4) for a variable density f. Afterwards, we will use these for a gradient descent-based optimization algorithm that can make use of automatic differentiation. Let us denote the objective function in (4) by

$$F\left(U,V,b_U,b_V\right) := - \sum_{(i,j):\,W_{ij}>0} \left(W_{ij} \log\left(f\left(X_{ij}\,|\theta_{ij},\vartheta\right)\right) - R_{ij}\right) \tag{6}$$

After taking partial derivatives and applying the chain rule, we obtain the following gradients (in matrix calculus notation) for every i for which there exists at least one j such that $W_{ij} > 0$ and every j for which exists at least one i such that $W_{ij} > 0$:

$$\frac{\partial}{\partial U_{i.}} F\left(U,V,b_U,b_V\right) = - \sum_{j:\,W_{ij}>0} \left(W_{ij} D_{ij} V_{j.} - \frac{\partial}{\partial U_{i.}} R_{ij} \right) \tag{7}$$

$$\frac{\partial}{\partial V_{j.}} F\left(U,V,b_U,b_V\right) = - \sum_{i:\,W_{ij}>0} \left(W_{ij} D_{ij} U_{i.} - \frac{\partial}{\partial V_{j.}} R_{ij} \right) \tag{8}$$

$$\frac{\partial}{\partial b_{U_{i.}}} F\left(U,V,b_U,b_V\right) = - \sum_{j:\,W_{ij}>0} \left(W_{ij} \widetilde{D}_{ij} - \frac{\partial}{\partial b_{U_{i.}}} R_{ij} \right) \tag{9}$$

$$\frac{\partial}{\partial b_{V_{j.}}} F\left(U,V,b_U,b_V\right) = - \sum_{i:\,W_{ij}>0} \left(W_{ij} \widetilde{D}_{ij} - \frac{\partial}{\partial b_{V_{j.}}} R_{ij} \right), \tag{10}$$

where the coefficients D_{ij} and $\widetilde{D}_{ij}$ are given by

$$D_{ij} = \frac{1}{f\left(X_{ij}\,|\theta_{ij},\vartheta\right)} \cdot \left.\frac{\partial}{\partial \theta} f\left(X_{ij}\,|\,\theta,\vartheta\right)\right|_{\theta=\theta_{ij}} \cdot \left.\frac{\partial}{\partial x} \tau\left(x, \mu + b_{U_{i.}} + b_{V_{j.}}\right)\right|_{x=U_{i.}V_{j.}^T} \tag{11}$$

$$\widetilde{D}_{ij} = \frac{1}{f\left(X_{ij}\,|\theta_{ij},\vartheta\right)} \cdot \left.\frac{\partial}{\partial \theta} f\left(X_{ij}\,|\,\theta,\vartheta\right)\right|_{\theta=\theta_{ij}} \cdot \left.\frac{\partial}{\partial y} \tau\left(U_{i.}V_{j.}^T, y\right)\right|_{y=\mu+b_{U_{i.}}+b_{V_{j.}}}, \tag{12}$$

where θ_{ij} is determined by (2) and $\frac{\partial}{\partial\theta} f\left(X_{ij}\,|\,\theta,\vartheta\right)\big|_{\theta=\theta_{ij}}$ means that the derivative of $f\left(X_{ij}\,|\,\theta,\vartheta\right)$ with respect to θ is evaluated at $\theta = \theta_{ij}$. If we use (5) for regularization, we furthermore have $\frac{\partial}{\partial U_{i.}} R_{ij} = 2\lambda U_{i.}$, $\frac{\partial}{\partial V_{j.}} R_{ij} = 2\lambda V_{j.}$, $\frac{\partial}{\partial b_{U_{i.}}} R_{ij} = 2\lambda b_{U_{i.}}$ and $\frac{\partial}{\partial b_{V_{j.}}} R_{ij} = 2\lambda b_{V_{j.}}$.

In order to solve (4) approximately, we use stochastic/mini-batch gradient descent with momentum. Gradient descent is based on the fact that the negative of a gradient of a multivariate differentiable function points in the direction of steepest descent, thus suggesting a good search direction for a minimum. Stochastic/mini-batch gradient descent are extensions of basic gradient descent that exhibit improved performance and are useful for big data sets. In this case, instead of looping over all the training data indices in a single step, one only loops successively in each step $s \in \mathbb{N}$ of the algorithm over one of some randomly selected disjoint subsets B_s whose union is the full training index set $\{(i,j)\,|\,W_{ij} > 0\}$ and repeats this after one complete pass through the training data. In the so-called "heavy-ball method" [10], an additional momentum term is introduced to increase the speed of convergence. This requires the determination of a suitable learning rate $\varepsilon_s > 0$ and momentum coefficient $\nu_s > 0$. Now, in our case this leads to the following update equations, that are repeated in each step s of the algorithm:[1]

[1] Here, $U^{(s-1)}, V^{(s-1)}, b_U^{(s-1)}, b_V^{(s-1)}$ mean that all the relevant rows/values of step $s-1$ are used. And formally we set $(-1) := (0)$ to make the notation consistent for step 1 of the algorithm.

$$U_{i.}^{(s)} := U_{i.}^{(s-1)} - \varepsilon_s \frac{\partial}{\partial U_{i.}} F(U, V, b_U, b_V)\Big|_{\substack{U=U^{(s-1)},V=V^{(s-1)},\\ b_U=b_U^{(s-1)},b_V=b_V^{(s-1)}}} \quad (13)$$
$$+ \nu_s \left(U_{i.}^{(s-1)} - U_{i.}^{(s-2)}\right)$$

$$V_{j.}^{(s)} := V_{j.}^{(s-1)} - \varepsilon_s \frac{\partial}{\partial V_{j.}} F(U, V, b_U, b_V)\Big|_{\substack{U=U^{(s-1)},V=V^{(s-1)},\\ b_U=b_U^{(s-1)},b_V=b_V^{(s-1)}}} \quad (14)$$
$$+ \nu_s \left(V_{j.}^{(s-1)} - V_{j.}^{(s-2)}\right)$$

$$b_{U_{i.}}^{(s)} := b_{U_{i.}}^{(s-1)} - \varepsilon_s \frac{\partial}{\partial b_{U_{i.}}} F(U, V, b_U, b_V)\Big|_{\substack{U=U^{(s-1)},V=V^{(s-1)},\\ b_U=b_U^{(s-1)},b_V=b_V^{(s-1)}}} \quad (15)$$
$$+ \nu_s \left(b_{U_{i.}}^{(s-1)} - b_{U_{i.}}^{(s-2)}\right)$$

$$b_{V_{j.}}^{(s)} := b_{V_{j.}}^{(s-1)} - \varepsilon_s \frac{\partial}{\partial b_{V_{j.}}} F(U, V, b_U, b_V)\Big|_{\substack{U=U^{(s-1)},V=V^{(s-1)},\\ b_U=b_U^{(s-1)},b_V=b_V^{(s-1)}}} \quad (16)$$
$$+ \nu_s \left(b_{V_{j.}}^{(s-1)} - b_{V_{j.}}^{(s-2)}\right)$$

These updates can be computed using the relations (7)–(10). If stochastic/mini-batch gradient descent is used instead of full gradient descent, the summation in (7)–(10) is done over all i respectively j with $(i,j) \in B_s$ instead of all i respectively j with $W_{ij} > 0$. Furthermore, often a constant learning rate ε and momentum coefficient ν can be used, as we do in our experiments. The first important aspect to note about these updates is the fact that they all have the same form for all possible densities f. At this point, the power of automatic differentiation can be utilized. Given selected functions f and τ, the partial derivatives $\frac{\partial}{\partial \theta} f(X_{ij} \mid \theta, \vartheta)\big|_{\theta=\theta_{ij}}$, $\frac{\partial}{\partial x} \tau(x, \mu + b_{U_{i.}} + b_{V_{j.}})\big|_{x=U_{i.}V_{j.}^T}$ as well as $\frac{\partial}{\partial y} \tau(U_{i.}V_{j.}^T, y)\Big|_{y=\mu+b_{U_{i.}}+b_{V_{j.}}}$ (and the partial derivatives of the R_{ij} if they are chosen to be of a different form than (5)) appearing in (11) and (12) can be determined automatically and efficiently by automatic differentiation. Thus, apart from specifying those functions no additional work for derivation is required from the user and the whole optimization can be done by a computer program. Regarding the initial values, we obtained good results by setting all $b_{U_{i.}}^{(0)}$ and $b_{V_{j.}}^{(0)}$ to zero and all vectors $U_{i.}^{(0)}$ and $V_{j.}^{(0)}$ as random perturbations around zero, with a positivity constraint for distributions for which only positive parameter values are allowed.

4.3 Generation of Predictions

After the model parameters have been estimated in the way described in the previous section, one can calculate statistics of interest and generate predictions for unknown ratings X_{ij}. Let us denote by $\widehat{X}_{ij}$ the estimate of X_{ij}. One reasonable choice would be to use the expected value (mean) of the fitted distribution. If we use the same notation for the corresponding random variable, we have

$$\widehat{X}_{ij} = \mathbb{E}[X_{ij}] = \int_{\mathbb{R}} x f(x \mid \theta_{ij}, \vartheta)\, dx \quad (17)$$

in the continuous case. In the discrete case the integral is replaced by a sum. In (17), θ_{ij} is given by (2), whereby for $U_{i.}$, $V_{j.}$, $b_{U_{i.}}$ and $b_{V_{j.}}$ the values are used that were determined by the algorithm in Section 4.2. However, using the expected value is not always the best choice, and the median of the distribution can be a better target in some applications, since it is more robust. While the sample mean is a minimizer of the mean square error, the sample median minimizes the mean absolute error. Thus, it is plausible that using the median of the fitted distribution instead of the mean will yield better results with respect to mean absolute error as a performance measure. And as we discuss below, in our application in which we deal with count data, mean absolute error is more suitable for evaluation purposes than root mean square error. In the continuous case, if we choose $\widehat{X}_{ij}$ to be the median of the distribution, we can instead calculate it by the following relation:

$$\int_{-\infty}^{\widehat{X}_{ij}} f(x \mid \theta_{ij}, \vartheta)\, dx = \frac{1}{2} \quad (18)$$

An analogous result applies for sums in case of a discrete density. Now the benefit of using an appropriate transformation function τ comes into play. For many distributions analytical expressions for the mean and the median dependent on the parameters are available. By a suitable choice of τ we can often use these and calculate the mean or the median easily and efficiently. In particular, let us define τ as a composition $\tau = g \circ l$ with functions $l : (x, y) \mapsto l(x, y)$ and $g : x \mapsto g(x)$. Hereby, the function l describes how the interplay between bias term and user-item interaction is modeled. The most straightforward choice is $l(x, y) := x + y$, meaning that the user-item interaction is modeled as an additive deviation from the bias baseline. A different ansatz could be, for example, $l(x, y) := \exp\left(\frac{x}{c}\right) \cdot y$, for some constant $c > 0$, whereby the user-item interaction is modeled as a multiplicative deviation from the bias term. In case no user-item interaction is present, i.e., $U_{i.}V_{j.}^T = 0$, both choices simplify to the bias term alone. The function g now has the purpose of being the solution function that is determined by solving the equation of the mean or the median, respectively, for θ_{ij} (i.e., the inverse function of the mean function or median function with respect to θ_{ij}). Therefore, based on the analytical expressions for the mean or median, respectively, that depend on θ_{ij}, we seek for g such that $l\left(U_{i.}V_{j.}^T, \mu + b_{U_{i.}} + b_{V_{j.}}\right)$ is identical to the target we are interested in (the mean or median, respectively). As a specific example consider the log-normal distribution, which we use in our experiments. In this case θ_{ij} is the log-scale parameter and dependent on this parameter, the median is given by $\exp(\theta_{ij})$. We choose $l(x, y) := x + y$ and thus we see that the function $g(x) := \log(x)$ satisfies $\exp\left(g\left(l\left(U_{i.}V_{j.}^T, \mu + b_{U_{i.}} + b_{V_{j.}}\right)\right)\right) = U_{i.}V_{j.}^T + \mu + b_{U_{i.}} + b_{V_{j.}}$, so that $U_{i.}V_{j.}^T + \mu + b_{U_{i.}} + b_{V_{j.}}$ indeed is the estimated user-item dependent median, whereby μ is the global median.

The role of g here is similar to the link function in GLMs, but in contrast to the latter it is not limited to natural exponential family distributions and is also allowed to be a map to a different target than the mean (like the median as discussed above).

Now, a big advantage of our approach is that by using computer algebra we can automate the determination of g, too. We only need to specify the expression for the target and by routines for the symbolical solution of equations we can obtain g automatically. In other cases, like when no such a solvable closed-form expression of the target is available, we can instead use numerical integration to approximately solve (17) or (18), respectively, to find $\widehat{X}_{ij}$.

4.4 Flexible Loss Functions as Special Cases

A conceptually different way to approach the problem of generating best recommendations is by using goal-oriented loss functions. In this use case we might not be interested in inferring the precise underlying distribution, but rather impose flexible losses in the form of cost functions that model the problem we have to solve. For example, our objective might arise from a business-oriented perspective. For instance, it might not be as important if an algorithm makes more errors on less valuable customers or products with low profit margin as long as it performs well from a business point of view. There has been related work, such as [1], where profit maximization is addressed, although not in a MF context. A related approach is to directly optimize for ranking functions. The idea behind this is that indicator functions which are hard to deal with can be approximated smoothly like in artificial neural networks, e.g., by a logistic function. There have been particular related approaches in the literature such as [14], in which mean reciprocal rank is addressed.

Problems of this kind can be described by the minimization of a certain distance function, which in turn can be seen as a special case of our framework. Suppose that we construct a distance function $d : \mathbb{R}^2 \to \mathbb{R}_0^+$, $(x, y) \mapsto d(x, y) \geq 0$ which is differentiable with respect to y for every fixed x. Assuming $d(x, x) = 0$ is plausible, but we do not restrict d to be a metric, so it does not have to fulfill symmetry or the triangle inequality. Our goal is then to minimize the deviation $d(X_{ij}, \theta_{ij})$ over all observations (i, j), with θ_{ij} given by (2). This can be described within our probabilistic framework by defining the artificially constructed density as

$$f(x \mid \theta_{ij}) := \frac{1}{C} \exp(-d(x, \theta_{ij})),$$

whereby we require $C := \int_{\mathbb{R}} \exp(-d(x, \theta_{ij}))\, dx < \infty$. So in this case (4) is equivalent to the following problem:

$$\underset{U,V,b_U,b_V}{\arg\min} \sum_{(i,j):\, W_{ij}>0} (W_{ij}\, d(X_{ij}, \theta_{ij}) + R_{ij}) \tag{19}$$

Again, while the approaches in the literature are focusing on particular losses and devise a corresponding algorithm manually, the key advantage of our framework is that one can just specify a loss and the optimization algorithm is created automatically.

Discussing and evaluating possibilities of such flexible loss function approaches is beyond the scope of this paper, but will be addressed in future work. Related to this approach are distributions which are closely connected to common losses, such as the Laplace distribution, which will also be investigated in the future.

5. EXPERIMENTAL EVALUATION

5.1 Implementation Details

We have developed our implementation in R whereby we used just-in-time compilation as well as C++ via the Rcpp library for the most computationally intensive part of our code in order to increase performance. For our implementation of automatic differentiation and the symbolic solution of equations, we used the interface to the Python computer algebra library SymPy. A promising alternative to SymPy is the investigation of Theano, which offers advantageous performance. However, its symbolic computing capabilities and its interface to R are still issues that have to be taken into consideration. In the experiments, we made use of several R built-in quantile functions as we describe in Section 5.3.

5.2 Experimental Setup

For the experimental evaluation of our proposed framework, we use a random sample of the commonly available "Echo Nest Taste Profile Subset". This data set consists of play count records of songs by users. In this case, the value X_{ij} represents the number of times user i listened to song j and can be seen as an implicit rating in the form of count data. We can assume that the higher a play count, the more a user likes the corresponding song. We created a sample by initially randomly selecting 20% of the users of this data set and then restricting to play count values between 3 and 300. The purpose of this filtering is to clean the data set from noise and outliers. Low play counts can occur, for instance, because a user is unaware which type of song is behind a link. Very high play counts, on the other hand, are likely the consequence of some automated mechanism like Web crawlers. Additionally, we filtered out all users and songs for which less than 10 play count records exist in order to strengthen the collaborative effect. After applying this preprocessing, we obtained a random sample consisting of 1,557,337 (user, song, play count)-triplets with 68,119 unique users and 34,032 unique songs. A histogram showing the frequency of the different play count values is depicted in Figure 1. The number of users depending on the number of observations (different songs) per user, as well as the number of songs depending on the observations per song are shown in Figure 2.

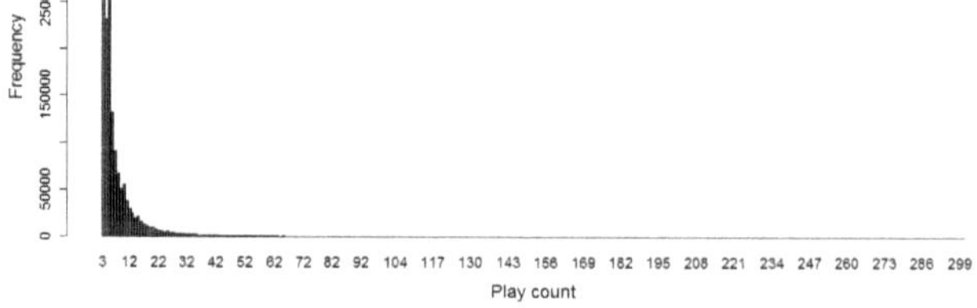

Figure 1: Frequencies of the play count values

We applied our proposed method for different distributions, namely the normal (corresponding to standard PMF), the Poisson, the gamma, the Pareto and the log-normal distribution. For the evaluation, we randomly split the data set into a training part used for model building and a validation

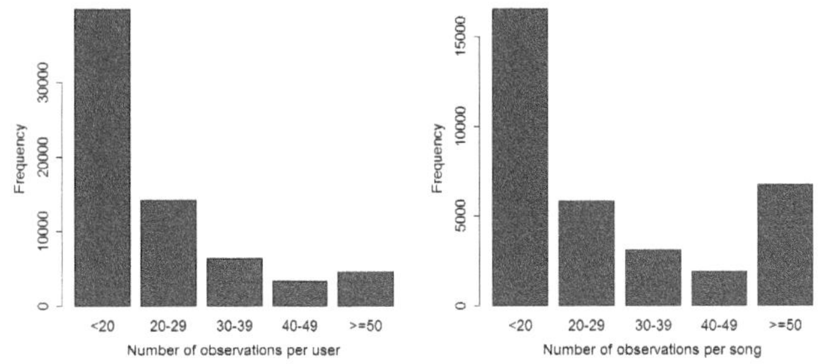

Figure 2: Number of observations per user and song

part used for testing purposes. We used 1, 200, 000 randomly chosen (user, song, play count)-triplets for the training part and the remaining 357, 337 for validation. For all distributions we used 4 randomly selected and equally sized batches. We determined the values of the learning rate ε, the momentum coefficient ν, the regularization parameter λ as well as hyperparameters for distributions which provided the best result on the validation set by the commonly used method of manually adapted grid search. This procedure consists of searching through the joint parameter space with refinements in regions in which good values were found. In the same manner, the initial values were selected as described in Section 4.2. We used the best values obtained for the comparison in the next section. We evaluated the performance of our method for all of the distributions with respect to the frequently used mean absolute error (MAE). If the number of all user-item pairs (i, j) in the validation index set $\mathcal{V}$ is denoted by N and the predicted value of every X_{ij} by $\widehat{X}_{ij}$, this is defined as $\text{MAE}\left(\widehat{X}\right) := \frac{1}{N} \sum_{(i,j)\in\mathcal{V}} \left|X_{ij} - \widehat{X}_{ij}\right|$. In our setting, this is a better choice than root mean square error (RMSE). While RMSE is suitable in cases where the rating range is small, such as 1–5 stars, it is not appropriate in the case of count data where the values can vary in several orders of magnitude. Since in this case the squaring in the RMSE definition implies that only small relative changes in the values can result in large errors.

5.3 Experimental Results

Here, we present the results we obtained in our experiments. We have tried various options and tunings for each of the distributions and report the best values we found. Figure 3 shows the performance with respect to MAE on the validation set for each of the distributions dependent on the epoch, whereby epoch refers to the number of full passes through the training data. The minimum MAE values are summarized in Table 1. The value for the mean corresponds to the MAE when predictions for the validation set are made based on the training data mean. The number of features k is 20 for all distributions. In the case of a normal distribution assumption, for which the mean is identical to the median, we used standard PMF as described in Section 3.1. The best parameter settings in this case are $\varepsilon = 1.7 \cdot 10^{-4}$, $\nu = 0.4$ and $\lambda = 0.25$, which we obtained by the grid search approach described in Section 5.2. Regarding the Poisson distribution, we found that it is beneficial to fit a shifted version by first subtracting the minimum play count value 3. This means that $f_{Pois}\left(X_{ij} - 3 \mid \theta_{ij} = U_{i.}V_{j.}^T + b_{U_{i.}} + b_{V_{j.}}\right)$ (with $\mu = 0$, since θ_{ij} does not correspond to the median in this case) is fitted to determine the parameters and herewith the median is generated by using R's `qpois(0.5,.)` to which 3 is added again for the predictions. In this case, the corresponding best parameter settings are $\varepsilon = 1.7 \cdot 10^{-3}$, $\nu = 0.4$ and $\lambda = 0.2$. For the gamma distribution we used the scale parameter as variable parameter θ_{ij} and treated the additional shape parameter κ as a hyperparameter, whereby the same form for θ_{ij} as in the Poisson case worked best. Analogously, we used the R function `qgamma` to predict each of the medians, since as in the case of a Poisson distribution no closed-form expression for the median exists. The respective best parameter settings are $\varepsilon = 6.7 \cdot 10^{-3}$, $\nu = 0.4$, $\lambda = 0.01$ and $\kappa = 1$. For the Pareto distribution once again the same ansatz for θ_{ij} worked best, this time representing the shape parameter, while we used a value of 3 for the scale parameter. This choice is plausible, because for this distribution the scale parameter is the minimum possible value and this is 3 for our preprocessed data set. Like for the previous distributions, we used R's corresponding function `qpareto` to calculate the medians. Here, the best parameter choices are $\varepsilon = 3.3 \cdot 10^{-4}$, $\nu = 0.4$, $\lambda = 0.15$. Finally, for the log-normal distribution we made use of the fact that in this case there exists a convenient closed-form expression for the median and we used the parameter transformation described in Section 4.3 with which the variable log-scale parameter θ_{ij} is identical to the median. Additionally, we found that using log-scaled biases leads to slight improvements of the MAE for this distribution, although it still performs better than the remaining distributions in the standard form without log-scaled biases. The corresponding parameter settings in this case are $\varepsilon = 1.7 \cdot 10^{-3}$, $\nu = 0.4$, $\lambda = 0.01$, whereby the additional shape parameter is 0.5. Also, if alternatively the same ansatz for θ_{ij} as for the other distributions is used and the predictions are analogously generated by the corresponding quantile function `qlnorm` instead of using the transformation function, it still performed better than the remaining distributions (MAE 3.9586). But using this transformation function approach improved the performance.

As we can see from the experimental results in Table 1, all distributions that are more common to model skewed count data show better performance than the standard PMF method which assumes a normal distribution. The different results for the four remaining distributions can be explained by their different tail characteristics. For instance, the Pareto distribution is a heavy-tailed power law distribution. For given (implicit) rating distributions with a higher average rating this would imply that high values still occur with relatively high probability. But according to the histogram in Figure 1, such high count values do not occur often. Therefore it is reasonable that the Pareto distribution performs worse than the other three distributions. In contrast, a log-normal distribution with a bit lower shape parameter (and thus lower variance) models these characteristics better. Of the four non-normal distributions, the Poisson and the gamma distribution are from the natural exponential family, while the Pareto and the log-normal distribution are not. As discussed in Section 2, previous approaches have been limited to natural exponential family distributions with one variable parameter. The fact that the best result is obtained for a log-normal distribution thus demonstrates that it is indeed worthwhile to consider more general distributions. Furthermore, with our framework it is

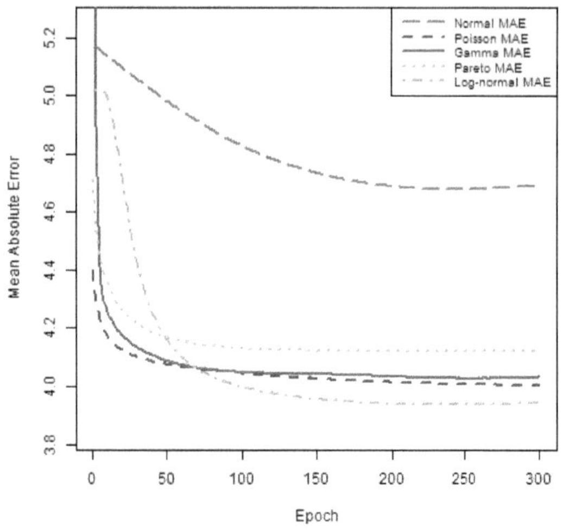

Figure 3: Mean absolute error performance

easy to use modified variants of usual distributions, like predicting the median of a shifted Poisson distribution, which is a different approach from what has been used previously in the literature and indeed turned out to be advantageous.

Table 1: MAE comparison for MF based methods

Method	Minimum MAE achieved
Normal distribution	4.6804
Poisson distribution	4.0038
Gamma distribution	4.0282
Pareto distribution	4.1208
Log-normal distribution	3.9366
Mean	5.1738

6. CONCLUSION

In this paper we have proposed a flexible framework for matrix factorization that allows the use of general distributions. The automatic derivation of the corresponding learning algorithm by means of techniques like automatic differentiation make our framework particularly lucrative in practice. In an application with quantitative implicit feedback we have shown that it is indeed worthwhile to consider broader classes of distributions while different choices can be tested easily and efficiently. Our method opens many directions for future work. This includes the investigation of more complex distributions with multiple parameters, for example in applications with explicit feedback where a normal distribution is likely to be outperformed. This could be the case in online dating, where distributions are often U-shaped, or in settings where the rating distributions are significantly skewed. Furthermore, as we described in Section 4.4, flexible cost functions can be used that allow, for instance, the consideration of business rules. A more extensive evaluation is also needed, e.g., with ranking measures. From a theoretical point of view we plan to extend our framework to allow for constrained optimization, full bayesian inference and Factorization Machines as a building block, whereby side information and temporal dynamics can be incorporated as well as a generalization to tensors. Additionally, we plan to derive theoretical statistical properties of our framework, including the generation of confidence bounds, as well as automated methods to preliminarily determine distributions that are likely to provide good results.

7. REFERENCES

[1] A. Azaria, A. Hassidim, S. Kraus, A. Eshkol, O. Weintraub, and I. Netanely. Movie recommender system for profit maximization. In *Proceedings of the 7th ACM conference on Recommender systems*, pages 121–128. ACM, 2013.

[2] J. Canny. Gap: a factor model for discrete data. In *Proceedings of the 27th annual international ACM SIGIR conference on Research and development in information retrieval*, pages 122–129, 2004.

[3] T. Chen, Z. Zheng, Q. Lu, W. Zhang, and Y. Yu. Feature-based matrix factorization. *arXiv preprint arXiv:1109.2271*, 2011.

[4] Y. Chen, M. Kapralov, J. Canny, and D. Pavlov. Factor modeling for advertisement targeting. In *Advances in Neural Information Processing Systems*, pages 324–332, 2009.

[5] C. Cheng, H. Yang, I. King, and M. R. Lyu. Fused matrix factorization with geographical and social influence in location-based social networks. In *AAAI'12: Proceedings of the 26th Conference on Artificial Intelligence*, pages 17–23, 2012.

[6] Y. Hu, Y. Koren, and C. Volinsky. Collaborative filtering for implicit feedback datasets. In *Proceedings of the 8th IEEE International Conference on Data Mining*, pages 263–272, 2008.

[7] Y. Koren, R. Bell, and C. Volinsky. Matrix factorization techniques for recommender systems. *Computer*, 42(8):30–37, 2009.

[8] H. Ma, C. Liu, I. King, and M. R. Lyu. Probabilistic factor models for web site recommendation. In *Proceedings of the 34th international ACM SIGIR conference on Research and development in Information Retrieval*, pages 265–274. ACM, 2011.

[9] J. Nocedal and S. J. Wright. *Numerical Optimization*. Springer, New York, 2nd edition, 2006.

[10] B. T. Polyak. *Introduction to optimization*. Optimization Software New York, 1987.

[11] S. Rendle. Factorization machines. In *Proceedings of the 10th IEEE International Conference on Data Mining*. IEEE Computer Society, 2010.

[12] S. Rendle. Factorization machines with libFM. *ACM Trans. Intell. Syst. Technol.*, 3(3):57:1–57:22, May 2012.

[13] R. Salakhutdinov and A. Mnih. Probabilistic matrix factorization. In *Advances in neural information processing systems 20*, pages 1257–1264, 2008.

[14] Y. Shi, A. Karatzoglou, L. Baltrunas, M. Larson, N. Oliver, and A. Hanjalic. Climf: learning to maximize reciprocal rank with collaborative less-is-more filtering. In *Proceedings of the sixth ACM conference on Recommender systems*, pages 139–146. ACM, 2012.

[15] A. P. Singh and G. J. Gordon. A unified view of matrix factorization models. In *ECML PKDD*, pages 358–373. Springer, 2008.

Speeding Up the Xbox Recommender System Using a Euclidean Transformation for Inner-Product Spaces

Yoram Bachrach
Microsoft Research

Yehuda Finkelstein
Microsoft R&D

Ran Gilad-Bachrach
Microsoft Research

Liran Katzir
Computer Science, Technion

Noam Koenigstein
Microsoft R&D

Nir Nice
Microsoft R&D

Ulrich Paquet
Microsoft Research

ABSTRACT

A prominent approach in collaborative filtering based recommender systems is using dimensionality reduction (matrix factorization) techniques to map users and items into low-dimensional vectors. In such systems, a higher inner product between a user vector and an item vector indicates that the item better suits the user's preference. Traditionally, retrieving the most suitable items is done by scoring and sorting all items. Real world online recommender systems must adhere to strict response-time constraints, so when the number of items is large, scoring all items is intractable.

We propose a novel order preserving transformation, mapping the maximum inner product search problem to Euclidean space nearest neighbor search problem. Utilizing this transformation, we study the efficiency of several (approximate) nearest neighbor data structures. Our final solution is based on a novel use of the PCA-Tree data structure in which results are augmented using paths one hamming distance away from the query (neighborhood boosting). The end result is a system which allows approximate matches (items with relatively high inner product, but not necessarily the highest one). We evaluate our techniques on two large-scale recommendation datasets, Xbox Movies and Yahoo Music, and show that this technique allows trading off a slight degradation in the recommendation quality for a significant improvement in the retrieval time.

Categories and Subject Descriptors

H.5 [**Information systems**]: Information retrieval—*retrieval models and ranking, retrieval tasks and goals*

Keywords

Recommender systems, matrix factorization, inner product search, fast retrieval

RecSys'14, October 6–10, 2014, Foster City, Silicon Valley, CA, USA.

ACM 978-1-4503-2668-1/14/10 ...$15.00.
http://dx.doi.org/10.1145/2645710.2645741.

1. INTRODUCTION

The massive growth in online services data gives rise to the need for better information filtering techniques. In the context of recommender systems the data consists of (1) the item catalog; (2) the users; and (3) the user feedback (ratings). The goal of a recommender system is to find for every user a limited set of items that have the highest chance to be consumed. Modern recommender systems have two major parts. In the first part, the learning phase, a model is learned (offline) based on user feedback[1]. In the second part, the retrieval phase, recommendations are issued per user (online). This paper studies the scalability of the retrieval phase (the second part) in massive recommender systems based on matrix factorization. Specifically, we introduce a new approach which offers a trade-off between running time and the quality of the results presented to a user.

Matrix Factorization (MF) is one of the most popular approaches for collaborative filtering. This method has repeatedly demonstrated better accuracy than other methods such as nearest neighbor models and restricted Boltzmann machines [2, 8]. In MF models, users and items are represented by latent feature vectors. A Bayesian MF model is also at the heart of the Xbox recommendation system [16] which serves games, movies, and music recommendations to millions of users daily. In this system, users and items are represented by (low-dimensional) vectors in $\mathbb{R}^{50}$. The quality of the match between a user u represented by the vector $\mathbf{x}_u$ and the item i represented by the vector $\mathbf{y}_i$ is given by the inner product $\mathbf{x}_u \cdot \mathbf{y}_i$ between these two vectors. A higher inner product implies a higher chance of the user consuming the item.

The Retrieval Problem: Ideally, given a user u represented by a vector $\mathbf{x}_u$, all the item vectors $(\mathbf{y}_1, \ldots, \mathbf{y}_n)$ are examined. For each such item vector $\mathbf{y}_i$, its match quality with the user $(\mathbf{x}_u \cdot \mathbf{y}_i)$ is computed, and the items sorted according to their match quality. The items with the highest match quality in the list are then selected to form the final list of recommendations. However, the catalog of items is often too large to allow an exhaustive computation of all the inner products within a limited allowed retrieval time.

The Xbox catalog consists of millions of items of various kinds. If a linear scan is used, millions of inner product computations are required for each single recommendation. The

[1] This phase cannot be done entirely offline when a context is used to issue the recommended items.

user vectors can take into account contextual information[2] that is only available during user engagement. Hence, the complete user vector is computed *online* (at runtime). As a result, the retrieval of the recommended items list can only be performed online, and cannot be pre-computed offline. This task constitutes the single most computational intensive task imposed on the online servers. Thereby, having a fast alternative for this process is highly desirable.

Our Contribution: This paper shows how to significantly speed up the recommendation retrieval process. The optimal item-user match retrieval is relaxed to an approximate search: retrieving items that have a high inner product with the user vector, but not necessarily the highest one. The approach combines several building blocks. First, we define a novel transformation from the inner product problem to a Euclidean nearest neighbor problem (Section 3). As a pre-processing step, this transformation is applied to the item vectors. During item retrieval, another transformation is applied to the user vector. The item with the smallest Euclidean distance in the transformed space is then retrieved. To expedite the nearest neighbor search, the PCA-Tree [21] data structure is used together with a novel neighborhood boosting scheme (Section 4).

To demonstrate the effectiveness of the proposed approach, it is applied to an Xbox recommendations dataset and the publicly available Yahoo Music dataset [8]. Experiments show a trade-off curve of a slight degradation in the recommendation quality for a significant improvement in the retrieval time (Section 5). In addition, the achievable time-accuracy trade-offs are compared with two baseline approaches, an implementation based on Locality Sensitive Hashing [1] and the current state of the art method for approximate recommendation in matrix-factorization based CF systems [13]. We show that for a given required recommendation quality (accuracy in picking the optimal items), our approach allows achieving a much higher speedup than these alternatives.

Notation: We use lower-case fonts for scalars, bold lower-case fonts for vectors, and bold upper-case fonts for matrices. For example, x is a scalar, $\mathbf{x}$ is a vector, and $\mathbf{X}$ is a matrix. Given a vector $\mathbf{x} \in \mathbb{R}^d$, let x_i be the measure in dimension i, with $(x_1, x_2, \ldots, x_d)^T \in \mathbb{R}^d$. The norm is denoted by $\|\cdot\|$; in Euclidean space $\|\mathbf{x}\| = \sqrt{\sum_{i=1}^{d} x_i^2}$. We denote by $\mathbf{x} \cdot \mathbf{y}$ a dot product (inner product) between $\mathbf{x}$ and $\mathbf{y}$. Finally, we use $\left(a, \mathbf{x}^T\right)^T$ to denote a concatenation of a scalar a with a vector $\mathbf{x}$.

2. BACKGROUND AND RELATED WORK

In this section we will explain the problem of finding best recommendations in MF models and review possible approaches for efficient retrieval of recommendations.

2.1 Matrix Factorization Based Recommender Systems

In MF models, each user u is associated with a user-traits vector $\mathbf{x}_u \in \mathbb{R}^d$, and each item i with an item-traits vector $\mathbf{y}_i \in \mathbb{R}^d$. The predicted rating of a user u to an item i is denoted by $\hat{r}_{ui}$ and obtained using the rule:

$$\hat{r}_{ui} = \mu + b_u + b_i + \mathbf{x}_u \cdot \mathbf{y}_i \,, \tag{1}$$

[2]The contextual information may include the time of day, recent search queries, etc.

where μ is the overall mean rating value and b_i and b_u represent the item and user biases respectively. The above model is a simple baseline model similar to [14]. It can be readily extended to form the core of a variety of more complex MF models, and adapted to different kinds of user feedback.

While μ and b_i are important components of the model, they do not effect the ranking of items for any given user, and the rule $\tilde{r}_{ui} = b_i + \mathbf{x}_u \cdot \mathbf{y}_i$ will produce the same set of recommendations as that of Equation 1. We can also concatenate the item bias b_i to the user vector and reduce our prediction rule to a simple dot product: $\tilde{r}_{ui} = \bar{\mathbf{x}}_u \cdot \bar{\mathbf{y}}_i$, where $\bar{\mathbf{x}}_u \triangleq (1,\ \mathbf{x}_u^T)^T$, and $\bar{\mathbf{y}}_i \triangleq (b_i,\ \mathbf{y}_i^T)^T$. Hence, computing recommendations in MF models amounts to a simple search in an inner product space: given a user vector $\bar{\mathbf{x}}_u$, we wish to find items with vectors $\bar{\mathbf{y}}_i$ that will maximize the inner product $\bar{\mathbf{x}}_u \cdot \bar{\mathbf{y}}_i$. For the sake of readability, from this point onward we will drop the bar and refer to $\bar{\mathbf{x}}_u$ and $\bar{\mathbf{y}}_u$ as $\mathbf{x}_u$ and $\mathbf{y}_i$. We therefore focus on the problem of finding maximal inner product matches as described above.

2.2 Retrieval of Recommendations in Inner-Product Spaces

The problem of efficient retreival of recommendations in MF models is relatively new, but it has been discussed in the past [10, 11, 13]. In real-world large scale systems such as the Xbox Recommender, this is a concrete problem, and we identified it as the main bottleneck that drains our online resources.

Previous studies can be categorized into two basic approaches. The first approach is to propose new recommendation algorithms in which the prediction rule is not based on inner-product matches. This was the approach taken by Khoshneshin et al. [10], who were first to raise the problem of efficient retrieval of recommendations in MF models. In [10] a new model is proposed in which users and items are embedded based on their Euclidean similarity rather than their inner-product. In a Euclidean space, the plethora of algorithms for nearest-neighbor search can be utilized for an efficient retrieval of recommendations. A similar approach was taken by [11] where an item-oriented model was designed to alleviate retrieval of recommendations by embedding items in a Euclidean space. While these methods show significant improvements in retrieval times, they deviate from the well familiar MF framework. These approaches which are based on new algorithms do not benefit the core of existing MF based recommender systems in which the retrieval of recommendations is still based on inner-products.

The second approach to this problem is based on designing new algorithms to mitigate maximal inner-product search. These algorithms can be used in any existing MF based system and require only to implement a new data structure on top of the recommender to assist at the retrieval phase. For example, in [13] a new IP-Tree data structure was proposed that enables a branch-and-bound search scheme in inner-product spaces. In order to reach higher speedup values, the IP-Tree was combined with spherical user clustering that allows to pre-compute and cache recommendations to similar users. However, this approach requires prior knowledge of all the user vectors which is not available in systems such as the Xbox recommender where ad-hoc contextual information is used to update the user vectors. This work was later continued in [18] for the general problem of maximal inner-product search, but these extensions showed effectiveness in high-dimensional sparse datasets which is not the case for vectors generated by a MF process.

This paper builds upon a novel transformation that reduces the maximal inner-product problem to simple nearest neighbor search in a Euclidean space. On one hand the proposed approach can be employed by any classical MF model, and on the other hand it enables using any of the existing algorithms for Euclidean spaces. Next, we review several alternatives for solving the problem in a Euclidean Space.

2.2.1 Nearest Neighbor in Euclidean Spaces

Locality Sensitive Hashing (LSH) was recently popularized as an effective approximate retrieval algorithm. LSH was introduced by Broder et al. to find documents with high Jaccard similarity[4]. It was later extended to other metrics including the Euclidean distance [9], cosine similarity [5], and earth mover distance [5].

A different approach is based on space partitioning trees: KD-trees [3] is a data structure that partitions $\mathbb{R}^d$ into hyper-rectangular (axis parallel) cells. In construction time, nodes are split along one coordinate. At query time, one can search of all points in a rectangular box and nearest neighbors efficiently. Several augmented splits are used to improve the query time. For example, (1) Principal component axes trees (PCA-Trees) transform the original coordinates to the principal components [21]; (2) Principal Axis Trees (PAC-Trees) [15] use a principal component axis at every node; (3) Random Projection Trees (RPT) use a random axis at each node [6]; and (4) Maximum Margin Trees (MMT) use a maximum margin axis at every node [20]. A theoretical and empirical comparison for some variants can be found [19].

Our approach makes use of PCA-trees and combines it with a novel neighborhood boosting scheme. In Section 5 we compare to alternatives such as LSH, KD-Trees, and PAC-Trees. We do not compare against MMT and RPT as we don't see their advantage over the other methods for the particular problem at hand.

3. REDUCIBLE SEARCH PROBLEMS

A key contribution of this work is focused on the concept of efficient reductions between search problems. In this section we formalize the concept of a search problem and show efficient reductions between known variants.

We define a search problem as:

DEFINITION 1. *A search problem $S(\mathcal{I}, \mathcal{Q}, s)$ consists of an instance set of n items $I = \{i_1, i_2, \ldots, i_n\} \in \mathcal{I}$, a query $\mathfrak{q} \in \mathcal{Q}$, and a search function*

$$s : \mathcal{I} \times \mathcal{Q} \to \{1, 2, \ldots, n\} \ .$$

Function s retrieves the index of an item in I for a given query $\mathfrak{q}$. The goal is to pre-process the items with $g : \mathcal{I} \to \mathcal{I}'$ such that each query is answered efficiently. The pre-processing g can involve a transformation from one domain to another, so that a transformed search problem can operate on a different domain. The following definition formalizes the reduction concept between search problems:

DEFINITION 2. *A search problem $S_1(\mathcal{I}, \mathcal{Q}, s_1)$ is reducible to a search problem $S_2(\mathcal{I}', \mathcal{Q}', s_2)$, denoted by $S_1 \leq S_2$, if there exist functions $g : \mathcal{I} \to \mathcal{I}'$ and $h : \mathcal{Q} \to \mathcal{Q}'$ such that*

$$j = s_1(I, \mathfrak{q}) \ \text{ if and only if } \ j = s_2(g(I), h(\mathfrak{q})) \ .$$

This reduction does not apply any constraints on the running time of g and h. Note that g runs only once as a pre-processing step, while h is applied at the query time. This yields a requirement that h has a $O(1)$ running time. We formalize this with the following notation:

DEFINITION 3. *We say that $S_1 \leq_{O(f(n))} S_2$ if $S_1 \leq S_2$ and the running time of g and h are $O(f(n))$ and $O(1)$ respectively.*

For a query vector in $\mathbb{R}^d$, we consider three search problems in this paper: **MIP**, the maximum inner product from n vectors in $\mathbb{R}^d$ ($\text{MIP}_{n,d}$); **NN**, the nearest neighbor from n vectors in $\mathbb{R}^d$ ($\text{NN}_{n,d}$); **MCS**, the maximum cosine similarity from n vectors in $\mathbb{R}^d$ ($\text{MCS}_{n,d}$). They are formally defined as follows:

Instance: A matrix of n vectors $\mathbf{Y} = [\mathbf{y}_1, \mathbf{y}_2, \ldots, \mathbf{y}_n]$ such that $\mathbf{y}_i \in \mathbb{R}^d$; therefore $\mathcal{I} = \mathbb{R}^{d \times n}$.

Query: A vector $\mathbf{x} \in \mathbb{R}^d$; hence $\mathcal{Q} = \mathbb{R}^d$.

Objective: Retrieve an index according to

$$s(\mathbf{Y}, \mathbf{x}) = \operatorname*{argmax}_i \mathbf{x} \cdot \mathbf{y}_i \qquad \text{MIP}_{n,d}$$

$$s(\mathbf{Y}, \mathbf{x}) = \operatorname*{argmin}_i \|\mathbf{x} - \mathbf{y}_i\| \qquad \text{NN}_{n,d}$$

$$s(\mathbf{Y}, \mathbf{x}) = \operatorname*{argmax}_i \frac{\mathbf{x} \cdot \mathbf{y}_i}{\|\mathbf{x}\| \, \|\mathbf{y}_i\|} \qquad \text{MCS}_{n,d} \ ,$$

where i indicates column i of $\mathbf{Y}$.

The following section shows how transformations between these three problems can be achieved with $\text{MCS}_{n,d} \leq_{O(n)} \text{MIP}_{n,d} \leq_{O(n)} \text{NN}_{n,d+1}$ and $\text{NN}_{n,d} \leq_{O(n)} \text{MCS}_{n,d+1} \leq_{O(n)} \text{MIP}_{n,d+1}$.

3.1 Order Preserving Transformations

The triangle inequality does not hold between vectors $\mathbf{x}$, $\mathbf{y}_i$, and $\mathbf{y}_j$ when an inner product compares them, as is the case in **MIP**. Many efficient search data structures rely on the triangle inequality, and if **MIP** can be transformed to **NN** with its Euclidian distance, these data structures would immediately become applicable. Our first theorem states that **MIP** can be reduced to **NN** by having an Euclidian metric in one more dimension than the original problem.

THEOREM 1. $\text{MIP}_{n,d} \leq_{O(n)} \text{NN}_{n,d+1}$

Proof: Let $\phi \triangleq \max_i \|\mathbf{y}_i\|$ and preprocess input with: $\tilde{\mathbf{y}}_i = g(\mathbf{y}_i) = \left(\sqrt{\phi^2 - \|\mathbf{y}_i\|^2}, \mathbf{y}_i^T\right)^T$. During query time: $\tilde{\mathbf{x}} = h(\mathbf{x}) = \left(0, \mathbf{x}^T\right)^T$. As

$$\|\tilde{\mathbf{x}}\|^2 = \|\mathbf{x}\|^2$$

$$\|\tilde{\mathbf{y}}_i\|^2 = \phi^2 - \|\mathbf{y}_i\|^2 + \|\mathbf{y}_i\|^2 = \phi^2$$

$$\tilde{\mathbf{x}} \cdot \tilde{\mathbf{y}}_i = \sqrt{\phi^2 - \|\mathbf{x}_i\|^2} \cdot 0 + \mathbf{x} \cdot \mathbf{y}_i = \mathbf{x} \cdot \mathbf{y}_i$$

we have

$$\|\tilde{\mathbf{x}} - \tilde{\mathbf{y}}_i\|^2 = \|\tilde{\mathbf{x}}\|^2 + \|\tilde{\mathbf{y}}\|^2 - 2\tilde{\mathbf{x}} \cdot \tilde{\mathbf{y}}_i = \|\mathbf{x}\|^2 + \phi^2 - 2\mathbf{x} \cdot \mathbf{y}_i \ .$$

Finally, as ϕ and $\mathbf{x}$ are independent of index i,

$$j = \operatorname*{argmin}_i \|\tilde{\mathbf{x}} - \tilde{\mathbf{y}}_i\|^2 = \operatorname*{argmax}_i \mathbf{x} \cdot \mathbf{y}_i \ .$$

■

Theorem 1 provides the main workhorse for our proposed approach (Section 4). In the remaining of this section, we present its properties as well the related transformations.

If it is known that the transformed $\tilde{\mathbf{Y}} = [\tilde{\mathbf{y}}_1, \tilde{\mathbf{y}}_2, \ldots, \tilde{\mathbf{y}}_n]$ is in a manifold, as given above, we might expect to recover $\mathbf{Y}$ by reducing back with $\mathrm{NN}_{n,d} \leq_{O(n)} \mathrm{MIP}_{n,d-1}$. However, in the general case the transformation is only possible by increasing the dimensionality by one again:

THEOREM 2. $\mathrm{NN}_{n,d} \leq_{O(n)} \mathrm{MIP}_{n,d+1}$

Proof: The preprocessing of the input: $\tilde{\mathbf{y}}_i = g(\mathbf{y}_i) = \left(\|\mathbf{y}_i\|^2, \mathbf{y}_i^T\right)^T$. During query time: $\tilde{\mathbf{x}} = h(\mathbf{x}) = \left(1, -2\mathbf{x}^T\right)^T$. We have $\tilde{\mathbf{x}} \cdot \tilde{\mathbf{y}}_i = \|\mathbf{y}_i\|^2 - 2\mathbf{x} \cdot \mathbf{y}_i$. Finally,

$$\begin{aligned} j &= \operatorname*{argmax}_i \tilde{\mathbf{x}} \cdot \tilde{\mathbf{y}}_i = \operatorname*{argmin}_i \|\mathbf{x}\|^2 + \|\mathbf{y}_i\|^2 - 2\mathbf{x} \cdot \mathbf{y}_i \\ &= \operatorname*{argmin}_i \|\mathbf{x} - \mathbf{y}_i\|^2 . \end{aligned}$$

■

MIP search can also be embedded in a **MCS** search by increasing the dimensionality by one:

THEOREM 3. $\mathrm{MIP}_{n,d} \leq_{O(n)} \mathrm{MCS}_{n,d+1}$

Proof: Preprocessing and query transformation are identical to Theorem 1. The preprocessing of the input: $\phi \triangleq \max_i \|\mathbf{y}_i\|$ and let $\tilde{\mathbf{y}}_i = g(\mathbf{y}_i) = \left(\sqrt{\phi^2 - \|\mathbf{y}_i\|^2}, \mathbf{y}_i^T\right)^T$. During query time: $\tilde{\mathbf{x}} = h(\mathbf{x}) = \left(0, \mathbf{x}^T\right)^T$. Finally,

$$j = \operatorname*{argmax}_i \frac{\tilde{\mathbf{x}} \cdot \tilde{\mathbf{y}}_i}{\|\tilde{\mathbf{x}}\| \, \|\tilde{\mathbf{y}}_i\|} = \operatorname*{argmax}_i \frac{\mathbf{x} \cdot \mathbf{y}_i}{\|\mathbf{x}\| \, \phi} = \operatorname*{argmax}_i \mathbf{x} \cdot \mathbf{y}_i .$$

■

However, **MCS** is simply **MIP** searching over normalized vectors:

THEOREM 4. $\mathrm{MCS}_{n,d} \leq_{O(n)} \mathrm{MIP}_{n,d}$

Proof: The preprocessing of the input: $\tilde{\mathbf{y}}_i = g(\mathbf{y}) = \frac{\mathbf{y}_i}{\|\mathbf{y}_i\|}$. During query time: $\tilde{\mathbf{x}} = h(\mathbf{x}) = \mathbf{x}$. Finally,

$$j = \operatorname*{argmax}_i \tilde{\mathbf{x}} \cdot \tilde{\mathbf{y}}_i = \operatorname*{argmax}_i \frac{\mathbf{x} \cdot \mathbf{y}_i}{\|\mathbf{x}\| \, \|\mathbf{y}_i\|} .$$

■

Our final result states that a **NN** search can be transformed to a **MCS** search by increasing the dimensionality by one:

THEOREM 5. $\mathrm{NN}_{n,d} \leq_{O(n)} \mathrm{MCS}_{n,d+1}$

Proof: Same reduction as in Theorem 1. The preprocessing of the input: $\phi \triangleq \max_i \|\mathbf{y}_i\|$ and $\tilde{\mathbf{y}}_i = g(\mathbf{y}_i) = \left(\sqrt{\phi^2 - \|\mathbf{y}_i\|^2}, \mathbf{y}_i^T\right)^T$. During query time: $\tilde{\mathbf{x}} = h(\mathbf{x}) = \left(0, \mathbf{x}^T\right)^T$. Thus by Theorem 1,

$$\begin{aligned} j &= \operatorname*{argmax}_i \frac{\tilde{\mathbf{x}} \cdot \tilde{\mathbf{y}}_i}{\|\tilde{\mathbf{x}}\| \, \|\tilde{\mathbf{y}}_i\|} = \operatorname*{argmax}_i \frac{\mathbf{x} \cdot \mathbf{y}_i}{\|\mathbf{x}\| \, \phi} = \operatorname*{argmax}_i \mathbf{x} \cdot \mathbf{y}_i \\ &= \operatorname*{argmin}_i \|\tilde{\mathbf{x}} - \tilde{\mathbf{y}}_i\|^2 . \end{aligned}$$

■

Next, we utilize Theorem 1 for speeding up retrieval of recommendations in Xbox and other MF based recommender systems.

Algorithm 1 TransformAndIndex($\mathbf{Y}$, d')

```
input: item vectors Y, depth d' ≤ d + 1
output: tree t
compute φ, μ, W
S = ∅
for i = 1 : n do
    ỹ_i = g(y_i) ; S = S ∪ ỹ_i
end for
return T ← PCA-Tree(S, d')
```

4. AN OVERVIEW OF OUR APPROACH

Our solution is based on two components, a reduction to a Euclidian search problem, and a PCA-Tree to address it. The reduction is very similar to that defined in Theorem 1, but composed with an additional shift and rotation, so that the **MIP** search problem is reduced to **NN** search, with all vectors aligned to their principal components.

4.1 Reduction

We begin with defining the first reduction function following Theorem 1. Let $\phi \triangleq \max_i \|\mathbf{y}_i\|$, and

$$\begin{aligned} \mathbf{y}_i^\star &= g_1(\mathbf{y}_i) = \left(\sqrt{\phi^2 - \|\mathbf{y}_i\|^2}, \mathbf{y}_i^T\right)^T \\ \mathbf{x}^\star &= h_1(\mathbf{x}) = \left(0, \mathbf{x}^T\right)^T , \end{aligned} \tag{2}$$

which, when applied to $\mathbf{Y}$, gives elements $\mathbf{y}_i^\star \in \mathbb{R}^{d+1}$. This reduces **MIP** to **NN**. As **NN** is invariant to shifts and rotations in the input space, we can *compose* the transformations with PCA rotation and still keep an equivalent search problem.

We mean-center and rotate the data: Let $\boldsymbol{\mu} = \frac{1}{n}\sum_i \mathbf{y}_i^\star$ be the mean after the first reduction, and $\mathbf{M} \in \mathbb{R}^{d+1 \times n}$ a matrix with $\boldsymbol{\mu}$ replicated along its columns. The SVD of the centered data matrix is

$$(\mathbf{Y}^\star - \mathbf{M}) = \mathbf{W}\mathbf{\Sigma}\mathbf{U}^T ,$$

where data items appear in the columns of $\mathbf{Y}^\star$. Matrix $\mathbf{W}$ is a $(d+1)$ by $(d+1)$ matrix. Each of the columns of $\mathbf{W} = [\mathbf{w}_1, \ldots, \mathbf{w}_{d+1}]$ defines an orthogonal unit-length eigenvector, so that each $\mathbf{w}_j$ defines a hyperplane onto which each $\mathbf{y}_i^\star - \boldsymbol{\mu}$ is projected. Matrix $\mathbf{W}$ is a *rotation* matrix that aligns the vectors to their principal components. [3] We define the centered rotation as our second transformation,

$$\begin{aligned} \tilde{\mathbf{y}}_i &= g_2(\mathbf{y}_i^\star) = \mathbf{W}^T(\mathbf{y}_i^\star - \boldsymbol{\mu}) \\ \tilde{\mathbf{x}} &= h_2(\mathbf{x}^\star) = \mathbf{W}^T(\mathbf{x}^\star - \boldsymbol{\mu}) . \end{aligned} \tag{3}$$

The composition

$$g(\mathbf{y}_i) = g_2(g_1(\mathbf{y}_i)), \quad h(\mathbf{x}) = h_2(h_1(\mathbf{x})) \tag{4}$$

still defines a reduction from **MIP** to **NN**. Using $\tilde{\mathbf{y}}_i = g(\mathbf{y}_i)$, gives us a transformed set of input vectors $\tilde{\mathbf{Y}}$, over which an Euclidian search can be performed. Moreover, after this transformation, the points are rotated so that their components are in decreasing order of variance. Next, we index the transformed item vectors in $\tilde{\mathbf{Y}}$ using a PCA-Tree data structure. We summarize the above logic in Algorithm 1.

[3]Notice that $\mathbf{\Sigma}$ is not included, as the Euclidian metric is invariant under rotations of the space, but not shears.

Algorithm 2 PCA-Tree($\mathcal{S}$, δ)

```
input: item vectors set S, depth δ
output: tree t
if δ = 0 then
    return new leaf with S
end if
j = d + 1 − δ  // principal component at depth δ
m = median({ỹ_ij for all ỹ_i ∈ S})
S_≤ = {ỹ_i ∈ S where ỹ_ij ≤ m}
S_> = {ỹ_i ∈ S where ỹ_ij > m}
t.leftChild = PCA-Tree(S_≤, δ − 1)
t.rightChild = PCA-Tree(S_>, δ − 1)
return t
```

4.2 Fast Retrieve with PCA-Trees

Building the PCA-Tree follows from a the KD-Tree construction algorithm on $\tilde{\mathbf{Y}}$. Since the axes are aligned with the $d+1$ principal components of $\mathbf{Y}^*$, we can make use of a KD-tree constriction process to get a PCA-Tree data structure. The top $d' \leq d+1$ principal components are used, and each item vector is assigned to its representative leaf. Algorithm 2 defines this tree construction procedure.

At the retrieval time, the transformed user vector $\tilde{\mathbf{x}} = h(\mathbf{x})$ is used to traverse the tree to the appropriate leaf. The leaf contains the item vectors in the neighborhood of $\tilde{\mathbf{x}}$, hence vectors that are on the same side of all the splitting hyperplanes (the top principal components). The items in this leaf form an initial candidates set from which the top items or nearest neighbors are selected using a direct ranking by distance.

The number of items in each leaf decays exponentially in the depth d' of the tree. By increasing the depth we are left with less candidates hence trading better speedup values with lower accuracy. The process allows achieving different trade-offs between the quality of the recommendations and an allotted running time: with a larger d', a smaller proportion of candidates are examined, resulting in a larger speedup, but also a reduced accuracy. Our empirical analysis (Section 5) examines the trade-offs we can achieve using our PCA-trees, and contrasts this with trade-offs achievable using other methods.

4.2.1 *Boosting Candidates With Hamming Distance Neighborhoods*

While the initial candidates set includes many nearby items, it is possible that some of the optimal top K vectors are indexed in other leafs and most likely the adjacent leafs. In our approach we propose boosting the candidates set with the item vectors in leafs that are on the "wrong" side in at most one of the median-shifted PCA hyperplane compared to $\tilde{\mathbf{x}}$. These vectors are likely to have a small Euclidean distance from the user vector.

Our PCA-Tree is a complete binary tree of height d', where each leaf corresponds to a binary vector of length d'. We supplement the initial candidates set from the leaf of the user vector, with all the candidates of leafs with a Hamming distance of '1', and hence examine candidates from d' of the $2^{d'}$ leafs. In Section 5.1.1 we show that this approach is instrumental in achieving the best balance between speedup and accuracy.

5. EMPIRICAL ANALYSIS OF SPEEDUP-ACCURACY TRADEOFFS

We use two large scale datasets to evaluate the speedup achieved by several methods:

1. **Xbox Movies** [12] – This dataset is a Microsoft propriety dataset consisting of 100 million binary $\{0,1\}$ ratings of more than 15K movies by 5.8 million users. We applied the method used in [12] to generate the vectors representing items and users.

2. **Yahoo! Music** [8] – This is a publicly available ratings dataset consisting of 252,800,275 ratings of 624,961 items by 1,000,990 users. The ratings are on a scale of 0-100. The users and items vectors were generated by the algorithm in [7].

From both datasets we created a set of item vectors and user vectors of dimensionality $d = 50$. The following evaluations are based on these vectors.

Speedup Measurements and Baselines.

We quantify the improvement of an algorithm A over another (naive) algorithm A_0 by the following term:

$$\text{Speedup}_{A_0}(A) = \frac{\text{Time taken by Algorithm } A_0}{\text{Time taken by Algorithm } A}. \tag{5}$$

In all of our evaluations we measure the speedup with respect to the same algorithm: a naive search algorithm that iterates over all items to find the best recommendations for every user (i.e. computes the inner product between the user vector and each of the item vectors, keeping track of the item with the highest inner product found so far). Thus denoting by T_{naive} the time taken by the naive algorithm we have: $T_{naive} = \Theta(\#\text{users} \times \#\text{items} \times d)$.

The state of the art method for finding approximately optimal recommendations uses a combination of IP-Trees and user cones [13]. In the following evaluation we dubbed this method *IP-Tree*. The IP-Tree approach assumes all the user vectors (queries) are computed **in advance** and can be clustered into a structure of user cones. In many real-world systems like the Xbox recommender the user vectors are computed or updated online, so this approach cannot be used. In contrast, our method does not require having all the user vectors in advance, and is thus applicable in these settings.

The IP-Tree method relies on an adaptation of the branch-and-bound search in metric-trees [17] to handle nearest neighbor search in inner-product spaces. However, the construction of the underlaying metric-tree data structure, which is a space partitioning tree, is not adapted to inner-product spaces (it partitions vectors according to Euclidean proximity). By using the Euclidean transformation of Theorem 1, we can utilize the data structures and algorithms designed for Euclidean spaces in their original form, without adaptations that may curb their effectiveness. Next, we show that our approach achieves a **superior computation speedup**, despite having no access to any prior knowledge about the user vectors or their distribution. [4]

[4]We focus on online processing time, i.e. the time to choose an item to recommend for a target user. We ignore the computation time required by offline preprocessing steps.

Theorem 1 allows using various approximate nearest-neighbor algorithms for Euclidean spaces, whose performance depends on the specific dataset used. We propose using PCA-Trees as explained in Section 4.2, and show that they have an excellent performance for both the Xbox movies and Yahoo! music datasets, consisting of low dimensionality dense vectors obtained by matrix factorization. A different and arguably more popular approach for finding approximate-nearest-neighbors in Euclidean spaces is Locality-Sensitive Hashing (LSH) [1]. In the evaluations below we also include a comparison against LSH. We emphasize that using both our PCA-Trees approach and LSH techniques is only enabled by our Euclidean transformation (Theorem 1).

Our approximate retrieval algorithms introduce a tradeoff between accuracy and speedup. We use two measures to quantify the quality of the top K recommendations. The first measure *Precision@K* denotes how similar the approximate recommendations are to the optimal top K recommendations (as retrieved by the naive approach):

$$Precision@K \triangleq \frac{|L_{rec} \cap L_{opt}|}{K}, \quad (6)$$

where L_{rec} and L_{opt} are the lists of the top K approximate and the top K optimal recommendations respectively. Our evaluation metrics only consider the items at the top of the approximate and optimal lists.[5]

A high value for *Precision* implies that the approximate recommendations are very similar to the optimal recommendations. In many practical applications (especially for large item catalogs), it is possible to have low *Precision* rates but still recommend very relevant items (with a high inner product between the user and item vectors). This motivates our second measure *RMSE@K* which examines the preference to the approximate items compared to the optimal items:

$$RMSE@K \triangleq \sqrt{\frac{1}{K}\sum_{k=1}^{K}\Big(L_{rec}(k) - L_{opt}(k)\Big)^2}, \quad (7)$$

where $L_{rec}(k)$ and $L_{opt}(k)$ are the scores (predicted ratings) of the k'th recommended item in the approximated list and the optimal list respectively. Namely, $L_{rec}(k)$ and $L_{opt}(k)$ are the values of inner products between the user vector and k'th recommended item vector and optimal item vector respectively. Note that the amount $\Big(L_{rec}(k) - L_{opt}(k)\Big)$ is always positive as the items in each list are ranked by their scores.

5.1 Results

Our initial evaluation considers three approximation algorithms: *IP-Tree*, *LSH*, and our approach (Section 4.2). Figure 1(a) depicts *Precision@10* for the Xbox Movies dataset (higher values indicate better performance). The *Precision* values are plotted against the average speedup values they enable. At very low speedup values the LSH algorithm shows the best trade-off between precision and speedup, but when higher speedup values are considered the LSH performance drops significantly and becomes worst. One possible reason for this is that our Euclidean transformation results in transformed vectors with one dimension being very large compared with the other dimensions, which is a difficult input distribution for LSH approaches.[6] In contrast, the tree-based approaches (IP-Tree and our approach) show a similar behavior of a slow and steady decrease in *Precision* values as the speedup increases. The speedup values of our approach offers a better precision-vs-speedup tradeoff than the IP-tree approach, though their precision is almost the same for high speedup values.

[5]Note that for this evaluation the *recall* is completely determined by the *precision*.

Method	Enabled by Theorem 1	Prior knowledge	Neighborhood boosting
IP-Tree	no	user vectors	not allowed
KD-Tree	yes	none	allowed
PCA-Tree	yes	none	allowed
PAC-Tree	yes	none	not allowed

Table 1: A summary of the different tree approaches. IP-Tree is the baseline from [13], which requires prior knowledge of the users vectors. All other approaches (as well as LSH) were not feasible before Theorem 1 was introduced in this paper.

Figure 1(b) depicts the *RMSE@10* (lower values indicate better performance) vs. speedup for the three approaches. The trend shows significantly superior results for our *PCA-Tree* approach, for all speedup values. Similarly to Figure 1(a), we see a sharp degradation of the *LSH* approach as the speedup increases, while the tree-based approaches show a trend of a slow increase in RMSE values as the speedup increases. We note that even for high speed-up values, which yield low precision rates in Figure 1(a), the RMSE values remain very low, indicating that very high quality of recommendations can be achieved at a fraction of the computational costs of the naive algorithm. In other words, the recommended items are still very relevant to the user, although the list of recommended items is quite different from the optimal list of items.

Figure 2 depicts *Precision@10* and *RMSE@10* for the Yahoo! Music dataset. The general trends of all three algorithms seem to agree with those of Figure 1: *LSH* starts better but deteriorates quickly, and the tree-based approaches have similar trends. The scale of the *RMSE* errors in Figure 1(b) is different (larger) because the predicted scores are in the range of 0-100, whereas in the Xbox Movies dataset the predictions are binary.

The empirical analysis on both the Xbox and Yahoo! datasets shows that it is possible to achieve excellent recommendations for very low computational costs by employing our Euclidean transformation and using an approximate Euclidean nearest neighbor method. The results indicate that tree-based approaches are superior to an LSH based approach (except when the required speedup is very small). Further, the results indicate that our method yields higher quality recommendations than the IP-trees approach [13]. Note that we also compared *Precision@K* and *RMSE@K* for other K values. While the figures are not included in this paper, the trends are all similar to those presented above.

5.1.1 *Comparing Different Tree Approaches*

A key building block in our approach is aligning the item vectors with their principal components (Equation 3) and using PCA-Trees rather than KD-Trees. Another essential

[6]The larger dimension is the auxiliary dimension $(\sqrt{\phi^2 - \|\mathbf{y}_i\|^2})$ in Equation 2.

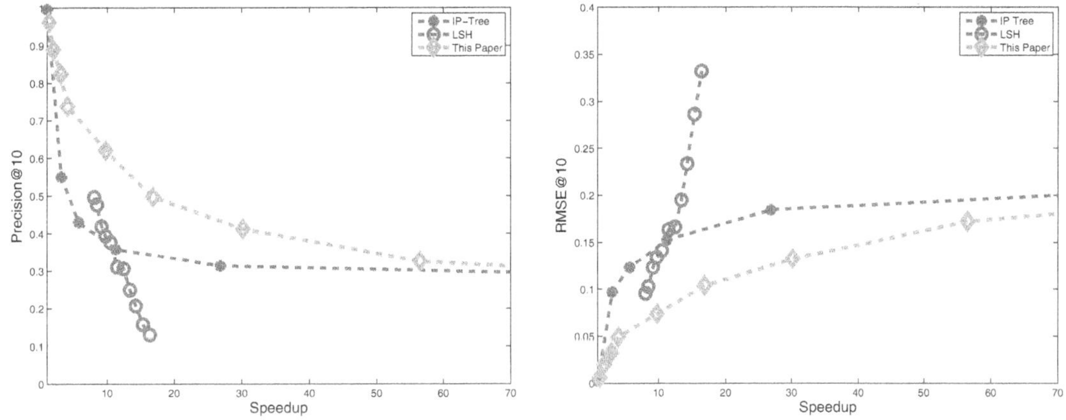

(a) Precision vs. Speedup

(b) RMSE vs. Speedup

Figure 1: Performance against speedup values for the Xbox Movies dataset top 10 recommendations

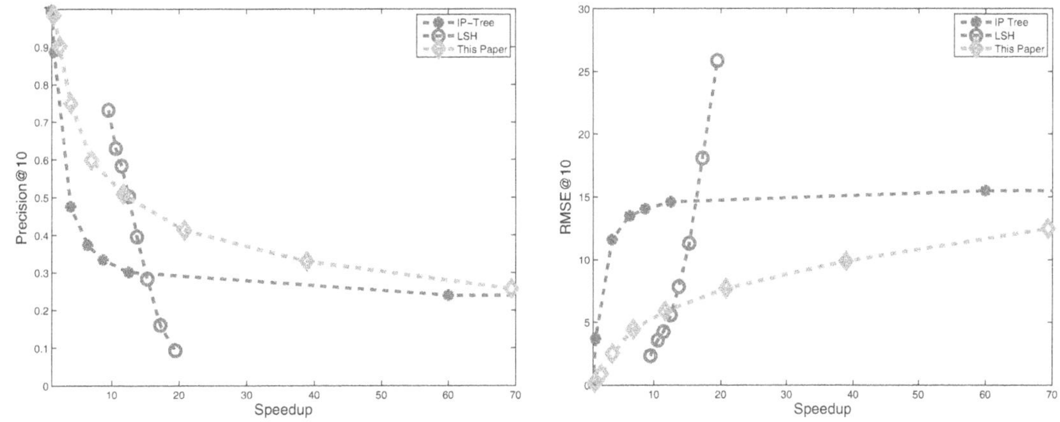

(a) Precision vs. Speedup

(b) RMSE vs. Speedup

Figure 2: Performance against speedup values for the Yahoo! Music dataset top 10 recommendations

ingredient in our approach is the neighborhood boosting of Section 4.2.1. One may question the vitality of PCA-Trees or the neighborhood boosting to our overall solution. We therefore present a detailed comparison of the different tree based approaches. For the sake of completeness, we also included a comparison to *PAC-Trees* [15]. Table 1 summarizes the different data structures. Except the IP-Tree approach, all of these approaches were not feasible before Theorem 1 was introduced in this paper. Note that neighborhood boosting is possible only when the tree splits are all based on a single consistent axis system. It is therefore prohibited in IP-Tees and PAC-Trees where the splitting hyperplanes are ad-hoc on every node.

We compare the approach proposed in this paper with simple KD-Trees, PAC-Trees, and with PCA-Trees without neighborhood boosting (our approach without neighborhood boosting). Figure 3 depicts *Precision@10* and *RMSE@10* on the Yahoo! Music dataset. As the speedup levels increase, we notice an evident advantage in favor of PCA aligned trees over KD-Trees. When comparing PCA-Trees without neighborhood boosting to PAC-Trees we see a mixed picture: For low speedup values PCA-Trees perform better, but for higher speedup values we notice an eminent advantage in favor of PAC-Trees. To conclude, we note the overall advantage for the method proposed in this paper over any of the other tree based alternatives both in terms of *Precision* and *RMSE*.

6. CONCLUSIONS

We presented a novel transformation mapping a maximal inner product search to Euclidean nearest neighbor search, and showed how it can be used to speed-up the recommendation process in a matrix factorization based recommenders such as the Xbox recommender system.

We proposed a method for approximately solving the Euclidean nearest neighbor problem using PCA-Trees, and empirically evaluated it on the Xbox Movie recommendations and the Yahoo Music datasets. Our analysis shows that our approach allows achieving excellent quality recommendations at a fraction of the computational cost of a naive approach, and that it achieves superior quality-speedup tradeoffs compared with state-of-the-art methods.

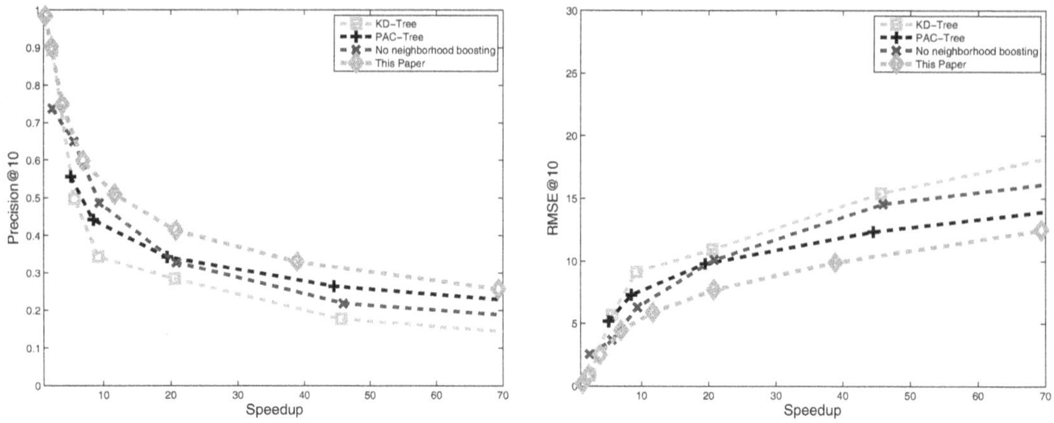

(a) Precision vs. Speedup

(b) RMSE vs. Speedup

Figure 3: Comparing tree based methods for the Yahoo! Music dataset top 10 recommendations

7. REFERENCES

[1] Alexandr Andoni and Piotr Indyk. Near-optimal hashing algorithms for approximate nearest neighbor in high dimensions. In *FOCS*, pages 459–468, 2006.

[2] Robert M. Bell and Yehuda Koren. Lessons from the netflix prize challenge. *SIGKDD Explor. Newsl.*, 2007.

[3] Jon Louis Bentley. Multidimensional binary search trees used for associative searching. *Commun. ACM*, 18(9):509–517, September 1975.

[4] Andrei Broder. On the resemblance and containment of documents. In *Proceedings of the Compression and Complexity of Sequences 1997*, pages 21–29, 1997.

[5] Moses S. Charikar. Similarity estimation techniques from rounding algorithms. In *Proceedings of the Thiry-fourth Annual ACM Symposium on Theory of Computing*, pages 380–388, 2002.

[6] Sanjoy Dasgupta and Yoav Freund. Random projection trees and low dimensional manifolds. In *Proceedings of the Fortieth Annual ACM Symposium on Theory of Computing*, pages 537–546, 2008.

[7] Gideon Dror, Noam Koenigstein, and Yehuda Koren. Yahoo! music recommendations: Modeling music ratings with temporal dynamics and item taxonomy. In *Proc. 5th ACM Conference on Recommender Systems*, 2011.

[8] Gideon Dror, Noam Koenigstein, Yehuda Koren, and Markus Weimer. The Yahoo! music dataset and KDD-Cup'11. *Journal Of Machine Learning Research*, 17:1–12, 2011.

[9] Piotr Indyk and Rajeev Motwani. Approximate nearest neighbors: Towards removing the curse of dimensionality. In *Proceedings of the Thirtieth Annual ACM Symposium on Theory of Computing*, pages 604–613, 1998.

[10] Mohammad Khoshneshin and W. Nick Street. Collaborative filtering via euclidean embedding. In *Proceedings of the fourth ACM conference on Recommender systems*, 2010.

[11] Noam Koenigstein and Yehuda Koren. Towards scalable and accurate item-oriented recommendations. In *Proc. 7th ACM Conference on Recommender Systems*, 2013.

[12] Noam Koenigstein and Ulrich Paquet. Xbox movies recommendations: Variational Bayes matrix factorization with embedded feature selection. In *Proc. 7th ACM Conference on Recommender Systems*, 2013.

[13] Noam Koenigstein, Parikshit Ram, and Yuval Shavitt. Efficient retrieval of recommendations in a matrix factorization framework. In *CIKM*, 2012.

[14] Yehuda Koren, Robert M. Bell, and Chris Volinsky. Matrix factorization techniques for recommender systems. *IEEE Computer*, 2009.

[15] James McNames. A fast nearest-neighbor algorithm based on a principal axis search tree. *IEEE Trans. Pattern Anal. Mach. Intell.*, 23(9):964–976, September 2001.

[16] Ulrich Paquet and Noam Koenigstein. One-class collaborative filtering with random graphs. In *Proceedings of the 22nd international conference on World Wide Web*, WWW '13, pages 999–1008, 2013.

[17] Franco P. Preparata and Michael I. Shamos. *Computational Geometry: An Introduction.* Springer, 1985.

[18] Parikshit Ram and Alexander Gray. Maximum inner-product search using cone trees. In *SIGKDD International Conference on Knowledge Discovery and Data Mining.* ACM, 2012.

[19] Parikshit Ram and Alexander G. Gray. Which space partitioning tree to use for search? In Christopher J. C. Burges, Léon Bottou, Zoubin Ghahramani, and Kilian Q. Weinberger, editors, *NIPS*, pages 656–664, 2013.

[20] Parikshit Ram, Dongryeol Lee, and Alexander G. Gray. Nearest-neighbor search on a time budget via max-margin trees. In *SDM*, pages 1011–1022. SIAM / Omnipress, 2012.

[21] Robert F. Sproull. Refinements to nearest-neighbor searching in k-dimensional trees. *Algorithmica*, 6(4):579–589, 1991.

Gradient Boosting Factorization Machines

Chen Cheng[1,2]*, Fen Xia[3], Tong Zhang[3], Irwin King[1,2], Michael R. Lyu[1,2]
[1] Shenzhen Key Laboratory of Rich Media Big Data Analytics and Applications,
Shenzhen Research Institute, The Chinese University of Hong Kong, Shenzhen, China
[2] Department of Computer Science and Engineering,
The Chinese University of Hong Kong, Shatin, N.T., Hong Kong
[3] Big Data Lab, Baidu Inc., No.10 Shangdi Street, Haidian, Beijing, China
{ccheng,king,lyu}@cse.cuhk.edu.hk {xlafen,tongzhang}@baidu.com

ABSTRACT

Recommendation techniques have been well developed in the past decades. Most of them build models only based on user item rating matrix. However, in real world, there is plenty of auxiliary information available in recommendation systems. We can utilize these information as additional features to improve recommendation performance. We refer to recommendation with auxiliary information as context-aware recommendation. Context-aware Factorization Machines (FM) is one of the most successful context-aware recommendation models. FM models pairwise interactions between all features, in such way, a certain feature latent vector is shared to compute the factorized parameters it involved. In practice, there are tens of context features and not all the pairwise feature interactions are useful. Thus, one important challenge for context-aware recommendation is how to effectively select "good" interaction features. In this paper, we focus on solving this problem and propose a greedy interaction feature selection algorithm based on gradient boosting. Then we propose a novel Gradient Boosting Factorization Machine (GBFM) model to incorporate feature selection algorithm with Factorization Machines into a unified framework. The experimental results on both synthetic and real datasets demonstrate the efficiency and effectiveness of our algorithm compared to other state-of-the-art methods.

Categories and Subject Descriptors

H.1.1 [**Models and Principles**]: Systems and Information Theory; J.4 [**Computer Application**]: Social and Behavior Sciences

Keywords

Gradient Boosting, Factorization Machines, Recommender Systems, Collaborative filtering

*The work was performed when the first author was an intern at Big Data Lab of Baidu Inc..

RecSys'14, October 6–10, 2014, Foster City, Silicon Valley, CA, USA.

ACM 978-1-4503-2668-1/14/10 ...$15.00.
http://dx.doi.org/10.1145/2645710.2645730.

1. INTRODUCTION

Recommendation systems have been well studied in the past decades. Most of them mainly focus on context unaware methods, e.g. only consider user and item interactions. Among them, matrix factorization methods [16, 27] have become popular due to their good performance and efficiency in dealing with larger dataset. These methods focus on approximating user item rating matrix using low rank representations, and use them to make further predictions. However, in real world scenarios, plenty of auxiliary information is available and is proved to be useful especially in large industry datasets. For example, in the Weibo celebrity recommendation scenario, both the user's and celebrity's meta data (such as age and gender), the popularity of a celebrity, the recent following behavior of the user, etc. can help make better recommendations. Recent work in KDDCup 2012 [1] [23, 7] show the effectiveness of utilizing auxiliary information for recommendation.

In regarding of utilizing auxiliary information, several methods have been studied to incorporate meta data (e.g., user profile, movie genre,etc.) [18, 30] and more general auxiliary information such as session information [32, 2, 14, 22, 25]. In these methods, auxiliary information is encoded as features and together with user and item they are mapped from feature space into a latent space. The Factorization Machine (FM) model [25] is currently a very strong and flexible method which easily incorporates any categorical features. However, it is common that there are tens of context features in real data. In FM, all features are assumed to be interacted with all other features. For example, assuming there are n features, then for a certain feature i, the latent vector $\boldsymbol{v}_i$ is shared with $n-1$ interaction features. It is not always the case that all the feature interactions are useful. Useless feature interactions will introduce noise in learning latent feature vector $\boldsymbol{v}_i$. Thus it is challenging to automatically select useful interaction features to reduce noise.

The most recent work in [6] introduced an automatic feature construction method in matrix factorization using gradient boosting. In their method, feature functions are constructed using greedy gradient boosting method and then incorporated into the matrix factorization framework. Different from their method, in our paper, we focus on selecting useful interaction features under factorization machines framework. At each step, we propose a greedy gradient boosting method to efficiently select interaction features, and then we additively optimize the selected latent vector by

[1]http://www.kddcup2012.org/

optimizing the residual loss. Another difference is that our method is more efficient in selecting categorical feature interactions compared to the binary decision tree construction algorithm in [6]. The contribution of our paper is summarized as follows:

- We propose an efficient feature interaction selection algorithm using gradient boosting which can reduce noise compared to factorization machines methods.
- We proposed a novel Gradient Boosting Factorization Machines Model (GBFM) by incorporating the feature selection algorithm with factorization machines into a unified framework.
- The experiment results in both synthetic and real data show the effectiveness of our proposed methods compared to factorization machines and other state-of-the-art methods.

The rest of the paper is organized as follows. Section 2 introduces the related work. Section 3 gives the details of our methods. Section 4 presents the experiment results and discussions. The paper is concluded in Section 5.

2. RELATED WORK

The work present in this paper is closely related to traditional matrix factorization models, context-aware recommendation and gradient boosting. In the following, we briefly review the related work.

2.1 Matrix Factorization

Matrix factorization techniques [29, 4, 16, 27, 2] have been shown to be particularly effective in recommender system as well as the well-known Netflix prize competitions[2]. They usually outperform traditional item-based methods [28]. The main idea behind matrix factorization is to learn two low rank latent matrices $U \in \mathbb{R}^{k\times m}$ and $V \in \mathbb{R}^{k\times n}$ to approximate the observed user item rating matrix $R \in \mathbb{R}^{m\times n}$ so that

$$R \approx U^T V, \tag{1}$$

where m, n are the number of users and items respectively and k is the dimension of low rank matrices.

We assume that the conditional distribution over the observed rating is:

$$p(R|U,V,\sigma_R^2) = \prod_{i=1}^{m}\prod_{j=1}^{n}[\mathcal{N}(R_{ij}|U_i V_j^T, \sigma_R^2)]^{I_{ij}^R}, \tag{2}$$

where $\mathcal{N}(x|\mu,\sigma^2)$ is the probability density function of the Gaussian distribution with mean μ and variance σ^2, and I_{ij}^R is the indicator function that is equal to 1 if user u_i rated item v_j and equal to 0 otherwise. The zero-mean spherical Gaussian priors are also placed on user and item latent feature vectors:

$$p(U|\sigma_U^2) = \prod_{i=1}^{m}\mathcal{N}(U_i|0,\sigma_U^2 \boldsymbol{I}), p(V|\sigma_V^2) = \prod_{j=1}^{n}\mathcal{N}(V_j|0,\sigma_V^2 \boldsymbol{I}), \tag{3}$$

[2]http://www.netflixprize.com

through a Bayesian inference, we have the following objective function:

$$\min_{U,V} \frac{1}{2}\sum_{i=1}^{m}\sum_{j=1}^{n} I_{ij}^R (R_{ij} - U_i V_j^T)^2 + \frac{\lambda_1}{2}\|U\|_F^2 + \frac{\lambda_2}{2}\|V\|_F^2. \tag{4}$$

The above equation can be easily solved either by stochastic gradient descent (SGD) or alternating least squares (ALS).

2.2 Context-aware recommendation

Most traditional matrix factorization method mainly analyze the user item rating matrix thus they are context unaware. Contextual information has proved to be useful in recommender systems and already have been widely studied. In order to incorporate auxiliary information, several variants of matrix factorization have been proposed. In [17, 33], temporal features are explored to help capture user preference more precisely. Socical [20, 13] or location information [35, 8, 9] also have been explored. The meta-data like user age or item genre are incorporated into the matrix factorization model [30, 18]. In addition to the meta-data which is attached to user or item itself, the context features include information attached to the whole recommendation event such as user's mood, day of the week, etc. as well.

The most basic approach for context aware recommendation is to conduct pre-filtering or post-filtering where a standard context-unaware method is applied [21, 1]. Baltrunas et al. [3] proposed a simple model that introduced a basis term for each context feature or item context interaction feature. Context information is encoded in these additional parameters. More generally, Karatzoglou et al. [14] proposed a multiverse recommendation model by modeling the data as a user-item-context N-dimension tensor. Then Tucker decomposition [31] is applied to factorize the tensor. However, the computation complexity of this model is $\Theta(k^m)$ where k is the dimension of low rank vectors and m is the number of features, which is intolerable in practice. Rendle et al. [25] proposed to apply factorization machines (FM) [22] to overcome the problem in Multiverse recommendation. They transform the recommendation data into a prediction problem and FM models all interactions between pairs of features with the target. They further proposed to deal with relational data in [24] through block structure within a feature which have repeating patterns.

The idea of tree based random partition has been explored in [36, 19]. Zhong et al. [36] assumed that contextual information is reflected by user and item latent vectors. In their method, the random tree partition is conducted to split the user item matrix by grouping users and items with similar contexts. Then matrix factorization is applied on the sub-matrices. Liu et al. [19] employ the similar idea but explicitly use context information to split the user item matrix into sub matrices according to specific context values. The prediction is the average values of each prediction from T generate decision trees. However, they fail to discuss how to select useful features especially when there are tens of features.

2.3 Gradient Boosting

Gradient Boosting have been successfully used in classifications [12] and learning to rank [34, 5]. In each step, gradient boosting greedily conducts coordinate descent in the function space to select a feature function. Chen et al. [6] proposed to use gradient boosting method to automatically

(a) Online rating example

	v_1	v_2	v_3	v_4	v_5	v_6
u_1		5	2		3	
u_2	4			3		4
u_3			2			2
u_4	5			3		
u_5		5	5			3

(b) User item rating matrix

	User			Movie				Mood			...	R
$\mathbf{x}^{(1)}$	1	0	0	1	0	0	0	1	0	0	...	4
$\mathbf{x}^{(2)}$	0	1	0	0	1	0	0	0	0	1	...	2
$\mathbf{x}^{(3)}$	1	0	0	0	1	0	0	0	1	0	...	5
$\mathbf{x}^{(4)}$	0	0	1	0	0	1	0	0	0	1	...	1

(c) Context-aware prediction

Figure 1: Context-aware recommendation

construct feature function for each user(item) latent vector at each step. Time dependent feature function and demographic feature function construction is discussed in their work. Different from their work, in our paper, we employ gradient boosting algorithm to find the best feature interaction at each step, then similar to gradient boosting, we additively optimize the latent feature vectors. Besides, in real world, there are many categorical features with large size, the binary tree splitting algorithm in their work is not efficient in deal with such features.

3. GRADIENT BOOSTING FACTORIZATION MACHINES

In this section, we first describe the context-aware recommendation problem we study in this paper and define the notations, and then we briefly review context-aware FMs which is closely related to our work. Then we present the details of our proposed Gradient Boosting Factorization Machines Model followed by complexity analysis and discussions.

3.1 Preliminaries and Problem Definition

Figure 1(a) shows an example of context-aware online rating system. Traditional recommendation systems consider only the user rating matrix 1(b) to make recommendations. However, rich context information is available and easy to obtain in real world. For example, in Fig. 1(a) we can easily get the rating time and the rating comments. These information provide a new information dimension for recommendation. We can encode the context information as well as user and item as either real value or categorical features, and the rating as the target value. In such way, we can transform the context aware recommendation into a prediction problem as shown in Fig.1(c). The figure shows an example about users $\mathcal{U}$ watch movies $\mathcal{I}$ in mood $\mathcal{M}$:

$$\begin{aligned}\mathcal{U} &= \{u_1, u_2, u_3\}\\ \mathcal{I} &= \{i_1, i_2, i_3, i_4\}\\ \mathcal{M} &= \{Happy, Normal, Sad\}\end{aligned}$$

Then the first tuple in Fig.1(c) states that user u_1 gave movie i_1 4 stars in a *Happy* mood.

Next we give the formal definition of context-aware recommendation problem. We denote the user set as $\mathcal{U}$ and the item set as $\mathcal{V}$. Assume there are another $m-2$ context features, we further denote the context features as $\mathcal{C}_3, \ldots, \mathcal{C}_m$. In fact, user and item can be regarded as the first and second "context" feature. For simplicity, we denote user set as $\mathcal{C}_1$ and item set as $\mathcal{C}_2$. In our paper, we consider only categorical features for simplicity, since in practice most features are categorical [23] and for real value features can also be segmented into categorical features. The training data can be encoded as feature vectors as shown in Fig 1(c) by transforming categorical features to indicator variables. We denote n_i as the number of different feature values for context feature $\mathcal{C}_i$. Each context feature set is $\mathcal{C}_i = \{c_{i,0}, \ldots, c_{i,n_i}\}$. We further denote the length of feature vector as d which equals to $n_1 + \ldots + n_m$. Training data is denoted as $\mathcal{S} = \sum_{i=1}^{N}(\mathbf{x}_i, y_i)$, where N is the total training instance number, $\mathbf{x}_i \in \mathbb{R}^d$, $y_i \in \mathbb{R}$ are feature vector and target value for instance i respectively. Our problem is to estimate the following rating function

$$\hat{y} : \mathbb{R}^d \to \mathbb{R}, \tag{5}$$

that minimize the following objective function:

$$\arg\min_{\Theta} \sum_{i=1}^{N} l(\hat{y}_i, y_i) + \Omega(\hat{y}), \tag{6}$$

where l is a differentiable convex loss function that measures the difference between the prediction rating $\hat{y}_i$ and the target rating y_i, Θ is parameter set to be estimated. The second term Ω measures the complexity of the model to avoid overfitting.

3.2 Context-aware FM

Factorization Machines [22] is a generic model class that subsumes many well-known recommendation methods including SVD++[16], matrix factorization [29] and PITF[26]. Rendle et al. [25] proposed to apply FM to solve context-aware recommendation problem and it has proven to be effective in KDDCup 2012 [23] as well.

In [25], factorization machines is restricted to be 2-way FMs. In such setting, the FM models all interactions between pairs of variables with the target including nested ones, by using factorized interaction parameters. The rating prediction function is:

$$\hat{y}(\mathbf{x}) := w_0 + \sum_{i=1}^{d} w_i x_i + \sum_{i=1}^{d} \sum_{j=i+1}^{d} \hat{w}_{i,j} x_i x_j. \tag{7}$$

From the perspective of classification problem, w_0 is the global bias, w_i is the weight for feature x_i and $\hat{w}_{i,j}$ is the weight for feature $x_i x_j$. We refer feature $x_i x_j$ as interaction feature which indicates the instance have both feature value x_i and x_j. For example, the first tuple in Fig. 1(c) one interaction feature is $u_1 v_1$ since we have user u_1 and item v_1 in the tuple.

The factorized parameters $\hat{w}_{i,j}$ is defined as:

$$\hat{w}_{i,j} := \langle \mathbf{v}_i, \mathbf{v}_j \rangle = \sum_{f=1}^{k} v_{i,f} \cdot v_{j,f}. \tag{8}$$

The model parameters Θ that need to be estimated are:

$$w_0 \in \mathbb{R},\ \mathbf{w} \in \mathbb{R}^d,\ \mathbf{V} \in \mathbb{R}^{d \times k}. \tag{9}$$

Note that the latent matrix $\mathbf{V}$ can be regarded as the concatenation of all m latent feature matrices $\mathbf{V}_i \in \mathbb{R}^{n_i \times k}, i = 1, \ldots, m$. The final objective function is

$$\arg\min_{\Theta} \sum_{i=1}^{N} l(\hat{y}(\mathbf{x}_i), y) + \sum_{\theta \in \Theta} \lambda_{(\theta)} \theta^2, \quad (10)$$

where $\lambda_{(\theta)}$ is the regularization parameters. In practice, l can be logit loss for binary classification problems:

$$l(\hat{y}, y) = \log(1 + \exp(-\hat{y}y)) \quad (11)$$

or least square loss for regression

$$l(\hat{y}, y) = (\hat{y} - y)^2. \quad (12)$$

In practice, it is not surprising that we can have tens of context features [3] and not all interaction features are useful for rating prediction. Note that FM models all pairwise interactions between context features, while the weight of interaction feature is defined in Eq. 8. The latent vector $\mathbf{v}_i$ is shared by all other feature vector $\mathbf{v}_j$ in order to estimate the feature weight $\hat{w}_{i,j}$. If the feature interaction feature $x_i x_j$ is not useful i.e. in practice, the estimate function $\hat{y}$ does not have the item $\hat{w}_{i,j} x_i x_j$, in such case, the estimation for parameter $\mathbf{v}_j$ and $\mathbf{v}_j$ will be affected. In order to effectively select "good" interaction features, we propose our Gradient Boosting Factorization Machines model.

3.3 Gradient Boosting Factorization Machines

3.3.1 GBFM Training

In this section, we present our proposed GBFM training algorithm. To relieve the problem in FM discussed in previous section, we borrow the idea of boosting methods [10] to select one interaction feature at each step and additively optimize the target function. The rating prediction function in our model is defined as:

$$\hat{y}_s(\mathbf{x}) := \hat{y}_{s-1}(\mathbf{x}) + \sum_{i \in \mathcal{C}_p} \sum_{j \in \mathcal{C}_q} \mathbb{I}[i, j \in \mathbf{x}] \langle \mathbf{V}_p^i, \mathbf{V}_q^j \rangle, \quad (13)$$

where s is the iteration step of the learning algorithm. At step s, we greedily select two interaction features $\mathcal{C}_p$ and $\mathcal{C}_q$ where $\mathbb{I}$ is the indicator function, the value is 1 if the condition holds otherwise 0. The feature selection algorithm we will introduce later. $\mathbf{V}_p \in \mathbb{R}^{n_p \times k}$ and $\mathbf{V}_q \in \mathbb{R}^{n_q \times k}$ are the low rank matrices for feature $\mathcal{C}_p$ and $\mathcal{C}_q$, k is the low rank dimension. After interaction features $\mathcal{C}_p$ and $\mathcal{C}_q$ are selected, we estimate the parameters $\mathbf{V}_p$ and $\mathbf{V}_q$ at step s. For example, at step s we select the interaction between user and item, we need to learn the low rank latent matrices $\mathbf{U}$ and $\mathbf{V}$. The objective function for estimate $\mathbf{V}_p, \mathbf{V}_q$ is:

$$\arg\min_{\mathbf{V}_p, \mathbf{V}_q} \sum_{i=1}^{N} l(\hat{y}_s(\mathbf{x}_i), y_i) + \|\mathbf{V}_p\|_F^2 + \|\mathbf{V}_q\|_F^2. \quad (14)$$

Assume we totally have S steps, we denote $\mathcal{C}_{sp}$ and $\mathcal{C}_{sq}$ as interaction feature selected at step s, then the final prediction function is:

$$\hat{y}_S(\mathbf{x}) = \hat{y}_0(\mathbf{x}) + \sum_{s=1}^{S} \sum_{i \in \mathcal{C}_{sp}} \sum_{j \in \mathcal{C}_{sq}} \mathbb{I}[i, j \in \mathbf{x}] \langle \mathbf{V}_{sp}^i, \mathbf{V}_{sq}^j \rangle, \quad (15)$$

[3] In KDDCup 2012 Task 1 we can easily extract around 20 features, there are more features in real industry world.

where $\hat{y}_0(x)$ is the initialized prediction function.

The details of the algorithm are shown in Algorithm 1.

Algorithm 1 Gradient Boosting Factorization Machines Model

1: **Input**: Training Data $\mathcal{S} = \{\mathbf{x}_i, y_i\}_{i=1}^N$
2: **Output**: $\hat{y}_S(x) = \hat{y}_0(x) + \sum_{s=1}^{S} \langle \mathbf{v}_{si}, \mathbf{v}_{sj} \rangle$
3: Initialize rating prediction function as $\hat{y}_0(x)$
4: **for** $s = 1 \to S$ **do**
5: Select interaction feature C_p and C_q from *Greedy Feature Selection Algorithm*
6: Estimate latent feature matrices $\mathbf{V}_p$ and $\mathbf{V}_q$
7: Update $\hat{y}_s(\mathbf{x}) := \hat{y}_{s-1}(\mathbf{x}) + \sum_{i \in \mathcal{C}_p} \sum_{j \in \mathcal{C}_q} \mathbb{I}[i, j \in \mathbf{x}] \langle \mathbf{V}_p^i, \mathbf{V}_q^j \rangle$
8: **end for**

3.3.2 Greedy Feature Selection Algorithm

In this section, we show how to effectively select "good" interaction features at each step which is the core part of our model. From the view of gradient boosting machine, at each step s, we would like to search a function f in the function space $\mathcal{F}$ that minimize the objective function:

$$\mathcal{L} = \sum_{i=1}^{N} l(\hat{y}_s(\mathbf{x}_i), y_i) + \Omega(f), \quad (16)$$

where $\hat{y}_s(\mathbf{x}) = \hat{y}_{s-1}(\mathbf{x}) + \alpha_s f_s(\mathbf{x})$. In our GBFM, the function f is set to factorized feature interactions like in FM. However, it is impossible to search all feature interactions to find the best (i.e. decrease the objective function most) due to high computation complexity. In order to find the desirable interaction features, we propose a greedy layer-wised algorithm to find the n-way interaction features. Our idea is as follows: there are n layers in total, at each layer, we greedily select the feature $\mathcal{C}_i$ that makes the objective function decrease fastest. At the end, we will get the n-way interaction feature. we heuristically assume that the function f has the following form:

$$f_l(\mathbf{x}) = \prod_{t=1}^{l} q_{\mathcal{C}_{i(t)}}(\mathbf{x}), \quad (17)$$

where $q_{\mathcal{C}_{i(t)}}(\mathbf{x})$ is the function learned at layer t with $i(t)$-th context feature selected. The function q maps latent feature vector $\mathbf{x}$ to real value domain. There are d elements in feature set, for each element we assign a weight w_{tj} to it. The function $q_{\mathcal{C}_{i(t)}}(\mathbf{x})$ is defined as:

$$q_{\mathcal{C}_{i(t)}}(\mathbf{x}) = \sum_{j \in \mathcal{C}_{i(t)}} \mathbb{I}[j \in \mathbf{x}] \cdot w_{tj}, \quad (18)$$

where $\mathbb{I}$ is the indicator function. Although the q looks very complex, in fact, in each instance there is only one non-zero element corresponding to feature $\mathcal{C}_{i(t)}$, the function value just takes the weight corresponding to the non-zero element. Take the instances in Fig. 1(c) for example again, suppose we select feature $\mathcal{C}_1$ at layer t, then the q function for first tuple is w_{t1}.

Searching function f to optimize the objective function in Eq. 16 can be hard for a general convex loss function l. The most common way is to approximate it by least-square minimization [11]. We denote the negative first derivative and the second derivative at instance i as g_i and h_i:

$$g_i = -\frac{\partial l(\hat{y}_s(x_i), y_i)}{\partial \hat{y}_s(x_i)}|_{\hat{y}_s(x_i)=\hat{y}_{s-1}(x_i)} \tag{19}$$

$$h_i = \frac{\partial^2 l(\hat{y}_s(x_i), y_i)}{\partial \hat{y}_s(x_i)^2}|_{\hat{y}_s(x_i)=\hat{y}_{s-1}(x_i)}. \tag{20}$$

The first part of Eq. 16 can be approximate as:

$$\begin{aligned} \mathcal{L} &= \sum_{i=1}^{N} l(\hat{y}_{s-1}(\mathbf{x}_i) + \alpha_s f_s(\mathbf{x}_i), y_i) \\ &\approx \sum_{i=1}^{N} l(\hat{y}_{s-1}(\mathbf{x}_i), y_i) - g_i(\alpha_s f_s(\mathbf{x}_i)) + \frac{1}{2} h_i(\alpha_s f_s(\mathbf{x}_i))^2 \end{aligned} \tag{21}$$

The Eq. 21 is equivalent to:

$$\mathcal{L}(f) = \sum_{i=1}^{N} h_i(g_i/h_i - f_s(\mathbf{x}_i))^2 + \Omega(f_s) \tag{22}$$

Replace the f_s function with the heuristic f defined in Eq. 18, we get the objective function for selecting n-way interaction features. Even using heuristic functions, finding the best interaction feature is still impossible. Instead, we learn the function f_l layer by layer. At layer t, we assume that the function $q_{\mathcal{C}_{i(1)}}, \dots, q_{\mathcal{C}_{i(t-1)}}$ have been learned, i.e. f_{t-1} has been learned. Suppose at layer t we select $i(t)$-th feature, then we have:

$$f_t(\mathbf{x}) = f_{t-1}(\mathbf{x}) \cdot q_{\mathcal{C}_{i(t)}}(\mathbf{x}). \tag{23}$$

Our problem is finalized to find the $i(t)$-th feature which:

$$\arg\min_{i(t)\in\{1,\dots,m\}} \sum_{i=1}^{N} h_i(\frac{g_i}{h_i} - f_{t-1}(\mathbf{x}_i) \cdot q_{\mathcal{C}_{i(t)}}(\mathbf{x}_i))^2 + \lambda \sum_{\theta\in\Theta} \theta^2, \tag{24}$$

where here we use L2-regularization to control the model complexity. To obtain the feature $i(t)$ minimize Eq. 24, we calculate the function q for all features. Without loss of generality, we assume the selected feature at layer t is $\mathcal{C}_{i(t)}$. The problem is actully transformed to estimating the weight for each $n_{i(t)}$ item in feature $\mathcal{C}_{i(t)}$. For a certain element j in $\mathcal{C}_{i(t)}$, we denote its corresponding weight as w_{ij}. The solution for w_{ij} is:

$$w_{ij} = \arg\min_{w} \sum_{i=1}^{N} h_i(g_i/h_i - f_{t-1}(\mathbf{x}_i) \cdot \mathbb{I}(j \in \mathbf{x}_i) \cdot w)^2 + \lambda w^2 \tag{25}$$

We denote $z_i = g_i/h_i$ and let

$$\begin{aligned} a &= \sum_{i=1}^{N}\sum_{j=1}^{d} \mathbb{I}(\mathbf{x}_j == \mathbf{z}_j) z_i h_i f_{t-1}(\mathbf{x}_i) \\ b &= \sum_{i=1}^{N}\sum_{j=1}^{d} \mathbb{I}(\mathbf{x}_j == \mathbf{z}_j) h_i (f_{t-1}(\mathbf{x}_i))^2 \end{aligned} \tag{26}$$

Then the solution for w_{ij} is:

$$w_{ij} = \frac{a}{b+\lambda}. \tag{27}$$

Note that although we need to calculate q function for all features, we can compute a, b for all features at the same time by scanning the training data just once. After we get the q function for all features, it is easy to select the best feature which satisfies Eq. 24. We repeat this process at each layer, at the end we can obtain the heuristic n-way interaction feature. Like FM, in our method, we consider 2-way interaction feature only. The details of the algorithm are shown in Algorithm 2.

Algorithm 2 Greedy Feature Selection Algorithm

Input: Training Data $\mathcal{S} = \{\mathbf{x}_i, y_i\}_{i=1}^{N}$,context feature set $\mathcal{C}$
Output: n-way interaction feature $\mathcal{C}_{i(1)}, \dots, \mathcal{C}_{i(n)}$.
for $l = 1 \to n$ **do**
  $\mathcal{A} = \emptyset$ // $\mathcal{A}$ is the set of context features already selected
  Maintain two vectors $\mathbf{a}$ and $\mathbf{b}$ for all categorical values in $\mathcal{C}$, both initialized to $\mathbf{0}$
  for $(\mathbf{x}_i, y_i)$ in $\mathcal{S}$ **do**
    compute *tempa* $= z_i h_i f_{t-1}(\mathbf{x}_i)$ and *tempb* $= h_i(f_{t-1}(\mathbf{x}_i))^2$
    for $j = 1 \to d$ **do**
      if $\mathbf{x}_{ij}$ is non-zero and not in $\mathcal{A}$ **then**
        add *tempa* to $\mathbf{a}_j$ and *tempb* to $\mathbf{b}_j$
      end if
    end for
  end for
  Compute weight for all categorical features in $\mathcal{C} - \mathcal{A}$ according to Eq. 25.
  Select the feature $\mathcal{C}_{i(l)}$ according to Eq. 24.
  Add feature $\mathcal{C}_{i(l)}$ into $\mathcal{A}$
end for

3.3.3 Complexity Analysis

The computation complexity for *Greedy Feature Selection Algorithm* is $\mathcal{O}(n \cdot N)$, where N is the training data size, n is the number of layers. At each layer, the q function can be computed though scanning the training dataset once as described in Algorithm 2. Then best feature selection according to Eq. 24 can also be carried out by the training dataset once. Usually, $n \ll N$, in 2-way FM, $n = 2$. So the computation cost for Algorithm 2 is $\mathcal{O}(N)$.

In Algorithm 1, the estimation for $\mathbf{V}_p$ and $\mathbf{V}_q$ is usually carried out by stochastic gradient descent (SGD). The complexity for this part is $\mathcal{O}(kN)$, where k is number of iterations. In total, the complexity for GBFM is $\mathcal{O}(SN + kSN)$, S is number of boosting steps as stated in the algorithm, the computation complexity is still linear to the number of training dataset.

In addition, GBFM can be speedup by multi-threading and parallelization. The computation of first and second derivative can be decoupled thus can be easily computed though multi-threading and distributed to a cluster of computers. The gradient of Eq. 14 also can be decoupled and parallelization is possible for Algorithm 1.

3.3.4 Discussions

We discuss the insights of our heuristic function f in Eq. 17 which is the key part of Algorithm 2 as well as the relationship between the proposed GBFM and other state-of-the-art methods. At last, we discuss some variants of our model.

Insights of heuristic function f: The main idea of our algorithm is that at each layer we greedily select a context feature $\mathcal{C}_i$ according to Eq. 24 and we compute the corresponding weight vector, e.g. $q_{\mathcal{C}_i}$. We can regard it as the low rank latent feature matrix for feature $\mathcal{C}_i$ like in FM with latent dimension $k = 1$. Then the heuristic function f is an intance of CANDECOMP/PARAFAC (CP) decomposition

[15] with $k = 1$. We greedily use this f function to choose the interaction feature. In practice, for large dataset in industry world, we can additively use this function f as the "weak learner" instead of $\langle \mathbf{V}_p, \mathbf{V}_q \rangle$, to quickly find useful interaction features since the computation cost is relatively low.

Relation to Factorization Machines: Factorization Machines is a strong baseline method for context-aware recommendation [25]. The main difference between our model and FM is that FM models all interactions between context features while our method only consider part of them. For example, in Fig. 1(c), we have 3 context features, the rating prediction function of FM is:

$$\begin{aligned} \hat{y}(\mathbf{x}(u, i, c_3)) &= w_0 + w_u + w_i + w_{c_3} + \langle \mathbf{v}_u, \mathbf{v}_i \rangle \\ &+ \langle \mathbf{v}_u, \mathbf{v}_{c_3} \rangle + \langle \mathbf{v}_i, \mathbf{v}_{c_3} \rangle. \end{aligned} \tag{28}$$

While in our GBFM, we may only consider the (user,item) and (user,mood) interaction pair. If the interaction feature (item,mood) is actually not useful, then the term $\langle \mathbf{v}_i, \mathbf{v}_{c_3} \rangle$ which is the weight for feature $\mathbf{x}_i \mathbf{x}_{c_3}$ will introduce noise for the prediction function. Another difference is that in our algorithm we additively learn the latent feature matrices which are not shared to compute other factorization weights. For example, in first step, we select (user,item) pair, then the second step we select (user,mood) pair, the latent feature matrix $\mathbf{V}_u$ is not the same. It may lose the advantage of generalization compared to FM, we can regard our GBFM as a feature selection algorithm and only model the interaction on selected features.

Relation to GBMF: Gradient Boosting Matrix Factorization [6] is the state-of-the-art model which is a general functional matrix factorization using gradient boosting. GBMF is under the framework of matrix factorization [27]. They assume that the user/item latent low rank matrix is functional, each time a function f is added to latent dimension $\mathbf{U}_k$. While our model is under the framework of factorization machines, we use gradient boosting to greedily select "good" interaction features. Another difference is the construction method of high-order categorical features. In our algorithm, we can efficiently find the "best" features according to Algorithm 2, while the binary splitting tree algorithm may fail for categorical features since the cost for finding the best binary split is exponential.

Variants of our GBFM: There are several variants of our proposed GBFM. In our paper, we only use the 2-way interaction feature like in FM. It can be easily extended to n-way FM by selecting n-way interaction feature. Since our model is an additive model, we can first consider linear features, i.e. 1-way feature, then 2-way interaction and more high order features. Another variant is that we can fully optimize the selected interaction features instead of additively optimize interaction features one by one, we refer this variant as GBFM-Opt. The difference between GBFM-Opt and FM is that GBFM-Opt only consider some "good" selected 2-way interaction features.

4. EXPERIMENTS

In this section, we empirically investigate whether our proposed GBFM can achieve better performance compared to other state-of-the-art methods with large number of context features. Furthermore we would like to examine whether the interaction features selected by our algorithm is more effective compared to pairwise interactions in FM.

4.1 Datasets

We conduct our experiments on two dataset: a synthetic dataset and a real world dataset, i.e., the Tencent Microblog[4].

Synthetic data: Since there are few public datasets that have many context features. We construct a synthetic dataset for comparison. The data generation process is as follows: assume we have m context features, each context feature $\mathcal{C}_i$ have n_i values, we generate the latent context features from zero-mean spherical Gaussian as follows:

$$\mathbf{V}_i^j \sim \mathcal{N}(\mathbf{0}_K, \sigma^2 \mathbf{I}_K),$$

where $j = 1, \ldots, n_i$, $\mathbf{0}_K$ is a K-dimension vector with all elements set to 0, and $\mathbf{I}_K$ is the $K \times K$ identity matrix. We also generate the weight vector all categorical feature values $\mathbf{w} \sim \mathcal{N}(\mathbf{0}_{d+1}, \sigma^2 \mathbf{I}_{d+1})$, where $d = \sum_{i=1}^m n_i$, we incorporate the global bias into the weight vector. Then we select several 2-way interaction features. We denote the interaction feature set as $\mathcal{F}$. Then the rating is obtained by rescale the sigmoid value to 1 to D by:

$$\begin{aligned} \hat{y}(\mathbf{x}) &= \sum_{i=0}^{d} w_i x_i + \sum_{(p_1,p_2)\in\mathcal{F}} \sum_{i\in\mathcal{C}_{p_1}} \sum_{j\in\mathcal{C}_{p_2}} \mathbb{I}[i,j \in \mathbf{x}] \langle \mathbf{V}_{p_1}^i, \mathbf{V}_{p_2}^j \rangle \\ \hat{y}(\mathbf{x}) &= \lceil g(\hat{y}) \times D \rceil, \end{aligned}$$

where D is the rating scale, $g(x) = 1/(1 + \exp(-x))$. In our experiment, we set number of context features $m = 10$, latent dimension $K = 5$, rating scale $D = 5$, feature value size $n_i = 1000$.

Table 1: Statistics of datasets

Dataset	# Users	#Items	#Observed Entries
Synethic data	1000	1000	16270
Tencent microblog	2.3 M	6095	73 M

Tencent microblog dataset: Tencent microblog is one of the largest social media services in China like Sina Weibo and Twitter. The dataset is designed for KDDCup 2012 competition and it contains the celebrity recommendation records of about 2.3 million users over a time period of about two months. In this dataset, the celebrities are regarded as items for recommendation. The system recommends a celebrity to a user at a certain time and the user's response is either "accept" or "reject". The dataset contains rich context information such as user's age, gender, item's category, time information, etc.. We can also extract the session information such as the number of recommendation records before current recommendation. The dataset splits into training and testing data by time. The test data furthermore splits into public and private set for independent evaluations. The dataset is extremely sparse with only about two positive records (e.g. accept the recommendation) for each user. Besides, nearly 70% of users in the test dataset are never occurred in the training data.

Table 1 shows the statistic for both our synthetic data and real data.

[4]http://kddcup2012.org/c/kddcup2012-track1/data

4.2 Setup and Metrics

We randomly remove 20% of dataset as testing data, and the remaining 80% data as the training for the synthetic data. We repeat the experiment 5 times and report the average results. For Tencent Microblog data, the dataset is already splitted into training and testing set. We further use 1/5 training data as validation data to tune parameters and we conduct the evaluation on pubic test dataset. We extract 18 features from the data, including user, item, tweets number, follower/followee number, tweet time etc. We treat all of the features as categorical features.

For synthetic dataset, we use two metrics, the Mean Absolute Error (MAE) and Root Mean Square Error (RMSE), to measure the prediction quality of different methods. MAE and RMSE are defined as follows:

$$MAE = \frac{\sum_i |\hat{y}(i) - y_i|}{N} \tag{29}$$

$$RMSE = \sqrt{\frac{\sum_i (\hat{y}(i) - y_i)^2}{N}}, \tag{30}$$

where N is the number of training instance.

For Tencent microblog data, MAP@k is used as the metric:

$$MAP@k = \sum_{i=1}^{N} ap@k_i / N, \tag{31}$$

where N is the number of users and $ap@k$ is the average precision at k for the user:

$$ap@k = \sum_{i=1}^{k} P(k)/(number\, of\, items\, clicked\, in\, m\, items) \tag{32}$$

where $P(k)$ is the precision at cut-off k in the item list.

4.3 Performance Comparsion

In our experiments, we compare the following methods:

- **PMF**: this method is well known in recommender systems and proposed in [27]. It only uses user-item matrix for recommendation.
- **Context-aware FM**: this method is proposed in [25]. It is a strong baseline method we introduced in Section 3.2.
- **GBFM**: this method is our newly proposed model which is described in Algorithm 1 and Algorithm 2.
- **GBFM-Opt**: this method is a variant of our GBFM which we discussed in Section 3.3.4. After S steps when the training process stops, we will obtain S interaction features. We fully optimize these S interaction features.

For GBFM, we use 1-way feature linear model as the initialized prediction function. Grid search is applied to find regularization parameter λ, and we set it to 0.1 for synthetic data and 0.8 for Tencent microblog data. The latent dimension k is set to 5 and 10 for synthetic data and Tencent microblog data respectively. We use square loss to train synthetic data and logit loss for Tencent microblog data. The detailed comparison results are shown in Table 2 and Table 3.

From the table, we can observe that:

Table 2: Results on Synthetic data in RMSE and MAE

Method	RMSE	MAE
PMF	1.9881	1.7650
FM	1.9216	1.6981
GBFM	1.8959	1.6354
GBFM-Opt	**1.8611**	**1.5762**

Table 3: Results on Tencent Microblog data in MAP

Method	MAP@1	MAP@3	MAP@5
PMF	22.88%	34.50%	37.95%
FM	24.36%	36.77%	40.32%
GBFM	24.62%	37.17%	40.90%
GBFM-Opt	**24.66%**	**37.23%**	**40.98%**

- Both our proposed GBFM and GBFM-Opt model achieve better performance on both synthetic data and Tencent microblog data in terms of all metrics compared with PMF and FM. On synthetic dataset, FM gives 0.066 reduction over PMF in terms of RMSE, and GBFM further gives 0.026 reduction over FM. Since the synthetic data is generated from part of 2-way feature interactions, the results reveal that our proposed GBFM can learn "good" interaction features. While on the Tencent microblog data, FM improves 2.25% in terms of MAP@3 compared to PMF. GBFM can still be able to improve the performance by 0.4%. This result verifies our assumption that selecting "good" features is better than considering all of pairwise interaction features.
- It is not surprising that the performance of FM, GBFM and GBFM-Opt is much better than PMF. It reveals the importance of utilizing auxiliary information on context-aware recommendation. It is even more critical on Tencent microblog data since most of users in test dataset do not exist in the training data which means PMF cannot deal with them at all.
- The performance of GBFM-Opt can illustrate whether the selected interaction features are useful for recommendation. We can observe that on both datasets GBFM-Opt can achieve even better performance than GBFM. On synthetic dataset, GBFM-Opt improves a lot (0.035) compared to GBFM in terms of RMSE while on Tencent microblog data GBFM-Opt is slightly better than GBFM. The results reveal that the features selected by our GBFM is quite useful compared to consider all the pairwise interactions. Further, recall the discussion we conducted in Section 3.3.4, compared to GBFM-Opt, GBFM loses the advantage of generalization, which may be the main reason why GBFM-Opt is better than GBFM. Compared to synthetic data, the Tencent microblog data is much sparser thus it is not easy to benefit from generalization which explains why GBFM-Opt only improves a little compared to GBFM.

5. CONCLUSION

In this paper, we have proposed a novel model called GBFM which incorporates feature interaction selection algorithm with Factorization Machines into a unified framework to solve context-aware recommendation problems. Experiments on both synthetic and real datasets show that our model can effectively select "good" interaction features and achieve better performance compared to other state-of-the-art methods.

There are several interesting directions worthy of considering in the further study: 1) we would like to explore how to find high order features, 2) we are interested to extend our GBFM with better high order feature selection algorithm. 3) it is also interesting to explore how to effectively deal with other features apart from categorical features.

6. ACKNOWLEDGEMENTS

The work described in this paper was fully supported by the National Grand Fundamental Research 973 Program of China (No. 2014CB340405 and No. 2014CB340401), the Research Grants Council of the Hong Kong Special Administrative Region, China (Project No. CUHK 413212 and CUHK 415113), and Microsoft Research Asia Regional Seed Fund in Big Data Research (Grant No. FY13-RES-SPONSOR-036).

7. REFERENCES

[1] G. Adomavicius, R. Sankaranarayanan, S. Sen, and A. Tuzhilin. Incorporating contextual information in recommender systems using a multidimensional approach. pages 103–145, 2005.

[2] D. Agarwal and B.-C. Chen. Regression-based latent factor models. In *KDD*, pages 19–28, 2009.

[3] L. Baltrunas, B. Ludwig, and F. Ricci. Matrix factorization techniques for context aware recommendation. In *RecSys*, pages 301–304, 2011.

[4] R. M. Bell and Y. Koren. Lessons from the netflix prize challenge. *SIGKDD Explorations*, 9(2):75–79, 2007.

[5] C. J. Burges. From ranknet to lambdarank to lambdamart: An overview. *Learning*, 11:23–581, 2010.

[6] T. Chen, H. Li, Q. Yang, and Y. Yu. General functional matrix factorization using gradient boosting. In *Proceedings of The 30th International Conference on Machine Learning*, pages 436–444, 2013.

[7] T. Chen, L. Tang, Q. Liu, D. Yang, S. Xie, X. Cao, C. Wu, E. Yao, Z. Liu, Z. Jiang, et al. Combining factorization model and additive forest for collaborative followee recommendation. *KDD CUP*, 2012.

[8] C. Cheng, H. Yang, I. King, and M. R. Lyu. Fused matrix factorization with geographical and social influence in location-based social networks. In *AAAI*, 2012.

[9] C. Cheng, H. Yang, M. R. Lyu, and I. King. Where you like to go next: Successive point-of-interest recommendation. In *Proceedings of the Twenty-Third international joint conference on Artificial Intelligence*, pages 2605–2611. AAAI Press, 2013.

[10] J. Friedman, T. Hastie, and R. Tibshirani. Special invited paper. additive logistic regression: A statistical view of boosting. *Annals of statistics*, pages 337–374, 2000.

[11] J. H. Friedman. Greedy function approximation: a gradient boosting machine. *Annals of Statistics*, pages 1189–1232, 2001.

[12] T. Hastie, R. Tibshirani, J. Friedman, T. Hastie, J. Friedman, and R. Tibshirani. *The elements of statistical learning*, volume 2. Springer, 2009.

[13] M. Jamali and M. Ester. A matrix factorization technique with trust propagation for recommendation in social networks. In *RecSys*, pages 135–142, 2010.

[14] A. Karatzoglou, X. Amatriain, L. Baltrunas, and N. Oliver. Multiverse recommendation: n-dimensional tensor factorization for context-aware collaborative filtering. In *RecSys*, pages 79–86, 2010.

[15] T. G. Kolda and B. W. Bader. Tensor decompositions and applications. *SIAM review*, 51(3):455–500, 2009.

[16] Y. Koren. Factorization meets the neighborhood: a multifaceted collaborative filtering model. In *KDD*, pages 426–434, 2008.

[17] Y. Koren. Collaborative filtering with temporal dynamics. In *KDD*, pages 447–456, 2009.

[18] N. D. Lawrence and R. Urtasun. Non-linear matrix factorization with gaussian processes. In *ICML*, page 76, 2009.

[19] X. Liu and K. Aberer. Soco: a social network aided context-aware recommender system. In *WWW*, pages 781–802, 2013.

[20] H. Ma, I. King, and M. R. Lyu. Learning to recommend with explicit and implicit social relations. *ACM TIST*, 2(3):29, 2011.

[21] U. Panniello, A. Tuzhilin, M. Gorgoglione, C. Palmisano, and A. Pedone. Experimental comparison of pre- vs. post-filtering approaches in context-aware recommender systems. In *RecSys*, pages 265–268, 2009.

[22] S. Rendle. Factorization machines. In *ICDM*, pages 995–1000, 2010.

[23] S. Rendle. Social network and click-through prediction with factorization machines. In *KDD-Cup Workshop*, 2012.

[24] S. Rendle. Scaling factorization machines to relational data. *PVLDB*, 6(5):337–348, 2013.

[25] S. Rendle, Z. Gantner, C. Freudenthaler, and L. Schmidt-Thieme. Fast context-aware recommendations with factorization machines. In *SIGIR*, pages 635–644, 2011.

[26] S. Rendle and L. Schmidt-Thieme. Pairwise interaction tensor factorization for personalized tag recommendation. In *WSDM*, pages 81–90, 2010.

[27] R. Salakhutdinov and A. Mnih. Probabilistic matrix factorization. In *NIPS*, 2007.

[28] B. M. Sarwar, G. Karypis, J. A. Konstan, and J. Riedl. Item-based collaborative filtering recommendation algorithms. In *WWW*, pages 285–295, 2001.

[29] N. Srebro, J. D. M. Rennie, and T. Jaakkola. Maximum-margin matrix factorization. In *NIPS*, 2004.

[30] D. H. Stern, R. Herbrich, and T. Graepel. Matchbox: large scale online bayesian recommendations. In *WWW*, pages 111–120, 2009.

[31] L. R. Tucker. Some mathematical notes on three-mode factor analysis. *Psychometrika*, 31(3):279–311, 1966.

[32] J. Weston, C. Wang, R. J. Weiss, and A. Berenzweig. Latent collaborative retrieval. In *ICML*, 2012.

[33] L. Xiong, X. Chen, T.-K. Huang, J. G. Schneider, and J. G. Carbonell. Temporal collaborative filtering with bayesian probabilistic tensor factorization. In *SDM*, pages 211–222, 2010.

[34] J. Xu and H. Li. Adarank: a boosting algorithm for information retrieval. In *Proceedings of the 30th annual international ACM SIGIR conference on Research and development in information retrieval*, pages 391–398. ACM, 2007.

[35] M. Ye, P. Yin, W.-C. Lee, and D. L. Lee. Exploiting geographical influence for collaborative point-of-interest recommendation. In *SIGIR*, pages 325–334, 2011.

[36] E. Zhong, W. Fan, and Q. Y. 0001. Contextual collaborative filtering via hierarchical matrix factorization. In *SDM*, pages 744–755, 2012.

Exploiting Temporal Influence in Online Recommendation

Róbert Pálovics[1,2] András A. Benczúr[1,3] Levente Kocsis[1,4]
Tamás Kiss[1,3] Erzsébet Frigó[1,2]
[1]Institute for Computer Science and Control, Hungarian Academy of Sciences (MTA SZTAKI)
[2]Technical University Budapest [3]Eötvös University Budapest [4]University of Szeged
{rpalovics, benczur, kocsis, kisstom, fbobee}@ilab.sztaki.hu

ABSTRACT

In this paper we give methods for time-aware music recommendation in a social media service with the potential of exploiting immediate temporal influences between users. We consider events when a user listens to an artist the first time and this event follows some friend listening to the same artist short time before. We train a blend of matrix factorization methods that model the relation of the influencer, the influenced and the artist, both the individual factor decompositions and their weight learned by variants of stochastic gradient descent (SGD). Special care is taken since events of influence form a subset of the positive implicit feedback data and hence we have to cope with two different definitions of the positive and negative implicit training data. In addition, in the time-aware setting we have to use online learning *and* evaluation methods. While SGD can easily be trained online, evaluation is cumbersome by traditional measures since we will have potentially different top recommendations at different times. Our experiments are carried over the two-year "scrobble" history of 70,000 Last.fm users and show a 5% increase in recommendation quality by predicting temporal influences.

Categories and Subject Descriptors

H.3.3 [**Information Storage and Retrieval**]: Information filtering; I.2.6 [**Artificial Intelligence**]: Learning

Keywords

temporal recommendation and evaluation; social influence; online matrix factorization; Last.fm; music recommendation

1. INTRODUCTION

Part of the appeal of Web 2.0 is to find other people who share similar interests. Last.fm organizes its social network around music recommendation: users may automatically share their listening habits and at the same time grow their friendship. Based on the profiles shared, users may see what artists friends really listen to the most.

In a recent paper [22], we proved the existence of the influence of friends on musical taste by carefully decoupling trends and homophily, the fact that friends are a priori more likely to have similar taste. In this paper we exploit the timely information gathered by the Last.fm service on users with public profile to exploit the potential influence between friends for recommendation. Last.fm's service is unique in that we may obtain a detailed timeline and catch immediate effects by comparing the history of friends in time and comparing to pairs of random users instead of friends.

As our main contribution, we give a matrix factorization mixture model for influence between friends that yield improved collaborative filtering methods. In the simplest setting, we may recommend a new artist a to a user u closely after a friend v listened to the same artist. When we turn to modeling the tensor data $< u, v, a >$ that may even involve the time elapsed since v listening to a, we face a very sparse problem. Hence instead of modeling the tensor, we flatten out along the variables and define three matrices in addition to single-variable effects similar to the ones defined by the centralization procedures of [4].

Since influence from friends has a very strong time dependence in that only the events of the last few hours or days may have an effect on the user behavior, in this paper we consider online learning with very strong time sensitivity. Compared to standard collaborative filtering methods, we process events only once and in the order they have appeared. As baseline we use online stochastic gradient descent (SGD) with high learning rate so that recent events have high contribution to the factor weights. The online factor model already incorporates not just popularity by using a high learning rate and involving an online updated item bias, but also part of friends' influence. Immediately after a user listens to an artist, the corresponding factor weights are relative strongly adjusted due to the high learning rate. If a friend has similar factor weights e.g. by homophily, the same artist will have high recommendation score after the learning step. The online factor model hence involves an implicit variant of an influence recommender by itself that we will further improve by a direct modeling of the influences.

To obtain the weighted combination of the baseline and the influence recommenders, we propose a new method for online learning user-dependent blending weights. If the derivatives of the individual models are available, a single SGD could optimize both the internal parameters and the blending weights. However as it turns out, the influence recom-

RecSys'14, October 6–10, 2014, Foster City, Silicon Valley, CA, USA.

http://dx.doi.org/10.1145/2645710.2645723.

mender requires a different set of implicit positive items and a procedure for generating a negative sample than the traditional online matrix factor model.

In our blend, we obtain a 5% of increase in quality, a strong result in view of the three-year Netflix Prize competition [6] to improve recommender quality by 10%. The fact that influences blend well with collaborative filtering and temporal effects prove that close events in the network bring in new information: friends' close events in the past can be exploited in a recommender system.

Finally, as part of our results, we introduce quality measures for time-aware recommender evaluation. As influence from friends has only a short, typically few hours effect, we retrain part of our models after each event and hence potentially give completely new top list of items for each event in the testing period. We highlight that discounted cumulative gain (DCG) computed individually for each event and averaged over time is an appropriate measure for real time recommender evaluation.

The rest of this paper is organized as follows. After describing our Last.fm data in Section 2, we explore for measurable signs of influence by friends in Section 3. Our main influence recommender is defined in Section 4, our online evaluation metric in Section 5, the online blending method in Section 6 and the baseline algorithms in Section 7. Finally we show our measurements for improved recommendation quality in Section 8.

1.1 Related results

The Netflix Prize competition [6] has recently generated increased interest in recommender algorithms in the research community and put recommender algorithms under a systematic thorough evaluation on standard data [5]. The final best results blended a very large number of methods whose reproduction is out of the scope of this paper.

Bonchi [7] summarizes the data mining aspects of research on social influence. He concludes that "another extremely important factor is the temporal dimension: nevertheless the role of time in viral marketing is still largely (and surprisingly) unexplored", an aspect that is key in our result. Notion of influence similar to ours is derived in [3, 8] for Flickr and Twitter cascades, respectively.

Closest to our results are the applications of network influence in collaborative filtering under the term of "social regularization" [18, 21, 25, 26]. These results add smoothing to make friends' model similar. We use social regularization as one baseline model in our experiments. In other results, only ratings and no social contacts are given [11], or in [13], both friendship and view information was present over Flickr, but the main goal was to measure the strength of the influence and no measurements were designed to separate influence from other effects.

Since our goal is to recommend different artists at different times, our evaluation must be based on the quality of the top list produced by the recommender. This so-called top-K recommender task is known to be hard [10]. A recent result on evaluating top-K recommenders is found in [9].

Music recommendation is considered in several results orthogonal to our methods that will likely combine well. Mood data set is created in [14]. Similarity search based on audio is given in [16]. Tag based music recommenders [12, 23] and many more, a few of them based on Last.fm tags, use annotation and fall into the class of content based methods as opposed to collaborative filtering considered in our paper [15, 19, 20].

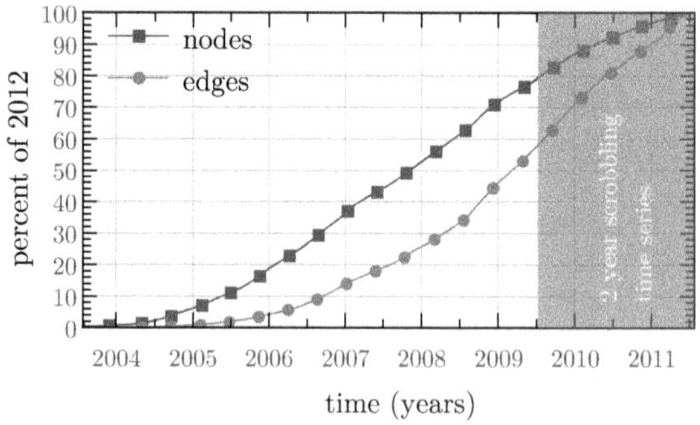

Figure 1: The number of the users and friendship edges in time as the fraction of the values at the time of the data set creation (2012).

2. THE LAST.FM DATA SET

Last.fm became a relevant online service in music based social networking. For registered users, it collects, "scrobbles"[1] what they have listened. Each user has its own statistics on listened music that is shown in her profile. Most user profiles are public, and each user of Last.fm may have friends inside the Last.fm social network. Therefore one relevant information for the users is that they see their own and their friends' listening statistics.

We investigate a data set that consists of the contacts and the implicit feedback timeline, the "scrobble history" of the users. Our goal is to exploit the influence of social contacts for recommendation. For privacy considerations, throughout our research, we selected an anonymous sample of users. Anonymity is provided by selecting random users while maintaining a connected friendship network. We set the following constraints for random selection:

- User location is stated in UK;
- Age between 14 and 50, inclusive;
- Profile displays scrobbles publicly (privacy constraint);
- Daily average activity between 5 and 500.
- At least 10 friends that meet the first four conditions.

The above selection criteria were set to select a representative part of Last.fm users and as much as possible avoid users who artificially generate inflated scrobble figures. In this anonymized data set of two years of artist scrobble timeline, edges of the social network are undirected and timestamped by creation date (Fig. 1). The number of users both in the time series and in the network is 71,000 with 285,241 edges; no edges are ever deleted from the network.

The time series contain 979,391,001 scrobbles from 2,073,395 artists and were collected between 01 January 2010 and 31 December 2011. The same user can scrobble an artist several times. The number of unique user-artist scrobbles is 57,274,158.

[1]The name "scrobbling" is a word by Last.fm, meaning the collection of information about user listening.

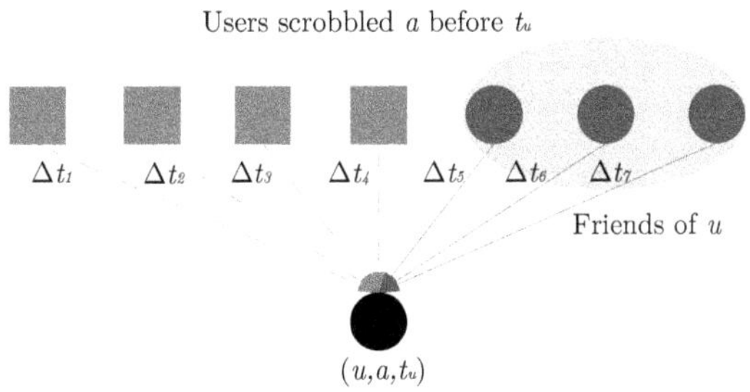

Figure 2: Potential influence on u by other users to scrobble (u, a, t_u).

3. NETWORK INFLUENCE

The key concept in this paper is a user v influencing another u to scrobble a. The sign of an influence is if u scrobbles artist a the first time at time t_u, after v last scrobbling the same artist at some time $t_v < t_u$ before. The time difference $\Delta t = t_u - t_v$ is the *delay*, as seen in Fig. 2. Our key assumption is that we observe such a subsequent first time scrobbling between non-friends only by coincidence while some of these events between friends are the result of certain interaction. Our goal is to prove that friends indeed influence each other and this effect can be exploited for recommendations.

Similar influence definitions are given in [3, 8, 13]. As detailed in [3], one main difference between these definitions is that in some papers t_v is defined as the first and not the last time when user v scrobbles a. The smaller the delay Δt between the scrobbles of v and u, the more certain we are that u is affected by the previous scrobble of v. The distribution of delay with respect to friends and non-friends will help us in determining the frequency and strength of influence over the Last.fm social network.

Out of the 57,274,158 first-time scrobbles of a certain artist a by some user, we find a friend who scrobbled a before 10,993,042 times (19%) in the whole time series and 4,203,109 times in the second year. Note that one user can be influenced by more friends, therefore the total number of influences is 24,204,977. If we only consider influences with delay less than one week, this number reduces to 4,625,141. Note that there is no influencing user for the very first scrobbler of a in the data set. For other scrobbles there is always an earlier scrobble by some other user, however, that user may not be a friend of u. Some of the observed subsequent scrobbles may result by pure coincidence, especially when a new album is released or the popularity of the artist increases for some other reason.

In order to quantify real influence within the set of subsequent first time scrobbles, our goal is to determine the probability that the subsequent scrobbles are result of influence. If we condition this probability for friends and by a limit t on the delay, we should obtain a monotonically decreasing function $\text{Infl}(t)$.

To formalize, let us consider the probability space of subsequent first time scrobbles among all users. Let I denote the event that an subsequent first time scrobble is the result of an influence. I^c is the opposite, no influence occurs. Coincidence or other, external reason such as the overall increase in popularity causes the subsequent first time scrobble in

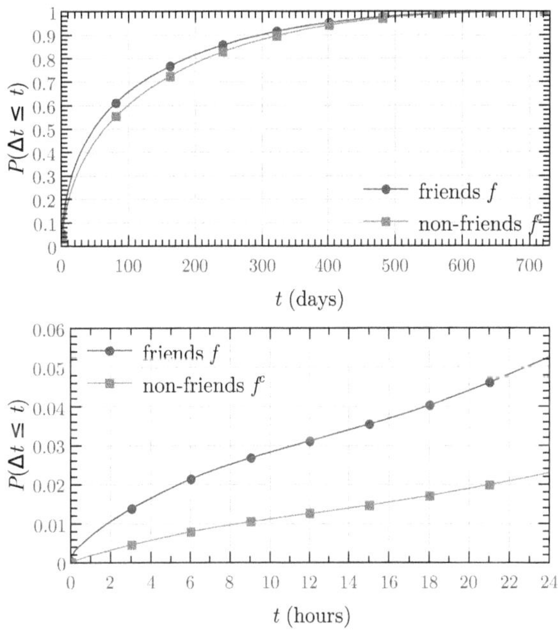

Figure 3: Fraction of subsequent first time scrobbles with delay $\Delta t \le t$ as the function of t, in case of friends ($P(\Delta t \le t \mid f)$) and non-friends ($P(\Delta t \le t \mid f^c)$) over the entire timeline (**top**) and the first 24 hours (**bottom**).

the time series. Let f denote events between friends and f^c between non-friends. Finally let $\Delta t \le t$ denote the set of events with delay at most t. With these notations,

$$\text{Infl}(t) = P(I \mid \Delta t \le t, f) = \quad (1)$$

$$= \frac{P(I, \Delta t \le t, f)}{P(\Delta t \le t, f)} = \frac{P(\Delta t \le t, I \mid f)P(f)}{P(\Delta t \le t \mid f)P(f)} \quad (2)$$

$$= \frac{P(\Delta t \le t, I \mid f)}{P(\Delta t \le t \mid f)} = \frac{P(\Delta t \le t \mid f) - P(\Delta t \le t, I^c \mid f)}{P(\Delta t \le t \mid f)}. \quad (3)$$

As non-friends f^c should not have any real influence on each other, we assume that

$$P(\Delta t \le t, I^c \mid f) \approx P(\Delta t \le t, I^c \mid f^c) = P(\Delta t \le t \mid f^c). \quad (4)$$

Using this approximation, we can compute the probability of influences between friends as in (1) by expanding (3),

$$\text{Infl}(t) = P(I \mid \Delta t \le t, f) \approx \frac{P(\Delta t \le t \mid f) - P(\Delta t \le t \mid f^c)}{P(\Delta t \le t \mid f)}. \quad (5)$$

By the above equation, the influence probability can be approximated by observing the cumulative density curves in Fig. 3. The estimate of this function as in (5) is shown in Fig. 4. As expected, $\text{Infl}(t)$ is a monotonically decreasing function of t. However, the decrease is slow unlike in some recent influence models that propose exponential decay in time [13]. Therefore, we approximate the influence probability with a slowly decreasing logarithmic function instead of an exponential decay,

$$\text{Infl}(t) = 1 - c \log t, \quad (6)$$

where c is a constant.

4. INFLUENCE BASED RECOMMENDATION

Based on the measurements in the previous section, we model the observed influences and give a method to apply for

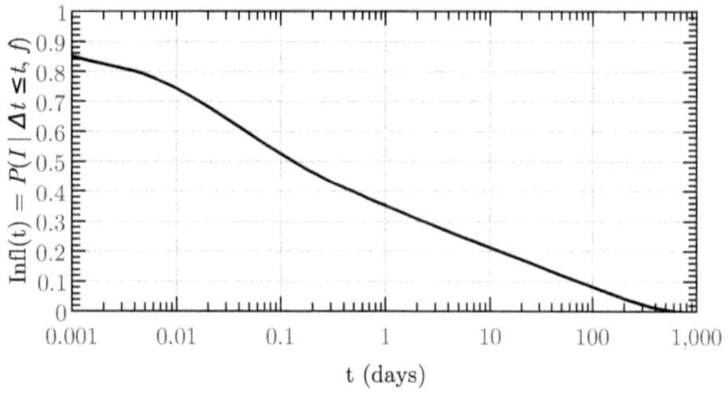

Figure 4: The influence probability approximated by equation (5), the ratio of increase among friends compared to non-friends very closely follows a logarithmic function of delay $\Delta t \leq t$.

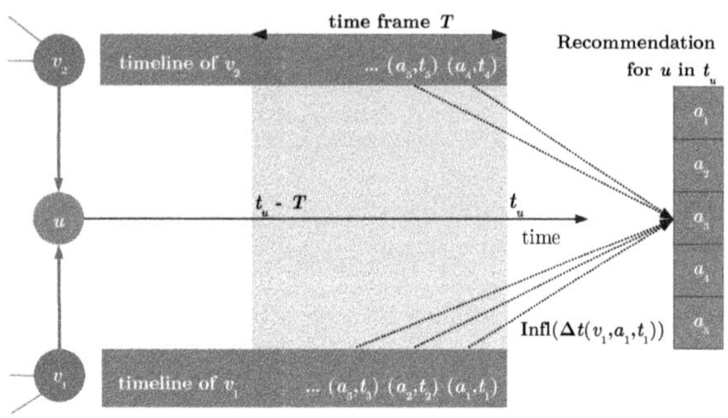

Figure 5: Scheme of the influence based recommender algorithm.

recommendation. Influence depends on time and no matter how relative slow, the influential power of a friend scrobbling an artist decays as time passes by. For this reason, the influence based recommender must learn online.

To formalize, let $v \xrightarrow{a;\Delta t \in \mathcal{T}} u$ denote the event that user u scrobbles artist a the first time in her time series, and Δt time after her friend v also scrobbled a. The time difference Δt is restricted to be in a time interval $\mathcal{T}$. As illustrated in Fig. 5, we would like to decompose the probability that $v \xrightarrow{a;\Delta t \in \mathcal{T}} u$ happens *and* the reason for this event is influence (I) between the users into a factor that only depends on Δt and another one that is independent of Δt. First we decompose the full event into a conditional probability as

$$P(I, v \xrightarrow{a;\Delta t \in \mathcal{T}} u) = P(I \mid v \xrightarrow{a;\Delta t \in \mathcal{T}} u) \cdot P(v \xrightarrow{a;\Delta t \in \mathcal{T}} u). \quad (7)$$

When a scrobble event happens at time exactly t after the scrobble of v, the interval becomes a point and hence we are looking for the derivative

$$\lim_{\tau \to 0} \left(P(I, v \xrightarrow{a;\Delta t \leq t+\tau} u) - P(I, v \xrightarrow{a;\Delta t \leq t} u) \right) / \tau. \quad (8)$$

We model the right hand side of (7), the "strength" of the influence between users u and v, independent of time as

$$f(v \xrightarrow{a} u) := P(v \xrightarrow{a;\Delta t \in \mathcal{T}} u) / |\mathcal{T}|, \quad (9)$$

hence by equation (7) we may divide the derivative (8) by $f(v \xrightarrow{a} u)$ to get

$$\lim_{\tau \to 0} \left(P(I \mid v \xrightarrow{a;\Delta t \leq t+\tau} u)(t+\tau) - P(I \mid v \xrightarrow{a;\Delta t \leq t} u)t \right) / \tau. \quad (10)$$

We model influence conditional probabilities by a global function for all users that depend only on the time Δt elapsed,

$$P(I \mid v \xrightarrow{a;\Delta t \leq t} u) \approx P(I \mid \Delta t \leq t, f). \quad (11)$$

By using our function in (5) and (6), equation (10) becomes

$$\lim_{\tau \to 0} \left((1 - c \log(t+\tau)) \cdot (t+\tau) - (1 - c \log t) \cdot t \right) / \tau \quad (12)$$

$$= 1 - c(1 + \log t). \quad (13)$$

Now we give our matrix factorization model for $f(v \xrightarrow{a} u)$. We decompose the model into seven terms that give a global model for one or more of the three variables u, v, a in $(v \xrightarrow{a} u)$. By replacing variables considered globally by $\bullet$ and noting that the last term with all three variables global is a constant, we get

$$\begin{aligned} f(v \xrightarrow{a} u) &\sim w_0 + w(\bullet \xrightarrow{\bullet} u) + w(v \xrightarrow{\bullet} \bullet) + w(\bullet \xrightarrow{a} \bullet) \\ &+ w(\bullet \xrightarrow{a} u) + w(v \xrightarrow{a} \bullet) + w(v \xrightarrow{\bullet} u). \end{aligned} \quad (14)$$

We have four global effects, a constant, an influencer, an influenced, and an artist, and three bivariate terms that can be modeled by matrix factorization as

$$\begin{aligned} f(v \xrightarrow{a} u) &\sim \alpha_0 + \alpha_1 b_v + \alpha_2 b_u + \alpha_3 b_a \\ &+ \vec{U}\vec{A} + \vec{A}'\vec{V} + \vec{U}'\vec{V}'. \end{aligned} \quad (15)$$

The three bias terms b_v, b_u and b_a correspond to the frequencies of user v influencing, user u being influenced and influences occurred with artist a. $\alpha_1, \ldots, \alpha_3$ are learned weights of the biases, and α_0 is the global learned bias. The six vectors correspond to six different latent vectors.

The final prediction score $\hat{r}$ is based on (8), by using (15) and (13) we can write it in a form

$$\begin{aligned} \hat{r}(u, a, t_u) &= \sum_{v \in n(u)} (\alpha_0 + \alpha_1 b_v + \alpha_2 b_u + \alpha_3 b_a \\ &+ \vec{U}\vec{A} + \vec{A}'\vec{V} + \vec{U}'\vec{V}')(1 - c(1 + \log(t_u - t_v))), \end{aligned} \quad (16)$$

where we sum up for all neighbors of u and t_v is when v last scrobbled a before t_u. For training, we only update $f(v \xrightarrow{a} u)$ by the actual positive events and a generated sample of negative events. In our algorithm we use SGD with respect to MSE to train the latent factors and the weights $\alpha_0, \ldots, \alpha_3$. Notice that the weight of the factor models is included within the factors, since the entire formula (15) is trained by a single SGD procedure. As we learn online, the weight of the effects are also trained by SGD and not by the least squares optimization procedure proposed in [4].

In an efficient implementation, since the expression (13) quickly decays with t, we only need to retrieve the past scrobbles of all friends of u. This step is computationally inexpensive unless u has too many friends, when the recommendation is noisy anyway. To speed up computations, we only consider influences with delay not more than a predefined time frame T and hence we set $c = 1/(1 + \log T)$. With a sufficiently small parameter of the time frame in the range of a few days, our algorithm can hence be implemented even to provide recommendations based on real time updated models.

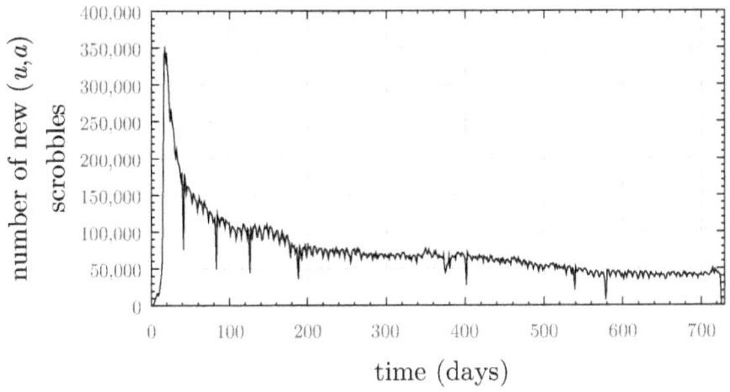

Figure 6: Number of new (u, a) scrobbles as the function of time.

5. ONLINE EVALUATION

Recommender systems in practice need to rank the best K items for the user. In this top-K recommendation task [10, 9] the goal is not to rate some of the individual items but to provide the best candidates. Despite the fact that only prediction for the top list matters in top-K evaluation, several authors propose models trained for RMSE with good top-K performance [17, 24] and hence we follow their approach.

In a time sensitive or online recommender that potentially retrains its model after each and every scrobble, we have to generate new top-K recommendation list for every single scrobble in the test period. The online top-K task is hence different from the standard recommender evaluation settings, since there is always a single item only in the ground truth and the goal is to aggregate the rank of these single items over the entire testing period. For our task, we need carefully selected quality metrics that we describe next.

Out of the two year scrobbling data, we use the full first year as training period. The second year becomes the testing period where we consider scrobbles one by one. We allow a recommender algorithm to use part or full of the data before the scrobble in question for training and require a ranked top list of artists as output. We evaluate the given single actual scrobble a in question against the recommended top list of length K. As seen in Fig. 6, by the second year, the number of first-time scrobbles stabilize around 50,000 a day after the artificial peak in the beginning caused by the lack of earlier data. For the reason of stability, we measure our recommender methods in Year 2 of the timeline.

One possible measure for the quality of a recommended top list of length K could be precision and recall [25, 26]. Note that we evaluate against a single scrobble. Both the number of relevant (1) and the number of retrieved (K) items are fixed. Precision is $1/K$ if we retrieve the single item scrobbled and 0 otherwise. Recall is 0 if we do not retrieve the single relevant item and 1 otherwise. The value of K that maximizes precision is the rank of the item scrobbled and hence "maximal precision" follows the function of $1/\text{rank}$.

Recently, measures other than precision and recall are preferred for measuring the quality of top-K recommendation [2]. The most common measure is NDCG that is a normalized version of the discounted cumulative gain (DCG) with threshold K

$$\text{DCG@K}(a) = \begin{cases} 0 & \text{if rank}(a) > K; \\ \dfrac{1}{\log_2(\text{rank}(a) + 1)} & \text{otherwise.} \end{cases} \quad (17)$$

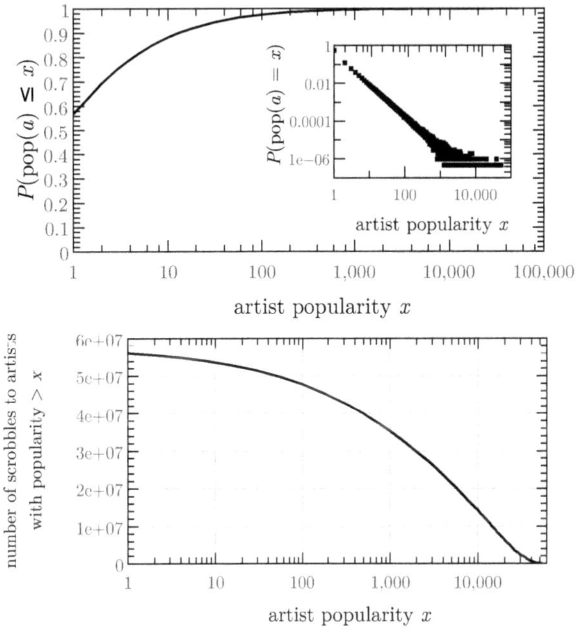

Figure 7: **Top:** Distribution of scrobble count to a given artist and the cumulative distribution. **Bottom:** Fraction of scrobbles for artists with popularity at least a given value x, as the function of x.

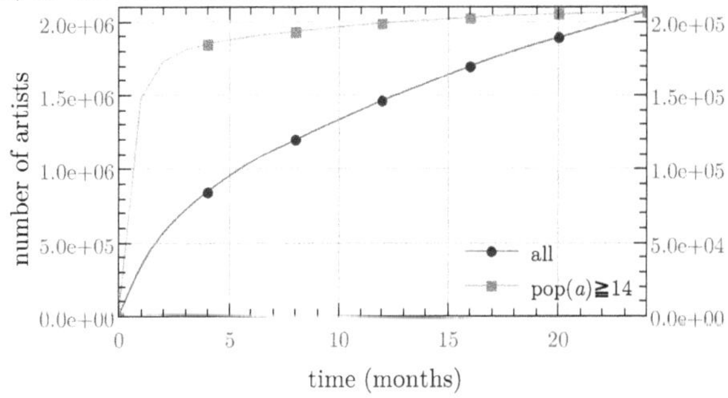

Figure 8: The number of different artists scrobbled before a given time in the two year period of the data set.

Since DCG is a slower decreasing function of the rank than what we observed for maximal precision, DCG is more advantageous since we have a large number of artists of potential interest to each user. Our choice is in accordance with the observations in [2] as well.

Note that in our unusual setting of DCG evaluation, there is a single relevant item and hence for example no normalization is needed as in case of the DCG measure. Also note that the DCG values will be small since the NDCG of a relative short sequence of actual scrobbles will roughly be equal to the sum of the individual DCG values. The DCG measured over 100 subsequent scrobbles of different artists cannot be more than the ideal DCG, which is $\sum_{i=1}^{100} 1/\log_2(i+1) = 20.64$ in this case (the ideal value is 6.58 for $K = 20$). Hence the DCG of an individual scrobble will on average be less than 0.21 for $K = 100$ and 0.33 for $K = 20$.

In our evaluation we discard infrequent artists from the data set both for efficiency considerations and due to the fact that our item based recommenders will have too little information on them. As seen in Fig. 7, top, the number of

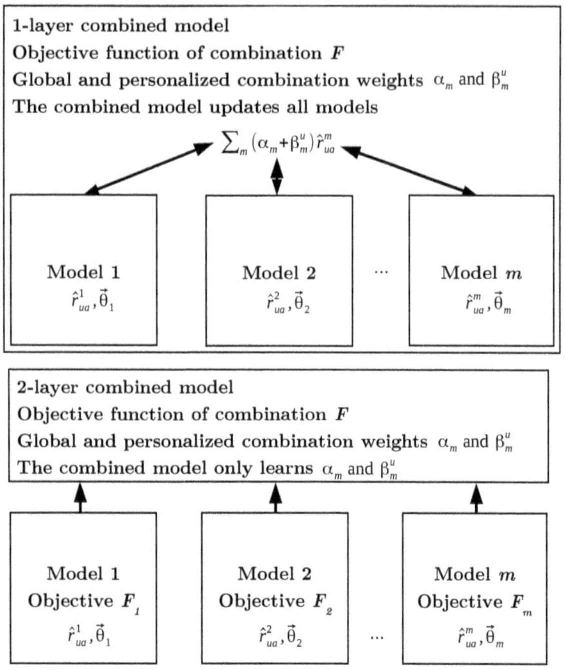

Figure 9: Scheme of the 1-layer(**top**) and 2-layer(**bottom**) online combination models.

artists with a given scrobble count follow a power-law distribution with near 60% of the artists appearing only once. While 90% of the artists gathered less than 20 scrobbles in two years, as seen in Fig. 7, bottom, they attribute to only less than 10% of the data set. In other words, by discarding a large number of artists, we only lose a small fraction of the scrobbles. For efficiency we only consider artists of frequency more than 14.

As time elapses, we observe near linear increase in the number of artists that appear in the data set in Fig. 8. This figure shows artists with at least 14 scrobbles separately. Their count grows slower but still we observe a large number of new artist that appear in time and exceed the minimum count of 14. Very fast growth for infrequent artists may be a result of noise and unidentified artists from e.g. YouTube videos and similar Web sources.

6. ONLINE BLENDING

We give two methods based on SGD that learn the online blending weight of recommender algorithms. Note that the algorithms may or may not themselves be based on SGD, i.e. the derivative of the individual models may or may not be available for the blending optimization procedure. Furthermore, we may blend methods with different definitions of the implicit feedback data sequence: the positive instances for the influence based recommender form a small subset of all the events and hence the influence recommender also needs different methods for generating negative training samples.

If the derivatives of the individual models are available for the top level optimizer, we may optimize in a single layer (top of Fig. 9) by minimizing

$$F(\hat{r}_{ua}) = F\left(\sum_m (\alpha_m + \beta^u_m)\hat{r}^m_{ua}\right), \qquad (18)$$

where we sum over all models m, and F is the error measure, MSE in our case. Notice that we learn a user dependent blending weight vector β^u_m, hence for example the blending of a k and a k' factorization will in theory have at most as high F as a single $k+k'$ one, and in our experience performed only slightly better.

We may take the derivatives for both the constants α and β and the individual model parameters $\vec{\theta}_m$:

$$\frac{\partial F}{\partial \vec{\theta}_m} = \frac{\partial F}{\partial \hat{r}_{ua}} \frac{\partial \hat{r}_{ua}}{\partial \hat{r}^m_{ua}} \frac{\partial \hat{r}^m_{ua}}{\partial \vec{\theta}_m} = \frac{\partial F}{\partial \hat{r}_{ua}} (\alpha_m + \beta^u_m) \frac{\partial \hat{r}^m_{ua}}{\partial \vec{\theta}_m}; \qquad (19)$$

$$\frac{\partial F}{\partial \alpha_m} = \frac{\partial F}{\partial \hat{r}_{ua}} \frac{\partial \hat{r}_{ua}}{\partial \alpha_m} = \frac{\partial F}{\partial \hat{r}_{ua}} \hat{r}^m_{ua}; \qquad (20)$$

$$\frac{\partial F}{\partial \beta^u_m} = \frac{\partial F}{\partial \hat{r}_{ua}} \frac{\partial \hat{r}_{ua}}{\partial \beta^u_m} = \frac{\partial F}{\partial \hat{r}_{ua}} \hat{r}^m_{ua}. \qquad (21)$$

If the derivatives are not available, the individual models are considered as black box for blending and we have to train in two layers (bottom of Fig. 9) and we may only use the last two derivatives (20) and (21).

If different models need different training samples, we cannot use the derivative (19) either. This is the case if we combine the baseline matrix factorization with the algorithm of Section 4. If the current positive event is not the result of an influence (i.e. not a first time scrobble or no friend scrobbling the same artist before), then we only update the baseline models. And if there is at least one possible influencer $v \xrightarrow{a} u$ for the current event (u, a), then we generate separate negative training instances for the baseline and the influence models. Notice that even a negative influence training data $v' \xrightarrow{a} u$ must satisfy that v' is a friend of u who scrobbled a and hence we usually have to choose from a restricted small set. Blending is meaningful only over this restricted set too, since for other events, the influence recommender has no t value in equation (16) to compute its prediction. Hence for blending, we have to use the same negative samples as for training the influence model.

7. MUSIC RECOMMENDATION BASELINE METHODS

We describe three baseline methods. The first one is based on dynamic popularity in Section 7.1. The second one in Section 7.2 is an online matrix factorization and the third one in Section 7.3 adds regularization over friendship as in [18].

All the methods discussed here are online algorithms, as opposed to the batch methods used in challenges such as Netflix. In some preliminary experiments the batch algorithms performed significantly worse in the online task compared to their online versions. We plan to compare the performance of batch and online versions of the algorithms in an online task more extensively in the future.

7.1 Dynamic popularity based recommendation

Given a predefined time frame T as in Section 4, at time t_u we recommend an artist based on the popularity in time not earlier than $t_u - T$ but before t_u. In our algorithm we update the counts and store artists sorted by the current popularity. In one time step, we may either add a new scrobble event or remove the earliest one, corresponding to a count increment

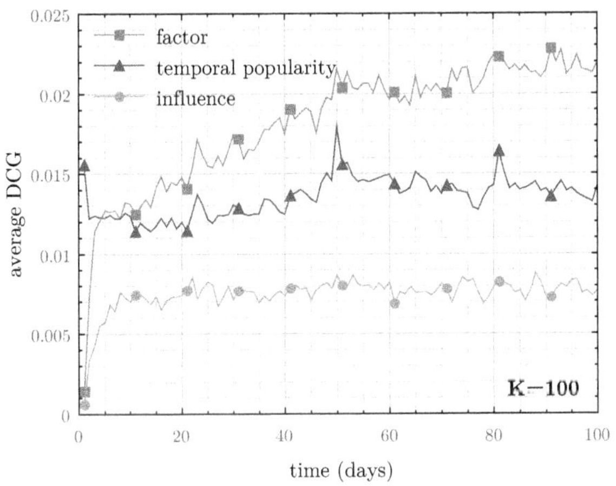

Figure 10: Online performance of the three different recommenders.

or decrement. For globally popular items, the sorted order can be maintained by a few changes in the order only.

7.2 Online matrix factorization

Stochastic gradient descent methods in batch setting may iterate several times over the training set until convergence. In an online setting [1], the model needs to be retrained after each new event and hence reiterations over the earlier parts of the data is ruled out. We may implement an online recommender algorithm by allowing a single iteration over the training data only, and this single iteration processes the events in the order of time. We used the first time scrobbles as positive training instances and generated negative training instances by selecting three random artists uniformly at the time when a user first scrobbled an artist.

Online recommenders seem more restricted than those that may iterate over the data set several times and one would expect inferior quality by the online methods. Online methods however have the advantage of giving much more emphasis on recent events. In some sense, the online methods may incorporate the notion of influence from Section 3: if friends have similar taste and hence similar factor weights, a friend scrobbling some artist a will in the near future strengthen the weight for this artist for all users who have similar taste.

7.3 Social regularization

Ma et al. [18] propose a method to implement constraints in a factor model based recommender algorithm for keeping the profile of friends similar. We implemented both the average-based and the individual-based regularization of [18] and found the latter superior, hence we use individual-based regularization in our experiments. Note that these algorithms have no knowledge of time and hence cannot incorporate our notion of subsequent first time scrobbles as in Section 3, even though they may work very well for other, non-first-time scrobbles that we do not consider in this paper.

8. EXPERIMENTS

In this section we describe the quality of our results for the second year testing period. Under various settings, we give daily average DCG@K defined by equation (17).

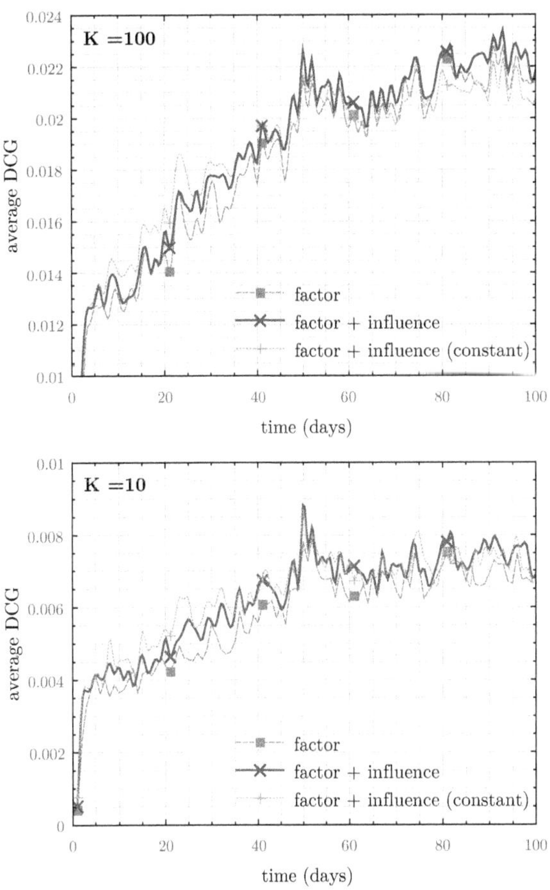

Figure 11: Combination of the influence and factor models.

Our experiments were carried out over the single core of an AMD based virtual server with 128GB RAM. On average, it took 28 minutes to process one day of scrobble history, update the online models and provide top-K recommendation corresponding to each user event.

Parameter K in equation (17) controls the length of the top list considered for evaluation. In other words, K can be interpreted as the size of the list presented to the user. Practically K must be small in order not to flood the user with information. We show results for $K = 10$ and 100. In Fig. 10, DCG@100 is shown for two baseline methods, matrix factorization and temporal popularity, as well as our influence model.

When combining variants of baseline and influence recommendation predictions, we observed that that social regularization did not improve matrix factorization and temporal popularity did not blend with online factorization. Indeed in Fig. 10 we may observe that peaks in temporal popularity performance immediately appear as peaks in matrix factorization performance, since online factorization learns temporal trends very well.

In Fig. 11, one can see that the online combination with influence recommendation improves over online matrix factorization both for DCG@10 and DCG@100. The average improvement is roughly 7% for DCG@10, and 3% for DCG@100. Over the same figure, we plot the performance of the constant term alone in equation (15). This simple recommender corresponds to adding up all the $(1 - c(1 + \log t))$ values for possible influencers without model building beyond learning the blending weight involved. At first this simple model blends best with the baseline, however, as the factor models get more training data, they become superior and the importance of the constant term α_0 in the model diminishes.

Conclusions

Based on a 70,000-entry sample of Last.fm users, we were able to exploit the effect of users influencing the taste of friends for improving the quality of music recommendation. Over static baseline recommenders, we achieved a 5% improvement in recommendation accuracy when presenting artists from friends' past scrobbles that the given user had never seen before.

Our system has very strong time-awareness: when we recommend, we look back in the near past and combine friends' scrobbles with the baseline methods. The influence from a friend at a given time is certain function of the observed influence in the past and the time elapsed since the friend scrobbled the given artist.

All of our methods learn online and provide top-K recommendation lists recomputed for every user query. Because of the inherent time dependence, we defined average DCG as our evaluation metric and gave a new online blending procedure that learns online user-dependent weights.

Acknowledgments

To the Last.fm team for preparing us this volume of the anonymized data set that cannot be efficiently fetched through the public Last.fm API.

The publication was supported by the KTIA_AIK_12-1-2013-0037 and the PIAC_13-1-2013-0205 projects. The projects are supported by Hungarian Government, managed by the National Development Agency, and financed by the Research and Technology Innovation Fund. Work conducted at the Institute for Computer Science and Control, Hungarian Academy of Sciences (MTA SZTAKI) was supported in part by the EC FET Open project "New tools and algorithms for directed network analysis" (NADINE No 288956), by the Momentum Grant of the Hungarian Academy of Sciences, and by OTKA NK 105645. Work conducted at the Technical University Budapest has been developed in the framework of the project "Talent care and cultivation in the scientific workshops of BME" project. This project is supported by the grant TÁMOP - 4.2.2.B-10/1–2010-0009. Work conducted at University of Szeged was partially supported by the European Union and the European Social Fund through project FuturICT.hu (grant no.: TAMOP-4.2.2.C-11/1/KONV-2012-0013).

9. REFERENCES

[1] J. Abernethy, K. Canini, J. Langford, and A. Simma. Online collaborative filtering. *University of California at Berkeley, Tech. Rep*, 2007.

[2] A. Al-Maskari, M. Sanderson, and P. Clough. The relationship between ir effectiveness measures and user satisfaction. In *Proc. 30th SIGIR*, pages 773–774. ACM, 2007.

[3] E. Bakshy, J. M. H., W. A. Mason, and D. J. Watts. Everyone's an influencer: quantifying influence on twitter. In *Proc. 4th WSDM*, pages 65–74. ACM, 2011.

[4] R. Bell and Y. Koren. Improved Neighborhood-based Collaborative Filtering. *KDD-Cup and Workshop*, 2007.

[5] R. Bell and Y. Koren. Lessons from the Netflix prize challenge. 2007.

[6] J. Bennett and S. Lanning. The netflix prize. In *KDD Cup and Workshop in conjunction with KDD*, 2007.

[7] F. Bonchi. Influence propagation in social networks: A data mining perspective. *IEEE Intelligent Informatics Bulletin*, 12(1):8–16, 2011.

[8] M. Cha, A. Mislove, B. Adams, and K. P. Gummadi. Characterizing social cascades in flickr. In *Proc. first workshop on Online social networks*, pages 13–18. ACM, 2008.

[9] P. Cremonesi, Y. Koren, and R. Turrin. Performance of recommender algorithms on top-n recommendation tasks. In *Proc. 4th RecSys*, pages 39–46. ACM, 2010.

[10] M. Deshpande and G. Karypis. Item-based top-n recommendation algorithms. *ACM TOIS*, 22(1):143–177, 2004.

[11] P. Domingos and M. Richardson. Mining the network value of customers. In *Proc. 7th SIGKDD*, pages 57–66. ACM, 2001.

[12] D. Eck, P. Lamere, T. Bertin-Mahieux, and S. Green. Automatic generation of social tags for music recommendation. *Advances in neural information processing systems*, 20:385–392, 2007.

[13] A. Goyal, F. Bonchi, and L. V. Lakshmanan. Learning influence probabilities in social networks. In *Proc. 3rd WSDM*, pages 241–250. ACM, 2010.

[14] X. Hu, M. Bay, and J. Downie. Creating a simplified music mood classification ground-truth set. In *Proc. 8th ISMIR*, 2007.

[15] R. Jäschke, L. Marinho, A. Hotho, L. Schmidt-Thieme, and G. Stumme. Tag recommendations in folksonomies. *PKDD*, pages 506–514, 2007.

[16] P. Knees, T. Pohle, M. Schedl, and G. Widmer. A music search engine built upon audio-based and web-based similarity measures. In *Proc. 30th SIGIR*, pages 447–454. ACM, 2007.

[17] Y. Koren. Factorization meets the neighborhood: a multifaceted collaborative filtering model. In *Proc. 14th SIGKDD*, pages 426–434. ACM, 2008.

[18] H. Ma, D. Zhou, C. Liu, M. R. Lyu, and I. King. Recommender systems with social regularization. In *Proc. 4th WSDM*, pages 287–296. ACM, 2011.

[19] B. Markines, C. Cattuto, F. Menczer, D. Benz, A. Hotho, and G. Stumme. Evaluating similarity measures for emergent semantics of social tagging. In *18th WWW*, pages 641–641. ACM, 2009.

[20] C. Marlow, M. Naaman, D. Boyd, and M. Davis. Ht06, tagging paper, taxonomy, flickr, academic article, to read. In *Proc. 17th Hypertext and Hypermedia*, pages 31–40. ACM, 2006.

[21] J. Noel, S. Sanner, K.-N. Tran, P. Christen, L. Xie, E. V. Bonilla, E. Abbasnejad, and N. Della Penna. New objective functions for social collaborative filtering. In *Proc. 21st WWW*, pages 859–868. ACM, 2012.

[22] R. Pálovics and A. A. Benczúr. Temporal influence over the last. fm social network. In *Proc. ASONAM*, pages 486–493. ACM, 2013.

[23] K. Tso-Sutter, L. Marinho, and L. Schmidt-Thieme. Tag-aware recommender systems by fusion of collaborative filtering algorithms. In *Proc. Symp. on Applied Computing*, pages 1995–1999. ACM, 2008.

[24] M. Weimer, A. Karatzoglou, and A. Smola. Adaptive collaborative filtering. In *Proc. 2nd RecSys*, pages 275–282. ACM, 2008.

[25] X. Yang, H. Steck, Y. Guo, and Y. Liu. On top-k recommendation using social networks. In *Proc. 6th RecSys*, pages 67–74. ACM, 2012.

[26] Q. Yuan, L. Chen, and S. Zhao. Factorization vs. regularization: fusing heterogeneous social relationships in top-n recommendation. In *Proc. 5th RecSys*, pages 245–252. ACM, 2011.

'Free Lunch' Enhancement for Collaborative Filtering with Factorization Machines

Babak Loni, Alan Said, Martha Larson, Alan Hanjalic
Multimedia Computing Group
Delft University of Technology, Netherlands
{b.loni, a.said, m.a.larson, a.hanjalic}@tudelft.nl,

ABSTRACT

The advantage of Factorization Machines over other factorization models is their ability to easily integrate and efficiently exploit auxiliary information to improve Collaborative Filtering. Until now, this auxiliary information has been drawn from external knowledge sources beyond the user-item matrix. In this paper, we demonstrate that Factorization Machines can exploit additional representations of information inherent in the user-item matrix to improve recommendation performance. We refer to our approach as 'Free Lunch' enhancement since it leverages clusters that are based on information that is present in the user-item matrix, but not otherwise directly exploited during matrix factorization. Borrowing clustering concepts from codebook sharing, our approach can also make use of 'Free Lunch' information inherent in a user-item matrix from an auxiliary domain that is different from the target domain of the recommender. Our approach improves performance both in the joint case, in which the auxiliary and target domains share users, and in the disjoint case, in which they do not. Although the 'Free Lunch' enhancement does not apply equally well to any given domain or domain combination, our overall conclusion is that Factorization Machines present an opportunity to exploit information that is ubiquitously present, but commonly under-appreciated by Collaborative Filtering algorithms.

Categories and Subject Descriptors

H.3.3 [**Information Search and Retrieval**]: Information Filtering

General Terms

Algorithms, Performance, Experimentation

1. INTRODUCTION

Factorization Machines (FMs) [8] are general models that factorize user-item collaborative data into real-valued feature vectors. FMs have recently attracted the attention of the recommender system community because of the ease and effectiveness with which they can integrate information from external sources, for example, context information [9]. However, until now, focus of FM approaches in the recommender system community has been on integrating new sources of information. In this paper, we investigate the potential of FMs to help us make the most of information that we already have. Because our approach makes use of information that is already present in the user-item matrix, it has the feel of delivering 'something for nothing.' In this spirit, we call our approach 'Free Lunch' enhancement of Factorization Machines.

RecSys'14, October 6–10, 2014, Foster City, Silicon Valley, CA, USA.

ACM 978-1-4503-2668-1/14/10 ...$15.00.
http://dx.doi.org/10.1145/2645710.2645771.

The specific 'Free Lunch' effect that we focus on in this paper arises from known, but under-appreciated information inherent in the user-item matrix. In general, conventional Collaborative Filtering (CF) approaches, including memory-based and model-based methods, exploit similarities that are based on sets of rated items. The information in user-item matrixes can, however, be repackaged to create other representations of items and users. Specifically, here, we investigate one such repackaging that views users and items in terms of their overall rating patterns. Overall rating patterns are expressed as rating histograms, which are 'trivial' in the sense that they require simple aggregation of information inherent in the user-item matrix. However, clustering these histograms creates user and item categories that constitute new representations of information that is not otherwise exploited by matrix factorization. In this paper, we introduce an approach that uses Factorization Machines to integrate these category labels into a Collaborative Filtering algorithms capable of improving recommendation performance. The approach reveals its full potential when used to exploit information not only from the user-item matrix of the target domain, but also information from the user-item matrix of auxiliary domains. In this respect it constitutes a simple, yet effective, method for Cross-Domain Collaborative Filtering.

2. BACKGROUND AND MOTIVATION

The 'Free Lunch' approach does not literally achieve something for nothing. Rather, as mentioned above, it takes advantage of an underexploited representation of users and items as rating histograms. A rating histogram encodes the normalized frequency with which a user assigns a certain rating or an item is assigned a certain rating. Upon first consideration, rating histograms appear to destroy the very connections between users and items that provide the basis for CF. Worse, they capture bias in user rating habits, e.g., the general tendency of individual users to assign very high or very low scores. It is exactly this bias that many similarity metrics seek to avoid. However, seen from a different perspective, rating habits have the ability to capture something about the 'rating style' of individual users or the 'style' of users who rate specific items. Ultimately, the success of our approach attests to the benefit of taking this perspective.

The perspective is supported by evidence from the literature that similarity of rating style is connected to similarity in taste in populations of consumers. For example, Tan and Neetessine [10] presents a study of the Netflix Prize data set that reveals patterns such as a tendency of people who give higher ratings to watch mainstream movies. In other words, users who are similarly "generous" or "stingy" with high ratings when rating movies, may actually have a tendency to prefer the same kind of movies. The basic insight of our approach is that such relationships already exist implicitly in the user item matrix, but are not exploited by conventional matrix factorization approaches. Note that we are not making a claim that rating histograms are optimally suitable for comparing users. Our 'Free Lunch' enhancement still stands to benefit from a weak indicator of similarity. Our position is if we can stand to benefit from this information, we should seize the opportunity. Note that using normalized rating histograms to represent users means that it is possible to calculate a similarity between two users who have not necessarily rated the same items. In cases where recommender systems must confront extremely sparse data conditions, weak indicators of similarity could prove to be particularly useful.

Use of clustering techniques in CF stretches back into early history of recommender systems, and includes many variants. In the earliest work, clustering was used to reduce dimensionality, focusing on standard representations of users as vectors of rated items. Also, clustering has been used as a way to integrate content into CF to create hybrid recommendation algorithms. For example, in Li and Kim's approach [5], content-based information about items is used to create item clusters, which are then represented in a cluster-based matrix to which CF approaches are applied on. The clustering in our work differs from previous uses of clustering for CF in that it relies on neither standard representations, nor or additional information about items or users, but rather uses new representations of existing information in order to create clusters.

Clustering has proven particularly useful in Cross-Domain Collaborative Filtering (CDCF) algorithms, algorithms that exploit one domain to make recommendations in another. Li et al. [4] proposed a clustering approach known as *codebook transfer* for CDCF. Their model tries to find similar rating patterns in different domains, and then transfer cluster-level patterns to improve recommendation in a target domain. The approach requires additional factorizations on auxiliary domains which makes it computationally more complex compared to a typical matrix factorization model. Our 'Free Lunch' enhancement approach also uses domain transfer based on clusters. However, where Li et al. [4] use conventional representations of users and items and co-clustering, our approach represents users and items in terms of rating histograms. Our approach incurs little computational burden with clustering. Rather, in 'Free Lunch' Enhancement, clustering is a pre-processing step, since it is performed off-line on individual domains and is not part of building the model.

Our previous work [7], established that FMs achieve state-of-the-art performance in CDCF, and can be straightforwardly applied in the case of joint domains, i.e., cases in which the target domain and the auxiliary domain do not share the same users. That work did not use clusters, but rather exploited individual ratings. In this work, we take FM performance as our baseline, and investigate how it can be improved by exploiting user and item clusters. Our proposed approach also applies to disjoint domains, i.e., domains that do not share users.

3. ENHANCEMENT APPROACH FOR FMS

This section provides the necessary background on FMs and explains the details of our 'Free Lunch' enhancement approach, that creates clusters using rating histograms for integration into FMs.

3.1 Factorization Machines

In contrast to typical Factorization techniques in which the interaction of users and items are represented by a matrix, in Factorization Machines [8] the interaction of a user and an item (i.e., when a user rates an item) is represented by a feature vector. To understand how FMs work, let us assume that the data of a rating prediction problem is represented by a set S of tuples $(\mathbf{x}, y)$ where $\mathbf{x} = (x_1, \ldots, x_n) \in \mathbb{R}^n$ is an n-dimensional feature vector representing user-item interaction and y is the rating value. Factorization machines model all interactions between features using factorized interaction parameters. The interactions can be between a pair of features, or it can even be between larger number of features. In this work, we adopted an FM model with order 2 where only the interactions between pairs of features are taken into account. This model can be represented as follows:

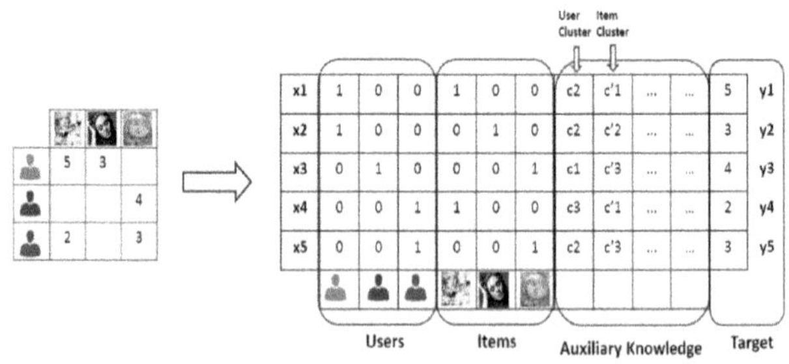

Figure 1: Encoding user and item clusters into user-item feature vectors.

$$\hat{y}(\mathbf{x}) = w_0 + \sum_{j=1}^{n} w_j x_j + \sum_{j=1}^{n} \sum_{j'=j+1}^{n} w_{j,j'} x_j x_{j'} \quad (1)$$

where w_j are model parameters and $w_{j,j'}$ are factorized interaction parameters and are defined as $w_{j,j'} = \mathbf{v}_j . \mathbf{v}_{j'}$ where $\mathbf{v}_j$ is k-dimensional factorized vector for feature j. For an FM with n as the dimensionality of feature vectors and k as the dimensionality of factorization, the model parameters that need to be learnt are $\Theta = \{w_0, w_1, \ldots, w_n, v_{1,1}, \ldots, v_{n,k}\}$.

The parameters of the model can be learnt by three different learning algorithms [8]: Stochastic Gradient Descent (SGD), Alternating Least-Squares (ALS) and Markov Chain Monte Carlo (MCMC) method. MCMC learning method proved fastest in our exploratory work and were adopted for our experiments.

3.2 Cluster Encoding

Factorization machines require the user-item interactions to be represented by a feature vector. This characteristic allows us to incorporate any additional knowledge in terms of real-valued features. We take this advantage of FMs into account and extend the user-item feature vectors with cluster level features which potentially can improve the rating prediction task.

In FMs, a standard rating prediction problem is represented by a target function $y : U \times I \rightarrow \mathbb{R}$. We represent each user-item interaction $(u, i) \in U \times I$ with a feature vector $\mathbf{x} \in \mathbb{R}^{|U|+|I|}$ with binary variables indicating which user rated which item. In other words, if user u rated item i the feature vector $\mathbf{x}$ is represented as:

$$\mathbf{x} = (\underbrace{0, \ldots, 0, 1, 0, \ldots, 0}_{|U|}, \underbrace{0, \ldots, 0, 1, 0, \ldots, 0}_{|I|}) \quad (2)$$

where non-zero elements correspond to user u and item i. The feature vector $\mathbf{x}$ can also be represented by its sparse representation $\mathbf{x}(u, i) = \{(u, 1), (i, 1)\}$.

Our cluster encoding algorithm extends the above feature vector by user and item clusters. Therefore, the target function would be

$y : U \times I \times C_u \times C_i \rightarrow \mathbb{R}$ where C_u and C_i are user and item cluster spaces. User and item clusters can also be drawn from other, auxiliary domains. In other words, the clusters that users and items belong to in auxiliary domains can also be identified and added to the feature vector. More specifically, we can represent the sparse form of a cluster-enhanced feature vector as follows:

$$\mathbf{x}(u, i) = \{(u, 1), (i, 1), (c_j(u), 1), (c_j(i), 1) : j = 1 \ldots m\} \quad (3)$$

where $c_j(u)$ and $c_j(i)$ are user and item cluster ids in domain j and m is the total number of domains.

Figure 1 illustrates our proposed approach to building feature vectors from a user-item matrix. For each rating, a binary feature vector is created in which the corresponding user and item are indicated by 1s and the remaining features are 0s. This feature vector is then extended by additional binary features which specify the user and item cluster in different domains. The rating values are specified as the output of each vector. Using FM we try to predict the output of the test samples.

3.3 Cluster Construction

Our clustering approach considers users with similar rating patterns to be similar, assigning them to the same cluster. In the context of our work, rating patterns are based on the histogram of rating values. More specifically a user u_j is represented by the feature vector $u_j = (u_{j1}, \ldots, u_{jp})$ where p is the upper bound of rating values in the dataset domain and u_{jk} is the number of items which are rated with value k by user u_j. Similarly, an item i_j can be represented by $i_j = (i_{j1}, \ldots, i_{jp})$. Given the above representations, we calculate user and item clusters using the K-means clustering algorithm. The distance between vectors is calculated based on Euclidean distance. We choose K-means due to its simplicity and efficiency, which distinguishes it from alternative clustering algorithms [1].

For cross-domain scenarios, we create clusters of users and items in auxiliary domains, and for each user and item in the target domain the most similar clusters are identified by measuring the distance of a user or an item to the center of clusters. The most similar clusters in the auxiliary domain are then used to extend the user-item feature vector in Equation 3.

4. EXPERIMENTS

In this section we explain the datasets and frameworks that we used and describe the experiments that we did with their results. We further analyze and discuss the results to find out whether the improvements obtained by our method is significant or not.

4.1 Datasets and Framework

We conducted our experiments on a dataset from Amazon [3] consisting of four joint domains, Movielens and Epinions datasets, each having a different set of users and items. The four domains in the Amazon dataset are books, music CDs, DVDs and video tapes. The Amazon dataset contains 7,593,243 ratings on a 1-5 scale provided by 1,555,170 users over 548,552 different products including 393,558 books, 103,144 music CDs, 19,828 DVDs and 26,132 VHS tapes. We use the Movielens 1 million dataset, which consists of 1,000,209 ratings on a 1-5 scale, 6,040 users and 3,883 items. The Epinions dataset contains 664,865 ratings also on a 1-5 scale, 49,289 users and 139,737 items. The data is split into a training set (75%) and a test set (25%).

We implemented our approach within our recommendation framework [6] using C#, which is built on top of two open source libraries for recommender systems: MyMediaLite [2], which implements the most common CF approaches, and LibFM [8], which implements FMs algorithms.

4.2 Results

We evaluated our 'Free Lunch' enhanced FM approach with respect to three different enhancement scenarios, and a range of different settings for the number of clusters, which were created with K-means clustering. Figures 2 and 3 present the performance of our approach on the Amazon Books and and the Amazon Music datasets in terms of Root Mean Square Error (RMSE). Each graph shows the performance of the dataset under our three scenarios: 1) Target domain clusters: user and item clusters from the same domain (i.e., a single target domain) are used to extend the feature vectors (i.e., Equation (3) with $j = 1$). 2) Target and joint auxiliary domain clusters: user and item clusters from a joint auxiliary domain are used (i.e., Equation (3) with $j > 1$). 3) Target and disjoint auxiliary domain clusters: user and item clusters from a disjoint auxiliary domain are used (i.e., users do not overlap). To show the effectiveness of our approach, we compare the performance of each scenario with a baseline in which no user or item clusters are used. In other words, for our baseline, the user-item interactions are simply represented by feature vectors as described in Equation (2). The results in Figure 2 and 3 demonstrate that our method outperforms the baseline on both datasets and in all three scenarios. The best performance is achieved on joint domains, which is not unexpected since the domains share users, and the auxiliary domain brings additional information about items rated by these users into play. What is more surprising is that clustering applied in the single domain case, or applied in the case of joint domains is able to come very close to the performance in the joint domains. Figures 2 and 3 also reveal that for all three scenarios, the performance also improves as the number of clusters is increased, until it reaches a point where there is no improvement, at $k = 10$.

We investigate the results achieved in the joint domain scenario with a statistical analysis of the results (in terms of RMSE). This analysis reveals that the improvements obtained for the Amazon Books dataset (Figure 2) when extended with clusters from Amazon Music are statistically significant ($p < 0.05$) regardless of the number of clusters used when compared to the results from the baseline (no clusters). However, a similar analysis of the results obtained for the Amazon Music dataset enriched with clusters from Amazon Book (Figure 3) does not point to significance ($p > 0.2$). We note that the performance of the joint and disjoint scenarios on each data set track the performance of the single domain scenario. This fact suggests that a strongly performing target domain is critical for the approach to benefit from joint domains. Strong performance of the target domain could be related to size, here, 400 thousand books vs.100 thousand music CDs.

Next we turn to investigate the 'target domain cluster' scenario involving a single domain in more detail. Table 1, summarizes the results from the Amazon Books and Amazon Music data set, and also reports further results calculated on the Movielens and Epinions datasets (both RMSE and MAE evaluation metrics). The performance on the different data sets is reported for k=10 clusters, the best condition determined in the previous experiment, and compared with the no-clustering baseline. These results confirm that the performance improvement delivered by 'Free Lunch' enhancement is not limited to Amazon data sets, but is achieved on other data sets as well. The relative improvement on the Amazon Book dataset (12% in terms of RMSE) is the largest. The relative greater improvement on the Amazon data set may be attributable to the fact that it is sparser than the Movielens or Epinions sets.

As the results in Table 1 show, the best improvement is achieved on the Amazon Book dataset (12% in terms of RMSE), while there

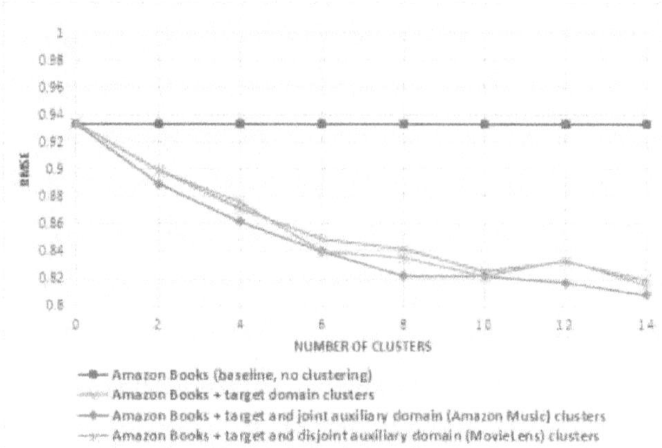

Figure 2: Performance of our proposed method on Amazon Books dataset based on different number of clusters and different enhancement scenarios. The baseline (no clusters) is represented by the straight line.

are less dramatic improvements on the Movielens and Epinions datasets. This can be due to the fact these datasets are denser compared to the Amazon dataset, implying that the underlying similarities between users and items are already well captured, and clustering information is of less importance. 'Free Lunch' enhancement can apparently contribute more to the rating prediction task in cases where datasets are sparse, meaning that additional representations of the information in the user-item matrix have more to contribute.

Table 1: Comparison of our cluster-enhanced approach with the no-cluster baseline

	No clusters		10 clusters	
Dataset	RMSE	MAE	RMSE	MAE
Amazon Books	0.933	0.841	0.825	0.778
Amazon Music	0.984	0.861	0.945	0.832
Movielens	0.936	0.862	0.890	0.838
Epinions	1.082	0.920	1.024	0.891

5. CONCLUSION AND OUTLOOK

We have presented a 'Free Lunch' enhancement approach that makes use of the ability of Factorization Machines to easily and effectively integrate additional information. Our approach demonstrates that it is not necessary to turn to outside resources to find additional information useful for improving Factorization Machines, but instead we can make better use of information already at hand. The larger message is that FM approaches that do not first attempt to maximize the benefit they can derive from information at hand, i.e., 'Free Lunch', are missing opportunities.

In this paper, we have focused on clusters formed using rating histograms. We show that this information can be used to improve rating prediction in cases where only a single, target domain is available, or in cases where an auxiliary domain (joint or disjoint with the target domain) is also available. Our future work will also investigate other possible types of 'Free Lunch' information. The list of sources that we are interested in ranges from popularity information to random assignment of users to user-groups. Further, we will work to make more detailed understanding of what makes a domain particularly a suitable target domain for 'Free Lunch' enhancement, and how to best identify useful auxiliary domains.

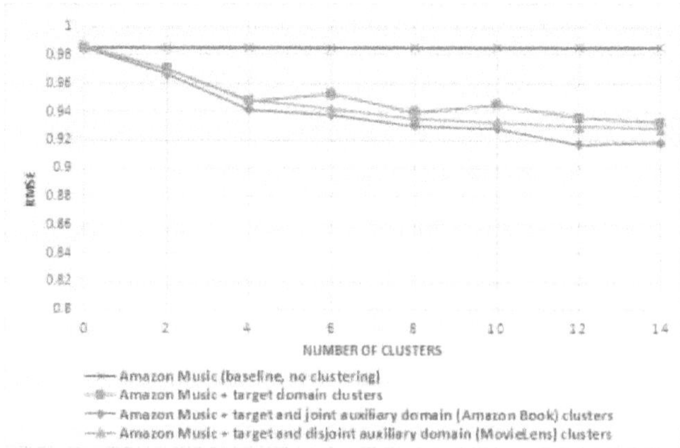

Figure 3: Performance of our proposed method on Amazon Music dataset based on different number of clusters and different enhancement scenarios. The baseline (no clusters) is represented by the straight line.

Acknowledgment

This research is supported by funding from two European Commission's 7th Framework Program projects under grant agreements no. 610594 (CrowdRec) and no. 601166 (PHENICX).

6. REFERENCES

[1] X. Amatriain, A. Jaimes, N. Oliver, and J. M. Pujol. Data Mining Methods for Recommender Systems. In F. Ricci, L. Rokach, B. Shapira, and P. B. Kantor, editors, *Recommender Systems Handbook*, chapter 2, pages 39–71. Springer US, 2011.

[2] Z. Gantner, S. Rendle, C. Freudenthaler, and L. Schmidt-Thieme. Mymedialite: a free recommender system library. RecSys '11. ACM, 2011.

[3] J. Leskovec, L. A. Adamic, and B. A. Huberman. The dynamics of viral marketing. *ACM Trans. Web*, 1(1), May 2007.

[4] B. Li, Q. Yang, and X. Xue. Can movies and books collaborate?: cross-domain collaborative filtering for sparsity reduction. IJCAI'09, 2009.

[5] Q. Li and B. M. Kim. Clustering approach for hybrid recommender system. In *Web Intelligence, 2003. WI 2003. Proceedings. IEEE/WIC International Conference on*, pages 33–38, Oct 2003.

[6] B. Loni and A. Said. Wraprec: An easy extension of recommender system libraries. In *Proceedings of 8th ACM International Conference of Recommender Systems*, RecSys '14, 2014.

[7] B. Loni, Y. Shi, M. Larson, and A. Hanjalic. Cross-domain collaborative filtering with factorization machines. In *Proceedings of the 36th European Conference on Information Retrieval*, ECIR '14, 2014.

[8] S. Rendle. Factorization machines with libfm. *ACM Trans. Intell. Syst. Technol.*, 3(3), May 2012.

[9] S. Rendle, Z. Gantner, C. Freudenthaler, and L. Schmidt-Thieme. Fast context-aware recommendations with factorization machines. SIGIR '11. ACM, 2011.

[10] T. Tan and S. Neetessine. Is Tom Cruise threatend? using Netflix Prize data to examine the long tail of electronic commerce. Technical report, University of Pennsylvania, Wharton Business School, 2009.

An Analysis of Users' Propensity toward Diversity in Recommendations

Tommaso Di Noia[1], Vito Claudio Ostuni[1], Jessica Rosati[1,2], Paolo Tomeo[1], Eugenio Di Sciascio[1]
[1] Polytechnic University of Bari – Via Orabona, 4 – 70125 Bari, Italy
[2] University of Camerino – Piazza Cavour 19/f – 62032 Camerino (MC), Italy
{firstname.lastname}@poliba.it

ABSTRACT

Providing very accurate recommendations to end users has been nowadays recognized to be just one of the main tasks a recommender systems must be able to perform. While predicting relevant suggestions, attention needs to be paid to their diversification in order to avoid monotony in recommendation. In this paper we focus on modeling users' inclination toward selecting diverse items, where diversity is computed by means of content-based item attributes. We then exploit such modeling to present a novel approach to re-rank the list of Top-N items predicted by a recommendation algorithm, in order to foster diversity in the final ranking. Experimental evaluation proves the effectiveness of the proposed approach.

Categories and Subject Descriptors

H.3.3 [**Information Systems**]: Information Search and Retrieval

Keywords

Recommender System; Diversity; MMR; ILD; Movielens

1. INTRODUCTION

The main task of a recommendation engine is typically to predict the ratings of unknown items for each user and recommend the top N items by considering the highest predicted ratings. As a result, in the recommender systems field new algorithms and approaches have been proposed over the years mainly devoted to maximizing recommendation accuracy. However, it has been recognized that improving only the predictive accuracy of recommendations is not enough to judge the effectiveness of a recommender system [4]. The most accurate recommendations for a user are often too similar to each other and attention has to be paid towards the goal of improving diversity in recommended items thus avoiding monotony. A number of works propose strategies to enhance the trade-off between accuracy and diversity, which however are not adaptive with respect to individual users' spontaneous needs [13, 12, 14]. Recently, the idea of exploiting the user profile in the diversification approach got ahead. In [11] the identification of diversity within the user profile is carried out through the extraction of user subprofiles to reflect the polyfacetic nature of user interests.

The main intuition behind our work is that some users may prefer diversification in suggestions while others may not. In addition, users could be inclined to diversifying only with respect to some specific item dimensions (e.g., item attributes as *director* and *year* in the movie domain) and not interested in diverse suggestions related to other ones (e.g. *genre* in the movie domain). Following this idea, in this paper we investigate *individual* diversity[1] taking into account user diversity needs over item attributes. As in [11], we consider the principle that good recommendations should be not only diverse, but they should also realize the diversity within the user interests and behaviour, to provide recommendations that embody a better fitted and more comprehensive view of user preferences. We propose an *adaptive attribute-based* diversification approach able to customize the degree of recommendation diversity of the *Top-N* recommendation list taking into account the inclination to diversity of the user over different content-based item dimensions. Specifically, we employ Entropy as a measure of the degree of diversity in the user preferences and use it in conjunction with user profile dimensions for calibrating the degree of diversification of the list. We apply our approach to the movie domain, considering what leads a user to choose a movie in a huge collection of items. Reasonably the choice of a user can be led by several factors, such as *genre*, *actor*, *director* and *year of release*. However not all these factors have the same influence on different users: by way of example, a user can be interested in a movie director more than in its genre. Analogously, a user can decide to cling to a particular director and accept to watch several genres. As a consequence we need to measure such differences, that is to show the different tendencies of each user in diversifying her choices, dealing separately with the significant movie attributes mentioned above. Differently from [11], where the movie genre is the only attribute used to characterize subprofiles, we analyze user propensity to diversify, in different ways, the *genre*, the *actor*, *director* or *year of release*. The selection of these attributes follows the results pointed out

RecSys'14, October 6–10, 2014, Foster City, Silicon Valley, CA, USA.

http://dx.doi.org/10.1145/2645710.2645774.

[1]In this paper by *individual* diversity we mean the degree of diversification in the recommendations provided to an individual user, in contrast to *aggregate* diversity of recommendations across all users [1].

in [6] where the authors show a correlation between personality factors (such as openness and conscientiousness) and the degree of diversification in the user choices with respect to such attributes[2]. The main contributions of this paper are:

- a representation of user's propensity in diversifying her choices. By looking at the user's profile we model her inclination to diversify the items she chooses in relation to the attributes describing items in the collection.
- an adaptive attribute-based re-ranking approach that takes into account individual diversity while suggesting new items to the user. The ranking of items suggested to the end user is computed by considering her personal propensity to diversify the items she selects. The approach has been experimentally evaluated in the movie domain proving its effectiveness.

The remainder of the paper is structured as follows: after reporting an overview of the diversity property in Section 2, we propose the details of our recommendation approach in Section 3 and the experimental results in Section 4. Conclusion and future work close the paper.

2. DIVERSITY IN RECOMMENDATION

The activity of a recommender system can be divided into two phases: firstly there is the prediction of the ratings for unrated items and secondly the items can be re-ranked to maximize user's utility. According to [1], in order to improve the diversity of recommendations it is possible to deal only with the second phase. The individual diversity can be increased through several heuristics. In this work we consider greedy heuristics, which look for an intermediate solution and have been demonstrated to be efficient and effective. Particularly, we borrow the greedy strategy presented in [11]. Hereafter we will use overlined bold capital letters to denote lists, e.g., $\overline{\mathbf{X}}$, and bold capital letters to represent the corresponding set of elements belonging to the list, e.g., $\mathbf{X}$. Let $\overline{\mathbf{P}} = \langle 1, ..., n\rangle$ be the recommendation list for user u generated using the predicted ratings and let us suppose we want to provide the user with the re-ranked list $\overline{\mathbf{S}}$ of recommendations, such that $\mathbf{S} \subset \mathbf{P}$ and whose length is $N \leq n$. The adopted greedy strategy can be explained through Algorithm 1.

Data: The original list $\overline{\mathbf{P}}$, $N \leq n$
Result: The re-ranked list $\overline{\mathbf{S}}$

1 $\overline{\mathbf{S}} = \langle\rangle$;
2 **while** $|\mathbf{S}| < N$ **do**
3 $\quad i^* = \underset{i \in \mathbf{P} \setminus \mathbf{S}}{\text{argmax}}\, f_{obj}(i, \overline{\mathbf{S}})$;
4 $\quad \overline{\mathbf{S}} = \overline{\mathbf{S}} \circ i^*$;
5 $\quad \mathbf{P} = \mathbf{P} \setminus \{i^*\}$
6 **end**
7 **return** $\mathbf{S}$.

Algorithm 1: The greedy strategy

At each step, we select the item which maximizes an objective function f_{obj} (line 3), which in turn can be defined to deal with the trade-off between accuracy and diversity, and we add it to the re-ranked list (line 4). In our work, we adopt the Maximal Marginal Relevance (MMR) [5], whose objective function is defined as:

$$f_{obj}(i, \overline{\mathbf{S}}) = \lambda \cdot r^*(u, i) - (1 - \lambda) \cdot \max_{j \in \mathbf{S}} sim(i, j) \quad (1)$$

where r^* is a function for rating estimation, sim a similarity measure on item pairs and the λ parameter lets to manage the accuracy-diversity balance.

3. ADAPTIVE DIVERSIFICATION

In the following we detail the *adaptive attribute-based* diversification model proposed in this paper. We provide a way to compute similarity that considers the diversification attitude of each user with respect to different item attributes (i.e. *year*, *genre*, *director* and *actors* in the movie domain). For each attribute $a \in \mathbf{A}$, we measure the user propensity towards diversity through Shannon's entropy, which is a two-dimensional measure, meaning that it reflects both the categories of classification and the distribution of elements within those categories. Shannon's entropy for user u and attribute a with k values can be computed as:

$$\mathcal{H}_a(u) = -\sum_{i=1}^{k} p_i \cdot \log_k p_i, \quad (2)$$

where p_i is the relative frequency of the i-th value (category) of a considering all the items (elements) belonging to the user profile (collection of the items rated by that user). Our model is adaptive in the way that it is based on the classification of users in four groups, referred to as *quadrants*, defined by considering as discriminating parameters the medians of the entropy distribution and user profile length distribution across all users. A separate classification is computed for each attribute describing the item. For example a user u is in the first quadrant for the *genre* attribute, if her entropy $\mathcal{H}_{genre}(u)$ is less than the median of the entropy computed across all users and she has a short user profile (her number of ratings is less than the median of users' ratings). The same user may belong to different quadrants in relation to different attributes. All the quadrants are defined as in Table 1.

The main modelling hypothesis behind this classification is the following. Users who have explored items with different characteristics in the past are willing to accept diverse recommendations. Given an attribute a, we interpret a high value of entropy as an attitude of the user to choose items with different values for a. Conversely, a low value of entropy is read as her willing to consider items similar for that attribute.

Of course, more groups can be defined thus identifying more than four quadrants. Nevertheless, we will show in our experimental section that already with such a coarse grained classification we obtain interesting results in terms of *precision* and *intra list diversity* (ILD) values.

The quadrants the user belongs to, potentially different for each item attribute, are used to define the similarity measure in Equation (1). Let us consider a user u and indicate with $\mathbf{A}$ the set of item attributes (for example in the movie domain $\mathbf{A} = \{year, genre, direction, starring\}$). We consider a function $q_u : \mathbf{A} \to \{1, 2, 3, 4\}$, which assigns, for each attribute, the quadrant to which user u belongs and then we define a quadrant weight $\omega_i \in [0, 1]$, with $i \in \{1, 2, 3, 4\}$. Taking into accounts such weights and set-

[2] In fact, in [6] the attribute *country* is considered too, but we prefer not considering it since in the dataset we use for our experiments *country* is specified for less than 10% of the items.

Profile Length	Entropy	
	Quadrant 1 Low Entropy Small Profile	**Quadrant 2** High Entropy Small Profile
	Quadrant 3 Low Entropy Large Profile	**Quadrant 4** High Entropy Large Profile

Table 1: Quadrants

ting $m = \max\{\omega_i \mid i = 1, 2, 3, 4\}$, the overall similarity between item i and item j in Equation (1), for the generic user u, becomes tailored to the quadrants she belongs to and is defined as:

$$sim(i, j) = \frac{\sum_{a \in \mathbf{A}} \omega_{q_u(a)} \cdot sim_a(i, j)}{m \cdot |\mathbf{A}|} \quad (3)$$

with $sim_a(i, j)$ being a similarity measure between i and j with respect to attribute a. The weights associated to user belonging quadrants influence the similarity score and hence the resulting objective function of MMR, with the consequence of varying the ILD of the recommendation list.
Specifically, the weights account for the user propensity in diversifying every single attribute, based on our modelling hypothesis. In fact, if a user is in the second or forth quadrant for a fixed attribute, then assigning a sufficiently big value to ω_2 and ω_4 corresponds to keeping a high value for the original similarity score and thus decreasing the overall value of $f_{obj}(i, \overline{\mathbf{S}})$ for the items i most similar to the ones already available in $\overline{\mathbf{S}}$. Those items are the ones whose number we want to reduce in $\overline{\mathbf{S}}$, in order to guarantee a high ILD value. Conversely, assigning low weights to the first and third quadrant (low weights for ω_1 and ω_3) results in a significant lowering of the original similarity score and hence in an increasing of the corresponding $f_{obj}(i, \overline{\mathbf{S}})$ values. This corresponds to foster items similar to the ones in the re-ranked list $\overline{\mathbf{S}}$.

4. EXPERIMENTS AND RESULTS

In order to test whether our proposal of using adaptive attribute-based recommendations is competitive, we carried out experiments on a subset of the well known `Movielens 1M`[3] dataset. The original dataset was enriched with further attribute information such as actors and directors extracted from `DBpedia`[4]. More details about this `DBpedia` enriched version of the dataset are available in [8]. We concentrated on users who gave at least fifty ratings: as a consequence, the final dataset contains 4297 users, 3689 items and 942590 ratings. We ordered the ratings by using the timestamps available in the dataset and built the training set by using, for each user, the first 60% of the ratings and the remaining 40% to build the test set. We compared our approach with two baselines: (i) recommendations generated considering the predicting ratings without any diversification strategy, denoted as *no-MMR*; (ii) recommendations computed by using Equation 1 without considering quadrants, wherein diversification is applied to all users, denoted as *MMR*. Hereafter we refer to our adaptive attribute-based diversification approach as *adaptiveMMR*. The main difference between *MMR* and *adaptiveMMR* is that the latter considers different values for each ω_i depending on the position, for each attribute, of the user in one of the four quadrants. We remark that the main insight behind *adaptiveMMR* is that the re-ranking is tailored to each user according to the idea that the diversification with respect to an attribute should be applied only for users who exhibited a propensity in diversifying such an attribute. Conversely, in *MMR*, diversification is applied indiscriminately to all users regardless of whether they are incline to diversifying their choices or not.
To compute values for *no-MMR* we adopted a generic user-based kNN Collaborative Filtering algorithm available in Apache Mahout[5] using Pearson correlation as similarity measure. Then, for each user we selected the top 200 recommendations generated by *no-MMR* to build the initial $\overline{\mathbf{P}}$ list used for performing the re-ranking as shown in Algorithm 1. In both *MMR* and *adaptiveMMR* the λ parameter was set to 0.5. As similarity measure for attribute a in (3), we decided to use the Jaccard index. Since the number of distinct attribute values was too large for the *year*, *actors* and *director* attributes, we divided movies in decades and performed a K-means clustering for actors and directors on the basis of their `DBpedia` categories. For both directors and actors we obtained 20 clusters. The number of values is 19 and 8 for *genre* and *year*, respectively.
For evaluating recommendation ranking accuracy and diversity we used the *TestItems* evaluation methodology presented in [3]. For measuring accuracy we used precision (P@k) and nDCG@k, while ILD@k was used for diversity. Furthermore we measured the balance between accuracy and diversity, as in [9], that is we standardized the metrics P@k and ILD@k in order to make the scales homogeneous and we computed the average. We indicate this combination metric as *avg(P,ILD)*. P@k is chosen instead of nDCG@k since they have a similar trend.
In the first part of the experiments we tested the validity of the modelling hypothesis behind our approach, that is users who have explored different items in the past are inclined to diversity. Specifically we compared the performances of the two baselines *no-MMR* and *MMR* on different groups of users considering those belonging to the same quadrant for at least three attributes as shown in Table 2. As expected, *MMR* dominates the *no-MMR* for quadrant 2 and 4 for both precision and ILD, demonstrating that users with high entropy benefit from diversification. In the other quadrants (1 and 3) there is a normal decrease of accuracy. Hence users with low entropy in their user profiles are not inclined to an uncontrolled diversification. This preliminary analysis supports the adoption of entropy as discriminant parameter for users' classification.
In order to test the effectiveness of *adaptiveMMR* we evaluated various combination of ω weights. Particularly, we conducted a grid search on ω, finding, as a first result, that our intuition of choosing small values for ω_1 and ω_3 and bigger ones for ω_2 and ω_4 is validated by accuracy and ILD results. Without such constraints, in fact, the accuracy values of *adaptiveMMR* get deeply worse. For lack of space we discuss here only three weights configurations $\langle\omega_1, \omega_2, \omega_3, \omega_4\rangle$ (adopting the notation introduced in Section 2 for lists), A, B and C, respectively given by A = $\langle 0, 0, 0, 1\rangle$, B = $\langle 0, 1, 0, 1\rangle$, C = $\langle 0.1, 1, 0.1, 0.75\rangle$. The values of list C have

[3]Available at `http://grouplens.org/datasets/movielens`
[4]`http://dbpedia.org`

[5]`http://mahout.apache.org`

	Quadrant 1 (1149 users)		*Quadrant 2* (469 users)		*Quadrant 3* (467 users)		*Quadrant 4* (1146 users)	
algorithm	P@10	ILD@10	P@10	ILD@10	P@10	ILD@10	P@10	ILD@10
no-MMR	**0.0455**	0.3890	0.0678	0.3663	**0.0904**	0.3961	0.1306	0.3544
MMR	0.0394	**0.4363**	**0.0706**	**0.4212**	0.0829	**0.4355**	**0.1325**	**0.4012**

Table 2: Accuracy and Diversity Results distributed among the different quadrants. *Quadrant 1* contains users belonging to Quadrant 1 for at least 3 attributes; analogously for the other quadrants (users who belong for each attribute to quadrant 2 are only 69, while those belonging always to quadrant 3 are 70).

algorithm	nDCG@10	P@10	ILD@10	avg(P,ILD)
no-MMR	0.0840	0.0842	0.3764	0.3019
MMR	0.0837^{a}	0.0827^{a}	$\mathbf{0.4236}^{a}$	0.5000
AdaptiveMMR-A	0.0851^{ab}	0.0849	0.3921^{ab}	0.6184
AdaptiveMMR-B	$\mathbf{0.0855}^{b}$	0.0850^{ab}	0.4049^{ab}	0.7592
AdaptiveMMR-C	0.0854^{ab}	$\mathbf{0.0852}^{b}$	0.4101^{ab}	**0.8561**

Table 3: Accuracy and Diversity Results on all users. The superscripts a and b indicate statistically significant differences (Wilcoxon signed rank with $p < 0.05$) with respect to the *no-MMR* and *MMR* algorithms, respectively.

been computed via grid search where we fixed ω_1 and ω_3 and varied ω_2 and ω_4 by considering a discretization step of 0.25. These configurations let us deal with emblematic situations and confirm our intuition on the importance of individual entropy values. In particular, configuration A acts on users who are in quadrant 4 for some attributes, configuration B on users belonging to quadrant 2 or quadrant 4, and configuration C imposes the constraints $\omega_1 < \omega_2$ and $\omega_3 < \omega_4$. The experimental results are shown in Table 3 and are relative to $k = 10$. With other values of k the results are analogous, so we omitted them for brevity. Consistently with the accuracy-diversity trade-off, the basic *MMR* approach improves the diversity by sacrificing the accuracy. *AdaptiveMMR*, compared to both *no-MMR* and *MMR*, gains the best balance between accuracy and diversity, represented by *avg(P,ILD)*, regardless of the aforementioned weights configurations. In terms of accuracy, *adaptiveMMR* out-performs *no-MMR* and *MMR*, while in terms of diversity, they perform better than *no-MMR*. Specifically, *adaptiveMMR-C* obtains the best results in terms of precision, diversity and their combination. Remarkably, the configuration C has an ILD value close to *MMR* but a significantly better accuracy values. The higher values of accuracy and diversity for *adaptiveMMR-B* and *adaptiveMMR-C* compared to *adaptiveMMR-A* suggest also that the diversification tendency, represented by entropy, should be considered even for users with a small profile length.

5. CONCLUSIONS AND FUTURE WORK

Computing effective recommendations calls for approaches taking into account not only accurate lists of results. Diversity in the final ranking plays an important role in the user satisfaction [4]. In this paper we focus on *individual* diversity. We firstly propose a novel approach to model users' propensity to accept diverse recommendations. The modeling hypothesis is that a user who selected many diverse items in the past is more willing to receive diverse recommendation. We then take into account the past diversification behaviour of each user and give the right weight to her attitude toward diversification with respect to each item attribute. This modelling is then exploited to re-rank the list of recommended items. An experimental evaluation in the movie domain on the `Movielens 1M` proved the effectiveness of the proposed approach. Experiments have been carried out considering the MMR criterion [5] and we are planning to test other criteria to diversify results in the final recommendation list such as IA-select [2] or xQuAD [10]. The usage of a more fine grained analysis on the user profile length, considering quantiles instead of medians will be also tested to evaluate how this affects final results. Moreover we are investigating how to apply our approach to estimate and detect peaks of interest as in [7].

Acknowledgements. The authors acknowledge partial support of PON01_00850 ASK-Health and PON02_00563_3470993 VINCENTE

6. REFERENCES

[1] G. Adomavicius and Y. Kwon. Improving aggregate recommendation diversity using ranking-based techniques. *IEEE TKDE*, 24(5):896–911, 2012.
[2] R. Agrawal, S. Gollapudi, A. Halverson, and S. Ieong. Diversifying search results. In *ACM WSDM '09*, pages 5–14, 2009.
[3] A. Bellogin, P. Castells, and I. Cantador. Precision-oriented evaluation of recommender systems: An algorithmic comparison. In *ACM RecSys '11*, pages 333–336, 2011.
[4] K. Bradley and B. Smyth. Improving Recommendation Diversity. In *Irish Conference in Artificial Intelligence and Cognitive Science*, pages 75–84, 2001.
[5] J. Carbonell and J. Goldstein. The use of mmr, diversity-based reranking for reordering documents and producing summaries. In *ACM SIGIR '98*, pages 335–336, 1998.
[6] L. Chen, W. Wu, and L. He. How personality influences users' needs for recommendation diversity? In *Extended Abstracts on Human Factors in Computing Systems*, CHI EA '13, pages 829–834, 2013.
[7] H. Khrouf and R. Troncy. Hybrid event recommendation using linked data and user diversity. In *ACM RecSys '13*, pages 185–192, 2013.
[8] V. C. Ostuni, T. Di Noia, E. Di Sciascio, and R. Mirizzi. Top-n recommendations from implicit feedback leveraging linked open data. In *ACM RecSys '13*, pages 85–92, 2013.
[9] U. Panniello, A. Tuzhilin, and M. Gorgoglione. Comparing context-aware recommender systems in terms of accuracy and diversity. *User Modeling and User-Adapted Interaction*, 24(1-2):35–65, 2014.
[10] R.L.T. Santos, C. Macdonald, and I. Ounis. Exploiting query reformulations for web search result diversification. In *WWW '10*, pages 881–890, 2010.
[11] S. Vargas and P. Castells. Exploiting the diversity of user preferences for recommendation. In *OAIR '13*, pages 129–136, 2013.
[12] M. Zhang. Enhancing diversity in top-n recommendation. In *ACM RecSys '09*, pages 397–400, 2009.
[13] M. Zhang and N. Hurley. Avoiding monotony: Improving the diversity of recommendation lists. In *ACM RecSys '08*, pages 123–130, 2008.
[14] C. Ziegler, S. M. McNee, J. A. Konstan, and G. Lausen. Improving recommendation lists through topic diversification. In *WWW '05*, pages 22–32, 2005.

Clinical Online Recommendation with Subgroup Rank Feedback

Yanan Sui
California Institute of Technology
1200 E California Blvd
Pasadena, CA, USA
ysui@caltech.edu

Joel Burdick
California Institute of Technology
1200 E California Blvd
Pasadena, CA, USA
jwb@robotics.caltech.edu

ABSTRACT

Many real applications in experimental design need to make decisions online. Each decision leads to a stochastic reward with initially unknown distribution. New decisions are made based on the observations of previous rewards. To maximize the total reward, one needs to solve the tradeoff between exploring different strategies and exploiting currently optimal strategies. This kind of tradeoff problems can be formalized as Multi-armed bandit problem. We recommend strategies in series and generate new recommendations based on noisy rewards of previous strategies. When the reward for a strategy is difficult to quantify, classical bandit algorithms are no longer optimal. This paper, studies the Multi-armed bandit problem with feedback given as a stochastic rank list instead of quantified reward values. We propose an algorithm for this new problem and show its optimality. A real application of this algorithm on clinical treatment is helping paralyzed patient to regain the ability to stand on their own feet.

Categories and Subject Descriptors

H.4 [**Information Systems Applications**]: Miscellaneous

Keywords

Clinical Recommendation, Exploration-Exploitation Tradeoff, Bandit Problem, Rank-Comparison

1. INTRODUCTION AND MOTIVATION

Our problem is motivated by clinical research which aims to recover motor function after severe spinal cord injury (SCI). Previous research [4] has shown that electrical stimulation applied to the spinal cord via electrodes arrays implanted in the epidural space over the lumbosacral area enables paralyzed patients to achieve full weight-bearing standing, improvements in stepping, and partial recovery of lost autonomic functions. The electrical stimulation must be coupled with physical therapy to realize the best outcome.

RecSys'14, October 6–10, 2014, Foster City, Silicon Valley, CA, USA.

ACM http://dx.doi.org/10.1145/2645710.2645773.

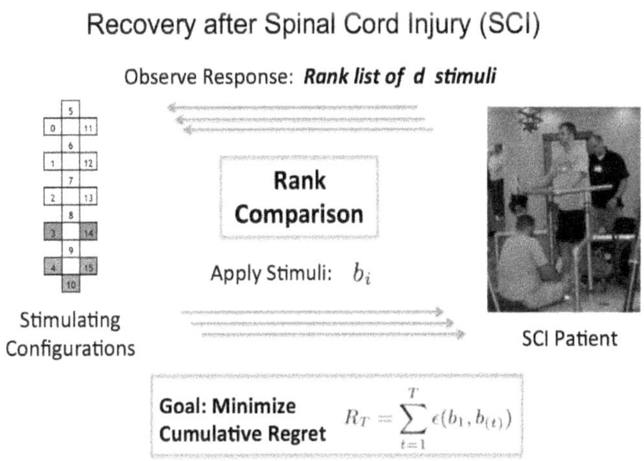

Figure 1: Clinical Treatment of Spinal Cord Injury

Stimulation consists of electrical pulse trains applied to selected electrodes. However, the optimal stimulus pattern (the choice of active electrodes and their polarity, the pulse amplitude and width, and the pulse train frequency) varies significantly across patients. And even for the same patient, the outcome of the same stimulus varies from trial to trial, and the optimal stimulation varies over time due to spinal cord plasticity. Hence, clinicians must determine the optimal stimulus for each patient under noisy and mildly non-stationary conditions. Currently, the search for the optimal stimulating parameters is a laborious and somewhat ad-hoc approach which consumes valuable clinician and patient time, and does not currently guarantee an optimal outcome.

Figure 1 shows the clinical treatment procedure for *stand-training*. During a treatment/optimization session, a new stimulus is recommended by our algorithm. The patient then attempts to stand using the given stimulus, and the observing clinicians then rank the patient's resulting performance. Using this noisy ranking as feedback, the algorithm continues to explore for the optimal stimulus while also exploiting currently good ones. The algorithm must spend significant time dwelling on good performing stimuli in order to provide the patient with a good therapeutic experience. Since clinical training has a fixed time horizon, we must also maximize total performance during the limited period within which we can search for the optimal solution.

This paper develops an algorithm to recommend optimal stimuli based on the general setting of multi-armed bandit problem. The classical bandit problem trades off between exploration and multi-armed bandit problem exploitation among a number of different arms, each having a quantifiable, but stochastic, reward with initially unknown distribution. The goal of a bandit algorithm is to maximize the total reward. Since its introduction by Robbins [5], bandit problems have been widely studied in many situations [2]. Many efficient algorithms have been developed based on the work of Auer et al., [1].

However, for our clinical problem, the patient's motor response to stimulation is hard to quantify. Neither video motion capture nor electromyograhic (EMG) recordings of muscle activity can yet provide a consistent and satisfactory measure of motor skill under stimulation. A good standing performance might map to numerous combinations of muscle activities, and it is not a stationary process. While the patient's performance under a specific stimulus is hard to quantify, it can be compared to others. In the clinical setting, we can obtain the ranking of a *group* of stimuli which are performed within the short time period of one training session. The *dueling bandit problem* [7] formalizes online learning problems with preference feedback instead of absolute rewards, and hence it can be used for problems with unquantifiable reward. The algorithm we propose in this paper is a variant of the dueling bandit problem which is dictated by the clinical demands of our application.

At the start of the optimization process, we have little information about the best stimulus for the patient, but we have often have a pool of possibly useful stimuli. Our approach is based on the idea of successively removing suboptimal arms [3] while keeping the optimal one(s) in the sample space. By setting proper confidence intervals, we can reach the optimal reward within the time horizon.

2. PROBLEM SETUP

The classical dueling bandit problem receives feedback in the form of a comparison between a pair of bandits in each test. When the size of the decision set, K, is large, it is unavoidable to carry out a very large number of tests before the algorithm converges to its optimal solution. In some applications like our clinical example, each test is expensive and time consuming. The number of tests - time horizon of an algorithm - is often predetermined by clinical conditions. It is infeasible to apply the dueling bandit algorithm directly.

However, our training and optimization procedure allows for patients to not only compare successive stimulations, but to also rank the performances for a modest-sized group of stimulations (the number which can be tested in one clinical session before the patient fatigues). Thus, feedback consists of a ranked list of at most d ($d < K$) chosen arms. More precisely, the feedback for each test consists of a combined scoring of 4 different standing criteria by the observing clinicians, and the combined score is used to rank the tests within one session. We show below that this feature helps us to reduce the total number of tests significantly, while also dovetailing well with current clinical practice.

Our procedure can be described as follows. There are K arms $\{b_1, \cdots, b_K\}$, and a total number of T tests to be performed. Each test physically corresponds to a ~90-second stimulation period with a specific stimulus (arm) chosen from the K arms. T is determined before we run the algorithm, and is generally assumed to be an integer multiple of d: $T = d * G$, where G is the number of ranking sessions, with each session producing a noisy ranked list of d arms.

Algorithm 1 Rank-Comparisons

Input: $\{b_1, ..., b_K\}$, d, G // *Total tests* $T = d \cdot G$
Input: $c_\delta(n) = \sqrt{(1/n)log(1/\delta)}$
Run: [Parameters-Initialization]
Run: [Active-Elimination]
return b^* // *Optimal arm*

Algorithm 2 Parameters-Initialization

Input: $\{b_1, ..., b_K\}$, d, G
Input: $c_\delta(n) = \sqrt{(1/n)log(1/\delta)}$
$W_1 \leftarrow \{b_1, ..., b_K\}$ // *set of active arms*
$\ell \leftarrow 1$ // *rounds*
$\forall b \in W_\ell$, $n_b \leftarrow 0$ // *comparisons*
$\forall b \in W_\ell$, $w_b \leftarrow 0$ // *priorities*
$\forall b \in W_\ell$, $\hat{P}_b \equiv w_b/n_b$, or 1/2 if $n_b = 0$
$n^* \equiv min_{b \in W_\ell} n_b$
$c^* \equiv c_\delta(n^*)$, or 1 if $n^* = 0$ // *confidence radius*
$g \leftarrow 0$ // *total number of ranks*
$T \leftarrow d \cdot G$
return all new parameters

We follow the the original notation of the dueling bandit problem [7]. For two arms b_i and b_j, where $i, j \in \{1, \cdots, K\}$, we write the comparison factor as:

$$\epsilon(b_i, b_j) = P(b_i \succ b_j) - 1/2$$

where $P(b_i \succ b_j)$ is the probability that b_i dominates b_j and $\epsilon(b_i, b_j) \in [-1/2, 1/2]$ represents the priority between b_i and b_j. We define $b_i \succ b_j \Leftrightarrow \epsilon(b_i, b_j) > 0$. We use the notation $\epsilon_{i,j} \equiv \epsilon(b_i, b_j)$ for convenience. Note that $\epsilon(b_i, b_j) = -\epsilon(b_j, b_i)$ and $epsilon(b_i, b_i) = 0$. We assume the distribution of reward for each arm is stationary so that all comparison factors converge in [-1/2,1/2]. We also assume *w.l.o.g.* that the bandits are indexed in preferential order $b_1 \succ b_2 \succ \cdots \succ b_K$ so that there is one preferred arm.

The total reward is defined in terms of regret as in the classical bandit problem setting. In the online setting, let $b_{(t)}$ be the arm chosen at test t. We define total regret as follows:

$$R_T = \sum_{t=1}^{T} \epsilon(b_1, b_{(t)})$$

The total regret $R_T = 0$ if we constantly choose $b_{(t)} = b_1$ during the experiment. $R_T = \Theta(T)$ is linear *w.r.t.* T if we constantly choose $b_{(t)} \in \{b_1, \cdots, b_K\}$.

We also inherit two important properties of the comparison factors from the original dueling bandit problem:

Strong Stochastic Transitivity. For any triplet of arms $b_i \succ b_j \succ b_k$, we assume $\epsilon_{i,k} \geq \max\{\epsilon_{i,j}, \epsilon_{j,k}\}$.

Stochastic Triangle Inequality. For any triplet of arms $b_i \succ b_j \succ b_k$, we assume $\epsilon_{i,k} \leq \epsilon_{i,j} + \epsilon_{j,k}$. This can be viewed as a diminishing returns property.

An optimal method is proposed for our problem which has a finite-time regret bound of order $O(\frac{K}{d} logT)$ where T is the time horizon.

3. ALGORITHM

Our *Rank-Comparison* algorithm (Algorithm 1), which is a modified version of "Beat-the-Mean" [8], is based on the idea of successively removing suboptimal arms while keeping

Algorithm 3 Active-Elimination

1: **Input:** $\{b_1, ..., b_K\}$, d, G
2: **Input:** parameters generated in [Parameters-Initialization]
3: **while** $|W_\ell| > 1$ and $g \leq G$ **do**
4:   **if** $|W_\ell| \geq d$ **then**
5:     select $b'_1, ..., b'_d \in W_\ell$ at random with no repeats
6:   **else**
7:     $r \leftarrow d\%|W_\ell|$
8:     $p \leftarrow (d - r)/|W_\ell|$
9:     select $b'_1, ..., b'_r \in W_\ell$ at random with no repeats. In addition, select each arm in W_ℓ p times
10:   **end if**
11:   test selected arms and get rank of the selection
12:   **for** all commutable pairs (b'_i, b'_j) in the selection **do**
13:     if $b'_i \succ b'_j$, $w_{b'_i} \leftarrow w_{b'_i} + 1$
14:     $n_{b'_i} \leftarrow n_{b'_i} + 1$
15:     **if** $\min_{b' \in W_\ell} \hat{P}_{b'} + c^* \leq \max_{b \in W_\ell} \hat{P}_b - c^*$ **then**
16:       $b' \leftarrow \arg\min_{b \in W_\ell} \hat{P}_b$
17:       $\forall b \in W_\ell$, delete comparisons with b' from w_b, n_b
18:       $W_{\ell+1} \leftarrow W_\ell \backslash \{b'\}$ *// update working set*
19:       $\ell \leftarrow \ell + 1$ *// new round*
20:     **end if**
21:   **end for**
22: **end while**
23: **return** $b^* = \arg\max_{b \in W_\ell} \hat{P}_b$

the optimal one(s) in the sample space. The inputs to *Rank-Comparison* are the K arms, the largest group size d, and total number of groups G: $T = d \cdot G$.

Parameters-Initialization (Algorithm 2) defines the set of active arms W_ℓ, whose size shrinks as more tests are completed. For each arm b, let n_b be the total number of comparisons between b and other arms, and let w_b be the total number of wins against all other arms. Let $\hat{P}_b$ be the empirical average of $P(b \succ b')$ for all b' in W_ℓ, and let $\hat{P}_{b,n}$ be the value of $\hat{P}_b$ after n comparisons between arm b and any other arms. Set the confidence interval of $P(b \succ b')$ as:

$$\hat{C}_{b,n} = (\hat{P}_{b,n} - c_\delta(n), \hat{P}_{b,n} + c_\delta(n))$$

where $c_\delta(n) = \sqrt{(1/n)log(1/\delta)}$, and δ is the confidence that $P(b \succ b')$ lies in $\hat{C}_{b,n}$. The function $c_\delta(n)$ decreases as the number of comparisons n increases. By properly setting parameter δ, the optimal reward can be reached within the fixed time horizon.

Active-Elimination (Algorithm 3) is the key part of *Rank-Comparison*. For each group of tests, d arms are randomly chosen from W_ℓ with no repeats when $d < |W_\ell|$. Otherwise, we pick each arm equally and pick the rest arms randomly according to lines 7-9 in Algorithm 3. The randomized selection method provides low-variance total regret. Each group of tests results in a ranking of d arms, which can be regarded as $d(d-1)/2$ comparisons among the d arms. For each arm b, the values of w_b, n_b and $\hat{P}_b$ are updated, as is the corresponding confidence radius c^*. For any pair of arms b and b', one dominates the other if their confidence intervals do not overlap, and the less superior arm is eliminated from W_ℓ. The algorithm runs until the time horizon $T = d \cdot G$ is reached, or only one active arm remains.

4. THEORETICAL RESULTS

The patients can rank performances d stimuli at most. For fixed time horizon T, choose the size of groups equals the maximum group size d. It will maximize the number of total comparisons extracted from the ranks, which is $d(d-1)/2$.

Let $\epsilon = \epsilon_{1,2}$ to be the comparison factor between the best and second best arms. Obviously, we have $\epsilon \leq \epsilon_{1,j}$ for all j. The upper bound of the expected total regret for *Rank-Comparison* is given in the theorem below.

THEOREM 1. *The expected regret generated by running Algorithm 1 is bounded from above by* $O(\frac{K}{\epsilon \cdot d} logT)$.

As compared to the classical dueling bandit regret bound of $O(\frac{K}{\epsilon} logT)$, *Rank-Comparison* has an extra divisor factor of d. This tighter bound is realized because for each group of d tests, order $O(d^2)$ comparisons are extracted from the ranking test. Recall that $R_T = 0$ if the optimal arm $b_{(t)} = b_1$ is constantly chosen, and $R_T = \Theta(T)$ is linear *w.r.t.* T if we constantly choose $b_{(t)} \in \{b_1, \cdots, b_K\}$. The factor $O(\frac{K}{\epsilon \cdot d} logT)$ lies in the region between 0 and $\Theta(T)$. As T increases, $O(\frac{K}{\epsilon \cdot d} logT)$ is significantly less than $\Theta(T)$.

By extending Theorem 4 of [7], we can form a lower bound on regret in expectation, as stated in Theorem 2, for any algorithm which solves the rank comparison problem. Which means no algorithm can achieve lower regret than *Rank-Comparison* in expectation.

THEOREM 2. *Any algorithm for the rank comparison problem has a regret bounded from below by* $\Omega(\frac{K}{\epsilon \cdot d} logT)$.

Notice that Theorem 2 lower bounds total regret on the same order as the upper bound in Theorem 1. So we have $\Omega(\frac{K}{\epsilon \cdot d} logT) = E[R_T] = O(\frac{K}{\epsilon \cdot d} logT)$, from which we can conclude that total regret is order $\Theta(\frac{K}{\epsilon \cdot d} logT)$ for *Rank-Comparison*.

Theorems 1 and 2, whose detailed proofs can be found in the supplementary [6], show that our algorithm is optimal in terms of the expected total regret.

Unlike the classical multi-armed bandit problem, which only focuses on expected total regret, many applications must constrain the regret's variation. In our context, if a stimulus optimization algorithm provides good results in the majority of patients, but bad results in a few, the variation is large. Such an algorithm is not practically useful, even if total regret is small. By randomizing the choice of arms within each test group, the randomized comparison strategy of *Rank-Comparison* provides low-variance regret in expectation.

5. EXPERIMENTS

We first evaluate the algorithm by simulation. The reward for each arm b_i is modeled as a Gaussian distribution with mean μ_i and standard deviation σ_i. All arms are independent with each other. Obviously, the distributions generated in this way satisfies the Strong Stochastic Transitivity and Stochastic Triangle Inequality. Then we sample the arms for each group and rank them by using the Rank-Comparison algorithm. We calculated the expected regret $r_t = R_t/t$ (instead of total regret R_t) where t is the number of tests. In the simulation, we consider the total number of arms is 10 and we can get rank list with dimension no larger than 5. The reward of each arm b_i follows a Gaussian distribution

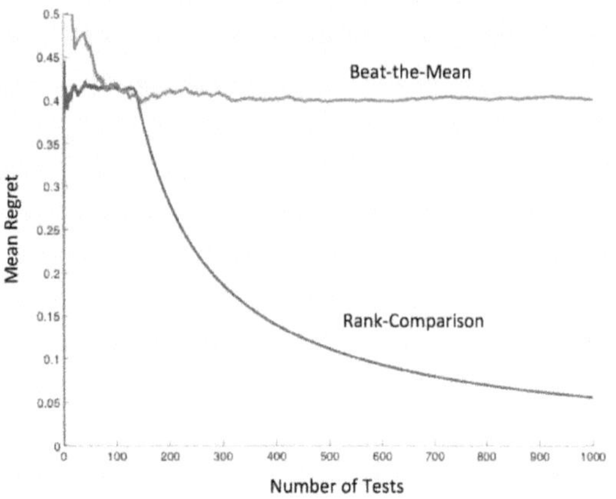

Figure 2: Mean Regret against Number of Tests

with mean $\mu_i \in [0, 1]$ and standard deviation $\sigma_i = 0.2$. Set the confidence parameter $\delta = 10^{-2}$.

Under this setting, the arms are hard to be distinguished from each other due to the large variances. Figure 2 shows the mean regret r_t vs. time t for *Rank-Comparison* (blue curve) and Beat-the-mean [8] (red curve) with fixed horizon $T = 1000$. Blue curve is the mean regret of *Rank-Comparison*, while the red curve is the mean regret of Beat-the-Mean algorithm. For both algorithms, the mean regret is high during exploration, and then drops quickly after the algorithms converge to the optimum. We can see that *Rank-Comparison* finds the optimum within 150 tests, and thereafter exploits it to reduce the mean regret. However, Beat-the-Mean did not converge to the optimum within the time horizon for the same parameter settings. We hypothesize that *Rank-Comparison* outperforms Beat-the-Mean because of the utility of finer feedback information.

We have applied *Rank-Comparison* to a SCI patient implanted with Medtronic electrode arrays (16 electrodes) driven by a Restore Advanced impulse generator. This system can apply more than 10^9 unique stimuli. Searching through the whole space of possible stimuli is neither feasible nor necessary for the clinical experiment.

For the first clinical treatment, the initial space for exploration is composed of around 20 stimuli. We have run *Rank-Comparison* for the stimuli recommendation. The algorithm has not converges to a single arm but has eliminated the majority of them. Since the number of current clinical tests is small, we have not seen the logarithmic convergence of the regret. The reason is that elimination precess is still ongoing and we are exploring more for the early experiments. We will keep running the *Rank-Comparison* algorithm on new clinical treatments.

6. DISCUSSION AND CONCLUSION

This paper proposed a *Rank-Comparison* algorithm to efficiently solve a specific bandit problem using subgroup rank feedback. This optimal strategy (Theorems 1 and 2) provides clinical recommendation which explore for optimal stimuli while exploiting high performing stimuli for SCI therapy. The main advantages of *Rank-Comparison* are:

- Fast convergence, which is a necessity for applications which are characterized by expensive explorations.
- low variance of the reward/regret (R_T), which guarantees that the approach performs uniformly on the majority of patients.

Rank-Comparison decomposes test group rankings into equally weighted comparisons. One might reasonably assume that arms far apart in rank may be more distinguishable than adjacent ones, and thus employ different confidence parameters as appropriate. This feature can reduce total regret under the same problem setting. From the clinical point of view, this method avoids the varying effect of human judgement by using robust comparisons instead of volatile quantitative values, which may be non-stationary in our application. However, the time varying characteristics of human motor performance due to fatigue in the short term, and spinal plasticity over the long term, is a real theoretical and clinical issue we must address.

Additionally, the classical bandit problem's assumption of independent arms does not hold for the spinal cord stimulation where anatomical principles and electrical properties suggest a coupling occurs. Using a measure of similarity between stimuli based on the physical properties, we can build a prior distribution on unknown arms to guide our search.

7. ACKNOWLEDGMENTS

This work was supported by the the Helmsley Foundation, the Christopher and Dana Reeve Foundation, and the National Institutes of Health (NIH).

8. REFERENCES

[1] P. Auer, N. Cesa-Bianchi, and P. Fischer. Finite-time analysis of the multiarmed bandit problem. *Machine learning*, 47(2-3):235–256, 2002.

[2] S. Bubeck and N. Cesa-Bianchi. Regret analysis of stochastic and nonstochastic multi-armed bandit problems. *Foundations and Trends in Machine Learning*, 5:1–122, 2012.

[3] E. Even-Dar, S. Mannor, and Y. Mansour. Pac bounds for multi-armed bandit and markov decision processes. In *Computational Learning Theory*, pages 255–270. Springer, 2002.

[4] S. Harkema, Y. Gerasimenko, J. Hodes, J. Burdick, C. Angeli, Y. Chen, C. Ferreira, A. Willhite, E. Rejc, R. G. Grossman, et al. Effect of epidural stimulation of the lumbosacral spinal cord on voluntary movement, standing, and assisted stepping after motor complete paraplegia: a case study. *The Lancet*, 377(9781):1938–1947, 2011.

[5] H. Robbins. Some aspects of the sequential design of experiments. *Bulletin of the American Mathematical Society*, 58(5):527–535, 1952.

[6] Y. Sui and J. Burdick. Bandit problem with subgroup rank feedback. *arXiv preprint arXiv:0971348*, 2014.

[7] Y. Yue, J. Broder, R. Kleinberg, and T. Joachims. The k-armed dueling bandits problem. *Conference on Learning Theory (COLT)*, 2009.

[8] Y. Yue and T. Joachims. Beat the mean bandit. In *Proceedings of the 28th International Conference on Machine Learning (ICML-11)*, pages 241–248, 2011.

Convex AUC Optimization for Top-N Recommendation with Implicit Feedback

Fabio Aiolli
University of Padova, Italy
aiolli@math.unipd.it

ABSTRACT

In this paper, an effective collaborative filtering algorithm for top-N item recommendation with implicit feedback is proposed. The task of top-N item recommendation is to predict a ranking of items (movies, books, songs, or products in general) that can be of interest for a user based on earlier preferences of the user. We focus on implicit feedback where preferences are given in the form of binary events/ratings. Differently from state-of-the-art methods, the method proposed is designed to optimize the AUC directly within a margin maximization paradigm. Specifically, this turns out in a simple constrained quadratic optimization problem, one for each user. Experiments performed on several benchmarks show that our method significantly outperforms state-of-the-art matrix factorization methods in terms of AUC of the obtained predictions.

Categories and Subject Descriptors

H.4 [**Information Systems Applications**]: Miscellaneous; H.3.3 [**Information Storage and Retrieval**]: Information Search and Retrieval

Keywords

Collaborative Filtering; Top-N Recommendation; Implicit Feedback; AUC optimization

1. INTRODUCTION

Collaborative filtering aims at improving customer experience in e-commerce applications. These techniques exploit the history of user interactions to improve future recommendations to users. Different types of interactions can be stored and used. For example, a user can be asked a vote, a rate, or a degree of satisfaction for some of the items available. The system can also keep the history of user purchases autonomously, browsing activity of the users, etc. The former case is commonly called *explicit feedback* while the latter is usually referred to as *implicit feedback*.

In a collaborative recommender system we have a set $\mathbb{U}$ of n users, a set $\mathbb{I}$ of m items, and a user-item rating matrix $\mathbf{R} = \{r_{ui}\} \in \mathbb{R}^{n \times m}$ representing, for any user and item, how much user u likes item i. In this paper, we assume implicit feedback and binary ratings, that is $r_{ui} \in \{0, 1\}$. A value $r_{ui} = 1$ means that the user u rated the item i, while a value $r_{ui} = 0$ means not availability of information about whether user u likes item i.

There are two principal recognized approaches to collaborative filtering [1]. On one hand, model-based collaborative filtering, a.k.a. matrix factorization (MF) aims at constructing a model of the matrix $\mathbf{R}$. There are several proposed methods of this type, including Bayesian models, clustering models, classification, and regression models. On the other side, there are memory-based (MB) collaborative filtering methods where similarities among users (or items) are computed on the basis of the training ratings and the prediction is made on the basis of these similarities.

As shown in this paper, the two approaches above can be seen in the same optimization framework where a matrix factorization has to be found. Specifically, in the memory based approaches, like user-based and item-based nearest neighbors, particular factorizations are fixed a-priori and no actual train needs to be performed.

Despite MF is recognized to be the state-of-the-art technique in collaborative filtering, typically much better than MB techniques, MF has some drawbacks that made it impractical and unsuccessful sometimes. First of all, training the corresponding model is computationally onerous and this fact is crucial when the size of the matrix $\mathbf{R}$ is very large. Second, since MF is typically modelled as a regression problem, then it seems unsuitable for implicit feedback tasks and some modifications to the original technique are needed [4]. Third, MF techniques typically solve the associated non convex minimization problem by using gradient descent algorithms which do not guarantee the convergence to a global minimum and, it is well known, the rate of convergence is quite low when near to local minima. Finally, the high number of parameters to optimize, the sparsity of the rating matrix, and no apriori knowledge available can possibly lead to overfitting and strong validation and/or early-stopping of the stochastic gradient descent is often necessary.

In this paper we propose a solution lying midway between the two extreme approaches of MB and MF. In particular, we cast the problem into a instance ranking one and we propose a convex quadratic optimization framework for the optimization of AUC.

2. TOP-N RECOMMENDATION

In the top-N recommendation setting, for each user u, there are available a subset $\mathbb{I}(u) \subset \mathbb{I}$ of items that have been rated by the user and the task is to predict a ranking of the items not yet rated such

RecSys'14, October 6–10, 2014, Foster City, Silicon Valley, CA, USA.
Copyright 2014 ACM 978-1-4503-2668-1/14/10 ...$15.00.
http://dx.doi.org/10.1145/2645710.2645770.

that most of another set $\bar{\mathbb{I}}(u) \subseteq \mathbb{I} - \mathbb{I}(u)$ of items are in the first N positions of the ranking. In this paper, we indicate as $\mathbb{U}(i) = \{u \in \mathbb{U} | i \in \mathbb{I}(u)\} \subset \mathbb{U}$ the subset of users that have rated the item i in the initial set and $\bar{\mathbb{U}}(i) = \{u \in \bar{\mathbb{U}} | i \in \bar{\mathbb{I}}(u)\} \subseteq \mathbb{U} - \mathbb{U}(i)$ the subset of users that have rated the item i in the test set. By construction, the sets are chosen such that $\mathbb{I}(u) \cap \bar{\mathbb{I}}(u) = \phi$. We also define $m_u^+ = |\mathbb{I}(u)|$ and $m_u^- = m - m_u^+$.

In the following we indicate by $\mathbf{R} = \{r_{ui}\} \in \mathbb{R}^{n \times m}$ the initial rating matrix such that $r_{ui} = 1$ whenever $i \in \mathbb{I}(u)$ and $r_{ui} = 0$ otherwise, and by $\bar{\mathbf{R}} = \{\bar{r}_{ui}\} \in \mathbb{R}^{n \times m}$ the test rating matrix such that $\bar{r}_{ui} = 1$ whenever $i \in \bar{\mathbb{I}}(u)$ and $\bar{r}_{ui} = 0$ otherwise.

3. COLLABORATIVE FILTERING

In this section, we consider a general framework where many different approaches can be cast. Let the matrix $\mathbf{W} \in \mathbb{R}^{n \times k}$ be the embedding of users in a factor space of dimension k with users representations $\mathbf{w}_u \in \mathbb{R}^k$ as rows. Similarly, let the matrix $\mathbf{X} \in \mathbb{R}^{k \times m}$ be the embedding of items in the same factor space with items representations $\mathbf{x}_i$ as columns. A recommendation is performed on the basis of the ranking induced by the following factorization:

$$\hat{\mathbf{R}} = \mathbf{W}\mathbf{X}$$

The factorization parameters are typically computed minimizing a functional

$$\mathcal{P}(\mathbf{R}, \mathbf{W}, \mathbf{X}) = \mathcal{L}(\mathbf{R}, \mathbf{W}\mathbf{X}) + \mathcal{R}(\mathbf{W}, \mathbf{X})$$

where $\mathcal{L}(\mathbf{R}, \mathbf{W}\mathbf{X})$ is the training loss, that is a measure of the discrepancy between the initial rating matrix and the obtained approximated matrix, and $\mathcal{R}(\mathbf{W}, \mathbf{X})$ is a regularization term.

Now, we review well known state-of-the-art methods in the framework above. We start with user-based NN and item-based NN prediction although in these cases there is a fixed embedding and no real training has to be performed.

User-based NN prediction.

In the user-based NN case the embedding is performed in $\mathbb{R}^n$, the space of users, according to:

$$\mathbf{w}_u^{(v)} = \begin{cases} s_{uv} & \text{if } v \in \text{NN}(u) \\ 0 & \text{otherwise} \end{cases}, \quad s_{uv} = \cos(\mathbf{r}_u, \mathbf{r}_v) = \frac{\mathbf{r}_u^\top \mathbf{r}_v}{||\mathbf{r}_u|| ||\mathbf{r}_v||}$$

$$\mathbf{x}_i^{(v)} = \frac{r_{vi}}{||\mathbf{r}_i||} \quad \text{i.e.} \quad \mathbf{x}_i = \frac{\mathbf{r}_i}{||\mathbf{r}_i||}$$

Item-based NN prediction.

In this case, the embedding is performed in $\mathbb{R}^m$, the space of items, according to:

$$\mathbf{w}_u^{(j)} = \frac{r_{uj}}{||\mathbf{r}_u||} \quad \text{i.e.} \quad \mathbf{w}_u = \frac{\mathbf{r}_u}{||\mathbf{r}_u||}$$

$$\mathbf{x}_i^{(j)} = \begin{cases} s_{ij} & \text{if } j \in \text{NN}(i) \\ 0 & \text{otherwise} \end{cases} \quad \text{and} \quad s_{ij} = \cos(\mathbf{r}_i, \mathbf{r}_j) = \frac{\mathbf{r}_i^\top \mathbf{r}_j}{||\mathbf{r}_i|| ||\mathbf{r}_j||}$$

Weighted Regularized Matrix Factorization (WR-MF).

In WR-MF, both the user embedding and the item embedding have to be trained. These embeddings are performed in a common space of dimension k, which is an external parameter, and the optimization problem consists of a regularized weighted squared loss

$$\mathcal{P}(\mathbf{R}, \mathbf{W}, \mathbf{X}) = \sum_{u \in \mathbb{U}} \sum_{i \in \mathbb{I}} c_{ui}(\hat{r}_{ui} - 1)^2 + \lambda(||\mathbf{W}||^2 + ||\mathbf{X}||^2)$$

where c_{ui} are apriori given weights for each (rated and unrated) item. The coefficients of positive feedback typically gets a greater value (see [6, 4]).

SLIM (Sparse Linear Method).

The method in [5] can be cast in our framework as well. In this case, the embedding is performed in item space ($k = m$). SLIM learns a sparse matrix $\mathbf{X} \in \mathbb{R}^{m \times m}$ by minimizing a least square loss $LS(\mathbf{R}, \mathbf{X}\mathbf{W})$ such that $x_{ij} \geq 0, x_{ii} = 0$. Specifically, the regularization term is $\mathcal{R}(\mathbf{W}, \mathbf{X}) = \frac{\beta}{2}||\mathbf{X}||_F^2 + \lambda||\mathbf{X}||_1$ where β, λ are two external parameters. The matrix $\mathbf{W}$ is fixed ($\mathbf{W} = \mathbf{R}$).

Bayesian Personalized Ranking (BPR).

The method in [7] learns the two embeddings in a factor space of dimension k (external parameter). The optimization problem is obtained by a Bayesian interpretation of AUC maximization and it is defined by:

$$\mathcal{P}(\mathbf{R}, \mathbf{W}, \mathbf{X}) = \sum_{u \in \mathbb{U}} \sum_{i \in \mathbb{I}} \ln(\sigma(\hat{r}_{ui} - \hat{r}_{uj})) + \lambda_w||\mathbf{W}||^2 + \lambda_x||\mathbf{X}||^2$$

where $\sigma(\cdot)$ is the sigmoid function and λ_w, λ_x are external parameters. The problem is clearly not convex and the training is performed by stochastic gradient descent.

4. MARGIN AND AUC OPTIMIZATION

As seen in the previous sections, typical approaches to collaborative filtering cast the problem of item recommendation as a regularized regression problem [4, 6, 5]. This means that they try to fit the matrix $\mathbf{R}$ with a regularized function that should predict values close to 1 for rated items and values close to 0 for unrated items. For the regression case, a natural choice of a loss to optimize is the least square loss. Even if this choice has been shown to be very good for explicit feedback, where the evaluation is usually performed with RMSE, this seems less suited to the implicit feedback setting where different ranking-based evaluation measure, like AUC, mean average precision, etc., are preferred.

In this paper, we propose a different paradigm inspired to preference learning and instance ranking [3] by considering preferences on pairs of items of a user. In particular, we consider a user preferring an item i over an item j ($i \succ_u j$) whenever the user u has rated item i but we have not information about the user preference on item j. Moreover, we assume that users act independently, that is, the fact that a user has ranked or not an item gives no additional information about what other users do. With this hypothesis any user can be modeled independently.

In our model a user ranks items based on the usual scoring function $\hat{r}_{ui} = \mathbf{w}_u^\top \mathbf{x}_i$ but with the additional constraint that the vectors $\mathbf{w}_u$ and $\mathbf{x}_i$ are enforced to be unitary norm vectors. Note that, given this assumption, we have $|\hat{r}_{ui}| \leq 1$ since $|\hat{r}_{ui}| \leq ||\mathbf{w}_u|| \cdot ||\mathbf{x}_i|| = 1$ always holds.

In the following, we focus on a fixed item representation, namely the same used by user-based NN method, i.e. $\mathbf{x}_i = \mathbf{r}_i / ||\mathbf{r}_i||$.

Given a user, we define the *margin* for a item pair (i, j) such that $i \succ_u j$, and we denote it by $\rho(i \succ_u j)$, as in the following:

$$\rho(i \succ_u j) = \frac{1}{2}(\hat{r}_{ui} - \hat{r}_{uj}) = \frac{1}{2}\mathbf{w}_u^\top(\mathbf{x}_i - \mathbf{x}_j).$$

Note that $-1 \leq \rho(i \succ_u j) \leq +1$ holds for any pair of items. The function $\rho(i \succ_u j)$ well approximates the indicator function $[\![\hat{r}_{ui} > \hat{r}_{uj}]\!]$ having value 1 when a pair is correctly ranked or 0 otherwise. In particular, we have that the margin is a non trivial lower bound of the indicator function:

$$-1 \leq \rho(i \succ_u j) \leq [\![\hat{r}_{ui} > \hat{r}_{uj}]\!] \leq +1.$$

Following the same line as in [2] we consider for each user u the following game. Let $\mathcal{P}_{min}$ (the nature), and $\mathcal{P}_{max}$ (the player). On each round of the game, $\mathcal{P}_{max}$ picks an hypothesis $\mathbf{w}_u$ such that $||\mathbf{w}_u|| = 1$, and simultaneously $\mathcal{P}_{min}$ picks a preference $i \succ_u j$. $\mathcal{P}_{max}$ wants to maximize its pay-off defined as the achieved margin on the pair of items which, in our setting, is defined by $\rho(i \succ_u j)$.

Let now be given a mixed strategy for the $\mathcal{P}_{min}$ player defined by two probability distributions: $\boldsymbol{\alpha}_u^+$, the probability of each positive item to be selected, and $\boldsymbol{\alpha}_u^-$ the corresponding probabilities for negative items. We can assume these probabilities can be marginalized as the associated events are independent. In other words, the probability to pick the pair $(i \succ_u j)$ is simply given by $\alpha_{ui}^+\alpha_{uj}^-$. Hence, the value of the game, i.e. the expected margin obtained in a game, will be:

$$\mathbb{E}_{\boldsymbol{\alpha}}[\rho] = \frac{1}{2} \sum_{i\in\mathbb{I}(u), j\notin\mathbb{I}(u)} \alpha_{ui}^+\alpha_{uj}^-(\mathbf{w}_u^\top\mathbf{x}_i - \mathbf{w}_u^\top\mathbf{x}_j)$$

When the player $\mathcal{P}_{min}$ is free to choose any possible strategy, the following problem is obtained that determines the equilibrium of the game, that is

$$(\mathbf{w}_u^*, \boldsymbol{\alpha}_u^*) = \arg \max_{||\mathbf{w}_u||=1} \min_{\boldsymbol{\alpha}\in\mathbb{C}(u)} \mathbb{E}_{\boldsymbol{\alpha}}[\rho]$$

where $\mathbb{C}(u) = \{\boldsymbol{\alpha} | \alpha_i \geq 0, \sum_{i\in\mathbb{I}(u)} \alpha_i = 1, \sum_{i\notin\mathbb{I}(u)} \alpha_i = 1\}$.

The expected margin can now be reformulated as follows:

$$\begin{aligned}
\mathbb{E}_{\boldsymbol{\alpha}_u}[\rho] &= \frac{1}{2}\sum_{i\in\mathbb{I}(u)}\sum_{j\notin\mathbb{I}(u)} \alpha_{ui}\alpha_{uj}(\hat{r}_{ui} - \hat{r}_{uj}) \\
&= \frac{1}{2}\Big(\sum_{i\in\mathbb{I}(u)} \alpha_{ui}\hat{r}_{ui} \underbrace{\sum_{j\notin\mathbb{I}(u)} \alpha_{uj}}_{=1} - \sum_{j\notin\mathbb{I}(u)} \alpha_{uj}\hat{r}_{uj} \underbrace{\sum_{i\in\mathbb{I}(u)} \alpha_{ui}}_{=1}\Big) \\
&= \frac{1}{2}\sum_{i\in\mathbb{I}} y_{ui}\alpha_{ui}\hat{r}_{ui} = \frac{1}{2}\sum_{i\in\mathbb{I}} y_{ui}\alpha_{ui}\mathbf{w}_u^\top\mathbf{x}_i \\
&= \frac{1}{2}\mathbf{w}_u^\top\mathbf{X}\mathbf{Y}_u\boldsymbol{\alpha}_u
\end{aligned}$$

where we set

$$\mathbf{y}_u : y_{ui} = \begin{cases} +1 & \text{if } i \in \mathbb{I}(u) \\ -1 & \text{if } i \notin \mathbb{I}(u) \end{cases} \quad \text{and } \mathbf{Y}_u = \text{diag}(\mathbf{y}_u).$$

Setting $\mathbf{v}_u = \mathbf{X}\mathbf{Y}_u\boldsymbol{\alpha}_u$, then the $\mathbf{w}_u$ maximizing the expected margin is simply defined by $\mathbf{w}_u^* = c\mathbf{v}_u$, where $c = ||\mathbf{v}_u||^{-1}$. Note that, since c depends on the user only, then the ranking of items induced by $\mathbf{w}_u^*$ is the same as the one induced by $\mathbf{v}_u$. Substituting back the obtained solution for $\mathbf{w}_u$, we obtain:

$$\begin{aligned}
\mathbb{E}_{\boldsymbol{\alpha}_u}[\rho] &= \frac{1}{2}\sum_{i\in\mathbb{I}} y_{ui}\alpha_{ui}\mathbf{w}_u^\top\mathbf{x}_i \\
&= \frac{1}{2||\mathbf{v}_u||}\sum_{i\in\mathbb{I}} y_{ui}\alpha_{ui}\mathbf{v}_u^\top\mathbf{x}_i \\
&= \frac{\mathbf{v}_u^\top\mathbf{v}_u}{2||\mathbf{v}_u||} = \frac{1}{2}||\mathbf{v}_u||
\end{aligned}$$

Every element of the set $\mathbb{C}(u)$ represents two points, one in the convex hull of positive items, that is $\mathbf{x}^+ = \sum_{i\in\mathbb{I}(u)} \alpha_{ui}\mathbf{x}_i$, and another in the convex hull of negative items, that is $\mathbf{x}^- = \sum_{j\notin\mathbb{I}(u)} \alpha_{uj}\mathbf{x}_j$, for any given user. It is possible to show that $\mathbf{v}_u$ corresponds to the vector starting from $\mathbf{x}^-$ and ending in $\mathbf{x}^+$, that is $\mathbf{v}_u = \mathbf{x}^+ - \mathbf{x}^-$. As shown above, the expected margin is proportional to the length of this vector.

Given the game defined above, we see now that the expectation of the margin is also a lower bound of the expected AUC obtained in the game for that user. In fact, given the probability distributions $\boldsymbol{\alpha} \in \mathbb{C}(u)$ we get:

$$\begin{aligned}
\text{AUC}_\alpha(u) &= \sum_{i\in\mathbb{I}(u), j\notin\mathbb{I}(u)} \alpha_{ui}\alpha_{uj}[\![\hat{r}_{ui} > \hat{r}_{uj}]\!] \\
&\geq \sum_{i\in\mathbb{I}(u), j\notin\mathbb{I}(u)} \alpha_{ui}\alpha_{uj}\rho(i \succ_u j) = \mathbb{E}_{\boldsymbol{\alpha}_u}[\rho]
\end{aligned}$$

As discussed in [2] for the classification case, the pure maximization of the minimum margin is not necessarily the best choice. Especially in our case, noise is always present in the negative set of items. For this, we consider two quadratic regularization terms that give a bias towards uniform solutions for $\boldsymbol{\alpha}$, namely $\alpha_{ui} = 1/m_u^+$ whenever $i \in \mathbb{I}(u)$ and $\alpha_{uj} = 1/m_u^-$ whenever $j \notin \mathbb{I}(u)$. In the experiments we will see that an imbalanced setting of these regularization parameters is crucial for the effectiveness of our method.

For each user, we define the following optimization problem with the aim to maximize the expected margin and the AUC lower bound:

$$\min_{\boldsymbol{\alpha}_u\in\mathbb{C}(u)} \mathcal{Q}(\boldsymbol{\alpha}_u) + \mathcal{R}(\boldsymbol{\alpha}_u)$$

where

$$\mathcal{Q}(\boldsymbol{\alpha}_u) = ||\mathbf{v}_u||^2 = \boldsymbol{\alpha}_u^\top\mathbf{Y}_u\mathbf{X}^\top\mathbf{X}\mathbf{Y}_u\boldsymbol{\alpha}_u$$

$$\mathcal{R}(\boldsymbol{\alpha}_u) = \lambda_p \sum_{i\in\mathbb{I}(u)} \alpha_{ui}^2 + \lambda_n \sum_{i\notin\mathbb{I}(u)} \alpha_{ui}^2$$

Rearranging the terms in matrix form we obtain:

$$\boldsymbol{\alpha}_u^* = \arg \min_{\boldsymbol{\alpha}_u\in\mathbb{C}(u)} \boldsymbol{\alpha}_u^\top \left(\mathbf{Y}_u\mathbf{X}^\top\mathbf{X}\mathbf{Y}_u + \boldsymbol{\Lambda}\right) \boldsymbol{\alpha}_u$$

where the diagonal matrix $\boldsymbol{\Lambda}$ is defined as follows:

$$\boldsymbol{\Lambda} : \boldsymbol{\Lambda}(i,j) = \begin{cases} \lambda_p & \text{if } i = j \text{ and } i \in \mathbb{I}(u) \\ \lambda_n & \text{if } i = j \text{ and } i \notin \mathbb{I}(u) \\ 0 & \text{otherwise} \end{cases}$$

This problem is convex quadratic and can be optimized with any tool for convex optimization. For our experiments, we used Python and the CVXOPT package[1].

Note that, when $\lambda_p, \lambda_n = +\infty$, it is possible to show that the optimization problem has a closed form solution, that is

$$\mathbf{w}_u \propto \frac{1}{m_u^+}\sum_{i\in\mathbb{I}(u)} \mathbf{x}_i - \frac{1}{m_u^-}\sum_{j\notin\mathbb{I}(u)} \mathbf{x}_j.$$

5. EXPERIMENTS

The datasets used for the evaluation have been extracted from MovieLens1M (ML1M), NetFlixSmall (NFS), BookCrossing (BX). All these datasets correspond to multi-value ratings that we converted into binary ratings (rated/non-rated). In particular we used the following three datasets[2]:

[1]M. S. Andersen, J. Dahl, and L. Vandenberghe. CVXOPT: A Python package for convex optimization, version 1.1.6. Available at cvxopt.org, 2013.

[2]http://www.math.unipd.it/~aiolli/DATA/RECSYS14/

Dataset	Our Method	WRMF
ML1M (3850,2273)	**0.89886**	0.88630
NFS (2979,2544)	**0.89550**	0.87309
BX (1609,1629)	**0.74200**	0.73932

Table 1: AUC comparisons. Our method vs. WRMF (in parenthesis the number of users and items of the subset).

$\lambda_p \setminus \lambda_n$	1	10	100	1000	10000
0.01	0.87751	0.89714	0.89768	0.89631	0.89612
0.1	0.87809	0.89762	0.89792	0.89646	0.89626
1	0.87961	**0.89886**	0.89779	0.89584	0.89557
10	0.87926	0.89764	0.89376	0.89065	0.89023
100	0.87897	0.89692	0.89178	0.88813	0.88763
1000	0.87903	0.89685	0.89151	0.88777	0.88727

Table 2: ML1M AUC results varying the external parameters

1. **ML1M**. The ML1M[3] dataset is a subset of the MovieLens1M movie-related data corresponding to users who rated from 20 to 500 items and items being rated by from 20 to 500 users.
2. **NFS**. The NFS dataset[4] is a subset of the NetFlixSmall movie-related data corresponding to users who rated from 20 to 500 items and items being rated by from 5 to 500 users.
3. **BX**. The BX[5] dataset is a subset of the BookCrossing book-related data corresponding to users who rated from 10 to 500 items and items being rated by from 10 to 500 users.

To evaluate the performance of the proposed method, and compare it with other methods, 5-fold cross-validation has been employed. We first compared all the state-of-the-art methods described in this paper (UserBased and ItemBased NN, WRMF, SLIM, and BPR). MyMediaLite[6] implementations of these methods has been used. WRMF performed similar to BPR and better than SLIM and it has been selected for direct comparison with our method (see Table 1). Note that this partially contradicts results presented in the original paper [5] where they were presented in terms of HR (leave-one-out). Worse performance of SLIM can be due to the fact that it is based on least-square/regression and does not weights differently positive (unambiguous) and negative (ambiguous) implicit feedback. From the table we can note that our method outperforms the state-of-the-art method in terms of AUC. We observed the same trend when using other top-N measures (e.g. map@10).

[3]http://grouplens.org/datasets/movielens/

[4]http://www.netflixprize.com/

[5]http://www.informatik.uni-freiburg.de/~cziegler/BX/

[6]http://mymedialite.net/

$\lambda_p \setminus \lambda_n$	1	10	100	1000	10000
0.01	0.85428	0.88473	0.89414	0.89466	0.89469
0.1	0.85400	0.88490	0.89440	0.89489	0.89492
1	0.85396	0.88590	0.89507	0.89547	**0.89550**
10	0.85220	0.88412	0.89388	0.89416	0.89415
100	0.85159	0.88357	0.89319	0.89469	0.89337
1000	0.85290	0.88358	0.89309	0.89327	0.89326

Table 3: NFS AUC results varying the external parameters

$\lambda_p \setminus \lambda_n$	1	10	100	1000	10000
0.01	0.69457	0.72075	0.73837	0.74087	0.74114
0.1	0.69483	0.72106	0.73867	0.74112	0.74175
1	0.69473	0.72165	0.73925	0.74175	**0.74200**
10	0.69244	0.71965	0.73751	0.74012	0.74039
100	0.69179	0.71893	0.73683	0.73939	0.73966
1000	0.69184	0.71897	0.73676	0.73931	0.73957

Table 4: BX AUC results varying the external parameters

Further analysis has been done to demonstrate the robustness of the proposed method with respect to the setting of external parameters. In Tables 2,3,4, the results obtained with different settings show that $\lambda_p \approx 1$, $\lambda_n \approx 1000$ always give good results and this is a great advantage of our method with respect to other state-of-the-art methods that typically are more sensitive to the external parameter setting and often require heavy parameter tuning to work well.

Finally, we can note that the results of our method tend to get worse for big λ_p values or small λ_n values. In the case of λ_p (unambiguous information parameter), smaller values allows the model to (safely) optimize the minimum margin in the training set. In the case of λ_n, small values tend to make the ambiguous information to be too relevant in the construction of the model and this introduces erroneous information in the final model estimate. On the other side, larger λ_n values tend to mitigate the negative effect of ambiguous information on the constructed model and this explains why so high values of λ_n are preferable in our context.

6. CONCLUSIONS AND FUTURE WORK

We presented an effective method for AUC optimization of top-N recommendation with implicit feedback. Future work will extend the method to learn in a principled way the user and item embeddings simultaneously.

7. REFERENCES

[1] F. Aiolli. Efficient top-n recommendation for very large scale binary rated datasets. In Q. Yang, I. King, Q. Li, P. Pu, and G. Karypis, editors, *RecSys*, pages 273–280. ACM, 2013.

[2] F. Aiolli, G. D. S. Martino, and A. Sperduti. A kernel method for the optimization of the margin distribution. In *ICANN (1)*, pages 305–314, 2008.

[3] F. Aiolli and A. Sperduti. A preference optimization based unifying framework for supervised learning problems. In J. Fürnkranz and E. Hüllermeier, editors, *Preference Learning*, pages 19–42. Springer-Verlag, 2010.

[4] Y. Hu, Y. Koren, and C. Volinsky. Collaborative filtering for implicit feedback datasets. In *ICDM*, pages 263–272, 2008.

[5] X. Ning and G. Karypis. Slim: Sparse linear methods for top-n recommender systems. In *ICDM*, pages 497–506, 2011.

[6] R. Pan, Y. Zhou, B. Cao, N. N. Liu, R. Lukose, M. Scholz, and Q. Yang. One-class collaborative filtering. In *ICDM*, 2008.

[7] S. Rendle, C. Freudenthaler, Z. Gantner, and L. Schmidt-Thieme. Bpr: Bayesian personalized ranking from implicit feedback. In *Proc. of the 25th Conference on Uncertainty in Artificial Intelligence (UAI)*, 2009.

Cross-domain Recommendations without Overlapping Data: Myth or Reality?

Paolo Cremonesi
Politecnico di Milano
Italy
paolo.cremonesi@polimi.it

Massimo Quadrana
Politecnico di Milano
Italy
massimo.quadrana@polimi.it

ABSTRACT

Cross-domain recommender systems adopt different techniques to transfer learning from source domain to target domain in order to alleviate the sparsity problem and improve accuracy of recommendations. Traditional techniques require the two domains to be linked by shared characteristics associated to either users or items. In collaborative filtering (CF) this happens when the two domains have *overlapping* users or item (at least partially). Recently, Li et al. [7] introduced *codebook transfer* (CBT), a cross-domain CF technique based on co-clustering, and presented experimental results showing that CBT is able to transfer knowledge between non-overlapping domains. In this paper, we disprove these results and show that CBT does not transfer knowledge when source and target domains do not overlap.

Categories and Subject Descriptors

H.3.3 [**Information Storage and Retrieval**]: Information Search and Retrieval—*Information filtering*

General Terms

Algorithms and theory

Keywords

Accuracy measures; Cold start; Matrix factorization; Ratings aggregation; Sparsity

1. INTRODUCTION

In 2009, Li et al. [7] proposed *codebook-transfer* (CBT), a cross-domain collaborative filtering (CF) recommender system based on co-clustering and tri-matrix factorization. The core of CBT is based on a two-step process: extraction of knowledge (the *codebook*) from the source domain and injection of knowledge in the target domain. Both steps are performed by using a constrained tri-matrix factorization. The injection phase is used to reduce the sparsity of the target domain. After the injection, traditional CF algorithms are trained on the target domain.

The Li et al. paper [7] claims that CBT is able to transfer learning from the source domain to the target domain even in the case of totally disjoint domains, i.e., domains without shared users or items. They prove this by comparing the accuracy of a traditional CF algorithm on the target domain before and after the injection of the codebook from the source domain. The algorithm adopted for the comparison is a user-based k-nearest-neighbors (kNN) collaborative filtering based on Pearson correlation. The comparison shows a significant increase of accuracy after the injection.

However, in this paper we provide an alternative explanation to the increase of accuracy experimented with CBT that does not involve transfer of knowledge between domains. The contributions of this paper are three-fold.

- First, we provide empirical evidence that CBT improves the accuracy of CF without transferring knowledge from source to target domain[1].
- Second, we show that the injection of the codebook in the target domain is equivalent to a two-matrix factorization algorithm without transfer of knowledge from the source domain.
- Third, as a consequence of this, we show that the increase of accuracy measured in [7] is due to a pitfall in the evaluation procedure as it compares a user-based kNN algorithm (before the injection) with a matrix-factorization algorithm (after the injection) and matrix-factorization is known to outperform kNN.

The rest of the paper is organized as follows. In Section 2, we introduce the cross-domain CF problem and describe the CBT algorithm. In Section 3, we show that the CBT algorithm does not transfer knowledge. Finally, the conclusions are given in Section 4.

2. CROSS-DOMAIN CF

Cross-domain CF systems aim to generate or enhance recommendations in a target domain by exploiting knowledge (mainly user preferences) from source domains. One of the motivating use cases of cross-domain recommendations is the well known cold-start problem, which prevents a recommender system from generating recommendations due to

[1] Code and datasets are available for download from: http://home.deib.polimi.it/cremones/recsys/cbt.zip

RecSys'14, October 6–10, 2014, Foster City, Silicon Valley, CA, USA.
Copyright 2014 ACM 978-1-4503-2668-1/14/10 ...$15.00.
http://dx.doi.org/10.1145/2645710.2645769.

the lack of sufficient information about a user or item. In a cross-domain setting, a recommender system may draw on information acquired from other domains to alleviate such problem. For instance, a user's preferred movie genres are likely to be derived accurately from her/his preferred literature genres. This example is based on the assumption that there are similarities or correspondences either between the user preferences or between the items in the source and target domains. Cross-domain recommender systems leverage these dependencies through considering, for example, overlaps between the observed user or item sets, similarities of item attributes, features of rated items, or correlations between user preferences in the domains. Then, they apply a variety of techniques for enriching the knowledge possessed by the target domain, and improving the quality of recommendations.

The research on cross-domain recommendation has generally aimed to exploit knowledge from a source domain $\mathcal{D}_S$, to perform or improve recommendations in a target domain $\mathcal{D}_T$. Respectively for such domains, let $\mathcal{U}_S$ and $\mathcal{U}_T$ be their sets of users, and let $\mathcal{I}_S$ and $\mathcal{I}_T$ be their sets of items. The users of a domain are those that have some ratings for items of the domain. In order to alleviate cold-start and sparsity problems in the target domain, cross-domain systems recommend items in the target domain by exploiting knowledge from both source and target domains, i.e., recommend items in $\mathcal{I}_T$ to users in $\mathcal{U}_S$ by exploiting knowledge about $\mathcal{U}_S \cup \mathcal{U}_T$ and/or $\mathcal{I}_S \cup \mathcal{I}_T$. In general, to perform this type of recommendation, some data relations or overlaps between domains are needed, and approaches aim to establish explicit or implicit knowledge-based links between the domains.

As discussed by Fernández-Tobías et al. [4], domains can be linked by means characteristics associated to users or items. Following the notation used in [4], let $\mathcal{X}^{\mathcal{U}}$ and $\mathcal{X}^{\mathcal{I}}$ be the sets of characteristics used to represent the users and items, respectively. The nature of these characteristics may be diverse, e.g. ratings, user demographics, item attributes. Two domains $\mathcal{D}_S$ and $\mathcal{D}_T$ are linked if $\mathcal{X}^{\mathcal{U}}_S \cap \mathcal{X}^{\mathcal{U}}_T \neq \varnothing$ or $\mathcal{X}^{\mathcal{I}}_S \cap \mathcal{X}^{\mathcal{I}}_T \neq \varnothing$, i.e., if there are user or item characteristics shared by the domains.

In collaborative filtering systems, the user preferences are usually modeled as a matrix $R \in \mathbb{R}^{|\mathcal{U}| \times |\mathcal{I}|}$, in which an element r_{ui} is the rating assigned by user u to item i. Users are described through the ratings they assign to items. Thus, $\mathcal{X}^{\mathcal{U}}_S = \mathcal{I}_S$ and $\mathcal{X}^{\mathcal{U}}_T = \mathcal{I}_T$. Similarly, items are described in terms of the ratings received by users, i.e., $\mathcal{X}^{\mathcal{I}}_S = \mathcal{U}_S$ and $\mathcal{X}^{\mathcal{I}}_T = \mathcal{U}_T$. Domains $\mathcal{D}_S$ and $\mathcal{D}_T$ overlap when $\mathcal{I}_S \cap \mathcal{I}_T \neq \varnothing$ or $\mathcal{U}_S \cap \mathcal{U}_T \neq \varnothing$. Figure 1 shows the four scenarios deriving by the combination of user and items overlapping in cross-domain CF as identified by Cremonesi et al. in [2]:

- *No overlap.* There is no overlap between users and items, i.e., $\mathcal{U}_{ST} = \mathcal{U}_S \cap \mathcal{U}_T = \varnothing$ and $\mathcal{I}_{ST} = \mathcal{I}_S \cap \mathcal{I}_T = \varnothing$.
- *User overlap.* There are some shared users who have preferences for items in both domains, i.e., $\mathcal{U}_{ST} \neq \varnothing$.
- *Item overlap.* There are shared items rated by users from both the domains, i.e., $\mathcal{I}_{ST} \neq \varnothing$.
- *User and item overlap.* There is overlap between both users and items, i.e., $\mathcal{U}_{ST} \neq \varnothing$ and $\mathcal{I}_{ST} \neq \varnothing$.

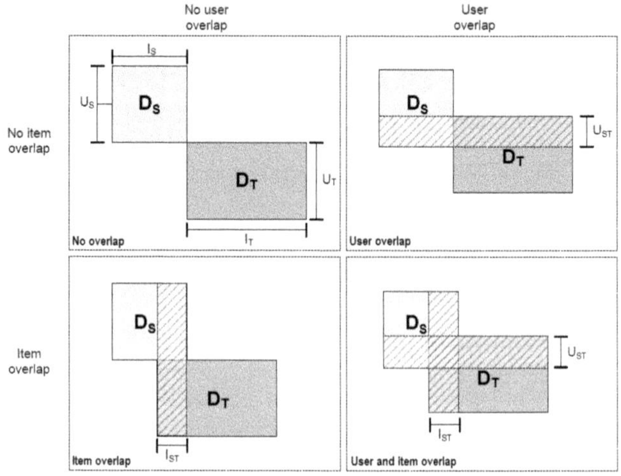

Figure 1: Scenarios of data overlap between user and item sets in two domains $\mathcal{D}_S$ and $\mathcal{D}_T$: *no overlap*, *user overlap*, *item overlap*, and *user and item overlap*.

2.1 The CBT algorithm

CBT is one of the recent CF methods based on rating pattern sharing which do not rely on any kind of overlap between domains [8, 7, 5]. The underlying hypothesis is that. even when users and items are different, related domains are likely to have user preferences sampled with the same population. Therefore, correlations may exist between preferences of groups of users for groups of items, which are referred to as the *rating patterns*. Rating patterns can act as a bridge that relates the involved domains, even though users and items may not overlap between the domains.

The CBT algorithm [7] extracts rating patterns from the source domain by simultaneously co-clustering users and items. Clustering is performed using a tri-factorization of the source rating matrix [3]. Then, knowledge is transferred through the *codebook*, a compact cluster-level matrix that is computed in the source domain taking the average rating of each user-item cluster. In the target domain, the sparse user-rating matrix is filled with ratings predicted using the shared codebook. The now filled user-rating matrix is then used to train a traditional CF algorithm.

The CBT algorithm consists of three steps: *codebook construction*, *target filling* and *CF training*.

In the **first step**, the source rating matrix R_S is factorized by using the orthogonal nonnegative matrix tri-factorization described in [3]

$$\min_{U_S \geq 0, V_S \geq 0, S \geq 0} \|R_S - U_S S V_S^\top\|_F^2 \qquad (1)$$
$$\text{s.t. } U_S^\top U_S = I, V_S^\top V_S = I$$

where $U_S \in \mathbb{R}_+^{n \times k}$, $V_S \in \mathbb{R}_+^{m \times l}$, $S \in \mathbb{R}_+^{k \times l}$, $\|\cdot\|_F^2$ is the Frobenius norm, n is the number of users, m the number of items, and k and l are the number of user and item clusters, respectively. Before the factorization, the zero elements of R_S are filled with the average user rating. After the factorization, matrices U_S and V_S are binarized to form two hard membership matrices. The codebook B is constructed as follows

$$B = [U_S^\top R_S V_S] \oslash [U_S^\top \mathbf{1}\mathbf{1}^\top V_S] \qquad (2)$$

where $\oslash$ is the entry-wise division and **1** is a vector of ones. The codebook contains the average rating of each co-cluster of users and items.

In the **second step**, the target rating matrix R_T is filled by expanding the values in the codebook. To this purpose, users and items in the target domains are first mapped to the co-clusters identified in the codebook by minimizing the following quadratic loss function

$$\min_{\substack{U_T \in \{0,1\}^{p \times k} \\ V_T \in \{0,1\}^{q \times l}}} \|R_T - U_T B V_T^\top\|^2 \quad (3)$$
$$\text{s.t } U_T\mathbf{1} = \mathbf{1}, V_T\mathbf{1} = \mathbf{1}$$

Each row in U_T or V_T is the cluster membership of the user or item. Note that, differently from what happens in the first step, the norm of this second minimization problem is computed only on the non-zero entries of the user-rating matrix. Once the user and item membership matrices U_T and V_T are obtained, all the zero elements of the target rating matrix R_T are filled with the appropriate elements of the codebook

$$R_T \leftarrow W \circ R_T + [\mathbf{1} - W] \circ \left[U_T B V_T^\top\right] \quad (4)$$

where $\circ$ denotes the entry-wise product and W is a binary mask of the same size as R_T used to mask zero elements.

In the **third step**, the filled target matrix can be used as the training data set for CF.

The authors performed experiments using a dense subset of the EachMovie dataset to compute the rating patterns, which were transferred to the more sparse MovieLens and BookCrossing datasets. They compared the accuracy of a traditional CF algorithm on the target domain with and without the transfer of the codebook from the source domain. The algorithm adopted for the comparison was a user-based k-nearest-neighbors (kNN) collaborative filtering based on Pearson correlation. According to the results, rating predictions were improved with the transfer of the codebook.

3. EVALUATION OF CBT

In this section we describe the methodology adopted to evaluate if the improvement of accuracy experimented by Li et al. in [7] with the CBT algorithm is due to a transfer of learning from source to target domain.

The CBT algorithm consists of three steps: (i) construction of the codebook from the source domain; (ii) filling of the missing ratings in the target domain by using the codebook; (iii) training a CF algorithm on the filled target domain. The goal of the second step is to reduce the sparsity on the target domain and to help the final CF algorithms in providing better recommendations.

We have modified the CBT algorithm by removing step (i) and by generating a codebook B that is not based on the source domain. In other words, we drop equations (1) and (2) and keep equations (3) and (4). We have tested three different methods to generate a "false" codebook:

- *Random* (RND): the codebook is created by randomly generating ratings uniformly distributed in the range $[3 \ldots 5]$.
- *Global Effects* (GE): the codebook is created by estimating ratings with the global effects $r_{ui} = \mu + \mu_u + \mu_i$ described in [6], where μ is the overall average rating of the target user-rating matrix R_T and $\mu_u + \mu_i$ are deviations of user u and item i from the average, respectively.
- *Asymmetric SVD* (AsySVD): the codebook is created by estimating ratings with the matrix-factorization algorithm *Asymmetric SVD* described in [6] and applied to the target user-rating matrix R_T.

With both GE and AsySVD, the numbers of user and item clusters in the codebook B is equal to the size of the target user-rating matrix R_T (i.e., each cluster is composed by one user and one item).

3.1 Results

In this section we present the quality of the different approaches on **three standard datasets**: *MovieLens* [1], *Netflix* [1] and *BookCrossing* [9]. All the datasets are publicly available. Ratings in the MovieLens and Netflix datasets are in a 1-5 scale. Ratings in the Book-Crossing dataset are in a 1-10 scale and have been normalized to a 1-5 scale. All the three datasets have been used as target domains, while only Netflix and MovieLens have been used as source domains. We performed in total **four experiments**, as each of the two source datasets has been used in conjunction with the remaining two datasets.

The evaluation has been performed with a methodology similar to the one adopted in the CBT paper [7]. We randomly selected 500 users with at least 40 ratings and 1000 items from each dataset. Each dataset has been used as either the source or the target domain. For each target dataset, 200 users have been randomly removed to form the test set. For each user in the test set, all but 15 ratings are randomly removed from her/his profile and used as ground truth for the evaluation of mean absolute error (MAE) and root mean squared error (RMSE). The evaluation has been performed 10 times, each time sampling a different set of test users. Results are reported in Table 1 and are the average over the 10 repetitions. For lack of space, not all the combination of source/target domains are reported. Each column refers to a different algorithm.

- kNN: user-based kNN with Pearson similarity. Recommendations are performed on the target domain, without using the source domain. The size of the neighborhood is $k = 20$ users. In order to improve the accuracy of recommendations, missing values in the user-rating matrix are filled in with average user rating.
- CBT: the codebook transfer method described in [7]. The number of both user and item clusters is 50.
- RND: the "false" codebook is filled with random ratings. The number of clusters is the same as with CBT.
- AsySVD: the "false" codebook is filled with ratings generated with the Asymmetric SVD matrix-factorization algorithm. The number of user and item clusters is equal to the size of the target user-rating matrix.
- GE: the "false" codebook is filled with ratings generated with the global effects method. The number of user and item clusters is equal to the size of the target user-rating matrix.

source: MovieLens → target: BookCrossing					
	kNN	CBT	RND	AsySVD	GE
MAE	0.5216	**0.5064**	**0.4963**	**0.5089**	**0.5109**
RMSE	0.4736	0.4492	**0.4380**	0.4556	0.4578
source: MovieLens → target: Netflix					
	kNN	CBT	RND	AsySVD	GE
MAE	0.7285	**0.7090**	**0.7047**	**0.7085**	**0.7124**
RMSE	0.8630	**0.8208**	**0.8149**	**0.8245**	**0.8313**
source: Netflix → target: BookCrossing					
	kNN	CBT	RND	AsySVD	GE
MAE	0.5580	**0.5456**	**0.5388**	**0.5474**	**0.5486**
RMSE	0.5437	**0.5231**	**0.5113**	**0.5269**	**0.5290**
source: Netflix → target: MovieLens					
	kNN	CBT	RND	AsySVD	GE
MAE	0.7640	**0.7446**	**0.7425**	**0.7397**	**0.7417**
RMSE	0.9388	**0.8988**	**0.8932**	**0.8915**	**0.8935**

Table 1: Accuracy of different methods. Bold numbers are significantly different from the baseline method kNN.

As expected, CBT clearly outperforms the baseline method for all the datasets. Surprisingly, the experiments with the random codebook present an accuracy which is identical to the accuracy of the CBT method, even in the lack of knowledge transfer from source to target domain.

4. DISCUSSION AND CONCLUSIONS

In this section we try to investigate the surprisingly results obtained by the random codebook. By design, the random codebook does not transfer any knowledge from the source domain into the target domain. Therefore, the increase of accuracy introduced by the random algorithm cannot be explained in terms of transfer of knowledge and we need to look for a different explanation.

The insight of the solution of this problem is from the second step of the CBT, described in (3). The goal of this step is to map users and items in the target domain to the clusters derived in the source domain (in the case of a codebook correctly created in the source domain). The structure of the optimization problem (3) closely resemble regularized SVD matrix-factorization, as the minimization is performed only on the non-zero elements of the user-rating matrix [6]:

$$\min_{U_T \geq 0, V_T \geq 0} \|R_T - U_T V_T^\top\|^2$$

The main differences are the constraints on the U_T and V_T matrices and the presence of the codebook B.

We believe that the second step of the codebook transfer, which is supposed to simply map users and item to clusters, is in fact equivalent to the training of a matrix-factorization algorithm, provided that matrix B (the codebook) has a wide enough range of ratings to account for the constraints imposed on U_T and V_T.

We also believe that the enrichment of the target domain performed by (4) is equivalent to performing recommendations with the trained matrix-factorization model.

We finally believe that the last step of the CBT method (i.e., running the kNN algorithm over the enriched target matrix) does not provide any additional improvement to the quality of the estimations, as it is well know in the literature that matrix-factorization CF outperform user-based CF in terms of accuracy [6]. Our believes are confirmed by the last two columns of Table 1, showing how codebooks created by running CF algorithms on the target domain still provide a significant reduction of the errors, even if the codebooks do not transfer any knowledge from the source domain. Our findings prove that the modified CBT method is able to improve the accuracy of recommendations even when there is no transfer of knowledge from the source domain, but they do not directly disprove that the CBT method is able to transfer knowledge between non-overlapping domains.

Still, by applying Occam's razor, we should prefer the more general explanation and derive the conclusion that *CBT is not able to transfer knowledge between non-overlapping domains, as the experimented increased accuracy is originated by the matrix-factorization performed by equations* (3) *and* (4).

5. REFERENCES

[1] P. Cremonesi, Y. Koren, and R. Turrin. Performance of recommender algorithms on top-n recommendation tasks. In *Proceedings of the Fourth ACM Conference on Recommender Systems*, RecSys '10, pages 39–46, New York, NY, USA, 2010. ACM.

[2] P. Cremonesi, A. Tripodi, and R. Turrin. Cross-domain recommender systems. In *Data Mining Workshops (ICDMW), 2011 IEEE 11th International Conference on*, pages 496–503. IEEE, 2011.

[3] C. Ding, T. Li, W. Peng, and H. Park. Orthogonal nonnegative matrix t-factorizations for clustering. In *Proceedings of the 12th ACM SIGKDD international conference on Knowledge discovery and data mining*, pages 126–135. ACM, 2006.

[4] I. Fernández-Tobías, I. Cantador, M. Kaminskas, and F. Ricci. A generic semantic-based framework for cross-domain recommendation. In *Proceedings of the 2nd International Workshop on Information Heterogeneity and Fusion in Recommender Systems*, pages 25–32. ACM, 2011.

[5] S. Gao, H. Luo, D. Chen, S. Li, P. Gallinari, and J. Guo. Cross-domain recommendation via cluster-level latent factor model. In *Machine Learning and Knowledge Discovery in Databases*, pages 161–176. Springer, 2013.

[6] Y. Koren. Factorization meets the neighborhood: a multifaceted collaborative filtering model. In *Proceedings of the 14th ACM SIGKDD international conference on Knowledge discovery and data mining*, pages 426–434. ACM, 2008.

[7] B. Li, Q. Yang, and X. Xue. Can movies and books collaborate? cross-domain collaborative filtering for sparsity reduction. In *IJCAI*, volume 9, pages 2052–2057, 2009.

[8] B. Li, Q. Yang, and X. Xue. Transfer learning for collaborative filtering via a rating-matrix generative model. In *Proceedings of the 26th Annual International Conference on Machine Learning*, pages 617–624. ACM, 2009.

[9] C.-N. Ziegler, S. M. McNee, J. A. Konstan, and G. Lausen. Improving recommendation lists through topic diversification. In *Proceedings of the 14th International Conference on World Wide Web*, WWW '05, pages 22–32, New York, NY, USA, 2005. ACM.

CSLIM: Contextual SLIM Recommendation Algorithms

Yong Zheng
Center for Web Intelligence
DePaul University
Chicago, Illinois, USA
yzheng8@cs.depaul.edu

Bamshad Mobasher
Center for Web Intelligence
DePaul University
Chicago, Illinois, USA
mobasher@cs.depaul.edu

Robin Burke
Center for Web Intelligence
DePaul University
Chicago, Illinois, USA
rburke@cs.depaul.edu

ABSTRACT

Context-aware recommender systems (CARS) take contextual conditions into account when providing item recommendations. In recent years, context-aware matrix factorization (CAMF) has emerged as an extension of the matrix factorization technique that also incorporates contextual conditions. In this paper, we introduce another matrix factorization approach for contextual recommendations, the contextual SLIM (CSLIM) recommendation approach. It is derived from the sparse linear method (SLIM) which was designed for Top-N recommendations in traditional recommender systems. Based on the experimental evaluations over several context-aware data sets, we demonstrate that CLSIM can be an effective approach for context-aware recommendations, in many cases outperforming state-of-the-art CARS algorithms in the Top-N recommendation task.

Categories and Subject Descriptors

H.3.3 [**Information Search and Retrieval**]: Information filtering

Keywords

Recommendation; Context; Context-aware recommendation; SLIM; Matrix Factorization

1. INTRODUCTION AND RELATED WORK

Context-aware recommender systems (CARS) are an extension of traditional recommender systems (RS) that adapt their recommendations to users' specific situations. The fundamental assumption of CARS is that a rating for an item is a function not just of the user and the item but also of the context in which the item is evaluated or used. A user's preferences on a given item may vary from context to context. For example, *companion* is an influential contextual variable in the movie domain; you may make a different decision in selecting movies if you intend to see the movie on a date, than if you plan on watching a movie with children.

Recent work has demonstrated that matrix factorization (MF) is an effective approach in recommendation. Extensions of standard matrix factorization approach have incorporated contextual variables, such as time-aware MF. Karatzoglou et al. [3] proposed to use tensor factorization (TF) to integrate context in recommendation. Their approach assumed that contexts are independent of other dimensions. But the computation cost in TF is prohibitive, increasing exponentially as the number of contextual variables increases. Another approach, context-aware matrix factorization (CAMF) [2] was developed to adapt to contextual recommendations by modeling contextual dependencies with the user or item dimensions. CAMF is based on traditional MF [4], where both users and items are represented by factor weightings in a matrix. Those CARS algorithms based on MF have been demonstrated to outperform the ones based on neighborhood collaborative filtering (e.g. differential context modeling [9, 10]).

Most recently, a new matrix factorization for traditional RS, called *sparse linear method (SLIM)* [5] was proposed and shown to be more accurate than the state-of-the-art MF algorithms in the top-N recommendation task. In this paper, we extend this work to create a contextual SLIM (CSLIM) model incorporating contextual conditions. We compare the performance of our proposed approaches to the state-of-the-art context-aware recommendation algorithms through extensive empirical evaluations on multiple data sets.

2. SLIM RECOMMENDER

Assume that there are M users, N items, and let us denote the associated 2-dimensional rating matrix by R. We use u_i to denote user i and t_j to denote the item j. An entry, $R_{i,j}$, in matrix R represents u_i's rating on t_j. A row vector in R representing u_i's ratings over all items is denoted by $R_{i,:}$, and $R_{:,j}$ denotes a column vector in R representing ratings on item t_j from all users.

Sparse linear method (SLIM) is an approach designed for top-N recommendations. It improves upon the traditional item-based K-nearest neighbor (ItemKNN) collaborative filtering by learning, directly from the data, a sparse matrix of aggregation coefficients that are analogous to the traditional item-item similarities [5].

In SLIM, the ranking score for user u_i on item t_j is represented by $\widehat{S}_{i,j}$, which is calculated by a sparse aggregation of the ratings on the other items that have been rated by u_i. We denote this approach as SLIM-I, since it assigns a N by N non-negative matrix W to represent the aggregation coefficients between each two items. Accordingly, $\widehat{S}_{i,j}$ can be estimated by Equation 1.

$$\widehat{S}_{i,j} = R_{i,:}W_{:,j} = \sum_{\substack{h=1 \\ h\neq j}}^{N} R_{i,h}W_{h,j}, \text{where } diag(W) = 0 \quad (1)$$

An example of how the SLIM-I approach works is provided in Figure 1. To estimate the ranking score of u_2 on item t_1, SLIM extracts u_2's ratings on the other items, and aggregates the ranking score by multiplying of those ratings by the corresponding coeffi-

RecSys'14, October 6–10, 2014, Foster City, Silicon Valley, CA, USA.

http://dx.doi.org/10.1145/2645710.2645756.

cients between the item t_1 and t_h (i.e. t_h belongs to the set of other items u_i has rated) in matrix W. The estimated ranking score will be used to rank the items to finally provide top-N recommendations. Similarly, a SLIM-U approach can be easily derived, where $\widehat{S}_{i,j}$ is calculated by a sparse aggregation of ratings on this specific item t_j but were given by other users, where W is a M by M non-negative matrix representing the coefficients between every two users. A similar example can be viewed in Figure 2.

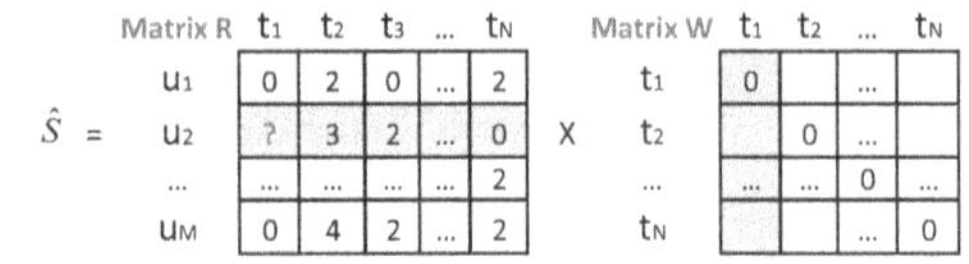

Figure 1: Example of SLIM-I

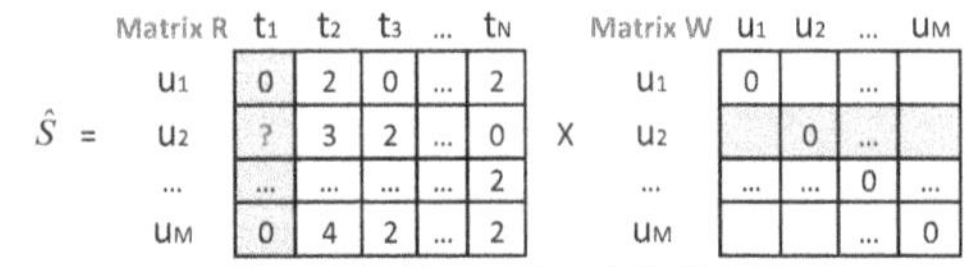

Figure 2: Example of SLIM-U

Traditional matrix factorization techniques, such as those proposed by Koren et al. [4], usually represent users and items by a set of weights on individual latent factors, and both the number of latent factors and training iterations are required to tune the model and find the optimal solution. In contrast to those approaches, the sizes of matrices R and W are fixed and there is only a single matrix, W, required to be learned in SLIM-I and SLIM-U.

3. CONTEXTUAL SLIM

Analogously to context-aware matrix factorization techniques [2], we propose to incorporate context into the SLIM approach for top-N recommendations. We refer to this as the contextual SLIM (CSLIM) approach. In the following, we use *contextual factor* to refer to the contextual variables such as "Time", "Location", and "Companion". The term *contextual condition* refers to a specific value in a contextual factor. For example, "weekend" and "weekday" are two contextual conditions for the "Time" contextual factor.

Assume there are F contextual factors and L contextual conditions in total in a context-aware data set, in addition to the M users and N items. The primary task in the CSLIM approach is to estimate the ranking score $\widehat{S}_{i,j,c}$ for user u_i on item t_j in context c. We use a binary vector, c = <$c_1, c_2, ..., c_L$>, to denote the contextual situation. For example, assume all contextual conditions with L=4 can be represent by {Time=*weekend*, Time=*weekday*, Location=*school*, Location=*home*}. Then, the vector c = <1, 0, 1, 0> indicates that the current contextual situation is {Time=*weekend*, Location=*school*}.

In CARS, users' preferences may vary from context to context for same item. Therefore, it is necessary to make predictions based on rating profiles in the same context c. Recall that the estimated ranking score matrix $\widehat{S}$ in SLIM-I is derived based upon the idea in ItemKNN – aggregation of users' ratings on other items. As a result, it is possible to estimate the ranking score $\widehat{S}_{i,j,c}$ by an aggregation of u_i' ratings on other items in the same contexts c. However, a context-aware data set, with multiple ratings for each item, is usually very sparse – it is not guaranteed that a user has rated other items in the same context c. In this case, we estimate u_i's rating on an item t_j in context c (i.e. $\widehat{R}_{i,j,c}$) based on the user's non-contextual rating on this item (i.e. $R_{i,j}$, ratings without considering contexts) and the aggregated contextual rating deviations (CRD, i.e., the rating deviations in different contextual conditions). Accordingly, we can build different CSLIM models based on how to estimate the CRD.

3.1 CSLIM-I Models

In this section, we present three CSLIM-I models based on how to estimate the CRD. First, we estimate contextual ratings (i.e. $\widehat{R}_{i,j,c}$) based on the non contextual rating $R_{i,j}$ and aggregated CRD. Specifically, we model CRD as the contextual rating deviations on items. In other words, we assume there is a rating deviation for each <item, context condition> pair. Thus, the predicted contextual rating $\widehat{R}_{i,j,c}$ can be computed as follows:

$$\widehat{R}_{i,j,c} = R_{i,j} + \sum_{l=1}^{L} D_{j,l}c_l \quad (2)$$

where R is the 2D non-contextual rating matrix. Typically, users may provide non-contextual ratings in addition to the ratings for an item in given contexts. But it is not necessary that both non-contextual ratings and contextual ratings are assigned to a same <user, item> entry. The average rating of each user on each item rated within multiple contexts can be added to the rating matrix R if there is no knowledge about the non-contextual ratings.

We build a $N \times L$ CRD matrix D where each row represents an item, and each column represents an individual contextual condition as shown in Figure 3. Thus, $D_{j,:}$ is a row in D representing CRD for the item t_j in L different contextual conditions.

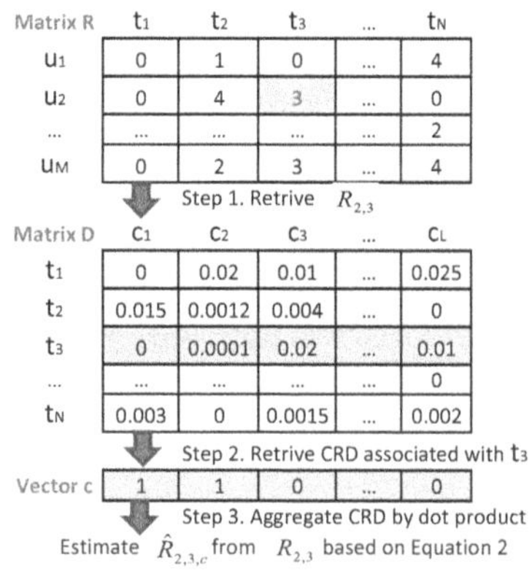

Figure 3: Example: Estimation of Contextual Rating

We can then use the SLIM-I approach to estimate the ranking score $\widehat{S}_{i,j,c}$ for user u_i on item t_j in contexts c. This is described in Equation 3, where t_h belongs to the set of items for which user u_i has provided non-contextual ratings (i.e. $R_{i,h} > 0$). The ranking score is estimated by an aggregation of user's ratings on other items in the same context c. We call this approach CSLIM-I-CI because the CRD are assumed for each <item, context condition> pair, and D is built as a CI matrix (i.e. columns and rows represent contexts and items respectively).

$$\widehat{S}_{i,j,c} = \sum_{\substack{h=1 \\ h \neq j}}^{N} \widehat{R}_{i,h,c} W_{h,j} = \sum_{\substack{h=1 \\ h \neq j}}^{N} (R_{i,h} + \sum_{l=1}^{L} D_{h,l}c_l) W_{h,j} \quad (3)$$

It is important to note that we set $h \neq j$ to avoid the model learning from u_i's non-contextual rating on t_j. Generally, the CSLIM-I-CI model will learn the parameters in D and W based on each entry of known contextual ratings $R_{i,j,c}$ in the training set, and make predictions only relying on three matrices: non-contextual rating matrix R, CRD matrix D, and the aggregation coefficient matrix W. Using squared error as the optimization criteria, the loss function with regularization terms can be described in Equation 4, which can be solved by stochastic gradient descent (SGD) approach. ∂ and β parameters are the learning rates. Both ℓ_F terms (e.g. $\|W\|_F^2$) and ℓ_1 terms (e.g. $\|W\|_1$) are included, where the ℓ_1 regularization term is usually applied for sparse models.

$$\underset{D,W}{Minimize}\ \frac{1}{2}\left\|R_{i,j,c}-\widehat{S}_{i,j,c}\right\|_F^2+\frac{\beta_1}{2}\|D\|_F^2+\frac{\beta_2}{2}\|W\|_F^2 + \partial_1\|D\|_1+\partial_2\|W\|_1 \quad (4)$$

In CSLIM-I-CI, D is modeled as a CI matrix, where the deviation is computed for each <item, context condition> pair. The deviations can also be considered for users – we assume there is a rating deviation for each <user, context condition> pair, where D results in a CU matrix (i.e. columns denote contexts and rows represent users). The latter model is called CSLIM-I-CU. In addition to these two approaches, the rating deviations can also simply be viewed as the deviations only associated with each contextual condition rather than as being paired with users or items. In this case, the CRD can be represented by a L-length vector d instead of a matrix D. We call this approach CSLIM-I-C. Note that the only difference among those three CSLIM-I models is the matrix D, while the matrix W is still the same – a $N \times N$ non-negative matrix of item-item coefficients.

3.2 CSLIM-U Models

Contexts can also be incorporated into the SLIM-U models. In this case, W is a $M \times M$ matrix representing user-user coefficients. The matrix D can be built using a similar approach as introduced in the CSLIM-I models. In other words, we can build three CSLIM-U models: CSLIM-U-CI, CSLIM-U-CU, CSLIM-U-C. The CSLIM-U-CU model, for example, utilizes user-based K-nearest-neighbor (UserKNN) collaborative filtering to estimate $\widehat{S}_{i,j,c}$ using a sparse aggregation of the ratings on item t_j in contexts c by other users who have rated it. Meanwhile, the CRD matrix D is modeled by a CU matrix which is of size $M \times L$, and W is a $M \times M$ non-negative matrix, with zero values in the diagonal, which is used to estimate coefficients between each pair of users. The loss function is the same as Equation 4 and the estimation for ranking score can be computed by Equation 5, where u_h belongs to the set of users who have rated item t_j except u_i. The parameters in matrices W and D can be updated in a similar way using SGD as the optimizer.

$$\widehat{S}_{i,j,c}=\sum_{\substack{h=1\\h\neq i}}^{M}\widehat{R}_{h,j,c}W_{i,h}=\sum_{\substack{h=1\\h\neq i}}^{M}(R_{h,j}+\sum_{l=1}^{L}D_{h,l}c_l)W_{i,h} \quad (5)$$

In a summary, CSLIM-I and CSLIM-U models utilize the intuitions behind ItemKNN and UserKNN, respectively, with the CRD matrix computed in one of three ways: CRD associated to each individual contextual condition, CRD associated with each <item, contextual condition> pair, or CRD associated with each <user, contextual condition> pair, which results in six CSLIM models.

3.3 Pros and Cons

In addition to the CRD matrix D, context-aware matrix factorization (CAMF) [2] has to also learn user and item matrices, as well as other parameters, such as user or item biases. In CSLIM, however, there is only one matrix W must be learned. The complexity of CSLIM models is associated with the number of users or items and the number of contextual conditions. For large-scale recommendations, contexts can be selected in advance based on contextual relevance [6], and feature selection [5] can also be applied to reduce the number of users or items, which was suggested in the original SLIM approach in order to deal with large W matrix.

Moreover, CSLIM helps alleviate the sparsity problem in contextual ratings by making use of the non-contextual ratings. In CSLIM, the contextual ratings are used to train the model, and the ranking score is estimated by the non-contextual ratings and the D and W matrices. The model can be trained and built incrementally with contextual ratings. It is a good solution for an application that has just started collecting context information.

CSLIM are based on co-ratings among items or users. Thus, this approach may be affected by the cold-start problem. For example, consider a situation where a user has no ratings or an item has not been rated before. This, of course, is a long-standing problem in recommender systems research. One possible solution is to use the item's or the user's average rating or even the global average rating in the data to fill the non-contextual rating matrix and then make predictions based on CSLIM models. Once a user has at least one contextual rating, CSLIM is able to learn the corresponding CRD to make recommendations in the future.

4. EXPERIMENTAL EVALUATIONS

4.1 Data Sets

We have evaluated our CSLIM models in five data sets [1]. For the reason of limited space, we just present the experimental results for three: *Food* [7], *Restaurant* [8] and *Music* [1] data sets. A summary of those data sets can be viewed in Table 1. For more information, please refer to the papers cited above.

Table 1: Context-aware Data Sets

	Food	Restaurant	Music
Non-contextual Ratings	N/A	50 users, 40 items 896 ratings	42 users, 140 items 930 ratings
Contextual Ratings	212 users, 20 items 6360 ratings	50 users, 40 items 1421 ratings	42 users, 140 items 3010 ratings
# of factors, F	2	2	8
# of conditions, L	7	5	34
Density	D_{cr}=12.5% D_{mr}=100%	D_{cr}=11.8% D_{mr}=39.6%	D_{cr}=5.7e-6 D_{mr}=100%
Rating Scale	1-5	1-5	1-5

We use two density metrics (see Equation 6) to describe the level of sparsity in the data. Assume there are F contextual factors, D_{cr} measures the density of contextual ratings, where $|\bullet|$ is used to measure the size of the user, item or context dimension. D_{mr} measures the density of multiple ratings in contexts based on unique <user, item> entries. D_{mr} = 100% indicates each unique <user, item> entry was given multiple ratings (i.e. more than one rating) in different contexts. Thus the Food and Music data are dense in multiple contextual ratings. Food data has no non-contextual ratings, so we use user's average rating on each item to fill the non-contextual rating matrix R. It is reliable, because D_{mr} = 100% in this data. Even if D_{mr} is small, we can still use average ratings to fill R. Because the diagonal values in W are 0s, the model will never make a prediction based on user's existing ratings on the item we'd like to predict.

$$D_{cr}=\frac{\text{\# of contextual ratings}}{|U|\,|I|\prod_{i=1}^{F}|C_i|},\ D_{mr}=\frac{\text{\# of entries was rated multiple times}}{\text{\# of unique entries in total}} \quad (6)$$

4.2 Evaluation Protocols

We compare the CSLIM algorithms with state-of-the-art context-aware recommendation algorithms, including TF [3], CAMF (i.e. CAMF-CI, CAMF-CU, CAMF-C) [2] and context-aware splitting approaches (CASA) using biased MF as the recommender (i.e. item splitting, user splitting and UI splitting) [11]. To better present the results based on CAMF and CASA, we just present the results by the best performing CASA and CAMF approaches. In addition, we include the original non-contextual SLIM algorithm.

Since SLIM was built for top-N recommendations, we evaluate CSLIM by comparing with baseline algorithms in the top-N

[1]Context-aware Data Repository, http://tiny.cc/contextdata

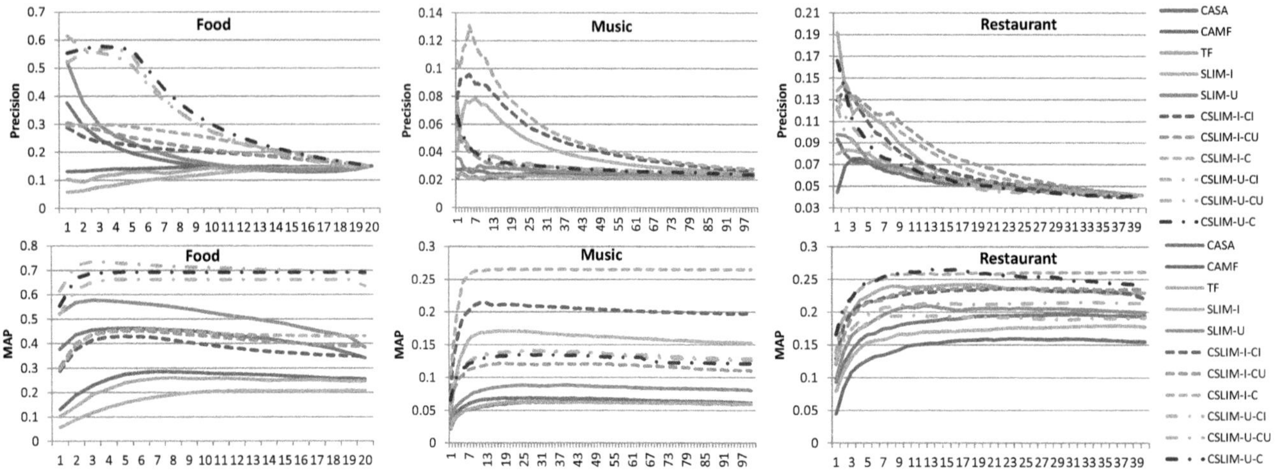

Figure 4: Results in Precision and MAP @ Top-N Recommendations (X-axis represents N; figures share same legends on the right)

recommendation task. We split the contextual ratings to 5 folds and measure the quality of recommendations using 5-fold cross validation across three metrics: precision, recall and mean average precision (MAP). Those metrics are measured using context as a parameter. Traditionally, precision is measured based on the hit ratio of relevant items in the top-N recommendation list. In CARS, we prefer to add contexts as additional constraints. Specifically, we provide a list of top-N recommended items for each <user, contexts> pair, instead of a single user. Then, we measure the hit ratio averaged by each context for each user. This type of evaluation has been used in prior research [11]. Recall and MAP can be measured in a similar manner. The resulting metric values are typically much smaller than the ones in traditional RS, because it is not very common for users to rate multiple items within a same context.

4.3 Experimental Results

The results in precision and MAP are shown in Figure 4. We did not show results for recall, since they are consistent with the ones in precision. As the results indicate, CSLIM approaches are able to significantly outperform the three baseline approaches (i.e. TF, CAMF, CASA), especially in the Food and Music data sets. Overall, the best performing CSLIM provides 102%, 23.7% and 320% improvement on precision@10 for the Food, Restaurant and Music data respectively, compared with the best performing baselines.

The original SLIM algorithms are able to outperform other baseline algorithms (i.e. CASA, CAMF, TF) in some cases, e.g. SLIM-I outperforms the other baseline algorithms in the music data. However, the best performing CSLIM always outperform the original SLIM algorithms in those context-aware data sets.

The ranking of the recommended items is another way of evaluating top-N recommendations, because a high-precision is not necessary to guarantee a good ranking. In terms of MAP, the results show a more significant gap between CSLIM and the baseline approaches. Some baseline approaches are able to outperform some CSLIM approaches in MAP. For example, CASA outperforms the CSLIM-I models in the Food data, and TF works better than some CSLIM-U models in the Restaurant data. But, we observe that the best performing CSLIM models can generally outperform the state-of-the-art context aware recommendation algorithms. Similar observation can be made in the other two data sets we evaluated, however, we did not present the results here due to limited space.

In our experiments, we also find that the performance of CSLIM is correlated with the D_{mr} value. A large D_{mr} value indicates users have multiple ratings on items in different contexts, where the parameters in both the CRD matrix D and coefficient matrix W will be learned in multiple times based on those dense entries and it is able to finally result in a more accurate ranking model for top-N context-aware recommendations.

5. CONCLUSION AND FUTURE WORK

In this paper, we successfully incorporate contexts into SLIM and develop several CSLIM algorithms, where they estimate the ranking score by the the intuition behind ItemKNN or UserKNN via the aggregation of users' estimated contextual ratings on items. CSLIM models are demonstrated to outperform the state-of-the-art CARS algorithms for top-N recommendations in our experiments. We also find that the performance of CSLIM is correlated with the density of multiple ratings in contexts. In our future work, we plan to incorporate the contexts into the coefficient matrix W, which helps estimate the coefficients between each contextual conditions and discover more insights about the contextual effects.

6. REFERENCES

[1] L. Baltrunas, M. Kaminskas, B. Ludwig, O. Moling, F. Ricci, A. Aydin, K.-H. Lüke, and R. Schwaiger. Incarmusic: Context-aware music recommendations in a car. In *E-Commerce and Web Technologies*, pages 89–100. Springer, 2011.

[2] L. Baltrunas, B. Ludwig, and F. Ricci. Matrix factorization techniques for context aware recommendation. In *ACM RecSys*, pages 301–304, 2011.

[3] A. Karatzoglou, X. Amatriain, L. Baltrunas, and N. Oliver. Multiverse recommendation: n-dimensional tensor factorization for context-aware collaborative filtering. In *ACM RecSys*, pages 79–86, 2010.

[4] Y. Koren, R. Bell, and C. Volinsky. Matrix factorization techniques for recommender systems. *IEEE Computer*, 42(8):30–37, 2009.

[5] X. Ning and G. Karypis. Slim: Sparse linear methods for top-n recommender systems. In *IEEE ICDM*, pages 497–506. IEEE, 2011.

[6] A. Odic, M. Tkalcic, J. F. Tasic, and A. Košir. Relevant context in a movie recommender system: Users' opinion vs. statistical detection. *RecSys Workshop on Context-Aware Recommender Systems*, 2012.

[7] C. Ono, Y. Takishima, Y. Motomura, and H. Asoh. Context-aware preference model based on a study of difference between real and supposed situation data. In *User Modeling, Adaptation, and Personalization*, pages 102–113, 2009.

[8] X. Ramirez-Garcia and M. Garca-Valdez. Post-filtering for a restaurant context-aware recommender system. In *Recent Advances on Hybrid Approaches for Designing Intelligent Systems*, volume 547, pages 695–707. Springer, 2014.

[9] Y. Zheng, R. Burke, and B. Mobasher. Differential context modeling in collaborative filtering. In *Proceedings of School of Computing Research Symposium*. DePaul University, Chicago IL, USA, 2013.

[10] Y. Zheng, R. Burke, and B. Mobasher. Recommendation with differential context weighting. In *The 21st Conference on User Modeling, Adaptation and Personalization*, pages 152–164, 2013.

[11] Y. Zheng, R. Burke, and B. Mobasher. Splitting approaches for context-aware recommendation: An empirical study. In *ACM SAC*, pages 274–279, 2014.

Dynamics of Human Trust in Recommender Systems

Jason L Harman
Dynamic Decision Making Laboratory
Carnegie Mellon University
5000 Forbes Ave.
412-268-6242
jharman@cmu.edu

John O'Donovan
Department of Computer Science
University of California
Santa Barbara, CA
805-451-9342
jod@cs.ucsb.edu

Tarek Abdelzaher
Department of Computer Science
University of Illinois at Urbana Champaign
217-265-6793
zaher@illinois.edu

Cleotilde Gonzalez
Dynamic Decision Making Laboratory
Carnegie Mellon University
5000 Forbes Ave.
412-268-6242
coty@cmu.edu

ABSTRACT

The trust that humans place on recommendations is key to the success of recommender systems. The formation and decay of trust in recommendations is a dynamic process influenced by context, human preferences, accuracy of recommendations, and the interactions of these factors. This paper describes two psychological experiments (N=400) that evaluate the evolution of trust in recommendations over time, under personalized and non-personalized recommendations by matching or not matching a participant's profile. Main findings include: Humans trust inaccurate recommendations more than they should; when recommendations are personalized, they lose trust in inaccurate recommendations faster than when recommendations are not personalized; and participants report less trust and lower overall ratings of personalized but inaccurate recommendations compared to not-personalized inaccurate recommendations. We make connections to the possible implications of these psychological findings to the design of recommender systems.

Categories and Subject Descriptors
[H.3.3] Information Storage and Retrieval: Information Search and Retrieval; [J.4] SOCIAL AND BEHAVIORAL SCIENCES
General Terms
Performance, Experimentation, Human Factors, Theory.
Keywords
Trust, decision making, cognitive processes

1. INTRODUCTION

Over the last 25 years, automated recommender systems (RS) have attempted to help users find the right information at the right time [15]. Recently, the social web has made massive amounts of user-provided content available for analysis, making the task of identifying reliable information sources increasingly difficult. In many cases, only a small window of information exists upon which a human can make a decision about whether or not to trust a recommendation and the RS that produced it. Furthermore, that window of information changes dynamically, and humans adapt their trust judgments and their preferences accordingly.

Quite recently, a number of researchers have argued that automated accuracy metrics are not enough for evaluation of RS [7, 14, 16]. A main reason is that the overall user experience with a RS should be accounted for. We believe that a key component of this overall user experience is the trust that humans place on the RS and its recommendations.

RecSys'14, October 6–10, 2014, Foster City, Silicon Valley, CA, USA.

http://dx.doi.org/10.1145/2645710.2645761

Trust in RS has been studied from the computational perspective [1, 12, 13] at the network [4], temporal [10], and algorithmic [14] levels. However, accounting for human trust in order to build RS that dynamically adjust to the human preferences and experiences is a challenge. This is largely due to the lack of research regarding how humans develop and adjust their trust in a RS. The current research is an interdisciplinary effort, bringing together behavioral and computer scientists, to collaborate on the development of recommender systems that are aware of and can adapt to the dynamics of human behavior.

This paper aims to provide generalizable scientific insight into the dynamics of human trust in RS. We use psychological experiments in simple learning paradigms to develop theoretical insights of the process of learning, choice, and trust that could inform the development of RS.

In Experiment 1, we look at the process of choosing among options of differing quality in the presence of accurate or inaccurate recommendations that are impersonal in terms of pre-defined human preferences. Results indicate that participants decrease their trust when the RS is inaccurate, yet even after extended practice with inaccurate recommendations, they continue to trust the RS more than they should objectively.

In Experiment 2, we add a richer context and personalized recommendations that match the user's profile exactly. As in Experiment 1, participants chose among options that differ in their outcome quality under accurate and inaccurate recommendations. Our results indicate that participants were able to abandon the inaccurate RS more rapidly than in Experiment 1. Furthermore, participants reported lower levels of trust and overall quality of the RS in the inaccurate condition compared to the first experiment.

We discuss implications of these findings and potential applications to the design of cognitively-aware RS.

2. BACKGROUND

Trust in recommendations systems has been approached mostly from a computational perspective. For example, early trust metrics for RS include Golbeck's metrics in social networks [4]; O'Donovan and Smyth [14] evaluated a trust model to accompany similarity scores in a collaborative filtering algorithm; and this model was extended by Liu [11] to account for temporal sequences. A common thread among these studies is that they evaluate trust in a RS using automated accuracy metrics while placing little attention to human-based trust decisions and to the role of trust from the overall human experience.

Beyond the computational approaches above, researchers have explored how contextual elements of RS influence trust. For example, Swearing and Sinha [16] examined interaction design for RS focusing on user requirements and available system features. They argue that a familiar recommendation can increase trust, and that transparency of the recommendation process plays an important role. These findings are supported by the psychology literature on conformity [1] where systems designed to help people make choices can actually change people's subjective opinions. Researchers also argue for the benefits of providing explanations to recommendations that may convince users to trust the system. Knijnenburg [9] and Bostandjiev [2] report similar findings using an interactive visual recommender system. Finally, Cosley et al. find that recommendations can influence users' ratings towards the predicted rating, whether it is an accurate one or not [3].

In contrast to all those past studies in RS, our approach highlights trust perceptions and actions that signal trust from the human perspective. We present experiments where humans make decisions about several sources in the presence of a recommender system that provides accurate or inaccurate recommendations. We aim at advancing the theoretical basis for building RS that account for the dynamics of human trust and preferences. Particularly, we are concerned with providing some theoretical basis for building RS that dynamically adapt to the preferences and changes in human trust. This is largely a challenge in the RS community. We believe that addressing this challenge can begin with knowledge about how humans adjust their preferences and how they learn to trust or not trust RS.

In what follows, we offer results from two psychological experiments where we used simplistic paradigms of decisions from experience (DFE) [5, 6], expanded to include simple accurate or inaccurate recommendations. DFE paradigms are designed to study how humans make small daily decisions that they face repeatedly. In these well studied paradigms, participants learn from making repeated choices under conditions of uncertainty, where explicit information about outcomes and the probabilities of good outcomes from different options is not descriptively provided but rather learned from experience. The most basic DFE paradigm is presented as a money machine, where participants choose between two unlabeled buttons over several trials, receiving feedback for each choice. The buttons provide feedback based on underlying outcome distributions and over time, participants learn through experience which button provides better outcomes on average [8]. Given the research summarized above, we expected that humans would trust inaccurate recommenders more than they should, but that with extended experience, they would learn to not trust inaccurate recommendations.

3. EXPERIMENTS

3.1 Experimental Paradigm

In our experimental paradigm, participants are presented with four options (represented as buttons on the screen) that they are asked to choose from. On each of 200 trials, participants choose one of the four options and receive feedback (positive or negative) from their selected option before moving to the next trial. Positive feedback is recorded and added to a running total which determines the participant's compensation at the end of the experiment. The four options varied in the frequency with which they provided a quality outcome as: .2, .4, .6, and .8 for the four respective buttons (presentation order and labeling were randomized). The feedback probability of the four options was determined through extensive pretesting to ensure that most participants would be able to learn to discriminate between the four buttons by the end of 200 trials.

On each trial, one or more options are recommended to the participant by an accurate (recommendations always led to a good quality outcome) or inaccurate (recommendations led to a good quality outcome only half of the time) recommender. Note that our definition of accuracy represents a probability, and differs from the typical rating-based concept of accuracy in RS, e.g., from [3]. Thus, for accurate recommendations, each chosen option that was recommended on a trial produced a positive outcome (and each source not recommended produces a negative outcome); and in the inaccurate condition, recommended options produced a positive outcome half of the time and a negative outcome half of the time (the same is true for options not recommended).

The primary dependent variables in each condition are proportion of recommendations followed (as a measure of trust in the recommendations), total outcome (sum of positive feedback), and choice proportion for each of the four options (as a measure of detection of more profitable options). After participants complete 200 trials, they answer questions designed to elicit their perceptions of both the recommender and the quality of outcomes from the four options, in addition to basic questions about trust and trust in RS.

3.2 Experiment 1

Two hundred participants completed Experiment 1 on Amazon MTurk; 80 participants were female with an overall mean age of 34.7.

Experiment 1 was designed as an abstract learning and trust experiment, similar to paradigms common in cognitive science [6]. The four options were labeled A-D and the outcome feedback was composed of 1 (positive) or 0 (negative). In the experimental instructions, participants were told that the study was designed to explore how intelligence analysts collect and acquire information, and that the four options could represent sources of information such as military reports or social media that could provide information at a given time that is useful or not useful. Additionally, participants were told that a RS would highlight specific sources on each trial that could provide useful information on that trial.

3.2.1 Results

The left side of Figure 1 plots the proportion of recommendations followed on each trial for the accurate and inaccurate conditions. In the accurate recommendation condition, participant immediately chose from the recommended options and continued to choose recommended options across the 200 trials. In the inaccurate recommendation condition, participants began choosing recommended options but decreased their choice of recommended options as trials progressed, choosing recommended options about 60% of the time by the end of the experiment, indicating that participants trust inaccurate recommendations more than they objectively should (50%).

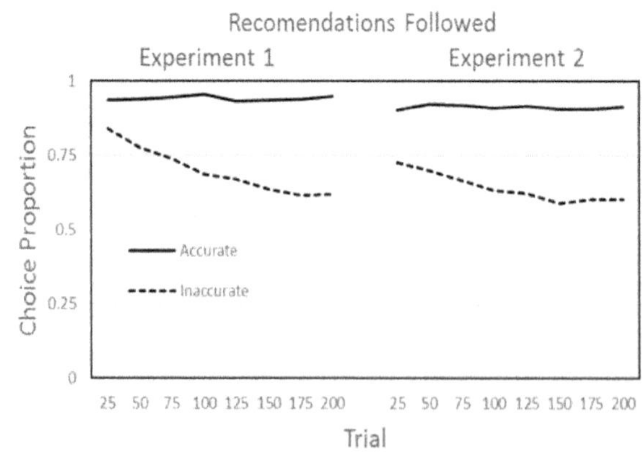

Figure 1. The proportion of choices from recommended options are plotted over time by condition (accurate recommender, inaccurate recommender) for each experiment.

Choice proportions for the four options in the accurate condition mirror the distribution of recommendations for each option (as recommendations were predominantly followed) with clear distinction between the high probability options and the low probability options. In the inaccurate condition, choice proportions between the four options (left side of Figure 2) differed across trials with participants choosing more from the best option, despite inaccurate recommendations.

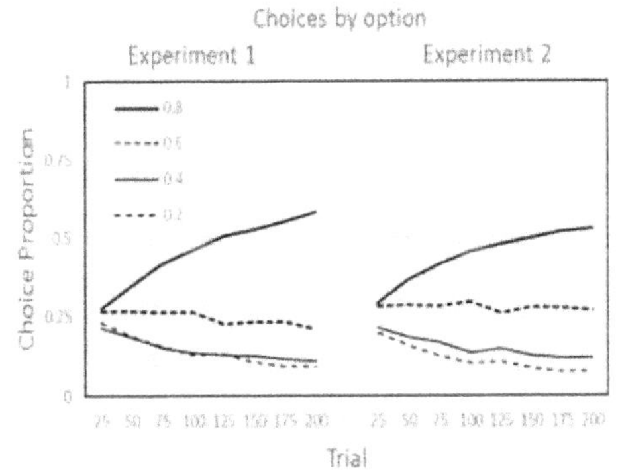

Figure 2. For the inaccurate recommender conditions only, the proportion of choices for each option (.8[best], .6, .4, .2[worst]) are plotted across time for each experiment.

3.3 Experiment 2

Experiment 2 was designed to provide personalized recommendations in a more detailed scenario. Two hundred participants completed Experiment 2 on Amazon MTurk (81 female participants, *M* age = 33.5). Participants were told that the experiment was designed to test a personalized social media app that provided recommendations on which venue to visit on a given night to have the best opportunity to meet a person they are compatible with. Before beginning the experiment, participants rated their preferences in a potential partner on three attributes with three levels in each attribute: attractiveness, education, and common interests. The participants' ratings were used to determine what feedback was considered a match (positive outcome) or not (negative outcome). The choice portion of Experiment 2 was identical in structure to Experiment 1 with two exceptions. First, the four options, instead of being labeled A-D, were labeled: Alpha Club, Beta Bar, Common Club, and Delta Bar. Second, the feedback was presented as the profile (levels of the three attributes represented by stars) of a person they meet. If the attribute levels were identical to the participant's stated preferences, it was considered a match and added to their total, which determined their monetary compensation at the end of the experiment.

3.3.1 Results

The right side of Figure 1 plots the proportion of recommendations followed in each trial for the accurate and inaccurate conditions. In the accurate recommendation condition, the proportion following recommendations mirrored that of Experiment 1. That is, people trusted and followed the recommendations almost all of the time. In the inaccurate recommendation condition, participants decreased their choice in the recommended options more over time. Compared to Experiment 1's results, the personalization with individual profiles led to participants abandoning recommendations more quickly, evident in the difference in recommendations followed in the first 25 trials (72% vs. 84% in Exp. 1). Yet, even in this case and after 200 trials, participants trusted the recommendations more than they should have (about 60% of the time by the end of the experiment).

Despite the difference in recommendations followed, the choice proportions between the four options in the inaccurate recommender condition (right side of Figure 2) is similar to the matching condition in Exp. 1, favoring the best option over time, and reducing the proportion of choices from the less favorable options over time. This is consistent with people learning the best experienced outcome from repeated trials [6].

3.4 Statistical comparisons

For each condition in both experiments, Table 1 shows the total proportion (and Standard Deviation) of the total number of choices made from recommended options, the final outcome (measure of overall performance), and the proportion of choices from the best option and the worst option. The accurate recommendations conditions did not differ from one another, and we focus our analysis on comparisons between the inaccurate conditions in Experiments 1 and 2.

The differences in behavior between the inaccurate conditions in Experiments 1 and 2 are significant for both the number of choices from recommended options (t (199) = 8.77, p < .001) and the obtained outcome (t (199) = 3.28, p < .001). There is no difference between the two groups in terms of choices from the best option 1 (t (199) = 0.69, p = .488) however the difference in choice proportion for the worst option is significant (t (199) = 3.18, p < .01).

Table 1. Mean (SD) dependent variables for each condition.

	Experiment 1		Experiment 2	
	Accurate	Inaccurate	Accurate	Inaccurate
Rec. followed	.94 (.02)	.70 (.09)	.91 (.02)	.60 (.07)
Outcome	.94 (.02)	.60 (.07)	.91 (.02)	.64 (.10)
Best Option	.47 (.06)	.46 (.10)	.45 (.06)	.44 (.27)
Worst Option	.28 (.05)	.14 (.05)	.29 (.05)	.11 (.08)

3.5 Contingent Trust Dynamics

To further explore the role of trust in choice behavior for the inaccurate conditions, we examined dynamic choice behavior in response to choosing a recommended option and receiving either a positive or negative outcome. We used two time points (trial 25 and trial 175) to explore early and late changes in trust and reactions to feedback. At each time point, we looked at participants who chose a recommended option and whether they received a positive outcome (the recommendation was correct) or whether they received a negative outcome (the recommendation was incorrect). We then calculated how many times participants chose a recommended option over the next ten trials to calculate the probability of choosing a recommended option after a successful or unsuccessful recommendation. These contingent choice dynamics are plotted in Figure 3 (the same analysis was performed using only the following trial and the following 25 trials, both of which produce the same results presented here).

Across both experiments there is a decrease in the probability of choosing a recommended option following either a successful or unsuccessful recommendation from time 1 to time 2 (Experiment 1: F (1,141) = 4.127, p < .05; Experiment 2: F (1, 96) = 71.13, p < .001). In Experiment 2, this main effect is in the presence of an interaction where the probability of choosing a recommended option after a successful recommendation is lower than after an unsuccessful recommendation at time 2 (F (1, 96) = 39.29, p < .001). This interaction did not reach significance in Experiment 1.

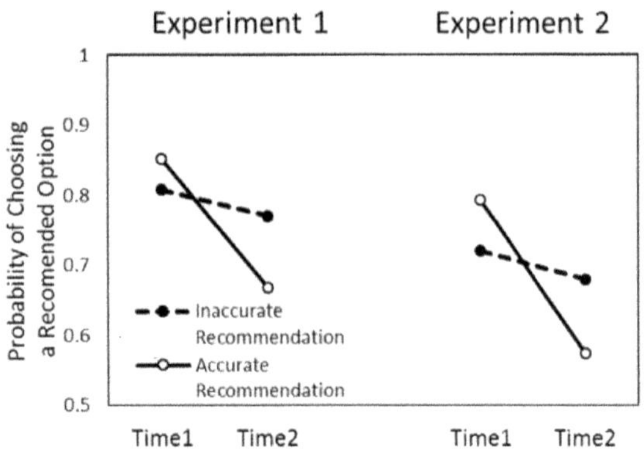

Figure 3. Probability of using the recommendation system after a correct or incorrect recommendation over time in the inaccurate recommendation condition.

3.6 Perception of the recommendations and accuracy

After the experiment, we asked participants to estimate out of ten recommendations, how many would be successful. We also asked them to rate, on a 1-5 scale, the quality of the RS and their trust in the recommendations.

Participants in the inaccurate condition of both experiments correctly estimated that the rate of accurate recommendations was about 50% (Experiment 1: M = 5.2/out of 10; SD=1.2; Experiment 2: M = 5.06, SD= 1.3). However, when asked for their opinion of the RS, participants in Experiment 2 rated it significantly worse than those in Experiment 1 (t (200) = 7.377, p < .001). Additionally, participants in the inaccurate condition of Experiment 2 reported trusting the recommendation system less than those in Experiment 1 (t (200) = 5.189, p < .001).

4. CONCLUSIONS

Several important conclusions arise from the results of these two experiments. First, humans trust recommendations, even when they are inaccurate, and they trust them more than they objectively should. This result agrees with Cosley et al.'s study [3], which found that people's opinions can be influenced based on what the RS predicts, regardless of predictive accuracy. However, in contrast to [3], we observe a difference between accurate and inaccurate conditions. Second, people lower their trust in the recommendations when they are inaccurate, but they do so more when recommendations are personalized. Third, people learn to select more accurate options even in the presence of inaccurate recommendations. And fourth, even when people are sufficiently aware of the inaccuracy of recommendations, participants feel more dissatisfied and trust the recommendations less when they are personalized.

In terms of insight for the design of real world RS, we believe that the results of these cognitive experiments are a step towards understanding when recommendation consumers are at higher risk of losing trust in a system's predictions, and conversely when their trust is high and they can be most influenced by the system's predictions.

5. ACKNOWLEDGMENTS

This work was partially supported by the U.S. Army Research Laboratory under Cooperative Agreement No. W911NF-09-2-0053 The views and conclusions contained in this document are those of the authors and should not be interpreted as representing the official policies, either expressed or implied by the U.S. Government. The U.S. Government is authorized to reproduce and distribute reprints for Government purposes notwithstanding any copyright notation here on.

6. REFERENCES

[1] S. E. Asch. Effects of group pressure upon the modification and distortion of judgments. In *Groups, leadership and men; research in human relations*, pages 177–190. Carnegie Press, Oxford, England, 1951.

[2] S. Bostandjiev, J. O'Donovan, and T. Höllerer. TasteWeights: A visual interactive hybrid recommender system. In *Proceedings of the Sixth ACM Conference on Recommender Systems*, pages 35–42. ACM, September 2012.

[3] D. Cosley, S. K. Lam, I. Albert, J. A. Konstan, and J. Riedl. Is seeing believing?: How recommender system interfaces affect users' opinions. In *Proceedings of the SIGCHI Conference on Human Factors in Computing Systems*, pages 585–592. SIGCHI, April 2003.

[4] J. A. Golbeck. Computing and applying trust in web-based social networks. PhD thesis, University of Maryland, 2005.

[5] C. Gonzalez. The boundaries of instance-based learning theory for explaining decisions from experience. In *Progress in Brain* Research, pages 73-98. Elsevier, Amsterdam, 2013.

[6] C. Gonzalez and V. Dutt. Instance-based learning: Integrating sampling and repeated decisions from experience. *Psych. Rev.*, 118(4): 523-551, October 2011.

[7] J. L. Herlocker, J. A. Konstan, L. G. Terveen, and J. T. Riedl. Evaluating collaborative filtering recommender systems. *ACM Trans. Inf. Syst.*, 22(1): 5–53, January 2004.

[8] R. Hertwig, G. Barron, E. U. Weber, and I. Erev. Decisions from experience and the effect of rare events in risky choice. *Psych. Sci.*, 15(8): 534-539, August 2004.

[9] B. P. Knijnenburg, S. Bostandjiev, J. O'Donovan, and A. Kobsa. Inspectability and control in social recommenders. In *Proceedings of the Sixth ACM Conference on Recommender Systems*, pages 43–50. ACM, September 2012.

[10] N. K. Lathia. Evaluating collaborative filtering over time. PhD thesis, University College London, 2010.

[11] D.-R. Liu, C.-H. Lai, and H. Chiu. Sequence-based trust in collaborative filtering for document recommendation. *Int. J. Hum.-Comput. Stud.*, 69(9): 587–601, August 2011.

[12] P. Massa and P. Avesani. Trust-aware recommender systems. In *Proceedings of the 2007 ACM Conference on Recommender Systems*, pages 17–24. ACM, October 2007.

[13] P. Massa and P. Avesani. Trust metrics in recommender systems. In *Computing with Social Trust*, J. Golbeck, Ed., pages 259–285. Springer, London, 2009.

[14] J. O'Donovan and B. Smyth. Trust in recommender systems. In *Proceedings of the 10th International Conference on Intelligent User Interfaces*, pages 167–174. ACM, January 2005.

[15] P. Resnick and H. Varian. Recommender systems. *Commun. ACM*, 40(3): 56–58, March 1997.

[16] K. Swearing and R. Sinha. Interaction design for recommender systems. In *Designing Interactive Systems 2002*. ACM, June 2002.

Eliciting the Users' Unknown Preferences

Julia Neidhardt
EC Group, TU Vienna
Favoritenstrasse 9-11
1040 Vienna, Austria
neidhardt@ec.tuwien.ac.at

Rainer Schuster
EC Group, TU Vienna
Favoritenstrasse 9-11
1040 Vienna, Austria
schuster@ec.tuwien.ac.at

Leonhard Seyfang
EC Group, TU Vienna
Favoritenstrasse 9-11
1040 Vienna, Austria
seyfang@ec.tuwien.ac.at

Hannes Werthner
EC Group, TU Vienna
Favoritenstrasse 9-11
1040 Vienna, Austria
werthner@ec.tuwien.ac.at

ABSTRACT

Personalized recommendation strongly relies on an accurate model to capture user preferences; eliciting this information is, in general, a hard problem. In the field of tourism this initial profiling becomes even more challenging. It has been shown that particularly in the beginning of the travel decision making process, users themselves are often not conscious of their needs and are not able to express them. In this paper, the basics of a picture-based approach are introduced that aims at revealing implicitly given user preferences. Based on a set of travel related pictures selected by a user, an individual travel profile is deduced. This is accomplished by mapping those pictures onto seven basic factors that reflect different travel behavioral aspects. Also tourism products can be represented by this seven factor model. Thus, this model constitutes the basis of our recommendation algorithm. First tests show that this non-verbal way of interaction is experienced as exiting and inspiring.

Categories and Subject Descriptors

G.3 [**Probability and Statistics**]: Multivariate statistics; H.1.2 [**Models and Principles**]: User/Machine Systems—*Human factors*; H.3.3 [**Information Storage and Retrieval**]: Information Search and Retrieval—*Selection process*

General Terms

Human Factors

Keywords

Picture-Based Recommender; Travel Personality; Implicit Preference Elicitation; Factor Analysis

RecSys'14, October 6–10, 2014, Foster City, Silicon Valley, CA, USA.

http://dx.doi.org/10.1145/2645710.2645767.

1. INTRODUCTION

In recent years, recommender systems have clearly moved into the center of attention. Especially in the context of the Web, they often support users in comparing a hardly comprehensible and understandable quantity of options. In this way, recommender systems form the basis of the success of a number of Websites and services.

A user model that is capable of capturing individual preferences and dislikes is of major importance to personalized recommendation. However, before being able to exploit knowledge about users' preferences, this information has to be provided to the system. Although there are some common strategies to accomplish this step such as asking the user either to rate some example items or to answer a number of questions, this initial profiling remains a challenging task [12].

In the context of tourism the elicitation of user preferences is even more difficult than in other domains. The tourism product itself is more complex and less tangible than books, movies or pieces of news [16]. Traveling is usually costly and time-consuming and so the average number of items rated by a user will be smaller than in domains with lower complexity, e.g., books or movies. However, the setting presented in this paper is even more complex. It has been shown that especially in the early phase of their travel decision making process, tourists might neither be aware of their needs nor be able to state them explicitly [19]. In general, traveling is an emotional experience, where preferences are difficult to characterize explicitly; they might rather be implicitly given. Thus, the preferences are not only unknown to the system but also unknown to the users.

In this paper, the basics of a picture-based approach to elicit user preferences are introduced. By addressing a non-verbal level, this approach aims at revealing travel preferences and needs that a user is not explicitly aware of. This is exclusively accomplished by asking the user to select a set of pictures that she or he considers pleasing when thinking of going on vacation. In a next step, those pictures are mapped onto seven basic factors that represent distinct touristic behavioral patterns. The individual travel profile of the user is then obtained as a mixture of those basic factors. Thus, our user model is "simply" constituted by a seven dimensional vector.

Figure 1: Picture selection – offline (left-hand side) and online (right-hand side).

To get a more comprehensive idea of a user's touristic personality, immediate vacation patterns (captured with the help of so-called tourist roles) as well as long-term behavior (captured with the help of personality traits) are taken into account. Based on all this, a computational model is developed that forms the core of a recommendation algorithm for tourism related products. However, unlike other approaches that are typically focusing on the attributes of these products, our model aims at abstracting from those attributes and reaching at a more comprehensive user-centric representation.

The remainder of the paper is organized as follows: Related work is discussed in Section 2. In Section 3 our approach is described in more detail. A short evaluation regarding user response is presented in Section 4; and, finally, in Section 5 conclusions are provided.

2. RELATED WORK

In [12] recommender systems are characterized as "software tools and techniques providing suggestions for items to be of use to a user". Such "items" are typically books or movies, but also more complex products can be within the scope of recommender systems. In the context of tourism content-based approaches (i.e., items are recommended that have similar attributes as items that the user has liked before) and/or knowledge based approaches (i.e., domain knowledge about a user's preferences with respect to the attributes of the items is deployed for recommendation) are regarded as appropriate techniques to predict whether an item is in fact useful to the user [2]. This is due to the fact that tourism can be seen as a domain with high risk (i.e., the price of the items is comparatively high), low churn (i.e., the value or relevance of items does not change so rapidly), low heterogeneity (i.e., needs that the items can satisfy are not so diverse), unstable preferences (i.e., user preferences in the past might not be valid anymore today) and explicit interaction style (i.e., a user needs to formulate an opinion or perform a search to add personal data). Furthermore, scrutability is required, which means that it should be transparent why a certain item is recommended by the system. Despite all these challenges, an increasing number of tourism-related Websites incorporate recommender systems [14].

A similar objective to the one of our work – providing a more sophisticated support in eliciting user needs and preferences – is followed by critique based recommendation methods (e.g., [11]; see [8] for a comprehensive overview). However, there the focus is on the conversational process, iteratively refining first results. Users do not specify their preferences from the early start, but follow several cycles. However, the system needs either some initial user input, e.g., by answering system's question, or an initial example. With the help of initial examples, e.g., shown as pictures of hotels as in [13], the user may iteratively explore the solution space in a graphical manner. This approach is similar to ours; however, their pictures "describe" products, whereas in our case pictures reflect touristic behavioral patterns.

The work of [10] focusing on the design of preference elicitation interfaces supports our approach. Their results show that a) low cognitive effort (e.g., using pictures) leads to a high user liking; b) affective feedback increases the willingness to spend more effort.

Since the 1970s research aims at relating touristic behavioral patterns to psychological needs and expectations. The work of Gibson and Yiannakis [4] has a high impact in this context. They extend a previously developed framework to measure touristic role preferences [18]. In the end, this framework comprises 17 tourist roles (namely *Action Seeker*, *Active Sport Tourist*, *Anthropologist*, *Archaeologist*, *Drifter*, *Educational Tourist*, *Escapist I and II*, *Explorer*, *High Class Tourist*, *Independent Mass Tourist I and II*, *Jetsetter*, *Organized Mass Tourist*, *Seeker*, *Sun Lover*, *Thrill Seeker*) to capture the range of touristic behavioral patterns. The association between these tourist roles and psychological needs is investigated for both genders over lifetime. Statistical evidence is given that touristic behavioral patterns are related to psychological needs and that they change during time.

In [1] a relation is established between these 17 tourist roles and representative, tourism-related photos, which implies that it is reasonable to assign tourist roles to people based on selected pictures. In [5] it is shown that 12 predefined travel personalities are distinguishable regarding travel style (e.g., variety seeking), travel motivations (e.g., social contacts) and travel values (e.g., active vs. passive).

Also in our approach, the tourist roles of Gibson and Yiannakis are chosen as starting point. However, focusing on

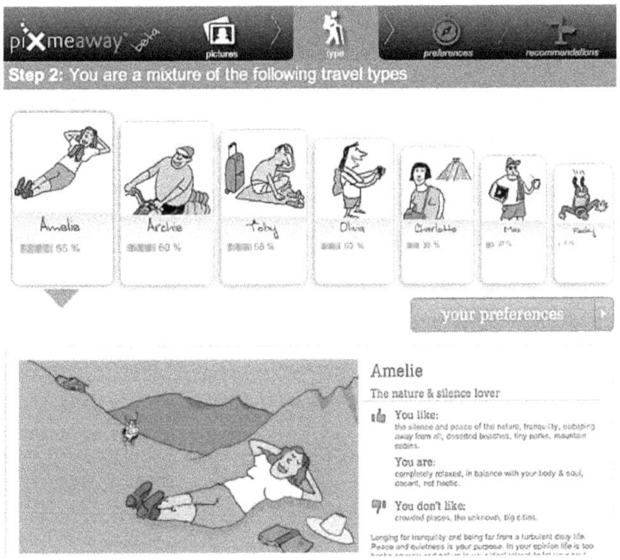

Figure 2: User interface – travel profile feedback.

what people are already doing, their model captures current vacation patterns. Our aim, on the other hand, is more particularly to predict what people might potentially enjoy. For this reason, also personality traits are included into our model. It is widely accepted that they facilitate the prediction of behavioral patterns over time and across situations [17]. Furthermore, statistical methods are deployed to reduce the number of factors of the model. This makes it computational more efficient and thus better applicable on a large scale.

3. FACTORS AND PICTURES

To develop our recommendation algorithm, the following steps were taken:

1. First, a questionnaire was developed taking into account both the 17 tourist types by Gibson and Yiannakis [4] and the "Big Five" personality traits (i.e., *extraversion, agreeableness, conscientiousness, neuroticism* and *openness*) [6]. For both, standard questions were available, which were phrased as statements that had to be rated on a five level scale. Also, it was asked for demographic information such as age and country. The questionnaire was made available online and offline. In total, 997 questionnaires were completed.

2. On this data that comprised 22 variables (i.e., 17 tourist roles plus five personality traits) a factor analysis was conducted that led to a seven factor solution. For those factors, suitable interpretations could be identified. They capture touristic behavioral aspects such as *connected and sun loving, educational, independent, culture loving, open minded and sportive, risk seeking* and *nature and silence loving.*

3. In a second study, an association between the seven factors and 102 travel related pictures was establish. Those pictures were preselected and evaluated in an interdisciplinary workshop with respect to their relationship to the before mentioned aspects. The pictures were physically arranged on a table in random order (see Figure 1, left-hand side). The participants (in total 105) had to select three to ten pictures that they found most appealing in the context of tourism. Then, they had to rank the selection. This study helped to reduce the number of pictures to 63, and led also to the insight that people tend to select at most seven pictures. Furthermore, the order of the final set was often reconsidered and changed. In the end, also these participants were asked to fill out the questionnaire (see step 1) to validate the association of both factors and pictures.

4. In a next step, 15 experts had to assign up to seven pictures to 10,835 touristic points of interest (POI) all over the world (Experts are frequent travelers who knew the respective POI). They also had to rank them according to their degree of association with the POI. In addition, for each POI and each factor, they had to assign a number from the interval [0, 1] expressing the extent to which in their opinion the POI represented the respective basic factor.

5. Then, the relations between factors and pictures were quantified. A multiple regression model of the form

$$f_j = b_{j0} + \sum_{i=1}^{63} b_{ji} x_i, \tag{1}$$

$j = 1, \ldots, 7$, was fitted for each factor. To calculate the coefficients b_{ji}, the assignments of the experts were used: Each f_j was set to the number assigned in step 4. Then, x_i was calculated as

$$x_i = 7 \cdot \frac{-k + n + 1}{\sum_{i=1}^{n} i} \tag{2}$$

if the i-th picture had been chosen and ranked on the k-th place, and 0 otherwise. The value of x_i does not only depend on rank k but also on the number of selected pictures n. With the x_i the coefficients b_{ji} were estimated using the least squares method.

6. Based on user u's picture choice, Equation 1 is used to calculate f_j^u, $j = 1, \ldots, 7$. Now, to recommend POIs to user u, the Euclidian metric $d : \mathbb{R}^7 \times \mathbb{R}^7 \to \mathbb{R}$

$$d(\mathbf{f^u}, \mathbf{f^p}) = \sqrt{\sum_{j=1}^{7} \left(f_j^u - f_j^p\right)^2}, \tag{3}$$

is applied. Here, $\mathbf{f^u}$ is representing the travel profile of user u and $\mathbf{f^p}$ the POI p. The scores f_j^p, $j = 1, \ldots, 7$ are the results of the assignments of the experts (see step 4).

This approach has been implemented and forms the core of the picture-based search and recommendation engine PixMeAway [9]. In Figure 1, right-hand side the interface for online picture selection is shown. It constitutes the first step of the customer's interaction with the system. The individual travel profile of the user is presented as a feedback with the help of comic characters; it is shown to what extend the preferences of the user align with each of those travel factors (see Figure 2). In a next step (not shown) users can indicate their preferences, such as time or point of departure. Then, the recommendations are displayed.

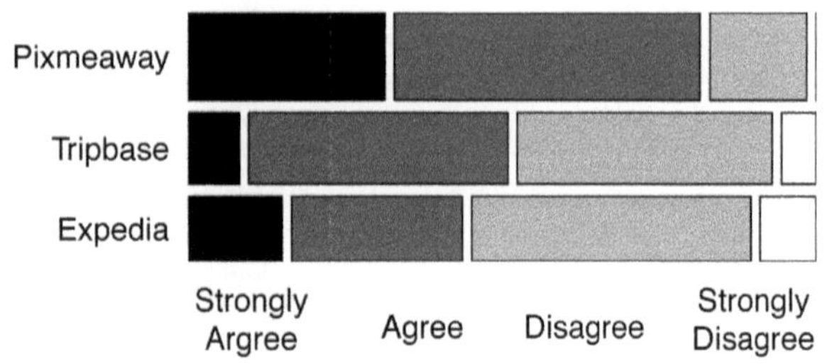

Figure 3: Mosaic plot: "The page is exciting" (based on [7]).

4. USER RESPONSE EVALUATION

In a first user study, aspects of the preference eliciting interface with respect to user liking were investigated [7]. In total, 110 participants were assigned to one of the following Websites in order to explore them: PixMeAway [9], Tripbase, a travel Website providing also recommendations [15], and Expedia, a traveling booking site [3]. After that, their experiences with respect to several emotional categories, such as inspiration, enjoyment, enthusiasm and interest were inquired using an online questionnaire. The main goal of this work was to study the impact of emotional and inspirational aspects of online travel portals on the overall satisfaction of users and their intention to revisit a Website rather than doing a "classical" evaluation measuring precision and recall (since at this stage users have no clear idea what they want).

The findings of this first analysis are promising. For the category excitement, the Kruskal-Wallis test detected significant differences between the distributions of the answers regarding the three Websites ($p < 0.001$). Here, 84 % of the participants agreed or strongly agreed that the experience with PixMeAway was exciting (see Figure 3). There are similar results for the categories inspiration, interest, enjoyment and pride. Furthermore, the study showed a significant correlation between inspiration and the intention to revisit a Website ($p < 0.01$) as well as between inspiration and satisfaction ($p < 0.001$).

5. CONCLUSIONS

In our approach a model space is designed that is based on tourist profiles rather than product properties. Users are mapped to this model by selecting a set of pictures. Also POIs can be integrated into this approach, hence a simple distance metric serves as core of the recommendation procedure. Basic user interactions are conducted in a non-textual manner and are experienced as exciting and inspiring.

Further research will include automated parameter optimization based on user feedback. Another focus will be a flexible administration of the picture set (i.e., exchange of pictures). Also the extension of the approach using other emotional objects such as sound samples is planned. Finally, text mining methods on object descriptions and reviews will be used to position the touristic object automatically in the presented model space.

6. REFERENCES

[1] H. Berger, M. Denk, M. Dittenbach, D. Merkl, and A. Pesenhofer. Quo vadis homo turisticus? towards a picture-based tourist profiler. *Information and Communication Technologies in Tourism 2007*, pages 87–96, 2007.

[2] R. Burke and M. Ramezani. Matching recommendation technologies and domains. In *Recommender Systems Handbook*, pages 367–386. Springer, 2011.

[3] Expedia, Inc. `http://www.expedia.at`, April 2014.

[4] H. Gibson and A. Yiannakis. Tourist roles: Needs and the lifecourse. *Annals of tourism research*, 29(2):358–383, 2002.

[5] U. Gretzel, N. Mitsche, Y.-H. Hwang, and D. R. Fesenmaier. Tell me who you are and i will tell you where to go: use of travel personalities in destination recommendation systems. *Information Technology & Tourism*, 7(1):3–12, 2004.

[6] O. P. John and S. Srivastava. The big five trait taxonomy: History, measurement, and theoretical perspectives. *Handbook of personality: Theory and research*, 2:102–138, 1999.

[7] W. Krinninger. Inspiration and information – critical factors to the success of travel platforms. Master's thesis, Vienna University of Economics and Business, November 2012.

[8] L. McGinty and J. Reilly. On the evolution of critiquing recommenders. In *Recommender Systems Handbook*, pages 419–453. Springer, 2011.

[9] Pixtri OG. `http://www.pixmeaway.com`, April 2014.

[10] A. Pommeranz, J. Broekens, P. Wiggers, W.-P. Brinkman, and C. M. Jonker. Designing interfaces for explicit preference elicitation: a user-centered investigation of preference representation and elicitation process. *User Modeling and User-Adapted Interaction*, 22(4-5):357–397, 2012.

[11] F. Ricci and Q. N. Nguyen. Acquiring and revising preferences in a critique-based mobile recommender system. *Intelligent Systems, IEEE*, 22(3):22–29, 2007.

[12] F. Ricci, L. Rokach, and B. Shapira. Introduction to recommender systems handbook. In *Recommender Systems Handbook*, pages 1–35. Springer, 2011.

[13] F. Ricci, K. Woeber, and A. Zins. Recommendations by collaborative browsing. In *Information and Communication Technologies in Tourism 2005*, pages 172–182. Springer, 2005.

[14] O. Stock, H. Werthner, and M. Zancanaro. Futuring travel destination recommendation systems. In *Destination Recommendation Systems: Behavioral Foundations and Applications*, pages 297–314. CAB International, 2006.

[15] Trip Technologies Inc. `http://www.tripbase.com`, April 2014.

[16] H. Werthner and F. Ricci. E-commerce and tourism. *Communications of the ACM*, 47(12):101–105, 2004.

[17] A. B. Woszczynski, P. L. Roth, and A. H. Segars. Exploring the theoretical foundations of playfulness in computer interactions. *Computers in Human Behavior*, 18(4):369–388, 2002.

[18] A. Yiannakis and H. Gibson. Roles tourists play. *Annals of tourism Research*, 19(2):287–303, 1992.

[19] A. H. Zins. Exploring travel information search behavior beyond common frontiers. *Information Technology & Tourism*, 9(3-4):3–4, 2007.

Emphasize, Don't Filter! Displaying Recommendations in Twitter Timelines

Wesley Waldner and Julita Vassileva
Department of Computer Science
University of Saskatchewan
Saskatoon, Saskatchewan, Canada
{w.waldner, julita.vassileva}@usask.ca

ABSTRACT

This paper describes and evaluates a method for presenting recommendations that will increase the efficiency of the social activity stream while preserving the users' accurate awareness of the activity within their own social networks. With the help of a content-based recommender system, the application displays the user's home timeline in Twitter as three visually distinct tiers by emphasizing more strongly those Tweets predicted to be more interesting. Pilot study participants reported that they were able to read the interesting Tweets while ignoring the others with relative ease and that the recommender accurately categorized their Tweets into three tiers.

Categories and Subject Descriptors

H.3.3 [**Information Storage and Retrieval**]: Information Search and Retrieval—*Information filtering;* H.5.2 [**Information Interfaces and Presentation**]: User Interfaces—*user-centered design.*

Keywords

Recommender Systems; Social Media; Twitter; Visualization

1. INTRODUCTION AND BACKGROUND

People have many different reasons for using Social networking sites (SNSs) like Twitter, Facebook, and Google+. Corporations use them to advertise, marketing companies use them to mine trends and opinions among demographic groups, and public figures use them to cultivate a greater following. Most people, however, use them at least in part for enjoyment and to stay connected to other people they already know in real life. Part of this experience is in sharing content with others, and part is in reading content shared *by* others. As the rates of usage of these applications grow, information overload, determining how best to recommend updates, and deciding how best to present those recommendations in social activity streams are becoming increasingly important problems.

The issue of recommendation in Twitter[1] timelines in particular has been tackled by Wang et al. [10] and Sriram [9], who used recommendations in an attempt to overcome information overload. In these cases, researchers used several machine-learning algorithms to classify Tweets into different categories based on topic or level of user interest. Abel et al. [1] also looked at recommendations in Twitter, using semantic enrichment to construct user models for personalized news recommendation. Much research has focused on improving the performance of different algorithms for recommendation, but unfortunately not enough has considered the user acceptance of these recommendations [4].

Most SNSs now use some form of recommender system to reduce the information overload, typically by filtering out posts that are predicted to be uninteresting. However, there are a number of problems with stream filtering:

- Recommenders are imperfect, so some interesting content will be missed.
- Recommenders tend to filter away anything that cannot be predicted as interesting based on the users' past behavior, and this can cause the user to miss potentially very important information (the "filter bubble" problem [7]).
- Often no indication is given that any content was hidden, and there is no way to view hidden content, such as in Facebook[2].
- If the hidden content *is* retrievable, it is often either not indicated or difficult to perceive where the content belongs in the stream chronologically. This can lead to an inaccurate perception of stream activity and relative quality of content.

TweetDeck[3] and Filttr[4] are Twitter applications that allow users to filter their streams by certain keywords, phrases, or authors, and Social Fixer[5] is a similar service created for Facebook. However, these services all require users explicitly to define filtering criteria, and while Filttr can show where posts have been filtered in the stream, each one must be expanded individually in order to be read. In addition, showing a filtered, uniform stream offers no flexibility for different reading situations: the user may want to spend more or less time reading than it would take to consume all unread items in his stream. As a result, it is unlikely that the n content items the user consumes are the n most interesting ones, even if the filtering recommender is perfect. So while stream filtering can help with information overload, stream efficiency still has much room for improvement. Even more importantly, stream filtering can ultimately result in decreased trust [6], which can make it less likely for users to return to the system for continued use [8].

The method for presenting recommendations in social activity streams described in this paper will increase efficiency of stream consumption while avoiding many of the drawbacks of stream filtering. Using this method, the user whose unaltered stream is

RecSys '14, October 6–10, 2014, Foster City, Silicon Valley, CA, USA.

ACM 978-1-4503-2668-1/14/10…$15.00.
http://dx.doi.org/10.1145/2645710.2645762

[1] https://twitter.com
[2] https://www.facebook.com
[3] https://tweetdeck.twitter.com/
[4] https://oauth.filttr.com
[5] http://socialfixer.com/

depicted in the Figure 1 example will easily be able to read only the interesting updates, while still knowing that there are seven updates (four interesting, three uninteresting) in total, being fully aware of where each update fits chronologically, and having an easy way to read the less interesting updates in context if desired.

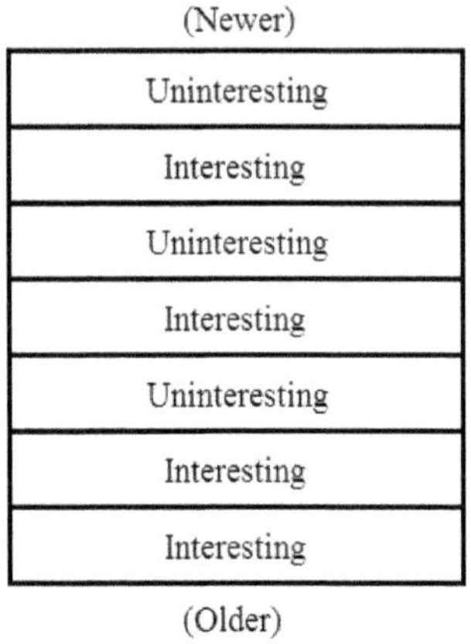

Figure 1. Simplified unfiltered social stream example

2. SOCIAL STREAM EMPHASIS

This paper presents an alternative to stream filtering that incorporates many of its strengths while avoiding its drawbacks. We chose Twitter because of the large amount of public updates available and the ease with which one can follow many other users to build a rich content stream. With the help of a content-based recommender system (RS), the social stream is displayed by emphasizing Tweets predicted to be most interesting and de-emphasizing Tweets predicted to be least interesting. In total, three distinct visual tiers are used, as shown in Figure 2.

2.1 Visual Design

Three tiers were chosen to keep the system very simple but to allow for more than a simple dichotomous differentiation. Having more tiers is advantageous because the user can move on from the top tier without needing to consume the most uninteresting content. Assuming equal distribution among tiers, offering a greater number of tiers provides the user with a greater degree of control over the quality of content he consumes. However, having too many tiers would prevent each tier from standing out in relation to the others, making it more difficult for the user to restrict his reading to a single tier.

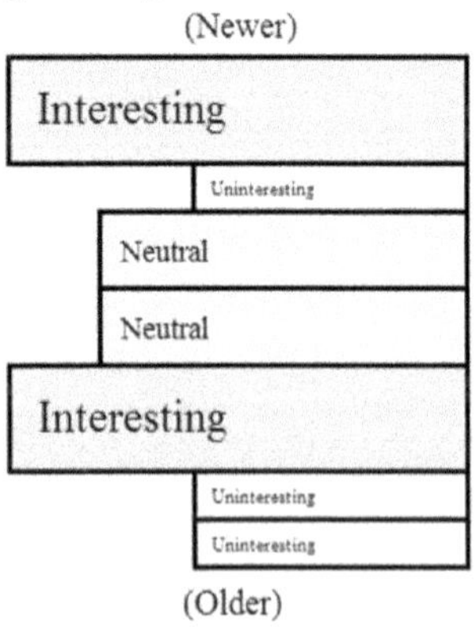

Figure 2. Recommendations in a social stream using emphasis

Depicting the three distinct tiers can be thought of as a problem in visualizing ordinal data. Mackinlay [5] provides a ranking of visual properties that are effective for such a task, and two of the top three have been chosen to enhance presentation of the three tiers: position and color saturation. The most highly-rated Tweets are shown furthest to the left and with a greater saturation of yellow than the others, while the lowest-rated Tweets are offset toward the right and have no colour at all. To add to the difference in emphasis, the size of both the text and the containing elements are increased for more highly-rated Tweets as well. This removes any ambiguity about which tier should draw the user's focus.

Besides offering a clear separation between tiers, the horizontal offsets make it easier for users to read through a particular tier while ignoring the less interesting ones. Additionally, the horizontal alignment of Tweets within a tier facilitates chronological consumption of a particular tier. The user's eye can return to a single reference point and scan up or down to find other Tweets within that tier.

2.2 User Ratings

All recommender systems need some way to make inferences about user preferences. In Twitter, a user's appreciation for a particular Tweet is explicitly indicated by "retweeting", or sharing with one's followers, or "favoriting", which is a public expression of interest. The potential downside to these actions is that they are completely public, which might be an incentive or deterrent to performing those actions in certain situations. For the purposes of training a recommender, it would be preferable to have private action so the user feels free to be completely honest. Twitter also does not provide a way to indicate disinterest in a Tweet.

To address these shortcomings, we propose private "like" and "dislike" features, used exclusively to train the recommender and to provide visual feedback by assigning "liked" updates automatically to the "interesting" tier and "disliked" updates automatically to the "uninteresting" tier. These two actions are denoted by familiar "thumbs-up" and "thumbs-down" icons.

3. IMPLEMENTATION

To demonstrate and experiment with this idea, we developed a web application that uses the Twitter API along with custom server and client software to present a custom social stream layout in the web browser. The software implementation of this application consists of three basic components: a client, server, and database. The server connects directly to the Twitter API and to the database and just sends the necessary updates to the client. A full-JavaScript technology stack was used, consisting of Node.js[6], Express[7], MongoDB[8], Socket.IO[9], and AngularJS[10].

3.1 Recommender

Users are given the ability to rate individual Tweets as "interesting" by clicking the "retweet", "favorite", or "like" icon, or to rate as "uninteresting" by clicking the "dislike" icon. After the user supplies 30 ratings, the recommender becomes active. Previous research on RSs for movies using both collaborative and content-based methods suggests that 10 ratings are enough [3], while Movielens.org requires at least 15[11]. However, in social activity streams, such a small number items from a single point in time may not be representative enough to attain an acceptable level of accuracy, so a slightly higher target was used for this application just to be sure.

---

[6] http://nodejs.org/

[7] http://expressjs.com/

[8] https://www.mongodb.org/

[9] http://socket.io/

[10] http://angularjs.org/

[11] http://movielens.org/join (accessed May 6, 2014)

The recommender uses a naïve Bayes classifier to predict whether unrated Tweets would be interesting to the logged-in user. Every ten minutes, the classifier is retrained using features from the rated Tweets stored in the database. Then all unrated Tweets are classified as interesting or uninteresting. The recommendation score is given by the following formula, where T is the Tweet being classified, I is the set of interesting Tweets, and U is the set of uninteresting Tweets:

$$score = \frac{P(T \in I)}{P(T \in I) + P(T \in U)} \qquad (1)$$

Tweets are assigned to one of three categories based on this score: Tweets with scores less than 1/3 are classified as "uninteresting", Tweets with scores greater than 2/3 are classified as "interesting", and the rest are classified as "neutral". The following features are included in the classification procedure:

- Content author and retweeter (if applicable)
- All hashtags and user mentions
- Tweet type(s): photo, link, retweet, reply, quote, manual retweet, comment
- Number of retweets and favorites
- Length of text
- Number of numeric digits

These features are all used to try to classify different types of Tweets. For example, a user may be partial to long Tweets with many numbers and no links that have been retweeted many times.

3.2 Client

The application's view consists of a linear vertical display of Tweets in chronological order, to remain consistent with the official Twitter client and thus familiar to users. Each Tweet is shown in its own rectangle (Figure 3). Embedded images can be expanded by clicking but are displayed as thumbnails by default, as showing the full images would add too much to the size of the Tweet, artificially increasing its visual prominence in the stream. Each Tweet appears differently depending on its recommendation score. In addition to the content-based RS, users can increase or decrease the relative influence of any of the users they follow by means of a "User Volume" feature. This feature can be accessed by hovering the cursor over a user's avatar and moving a slider to the left or to the right. Since there are three recommendation levels, which can be thought of as −1, 0, and +1, influence can be changed from a minimum value of −2 to a maximum of +2. For example, if a level of −1 is chosen then all Tweets from this user, unless explicitly rated, will appear as one level lower than the rating they were given by the RS, to a minimum level of −1.

Figure 3. User interface with all three recommendation tiers

Tweets that have been retweeted, favorited, or liked are displayed in the "interesting" tier regardless of their actual recommendation score. However, to distinguish these Tweets from ones that were merely recommended as interesting, a small vertical bar is displayed at the left-hand side of the Tweet element.

4. PILOT STUDY

4.1 Goals

The primary goal of this evaluation was to determine the suitability of the design for presenting recommendations in a social stream. Most importantly, we want to know whether it is easy to ignore de-emphasized content, because this design otherwise may not be a reasonable alternative to stream filtering. Of secondary interest was the accuracy of the RS. The current implementation was not expected to perform exceptionally well, but it should perform well enough to gain the user's trust. If users do not trust the recommender at all, they will not gain anything by reading only the recommended Tweets.

4.2 Procedure

12 participants were recruited for this pilot study using word of mouth through extended Facebook and Twitter friend networks. Participants ranged from expert to casual Twitter users. Five of them only read their Twitter timelines a few times a month, while seven do so several times per day, and the other about once a day. Follow network sizes were distributed evenly between 10 and 500 friends.

Initial instruction informed users of the purpose of the study and that they would be testing a prototype of a system that presents recommendations in a Twitter timeline. Estimated time to complete the study, including the final questionnaire, was 20–30 minutes. Upon logging in, users received further instruction. After reading about the purpose of the application and a brief explanation of the recommender and the different rating tiers, users were asked to complete the following tasks:

1. ***Rate 30 Tweets***: Required to train the recommender.
2. ***Tiered Reading***: Once the recommender is active, read through the timeline one tier at a time.
3. ***Normal Reading***: Read through everything chronologically.
4. ***Survey***: A link to an external survey is provided in the top bar of the application after the recommender is activated.

4.3 Results

The survey consisted of a questionnaire. The questions were broken down into the following categories: Twitter usage, recommendation presentation, recommender performance, and design feedback. The results for categories 2 and 3, which were on a six-point Likert scale, are outlined in the following sections.

4.3.1 Recommendation Presentation

Users were asked how easy it was to accomplish three objectives in the tiered and normal reading tasks.

More than half of the participants said that it was "very easy" to read only the most emphasized Tweets, and all but one said it was more than "somewhat" easy. Ignoring only the most de-emphasized Tweets was more difficult, while consuming the entire stream chronologically was rated as the most difficult task, though all tasks had generally positive responses.

Table 1. Recommendation presentation responses

Objective	1	2	3	4	5	6
Read Emphasized	-	-	-	1	4	7
Ignore De-emphasized	-	-	2	3	3	4
Read All	-	-	3	1	6	2

The difficulty of the "Read All" objective is least relevant because users were able to disable the visualization styles altogether in the application settings. These results suggest that this method of recommendation presentation could be a viable alternative to stream filtering, given an accurate recommender. It may even be applicable to other unrelated tasks where users are required to consume large amounts of information of varying priority levels.

4.3.2 Recommender Performance

Users were asked to rate the recommender's performance in placing unrated Tweets into the highest and lowest tiers.

Table 2. Recommender performance responses

Accuracy	1	2	3	4	5	6
Interesting	-	-	-	6	4	2
Uninteresting	-	-	-	4	6	2

This very simple subjective evaluation showed slightly better results than expected. It is very possible that an unbiased test of RS accuracy using pre-determined ratings in training and testing sets and cross-validation would tell a different story and that users are more forgiving of recommendations that are slightly off or just better than the alternative. At the same time, user perception of recommendation accuracy reveals more about trust than objective measures of precision and recall. User preferences would be quite easily inferred by the naïve Bayes classifier if the user follows others who tweet about only a narrow range of topics. To get a more reliable indication of RS performance using this subjective method of testing, a larger sample size is needed.

4.3.3 Design Feedback

Users were finally asked to rate the helpfulness of the "User Volume" feature and to give open-ended feedback about the user interface and application features.

Table 3. User volume helpfulness responses

	1	2	3	4	5	6
User Volume	-	1	-	3	7	1

Tweet interest can sometimes fluctuate greatly even within the set of Tweets from a given user. Because of this fact, it was unclear how helpful the user volume feature would be. However, the responses indicate that the feature was indeed useful and that users would like to see the feature expanded to be more flexible.

The main theme of the open-ended feedback responses was that participants wanted more manual customization options. While it is desirable to automate the recommendation process as much as possible, allowing users to choose from different colour, size, and position options one time would add much to the user experience without taking away from the application's benefits.

4.4 Limitations

The greatest drawback to this pilot study was the limited sample size. As well, most of the questions asked in the questionnaire were subjective and may have been positively biased. Future experiments will be designed to try to minimize this effect.

5. RELATED WORK

Some of the drawbacks of social activity stream filtering have been addressed in Madmica [6]. The filter bubble visualization in this SNS allows users to view which updates have been hidden, and it also gives control to show or hide posts on certain topics from certain users. However, it remains difficult to get a sense of where posts belong in the context of the social stream without restoring them to a visible status.

The Comtella discussion forum [11] was the original inspiration for the strategy of presenting recommendations without filtering. In this system, recommendations are made collaboratively by and for other members of the community. The most recommended posts are shown in a brighter colour and with larger text in order to be visually attractive and more noticeable. However, the horizontal offset was not employed in this system, and the method of collaborative recommendations used within this closed community is not replicable in the vast open world of Twitter.

6. CONCLUSION AND FUTURE WORK

This short paper proposes to solve the problems related to user awareness and control of information filtering in social network activity streams by visually emphasizing the recommendations within the full stream. In this way nothing is hidden, and the user gains awareness and control of the recommendations. Results from the pilot study suggest that the idea does have merit and that further study would be worthwhile. The next step is to address the user feedback received and perform a larger-scale experiment to compare user trust, satisfaction, and subjectively reported recommender accuracy in two systems: one using stream filtering to hide the least interesting updates and the other using the recommendation emphasis design described in this paper.

7. REFERENCES

[1] Abel, F., Gao, Q., Houben, G., Tao, K. (2011). "Analyzing User Modeling on Twitter for Personalized News Recommendations." *Proceedings, 19th Int. Conf. on User Modeling, Adaptation and Personalization, UMAP'11*, 1–12.

[2] Adomavicius, G. & Tuzhilin, A. (2005). "Toward the Next Generation of Recommender Systems: A Survey of the State-of-the-Art and Possible Extensions. *IEEE Transactions on Knowledge and Data Engineering*, 17 (6), 734–749.

[3] Cremonesi, P., Garzotto, F., & Turrin, R. (2012). "User Effort vs. Accuracy in Rating-based Elicitation." *Proceedings, 6th ACM Conference on Recommender Systems, RecSys '12*, 27–34.

[4] Konstan, J. & Riedl, J. (2010). "Recommender Systems: From Algorithms to User Experience." *User Modeling and User-Adapted Interaction*, 22 (1–2), 101–123.

[5] Mackinlay, J. (1986). "Automating the design of graphical presentations of relational information." *ACM Transactions on Graphics*, 5 (2), 110–141.

[6] Nagulendra, S. & Vassileva, J. (2013). "Providing Awareness, Understanding and Control of Personalized Stream Filtering in a P2P Social Network." *Proceedings, 19th Int. Conf., CRIWG 2013, Wellington, New Zealand*, 61–76.

[7] Pariser, E. (2011). *The Filter Bubble: What the Internet Is Hiding from You*. New York: Penguin Press.

[8] Pu, P. & Chen, L. 2006. "Trust Building with Explanation Interfaces." *Proceedings, 11th Int. Conf. on Intelligent User Interfaces*, 93–100.

[9] Sriram, B. (2010). "Short Text Classification in Twitter to Improve Information Filtering." M.Sc. thesis, The Ohio State University.

[10] Wang, Y., Zhang, J., & Vassileva, J. (2010). "Towards Effective Recommendation of Social Data across Social Networking Sites." *Proceedings, 14th Int. Conf., AIMSA 2010*, 61–70.

[11] Webster, A. & Vassileva, J. (2006). "Visualizing Personal Relations in Online Communities." *Proceedings, 4th Int. Conf., AH 2006*, 223–233.

Implicit vs. Explicit Trust in Social Matrix Factorization

Soude Fazeli
Open Universiteit Nederland (OUNL)
6401 DL Heerlen
The Netherlands
soude.fazeli@ou.nl

Babak Loni
Delft University of Technology
2628 CD Delft
The Netherlands
b.loni@tudelft.nl

Alejandro Bellogin
Universidad Autónoma de Madrid
28049 Madrid
Spain
alejandro.bellogin@uam.es

Hendrik Drachsler
Open Universiteit Nederland (OUNL)
6401 DL Heerlen
The Netherlands
hendrik.drachsler@ou.nl

Peter Sloep
Open Universiteit Nederland (OUNL)
6401 DL Heerlen
The Netherlands
peter.sloep@ou.nl

ABSTRACT

Incorporating social trust in Matrix Factorization (MF) methods demonstrably improves accuracy of rating prediction. Such approaches mainly use the trust scores explicitly expressed by users. However, it is often challenging to have users provide explicit trust scores of each other. There exist quite a few works, which propose Trust Metrics (TM) to compute and predict trust scores between users based on their interactions. In this paper, we first evaluate several TMs to find out which one can best predict trust scores compared to the actual trust scores explicitly expressed by users. And, second, we propose to incorporate these trust scores inferred from the candidate TMs into social matrix factorization (MF). We investigate if incorporating the implicit trust scores in MF can make rating prediction as accurate as the MF on explicit trust scores. The reported results support the idea of employing implicit trust into MF whenever explicit trust is not available, since the performance of both models is similar.

Categories and Subject Descriptors

H.3.3 [Information Search and Retrieval]: Information filtering

General Terms

Algorithms, Performance, Experimentation

Keywords

recommender system, matrix factorization, implicit trust, social network, rating, similarity

1. INTRODUCTION

Quite a few works discuss incorporating social trust in Matrix Factorization (MF), which proved to improve rating prediction accuracy [5, 8]. Such approaches assume that users themselves explicitly express the trust scores. Examples of well-known and publicly available datasets are Epinions and FilmTrust. However, there are still certain issues with this kind of trust scores. First, it is often very challenging to have users giving trust scores of each other. Second, even these publicly available datasets for trust only provide trust relations in binary format (0/1), usually, and as stated in the literature, because of privacy concerns. Therefore, trust relations will all be considered equal and we will ignore the fact that users can have different levels of trust of each other.

In contrast, implicit trust scores may be predicted based on the users' interaction histories. This is also true in the context of real life scenarios. People often tend to share and interact with people they trust. Nevertheless, it is still an open problem how to compute and predict trust between users more accurately and effectively. In this paper:

First, we evaluate several well-known Trust Metrics (TM) to find out which one is closest to the real, explicit scores, and therefore, can make the most accurate trust prediction.

Second, we try to incorporate the candidate TMs in the MF to answer this research question: *Can we incorporate implicit trust into social matrix factorization when explicit trust relations are not available?*

The rest of the article is organized as follows: Section 2 presents a brief review of the existing TMs. Section 3 provides the problem definition for MF. Our proposed approach is presented in Section 4. Section 5 presents the results and discussions. Finally, we conclude by giving an overview of further work in Section 5.

2. FROM RATINGS TO TRUST

Trust is known to be a complex and ambiguous concept in various domains. However, in recommender systems it is a fairly simple and precise notion: it is correlated with similarity of interests and preferences of users sharing the same items. Guo [2] presents this definition for trust in recommender systems: "Trust is defined as one's belief towards the ability of others in providing valuable ratings". In general, trust has a number of distinct properties [3]:

- Asymmetry. Trust is personal and subjective. People might have different opinions about a particular person based on their background and experiences with that person. If user Alice trusts Bob, Bob does not necessarily trust Alice.
- Transitivity. A very useful property of trust in recommender systems is transitivity; by and large, it holds in real life scenarios as well. People tend to trust friends of a friend more so than strangers. So, if Alice

RecSys '14, October 06 - 10 2014, San Jose or vicinity, CA, USA

ACM 978-1-4503-2668-1/14/10 $15.00.
http://dx.doi.org/10.1145/2645710.2645766

trusts Bob, and Bob trusts Carol, Alice is likely to trust Carol too. This property helps to identify new neighbors (likeminded users) for a target user by propagating trust in social networks and thus, to improve performance of recommender systems.

- Dynamicity. Trust between two persons often gradually develops and changes over time. In recommender systems, trust grows over time as two users share more opinions on common items.
- Context dependence. Trust can depend strongly on the context in which it has formed. The context in recommender systems can refer to the type of the items users give ratings to or to other specific properties in the user or item profile.

Table 1. Trust prediction metrics

Trust metric	Computation function
O'Donovan & Smyth (TM1) [9]	$t_{u,v} = \frac{\lvert CorrectSet(v) \rvert}{\lvert RecSet(v) \rvert}$ $correct(r_{u,i}, r_{v,i}) \leftrightarrow \lvert p_{u,i} - r_{u,i} \rvert$
Lathia et al. (TM2) [7]	$t_{u,v} = \frac{1}{\lvert I_{u,v} \rvert} \sum_{i \in I_{u,v}} (1 - \frac{\lvert r_{u,i} - r_{v,i} \rvert}{r_{max}})$
Hwang & Chen (TM3) [4]	$t_{u,v} = \frac{1}{\lvert I_{u,v} \rvert} \sum_{i \in I_{u,v}} (1 - \frac{\lvert p_{u,i} - r_{u,i} \rvert}{r_{max}})$ $p_{u,i} = r_u + (\bar{r}_{v,i} - \bar{r}_v)$
Shambour & Lu (TM4) [12]	$t_{u,v} = \frac{\lvert I_{u,v} \rvert}{\lvert I_u \cup I_v \rvert} (1 - \frac{1}{\lvert I_{u,v} \rvert} \sum_{i \in I_{u,v}} \left(\frac{p_{u,i} - r_{u,i}}{r_{max}}\right)^2)$ $p_{u,i} = r_u + (\bar{r}_{v,i} - \bar{r}_v)$
Papagelis et al. (TM5) [10]	$t_{u,v} = \begin{cases} s_{u,v}, if\ s_{u,v} > \theta_s, \lvert I_{u,v} \rvert > \theta_I \\ 0, \quad otherwise; \end{cases}$ $s_{u,v} = \frac{\sum_i (\bar{r}_{u,i} - \bar{r}_u)(\bar{r}_{v,i} - \bar{r}_v)}{\sqrt{\sum_i (\bar{r}_{u,i} - \bar{r}_u)^2} \sqrt{\sum_i (\bar{r}_{v,i} - \bar{r}_v)^2}}$

Table 1 presents several trust metrics that compute trust scores between users based on their rating data. For all trust metrics in this table, *U*, *I*, and *R* are sets of users, items, and ratings, respectively. The trust values between two users *u* and *v* ($t_{u,v}$) are inferred based on their co-rated items ($I_{u,v}$). We use $p_{u,i}$ as the predicted rating value for a user *u* on an item *i*. The average of ratings for user *u* is denoted by $\bar{r}_u$ for all the items rated by user *u*. Finally, r_{max} is the maximum value of ratings.

As for O'Donovan & Smyth [9] (TM1 in Table 1), the *CorrectSet(v)* is the set of correct ratings given by the user *v*, and *RecSet(v)* is the whole set of recommendations made for user *v*. Moreover, in the trust metric proposed by Papagelis et al. [10] (TM5 in Table 1), the similarity threshold (θ_s) is set to ensure that the inferred trust is transitive only when the two users *v* and *u* are highly correlated. Moreover, when the number of co-rated items between the users *v* and *u* is too small, there might be a risk that the inferred trust value is less reliable. Hence, Papagelis et al. [10] sets a threshold (θ_I) to address this as well.

As indicated, we will first evaluate the trust metrics in Table 1 by comparing the trust scores generated by them with the grounded trust scores explicitly expressed by users. We do this to find out which of these trust metrics can best predict the trust scores between users. The trust metrics presented in Table 1 are all based on differences between a user's ratings and its neighbors' ratings. Therefore, for all of them, similarity is an emergent property of the trust relationship and not necessarily the cause of it. So, they all are asymmetric and transitive. However, none of them provides dynamicity and context-dependence.

3. SOCIAL MATRIX FACTORIZATION

In recommender systems, we have a set of users $\{u_1, ..., u_N\}$ and set of items $\{i_1, ... i_M\}$. The rating matrix $R = [R_{u,i}]_{N \times M}$ provide the ratings given by users to items. Therefore, $R_{u,i}$ is the rating of user u to item i. The ratings are often on a five-star scale. The recommender system's task is then to predict the rating a user u would give to an item i whenever $R_{u,i}$ is unknown. In this paper, we follow the basic idea of the social matrix factorization (SocialMF) method [5] to learn the latent features of both users and items more precisely when trust information between users is available. Let us assume $U \in R_{K \times N}$ and $V \in R_{K \times M}$ be latent user and item feature matrices, with column vectors U_u and V_i representing K-dimensional user-specific and item-specific latent feature vectors of users u and item i, respectively. The goal of matrix factorization is to learn these latent features and, subsequently, to employ them for making rating predictions [6].

Now assume that $T_{u,v}$ denotes the trust value between users u and v. Therefore, matrix $T = [T_{u,v}]_{N \times N}$ represent all trust scores between users. Note that T is asymmetric in general. The SocialMF model [5] exploits these trust scores to learn the latent features more precisely. As the trust scores are incorporated into SocialMF, the loss function is defined as follows [5]:

$$L(R,T,U,V) = \frac{1}{2} \sum_{u=1}^{N} \sum_{i=1}^{M} I_{u,i}^{R} (R_{u,i} - g(U_u^T V_i))^2 + \frac{\lambda_U}{2} \sum_{u=1}^{N} U_u^T U_u + \frac{\lambda_V}{2} \sum_{i=1}^{M} V_i^T V_i + \frac{\lambda_T}{2} \sum_{u=1}^{N} ((U_u - \sum_{v \in N_u} T_{u,v} U_v)^T (U_u - \sum_{v \in N_u} T_{u,v} U_v)) \quad (1)$$

Where g(.) is a logistic normalization function and λ_U, λ_V, λ_T are biases for user, item and trust, respectively. The model learns the latent features using a gradient descent method.

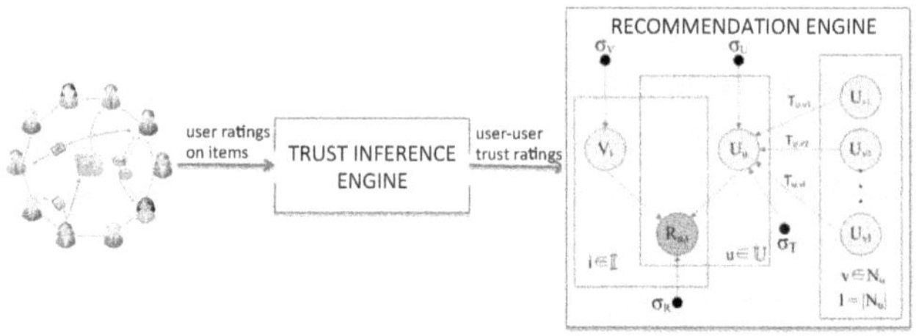

Figure 1. Our proposed approach based on the SocialMF model

4. A TRUST-AWARE SOCIAL MF

As mentioned before, each of the trust-aware recommenders and the social MF alone proved to improve accuracy of ratings prediction. In this paper, we propose to incorporate implicit trust scores between users in the social MF in order to boost performance of model-based recommender systems. Figure 1 shows how we want to combine inferred trust scores based on user ratings on items, with the social MF. As shown in Figure 1, the approach we propose consists of two main modules: a trust inference engine and a recommendation engine. The trust inference engine takes user ratings on items as input and computes the trust scores between users using any of the trust metrics in the literature (such as those presented in Table 1). Then, the recommendation engine generates rating predictions by employing the SocialMF method [5], using the inferred trust scores instead of the explicit ones.

5. EXPERIMENT

We used the Epinions[1] dataset, which includes 49,290 users who rated a total of 139,738 different items, 664,824 reviews, and 487,181 issued trust statements. Our experiment consists of two steps. First, we evaluate the trust metrics in Table 1, by comparing the trust scores generated by them with the ground trust scores explicitly expressed by users (Table 2). Second, we incorporate the trust scores generated by the trust metrics, into the SocialMF as described in the previous section (Table 3).

5.1 Evaluating trust ratings predictions

Here, we present results of an evaluation of the trust metrics presented in Section 2. For each metric, we have measured how relevant a user's ranking (composed of other users, and sorted according to the trust scores produced by the metrics) is, compared against the ground truth scores available in Epinions dataset. Specifically, four metrics commonly used in Information Retrieval are presented: normalized discounted cumulative gain (nDCG), precision (P), recall (R), and reciprocal rank (MRR) [1]. Table 2 shows the results for these metrics; along with the user coverage (Cvg) measured as the number of users for which a metric is able to infer trust values.

Table 2. Comparing the inferred trust scores (implicit) with the ground trust scores (explicit)

Trust metric	nDCG@10	nDCG	P@10	R@10	MRR	Cvg
O'Donovan & Smyth [9] (TM1)	0.007	0.008	0.007	0.001	0.022	98.8%
Lathia et al. [7] (TM2)	0.004	0.008	0.004	0.001	0.014	99.7%
Hwang & Chen [4] (TM3)	0.006	0.009	0.005	0.001	0.020	100%
Shambour & Lu [12] (TM4)	0.006	0.009	0.005	0.001	0.017	100%
Papagelis et al. [10] (TM5)	0.028	0.007	0.024	0.003	0.071	9.5%

As Table 2 shows, there is an important tradeoff between accuracy and coverage: whereas Papagelis et al. (TM5) has high precision and MRR values, its coverage is too low. It is also important to note the difference in performance at varying cutoffs: although Papagelis et al. perform well at smaller cutoffs (nDCG@10), its performance is worse when the whole ranking is considered (nDCG); in particular, this metric is not the best performing one, but more complex metrics like Hwang & Chen (TM3) and Shambour & Lu (TM4) obtain better performance in the long term.

Assuming we are interested in metrics with high user coverage and good performance at small cutoffs, our results suggest O'Donovan and Smyth (TM1) is the best candidate. This is due to a good tradeoff this metric presents between the different aspects measured over the trust metrics from Table 1.

[1] http://www.trustlet.org/wiki/Epinions_dataset

5.2 Evaluating accuracy of ratings prediction

In this section, we present results on accuracy of rating prediction in terms of RMSE (Root Mean Square Error) and MAE (Mean Absolute Error), which are common metrics used when evaluating MF methods. We set the number of latent features k to be equal to 5 and 10; as suggested in the literature on social MF [5, 8]. For testing our model, 80% of the data was randomly selected and assigned to training set and the rest was considered as test set. We compare our approach with two state-of-the-art approaches: Probabilistic MF (PMF) [11] and an approach using only trust information, SocialMF [5]. For all the methods used, we set optimal parameters recommended in the literature, as indicated in Table 3. For PMF and SocialMF, we adopt the implementations provided by the MyMediaLite framework[2].

Table 3. Performance comparison of the SocialMF using implicit trust against the baselines (the lower, the better); lowest values for each k in bold face and best values underlined.

	RMSE		MAE	
Method/k	**k=5**	**k=10**	**k=5**	**k=10**
PMF	1.1741	1.1705	0.9471	0.9507
SocialMF-explicit trust	1.0956	**1.0934**	0.9161	**0.9154**
SocialMF-TM1: O'Donovan & Smyth [9]	<u>**1.0926**</u>	1.1003	<u>**0.9145**</u>	0.9170
SocialMF-TM2: Lathia et al. [7]	1.0968	1.1005	0.9160	0.9175
SocialMF-TM3: Hwang & Chen [4]	1.0947	1.1006	0.9154	0.9174
SocialMF-TM4: Shambour & Lu [12]	1.0952	1.0990	0.9153	0.9167
SocialMF-TM5: Papagelis et al. [10]	1.0970	1.1065	0.9150	0.9186

Table 3 presents the results of comparing the SocialMF on implicit trust scores, explicit trust scores, and PMF. Based on the results, all SocialMFs that incorporates implicit trust outperforms the PMF; the largest difference is 8.2% and smallest difference is 7.7%.

In general, the results of SocialMF on implicit trust (for all TMs) are quite similar to the results of SocialMF using explicit trust. As the table shows, the SocialMF on implicit trust inferred by O'Donovan and Smyth's (TM1) (RMSE=1.0926; MAE=0.9145) can perform as accurate as the SocialMF with explicit trust (1.0956; k=5). The results show that SocialMF on implicit trust can achieve quite the same results as the SocialMF on explicit trust; with the difference in range of {-0.016%,+0.4%}. Regarding our research question in Section 1, we may safely conclude that the implicit trust can be incorporated into the social matrix factorization whenever explicit trust is not available. Moreover, the results in Table 3 conform to the results presented in the previous section (Table 2) where TM1 was selected as the best candidate for inferring trust scores.

[2] www.mymedialite.net

5.3 Impact of social regulation (λ_T) on results

As described in Section 3, our model has a parameter λ_T that indicates the impact of social trust scores in the trust learning process. To analyze how sensitive our model is to this parameter, Figure 2 shows the effect of changing the value of λ_T in the range of [0, 3], specifically, we show the RMSE of the SocialMF model for different values of this parameter. As shown in this figure, λ_T =1 seems to be a good candidate for our experiment since the SocialMF model provides the lowest RMSE at this value.

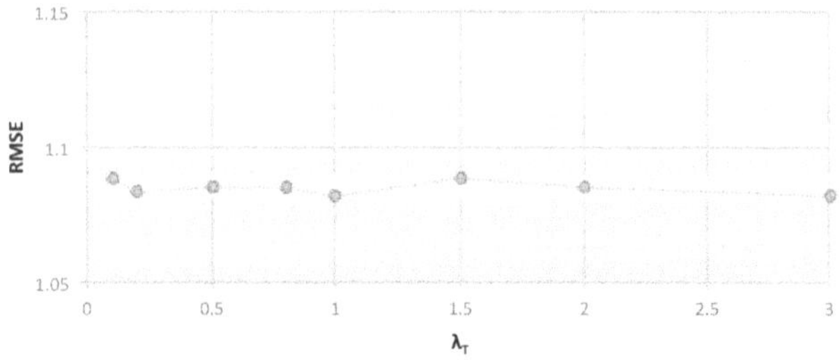

Figure 2. Effect of changes in social regulations on the RMSE

6. CONCLUSION AND FUTURE WORK

In this paper, we addressed the following research question: *Can we incorporate implicit trust into social matrix factorization when explicit trust relations are not available?* For this, we have investigated which trust metric can provide us with the most accurate trust scores in comparison with the explicit trust scores given by users themselves. Our results show that there is a trade-off between accuracy and coverage, but that the metric defined by O'Donovan and Smyth in [9] performs best. Then, we incorporated these inferred trust scores into a social matrix factorization recommender. The results show that the social MF with implicit trust outperforms one of the baselines (PMF) and performs in ways similar to the SocialMF using explicit trust. A clear advantage of this result is that, since we often have no trust scores explicitly given by users in social networks, we can overcome this problem by using implicit (or inferred) trust scores and incorporate them into the recommender. In the future, we aim to define and infer trust scores taking into account context data of users rather than their ratings only. We also want to evaluate additional dimensions of recommendation quality, such as diversity, novelty or serendipity.

7. ACKNOWLEDGEMENT

This paper is part of a doctoral study funded by NELLL (the Netherlands Laboratory for Lifelong Learning) and the Open Discovery Space project. Open Discovery Space is funded by the European Union (EU) under the ICT theme of the 7th Framework Programme for R&D. This document does not represent the opinion of the EU, and the EU is not responsible for any use that might be made of its content. This work has been also partially supported by the EU FP7 LACE project and the Spanish Ministry of Science and Innovation (TIN2013-47090-C3-2).

8. REFERENCES

[1] Baeza-Yates, R.A. and Ribeiro-Neto, B.A. 2011. *Modern Information Retrieval - the concepts and technology behind search, Second edition*. Pearson Education Ltd., Harlow, England.

[2] Guo, G. 2013. Integrating trust and similarity to ameliorate the data sparsity and cold start for recommender systems. *In Proceedings of the 7th ACM Conference on Recommender Systems (RecSys)* (2013).

[3] Guo, G., Zhang, J., Thalmann, D., Basu, A. and Yorke-smith, N. 2014. From Ratings to Trust□: an Empirical Study of Implicit Trust in Recommender Systems. *Symposium on Applied Computing - Recommender Systems 2014* (2014).

[4] Hwang, C.-S. and Chen., Y.-P. 2007. Using trust in collaborative filtering recommendation. *In New Trends in Applied Artificial Intelligence*. (2007).

[5] Jamali, M. and Ester, M. 2010. A Matrix Factorization Technique with Trust Propagation for Recommendation in Social Networks Categories and Subject Descriptors. *Proceedings of the fourth ACM conference on Recommender systems* (2010), 135–142.

[6] Koren, Y., Bell, R. and Volinsky, C. 2009. Matrix factorization techniques for recommender systems. *IEEE Computer*. (2009), 30–37.

[7] Lathia, N., Hailes, S. and Capra, L. 2008. Trust-Based Collaborative Filtering. *Trust Management II, IFIP Advances in Information and Communication Technology*. 263/2008, (2008).

[8] Ma, H., Yang, H., Lyu, M.R. and King, I. 2008. SoRec. *Proceeding of the 17th ACM conference on Information and knowledge mining - CIKM '08* (New York, New York, USA, Oct. 2008), 931.

[9] O'Donovan, J. and Smyth, B. 2005. Trust in recommender systems. *Proceedings of the 10th international conference on Intelligent user interfaces* (2005), 167–174.

[10] Papagelis, M., Plexousakis, D. and Kutsuras, T. 2005. Alleviating the sparsity problem of collaborative filtering using trust inferences. *In Trust management*. (2005).

[11] Salakhutdinov, R. and Mnih., A. Probabilistic matrix factorization. *In NIPS 2008*. 20.

[12] Shambour, Q. and Lu. A, J. 2012. Trust-semantic fusion-based recommendation approach for e-business applications. *Decision Support Systems*. 54 (2012), 768–780.

Modeling the Dynamics of User Preferences in Coupled Tensor Factorization

Dimitrios Rafailidis*
Department of Informatics
Aristotle University of Thessaloniki
Thessaloniki, Greece
draf@csd.auth.gr

Alexandros Nanopoulos
School of Management
Catholic University of Eichstät-Ingolstadt
Ingolstadt, Germany
alexandros.nanopoulos@ku.de

ABSTRACT

In several applications, user preferences can be fairly dynamic, since users tend to exploit a wide range of items and modify their tastes accordingly over time. In this paper, we model continuous user-item interactions over time using a tensor that has time as a dimension (mode). To account for the fact that user preferences are dynamic and change individually, we propose a new measure of user-preference dynamics (UPD) that captures the rate with which the current preferences of each user have been shifted. We generate recommendations based on factorizing the tensor, by weighting the importance of past user preferences according to their UPD values. We additionally exploit users' side data, such as demographics, which can help improving the accuracy of recommendations based on a coupled, tensor-matrix factorization scheme. Our empirical evaluation uses a real data set from last.fm, which allows us to demonstrate that user preferences can become very dynamic. Our experimental results show that the proposed method, by taking into account these dynamics, outperforms several baselines.

Categories and Subject Descriptors

H.2.8 [**Information Systems Applications**]: Miscellaneous

Keywords

Preference dynamics; Coupled tensor factorization.

1. INTRODUCTION

Users may change their interest over time, especially in applications where they interact customarily with a wide range of items when consuming news or music online. For this reason, recent research started to incorporate temporal effects into model-based collaborative filtering [2, 6, 8], by observing drifts in rating behavior and modeling the way user and item characteristics change over time (e.g., users liking cartoons when they are young, but disliking them when growing up). However, such approaches do not take into account the facts that in several applications: (i) users interact continuously with items over time [3], e.g., when consuming music online or purchasing several categories of retail products (e.g., household items); or (ii) that implicit quantitative feedback may be provided by users, such as the number of times they listened to a song or downloaded a video within a time period (in contrast, [3] focused on explicit feedback in the form of ratings).

Continuous user-item interactions over time can be captured with a sparse tensor whose dimensions (modes) correspond to user, items, and time. Each non-empty tensor cell can record explicit or implicit (quantitative) feedback within the given period. For instance, Xio et al. [7] used a Bayesian probabilistic tensor factorization model for movie recommendation. Spiegel et al. [5] used tensor factorization on evolving data with different time-periods being modeled as time slices in the tensor. They proposed the use of a Smoothing Factor (SF), by exponentially decreasing the importance of past preferences. Nevertheless, these approaches ignore the fact that changes in user preferences can vary individually, i.e., some users' tastes may be very volatile whereas others may keep their tastes relatively stable over time.

In this paper, we follow the aforementioned approaches and model varying user preferences with tensors. We consider individual changes in preferences based on a new measure of user-preference dynamics (UPD) that captures the rate with which the current preferences of each user have shifted compared to his past preferences. Recommendations are generated based on tensor factorization, by weighting the importance of past user preferences according to their UPD values. Motivated by recent research on auxiliary information (a.k.a. side information) [4], we examine users' side data, such as demographics, to improve the recommendation accuracy based on a coupled tensor factorization model, which captures shared latent factors across the time-varying user preference data and the side information about the users. Our empirical evaluation uses a real data set from last.fm, which demonstrates that user preferences can become very dynamic. Our experimental results show that the proposed method outperforms several baselines.

2. THE PROPOSED MODEL

The inputs of the proposed model are (1) a third-order tensor $\mathcal{X} \in \mathbb{R}^{|U|\times|I|\times|T|}$, where U, I and T denote the sets

*Also with the Comp. Science Dept. of Cyprus Univ.

RecSys'14, October 6–10, 2014, Foster City, Silicon Valley, CA, USA.

http://dx.doi.org/10.1145/2645710.2645758 .

of users, items and time-periods, respectively and each non-empty tensor cell $\mathcal{X}(u,i,t)$ contains the number of interactions of user $u \in U$ to item $i \in I$ at the time-period $t \in T$; (2) an auxiliary matrix $Y \in \mathbb{R}^{|U|\times|D|}$ of users' side information with a set of D attributes, coupled in the user dimension (mode) U of tensor $\mathcal{X}$; and (3) the rank R of $\mathcal{X}$. Firstly, we model the temporal and users' side information (Section 2.1), and then the proposed model reweigh the past interactions of tensor $\mathcal{X}$ based on the users' recent interaction behavior to items(Section 2.2). The output of the proposed model is a low rank R approximation of $\mathcal{X}$, denoted by $\hat{\mathcal{X}}$, using a CANDECOMP/PARAFAC (CP) decomposition (Section 2.3).

2.1 Modeling Changing User Preferences and Side Information

Each non-empty tensor cell $\mathcal{X}(u,i,t)$ contains the number of interactions of user u to item i at the time period t (assuming implicit quantitative feedback). The time period can be days, months, semiannuals (i.e., 6 months), or whole years, corresponding to the $|T|$ different time slices $|U| \times |I|_t$ of tensor $\mathcal{X}$, with $t \in 1 \dots |T|$. The choice of the time period mainly depends on the application of the recommender system. This means that the test time period, e.g., the test month where the personalized recommendations have to be generated, is included in the last time slice $|U| \times |I|_{|T|}$, e.g., the current semiannual, of the tensor $\mathcal{X}$.

With respect to the users' side information the u-th, $u \in U$, row of the auxiliary matrix Y corresponds to the set D of attributes of user u. In case of numerical attributes, e.g., age, we perform an equal-width binning, where for each numerical entry in the matrix Y we store the respective number of the bin. In the case of categorical attributes, such county and gender, we calculate the c distinct categorical values and then we create a binary vector $\mathbf{c}_i \in \mathbb{R}^{c \times 1}$, where 1 denotes the categorical attribute of user u_i. Finally, we append the transformed numerical and categorical attributes to generate the final $|D|$ attributes in matrix Y.

2.2 Users Preference Dynamics (UPD)

Given a test period $t+1$ within the current/last time slice $|U| \times |I|_{|T|}$ of the tensor $\mathcal{X}$, e.g., the test month in the last semiannual, for each user u we calculate the UPD_u value as follows:

$$\text{UPD}_u = 1 - \frac{|I^u_{cur} \cap I^u_{prev}|}{|I^u_{cur} \cup I^u_{prev}|} \quad (1)$$

where $I^u_{cur} \subseteq I$ denotes the set of items that user u has interacted at the current/last time slice $|U| \times |I|_{|T|}$ of $\mathcal{X}$ and $I^u_{prev} \subseteq I$ is the union set of the items that user u has interacted at all the previous time slices $|U| \times |I|_t$, with $t = 1 \dots |T| - 1$. The numerator of the fraction in Eq. 1 is the number of common items that user u has interacted at the current and the previous time periods, whereas the denominator of the fraction is the number of the distinct items that user u has interacted overall. According to Eq. 1, low UPD_u values indicate that user u preserved his preferences, whereas high ones correspond to users' u high tendency to change his preferences at the current time period (the $|T|$-th time slice of $\mathcal{X}$). After calculating the $|U|$ different UPD values, we decrease the weights of each interaction of user u at the $|T| - 1$ different past time slices $|U| \times |I|_t$, by multiplying them with the smoothing factor $sf_u = 1 - \text{UPD}_u$, as follows $\forall u \in U$ and $|T| > 1$[1]:

$$\mathcal{X}(u,i,t) := sf_u * \mathcal{X}(u,i,t) \quad (2)$$

$$\text{with } t = 1, \dots, |T| - 1 \text{ and } i \in I^u_{prev}$$

We have to mention that the smoothing factor sf_u is different for each user u, depending on the users' current interaction behavior to items within the current time period. This comes in contrast to several works such as [5], where the smoothing factor is applied in an non-personalized way. The outcome of this process is the recalculation of the respective entries (number of interactions) of $\mathcal{X}$ based on Eq. 2.

2.3 The Low Rank R Approximation Of The Tensor $\mathcal{X}$

In our model we used the CP decomposition of $\mathcal{X}$ with the recalculated entries based on Eq. 2. To generate the output of the proposed model, we calculate the $\hat{\mathcal{X}}$ low rank R approximation as follows:

$$\hat{\mathcal{X}} = \sum_{r=R}^{R} \mathbf{u}_r \circ \mathbf{i}_r \circ \mathbf{t}_r \quad (3)$$

where $\circ$ is the outer product operation and $\mathbf{u}_r$, $\mathbf{i}_r$, $\mathbf{t}_r$ are the respective user, item, time vectors of the r-th component. The goal of the proposed model is to minimize the low rank approximation error $||\mathcal{X} - \hat{\mathcal{X}}||^2_F$, where $||\cdot||_F$ indicates the Frobenius norm. The R component of a tensor $\mathcal{X}$ and the auxiliary matrix Y is defined as:

$$f(A,B,C,V) = ||\mathcal{X} - [A,B,C]||^2 + ||Y - AV^T||^2 \quad (4)$$

where matrices $A \in \mathbb{R}^{|U|\times R}$, $B \in \mathbb{R}^{|I|\times R}$ and $C \in \mathbb{R}^{|T|\times R}$ are the factor matrices of $\mathcal{X}$, extracted by CP; matrices A and $V \in \mathbb{R}^{|D|\times R}$ are the factor matrices extracted from matrix Y (with users' side information) by a matrix factorization technique. Also, in Eq. 4 we use the notation $\hat{\mathcal{X}} = [A,B,C]$ to denote the low rank approximation based on the CP model. Our goal is to calculate the matrices A, B, C and V that minimize the objective function of Eq. 4. In order to solve the minimization problem we used the CMTF-OPT algorithm of the CMTF toolbox[2], which also handles missing data, since $\mathcal{X}$ is usually sparse.

The final top-k recommendations for each user u at the current test time-period t are generated by ordering in descending order the entries of $\hat{\mathcal{X}}(u,:,t)$, i.e. the respective column of items with indices $u \in U$ and t within the current/last time slice of $\hat{\mathcal{X}}$. Thus, the outcome of the proposed model is the respective top-k (recommended) items.

3. EXPERIMENTS

3.1 The last.fm Dataset

In our experiments, we used the last.fm Dataset - 1K users[3] which contains the listening habits for $|U|$=992 users. The dataset consists of tuples in the form of user-artist-song-timestamp over 54 months (till May, 5th 2009). In to-

[1]For $|T|$=1, $\forall u \in U$ $sf_u = 1$

[2]`www.models.life.ku.dk/joda/CMTF_Toolbox/`

[3]`www.dtic.upf.edu/~ocelma/MusicRecommendationDataset/`

tal, there are $|I|$=176,948 artists[4] and 19,150,868 listening events, corresponding to track-listenings. The distribution of the listening events is presented in Figure 1. In our experiments, we split the dataset into 9 time periods (time slots $S_1 \dots S_9$), corresponding to 9 semiannuals. Thus, we have $|T|$=9 different time slices in the tensor, where each slice corresponds to a six-months period. In this dataset, users' side information is also available, including age, gender, country (with missing values, however). Users in this dataset come from 68 different countries. Since gender and country are categorical values, we used the transformation technique of Section 2.1 to generate $|D| = 71$ attributes in total.

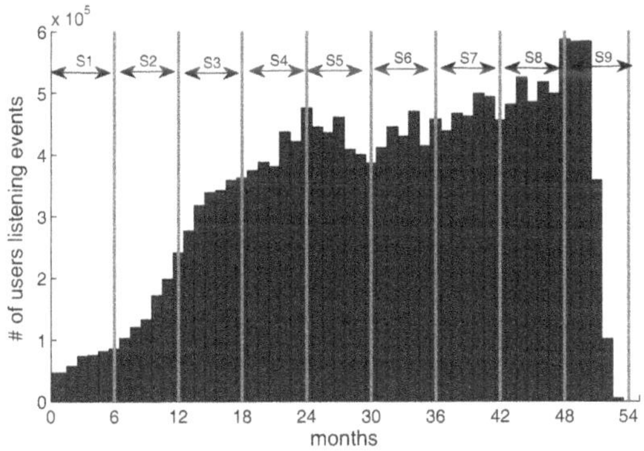

Figure 1: Users listening events (track-listenings) in the last.fm dataset.

3.2 Evaluation Protocol

Tuples were transformed in the form of user-artist-time slot-# of listening events, corresponding to how many times (number of interactions) a user has listened tracks of an artist within the time slot. In doing so, we generated 2,963,653 tuples. Given a set of training months the goal of the proposed model is to perform top-k artist recommendation for a user at a test month. In our experiments we used a time window equal to semiannual, where as training set we considered all the past months of the previous semiannuals and the first five months of the current semiannual. The goal is to predict the artists that each user is going to listen at the last (6-th) test month of the current semiannual. Therefore, we have nine different test sets of tuples at test months 6, 12, 18, 24, 30, 36, 42, 48 and 54, denoted by red lines in Figure 1, and nine different training sets of tuples at the respective past months. Since we noticed in the dataset that each user does not listen to more than 100 artists for a test month, in our experiments we report Average Recall (AR), with k=100 artists.

3.3 Preference Dynamics

In Figures 2 and 3, we group users from the test months into 3 different groups based on their listening events and their UPD value (Eq. 1), respectively. From Figure 2 we can observe that users increase the number of their listening events over time. The evolution of the 3 different groups based on the UPD metric in Figure 3 shows that users tend to significantly shift their preferences over time, since the percentage of users in the group UPD ≥ 0.75 is highly increased over time. According to Eq. 1, the user group with UPD ≥ 0.75 contains the users at the test months that have listened more than a 75% percentage of new artists than they have listened at the past months. An interesting observation is that we have a critical point at 18 months, where users start to significantly shift their preferences, denoted by the starting point of the high increase of the percentage of users in group UPD ≥ 0.75 and the starting point of the high decrease of groups UPD ≤ 0.5 and $0.5 <$ UPD < 0.75 .

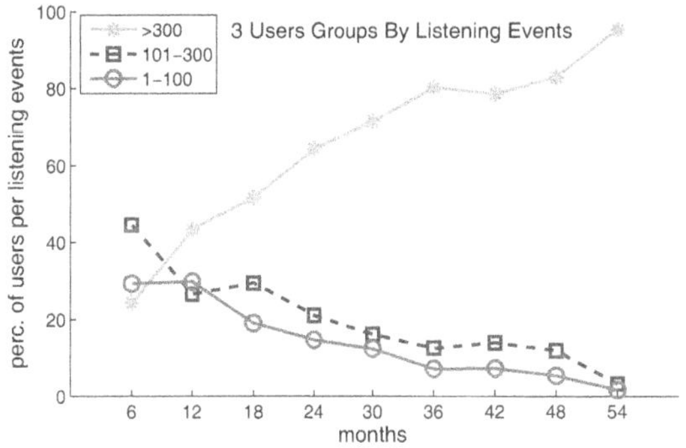

Figure 2: The evolution of the 3 different users groups based on the listening events.

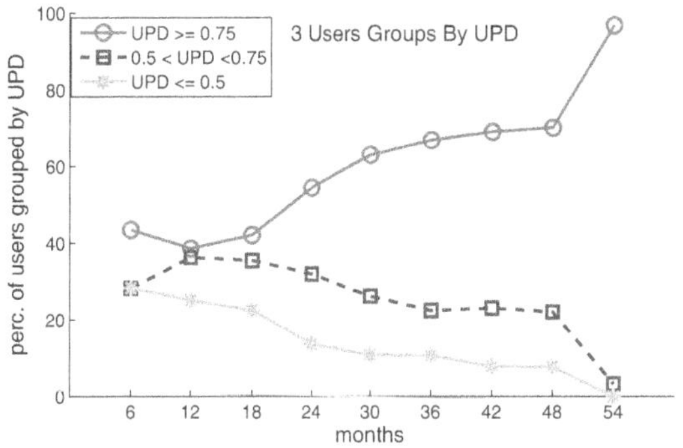

Figure 3: The evolution of the 3 different users groups based on UPD.

3.4 Settings

In our experiments, we evaluated the proposed model, by considering (a) only the modeling of side information with the CP decomposition, performing thus Coupled Tensor Factorization (**CTF**) and (b) the combination of side information with the weighting scheme based on UPD in Eq. 1 and 2 (**UPD-CTF**). As competitive methods we consider the **TF** method of [1] and the **SF** method of [5]. For **SF**, we varied the smoothing factor from 0.1 to 0.9 and selected the value 0.3 as best performing. Lower values of the smoothing factor mean that the SF method down-weigh more the past preferences, in our case listening events. As **baseline** method, we used the most-popular artists methods, which recommends the top-k most popular artists for each user within the training months.

Since determining the rank R of the tensor is a NP-problem, we varied R by 5, 10, 15 and 20. We concluded to R=15, since a further increase of rank R results in a higher computational cost without paying off in terms of recommendation accuracy. TF and SF method have similar computational complexities, whereas CTF and UPD-CTF have higher com-

[4]To remove extreme sparsity for artists, we applied the p-core filtering technique, with p =0.2%$|I|$.

putational complexity for the required coupling of matrix Y with the users' side information. For the methods (a) with and (b) without the coupling the computational times (for R=15) are 126 and 432 secs, respectively (on a Windows 7 PC with Intel core i7 2700K at 3.50 GHz, 8GB Ram).

3.5 Results

The results on the nine test months are presented in Figure 4. The proposed UPD-CTF method outperforms TF, SF and the baseline, because it captures users' preference dynamics in a personalized way and also incorporates auxiliary information. Using paired t-test we found that the difference between the reported results for the proposed UPD-CTF method against the competitive approaches is statistically significant at level 0.05. An important observation is that after the critical point of 18 months, where users start to significantly shift their preferences (see description in Section 3.3), the accuracy of TF and SF starts to decrease fast, even lower than the baseline method. This happens because both methods neither handle the users' personalized preference dynamics nor use auxiliary information. Finally, an interesting observation is that, despite the fact that CTF does not handle users' preference dynamics, it preserves the recommendation accuracy relatively high, which means that users' auxiliary information plays a crucial role in recommender systems.

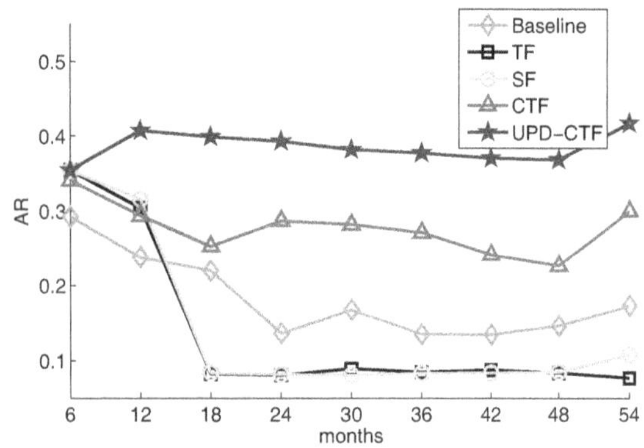

Figure 4: Methods comparison.

In Table 1 we report the performance of the examined methods separately for the three users groups based on UPD for the test months 12 and 54. We selected these months because they are before and after the critical point of 18 months, where the users preference dynamics (UPD) start to change significantly. As expected the baseline method performs worse in the case of users in the groups of UPD $\geq$ 0.75 and 0.5 $<$ UPD $<$ 0.75 than users in group UPD $\leq$ 0.5, since in the latter group we have users that remain stable to their preferences over time. Additionally, the proposed UPD-CTF method preserves the recommendation accuracy high in all 3 different groups of users based on UPD, by handling the users' preferences dynamics and exploiting side information.

4. CONCLUSIONS

We modeled users preference dynamics and users' side information in coupled tensor factorization. Our experiments showed that the proposed model can achieve significant improvement in recommendation accuracy against competitive

Table 1: Methods performance for the 3 different users groups based on UPD (test months 12 and 54).

12 months	UPD $\geq$ 0.75	0.5 $<$ UPD $<$ 0.75	UPD $\leq$ 0.5
Perc. users	38.6%	36.28%	25.12%
Baseline	0.21 ± 0.02	0.24 ± 0.09	0.26 ± 0.06
TF	0.30 ± 0.13	0.32 ± 0.08	0.27 ± 0.11
SF	0.31 ± 0.13	0.34 ± 0.09	0.28 ± 0.13
CTF	0.27 ± 0.12	0.31 ± 0.08	0.26 ± 0.12
UPD-CTF	$\mathbf{0.41 \pm 0.11}$	$\mathbf{0.42 \pm 0.06}$	$\mathbf{0.4 \pm 0.08}$
54 months			
Perc. users	96.77%	3.23%	0%
Baseline	0.16 ± 0.09	0.30 ± 0.12	N/A
TF	0.09 ± 0.08	0.06 ± 0.05	N/A
SF	0.11 ± 0.06	0.07 ± 0.07	N/A
CTF	0.32 ± 0.12	0.34 ± 0.08	N/A
UPD-CTF	$\mathbf{0.43 \pm 0.09}$	$\mathbf{0.42 \pm 0.11}$	N/A

methods. This happens because our model considers continuous user-item interactions over time, by capturing the rate with which user preferences change, and also exploits user's side information. Since for each test time-period we have to recalculate the approximation of the tensor offline, we plan to extend the proposed model to incremental tensor factorization techniques. Another research direction is to address the cold-start problem when computing change rates for users without adequate number of interactions.

5. REFERENCES

[1] D. M. Dunlavy, T. G. Kolda, and E. Acar. Temporal link prediction using matrix and tensor factorizations. *TKDD*, 5(2):10, 2011.

[2] Y. Koren. Collaborative filtering with temporal dynamics. In *Proceedings of KDD*, pages 447–456, 2009.

[3] N. Lathia, S. Hailes, L. Capra, and X. Amatriain. Temporal diversity in recommender systems. In *Proceedings of the 33rd International ACM SIGIR Conference on Research and Development in Information Retrieval*, SIGIR '10, pages 210–217, 2010.

[4] A. Narita, K. Hayashi, R. Tomioka, and H. Kashima. Tensor factorization using auxiliary information. In *Proceedings of ECML/PKDD*, 2011.

[5] S. Spiegel, J. H. Clausen, S. Albayrak, and J. Kunegis. Link prediction on evolving data using tensor factorization. In *PAKDD Workshops*, pages 100–110, 2011.

[6] L. Xiang and Q. Yang. Time-dependent models in collaborative filtering based recommender system. In *Proceedings of the 2009 IEEE/WIC/ACM International Joint Conference on Web Intelligence and Intelligent Agent Technology - Volume 01*, pages 450–457, 2009.

[7] L. Xiong, X. Chen, T.-K. Huang, J. G. Schneider, and J. G. Carbonell. Temporal collaborative filtering with bayesian probabilistic tensor factorization. In *Proceedings of the SIAM International Conference on Data Mining*, pages 211–222, 2010.

[8] C. Zhang, K. Wang, H. Yu, J. Sun, and E.-P. Lim. Latent factor transition for dynamic collaborative filtering. In *Proceedings of the SIAM International Conference on Data Mining*, SDM '14, pages 452–460, 2014.

Multi-Criteria Journey Aware Housing Recommender System

Elizabeth M. Daly, Adi Botea, Akihiro Kishimoto, Radu Marinescu
Smart Cities Technology Centre
IBM Research - Ireland
{dalyeliz, adibotea, akihirok, marinrad}@ie.ibm.com

ABSTRACT

Recommender systems can be employed to assist users in complex decision making processes. This paper presents a multi-criteria housing recommender system which takes into account not just features of a home, such as rent, but also the transportation links to user specified locations. First, we describe an efficient multi-hop journey time calculator. Second, we introduce a mechanism to find the optimal solutions for multi-criteria evaluation, where a balanced trade-off between the target goals is found. Finally, we present a user study to demonstrate the potential of such a system.

Categories and Subject Descriptors

H.4 [**Information Systems Applications**]: Miscellaneous

General Terms

Algorithms, Decision-Support

Keywords

Recommender Systems; Multi-criteria; Public Transportation

1. INTRODUCTION

Recommender systems may assist users in the decision-making process and have been employed in a wide variety of domains from product recommendations [9], to music and movies, to social connections [2] and city events [7]. More recently, recommender systems have been applied to more complex tasks such as trip planning [8] and journey planning [10] in the area of tourism.

Recommender systems can be extremely valuable in domains which require a great deal of computation in order to evaluate candidate solutions and assist a user in decision making in the face of an abundance of options. Housing selection presents an interesting challenge, due to a combination of two reasons. First off, there can be many candidate houses to consider. Secondly, evaluating one house needs to consider multiple factors. Besides traditional factors, such as cost, number of bedrooms, and housing type, one needs to take into account where they travel to and from (i.e. their geographic requirements), when they travel (e.g. rush-hour or day time) and how frequently they intend to travel. These many dimensions may make it difficult for users to reason about, when evaluating a home in order to find the optimum location depending on their individual needs.

Journey planning and route recommendations have become increasingly popular in the tourism domain. Tumas and Ricci present a personalised route recommendation system using a combination of walking and public transportation to support tourists taking into account user preferences [10]. Garcia et. al. integrate public transportation and real-time scheduling and in order to design tourist trails [3]. Lathia and Capra leverage user travel patterns to recommend public transportation tickets to minimise the cost to the passenger [5].

The deployment of recommender systems for the purpose of home finding is less studied due to the increased complexity and the higher risk associated with such decisions [4]. However, recent work has begun to explore this application domain. Wang et. al. propose a collaborative filtering approach to recommending housing using a person's attributes such as gender, age and profession [11]. Yang et. al. developed a real-estate recommendation system employing case-based reasoning to match user wish lists to homes on the basis of location, attributes such as number of bedrooms and bathrooms and property price [12]. Our work focuses on evaluating the utility of providing users with transportation related information when selecting a home and presenting options that optimize their choice across multiple criteria.

2. HOUSING RECOMMENDER

Our JOURA (Journey-Aware) Housing Recommender System combines multi-modal journey planning with a multi-objective constraint optimization engine in order to recommend available homes. The map interface allows users to view available homes based on their geographic location. Users can input a number of target locations that they wish to be accessible through public transportation from their home. For instance, the work place can be one of the selected target locations. Once users have selected their target locations, the journey planner is queried to calculate the travel times from each target location to each home over the course of the day. For the purposes of this paper the chosen times of day are 8am, 12pm, 4pm and 8pm.

2.1 System Overview

The JOURA Housing Recommender System consists of three main components:

- **User Profile.** Users specify target locations that they are interested in travelling to on a regular basis and therefore would like to be considered when recommending a home.

RecSys'14, October 6–10, 2014, Foster City, Silicon Valley, CA, USA.

http://dx.doi.org/10.1145/2645710.2645764.

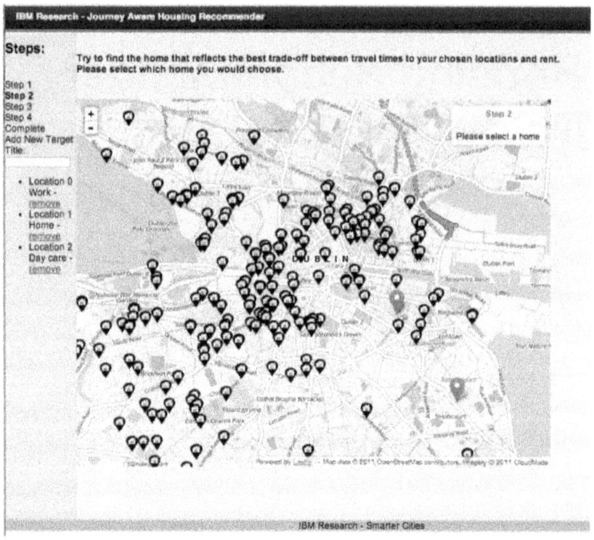

Figure 1: JOURA Recommender System

- **Journey Planner.** A journey planning system is used to compute travel times between relevant pairs of locations, such as a candidate house and a work place. The input required to the planning system includes knowledge about the public transport network, called a *network snapshot*, and a *journey plan request*. These are described in the next section.

- **Optimisation Component.** In order to recommend the optimum homes based on the criteria of travel times and rental price, a depth-first heuristic search algorithm is used to approximate the set of Pareto optimal solutions taking into account the multi-objective constraints.

2.2 Computing Journey Travel Times

Though services exist such as Google Maps to provide estimated travel times using public transportation, it is important to note these services typically provide point-to-point travel times, working for one origin–destination (OD) pair at a time. For the purposes of evaluating many OD pairs, to support a real-time service taking into account user preferences, we employ a customized journey computation solution. This generalisation allows to greatly improve the computational speed. For instance, it allows to compute multiple journey plans, from one target location to many candidate houses, with one Dijkstra search.

The public transport data is represented in the GTFS format. [1] It includes knowledge about stops, routes and scheduled vehicle trips that follow a timetable. Stop details include their location (as latitude and longitude coordinates), their name and a unique id. Each trip belongs to a given route and represents the actual trip of a vehicle (e.g., bus) through an ordered sequence of stops. For each stop along the trip, the arrival and the departure time are provided as part of the GTFS data.

A standard journey plan request specifies the origin of a journey, the destination, and the start or the arrival time. We generalize this to be able to specify multiple OD pairs. We take into account so-called quotas, which are maximum acceptable values for parameters such as the total walking time and the number of hops (legs) in the journey. Additional constraints specify what transport modes can be considered in a given journey.

[1] `https://developers.google.com/transit/gtfs/`

Journey plans are computed by searching in a state space whose states and transitions are defined as follows. A state $s = (l, t, q)$ is a vector containing a *relevant location* l, a time t when the traveller arrives at that location, and the quotas q available in that state. Relevant locations include all stops, all candidate houses, and the target locations indicated by a user, such as a work place or a school. As defined here, the set of relevant locations is much smaller than the set of all intersections in a city, which leads to a corresponding reduction in the computational effort needed to obtain journey plans. Transitions between states include walking actions and public-transport riding actions. Quotas q get updated after each application of an action. Every such an action updates the number of hops by 1. Walking actions update the walking time quota by an amount equivalent to the duration of the walking hop at hand.

The number of relevant locations on a map is reasonably small. For example, in Dublin, our GTFS data[2] contains 4,739 bus stops. However, the state space can be much larger, due to constraints such as bus schedules and quotas. For each bus stop, there can be many states in the search space, each having a different combination of quotas (e.g., max walking time and max number of hops allowed in a journey from that state to the destination). Such combinatorial blow-ups make table-based approaches including the Floyd-Warshall algorithm infeasible in terms of both time complexity and memory requirements.

In calculating travel times, our approach relies on the fact that there are many more houses than user specified target locations (hundreds of houses versus a few target locations). One invocation of the Dijkstra's algorithm computes optimal travel times from one user specified location to all houses, for one departure time. Given one user-specified target location, several runs of Dijkstra's algorithm are performed with different departure times. The travel times are averaged for each pair of a user specified location and a house. This process is repeated for every user-specified location.

Our implementation of Dijkstra's algorithm uses a priority queue to select the best state to examine next. It dequeues the best state s from the priority queue, generates successors of s, saves s in a hash table called the closed list, and enqueues theses successors in the priority queue. These procedures are repeated until the algorithm either reaches all houses or proves that it cannot reach some houses without exceeding the available quotas specified by the user.

2.3 Pareto Optimal Solution for Multi-Criteria Evaluation

In many real-world situations, a decision maker has more than one objective. In the case of housing, examples of such objectives include the rent and the travel times to a few user-specified target locations. Each of these criteria has a different scale and therefore mapping these objectives to a single utility scale can be problematic, since the decision maker may be unwilling or unable to provide precise trade-offs between objectives [1].

As a result, it is natural to consider multi-attribute or multi-criteria utility functions to cope with multiple and non-commensurate utility scales on which the decision maker's preferences are expressed.

Given p attributes, a *multi-attribute utility value* is characterized by a vector $\vec{u} = (u_1, \ldots, u_p) \in \mathbb{R}^p$, where u_i represents the utility with respect to attribute $i \in \{1, \ldots, p\}$. Given $\vec{u}, \vec{v} \in \mathbb{R}^p$, we say that $\vec{u}$ *Pareto dominates* $\vec{v}$ (denoted $\vec{u} \succcurlyeq \vec{v}$) iff $\forall i \in \{1, \ldots, p\}$ $u_i \geq v_i$. As usual, the symbol $\succ$ refers to the asymmetric part of $\succcurlyeq$, namely $\vec{u} \succ \vec{v}$ iif $\vec{u} \succcurlyeq \vec{v}$ and it is not the case that $\vec{v} \succcurlyeq \vec{u}$. Given a finite set of utility vectors $\mathcal{U} \subseteq \mathbb{R}^p$, we define

[2] Downloaded from `http://dublinked.ie`.

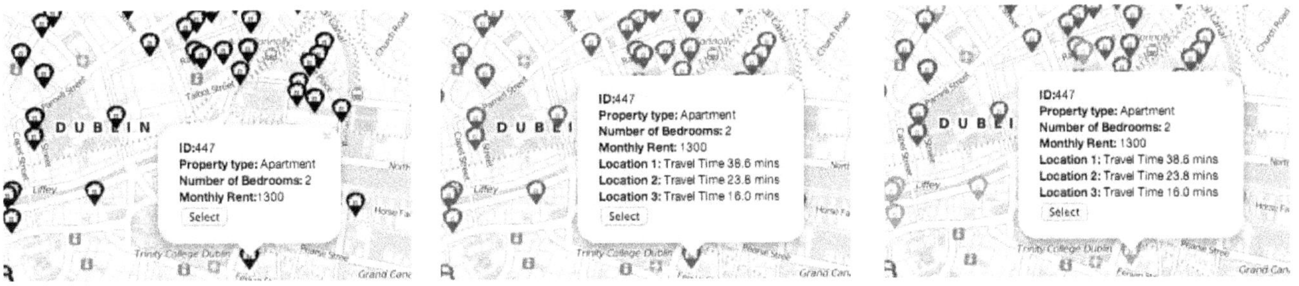

(a) Step 1. Rent information available.

(b) Step 2. Travel times added as relevant information.

(c) Step 3. Houses on the pareto-optimal frontier highlighted in blue.

Figure 2: Main steps of the user study

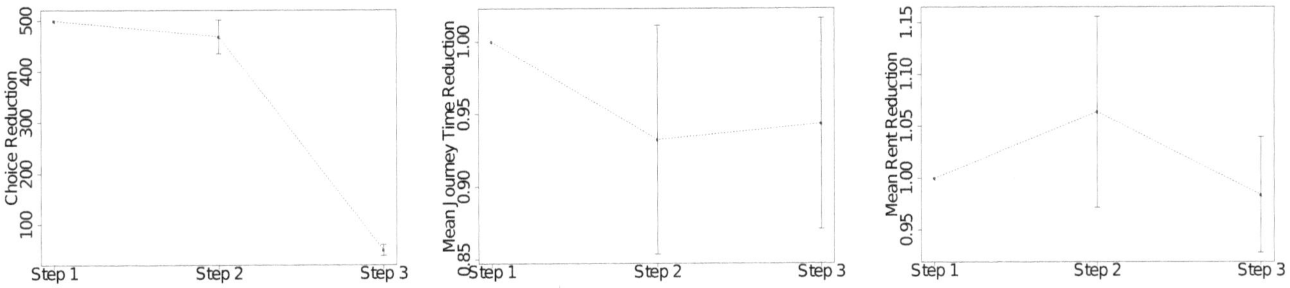

(a) Choice Reduction

(b) Normalized Journey Times Savings

(c) Normalized Rent Savings

Figure 3: User Choice Optimization at each step. Journey times and rent are normalized by the user selection at step 1

the *maximal set*, denoted by $\max_{\succcurlyeq}(\mathcal{U})$, to be the set consisting of the undominated elements in $\mathcal{U}$, i.e., $\max_{\succcurlyeq}(\mathcal{U}) = \{\vec{v} \in \mathcal{U} \mid \nexists \vec{v} \in \mathcal{U}, \vec{v} \succ \vec{u}\}$. Computing $\max_{\succcurlyeq}(\mathcal{U})$ is quadratic in the size of $\mathcal{U}$.

In general, the Pareto ordering may lead to relatively large maximal sets and yet be useful to make an informed decision. Therefore, the decision maker may be happy to allow some additional trade-offs between attributes. Based on previous work by Marinescu et al. [6], we consider a set Θ of vector pairs of the form $(\vec{u}, \vec{v})$, where $\vec{u}, \vec{v} \in \mathbb{R}^p$ and $\vec{u} \succcurlyeq \vec{v}$. Such trade-offs may be elicited using some structured method, or in a more *ad hoc* way. The input preferences Θ (if consistent) give rise to a relation $\succcurlyeq_\Theta$ which may induce a much stronger ordering than the weak Pareto ordering. However, computing the maximal set with respect to $\succcurlyeq_\Theta$ is more involved and requires solving a linear program representing Θ [6].

In JOURA, each candidate housing location is associated with a four-attribute value representing the rent of that house and the average travel times from the house to each of the three target locations. The solution recommended by the system is the set of undominated housing locations. If additional trade-offs are elicited (e.g., one prefers to travel 15 more minutes to the first target location to decrease the rent by 100 euros) then the subset of candidate houses can be reduced even further, to the set of optimal (i.e., non-dominated) housing locations to account for the trade-offs.

3. EVALUATION - USER STUDY

To test the effectiveness of the JOURA system we created a web application to allow users to view a selection of available homes throughout Dublin. The purpose of this study was to better understand the effect of a) showing travel times to users and b) providing a recommended subset of the homes that reflect an optimal trade-off across multiple criteria. For the purpose of this study we limited our criteria to rent and travel times, all homes were displayed as 2 bedroom apartments to control for other preferences. When the journey times are calculated, the maximum walking time is set to 15 minutes, and the maximum number of hops is set to 5. The Dublin public transportation data that we used contains 4,739 bus stops and 120 bus routes. Each route is served by multiple trips, at different times of the day, for a total of 16,777 trips per day.

We recruited 20 participants, all working and living in Dublin. Users were asked to select three target locations of interest and in real time the journey times between each candidate home and the targets were computed. The users were then guided through a three step process where they could select from 500 homes located in various parts of the city. Each step provided more information to the users, with the benefits of a more informed decision and, in the case of the third step, a significantly simpler decision process for the user, as a result of filtering away dominated candidate houses. Clicking on a home allows the user to see the details of that home available at a given step (e.g., rent at Step 1).

- **Step 1:** In order to understand where a user would select a house based purely on their own knowledge of the city we first ask users to select a home they felt provided the best trade-off between rent and accessibility to their chosen locations. A user was given only basic information about the home and the rent, as shown in Figure 2 a). The user could select a home where the details remain displayed to the right of the map, in order to support the user comparing different options before making their final selection.

- **Step 2:** Users are provided with additional information where the journey times to each of their chosen locations is shown to the user, as seen in Figure 2 b).
- **Step 3:** Finally, as shown in Figure 2 c), non-dominated homes, which best reflect a trade-off between journey times and rent, are highlighted in blue. As all homes remain visible, users were still given the option of choosing a non-optimal home if desired.

3.1 Choice Reduction

Navigating through the complete set of available homes is a time consuming task for the user, particularly when processing several criteria at once. Algorithmically however, it is very efficient to compute homes that reflect a trade-off and therefore narrowing down the selection process for the user.

Figure 3 a) shows the reduction in the number of homes a user needs to evaluate at each step in the process. There is a small reduction from step 1 to step 2 where some homes are inaccessible through public transportation links due to the constraints of the maximum walking time and maximum number of hops. The reduction in step 3 includes only the recommended options, even though all options were available to the user. At the final stage an average of 50 homes were included in the recommended subset. This 10-fold reduction allows the users to focus on a much smaller set of candidate homes, under the guarantee that each house filtered out is dominated on all four criteria by at least one house in the preserved subset.

3.2 Effectiveness of Recommendations

Overall, 90% of the participants had chosen a house that was included in the recommended subset by the end of the experiment. However, 45% of the users did not change their selection between step 1 and step 3. When examining whether their original selection was included in the recommended subset, in 77.77% of the instances the house was included in the final recommendations meaning the user had already selected a home that represented a valid trade-off between their goals of travel times and rent.

3.3 Journey Times Savings

Figure 3 b) shows the normalized travel time reduction for users as they progress through the user study. The confidence intervals are quite large, this is a result of 45% of the users selecting the same home for each step, resulting in zero savings. For the remaining users however we do see a reduction in overall travel time between step 1 and step 2. Interestingly there is a slight increase in overall travel time between step 2 and step 3 as users are shown the recommended options. This is due to a reduction in rent at the final step where the users make a compromise of a slight increase in travel time for a lower rent.

3.4 Rent Savings

Figure 3 c) shows the normalized rent reductions for users at each step. As can be seen at step 2, when users are shown information about journey times they optimize for travel times and have trouble optimizing their selection over multiple different criteria. At step 3 however, we see that when they are presented with the optimal recommendations, the users select a better trade-off across the goals of reduced rent and journey times.

4. CONCLUSION

In real life, travel times to relevant destinations, such as a workplace, play an important role in the overall evaluation of a house to purchase or rent. For instance, houses located in the proximity of main transportation routes, such as a metro line, might be seen as more suitable to one's mobility needs. In this work we have focused on incorporating public transportation links and user journey requirements into a housing recommender system.

Clearly, selecting a home is affected by more factors besides the set considered in this work (e.g., rent and travel times to a few selected locations). In future work, we plan to integrate additional environmental factors, such as security, amenities, and convenience facilities.

5. REFERENCES

[1] T. Brink, R. Keeney, and H. Raiffa. Decisions with multiple objectives, preferences and value tradeoffs. *Behavioral Science*, 39(2):169–170, 1994.

[2] J. Chen, W. Geyer, C. Dugan, M. Muller, and I. Guy. Make new friends, but keep the old: Recommending people on social networking sites. In *Proceedings of the SIGCHI Conference on Human Factors in Computing Systems*, CHI '09, pages 201–210, New York, NY, USA, 2009. ACM.

[3] A. Garcia, P. Vansteenwegen, O. Arbelaitz, W. Souffriau, and M. T. Linaza. Integrating public transportation in personalised electronic tourist guides. *Computers & Operations Research*, 40(3):758–774, 2013.

[4] J. A. Konstan and J. Riedl. Recommender systems: from algorithms to user experience. *User Modeling and User-Adapted Interaction*, 22(1-2):101–123, 2012.

[5] N. Lathia and L. Capra. Mining mobility data to minimise travellers' spending on public transport. In *Proceedings of the 17th ACM SIGKDD international conference on Knowledge discovery and data mining*, pages 1181–1189. ACM, 2011.

[6] R. Marinescu, A. Razak, and N. Wilson. Multi-objective influence diagrams. In *Proceedings of the Twenty-Eighth Conference Annual Conference on Uncertainty in Artificial Intelligence (UAI-12)*, pages 574–583, Corvallis, Oregon, 2012. AUAI Press.

[7] D. Quercia, N. Lathia, F. Calabrese, G. Di Lorenzo, and J. Crowcroft. Recommending social events from mobile phone location data. In *Data Mining (ICDM), 2010 IEEE 10th International Conference on*, pages 971–976, 2010.

[8] F. Ricci and F. del Missier. Designing personalized user experiences in ecommerce. chapter Supporting Travel Decision Making Through Personalized Recommendation, pages 231–251. Kluwer Academic Publishers, Norwell, MA, USA, 2004.

[9] J. B. Schafer, J. A. Konstan, and J. Riedl. E-commerce recommendation applications. In *Applications of Data Mining to Electronic Commerce*, pages 115–153. Springer US, 2001.

[10] G. Tumas and F. Ricci. Personalized mobile city transport advisory system. In *ENTER*, pages 173–183. Springer, 2009.

[11] L. Wang, X. Hu, J. Wei, and X. Cui. A collaborative filtering based personalized top-k recommender system for housing. In *Proceedings of the 2012 International Conference of Modern Computer Science and Applications*, pages 461–466. Springer, 2013.

[12] X. Yuan, J.-H. Lee, S.-J. Kim, and Y.-H. Kim. Toward a user-oriented recommendation system for real estate websites. *Information Systems*, 38(2):231 – 243, 2013.

PERSPeCT: Collaborative Filtering for Tailored Health Communications

Roy J. Adams
School of Computer Science
UMass Amherst
rjadams@cs.umass.edu

Rajani S. Sadasivam
Department of Quantitative Health Sciences
UMass Medical School

Kavitha Balakrishnan
Department of Quantitative Health Sciences
UMass Medical School

Rebecca L. Kinney
Department of Quantitative Health Sciences
UMass Medical School

Thomas K. Houston
eHealth QUERI
Bedford VA Medical Center
UMass Medical School

Benjamin M. Marlin
School of Computer Science
UMass Amherst

ABSTRACT

The goal of computer tailored health communications (CTHC) is to elicit healthy behavior changes by sending motivational messages personalized to individual patients. One prominent weakness of many existing CTHC systems is that they are based on expert-written rules and thus have no ability to learn from their users over time. One solution to this problem is to develop CTHC systems based on the principles of collaborative filtering, but this approach has not been widely studied. In this paper, we present a case study evaluating nine rating prediction methods for use in the *Patient Experience Recommender System for Persuasive Communication Tailoring*, a system developed for use in a clinical trial of CTHC-based smoking cessation support interventions.

Categories and Subject Descriptors

H.3.3 [**INFORMATION STORAGE AND RETRIEVAL**]: Information Search and Retrieval

Keywords

Recommender systems; tailored health communications

1. INTRODUCTION

Computer tailored health communications (CTHC) systems aim to elicit healthy behavior changes by sending motivational messages personalized to individual patients. Current CTHC systems start by creating a pool of messages and a fixed set of theory-driven, expert-written rules that relate the characteristics of messages to the characteristics of the patients [4]. When a new patient is enrolled in the system, a baseline patient profile is collected that includes demographic information and assessments of the relevant tailoring characteristics. Messages are then selected for the patient on the basis of the patient's characteristics and the expert-derived message selection rules.

CTHC systems have been deployed to address a range of high-profile health problems including supporting smoking cessation [12]. One prominent weakness of many existing CTHC systems is that they do not solicit feedback from their users and thus have no ability to learn over time. The fixed rules these systems are based on may fail to account for socio-cultural concepts that have intrinsic importance to the targeted population, thus limiting their success [1].

One solution to this problem is to develop CTHC systems based on the principles of collaborative filtering. In electronic commerce settings, collaborative filtering recommender systems have been successfully used to derive personalized recommendations for items like books or movies based on implicit or explicit feedback about the items collected from an online community of users. The promise of collaborative filtering-based recommendation in the CTHC setting derives from its ability to learn associations between types of patients and types of messages directly from data, allowing the CTHC system to adapt to individual users over time [9].

Collaborative filtering in the CTHC setting presents a number of challenges. Our prior work has addressed the problem of defining semantics for explicit feedback ratings in the CTHC setting as a precursor to developing the *Patient Experience Recommender System for Persuasive Communication Tailoring* (PERSPeCT) [5]. The PERSPeCT system will use collaborative filtering-based rating prediction to drive the personalized selection of smoking cessation support messages that are currently in use in a deployed expert system operated through our online smoking cessation support portal, decide2quit.org.

The primary challenge faced by PERSPeCT is the need to construct a system with maximal accuracy in the small data regime. In this case study, we present an empirical evaluation of nine classical and state of the art rating prediction methods applied to the novel problem of predicting smoking cessation support message ratings. We begin by reviewing the problem of rating semantics in the CTHC setting. We then present the details of a new data set collected

RecSys'14, October 6–10, 2014, Foster City, Silicon Valley, CA, USA.

ACM 978-1-4503-2668-1/14/10
http://dx.doi.org/10.1145/2645710.2645768.

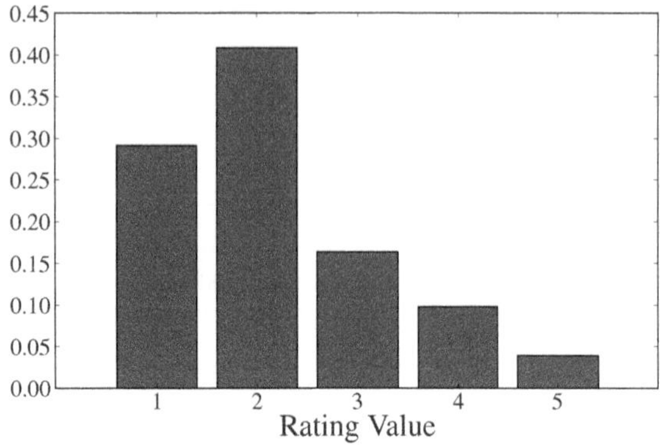

Figure 1: The marginal distribution over ratings.

to bootstrap collaborative filtering model learning and selection for PERSPeCT and provide a brief overview of the models evaluated in our study. Finally, we describe our results, which underscore the importance of Bayesian methods in small data regimes and surprisingly show that the inclusion of patient and message features has no marginal benefit in addition to the available rating information.

2. STUDY DESIGNS & DATA COLLECTION

To date, two studies have been performed to guide the design of PERSPeCT. The first study was designed to inform the choice of rating semantics, which was a significant open question resulting from the differing goals of e-commerce recommender systems (recommending items that users will like) and CTHC systems (selecting messages to promote healthy behavior changes for individual patients).

To address this issue, four candidate factors including how much the message influenced the user not to smoke, how much the message effected the subject emotionally, how relevant the message was to the subject, and how much the user liked the message were identified. To assess the differences between these factors, we collected a novel multi-factor rating data set consisting of ratings for all four message factors collected from 100 study participants. Each participant provided ratings on a 5-point scale for each of five unique messages drawn randomly from a 50 message subset of all messages available on decide2quit.org. The results showed that the ratings for each of the four factors were highly correlated, rendering the collection of all four ratings for each message unnecessary. These results are presented in detail in our prior work [5], which also includes ratings analysis and a small-scale rating prediction feasibility study.

Following the completion of the rating semantics study, a second study was performed to collect a larger rating data set to bootstrap the learning and evaluation of collaborative filtering models for PERSPeCT. We collected ratings of both influence and relevance from a total of 846 users with respect to all 261 actively used messages from decide2quit.org. Each study participant was asked to rate 20 messages. This resulted in a total of 16920 ratings, yielding a data density of 7.7%. Subjects also supplied demographic data and values for a variety of tailoring variables related to smoking behavior including number of cigarettes smoked per day and readiness to quit. Study subjects were recruited through a mix of local and online sources and received a $50 incentive.

The marginal distribution of influence ratings for this data set is shown in Figure 1. In the remainder of this paper, we present the first empirical analysis of influence rating prediction using the data collected in this second study.

3. METHODS AND MODELS

Baselines: Our evaluation includes a number of common baselines including predicting the global mean rating (Global Mean) and the item mean rating (Item Mean). The item mean model includes smoothing hyperparameters that pull the means toward the global mean. We also include a simple additive model that learns an optimal additive combination of ℓ_2 regularized user and item bias terms.

KNN: User and item-based K-Nearest Neighbors are classical models in collaborative filtering. A user-based KNN model works by predicting user u's rating for item i as a weighted sum of other users' ratings of i, where the weights are a similarity measure. Following [2], we used Pearson Correlation between ratings on co-rated items, adjusted to account for the number of co-rated items. KNN models have two hyperparameters: the neighborhood size, K, and the weight for pairs with few shared ratings.

PMF: Probabilistic Matrix Factorization represents each user and item as a K-dimensional vector with a multivariate normal prior. User u's rating for item i is then a normal random variable with mean equal to the inner product of u's and i's factors. The user and item factors can be learned using standard numerical optimization techniques [8]. Additionally, global, user, and item biases can be added to the model with little additional complexity. The hyperparameters in PMF include the ℓ_2 regularization parameters for the user/item biases and factor matrices, as well as the dimensionality of the model K.

BPMF: Bayesian Probabilistic Matrix Factorization extends PMF by adding Normal-Wishart hyper-priors to the mean and covariance matrices of the user and item factors and replaces learning the primary parameters with optimization by full Bayesian inference using Gibbs sampling [7].The hyperparameters in BPMF include the parameters for the Normal-Wishart hyper-priors, the rating noise variance, and the dimensionality of the factors.

PMF-F/BPMF-F: A simple way to incorporate user and item side-information into both of the previous models is to add linear regression terms to the models. In PMF, the feature weights can be ℓ_2 regularized and estimated along with all of the other parameters. In BPMF, the individual feature weights are given normal priors with zero mean and tunable variance and added to the Gibbs sampling routine.

CMF: Collective Matrix Factorization jointly factorizes the rating matrix and a related feature matrix into a set of user, item, and feature factors [10]. In our case, the item factors are shared between the two factorizations and allow information to flow between the feature and ratings matrices. A hyperparameter, α, balances the importance of the reconstruction error on the ratings against the reconstruction error on the features. Parameters in this model are learned via numerical optimization as in PMF. The hyperparameters in CMF are the same as those in PMF plus α and an ℓ_2 regularization parameter for the feature factors.

BCMF: Bayesian Collective Matrix Factorization extends CMF in the same way that BPMF extends PMF, with Normal-Wishart hyper-priors on the user, item, and feature hyperparameters [11]. The same distributions as in BPMF are involved, so we used a similar Gibbs sampler to run inference in this model. We used the same Normal-Wishart parameters as in BPMF and the the only additional hyperparameter is a noise variance parameter for the features.

HFT: In addition to the user demographics and theory based message codings, the text of the messages themselves can be used as features. Similar to CMF, the recently introduced Hidden Factors as Topics model incorporates text by jointly fitting a PMF model to the ratings data and a latent Dirichlet allocation (LDA) model to the message text where a softmax transformation of the item factor is used as the distribution over topics [6]. The model is trained by alternating numerical optimization of the user/item factors and topic specific distributions over words and sampling the topic assignments for individual words. The only additional hyperparameter is similar to α in CMF and balances the importance of the LDA portion of the model.

4. PROTOCOLS AND METRICS

The fielded PERSPeCT system will select messages for users based on their predicted influence ratings. One previously unseen message will be selected and sent per day for each user. The system will initially be evaluated on its ability to select messages that are rated higher on average than messages selected by an existing expert system. These design factors are reflected in our evaluation methodology as described below. All methods were implemented by the authors using Python with the exception of HFT, for which we use the originally published code [6].

Empirical Protocol: We use a strong-generalization protocol that evaluates the ability of the system to generalize to non-training users, which better matches our application. This involves completely separating test users from train users, learning a model using all of the train users' ratings, freezing all non-user-specific parameters, and finally training the user-specific parameters (e.g. user factors and biases in PMF) on a subset of each test user's observed ratings. To implement this protocol, we first divided the users randomly into five folds and then generated three random train and validation sets for each test fold. We further divided each test user's ratings into five folds. To evaluate each method's performance given varying levels of information about a test user, we evaluated all methods with 5, 10 and 16 of each test user's ratings available for inference and learning of user-specific parameters. Each test user has a constant set of 4 test ratings per test fold. The validation sets were used to set the hyper-parameters of each method (e.g. K in KNN). Exhaustive grid search was used and the hyper-parameter ranges were iteratively extended to ensure that no selected hyperparameter values occurred at the endpoints of the search intervals.

Performance Metrics: In evaluating rating prediction methods, we considered a range of standard performance metrics including root mean squared error (RMSE), Kendal's Tau-b (KTAU-b), and normalized discounted cumulative gain (NDCG) to analyze rating prediction and ranking performance. We also evaluate some less common metrics including the fraction of times a test item with the maximal rating is ranked first (Hit Rate), the absolute difference between the maximum test item rating and the rating of the top ranked test item (Top Loss), and the average rating of the top-ranked test items (Avg. Top). We report averages for these metrics over all test folds.

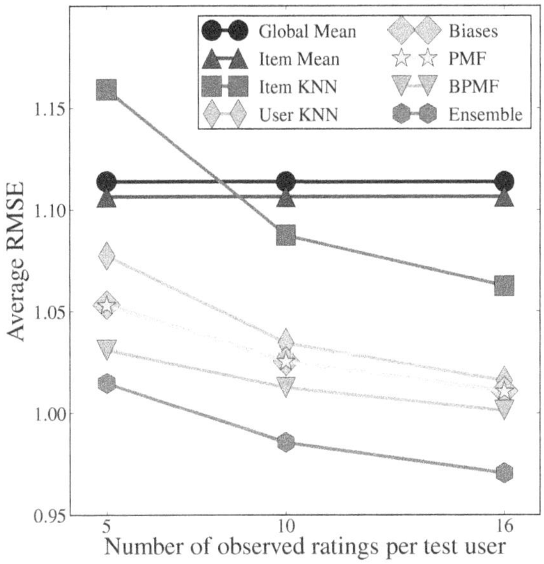

Figure 2: Average RMSEs for all models without features using 5, 10, and 16 training examples.

5. EXPERIMENTS AND RESULTS

In this section, we present an empirical evaluation of the methods described in the previous section applied to the prediction of the influence ratings collected in our second PERSPeCT study.

Pure Methods: The average test performance for all collaborative filtering models based on 10 test user observations is reported in Table 1 along with standard errors. In terms of RMSE, the best performing pure (Type P) collaborative filtering method is BPMF, with an RMSE of 1.001. The absolute performance gap between BPMF and the other base methods is small, ranging between 1 and 10 percent improvement. However, the RMSE gap between BPMF and all the other pure methods is statistically significant at the $p = 0.01$ level as determined by a paired t-test with Bonferroni correction. Figure 2 shows the performance of each of the pure collaborative filtering methods across 5, 10 and 16 observed ratings per test user. We can see that the performance gap is larger with fewer observed ratings, which highlights the superiority of Bayesian models in small data settings. Further investigation showed that BPMF was able to effectively use more factors than PMF. Across all runs, BPMF selected between 4 and 7 factors, while PMF selected only 1 or 2 factors. This highlights the ability of Bayesian methods to learn richer models while avoiding over fitting problems that effect optimization-based approaches in small data settings. A surprising finding is that many methods, including PMF, perform worse or no better than the Biases baseline approach in terms of RMSE. This indicates the difficulty of extracting useful structure in the small data setting. In general, the performance gap is much smaller with respect to the ranking metrics; however, BPMF is always either the best model or statistically indistinguishable from the best model.

Ensemble Methods: The Netflix competition demonstrated the success of ensemble methods which aggregate the predictions of a number of distinct models [3]. To evaluate ensemble methods in our context, we considered combing the results of the best neighborhood-based method (user

Model	Type	RMSE	KTAU-b	NDCG	Hit Rate	Avg. Top	Top Loss
Global Mean	P	1.114 ± 0.019	0.000 ± 0.000	0.876 ± 0.002	0.000 ± 0.000	2.302 ± 0.032	0.851 ± 0.009
Item Mean	P	1.106 ± 0.019	0.105 ± 0.013	0.894 ± 0.004	0.552 ± 0.012	2.158 ± 0.042	0.706 ± 0.031
Biases	P	1.026 ± 0.014	0.113 ± 0.013	0.895 ± 0.004	0.561 ± 0.014	2.142 ± 0.050	0.690 ± 0.031
Item KNN	P	1.088 ± 0.015	0.078 ± 0.008	0.889 ± 0.003	0.525 ± 0.011	2.201 ± 0.027	0.749 ± 0.020
User KNN	P	1.035 ± 0.012	0.000 ± 0.000	0.876 ± 0.002	0.000 ± 0.000	2.302 ± 0.032	0.851 ± 0.009
PMF	P	1.025 ± 0.014	0.112 ± 0.013	0.895 ± 0.004	0.561 ± 0.014	2.141 ± 0.048	0.689 ± 0.031
BPMF	P	1.013 ± 0.013	0.112 ± 0.014	0.895 ± 0.004	0.560 ± 0.014	2.144 ± 0.047	0.692 ± 0.033
PMF-F	H	1.022 ± 0.013	0.112 ± 0.013	0.895 ± 0.004	0.561 ± 0.013	2.144 ± 0.050	0.692 ± 0.032
BPMF-F	H	1.013 ± 0.013	0.113 ± 0.013	0.896 ± 0.004	0.564 ± 0.013	2.134 ± 0.043	0.682 ± 0.027
CMF	H	1.035 ± 0.012	0.105 ± 0.013	0.894 ± 0.004	0.557 ± 0.012	2.146 ± 0.047	0.694 ± 0.028
BCMF	H	1.012 ± 0.013	0.108 ± 0.011	0.894 ± 0.003	0.559 ± 0.009	2.152 ± 0.039	0.701 ± 0.026
HFT	H	1.031 ± 0.012	0.110 ± 0.014	0.895 ± 0.004	0.559 ± 0.014	2.140 ± 0.051	0.688 ± 0.032

Table 1: Predictive performance for pure (P) and hybrid (H) models with 10 observed ratings per test user.

KNN) and the best matrix factorization method (BPMF) using an unweighted average of their predictions. The average RMSE at each training data size is shown in Figure 2. With 10 test user observations, the ensemble method has an average RMSE of 0.986, approximately 3% better than the best pure method, BPMF. This confirms the utility of ensemble methods in the small data regime.

Hybrid Methods: The models indicated as hybrid (Type H) in Table 1 include features in various ways. The best performing of these models in terms of RMSE is BCMF, however, its performance is statistically indistinguishable from BPMF. In fact, PMF with linear features, CMF, BPMF with linear features, and BCMF are all very close in performance to their counterparts that do not include features. Finally, the addition of text features through HFT also results in performance that is slightly worse than PMF, the corresponding base model. Interestingly, these results indicate that the demographic and behavioral theory-based features, which are currently the basis for assigning messages to users in an existing expert system, do not add any information over ratings alone within the state-of-the-art modeling frameworks we have investigated. To further investigate this finding, we evaluated the mutual information between the rating values and each of the patient and message features. The results showed a maximum absolute mutual information value of 0.027 for patient features and 0.002 for message features. These values are remarkably low and explain why the features do not result in a significant boost in performance.

6. CONCLUSIONS

In this paper we have described PERSPeCT, a novel collaborative filtering-based computer tailored health communications (CTHC) system targeted at the smoking cessation support domain. Our primary contribution is an evaluation of a wide range of classic and state-of-the art collaborative filtering methods including pure methods, ensemble methods, and hybrid methods in a new and important small-data domain. Due to the success of Bayesian Probabilistic Matrix Factorization (BPMF) as the best single model identified in our evaluation, a pure BPMF-based instance of PERSPeCT is currently being deployed and evaluated relative to our existing expert system through a randomized control trial to determine its effectiveness in an online message selection context. The online evaluation of ensemble methods is reserved for future work and future versions of PERSPeCT will be evaluated based on patient outcomes.

Acknowledgments

This work is supported by the Patient Centered Outcomes Research Institute (1IP2P1000582) and the University of Massachusetts Center for Clinical and Translational Sciences (UL1TR000161). Dr Sadasivam is also funded by a National Cancer Institute Career Development Award (K07CA172677).

7. REFERENCES

[1] K. Ashing-Giwa. Health behavior change models and their socio-cultural relevance for breast cancer screening in african american women. *Women Health*, 28(4):53–71, 1999.

[2] J. L. Herlocker, J. A. Konstan, A. Borchers, and J. Riedl. An algorithmic framework for performing collaborative filtering, 1999.

[3] M. Jahrer, A. Töscher, and R. Legenstein. Combining predictions for accurate recommender systems. In *Proceedings of the 16th ACM SIGKDD*, pages 693–702. ACM, 2010.

[4] M. Kreuter. *Tailoring health messages : customizing communication with computer technology.* LEA's communication series. L. Erlbaum, Mahwah, N.J., 2000.

[5] B. Marlin, R. Adams, R. Sadasivam, and T. Houston. Towards collaborative filtering recommender systems for tailored health communications. In *Proceedings of the AMIA 2013 Annual Symposium*, pages 1600–1607, 2013.

[6] J. McAuley and J. Leskovec. Hidden factors and hidden topics: understanding rating dimensions with review text. In *Proceedings of the 7th ACM conference on Recommender systems*, pages 165–172. ACM, 2013.

[7] R. Salakhutdinov and A. Mnih. Bayesian probabilistic matrix factorization using markov chain monte carlo. pages 880–887. ACM, 2008.

[8] R. Salakhutdinov and A. Mnih. Probabilistic matrix factorization. *Advances in neural information processing systems*, 20:1257–1264, 2008.

[9] T. Segaran. *Programming collective intelligence : building smart web 2.0 applications.* O'Reilly, Beijing ; Sebastapol CA, 1st edition, 2007.

[10] A. P. Singh and G. J. Gordon. Relational learning via collective matrix factorization. In *Proceedings of the 14th ACM SIGKDD*, pages 650–658. ACM, 2008.

[11] A. P. Singh and G. J. Gordon. A bayesian matrix factorization model for relational data. In *Proceedings of the 26th Conference on Uncertainty in Artificial Intelligence*, 2010.

[12] V. J. Strecher, J. B. McClure, G. L. Alexander, B. Chakraborty, V. N. Nair, J. M. Konkel, S. M. Greene, L. M. Collins, C. C. Carlier, C. J. Wiese, R. J. Little, C. S. Pomerleau, and O. F. Pomerleau. Web-based smoking-cessation programs: results of a randomized trial. *Am J Prev Med*, 34(5):373–81, 2008.

Preference Elicitation for Narrowing the Recommended List for Groups

Lihi Naamani-Dery[1,3], Meir Kalech[2], Lior Rokach[2,3], Bracha Shapira[2,3]

[1]Department of Industrial Engineering and Management at Ariel University, [2]Department of Information Systems Engineering at Ben-Gurion University, [3]Telekom Innovation labs at Ben-Gurion University

{ln,kalech,liorrk,bshapira}@bgu.ac.il

ABSTRACT

A group may appreciate recommendations on items that fit their joint preferences. When the members' actual preferences are unknown, a recommendation can be made with the aid of collaborative filtering methods. We offer to narrow down the recommended list of items by eliciting the users' actual preferences. Our final goal is to output top-k preferred items to the group out of the top-N recommendations provided by the recommender system ($k < N$), where one of the items is a *necessary* winner. We propose an iterative preference elicitation method, where users are required to provide item ratings per request. We suggest a heuristic that attempts to minimize the preference elicitation effort under two aggregation strategies. We evaluate our methods on real-world Netflix data as well as on simulated data which allows us to study different cases. We show that preference elicitation effort can be cut in up to 90% while preserving the most preferred items in the narrowed list.

Categories and Subject Descriptors

H.3.3 1 [**Information Storage and Retrieval**]: Information Search and Retrieval

General Terms

Algorithms, Human Factors, Experimentation

Keywords

Preference Elicitation, Group Recommender Systems

1. INTRODUCTION

Group recommendation may be useful in various common daily scenarios. For example, a group who wishes to dine together may appreciate recommendations on relevant restaurants that fit their joint preferences [11]. Given the list of recommended restaurants, the group's members often interact among themselves to narrow down the possible options and choose a restaurant [10]. When the members' actual preferences regarding the recommended items are known, some aggregation strategy can be used to compute the most preferred restaurant out of the list of recommended items. However, often full preferences are not readily available, mainly because it can be tiresome or difficult for users to determine all of their preferences in advance. Consider for example a setting of 30 optional dinner locations for a group. The group members might be reluctant to provide input on each of the restaurants.

RecSys'14, October 6–10, 2014, Foster City, Silicon Valley, CA, USA.

http://dx.doi.org/10.1145/2645710.2645760

The problem we investigate in this paper is how to narrow down the list of items recommended by the system by eliciting the users' actual preferences. Since preference elicitation requires time and effort, the goal is to stop elicitation as soon as possible. We borrow from the closely related domain of social choice [2], where preference elicitation has been examined under different voting protocols. In the worst case for most voting protocols all the preferences are needed in order to determine a winner [3]. However, in practice it has been shown that the required information for determining a winner can be cut in more than 50% [6, 8, 10]. Given partial preferences, it is possible to define the set of *necessary* winners, i.e., items which must necessarily win given a certain aggregation strategy, as well as the set of possible winners, i.e., items which can still possibly win [7]. These definitions enable the elicitor to determine whether enough information about the users' preferences is available, and iteratively request for more user ratings. Once a necessary item is identified, it is recommended to the group. An additional benefit of this process is that the output is not a predicted item, but rather an item that *certainly* fits the group's joint preferences.

Although outputting a definite winner is the most accurate result, there are advantages in providing top-k items (where one of them is a necessary winner) out of the top-N recommendations list ($k < N$). Less elicitation effort is required for outputting top-k items than for outputting one necessary winner (i.e., $k = 1$). Thus issues such as elicitation costs are reduced. Also, users might prefer to receive a few options rather than just one. Thus, if a certain alternative is unavailable, the group can quickly switch to another alternative without applying an additional preference elicitation process. For example, if the system recommends only a fish restaurant as the winner item, but one of the group members dislikes fish, the group might prefer to switch to another alternative recommended by the system rather than to perform another elicitation round.

Of course, the top-k winners list depends on the applied aggregation strategy. The aggregation strategy should be a fair one. In his famous work, Arrow shows that there is no perfect aggregation system [1]. One of the major differences between aggregation strategies is the social environment in which they are used. The emphasis can be either on mindfulness toward the individual user or on mindfulness toward the majority of the group [5]. Two state-of-the-art aggregation strategies that hold this tension in between are the *Majority Based Strategy* and the *Least Misery Strategy*. In the *Majority Based Strategy* the users' ratings of the different items are aggregated and the item with the highest total value is the winner. In the *Least Misery Strategy* the chosen item cannot be the least preferred by any of the users [9]. Preferences elicitation methods usually assume that the Majority based strategy is employed [6, 8, 10]. We show that the aggregation strategy affects the effort required in the preference elicitation and evaluate two state-of-the-art aggregation strategies.

Our final goal is to output top-k preferred items to the group out of the top-N recommendations provided by the recommender system (k<N), where one of the items is a *necessary* winner. We propose an iterative preference elicitation method, where users are required to provide item ratings per request. We suggest a heuristic that attempts to minimize the preference elicitation effort under two aggregation strategies, while still outputting a necessary winner. We evaluate our methods on real-world Netflix data as well as on simulated data which allows us to study different cases. We show that the preference elicitation effort can be cut in up to 90% in some cases.

We focus on the Range voting protocol which requires users to submit ratings to items. Applications that ask for ratings are quite common, for example Amazon and Netflix[1]. We assume that users' preferences are unknown in advance, but can be acquired during the process, i.e., if a user is asked for her preference on an item she is able to submit it. We also assume a user submits her true preferences and thus in this paper we do not consider manipulation. Lastly, we assume an approximate distribution of each user's preferences for each item exists, as in [10].

2. RELATED WORK

Both [9] and [13] study how different strategies affect group members. However, the aggregation strategies have not been studied in the context of *preference elicitation*. Practical preference elicitation is gaining interest recently. In [6] it is assumed that each user holds a predefined decreasing order of the preferences. In an iterative process, the users are requested to submit their highest preferences; the request is for the rating of one item from all the users. However, requiring the users to predefine their preferences can be inconvenient to the users. In [10] two practical heuristics that attempt to minimize preference elicitation effort are presented for the Range voting protocol. However both output one definite item and not top-k items. In [8] a practical elicitation process is proposed for the Borda voting protocol. The output is multiple winners. However the authors did not consider the Range protocol. In all of the above, the authors considered only the majority based aggregation strategy. The algorithm proposed in [8] lacks details and the authors did not provide us with explanations so we cannot expand it to the Least Misery strategy or to the Range voting protocol. In this paper we expand the preference elicitation algorithm for the Range voting protocol suggested in [10]. To the best of our knowledge the issue of preference elicitation and returning one or more items under the Least Misery strategy has not been investigated before.

3. MODEL DESCRIPTION

Let us define a set of users (voters) as $V = \{v_1, v_2, \ldots, v_m\}$ and a set of candidate items as $C = \{c_1, c_2, \ldots, c_n\}$. When queried, the users assign ratings to the items from a discrete domain of values $D = \{d_{min}, \ldots, d_{max}\}$ where d_{min} and d_{max} are the lowest and highest values, respectively. User v_i's preferences are represented by the rating function $value: VxC \rightarrow D$. For abbreviation we denote q_j^i as a single preference of v_i for a single item c_j. The user-item rating q_j^i is not necessarily known to the voting center. Let $O^i = \{q_p^i, \ldots, q_t^i\}$ represent the set of user v_i responses to queries. Note that this set does not necessarily contain all the items. $O^A = \{O^1, \ldots, O^m\}$ is a set of O^i sets. In an iterative process, in each round one user is queried for her ratings on one item. The preferences are aggregated according to a predefined aggregation strategy. The process terminates once a predefined termination condition is reached.

We denote the applied aggregation strategy str. The item score depends on the strategy used. As mentioned, in the Majority based aggregation strategy the mindfulness is towards the majority of the group. The user rating for an item are added: $s_{majority}(c_j) = \sum_{i\in=\{1,\ldots,m\}} q_j^i$. Although the Majority Based Strategy is fairly common, a disadvantage of this strategy is that it can be unfair towards users with the minority view. In fact, the authors in [14] state that their system works well for a homogenous group. However, when the group is heterogeneous, dissatisfaction of the minority group occurs. In the Least Misery strategy, the chosen item cannot be the least preferred by any of the users. The items score is the score of the least preferred item:$s_{least}(c_i) = \min_{i\in=\{1,\ldots,m\}} q_j^i$. An implementation can be found in [12] for example. The disadvantage is that the minority opinion can dictate the group – if all users but one really want some item to win, it will not be chosen [9].

Let k be the number of alternatives that will be presented to the group members. When given a set of responses to queries O^A, the goal is to determine whether the iterative process can be terminated. The termination condition is that the winner item is definitely one of the k items. The function $pmax^A(c_j, O^A)$ computes the possible maximum rating for item c_j, given the known user preferences. Similarly, the function of the possible minimum rating is $pmin^A(c_j, O^A)$.

Definition 1. *(Possible Maximum): given the set of responses O^A and an aggregation strategy str, the possible maximum score of candidate c_j, denoted $pmax^A(c_j, O^A)$, is computed as follows:*

$$pmax^A(c_j, O^A, str) = \begin{cases} \sum_{i\in 1..m} pmax^i(c_j, O^i) & str = majority \\ min_i\left(pmax^i(c_j, O^i)\right) & str = least\ misery \end{cases}$$

$$where\ pmax^i(c_j, O^i) = \begin{cases} d_g & if\ \exists q_p^i = d_g \in O^i \\ d_{max} & otherwise \end{cases}$$

Definition 2. *(Possible Minimum): given the set of responses O^A and an aggregation strategy str, the possible minimum score of candidate c_j, denoted $pmin^A(c_j, O^A)$ is computed as follows:*

$$pmin^A(c_j, O^A, str) = \begin{cases} \sum_{i\in 1..m} pmin^i(c_j, O^i) & str = majority \\ min_i\left(pmin^i(c_j, O^i)\right) & str = least\ misery \end{cases}$$

$$where\ pmin^i(c_j, O^i) = \begin{cases} d_g & if\ \exists q_p^i = d_g \in O^i \\ d_{min} & otherwise \end{cases}$$

A necessary winner NW is a set of items whose possible minimum aggregated rating is equal or greater than the possible maximum aggregated rating of all the others. Formally:

Definition 3. *(Necessary Winners set):* $NW = \{c_i | pmin^A(c_i, O^A) \geq pmax^A(c_j, O^A)\ \forall c_j \in C \backslash c_i\}$

Although the necessary winner set may contain more than one item, we assume that there is only one necessary item. In the case of a few winning items, the first item is selected lexicographically. In order to decide on the next query, the elicitor considers the rating distribution of the user-item preferences. The distribution can be inferred from rankings of similar users using collaborative filtering methods [10]. Formally the rating distribution is:

Definition 4. *(Rating Distribution): the voting center considers q_j^i as a discrete random variable distributed according to some rating distribution vd_j^i, such that $vd_j^i[d_g] \equiv P_r(q_j^i = d_g)$.*

Where $vd = \{vd_1^1, vd_2^1, \ldots vd_m^1, vd_1^2, vd_2^2, \ldots, vd_m^2, \ldots, vd_m^n\}$ is the set of all the rating probability distributions.

[1] www.amazon.com, www.netflix.com

The example presented in Table 1 shows the rating distribution of three users for two items in the domain $D = \{1,2,3\}$. E.g., the probability that v_1 will assign a rate of 1 to item c_1 is 0.2.

We assume independence between the probability distributions. While the independence assumption is naive, it can be used for approximating the actual probability. An attempt to address dependency will yield probabilities that are too complex for a system. When facing the tradeoff between the models accuracy and practicality, we chose to model a practical system. However, note that the precise probability value is not required if the queries are still sorted correctly according to the value of the information they hold (their informativeness). In the closely related domain of machine learning, a similar naive assumption is known to provide accurate classification, though the independence assumption is not always true [4]. We therefore argue that the decrease of accuracy, if at all exists, is not significant.

The initial rating distribution is calculated before the heuristics are applied. Both heuristics iteratively reveal one new rating upon request. This allows updating the distribution every time a new rating is added. The accuracy is expected to grow with the number of ratings acquired. Note that the proposed algorithm can be used when no history of ratings is available (this is known as cold start). In such a case, the initial distribution will be uniform, and will be updated as we proceed.

Table 1. Rating distribution of 3 users, $V = \{v_1, v_2, v_3\}$

	v_1		v_2		v_3	
	c_1	c_2	c_1	c_2	c_1	c_2
$d_1 = 1$	0.2	0.2	0.4	0.5	0.3	0.7
$d_2 = 2$	0.2	0.2	0.3	0.2	0.3	0.1
$d_3 = 3$	0.6	0.6	0.3	0.3	0.4	0.2

4. The Preference Elicitation Heuristic

The Extended Dynamic Information Gain (*EDIG*) Heuristic is an iterative algorithm based on the DIG algorithm proposed in [10]. It uses a greedy calculation in order to select a query out of the possible $m \times n$ queries. The chosen query is the one that maximizes the information gain. The information gain of a specific query is the difference between the prior and the posterior probability of the candidates to win given the possible responses to the query. The algorithm terminates once a winner is within the requested top-k items. In order to select a query, the heuristic calculates the information gained from each one of the optional queries and then selects the one that maximizes it. To compute the information gain, the winning probability of each item is calculated. The score s that the candidate can achieve depends on the strategy:

$$S = \begin{cases} \{n \cdot d_{min}, \dots, s_{majority}, \dots, n \cdot d_{max}\} & if\ str = majority \\ \{d_{min}, \dots, s_{least}, \dots, d_{max}\} & if\ str = least \end{cases}$$

Let us denote the probability an item has a certain score $Pr(c_j = s)$. The probability of an item to win is:

Definition 5. *(Item Winning Probability): Under the independence of probabilities assumption, the probability that item c_j is a winner is the aggregation of c_j's probabilities to win over the possible ratings s:* $Pr(NW = c_j) = \sum_{s \in S, i \neq j} \Pr(c_j = s \wedge \forall\ c_i < s) = \sum_{s \in S} \Pr(c_j = s) \cdot \prod_{\forall i \neq j} \Pr(c_i < s)$

To compute the probability that an item will receive the score s, and to compute the probability that an item will receive a score of at most s, for the majority based strategy we use:

$$Pr(c_j = s) = \sum_{x=d_{min}}^{d_{max}} \left(\prod_{i=1}^{n-1} Pr(q_i^j = s - x) \cdot Pr(q_n^j = x) \right)$$

$$Pr(c_j < s) = \sum_{x=\min(S)}^{s-1} Pr(c_j = x)$$

For the Least Misery strategy we use:

$$Pr(c_j = s) = min_{x \in S} \left(\prod_{i=1}^{n-1} Pr(q_i^j = s - x) \cdot Pr(q_n^j = x) \right)$$

$$Pr(c_j < s) = min_{x \in S} Pr(c_j = x)$$

Next, the heuristic calculates the information gain of the $m \times n$ possible queries. The information gain of a query is the difference between the prior entropy and the posterior entropy, given the possible responses to the query:

$$H(NW) = -\sum_{j-1}^{m} Pr(NW = c_j) \cdot \log\left(Pr(NW = c_j)\right)$$

Definition 6. *(Information Gain): The Information Gain (IG) of a query is:* $IG(NW|q_j^i) = H(NW) - \sum_{g=min}^{max} H(NW|q_j^i = d_g) \cdot Pr(q_j^i = d_g)$ *where* $H(NW|q_j^i = d_g)$ *represents the entropy of NW given the possible values by querying user v_i on item c_j.*

The query that maximizes the information gain is selected: $argmaxIG_{i,j}(NW|q_j^i)$. The query selection process continues until the termination condition is reached.

5. EVALUATION

We examine the performance of the EDIG algorithm, under two aggregation strategies: Majority and Least Misery. The tradeoff between the number of items outputted (top-k) to the group and the number of preference elicitation required is investigated. Performance is measured in terms of elicitation effort, i.e., the required number of queries (requests for the user to provide ratings), in order to reach the termination condition. As mentioned in the related work, to the best of our knowledge there are no other algorithms that operate (or can be expanded to operate) under the same settings. Therefore the baseline for measuring the effectiveness of our method is a random procedure (RANDOM), which randomly selects the next query. To account for the randomness in RANDOM, each experiment was repeated 20 times.

We present an evaluation on simulated data as well as on a real-world dataset, the Netflix prize dataset. The Netflix dataset (http://www.netflixprize.com) consists of ~100,000 users and ~16,000 items. We consider a setting of a group of 10 members and 10 items. The users in the group are drawn randomly from a subset of Netflix where all users gave rating to 100 items. 90 items are used to create the initial rating distribution. The 10 remaining items are the items in question. To account for randomness, each experiment was repeated 10 times.

We simulate a cold start scenario where no history of ratings is available. We consider a setting of a group of 10 members and 10 items where the users rate their preferences on a scale of 1-4. We set the user-item distribution to a Uniform distribution. For example, the initial distribution for any user-item pair is: {0.25,0.25,0.25,0.25}, indicating that item c_j has a 25% probability to be rated 1-4 by user v_i. Similarly, we simulated a problem where one item is suspected to be more favorable and has a skewed distribution skewed to the right (Right-Skew), and a problem where one item is suspected to be less favorable and has a distribution skewed to the left (Left-Skew). The distribution values for the right and left skews were set to: {0.011,0.011,0.147,0.832} and {0.832, 0.147,0.011,0.011}. In all cases, we cast lots to set the user-item ratings. To account for randomness, each experiment was repeated 10 times.

We compared the two strategies: Majority (MAJ) and Least Misery (LM) combined with EDIG and RANDOM heuristics. We examined different termination conditions, from $k = 1$, i.e., requiring one definite winner, to $k = 9$, i.e., requiring the winner to be one of the top 9 items. The results on the Netflix data are displayed in Figure 1. Axis x presents the termination condition k=1,...,10, Axis y presents the number of queries required in order to find a winner within the top-k. As expected, all combinations (of heuristics with strategies) drop in the amount of elicitation effort required as the termination condition includes a larger number of k items. The best results are received for EDIG combined with MAJ strategy. This combination reduces the elicitation effort in up to 35%. All the results were found significant with a 95% confidence level using a one-tailed t-test.

Table 2. Preference Elicitation effort on simulated data

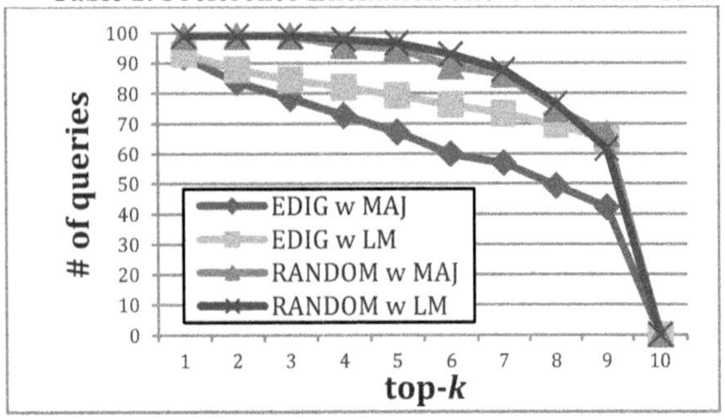

Figure 1. Preference Elicitation effort on the Netflix dataset

	Right-Skew		Uniform		Left-Skew	
topk	MAJ	LM	MAJ	LM	MAJ	LM
1	27.7	83	79.7	61.9	83	42.2
2	26.1	67.8	75.7	44.5	76.1	35.3
3	24.7	54.5	72.7	38.7	69.4	27.7
4	23.2	44.1	70.1	32.6	65.5	21.2
5	21.2	35.9	65.2	24.2	61.6	15.5
6	19.3	28.9	59.7	18.4	59.6	9.8
7	17.4	23.9	55.5	13.7	55.5	6.6
8	15.2	17.3	50.3	7.5	49.6	3.4
9	12	14.7	35.1	2.3	39.3	0.2

For the simulated data with different skewness levels: Right-Skew, Uniform (cold-start problem) and Left-Skew, EDIG significantly outperformed RANDOM with a confidence level of 95% using a one-tailed t-test. For a cold-start problem (Uniform skewness, columns 4-5 in Table 2) LM outperforms MAJ reducing the preference elicitation effort in 22%-93%. For a Left-Skew (columns 6-7 in Table 2), again LM outperforms MAJ for every k. The trend changes for the Right-Skew (columns 2-3). Here MAJ outperforms LM. All of these results were found significant with a confidence level of 95% using a one-tailed t-test. The results indicate that it is advised to consider the users assumed behavior. If the user preferences are assumed to be skewed towards some favorable item, as is the case with the Netflix dataset and with the simulated data with a right skew, it is best to use a heuristic that employs the Majority based strategy. If the results are uniformly skewed or it is assumed that some item or items are less preferred (left skew), it is best to choose a heuristics that employs the Least Misery strategy. Reducing the preference elicitation effort can also be achieved by changing the preference elicitation termination condition and requiring a winning item within top k instead of a definite item.

6. CONCLUSIONS

We propose an iterative preference elicitation method, where users are required to provide item ratings per request. We suggest a heuristic that attempts to minimize the preference elicitation effort under two aggregation strategies. The goal is to output top-k preferred items, where one of the items is a *necessary* winner, out of the top-N recommendations provided to the group by the recommender system ($k < N$). We show that the aggregation strategy affects the effort required in the preference elicitation and evaluate two state-of-the-art aggregation strategies. We demonstrate that the preference elicitation effort can be cut in up to 90% in some cases, while a necessary winner is still outputted. Since different aggregation strategies are used in different situations, in the future we plan to investigate other aggregation strategies and heuristics that combine a few strategies.

7. REFERENCES

[1] Arrow, K. J. 1951. *Social Choice and Individual Values.* Cowles Foundation, New Haven.

[2] Brandt, F., Conitzer, V. and Endriss, U. Computational social choice. 2013. In Weiss, G. ed. *Multiagent Systems.* MIT Press.

[3] Conitzer, V. and Sandholm, T. 2005. Communication complexity of common voting rules. In *Proceedings of the 6th ACM conference on Electronic commerce.* ACM, 78-87.

[4] Domingos, P. and Pazzani, M. 1997. On the optimality of the simple Bayesian classifier under zero-one loss. *J. Mach. Learning*, 29, 2, 103-130.

[5] Jameson, A. and Smyth, B. 2007. Recommendation to groups. *The adaptive web*, 596-627.

[6] Kalech, M., Kraus, S., Kaminka, G. A. and Goldman, C. V. 2011. Practical voting rules with partial information. *J. Auton. Agents Multi-Agent Syst.*, 22, 1, 151-182.

[7] Konczak, K. and Lang, J. Voting procedures with incomplete preferences. 2005. In *Proceedings of the 19th IJCAI.* Edinburgh. .

[8] Lu, T. and Boutilier, C. Multi-winner Social Choice with Incomplete Preferences. 2013. *Proceedings of IJCAI-13.* 263-270.

[9] Masthoff, J. 2011. Group recommender systems: Combining individual models. *Recommender Systems Handbook*, 677-702.

[10] Naamani Dery, L., Kalceh, M., Rokach, L., Shapira, B. 2014. Reaching a Joint Decision with Minimal Elicitation of Voter Preferences. Information Sciences, Vol.278, 466-487.

[11] Naamani Dery, L., Kalech, M., Rokach, L. and Shapira, B. 2010. Iterative voting under uncertainty for group recommender systems. In *Proceedings of the 4th ACM RECSYS.* 265-268.

[12] O'connor, M., Cosley, D., Konstan, J. A. and Riedl, J. 2001. PolyLens: a recommender system for groups of users. In *proceedings of ECSCW 2001.*199-218.

[13] Senot, C., Kostadinov, D., Bouzid, M., Picault, J. and Aghasaryan, 2011. Evaluation of group profiling strategies. In *Proceedings of the 22nd AAAI.* AAAI Press, 2728-2733.

[14] Yu, Z., Zhou, X., Hao, Y. and Gu, J. 2006. TV program recommendation for multiple viewers based on user profile merging. *User Modeling and User-Adapted Interaction,* 16,63-82.

Recommendation-based Modeling Support for Data Mining Processes

Dietmar Jannach
TU Dortmund, Germany
dietmar.jannach@tu-dortmund.de

Simon Fischer
RapidMiner GmbH, Germany
sfischer@rapidminer.com

ABSTRACT

RapidMiner is a software tool that allows users to define data mining processes based on a visual model and implements a variety of so-called "operators" for data extraction, manipulation, model learning and analysis. The large number of available operators can however make it challenging for the process designer to find the appropriate operators for the problem at hand. At the same time, some operators are only meaningful when combined with certain others.

In this work, we evaluate different strategies of recommending additional operators to the user during the design of the process. The recommendation models are learned using a pool of several thousand existing data mining processes and evaluated in an offline experiment. The results indicate that good predictive accuracy can already be achieved with comparably simple co-occurrence based algorithms.

Categories and Subject Descriptors

H.3.3 [**Information Search and Retrieval**]: Information filtering

Keywords

Recommender Systems; Evaluation; Process Modeling

1. INTRODUCTION

Practical data mining processes typically consist of several sequential steps including, for example, data-preprocessing, feature selection, model learning or performance evaluation. RapidMiner [9] is an open source software tool that supports the visual design as well as the execution of data mining and analytics processes[1]. A data mining process in RapidMiner consists of a number of process steps (called "operators") and connections between them. The operators implement some pre-defined functionality and the connections represent data flows. Figure 1 shows a fragment of a process designed in RapidMiner.

[1] `http://www.rapidminer.com`

RecSys'14, October 6–10, 2014, Foster City, Silicon Valley, CA, USA.
Copyright 2014 ACM 978-1-4503-2668-1/14/10 ...$15.00.
http://dx.doi.org/10.1145/2645710.2645755.

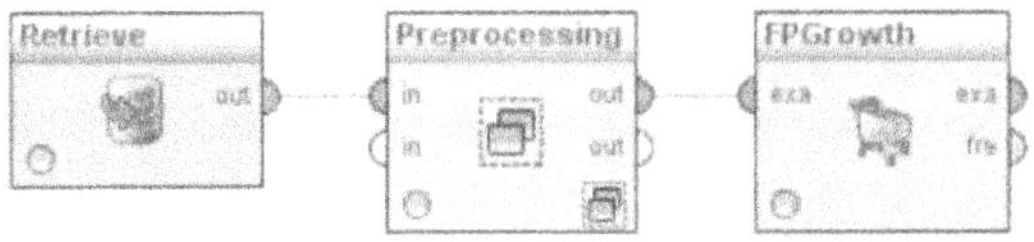

Figure 1: A process fragment.

While the graphical editor makes it easy for the designer to construct and test the process on a visual level, the design of a data mining process can still be challenging. First, process developers can be easily overwhelmed by the huge number of pre-implemented operators. Depending on the number of installed add-ons and custom extensions, the pool of available operators can comprise several hundred items. Second, some operators are only meaningful when combined with others or require that the data is transformed before it can be fed into the operator. In the example in Figure 1, for example, the frequent itemset mining operator FP-Growth is typically followed by an association rule generation operator. Likewise, the data that is fed into FP-Growth has in many application scenarios to be first transformed into a format that is suitable for itemset mining, e.g., by pivoting.

In this paper, we design and evaluate different strategies to automatically recommend additional operators to the user during the modeling process. Overall, the recommendations should make the modeling process easier for the developer by pointing him to relevant additional operators and at the same time help him avoid errors that can occur when a required step is missing in the model.

Our evaluation is based on an offline experimental design and a pool of several thousand data mining processes that were developed with RapidMiner. The algorithms tested so far are mainly based on the identification of operator co-occurrence patterns in the pool of existing processes. To compare the different strategies, we use an evaluation protocol in which we hide different operators from the processes in the test set and calculate the recall (hit rate) and the mean reciprocal rank measure for the top-n recommendation lists.

In the following sections, we will first describe the data set and the tested algorithms and then present the results of the experimental evaluation. The paper ends with a discussion of related approaches and an outlook on future works, which will in particular include user and field studies that will be conducted using a fully-functional plug-in to the RapidMiner system that has already been developed.

2. EXPERIMENTAL SETUP

2.1 Dataset

We created a collection of 6,520 data mining processes using different sources including, for example, a number of publicly posted processes on the "myexperiment" Web site[2] or other forums. The original dataset was even larger, but we applied a very strict strategy with respect to duplicates in that we removed all processes that contained the same sequence of internal operator IDs. Processes consisting of only one single process step were also removed. Table 1 shows some statistics of the dataset.

Number of processes:	6,520
Average number of operators per process:	15.5
Median number of operators per process:	10
Number of different operators:	871

Table 1: Dataset characteristics

Note that the mean and median of the number of operators per process include the operators appearing in subprocesses; when counting the different operators, we also included user-developed operators that are not contained in RapidMiner.

An important aspect in that context is that the distribution of how often the individual operators appear in the processes is highly skewed (see Figure 2).

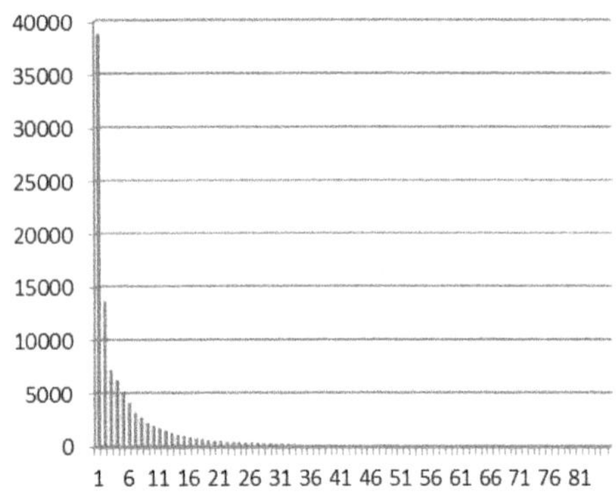

Figure 2: Distribution of operators.

To visualize the distribution, we have sorted the operators by their frequency (popularity) of appearance in the data and grouped them into bins, each containing 10 operators. The first bin therefore contains the 10 most frequently used operators. These operators appear more than 35,000 times in the processes and correspond to very general tasks like data import, data sampling, or the computation of derived attribute values. On the other hand, more than 400 operators were used less than 10 times.

2.2 Measurement method

We split the processes into training and test sets and applied a five-fold cross-validation procedure. To evaluate the accuracy of the recommendations, we removed individual operators from each process in the test set and the task of the recommender was to predict the hidden operator given the processes in the training set and the non-hidden elements of the current process. Given a top-n list of recommendations, we then determined the *recall* and the *mean reciprocal rank* (MRR) measures and averaged the values over all tested processes.

We evaluated several schemes of "hiding" elements including the selection of a random element, the selection of the first or last element, or the selection of the second to last element. Predicting the first is in our view not particularly interesting, because the first operation is typically related to data import and might be obvious. Beside the strategy of leaving out one single element, we also evaluated different "given-n" scenarios to simulate an incremental modeling process.

2.3 Algorithms

We evaluated the following recommendation strategies. Most of them rely on techniques to identify co-occurrence patterns in the data. We will discuss alternative approaches later on in Section 4.

MostFreq:	This baseline method recommends the most frequently used operators. Given the skewedness of the data, this can be a simple yet effective strategy.
CoOccur:	A recommendation strategy based on the conditional probabilities of the co-occurrence of two items.
AssocRules:	An association rule mining approach using FP-Growth [3]. The item ranking is based on the confidence of the applicable rules for a given test process.
CFP-Growth:	An association rule mining approach designed for finding itemsets and rules for "rare items" [4], which are quite common in our dataset.
SeqPatterns:	In order to be able to take the order of operators into account, a recent sequential pattern mining technique was included in the evaluation [2].
kNN:	A k-nearest-neighbors (kNN) approach in which we used cosine similarity as a distance measure and the usual weighted prediction scheme.
kNN-BPR:	Considering processes as users and operators and items, we train a Bayesian Personalized Ranking (BPR) model [10]. Predictions are made as in the kNN method with the difference that predictions are based on weighted BPR scores.

Table 2: Evaluated algorithms.

We implemented all algorithms in a Java-based evaluation framework. For the association rule mining approaches, we used the implementations from the SPMF-Framework[3]. Note that modern techniques for personalized recommendations based on matrix factorization cannot be directly applied in our setting, since the recommendations are only dependent on the current process and not the past processes modeled by a specific user.

[2] http://www.myexperiment.org

[3] http://www.philippe-fournier-viger.com/spmf/

3. RESULTS

Accuracy and coverage.

Table 3 summarizes the recall, MRR and coverage results for the setting in which the second to last element was hidden from each process in the test set[4]. When an algorithm places the hidden element of a process in the top-n list, recall is 1 and otherwise 0; the MRR in addition takes the position of the "hit" into account. The overall ranking of the algorithms was similar when a different strategy of hiding elements (like "first", "random", "last element") was applied.

Algorithm	Recall	MRR	Cov.	RecTime
kNN	**0.67**	**0.55**	1.00	20.9 ms
CoOccur	0.60	0.32	0.98	<1 ms
kNN-BPR	0.59	0.34	1.00	20.6 ms
SeqPatterns	0.58	0.34	0.99	16.7 ms
CFP-Growth	0.53	0.30	0.98	29.0 ms
AssocRules	0.50	0.30	0.98	4.75 ms
MostFreq	0.40	0.14	1.00	<1 ms

Table 3: Recall and MRR (top-10).

The results show that the kNN method with an empirically determined neighborhood size of 10 outperforms all other methods in terms of recall, and even more strongly in terms of the MRR. In our experiments, we used a typical top-n list length of 10, assuming that users will be willing to inspect up to 10 items. Experiments with shorter list sizes (e.g., 3) did not lead to different rankings of the algorithms. Quite interestingly, the simple CoOccur method works better in terms of recall than the association rules techniques. Co-occurrences of two elements[5] therefore seem very common in this domain.

The different association rule mining approaches outperform the basic frequency-based approach. The sequential pattern mining technique worked best among them, which indicates that the sequence of the operators is actually relevant. Mining rules for infrequent items is slightly more effective than the standard FP-Growth algorithm.

Recommending the most frequent items leads to recall values that were expected based on the data distribution shown in Figure 2. The coverage is high for all tested approaches.

Overall, the measurements show that in particular the neighborhood-based method is promising and was able to place the hidden item into the top-10 list in 2 out of 3 cases.

Parameter settings and running times.

A drawback of association rule mining techniques is that finding good threshold values for minimum support and confidence is tedious. Our experiments showed that lower values – e.g., minSup=0.02, minConf=0.02 for FP-Growth – led to the best results. When the values where further lowered, both the running times and memory consumption increased dramatically. For more sophisticated algorithms like CFP-Growth even more parameters have to be found.

The running times for prediction are crucial in our application since immediate feedback has to be provided during the interactive modeling process. In the right-most column of Table 3, we show the required computation times for generating one recommendation list[6]. The best-performing kNN approach needed about 20ms to produce a recommendation using a compact bitset-based representation of the training processes. The performance of the rule-based approaches is better and depends on the number of rules (ranging, e.g. up to over 400,000 for CFP-Growth). Further improvements can however be achieved through better engineering.

Given-N evaluation.

To estimate how much information the algorithms need to be able to predict suitable operators during the incremental design of a process, we used a *given-n* protocol in which we removed all but the first $n+1$ elements in each process and hid the last element. Table 4 shows the results for different configurations in the form of *recall/MRR* at list length 10.

Algorithm	Given-1	Given-3	Given-5
kNN	0.39/0.14	**0.59/0.29**	**0.57/0.29**
CoOccur	0.44/0.17	0.49/0.21	0.49/0.21
kNN-BPR	**0.47/0.17**	0.52/0.21	0.55/0.21
SeqPatterns	0.40/0.15	0.45/0.20	0.47/0.20
CFP-Growth	0.33/0.12	0.40/0.18	0.39/0.18
AssocRules	0.31/0.11	0.41/0.19	0.40/0.18
MostFreq	0.38/0.14	0.33/0.31	0.31/0.12

Table 4: Different given-n configurations.

The results show that already for the extreme "cold-start" situation when the process only contains one element, several techniques are better than the frequency-based method. Due to the lack of suitable neighbors, the kNN method is not the best choice in the beginning. Very quickly, however, the method works again better than the others[7].

4. RELATED WORK

The recommendation of operators for data mining processes has to the best of our knowledge not been explored before. However, some proposals to provide recommendation support in the context of general business process modeling can be found in the literature. A classification of such approaches was proposed by Kluza et al. in [5]. According to their classification scheme, our work would fall into the category of single-element structural recommendation; the *given-N* simulation described in the previous section would correspond to a "forward-completion" technique.

In the work presented in [6] the goal is to support process designers during modeling by automatically ranking existing process fragments from a given repository of past processes. Technically, their approach is mainly based on frequency patterns and on matching the textual annotations (tags) of past processes with the currently modeled process using the typical vector space model for document encoding.

In [8], Matejka et al. explored automated command recommendation for the AutoCAD system based on command usage frequencies and nearest-neighbor methods. In contrast to our work, their algorithms produced personalized

[4]The selection was done heuristics-based since this element is not always unique because, e.g., of parallelism.

[5]E.g., X-Validation/Apply Model, Process Documents/ Filter stop words, kMeans/Normalization.

[6]For the experiments, we used a Laptop computer with an Intel i7 CPU and 8GB of RAM.

[7]Note that the absolute recall/MRR values cannot be compared on an absolute scale across the different configurations as there are processes that have less than, e.g., 5 operators.

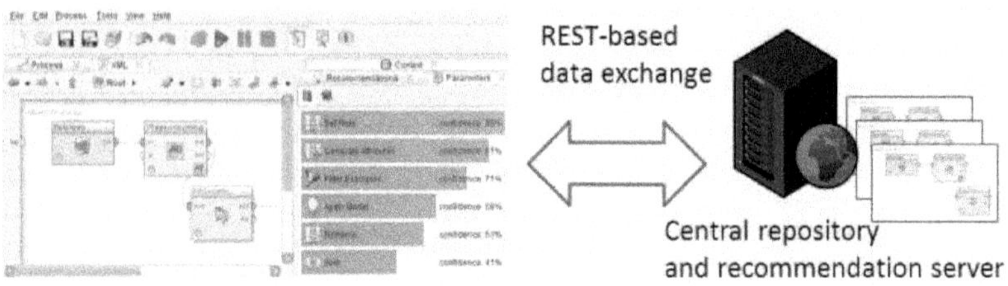

Figure 3: Architecture of recommendation system in RapidMiner.

recommendations, whereas our approach focuses on operators that are relevant in the current modeling context.

In the area of service-oriented architectures, the recommendation of suitable Web Services (e.g., for the purpose of service discovery or as a replacement of a broken services), has for example been explored in [1]. Their approach is based on the identification of patterns in past processes that are *structurally* similar to certain fragments of the currently developed process. Structural similarity is also the basis for recommendations in the more recent approach presented in [7]. Zheng et al. in [11], in contrast, proposes a collaborative filtering approach to Web Service recommendation, where the goal is to predict the expected Quality of Service (QoS) of several alternative services that can be included in a process. The input to the calculations consists of a record of past QoS levels achieved by the individual services and the goal is therefore quite different from our work.

Overall, there are two general schemes for recommendation-based modeling support which we see to be orthogonal to our co-occurrence based approaches: structural matching and "semantic"-based retrieval and ranking. Both schemes seem to be applicable in our application scenario and will be explored in our future work. Semantic information is for example available in the form of operator documentation or the in the names given by users to the process steps in their models. Structural patterns like sub-processes for cross-validation schemes or are also common in the domain.

In [6], the recommendation technique was implemented in a visual modeling editor and evaluated through laboratory studies that aimed to assess the effect of the tool on the modelers. In particular, the goal was to determine, among other aspects, if users will actually use the tool's recommendation and re-use existing fragments more often, if the tool support helps them build their models faster, if the resulting model quality is higher, and to which extent the effect depends on the experience of the modelers.

Our own work so far is based on an offline experimental design and our results indicate that our recommendation schemes can be helpful to users in different ways. In order to validate this hypothesis, we are currently preparing user and field studies in the sense of [6]. Specifically, a fully-functional plug-in component to the RapidMiner system has been developed which interacts with a central recommendation server that hosts the repository of past processes (Figure 3). So far, however, only a preliminary and informal pilot study with expert users has been made.

5. CONCLUSION

We have presented the results of an experimental analysis regarding the suitability of different algorithmic strategies for providing recommendation support for the end user during process modeling. The results indicate that co-occurrence based schemes can lead to good results in this application domain and the hybrid designs are advisable in cold-start situations. Our future works comprise (a) the evaluation of alternative approaches based on structural and semantic information, (b) an investigation of the applicability of existing process-mining techniques, as well as (c) systematic evaluations with real users.

6. REFERENCES

[1] N. Chan, W. Gaaloul, and S. Tata. Composition context matching for web service recommendation. In *Proc. IEE SCC 2011*, pages 624–631, 2011.

[2] P. Fournier-Viger, U. Faghihi, R. Nkambou, and E. M. Nguifo. CMRules: Mining sequential rules common to several sequences. *Knowledge-Based Systems*, 25(1):63 – 76, 2012.

[3] J. Han, J. Pei, Y. Yin, and R. Mao. Mining frequent patterns without candidate generation: A frequent-pattern tree approach. *Data Mining and Knowledge Discovery*, 8(1):53–87, 2004.

[4] Y.-H. Hu and Y.-L. Chen. Mining association rules with multiple minimum supports: a new mining algorithm and a support tuning mechanism. *Decis Support Syst*, 42(1):1 – 24, 2006.

[5] K. Kluza, M. Baran, S. Bobek, and G. J. Nalepa. Overview of recommendation techniques in business process modeling. In *Proc. KESE 2013*, 2013.

[6] A. Koschmider, T. Hornung, and A. Oberweis. Recommendation-based editor for business process modeling. *Data and Knowledge Engineering*, 70(6):483–503, 2011.

[7] Y. Li, B. Cao, L. Xu, J. Yin, S. Deng, Y. Yin, and Z. Wu. An efficient recommendation method for improving business process modeling. *IEEE Trans Industr Informatics*, 10(1):502–513, 2014.

[8] J. Matejka, W. Li, T. Grossman, and G. W. Fitzmaurice. CommunityCommands: command recommendations for software applications. In *Proc. UIST '09*, pages 193–202, Victoria, BC, Canada, 2009.

[9] I. Mierswa, M. Wurst, R. Klinkenberg, M. Scholz, and T. Euler. Yale: Rapid prototyping for complex data mining tasks. In *Proc. KDD '06*, pages 935–940, 2006.

[10] S. Rendle, C. Freudenthaler, Z. Gantner, and L. Schmidt-Thieme. BPR: Bayesian personalized ranking from implicit feedback. In *Proc. UAI '09*, pages 452–461, Montreal, Canada, 2009.

[11] Z. Zheng, H. Ma, M. Lyu, and I. King. WSRec: A collaborative filtering based web service recommender system. In *Proc. ICWS 2009*, pages 437–444, 2009.

Scalable Audience Targeted Models for Brand Advertising on Social Networks

Kunpeng Zhang
Department of Information and Decision Sciences
University of Illinois at Chicago
Chicago, IL USA
kzhang6@uic.edu

Aris Ouksel
Department of Information and Decision Sciences
University of Illinois at Chicago
Chicago, IL USA
aris@uic.edu

Shaokun Fan
Department of Computer Information and Decision Management
West Texas A&M University
Canyon, Texas USA
fsk1234@gmail.com

Hengchang Liu
School of Computer Science and Technology
University of Science and Technology of China
Suzhou, Jiangsu China
hcliu@ustc.edu.cn

ABSTRACT

People are using social media to generate, share, and communicate information with each other. Finding actionable insights from such big data has attracted a lot of research attentions on, for example, finding targeted user groups based on their historical on-line activities. However, existing machine learning algorithms fail to keep up with the increasing large data volume. In this paper, we develop a scalable regression-based algorithm called distributed iterative shrinkage-thresholding algorithm (DISTA) that can identify potential users. Our experiments conducted on Facebook data containing billions of users and associated activities show that DISTA with feature selection not only enables on-line audience-targeted approach for precise marketing but also performs efficiently on parallel computers.

Categories and Subject Descriptors

H.2.8 [**Information Systems**]: Database Applications—*Data mining*; G.1.6 [**NUMERICAL ANALYSIS**]: Optimization—*Unconstrained optimization*

Keywords

Social brand; feature selection; DISTA; advertising

1. INTRODUCTION

Most social platforms, such as Facebook, Twitter, Youtube, and Amazon.com, have mechanisms allowing users to generate, share, and communicate with each other for their interested topics. For example, users can give rating scores and leave their reviews on products they purchased. People can also "like" or make comments on social brands (e.g. celebrities, institutes, organizations, companies, and products). Analyzing these user-generated contents to find actionable insights can help users make informed decisions, which has attracted a lot of attention in research. Research in social media data analysis falls into two categories. The first one is from the text-mining perspective: text sentiment analysis for decision making [4]; the second one is from the social network perspective: study of static and dynamic properties of networks [5].

Recently, the trend to social content-driven advertising is becoming increasingly evident in business management. Finding targeted audience for precise on-line advertising based on user historical behaviors is one of the most important marketing tasks. BIA/Kelsey's study estimates that the social advertising revenues in the U.S. will grow over 3 billion dollars by 2017 [1]. Machine-learning methods have been widely used, for example, for building a predictive model based on users' profile, historical activities, and social networking information. Many psychological and sociological models were also proposed to build user sociality from user access log data so that they can be used to guide marketing managers to find their targeted audience. In this work, we focus on user preference prediction on social brands.

However, there are some challenges given the big size of the training samples and the large number of training features. First, existing feature selection algorithms is infeasible and inefficient, which motivates us to find a scalable solution. Secondly, implementing distributed algorithms to efficiently and accurately learn predictive models is also not straightforward. To address the first challenge, we implement a MapReduce-based Apriori algorithm to find a given brand the group of correlative brands that share the most user activities. The identified brands will be used as the selected features in the model learning. To solve the second problem, we implement a distributed regression-based algorithm called iterative shrinkage-thresholding algorithm

RecSys'14, October 6–10, 2014, Foster City, Silicon Valley, CA, USA.
Copyright 2014 ACM 978-1-4503-2668-1/14/10 ...$15.00.
http://dx.doi.org/10.1145/2645710.2645763.

(DISTA), a stochastic optimization algorithm that can handle a large amount of training instances. The experiments show that our DISTA can get up to 16% increase of accuracy by incorporating our feature selection strategy comparing to other baselines.

2. PROBLEM STATEMENT

Our problem is a typical classification in machine learning domain. The training features are social brands (b_1, b_2, ..., b_n) and the value of each feature is the number of historical activities a user had on the corresponding brands (e.g. the number of likes, the number of comments, or both). The target brand (b_t) is labeled in a binary form: 1 if a user is interested in this brand, 0 otherwise. Before mathematically formulating this problem, we define the terms of social brands and activity matrix used in this paper.

A social brand is an entity in the social network that allows other users to leave comments on its page. Examples are companies, organizations, individuals, or consumer products. The activity matrix is represented as the following.

$$A = \begin{array}{c} \\ u_1 \\ u_2 \\ \vdots \\ u_m \end{array} \begin{array}{c} \begin{array}{ccccc} b_1 & b_2 & \cdots & b_n & b_t \end{array} \\ \begin{pmatrix} x_{11} & x_{12} & \cdots & x_{1n} & 1 \\ x_{21} & x_{22} & \cdots & x_{2n} & 1 \\ \vdots & \vdots & \ddots & \vdots & \vdots \\ x_{m1} & x_{m2} & \cdots & x_{mn} & 0 \end{pmatrix} \end{array}$$

where u_i is the ith user; b_j is the jth brand; The entry x_{ij} is the number of activities made by i^{th} user on brand j. $x_{ij} = like_{ij} + comment_{ij}$, where $like_{ij}$ is the number of likes user i gave to all posts initiated by brand j and $comment_{ij}$ is the number of comments made by user i on brand j.

To obtain the kth user's preference on a specified target brand b_t, we calculate P_{kt}.

$$P_{kt} = A_k * \alpha = \alpha_1 x_{k1} + \alpha_2 x_{k2} + \cdots + \alpha_i x_{ki} + \cdots + \alpha_n x_{kn}$$

where A_k is the kth row of activity matrix A. $P_{kt} \in [0, 1]$ is the output value for the target brand b_t, representing the preference on brand t of the kth user; $\alpha = [\alpha_1, \alpha_2, \cdots, \alpha_n]^T$; All these x_{ki} are given for a testing user and all α_i obtained through the training process, which involves solving the following convex optimization problem.

$$min_\alpha f(\alpha) + \lambda\|\alpha\|_1 = min_\alpha \|A\alpha - b_t\|_2^2 + \lambda\|\alpha\|_1 \qquad (\star)$$

where α is a vector of n dimensions; b_t is a vector of the targeted brand t of n dimensions; λ is a constant and $\|\alpha\|_1$ is the l_1-norm of the parameter vector. $\|\alpha\|_1 = \sum|\alpha_1| + |\alpha_2| + \ldots + |\alpha_n|$.

In this work, we used Facebook Graph API to download social brand data from Facebook. The data covers many different categories, including sports, movies, politics, fast-food, and many others. The first issue we need to handle is feature selection, because not all brands in the feature set are related to the targeted brand. We start with selecting top related brands to reduce the size of the activity matrix A. The method we use here is association rule mining to find patterns like "$b_i \Rightarrow b_t$" with high confidence scores. In the next section, we will discuss a MapReduce-based technique to find top k other brands ($b_1, b2, \ldots, b_k$) in terms of confidence score with the pattern of "$b_i \Rightarrow b_t$". Then the size of the new activity matrix A' is significantly reduced from $m * n$ to $u * k$ ($k << n$ and u is the number of users having activities on at least one of top k brands, $u << m$). The next step is the binary classification problem to identify potential users.

3. METHODOLOGY

In this section, we describe our distributed iterative shrinkage-thresholding algorithm. In addition, to address the large data volume challenge in feature selection, we use MapReduce-based Apriori to select top associated brands.

3.1 Feature Selection

As most of the features/brands are not closely related to the targeted brand, removing irrelevant features during the learning can not only reduce the size of training data, but also help mitigate bias. In this work, we use a distributed Apriori algorithm to select top brands (features) based on the confidence score of associated rules like "$b_i \Rightarrow b_t$". Before diving into the details, we first describe the data we collect from the Facebook.

Data Preparation For the public social brands, users can like or make comments on campaigns posted by brand administrators. In this work, we assume that a user is interested in a brand if he/she makes positive comments on it or likes campaigns on that brand. OpinionFinder [6] is used to identify sentiments. We consider likes and comments as user activities, which can be represented as a 3-tuple: $[user_{id}, brand_{id}, \#\_of\_activities]$. We then combine all activities across all brands for each user. After this process, each user is described with the format of $<user_{id}$ DEL $b_1|w_1, b_2|w_2, \cdots, b_i|w_i, \cdots>$, where b_i is the ith brand and w_i is the corresponding number of activities, DEL could be any delimiter.

Confidence score: The goal here is to find the frequent pattern "$b_i \Rightarrow b_t$" based on a large amount of user historical activities across brands. Two-itemset (I_x, I_y) Apriori ("$I_x \Rightarrow I_y$") indicates their correlation. Here, I_x could be any brand $b_i \in \{n$ features: $b_1, b_2, \ldots, b_n\}$ except the target brand, I_y is the target brand b_t. We choose top k brands based on the confidence score of the pattern "$b_i \Rightarrow b_t$". The confidence is calculated using the following equation.

$$Conf(b_i \Rightarrow b_t) = \frac{Support(b_i, b_t)}{Support(b_i)}$$

Where $Support(X)$ is the occurrence frequency of X. In our case, it is the number of users who have activities on both brands b_i and b_t for $Support(b_i, b_t)$, on brand b_i only for $Support(b_i)$. The key sketchlon of the MapReduce-based algorithm of calculating confidence score (CSC) is shown in Algorithm 1.

3.2 DISTA: Distributed Iterative Shrinkage-Thresholding Algorithm

Given large amounts of user historical activities, a very intuitive way to solve the problem mentioned in ($\star$) is building a regression model. We intend to develop our model to have the following two properties: (1) less sensitive to outliers, and (2) can promote sparse solutions because most of the features are irrelevant to the class/label, even using top k features after feature selection. Consider the unconstrained minimization problem of a continuously differentiable function $f(\alpha)$: $R^n \to R$: $min\{f(\alpha), \alpha \in R^n\}$ ($\triangle$). One of the simplest methods for solving ($\triangle$) is the gradient descent algorithm which generates a sequence of α^k via

Algorithm 1 CSC. *al*: an activity list for a user

map function:
for all $b_i \in al$ **do**
  if $b_t \in al$ **then**
    output $<(b_i, b_t), \mathbf{1}>$;
  end if
  output $<b_i, \mathbf{1}>$;
end for

reduce function:
for all keys: (b_i, b_t) and b_i **do**
  sum all values $\rightarrow S_{it}$ or S_i;
end for

for all $b_i \Rightarrow b_t$ sequentially **do**
  $Conf(b_i \Rightarrow b_t) = S_{it}/S_i$;
end for

$\alpha^k = \alpha^{k-1} - t^k \nabla f(\alpha^{k-1})$ $(\diamondsuit)$, where $\alpha^0 \in R^n$, $t^k > 0$ is a suitable step size. It is very well known [3] that the gradient iteration in $(\diamondsuit)$ can be viewed as a proximal regularization of the linearized function f at α^{k-1}, and written equivalently as $argmin_\alpha\{f(\alpha^{k-1}) + \nabla f(\alpha^{k-1})^T(\alpha - \alpha^{k-1}) + \frac{1}{2t^k}\|\alpha - \alpha^{k-1}\|_2^2\}$. Adopting this same basic gradient idea to the non-smooth l_1 regularized problem: $min\{f(\alpha)+\lambda\|\alpha\|_1 : \alpha \in R^n\}$. It leads to the iterative scheme: $\alpha^k = argmin_\alpha\{f(\alpha^{k-1})+ \nabla f(\alpha^{k-1})^T(\alpha - \alpha^{k-1}) + \frac{1}{2t^k}\|\alpha - \alpha^{k-1}\|_2^2 + \lambda\|\alpha\|_1\}$. α^k can be solved as: $\alpha^k = T_{\lambda t^k}\{\alpha^{k-1} - t^k\nabla f(\alpha^{k-1})\}$, where $T_x(\cdot) : R^n \rightarrow R^n$ is the shrinkage soft threshold; $T_x(y) = (|y| - x)^+ sign(y)$, where $(Y)^+ = max\{0, Y\}$ and $sign$ is the sign function. Therefore, $\alpha^k = (|\alpha^{k-1} - t^k\nabla f(\alpha^{k-1})| - \lambda t^k) sign(\alpha^{k-1} - t^k\nabla f(\alpha^{k-1}))$

THEOREM 1. α^k ***is separable to calculate. Since the*** l_1 ***norm is separable, the computation of*** α^k ***reduces to solving a one-dimensional minimization problem for each of its components.***

Proof: α^k is equivalent to $argmin_\alpha\{\frac{1}{2t^k}\|\alpha - \alpha^{k-1} + t^k\nabla f(\alpha^{k-1})\|_2^2 + \lambda\|\alpha\|_1\}$ after ignoring constant terms, because:

$$\begin{aligned}\alpha^k &= argmin_\alpha\{\tfrac{1}{2t^k}(\|\alpha - \alpha^{k-1}\|_2^2 + 2t^k\nabla f(\alpha^{k-1})^T(\alpha - \alpha^{k-1}) \\ &\quad +(t^k)^2\|\nabla f(\alpha^{k-1})\|_2^2) + \lambda\|\alpha\|_1\} \\ &= argmin_\alpha\{\tfrac{1}{2t^k}(\|a\|_2^2 - 2a^Tb + \|b\|_2^2) + \lambda\|\alpha\|_1\} \\ &= argmin_\alpha\{\tfrac{1}{2t^k}\|\alpha - \alpha^{k-1} + t^k\nabla f(\alpha^{k-1})\|_2^2 + \lambda\|\alpha\|_1\} \\ &= argmin_\alpha\{\tfrac{1}{2t^k}\|\alpha - c\|_2^2 + \lambda\|\alpha\|_1\} \\ &= argmin_\alpha\{\tfrac{1}{2t^k}\textstyle\sum_{i=1}^n(\alpha_i - c_i)^2 + \lambda|\alpha_i|\}\end{aligned}$$

where $a = \alpha - \alpha^{k-1}$, $b = t^k\nabla f(\alpha^{k-1})$, and $c = \alpha^{k-1} - t^k\nabla f(\alpha^{k-1})$. t^k is the step length. From this derivation, we could see that we can minimize each component of α separately. This also provides our opportunities of distributed computing. Therefore,

$$\alpha_i^k = (|\alpha_i^{k-1} - t^k\nabla f(\alpha_i^{k-1})| - \lambda t^k) sign(\alpha_i^{k-1} - t^k\nabla f(\alpha_i^{k-1})) \blacksquare$$

There are still some key points that need to be addressed, including: (I) step length. Usually, we use $t^k = \frac{1}{L}$ as the step length where L is the lipschitz continuity. In this work, we set L to $\|A^TA\|_2$. (II) Stopping condition. We use the following criteria to stop the iterative learning process.

$$\frac{\|\alpha^{k+1} - \alpha^k\|_F^2}{\|\alpha^k\|_F^2} \leq \epsilon$$

where $\|X\|_F$ is called the Frobenius norm and $\|X\|_F = \sqrt{\sum_{i=1}^m\sum_{j=1}^n |x_{ij}|^2}$. (III) Convergence. Previous work has show ISTA algorithm behaves like: $f(\alpha^k) - f(\alpha^\star) \simeq \mathcal{O}(1/k)$ ($\alpha^\star$ is the optimal value of α), namely, shares a sublinear global rate of convergence. In [2], authors proved the converge in function values as $\mathcal{O}(1/k^2)$, where k is the iteration counter. (IV) Backtracking. There are a number of different accelerated backtracking schemes and these are made under different criteria for the same reason. We use one of the simpler schemes - line search backtracking. Algorithm 2 describes the learning process of DISTA.

Algorithm 2 DISTA: Distributed Iterative Shrikage-Thresholding Algorithm with Line Search Backtracking

choose β, such that $0 < \beta < 1$;
$t^0 = 1$;
repeat
  $t^k = t^{k-1}$;
  for all i such that $1 \leq i \leq n$ **do**
    {distributed computing of α_i as indicated in $\blacksquare$}
    $\alpha_i^+ = T_{\lambda t^k}\{\alpha_i^{k-1} - t^k\nabla f(\alpha_i^{k-1})\}$;
  end for
  while $(f(\alpha^+) > f(\alpha^{k-1}) + \nabla f(\alpha^{k-1})^T(\alpha^+ - \alpha^{k-1}) + \frac{1}{2t^k}\|\alpha^+ - \alpha^{k-1}\|_2^2)$ **do**
    {line search backtracking step}
    $t^k = \beta t^k$;
    for all i such that $1 \leq i \leq n$ **do**
      $\alpha_i^+ = T_{\lambda t^k}\{\alpha_i^{k-1} - t^k\nabla f(\alpha_i^{k-1})\}$;
    end for
  end while
until the stopping criteria meets
return α^+;

4. EXPERIMENTS AND RESULTS

In this section, we first describe the structure of data used in our experiments. As the social media data is generated by the public, there are many noisy factors. It is necessary to filter out spams to obtain a high-quality data for producing unbiased results. Then, we discuss the experimental results of feature selection and DISTA under different parameter settings and compare them with some baselines.

4.1 Experimental Data and Cleaning

On Facebook, the largest and most popular social network platform, many companies, organizations, and individuals build their own pages to communicate with social users (fans), which generates an extensive amount of networked and textual information. In this paper, we mainly consider social brands as our target objects. We use Facebook Graph API to download the available activities made on brand side such as posts and user side, such as comments on posts, likes on posts, and public profiles. We have designed some rules to filter out spam users and their activities in our previous work, such as users having an abnormal amount of brand accesses (e.g. >100). Table 1 describes the cleaned data used in our experiments. For labels in the training dataset, we consider users who make all positive comments on the target brand as positive samples and negative comments as negative samples.

4.2 Experimental Results

The input data used in our experiments is big. Using single machine to do feature selection, and regression model

Table 2: The comparison of classification accuracy using DISTA between with and without incorporating feature selection under different size of training sets with three baselines. All these results are average accuracy on 10 target brands.

		Classification Accuracy			
Row Normalization	Model	Without Feature Selection		With Feature Selection	
		Size (10,000)	Size (20,000)	Size (10,000)	Size (20,000)
No	Naive Bayes	55.52%	57.30%	58.82%	55.44%
	SVM	61.31%	60.52%	63.04%	56.62%
	Logistic Regression	70.14%	70.10%	71.18%	79.58%
	DISTA	**72.07%**	**73.14%**	**77.58%**	**81.68%**
Yes	Naive Bayes	68.95%	71.04%	86.65%	86.24%
	SVM	77.53%	79.76%	**87.89%**	88.52%
	Logistic Regression	76.70%	79.50%	86.78%	88.07%
	DISTA	**80.32%**	**80.50%**	81.76%	**89.25%**

Table 1: Data descriptions after cleaning.

# of unique users	97,699,832
# of social brands	7,580
# of the triple (user, page, comments)	102,517,478
# of the triple (user, page, likes)	192,442,757
The number of total post likes	5,275,921,875

Table 3: Top 5 associated brands sorted by the confidence score of the rule: "$b_i \Rightarrow Nordstrom$"

Rank	Brand Name (b_i)	Confidence Score
1	NORDSTROM RACK	0.288
2	NEIMAN MARCUS	0.225
3	HAUTELOOK	0.185
4	SAKS FIFTH AVENUE	0.181
5	LORD & TAYLOR	0.169

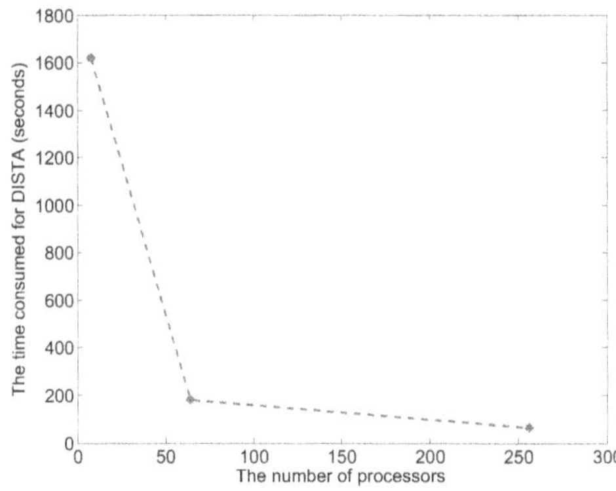

Figure 1: The time (seconds) consumed for DISTA on different number of processors.

building is infeasible. In fact, we could not finish the job within 10 hours using only single machine. Hence, we conduct our experiments on a Hadoop-based environment which has 10 machines. Each machine has 8 compute processors. We randomly select 10 different target brands in our experiments. Table 3 shows top 5 correlated brands to the target brand "Nordstrom" in terms of the confidence score. Table 2 compares the performance of using DISTA between with and without incorporating this feature selection strategy under different size of training sets with three other baselines. It shows that with our feature selection strategy can obtain up to 16% increase of accuracy and also always beat without incorporating feature selection.

To build the model, we used the training dataset of size 10,000 positive instances and 10,000 negative instances. We use 10-fold cross validation. For such training sets, it takes a long time to finish learning. But our DISTA learning algorithm significantly speeds it up, as shown in Figure 1.

5. CONCLUSION AND FUTURE WORK

In this work, we build a user predictive model based on their historical behaviors on social media for on-line advertising. We implemented a distributed Apriori feature selection for reducing the training dataset. In addition, we implemented a distributed iterative shrinkage thresholding model to predict user's preference. The experiments conducted on Facebook data has shown that all proposed techniques in this work are scalable and efficient for social audience-targeted advertising. Future work includes deeply understanding and incorporating semantics of user-generated contents; finding more accurate and fast predictive learning algorithms.

6. REFERENCES

[1] `http://www.biakelsey.com/index.asp`.

[2] Amir Beck and Marc Teboulle. A fast iterative shrinkage-thresholding algorithm for linear inverse problems. *SIAM J. Img. Sci.*, pages 183–202, 2009.

[3] Jian-Feng Cai, Emmanuel J. Candès, and Zuowei Shen. A singular value thresholding algorithm for matrix completion. *SIAM J. on Optimization*, 20(4):1956–1982, 2010.

[4] Bing Liu. *Sentiment Analysis and Opinion Mining*. Synthesis Lectures on Human Language Technologies. Morgan & Claypool Publishers, 2012.

[5] Jie Tang, Tiancheng Lou, and Jon Kleinberg. Inferring social ties across heterogenous networks. In *WSDM*, pages 743–752, New York, USA, 2012.

[6] Theresa Wilson, Paul Hoffmann, Swapna Somasundaran, Jason Kessler, Janyce Wiebe, Yejin Choi, Claire Cardie, Ellen Riloff, and Siddharth Patwardhan. Opinionfinder: A system for subjectivity analysis. In *Proceedings of HLT/EMNLP on Interactive Demonstrations*, pages 34–35, 2005.

Social Collaborative Filtering for Cold-start Recommendations

Suvash Sedhain*
ANU/NICTA and Kobo Inc.
Canberra, Australia
suvash.sedhain@anu.edu.au

Scott Sanner
NICTA/ANU
Canberra, Australia
ssanner@nicta.com.au

Darius Braziunas
Kobo Inc.
Toronto, Canada
dbraziunas@kobo.com

Lexing Xie
ANU/NICTA
Canberra, Australia
lexing.xie@anu.edu.au

Jordan Christensen
Kobo Inc.
Toronto, Canada
jchristensen@kobo.com

ABSTRACT

We examine the cold-start recommendation task in an online retail setting for users who have not yet purchased (or interacted in a meaningful way with) any available items but who have granted access to limited side information, such as basic demographic data (gender, age, location) or social network information (Facebook friends or page likes). We formalize neighborhood-based methods for cold-start collaborative filtering in a generalized matrix algebra framework that does *not* require purchase data for target users when their side information is available. In real-data experiments with 30,000 users who purchased 80,000+ books and had 9,000,000+ Facebook friends and 6,000,000+ page likes, we show that using Facebook page likes for cold-start recommendation yields up to a 3-fold improvement in mean average precision (mAP) and up to 6-fold improvements in Precision@k and Recall@k compared to most-popular-item, demographic, and Facebook friend cold-start recommenders. These results demonstrate the substantial predictive power of social network content, and its significant utility in a challenging problem – recommendation for cold-start users.

Categories and Subject Descriptors

H.4 [**Information Search and Retrieval**]: Information Filtering

General Terms

Algorithms; Experimentation; Performance

Keywords

Recommender systems; Cold-start problem

*Parts of this work were done while the first author was an intern at Kobo Inc.

RecSys'14, October 6–10, 2014, Foster City, Silicon Valley, CA, USA.

ACM 978-1-4503-2668-1/14/10 ...$15.00.
http://dx.doi.org/10.1145/2645710.2645772 .

1. INTRODUCTION

The user cold-start problem concerns the task of recommending items to users who have not previously purchased or otherwise expressed meaningful preferences towards any items under consideration for recommendation. Addressing the cold-start problem can be important for first-time user engagement and retention and is therefore of critical significance in settings such as online retail.

While traditional collaborative filtering methods [1, 6] often provide strong recommendation performance once a user has made a few item purchases or preference judgments, they cannot be used in the cold-start setting when there are no user interactions with items. Content-based and user-based filtering [3] approaches may recommend solely based on user and item features in the absence of direct purchase or preference information over items; however, these methods typically provide very coarse approximations of content types (e.g., genre, author) and user profiles (e.g., gender, age, and location) and often only do marginally better than recommendation based solely on item popularity, as we show for the case of user-based demographic data in Section 4.

Recent years have seen the advent of social extensions of collaborative filtering [5] and efforts to leverage rich user information from Facebook and other social networks for predicting users' latent traits [2] and for recommendation [8, 10]. In the cold-start setting, Lin *et al* [4] leveraged social information for the *item* cold-start recommendation problem (where an item has not been previously purchased or rated by anyone), e.g., recommending new apps by leveraging Twitter feedback on an app's developer even though the app itself may be yet unrated.

Here, we propose to directly leverage user's social network content such as Facebook friends and page likes in a novel extension of item-based collaborative filtering formalized in a generalized matrix algebra framework. This framework does *not* require item purchase or preference data for target users and hence addresses the *user* cold-start problem.

We experiment with a subset of data from Kobo Inc. that contains 30,000 users who purchased 80,000+ ebooks and had 9,000,000+ Facebook friends and liked 6,000,000+ pages. We demonstrate that using Facebook page likes for cold-start recommendation yields up to a 3-fold improvement in mean average precision (mAP) and up to 6-fold improvements in Precision@k and Recall@k when compared to most-popular-item, demographic, and Facebook friend cold-

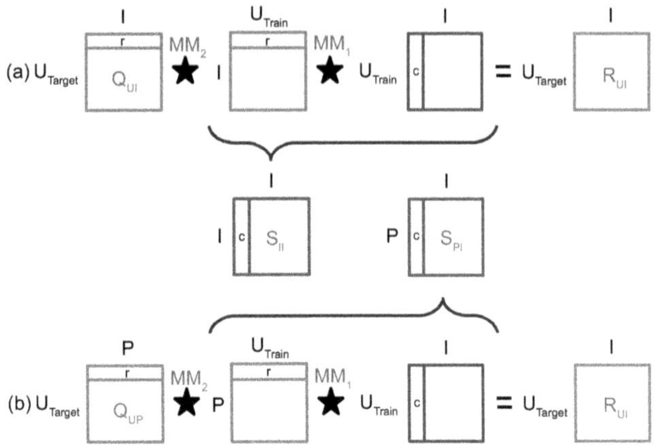

Figure 1: (a) A matrix algebra view of standard item-item neighborhood-based recommendation and (b) a variation for social cold-start recommendation that instead uses page-item similarity and does not require item purchase information for target users. U represents the user dimension (subdivided into train and test users), I the item dimension, and P the user's personal information dimension (demographics, friends, or page likes). The ★ operators annotated by MM_1 and MM_2 denote *generalized* matrix multiplication, permitting *any* similarity metric over two vectors in place of the usual inner product.

start recommendation approaches. These results demonstrate the substantial predictive power of social network content when leveraged in our novel social collaborative filtering framework for cold-start recommendation.

2. BACKGROUND AND CONTRIBUTION

We begin our discussion with a brief technical review of neighborhood-based collaborative filtering methods as viewed from a generalized matrix algebra framework and then discuss our extensions of this framework to a social collaborative filtering approach for cold-start recommendation.

2.1 Item-based Recommendation

We refer the reader to Figure 1(a) which shows a matrix view of item-based collaborative filtering [7]. Here Q_{UI} denotes a matrix of user-item purchases (users in rows, items in columns) for a set of target users $U_{Target} = \{u_1, u_2, \dots, u_m\}$ and a set of items $I = \{i_1, i_2, \dots, i_n\}$. For any $u \in U_{Target}$ and $i \in I$, we define

$$Q_{u,i} = \begin{Bmatrix} 1 & \textit{if } u \text{ purchased } i \\ 0 & \textit{otherwise} \end{Bmatrix}$$

For a set of training users U_{Train} (potentially overlapping with U_{Target}) and analogous definitions of the remaining matrices on the LHS of the equality in Figure 1(a), we can apply operator ★ annotated by MM_1 (e.g, matrix multiplication) to obtain S_{II}, where for items $i \in I$ and $j \in I$, S_{ij} represents an item-item similarity between i and j. Finally, applying operator MM_2 to compute $Q_{UI}{\star}S_{II}$ yields a recommendation matrix R_{UI} where for each target user $u \in U_{Target}$ and item $i \in I$, R_{ui} represents a real-valued rating. Given R_{ui} and sorting items in descending order for each u yields a ranked list of most- to least-recommended items for user u.

By permitting definitions for the ★ operators MM_1 and MM_2 other than standard matrix multiplication, we define a generalized matrix algebra framework for recommendation that can recover many existing frameworks when the operators are defined appropriately. For example, in order to recover a version of item-based collaborative filtering [7], one could use cosine similarity in place of the inner product for MM_1. In general, we explore the following similarity metrics $Sim(\boldsymbol{r}, \boldsymbol{c})$ for the row $\boldsymbol{r}$ and column $\boldsymbol{c}$ vectors used to define ★ in MM_1 and MM_2 (they need not be the same):

- **IP:** Standard matrix multiply inner product given by
$$Sim(\boldsymbol{r}, \boldsymbol{c}) = \langle \boldsymbol{r}, \boldsymbol{c} \rangle.$$
- **BinIP:** For $\tau \in \mathbb{R}$, a binary thresholded version of the inner product given by
$$Sim(\boldsymbol{r}, \boldsymbol{c}) = \begin{cases} 1 & \textit{if } \langle \boldsymbol{r}, \boldsymbol{c} \rangle > \tau \\ 0 & \textit{otherwise} \end{cases}.$$
- **LogIP:** A logarithm of the inner product
$$Sim(\boldsymbol{r}, \boldsymbol{c}) = \log \langle \boldsymbol{r}, \boldsymbol{c} \rangle.$$
- **Cos:** Cosine similarity which is obtained by an inner product of two L_2 normalized vectors equivalent to
$$Sim(\boldsymbol{r}, \boldsymbol{c}) = \frac{\langle \boldsymbol{r}, \boldsymbol{c} \rangle}{\|\boldsymbol{r}\| \|\boldsymbol{c}\|}.$$

While there are alternate similarity metrics that can be considered (e.g., Pearson Correlation Coefficient in general and Jaccard in the special case of binary vectors), the above metrics worked best for our cold-start evaluation.

2.2 Social Cold-start Recommendation

Returning to our discussion of Figure 1(a), since Q_{UI} requires item interaction information for the target users U_{Target}, item-based collaborative filtering is not applicable in the cold-start case. However, if we view the purchased subset of items I simply as user attributes and extend this attribute set to other non-item personal attributes P (e.g., demographics, Facebook friends, or page likes) then for users U_{Target} we can substitute P for I to obtain Figure 1(b).

More formally, we define $P = \{p_1, p_2, \dots, p_l\}$ as a set of attributes for user demographic traits (gender, age group, location), Facebook friends, or Facebook page likes. Then we define the matrices in Figure 1(b) analogous to 1(a) where the first two matrices replace dimensions over I with dimensions over P. Thus for Q_{UP} and any $p \in P$ (e.g., page likes) and $u \in U_{Target}$, $Q_{up} = 1$ if u had attribute p (e.g., u liked p) and $Q_{up} = 0$ otherwise. Defining the second matrix analogously, we apply MM_1 ★ to obtain S_{PI} which relates personal attributes P to preferences over items I. And finally $Q_{UP}{\star}S_{PI}$ yields recommendation matrix R_{UI} analogous to Figure 1(a) except that in 1(b), no interactions on I were required for the target recommendation users U_{Target}, thus making 1(b) applicable in the cold-start case.

While this recommender can use both social (e.g. friends, page likes) and non-social (e.g. demographics) information to define P, we note that our experimental evaluation in Section 4 shows that page likes provide an exceptionally strong signal for cold-start recommendation. These results lead us to focus on the contribution of this novel cold-start recommender in conjunction with social data.

	Most Popular		Demographics		Friend Network		Page Likes	
k	Precision	Recall	Precision	Recall	Precision	Recall	Precision	Recall
@1	0.006+/-0.003	0.006+/-0.003	0.014+/-0.004	0.014+/-0.004	0.014+/-0.006	0.014+/-0.006	**0.038+/-0.015**	**0.038+/-0.015**
@3	0.008+/-0.003	0.023+/-0.010	0.010+/-0.003	0.031+/-0.008	0.011+/-0.004	0.032+/-0.012	**0.025+/-0.010**	**0.076+/-0.029**
@5	0.008+/-0.004	0.039+/-0.019	0.010+/-0.004	0.050+/-0.018	0.009+/-0.003	0.044+/-0.016	**0.023+/-0.009**	**0.117+/-0.044**
@10	0.007+/-0.003	0.074+/-0.034	0.008+/-0.003	0.083+/-0.029	0.006+/-0.002	0.062+/-0.022	**0.017+/-0.006**	**0.173+/-0.059**
@20	0.006+/-0.003	0.120+/-0.067	0.006+/-0.003	0.125+/-0.051	0.004+/-0.001	0.078+/-0.025	**0.010+/-0.003**	**0.205+/-0.063**
mAP	0.026+/-0.011		0.035+/-0.010		0.029+/-0.010		**0.075+/-0.025**	

Table 1: Comparison of Most Popular baseline with various cold-start recommender systems.

	IP-IP		LogIP-IP		BinIP-IP		Cos-IP	
k	Precision	Recall	Precision	Recall	Precision	Recall	Precision	Recall
@1	0.027+/-0.013	0.027+/-0.013	**0.030+/-0.012**	**0.030+/-0.012**	0.028+/-0.012	0.028+/-0.012	**0.030+/-0.012**	**0.030+/-0.012**
@3	0.018+/-0.007	0.053+/-0.020	0.020+/-0.008	0.061+/-0.023	**0.022+/-0.009**	**0.066+/-0.026**	**0.022+/-0.008**	**0.066+/-0.024**
@5	0.017+/-0.006	0.086+/-0.032	0.019+/-0.008	0.097+/-0.038	**0.020+/-0.008**	**0.102+/-0.040**	**0.020+/-0.008**	**0.102+/-0.038**
@10	0.014+/-0.005	0.136+/-0.047	**0.015+/-0.005**	0.148+/-0.050	**0.015+/-0.005**	0.153+/-0.051	**0.015+/-0.005**	**0.154+/-0.052**
@20	0.009+/-0.003	0.181+/-0.060	0.009+/-0.003	0.185+/-0.061	0.009+/-0.003	0.186+/-0.060	**0.010+/-0.003**	**0.191+/-0.060**
mAP	0.057+/-0.019		0.062+/-0.021		0.063+/-0.022		**0.065+/-0.021**	

Table 2: Performance of Page Likes Recommender for $\mathrm{MM}_1 \in \{$IP, LogIP, BinIP, Cos$\}$, $\mathrm{MM}_2 =$ IP.

	IP-Cos		LogIP-Cos		BinIP-Cos		Cos-Cos	
k	Precision	Recall	Precision	Recall	Precision	Recall	Precision	Recall
@1	0.031+/-0.014	0.031+/-0.014	0.031+/-0.013	0.031+/-0.013	0.030+/-0.014	0.030+/-0.014	**0.038+/-0.015**	**0.038+/-0.015**
@3	0.021+/-0.008	0.064+/-0.023	0.022+/-0.008	0.065+/-0.023	0.021+/-0.008	0.063+/-0.024	**0.025+/-0.010**	**0.076+/-0.029**
@5	0.020+/-0.008	0.100+/-0.039	0.020+/-0.008	0.101+/-0.038	0.020+/-0.007	0.100+/-0.037	**0.023+/-0.009**	**0.117+/-0.044**
@10	0.015+/-0.005	0.151+/-0.052	0.015+/-0.005	0.153+/-0.052	0.016+/-0.005	0.159+/-0.055	**0.017+/-0.006**	**0.173+/-0.059**
@20	0.010+/-0.003	0.193+/-0.061	0.010+/-0.003	0.193+/-0.061	0.010+/-0.003	0.202+/-0.063	0.010+/-0.003	**0.205+/-0.063**
mAP	0.065+/-0.022		0.065+/-0.022		0.065+/-0.021		**0.075+/-0.025**	

Table 3: Performance of Page Likes Recommender for $\mathrm{MM}_1 \in \{$IP, LogIP, BinIP, Cos$\}$, $\mathrm{MM}_2 =$ Cos.

3. EXPERIMENTAL SETUP

The dataset we use in this study comes from Kobo Inc., a major online ebook retailer with more than 20 million readers. It contains an anonymized dataset of ebook purchases and Facebook friends and page likes for a random subset of 30,000 Kobo users; these users purchased more than 80,000 books, had over 9 million friends and liked about 6 million pages. We subsample pages by including only those pages liked by at least 5 people and not more than 5,000 people, which reduces the number of unique pages to about 600,000. The dataset also includes basic user demographics, namely age group, gender and location.

We split the dataset into 10 temporally divided train and test folds. To prepare the training dataset, we include all the user-item data prior to a specific date, starting from June 2012 and incremented by a month in each fold. The test set includes the first purchase of all new users in the following month when the user had at least 10 page likes.

We can obtain different social cold-start recommenders by choosing the similarity metrics (**IP, LogIP, BinIP, Cos**) used for both MM_1 and MM_2 in Figure 1(b). We express the choices in the order of MM_1-MM_2 and show evaluations for the following eight possibilities (the remaining possibilities did not approach the best result reported among these eight):

- $\mathrm{MM}_2 =$ **IP**, $\mathrm{MM}_1 \in \{$**IP, LogIP, BinIP, Cos**$\}$
- $\mathrm{MM}_2 =$ **Cos**, $\mathrm{MM}_1 \in \{$**IP, LogIP, BinIP, Cos**$\}$

We used the threshold $\tau = 2$ for **BinIP**.

We compare the popularity-based baseline with three cold-start collaborative filtering recommender systems defined in Section 2.2, all using respective P as defined below and **Cos-Cos** similarities unless otherwise specified:

- **Most popular** baseline recommends the most popular items in the dataset in order of popularity. While this is a non-personalized recommender, it is often used in the cold-start setting.
- **Demographics** defines P as the set of binary attribute dimensions for a user's gender, age-group and location. Here, we use 10 different disjoint age group indicators, each with a range of 10 years. Every unique location gets its own binary attribute.
- **Friends** defines P as the set of binary attribute dimensions for Facebook friends and assumes that all users are friends with themselves.
- **Page Likes** defines P as the set of binary attributes for Facebook page likes.

In all of the experiments, we report Precision@k, Recall@k and mean average precision (mAP@100)[1] using 10-fold cross validation and provide standard error bars corresponding to 95% confidence intervals.

4. RESULTS AND ANALYSIS

In Table 1, we compare our most popular baseline with three variants of our cold-start approach. Here, we see that social cold-start collaborative filtering using **Page Likes** yields up to a 3-fold improvement in mean average precision (mAP) and up to 6-fold improvements in Precision@k and Recall@k when comparing to **Most Popular**, **Demographic**, and Facebook **Friend Network** recommenders.

[1]As defined in `https://www.kddcup2012.org/c/kddcup2012-track1/details/Evaluation` and used as a surrogate measure of area under the precision/recall curve.

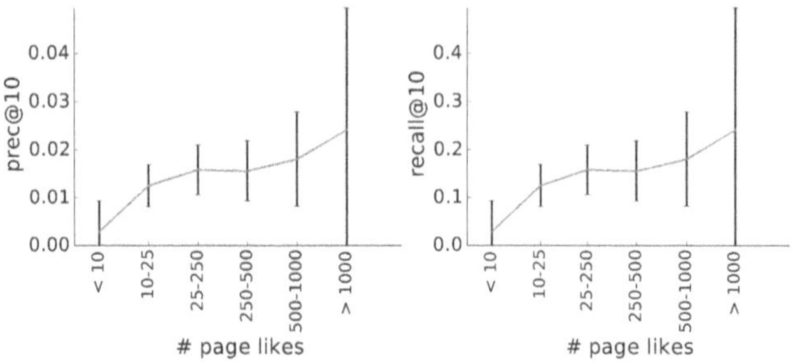

Figure 2: Performance of the Page Likes recommender for users vs. different numbers of page likes.

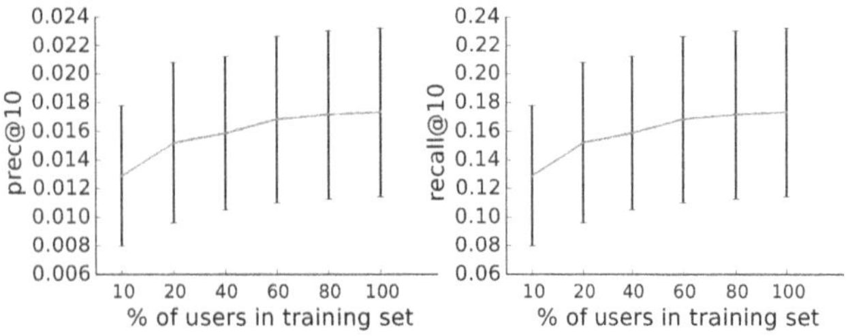

Figure 3: Performance of the Page Likes recommender vs. the percentage of users in U_{Train} used.

To assess whether **Cos-Cos** is indeed the best choice for MM_1-MM_2, we evaluate variants as previously described in Tables 2 and 3 and show that **Cos-Cos** is the best method for social cold-start recommendation with **Page Likes**. We remark that **Cos-Cos** likewise performed best among **Demographics** and the **Friend Network**.

To conclude our analysis we focus on the best performing **Page Likes** social cold-start recommender and investigate its performance as a function of different key quantities:

How does performance vary vs. the number of page likes for a target user? The number of page likes varies from user to user. Thus we divide users in U_{Target} into six categories based on the number of pages they have liked and evaluate the performance on each user category. Figure 4 shows that performance increases as the number of user page likes increases. However, the variance for users with the largest number of page likes is much higher, indicating that a lack of selectiveness with page likes can lead to high noise when using this information for cold-start recommendation.

How does performance vary vs. the number of users and pages in the training set? To analyze this for the number of users, we randomly select $x\%$ of users from U_{Train} and show the cold-start performance vs. x in Figure 4. This figure shows that the performance steadily increases with the number of users, but with diminishing returns beyond 80% of the users. Similarly, we randomly select $x\%$ of the dimensions in P and show the cold-start performance vs. x in Figure 4. This figure shows that the performance increases gradually with the number of pages but with less increase in improvement once 40% of the pages in P are used.

5. CONCLUSION

We defined a novel social collaborative filtering framework that generalizes standard item-based collaborative filtering

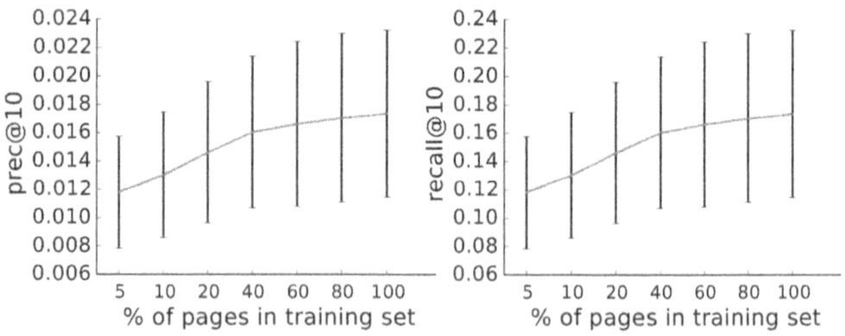

Figure 4: Performance of the Page Likes recommender vs. the percentage of pages in P used.

to the cold-start recommendation setting. When used in conjunction with Facebook page likes data for each user, this approach substantially outperformed cold-start recommenders based on popular items, demographics, and the Facebook friend network. Overall, these results demonstrate the substantial power of Facebook page likes when leveraged to address the user cold-start recommendation problem in a social collaborative filtering framework. Future work may explore whether this work can be extended with learning-based techniques such as *collective matrix factorization* [9].

6. ACKNOWLEDGMENTS

NICTA is funded by the Australian Government as represented by the Department of Broadband, Communications and the Digital Economy and the Australian Research Council through the ICT Centre of Excellence program. This research was supported in part by Australian Research Council project DP140102185.

7. REFERENCES

[1] R. M. Bell and Y. Koren. Scalable collaborative filtering with jointly derived neighborhood interpolation weights. In *ICDM-07*, 2007.

[2] M. Kosinski, D. Stillwell, and T. Graepel. Private traits and attributes are predictable from digital records of human behavior. In *PNAS-13*, volume 110, 2013.

[3] K. Lang. NewsWeeder: Learning to filter netnews. In *ICML-95*, 1995.

[4] J. Lin, K. Sugiyama, M.-Y. Kan, and T.-S. Chua. Addressing cold-start in app recommendation: Latent user models constructed from twitter followers. In *SIGIR-13*. 2013.

[5] H. Ma, H. Yang, M. R. Lyu, and I. King. Sorec: Social recommendation using probabilistic matrix factorization. In *CIKM-08*, 2008.

[6] P. Resnick and H. R. Varian. Recommender systems. *Communications of the ACM*, 40, March 1997.

[7] B. Sarwar, G. Karypis, J. Konstan, and J. Riedl. Item-based collaborative filtering recommendation algorithms. In *WWW-01*, 2001.

[8] S. Sedhain, S. Sanner, L. Xie, R. Kidd, K.-N. Tran, and P. Christen. Social affinity filtering: Recommendation through fine-grained analysis of user interactions and activities. In *COSN-13*, 2013.

[9] A. P. Singh and G. J. Gordon. Relational learning via collective matrix factorization. In *KDD-08*, 2008.

[10] Y. Zhang and M. Pennacchiotti. Predicting purchase behaviors from social media. In *WWW-13*, 2013.

Switching Hybrid for Cold-Starting Context-Aware Recommender Systems

Matthias Braunhofer
Free University of Bolzano
Piazza Domenicani 3
Bolzano, Italy
mbraunhofer@unibz.it

Victor Codina
Technical University of Catalonia
Jordi Girona 1-3
Barcelona, Spain
vcodina@lsi.upc.edu

Francesco Ricci
Free University of Bolzano
Piazza Domenicani 3
Bolzano, Italy
fricci@unibz.it

ABSTRACT

Finding effective solutions for cold-starting Context-Aware Recommender Systems (CARSs) is important because usually low quality recommendations are produced for users, items or contextual situations that are new to the system. In this paper, we tackle this problem with a switching hybrid solution that exploits a custom selection of two CARS algorithms, each one suited for a particular cold-start situation, and switches between these algorithms depending on the detected recommendation situation (new user, new item or new context). We evaluate the proposed algorithms in an off-line experiment by using various contextually-tagged rating datasets. We illustrate some significant performance differences between the considered algorithms and show that they can be effectively combined into the proposed switching hybrid to cope with different types of cold-start problems.

Categories and Subject Descriptors

H.3.3 [**Information Storage and Retrieval**]: Information Search and Retrieval—*information filtering*

Keywords

Context-Aware Recommender Systems; Cold-Start Problem; Switching Hybrid System

1. INTRODUCTION

Context-Aware Recommender Systems (CARSs) are a special type of Recommender Systems (RSs) that aim at generating more accurate recommendations by exploiting not only the traditional user and item dimensions but also relevant contextual information (e.g., time, weather, location) in the recommendation process [1]. Context management aggravates the cold-start, i.e., dealing with new users and new items, which is affecting traditional RSs; in CARSs it does not suffice to have enough ratings for users and items, it is also necessary a sufficient number of ratings in the various contextual situations the system may be requested to operate: the new context problem.

In this paper, we analyse the cold-start situations that can be observed in CARSs. In particular, we deal with: (i) the new user problem, which occurs when a new user is added to a CARS and there is not enough information about the user's preferences to make good suggestions; (ii) the new item problem, which refers to new items introduced into a CARS and that can not be recommended until some users have rated them; and (iii) the new context problem, which was not specifically considered so far, and relates to the difficulty of accurately recommending items to users under new contextual situations.

We have tackled the above mentioned problems with two novel CARS algorithms namely, demographics-based CAMF-CC and content-based CAMF-CC, which are hypothesised to perform better in one or more of the above considered cold-start cases, and a switching hybrid combination [5], named SHCA. SHCA switches between these two depending on the target recommendation situation. These three algorithms are compared with two state of the art CARS algorithms: CAMF-CC, which is a variant of Context-Aware Matrix Factorisation (CAMF) [3] and SPF (Semantic Pre-Filtering) [6]. We have evaluated all the considered algorithms in an off-line experiment on some contextually-tagged rating datasets, i.e., datasets of ratings for items tagged with the contextual situations of the user while experiencing the rated item. Results from this study show that, as conjectured, there exist some significant performance differences between the algorithms across the individual cold-start cases, and that the proposed switching hybrid provides a more robust solution to the identified cold-start situations.

2. RATING PREDICTION MODELS

This section describes the four CARS algorithms (two state of the art and two novel) and the switching hybrid solution that we have tested in cold-start situations. The $|Users| \times |Items| \times |Context|$ rating tensor is denoted as R, where $|Users|$ is the number of users, $|Items|$ is the number of items, and $|Context|$ is the number of contextual situations. The tensor entry $r_{uic_1,\ldots,c_k}$ is the rating of user u on item i in the contextual situation described by the contextual conditions $c_1, \ldots, c_k$, and c_j is the index of the contextual condition for factor j (e.g., the index of condition "sunny" for the "weather" contextual factor).

RecSys'14, October 6–10, 2014, Foster City, Silicon Valley, CA, USA.

http://dx.doi.org/10.1145/2645710.2645757.

2.1 CAMF-CC

CAMF-CC (Context-Aware Matrix Factorisation for item categories) is a variant of CAMF [3] that extends standard Matrix Factorisation (MF) by incorporating baseline parameters for each contextual condition and item category. It models how the ratings of items belonging to a specific category are affected by the contextual conditions. We have chosen that particular CAMF variant since it was shown to outperform other CAMF variants in terms of Mean Absolute Error (MAE) [3]. Given a user u, an item i, a contextual situation $c_1, ..., c_k$ and the set of categories $T(i)$ associated to item i, it predicts ratings using the following rule:

$$\hat{r}_{uic_1,...,c_k} = q_i^\top p_u + \mu + b_i + b_u + \sum_{t \in T(i)} \sum_{j=1}^{k} b_{tc_j} \quad (1)$$

where q_i and p_u are the latent factor vectors associated to the item i and user u, respectively. μ is the overall average rating, and b_i, b_u and b_{tc_j} are the baseline parameters for item i, user u, and item category-contextual condition pair tc_j, respectively. We learned the model parameters by minimising the associated regularised squared error function.

2.2 Semantic Pre-Filtering

Semantic Pre-Filtering (SPF) [6] is a pre-filtering method [1] that, given a target contextual situation, uses a standard MF model learnt on all the ratings tagged with contextual situations equal or similar to the target one. SPF is conjectured to better perform in cold-start situations because it is able to reuse ratings tagged with contexts that, although syntactically different, they influence the users' ratings similarly. Thus, SPF can build more robust local MF models. In our work, we used the particular SPF variant described in [6], which models contextual conditions as their per-item aggregated impact in combination with Singular Value Decomposition (SVD).

2.3 Content-based CAMF-CC

We conjecture that CAMF-CC may fail to provide accurate recommendations for items that have received few or no ratings (i.e., new item problem). The reason is that CAMF-CC, in order to create profiles for items, relies exclusively on explicit ratings. Content-based CAMF-CC, which we propose here, addresses this problem by taking into account item attributes, for instance, the type of a place of interest (POI), the actors or the genre of a movie, in addition to user ratings. A distinct factor vector x_a for each item's attribute $a \in A(i)$ models how an item's attribute influences the item's rating $\sum_{a \in A(i)} x_a$:

$$\hat{r}_{uic_1,...,c_k} = (q_i + \sum_{a \in A(i)} x_a)^\top p_u + \mu + b_i + b_u + \sum_{t \in T(i)} \sum_{j=1}^{k} b_{tc_j} \quad (2)$$

2.4 Demographics-based CAMF-CC

Content-based CAMF-CC doesn't explicitly tackle the new user problem. Hence, we propose also a demographics-based CAMF-CC variant that addresses this problem by profiling users through known users attributes, such as gender, age group, personality traits, and so on. A distinct factor vector y_a is used to describe a user through the set of user-associated attributes $\sum_{a \in A(u)} y_a$. By enhancing the user representation demographics-based CAMF-CC predicts ratings using the following rule:

$$\hat{r}_{uic_1,...,c_k} = q_i^\top (p_u + \sum_{a \in A(u)} y_a) + \mu + b_i + b_u + \sum_{t \in T(i)} \sum_{j=1}^{k} b_{tc_j} \quad (3)$$

2.5 Switching Hybrid - SHCA

We finally propose here SHCA, a switching hybrid algorithm that combines the conjectured strengths of the two previously described novel CARS algorithms: content-based CAMF-CC and demographics-based CAMF-CC. SHCA uses content-based CAMF-CC when it is requested to predict a rating for a new item, while it uses demographics-based CAMF-CC when predicting a rating for a new user or a new contextual situation. When a mixture of the elementary cold-start situations is detected, SHCA computes the predicted rating by averaging the predictions of the two constituent algorithms. For instance, the predictions for a rating that is both for a new user and a new item is the average of the ratings estimated by demographics-based CAMF-CC and content-based CAMF-CC. SHCA is expected to better tackle all kinds of cold-start situations found in CARSs. More adaptive combinations of elementary CARS algorithms will be considered in future work.

3. EXPERIMENTAL EVALUATION

We present here the evaluation of the aforementioned CARS algorithms, compared with a baseline Matrix Factorisation (MF) algorithm [10]. We first describe the datasets used in the evaluation, then the experimental design, and finally we present and discuss the obtained results.

3.1 Datasets

We have used three contextually-tagged rating datasets with different characteristics: *STS* [8]; *CoMoDa* [11]; *Music* [2]. Table 1 provides some descriptive statistics of these datasets. We note that there are only a few contextually-tagged rating datasets available, and these are amongst the more popular ones.

Table 1: Datasets' characteristics

Dataset	STS	CoMoDa	Music
Domain	POIs	Movies	Music
Rating scale	1-5	1-5	1-5
Ratings	2,534	2,296	4,012
Users	325	121	43
Items	249	1,232	139
Contextual factors	14	12	8
Contextual conditions	57	49	26
Contextual situations	931	1,969	26
User attributes	7	4	10
Item features	1	7	2

3.2 Evaluation Procedure

Our experiment involved three separate test cases, one for each of the three cold-start situations being addressed. In the first test case, we measured the algorithms' performance for new users by carrying out a ten-fold cross-validation scheme as follows. First, we shuffled the set of users in the whole rating dataset and split it into ten (roughly) equally sized subsets. Then, in each cross-validation iteration, we used the ratings coming from nine merged user subsets as training set to build the models and the remaining ones as testing set. In this way, the testing set contains users with no ratings in the training set (new users). Finally, for each of the ten iterations, we computed the Mean Absolute Error (MAE) of the models, which were then averaged over all iterations to obtain more reliable results.

In addition, we measured the normalised Discounted Cumulative Gain_1 (nDCG_1) for each evaluation run, using the test procedure described in [12]. We also calculated nDCG_k, $k = 2, \dots 5$, but for lack of space and since they gave similar results we do not report them.

An identical procedure was used when assessing models' performance on new items and new contextual situations, respectively. The only difference was that here cross-validation was performed on the set of items and contextual situations rather than the set of users. In principle, our evaluation procedure could also be used for assessing the models' performance on mixtures of cold-start cases, by cross-validating on user-item, user-context, item-context and user-item-context tuples. This would be interesting since the proposed hybrid algorithm SHCA is expected to handle this kind of mixed cases. However, we did not assess these performances because the available rating datasets are not large and dense enough to perform this fine-grained analysis. Another aspect not considered here is that there exist various degrees of coldness; but we focused on really cold users, items and contextual situations, i.e., without any observed rating.

3.3 Evaluation Results

The obtained results are summarised in Table 2. Not considering SHCA, which is discussed at the end of this section, it can be noted that demographics-based CAMF-CC performed very well in the new user situation. This supports our hypothesis that in this case CAMF-CC can be improved by using user attributes. The weaker performance of demographics-based CAMF-CC on the *Music* dataset may be explained by noting that, differently from the other datasets, where attributes like age, gender, user personality and zip code are available, here only the users' evaluations of the music genres (e.g., user u likes pop music, giving it five out of five stars) are available.

Regarding the new item scenario, we can observe, as conjectured, the excellent performance of content-based CAMF-CC, if compared to the other non-hybrid algorithms. It is effective in this situation because it profiles items also using the available metadata. In the new context scenario, again the demographics-based CAMF-CC is the best. We note that SPF performs very badly in the *Music* dataset because here contextual situations are made up of only one contextual condition. This makes it impossible for SPF to correctly compute similarities between contextual situations.

Finally, if we now focus on the results obtained by the proposed switching hybrid approach SHCA, it can be seen that it is able to correctly exploit the strengths (and avoid the weaknesses) of the elementary algorithms in all the individual cold-start cases. In all cases, except for the new user scenario in the *Music* dataset, it is the best or second best performing algorithm. This illustrates that SHCA, and likely a more adaptive version of it, can become a viable and flexible solution for cold-starting CARSs if an adequate set of elementary (non-hybrid) models are available.

4. RELATED WORK

So far, only little research has been conducted specifically on the cold-start problem for CARSs. One direct approach to this problem is to acquire additional information about the users, items or contextual situations. However, acquiring such information usually requires some additional effort of the users and/or service providers. This effort can be mitigated by employing an Active Learning (AL) strategy [8] or a cross-domain recommendation technique [9]. Another alternative, which we considered in our work, is to exploit a set of metadata describing the users and items (e.g., demographics and item descriptions), and to utilise them in a hybrid CARS in order to overcome the new user and new item problem, respectively [14].

Switching hybrid, as described, e.g., in [7], was used in traditional RSs, i.e., non context-aware. From these approaches we borrowed the idea of selecting and applying the best performing recommender among a set of candidate models, based on the current recommendation situation, and hence avoiding problems specific to a particular recommendation algorithm.

Instead of acquiring new preference data or metadata, one can try to better process the existing preference data. In fact, an example of such approach is SPF [6], which we have evaluated in this paper. SPF tries to deal with the cold-start problem in CARSs by using in the recommendation process, not only contextual ratings that exactly match the target context, but also those that were provided in semantically equivalent contexts. But, as we have shown in this paper, SPF may fail to reliably assess the situation-to-situation similarity in cold-start scenarios.

5. DISCUSSION

We must observe that the off-line evaluation of cold-start performance of CARSs is a complex task. This is mainly due to the lack of large (enough) contextually-tagged rating datasets, which hinders a one-to-one application of the cold-start evaluation protocols proposed before for traditional RSs. For instance, the evaluation schema presented in [12] that splits user ratings into four partitions (i.e., recommendation on existing items for existing users, recommendation on existing items for new users, recommendation on new items for existing users, and recommendation on new items for new users) by randomly selecting half of the users (items) as new users (items) and the rest as existing users (items) can only be applied to very large and dense contextually tagged rating datasets. Otherwise the partitions (i.e., eight in the case of a CARS) will be filled with no or few ratings, or even worse, with "wrong" ratings as the corresponding training ratings might not be available.

Similar limitations apply to the testing methodology illustrated in [13] when trying to extend it and evaluate the system performance not only on new items (the case considered in their work) but also on new users and new contexts. Unfortunately, the standard large-scale datasets used for non context-aware RS research (e.g., MovieLens[1] and LibraryThing[2]) are of limited use here since they do not provide either contextual tags, or user/item attributes, or both.

[1]MovieLens: http://grouplens.org/datasets/movielens/
[2]LibraryThing: https://www.librarything.com

Table 2: Results in terms of MAE and nDCG$_1$ (boldface indicates significant improvements over the baseline MF model with $p < 0.05$; underline means same or better performance of SHCA over all CARS algorithms)

Cold-start case	Algorithm	STS		CoMoDa		Music	
		MAE	nDCG$_1$	MAE	nDCG$_1$	MAE	nDCG$_1$
Recommendation for new users	MF	1.035	0.650	1.044	0.633	1.349	0.351
	CAMF-CC	**0.999**	0.646	0.895	0.548	**1.263**	**0.442**
	SPF	**1.000**	**0.682**	**0.815**	0.630	**1.259**	**0.480**
	Content-based CAMF-CC	1.020	0.641	1.054	**0.692**	2.327	0.397
	Demogr.-based CAMF-CC	**0.997**	0.679	**0.803**	**0.711**	1.307	**0.421**
	SHCA	**0.997**	**0.681**	**0.837**	0.694	1.307	**0.421**
Recommendation for new items	MF	1.056	0.322	0.985	0.242	1.227	0.188
	CAMF-CC	**0.970**	**0.541**	**0.884**	**0.605**	**1.195**	**0.493**
	SPF	**0.984**	**0.597**	**0.837**	**0.288**	1.258	**0.545**
	Content-based CAMF-CC	**0.935**	**0.655**	**0.783**	**0.747**	**1.187**	**0.515**
	Demogr.-based CAMF-CC	**0.941**	**0.552**	**0.868**	**0.743**	1.434	**0.494**
	SHCA	**0.930**	**0.649**	**0.779**	**0.749**	**1.186**	**0.515**
Recommendation under new contexts	MF	0.907	0.711	0.893	0.653	0.817	0.735
	CAMF-CC	**0.868**	0.714	**0.820**	0.680	0.796	0.715
	SPF	**0.854**	**0.745**	**0.807**	0.653	1.009	0.679
	Content-based CAMF-CC	**0.863**	**0.746**	**0.745**	**0.773**	1.108	0.630
	Demogr.-based CAMF-CC	**0.848**	**0.768**	**0.810**	**0.759**	**0.759**	0.747
	SHCA	**0.848**	**0.766**	**0.771**	**0.771**	**0.759**	0.747

6. CONCLUSIONS AND FUTURE WORK

In this study we focused on cold-starting CARSs, i.e., dealing with a lack of ratings for users, items or contextual situations. We have compared (off-line) four CARS algorithms, two state of the art and two novel, which we conjectured to perform well in these scenarios, and a novel switching hybrid approach. We have shown that the two novel CARS algorithms and their hybrid combination (SHCA) successfully deal with all the considered cold-start problems. We have also shown that the new context scenario is the hardest and more research is required to effectively solve it.

Cold-start in CARSs is still a new and poorly explored topic, and there are several research questions that deserve future work. For instance, can the elementary (non-hybrid) CARS algorithms be adaptively combined based on ratings gathered from users [4]? Additionally, how will the proposed algorithms perform on larger contextually-tagged rating datasets? Our results offer an initial support to the conjecture that a switching hybrid approach can be a viable solution to the cold-start problem in CARSs.

7. REFERENCES

[1] G. Adomavicius, B. Mobasher, F. Ricci, and A. Tuzhilin. Context-aware recommender systems. *AI Magazine*, 32(3):67–80, 2011.

[2] L. Baltrunas, M. Kaminskas, B. Ludwig, O. Moling, F. Ricci, A. Aydin, K.-H. Lüke, and R. Schwaiger. Incarmusic: Context-aware music recommendations in a car. In *E-Commerce and Web Technologies*, pages 89–100. Springer, 2011.

[3] L. Baltrunas, B. Ludwig, and F. Ricci. Matrix factorization techniques for context aware recommendation. In *Proceedings of RecSys'11*, pages 301–304. ACM, 2011.

[4] M. Braunhofer. Hybridisation techniques for cold-starting context-aware recommender systems. In *Proceedings of RecSys'14, Doctoral Symposium*. ACM, 2014.

[5] R. Burke. Hybrid web recommender systems. In *The Adaptive Web*, pages 377–408. Springer Berlin / Heidelberg, 2007.

[6] V. Codina, F. Ricci, and L. Ceccaroni. Local context modeling with semantic pre-filtering. In *Proceedings of RecSys'13*, pages 363–366. ACM, 2013.

[7] M. Ekstrand and J. Riedl. When recommenders fail: predicting recommender failure for algorithm selection and combination. In *Proceedings of RecSys'12*, pages 233–236. ACM, 2012.

[8] M. Elahi, M. Braunhofer, F. Ricci, and M. Tkalcic. Personality-based active learning for collaborative filtering recommender systems. In *AI* IA 2013: Advances in Artificial Intelligence*, pages 360–371. Springer, 2013.

[9] M. Enrich, M. Braunhofer, and F. Ricci. Cold-start management with cross-domain collaborative filtering and tags. In *E-Commerce and Web Technologies*, pages 101–112. Springer, 2013.

[10] Y. Koren and R. Bell. Advances in collaborative filtering. In *Recommender Systems Handbook*, pages 145–186. Springer, 2011.

[11] A. Odić, M. Tkalčič, J. F. Tasič, and A. Košir. Predicting and detecting the relevant contextual information in a movie-recommender system. *Interacting with Computers*, 25(1):74–90, 2013.

[12] S.-T. Park and W. Chu. Pairwise preference regression for cold-start recommendation. In *Proceedings of RecSys'09*, pages 21–28. ACM, 2009.

[13] A. I. Schein, A. Popescul, L. H. Ungar, and D. M. Pennock. Methods and metrics for cold-start recommendations. In *Proceedings of the 25th annual international ACM SIGIR conference on Research and development in information retrieval*, pages 253–260. ACM, 2002.

[14] W. Woerndl, M. Brocco, and R. Eigner. Context-aware recommender systems in mobile scenarios. *International Journal of Information Technology and Web Engineering (IJITWE)*, 4(1):67–85, 2009.

Using Graded Implicit Feedback for Bayesian Personalized Ranking

Lukas Lerche
TU Dortmund, Germany
lukas.lerche@tu-dortmund.de

Dietmar Jannach
TU Dortmund, Germany
dietmar.jannach@tu-dortmund.de

ABSTRACT

In many application domains of recommender systems, explicit rating information is sparse or non-existent. The preferences of the current user have therefore to be approximated by interpreting his or her behavior, i.e., the implicit user feedback. In the literature, a number of algorithm proposals have been made that rely solely on such implicit feedback, among them Bayesian Personalized Ranking (BPR).

In the BPR approach, pairwise comparisons between the items are made in the training phase and an item i is considered to be preferred over item j if the user interacted in some form with i but not with j. In real-world applications, however, implicit feedback is not necessarily limited to such binary decisions as there are, e.g., different types of user actions like item views, cart or purchase actions and there can exist several actions for an item over time.

In this paper we show how BPR can be extended to deal with such more fine-granular, graded preference relations. An empirical analysis shows that this extension can help to measurably increase the predictive accuracy of BPR on realistic e-commerce datasets.

Categories and Subject Descriptors

H.3.3 [**Information Search and Retrieval**]: Information filtering

Keywords

Recommender Systems; Implicit Feedback; Evaluation

1. INTRODUCTION

Most of the published Collaborative Filtering (CF) recommendation approaches aim to identify patterns of user preferences within a set of *explicit item ratings* provided by a larger user community. In practice, however, this form of explicit feedback from the users in many application domains is very sparse, limited to dominantly positive or positive-only statements, or even non-existent.

RecSys'14, October 6–10, 2014, Foster City, Silicon Valley, CA, USA.
Copyright 2014 ACM 978-1-4503-2668-1/14/10 ...$15.00.
http://dx.doi.org/10.1145/2645710.2645759.

Correspondingly, a number of proposals have been made in the literature to exploit *implicit user feedback* in the recommendation process, e.g., [3, 7, 8, 10]. In these cases, a user's true preferences are estimated by interpreting his or her behavior. On an online shop, for example, one will typically interpret user actions like an item purchase or viewing an item for some time as a sign of interest in the item.

Bayesian Personalized Ranking (BPR) [10] is a comparably recent CF method designed to deal with implicit-only feedback. One particularity of BPR when compared, e.g., to the highly accurate SVD++-based method [3] is that it directly aims to optimize a ranking criterion, whereas SVD++ primarily aims to minimize the prediction error. Therefore, BPR can be considered to fall into the class of "learning-to-rank" methods [2] which – due to their design – are typically able to outperform methods designed for error-minimization on *rank measures* like precision, recall or nDCG.

In the BPR approach, the input consists of a user-item rating matrix, which however only captures positive interactions (unary feedback), i.e., there is a "one" whenever a user i has interacted with item j. At its core, BPR uses the pairwise preferences derived from the implicit ratings to optimize an AUC-like ranking criterion and Rendle et al. show how this optimization can be applied to two typical classes of recommendation models (kNN and matrix factorization).

One limitation of the basic BPR model is that it only supports discrete, unary feedback. In practice, however, some types of user interactions might be considered stronger indicators of interest than others. A purchase action might be stronger than a view action; multiple clicks on an item might be more indicative than a single click; finally, a recent view action might be more relevant than one in the past.

In this work, we propose an extension to BPR (called BPR++), which is designed to take various forms of such graded implicit feedback into account. The main idea is to first derive additional pairwise preferences from the data using the available "importance" information and – in the optimization phase – bias the optimization procedure to draw a certain amount of samples from these additionally available data points. In the next section, we describe the approach in more detail before we present results of an experimental evaluation with different datasets.

2. EXTENDING BPR

2.1 Generation of preference relations

In BPR, the first task is to derive pairwise item preferences from the unary feedback. The set of available items is denoted as I. For each user u, we are given a set of items I_u^+, containing those items of I for which a (positive) implicit feedback action was observed. User-specific item preferences are triples of the form (u, i, j), which express the fact that user u prefers item i over item j. The set of derived preference relations D_S, i.e., the training data used for optimization later on, is defined as follows.

$$D_S := \{(u, i, j) \mid i \in I_u^+ \wedge j \in I \backslash I_u^+\}$$

Using this approach, we can encode single, positive-only statements like non-repeated item purchases or "like" statements on social platforms. The user actions that can be used to assess preference profiles can however be richer in reality and may include, for example, the following:

1. In the logs of online shops, we typically can find view, add-to-cart, add-to-wishlist, or purchase actions, which can correspond to interest indicators of different strengths. In an even more fine-grained setting, the individual viewing times could be taken into account.
2. Recency of events and temporal aspects could be considered as carrying information about (recent) user preferences.
3. There are specific relationships between the users, e.g., in the form of social network connections [5], or between items that share similar characteristics.

In this paper, we therefore propose a generic extension of BPR regarding the way the set D_S is derived. In the original BPR formulation, a preference can only be derived if there is an implicit rating for i and none of j (e.g., because the user only viewed item i). If, for example, the user viewed i three times and j one time, nothing can be said about the preference. Since the number of views can be an interest indicator, we introduce a preference weight function $pweight(u, i)$ for user actions instead of the binary decision of [10].

We assume that $pweight(u, i)$ returns a positive number if an interaction between u and i exists, and 0 otherwise. A preference tuple (u, i, j) is therefore inferred whenever $pweight(u, i) > pweight(u, j)$ holds. Generally, the *pweight* function can encode arbitrary types of information, including, e.g., the time or recency aspects as mentioned above. The extended set of preference relations D_S^{++} for each user u is defined as follows:

$$D_S^{++} := \{(u, i, j) | pweight(u, i) > pweight(u, j), i \in I, j \in I\}$$

Consider the example in Figure 1. Let us assume that we have information about how often a user viewed an item as well as the time point of the latest view action for each item. User u_1 has both viewed item i_1 and item i_2. In the original BPR formulation, no preference could be derived. Here, however we could design a function *pweight* that returns a higher value for i_1 because of the higher number of interactions. Likewise, the function could return a slightly higher preference value for item i_1 also for user u_2 because of the more recent view event. A weighted combination of these aspects inside *pweight* is also possible. For user u_3, both the original and adapted BPR version would derive a preference for i_1. Generally, how *pweight* is defined depends on the application domain and the characteristics of the available data. Meta-data features or social network information could for example be used as done, e.g., in [5] or [7]. The chosen *pweight* function in any case however has to be carefully designed and thoroughly evaluated.

User \ Item	i_1	i_2
u_1	2 (t=10)	1 (t=10)
u_2	1 (t=12)	1 (t=10)
u_3	1 (t=12)	?

Table 1: Implicit feedback database.

2.2 Biased sampling

In the learning phase of BPR, Rendle et al. proposed to use a random bootstrap stochastic gradient descent approach to choose triples from D_S to learn the model, since using all $O(|U| \cdot |I|^2)$ triples is in general not feasible. When using the same random sampling in the `BPR++` approach, most of the time only triples from the original BPR formulation would however be considered. The reason is that the number of additional data tuples (u, i, j) in D_S^{++} can be fairly small when compared to the number of triples in D_S, because additional tuples are only generated when the user has interacted both with the items i and j.

We therefore extend the training algorithm of `BPR++` with a parameter β that expresses the probability of taking a sample from the additional tuples in D_S^{++}. Finding a suitable value for β is crucial for the effectiveness of the approach and its value has to be determined empirically for a given data set. The modification to the learning procedure of [10] is shown in lines 4-6 in Figure 1.

1: **procedure** LearnBPR++(D_S,Θ)
2: initialize Θ
3: **repeat**
4: r = random(0,1)
5: **if** $r \leqslant \beta \wedge D_S^{++} \backslash D_S \neq \varnothing$ **then**
6: draw (u,i,j) from $D_S^{++} \backslash D_S$
7: **else**
8: draw (u,i,j) from D_S
9: **end if**
10: $\Theta \leftarrow \Theta + \alpha \left(\frac{e^{-\hat{x}_{uij}}}{1+e^{-\hat{x}_{uij}}} \cdot \frac{\partial}{\partial \Theta} \hat{x}_{uij} - \lambda_\Theta \cdot \Theta \right)$
11: **until** convergence
12: **return** $\hat{\Theta}$
13: **end procedure**

Figure 1: Learning algorithm with biased sampling.

3. EXPERIMENTAL EVALUATION

To determine to which extent the consideration of different types of feedback helps to improve the prediction accuracy of BPR, we conducted experiments on different data sets and, correspondingly, different types of additional information. The accuracy was measured in terms of precision and recall[1]. We used two datasets consisting of navigation log data from real online shops as well as one of the MovieLens datasets. Table 2 shows the basic statistics of the datasets.

Overview of datasets.

Zalando: A dataset from Zalando[2], a large online retailer for fashion products, that has been sampled from log data in

[1]Additional MRR measurements were in line with these results for all datasets and are therefore not reported here.
[2]http://www.zalando.de

such a way that no conclusions on visitor data or true business figures of the company can be drawn. The logged and session-numbered interactions have different types (view, purchase, wish, put-in-cart), where the majority of the events are item views. We created a subset for which there are at least 10 interactions per user and item.

Tmall: A similar but smaller anonymized dataset from a shopping portal[3] containing user interactions of different types. For each of the actions, a time stamp is available.

MovieLens: We created a subset of "heavy users" of MovieLens using the 10 million ratings dataset as a basis.

Dataset	Zalando	Tmall	MovieLens
users	12,724	884	17,107
items	20,596	9,531	963
interactions	2,021,716	182,879	3,601,968
sparsity	0.008	0.022	0.219
interactions/user	159	207	211
interactions/item	98	19	3,740

Table 2: Dataset characteristics.

BPR++ variants and measurement method.

Depending on the available data, we used the following comparably simple variants of `BPR++` and varied the interpretation of $pweight(u, i)$ correspondingly.

`BPR++(T)`: Items with which the user interacted more recently are considered to be more relevant. $pweight(u, i)$ corresponds to the time stamp or session number of the last interaction of user u with item i.

`BPR++(N)`: Items with which the user interacted more often are considered to be preferred. $pweight(u, i)$ corresponds to the number of interactions of user u with item i.

The time-based and interaction-count based versions were tested for the shop datasets. For the MovieLens dataset, we used the rating values as a preference indicator.

`BPR++(R)`: Higher rated items are more relevant. $pweight(u, i)$ corresponds to the rating of user u for item i.

In our evaluation, we compared `BPR++` with the original BPR implementation[4], FunkSVD[5] with 50 latent features, and item-to-item collaborative filtering with the cosine similarity measure (Item-KNN). The number of optimization rounds for the BPR-based methods was varied in the tests to analyze the convergence and possible overfitting behavior of `BPR++`. We have empirically evaluated different values for β and determined a fixed value $\beta = 0.75$ in all our experiments as it led to overall high results and enables comparability between the different $pweight(u, i)$ functions[6].

For the online shop datasets we created one time-based 80/20 train-test split. Since cross-validation is not possible due to the unique time-based ordering, we randomly created ten 90% sub-samples of the splits and repeated the experiments to factor out random effects. For the MovieLens dataset we used standard 5-fold cross-validation.

[3]Tmall Rec. Prize 2014 & TianChi Open Data Project

[4]We used matrix factorization, uniform sampling, 100 latent features, $\alpha = 0.05$, $\lambda_W = \lambda_{H+} = 0.0025$, $\lambda_{H-} = 0.00025$

[5]http://sifter.org/~simon/journal/20061211.html

[6]Optimizing β for the different datasets and $pweight(u, i)$ functions is beyond the scope of this paper.

Precision@10 and Recall@10 were used as accuracy measures. An item was considered relevant when it was actually purchased (shop data) or rated higher than the user's average (MovieLens). Items that were previously bought or rated were not recommended for the Zalando and movie dataset. Since in the *Tmall* scenario rather families of items than individual items are recommended, we allowed "repeated recommendations" for this dataset.

4. RESULTS

Zalando: Table 3 shows precision and recall for the Zalando dataset after n optimization rounds[7]. The time-based variant `BPR++(T)` helps to increase both precision and recall which indicates that the recency of the interactions is relevant in the domain. The `BPR++(N)` variant in contrast led to results that were worse than the original BPR method, which is possibly caused by recency effects. Since `BPR++(N)` ignores the interaction time, the focus on items that are no longer relevant for the user might be too strong. Systematic tuning of β might help to mitigate this effect.

#it	`BPR++(T)`	`BPR++(N)`	BPR
1	0.005/0.024	0.004/0.020	0.002/0.009
10	0.044/0.193	0.025/0.113	0.033/0.149
50	0.064/0.268	0.037/0.163	0.048/0.209
100	0.068/0.285	0.041/0.177	0.051/0.221
150	0.070/0.289	0.042/0.183	0.054/0.230
200	**0.071/0.293**	0.043/0.186	0.054/0.231

Table 3: Precision@10/Recall@10 for *Zalando*

Tmall: The results for the *Tmall* shown in Table 4 corroborate the findings made for the Zalando dataset. Taking recency of events into account (`BPR++(T)`) helps to improve the accuracy both in terms of precision and recall. Considering the number of interactions for each item as preference indicators (`BPR++(N)`) leads to faster convergence – which can be considered a highly desirable characteristic for large datasets – but not to better overall results. Again, Funk-SVD, item-kNN, and popularity-based ranking performed worse.

#it	`BPR++(T)`	`BPR++(N)`	BPR
1	0.041/0.252	0.030/0.183	0.020/0.118
10	0.075/0.457	0.051/0.314	0.045/0.277
50	0.085/0.513	0.056/0.343	0.056/0.341
100	0.087/0.521	0.057/0.344	0.056/0.341
150	**0.088/0.522**	0.058/0.352	0.059/0.362
200	0.087/0.521	0.058/0.350	0.059/0.360

Table 4: Precision@10/Recall@10 for *Tmall*

MovieLens: The results for the MovieLens data are shown in Table 5. The rating-based variant of `BPR++` performed best already after only 10 iterations. With an increasing number of iterations, there is however a tendency of overfitting[8].

[7]Results for Funk-SVD, item-kNN, and popularity-based ranking are omitted, since they never exceeded the value 0.001 for precision and recall.

[8]The results obtained for the original BPR are comparable to the results reported at `http://mymedialite.net/examples/item_recommendation_datasets.html`. Item-kNN and popularity-based ranking led to lower results than FunkSVD and are therefore again omitted here.

#it	BPR++(R)	BPR	FunkSVD
1	0.368/0.171	0.331/0.153	0.092/0.040
10	**0.398/0.191**	0.354/0.169	0.212/0.096
50	0.387/0.186	0.341/0.163	0.164/0.072
100	0.387/0.186	0.336/0.161	0.145/0.061
150	0.382/0.183	0.342/0.164	0.144/0.060
200	0.384/0.184	0.342/0.165	0.140/0.058

Table 5: Precision@10/Recall@10 for MovieLens

We made additional experiments in which we used the non-filtered MovieLens dataset. In these scenarios, the results of BPR++(R) were however worse than when the original BPR method was used. Overall, our results show that additional preference indicators and graded forms of implicit feedback can help to increase the prediction accuracy of BPR[9]. The choice of the additional preference signals however depends on the domain. Using frequency information as an indicator for preference strength did for example not lead to better results in the Zalando scenario but actually led to a deterioration of the results.

So far, we have only considered one additional factor at a time to derive pairwise item preferences. On principle, multiple types of information could be incorporated in parallel, which should help us to achieve a higher density of the preference matrix. One particular question here is how to deal with situations when the preference statements that were derived from different information sources are conflicting. The design and evaluation of such hybrid methods and the analysis of factors like diversity and potential popularity-biases are part of our ongoing work.

5. RELATED WORK

BPR falls into the category of "one-class collaborative filtering" approaches and is able to make inferences from positive-only feedback (interpreted user actions). At the same time, with the AUC-like optimization criterion, BPR can be considered as a "learning-to-rank" approach. Another learning-to-rang technique is xCLiMF [11] which uses a graded relevance scale and optimizes a rank criterion, in that case the Expected Reciprocal Rank.

In recent years, a number of techniques have been developed to better deal with implicit user feedback, among them the SVD++ method, which integrates both implicit and explicit feedback in a matrix factorization model [3]. In [7], Manzato shows how to integrate additional information about item content into SVD++. In [4], the SVD++ model is extended to be able to deal with temporal dynamics. In our work, we have shown how time and recency information can be incorporated into the BPR method. In contrast to other time-aware CF methods, considering temporal aspects is however only one possible way of incorporating graded relevance feedback. Using interaction counts on items was explored as another possible form of graded feedback in our paper. This is partially similar to the probabilistic method presented in [6], which can use interaction frequency information when learning a preference profile.

Extensions to the basic BPR scheme have for example been proposed in [1], [5], or [9]. In [1], a strategy that weights the impact of negative items based their global popularity is introduced. In [5], the authors integrate additional information – in that case social network information – into BPR. Different to our work, their method directly influences the weight learning approach. In [9], an alternative sampling strategy was proposed that aims to statically or adaptively determine the most informative pairs.

[9]The differences of the best BPR++ results and the BPR results were statistically significant ($p<0.01$) for all datasets.

6. CONCLUSIONS AND OUTLOOK

In this work we propose to incorporate implicit feedback signals at a more fine-grained level in the personalized ranking process. The approach therefore allows us to differentiate between arbitrary types of feedback, e.g., take time and recency aspects into account. An experimental evaluation shows that for the considered domains the retrieval accuracy can be improved and faster convergence can be achieved when compared to the original BPR approach. In our future work, we plan to explore additional ways of combining the different types of user feedback in a hybrid approach, further investigate temporal effects and also look at other characteristics of the generated recommendation lists such as diversity and popularity biases.

7. REFERENCES

[1] Z. Gantner, L. Drumond, C. Freudenthaler, and L. Schmidt-Thieme. Bayesian personalized ranking for non-uniformly sampled items. *JMLR*, 18:231–247, 2012.

[2] A. Karatzoglou, L. Baltrunas, and Y. Shi. Learning to rank for recommender systems. In *Proc. RecSys '13 (Tutorials)*, pages 493–494, 2013.

[3] Y. Koren. Factorization meets the neighborhood: a multifaceted collaborative filtering model. In *Proc. KDD '08*, pages 426–434, 2008.

[4] Y. Koren. Collaborative filtering with temporal dynamics. *Commun. ACM*, 53(4):89–97, 2010.

[5] A. Krohn-Grimberghe, L. Drumond, C. Freudenthaler, and L. Schmidt-Thieme. Multi-relational matrix factorization using bayesian personalized ranking for social network data. In *Proc. WSDM '12*, pages 173–182, 2012.

[6] H. Ma, C. Liu, I. King, and M. R. Lyu. Probabilistic factor models for web site recommendation. In *Proc. SIGIR '11*, pages 265–274, 2011.

[7] M. G. Manzato. gSVD++: Supporting implicit feedback on recommender systems with metadata awareness. In *Proc. SAC '13*, pages 908–913, 2013.

[8] D. Oard and J. Kim. Implicit feedback for recommender systems. In *Proc. AAAI'98 Workshop on RS*, pages 81–83, 1998.

[9] S. Rendle and C. Freudenthaler. Improving pairwise learning for item recommendation from implicit feedback. In *Proc. WSDM '14*, pages 273–282, 2014.

[10] S. Rendle, C. Freudenthaler, Z. Gantner, and L. Schmidt-Thieme. BPR: Bayesian personalized ranking from implicit feedback. In *Proc. UAI '09*, pages 452–461, 2009.

[11] Y. Shi, A. Karatzoglou, L. Baltrunas, M. Larson, and A. Hanjalic. xCLiMF: optimizing expected reciprocal rank for data with multiple levels of relevance. In *Proc. RecSys '13*, pages 431–434, 2013.

Inferring User Interests in the Twitter Social Network

Parantapa Bhattacharya
IIT Kharagpur, India
MPI-SWS, Germany

Muhammad Bilal Zafar
MPI-SWS, Germany

Niloy Ganguly
IIT Kharagpur, India

Saptarshi Ghosh
MPI-SWS, Germany

Krishna P. Gummadi
MPI-SWS, Germany

ABSTRACT

We propose a novel mechanism to infer topics of interest of individual users in the Twitter social network. We observe that in Twitter, a user generally follows *experts* on various topics of her interest in order to acquire information on those topics. We use a methodology based on social annotations (proposed earlier by us) to first deduce the topical expertise of popular Twitter users, and then transitively infer the interests of the users who follow them. This methodology is a sharp departure from the traditional techniques of inferring interests of a user from the tweets that she posts or receives. We show that the topics of interest inferred by the proposed methodology are far superior than the topics extracted by state-of-the-art techniques such as using topic models (Labeled LDA) on tweets. Based upon the proposed methodology, we build a system **Who Likes What**, which can infer the interests of *millions of Twitter users*. To our knowledge, this is the first system that can infer interests for Twitter users at such scale. Hence, this system would be particularly beneficial in developing personalized recommender services over the Twitter platform.

Categories and Subject Descriptors: H.3.3 [Information Search and Retrieval]: selection process; H.3.5 [On-line Information Services]: Web-based services

Keywords: Twitter, user interests, Lists, Labeled LDA.

1. INTRODUCTION

The Twitter microblogging site is increasingly being used to discover current information on various topics of one's interest. Many personalized search and recommender systems are being developed to help Twitter users find content that is of interest to them. These systems [3, 6] use a variety of methods ranging from traditional *collaborative filtering* (or variants such as co-factorization machines [5]) to more recent *social recommendations* [2], where the items to be recommended to a user u are drawn from her social network neighborhood. Another approach is *topical recommendations* [7], where a user's topics of interest are first inferred and then leveraged to generate personalized recommendations consisting of items related to those topics. In this paper, we focus on topical recommendations, which have received comparatively less attention in the existing literature.

A key challenge for topical recommendation systems is to accurately infer the topics of interest for an individual user. All prior studies attempted to infer topics of interest from the contents of *tweets*. Most studies inferred interests of user u from the tweets posted by u herself [7, 8], using techniques such as topic models (e.g., Labeled Latent Dirichlet Allocation [8], which is a supervised version of LDA). Some approaches also used the tweets posted by the users whom u follows, i.e., the tweets received by u [2]. However, tweets often contain conversations about mundane daily activities of users [10, 11], making it difficult to identify meaningful topics from tweets.

In this paper, we propose a novel methodology for inferring the topics of interests of a given Twitter user u. Our methodology discovers u's interests from the topical expertise of the users whom u follows (i.e., u's followings). The topical expertise of u's followings are, in turn, inferred from social annotations (collected via the Twitter Lists feature [1]) using a methodology developed in our prior work [4, 10]. We compare the topics of interest inferred for a given user by our methodology with those extracted by a state-of-the-art technique – using supervised topic models (Labeled LDA) on the tweets that are either posted by or received by the given user. We find that topics inferred by our methodology are far superior to the topics inferred from the content of tweets, both in terms of accuracy of the topics, and the completeness with which the interests of a user are identified.

Another important advantage of our methodology is that it can be used to infer interests for any Twitter user who follows a few known topical experts. Using this methodology, we developed and publicly deployed a **Who Likes What** system (`http://twitter-app.mpi-sws.org/who-likes-what/`). We used our system to infer the interests of about *30 million Twitter users*, which is many orders of magnitude more than what prior studies could achieve. Our system – the first one to discover user-interests in Twitter *at scale* – can potentially be a fundamental building block for future designers of content or friend recommendation services over the Twitter platform.

RecSys'14, October 6–10, 2014, Foster City, Silicon Valley, CA, USA.

ACM 978-1-4503-2668-1/14/10 ...$15.00.
http://dx.doi.org/10.1145/2645710.2645765.

2. INFERRING USER INTERESTS

In this section, we first propose a novel methodology for inferring the topical interests of users in Twitter and then discuss some alternative state-of-the-art methodologies.

2.1 Proposed methodology

For a given Twitter user u (whose interests are to be inferred), our methodology consists of the following two steps. First, we check which other users u is following, i.e., users from whom u is interested in receiving information. Second, we identify the topics of expertise of those users (whom u is following) to infer u's interests, i.e., the *topics* on which u is interested in receiving information.

Inferring topical expertise using Twitter Lists: Lists are an organizational feature, by which users can group experts on topics that interest them [1]. To create a List, a user specifies a name and an optional description, and then adds other users as members of the List; for instance, a user can create a List named "Music and musicians", and add accounts such as Lady Gaga, Katy Perry, Yahoo Music.

In our prior work [4, 10], we proposed a methodology for utilizing List names and descriptions to discover the topical expertise of popular users in Twitter. To identify topics of expertise of a user v (whom u has subscribed to), we collect the Lists which have v as a member, and extract the most common terms that appear in the names and descriptions of the Lists. We identify v as an expert on a topic t if and only if v has been listed on t at least 10 times, i.e., if the term t appears at least 10 times in the names or descriptions of the Lists containing v.[1] Similar to [4, 10], we considered as topics only unigrams (single words such as 'politics', 'music') and bigrams (two words which frequently occur together, e.g., 'social media', 'video game', 'bay area') which are identified as *nouns* or *adjectives* by a standard part-of-speech tagger. Our prior work [4, 10] has shown that this methodology accurately infers the topics of expertise of millions of popular users in Twitter. For instance, some topics of expertise of the user-account @BarackObama, as inferred by the above methodology, are 'politics', 'celebs', 'government', and so on. Similarly, some topics inferred for the user account @linuxfoundation are 'tech', 'linux', 'software', 'computer', and 'developer' (see [4, 10] for more examples).

Inferring user interests: For the given user u (whose interests are to be inferred), we use the above List-based methodology to identify the topics of expertise of those to whom u has subscribed. Intuitively, if a user subscribes to tweets from several experts on a certain topic, then the user is likely to be interested in that topic. We considered u to be interested in topic t if and only if u subscribes to at least 3 experts on topic t. Thus, we obtain an *interest vector* for u, which is a ranked list of topics, ranked on the basis of the number of experts on a topic whom u subscribes to.

2.2 Alternative methodologies

As stated earlier, prior attempts to infer interests of a given user u rely on the tweets posted by either u herself [7, 8], or by the users whom u follows [2]. Hence, for a given user u, we collected two sets of tweets – (i) **self-tweets:** up to 3,200 most recent tweets *posted by* u herself[2], and (ii) **received-tweets:** the most recent tweets *received by* u, i.e., up to 3,200 most recent tweets posted by the users whom u follows. We pre-process the tweets by removing a standard set of stopwords, URLs and @user mentions. Thereafter, we apply Labeled Latent Dirichlet Allocation (L-LDA) to infer latent topics from the two tweet-sets.

L-LDA [9] is a supervised version of the popular LDA topic model, and has recently been used by several studies to infer topics from tweets [8]. L-LDA requires each document (tweet) to be tagged with zero or more 'labels'. Similar to LDA, each topic inferred by L-LDA is a distribution over the set of distinct terms in the corpus, and each document is a distribution over the topics. However, unlike LDA, each topic discovered by L-LDA maps to one of the labels specified in the input [9].

Following the methodology in [8], we used as the input labels for a given set of tweets, the K most frequent hashtags contained in that tweet-set. For instance, for the self-tweets of user u, the labels are the top K hashtags that are most frequently tweeted by u. Similarly, for the received-tweets of u, the labels are the top K hashtags that were tweeted most frequently by the users whom u follows. Then we use L-LDA to infer K topics for each of the tweet-sets.[3]

3. EVALUATION

We now evaluate the comparative performance of the above three methodologies. Each methodology potentially infers several hundreds of topics for a given user; since it is difficult to evaluate so many topics, we decided to focus on the top 20 topics of interest inferred for a given user.

For the proposed List-based methodology, we consider the top 20 topics in the interest vector for u, i.e., the 20 topics on which u follows most number of topical experts. For the L-LDA-based methods, we use $K = 20$, i.e., we use the top 20 hashtags in a tweet-set as the input labels to L-LDA, so that L-LDA infers 20 topics. Each topic inferred by L-LDA is a probability distribution over the set of distinct terms in the corpus, and the terms within a topic are ranked according to a probability score. We select from each topic the term with the highest probability score assigned by L-LDA, so that we have 20 terms representing the 20 topics inferred for a user.

Thus, for a given user, we have three sets of 20 topics each: (i) **List-topics:** inferred using the proposed methodology, (ii) **self-llda:** inferred using L-LDA on the tweets posted by the user herself, and (iii) **received-llda:** inferred using L-LDA on the set of tweets received by the user.

To evaluate the quality of these topic-sets, one needs to compare the inferred topics with some *ground truth*, i.e., known interests for some specific Twitter users. Since such ground truth is difficult to obtain for random Twitter users, we adopt two strategies for our evaluation, as described in Section 3.1 and Section 3.2 below.

3.1 Using declared interests of users

Methodology: We focus on some well-known Twitter users who have indicated some topics of their interest in their 'bio' (short autobiography written by a user in her account

[1]The threshold 10 is selected based on the observations in our prior studies [4, 10].

[2]One can obtain at most the 3,200 most recent tweets of a user through the Twitter API.

[3]Similar to [8], we set the parameters of L-LDA as $\alpha = 0.167$ and $\beta = 0.001$. The number of topics K was set to 20.

User, with extracts from bio	Top topics of interest, inferred by different methodologies		
	List-topics (proposed)	self-llda	received-llda
Michelle Zhou: into interior design, love shopping & food ...	interior design, decor, fashion, shopping, lifestyle, travel, drinks, hotel	design, system, night, check, gatos, food	#theskenstheory, #fashionstar, win, gardening, daily, love
Erin Marshall: sharing my life in fashion, fun ... Love red lipstick, high heels	fashion, fun, style, fashion designers, beauty	wedding, seatle, cute, today, thanks, love	seattle, obama, #fashion, wedding, thanks, wine
Jesse Millar: Computer sc. student, addicted to programming, game design	developers, game dev, technology, games	awesome, love, last, photo, time, week	games, time, app, thanks, years
Mattia Pontacolone: loves social media, mobile, web apps and start-ups	technology, social media, marketing, startup,	google, facebook, iphone, mayors, love, days	#ted, obama, facebook, thanks, books, new
Cege Smith: Obsessed with The Vampire Diaries, Cult, and Being Human. Author ...	authors, publishing, writing, vampirediaries, writing resources	#ghost, #halloween, #paranormal, #vampires, writers, #amreading	#fantasy, #amwriting, #mystery, #books, #wlcauthor, #horror

Table 1: Examples of top topics of interest inferred by the three methodologies, for some well-known Twitter users who declare their interests in their bio. All topics are case-folded to lower case.

profile). Specifically, we looked for well-known users (researchers, writers, politicians) whose bio contains a phrase such as "like <topic>" or "love <topic>", or some similar phrases. We then check whether the top topics inferred by the various methodologies for these users include the interests declared by the users themselves.[4]

Results: For almost all the users we studied, the topics inferred by the proposed methodology matched the interests declared in the account bio. Table 1 shows the declared interests for some well-known users (as given in their bio) and the top topics of interest inferred by the three methodologies. It is evident that the List-topics (inferred using the proposed methodology) capture a large fraction of the topics of interest stated by the users themselves. For instance, *Michelle Zhou*, one of the General Chairs of the RecSys 2014 conference, mentions in her Twitter bio – "into interior design, love shopping & food". We find that her List-topics include 'interior design' and 'shopping' as well as topics such as 'drinks' and 'hotel' which are closely related to food. Even in the cases where the List-topics do not include the specific interests mentioned by the user (e.g., 'love red lipstick, high heels for user *Erin Marshall*), the List-topics are very relevant broader topics such as 'fashion' and 'style'.

On the other hand, most of the topics inferred using L-LDA on tweets (self-llda and received-llda) are much less relevant to the interests of the users. In fact, several of the terms extracted from the tweets are about recent events (e.g., 'wedding', 'halloween') or are globally popular topics (e.g., 'obama' and 'facebook') which are likely to be posted by the masses.

3.2 Using human feedback

Methodology: Since the interests of a certain user are best known to that user herself, one of the best ways of evaluating the quality of inferred interests is through direct human feedback. We selected 10 volunteers to give us feedback about the quality of the interests inferred for them. The volunteers, all of whom actively use Twitter, are researchers at the home institutions of the authors of this paper (but none of them is an author of this paper herself). Each evaluator was shown the top 20 topics inferred for him / her by the three methodologies. To prevent bias in judgment, the topic-sets were anonymized, i.e., the evaluator was not told which topic-set is from which methodology. Then the evaluator was asked to *rank the three topic-sets* with respect to (i) accuracy, and (ii) completeness of the inferred topics of interest. Note that both *accuracy* (how correct the inferred interests were, analogous to *precision*) and *completeness* (whether a large fraction of the user's interests could be inferred, analogous to *recall*) are important aspects which determine the quality of a set of inferred topics of interest.

Eval. id	list-topics		self-llda		received-llda	
	Acc	Com	Acc	Com	Acc	Com
1	1	1	2	2	3	3
2	1	1	3	3	2	2
3	1	1	3	3	2	2
4	2	1	1	2	3	3
5	1	1	3	3	2	2
6	1	1	3	3	2	2
7	1	2	2	3	2	1
8	1	1	3	3	2	2
9	1	1	2	2	3	2
10	1	1	2	2	3	3

Table 2: Rankings given by 10 evaluators to the topics inferred for their own Twitter accounts by three methodologies. Rankings are based on two aspects: accuracy (Acc) and completeness (Com) of the inferred topics.

Results: Table 2 summarizes the rankings given by the 10 evaluators to the topic-sets inferred by the three methodologies. *All except one of the evaluators ranked* **list-topics** *as the most accurate.* Between the two LLDA-based methodologies, the *received-llda* set (obtained using L-LDA on the tweets received by a user) was ranked better than self-llda by a majority of the evaluators. The results for completeness were very similar – all except one evaluator ranked **list-topics** as the best, and received-llda was ranked higher than self-llda by most evaluators.

These results clearly indicate that the topics of interest inferred by the proposed methodology are far superior than topics inferred from the contents of tweets. This is because tweets primarily contain day-to-day conversations [10, 11], which makes it difficult to identify meaningful topics even when using state-of-the-art techniques such as L-LDA.

4. THE WHO-LIKES-WHAT SYSTEM: INFERRING USER INTERESTS AT SCALE

Having established the accuracy of the proposed methodology, we used the methodology to develop a system for large-scale discovery of user-interests in Twitter.

[4]Note that only 22% of Twitter users have a bio on their profile, with only 3% having phrases "like <topic>" or "love <topic>". Thus, while this method is good for validating interests, it is not suitable for inferring user interests at scale.

Large-scale inference of user-interests: Given the restrictions on using the Twitter API, it is infeasible to crawl data of all 600 million users presently using Twitter. Hence, we started crawling user-accounts in the chronological order of their account creation date, and were able to gather data for about 38.4 million users. Using the proposed methodology, we could infer as many as 36,481 distinct topics of interest, for as many as 29.7 million of these users (i.e., 77.25% of all users whose data we could gather).[5] These numbers show that apart from being accurate, the proposed methodology also has very high *coverage*, i.e., it can be used to infer topics of interest for a large fraction of active Twitter users, which is several orders of magnitude larger than what any of the prior studies of inferring user-interests could achieve.

We have developed a novel Web-based system called **Who Likes What** (deployed at `http://twitter-app.mpi-sws.org/who-likes-what/`), where one can enter the name of any Twitter user, and see word clouds containing the top interests inferred for the given user. We invite readers to use the system for themselves. To our knowledge, this is the first system which can infer user-interests in Twitter at the scale of millions of users.

Differentiating between general and niche topics: During our evaluation using human feedback (see Section 3.2), some evaluators commented that though the top inferred topics accurately captured their broad interests, the topics were sometimes too general. They preferred to see more specific interests, such as 'machine learning' or 'big data' instead of 'science' or 'technology'. We observed that the more specific interests are indeed inferred by the proposed methodology; however, these specific interests were not getting included in the top 20 topics (ranked according to the number of topical experts that a user follows) that were initially shown to the evaluators.

To take this feedback into account, we classified topics into two categories based on their generality, which we estimate by the global number of users who are interested in a topic. Out of the 36 thousand distinct topics inferred (as stated above), we consider the top five percentile of topics as 'general' topics (on which there are thousands of interested users), and the rest of the less popular topics as 'niche' topics. Table 3 shows the general and niche interests for some volunteers who participated in the evaluation.

For a given user, **Who Likes What** shows three word clouds – one showing the top topics considering all inferred interests of the user, the second one showing only the top general topics, and the third showing only the top niche topics of interest. The evaluators were later shown the three word clouds inferred for their accounts, and the *niche* word cloud was unanimously voted as the best by all evaluators.

Eval. id	Top general interests	Top niche interests
1	technology, movies, geek	star trek, programmers, pythonistas, vim
2	technology, politics, science	machine learning, big data, networks
3	football, sports, technology	barcelona, soccer, premier league, la liga
6	football, sports, world, motor sport	man utd, epl, formula1, premier league
10	developers, technology, programmers	haskell, scala, functional programming

Table 3: Examples of general and niche topics of interests for some of the evaluators.

5. CONCLUSION

We developed a novel methodology to infer topics of interests of users in the Twitter social network. Comparison with topics extracted by content-based techniques reveals interesting insights – besides observing that the proposed technique is much superior, we also find that the tweets which a user *receives* are a better indicator of her interests, than the tweets she herself posts. Our findings imply that (i) using social signals can lead to better discovery of user-interests than content-based methods, and (ii) interests are passive traits of users, and inferring them from the user's activity (tweets posted) may be misleading. We also developed a complete system which can infer interests of millions of Twitter users. The potential of such a system is enormous – several topical search / recommender applications can be built using *Who Likes What* as a foundation structure, and our future plan is to develop such systems over the Twitter platform.

Acknowledgment: This research was supported in part by a grant from the Indo-German Max Planck Centre for Computer Science (IMPECS). P. Bhattacharya was supported by a fellowship grant from Tata Consultancy Services.

6. REFERENCES

[1] Twitter help center: how to use Twitter lists. `http://bit.ly/how-to-use-twitter-lists`.

[2] J. Chen, R. Nairn, L. Nelson, M. Bernstein, and E. H. Chi. Short and tweet: experiments on recommending content from information streams. In *ACM SIGCHI*, 2010.

[3] E. Diaz-Aviles et al. What is Happening Right Now ... That Interests Me?: Online Topic Discovery and Recommendation in Twitter. In *ACM CIKM*, 2012.

[4] S. Ghosh, N. Sharma, F. Benevenuto, N. Ganguly, and K. Gummadi. Cognos: crowdsourcing search for topic experts in microblogs. In *ACM SIGIR*, 2012.

[5] L. Hong, A. S. Doumith, and B. D. Davison. Co-factorization Machines: Modeling User Interests and Predicting Individual Decisions in Twitter. In *ACM WSDM*, 2013.

[6] Y. Kim and K. Shim. TWITOBI: A Recommendation System for Twitter Using Probabilistic Modeling. In *IEEE ICDM*, 2011.

[7] M. Michelson and S. A. Macskassy. Discovering users' topics of interest on Twitter: a first look. In *ACM Workshop on Analytics for Noisy Unstructured Text Data*, 2010.

[8] R. Ottoni et al. Of Pins and Tweets: Investigating how users behave across image- and text-based social networks. In *AAAI ICWSM*, 2014.

[9] D. Ramage, D. Hall, R. Nallapati, and C. D. Manning. Labeled LDA: A Supervised Topic Model for Credit Attribution in Multi-labeled Corpora. In *EMNLP*, 2009.

[10] N. Sharma, S. Ghosh, F. Benevenuto, N. Ganguly, and K. Gummadi. Inferring Who-is-Who in the Twitter Social Network. In *Workshop on Online Social Networks*, 2012.

[11] C. Wagner, V. Liao, P. Pirolli, L. Nelson, and M. Strohmaier. It's not in their tweets: modeling topical expertise of Twitter users. In *IEEE SocialCom*, 2012.

[5] Of the rest 22.75% users, whose interests we could not infer, 95% follow less than 2 users (with 83% following zero users), and have posted less than 10 tweets in their entire lifetime. Thus, almost all those users for whom our methodology fails to infer interests are *inactive* users.

Aspect-Based Opinion Mining and Recommendation System for Restaurant Reviews

Vaishak Suresh
Computer Engineering Department
San Jose State University
San Jose, CA, 95192

Syeda Roohi
Computer Engineering Department
San Jose State University
San Jose, CA, 95192

Magdalini Eirinaki
Computer Engineering Department
San Jose State University
San Jose, CA, 95192

ABSTRACT

The success of a product/service in e-commerce largely depends on the user reviews. A product/service that has a higher average review or rating usually gets picked against a similar product/service with less favorable reviews. Reviews usually have an overall rating, but most of the times there are sub-texts in the review body that describe certain features/aspects of the product. This demonstration presents a system that extracts aspect-specific ratings from reviews and also recommends reviews to users based on their and other users' rating patterns.

Categories and Subject Descriptors

H.3.5 [**Information Storage and Retrieval**]: Online information Services

Keywords

Recommendation Engine; feature ranking; sentiment analysis

1. INTRODUCTION

With more and more businesses selling their products or advertising their services online, customers rely on word of mouth in the form of customer reviews to make their decisions. Most of the current websites that feature product/service reviews list these reviews in reverse chronological order, or by employing heuristic metrics (e.g. ranking higher reviews of "super users", i.e. users with many reviews). However, such a generic ranking requires from users to read or at least scan the tens or hundreds of reviews for one product/service.

Moreover, different people value different qualities of the same product/service. For example, when searching for a good Italian restaurant, one user might value the wine list of a place, while another might prefer restaurants that are family-friendly. Ideally, users would like to be presented with only these reviews that highlight the qualities of a product/service that they value.

In this work, we propose a system that automatically generates personalized review recommendations using two different approaches. Firstly, drawing inspiration from traditional collaborative filtering systems, the system generates user rating profiles and tailors the list of reviews to the preferences of each user. Secondly, we employ aspect-based opinion mining to identify the important features highlighted in each review. As opposed to traditional sentiment analysis, which provides an overall picture of whether a review is positive or negative, aspect-based opinion mining provides a fine-grain analysis of both sentiment and strength of the review [1]. Given a predetermined set of features for a particular domain, results from aspect-based opinion mining can be used to rank/sort the reviews based on the aspect the users are most interested in. The proposed system displays a personalized list of reviews for the same product/service tailored to the preferences of each user. We demonstrate our system using real-life reviews from Yelp.

RecSys '14, Oct 06-10 2014, San Jose or vicinity, CA, USA
ACM 978-1-4503-2668-1/14/10.
http://dx.doi.org/10.1145/2645710.2645716

2. SYSTEM OVERVIEW

The system architecture is shown in Figure 1. It comprises two main modules, an offline processing module, where the user profiles are being generated and the feature extraction and rating happens, as well as an online module, that generates real-time recommendations. The prototype uses user review data from Yelp[1]. The dataset contains user information, business information and user reviews in the form of JSON objects. These objects are stored on MongoDB, a NoSQL database. A brief overview of the system is provided in what follows. For more details please refer to [2].

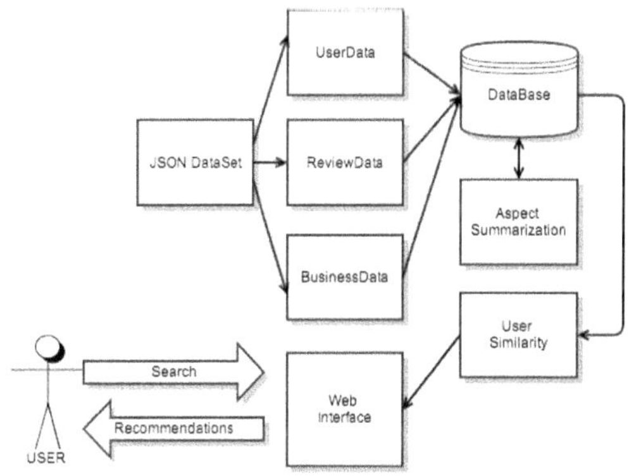

Figure 1: System Architecture

2.1 Offline Processing

2.1.1 Aspect Summarization

This module aims at extracting the important features from each review, along with their polarity weight. To perform this we employ the subjectivity lexicon [3] in order to map weak and strong positive and negative to numeric values (ranging from -4 to +4). Using a master list of positive and negative opinion words

[1] http://www.yelp.com/dataset_challenge/

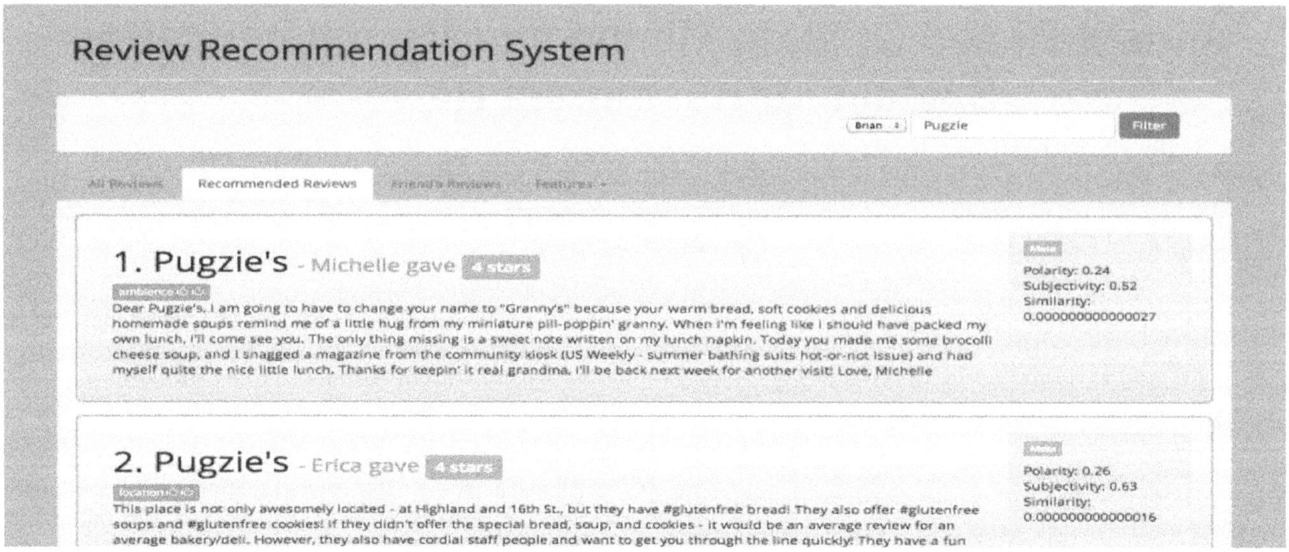

Figure 2: Client application - personalized recommended reviews

from opinion lexicon [1] we created a list of negation words (not, no, nothing etc.) which inverse the sentiment, and positive words (too, very, so, etc.), which increase the intensity of the sentiment. Each review is POS tagged using the default tagger from NLTK[2] python package, which uses the Treebank corpus for training the model. These three inputs are subsequently fed to our algorithm that generates as output an opinion score for each feature identified in a review [2]. In this work we assume that the product aspects are predetermined.

2.1.2 User preference generation

The front-end of the application acts as a REST client and sends request to the RESTful server written using Jersey[3] to recommend reviews. We employ a user-based collaborative filtering technique where user profiles consist of all their star ratings in past reviews. The RESTful service uses MongoDBDataModel API from Mahout to build a model based on the ratings of all the users. User similarity is calculated using the Pearson correlation coefficient.

2.2 Online Recommendations

This step is used to rank and recommend reviews. The client is a Django-based Python Web application that consumes the recommendations in the form of a RESTful response from the engine. When a given user searches for a specific restaurant, the recommendation engine computes the similarity of the current user with all the reviewers of the particular business and ranks and presents the related reviews in descending order of similarity. As a result, each user will be presented with a different set of reviews for the same business. The interface allows the end user to get the gist of the reviews without the need to read the entire review text. For each review, the overall star rating as well as the most important aspects of each review, are prominently shown. The aspects are intuitively marked as strong/weak positive/negative, by using colors and thumbs up/down images[4]. A sample result set is shown in Figure 2. For demonstration purposes, each review is accompanied by some metrics showing the calculated polarity and subjectivity of the review [1] as well as the similarity of each reviewer to the user (similarity is very low as the utility matrix is very sparse). The end user may further filter the personalized list of reviews by filtering only those that come from his/her friends (in a virtual social network setting), or by feature (e.g. location, food, etc.).

3. DEMONSTRATION SCENARIO

We will demonstrate the prototype by employing different users with different ratings and show how their review recommendations differ for the same businesses. The audience will be also shown some back-end details on how the user similarity is calculated. A screencast of the prototype is available at: http://youtu.be/vMz5CobpIw4.

4. CONCLUSIONS

The amount of online reviews for products and services has grown to such extend that often makes it impossible to read all of them. In this work we propose a system that personalizes the order in which the reviews are shown and provides an intuitive interface that allows the users to see the important aspects of each review in a glimpse. As part of our future work we plan to integrate further these two types of recommendations and enhance them by introducing trust-based and reputation metrics.

5. REFERENCES

[1] Bing Liu, *Sentiment Analysis and Opinion Mining,* Morgan & Claypool Publishers, May 2012

[2] Syeda Roohi, Vaishak Suresh, *Aspect based Opinion Mining and Recommendation System for Reviews,* Technical Report, San Jose State University, May 2014, available at: http://www.engr.sjsu.edu/meirinaki/papers/SyedaRoohi_VaishakSuresh_295B_Report.pdf

[3] Theresa Wilson, Janyce Wiebe, and Paul Hoffmann, *Recognizing Contextual Polarity in Phrase-Level Sentiment Analysis.* Proc. of HLT-EMNLP-2005

[2] http://www.nltk.org

[3] https://jersey.java.net/

[4] The same aspect might appear in more than one reviews and one review might contain more than one aspects.

Configuring and Monitoring Recommender System as a Service

David Ben-Shimon &
Alexander Tsikinovsky
YooChoose Labs Ltd
Hagoren 6, Omer 84965, Israel
{david.ben-shimon, alexander.tskinovsky} @yoochoose.com

Michael Friedmann &
Johannes Hörle
YooChoose GmbH, Bonner 484, Cologne 50968, Germany
{michael.friedmann, johannes.hoerle} @yoochoose.com

ABSTRACT
Many small and medium e-commerce retailers and publishers use recommender systems (RS) to personalize the website content. Many of them do not have an on premise solution for doing that, but rather contact a company that delivers the RS as a service to their website. The service is then responsible for collecting and storing the data, building recommendation models, and answering recommendation requests.

Once the integration to such a service is done, the e-commerce retailer still wish to have some control on the service. Control that allows him to configure the recommendation models, turn off/on the service, apply filters on recommendations, define fallback models and more. In this demo we provide an overview of a real backend system which enables to a typical website owner exactly these capabilities. Capabilities for controlling the RS service in terms of configuration, management and monitoring.

Categories and Subject Descriptors
H.5 **Information interfaces and presentation: Miscellaneous**

General Terms
Recommender System as a Service, Configuration, API

Keywords
Recommender System as a Service; Configuration; Management; Graphic User Interface

1. INTRODUCTION
Many e-commerce businesses record activities of users in order to enable personalization of the content and recommend items to view or to purchase. Such personalization is expected to improve the user experience and satisfaction and to increase the revenue of the e-business.

The decision of an e-business to apply personalization and integrate recommendations into their existing systems can be challenging and even risky, as the expected return on investment is difficult to predict. The required knowledge, expertise, and resources needed for implementing a personalized recommender system may be beyond the reach of medium and small e-businesses. To minimize the investment and risk, many small or medium e-businesses prefer to purchase the recommender system as a service [1] [4]. The providers of such services are called RS providers. Such services allow the e-businesses to request recommendations for the active user through a remote server, which is not owned or operated by the e-business owner. These services can be purchased and activated rapidly. They can also be turned off without any major cost in case of an unsuccessful deployment that does not withstands the goals of the e-business owner. Thus, such services reduce the required initial investment and represent very little risk to the e-business. The Integration to such a services is usually done via a REST API [3] which is provided by the RS provider, or could be done automatically if the required RS services are limited[1]. Once the integration is done the website is sending user activities to the service, the service is building recommendation models based on that, and then is able to respond to online recommendation requests out from the models.

RecSys '14, October 6–10, 2014, Foster City, Silicon Valley, CA, USA.
ACM 978-1-4503-2668-1/14/10.
http://dx.doi.org/10.1145/2645710.2645713

In order to be able to serve many types of potential customers the RS provider builds the service so it could be configured and adapted for many type of customers i.e. retailers, publishers etc. This includes the ability to support the building of several type of models i.e. Collaborative Filtering (CF), Content Based (CB), Popularity etc., supporting recommendations for different item types such as products, images, movies, article and more. Additionally there is an option to define fallback models. Fallback models are models that deliver recommendations when the preferred primary model cannot deliver recommendations from whatever reason. Additional aspects related to possible configurations exist but are not discussed here. Such a service is also working with default values so it can work smoothly, tough not ideally, in case no configuration has been provided.

Many customers that are connected to the service wish to have the ability to control the service generally and these aspects specifically. In this demo we provide an insight on a real productive application that enables each customer, which is connected to service of the RS provider, to configure and manage the service via a graphic user interface according to his needs and understanding.

2. CONFIGURING AND MANAGING THE SERVICE
As mentioned above the website is integrating the service via REST API. This integration then enables the service to do three main things. First, to collect and store the desired activities of the end users; the storage is in the RS provider servers. Second, once enough data has been collected, the service is building recommendation models using the model-based [2] approach. Third, the service is ready to answer recommendation requests very fast, so given a user, item or any preconfigured type of input, the service provides in return a list of recommendations using JSON or XML format. For more details on how to build such a service see the Netflix tutorial [5].

We now wish to define a new concept that we use in our system and is called *scenario*. Scenario is an abstract phrase that encapsulates within it all the information that the system needs in order to deliver recommendations according to some specific customers' expectations. From the customer perspective it could be viewed as a component that is responsible to populate a certain box/area in the GUI with recommendations.

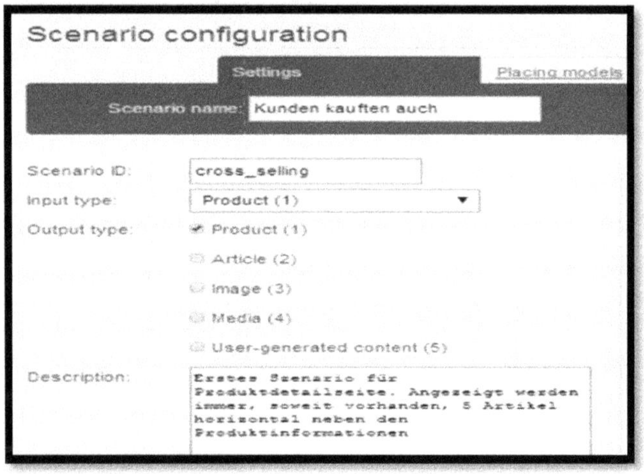

Figure 1. Snapshot of scenario configuration

Figure 1 provides a snapshot from the system when a new scenario is about to be generated by the customer. The customer needs to give a name to the scenario and to define the item type of the input and the output. I.e. the model is based on buying events of products and also recommends products. Description is not mandatory. Customers can apply filters on the recommendations. Filters are rules which work on the scenario and restrict the scenario from delivering certain items. I.e. do not recommend to the user items he already purchased in the past. This filter for instance may be valid in many stores but in an online grocery it is not. Once the customer provides these details for the scenario, he now has to define the recommendation models that has to be built for this scenario.

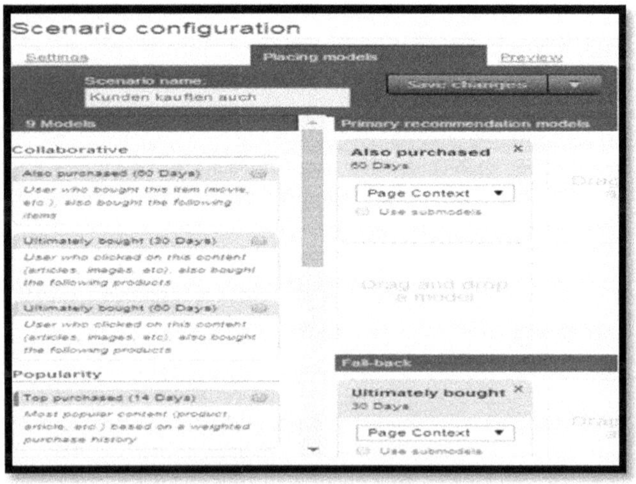

Figure 2. Placing models in the scenario

Figure 2 provides a snapshot of placing models inside a scenario. Here the customers decides what will be the type of the models, i.e. whether the recommendations will come from memory-based CF model, popularity model and the like. The customer also defines here the ranking of the models; meaning what is the primary model and which models serve as fallback and in what order. There is also the ability to configure recommendation list which is generated from more than one model. All this information is required for building the desired models and serving the requests from this scenario properly. Functionalities like defining AB tests, previewing recommendations, applying sophisticated filters and more, are also available but are not presented here. Finally whenever the customer enters the system he gets statistics of the service. Figure 3 provides a snapshot of this information. For instance the customer can view the statistics on the clicks, purchases, recommendation requests, AB test results and more.

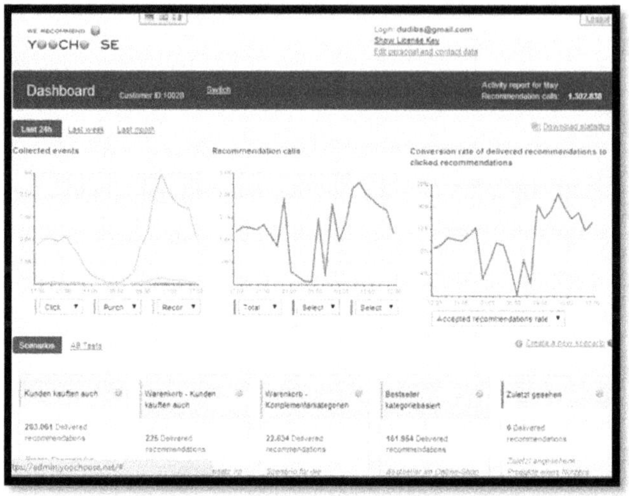

Figure 3. Overview on the entire service

3. SUMMARY

In this demo we provide an insight on how customers of a recommender system as a service can configure and manage the service. Part of the customers do not want to be involved in this configuration but some of them are eager for such a dashboard application to manage and configure the service for various reasons.

4. REFFERNCES

[1] Ben Shimon, D., Friedman, M., Hoerle, J., Tsikinovsky, A., Gude, R., & Alukhanov, R. (2014, February). Deploying recommender system for the masses. In Proceedings of the companion publication of the 19th international conference on Intelligent User Interfaces (pp. 1-4). ACM.

[2] Breese, J. S., Heckerman, D., & Kadie, C. (1998, July). Empirical analysis of predictive algorithms for collaborative filtering. In Proceedings of the Fourteenth conference on Uncertainty in artificial intelligence (pp. 43-52). Morgan Kaufmann Publishers Inc.

[3] Masse, M. (2011). REST API design rulebook. " O'Reilly Media, Inc.".

[4] Ronen, R., Koenigstein, N., Ziklik, E., Sitruk, M., Yaari, R., & Haiby-Weiss, N. (2013, October). Sage: recommender engine as a cloud service. In Proceedings of the 7th ACM conference on Recommender systems (pp. 475-476). ACM.

[5] http://recsys.acm.org/2012/tutorials.html#building

Content Ordering Based On Commuting Patterns

Travis Gingerich
Microsoft Corp.
Mountain View, CA
travisgi@microsoft.com

Omar Alonso
Microsoft Corp.
Mountain View, CA
omalonso@microsoft.com

ABSTRACT

Recommender systems take into account a wide range of information about both an individual user and other users' preferences in order to provide relevant content. However, one source of information that appears to be under-utilized is contextual information about the user's trajectory: where they are currently located, and where they are traveling to. We demonstrate a system that recommends the reading order of Twitter content based on the user's planned travel.

Categories and Subject Descriptors

H.4 [**Information Storage and Retrieval**]: Miscellaneous

1. INTRODUCTION

Recommender systems take into account a wide range of information about both an individual user and other users' preferences in order to provide relevant content; however, traditional content-based and collaborative filtering-based systems tend to rely on static user models [1]. As such there has been an increase in interest in context-aware recommender systems. One source of information that appears to be under-utilized is contextual information about the user's current travel. While there is previous work on recommendations from location-based social networks [2], little work has been done exploring trajectories.

With the current rising popularity of intelligent personal assistants such as Microsoft's Cortana and Google Now, mobile devices are increasingly aware of the context in which they are used. In particular, these assistants track users' daily commute patterns and also scheduled appointments, giving a wealth of contextual information that can be used to provide better content recommendation across a wide variety of content types. Our motivating scenario is as follows: a user commutes from home to work using public transportation and would like to consume relevant content as he/she travels to the destination. We are interested in exploring the *directionality* criterion, which assumes that users may be interested in entities that are on the future path rather than those that have been passed [3].

In this paper we present a recommender system that takes into account a user's current location and travel trajectory and provides a recommended reading order of their Twitter home stream (the stream containing all tweets and retweets from accounts the user follows). This ranking can be combined with a score from a rudimentary user model based on the user's tweets and favorite tweets to provide an alternative and personalized way to consume content apart from a strictly chronological ordering. Twitter is a source particular conducive to this location- and travel-aware ranking as many tweets contain hyperlocal content. While currently accessible through a browser, integration with an intelligent personal assistant is the intended use case for this ranking.

2. DEMO OVERVIEW

In this section we describe the main characteristics of the system. All content used by the system is obtained from the Twitter API[1].

2.1 Generating user model

The user model takes into account any tweets the user authored, retweeted, or marked as a favorite. Each tweet is stemmed using an implementation of the Porter stemmer, and the model consists of a vector of stemmed term frequencies. There are clearly many additional ways in which this model could be improved, but this serves as a proof of concept to show the feasibility of incorporating information about user travel with a content-based recommendation system.

2.2 Data processing

The application reads and stores tweets from the user's home stream over the most recent 5 hours. In order to take into account the user's travel, tweets must be mapped to particular locations. A relatively small number of tweets are geo-tagged or linked to a geo-tagged place by the tweet author. However, many account profiles have loosely-structured location information, and many tweets contain mentions of particular locations. We use an in-house named entity recognition system to identify locations, and map these and location information from the account profile to geographic coordinates using Bing Maps' geocoding API[2].

RecSys'14, October 6–10, 2014, Foster City, Silicon Valley, CA, USA.
ACM 978-1-4503-2668-1/14/10.
http://dx.doi.org/10.1145/2645710.2645715 .

[1]https://dev.twitter.com/docs
[2]http://msdn.microsoft.com/en-us/library/ff701713.aspx

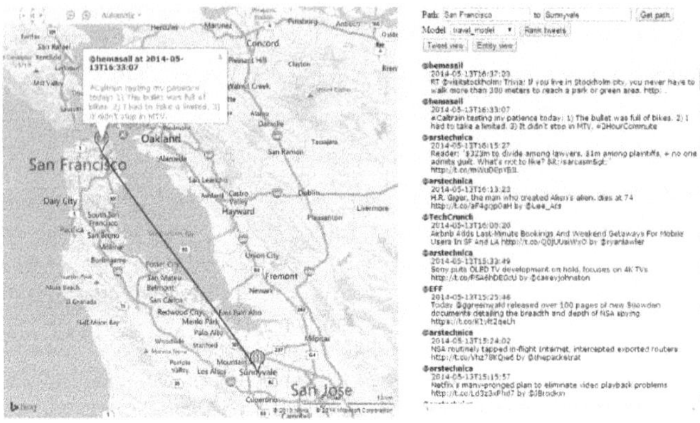

Figure 1: As the user travels from San Francisco to Sunnyvale, tweets near their current location in San Francisco are ranked higher than those closer to their destination.

2.3 Recommending a reading order

The demo uses two models. The first model (the "travel" model) asks the user to provide his/her current location and destination, and provides a reading order based on how each tweet falls along the user's approximate trajectory. For example, in Figure 1 the user is traveling between San Francisco and Sunnyvale. The trajectory is modeled as a straight line between the origin and destination. For each tweet, the ranking function identifies the closest point along this line to the tweet; tweets that fall at the user's current location along the line are given the highest score, and tweets closest to the destination are given a lower score. In this example, the user is currently in San Francisco, so tweets in the vicinity rank higher than those tweets that are located closer to the user's destination in Sunnyvale. This corresponds to the order in which the user will pass by the tweets' locations while traveling. The score of each tweet is penalized by exponential decay functions based on how far the tweet's location is from the closest point on the path, and the age of the tweet; this ensures that tweets that will fall in the user's vicinity rank higher than those that fall far away from the path, and that possibly stale tweets will be less likely to score highly. The equation is defined as: $score = \left(2 - \frac{d_1}{\text{path length}}\right) * e^{-\lambda_1 d_2 - \lambda_2 \alpha}$; d_2 is the distance from the closest point along the path to the tweet's location, d_1 is the distance from the start of path to that closest point, and α is the age of the tweet. λ_1 and λ_2 are configurable parameters that can be tuned to adjust how much tweets are penalized based on their age and distance from the path of travel.

The second model (the "blended" model) combines the score from the travel model with a score computed from the basic user model created for each user. The user model score is calculated using cosine similarity between the user model vector and a document vector derived from each tweet. As explained above, the user model consists of a vector in which the value for each token is the term frequency across tweets the user authored, retweeted, or marked as favorite: $w_{term,usermodel} = count(term)$. The tweet is modeled as a vector consisting of term frequencies, weighted by the inverse document frequency of the term (as seen across all tweets the system has consumed from the user's home stream): $w_{term,usermodel} = count(term) * \log(N/df_{terms})$ where N is the total number of tweets consumed from the stream and df_{terms} is the document frequency of the term across those tweets. The final score is the dot product between the two vectors:

$$score_{usermodel} = \sum_{term \in tweet} w_{term,usermodel} * w_{term,tweet}$$

The blended score is a linear combination of the user model and travel model scores:

$$score_{blended} = c_1 * score_{usermodel} + c_2 * score_{travel}$$

where c_1 and c_2 are parameters that adjust the relative importance of the user and travel models. The results are displayed using the same interface as the travel model. A video demonstrating the user interface is available online[3].

3. CONCLUSIONS AND FUTURE WORK

In addition to a web interface, the recommender system is also integrated with the yet-to-be-released Cortana intelligent personal assistant, providing the system a means to obtain information about commute patterns without requiring explicit user input. It is worth noting that this recommender system is not only limited to Twitter content; it can be applied to any content that has strong ties to a particular location, such as news or venues. The system we have presented here is a proof of concept showing how information about a user's travel plan can be taken into account to provide more relevant content ordering.

4. REFERENCES

[1] Gediminas Adomavicius, Bamshad Mobasher, Francesco Ricci, and Alexander Tuzhilin. Context-Aware Recommender Systems. *AI Magazine* 32(3), 2011, 67–80 .

[2] Max Sklar, Blake Shaw, and Andrew Hogue. Recommending Interesting Events in Real-time with Foursquare Check-ins. *Proc. of RecSys*, 2012, 311–312.

[3] Stefano De Sabbata and Tumasch Reichenbacher. Criteria for Geographic Relevance: An Experimental Study. *Int. Journal of Geographical Information Science*, 26(8), 2012, 1495–1520.

[3]http://aka.ms/bf3npo

Cosibon: An E-Commerce like Platform Enabling Bricks-and-Mortar Stores to use Sophisticated Product Recommender Systems

Thorben Keller*
Cosibon AG
Dufourstrasse 40a
9000 St. Gallen, Switzerland
thorben.keller@cosibon.com

Matthias Raffelsieper
Cosibon AG
Dufourstrasse 40a
9000 St. Gallen, Switzerland
matthias.raffelsieper@cosibon.com

ABSTRACT

Compared to online-retailers, bricks-and-mortar stores have only limited possibilities to understand consumer preferences, their intentions, and their feedback. The first are able to evaluate clickstream data collected on their webpages alongside the actual purchase data to put together a comprehensive view on individual customers. Bricks-and-mortar stores on the other hand have to rely solely on the evaluation of scanner data collected at the point of sale (POS). Thus, akin to the *Event Horizon* in physics, describing the boundary beyond which events are unobservable, we introduce the term *Receipt Horizon* to describe the natural boundary beyond which a retailing company is unable to observe the behavior of individual customers. In this demo paper we present our comprehensive approach on how bricks-and-mortar stores can go beyond the Receipt Horizon. We demonstrate how existing customer loyalty programs can be leveraged by an extensive mobile app, transferring proven e-commerce concepts to physical retailers and collecting numerous novel information about consumers.

Categories and Subject Descriptors

H.2.8 [**Database Management**]: Database Applications—*Data Mining*

Keywords

Recommender system; Bricks-and-Mortar Stores; e-Commerce

1. INTRODUCTION

Several information sources influence a consumer's purchase decision including personal information from family, friends, other customers, or renowned experts, and impersonal information from automatic recommender systems or independent research institutes. All of these have an impact on the consumers preferences. However, as stated in [1], "person-to-person communication is more effective than impersonal media sources in changing opinions and transmitting information". Furthermore, customer reviews and word-of-mouth play an important role in shaping consumer attitudes. It is well known that word-of-mouth has a significant impact on customers decision's about purchases. Hence, it follows that the more information sources are available to a recommender system, the better the recommendations will be and improvement leads to greater value for consumers in terms of higher decision making quality. Therefore, online retailers like Amazon.com provide their customers with an extensive platform which serves not only as a POS but also as a comprehensive source of information for both consumers and the retailer. While the consumer uses the information and browses the website to find the most suitable products for her individual needs the retailer is able to keep track of the clickstream data which represents the path a consumer took through the site. Even if the shop visits did not lead to an actual purchase the customer still left some foot prints. The additional knowledge about the product pages visited, the recommendations considered, and the time spent on the website serve as valuable input to improved recommender systems. By nature, bricks-and-mortar stores do not have access to such information as they are missing (1) a comparable data collection platform and (2) a comparable customer interaction platform.

They are thus bound to the analysis of pure purchase data and struggle to keep up with online retailers to provide customers with a comparably exciting shopping experience.

2. THE RECEIPT HORIZON

Following the definition of the Event Horizon in physics, describing the boundary beyond which occurrence and form of events are not observable by an individual in the current space-time continuum, we introduce the term *Receipt Horizon* to describe the natural boundary beyond which a retailing company is unable to observe the behavior of individuals within its customer base. The Receipt Horizon can be interpreted as the border between in-store and outside-store. Everything that happens outside of the store is hidden from the retailer's perception and thus cannot be used for anything.

*Dr. Keller is a former Senior Consultant at IBM, founder and CEO of Cosibon AG

RecSys'14, October 6–10, 2014, Foster City, Silicon Valley, CA, USA.
ACM 978-1-4503-2668-1/14/10.
http://dx.doi.org/10.1145/2645710.2645711 .

2.1 Going beyond the Receipt Horizon

In this section we demonstrate how we are able to go beyond the Receipt Horizon by transferring proven e-commerce concepts to bricks-and-mortar stores. The traditional process at the POS is as follows: As soon as a customer has collected all goods she approaches the POS and identifies herself using her personal loyalty card. Subsequently, after all products have been scanned, she receives her paper-based purchase receipt. We believe that the value of receipts is highly underestimated and can be remodeled as an interactive link between consumers and retailers. Accordingly, we put the receipt to the center of our considerations and move the entire process at the POS to a smartphone app. First, we replace the physical, plastic made loyalty card by a screen in the app showing the same barcode. Second, instead of, or in addition to, the paper receipt we send a digital version to the customer's smartphone. The process is implemented in real time, transferring the receipt to the smartphone within a few seconds. Finally, the smartphone app stores the personal receipts and offers a number of customer relevant information about the purchases. The mobile app eventually serves as a comprehensive platform that allows us to collect the same valuable information about consumers' intentions, preferences, and feedback. Using the same clickstream analysis techniques as that of successful online retailers we track every movement within the app.

2.2 Current state of the system

We have already managed to implement an extensive smartphone app that allows us to perform various experiments in the field of product recommendations. The main features include the mobile loyalty card, interactive digital receipts and product pages, as well as a complete social network where customers can connect to friends, share product recommendations, or upload purchase pictures and comment via Facebook and Twitter. The individual items on the digital receipt are linked to individual product pages, where the consumer has access to a lot of additional information. Those include basic information like a description and, if applicable, ingredients but also information that the customer in bricks-and-mortar stores currently has no access to, like popularity information, insights about which friends buy or recommend the product, and average user ratings and customer comments. This product information is also available outside the store: By scanning a product's barcode all of this information can be accessed, too. So not only the products finally bought by the customer are available for analysis, but also those that were only investigated. At various places within the app users have access to personal recommendations, which themselves are of high interest as we can easily measure the success of arbitrary recommendation algorithms. We furthermore added some more features like shopping lists, information about current promotions, and several cross and upselling techniques modeled on successful online retailers. Of particular interest is the tracking of interaction among customers and retailers. App users can send each other messages, recommend products to their friends, share their own purchases, or comment on other people's purchases using a FourSquare like stream. They can also interact with the retailing company by rating the shopping experience and give qualified feedback about the shopping experience right after receiving the receipt. On the product level they can rate and comment on every single product. Over the past few months of our pilot project together with a European Retailer it was shown that we track about 100-200 user interactions between every two shop visits. It should be highlighted that all person-to-person recommendations, comments, ratings, feedback etc. are directly liked to actual purchases and thus result in data of highest quality.

3. RESEARCHING ADVANCED PRODUCT RECOMMENDATION AND BEHAVIOR PREDICTION ALGORITHMS

Due to space limitations we are not able to give detailed insights into all of our current research projects. Thus, we briefly describe only our major research topic, the improvement of our product recommendation algorithms, some of which have never been deployed in bricks-and-mortar stores before. Currently there are different recommender systems implemented. The first one, is similar to Amazon's Movers & Shakers algorithm. Customers get recommendations based on the changes in popularity of products. The second one suggests products based on the customer's personal purchase history and some other factors. The third feature is not an actual algorithm but more a feature, allowing customers to send personal products recommendations to their friends right over the app. Regarding the first two algorithms we are researching different techniques of how to improve those algorithms even further by integrating additional knowledge about individual customers that is currently unavailable to physical retailers. The third type of recommendations will be used to construct a unique ground-truth for future recommendation algorithms, since we claim that people bother their friends mainly with product recommendations which they know is of high interest for their addressee. We will thus be investigating several machine learning algorithms to understand inter-personal recommendations and to build truly next generation algorithms aside of purchase histories and pure product features. The success of our experiments is immediately observable as we have direct access to the purchase data as well and thus can evaluate which products were actually recommended to which customer using which algorithm and were eventually purchased. We are also able to measure the time-to-conversion and contact-to-conversion. Consequently we are also able to use all the data collected to implement an extensive customer behavior prediction system. To our knowledge, the amount of collectable data and the quality of the data outperforms any other research in the field of product recommendations for bricks-and-mortar stores.

As stated in the beginning, traditional retailing companies have absolutely no insights into the inter-person communication between their customers and are lacking a useful data collection and customer interaction platform. We have given consumers a tool in hand where they can interact with each other and retailers are given a tool where they can, for the first time, observe and evaluate customer behavior beyond the Receipt Horizon.

4. REFERENCES

[1] M. Gilly and J. Graham. A dyadic study of interpersonal information search. *Journal of the Academy of Marketing Science*, 21.

Focal: a Personalized Mobile News Reader

Florent Garcin Frederik Galle Boi Faltings

Artificial Intelligence Lab
Ecole Polytechnique Fédérale de Lausanne
Switzerland
firstname.lastname@epfl.ch

ABSTRACT

Traditionally in mobile apps, news articles and recommendations are presented to the users as an ordered list. This ordering often reflects the freshness of the stories. Although most users are satisfied with such presentation, some users have different expectations and want to read stories related to some specific topics.

In this demo, we depart from the classic list-view layout and aim at exploring other ways to present news stories to the users. We introduce *Focal*, a personalized mobile news reader, which implements a fisheye-inspired interface. We briefly describe its system architecture and interface.

Categories and Subject Descriptors

H.3.3 [**Information Storage and Retrieval**]: Information Search and Retrieval—*Information filtering*

Keywords

recommender system; news; mobile; interface

1. INTRODUCTION

The proliferation of online news creates a need for filtering interesting articles. Most mobile news apps present to the users articles and their associated recommendations as an ordered list. The ordering often reflects one dimension of the articles such as the freshness. However, news articles have more than one dimension like popularity or relevance [3].

Although most users are satisfied with such presentation, some users have different expectations and want to read news that are either popular, or related to some specific topics. It is thus desirable to have a single interface that captures all these dimensions at a glance [6].

A list-view interface constrains the users into extensive scrolling while browsing the list. In addition, items at the bottom have a smaller chance of being clicked [1]. As a result, researchers have looked at the issue of visualization of recommendations, but they have mainly focused on product recommendations [5, 6]. The news domain has specific challenges: it is very dynamic. News stories are subject to trends and reader preferences change over time.

To this end, we present *Focal*, a personalized mobile news reader. Focal displays stories with a fisheye-inspired interface [2]. The key idea of Focal is to build a graph of the current news articles, and focus on a region of this graph depending on the preferences of the user.

We believe that such an interface is more intuitive for browsing and reading news stories. Thus, we aim at comparing the classic list-view interface to our graph-based one. We also plan to evaluate different recommender algorithms in order to identify which ones fit the best the application of mobile news recommendations.

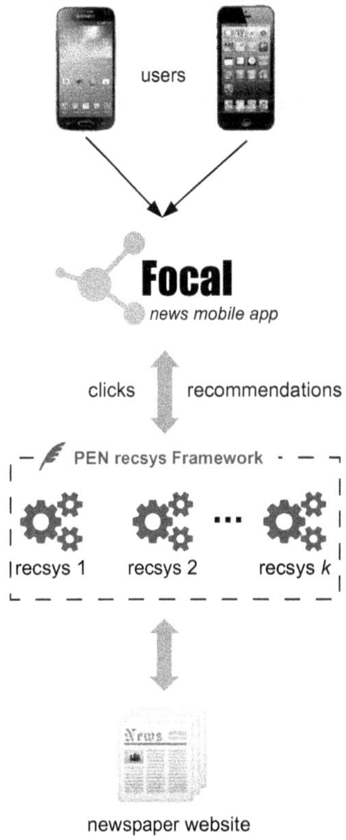

Figure 1: System architecture and components.

RecSys'14, October 6–10, 2014, Foster City, Silicon Valley, CA, USA.
ACM 978-1-4503-2668-1/14/10.
http://dx.doi.org/10.1145/2645710.2645714.

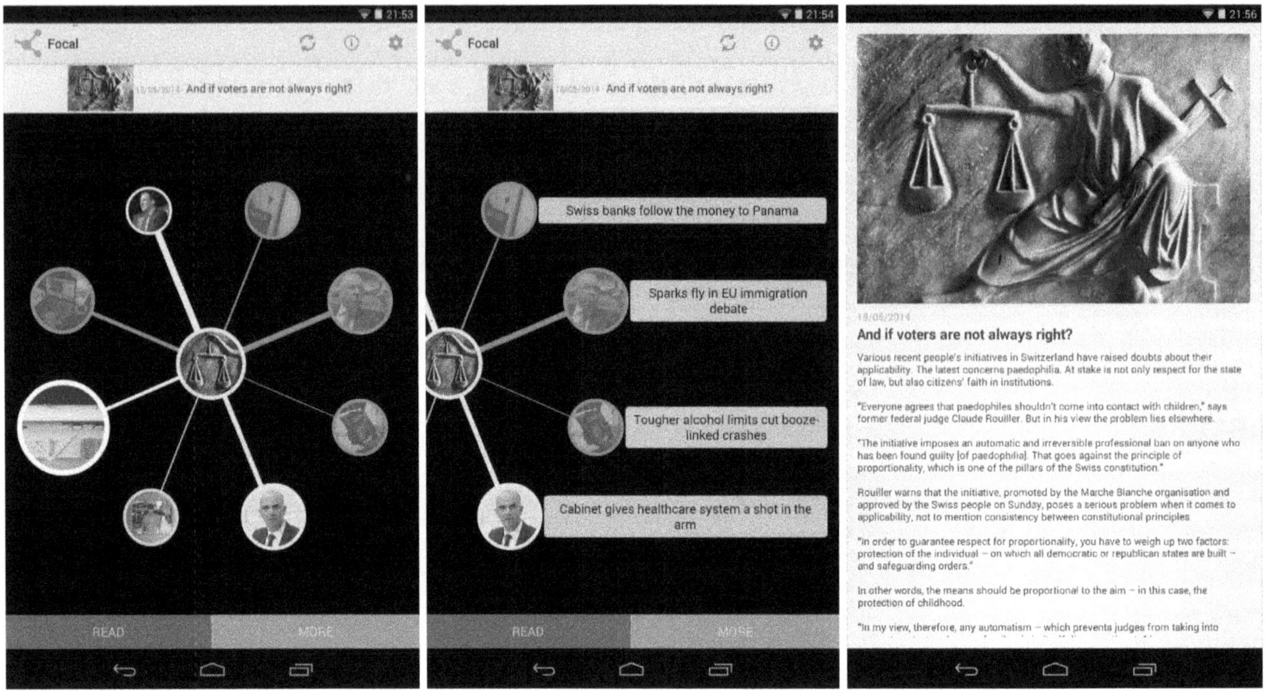

(a) main panel | (b) main panel with slide to left | (c) reading panel

Figure 2: Screenshots of Focal.

2. SYSTEM ARCHITECTURE

Figure 1 gives a brief overview of the main components interacting with Focal. When a user clicks on a news story, Focal sends the click to the PEN recsys framework [4]. The PEN recsys framework will assign randomly a recommender system and provide recommendations. It has a set of implemented recommender algorithms which are designed to take into account one or many dimensions of the news domain. For instance, a content-based recommender will only take into account the relevance between stories, while others recommend only the most popular articles. The PEN recsys framework also periodically gets the latest stories from the newspaper website. This architecture is very flexible and can be adapted to multiple news sources.

3. DESIGN AND INTERFACES

Figure 2(a) shows Focal's main panel. The user can easily recognize the 3 dimensions of a story: freshness, popularity and relevance.

Freshness is illustrated as the transparency of the node. When a node is very transparent, the associated story is old. *Popularity* is modelled as the size of the node. A large node represents a very popular story. *Relevance* is designed as the thickness of the edges between two articles. When an edge is very thick, the two associated stories have a high relevance.

A picture may not always be representative of the topic of a story. Thus, it is possible to slide the graph to the right or left such that story titles will appear (see Figure 2(b)). Finally, the user can double-tap on the node or tap on the read button to access the reading panel (Figure 2(c)). The *more* button moves the selected story to the central node and generates new recommendations. That way, the user moves the focus to another region of the news graph. Hence, a user browses the news like performing a walk through a graph of recommended stories.

4. CONCLUSION

We presented *Focal*, a personalized mobile news reader which displays stories as a fisheye-inspired interface. Focal captures the multiple dimensions of news stories into one single interface.

At the time of writing, we are conducting a user study to compare the different layouts (list vs graph). We plan to improve Focal based on the feedback of this user study. Finally, we want to evaluate the performance of different recommender systems when using Focal, and see which dimensions are the most important to the users.

5. REFERENCES

[1] N. Craswell, O. Zoeter, M. Taylor, and B. Ramsey. An experimental comparison of click position-bias models. In *Conf. on Web Search and Data Mining*, pages 87–94, 2008.

[2] G. Furnas. Generalized fisheye views. In *Conference on Human Factors in Computing Systems*, pages 16–23, 1986.

[3] F. Garcin, C. Dimitrakakis, and B. Faltings. Personalized news recommendation with context trees. In *Conference on Recommender Systems*, pages 105–112, 2013.

[4] F. Garcin and B. Faltings. Pen recsys: a personalized news recommender systems framework. In *News Recommender Systems Workshop*, pages 3–9, 2013.

[5] P. Janecek and P. Pu. Opportunistic search with semantic fisheye views. In *Web Information Systems*, pages 668–680. Springer, 2004.

[6] M. Kagie, M. van Wezel, and P. Groenen. Map based visualization of product catalogs. In *Recommender Systems Handbook*, pages 547–576. Springer, 2011.

RiVal – A Toolkit to Foster Reproducibility in Recommender System Evaluation

Alan Said
TU-Delft
The Netherlands
alansaid@acm.org

Alejandro Bellogín
Universidad Autónoma de Madrid
Spain
alejandro.bellogin@uam.es

ABSTRACT

Currently, it is difficult to put in context and compare the results from a given evaluation of a recommender system, mainly because too many alternatives exist when designing and implementing an evaluation strategy. Furthermore, the actual implementation of a recommendation algorithm sometimes diverges considerably from the well-known ideal formulation due to manual tuning and modifications observed to work better in some situations. RiVal – a recommender system evaluation toolkit – allows for complete control of the different evaluation dimensions that take place in any experimental evaluation of a recommender system: data splitting, definition of evaluation strategies, and computation of evaluation metrics. In this demo we present some of the functionality of RiVal and show step-by-step how RiVal can be used to evaluate the results from any recommendation framework and make sure that the results are comparable and reproducible.

Categories and Subject Descriptors

H.3.3 [**Information Storage and Retrieval**]: Information Search and Retrieval - Information filtering; H.5.1 [**Multimedia Information Systems**]: Evaluation/methodology

General Terms

Experimentation; Documentation; Measurement; Performance

Keywords

Recommender Systems; Evaluation; Benchmarking; Reproducibility; Recommendation Frameworks; Experiments

1. RECOMMENDATION AND EVALUATION

The recommender system research community has access to multiple open source recommendation frameworks, e.g. Apache Mahout[1], LensKit[2], MyMediaLite[3]. One of the emerging problems with having many recommendation frameworks is the difficulty when comparing results across frameworks, i.e. the reported accuracy of an algorithm in one framework will often differ from the same algorithm in a different framework. There are multiple causes for this, some of these are related to minor differences in algorithmic implementation, data management, and evaluation [1]. An example of this is shown in Table 1 which illustrates the different RMSE and nDCG values obtained through each framework's internal evaluation mechanisms (under the same evaluation conditions) using the same algorithms in Apache Mahout (AM), LensKit (LK) and MyMediaLite (MML) on the same dataset – Movielens100k. The table highlights the vast differences between the different frameworks showing that the same algorithm, dataset, and metric can differ several orders of magnitude across frameworks.

This demonstration shows a cross-framework recommender system evaluation toolkit – RiVal[4]. RiVal provides a transparent evaluation setting, allowing the practitioner complete control of the various evaluation settings.

(a) nDCG for AM and LK

Alg.	F.W.	nDCG
Item-based	AM	0.005169231
	LK	0.924546132
SVD 50	AM	0.105427298
	LK	0.943464094
User-based	AM	0.169295451
	LK	0.948413562

(b) RMSE for LK and MML.

Alg.	F.W.	RMSE
Item-based	LK	1.05018614
	MML	0.92933246
SVD 50	LK	1.01209290
	MML	0.93074012
User-based	LK	1.02545490
	MML	0.93419026

Table 1: Root-mean-square error (RMSE) and normalized Discounted Cumulative Gain (nDCG) for item-based and user-based (kNN, k=50) collaborative filtering algorithms using Pearson correlation, and matrix factorization (50 dimensions, FunkSVD in Mahout and Lenskit; SVD++ in MyMediaLite).

2. RIVAL – A TOOLKIT FOR EVALUATION

RiVal is an open source Java toolkit which allows for fine-grained control of the complete evaluation methodology. We have defined the following four stages in the recommendation-evaluation process *i) data splitting*; *ii) item recommendation*; *iii) candidate item generation*; *iv) performance measurement*.

[1]`http://mahout.apache.org`
[2]`http://lenskit.grouplens.org`
[3]`http://mymedialite.net`
[4]`http://rival.recommenders.net`

RecSys'14, October 6–10, 2014, Foster City, Silicon Valley, CA, USA.

ACM 978-1-4503-2668-1/14/10.
http://dx.doi.org/10.1145/2645710.2645712 .

Since RiVal is not a recommendation framework, step (*iii*) is not performed by RiVal, but can be performed by any of the three integrated frameworks (Mahout, LensKit and MyMediaLite), or outside of the RiVal pipeline. In this case, steps (*i*), (*iii*), and (*iv*) are performed in the toolkit, whereas in step (*ii*), the preferred recommendation framework is given the data splits generated in the previous step and the recommendations produced by the framework are then given as input to step (*iii*) of RiVal.

The toolkit can either be used as Maven dependencies, or ran as a standalone program for each of the steps. When running the toolkit in standalone mode, the type of evaluation to perform, recommendation algorithms, and framework to use are specified in property files which instantiate the necessary setup and execute each step. Listing 1 shows an example of a configuration file which sets up RiVal to prepare a set of datasets to perform cross validation on. The configuration instantiates the MovielensParser, which assumes the input data has a structure similar to the Movielens datasets (tab- or colon-separated columns). The resulting data splits will be written in the `ml100kcv` folder, separating training and test files through prefixes and/or suffixes, e.g. `mov100k_fold_1_global.train` would be the training file for the first cross validation fold.

Listing 1: Example of data splitter configuration

```
dataset.file=dataset.csv
dataset.parser=net.recommenders.rival.split.\
        parser.MovielensParser
dataset.splitter=net.recommenders.rival.split.\
        splitter.CrossValidationSplitter
split.peruser=false
split.seed=2014
split.cv.nfolds=5
split.output.folder=./ml100kcv/
split.training.prefix=mov100k_fold
split.test.prefix=mov100k_fold
split.training.suffix=_global.train
split.test.suffix=_global.test
```

Analogously, Listing 2 shows an example configuration of a recommendation step performing user-based recommendation using cosine similarity with a neighborhood size set to 50 with the LensKit recommendation framework. The evaluation step, which encompasses both candidate item generation and performance measurement is configured in a similar fashion (not included here due to space constraints). Examples of all configurations are found in the source code of RiVal[5].

Listing 2: Example of recommendation configuration

```
recommender=org.grouplens.lenskit.knn.user.\
        UserUserItemScorer
similarity=org.grouplens.lenskit.vectors.\
        similarity.CosineVectorSimilarity
neighborhood=50
training=./trainset.scv
test=./testset.csv
output=./results.csv
framework=lenskit
```

An example of an evaluation (RMSE) performed on a set of different algorithms (user/item-based CF, SVD), a

[5]`http://github.com/recommenders/rival`

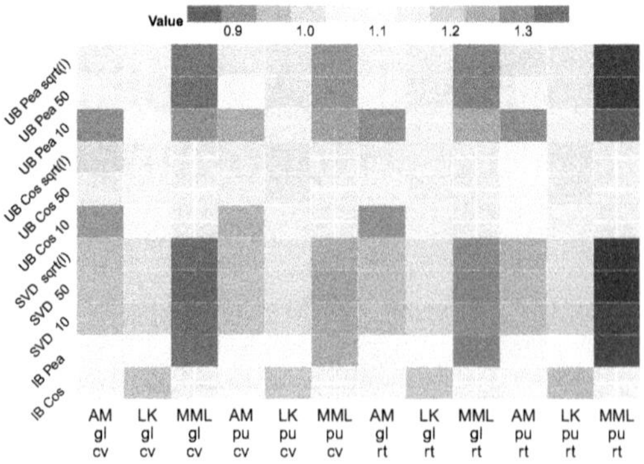

Figure 1: RMSE for a controlled evaluation. IB and UB refer to item- and user-based respectively; Pea and Cos to Pearson and Cosine; gl and pu to global and per user splitting; cv to cross validation and rt to ratio; and AM, LK, MML to the frameworks. (NB: To be viewed in color.)

set of different data splits (cross-validation, per-user, global random) and frameworks (Mahout, LensKit, MyMediaLite) is shown in Fig. 1. The figure highlights that not only does the internal evaluation of each framework differ, even when the evaluation is fully controlled, the results should not be directly compared across frameworks.

3. DEMONSTRATION

In the demonstration, we will be showing how to quickly set up RiVal and run cross-framework comparison (benchmarking) using LensKit, MyMediaLite, and Mahout as recommendation frameworks. Each step in the evaluation protocol (data splitting, recommendation, candidate item generation, performance measurement) will be shown in detail and comparisons across frameworks and different evaluation strategies will be shown in order to highlight the importance of a transparent evaluation setup.

We will also be showing the evaluation setup used by all participants in the 2014 ACM RecSys Challenge[6] as RiVal is the tool used by both participants and organizers in order to measure the performance of the algorithms developed in the scope of the challenge.

4. ACKNOWLEDGMENTS

This work was partly carried out during the tenure of an ERCIM "Alain Bensoussan" Fellowship Programme. The research leading to these results has received funding from the European Union Seventh Framework Programme (FP7/2007-2013) under grant agreements n°246016 and n°610594, and the Spanish Ministry of Science and Innovation (TIN2013-47090-C3-2).

5. REFERENCES

[1] A. Said and A. Bellogín. Comparative recommender system evaluation: Benchmarking recommendation frameworks. In *Proceedings of the 8th ACM Conference on Recommender Systems*, RecSys, New York, NY, USA, 2014. ACM.

[6]`http://2014.recsyschallenge.com`

System U: Automatically Deriving Personality Traits from Social Media for People Recommendation

Hernan Badenes[1], Mateo N. Bengualid[1], Jilin Chen[2], Liang Gou[2], Eben Haber[2], Jalal Mahmud[2], Jeffrey W Nichols[2], Aditya Pal[2], Jerald Schoudt[2], Barton A Smith[2], Ying Xuan[2], Huahai Yang[2], Michelle X. Zhou[2]

[1]IBM, Buenos Aires, Argentina, {hbadenes, bengualí}@ar.ibm.com

[2]IBM Research – Almaden, San Jose, CA, USA, {jilinc, lgou, ehaber, jumahmud, jwnichols, apal, jschoudt, barton.smith, yxuan, hyang, mzhou }@us.ibm.com

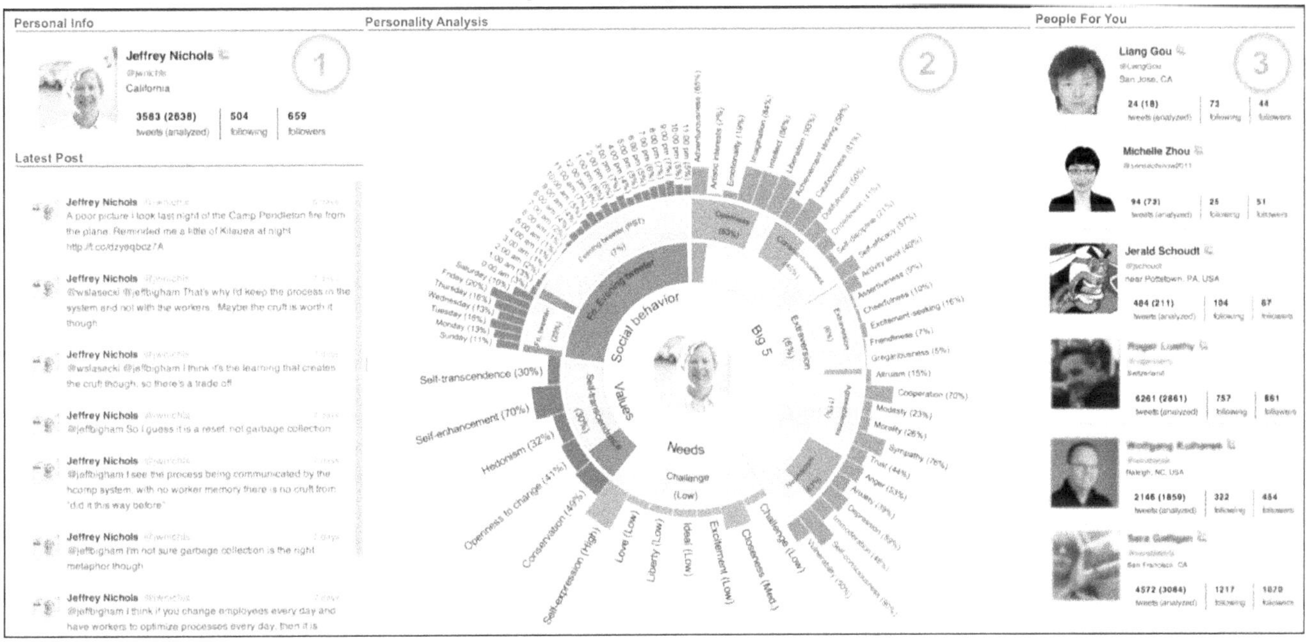

Figure 1: System U interface: (1) Basic information of a Twitter user and recent tweet posts from this user; (2) A visualization of personality portrait, including Big Five personality [8], fundamental needs [7], and human values [1]; (3) A panel showing recommended people for different tasks.

ABSTRACT

This paper presents a system, System U, which automatically derives people's personality traits from social media and recommends people for different tasks. The system leverages linguistic signals appearing in a person's social media activities to compute the personality portraits including Big Five personality, fundamental needs and basic human values. This system and technology can be used in a wide variety of personalized applications, such as recommending people to answer questions.

Categories and Subject Descriptors

H.1.2 User/Machine Systems: Human factors.

Keywords

System U; Big Five personality; basic human values; fundamental needs; social media; recommendation system.

RecSys '14, October 6–10, 2014, Foster City, Silicon Valley, CA, USA.
ACM 978-1-4503-2668-1/14/10.
http://dx.doi.org/10.1145/2645710.2645719

1. INTRODUCTION

People have different personality traits, such as openness to experience new activities, needs of closeness with families. Psychology and Behavioral Economic studies show that personality influences a person's behavior in the real world, e.g. occupational proficiency [2] and economic decisions [7]. However, it is impractical to obtain these traits for a large population with traditional psychometric surveys and tests.

Fortunately, a number of studies show personality traits can be detected from individuals' language use based on psycholinguistic analysis [2][3][8]. For example, the agreeableness of a person is highly correlated with their language choices of inclusive words, such as with, together, and us. Meanwhile, the public footprints left in social media offers us an opportunity to derive people' personality traits at scale.

In this paper, we demonstrate a system, System U, which automatically derives people's personality traits from social media with psycholinguistic analysis. We currently focus on three types of traits, including Big Five personality [2][8], fundamental needs [7] and human values [1]. We present the system architecture, key technologies and user interfaces. We also show how these traits can be used to recommend people who share similar interests.

2. SYSTEM OVERVIEW

2.1 System Architecture

Figure 2 shows the system architecture of System U. The social media crawlers first obtain people's public digital footprints (tweets, blogs and Facebook updates etc.), from various social media sources. This content is saved to a storage layer for later analysis. The module of people analytics then computes three types of traits from the textual content, and there are three models including Big Five personality, basic human values, and fundamental needs in this module. With the computed traits, the module of people recommender can suggest a group of people who can help on certain tasks. Also, some other personalization modules can be plugged into this to offer individualized services by leveraging the derived personality traits. Finally, the user interface allows users to interact with the personality traits and personalized services through interactive visualization.

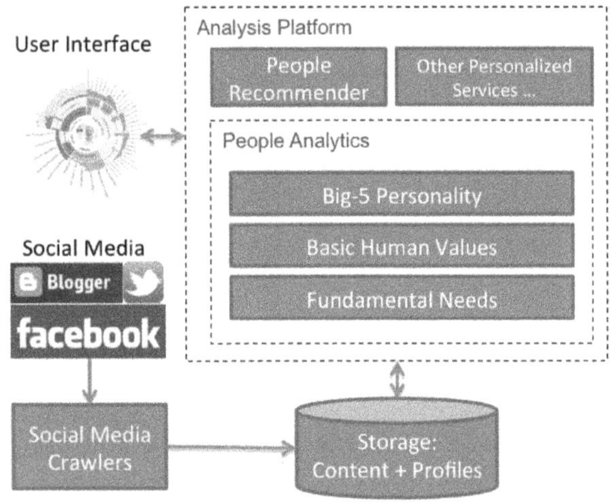

Figure 2. The system architecture of System U.

2.2 People Analytics

We currently model three types of personality traits with a lexicon-based, psycholinguistic analysis, including Big Five personality, basic human values, and fundamental needs. The first model is Big Five personality that consists of five unique and enduring personality characteristics, including *Openness*, *Conscientiousness*, *Extraversion*, Agreeableness, and *Neuroticism*. It influences one's life from many aspects, including job proficiency and team performance [2][8]. The second model concerns a person's fundamental needs with 12 dimensions (6 of them are currently shown in System U), which often influences one's brand and product choices [7]. The last one is the basic values model capturing people's beliefs and motivators along five major dimensions [1].

A lexicon-based analysis is used to build the trait models by analyzing correlations between personality traits and the usage of certain words or word categories. Specifically, our Big Five personality and basic values [6] use words and word categories derived from the LIWC dictionary [6], and our needs model [7] uses a custom dictionary. We developed a custom dictionary with a hybrid empirical and computational approach. The idea is to analyze the correlation of set of words extracted from written samples with each trait dimension by feature-based, statistical models. The extracted words construct a custom dictionary. More details can be found in [1][7].

2.3 People Recommender

A people recommender is designed to suggest a group of people who can help on certain tasks by assessing the task suitability of an individual. These tasks include finding

- Answerers to questions: We built a smart social QA system that automatically routes questions to suitable employees who are willing, able, and ready to provide answers. Our optimization-based approach also recommends both top-matched active (seed) and inactive (prospect) answerers for a given question [5].
- Information Spreaders: We built a recommendation system that actively identify and engage the right strangers at the right time on social media to help effectively propagate intended information within a desired time frame [4].

2.4 User Interface

The user interface of System U is shown in Figure 1. It includes three panels of user twitter information, derived personality portrait, and recommended people. Specifically, Panel 1 shows basic information of a Twitter user, including recent tweet posts from this user. Panel 2 shows a visualization of personality portrait, including Big Five personality, fundamental needs, human values and social activities. The visualization enables users to expand a trait of interest to see subtraits. For example, a user can have a better understanding of "*Neuroticism*" by expanding this sector to look at its subtraits, such as "*Anxiety*", "*Anger*", "*Depression*" and "*Self-consciousness*". Panel 3 shows a list of people who are recommended for certain tasks.

3. CONCLUSION

In this paper, we present a system, System U, which automatically derives people's personality traits, including Big Five personality, basic human values, and fundamental needs, from social media. We also demonstrate the capability of applying such technology for various potential personalized services such as recommending people to answer questions.

4. REFERENCES

[1] Chen, J., Hsieh, G., Mahmud, J., & Nichols, J.:. Understanding individuals' personal values from social media word use. *CSCW'14.*

[2] Golbeck, J., Robles, C., Edmondson, M., &Turner, K.: Predicting personality from twitter.*SocCom'11*, 149-156.

[3] Gou, L., Zhou, M. X., & Yang, H: KnowMe and ShareMe: Understanding Automatically Discovered Personality Traits from Social Media and User Sharing Preferences. *CHI'14.*

[4] Lee, K., Mahmud, J., Chen, J., Zhou, M.X., Nichols, J.: Who will retweet this?: Automatically Identifying and Engaging Strangers on Twitter to Spread Information. *IUI'14*: 247-256

[5] Luo, L, Wang, F., Zhou, M.X., Pan, Y., Chen, H.: Who have got answers?: growing the pool of answerers in a smart enterprise social QA system. *IUI'14*: 7-16.

[6] Pennebaker, J. W., Francis, M. & Booth, R.: Lin-guistic inquiry and word count: LIWC 2001.

[7] Yang, H., & Li, Y. Identifying user needs from social media. *IBM Tech. Report'13.*

[8] Yarkoni, T.: Personality in 100,000 Words: A large-scale analysis of personality and word use among bloggers. *Journal of Research in Personality*, 44, 363-373, 2010.

Tell Me Where to Go and What to Do Next, but Do Not Bother Me

Hongwei Liu
Northeastern University
Shenyang, China
hongweiliu@research.neu.edu.cn

Gang Wu
Northeastern University
Shenyang, China
wugang@ise.neu.edu.cn

Guoren Wang
Northeastern University
Shenyang, China
wanggr@mail.neu.edu.cn

ABSTRACT

In this demonstration, we present a system that recommends to the user the locations and activities she/he might be interested in according to history GPS trajectories and public places of interest (POI) data. Its innovation lies in the acceptable performance of recommendations in cases where no user comments on activity types are available. Such situations are more realistic considering the restrictions on mobile devices' abilities, users' privacies, or business secret. For this purpose, we first extract stay points according to uses' trajectories, and label them with the top-k common activities which have the most possibility in terms of the POI dataset. Then, by taking stay points as observations, and activities as hidden states, a Hidden Markov model is built to learn the transfer possibilities between activities and the generation probabilities between activities and stay points. Finally, with the obtained model, our system can perform two types of recommendation, i.e. the history based recommendation and the similarity based recommendation. The results of former type are those stay points from user's own history positions. While, the latter one conducts collaborative filtering by taking history based recommendation results from similar users. The demonstration shows the running effects of the implemented prototype system, in which the Microsoft GeoLife trajectories dataset and the "DianPing.com" POI dataset were loaded. The preliminary experimental results demonstrate the feasibility.

Categories and Subject Descriptors

H.3.4 [**Systems and Software**]:

General Terms

World Wide Web (WWW).

Keywords

LBS; Recommendation; Hidden Markov Model

1. INTRODUCTION

It would be really embarrassing if we totally have no idea of where to go and what to do next when hanging out with best friends. Nowadays location-based recommender system may be helpful in this situation because of its ability in mining users' life patterns (e.g. behaviors and preferences) from the history trajectories [1]. With the help of additional information like places of interest (POI) or even user comments, location-based recommenders can recommend possible activities as well as interesting locations.

RecSys '14, October 6–10, 2014, Foster City, Silicon Valley, CA, USA.
ACM 978-1-4503-2668-1/14/10.
http://dx.doi.org/10.1145/2645710.2645718

The traditional approaches for recommending locations try to choose statistically popular neighboring locations that extracted from all the users' trajectories [2]. Such approaches do make sense for recommending locations that are general-purpose (touring sequences are suitable for most of the common tourists) and coarse-grained with apparent boundary (tourist attractions like the Forbidden City). As users' life patterns are not taken into consideration in these approaches, personalized recommending results are still not available. Obviously, involving the user's actively specified activities for certain locations (e.g. shopping at the shopping mall, eating in the restaurant, or seeing a movie in the cinema) or alternatively employing places of interests (POI) data may improve the performance of recommendations. In this way, the user's life patterns could be learnt and used for future locations and activities recommendation.

However, people are always lazy or unwilling to share their actual activities by writing comments though equipping GPS devices e.g. smart phones are very common. Moreover, there are other more cases make user involved labeling of activities not available like restrictions on mobile devices' abilities, users' privacies, or business secret. Therefore, a new question emerges that is it possible to perform location and activity recommendations only depending on trajectories and POI data? In this demonstration (http://www.neunavy.com:8088), we try to positively answer the question by proposing an approach that recommends locations and activities with GPS trajectories and places of interest when no user comments are available.

Our system consists of four stages. 1) Firstly, as the basis of the location-based recommendation, stay points are extracted offline according to uses' trajectories. After the stage of Stay Point Extraction, the output is a sequence of stay points. 2) Then, we label the stay points with the semantics from a POI category dataset, Dianping.com which is the most famous Yelp like web site in China containing more than 6 million of local businesses covering 10 categories (food, entertainment, shopping, beauty, wedding, family, sports, hotel, automotive, and local services). According to the API of DianPing.com, a query to the possible activities given the GPS coordinates of a stay point will return a list of candidates. We evaluate the most likely top-k activities by the value of each label. In this way, after Location-Semantics Information Extraction, each stay point may have k activities. Therefore, the output is changed to a sequence of stay points with possible activities. 3) Next, we exploit HMM (Hidden Markov Model) to find a sequence of activities that most likely explain the observed sequence of stay points. Here, we regard a stay point as an observation and an activity as a hidden state. As we know, HMM is a double stochastic process, which can be represented as $\lambda = (N, M, \pi, A, B)$. To create the HMM, we need to prepare the basic parameters such as the number M of observations, the number N of the hidden states, the transfer matrix of the hidden states A, the confuse matrix between of hidden states and observations B, and the initial hidden state vector π . Then we can train the HMM for each user with all of her/his semantic sequences offline. 4) Finally, after the data modeling and the parameters learning, a HMM based recommender is available for recommending locations and activities according to each user's preferences. Two types of recommendations can be performed in terms of the differences of the results. They are History Based Recommendation and Similarity Based Recommendation. The results of former type are those stay points from user's own history positions. While, the latter one conducts collaborative filtering by taking history based recommendation results from similar users.

2. SYSTEM DESCRIPTION

2.1 Application View

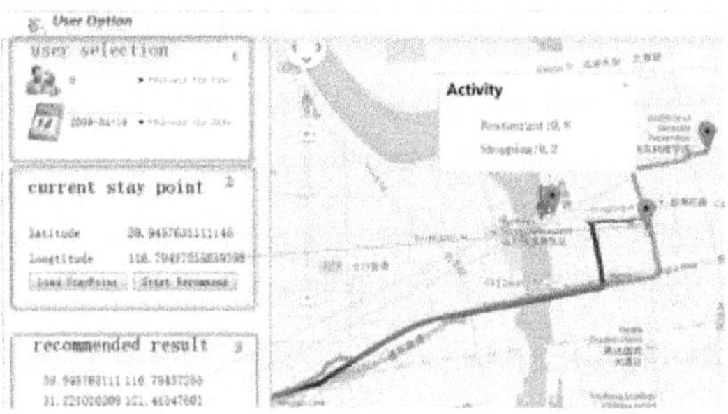

Figure. 1. The Overview of the Application

Figure 1 shows the user interface of our demo Web application. The left side of the user interface consists of three parts, 1) User Selection, in which the user can browse their own history trajectories by selecting different date. After the selection, the right side of the user interface will show all the trajectories of the date with different colors on the map; 2) Current Stay Point, shows the GPS coordinates of the stay point selected on the map by which our system can recommend the next possible stay points; 3) Recommended Results, gives the recommendation stay points based on the current stay point or any user mouse selection on the map. A map is displayed on the right side of the user interface on which several parts of trajectories in one day are represented as consecutive curved lines in different colors. The red and purple balloons stand for the current stay point and the recommended stay points respectively. The possible activities associated with a specific recommended stay point and corresponding probabilities are listed in a popup menu near the stay point.

In Section 2.2 and 2.3, we exemplify the two types of recommendations provided in our system, i.e. the history based recommendation and the similarity based recommendation. According to our extensive analysis on the GPS trajectory data, the POI data, and common user behaviors, we got an interesting finding that usually the history based recommendation is effective on workdays while the similarity based recommendation is meaningful on weekends. The reason is that our behavior on workdays is quite regular while we would like to try different activities during weekends.

2.2 History Based Recommendation

For example, as shown in Figure 2, at the beginning of the trajectory the user (id 0 of GeoLife, and date 2009-05-15) might in his dormitory which is a history stay point in our system marked with red ball in Figure 2. Based on the current stay point and the GPS signal of user's current movement, our system try to guess what he has done in current stay point (in this example is break) and infer what he will do next. Taking into account that it was workday afternoon and his history trajectories, as a result, our system recommended the user to go to swimming pool for swimming. After a period of swimming, the user might get out of the swimming pool, because of the prior stay point is in the dormitory, and according to the same situation of the history trajectories, our system guess the would go to her/his laboratory for work.

Figure. 2. The trajectory of the workday

2.3 Similarity Based Recommendation

Another example is the same user's trajectory on weekends (2008-10-23), which is shown in Figure 3.

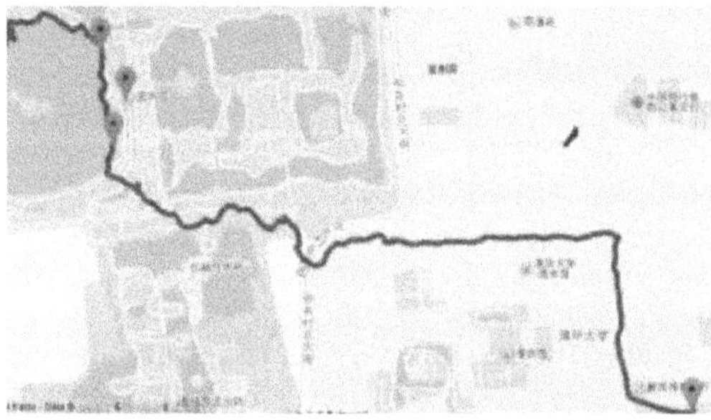

Figure. 3. The trajectory of the weekends

At the beginning of the trajectory the user was in the Concert Hall, and maybe accompanied with the boyfriend or girlfriend. We believe that during the weekend, the university's Concert Hall must be welcomed.

After enjoying some music, the user left the hall. Taking into account that the day was weekend and maybe some friends were together with the user, it was quite different from the workdays. So trying to recommend based on his history trajectories may not work well. Therefore, our system tried to recommend based on the same situation of other users in the system having similar history activities and the GPS signal of the user's movement. Finally, our system inferred that the user might tour the famous sight spot near the university, i.e. the Summer Palace.

3. ACKNOWLEDGMENTS

This project is supported by NSFC (Grant No. 61332006, 61370154, 61025007, 61328202); State Key Development Program for Basic Research of China (Grant No. 2011CB302200-G); National High Technology Research and Development Program of China (Grant No.2012AA011004).

4. REFERENCES

[1] Bao J, Zheng Y, Wilkie D, et al. A Survey on Recommendations in Location-based Social Networks [J]

[2] Zheng Y, Zhang L, Xie X, et al. Mining interesting locations and travel sequences from GPS trajectories[C]. ACM, 2009: 791-800.

WrapRec: An Easy Extension of Recommender System Libraries

Babak Loni, Alan Said
Multimedia Computing Group
Delft University of Technology, Netherlands
{b.loni, a.said}@tudelft.nl

ABSTRACT

WrapRec is an easy-to-use Recommender Systems toolkit which allows users to easily implement or wrap recommendation algorithms from other frameworks. The main goals of WrapRec are to provide a flexible I/O, evaluation mechanism and code reusability. WrapRec provides a rich data model which makes it easy to implement algorithms for different recommender system problems, such as context-aware and cross-domain recommendation. The toolkit is written in C# and the source code is publicly available on Github under the GPL license.

Categories and Subject Descriptors

H.3.3 [**Information Search and Retrieval**]: Information Filtering

Keywords

Recommender Systems; Open Source Library

1. INTRODUCTION

Personalized recommender systems are becoming very popular in online marketing, social networks and mobile applications. RecSys and machine learning communities have developed several successful libraries for recommender systems such as *MyMediaLite*[1], *Apache Mahout*[2] and *LensKit*[3].

Most of existing libraries require specific data formats, usually as text files, and are not flexible enough to support new data formats. Data processing is an important step in recommender systems which are usually neglected in current RecSys libraries. The existing frameworks usually require the users to provide the data in a specific format, and similarly they output results in a specific format. As an example consider that a user has a data source with a particular format which is not supported by the existing toolkits. A common practice to use this data is to convert to a format which is supported by the toolkit and then run the experiment on the converted data. Now, if the user wants to repeat the experiment for many different scenarios, usually the data preprocessing is done by an external application in a semi-manual way which makes the usage of toolkits difficult and error prone.

WrapRec is a toolkit, with defined routines. It allows users to incorporate any data processing steps easily into the experiment, without requiring to change the underlying algorithms. The toolkit is a wrapper around existing libraries, which allows them to be plugged into the system. The main goal of the toolkit is to provide high-level interfaces for low-level services to make it easier to run RecSys algorithms. WrapRec's solution to this goal is to provide a rich data object model to make data access flexible and safe. This feature makes it easier to implement algorithms which rely on multiple data sources such as context-aware and cross-domain recommendation scenarios. Furthermore, WrapRec provides high level interfaces to potential algorithms that can be wrapped into the toolkit. Similarly an abstraction layer for evaluation of algorithms is defined in the toolkit to implement custom evaluators and re-use evaluation logics for different RecSys algorithms.

2. OVERVIEW OF THE TOOLKIT

The WrapRec toolkit consists of three main components: Data Layer, Recommendation Engine and Evaluation Pipeline. The components are made independent of each other, meaning they can be modified and extended without requiring to change other components. Figure 1 illustrates the high level architecture of the toolkit. Below, we briefly describe each component:

- **Data Layer**: This component provides a common data interface, regardless of the underlying format of the data source. If users want to read a custom data format, they need to implement an interface which reads the data and converts it into the common data objects. This feature makes it possible to run different experiments without requiring to change the underlying algorithms or evaluation mechanism. Furthermore, the toolkit is able to represent the data objects within a context which enables the consumer of data to take advantage of the C# language and issue LINQ (Language Integrated Queries) on data. This feature enables users to write an integrated query, select a custom subset of data and pass it to the other components of the system.

[1]`http://mymedialite.net`
[2]`http://mahout.apache.org`
[3]`http://lenskit.grouplens.org`

RecSys'14, October 6–10, 2014, Foster City, Silicon Valley, CA, USA.
ACM 978-1-4503-2668-1/14/10.
http://dx.doi.org/10.1145/2645710.2645717.

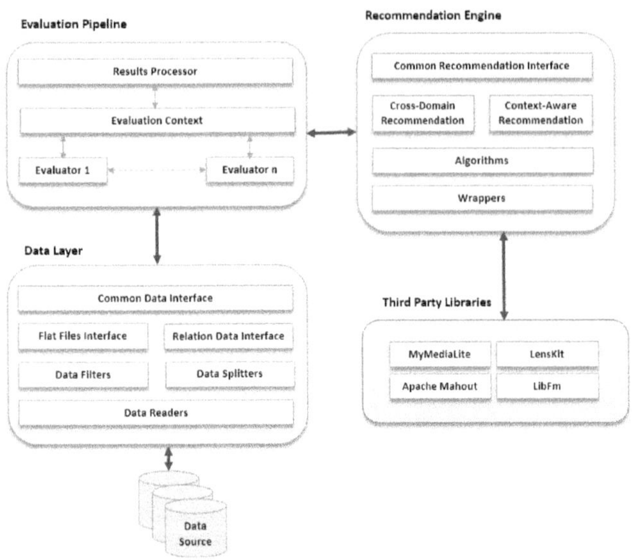

Figure 1: The overall architecture of WrapRec.

- **Recommendation Engine**: This component is the core of the toolkit. It provides common interfaces to RecSys algorithms. The focus of this component is not to implement the RecSys algorithms, but to provide a common interface to different algorithms that are implemented in various libraries. If users want to use an algorithm from existing libraries, they need to wrap the functionality of the third party libraries into the toolkit. Currently, the toolkit provides wrapper classes for MyMediaLite [1] (written in C#) and LibFM [2] (written in C++). This component also provides interfaces to implement Cross-Domain and Context-Aware recommendation algorithms.
- **Evaluation Pipeline**: WrapRec provides evaluation services based on the pipeline design pattern[4]. This enables the evaluator objects to share their results on a context object and thus improve the performance and re-usability of code. Pipeline-based evaluation allows users to re-use the evaluation logic for different RecSys algorithms since the evaluators only talk with high level data objects which are independent of the algorithms.

3. HOW TO USE THE TOOLKIT

The current version of WrapRec is implemented as a .Net library which can be added to a .Net project and be called through its public APIs. The WrapRec toolkit can be easily installed in a .Net project by installing its package through the *Nuget*[5] package management system, or by adding the library file directly to the references of the project. The source code of the toolkit is publicly available under GPL license on Github[6].

A major goal of WrapRec is to be easy to use. Based on the architecture of the system, to run a RecSys experiment users need to define three main objects: a data interface, an algorithm interface and an evaluation pipeline. More advance scenarios can be defined by extending each of the mentioned three objects. Listing 1 lists a simple RecSys experiment which trains a model on the Movielens 1M dataset[7] using MyMediaLite's rating prediction algorithms. The model is then tested using two evaluation metrics on 30% of the data.

Listing 1: Sample three step code to run a recommender system experiment

```
// step 1: dataset
var data = new Dataset<ItemRating>(new
     MovieLensReader("data.dat"), 0.7);

// step 2: recommender
var recommender = new MediaLiteRatingPredictor(new
     MatrixFactorization());

// step3: evaluation
var ep = new EvaluationPipeline(new
     EvalutationContext(recommender, data));

ep.Evaluators.Add(new RMSE());
ep.Evaluators.Add(new MAE());

// run the experiments
ep.Run();
```

Each of the three steps in the above example can be extended without modifying other steps. For example, to read a dataset with a different format, a different dataset reader needs to be defined in step 1. More advanced scenarios and samples can be found in the online documentation of the toolkit.

4. OUTLOOK

In this demo paper, we briefly introduced an open source RecSys toolkit that can be used for various purposes. The toolkit is currently available on Github and is in active development. The current version of the toolkit is available as a Nuget library and can be easily installed in any .Net project. In the future, we plan to further integrate this project with MyMediaLite and other existing libraries to take the advantages of the existing frameworks more.

Acknowledgment

This research is supported by funding from two European Commission's 7th Framework Program projects under grant agreements no. 610594 (CrowdRec) and no. 601166 (PHENICX).

5. REFERENCES

[1] Z. Gantner, S. Rendle, C. Freudenthaler, and L. Schmidt-Thieme. MyMediaLite: A free recommender system library. In *Proceedings of the 5th ACM Conference on Recommender Systems (RecSys 2011)*, 2011.

[2] S. Rendle. Factorization machines with libfm. *ACM Trans. Intell. Syst. Technol.*, 3(3), May 2012.

[4] msdn.microsoft.com/en-us/library/ff963548.aspx

[5] http://www.nuget.org/

[6] https://github.com/babakx/WrapRec

[7] http://grouplens.org/datasets/movielens/

Workshop on New Trends in Content-based Recommender Systems (CBRecSys 2014)

Toine Bogers
Department of Communication and Psychology
Aalborg University Copenhagen
2450 Copenhagen, Denmark
toine@hum.aau.dk

Marijn Koolen
Institute for Logic, Language and Computation
University of Amsterdam
Amsterdam, The Netherlands
marijn.koolen@uva.nl

Iván Cantador
Escuela Politécnica Superior
Universidad Autónoma de Madrid
28049 Madrid, Spain
ivan.cantador@uam.es

ABSTRACT

While content-based recommendation has been applied successfully in many different domains, it has not seen the same level of attention as collaborative filtering techniques have. However, there are many recommendation domains and applications where content and metadata play a key role, either *in addition to* or *instead of* ratings and implicit usage data. For some domains, such as movies, the relationship between content and usage data has seen thorough investigation already, but for many other domains, such as books, news, scientific articles, and Web pages we still do not know *if* and *how* these data sources should be combined to provided the best recommendation performance. The *CBRecSys 2014* workshop aims to address this by providing a dedicated venue for papers dedicated to all aspects of content-based recommendation.

Categories and Subject Descriptors

H.3.3 [**Information Storage and Retrieval**]: Information Search and Retrieval—*information Filtering*; D.2.8 [**Software Engineering**]: Metrics—*performance measures*

General Terms

Algorithms, Experimentation, Human Factors, Theory

Keywords

recommender systems, content-based recommendation, text reviews, user-generated content, implicit feedback, semantics, context

1. MOTIVATION AND GOALS

While content-based recommendation has been applied successfully in many different domains [2], it has not seen the same level of attention as collaborative filtering techniques have. In recent years, competitions like the Netflix Prize[1], CAMRA[2], and the Yahoo! Music KDD Cup 2011 [1] have spurred on advances in collaborative filtering and how to utilize ratings and usage data. However, there are many recommendation domains and applications where content and metadata play a key role, either *in addition to* or *instead of* ratings and implicit usage data. For some domains, such as movies, the relationship between content and usage data has seen thorough investigation already (e.g. [3]), but for many other domains, such as books, news, scientific articles, and Web pages we still do not know *if* and *how* these data sources should be combined to provided the best recommendation performance.

The *CBRecSys 2014* workshop aims to address this by providing a venue for papers dedicated to all aspects and new trends of content-based recommendation. This would include both recommendation in domains where textual content is abundant (e.g. books, news, scientific articles, jobs, educational resources, and Web pages) as well as dedicated comparisons and combinations of content-based techniques with collaborative filtering approaches.

[1] http://www.netflixprize.com/
[2] http://www.dai-labor.de/camra2010/

RecSys'14, Oct 06–10 2014, San Jose or vicinity, CA, USA.
ACM 978-1-4503-2668-1/14/10
http://dx.doi.org/10.1145/2645710.2645784.

2. TOPICS OF INTEREST

Relevant topics of the workshop include:

- Developing novel recommendation approaches
  - Hybrid strategies combining content-based and collaborative filtering recommendations
  - Content-based approaches to cross-system and cross-domain recommendation
  - Latent factor models for content-based and hybrid recommendation
- Exploiting user-generated content for recommendation
  - Mining microblogging data in content-based recommender systems
  - Social tag-based recommender systems
  - Exploiting Semantic Web and Linked Open Data in content-based recommender systems
- Processing text reviews
  - Estimating (implicit) ratings associated with text reviews
  - Opinion mining and sentiment analysis of text reviews to support content-based recommendation
  - Extracting user personality traits and factors from text reviews for recommendation

- Mining contextual data from content
  - Extraction of contextual signals from textual content for recommendation
  - Incorporating the temporal dimension in content-based recommendation
  - Mood-based recommender systems
- Addressing limitations of recommender systems
  - Addressing the cold-start problem with content-based recommendation approaches
  - Increasing diversity of content-based recommendations
  - Providing novelty in content-based recommendations

In particular, papers submitted to the the workshop have focused on the following topics. Several papers present hybrid systems combining collaborative filtering and content-based recommendation, finding them complementary, with content-based recommendation components especially suitable for tackling the cold-start problem. Other papers investigate how different content features can be used for similarity measures and explore ways to identify which features are the most relevant for a given context. Some papers present approaches to mine user reviews for inferring user preferences on specific attributes of items, essentially deriving more structured feature information from unstructured text. Finally, several papers look at semantic frameworks and Linked Open Data to measure item similarity across different domains.

3. CHALLENGE ON BOOK RECOMMENDATION

To facilitate exploration of the above mentioned topics, the workshop features an in-workshop challenge on book recommendation. This challenge focuses on recommending new, interesting books to LibraryThing users based on usage data (which books they have added to their collection) and content-based information about the books available in LibraryThing. The rich textual nature of the task makes the challenge an excellent venue to revisit questions about the benefits of content-based filtering vs. collaborative filtering, and metadata versus ratings information. At the workshop the evaluation results of the challenge were presented.

3.1 Dataset

For this challenge, a large dataset containing user profiles with book ratings and tags, and 2.8 million book descriptions with library metadata, user ratings, tags, and reviews from Amazon and LibraryThing was be made available.

The dataset for the book recommendation challenge is comprised of two parts: usage data and book metadata. The first part of the dataset for book recommendation is a log of usage data: who added which books to their collection at what point in time. In addition to this, ratings and tags assigned to books are also included in the usage dataset (where available). The user profiles in this data set contain a total number of 1,830,958 unique books added by 78,633 different LibraryThing users, anonymized through different privacy-preserving measures. This usage data serves as the main data source for evaluating our challenge, which is described in more detail in Section 3.2.

The second part of our challenge dataset for book recommendation is a collection of metadata records for 2.8 million books cataloged on LibraryThing. This collection was crawled from Amazon and LibraryThing by the University of Duisburg-Essen in early 2009. From Amazon, there is formal metadata like book title, author, publisher, publication year, library classification codes, Amazon categories, and similar product information, as well as user-generated content in the form of user ratings and reviews. From LibraryThing, there are user tags and user-provided metadata on awards, book characters and locations, and blurbs. This part of the challenge data has been used successfully for more retrieval-oriented challenges at the INEX 2011–2014 Social Book Search tracks[3].

3.2 Evaluation

The evaluation of the book recommendation challenge follows the familiar *backtesting* paradigm, where a small number of randomly selected books is withheld for each user with the remaining data to be used as training material. If a user?s withheld items are predicted at the top of the ranked result list, i.e., if the algorithm is able to correctly predict the user?s interest in those withheld items, then the algorithm has performed well. The main evaluation metric used in the challenge is the ranking-based metric NDCG@10, as ratings information is sparse in the usage data.

To make evaluation easier for challenge participants and to reduce the possibility of over-fitting, we divided the usage data into a training and a validation set. The training material contains 90% of the user profiles and is meant for training the participants' recommendation algorithms. To aid in the learning and parameter optimization phase on the training material, we performed 10-fold cross-validation on the training set. This resulted in 10 training and test sets, one for each of the folds. We encouraged all participants to use these 10 folds to train their system, so the results of the training phase are directly comparable among participants.

The validation set contains the remaining 10% of the user profiles (or 7863 users) and was released at a later date its aim was to produce the final comparison of the different submitted approaches. This validation set contains a set of users that are not included in the original training material to avoid over-fitting. To allow participants to train their systems on these new users as well, we also released a small amount of extra training material corresponding to the users near the end of the challenge.

4. WEBSITE AND PROCEEDINGS

The workshop material (list of accepted papers, invited talk, and the workshop schedule) ca be found on the CBRecSys 2014 workshop website at `http://ir.ii.uam.es/cbrecsys2014/`. The proceedings are published as a CEUR Workshop Proceedings volume.

5. REFERENCES

[1] G. Dror, N. Koenigstein, Y. Koren, and M. Weimer. The Yahoo! Music Dataset and KDD-Cup '11. In *JMLR Workshop and Conference Proceedings*, volume 18 of *Proceedings of KDD Cup 2011*, pages 3–18, 2012.

[2] P. Lops, M. de Gemmis, and G. Semeraro. Content-based Recommender Systems: State of the Art and Trends. In *Recommender Systems Handbook*, pages 73–105. 2011.

[3] I. Pilászy and D. Tikk. Recommending New Movies: Even a Few Ratings Are More Valuable Than Metadata. In *RecSys '09: Proceedings of the Third ACM Conference on Recommender Systems*, pages 93–100. ACM, 2009.

[3] `https://inex.mmci.uni-saarland.de/tracks/books/`

Overview of ACM RecSys CrowdRec 2014 Workshop:

Crowdsourcing and Human Computation for Recommender Systems

Martha Larson
Delft University of Technology
m.a.larson@tudelft.nl

Paolo Cremonesi
Politecnico di Milano
paolo.cremonesi@polimi.it

Alexandros Karatzoglou
Telefonica Research
alexk@tid.es

ABSTRACT

The CrowdRec workshop brings together the recommender system community for discussion and exchange of ideas. Its goal is to allow the potential of human computation and crowdsourcing to be exploited fully and sustainably, leading to the development of improved recommendation and information filtering technologies. Currently, the complete range of possible intelligent contributions that recommender systems could elicit from users is under-explored, and its full extent is unknown. Critical questions addressed in the workshop include how to: formulate crowdtasks, match tasks with crowdmembers, ensure the quality of crowd input, and integrate feedback from the crowd in an optimal manner to improve recommendation. Further, crowdsourcing can also be exploited for system design and system evaluation.

Categories and Subject Descriptors

H.3.3 [**Information Storage and Retrieval**]: Information Search and Retrieval—Information Filtering

General Terms

Algorithms, Design, Experimentation, Human Factors.

Keywords

human computation, human intelligence, crowdsourcing, recommender systems

1. INTRODUCTION

Recommender systems stand to benefit greatly if they would be able to call actively on intelligent human input specifically at those moments and for those purposes that it is most needed. This is the vision pursued by the CrowdRec workshop. The workshop is dedicated to new approaches to information filtering and recommendation technologies that make use of human intelligence, but also take advantage of human plurality, i.e., contributions from a large number of crowdmembers.

RecSys'14, October 6–10, 2014, Foster City, Silicon Valley, CA, USA.
ACM 978-1-4503-2668-1/14/10.
http://dx.doi.org/10.1145/2645710.2645783.

The aim of the CrowdRec workshop is to provide a forum within the recommender system community that can foster the development of new ideas and best practices for making use of crowdsourcing to improve the performance of recommendation technology.

The recommender system community faces a number of key challenges if human intelligence is to be actively exploited by algorithms and systems. These include recruitment of crowdmembers (e.g., identifying users with the appropriate expertise), providing effective explanations of tasks for the crowd (i.e., good task design), controlling noise and quality of the crowd input, designing incentive structures that encourage serious work, and ethical treatment of crowdmembers, including protecting personal or privacy-sensitive information, and appropriate compensation for their efforts. Further, crowdsourcing platforms can also be used to design and evaluate recommender systems. Large-scale commercial crowdsourcing platforms make it possible to directly question a large number of people concerning their preferences for system design, and their impressions of system results and result presentation. Finally, recommender systems have an important role within crowdsourcing systems. Crowdsourcing systems can operate efficiently at large scale if they are able to offer tasks to users that fit their interests and are also well suited to their ability.

2. HUMAN INTELLIGENCE AND RECSYS

Increasingly in our digital age, when information-related tasks need to be carried out, we turn to 'The Crowd' rather than to a dedicated pool of specialized employees. In 2006, Jeff Howe introduced the notion of outsourcing tasks to the crowd, with the article 'The Rise of Crowdsourcing' [8]. He defines crowdsourcing as, '...the act of taking a job traditionally performed by a designated agent (usually an employee) and outsourcing it to an undefined, generally large group of people in the form of an open call' [7]. Under this definition, crowdsourcing is a useful means of accomplishing a task that would need to be carried out anyway. We push beyond this view and point out that the existence of crowdsourcing as a paradigm, and also the growth of social networks and large commercial crowdsourcing platforms, significantly changes the playing field. In particular, these developments open up the possibility for new tasks, that are helpful for recommender systems, but never would have originally been created, were 'The Crowd' not available to tackle them.

Human computation and crowdsourcing are both techniques that take advantage of the intelligence of human contributors. However, an important distinction exists between the two. According to Quinn and Bederson [9], human computation is human intelligence applied to solve problems that might someday be solvable by computers. This view underlies the concept of 'Artificial Artificial Intelligence', the tagline for the large commercial crowdsourcing platform Amazon Mechanical Turk (https://www.mturk.com). The CrowdRec workshop strives to push beyond this view, to look at systems in which human contributions are valuable exactly because they are uniquely human, e.g., taste decisions that are only meaningful because they were made by a human being.

Quinn and Bederson [9] identify computational control of human intelligence as another aspect of human computation. Under this view, human computation occurs when a computational system or a process directs human contributions. Human computation in recommender systems represents, in this respect, a closed loop, since ultimately the behavior of a recommender system should be driven by the needs and preferences of its human users.

3. ON CROWDSOURCING WORKSHOPS

The CrowdRec Workshop series was established in 2013 with the first edition of the workshop held at ACM RecSys 2013 [6]. Motivation to found the workshop series arose from examples in other research communities, each which derived benefit from using workshops to develop and support their individual disciplines in successfully and sustainably exploiting the crowdsourcing paradigm. Particularly relevant to recommender systems are the closely related communities who research and develop systems that allow users to interact with information. In this section, we mention some selected examples of the previous workshops that have contributed to other communities.

The Information Retrieval community has led the way to applying crowdsourcing techniques and large commercial crowdsourcing platforms to the problem of evaluating algorithms and systems. The 'Crowdsourcing for Search Evaluation Workshop' [2] was held at the ACM SIGIR Conference on Research and Development in Information Retrieval in 2010. Topics included techniques for the development of data sets needed for evaluation of information retrieval systems, and for the development of models capable of predicting user interest in specific content. In the years that followed, other workshops expanded the topic to include techniques for directly eliciting contributions from 'The Crowd' for the purposes of data mining and information retrieval. Specifically, we mention the 'Crowdsourcing for Search and Data Mining Workshop' [3] at the 2011 ACM International Conference on Web Search and Data Mining, and the 'Crowdsourcing Web Search Workshop' [1] held at the 2012 International World Wide Web Conference. The multimedia community has also used workshops to help to foster the growth of crowdsourcing techniques, for the purposes of system design, data set creation, evaluation, and user studies. Workshops were held at ACM Multimedia 2012 and 2013 [4, 5], with another planned for 2014.

These workshops have revealed that it takes a great deal of continuous effort in order to develop the viable concepts and the best practices necessary to ensure that a research area is able to achieve maximum benefit from crowdsourcing. Crowdsourcing involves human systems, which are notoriously complex and delicate. In any given area, the opportunities to apply crowdsourcing cover a large number of diverse angles, for example, from annotation to evaluation. Workshops like CrowdRec help a community to realize these opportunities in their research and development activities.

4. CONCLUDING REMARKS

The term 'crowdsourcing' is sometimes used in a broad sense when a system exploits information from a group of people large enough to be considered a crowd. Under this view, conventional collaborative filtering recommender systems can be considered crowdsourcing, since they exploit information from a large number of users in the form of ratings, views, or other interaction data. The specific focus of the CrowdRec Workshop, however, is going beyond recommender systems that passively collect information on user behavior, to active systems that reach out to 'The Crowd', eliciting the intelligent information necessary to improve recommendations.

5. ACKNOWLEDGMENTS

Thank you to the authors, presenters, and reviewers for making this workshop possible. The organizers would also like to acknowledge the support of European Community's Seventh Framework Programme (FP7/2007-2013) under grant agreement 610594.

6. REFERENCES

[1] R. A. Baeza-Yates, S. Ceri, P. Fraternali, and F. Giunchiglia. Proceedings of CrowdSearch 2012: Workshop on Crowdsourcing Web Search at WWW 2012. http://ceur-ws.org/Vol-842, 2012.

[2] V. Carvalho, M. Lease, and E. Yilmaz. CSE 2010: Crowdsourcing for Search Evaluation Workshop at ACM SIGIR 2010. http://www.cs.cmu.edu/~vitor/papers/CSE2010-Proceedings.pdf, 2010.

[3] V. Carvalho, M. Lease, and E. Yilmaz. CDSM 2011: Workshop on Crowdsourcing for Search and Data Mining at WSDM 2011. http://ir.ischool.utexas.edu/csdm2011/proceedings.html, 2011.

[4] K.-T. Chen, W.-T. Chu, and M. Larson. ACM Multimedia 2013 Workshop on Crowdsourcing for Multimedia. In *Proceedings of ACM MM '13*, pages 1089–1090, 2013.

[5] K.-T. Chen, W.-T. Chu, M. Larson, and W. T. Ooi. ACM Multimedia 2012 Workshop on Crowdsourcing for Multimedia. In *Proceedings of ACM MM '12*, pages 1505–1506, 2012.

[6] K.-T. Chen, I. King, C. M. Au Yeung, and O. Alonso. CrowdRec 2013: Workshop on Crowdsourcing and Human Computation for Recommender Systems at ACM RecSys 2013. http://crowdrec2013.noahlab.com.hk/programme, 2013.

[7] J. Howe. Crowdsourcing. http://crowdsourcing.typepad.com.

[8] J. Howe. The rise of crowdsourcing. *Wired Magazine*, 14(6), 2006.

[9] A. J. Quinn and B. B. Bederson. Human computation: A survey and taxonomy of a growing field. In *Proceedings of ACM CHI '11*, pages 1403–1412, 2011.

RecSys'14 Joint Workshop on Interfaces and Human Decision Making for Recommender Systems

Nava Tintarev
Dept. of Computer Science,
University of Aberdeen, UK
n.tintarev@abdn.ac.uk

John O'Donovan
Dept. of Computer Science,
University of California,
Santa Barbara, USA
jod@cs.ucsb.edu

Peter Brusilovsky
School of Information Sciences,
University of Pittsburgh, USA
peterb@pitt.edu

Alexander Felfernig
Institute for Software Technology,
Graz University of Technology, Austria
alexander.felfernig@ist.tugraz.at

Giovanni Semeraro
Dept. of Computer Science,
University of Bari "Aldo Moro", Italy
giovanni.semeraro@uniba.it

Pasquale Lops
Dept. of Computer Science, University of Bari "Aldo Moro", Italy
pasquale.lops@uniba.it

ABSTRACT
As an interactive intelligent system, recommender systems are developed to give predictions that match users preferences. Since the emergence of recommender systems, a large majority of research focuses on objective accuracy criteria and less attention has been paid to how users interact with the system and the efficacy of interface designs from the end-user perspective. The field has reached a point where it is ready to look beyond algorithms, into users interactions, decision-making processes and overall experience. Accordingly, the goals of this workshop (IntRS@RecSys) are to explore the human aspects of recommender systems, with a particular focus on the impact of interfaces and interaction design on decision-making and user experiences with recommender systems, and to explore methodologies to evaluate these human aspects of the recommendation process that go beyond traditional automated approaches.

Categories and Subject Descriptors
H3.3 **[Information Search and Retrieval]**; H.4.2 **[Decision Support Systems]** H5.2 **[Information Interfaces and Presentation]**

General Terms
Algorithms, Experimentation, Human Factors, Human-Computer Interaction

Keywords
Recommender Systems; Decision Making; User Interfaces; Interaction; Decision Psychology; Recommender Algorithms; Decision Biases

RecSys14, October 6-10, 2014, Foster City, Silicon Valley, CA, USA.
ACM 978-1-4503-2668-1/14/10.
http://dx.doi.org/10.1145/2645710.2645787

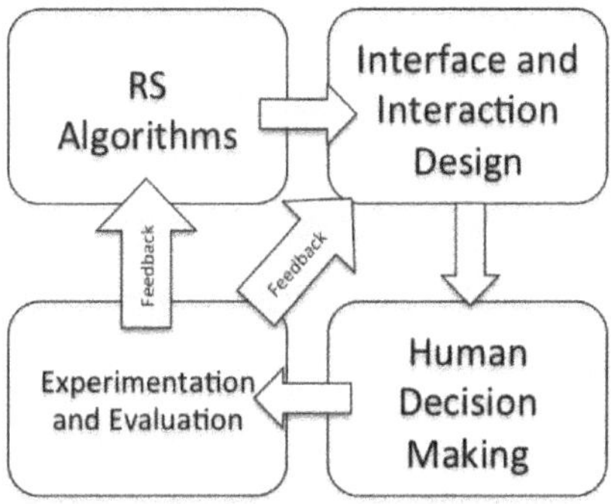

Fig 1: Overview of interactions between key workshop themes.

1. OVERVIEW AND MOTIVATION
This workshop integrates different theories of human decision making into the construction of recommender systems, as illustrated in Fig 1. In recent RecSys conferences, we have seen an emerging research theme on the impact of interfaces on decision support, satisfaction and overall user experience with the recommender system (RS). For this, and related workshops from previous years, the aim has been to bring together researchers and practitioners around the topics of designing and evaluating novel intelligent interfaces for recommender systems. Another has been to foster an interdisciplinary community with a focus on decision-making and on the related interface design issues for recommender systems and promoting collaboration opportunities between researchers and practitioners.

The workshop covers three interrelated themes: a) user interfaces (e.g. visual interfaces, explanations), b) interaction, user modeling and decision-making (e.g. decision theories, argumentation, detection and avoidance of biases), and c) evaluation (e.g. case studies and empirical evaluations).

This workshop is a follow up on the successful workshops at RecSys in previous years:

- Workshop on Human Decision Making in Recommender Systems (Decisions) 2013[1], 2012[2], and 2011[3].
- Workshop on Interfaces for Recommender Systems (InterfaceRS) 2012[4].

2. TOPICS OF INTEREST

The following list outlines core topics of interest.

User Interfaces

- Visual interfaces for recommender systems
- Explanation interfaces for recommender systems
- Collaborative multi-user interfaces (e.g., group decision making in e-tourism)
- Spoken and natural language interfaces
- Trust-aware interfaces
- Social interfaces
- Context-aware interfaces
- Ubiquitous and mobile interfaces
- Conversational interfaces
- Example- and demonstration-based interfaces
- New approaches to designing interfaces for recommender systems
- User interfaces for decision making (e.g., decision strategies and user ratings)

Interaction, user modeling and decision-making

- Cognitive Modeling for recommender systems
- Human-recommender interaction
- Controllability, transparency and scrutability
- Decision theories in recommender systems (e.g., priming, framing, and decoy effects)
- Preference detection (e.g., eye tracking for automated preference detection)
- The role of emotions in recommender systems (e.g., emotion-aware recommendation)
- Trust inspiring recommendation (e.g., explanation-aware recommendation)
- Argumentation and Persuasive recommendation (e.g., argumentation-aware recommendation)
- Cultural differences (e.g., culture-aware recommendation)
- Mechanisms for effective group decision making (e.g., group recommendation heuristics)
- Decision theories for effective group decision making (e.g., hidden profile management)
- Detection and avoidance of decision biases (e.g., in item presentations)

Evaluation

- Case studies
- Empirical studies and evaluations of new interfaces
- Empirical studies and evaluations of new interaction designs
- Evaluation methods and metrics (e.g., evaluation questionnaire design)

3. WORKSHOP FORMAT

The workshop started with a short general introduction to the workshop themes by the organizers. This was followed by oral presentation of accepted papers listed at the link below. Presentations were grouped into sessions based on the subthemes of the workshop. Julita Vassileva gave a keynote presentation titled *Visualization and User Control of Recommender Systems*. After each presentation and session, time was allocated for general discussion and feedback.

4. FURTHER INFORMATION

The workshop material including list of accepted papers, invited talk and workshop schedule are available at the IntRS@RecSys 2014 webpage: http://recex.ist.tugraz.at/intrs2014/ and via the workshops section on the main conference website: http://recsys.acm.org/recsys14/workshops/

[1] http://recex.ist.tugraz.at/RecSysWorkshop/

[2] http://recex.ist.tugraz.at/RecSysWorkshop2012

[3] http://recex.ist.tugraz.at:8080/RecSysWorkshop2011

[4] https://homepages.abdn.ac.uk/n.tintarev/pages/InterfaceRS/

Second Workshop on Large-Scale Recommender Systems: Research and Best Practice (LSRS 2014)

Tao Ye
Pandora Inc.
2101 Webster St., 16th Fl
Oakland, CA 94612
(+1) 510-451-4100
tye@pandora.com

Danny Bickson
GraphLab Inc.
4000 Mason Rd
Seattle, WA 98195
(+1)425-615-3777
bickson@graphlab.com

Qiang Yan
Alimama Inc, Alibaba Group
12#, West DaWang Rd
Chaoyang district, Beijing, China
100022
(+86)10-80775638
scmyyan@gmail.com

ABSTRACT
With the increase of data collected and computation power available, modern recommender systems are ever facing new challenges. While complex models are developed in academia, industry practice seems to focus on relatively simple techniques that can deal with the magnitude of data and the need to distribute the computation. The workshop on large-scale recommender systems (LSRS) is a meeting place for industry and academia to discuss the current and future challenges of applied large-scale recommender systems.

Categories and Subject Descriptors
H.2.8 [Database Management]: Database Applications – *data mining*. H.3.4 [Database Management]: System and Software – *distributed systems*.

Keywords
Recommendation systems, big data.

1. BACKGROUND AND MOTIVATION
As we enter the era of Big Data, the modern Recommender System faces greatly increased data volume and complexities. Previous computational models and experience on small data may not hold today, thus, how to build an efficient and robust system has become an important issue for many practitioners. Meanwhile, there is an increasing gap between academia research of recommendation systems focusing on complex models, and industry practice focusing on solving problems at large scale using relatively simple techniques.

RecSys'14, October 06–10 2014, Foster City, Silicon Valley, CA, USA.
ACM 978-1-4503-2668-1/14/10.
http://dx.doi.org/10.1145/2645710.2645785

Chances favor connected minds. The motivation of this workshop is to bring together researchers and practitioners working on large-scale recommender system in order to: (1) share experience, techniques and methodologies used to develop effective large-scale recommender, from architecture, algorithm, programming model, to evaluation (2) identify key challenges and promising trends in the area, and (3) identify collaboration opportunities among participants.

2. OBJECTIVES
This workshop aims to foster discussions in several fields that are of interest to our growing community of recommendation system builders. On the practical side, we would like to encourage sharing of architecture best practices in large-scale recommender systems as they are practiced in industry, as well as particular challenges and pain points. We hope this will guide future research that is system aware. On the research side, we focus on bringing in ideas and evaluations on scaling beyond the current generation of big data systems, with improved recommendation metrics. We believe the brightest minds from both sides will mutually benefit from the discussions and accelerate problem solving.

3. TOPICS OF INTEREST
We solicited submissions from industrial level recommendation system practitioners in either a short paper or slides formats on large scale system practice, as well as from recommendation systems researchers on their new research related to system aspect of recommendation with Big Data.

We focused on the following topics:

Systems of Large-scale RS:

- Architecture
- Programming Model
- Distributed systems, , multicore and GPU implementation
- Real-time recommendation
- Online learning for recommendation
- Scalability and Robustness

Data & Algorithms in Large-scale RS:

- Big data processing in offline/near-line/online modules

- Streaming data for recommendation
- Data platforms for recommendation
- Large, unstructured and social data for recommendation
- Heterogeneous data fusion
- Sampling techniques
- Parallel algorithms
- Incremental algorithms
- Algorithm validation and correctness checking

Application & Evaluation of Large-scale RS:

- Recommendation on mobile devices
- Explanations in Large-scale RS
- Anti-attack of Large-scale RS
- Large data and privacy issue
- Evaluation methodology
- Large user studies
- Measurement platforms
- Visualization

4. PROGRAM COMMITTEE

We are grateful for the help of our program committee to review submissions:

Jan Neumann, Comcast
Sebastian Schelter, TU Berlin
Sean Owen, Cloudera
Royi Ronen, Microsoft
Nikolas Vasiloglou, Ismion
Mohan Reddy, The Hive
Noam Koenigstein, Microsoft
Demian Bellumio, Senzari
Tal Kedar, Sears
Assaf Araki, Intel
Quan Yuan, Taobao
Baldo Faieta, Adobe
Nicholas Jing Yuan, Microsoft Research
Tao Zhou, UESTC
Yong Liu, NYU/Polyptych
Lei Tang, Walmart Labs
Jason Zhao, Douban
Dionysios Logothetis, Telefonica I+D
Justin Basilico, Netflix
Chih-Jen Lin, National Taiwan University
Valery Rashkov, Pandora
Joaquin Delgado, OnCue TV - Verizon Communications
Aapo Kyrola, Facebook

5. WORKSHOP FORMAT

The workshop will feature one keynote and three presentation sessions. We expect one presentation session to come from submitted papers and another two shorter sessions from invited talks.

6. ACKNOWLEDGMENTS

We thank the RecSys 2014 organizing committee for giving us the opportunity to host this workshop in conjunction with RecSys 2014.

Recommender Systems Challenge 2014

Alan Said[1], Simon Dooms[2], Babak Loni[1], Domonkos Tikk[3]
[1]TU-Delft, The Netherlands
[2]Ghent University, Belgium
[3]Gravity R&D, Hungary
alansaid@acm.org, simon.dooms@intec.ugent.be,
b.loni@tudelft.nl, domonkos.tikk@gravityrd.com

ABSTRACT

The 2014 ACM Recommender Systems Challenge invited researchers and practitioners to work towards a common goal, this goal being the prediction of users engagement in movie ratings expressed on Twitter. More than 200 participants sought to join the challenge and work on the new dataset released in its scope. The participants were asked to develop new algorithms to predict user engagement and evaluate them in a common setting, ensuring that the comparison was objective and unbiased, within the challenge.

Categories and Subject Descriptors

D.2.8 [**Software Engineering**]: Metrics - complexity measures, performance measures; H.3.3 [**Information Storage and Retrieval**]: Information search and retrieval - information filtering, relevance feedback; H.3.4 [**Information Technology and Systems Applications**]: Decision support; H.3.5 [**Online Information Services**]: Data Sharing; H.5.1 [**Multimedia Information Systems**]: Evaluation/methodology

General Terms

Algorithms; Design; Experimentation; Human Factors; Measurement

Keywords

Recommender Systems; Dataset; Challenge; Competition; Context-aware; Benchmarking

1. INTRODUCTION

The recommender systems community has a long standing tradition of organized benchmarking events, the most prominent one being the Netflix Prize[1]. Benchmarking events serve the purpose of creating a focused attempt at solving a predefined problem. By providing a dataset, a certain setting and the means of evaluation, participants only have to focus on algorithmic performance as everything else is already provided.

The 2014 edition of the RecSys Challenge was the fifth annual ACM RecSys competition, and the first of the RecSys Challenges to focus on *user engagement*. Previous challenges had focused on movie rating prediction [1, 6], scientific paper recommendation and user targeting [4], as well as point-of-interest recommendation [2]. In recent years, the recommender systems community has put considerable focus on the users of these systems, which is also reflected in the context of the Challenge.

For the 2014 edition, an extended version of the MovieTweetings dataset [3] was used. MovieTweetings contains movie ratings expressed by Twitter users who have tied their IMDb accounts to their Twitter account. The dataset contains the expected information found in a movie rating dataset, i.e. the user-movie rating matrix, timestamps, etc. This extended dataset also includes the interactions given to tweets that express ratings, i.e. the number of favorites and retweets each of the tweets containing movie ratings got from other users. This engagement could be considered as an additional signal reflecting e.g., the importance of a given rating with respect to other provided ratings.

Participants were asked to rank a given number of ratings within tweets by their predicted engagement for which we used the sum of the number of retweets and favorite counts as a proxy. The goal of the challenge is to provide insight on user interaction behavior with publicly posted ratings and to learn how being able to predict user engagement may be used for the benefit of recommender systems and its users.

2. DATASET & EVALUATION

For the purpose of the challenge, the MovieTweetings dataset was extended with additional meta-data from Twitter API. Therefore, besides the typical rating information consisting of user ids, item ids, ratings and timestamps, also many other types of data such as location and user profile information were available. The dataset contained 212.857 tweets collected over a period of 13 months and was chronologically split up in a training set (80% of the data), a test set (10% of the data) and an evaluation set (the remaining 10%). While the training set contained all data, the *retweet_count* and *favorite_count* data fields were removed in the test and evaluation set. Participants were given the training and test set to allow them to train their models and evaluate their

[1]`http://www.netflixprize.com`

RecSys'14, October 6–10, 2014, Foster City, Silicon Valley, CA, USA.
ACM 978-1-4503-2668-1/14/10.
http://dx.doi.org/10.1145/2645710.2645779 .

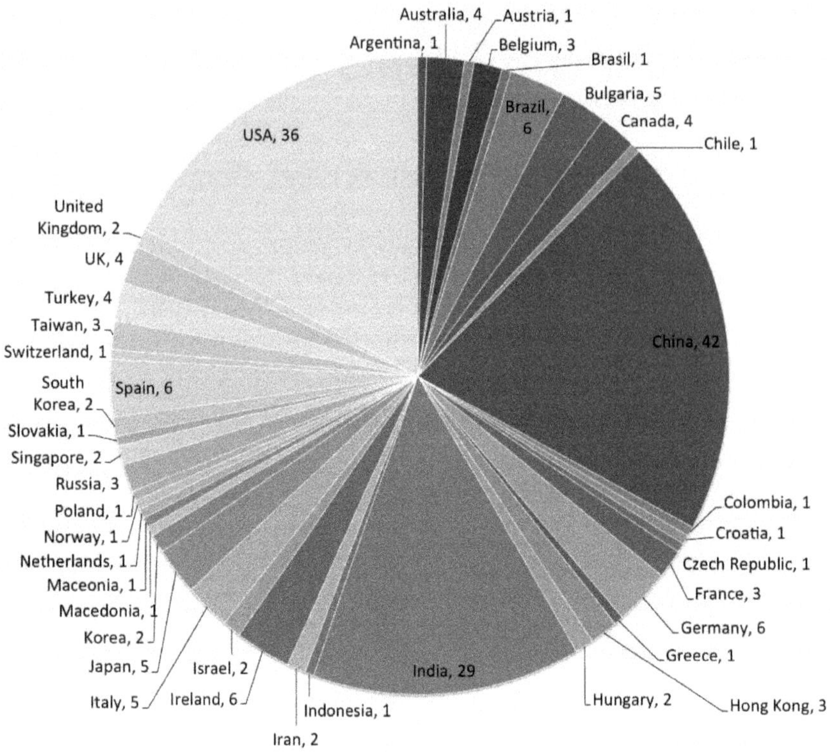

Figure 1: The distribution of participants by country. Note that some team did not state their country and have been omitted in the figure.

results. Final evaluation was however performed by the organizers using the private evaluation set.

For the evaluation the *NDCG@10* metric – as available in the Rival evaluation framework [2] – was chosen [5]. The metric expresses how well the challenge participants were able to capture the amount of interaction and engagement that each of the tweets in the test set obtained. This is done by comparing the ranked list generated by participant's algorithm to the ground truth that we provided in the dataset. For each user the true ranked list is considered to be a ranked list of tweets ordered by their *engagement* in descending order.

3. OVERVIEW

The challenge attracted more than 200 teams of international participants, Figure 1 shows the distribution of teams by country. All participating teams were invited to update the challenge leaderboard in order to allow the other teams to compare their current results. The challenge workshop took place on October 10, 2014. At the workshop, participants presented their approaches and discussed methods and possibilities of predicting user engagement.

Acknowledgments

The research leading to these results has received funding from the European Union Seventh Framework Programme (FP7/2007-2013) under grant agreement n°610594.

[2]http://rival.recommenders.net

4. REFERENCES

[1] Gediminas Adomavicius, Alexander Tuzhilin, Shlomo Berkovsky, Ernesto W. De Luca, and Alan Said, 'Context-awareness in recommender systems: Research workshop and movie recommendation challenge', in *Proceedings of the Fourth ACM Conference on Recommender Systems*, RecSys '10, pp. 385–386, New York, NY, USA, (2010). ACM.

[2] Jim Blomo, Martin Ester, and Marty Field, 'Recsys challenge 2013', in *Proceedings of the 7th ACM Conference on Recommender Systems*, RecSys '13, pp. 489–490, New York, NY, USA, (2013). ACM.

[3] Simon Dooms, Toon De Pessemier, and Luc Martens, 'Movietweetings: a movie rating dataset collected from twitter', in *Workshop on Crowdsourcing and Human Computation for Recommender Systems, CrowdRec at RecSys 2013*, (2013).

[4] Nikos Manouselis, Alan Said, Domonkos Tikk, Jannis Hermanns, Benjamin Kille, Hendrik Drachsler, Katrien Verbert, and Kris Jack, 'Recommender systems challenge 2012', in *Proceedings of the Sixth ACM Conference on Recommender Systems*, RecSys '12, pp. 353–354, New York, NY, USA, (2012). ACM.

[5] Alan Said and Alejandro Bellogín, 'Rival – a toolkit to foster reproducibility in recommender system evaluation', in *Proceedings of the 8th ACM Conference on Recommender Systems*, RecSys '13, New York, NY, USA, (2014). ACM.

[6] Alan Said, Shlomo Berkovsky, Ernesto William De Luca, and Jannis Hermanns, 'Challenge on context-aware movie recommendation: Camra2011', in *Proceedings of the Fifth ACM Conference on Recommender Systems*, RecSys '11, pp. 385–386, New York, NY, USA, (2011). ACM.

Controlled Experimentation in Recommendations, Ranking & Response Prediction

Ya Xu
LinkedIn Corp.
2029 Stierlin Ct,
Mountain View, CA 94043
+1.650.644.5597
xulongya@gmail.com

Rajesh Parekh
Groupon Inc.
3101 Park Blvd.,
Palo Alto, CA 94306
+1.650.793.0243
rgparekh@gmail.com

Juliette Aurisset
Netflix Inc.
745 Coleman Ave,
Menlo Park, CA 94025
+1.650.430.6975
juliette.aurisset@gmail.com

ABSTRACT
In this workshop, we have several leading industry experts sharing their knowledge and experiences on how online controlled experiments are used in their applications. The individual talks are followed by a panel discussion.

Categories and Subject Descriptors
G.3 [Probability and Statistics/Experimental Design]: controlled experiments, randomized experiments, A/B testing

General Terms
Measurement, Design, Experimentation

Keywords
Controlled experiments; A/B testing; experimental design; experiment systems; online experiments

Workshop Summary
Controlled experimentation, also called A/B testing, is providing the structure and moulding for future innovations in Recommender Systems, Search Ranking, Online Advertising and an array of other response prediction applications. Consumer facing web technology companies, including Amazon, Facebook, Google, Groupon, LinkedIn, Microsoft, Netflix, Yahoo, and countless others often utilize online controlled experiments for testing out new product strategies and approaches. Experimentation is the gold standard for leveraging the overwhelming growth of these sectors by consistently guiding the companies' data-driven analysis and decisions.

The theory of controlled experiment is simple and dates back to Sir Ronald A. Fisher's experiments at the Rothamsted Agricultural Experimental Station in England in the 1920s. However, the deployment and mining of online controlled experiments in practice and at scale can be very complex and challenging. As experimentation gained in popularity, so did the need for properly designing, managing and analyzing experiments, including avoiding pitfalls that can lead to bad and often catastrophic decisions for the aforementioned applications. On the other hand, scientifically instrumented, statistically validated and empirically endorsed approaches lead to a very structured whetting of algorithms, user interfaces and strategies at a brisk pace which is crucial to keep the innovation momentum going and critical for long term success of these applications.

In this workshop, we'll invite several leading industry experts to talk about their personal experiences on how online experiments are used in ranking for recommender systems, advertising and search applications. Each expert will contribute key lessons, challenges and best practices from their domain and bring to the workshop their years of experience designing and analyzing experiments. This is invaluable given that first-hand accounts discussed at length from so many diverse areas are seldom found in one setting. We will also get a chance to compare experimentation systems used at different companies and identify challenges and trends common to all.

For more information, such as speakers and topics, please check our webpage at http://data.linkedin.com/recsys14-workshop-controlled-experimentation

RecSys'14, October 6–10, 2014, Foster City, Silicon Valley, CA, USA.
ACM 978-1-4503-2668-1/14/10.
http://dx.doi.org/10.1145/2645710.2645781

First Workshop on Recommendation Systems for Television and Online Video (RecSysTV 2014)

Danny Bickson
Graphlab Inc
4000 Mason Rd
Seattle, WA 98195
+1 (425) 615-3777
bickson@graphlab.com

John Hannon
Boxfish
433 Hamilton Ave
Palo Alto, CA 94301
+1 (650) 924-9278
john@boxfish.com

Jan Neumann, Hassan Sayyadi
Comcast Labs
1110 Vermont Ave NW
Washington, DC 20005
+1 (202) 360-3940
{jan_neumann,hassan.sayyadi}@cable.comcast.com

ABSTRACT
For many households the television is the central entertainment hub in their home, and the average TV viewer spends about half of their leisure time in front of a TV. At any given moment, a costumer has hundreds to thousands of entertainment choices available, which makes some sort of automatic, personalized recommendations desirable to help consumers deal with the often overwhelming number of choices they face. The First Workshop on Recommendation Systems for Television and Online Video aims to offer a place to present and discuss the latest academic and industrial research on recommendation systems for this challenging and exciting application domain.

Categories and Subject Descriptors
H.2.8 [**Database Management**]: Database Applications – *data mining*. I.2.10 [**Artificial Intelligence**]: Vision and Scene Understand – *video analysis*, Implementation - *interactive systems*.

General Terms
Algorithms, Measurement, Performance, Design, Experimentation, Human Factors.

Keywords
Recommendations, big data, television, movies, video-on-demand.

1. BACKGROUND AND MOTIVATION
For many households the television is still the central entertainment hub in their home and the average TV viewer spends about half of their leisure time in front of a TV (3-5 hours/day).

At any given moment, a costumer has hundreds to thousands of entertainment choices available, which makes some sort of automatic, personalized recommendations desirable to help consumers deal with the often overwhelming choices they face.

RecSys'14, Oct 06-10 2014, Foster City, Silicon Valley, CA, USA
ACM 978-1-4503-2668-1/14/10.
http://dx.doi.org/10.1145/2645710.2645782

TV and online video recommendation systems face a number of unique challenges, for example, the content available on TV is constantly changing and often only available once, which leads to severe cold start problems.

Frequently, we also consume our entertainment in groups of varying compositions (individual vs household vs group of friends) which makes building taste profiles and modeling consumer behavior very challenging,

Recommendation systems for television and online video also have to address a number of very different consumption patterns, such as actively browsing through a list of personalized Video on Demand choices that match our current mood, compared to enjoying a "lean back experience" where a recommendation systems playlists a stream of TV shows from our favorite channels for us.

The unique challenges and wide-ranging applications of recommender systems in this domain motivated us to organize this workshop to bring together researchers from industry and academy in order to identify and share the key challenges, approaches and solutions of the field.

2. OBJECTIVES
The objective of this workshop is to encourage discussions among the researchers in the field, disseminate the latest approaches and encourage future collaboration among the participants. We believe that all participants will mutually benefit from the workshop activities and hopefully this will accelerate progress towards creating better recommendation systems for television and online video in the future.

3. TOPICS OF INTEREST
We solicited contributions from industrial and academic researchers on novel approaches to challenges found in the TV and online video recommendations space. Authors submitted both long and short papers focused on the following topics:

Context-aware TV and online video recommendations

- Leveraging contextual viewing behavior, e.g. device specific recommendations
- Mood based recommendations
- Group recommendations

User modeling & leveraging user viewing and interaction behavior

- How can social media improve TV recommendations
- Cross-domain recommendation algorithms (linear TV, video on demand, DVR, gaming consoles)
- Multi-viewer profile separation

Content-based TV and online video recommendations

- Analysis techniques for video recommendations based on video, audio, or closed caption signals
- Utilization of external data sources (movie reviews, ratings, plot summaries) for recommendations

Other topics related to TV and online video recommendations

- Video play listing
- Linear TV usage and box office success prediction
- Personalized advertisement recommendations
- Recommendations of 2nd screen web content
- Recommendations of short form videos (previews, trailers, music videos)

4. PROGRAM COMMITTEE

We thank the program committee for their help with reviewing the submissions:

Justin Basilico, Netflix

Balázs Hidasi, GravityR&D

Craig Carmichael, Rovi

Emanuele Coviello, Keevio

Pádraig Cunningham, Insight Centre for Data Analytics

Joaquin Delgado, OnCue TV (Verizon)

Diana Hu, OnCue TV (Verizon)

Ben Jordan, Univ. of Minnesota

Brendan Kitts, Adap.tv (AOL)

Noam Koenigstein, Microsoft

Gert Lanckriet, UC San Diego

Hayim Makabee, Yahoo! Labs

Tom Rampley, Dish Network

Royi Ronen, Microsoft

Barry Smyth, Insight Centre for Data Analytics

Domonkos Tikk, GravityR&D

Ari Tuchman, quantiFind

Udi Weinsberg, Technicolor Labs

Esti Widder, Viaccess-Orca

Ho-Hsiang Wu, Rd.io

Dávid Zibriczky, ImpressTV

Jiayu Zhou, Samsung Research

5. WORKSHOP FORMAT

The workshop will consist of several key note and presentation sessions with contributions from both academic and industrial researchers. We will also have an industrial demo session to demonstrate the latest state of the art systems in the area of TV and online video recommendations.

6. ACKNOWLEDGEMENTS

We thank the RecSys 2014 organizing committee for giving us the opportunity to host this workshop in conjunction with RecSys 2014 and our companies Boxfish, Comcast, and Graphlab for supporting this event.

.

REDD 2014 – International Workshop on Recommender Systems Evaluation: Dimensions and Design

Panagiotis Adamopoulos
New York University
44 West Fourth Street
New York, NY 10012, USA
padamopo@stern.nyu.edu

Alejandro Bellogín,
Pablo Castells
Univ. Autónoma de Madrid
Fco. Tomás y Valiente 11
Madrid, 28049 Spain
alejandro.bellogin@uam.es
pablo.castells@uam.es

Paolo Cremonesi
Politecnico di Milano
Via Ponzio 34/5
Milan, Italy
paolo.cremonesi@polimi.it

Harald Steck
Netflix, Inc.
100 Winchester Circle
Los Gatos, CA 95032, USA
hsteck@netflix.com

ABSTRACT
Evaluation is a cardinal issue in recommender systems; as in any technical discipline, it highlights to a large extent the problems that need to be solved by the field and, hence, leads the way for algorithmic research and development in the community. Yet, in the field of recommender systems, there still exists considerable disparity in evaluation methods, metrics and experimental designs, as well as a significant mismatch between evaluation methods in the lab and what constitutes an effective recommendation for real users and businesses. Even after the relevant quality dimensions have been defined, a clear evaluation protocol should be specified in detail and agreed upon, allowing for the comparison of results and experiments conducted by different authors. This would enable any contribution to the same problem to be incremental and add up on top of previous work, rather than grow sideways. The REDD 2014 workshop seeks to provide an informal forum to tackle such issues and to move towards better understood and shared evaluation methodologies, allowing one to leverage the efforts and the workforce of the academic community towards meaningful and relevant directions in real-world developments.

Categories and Subject Descriptors
H.3.3 [**Information Search and Retrieval**]: *Information filtering*

General Terms
Algorithms, Measurement, Performance, Experimentation, Standardization, Theory

Keywords
Utility, evaluation, methodology, metrics, recommender systems

1. INTRODUCTION
Thoughtful evaluation of recommender systems is a key challenge, as it guides algorithmic research and development [3,9]. In the community there is, however, considerable disparity in evaluation methods, metrics and experimental designs, as well as a significant mismatch between evaluation methods in the lab and what constitutes an effective recommendation for real users and businesses [5,6,9,11,12,13,15].

RecSys'14, October 6–10, 2014, Foster City, Silicon Valley, CA, USA.
ACM 978-1-4503-2668-1/14/10.
http://dx.doi.org/10.1145/2645710.2645780

On the one hand, REDD 2014 places a specific focus on the identification and measurement of different recommendation quality dimensions that go beyond the monolithic concept of simply matching user preferences. Novelty and diversity, for instance, have been recognized as key perspectives of the utility of recommendations for users in real-world scenarios, with a direct positive effect on business performance [1,2,4,7,8,10,14]. Considering the business perspective, performance metrics related to sales, revenues, and user engagement along the recommendation funnel should also be used. Additionally, from an engineering point of view, aspects such as efficiency, scalability, robustness and user interface design are typically major concerns; often prioritized over the effectiveness of the internal algorithms at the core of the system.

On the other hand, once a relevant quality dimension has been defined, a clear evaluation protocol should be specified in detail. This is essential for reproducibility of experiments. Moreover, it enables different authors to build on top of other researchers' previous works. Even when measuring recommendation accuracy, researchers and practitioners are still often faced with experimental design questions for which there are not always precise and consensual answers. Therefore, there remains room for further methodological development and convergence, which motivates this workshop.

2. SCOPE AND GOALS
REDD 2014 gathered researchers and practitioners interested in better understanding the unmet needs in the field in terms of evaluation methodologies and experimental practices. The workshop provided an informal setting for exchanging and discussing ideas as well as sharing experiences and viewpoints. REDD sought to identify and better understand the current gaps in recommender system evaluation methodologies, help lay directions for progress in addressing them, and foster the consolidation and convergence of experimental methods and best practices.

Specific questions raised and addressed by the workshop include, among others, the following:

- What are the unmet needs and challenges for evaluation in the Recommender Systems field? Where do we stand? What changes would we like to see? How could we speed up progress?

- What relevant recommendation utility and quality dimensions should be considered? How can they be captured and measured? How should evaluation methods be designed to effectively evaluate such dimensions?
- How can metrics become more clearly and/or formally related to the task, contexts, and goals for which a recommender application is deployed?
- How should IR metrics be applied to recommendation tasks? What aspects require adjustment or further clarification? What further methodologies should we draw from other disciplines (e.g., HCI, Machine Learning, etc.)?
- What biases and noise should experimental design typically watch for?
- Can we predict the success of a recommendation algorithm with offline experiments? What offline metrics correlate better and under which conditions?
- What are the outreach and limitations of offline evaluation? How can online and offline experiments complement each other?
- What type of public datasets and benchmarks would we want to have available, and how can they be built?
- How can the recommendation effect be traced on business outcomes?
- How should the academic evaluation methodologies improve their relevance and usefulness for industrial settings?
- How can we promote reproducibility of recommender systems methods?
- How do we envision the evaluation of recommender systems in the future?

3. COVERED TOPICS

The accepted papers and the discussions held at the workshop addressed, among others, the following topics:

- Evaluation methodology
- Experimental design
- Open evaluation platforms and infrastructures
- Recommendation quality dimensions: accuracy, novelty, diversity, unexpectedness, serendipity, coverage, risk, robustness, usability, explanations, persuasiveness, etc.
- Evaluating for efficiency and scalability
- Definition and assessment of evaluation metrics
- Matching metrics to tasks, needs, and goals
- Business-oriented evaluation
- Offline and online evaluation
- Datasets and benchmarks

The workshop opened with a keynote talk, followed by the presentation of accepted papers and open discussions. The accepted papers and a summary of discussions are available in the workshop proceedings, which can be reached from the workshop website at http://ir.ii.uam.es/redd2014.

4. REFERENCES

[1] Adamopoulos, P. and Tuzhilin, A. On unexpectedness in recommender systems: Or how to better expect the unexpected. *ACM TIST*.

[2] Adomavicius, G. and Kwon, Y. Improving aggregate recommendation diversity using ranking-based techniques. *IEEE TKDE*, 24(5):896 –911, 2012.

[3] Breese, J. S., Heckerman, D., and Kadie, C. Empirical analysis of predictive algorithms for collaborative filtering. *14th Conf. on Uncertainty in Artificial Intelligence (UAI 1998)*, 43-52, 1998.

[4] Celma, O. and Herrera, P. A New Approach to Evaluating Novel Recommendations. *2nd ACM International Conference on Recommender Systems (RecSys 2008)*, 179-186, 2008.

[5] Cremonesi, P., Garzotto, F., Negro, S., Papadopoulos, A. V., and Turrin, R. Comparative evaluation of recommender system quality. *ACM Conference on Human Factors in Computing Systems (CHI 2011)*, 1927-1932, 2011.

[6] Cremonesi, P., Koren, Y., and Turrin, R. Performance of Recommender Algorithms on Top-N Recommendation Tasks. *4th ACM International Conference on Recommender Systems (RecSys 2010)*, 39-46, 2010.

[7] Fleder, D. M. and Hosanagar, K. Blockbuster Culture's Next Rise or Fall: The Impact of Recommender Systems on Sales Diversity. *Management Science,* 55(5):697-712, 2009.

[8] Ge, M., Delgado-Battenfeld, C. and Jannach, D. Beyond accuracy: Evaluating recommender systems by coverage and serendipity. *4th ACM International Conference on Recommender Systems (RecSys 2010)*, 257-260, 2010.

[9] Herlocker, J. L., Konstan, J. A., Terveen, L. G., and Riedl, J. T. Evaluating collaborative filtering recommender systems. *ACM Trans. on Information Systems,* 22(1):5-53, 2004.

[10] Lathia, N., Hailes, S., Capra, L., and Amatriain, X. Temporal Diversity in Recommender Systems. *33rd International ACM SIGIR Conference on Research and Development in Information Retrieval (SIGIR 2010)*, 210-217, 2010.

[11] McNee, S. M., Riedl, J., and Konstan, J. A. Being Accurate is Not Enough: How Accuracy Metrics have hurt Recommender Systems. *ACM Conf. on Human Factors in Computing Systems (CHI 2006)*, 1097-1101, 2006.

[12] Shani, G. and Gunawardana, A. Evaluating Recommendation Systems. In Ricci, F. et al (Eds.), *Recommender Systems Handbook*, pages 257-297. Springer, 2011.

[13] Steck, H. Training and Testing of Recommender Systems on Data Missing Not At Random. *16th ACM International Conference on Knowledge Discovery and Data Mining (KDD 2010)*, 713-722, 2010.

[14] Vargas, S. and Castells, P. Rank and Relevance in Novelty and Diversity Metrics for Recommender Systems. *5th ACM International Conference on Recommender Systems (RecSys 2011)*, 109-116, 2011.

[15] Voorhees, E. M. and Harman, D. K. *TREC: Experiment and Evaluation in Information Retrieval*. The MIT Press, 2005.

The Sixth ACM RecSys Workshop on Recommender Systems and the Social Web

Dietmar Jannach
Dept. of Computer Science
TU Dortmund, Germany
dietmar.jannach@udo.edu

Jill Freyne
CSIRO ICT Center
Australia
Jill.Freyne@csiro.au

Werner Geyer
IBM Research
Cambridge, MA,USA
werner.geyer@us.ibm.com

1. WORKSHOP SUMMARY

The emergence of what is called the social web and the continuing stream of new applications and community-based platforms including Facebook, Twitter, LinkedIn and others had a substantial impact on recommender systems research and practice over the last years in different ways.

First, today's web users are more willing to share more about themselves than before the Web 2.0, thus providing more information sources that can be leveraged in the user modeling and recommendation process. Furthermore, the newly available information sources can not only be used to optimize the recommendations for an individual user, but can also help to identify more general patterns and trends in the behavior of the community that can be exploited by other applications.

Second, personalization, information filtering and recommendation are often the central functionality of many of these social web based applications. On typical social networks, users for example get recommendations for news to read, songs to listen to, groups to join, friends to follow, people to connect or jobs that might be interesting.

These developments lead to different challenges to be addressed in recommender systems research. On the one hand, for example, the question arises of how to effectively combine the huge variety of information sources for improved recommendations. On the other hand, regarding the new opportunities for applying recommender systems in social web environments, in many cases new techniques are required to address the particularities of the domain or to deal with scalability issues.

The *ACM RecSys 2014 Workshop on Recommender Systems and the Social Web* aims to be a platform for researchers from academia and industry as well as for practitioners to present and discuss the various challenges and possible solutions related to all aspects of social web recommendations. The call for papers correspondingly covered a variety of topics in this area including all sorts of applications of recommender systems technology and their interfaces; collective knowledge creation and topic emergence; context-aware and group recommendation approaches; and case studies and empirical evaluations.

This year's workshop was already the sixth in a series of successful workshops co-located with the ACM Conference on Recommender Systems since 2009. Again, we received several submissions from researchers from academia and industry which were thoroughly reviewed and selected for presentation at the workshop by a program committee of international experts in the field.

The papers submitted to the workshop addressed a number of different topics and put forward novel proposals to build social web recommender system. In the context of applying recommendation technology to information personalization and resource ranking problems in Social Web environments, the submitted papers for example dealt with the problem of ranking community-provided product reviews based on opinion mining or with the recommendation of friends on social networks. As an example of how to leverage Social Web information to build better systems, one of the works proposed to analyze the characteristics of publicly shared music playlists to better understand how future music recommendation systems should be designed. Finally, another contribution from industry addressed challenges and lessons learned when building large-scale collaborative filtering solutions on Social Web platforms in a real-world environment.

RecSys'14, October 6–10, 2014, Foster City, Silicon Valley, CA, USA.
ACM 978-1-4503-2668-1/14/10.
http://dx.doi.org/10.1145/2645710.2645786.

2. ADDITIONAL AUTHORS

Ido Guy, Yahoo! Labs, Israel,
`idoguy@yahoo.com`
Andreas Hotho, Universität Würzburg, Germany,
`hotho@informatik.uni-wuerzburg.de`
Bamshad Mobasher, DePaul University, USA,
`mobasher@cs.depaul.edu`

3. WORKSHOP WEB SITE

The workshop web site can be found at:
`http://ls13-www.cs.uni-dortmund.de/homepage/rsweb2014`

Categories and Subject Descriptors

H.3.3 [**Information Search and Retrieval**]; H.4.2 [**Decision Support Systems**]

Keywords

Recommender Systems; Personalization; Social Web

The Recommender Problem Revisited

[Tutorial]

Xavier Amatriain
Netflix
100 Winchester Cr.
Los Gatos, CA, USA
xavier@netflix.com

1. ABSTRACT

In 2006, Netflix announced a $1M prize competition to advance recommendation algorithms. The recommendation problem was simplified as the accuracy in predicting a user rating measured by the Root Mean Squared Error (RMSE). While that formulation helped get the attention of the research community in the area, it may have put an excessive focus on what is simply one of the many possible approaches to recommendations.

In this tutorial we will describe different components of modern recommender systems such as: personalized ranking, similarity, explanations, context-awareness, or search as recommendation. We will use the Netflix use case as a driving example of a prototypical industrial-scale recommender system that has evolved from focusing on rating prediction to full page optimization. We will also review the usage of modern algorithmic approaches that include algorithms such as Factorization Machines[9], Restricted Boltzmann Machines [10], SimRank [7], Deep Neural Networks, or Listwise Learning-to-rank [6, 12, 11].

The original recommendation problem was formulated around the existence of explicit user ratings. However, recommender systems can be built using different kinds of data including implicit behavioral data, social connections, or demographics. In this tutorial we will review the usage of different data types and discuss what the availability of Big Data has brought into the research area.

Finally, and also related to the availability of large quantities of data, we will talk about how system and architectural decisions play a role in understanding the recommender problem.

This tutorial is in part based on recent publications by the author [5, 1, 8, 2, 4, 3]

2. BIO

Xavier Amatriain (PhD) is Director of Algorithms Engineering at Netflix. He leads a team of researchers and engineers designing and implementing the next wave of machine learning approaches to power the Netflix product. Previous to this, he was a Researcher in Recommender Systems, and neighboring areas such as Data Mining, Machine Learning, Information Retrieval, and Multimedia. He has authored more than 50 papers including book chapters, journals, and articles in international conferences. He was General Chair for the 2010 ACM Recommender Systems Conference. He is often invited speaker at conferences, universities, and companies. He has also lectured in different universities including the University of California Santa Barbara and UPF in Barcelona, Spain, where he is originally from.

RecSys'14, October 6–10, 2014, Foster City, Silicon Valley, CA, USA.
ACM 978-1-4503-2668-1/14/10.
http://dx.doi.org/10.1145/2645710.2645775.

3. REFERENCES

[1] X. Amatriain, A. Jaimes, N. Oliver, and J. M. Pujol. Data Mining Methods for Recommender Systems. In Francesco Ricci, Lior Rokach, Bracha Shapira, and Paul B. Kantor, editors, *Recommender Systems Handbook*, chapter 2, pages 39 71. Springer US, Boston, MA, 2011.

[2] Xavier Amatriain. Building industrial-scale real-world recommender systems. In *Proceedings of the sixth ACM conference on Recommender systems*, pages 7–8. ACM, 2012.

[3] Xavier Amatriain. Beyond data: from user information to business value through personalized recommendations and consumer science. In *Proceedings of the 22nd ACM international conference on Conference on information & knowledge management*, pages 2201–2208. ACM, 2013.

[4] Xavier Amatriain. Big & personal: data and models behind netflix recommendations. In *Proceedings of the 2nd International Workshop on Big Data, Streams and Heterogeneous Source Mining: Algorithms, Systems, Programming Models and Applications*, pages 1–6. ACM, 2013.

[5] Xavier Amatriain. Mining large streams of user data for personalized recommendations. *ACM SIGKDD Explorations Newsletter*, 14(2):37–48, 2013.

[6] Z. Cao and T. Liu. Learning to rank: From pairwise approach to listwise approach. In *In Proceedings of the 24th ICML*, pages 129–136, 2007.

[7] Glen Jeh and Jennifer Widom. Simrank: A measure of structural-context similarity. In *Proceedings of the Eighth ACM SIGKDD International Conference on*

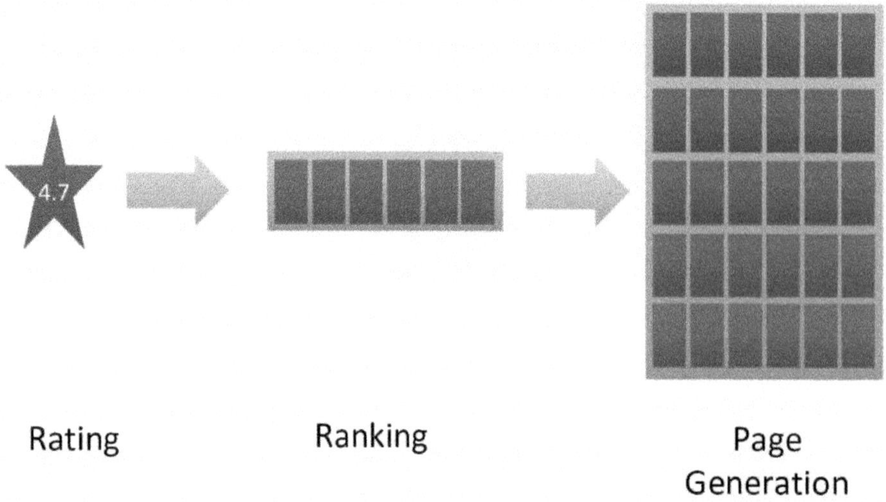

Figure 1:

Knowledge Discovery and Data Mining, KDD '02, pages 538–543, New York, NY, USA, 2002. ACM.

[8] Alexandros Karatzoglou, Xavier Amatriain, Linas Baltrunas, and Nuria Oliver. Multiverse recommendation: n-dimensional tensor factorization for context-aware collaborative filtering. In *Proceedings of the fourth ACM conference on Recommender systems*, pages 79–86. ACM, 2010.

[9] S. Rendle. Factorization Machines. In *Proc. of 2010 IEEE ICDM*, pages 995–1000. IEEE, December 2010.

[10] R. Salakhutdinov, A. Mnih, and G. E. Hinton. Restricted Boltzmann machines for collaborative filtering. In Zoubin Ghahramani and Zoubin Ghahramani, editors, *Proc of ICML '07*, volume 227 , of *ACM International Conference Proceeding Series* pages 791–798, New York, NY, USA, 2007. ACM.

[11] Y. Shi, A. Karatzoglou, L. Baltrunas, M. Larson, A. Hanjalic, and N. Oliver. TFMAP: optimizing MAP for top-n context-aware recommendation. In *Proc. of the 35th SIGIR*, SIGIR '12, pages 155–164, New York, NY, USA, 2012. ACM.

[12] Ming Tan, Tian Xia, Lily Guo, and Shaojun Wang. Direct optimization of ranking measures for learning to rank models. In *Proceedings of the 19th ACM SIGKDD International Conference on Knowledge Discovery and Data Mining*, KDD '13, pages 856–864, New York, NY, USA, 2013. ACM.

Personalized Location Recommendation on Location-based Social Networks

Huiji Gao
Computer Science and Engineering
Arizona State University
Tempe, AZ, USA
Huiji.Gao@asu.edu

Jiliang Tang
Computer Science and Engineering
Arizona State University
Tempe, AZ, USA
Jiliang.Tang@asu.edu

Huan Liu
Computer Science and Engineering
Arizona State University
Tempe, AZ, USA
Huan.Liu@asu.edu

ABSTRACT

Personalized location recommendation is a special topic of recommendation. It is related to human mobile behavior in the real world regarding various contexts including spatial, temporal, social, and content. The development of this topic is subject to the availability of human mobile data. The recent rapid growth of location-based social networks has alleviated such limitation, which promotes the development of various location recommendation techniques. This tutorial offers an overview, in a data mining perspective, of personalized location recommendation on location-based social networks. It introduces basic concepts, summarizes unique LBSN characteristics and research opportunities, elaborates associated challenges, reviews state-of-the-art algorithms with illustrative examples and real-world LBSN datasets, and discusses effective evaluation methods.

Keywords

Location Recommendation, Location-Based Social Networks, Personalization

1. TUTORIAL DESCRIPTION

The rapid growth of cities is accompanied with an increasing number of locations with specific functions, e.g., restaurants, theaters, and hotels, to enrich people's life and entertainment, providing us with more choices of life experience than before. Generally, people are willing to explore a city and its neighborhood, and go to a "new" place which he has never visited before. These activities involve a decision making process related to the user's personal interests w.r.t. the various choices of POIs. In the meantime, how to efficiently make a satisficing decision among a large number of POIs becomes a challenging problem for the user, usually referred to as "choice paralysis".

Addressing such a problem corresponds to a task named location recommendation, which aims to help users filter out uninteresting POIs and save their time in decision making. By observing a user's visiting history, applications in this area focus on discovering user's check-in interests and recommending locations to him which could most likely match his interests. Location recommendation is getting popular in recent years due to the fast development of location-based social networking services. Given various techniques focusing on different facets of location-based social networking data, it is time for researchers to be informed of new development of location-based social networking services and related recommendation techniques.

RecSys'14, October 6–10, 2014, Foster City, Silicon Valley, CA, USA.
ACM 978-1-4503-2668-1/14/10.
http://dx.doi.org/10.1145/2645710.2645776.

Targeted Audience

The tutorial is suitable for academic and industrial researchers, graduate students, and practitioners who want to learn concepts and principles of the location recommendation techniques w.r.t. spatial, temporal, social, and content aspects of location-based social network data. No specific prerequisite is required, but some basic knowledge of data mining and recommender systems will help.

2. PRESENTERS' BIOGRAPHY

Huiji Gao is a Ph.D. candidate of Computer Science and Engineering at Arizona State University. He obtained his B.S. and M.S. at Beijing University of Posts and Telecommunications in 2007 and 2010, respectively. He was awarded the 2014 ASU Graduate Education Dissertation Fellowship, the 2014 ASU Presidentâs Award for Innovation, the 3rd Place Dedicated Task 2 Next Location Prediction of Nokia Mobile Data Challenge 2012, and various Student Travel Awards and Scholarships. His research interests include social computing, crowdsourcing for disaster management system, recommender systems, and mobile data mining on location-based social networks. He has published innovative works in highly ranked journals and top conference proceedings such as DMKD, IEEE Intelligent Systems, SIGKDD, CIKM, WWW, RecSys, WSDM, ICWSM, ICDM, and IJCAI. He has interned in IBM Research Almaden in 2013 and LinkedIn in 2014. Updated information can be found at `http://www.public.asu.edu/~hgao16`.

Jiliang Tang is a senior PhD student of Computer Science and Engineering at Arizona State University. He obtained his Master degree in Computer Science and Bachelor degree in Software Engineering at Beijing Institute of Technology in 2008 and 2010, respectively. He was awarded the 2014 ASU President's Award for Innovation, Best Paper Shortlist in WSDM13, the 3rd Place Dedicated Task 2 Next Location

Prediction of Nokia Mobile Data Challenge 2012, University Graduate Fellowship, and various Student Travel Awards and Scholarships. His research interests are in computing with online trust and distrust, recommendation, mining social media data, data mining and feature selection. He co-presents two tutorials in KDD2014 and WWW2014, and has published innovative works in highly ranked journals and top conference proceedings such as IEEE TKDE, ACM TKDD, DMKD, ACM SIGKDD, SIGIR, WWW, WSDM, SDM, ICDM, IJCAI, AAAI, and CIKM. He also worked as a research intern in Yahoo!Labs in 2013. Updated information can be found at `http://www.public.asu.edu/~jtang20`.

Huan Liu is a professor of Computer Science and Engineering at Arizona State University. He obtained his Ph.D. in Computer Science at University of Southern California and B.Eng. in Computer Science and Electrical Engineering at Shanghai JiaoTong University. Before he joined ASU, he worked at Telecom Australia Research Labs and was on the faculty at National University of Singapore. He was recognized for excellence in teaching and research in Computer Science and Engineering at Arizona State University. His research interests are in data mining, machine learning, social computing, and artificial intelligence, investigating problems that arise in many real-world, data-intensive applications with high-dimensional data of disparate forms such as social media. His well-cited publications include books, book chapters, encyclopedia entries as well as conference and journal papers. He serves on journal editorial boards and numerous conference program committees, and is a founding organizer of the International Conference Series on Social Computing, Behavioral-Cultural Modeling, and Prediction (`http://sbp.asu.edu/`). He is an IEEE Fellow and an ACM Distinguished Scientist. Updated information can be found at `http://www.public.asu.edu/~huanliu`.

3. TUTORIAL OUTLINE

1. Introduction
2. LBSN Data Properties
    - W^4: LBSN Information Layout
    - Sparse Data in Large-Scale
    - Socio-Spatial Properties
    - Temporal Dynamics
    - Semantic Indications
3. Discovering Human Mobile Patterns from LBSN Data
    - Lévy Flight of Check-ins
    - Inverse Distance Rule on Social Connections
    - Temporal Periodic Patterns
    - Multi-Center Check-in Distribution
4. Existing Recommender Systems
    - Memory-Based Collaborative Filtering
    - Model-Based Collaborative Filtering
    - Hybrid Collaborative Filtering
5. Location Recommendation with LBSN Information
    - Geographical Influence
    - Social Correlations
    - Temporal Patterns
    - Content Indications
    - Hybrid Models
6. Evaluation Metrics
7. Conclusions and Discussion

4. TUTORIAL HOMEPAGE

`http://www.public.asu.edu/~hgao16/recsys2014.html`

5. ACKNOWLEDGMENTS

This work is supported, in part, by ONR, NSF, and ARO.

6. REFERENCES

[1] J. Chang and E. Sun. Location 3: How users share and respond to location-based data on social networking sites. *ICWSM*, 2011.

[2] C. Cheng, H. Yang, I. King, and M. Lyu. Fused matrix factorization with geographical and social influence in location-based social networks. *AAAI, Toronto, Canada*, 2012.

[3] Z. Cheng, J. Caverlee, K. Lee, and D. Sui. Exploring millions of footprints in location sharing services. In *ICWSM*, 2011.

[4] E. Cho, S. Myers, and J. Leskovec. Friendship and mobility: user movement in location-based social networks. In *ACM SIGKDD*. ACM, 2011.

[5] H. Gao and H. Liu. Data analysis on location-based social networks. In *Mobile Social Networking*, pages 165–194. Springer, 2014.

[6] H. Gao, J. Tang, X. Hu, and H. Liu. Exploring temporal effects for location recommendation on location-based social networks. In *ACM RecSys*, pages 93–100. ACM, 2013.

[7] H. Gao, J. Tang, and H. Liu. Exploring social-historical ties on location-based social networks. In *ICWSM*, 2012.

[8] H. Gao, J. Tang, and H. Liu. Addressing the cold-start problem in location recommendation using geo-social correlations. *DMKD*, pages 1–25, 2014.

[9] B. Hu and M. Ester. Spatial topic modeling in online social media for location recommendation. In *ACM RecSys*, pages 25–32. ACM, 2013.

[10] S. Scellato, A. Noulas, R. Lambiotte, and C. Mascolo. Socio-spatial properties of online location-based social networks. *ICWSM*, 11, 2011.

[11] M. Ye, P. Yin, W. Lee, and D. Lee. Exploiting geographical influence for collaborative point-of-interest recommendation. In *ACM SIGIR*, pages 325–334, 2011.

[12] Q. Yuan, G. Cong, Z. Ma, A. Sun, and N. M. Thalmann. Time-aware point-of-interest recommendation. In *ACM SIGIR*, pages 363–372. ACM, 2013.

[13] V. W. Zheng, Y. Zheng, X. Xie, and Q. Yang. Collaborative location and activity recommendations with gps history data. In *WWW*, pages 1029–1038. ACM, 2010.

Tutorial on Cross-domain Recommender Systems

Iván Cantador
Departamento de Ingeniería Informática
Universidad Autónoma de Madrid
28049 Madrid, Spain
ivan.cantador@uam.es

Paolo Cremonesi
Dipartimento di Elettronica, Informazione e Bioingegneria
Politecnico di Milano
20133 Milan, Italy
paolo.cremonesi@polimi.it

ABSTRACT
Cross-domain recommender systems aim to generate or enhance personalized recommendations in a target domain by exploiting knowledge (mainly user preferences) form other source domains. This may beneficial for generating better recommendations, e.g. mitigating the cold-start and sparsity problems in a target domain, and enabling personalized cross-selling for items from multiple domains. In this tutorial, we formalize the cross-domain recommendation problem, categorize and survey state of the art cross-domain recommender systems, discuss related evaluation issues, and outline future research directions on the topic.

Categories and Subject Descriptors
H.1.2 [**Models and Principles**]: User/Machine Systems – *human information processing*. H.3.3 [**Information Storage and Retrieval**]: Information Search and Retrieval – *information filtering*. H.4.2. [**Information Systems Applications**]: Types of Systems – *decision support*.

General Terms
Algorithms, Experimentation, Human Factors, Performance.

Keywords
Recommender Systems, Cross-Domain Recommendation, Cross-Selling, Knowledge Transfer.

1. INTRODUCTION
The majority of recommender systems offer recommendations for items belonging to a single domain. For instance, Netflix recommends movies and TV programs, and Last.fm recommends songs and music albums. These domain-specific systems have been successfully deployed by numerous websites, and the single-domain recommendation functionality is not perceived as a limitation but rather pitched as a focus on a certain market.

Large e-commerce sites like Amazon and eBay, however, often store user feedback for items from multiple domains, and in social networks users often provide feedback for a variety of topics. It may, therefore, be beneficial to leverage all the available user data provided in various domains and systems, in order to generate more encompassing user models and better recommendations. Instead of treating each domain or item type independently, knowledge acquired in a *source* domain could be exploited in another, *target* domain. The research challenge of transferring the knowledge, and the business potential of delivering recommendations spanning across multiple domains, have triggered an increasing interest in the so-called cross-domain recommender systems.

RecSys '14, Oct 06-10 2014, San Jose or vicinity, CA, USA.
ACM 978-1-4503-2668-1/14/10.
http://dx.doi.org/10.1145/2645710.2645777

2. OUTLINE AND TOPICS
2.1 Formulation of the Cross-Domain Recommendation Problem
In the literature authors have considered several notions of domains. For instance, some have treated items like *movies* and *books* as belonging to different domains, while others have considered items such as *action movies* and *comedy movies* as distinct domains. In the tutorial, we discuss different definitions of domain according to the attributes and types of recommended items, distinguishing between four levels, namely (i) item attribute, (ii) item type, (iii) item, and (iv) system level. We also consider the type of user feedback, evaluation scale, and context used by the recommender to explain the notion of domain.

The research on cross-domain recommendation generally aims to exploit knowledge from a source domain $\mathcal{D}_S$ to perform or improve recommendations in a target domain $\mathcal{D}_T$. Let $\mathcal{U}_S$ and $\mathcal{U}_T$ be their sets of users, and let $\mathcal{I}_S$ and $\mathcal{I}_T$ be their sets of items. The users of a domain are those who expressed preferences (ratings, reviews, tags, or consumption logs) for the domain items. The items of a domain do not necessarily have preferences from users of the domain, but may have content-based features that establish their belonging to the domain. Analyzing the literature, we observe that the addressed tasks are diverse, and a consensual definition of the cross-domain recommendation problem has not been formulated yet. Sorted in increasing order of complexity, we distinguish between the following three recommendation tasks:

- **Multi-domain recommendation**: recommend items in both the source and target domains, i.e., recommend items in $\mathcal{I}_S \cup \mathcal{I}_T$ to users in $\mathcal{U}_S$ (or, equivalently, in $\mathcal{U}_T$ or $\mathcal{U}_S \cup \mathcal{U}_T$).
- **Linked-domain recommendation**: recommend items in the target domain by exploiting knowledge from the source and target domains, i.e., recommend items in $\mathcal{I}_T$ to users in $\mathcal{U}_S$ by exploiting knowledge about $\mathcal{U}_S \cup \mathcal{U}_T$ and/or $\mathcal{I}_S \cup \mathcal{I}_T$.
- **Cross-domain recommendation**: recommend items in the target domain by exploiting knowledge from the source domain, i.e., recommend items in $\mathcal{I}_T$ to users in $\mathcal{U}_S$ by exploiting knowledge about $\mathcal{U}_S$ and/or $\mathcal{I}_S$.

In the tutorial, we detail the above recommendation tasks.

2.2 Categorization of Cross-domain Recommender Systems
The cross-domain recommendation problem has been addressed from various perspectives in different research areas. It has been faced by means of user preference aggregation and mediation strategies for the cross-system personalization problem in *user modeling* [1][2][8], as a potential solution to mitigate the cold-start and sparsity problems in *recommender systems* [3][9][10], and as a practical application of knowledge transfer in *machine learning* [5][6][7]. This has entailed the development of a wide array of approaches, which in many cases are difficult to compare due to

e.g., the user preferences they use, the cross-domain scenarios they deal with, and the algorithms on which they are based.

In the tutorial, we discuss different categories of cross-domain recommendation techniques proposed in the literature. Then, aiming to reconcile these categories in a way that captures and unifies their core ideas, we present a categorization focused on the exploitation of knowledge in cross-domain recommendation, which dictates the following two-level taxonomy:

Aggregating knowledge. Knowledge from various source domains is aggregated to perform recommendations in a target domain. Three use cases are considered:

- ***Merging user preferences***: the aggregated knowledge consists of user preferences, e.g., ratings, tags, transaction logs, and click-through data.
- ***Mediating user modeling data***: the aggregated knowledge comes from user modeling data exploited by various recommender systems, e.g., user similarities and user neighborhoods.
- ***Combining recommendations***: the aggregated knowledge is composed of single-domain recommendations, e.g. rating estimations and rating probability distributions.

Linking and transferring knowledge. Knowledge linkage or transfer between domains is established to support recommendations. Three variants are considered:

- ***Linking domains***: linking domains by a common knowledge, e.g., item attributes, association rules, semantic networks, and inter-domain correlations.
- ***Sharing latent features***: the source and target domains are related by means of implicit latent features.
- ***Transferring rating patterns***: explicit or implicit rating patterns from source domains are exploited in the target domain.

2.3 Evaluation of Cross-domain Recommender Systems

Whether a cross-domain recommender system is good or bad cannot be evaluated without taking into account for what it is intended. The nature of the evaluation must be connected to the purpose for which the recommendations are required. Thus, in the tutorial. we first describe the cross-domain **recommendation goals** addressed in the literature:

- **Addressing the new user problem**. This may be solved by exploiting the user's preferences collected in a different source domain.
- **Addressing the new item problem**. This is particularly evident when cross-selling new products from different domains.
- **Improving accuracy**. Data collected outside the target domain can increase the rating density and upgrade the recommendation quality.
- **Improving diversity**. The diversity of recommendations can be improved by considering multiple domains, as this may provide a better coverage of the range of user preferences.
- **Enhancing user models**. The main goal of cross-domain user modeling applications is to enhance user models. Achieving this goal may have personalization-oriented benefits such as discovering new user interests for the target domain, enhancing similarities between users and items, and measuring vulnerability in social networks.

Based on these goals, in the tutorial we discuss **evaluation scenarios**, **methodologies** and **metrics**.

2.4 Future Research on Cross-domain Recommendation

One interesting issue that deserves more attention in future work is the synergy between cross-domain and **context-aware recommendations**: different contexts (e.g. location, time, and mood) can be treated as different domains, and context can be treated as a bridge between different domains.

Another important issue concerns the **evaluation metrics** adopted. A common practice with cross-domain recommender systems is to evaluate their relevance through prediction metrics such as MAE and RMSE. However, the true advantage of cross-domain recommendations is not necessarily in their accuracy, but rather in their novelty and diversity, which may lead to a higher satisfaction and utility for the user.

A third open research issue refers to the usage of cross-domain recommender systems for reducing the **user model elicitation** effort. Cross-domain recommender systems could be used as alternative elicitation tools able to build detailed user profiles without or mitigating the need to collect explicit user preferences in cold-start situations.

3. REFERENCES

[1] Abel, F., Helder, E., Houben, G.-J., Henze, N., Krause, D. 2013. Cross-system User Modeling and Personalization on the Social Web. *User Modeling and User-Adapted Interaction*, 23(2-3), pp. 169-209.

[2] Berkovsky, S., Kuflik, T., Ricci, F. 2008. Mediation of User Models for Enhanced Personalization in Recommender Systems. *User Modeling and User-Adapted Interaction*, 18(3), pp. 245-286.

[3] Cremonesi, P., Tripodi, A., Turrin, R. 2011. Cross-domain Recommender Systems. *Proc. of the 11th IEEE International Conference on Data Mining Workshops*, pp. 496-503.

[4] Fernández-Tobíias, I., Cantador, I., Kaminskas, M., Ricci, F. 2012. Cross-domain Recommender Systems: A Survey of the State of the Art. *Proc. of the 2nd Spanish Conference on Information Retrieval*, pp. 187-198.

[5] Gao, S., Luo, H., Chen, D., Li, S., Gallinari, P., Guo, J. 2013. Cross-Domain Recommendation via Cluster-Level Latent Factor Model. *Proc. of the 17th and 24th European Conference on Machine Learning and Knowledge Discovery in Databases*, pp. 161-176.

[6] Li, B., Yang, Q., Xue, X. 2009. Can Movies and Books Collaborate? Cross-domain Collaborative Filtering for Sparsity Reduction. *Proc. of the 21st International Joint conference on Artificial Intelligence*, pp. 2052-2057.

[7] Pan, W., Xiang, E. W., Liu, N. N., Yang, Q. 2010. Transfer Learning in Collaborative Filtering for Sparsity Reduction. *Proc. of the 24th AAAI Conf. on Artificial Intelligence*, pp. 210-235.

[8] Shapira, B., Rokach, L., Freilikhman, S. 2013. Facebook Single and Cross Domain Data for Recommendation Systems. *User Modeling and User-Adapted Interaction*, 23(2-3), pp. 211-247.

[9] Shi, Y., Larson, M., Hanjalic, A. 2011. Tags as Bridges between Domains: Improving Recommendation with Tag-induced Cross-domain Collaborative Filtering. *Proc. of the 19th International Conference on User Modeling, Adaption, and Personalization*, pp. 305-316.

[10] Tiroshi, A., Berkovsky, S., Kaafar, M. A., Chen, T., Kuflik, T. 2013. Cross Social Networks Interests Predictions Based on Graph Features. *Proc. of the 7th ACM Conference on Recommender Systems*, pp. 319-322.

Social Recommender System Tutorial

Ido Guy
Yahoo! Labs Israel
Matam Park
Haifa 31905, Israel
idoguy@acm.org

Werner Geyer
IBM Research Cambridge
1 Rogers Street,
Cambridge, MA 02142, USA
werner.geyer@us.ibm.com

ABSTRACT
In recent years, with the proliferation of the social web, users are increasingly exposed to social overload and the designers of social web sites are challenged to attract and retain their user basis. Social recommender systems are becoming an integral part of virtually any leading website, playing a key factor in its success: First, they aim to address the overload problem by helping users to find relevant content. Second, they can provide recommendations for content creation, increasing participation and user retention. In this tutorial, we will review the broad domain of social recommender systems, their application for the social web, the underlying techniques and methodologies; the data in use, recommended entities, and target population; evaluation techniques; and open issues and challenges.

Categories and Subject Descriptors
H.3.3 Information Search and Retrieval – *Information filtering*

General Terms
Algorithms, Measurement, Human Factors.

Keywords
Recommender systems; social media; social networks; social web; social recommender systems; web 2.0

1. INTRODUCTION
While the abundance and popularity of social media sites allow people to leave and share their own digital footprints, they overwhelm the users with mountains of information and hence pose a great challenge for users to find relevant information. Social Recommender Systems aim to alleviate information overload by presenting the most attractive and relevant content, often using personalization techniques adapted for the specific user. At the same time, the proliferation of social web sites creates new challenges for user engagement and retention, as there is increased competition between social media sites. Social recommender systems can be leveraged to incentivize content creation and user engagement.

RecSys'14, October 6–10, 2014, Foster City, Silicon Valley, CA, USA.
ACM 978-1-4503-2668-1/14/10.
http://dx.doi.org/10.1145/2645710.2645778

In this tutorial, we will discuss the key motivations for social media sites to apply recommendation techniques and review the fundamental recommendation approaches. We will then present the key categories of social recommender systems, both in terms of the recommended entities and target audience. Following, we will review methods for handling the cold start problem, incorporating trust and reputation, and providing useful explanations for the recommendation decision of suggested items. We will then discuss evaluation techniques, with emphasis on the pros and cons of each method. We will also review emerging social recommender system domains, such as persuasive technologies and stream personalization methods. Finally, we will summarize by discussing open issues and challenges in the field.

Related tutorials were given at WWW 2011 and WWW 2014 as half-day (3 hours) tutorials [11][12].

2. OUTLINE
- Introduction to Social Recommender Systems
  - Social overload & user engagement
  - Social recommender examples
- The Cold Start Problem
  - Of new items
  - For new users
  - For tags
- Trust, Reputation, and Influence
  - Trust-aware recommender systems
  - Reputation-aware recommender systems
- Explanations and Evidence
- Evaluation Methods
  - Offline methods
  - User surveys
  - Live systems
- Emerging Domains
  - Persuasion and user engagement for content creation
    - Theories
    - Examples
  - Social Streams
    - User modeling based on social stream
    - Social Stream personalization
- Summary and Future Directions

3. PRESENTERS
Ido Guy is a principal research engineer at Yahoo! Labs Israel, focusing on analysis of large-scale social data. Prior to joining Yahoo!, Ido was a senior technical staff member and manager of the Social Technologies and Analytics group at the IBM Haifa Research Lab. Under his management, the group developed and

studied technologies in which people play a central role. Ido's main area of research is social media, with special focus on social network mining and analysis and on recommender systems. He has published over 40 conference and journal papers, spanning the fields of Human-Computer Interaction, Information and Knowledge Management, and Data Mining. In recent years, Ido has been particularly active in the area of Social Recommender Systems, publishing key papers on people recommendation ([2], [14], [15]) social content recommendation ([8], [16], [17], [18]), and activity stream filtering [13]. He is co-chair of the Workshop on Social Recommender Systems (held at IUI 2010, CSCW 2011, UMAP 2012, and WWW 2013-4), co-chair of the 2011, 2013, and 2014 workshop on Recommender Systems and the Social Web (all held at RecSys), and a guest editor of two ACM TIST special issues on Social Recommender Systems (2011 and 2013). Ido has also served as the program co-chair of the 2012 ACM conference on Recommender Systems (RecSys 2012).

Werner Geyer is a Research Manager of the Data Science User Experience (DUX) team at the IBM Cambridge Research Lab. His research focuses on social collaboration, recommender systems, and social media analytics. He has more than 10 years of experience in designing, building, and testing large scale software systems, deployed internally in IBM and externally on the Internet. He has more than 70 peer-reviewed publications at international conferences and journals in the fields of HCI, CSCW, Social Media and Recommender Systems ([1],[2],[3],[4],[5],[6],[7],[8],[9],[10] & [19]). He has been co-organizing a series of workshops on Social Recommender systems at ACM RecSys (2009, 2010, 2011, 2013), and was a co-organizer and senior program committee member of the ACM RecSys 2012. He is program committee member and reviewer for major conferences in the fields of HCI, CSCW, and Social Media. He has co-authored more than 27 patents, his research has impacted IBM social media products such as IBM Connections.

4. REFERENCES

[1] Ahn, H., Geyer, W., Dugan, C., Millen, D.R. "How Incredibly Awesome!" — Click Here to Read More. *Proc ICWSM '10,* Washington, DC, May 23 – 26, 2010, AAAI Press,Menlo Park, CA.

[2] Chen, J., Geyer, W., Dugan, C., Muller, M., Guy, I. 2009. "Make New Friends, but Keep the Old" – Recommending People on Social Networking Sites. *In Proc CHI '09*. ACM, New York, NY.

[3] Daly, E., Geyer, W. 2011. Effective event discovery: using location and social information for scoping event recommendations. *In Proc RecSys '11*. ACM, New York, NY, USA, 277-280

[4] Daly, E., Geyer, W., Millen, D.R. 2010. The network effects of recommending social connections. *Proc ACM RecSys '10*. ACM, New York, NY, USA, 301-304.

[5] Dugan, C., Geyer, W., Millen, David R. 2010. Lessons Learned from Blog Muse: Audience-based Inspiration for Bloggers. *Proc CHI '10*. ACM, New York, NY.

[6] Dugan, C., Muller, M., Millen, D. R., Geyer, W., Brownholtz, B., and Moore, M. 2007. The dogear game: a social bookmark recommender system. In Proc GROUP '07. ACM, New York, NY, 387-390.

[7] Freyne, J., Berkovsky, S., Daly, E., Geyer, W. 2010. Social networking feeds: recommending items of interest. *Proc ACM RecSys '10*. ACM, New York, NY, USA, 277-280.

[8] Freyne, J., Jacovi, M., Guy, I., and Geyer, W. 2009. Increasing engagement through early recommender intervention. In *Proc RecSys '09*. ACM, New York, NY, 85-92.

[9] Geyer, W., Dugan, C. 2010. Inspired by the Audience – A Topic Suggestion System for Blog Writers and Readers. *Proc CSCW '10*. ACM, New York, NY.

[10] Geyer, W., Dugan, C., Millen, D. R., Muller, M., and Freyne, J. 2008. Recommending topics for self-descriptions in online user profiles. In *Proc RecSys '08*. ACM, New York, NY, 59-66.

[11] Guy, I. Tutorial on Social Recommender Systems. *Proc. WWW '14 (Companion)*, 195-196.

[12] Guy, I. & Carmel, D. 2011. Social Recommender Systems. *Proc. WWW '11*, 283-284.

[13] Guy, I., Ronen, I., & Raviv, A. 2011. Personalized activity streams:sifting through the "river of news". Proc. *RecSys '11*, 181-188.

[14] Guy, I., Ronen, I., & Wilcox, E. 2009. Do you know? recommending people to invite into your social network. *Proc. IUI '09*, 77-86.

[15] Guy, I., Ur, S., Ronen, I., Perer, A., & Jacovi, M. 2011. Do you want to know? recommending strangers in the enterprise. *Proc. CSCW '11*, 285-294.

[16] Guy, I., Zwerdling, N., Carmel, D., Ronen, I., Uziel, E., Yogev, S.,& Ofek-Koifman, S. 2009. Personalized recommendation of social software items based on social relations. *Proc. RecSys '09*, 53-60.

[17] Guy, I., Zwerdling, N., Ronen, I., Carmel, D., & Uziel, E. 2010. Social media recommendation based on people and tags. *Proc. SIGIR '10*, 194-201.

[18] Ronen, I., Guy, I., Kravi, E., & Barnea, M. 2014. Recommending social media content to community owners. *Proc. SIGIR '14*, 243-252.

[19] Vatturi, P. K., Geyer, W., Dugan, C., Muller, M., and Brownholtz, B. 2008. Tag-based filtering for personalized bookmark recommendations. *In Proc CIKM '08*. ACM, New York, NY, 1395-1396.

Hybridisation Techniques for Cold-Starting Context-Aware Recommender Systems

Matthias Braunhofer
Free University of Bolzano
Piazza Domenicani 3
Bolzano, Italy
mbraunhofer@unibz.it

ABSTRACT

Context-Aware Recommender Systems (CARSs) suffer from the cold-start problem, i.e., the inability to provide accurate recommendations for new users, items or contextual situations. In this research, we aim at solving this problem by exploiting various hybridisation techniques, from simple heuristic-based solutions to complex adaptive solutions, in order to take advantage of the strengths of different CARS algorithms while avoiding their weaknesses in a given (cold-start) situation. Our initial research based on offline experiments using various contextually-tagged rating datasets has shown that basic CARS algorithms perform very differently in different recommendation scenarios, and that they can be effectively hybridised to achieve an overall optimal performance. Further research is now required to find the optimal method for hybridisation.

Categories and Subject Descriptors

H.3.3 [**Information Storage and Retrieval**]: Information Search and Retrieval—*information filtering*

Keywords

Context-Aware Recommender Systems; Cold-Start Problem; Hybrid System

1. INTRODUCTION

Context-Aware Recommender Systems (CARSs) have been developed using several algorithms to provide users with recommendations based on additional context information besides the typical user and item information. Roughly, they can be divided into three categories [1], namely contextual pre-filtering, contextual post-filtering and contextual modelling, depending on the recommendation stage where the available contextual information is used. However, to the best of our knowledge, none of the proposed approaches is specifically addressing all kinds of cold-start problems occurring in CARSs, i.e., the new user, new item and new context problems.

While hybrid RSs are a well-accepted technique to deal with cold-start issues in traditional Recommender Systems (RSs), they have not yet systematically been applied to CARSs. Hybrid RSs combine in different ways several recommendation techniques, each of which has its own strengths and weaknesses, to achieve overall peak performance [7]. For instance, the new item problem, which is tampering with pure Collaborative Filtering (CF), can be avoided by relying on a content-based component. Similarly, demographic approaches void the requirement of a history of user ratings needed by both CF and content-based techniques, and hence can be employed to alleviate the new user problem.

In our work, we extend this idea to deal with cold-start situations occurring in CARSs. In particular, we deal with: (i) the new user problem, which refers to the problem of providing relevant recommendations to new users with no rating history; (ii) the new item problem, which denotes the difficulty of accurately recommending items that are new to the system; (iii) the new context problem, which has not been explored in detail so far, and occurs when the system is requested to produce recommendations under new contextual situations; and finally (iv) the possible mixtures of the aforementioned problems.

We hypothesise that these problems can effectively be alleviated by hybrid approaches that combine the rating predictions from different CARS algorithms into one overall prediction. By combining multiple basic recommenders, which can be done using different techniques that range from simple heuristics to more complex adaptive algorithms, the resulting hybrid should be able to produce meaningful recommendations also in cold-start situations when the basic recommenders alone would fail.

We define the following research questions:

- Which basic CARS algorithms should be combined into a hybrid?
- How should the basic CARS algorithms be hybridised to handle the various cold-start situations?
- Which evaluation protocols and datasets should be used to measure the cold-start performance of the considered CARS algorithms?

To address the above stated research questions, we will design, develop and test novel hybridisation techniques for combining the predictions of a suite of CARS algorithms, which can then be used for effectively cold-starting CARSs.

RecSys'14, October 6–10, 2014, Foster City, Silicon Valley, CA, USA.
Copyright 2014 ACM 978-1-4503-2668-1/14/10 ...$15.00.
http://dx.doi.org/10.1145/2645710.2653360.

2. RELATED WORK

While there has been a lot of research on the cold-start problem for traditional RSs [17, 14], only few studies have examined it specifically for CARSs. One direct approach is to exploit additional information about the users, items or contextual situations in the recommendation process. But acquiring this information is a non-trivial task that requires substantial effort from the users and/or service providers. It can be obtained efficiently, for example, by employing an Active Learning (AL) strategy [10] or a cross-domain recommendation technique [11]. Another way more closely related to our research is by profiling users and items through attributes (e.g., demographics and item descriptions), and by using them to develop a hybrid CARS for overcoming the new user and new item problem [18]. There are several different hybridisation methods for traditional RSs [7]. Two of the most prominent ones, which inspired our work, are weighted and switching. A weighted hybrid recommender, as illustrated, for instance, in [5, 12], is one that aggregates the rating predictions of all available recommendation techniques into a single value by using a selected aggregation method [13]. On the other hand, a switching hybrid, as described, e.g., in [9, 4], chooses the best-performing algorithm for recommendation depending on the current recommendation situation. Switching hybrid can be considered a special case of weighting where a weight of 1 is assigned to the selected recommender, and 0 is assigned to all remaining ones.

Rather than relying on new ratings data or metadata, one can also try to better use the existing ratings data. One example of such approach is Differential Context Weighting (DCW) [19], which aims at alleviating the cold-start problems caused by exact pre-filtering [1] by weighting contextual ratings based on their similarity to a given target context. Another similar method, which we considered in our work, is Semantic Pre-Filtering (SPF) [8]. Also SPF exploits, in the recommendation process, not only contextual ratings that exactly match the target context but also those there were acquired in semantically similar contexts.

3. RATING PREDICTION MODELS

All the basic CARS algorithms as well as the hybrid solutions that we have considered so far in our research operate on a $|Users| \times |Items| \times |Context|$ user-item-context rating tensor denoted as R. The tensor entry $r_{uic_1,...,c_k}$ is the rating of the user u on the item i in the contextual situation described by the contextual conditions $c_1, ..., c_k$, and c_j is the index of the contextual condition for factor j (e.g., the index of condition "sunny"' for the "weather" contextual factor). More details about the specific algorithms are given below.

3.1 Basic Rating Prediction Models

We have considered four basic CARS algorithms. *CAMF-CC* (Context-Aware Matrix Factorisation for item categories) denotes a variant of CAMF [3] that extends standard Matrix Factorisation (MF) by incorporating baseline parameters for each contextual condition and item category in order to model how the ratings of items belonging to a specific category are affected by the contextual conditions.

SPF (Semantic Pre-Filtering) [8] is a pre-filtering algorithm that, given a target contextual situation, uses a standard MF model learnt from all ratings tagged with contextual situations identical or semantically equivalent to the target one. SPF is expected to perform well in cold-start situations since it reuses ratings tagged with contexts that, notwithstanding they are syntactically different, they actually influence in a similar way the users' ratings.

Content-based CAMF-CC is a novel variant of CAMF-CC that we have designed to tackle the new item problem of CAMF-CC. It extends CAMF-CC by incorporating additional factor vectors for describing an item also through a set of item-associated attributes, such as the type of a place of interest (POI) and the actors or the genre of a movie.

Finally, *Demographics-based CAMF-CC* is another variant of CAMF-CC that we propose for tackling the new user problem associated to CAMF-CC. It enhances the user representation by profiling users with additional factor vectors corresponding to known user attributes (demographics), for instance, gender, age group and personality traits.

3.2 Hybrid Rating Prediction Models

Moreover, we have designed two hybridisation techniques that we compare here with a baseline, namely *Average Weighted*, which combines individual basic CARS algorithms simply by taking the average of their predicted ratings. The first technique, called *Heuristic Switching*, was proposed by us in [6] and uses a stable heuristic in order to switch between the various basic algorithms depending on the encountered cold-start situation. It selects content-based CAMF-CC when requested to predict a rating for a new item, while it selects demographics-based CAMF-CC when predicting a rating for a new user or a new contextual situation. When a mixture of elementary cold-start cases is detected, it computes the predicted rating by averaging the predictions of the two constituent algorithms.

The second one, *Adaptive Weighted* refers to a novel adaptive weighted hybrid CARS algorithm. It extends the two-dimensional adaptive RS presented in [5], and builds for each basic CARS algorithm a new user-item-context error tensor whose entries are the known deviations (errors) of the CARS predictions from the true ratings. Then, it trains a separate CARS error prediction model for each of these error tensors, and combines all the considered basic CARS differently for each user-item-context setting by weighting each of them inversely proportional to its predicted error on that particular setting. As error prediction model, we chose a new variant of CAMF that is conceptually similar to the one illustrated in [11] and that uses latent factor vectors for modelling contextual conditions, rather than scalar numbers, as in original CAMF. It leverages latent correlations and patterns between users, items as well as contexts in the data, and hence is well-suited to produce error predictions. Given a user u, an item i, the subset of item-related contextual conditions IC and the subset of user-related contextual conditions UC, it predicts errors using the following rule:

$$\hat{e}_{uic_1,...,c_k} = (q_i + \sum_{c_i \in IC} x_{c_i})^\top (p_u + \sum_{c_u \in UC} y_{c_u}) + \bar{e_i} + b_u, \quad (1)$$

where q_i, p_u, x_{c_i} and y_{c_u} are the latent factor vectors associated to item i, user u, item-related contextual condition c_i and user-related contextual condition c_u, respectively, $\bar{e_i}$ is the average prediction error for item i, and b_u is the bias associated to user u. The model parameters are learnt by minimising the associated regularised squared error function through stochastic gradient descent.

4. EVALUATION AND RESULTS

This section describes the datasets, the evaluation procedure and the results of an offline experiment that we conducted to compare the cold-start performance of the aforementioned CARS algorithms.

4.1 Datasets

For the experiment, we have considered three contextually-tagged datasets of ratings with different characteristics: *STS* [10], *CoMoDa* [15] and *Music* [2]. Table 1 provides some descriptive statistics of these datasets. We note that finding a suitable dataset for our evaluation purposes is not a trivial task because most of the standard datasets available for RS research can not be used as they are either too small, too sparse or they do not provide contextual tags and user/item attributes.

Table 1: Datasets' characteristics

Dataset	STS	CoMoDa	Music
Domain	POIs	Movies	Music
Rating scale	1-5	1-5	1-5
Ratings	2,534	2,296	4,012
Users	325	121	43
Items	249	1,232	139
Contextual factors	14	12	8
Contextual conditions	57	49	26
Contextual situations	931	1,969	26
User attributes	7	4	10
Item features	1	7	2

4.2 Evaluation Procedure

We ran experiments for three separate test cases, one for new users, one for new items, and one for new contextual situations. Below, we describe the adopted testing procedure (i.e., ten-fold cross-validation test) for new users. The testing procedures for new items and new contextual situations were identical, except that here cross-validation was performed on the set of items and contextual situations rather than the set of users.

1. Divide the users into ten cross-validation folds (groups) at random.
2. For each fold $k = 1, 2, ..., 10$
   (a) Use all the ratings except those coming from users in fold k in order to build the prediction models.
   (b) Using the trained models, calculate the Mean Absolute Error (MAE) and normalised Discounted Cumulative Gain (nDCG) (measured according to the test procedure described in [16]) on the test ratings for the users in fold k. In this way, the models are tested on ratings coming from users with no ratings in the training set (new users).

The MAE and nDCG estimates from step 2(b) are then averaged over all 10 folds, to produce cross-validation estimates of the MAE and nDCG.

The above evaluation procedure could also be used for determining the models' performance on mixtures of elementary cold-start cases, simply by cross-validating on user-item, user-context, item-context and user-item-context tuples. However, we have not considered this yet, and it is left for future work. Another aspect not dealt with the above test procedure is the fact that there exist various degrees of coldness; currently we test the models' performance on really cold users, items and contextual situations, i.e., without any observed rating.

4.3 Obtained Results

The results, which are summarised in Table 2, reveal some significant performance differences between the individual basic CARS algorithms across the different cold-start cases. For the new user situation, we observed the best overall performance for demographics-based CAMF-CC, which is consistent with our hypothesis since it profiles users not only in terms of explicit ratings, but also through known user attributes (i.e., demographics).

In the new item situation, we found content-based CAMF-CC to be the best-performing CARS algorithm, thus also supporting our hypothesis. It works by incorporating item metadata into the CAMF-CC model, and hence can produce relevant recommendations also in the case when no ratings for the items are available.

Finally, regarding the new contextual situation scenario, we again observed the best performance of demographics-based CAMF-CC. Interestingly, we found a poor performance of SPF, especially for the Music dataset, which is due to the fact that here contextual situations are made up of only one contextual condition, thus making it impossible for SPF to correctly calculate similarities between contextual situations.

Considering the results for the hybrid CARS algorithms, we found that hybridisation techniques, including the simple Average Weighted method, can indeed improve performance in both MAE and nDCG in the different cold-start cases. In almost all cases, they outperformed the state-of-the-art CARS algorithms (i.e., CAMF-CC and SPF), thus easing the problem of model selection. This shows that our first developed hybridisation techniques, and likely more sophisticated follow-up versions, can provide an efficient solution for the cold-start problem in CARSs.

5. CONCLUSIONS AND FUTURE WORK

In the present research, we are trying to tackle the cold-start problems (i.e., new user problem, new item problem and new context problem) of CARSs by developing novel hybrid recommendation techniques that exploit different CARS algorithms, and adaptively use these algorithms for rating prediction depending on their strengths and weaknesses in a given (cold-start) situation. This is a new topic and little or no research has been conducted specifically in this direction.

As future work, we plan to first continue our offline experiments, trying to extend our analysis to mixtures of elementary cold-start cases as well to different levels of cold-start. Secondly, it is necessary to try out further hybridisation techniques proposed in the research literature before [13], and to identify the best-performing one for cold-start purposes. Finally, we plan to integrate the developed hybrid CARS algorithm into our STS Android app [10] so that we can perform a live user study and compare the users' perceived recommendation quality and choice satisfaction of our proposed algorithm against another state-of-the-art CARS algorithm (e.g., CAMF-CC or SPF).

Table 2: Results in terms of MAE and $nDCG_1$ (bold-face indicates significant improvements over both CAMF-CC and SPF with $p < 0.05$)

Cold-start case	Algorithm	STS		CoMoDa		Music	
		MAE	$nDCG_1$	MAE	$nDCG_1$	MAE	$nDCG_1$
Recommendation for new users	CAMF-CC	0.999	0.646	0.895	0.548	1.263	0.442
	SPF	1.000	0.682	0.815	0.630	1.259	0.480
	Content-based CAMF-CC	1.020	0.641	1.054	**0.692**	2.327	0.397
	Demogr.-based CAMF-CC	0.997	0.679	0.803	**0.711**	1.307	0.421
	Average Weighted	0.990	0.671	0.828	**0.715**	1.338	0.460
	Heuristic Switching	0.997	0.681	0.837	0.694	1.307	0.421
	Adaptive Weighted	0.990	0.673	0.832	**0.719**	1.285	0.470
Recommendation for new items	CAMF-CC	0.970	0.541	0.884	0.605	1.195	0.493
	SPF	0.984	0.597	0.837	0.288	1.258	0.545
	Content-based CAMF-CC	**0.935**	0.655	**0.783**	**0.747**	1.187	0.515
	Demogr-based CAMF-CC	**0.941**	0.552	0.868	**0.743**	1.434	0.494
	Average Weighted	**0.939**	**0.696**	**0.784**	**0.750**	1.238	**0.600**
	Heuristic Switching	**0.930**	0.649	**0.779**	**0.749**	1.186	0.515
	Adaptive Weighted	**0.939**	0.676	**0.781**	**0.757**	1.253	**0.592**
Recommendation under new contexts	CAMF-CC	0.868	0.714	0.820	0.680	0.796	0.715
	SPF	0.854	0.745	0.807	0.653	1.009	0.679
	Content-based CAMF-CC	0.863	0.746	**0.745**	**0.773**	1.108	0.630
	Demogr-based CAMF-CC	0.848	0.768	0.810	**0.759**	**0.759**	**0.747**
	Average Weighted	**0.830**	**0.786**	**0.736**	**0.773**	0.900	0.746
	Heuristic Switching	0.848	0.766	**0.771**	**0.771**	**0.759**	**0.747**
	Adaptive Weighted	**0.829**	**0.786**	**0.733**	**0.777**	0.871	**0.758**

6. REFERENCES

[1] G. Adomavicius, B. Mobasher, F. Ricci, and A. Tuzhilin. Context-aware recommender systems. *AI Magazine*, 32(3):67–80, 2011.

[2] L. Baltrunas, M. Kaminskas, B. Ludwig, O. Moling, F. Ricci, A. Aydin, K.-H. Lüke, and R. Schwaiger. Incarmusic: Context-aware music recommendations in a car. In *E-Commerce and Web Technologies*, pages 89–100. Springer, 2011.

[3] L. Baltrunas, B. Ludwig, and F. Ricci. Matrix factorization techniques for context aware recommendation. In *Proceedings of RecSys'11*, pages 301–304. ACM, 2011.

[4] D. Billsus and M. J. Pazzani. User modeling for adaptive news access. *User modeling and user-adapted interaction*, 10(2-3):147–180, 2000.

[5] O. F. Bjørkøy. Adaptive aggregation of recommender systems. 2011.

[6] M. Braunhofer, V. Codina, and F. Ricci. Switching hybrid for cold-starting context-aware recommender systems. In *Proceedings of RecSys'14*. ACM, 2014.

[7] R. Burke. Hybrid web recommender systems. In *The adaptive web*, pages 377–408. Springer, 2007.

[8] V. Codina, F. Ricci, and L. Ceccaroni. Local context modeling with semantic pre-filtering. In *Proceedings of RecSys'13*, pages 363–366. ACM, 2013.

[9] M. Ekstrand and J. Riedl. When recommenders fail: predicting recommender failure for algorithm selection and combination. In *Proceedings of RecSys'12*, pages 233–236. ACM, 2012.

[10] M. Elahi, M. Braunhofer, F. Ricci, and M. Tkalcic. Personality-based active learning for collaborative filtering recommender systems. In *AI* IA 2013: Advances in Artificial Intelligence*, pages 360–371. Springer, 2013.

[11] M. Enrich, M. Braunhofer, and F. Ricci. Cold-start management with cross-domain collaborative filtering and tags. In *E-Commerce and Web Technologies*, pages 101–112. Springer, 2013.

[12] J. Gemmell, T. Schimoler, B. Mobasher, and R. Burke. Hybrid tag recommendation for social annotation systems. In *Proceedings of the 19th ACM international conference on Information and knowledge management*, pages 829–838. ACM, 2010.

[13] M. Jahrer, A. Töscher, and R. Legenstein. Combining predictions for accurate recommender systems. In *Proceedings of the 16th ACM SIGKDD international conference on Knowledge discovery and data mining*, pages 693–702. ACM, 2010.

[14] X. N. Lam, T. Vu, T. D. Le, and A. D. Duong. Addressing cold-start problem in recommendation systems. In *Proceedings of the 2nd International Conference on Ubiquitous Information Management and Communication*, ICUIMC '08, pages 208–211, New York, NY, USA, 2008. ACM.

[15] A. Odić, M. Tkalčič, J. F. Tasič, and A. Košir. Predicting and detecting the relevant contextual information in a movie-recommender system. *Interacting with Computers*, 25(1):74–90, 2013.

[16] S.-T. Park and W. Chu. Pairwise preference regression for cold-start recommendation. In *Proceedings of RecSys'09*, pages 21–28. ACM, 2009.

[17] A. I. Schein, A. Popescul, L. H. Ungar, and D. M. Pennock. Methods and metrics for cold-start recommendations. In *Proceedings of the 25th ACM SIGIR conference on Research and development in information retrieval*, pages 253–260. ACM, 2002.

[18] W. Woerndl, M. Brocco, and R. Eigner. Context-aware recommender systems in mobile scenarios. *International Journal of Information Technology and Web Engineering (IJITWE)*, 4(1):67–85, 2009.

[19] Y. Zheng, R. Burke, and B. Mobasher. Recommendation with differential context weighting. In *User Modeling, Adaptation, and Personalization*, pages 152–164. Springer, 2013.

Moving beyond Linearity and Independence in Top-N Recommender Systems

Evangelia Christakopoulou
Email: evangel@cs.umn.edu

ABSTRACT

This paper suggests a number of research directions in which the recommender systems can improve their quality, by moving beyond the assumptions of linearity and independence that are traditionally made. These assumptions, while producing effective and meaningful results, can be suboptimal, as in lots of cases they do not represent the real datasets. In this paper, we discuss three different ways to address some of the previous constraints. More specifically, we focus on the development of methods capturing higher-order relations between the items, cross-feature interactions and intra-set dependencies which can potentially lead to a considerable enhancement of the recommendation accuracy.

1. INTRODUCTION

During the last years, the area of top-N recommendation has received great attention and become widespread [3]. The methods developed [7, 8, 10, 11, 13, 14] provide better recommendations as the years go by. However, there are still some simplifications assumed that might not always represent reality. When this is the case, the methods developed clearly suffer from the ignorance of this valuable information, that is anyway present in the dataset.

The first assumption that is commonly made is the one of independence. In a k-nearest neigbors system [8], it is assumed that every item that the user has purchased independently contributes to the rating score that the user would give to another target item. This assumption holds in a lot of commercial modern systems, like the ones suggesting a set of songs to a user, based on his listening history [5].

Moving beyond independence, the vast majority of recommender systems developed are still simple; they mostly create linear models. An example of this is a modern top-N recommendation method [11] that performs better than other algorithms and it is based on a linear regression model. In the same way, when side information is taken into account, it still exploits linear relations between the features [4, 12, 17].

RecSys'14 October 06 - 10 2014, Foster City, Silicon Valley, CA, USA

ACM 978-1-4503-2668-1/14/10 ...$15.00.
http://dx.doi.org/10.1145/2645710.2653361

We think that these assumptions while providing us with easy-to-interpret and simple models, they set a limit to the capabilities of recommender systems. By allowing recommender systems to develop more complex methods that will better capture real-life data, we may be able to get more effective and powerful recommendations. It should be noted that such approaches have already been introduced [15, 16] for rating prediction methods. However, this is not the case for top-N recommendation methods. Also, it has been shown [7] that top-N recommendation methods and rating prediction methods exhibit different characteristics, so a simple extension would not suffice. Towards this direction, in this work, we will investigate the following research questions:

- Do higher-order relations exist in the rating information in datasets, beyond pairwise associations? If yes, which is the best way to incorporate them?
- Which is the best way to incorporate side information, apart from a linear model? Is cross-feature interaction present? How can we best model it?
- In top-N recommendation lists, it is assumed that every item in the list is the best possible, independent of the others, without however guaranteeing the best possible list. How can we optimize this, so that the overall list is the best?

The way we have addressed or plan to address the above research questions is analyzed in the following sections. Initial results [6] show that more complex interactions exist in the datasets and when taken into account, they can improve the recommendation quality.

2. HIGHER-ORDER RELATIONS

Current top-N recommendation methods compute the recommendations by taking into account only relations between pairs of items. However, when higher-order relations between items exist, the above approach is suboptimal. In [6], we propose a way (HOSLIM) to incorporate higher-order relations in recommender systems.

More specifically, we first verify the existence of higher-order relations in real-world datasets, by measuring how prevalent are the itemsets with strong association beyond the items that comprise it (beyond pairwise associations). We use different metrics to measure the strength of the associations and different ways to measure how well the itemsets with strong association cover the datasets. From our analysis, we conclude that the presence of higher-order relations in different real-world datasets is clear and it cannot be ignored.

We then specify the itemsets, i.e. the sets of items that are co-purchased by at least σ users in the dataset. We compute the likelihood that a user will buy a specific item as a sparse aggregation of both the items and the itemsets purchased by the user. Our method builds upon the SLIM method [11] which estimates the rating that a user would give to an item as a sparse aggregation of the items rated by the user:

$$\tilde{R} = RS, \tag{1}$$

where R is the user×items rating matrix and S is the sparse aggregation coefficient matrix learned, that represents the similarities between the items.If R' denotes the users×itemsets matrix containing the information whether a user purchased all the items constituting an itemset, then the model proposed by our apporach is:

$$\tilde{R} = RS + R'S'. \tag{2}$$

The sparse matrix representing the similarities between items and itemsets (S') as well as S are learned, by solving an l_1 and l_2 regularized optimization problem. These matrices are used during the prediction time, in order to recommend the best top-N items to a user, by taking into account the higher-order information captured by the itemsets-items interaction.

After doing a full parameter study, exploring different levels of sparsity as well as different values of support threshold, we saw that the proposed method outperforms a variety of other top-N recommendation methods: the traditional and popular k-nearest neighbors [8], SLIM which is a modern top-N recommendation method outperforming the rest of the existing top-N methods [11] and HOKNN, which is the method that was the first to incorporate itemsets into the recommendation [8]. On top of that, we showed that there is a strong positive correlation between the existence of higher-order relations in a dataset and the performance of the proposed method, which demonstrates that our method can indeed capture effectively the existence of higher-order information and use it to improve the recommendation quality. In addition, we suggested a constrained version of our method, which controls the complexity and provides more efficient recommendations. By introducing this constraint, the recommendation performance is either not affected at all in some cases, or slightly decreased but still higher than the performance of the competing methods. In this way, our method can be easily used in order to provide good-quality recommendations fast.

The main purpose of this work was to answer the research question whether higher-order information exists in real-world datasets and whether incorporating it could help the recommendation quality. The take-away message was that by coupling the incorporation of higher-order associations (when they do exist) with a state-of-the-art top-N method, the quality of the recommendations made is improved beyond the current best results.

3. CROSS-FEATURE INTERACTIONS

Modern recommender systems in general also have side information, except from the traditional rating data. Side information could be user-based, like user demographics (e.g. age, gender, ethnicity, country of residence, user interests), or item-based (e.g.product characteristics), or both. A lot of recommender systems also have reviews , which are associated with the ratings themselves. By aggregating all the reviews written about a specific item, we have item side information and similarly by aggregating all the reviews written by a specific user, we have user side information. Different recommendation methods [4,12,17,19] take into account side information, as it enriches the ratings with additional features which if used properly can help improve the recommendation quality.

The existing approaches for incorporating side information exploit linear relations between the features. This means that the rating a user would give to an item is predicted as a linear combination of the different features of the user/item side information. However, these methods do not incorporate the interaction between the features. For example, let's suppose that a user is interested in articles related to 'Recommender Systems'. This feature is indicative of the fact that he will like articles related to 'Collaborative Filtering' or 'Matrix factorization'. Such cross-feature interactions are often not explicitly modeled by the methods.

In the work we are planning to do, we would like to better capture such cross-feature interactions, in the form of a bilinear model. More specifically, if I (items×item-features) is the matrix capturing item-side information, we will learn a matrix F (item-features×item-features) that will capture the cross-feature interaction. Specifically, the model used to estimate the ratings that users will give to items will be:

$$\tilde{R} = RIFI^T. \tag{3}$$

It is worth noting that RI basically represents the user side information, as for every user, his side information is the aggregation of the item side information of the items he rated.

In the same way, we can also incorporate user side information, too. If U (users×user-features) is the matrix capturing user-side information, then we can learn a matrix W (user-features×user-features) that will also capture the cross-feature interaction, for the user side now. Then, the model will be:

$$\tilde{R} = UWU^T R. \tag{4}$$

We can either use Equations 3 and 4 individually, or we can combine them (depending on how sparse our datasets are) to get

$$\tilde{R} = \alpha RIFI^T + (1-\alpha)UWU^T R, \tag{5}$$

where α denotes the strength of the user vs item side information.

In order to produce better quality results, apart from the side information, we can also incorporate a collaborative filtering component, which will take into account only the rating information. Different models can be used to include the rating information, but we will use the SLIM model [11] which estimates the rating that a user would give to an item as a sparse aggregation of the items rated by the user, described in Equation 1. Then by combining Equations 1 and 5, we get:

$$\tilde{R} = \gamma RS + \alpha RIFI^T + (1 - \alpha - \gamma)UWU^T R, \quad (6)$$

where γ is also a parameter.

For a more complete model, we can also include the linear side information. In [12], it was shown that the best method is a collective approach in which it is assumed that there exist correlations between users' copurchase behaviors on two items and the similarity of those items' side information. Thus, the weight matrix S that represents the weights on the ratings should also represent the weights on the features of the side info. In other words, S should satisfy $\tilde{R} = RS$, as well as $\tilde{I} = IS$.

Finally, in order to tie all the pieces together and in order to get the best possible results, since we took into account the cross-feature interactions, apart from the linear part, we can also take into account the higher-order rating information, apart from the linear part. Then, Equation 6 combined with Equation 2 becomes:

$$\tilde{R} = \gamma(RS + R'S') + \alpha RIFI^T + (1 - \alpha - \gamma)UWU^T R. \quad (7)$$

4. INTRA-SET DEPENDENCIES

Top-N recommender systems provide a list of N items, in which the user will be likely interested in. The items that are recommended are the ones that have the highest scores. However, this does not guarantee that the list as a whole is the best possible, even though the individual items are [2,9]. The reason is that the individual items could be very similar. For example, if the item with the highest score for a user is the book 'Alice in Wonderland' and there are two different versions of this book, a paperback and a hard one, then normally these two different versions have very high scores, so there is a high probability that they will end up both being recommended to the user, resulting in the user losing another meaningful recommendation.

This happens a lot, in many recommender systems. One example is music playlists, when the same artist's songs are recommended again and again, or even worse all the versions of the same song are played. Another example is groceries recommendation, when let's say a user is recommended both yellow and green bananas. Finally, another example is the advertisements in a commercial break, that are played in a row.

We propose to stop recommending every item in the list independently but instead follow a set-recommendation approach that will take into account the intra-set dependencies. In order to do this, we will use the side information of the items. For every item, we will find its k-nearest neighbors, in terms of side information features. Very similar items share a lot of the same intrinsic properties, that are encoded in side information. A very high similarity value threshold with the item in question will be imposed. If no neighbors exceeding this high threshold are found for an item, this is acceptable, as we would not like a system that probably eliminates items of importance to the user.

More analytically, top-N recommendation methods create an ordered list of all items for every user. This list is ordered according to how likely a user is to buy this item. The top-N items of this list are provided to the user. In our proposed method, for the first item in the top-N list, the k nearest neighbors of that item are removed from the set of potential candidate items recommended to the user. If the top-N list contained none of these neighbors, nothing changes. If the top-N list contained one or more of these neighbors, then the overall list of items is shifted one or more positions respectively, resulting in a different set of N items being on the top, thus having a new top-N list. The same procedure is done for the second, the third until the Nth item in the list. In the end, the top-N list provided to the user will provide only high-quality recommendations, without two or more items in the list being extremely similar.

The existing methods [18] try to tackle the above problem, in training time, having the users create collections. However, in the vast majority of systems, this is not the default user behavior. Users usually like or buy some items, without creating explicit collections. We believe that it is important in order to address the problem, not to modify user behavior. In order to do this, we will change the prediction part of the model, and not the learning part.

Other existing methods [1,2] focus on diversity or creating non-obvious recommendations. However, our primary goal is the recommendation quality, so we are totally fine if the recommendations made are not the most unexpected or diverse to a user. In the trade-off diversity vs accuracy, they choose diversity, by making sure that the accuracy does not fall down a prespecified threshold. However, we focus on accuracy. Also, by eliminating only items that it is really crucial to be removed, in order to avoid a repetitive list, we manage to present additional items, that might be of interest to a user, thus potentially even improving the accuracy. Also, in [1], the approach presented will be tried in the context of a massive open online course, but we will try it on a wide variety of datasets that may have different characteristics from an online course. For example, in an online course, there is the notion of prerequisites that will be taken into account, but in other datasets like groceries, this notion does not exist, so we should provide good-quality, diverse recommendations without the help of this notion.

5. CONCLUSION

In this work, we wish to evolve recommender systems to a stage in which the methods developed will not rely on over-simplifications, such as linearity and independence. These assumptions are commmonly made in the methods developed in recommender systems. Based on these assumptions, we can get recommendation results that are general and in some cases sufficient.

However, in a lot of real-world datasets, these assumptions do not hold, resulting in the methods relying on those to underperform. In order to improve the recommendation quality, we think that we should make full use of the different data we have available and learn the more complex relations that might characterize them. The ultimate goal is to develop more sophisticated and realistic models that will improve the recommendation quality.

Towards this direction, in this extended abstract, we suggest three different ways in which this can be achieved. First, we suggest taking into account the higher-order relations in users' rating data. The existing recommender systems compute pairwise associations. However, in real life, purchasing a subset of items in a set might significantly increase the likelihood of purchasing the rest (e.g. in a grocery store users tend to buy items that form the ingredients in recipes). Also, we suggest finding the cross-feature interactions, as many approaches for incorporating side information exploit only linear relations between the features. Finally, we propose developing set recommendation algorithms, that will take into account the intra-set dependencies. In this way, we will predict a set of items such that the overall quality of the set will not just be the sum of the quality values of its members.

6. ACKNOWLEDGMENT

This work was supported in part by NSF (IOS-0820730, IIS-0905220, OCI-1048018, CNS-1162405, and IIS-1247632) and the Digital Technology Center at the University of Minnesota. Access to research and computing facilities was provided by the Digital Technology Center and the Minnesota Supercomputing Institute.

7. REFERENCES

[1] Panagiotis Adamopoulos. Beyond rating prediction accuracy: on new perspectives in recommender systems. In *Proceedings of the 7th ACM conference on Recommender systems*, pages 459–462. ACM, 2013.

[2] Gediminas Adomavicius and YoungOk Kwon. Improving aggregate recommendation diversity using ranking-based techniques. *Knowledge and Data Engineering, IEEE Transactions on*, 24(5):896–911, 2012.

[3] Gediminas Adomavicius and Alexander Tuzhilin. Toward the next generation of recommender systems: A survey of the state-of-the-art and possible extensions. *Knowledge and Data Engineering, IEEE Transactions on*, 17(6):734–749, 2005.

[4] Deepak Agarwal and Bee-Chung Chen. Regression-based latent factor models. In *Proceedings of the 15th ACM SIGKDD international conference on Knowledge discovery and data mining*, pages 19–28. ACM, 2009.

[5] Fabio Aiolli. A preliminary study on a recommender system for the million songs dataset challenge. *PREFERENCE LEARNING: PROBLEMS AND APPLICATIONS IN AI*, page 1, 2012.

[6] Evangelia Christakopoulou and George Karypis. Hoslim: Higher-order sparse linear method for top-n recommender systems. In *Advances in Knowledge Discovery and Data Mining*, pages 38–49. Springer, 2014.

[7] Paolo Cremonesi, Yehuda Koren, and Roberto Turrin. Performance of recommender algorithms on top-n recommendation tasks. In *Proceedings of the fourth ACM conference on Recommender systems*, pages 39–46. ACM, 2010.

[8] Mukund Deshpande and George Karypis. Item-based top-n recommendation algorithms. *ACM Transactions on Information Systems (TOIS)*, 22(1):143–177, 2004.

[9] Derek L Hansen and Jennifer Golbeck. Mixing it up: recommending collections of items. In *Proceedings of the SIGCHI Conference on Human Factors in Computing Systems*, pages 1217–1226. ACM, 2009.

[10] Yifan Hu, Yehuda Koren, and Chris Volinsky. Collaborative filtering for implicit feedback datasets. In *Data Mining, 2008. ICDM'08. Eighth IEEE International Conference on*, pages 263–272. IEEE, 2008.

[11] Xia Ning and George Karypis. Slim: Sparse linear methods for top-n recommender systems. In *Data Mining (ICDM), 2011 IEEE 11th International Conference on*, pages 497–506. IEEE, 2011.

[12] Xia Ning and George Karypis. Sparse linear methods with side information for top-n recommendations. In *Proceedings of the sixth ACM conference on Recommender systems*, pages 155–162. ACM, 2012.

[13] Rong Pan, Yunhong Zhou, Bin Cao, Nathan Nan Liu, Rajan Lukose, Martin Scholz, and Qiang Yang. One-class collaborative filtering. In *Data Mining, 2008. ICDM'08. Eighth IEEE International Conference on*, pages 502–511. IEEE, 2008.

[14] Steffen Rendle, Christoph Freudenthaler, Zeno Gantner, and Lars Schmidt-Thieme. Bpr: Bayesian personalized ranking from implicit feedback. In *Proceedings of the Twenty-Fifth Conference on Uncertainty in Artificial Intelligence*, pages 452–461. AUAI Press, 2009.

[15] Steffen Rendle and Lars Schmidt-Thieme. Online-updating regularized kernel matrix factorization models for large-scale recommender systems. In *Proceedings of the 2008 ACM conference on Recommender systems*, pages 251–258. ACM, 2008.

[16] Ruslan Salakhutdinov, Andriy Mnih, and Geoffrey Hinton. Restricted boltzmann machines for collaborative filtering. In *Proceedings of the 24th international conference on Machine learning*, pages 791–798. ACM, 2007.

[17] Ajit P Singh and Geoffrey J Gordon. Relational learning via collective matrix factorization. In *Proceedings of the 14th ACM SIGKDD international conference on Knowledge discovery and data mining*, pages 650–658. ACM, 2008.

[18] Greg Walsh and Jennifer Golbeck. Curator: a game with a purpose for collection recommendation. In *Proceedings of the SIGCHI Conference on Human Factors in Computing Systems*, pages 2079–2082. ACM, 2010.

[19] Shuang-Hong Yang, Bo Long, Alex Smola, Narayanan Sadagopan, Zhaohui Zheng, and Hongyuan Zha. Like like alike: joint friendship and interest propagation in social networks. In *Proceedings of the 20th international conference on World wide web*, pages 537–546. ACM, 2011.

Enhancing Personalization and Learner Engagement through Context-aware Recommendation in TEL

Betty Mayeku
University of Goettingen
Institute of Computer Science
Goldschmidtstr. 7, 37077, Goettingen Germany
betty.mayeku@informatik.uni-goettingen.de

ABSTRACT

Providing a personalized learning experience that caters for individual learner's needs within the learner's context of use is crucial in achieving effective learning in a technology enhanced learning (TEL) environment. However, achieving personalization amidst diverse and rich environment within which learning takes place still remains a major challenge. Though adaption has been proposed to provide learners with learning experiences that are tailored to their particular educational needs, however, one of its limitation is user involvement. Absolute machine control is not always desirable considering the intellectual presence of human-beings. Furthermore learner engagement is one of crucial elements for realizing effective learning. Therefore, this study aims at exploring how context-awareness can support a personalized and engaged learning experience. The study in particular proposes the use of context-aware recommendation mechanism and the consideration of learner's preference to learning as approaches for achieving personalization and learner engagement.

Categories and Subject Descriptors

K.3 [**Computers and education**]: Miscellaneous; H.4 [**Information systems applications**]: Miscellaneous; H.3.4 [**Systems and Software**]: Current awareness systems - *context-aware systems, Recommender systems*

Keywords

Context; Personalization; Context-aware recommender; Adaptation; TEL; Learner preference; Learner engagement

1. INTRODUCTION

Context plays an important role not only in learning but also in the design of effective and efficient technology enhanced learning (TEL) systems. Learning always occurs in context [7]. It is impossible as [7] further notes, to separate the learner, the material to be learned and the context in which learning occurs. In addition, learner needs differ from learner to learner due to individual differences. As a result, context in which learning occurs may vary from learner to learner due these individual differences. Therefore, it is the authors' belief that providing learning experience that caters for individual learner's needs within the learner's context of use is crucial in achieving effective learning in a TEL environment. However, with learning taking place in extremely diverse and rich environments especially with the current integration of mobile and pervasive & ubiquitous technologies in TEL, how to offer personalized learning experience that caters for individual learner's needs from a potentially overwhelming variety of choices can be a daunting task.

RecSys'14, October 6–10, 2014, Foster City, Silicon Valley, CA, USA.
Copyright 2014 ACM 978-1-4503-2668-1/14/10…$15.00.
http://dx.doi.org/10.1145/2645710.2653362

2. PERSONALIZATION & LEARNER ENGAGEMENT

The notion of adaption has widely been proposed as an approach that can provide learners with learning experiences that are tailored to their particular educational needs and personal characteristics [4]. Though this notion aims at enhancing the end-user experience by enabling entities in the user's environment to intelligently adapt to the active situation without any end-user involvement [6], however, on the other hand, absolute machine control as manifested by the mainstream pervasive computing is not always desirable. This is not only because of the fact that software intelligence remains insufficient to enumerate and address all eventualities as [6] argues, but most importantly because of the intellectual presence of human-beings. The conceptual body of literature suggests that user engagement is one of crucial elements for realizing successful systems. For this purpose, learner situation awareness, self-expressiveness and involvement hold a crucial role in TEL systems. TEL should not only generate good learning outcomes, but also better engage learners in the learning process. From engaged learning perspective, truly engaged learners are behaviorally, intellectually, and emotionally involved in their learning tasks [5]. Therefore there is need for an efficient approach to employ technology without compromising learner intelligence but ensuring learner engagement. In this study, we argue that, a) giving the learner freedom to choose rather than automatic decision making for the learner and b) the focus being on the learner as the core entity may contribute greatly in providing a personalized and engaged learning experience. In order to achieve this, the authors propose among other approaches, the use of context-aware recommendation approach and the consideration of learner's preference to learning.

2.1 Why learner preference?

The preference of each user is different according to user context and profile. Therefore reflecting on learning preferences is an important key for reaching diverse individual learner needs and providing personalized services. Preference not only allow the learners to choose what accommodates their multiple needs depending on places and spaces across time or their present learning situation, but also better engage them in the learning process.

2.2 Why context-aware recommender?

Apart from facilitating the identification and retrieval of suitable resources from a potentially overwhelming variety of choices, recommender systems in TEL offer a promising approach that gives the user (learner) the power to decide based on their preference. This does not only enhance learner involvement in the learning process but offer a platform for personalized learning.

In the TEL domain, a number of recommender systems have been introduced. A survey of recommender systems in TEL by [2] indicates that most of these systems suggest learning resources. Other systems that have been introduced include course recommenders and systems that suggest people who can help with a learning activity. However, according to the authors' knowledge, so far, recommendation of learning activities is an area that has not yet been explored. Hence the focus of this study.

Another aspect worth noting are the particularities of TEL for recommendation. This area as [8] points out, offers some specific characteristics that are not met by today's general purpose recommendation approaches. For example, the information retrieval goals that TEL recommenders try to achieve are often different to the ones identified in other systems [2]. Others include usage data availability, heterogeneity in learner needs [8] and pedagogical issues [2] among others. Therefore, in order to make recommendation tailored to individual learner needs, hence personalize the learning experience, there is need as [8] notes, to take the context of the learner into account in a much more specific way than applied in today's recommendation approaches. Relevant contextual information does matter and as [1] notes, it is important to take this information into account when providing recommendations. This study attempts to employ context-aware recommendation approach towards achieving personalization within a sound pedagogical framework.

3. PRINCIPAL CONTRIBUTIONS

The main contributions of the study will be:

a) To formulate a framework as a platform for integrating pedagogy and technology in context aware learning environment

b) To explore how learning preference as context in which learning occurs can personalize learning experience

c) To explore how personalization can be enhanced through context-aware recommendation process.

d) To implement a context-aware recommender system within the formulated pedagogical framework in (a)

4. METHODOLOGY

So far, (a) and (b) have been covered to some extent in the study. (An overview of the contribution is presented in Fig 1. Refer to [3] for detailed explanation). Fig. 1 illustrates how learning preference can be integrated into the [3] formulated pedagogical framework at the contextual level under the learner context. The framework provides possibility to consider a wide variety of context. The context-aware adaptation & personalization layer acts as the mediator between the context and learning activities. At the moment the authors are in the process of implementing the context-aware recommender system within the proposed framework. A draft overview of the system architecture is presented in Fig.2. The context-aware adaptive and personalization engine of the system comprises of two major components namely; (a) Activity recommender component that recommends a learning activity based on the learner's contextual information and (b) a grouping component for collaborative activities. The grouping component should be able to recommend collaborative partners based on learner's preference as context.

One of the advantages of using the formulated framework is that it can allow one to focus on either one aspect of contextual information (like learner's sociological preference etc) or several contextual information and dimensions (e.g device, connectivity, location, preference e.t.c) all together. This attribute makes this framework to be an ideal framework within which a TEL context-aware recommendation system can be implemented. Furthermore this attribute enables the authors to carefully implement one contextual aspect at a time. At the moment, the authors' are focusing on sociological preference (Fig.1). This will enable the incorporation of collaborative activities as well as apply peer to peer teaching/learning approach. An approach that is employed in the study to enhance learner engagement. Another advantage of the framework is that it can be easily integrated in an existing learning management system (LMS). The system to be developed in this study is intended to be integrated in Canvas Instructure LMS for testing. An approach that makes this study unique from other studies in this area.

In the recommendation process, one of the approach the study has adapted for offering recommendation is contextual preference elicitation and estimation approach. Implicit methods are used to capture contextual information from computing and physical context categories while the learner contextual information especially preferences is inferred by analyzing the learner's interactions with the system.

The system is intended to be tested for 'learning Germany (for beginners)' as the subject domain to enable the authors to fully utilize the environmental awareness (environmental context). In brief, this is how the system is intended to work: Based on the contextual information of the learner for example location, social preference e.t.c, appropriately designed learning activity (s) is/are recommended to the learner; based on the learner's choice, appropriate collaborative partners are recommended for the collaborative activity; then predicting learning pattern in relation to previous learner behavior and contextual information, appropriate learning activities and collaborative partners are further recommended.

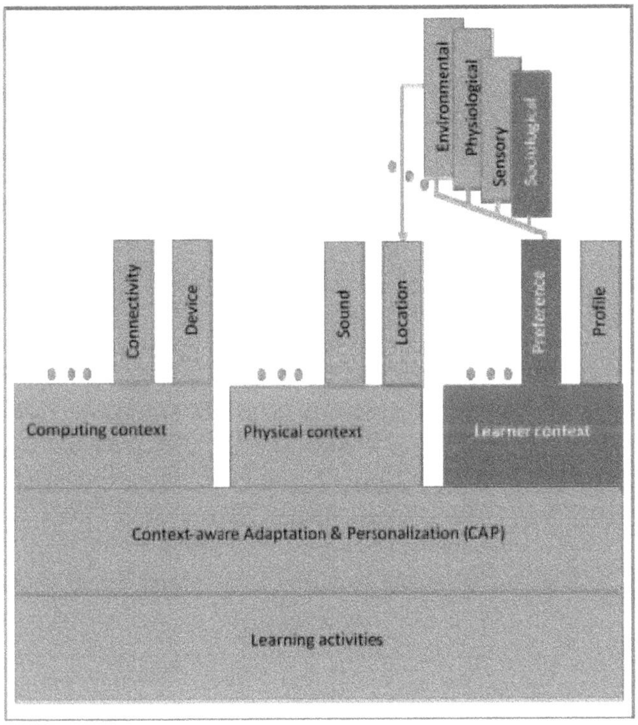

Fig 1: Learning preference as context within [3] Framework

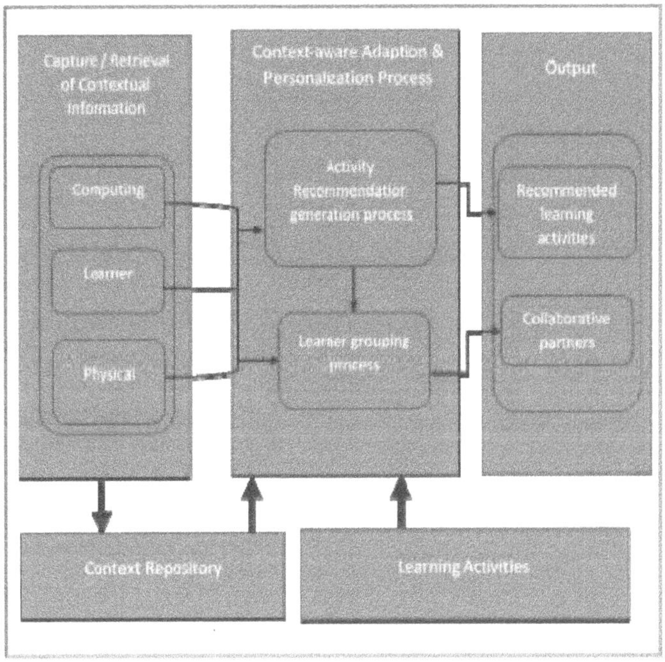

Fig.2. System Architecture

5. CONCLUSION

Context in which learning occurs vary from learner to leaner due to individual differences. Therefore, providing learning experiences that are tailored to learner's individual needs within the learner's context of use, as well as involving learners in the learning process may contribute greatly in achieving effective learning in a TEL environment. Therefore this study aims at how context-awareness can explored to support a personalized and engaged learning experience amidst diverse and rich environment within which learning takes place. The study proposes the use of recommendation approaches for achieving personalization and learner engagement.

6. ACKNOWLEDGMENTS

The author would like to acknowledge the input and guidance provided by Dieter Hogrefe, Ulrike Lucke, Eckart Modrow and Kerstin Strecker toward the undertaking of the research work summarized here. The author also thanks the German Academic Exchange Service (DAAD) & the Kenya National Council for Science and Technology (NCST) for the financial support that has made it possible to undertake this study.

7. REFERENCES

[1] Adomavicius, G., & Tuzhilin, A. 2011. Context-Aware Recommender Systems. In F. R. Ricci, *Recommender Systems Handbook* (pp. pp 217-253). Online: Springer US.

[2] Manouselis, N., Drachsler, H., Vuorikari, R., & Hummel, H. 2011. Recommender Systems in Technology Enhanced Learning. In L. R. Francesco Ricci, *Recommender Systems Handbook* (pp. pp 387-415). Online: Springer US.

[3] Mayeku, B., & Hogrefe, D. 2013. Toward a Conceptual Framework for Integrating Pedagogy and Technology in a Pervasive DL Environment. *E-Learn.* Las Vegas.

[4] Sampson, D. G., & Zervas, P. 2013. Context Aware Adaptive and Personalized Mobile Learning. *3rd International Conference for E-Learning and Distance Education.* Riyadh.

[5] Shen, L., Wang, M., & Shen, R. 2009. Affective e-Learning: Using "Emotional" Data to Improve Learning in Pervasive. *International Forum of Educational Technology & Society (IFETS).*, 12 (2), 176–189.

[6] Soylu, A. 2012. Exploiting Metadata, Ontologies and Semantics to Design/Enhance New End-User Experiences for Adaptive Pervasive Computing Environments. Leuven: Katholieke Universiteit Leuven.

[7] Uden, L. 2007. Activity theory for Designing Mobile Learning. *International Journal of Mobile Learning and Organization.*, Vol. 1 No.1.

[8] Verbert, K., Manouselis, N., Ochoa, X., Wolpers, M., Hendrik Drachsler, I. B., & Duval, E. 2012. Context-aware Recommender Systems for Learning: a Survey and Future Challenges. *Journal of Latex Class Files.*

Improving Recommender Systems: User Roles and Lifecycles

Tien T. Nguyen
GroupLens Research
Computer Science and Engineering - University of Minnesota
tien@cs.umn.edu

ABSTRACT

In the era of big data, it is usually agreed that the more data we have, the better results we can get. However, for some domains that heavily depend on user inputs (such as recommender systems), the performance evaluation metrics are sensitive to the amount of noise introduced by users. Such noise can be from users who only wanted to explore the systems, and thus did not spend efforts to provide accurate inputs. Noise can also be introduced by the methods of collecting user ratings. In my dissertation, I study how user data can affect prediction accuracies and performances of recommendation algorithms. To that end, I investigate how the data collection methods and the life cycles of users affect the prediction accuracies and the performance of recommendation algorithms.

Categories and Subject Descriptors

H.1 [**Information Systems**]: Personalization, Recommender systems; H.1 [**Human-centered computing**]: Collaborative filtering

Keywords

recommender system; noise; recommendation accuracy

1. INTRODUCTION & MOTIVATION

For recommender systems, especially those that use collaborative filtering algorithms, having sufficient data to build recommendation models is crucial. However, research has shown that noise exists in user ratings as evidenced by the inconsistencies observed when users rerated items [11]. Hence, more data may lead to more noise.

Noise in user rating data can be classified as **natural noise** and **malicious noise** [19]. Natural noise is noise generated by the methods recommender systems use to collect data about user preference. Malicious noise is noise deliberately injected into recommender systems for certain purposes.

RecSys'14, October 6–10, 2014, Foster City, Silicon Valley, CA, USA.
ACM 978-1-4503-2668-1/14/10ÂĔ15.00.
*http://dx.doi.org/*10.1145/2566486.2568012.

To address natural noise in user rating, and thus to improve recommendation accuracies, researchers have proposed several frameworks to minimize the effect of natural noise on recommendation accuracies. Amatriain et al. [2, 3] proposed methods to quantify the noise in user ratings, and algorithms to reduce natural noise via user re-ratings. My previous work [18] suggested that we could improve the rating interfaces to reduce the noise introduced by users.

On the other hand, several researchers have investigated the effects of malicious data (thus malicious noise) on recommender algorithms, and how recommender systems can deal with malicious data. Lam et al. [15] found that certain recommendation algorithms (such as item-item) were less affected by malicious data than others (such as user-user). Chirita et al. [5] proposed algorithms to detect and remove malicious data generated by malicious users, maintaining recommendation quality.

In my dissertation, I examine how to improve recommendation accuracies from a different angle. First, I look at methods to collect rating data, and the effects of those methods on recommendation quality. Second, I look at the life cycles of users, and their effects on the recommendation quality. Thus, I seek to answer these following research questions:

1. How can we modify rating interfaces to reduce natural noise from user ratings?
2. Do we lose any information when we use the rating data of committed users in lieu of rating data of all users?
3. Are the recommendation accuracies reduced when using only rating data produced by committed users?

2. RELATED WORK

Noise exists in user ratings and causes *magic barrier* [10], the minimum of prediction errors recommendation algorithms can obtain. To address the noise, researchers proposed approaches in user interface design, data analyses, and algorithms to detect and reduce noise [13, 18, 3, 19].

From the user interface perspectives, researchers looked into the literature for the process of preference construction and elicitation. They found that external factors such as anchoring effects and manipulated predictions had a strong influence on user preferences [1, 6]. They also found that users found it difficult and demanding to convert their preferences to the provided rating scales. This difficulty results in noise in user ratings [19].

From the data analytic and algorithmic approaches, researchers proposed several frameworks to estimate and minimize the amount of natural noise appeared in user ratings. Nguyen et al. [18] proposed a framework to estimate the upper limit of the amount of the true rating noise in a given set of ratings. They suggested that the upper limit was the conditional entropy between two sets of ratings and re-ratings. O'Mahony et al. [19] proposed that we could estimate the amount of the natural noise in user ratings by computing the probability distributions of the consistency between the actual and predicted ratings. This consistency, in turn, was the normalized Mean Absolute Error between the actual and predicted ratings. Said et al. [21] proposed a framework based on the empirical risk minimization principle in statistical learning to estimate the magic barrier, the optimal RMSE a recommendation algorithm can achieve.

Researchers also investigated the effect of deliberately injected malicious noise. O'Mahony et al. [19] proposed a framework based on signal detection theory to detect users who purposely introduced malicious noise into recommender systems. Lam et al. [15], when studying different ways to inject malicious data, found that the item-item algorithm was more resistant to shilling attacks than the user-user algorithm.

Although researchers also investigated the effect of recommender systems on users such as [17, 20, 8, 9], there is less research on understanding the life-cycles of users in recommender systems, and their effects on prediction accuracies. Hence, in this this thesis, I investigate the effects of rating collecting methods, and the user life cycles on the prediction accuracies in recommender systems.

In the next section, I briefly discuss what I have done. I describe my on going research and future directions about the effect of user life-cycles on prediction accuracies.

3. RATING SUPPORT INTERFACE

To answer the first research question, in the rating support interface project [18], I looked at how the methods of collecting user ratings affected the prediction accuracies. To that end, I developed three novel rating support interfaces: a tag interface, an exemplar interface, a tag + exemplar interface.

The tag interface provided users a personalized form of memory support, helping users remember what the movies being rated are about. The exemplar interface provided an anchoring support (rating support) by showing an exemplar: the most similar movie (to the movie being rated) a user previously rated at the hovered rating star. The tag + exemplar interface provided both memory support and rating support by combining the features of the above two interfaces. With this interface, users recalled not only what movies were about, but also what movies they previously rated at a particular rating.

I ran a between-subject experiment from March 21st 2013 until April 25th 2013 with a baseline as a rating interface without any support. 38,586 ratings from 386 users were collected for the analyses. I found that the exemplar interface helped users rate more consistently. Moreover, the exemplar interface achieved the lowest magic barrier, and lowest actual RMSEs. It also had the lowest upper limit of rating noise. From the qualitative analyses (via survey questions), I found that users liked all the rating interfaces that provided the rating support (as in the exemplar interface), since the users perceived these interfaces were more useful than the baseline interface.

4. COMMITTED USERS IN RECOMMENDER SYSTEMS: A SAFE HAVEN

After investigating how I could enhance rating interfaces to reduce the noise in the collected data, I have analyzed the effect of user life-cycles on the prediction accuracies. I observe that there are two types of users: committed users and uncommitted users. The committed users are those who plan to use recommender systems in a long term, and for their own benefits. Thus, their ratings are more stable and valuable than those of the uncommitted users, who perhaps want to just explore the systems. Thus, I pose a research question whether we can use only the rating data provided by committed users as representative data of the population when building prediction model. To help readers follow my proposal, I call the rating data provided by the committed users 'partial data'.

For this study, I analyze 57,339 MovieLens users collected from 2007-12-19 to 2013-11-20[1]. All these users had their first MovieLens visit in the said period.

Before I define committed users and uncommitted users, I first define an activity session as *a sequence of activities made by a user where the time difference of any two continuous activities is less than or equal to one hour* [2].

I compute the survival probability distribution, a well-known technique in survival analyses [12], as a proxy to determine how committed users were. The survival probability at the nth session is defined as the probability that users continue using the system after the nth session. Mathematically, if P_n is the survival probability at the nth session, and C_n is the number of users who survive at the nth session, then:

$$P_n = \frac{C_n}{C_{n-1}} P_{n-1}$$

Figure 1 shows the survival probability until the 70th activity sessions. I observe that the survival probability drops significantly in the first 10th sessions, and asymptotically approaches a stable straight line afterward. I classify users who had at least 10 sessions committed users, and users who did not uncommitted users. Table 1 shows that approximately only 10% of users who registered with MovieLens committed at least 10 sessions. These committed users rated 20,221 distinct movies (30.1% higher than that of the uncommitted users). However, the committed users only provide 1,754,516 ratings (approximately 31% less than that of the uncommitted users).

I examine the trade-offs and benefits when using only rating data of the committed users (partial data) to feed into recommendation algorithms. In the next section, I describe my analyses to answer the second and the third research questions mentioned in the introduction. Note that in this study, I only evaluate the prediction accuracies for these 5,748 committed users.

[1]I remove users who are our lab-mates and those whom MovieLens recruited for testing purposes.

[2]I discuss why I choose one hour cut-off in an up-coming paper due to the limited space I have here.

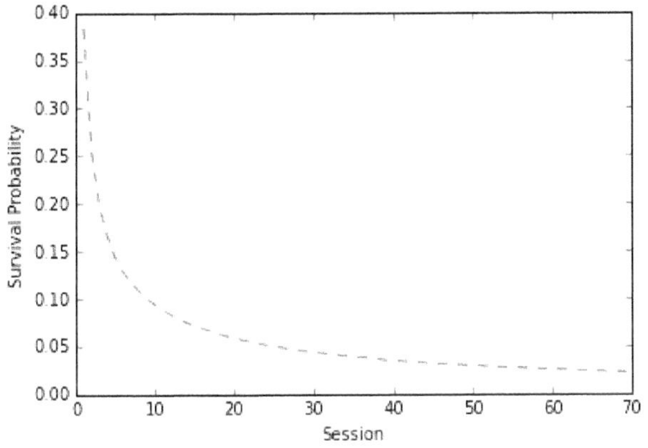

Figure 1: The survival probability.

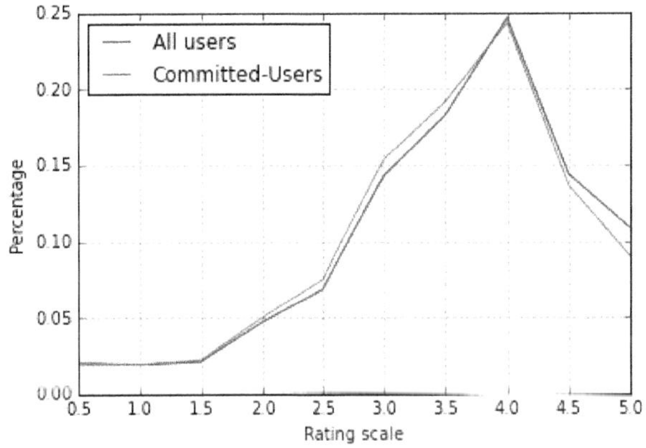

Figure 2: The rating distributions of two datasets.

	At most 9 sessions	At least 10 sessions
# Users	51,591	5,748
# Movies	15,499	20,221
# Movies	2,531,243	1,754,516

Table 1: The number of distinct users, distinct rated movies and the number ratings of two groups of users who committed at most 9 sessions (uncommitted users) and who committed at least 10 sessions (committed users).

4.1 Estimating information lost using Kullback - Leibler divergence

In the section 3, I discussed the results for the first research question. In this section, I discuss my approach to address the second research question. First, I compute the Kullback-Leibler (KL) divergence. The KL divergence, denoted as $D_{KL}(P||Q)$, measures how much information is lost when using the Q to approximate P [14]. The amount of information lost can be translated as the similarity of the two distributions. Mathematically, we can express the Kullback-Leibler divergence as:

$$D_{KL}(P||Q) = \sum_i log(\frac{P(i)}{Q(i)}) \times P(i) \quad (1)$$

where P and Q are two probability distributions.

The KL divergence is widely used to measure the similarity of any two distributions of data on various domains such as in detecting topics [16], building a user recommendation framework in social tagging system [22], and (most relevant to my research) predicting recommender system performances [4].

In this study, I am interested in how much information is lost when I use the rating distribution of the committed users as an approximation of the rating distribution of all users (as shown in figure 2). Let P be the rating distribution of all users, and Q be the rating distribution of the committed users. I measure the Kullback-Leibler divergence of Q from P. Based on formula 1, I compute the KL divergence, $D_{KL}(P||Q)$, is about 0.008 bit. This 0.008 bit suggests that if I use the rating distribution of the committed users to approximate the rating distribution of all users, it is required to use extra 0.008 bit to encode the distribution due to the loss of information. However, Kluver et al. [13] suggested that there was approximately 1.7 bits per rating for a 10 rating-scale. Thus 0.008 is about 0.47% of bits per rating for a 10 rating scale.

With this small amount of percentage, I conclude that the amount of information lost when I use only the data of the committed users as representative data for the rating distribution of all users is not significant.

4.2 Evaluating recommendation accuracies

In this section, I discuss my third research question: how the performances of recommendation algorithms are on the different data sets.

To evaluate the performances, I use lenskit [7] to compute the RMSE and nDCG per user for 5,747 [3] users who committed at least 10 sessions. I keep most of the default configurations of lenskit, except the RMSE and nDCG configurations. I compute per-user RMSE and nDCG instead of the aggregated RMSE and nDCG. I focus only on the following three algorithms: ItemItem, SVD, and PersMean.

Algorithms\Dataset	All data	Partial data
ItemItem	0.69 (0.18)	0.67 (0.17)
SVD	0.65 (0.17)	0.67 (0.18)
PersMean	0.78 (0.23)	0.78 (0.23)

Table 2: The average RMSE per user for each algorithm when running different datasets. In the brackets are the standard deviation (std).

Tables 2 and 3 show the average RMSE, and average nDCG per user when I evaluate the performances of the three algorithms on the two data sets. I observe that there is no significant difference in the performances of the three algorithms (in both RMSE and nDCG measures). Furthermore, as shown in table 4, I observe that the running times for both testing and building of all the algorithms when using partial data are faster than when using all data [4].

[3]One user is removed from this analysis because he did not rate more than 15 movies, the minimum number of ratings required for the cold start process.

[4]At this moment, I am not able to report the consumed memory since Lenskit does not generate a report for this metric.

Algorithms\Dataset	All data	Partial data
ItemItem	0.98 (0.02)	0.97 (0.02)
SVD	0.98 (0.01)	0.98 (0.02)
PersMean	0.97 (0.02)	0.97 (0.02)

Table 3: The median nDCG per user for each algorithm when running different data sets. In the brackets are the standard deviation (std).

Algorithms	Building Time	Testing Time
All data & ItemItem	922.29	58.13
All data & SVD	349.19	9.32
All data & PersMean	6.50	10.72
Partial data & ItemItem	493.48	56.41
Partial data & SVD	109.00	8.60
Partial data & PersMean	3.30	10.89

Table 4: Building time and testing time (in second) reported by Lenskit when running with all data and the committed users' (partial data).

5. DISCUSSION, AND FUTURE WORK

I set out to better understand the effect of rating interfaces and the roles of user life-cycles on prediction accuracies. I find that enhancing a rating interface with rating support helps to reduce the noise in user ratings, and improve the prediction accuracies. I also find that the recommendation algorithms produce the same prediction quality with partial data as with all data. I also observe that using the rating distribution of the committed users to approximate the rating distribution of all users does not lead to significant loss of information.

These findings suggest that we can use a substantially less data to achieve the same accuracy as when we use all available data, and that we can improve the rating interfaces to improve the quality of the rating data. Furthermore, our findings have an implication for practical uses. With the substantially less data, the algorithms can run faster, and consume less memory.

My work is not without limitations. First, due to the space limitation, I am only able to report the results on the subset of users of interests. In the future work, I plan to randomly select users, regardless of how committed they are [5], and evaluate the accuracy of the recommendation algorithms on these randomly selected users. Second, I have not explored the maximum amount of data I can ignore while keeping an adequate level of prediction accuracies. To discover this threshold, more data analyses must be done.

6. ACKNOWLEDGEMENT

I thank my advisor, Professor Joseph A. Konstan, for his advice and guidances.

[5]However, they must provide a sufficient ratings to pass the cold-start problem

7. REFERENCES

[1] G. Adomavicius, J. Bockstedt, S. Curley, and J. Zhang. Recommender systems, consumer preferences, and anchoring effects. In *RecSys 2011 Workshop on Human Decision Making in Recommender Systems*, pages 35–42, 2011.

[2] X. Amatriain, J. M. Pujol, and N. Oliver. I like it... i like it not: Evaluating user ratings noise in recommender systems. In *UMAP 2009*, pages 247–258.

[3] X. Amatriain, J. M. Pujol, N. Tintarev, and N. Oliver. Rate it again: increasing recommendation accuracy by user re-rating. In *Proc RecSys 2009*, pages 173–180.

[4] A. Bellogín. Predicting performance in recommender systems. In *Proc. RecSys 2011*, pages 371–374.

[5] P.-A. Chirita, W. Nejdl, and C. Zamfir. Preventing shilling attacks in online recommender systems. In *Proc. WIDM 2005*, pages 67–74.

[6] D. Cosley, S. K. Lam, I. Albert, J. A. Konstan, and J. Riedl. Is seeing believing?: how recommender system interfaces affect users' opinions. In *Proc. CHI 2003*, pages 585–592, 2003.

[7] M. D. Ekstrand, M. Ludwig, J. A. Konstan, and J. T. Riedl. Rethinking the recommender research ecosystem: reproducibility, openness, and lenskit. In *Proc. RecSys 2011*, pages 133–140.

[8] D. Fleder and K. Hosanagar. Blockbuster culture's next rise or fall: The impact of recommender systems on sales diversity. *Management science*, 55(5).

[9] D. Fleder, K. Hosanagar, and A. Buja. Will the global village fracture into tribes: Recommender systems and their effects on consumers. *Avai. at SSRN 1321962.*

[10] J. L. Herlocker, J. A. Konstan, L. G. Terveen, and J. T. Riedl. Evaluating collaborative filtering recommender systems. *ACM TOIS 2004.*

[11] W. Hill, L. Stead, M. Rosenstein, and G. Furnas. Recommending and evaluating choices in a virtual community of use. In *Proc. CHI 1995*, pages 194–201.

[12] D. W. Hosmer Jr, S. Lemeshow, and S. May. *Applied survival analysis: regression modeling of time to event data*, volume 618. John Wiley & Sons, 2011.

[13] D. Kluver, T. T. Nguyen, M. Ekstrand, S. Sen, and J. Riedl. How many bits per rating? In *RecSys 2012.*

[14] S. Kullback and R. A. Leibler. On information and sufficiency. *The Annals of Mathematical Statistics*, pages 79–86, 1951.

[15] S. K. Lam and J. Riedl. Shilling recommender systems for fun and profit. In *Proc. WWW 2004*, pages 393–402, 2004.

[16] V. Lavrenko, J. Allan, E. DeGuzman, D. LaFlamme, V. Pollard, and S. Thomas. Relevance models for topic detection and tracking. In *Proc. HLT 2002.*

[17] T. T. Nguyen, P.-M. Hui, F. M. Harper, L. Terveen, and J. A. Konstan. Exploring the filter bubble: the effect of using recommender systems on content diversity. In *Proc. WWW 2014*, pages 677–686, 2014.

[18] T. T. Nguyen, D. Kluver, T.-Y. Wang, P.-M. Hui, M. D. Ekstrand, M. C. Willemsen, and J. Riedl. Rating support interfaces to improve user experience and recommender accuracy. In *Proc. RecSys 2013*, pages 149–156, 2013.

[19] M. P. O'Mahony, N. J. Hurley, and G. Silvestre. Detecting noise in recommender system databases. In *Proc IUI 2006*, pages 109–115.

[20] E. Pariser. *The filter bubble: What the Internet is hiding from you.* Penguin UK, 2011.

[21] A. Said, B. J. Jain, S. Narr, and T. Plumbaum. Users and noise: The magic barrier of recommender systems. In *UMAP 2012*, pages 237–248.

[22] T. C. Zhou, H. Ma, M. R. Lyu, and I. King. Userrec: A user recommendation framework in social tagging systems.

Modeling the Effect of People's Preferences and Social Forces on Adopting and Sharing Items

Amit Sharma
Dept. of Computer Science
Cornell University, Ithaca, NY USA
asharma@cs.cornell.edu

ABSTRACT

Recommender systems within social networks face three distinct challenges: suggesting what to consume/adopt, what to share and who to share it with. For all three cases, my and others' research work shows that people's decisions to adopt and share depend not only on their preferences for items, but also on social forces such as influence, conformity and identity management. Modeling the combined effects of people's preferences and social forces can lead to socially-aware recommender algorithms and interfaces as well more accurate models of information diffusion.

I take a bottom-up approach to understanding how items are shared or adopted in a social network. First, I conduct behavioral experiments that give insights about, and allow to model the processes by which people decide to share or adopt items. Second, I use data from multiple social networking websites to validate and extend these models and develop tractable algorithms to predict people's decisions on items.

This paper presents preliminary models for adoption and sharing along with future directions towards more accurate models. Results of my current work indicate that people consider their own preferences for items more than the recipients' when sharing and share only highly liked items. When adopting, people's preferences towards items matter, but so do annotations that accompany recommendations based on social influences; I show how their relative effects can be modeled as a mixture distribution.

Categories and Subject Descriptors: H.1.2 [Models and Principles]: User/machine systems—*Human Factors*; H.3.3[Information Storage and Retrieval]: Information Search and Retrieval—*Information filtering*

Keywords: Social networks; Information diffusion; User preferences

1. INTRODUCTION

People curate online social networks to discover, consume and share items such as URLs (Twitter), music (Last.fm), movies (Flixster), books (Goodreads) pictures (Flickr), products (Etsy) and even code (Github). Many of these websites have millions of users and typically use recommender systems to help users sift through vast amounts of content.

However, while recommender models have been proposed that account for homophily within social networks [17, 9], how social forces such as influence, conformity or management of interpersonal relationships affect adoption and sharing in these networks is less understood. Studying the factors that affect people's decision to adopt or share items can lead to recommendation algorithms and interfaces that better support user goals, for example, suggesting who to share an item with, or displaying effective social annotations for an item that helps users in evaluating it.

Further, understanding the combined effect of people's preferences and social forces on their decisions would also lead to more accurate models of information diffusion within social networks. Buoyed by the abundance of data due to online networks, recent years have seen studies of diffusion which track topics, analyze the underlying network structure, or study the spread of items in social networks such as Twitter, Digg, Flickr and Flixster. The models that explain how these items are adopted and shared, however, are inspired from other settings such as the spread of diseases, interaction of particles [5], or the copying of behavior within a mob [6], and are inadequate to explain the observed adoption behavior in social media [4].

Current models are inadequate, in large part, because they fail to recognize that adopting and sharing items are two distinct, deliberate, socially-embedded actions that also depend on people's preferences for items. Unlike diseased individuals or mob actors, people in an online social network can voluntarily decide what activities or items to share and to whom. For instance, what gets shared to whom depends on factors such as a sharer's propensity to share, relations between the sharer and the recipient including tie strength, and people's motivations for sharing such as the need to express oneself, provide information, demonstrate expertise or help others [14]. System interfaces also matter; my past research has shown how Liking a movie on Facebook, an activity that gets shared automatically has a different connotation and usage among people than private actions such as rating a movie [11]. As another example showing the distinction between adoption and sharing, a recent study of web traffic[1] found little correlation between number of shares for a URL and whether people saw its contents fully.

RecSys'14, October 6–10, 2014, Foster City, Silicon Valley, CA, USA.

http://dx.doi.org/10.1145/2645710.2653364.

[1]http://blog.chartbeat.com/2013/10/28/understanding-traffic-sources-part-3-social-traffic/ [Accessed May 2014]

These observations suggest a new perspective for designing recommender systems and modeling diffusion in social networks, which takes into account people's preferences and social forces around sharing and adopting items. A key challenge in this work is to model the processes by which people make decisions for sharing and adoption. While observed activities like liking and sharing expose the *results* of people's decisions, they conceal the *processes* by which people arrive at their decision for an item.

To better understand these processes, I will employ a multi-method approach. I will use behavioral experiments to develop a qualitative understanding and build individual-level *process models* of how people think about, adopt and share items. In addition, I plan to analyze large-scale data from online social networks to validate and extend the above models, compare them across domains and simulate item diffusion through social networks.

2. BACKGROUND

My work marries research on recommendation systems, studying social influences in networks, and information diffusion towards understanding adoption and sharing of items in social networks. User modeling work from the recommender systems literature helps in modeling the preference of users towards different items. Theories and empirical studies of influence in social networks provide a guiding basis for including social factors in process models for sharing and adoption.

Recommender systems and social factors

Recent works on recommendation in social networks incorporate intuitive social signals (such as people connected to each other are likely to be similar) into their recommendation models [9, 17, 15]. Alternatively, users' preference can also be learned from just their social neighbors' data [7, 11]. The gains of using social information, however, are often small (except for cold-start users) and vary with different networks [1, 13].

A possible reason is that the impact of social factors is complex; it varies with people, item domains and the relationship between the sharer and the receiver [12]. For example, exposure to additional information such as the number of people who have adopted an item [12] or its predicted rating for a person [2] influences how people make decisions about items. Thus, developing a deeper understanding of how theories of social influences from sociology and social psychology impact people's decisions about item recommendations can be useful.

However, most of the work on understanding influence in social networks concerns imitation actions, such as when people tweet the same URL on Twitter after a followee's tweet mentioning it. One of the problems with measuring influence this way is that it is hard to know whether the imitation was because of influence or homophily ('imitator' discovered the URL independently), or which followee was the influencer in case of multiple followee's tweets with the same URL.

Developing fine-grained measures of influence will help in correctly estimating influence due to social neighbors. For example, Tang et al. measure group conformity of a user by incorporating pairwise similarities in adoption with users and aggregating it over all users in a group [16]. In addition, behavioral experiments where we can control the exposure to an item will help in correctly identifying influence effects.

Information diffusion models

While recommender models present techniques for predicting which items will be adopted or shared, research on information diffusion presents generative models for how items are adopted or shared [8, 4]. Two broad classes of diffusion models have emerged: threshold and dynamic cascade. Threshold models [6] assume that each person has a threshold for adopting an item which is met or not based on his social neighbors who have already adopted an item. In the simplest and most popular version of the model (Linear Threshold model), the effect of social neighbors is modeled as the total number of neighbors who has adopted an item.

Dynamic cascade models, on the other hand, assume a *push-based* transmission between people, based on work in interacting particle systems. After adopting an item, an individual transmits the item to his social connections based on the probability of transmission to each of his connections [5]. In the simplest cascade model called Independent Cascade, these probabilities of transmission are independent of each other and each adopter makes only one attempt to transmit the item to a neighbor.

Many extensions of these two basic models have been proposed. Still, diffusion models suffer from two limitations. First, they assume that adopted items automatically become candidates for sharing which would be true for involuntarily shared items such as diseases or computer viruses, but not for consciously shared items in social networks. Another limitation of these models is that they are item-agnostic. That is, given a social network, success or failure of the diffusion process between any two individuals is independent of the item being diffused. This means that they cannot account for effects due to people's preferences for items, as recommender systems are well-suited to do.

Connecting recommendation and diffusion models

Combining learnings from both communities—preference learning techniques from recommender systems and generative process models from diffusion—provides a promising research direction [10]. In particular, analyzing *micro-level* dynamics of adoption and sharing, as opposed to population-level dynamics in social networks, can help in answering questions such as when is a user more likely to adopt or share a particular item, and which users are more likely to be influenced by it? I next describe my progress on these questions.

3. CURRENT WORK: MICRO-LEVEL PROCESS MODELS

The main thrust of my thesis is to identify the factors that impact people's sharing and adopting decisions, estimate their relative impact, and use this knowledge to model people's decision processes around items. Discriminative versions of such *process models* are used in predicting sharing or adoption activity, while generative versions of process models become useful in building diffusion models as proposed in Section 4.3.

3.1 Activity: Modeling Adoption

My first study on modeling how additional social information affects people's likelihood of trying recommended items provides an example methodology that uses social annotations to trigger and measure social influence [12]. Many websites explain their recommendations with social information, such as "Amit likes it" or "10 of your friends like it". I conducted an experiment with 237 participants, where participants were shown musical artist recommendations along with social annotations and asked to rate their likelihood of trying them out.

The results showed that the effect of annotations that embody social influence (using names of close friends) exceeds that of annotations that work through social proof or conformity (using raw numbers of people). Still, an analysis of ratings and people's responses revealed that people's own preferences and attitudes toward the recommended artists based on artist information such as name, genre, and album covers exerted a large influence on their decision-making. I formalized these notions through a generative mixture model of rating that combines a user's own expectation of liking an item (as an exponential distribution) with additional social information (as a gaussian distribution). The relative effect of these distributions was moderated by a parameter that represents each user's *susceptibility* to social information.

3.2 Activity: Modeling Sharing

Apart from adoption, the other building block of diffusion at the micro-level is the process of sharing items to one's social connections. To model how people's preferences affect which items they share, I conducted a paired study in which participants rate and share movies to their partners from a set of movies shown to them. The set of available movies for a pair is selected from a mix of computed recommendations for each user, so that users have a chance to recommend items that are likely to align with their own preferences as well as their partner's.

Results from the study indicate that a person's own rating is the dominant factor for choosing which items to share. Users tend to share movies that they liked themselves and only sometimes consider recipients' interests. Nevertheless, we find that shared movies are rated comparably by recipients to algorithmically recommended movies, which shows that users are able to capture some of the recipients' preferences. These two seemingly contrarian results suggest a probable process model for selecting an item to share: people share items from a collection that they know about and likely have a strong feeling for, but they personalize their choice of the item based on the recipient. Experiment data also shows that users have different rates of sharing, suggesting that this model would need to account for people's sharing *propensity* too.

Finally, I show that machine learning models that use the sender's and recipient's preferences can (noisily) predict which specific items are shared. A classifier using past movie Likes of the sender and recipient, and differences in people's sharing propensity can predict shared items with more than 70% precision.

4. PROPOSED NEXT STEPS

4.1 Overview of the data

To adapt these process models for large-scale online data, I plan to collect data through public APIs of popular social networks. I will analyze data from a broad range of online activities such as consuming content (books, music), selling products, writing code and sharing links. I will collect some of these data myself (Last.fm, Goodreads, Etsy and Github), others are already available (Flickr, Flixster, Digg and Twitter). Each of these datasets contains timestamped data about people's Likes or Favorites, their friend connections, and (if available) their exposure to different items.

Domain	Friends	Adopt Action	Share Action
Last.fm	Undirected	Listen to song	Favorite
Goodreads	Undirected	Add to shelf	Review, rate
Etsy	Directed	Add to list	Favorite
Github	Directed	Contribute code	Favorite

Table 1: Properties of the datasets that I propose to study. Plausible adopt and share actions are determined based on an observation of user activity and the specific design of system interfaces.

Table 1 shows a qualitative comparison of some of these datasets. I have specified plausible adopt and share actions for these data based on observation of user activity and design of the system interfaces (for example, which activities get shared to others). Note how I have chosen Favorite action on some domains as a share action, even though the standard interpretation of the term may consider it closer to adoption. The reason is that in these domains, Favorite actions of followees or friends are highlighted in the feed, while other actions are not; thus giving them a share-like connotation [11].

4.2 Computing sharing and influence proxies on datasets

Reasonable proxies for exposure to social information and sharing will help me verify the process models proposed in my earlier work. This would require estimating factors such as an individual's susceptibility for adoption (baseline probability of adopting items), preferences for items, and social influence effects between any pair of connected people. Using the speed at which a person's preferences tend to come to resemble their neighbors' will give useful estimates of susceptibility, first overall (combining all neighbors) and then per-individual. Preferences of people for items can be readily learned through collaborative filtering using past adoptions.

Proxying influence effects due to exposure to social information is harder using offline datasets that provide only preference information. Past work on modeling influence effects of social neighbors have used all the neighbors [3], the first one or the last one who adopt an item as a proxy for exposure. To account for influence at a finer level, I will use tie strength and preference similarity measures to assign individual neighbors with weighted scores of influence for an individual. Instead of using raw number of neighbors, social exposure could also be estimated similarly as a tie-strength weighted sum of exposure due to each of the neighbors who adopted an item.

It may not be possible to accurately account for influence effects in the data, but reasonable proxies will provide bounds for the amount of influence in each dataset. I will evaluate proposed models of influence by comparing their performance on predicting whether a user will adopt an item or not, in a typical machine learning train-test framework.

4.3 Developing fine-grained diffusion models

Process models for how people share and adopt items can also be combined to yield new diffusion models which incorporate sharing and adopting as two separate decisions. Here I discuss a candidate diffusion model and propose ways to evaluate it.

Proposed diffusion model. The diffusion process proceeds in discrete steps, each of which consists of a share step and a adoption step. In the beginning, each person has some preferences for items. At each step, some people choose items to share and others choose which items to adopt. People decide whether to share a specific item or not based on their process model for sharing. Similarly, adoption decisions for items are based on their process model for adoption. Note an important difference from previous diffusion models: under this model, all adopted items may not be candidates for sharing, and similarly, all shared items may not be adopted.

The main question, then, is how to operationalize process models for adoption and sharing. In most diffusion models, sharing and adoption parameters are set uniformly [8] or learnt from population-level data [3]. The process models that I will build based on observed behavior of individuals and dyads will offer a data-driven and explainable approach to estimate these parameters.

Based on the results in Section 3.1, the process model for adoption posits that people adopt items because of the combined effect of social influences and their preferences. The probability of adoption for an item by a person can be computed using the methods I described earlier to estimate the effect of preferences and social influences, weighted by a person's estimated susceptibility to social influences. Then, at each adopt step, a person decides to adopt or not based on this computed probability. A similar share step can be constructed by considering the relative impact of senders' and recipients' preferences.

Although I focus on how people interact with items from their social neighbors, not all adoption events are based on explicit in-network sharing. Thus, the process models should also allow for spontaneous adoption of items, which constitutes much of the "dark matter" of adoptions that are not explained by traditional diffusion models [4]. This could be accounted for by allowing adoption for items which are not explicitly shared and using item-item recommendation algorithms that help estimate compatibility with preferences. That is, when compatibility with own preference is high, people may choose to adopt an item that matches their preferences even when it is not shared to them.

Evaluation. The models I build will be evaluated in two ways. First, I will simulate the diffusion of items using my model and test how resultant spread of items across the social network compares with that found in the real-world datasets listed in Section 4.1. My earlier work on comparing assortativity or clustering of preference in social networks will provide useful metrics to compare simulated and real distribution of items in the social network [13].

Second, I will use the model to predict people's actions on sharing and adoption. Starting from a given timestamp in a dataset, I will investigate how well the model can predict people's specific shares and adoptions and compare it to prior diffusion models and recommendation algorithms proposed for social networks.

5. CONTRIBUTIONS

Proposed work connects and extends research on social influences, preference modeling and information diffusion and presents a concise mathematical framework for modeling sharing and adopting decisions, which can be used for recommendation tasks within a social network as well as for understanding how information (ideas, products etc.) spreads in social networks.

As a contribution to the research community, I will release the datasets and code used in my research for academic use, and hope that they will start off further inquiries into learning about people's decisions around items in social networks. Finally, through my multi-methods research paradigm, I hope to demonstrate how iterating between data mining and behavioral exploration can be a viable methodology for modeling online user behavior.

Acknowledgments

This work was supported by the National Science Foundation under grant IIS 0910664.

6. REFERENCES

[1] O. Arazy, N. Kumar, and B. Shapira. A theory-driven design framework for social recommender systems. In *Journal of the Assoc. for Info. Sys.*, 2010.

[2] D. Cosley, S. K. Lam, I. Albert, J. A. Konstan, and J. Riedl. Is seeing believing? How recommender system interfaces affect users' opinions. In *Proc. CHI*, pages 585–592, 2003.

[3] D. Crandall, D. Cosley, D. Huttenlocher, J. Kleinberg, and S. Suri. Feedback effects between similarity and social influence in online communities. In *Proc. KDD*, 2008.

[4] S. Goel, D. J. Watts, and D. G. Goldstein. The structure of online diffusion networks. In *Proc. ACM Electron. Commerce*, EC '12, 2012.

[5] J. Goldenberg, B. Libai, and E. Muller. Talk of the network: A complex systems look at the underlying process of word-of-mouth. *Marketing Letters*, 2001.

[6] M. Granovetter and R. Soong. Threshold models of diffusion and collective behavior. *Journal of Mathematical sociology*, 9(3):165–179, 1983.

[7] I. Guy, M. Jacovi, A. Perer, I. Ronen, and E. Uziel. Same places, same things, same people? Mining user similarity on social media. In *Proc. CSCW*, 2010.

[8] D. Kempe, J. Kleinberg, and É. Tardos. Maximizing the spread of influence through a social network. In *Proc. KDD*, 2003.

[9] H. Ma, D. Zhou, C. Liu, M. R. Lyu, and I. King. Recommender systems with social regularization. In *Proc. WSDM*, 2011.

[10] Y. Pan, F. Cong, K. Chen, and Y. Yu. Diffusion-aware personalized social update recommendation. In *Proc. RecSys*, 2013.

[11] A. Sharma and D. Cosley. Network-centric recommendation: Personalization with and in social networks. In *Proc. IEEE SocialCom*, 2011.

[12] A. Sharma and D. Cosley. Do social explanations work? Studying and modeling the effects of social explanations in recommender systems. In *Proc. WWW*, 2013.

[13] A. Sharma, M. Gemici, and D. Cosley. Friends, strangers, and the value of ego networks for recommendation. In *Proc. ICWSM*, 2013.

[14] D. S. Sundaram, K. Mitra, and C. Webster. Word-of-mouth communications: a motivational analysis. *Advances in consumer research*, 1998.

[15] P. Symeonidis, E. Tiakas, and Y. Manolopoulos. Product recommendation and rating prediction based on multi-modal social networks. In *Proc. RecSys*, 2011.

[16] J. Tang, S. Wu, and J. Sun. Confluence: Conformity influence in large social networks. In *Proc. KDD*, 2013.

[17] X. Yang, H. Steck, Y. Guo, and Y. Liu. On top-k recommendation using social networks. In *Proc. RecSys*, RecSys '12, 2012.

Choicla: Towards Domain-Independent Decision Support for Groups of Users

Martin Stettinger
Institute for Software Technology
Graz University of Technology
Inffeldgasse 16b - 8010 Graz, Austria
martin.stettinger@ist.tugraz.at

ABSTRACT

Group recommendation technologies have been successfully applied in domains such as interactive television, music, and tourist destinations. Existing technologies are focusing on specific domains and do not offer the possibility of supporting different kinds of decision scenarios. The *Choicla* group decision support environment advances the state of the art by supporting decision scenarios in a domain-independent fashion. In this paper we give an overview of the *Choicla* environment and report the results of a first user study which focused on system usability.

Categories and Subject Descriptors

D.2 [**Software engineering**]: Design Tools and Techniques; H.5 [**Information Interfaces and Presentation (I.7)**]: User Interfaces (D.2.2, H.1.2, I.3.6)

General Terms

Algorithms; Human Factors; Experimentation

Keywords

Recommender Systems, Group Recommendation, Group Decision Making, Group Decision Tasks, Decision Technologies

1. INTRODUCTION

Decisions in everyday life often come up in groups, for example, a decision about the destination for the next holidays or a decision about which restaurant to choose for a dinner. The quality of a group decision can be negatively influenced by various factors. For example, knowledge about the preferences of other users in early phases of a decision process can lead to sub-optimal decision outcomes [9]. Anchoring effects [5] cause decisions which are biased by the voting of the first preference-articulating person. Furthermore, the non-inclusion of explanations can lead a lower level of trust in recommendations [2]. The outcome of a decision can also be influenced by the fact that single persons have to take a decision in place of persons who are not available for a meeting. In many cases, decision processes are not open in the sense that it is impossible to easily integrate new decision alternatives or change the individual preferences within the scope of a decision process - both aspects can lead to low-quality decision outcomes [10]. Finally, after taking a decision, the criteria for the decision often remain unclear since there is no explanation of the outcome.

There exist a couple of online tools which support different types of decision scenarios. *Dotmocracy*[1] is a method for collecting and visualizing the preferences of a large group of users. It is related to the idea of participatory decision making – it's major outcome is a graph type visualization of the group-immanent preferences. Doodle[2] focuses on the aspect of coordinating appointments. Similarly, VERN [14] is a tool that supports the identification of meeting times based on the idea of unconstrained democracy where individuals are enabled to freely propose alternative dates themselves. Compared to *Choicla*[3] these tools are not able to customize their decision processes depending on the application domain and are also focused on specific tasks. Furthermore, no concepts are provided which help to improve the overall quality of group decisions, for example, in terms of integrating explanations, recommendations for groups, and consistency management for user preferences.

One major goal of the *Choicla* environment is to facilitate group decision making and improve the overall quality of decision outcomes. The idea of this environment is to support definitions of different types of decision tasks in a domain-independent fashion while taking into account the above mentioned risk factors. In order to achieve this goal, *Choicla* builds upon group recommendation algorithms [8] which are used for determining alternative solutions for the participants of a group decision process. A typical scenario for the application of *Choicla* technologies is the decision about which restaurant to select for a dinner or - in a scientific community - a decision regarding the selection of the destination of next year's conference. Other objectives of *Choicla* are (1) to increase fairness within long term decisions and (2) to support decisions related to complex products or services.

The remainder of this paper is organized as follows. In Section 2 we provide insights to (1) the *Choicla* modelling process where participants can design decision tasks from scratch and (2) the intelligent management of already cre-

RecSys'14, October 6–10, 2014, Foster City, Silicon Valley, CA, USA.

ACM 978-1-4503-2668-1/14/10 ...$15.00.
http://dx.doi.org/10.1145/2645710.2653365 .

[1]dotmocracy.org.
[2]doodle.com.
[3]www.choicla.com.

ated decision apps. In the Section 3 we report the results of a first empirical study conducted with the goal of estimating the current status of *Choicla* in terms of usability. We then discuss future work (Section 4) and thereafter conclude the paper (Section 5).

2. CHOICLA DECISION SUPPORT

Because decision scenarios differ, a variety of parameters is needed to specify all relevant properties of a decision task. We will now discuss basic parameters (features) which can be configured (modelled) by the creator of a decision task. In this context we refer to the example features depicted in Figure 1.

2.1 Choicla Creation Process

Decision scenarios can differ from each other in terms of their process design. Some decision scenarios rely on a preselected decision heuristic that defines the criteria for taking the decision, for example, a group decides to use majority voting for deciding about the next restaurant visit. The design of decision tasks (the underlying process) can be interpreted as a configuration problem (see [12]). The major advantage of this approach is that making the process design of decision tasks configurable introduces the flexibility that is needed due to the heterogeneity of decision problems. This way we are able to build a software product line that is flexible with regard to the implementation (generation) of problem-specific decision applications.

Management of Decision Alternatives. There are different possibilities to support the management of decision alternatives within the scope of a decision task. *First*, only the creator of a decision task is allowed to add alternatives – this could be the case if a person is interested to know the opinions of his/her friends about a certain set of alternatives (e.g., alternative candidates for the next family car). Another related scenario are so-called "Micro-Polls" where the creator is only interested in knowing the preference distribution of a larger group of users. *Second*, in some scenarios it should be possible that all decision makers can add alternatives – a typical example of such a scenario is the group-based decision regarding a holiday destination or a hotel [6]. In this context, each user should be allowed to add relevant alternatives. An example scenario of the *third* case (only external users can add alternatives) is the support of group-based personnel decisions – in this context it should be possible that persons apply for a certain position (the application itself is interpreted as the addition of a new alternative to the decision task). Another related example is the selection of the next conference location where proposers submit their material.

Preference Visibility. The visibility of individual preferences of the other participants involved in a decision process can have an impact on decision quality (see [3] and [6]). There exist decision scenarios where all participants should exactly know who entered a rating. If, for example, a date for a business meeting is the decision task it is essential to find a date where all managers can attend the meeting and therefore it is important to know the individual preferences of the participants in that case. But there are decision scenarios where full preference visibility can lead to disadvantages for some participants but some kind of transparency of the preferences is helpful to achieve a reasonable decision. In such cases a summary of all given preferences regarding an alternative is a way to support decision makers (participants). A summary prevents all participants from statistical inferences but still can help participants who are unsure about which rating to select.

Explanations. Explanations can play an important role in decision tasks since they are able to increase the trust of users in the outcome of a decision process [2]. When designing a decision task in *Choicla*, explanations can be selected as a feature of the decision process. In the current version of *Choicla*, explanations are supported by simply allowing the creator of the decision process to include textual argumentations as to why a certain decision alternative has been selected as "the final decision".

Recommendation Support. In the context of group decision tasks an essential aspect is the aggregation function (recommendation heuristic). Aggregation functions can help to foster consensus in a group decision process. Furthermore, user studies show that these functions also help to increase the degree of the perceived decision quality (see, for example [3]). Preferences of individual users can be aggregated in many different ways and there exists no standard heuristic which fits for every decision scenario. To support groups of users in different scenarios, the selection of recommendation heuristics is a necessary feature which has to be configured by the creator of a decision task. Due to space limitations we only describe selected aggregation heuristics below. For an overview of basic aggregation heuristics, such as *Majority Vote (MAJ)*, *Average Vote (AVV)*, *Least Misery (LMIS)*, and *Most Pleasure (MPLS)* which are also already available in the *Choicla* environment we refer to Masthoff [8].

Group Distance (GD) (see Formula 1) returns the value d as group recommendation which causes the lowest overall change of the individual user preferences. For example, the GD d value for s = *North & South* (see Table 1) in *Dec. Sit. 1*[4] is 5 (or, alternatively 4).

$$GD(s) = minarg_{(d\in\{1..5\})}\left(\sum_{u\in Users}|eval(u,s)-d|\right) \quad (1)$$

An example of a meta-aggregation function included in *Choicla* is Ensemble Voting. *Ensemble Voting* (see Formula 2) determines the majority of the results of the individual voting strategies H = {MAJ, AVV, LMIS, MPLS, GD}. For example, the ensemble-based majority voting for *North & South* in *Dec. Sit. 1* is 5.

$$ENS(s) = maxarg_{(d\in\{1..5\})}\left(\#\left(\bigcup_{h\in H} eval(h,s)=d\right)\right) \quad (2)$$

To achieve fairness among all group members in long term scenarios (e.g., recurring decision tasks), we developed a modified version of the *Group Distance* algorithm (see Formula 4), where all past decisions influence the actual recommendation. A user-weighting $w(u)$ is used to ensure that users whose individual ratings often differ from related decisions (represented by $distance(u)$), are privileged.

$$w(u) = \frac{1}{\frac{1}{\sum distances(u)+1}} \quad (3)$$

$$GD'(s) = minarg_{(d\in\{1..5\})}\left(\sum_{u\in Users} w(u) * |eval(u,s)-d|\right) \quad (4)$$

[4] *Dec. Sit. n* denotes a specific decision situation in recurring decision tasks.

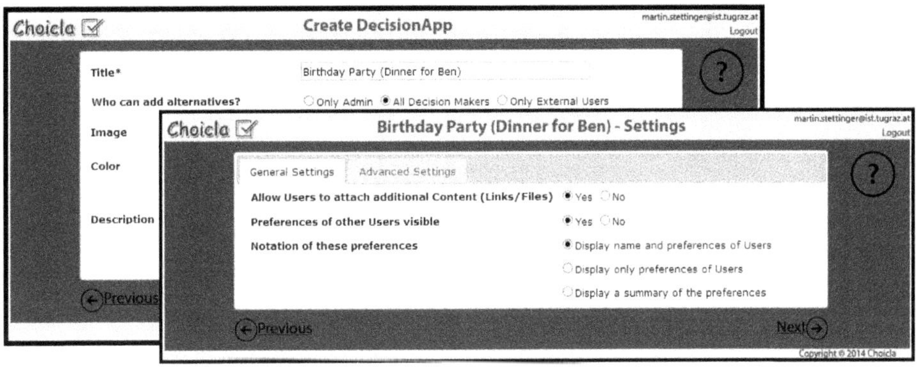

Figure 1: *Choicla*: definition of a decision task. Basic settings & further configurable features.

		North& South	Trattoria	El Gaucho	La Botte
Dec. Sit. 1	Martin	5	3	4	4
	Dave	2	3	5	3
	George	5	3	3	3
	Ben	4	3	4	4
	Rec. GD	**5**	3	4	4
Dec. Sit. 2	Martin	5	2	2	4
	Dave	3	3	4	2
	George	4	3	3	3
	Ben	4	4	3	5
	Rec. GD	4	3	3	**4**
Dec. Sit. 3	Martin	5	3	4	3
	Dave	3	5	3	3
	George	4	3	4	5
	Ben	4	4	5	5
	Rec. GD′	4	**5**	4	3

Table 1: User-specific ratings with regard to the available decision alternatives (restaurants) in recurring decision situations. The group recommendation is marked bold in the corresponding decision situation.

If we look at the example in Table 1 we notice that in *Dec. Sit. 3* the group recommendation is *Trattoria* although the individual aggregation heuristics [8] would calculate a different group recommendation. *Dec. Sit. 1 and 2* are responsible for a user-weighting in *Dec. Sit. 3* which leads to this recommendation. The used weights of the participants calculated by Formula 3 in *Dec. Sit. 3* are the following: **Martin:** 1, **Dave:** 6, **George:** 2, and **Ben:** 3. *Dave* has the highest weight in *Dec. Sit. 3.* This approach allows to achieve fairness among the group members in long term decisions - further related aspects will be discussed in Section 4.

2.2 Choicla Decision Apps

After the creation process has been finished the creator of the decision task sees a corresponding decision app directly on his home screen. Such an app also shows up on the home screen of the invited participants after an invitation has been accepted by a user. There is a tab *DecisionApp Store* where publicly available decision apps can be searched and installed on the personal *Home Screen.* With this, frequent decision tasks such as scheduling decision tasks do not have to be created from scratch every time. The decision process can be triggered right after the download of a decision app. The mentioned reuse has the potential to reduce the entry barrier for using *Choicla* and to make the interaction straightforward – especially for people who want to start a decision process quickly. Another tab *Create DecisionApp* allows a user to design a completely new decision app from scratch.

Due to the fact that many decision tasks occur regularly – for example, a group of friends watches a movie in the cinema once a month – a concept is needed to manage a potentially large number of decision tasks. To keep the decision tasks manageable, every decision app consists of a variable number of instances. This mechanism offers the possibility of an exact documentation of all past decisions and is also a basis for supporting recurring decision tasks - related aspects will be discussed in Section 4.

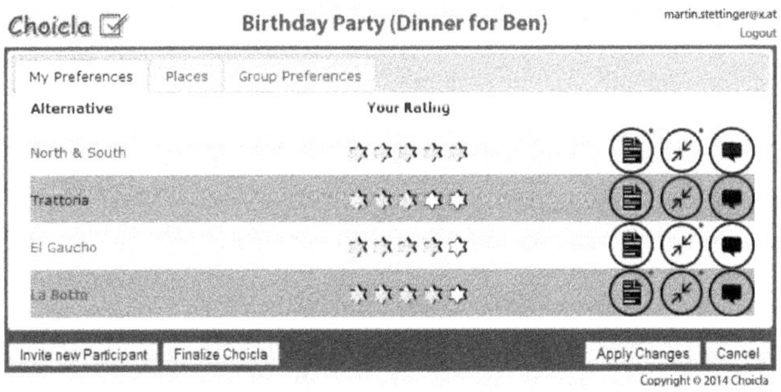

Figure 2: *Choicla*: example of individual ratings. Each user can take a look at geographical information of the alternatives and the current recommendation and adapt his/her preferences if needed.

3. USER STUDY

In order to evaluate the *Choicla* group decision environment, we conducted a first small-scale user study. In this study we made the software accessible to ten persons outside our university who were not aware of the fact that the system has been developed at our university. Each of these participants defined a decision task with the support of the *Choicla* environment and then made accessible the decision task to a group of other persons. The average number of persons participating in a decision scenario was around 5. The overall number of users who interacted with *Choicla* within the scope of our study was N=48 (38% female, 62% male). Within the scope this empirical study we could gain a first evidence that users consider the current version of the system applicable and can imagine to apply *Choicla* functionalities in various domains. For an in-depth discussion of this user study we refer to [13].

4. FUTURE WORK

Our future work will focus on the analysis of further application domains for the *Choicla* technologies. Our vision is to make the design (implementation) of group decision tasks as simple as possible. The resulting decision task should be easy to handle for users and make group decisions in general more efficient. We will also focus on the analysis of decision phenomena within the scope of group decision processes. Phenomena such as decoy effects [4] and anchoring effects [5] are well known for single-user cases but are not investigated in group-based decision scenarios.

In scenarios where all possible decision alternatives are not available from the beginning the possibility of adding new decision alternatives is imperative, but can also induce biases. The *assimilating effect* describes the fact that individuals are motivated to reduce psychological incongruity or discrepancy that is very likely to arise if new information is added to a present perception [11]. As discussed in [7] this effect is intensified if there is a high group cohesion, because the fear of exclusion from the group is higher. To reduce this effect, a special way of preference visibility can be included in future versions of *Choicla*. Such a mechanism could, for example, provide only insights to the preferences of other users for those participants who completed the individual rating of alternatives. A research question in this context is if such mechanisms can increase the willingness of participants to articulate their real preferences.

Another research direction is the support of long term decisions [1] (see Section 2). Fairness is an important issue in this context - the degree of perceived fairness influences the willingness of group members to accept compromises in the resolution of conflicts of opinions and also their trust in other group members [7].

The investigation in which way recommendations need to be structured to achieve consensus more quickly within a group of users is another issue for future work. In this context we will also focus on the development of further group recommendation heuristics to achieve a high level of fairness.

Finally, one of our major goals is also to make the *Choicla* datasets available to the research community in an anonymized fashion for experimentation purposes.

5. CONCLUSIONS

In this paper we gave a short introduction to *Choicla* which supports the flexible design and execution of different types of group decision tasks. Compared to existing group decision support approaches, *Choicla* provides an end user modelling environment which supports an easy development and execution of group decision tasks. We also discussed further research directions which can help to extend the available functionality of the *Choicla* environment.

6. REFERENCES

[1] D. Ariely and D. Zakay. A timely account of the role of duration in decision making. *Acta Psychologica*, 108(2):187 – 207, 2001. Time, Judgement and Decision Making.

[2] A. Felfernig, B. Gula, and E. Teppan. Knowledge-based Recommender Technologies for Marketing and Sales. *International Journal of Pattern Recognition and Artificial Intelligence (IJPRAI)*, 21(2):1–22, 2006.

[3] A. Felfernig, C. Zehentner, G. Ninaus, H. Grabner, W. Maalej, D. Pagano, L. Weninger, and F. Reinfrank. Group decision support for requirements negotiation. In L. Ardissono and T. Kuflik, editors, *Advances in User Modeling*, volume 7138 of *Lecture Notes in Computer Science*, pages 105–116. Springer Berlin Heidelberg, 2012.

[4] J. Huber, J. Payne, and C. Puto. Adding Asymmetrically Dominated Alternatives: Violations of Regularity and the Similarity Hypothesis. *The Journal of Consumer Research*, 9(1):90–98, 1982.

[5] K. Jacowitz and D. Kahneman. Measures of Anchoring in Estimation Tasks. *Personality and Social Psychology Bulletin*, 21(1):1161–1166, 1995.

[6] A. Jameson. More than the sum of its members: challenges for group recommender systems. In *Proceedings of the working conference on Advanced visual interfaces*, AVI '04, pages 48–54, New York, NY, USA, 2004. ACM.

[7] E. Lind, L. Kray, and L. Thompson. Primacy effects in justice judgments: Testing predictions from fairness heuristic theory. *Organizational Behavior and Human Decision Processes*, 85(2):189 – 210, 2001.

[8] J. Masthoff. Group Recommender Systems: Combining Individual Models. *Recommender Systems Handbook*, pages 677–702, 2011.

[9] A. Mojzisch and S. Schulz-Hardt. Knowing other's preferences degrades the quality of group decisions. *Journal of Personality & Social Psychology*, 98(5):794–808, 2010.

[10] E. Molin, H. Oppewal, and H. Timmermans. Modeling Group Preferences Using a Decompositional Preference Approach. *Group Decision and Negotiation*, 6:339–350, 1997.

[11] M. Neale, L. Ross, and J. Curhan. Dynamic Valuation: Preference Changes in the Context of Face-to-face Negotiation. *Journal of Experimental Social Psychology*, 40(2):142–151, 2004.

[12] M. Stettinger, A. Felfernig, G. Ninaus, M. Jeran, S. Reiterer, and G. Leitner. Configuring decision tasks. Technical report, Graz University of Technology, 2014.

[13] M. Stettinger, G. Ninaus, M. Jeran, F. Reinfrank, and S. Reiterer. We-decide: A decision support environment for groups of users. In M. Ali, T. Bosse, K. Hindriks, M. Hoogendoorn, C. Jonker, and J. Treur, editors, *Recent Trends in Applied Artificial Intelligence*, volume 7906 of *Lecture Notes in Computer Science*, pages 382–391. Springer Berlin Heidelberg, 2013.

[14] S. Yardi, B. Hill, and S. Chan. VERN: Facilitating Democratic group Decision Making Online. In *International ACM SIGGROUP Conference on Supporting Group Work (GROUP 2005)*, pages 116–119, Sanibel Island, Florida, USA, 2005. ACM.

Weighted Hybrid Recommendation for Heterogeneous Networks

Fatemeh Vahedian
Center for Web Intelligence, Depaul University, Chicago, IL 60604
fvahedia@cs.depaul.edu

ABSTRACT

Social media sites accumulate a wide variety of information about users: likes and ratings, friend and follower links, annotations, posts, media uploads, just to name a few. Key challenges for recommender systems research are (a) to synthesize of all of this data into an integrated recommendation model and (b) to support a wide variety of recommendation types simultaneously (items, friends, tags, etc.) One approach that has been explored in recent research is to view this multi-faceted data as a heterogeneous network and use network-based methods of generating recommendations. However, most such approaches involve computationally-intensive model generation resulting in a single-purpose recommender system. Our approach is to create a component-based hybrid model whose components can be reused for multiple recommendation tasks. In this paper, we show how this model can be applied to heterogeneous networks.

1. INTRODUCTION

Social media sites are an important element of today's Internet, drawing millions of users each day. The wealth of information found in these sites makes recommender systems essential. Such sites often must integrate recommendations of many types: for content, for like-minded users, for appropriate tags, etc. Our approach, called the Weighted Hybrid of Low-Dimensional Recommenders (WHyLDR) is designed to support the flexible creation and rapid deployment of a wide variety of recommenders in a heterogeneous environment. We have demonstrated its effectiveness in prior work focusing on social tagging systems [8, 7, 6, 3].

Compared to a homogeneous network of uniform node and edge types, a heterogeneous network is defined by a diversity of objects and relations, three examples of these networks can be seen in Figure 1. The diversity of nodes in heterogeneous networks means that different types of relations can be imagined between nodes.

The wide variety of relations in a social media site supports many recommendation types. One obvious use of the Yelp network is for recommending new businesses to users, but there are a variety of other possible recommendation tasks. Recommending other users to befriend, recommending locations, and recommending categories are all user-focused recommendation tasks. A site like Yelp may also be interested in recommending users to businesses for advertising or marketing purposes. In addition, a user may wish to constrain the recommendations in various ways: looking for a recommended business in a particular category or in a particular location, for example.

What is needed for complex social media sites is a recommendation technique that is responsive to both the complexity of heterogeneous data and the multiplicity of recommendation tasks. The WHyLDR model has been shown to meet both of these needs in the area of social tagging systems, performing basic recommendation tasks with accuracy surpassing that of single-purpose model-based techniques such as tensor factorization, and also supporting a wide variety of recommendation tasks [8].

As in other work with heterogeneous networks [10], the WHyLDR model views the network structure as a set of mappings, or projections from nodes to nodes: $proj_A(n) \rightarrow \{m_0, m_1, ..., m_i\}$ where A is a set of paths, n is a starting node and the ms are nodes reachable from n via some path in A. Sets of paths that pass from one type of node to another over specific categories of edges are known as meta-paths. Table 1 show example of some meta-paths in different heterogeneous networks. Each such projection induces a different profile for user. Using such profiles, we can build standard collaborative filtering components to select neighbors of users and generate recommendations. Individually such components may be relatively weak. However, as we have shown in prior work and confirm here, ensembles of such components can be effective.

It is not obvious that extended meta-paths will yield useful user profiles. However, our prior work with WHyLDR systems for social tagging has shown that, in some cases, components built from longer meta-paths may make a larger contribution to a recommendation hybrid than their more narrowly-focused subsets. Judicious exploration of the meta-path space is therefore important for hybrid construction.

A heterogeneous network is one where there are multiple object types and/or multiple edge types – typically both. The network schemas of the three datasets shown in Figure 1 give overviews of their respective heterogeneous networks by indicating the different object types and the relations that exist between them. A meta-path in a heterogeneous network is a path over the network schema, a sequenced

RecSys'14, October 6–10, 2014, Foster City, Silicon Valley, CA, USA.

ACM 978-1-4503-2668-1/14/10 ...$15.00.
http://dx.doi.org/10.1145/2645710.2653366 .

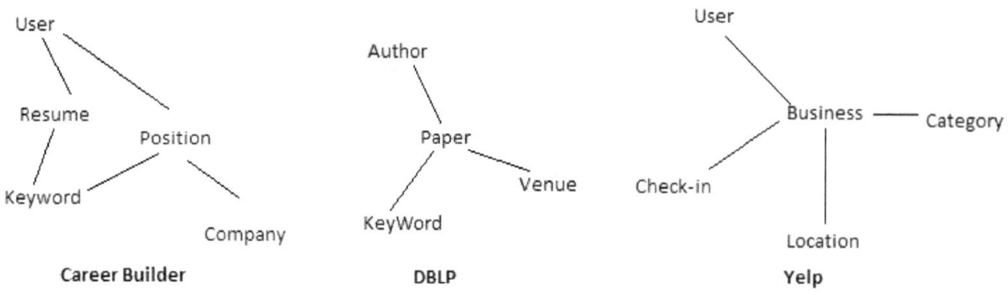

Figure 1: dataset network schema

composition of relations between two object types. Table 1 shows meta-path examples in these networks.

Table 1: Meta-path example in heterogeneous networks

dataset	Meta-paths
DBLP	paper→paper, paper→venue, paper→author, paper→author→paper, author→paper→venue
Career Builder	user→position, user→position→company, user→resume→keyword
Yelp	user→business, user→business→category, user→business→location, user→business→category→business

- DBLP: The Digital Bibliography and Library Project which is a collection of bibliographic information on major computer science journals and proceedings.There are a number of recommendation tasks relevant to this data set. One obvious recommendation task is co-author recommendation, also we can recommend publication venue to authors, paper citation recommendation could be another task is this network.

- Career-Builder: This dataset contains the profiles for job hunter, including education history, previous positions, and location. the main task in this network is to recommend job to user, we can add recommending users to companies that have open positions.

- Yelp: The academic version of Yelp dataset [1]. A variety of types of recommendation can be performed in such a network. Obviously, the recommendation of businesses to users is one, but one can also imagine recommending users to businesses for marketing purposes, recommending categories, even recommending particularly informative reviews. In this paper, all results and experimentations are based on this dataset.

2. CONSTRUCTING THE HYBRID

A weighted hybrid recommender is a system comprised of multiple recommendation components, each of which returns a real-valued score for a combination of user and item. The scores from all the components are combined in a weighted sum [2]. More formally, $s(u,i) = \sum_j \alpha_j s_j(u,i)$ where $s(u,i)$ is the score computed for a user-item combination, $s_j(u,i)$ is the score computed by the jth component, and α_j is the weight associated with the jth component.

The components and the weights are therefore the building blocks needed. The weights are learned through an optimization procedure as discussed below. The components are a function of the recommendation task and the structure of the network.

2.1 Components

WHyLDR components are built on two-dimensional matrices familiar to users of collaborative recommendation [5]. A user-based matrix is one in which the rows are users and the columns are information about user interests. Users are compared on the basis of their profiles and peer users form a neighborhood from which information about unknown items can be extrapolated.[1]

Three types of recommendation component can be considered in a our model. First, user-based KNN models which are constructed based on meta-paths starting from user node. An item-based version of this idea is also well-known. We can follow the meta-path starting from item to create a profile of each item in terms of the users who have rated it then applying a KNN method to make item-based recommendation.

A third type of low-dimensional recommender can also be constructed in which there are two matrices: one for users and one for item with the same columns. Users and item can therefore be compared directly using any one of a number of metrics. We use cosine similarity, so these are the cosine metrics.

Table 2: Recommendation components based on meta-paths

Type	Meta-paths
User-based	UB, UBC, UBL, UBH, UBCB, UBLB, UBHB
Item-based	BU, BL, BC, BH, BLBC, BLBU, BUBU, BUBL
Cosine	UBC, UBH

2.2 Hybrids

One outcome of our prior research on social tagging systems was some surprising trends in the behavior of components formed from long meta-paths. We expected that a component with a long meta-path (for example, ABCD) would be a less effective contributor to the overall recommender than its prefix meta-paths (AB or ABC). Usually

[1]All of the optimizations that have been applied to collaborative recommenders can therefore be applied to the individual WHyLDR components, for example, matrix factorization.

this was the case, but there were important exceptions [4]. Here we investigated this phenomenon by building a number of hybrids, incorporating successively longer meta-paths.

We divided the components into user-based and item-based and by path length (1, 2, and 3) and assembled the following hybrids:

- HM-1: User-based and item-based, paths of length 1 plus popularity
- HM-2: HM-1 plus user-based and item-based, paths of lengths 2
- HM-3: HM-2 plus cosine, paths of length 2
- HM-4: HM-3 plus user-based, paths of length 3
- HM-5: HM-4 plus item-based, paths of length 3

Table 3 gives the component breakdown of each hybrid by meta-path.

3. CONTROLLING COMPONENT GENERATION

There is no requirement that meta-paths be simple: nodes and edges can be revisited, as seen in components like kNN_{UBLB}. Component generation is therefore in principle an unbounded process. There are significant computational costs in generating components and in optimizing a hybrid with a large number of components. In addition, some components may make only a minor contribution to performance. It is therefore important to control this process – ideally, we would like to be able to estimate in advance what components are likely to make a substantial contribution and be able to trade off expected accuracy against the computational costs of adding another component.

As part of our experiments with this data, we used mutual information related to each meta-path to estimate the utility of recommendation components. For a given two-dimensional projection AB, the mutual information can be calculated as

$$I(A, B) = H(A) - H(A|B)$$

where $H(A)$ is entropy of dimension A and $H(A|B)$ is the conditional entropy.Entropy is calculated as

$$H(A) = -\sum_i p(a_i) log(p(a_i))$$

The entropy is therefore a function of the probability of occurrence of nodes in each dimension. In our networks, we define probability of node a_i from dimension A as

$$p(a_i) = \frac{Degree(a_i)}{\sum_i Degree(a_i)}$$

Conditional entropy measures the uncertainty of one dimension given another dimension. Considering an AB projection of a network, we make use of a two-dimension matrix to calculate probability of dimension B given A $P(B|A)$ as follows. The likelihood of reaching node b in dimension B is considered to be the fraction of paths from node a leading to node b out of all possible paths from node a. The conditional probability is therefore calculated as

$$P(b_i|a_j) = \frac{\#path(a_j \rightarrow b_i)}{\sum_i \#path(a_j \rightarrow b_i)}$$

For example, consider the user-business meta-path and associated recommendation component. The values for $H(U)$ and $H(U|B)$ can be calculated using the formulas above. If these values were roughly the same then the $I(U, B)$ will be around zero. This suggests that the meta-path does not add much information beyond what is already contained in the U dimension and that the UB meta-path is unlikely to give any additional contribution. The same principle can be applied to any user-based or item-based component.

To test this hypothesis, we measure the correlation between mutual information and the weight of components in the hybrid. If our information metric is a good measure of component contribution, we should expect a positive correlation between it and the weight of the corresponding component in the hybrid model.

4. RESULTS

For the experiments reported here, we used the **Yelp** dataset, Following the methodology [4] to build recommender models. Also we make use of Particle Swarm Optimization (PSO) [9] to learn α values for the weighted hybrid model. Figure 2 shows the recall-precision curve for the top individual recommendation component (kNN_{UB}) and the five hybrids. The HM-1 and HM-2 models do not show significant improvement over kNN_{UB} method, but the other three larger hybrids do show significant improvements over the simple collaborative component. The HM-5 hybrid, which incorporates all the components, is dominant. The effect of each

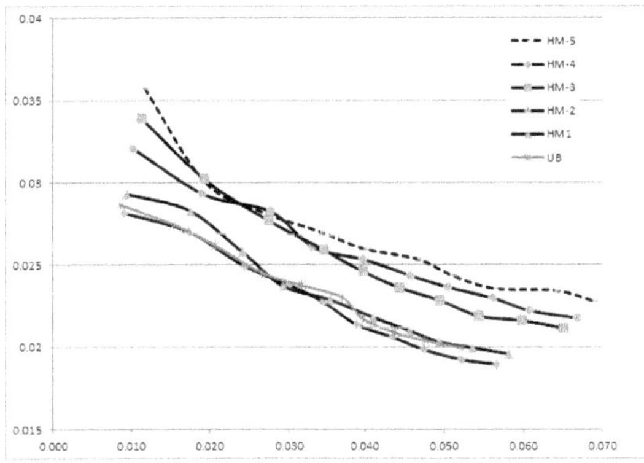

Figure 2: Recall vs. Precision

dimension of the network can be seen in the average learned α weights shown in Figure 3. Here the components with the largest contribution are colored red, fading to pink for those with a lower α value. The white cells are components not present in a particular hybrid. Unlike some of the our other datasets where overall popularity had minimal utility, the non-personalized popularity method contributes relatively strongly in HM-1, on par with location (kNN_{BL} component). However, we can see its contribution decreases in the models including longer meta-paths, as this popularity comes to be represented through particular paths. kNN_{BU} is the strongest contributor in all hybrid models, with kNN_{UB} placing second. This may be because part of the effectiveness of kNN_{UB} is due to a popularity effect. As noted above, location has a strong effect in the hybrid models. The kNN_{UBL} component makes a good contribution in HM-3. Its contribution decreases in HM-4 and HM-5, no doubt because these

Table 3: Component composition of the hybrid models

	UB + BU + BC BH + BL	UBC + UBL + UBH	UBCB + UBHB + UBLB	Cos-UBC + Cos-UBH	BLBC + BLBU + BUBL + BUBU
HM-1	X				
HM-2	X	X			
HM-3	X	X		X	
HM-4	X	X	X		
HM-5	X	X	X	X	X

models include kNN_{UBLB} a meta-path-based component that also incorporates location information.

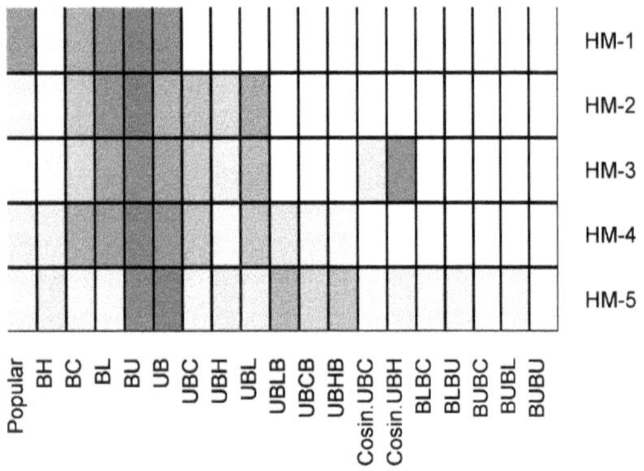

Figure 3: Heatmap of α values

Table 4: Correlation between mutual information and α values

Model	HM-1	HM-2	HM-3	HM-4	HM-5
Correlation	0.788	0.523	0.587	0.90	0.627

Table 4 shows the correlation between the mutual information measure described above and the learned α values in the various hybrids.[2] The strong correlations (all greater than 0.50) suggest that this metric may be a useful way to estimate the value of different components in a hybrid. We intend to make use of this finding in future work.

5. CONCLUSIONS

A key challenge in social media recommendation is to integrate the different types of information available in such systems to enhance recommendations and to offer recommendations of multiple types. In this work, we describe the WHyLDR approach that constructs a linear-weighted hybrid model from simple two-dimensional components based on meta-path traversals of a social media network. These components are then combined using weights learned through optimization. WHyLDR hybrids have been shown to be successful in social tagging applications. In addition to its effectiveness and simplicity, this approach has the benefit of creating re-usable components that can be applied to multiple recommendation tasks (e.g. friend recommendation or user recommendation for marketing).

As there are an unbounded number of possible components, our work raises the question of how to choose components for a hybrid and when to stop adding to it. Our study correlating mutual information with the α values optimized for each hybrid suggest that we may be able to use this measure or a similar one to control hybrid construction. Open questions include how to predict the contribution of components involving multiple paths (such as the cosine components) and how to factor in the influence of the recommendation task.

[2]This calculation did not include the cosine-based components.

6. ACKNOWLEDGMENTS

I would like to thank my advisor Professor Robin Burke for his support, guidance and valuable feedback.

7. REFERENCES

[1] https://www.yelp.com/academic_dataset.

[2] R. Burke. Hybrid recommender systems: Survey and experiments. *User Modeling and User-Adapted Interaction*, 12(4):331–370, 2002.

[3] R. Burke and F. Vahedian. Social web recommendation using metapaths. In *RSWeb@RecSys*, 2013.

[4] R. Burke, F. Vahedian, and B. Mobasher. Hybrid recommendation in heterogeneous networks. In *Proceedings of the 22nd Conference on User Modeling, Adaptation and Personalization*, 2014, to appear.

[5] C. Desrosiers and G. Karypis. A comprehensive survey of neighborhood-based recommendation methods. In F. Ricci, L. Rokach, B. Shapira, and P. B. Kantor, editors, *Recommender Systems Handbook*, pages 107–144. Springer, 2011.

[6] J. Gemmell, T. Schimoler, B. Mobasher, and R. Burke. Recommendation by example in social annotation systems. *E-Commerce and Web Technologies*, pages 209–220, 2011.

[7] J. Gemmell, T. Schimoler, B. Mobasher, and R. Burke. Tag-based resource recommendation in social annotation applications. *User Modeling, Adaption and Personalization*, pages 111–122, 2011.

[8] J. Gemmell, T. Schimoler, B. Mobasher, and R. Burke. Resource recommendation in social annotation systems: A linear-weighted hybrid approach. *Journal of Computer and System Sciences*, 78(4):1160–1174, 2012.

[9] J. Kennedy and R. C. Eberhart. Particle swarm optimization. In *Proceedings of the IEEE International Conference on Neural Networks*, pages 1942–1948, 1995.

[10] Y. Sun and J. Han. *Mining Heterogeneous Information Networks: Principles and Methodologies*. Synthesis Lectures on Data Mining and Knowledge Discovery. Morgan & Claypool Publishers, 2012.

Browser-Oriented Universal Cross-Site Recommendation and Explanation based on User Browsing Logs

Yongfeng Zhang
Department of Computer Science and Technology
Tsinghua University, Beijing, 100084, China
zhangyf07@gmail.com

ABSTRACT

Our research aims to bridge the gap between different websites to provide cross-site recommendations based on browsers. Recent advances have made recommender systems essential to various online applications, such as e-commerce, social networks, and review service websites. However, practical systems mainly focus on recommending inner-site homogeneous items. For example, a movie review website usually recommends other movies within the site when a user has enjoyed a movie online. However, it would be exciting if the system recommends some attractive products related to this movie from some e-commerce websites like Amazon or eBay.

Such an ability to provide heterogeneous cross-site recommendations may shed light on brand new and promising business models, which could benefit both the online shops in expanding the marketing efforts, and the online users in discovering items of interest from a wider scope. In this research, we propose and formalize the problem of universal recommendation, record and analyze user browsing actions in web browsers, and provide browser-oriented cross-site recommendations when the users are surfing online.

Categories and Subject Descriptors

H.3.3 [**Information Storage and Retrieval**]: Information Filtering; H.3.5 [**Online Information Services**]: Web-based services

Keywords

Recommender Systems; Collaborative Filtering; Browser Logs; Block Diagonal Form; Matrix Factorization

1. INTRODUCTION

With the development of Collaborative Filtering (CF) [15], the last few years have seen an increasingly important role that Recommender Systems (RS) [13] play in many online applications, such as product recommendation in Amazon, and friend recommendation in Facebook.

However, most practical recommender systems aim to provide inner-site homogeneous items according to the preferences of the target users, for example, to recommend similar videos when the user has watched a video online. Although intuitional and reasonable, the inner-site homogeneous recommendation paradigm is far from the tremendous benefits that recommender systems can bring into the Web.

The ability to recommend cross-site heterogeneous items benefits both the online businesses and the users. For example, after a user has finished watching the film *Titanic* on a video sharing website like YouTube, in which case it could be possible that she has been moved to tears, recommending an *Ocean Heart* necklace product from the online shopping website Amazon can be just no better.

The problem of cross-site recommendation is different from, but closely related to the problem of cross-domain recommendation, which attempts to provide recommendations of items in a target domain (e.g. books), by taking advantages of the user behaviours from other domains (e.g. movies or musics) [6, 19, 20]. Usually, recommendations are also provided in different domains simultaneously [14, 2].

However, an important problem troubling cross-domain recommendation in practice is the lack of inter-domain user behaviours, such as ratings, implicit feedbacks, or user-generated contents. This problem makes it even more difficult to conduct cross-site recommendation, because it is usual that the information of cross-site user behaviours may not even exist.

Fortunately, the vast amount of cross-site user browsing logs recorded by web browsers can serve as a kind of general inter-site relations in cross-site recommender systems. For example, a user who has finished watching the film *Titanic* on YouTube might continue to search for an *Ocean Heart* necklace from Amazon. By leveraging the wisdom of crowds and conducting CF according to the vast amount of similar browsing patterns, we can extract the hidden relationships between the heterogeneous items from different websites.

Web browser as the interface of browsing the internet can also serve as a platform of providing recommendations to the users. Due to the restrictions on security considerations, it is usually difficult for a web page to collect user browsing histories of other websites, which further makes it difficult for them to provide cross-site recommendations. However, such recommendations can be provided by the browser directly, which (if licenced by the user) is able to track the user browsing behaviors on different websites, and thus to provide recommended items from other websites according to the current browsing item and the preferences of the user.

In this research, we propose the problem of cross-site recommendation, and make it clear the similarities and differences between cross-site and cross-domain recommendation. We formalize the problem in a general and unified framework based on the Bordered Block Diagonal Form (BBDF) [25, 26, 24] structure of user-item relation matrices, and conduct cross-site recommendation with user browsing logs collected from web browsers.

RecSys'14, October 6–10, 2014, Foster City, Silicon Valley, CA, USA.

ACM 978-1-4503-2668-1/14/10 ...$15.00.
http://dx.doi.org/10.1145/2645710.2653367.

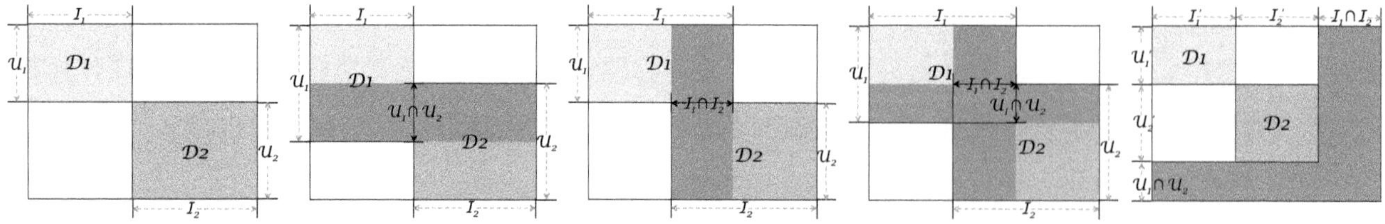

(a) No overlap (b) User overlap (c) Item overlap (d) User&Item overlap (e) BBDF structure

Figure 1: The user set and item set of two different domains may exhibit four relationships: (a) No common users or items; (b) Exist common users but no common items; (c) Exist common items but no common users; and (d) Exist both common users and items. The four relationships can be generalized into a unified bordered block diagonal form structured matrix (e) by permuting the common users/items to borders.

In the following part, we review some related work in Section 2, and introduce some of our research progress to date on cross-site recommendation in Section 3. We make further discussions, conclude the paper, and point out some of the future research directions in Section 4.

2. RELATED WORK

The most closely related research field is cross-domain personalized recommendation [2], which has been attracting the attention from research community over the past few years. One of the first studies was that presented by Winoto and Tang in [19], attempting to uncover the association between user preferences on related items across domains. They also discussed about the appropriate evaluation methods for cross-domain recommender systems.

The research of cross-domain recommendation has since then been driven into two main directions. One is to discover domain relations by Collaborative Filtering (CF) [6, 14, 7, 9, 27, 4, 5], and the other is to leverage various inter-domain content information [20, 18, 10, 1, 3, 16, 22].

One of the key techniques for CF approaches is Transfer Learning [8, 7, 9] and various of its extensions or variations. Singh [14] proposed Collective Matrix Factorization (CMF) to estimate the relations of multiple entities by factorizing several matrices simultaneously while sharing parameters in the latent space. Li [6] attempted to transfer user-item rating patterns from an auxiliary matrix in another domain to the target domain through Codebooks. Hu [5] and Zhao [27] extended transfer learning to triadic factorization and active learning for cross-domain recommendation, respectively. Gao [4] investigated cluster-level latent factor models to learn the common rating patterns shared across domains.

An important problem CF faces is data sparsity [4, 16, 9]. To alleviate the problem in a more direct way, researchers have been seeking the possibility of leveraging inter-domain relations and contents for cross-domain recommendations.

Shi [20] and Yang [22] made use of user generated tags as the bridge between domains to improve the performance. Chen [1] and Roy [10] used social relationships to recommend between domains in social media. More recently, Tobias [3, 18] attempted to leverage semantic network to discover the semantic-level relationships between objectives from different domains to make more informed recommendations.

The approach of leveraging inter-domain contents could be effective in specific applications. However, a key problem of such approaches is that the inter-domain information may be absent in many cases, and a substantial amount of manual work may have to be performed in order to align the content from different domains.

3. RESEARCH PROGRESS TO DATE

In this section, we introduce some of the current research progress on the topic of cross-site recommendation. We first review the four kinds of user-item relations in cross-domain recommendation, and further generalize them into a unified Bordered Block Diagonal Form (BBDF) structure [25, 24] to formalize the cross-site recommendation problem. User browsing logs are then integrated into this framework to serve as cross-site user and item relations. Besides, we further provide feature-level recommendation explanations [23] based on phrase-level sentiment analysis [21, 17] to improve the persuasiveness of cross-site recommendations.

3.1 Bordered Block Diagonal Forms

In cross-domain recommendation, the relationship between users and items from different domains can be generally classified according to their overlaps [2]. Without loss of generality, we consider the relationship between two domains. According to whether there exist common users (or items) between the user sets (or items sets) of the domains, there can be four kinds of relationships between the two domains, namely, no overlap users or items (Fig.1(a)), overlap users only (Fig.1(b)), overlap items only (Fig.1(c)), and both overlap users and items (Fig.1(d)).

It is important to note that, the four kinds of relationships can be generalized into a unified BBDF matrix structure by permuting the common users and items (if they exist) of the two domains to matrix borders [25, 24], as shown in Fig.1(e). The row and/or column borders in the BBDF structure may be absent if there is no common user and/or item between the two domains, respectively.

In the case of cross-site recommendation, the existence of common users and/or items may depend on the type of websites as well as the user and item information collected by the browsers. For example, two e-commerce websites like Amazon and eBay may contain a well amount of similar or even the same online products. By aligning the products from the two websites, we may extract the common items to serve as cross-site relations in personalized recommendation. However, an e-commerce website may hardly contain any common item with a video sharing website like YouTube, which leads to the absence of such cross-site item relations. Similarly, a substantial amount of users own accounts on many online service websites like Facebook, Twitter and Amazon. By user account alignment, we can extract the underlying common users among the websites, which also serve as the cross-site relationships.

In many common cases however, there could be no common users or items between different websites, which leaves us with two independent domains as shown in Fig.1(a), and thus there is no row or column border in Fig.1(e). Such a case also makes it difficult or even impossible to make cross-site recommendation if no external information is provided.

3.2 Browser-Oriented Recommendation

Cross-site recommendations can be best provided by web browsers. Traditional recommender systems are usually embedded in various online applications, like the product recommendation in e-commerce websites, and the friend recommendation in social networks. However, it is usually difficult for these web applications to collect user and item information from other sites, and such technical difficulties prevent them from providing cross-site recommendations. Besides, from a business perspective, some web service providers may be unwilling to present cross-site recommendations due to the business competitions, although a product from another website may better meet the current user need.

However, the cross-site recommendations can be provided beyond the websites and by the web browser directly [23], as shown in Fig.2. Besides, by tracking the user browsing actions across various websites during a period of time, the browser can better understand user needs than each single website, thus to make more informed recommendations. Additionally, the web browser logs can be easily integrated into the unified BBDF structure for cross-site recommendation. In the following sections, we discuss about the ways to incorporate browser logs, as well as the approaches to conduct CF on the BBDF structure to generate the recommendations.

3.3 Incorporating Browser Logs

We collected a vast amount of real user browsing logs from a commercial web browser, including 2.1 million users and 24 million web items (i.e. distinct urls). The browsing actions include visit time, duration, click position, and page title, etc, which makes it possible for us to analyze the user behaviours and preferences in real-world scenarios.

The browser logs provide a general way to construct inter-site relations by recovering the row borders (user relations) and column borders (item relations). Given an user-item relation matrix of two websites without any overlap users or items (as in Fig.1(a)), we adopt the following four approaches to recover the cross-site relations (as in Fig.1(e)):

1. Common user identification: The browser can identify that two user IDs from different websites actually correspond to the same user when she signs in on the websites. In such a case, the row vectors from different domains in Fig.1(a) that correspond to the same user are merged and permuted to serve as a row border.

2. Common item identification: We also merge two column vectors and permute them to border when the corresponding items are identified as the same one. For example, when a user follows an account on Twitter, we can also recommend her to follow the same account on Facebook.

3. Auxiliary users: Some browser users never sign in on the concerned websites, and thus it is difficult to map them to the existing user IDs of these sites. However, they can be appended to the BBDF structured relation matrix as row borders to help discover the item relations.

4. Auxiliary items: Symmetrically, we append the unmapped web items to the BBDF structure as column borders, and they help to estimate the collaboration relationship among the users.

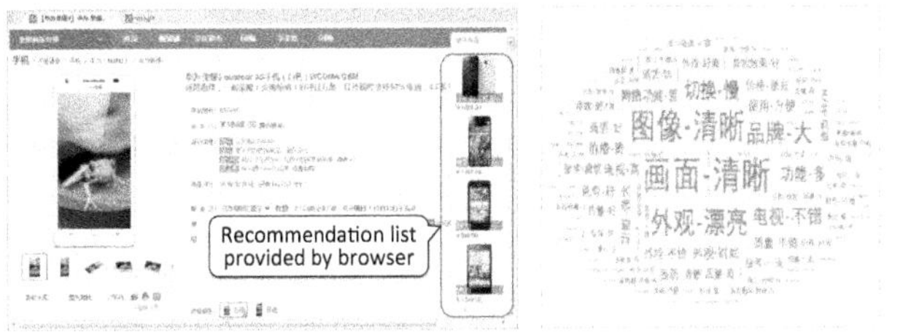

(a) In browser recommendation (b) Explanations

Figure 2: (a) Cross-site recommendations can be provided by browser plugins directly, beyond the specific website that the user is currently browsing. (b) The browser can also provide intuitional recommendation explanations, e.g., a feature word cloud.

Once the user and item information mined from browser logs is integrated into the BBDF structure and properly normalized, the cross-site relations (i.e. matrix borders) make it possible to conduct CF for personalized recommendation.

3.4 Localized Matrix Factorization

Our preliminary work on Localized Matrix Factorization (LMF) [26] provides a theoretical paradigm for conducting CF with matrix factorization techniques on the BBDF structured matrices. In this research, we adopt the LMF framework to make cross-site predictions and recommendations.

Matrix Factorization (MF) techniques have proved to be effective and efficient in modeling the hidden relationships of users and items in a latent factor space. However, MF algorithms fail to make cross-site predictions if there is no border in the BBDF structure as in Fig.1(a) [26, 25]. The reason is similar to that of the neighbourhood-based approaches, for which it would be impossible to compute the user similarities if there is no overlap item between two row vectors. As a result, the essence of incorporating bowser logs to recover the borders lies in that, it bridges the users and items across different sites, which makes it possible to model the relations in a common latent factor space.

The LMF framework is capable of integrating any decomposable MF algorithm, including many of the commonly used approaches, such as Singular Value Decomposition, Nonnegative Matrix Factorization, and Probabilistic Matrix Factorization. Besides, the framework can be easily parallelized to tackle the vast amount of cross-site user feedbacks.

3.5 Recommendation Explanation

Providing appropriate recommendation explanations could be more important in cross-site recommendation than inner-site recommendations, because it might be difficult for users to understand why a heterogeneous item is recommended instead of a similar product. Persuasive and informative explanations also attract the attention of users and guide the users across various websites that we expect them to visit. The ability to guide user browsing actions during the browsing process is of key importance for web browsers to gain the initiative in web economy.

Our preliminary work on Explicit Factor Models (EFM) [23] leverages phrase-level sentiment analysis to provide feature-level explanations by telling the user which feature of the recommended item may attract her. Practical online experiments verified the persuasiveness of the explanations. In this research, we further develop the idea of feature-level explanation by extracting item features from different websites and domains. Except for conducting phrase-level sentiment analysis on user reviews, the features can also be extracted from various other information sources, such as tags, metadata, and wikipedia categorization pages, etc.

3.6 Experimentation and Evaluation

Many commonly used evaluation metrics mainly focus on the precision of rating prediction or top-k recommendation, including MAE, RMSE, MRR, Precision@k, Recall@k and F-Measure, etc [11]. However, it is widely considered that the advantage of cross-domain/site recommendation may not be the improvement in accuracies, but the added novelty and diversity of the recommendations, which may offer better satisfaction and utility to the users [12, 11]. In this context, the recently proposed novelty and diversity metrics could also be taken into consideration [11].

Besides, we can perform online evaluation with large-scale practical users in real-world scenarios, which is a more flexible way to evaluate the performance of cross-site recommendation and explanation, and to conduct comparative studies with traditional inner-site recommendations.

4. CONCLUSIONS AND RESEARCH PLAN

Cross-site recommendation is more than a site-wide view of cross-domain recommendation. The research of cross-site recommendation touches various important and cutting-edge problems of recommender systems, *e.g.*, the problems of code-start, novelty, explanations, transfer-learning, data integration, and recommender interfaces. This makes cross-site recommendation a promising task to integrate and extend the research achievements of personalized recommendation. Besides, the browser-oriented recommendation may also bring brand new business models to the Web.

In the previous studies, we have formalized cross-site recommendation in a unified BBDF framework, investigated the feature-level explanation of recommendation based on sentiment analysis, and designed browser-based recommendation interfaces. Both offline and online experimental results verified the effectiveness and efficiency of our proposed methods in [26, 25, 24, 23, 21]. However, these are still preliminary studies of cross-site recommendation, and there is much room for improvement. Some of the key problems to investigate in the future includes: Integrating (perhaps inconsistent) data from different websites into the unified BBDF framework; Extracting explicit features from different information sources for explainable recommendations; Understanding the user needs during the browsing process; and designing appropriate metrics as well as online experiments for the evaluation of cross-site recommendations.

Acknowledgment

I sincerely thank my supervisors Professor Shaoping Ma, Min Zhang and Yiqun Liu for the consistent support and mentoring during my research, and special thanks to Prof. Yi Zhang of UCSC and Prof. Min-Yen Kan of NUS for the fruitful discussions and valuable suggestions.

5. REFERENCES

[1] W. Chen, W. Hsu, and M. L. Lee. Making recommendations from multiple domains. *KDD*, 2013.

[2] P. Cremonesi, A. Tripodi, and R. Turrin. Cross-Domain Recommender Systems. *The 11th IEEE International Conference on Data Mining Workshops*, 2011.

[3] I. Fernandez-Tobias. Mining Semantic Data, User Generated Contents and Contextual Information for Cross-Domain Recommendation. *UMAP*, 2013.

[4] S. Gao, H. Luo, D. Chen, S. Li, P. Gallinari, and J. Guo. Cross-Domain Recommendation via Cluster-Level Latent Factor Model. *ECML*, 2013.

[5] L. Hu, J. Cao, G. Xu, L. Cao, Z. Gu, and C. Zhu. Personalized Recommendation via Cross-Domain Triadic Factorization. *WWW*, pages 595–605, 2013.

[6] B. Li, Q. Yang, and X. Xue. Can Movies and Books Collaborate? Cross-Domain Collaborative Filtering for Sparsity Reduction. *IJCAI*, pages 2052–2057, 2009.

[7] B. Li, Q. Yang, and X. Xue. Transfer Learning for Collaborative Filtering via a Rating-Matrix Generative Model. *ICML*, pages 617–624, 2009.

[8] S. J. Pan and Q. Yang. A Survey on Transfer Learning. *TKDE*, 22(10):1345–1359, 2010.

[9] W. Pan, N. N. L. Evan W. Xiang, and Q. Yang. Transfer Learning in Collaborative Filtering for Sparsity Reduction. *AAAI*, pages 230–235, 2011.

[10] S. D. Roy, T. Mei, W. Zeng, and S. Li. SocialTransfer: Cross-Domain Transfer Learning from Social Streams for Media Applications. *MM*, 2012.

[11] S. Vargas, P. Castells. Rank and Relevance in Novelty and Diversity Metrics for Recommender Systems. *RecSys*, 2011.

[12] G. Shani and A. Gunawardana. Evaluating Recommender Systems. *Recommender Systems Handbook*, 2011.

[13] Y. Shi, M. Larson, and A. Hanjalic. Collaborative Filtering beyond the User-Item Matrix: A Survey of the State of the Art and Future Challenges. *ACM Comp. Surv.*, 47(1), 2014.

[14] A. P. Singh and G. J. Gordon. Relational Learning via Collective Matrix Factorization. *KDD*, 2008.

[15] X. Su and T. M. Khoshgoftaar. A Survey of Collaborative Filtering Techniques. *Advances in AI*, 2009(4), 2009.

[16] S. Tan, J. Bu, X. Qin, C. Chen, and D. Cai. Cross domain recommendation based on multi-type media fusion. *Neurocomputing*, pages 124–134, 2014.

[17] Y. Tan, Y. Zhang, M. Zhang, Y. Liu, and S. Ma. A Unified Framework for Emotional Elements Extraction based on Finite State Matching Machine. *NLPCC*, 400:60–71, 2013.

[18] I. F. Tobias, M. Kaminskas, I. Cantador, and F. Ricci. A Generic Semantic-based Framework for Cross- Domain Recommendation. *HetRec*, pages 25–32, 2011.

[19] P. Winoto and T. Tang. If You Like the Devil Wears Prada the Book, Will You also Enjoy the Devil Wears Prada the Movie? A Study of Cross-Domain Recommendations. *New Generation Computing*, 26(3):209–225, 2008.

[20] Y. Shi, M. Larson, A. Hanjalic. Tags as Bridges between Domains: Improving Recommendation with Tag-Induced Cross-Domain Collaborative Filtering. *UMAP*, 2011.

[21] Y. Zhang, H. Zhang, M. Zhang, Y. Liu, S. Ma. Do Users Rate or Review? Boost Phrase-level Sentiment Labeling with Review-level Sentiment Classification. *SIGIR*, 2014.

[22] D. Yang, Y. Xiao, Y. Song, J. Zhang, K. Zhang, and W. Wang. Tag Propagation Based Recommendation across Diverse Social Media. *WWW*, 2014.

[23] Y. Zhang, G. Lai, M. Zhang, Y. Zhang, Y. Liu, and S. Ma. Explicit Factor Models for Explainable Recommendation based on Phrase-level Sentiment Analysis. *SIGIR*, 2014.

[24] Y. Zhang, M. Zhang, Y. Liu, and S. Ma. A General Collaborative Filtering Framework based on Matrix Bordered Block Diagonal Forms. *Hypertext*, 2013.

[25] Y. Zhang, M. Zhang, Y. Liu, and S. Ma. Improve Collaborative Filtering Through Bordered Block Diagonal Form Matrices. *SIGIR*, 2013.

[26] Y. Zhang, M. Zhang, Y. Liu, S. Ma, and S. Feng. Localized Matrix Factorization for Recommendation based on Matrix Block Diagonal Forms. *WWW*, 2013.

[27] L. Zhao, S. J. Pan, E. W. Xiang, E. Zhong, Z. Lu, and Q. Yang. Active Transfer Learning for Cross-System Recommendation. *AAAI*, 2013.

Deviation-Based and Similarity-Based Contextual SLIM Recommendation Algorithms

Yong Zheng
Center for Web Intelligence
DePaul University
Chicago, Illinois, USA
yzheng8@cs.depaul.edu

ABSTRACT

Context-aware recommender systems (CARS) have been demonstrated to be able to enhance recommendations by adapting users' preferences to different contextual situations. In recent years, several CARS algorithms have been developed to incorporated into the recommender systems. For example, differential context modeling (DCM) was modified based on traditional neighborhood collaborative filtering (NBCF), context-aware matrix factorization (CAMF) coupled contextual dependency with the matrix factorization technique (MF), and tensor factorization directly models contexts as additional dimensions in the multi-dimensional space, etc. CAMF works well but it is difficult to interpret the latent features in the algorithm. DCM is good for explanation but it may only work well on data sets with dense contextual ratings. Recently, we successfully incorporate contexts into Sparse LInear Method (SLIM) and develop contextual SLIM (CSLIM) recommendation algorithms which take advantages of both NBCF and MF. CSLIM are demonstrated as more effective and promising context-aware recommenders. In this work, we provide the introduction on the framework of the CSLIM algorithms, present the current state of the research, and discuss our ongoing future work to develop and improve our CSLIM models for context-aware recommendations.

Categories and Subject Descriptors

H.3.3 [**Information Search and Retrieval**]: Information filtering

Keywords

Recommendation; Context; Context-aware recommendation; SLIM; Matrix Factorization

1. INTRODUCTION AND MOTIVATIONS

In contrast to traditional recommender systems (RS), context-aware recommender systems (CARS) adapt the recommendations to users' specific situations. The fundamental assumption of CARS is that a rating for an item is a function not just of the user and the item but also of the context in which the item is evaluated or used. User's preferences on a given item may vary from context to context. For example, *companion* is an influential contextual variable in the movie domain; you may make a different decision in selecting movies if you intend to see the movie on a date, than if you plan on watching a movie with children.

RecSys'14, October 6–10, 2014, Foster City, Silicon Valley, CA, USA.

http://dx.doi.org/10.1145/2645710.2653368.

Incorporating contexts into recommendation algorithms is an important research problem in CARS. Several CARS algorithms have been developed by incorporating contexts in different ways: Differential context modeling (DCM) [11] is one approach coupled with the traditional neighborhood-based collaborative filtering (NBCF), where contexts are considered as constraints to be applied to different functional components in NBCF. Extensions of standard matrix factorization (MF) approach have incorporated contextual variables too, such as time-aware MF [3] and context-aware matrix factorization (CAMF) [2]. CAMF works well in context-aware recommendation, but it is difficult to interpret the latent features in the algorithm. DCM is good for explanation but it may only work well on context-aware data sets with dense contextual ratings. Thus, it is important to develop one contextual algorithm taking the advantages of both NBCF and MF – working well in contextual recommendation and also easy to interpret the contextual effects.

Sparse LInear Method (SLIM) is a version of an approach designed for top-N recommendation in the traditional RS, where it utilizes the intuition of item-based K-nearest neighbor (ItemKNN) collaborative filtering and make use of the learning process in MF techniques to estimate the coefficients between every two items, which is demonstrated as a more effective recommender than the state-of-the-art recommendation algorithms. In this paper, we propose to incorporate contexts into SLIM and develop contextual SLIM (CSLIM) recommendation algorithms which are demonstrated as more promising models for top-N context-aware recommendation compared with the state-of-the-art CARS algorithms. Typically, contextual ratings can be estimated by a deviation-based [15] or similarity-based way. In this paper, we mainly introduce how to utilize those two ways to build the CSLIM algorithms, present the preliminary results and also discuss our ongoing work, as well as the challenges in the future.

The remainder of this paper is organized as follows. Section 2 positions related work in CARS domain. Section 3 introduces the SLIM approach and Section 4 shows our current state of our research on developing deviation-based CSLIM algorithms. Section 5 presents our ongoing work and challenges on a general CSLIM model, where other possible models, such as similarity-based CSLIM approaches are also introduced and discussed. Finally, conclusions are made in the Section 6.

2. RELATED WORK

Traditional recommendation problem can be modeled as a two-dimensional (2D) prediction – R: *Users* $\times$ *Items* $\rightarrow$ *Ratings*, while

CARS try to additionally incorporate contexts to estimate user preferences using a "*multidimensional*" rating function – *R*: *Users* $\times$ *Items* $\times$ *Contexts* $\rightarrow$ *Ratings* [1]. In the following section, we mainly introduce the development of CARS algorithms base on collaborative filtering (CF), including both the traditional neighborhood-based collaborative filtering (NBCF) based and matrix factorization (MF) based approaches.

Differential context modeling (DCM) [11] is one approach coupled with NBCF, and there are two series of approaches in DCM: differential context relaxation (DCR) [9, 10] and differential context weighting (DCW) [12]. In DCM, contexts are considered as constraints being applied to different functional components in NBCF, where DCR uses a relaxation strategy and DCW tries to weight the importance of each context dimension. Those models are good for explanations, where we have demonstrated this benefit by explaining the emotional effects in recommender systems [13]; however, DCM may only work well in the context-aware data sets with dense contextual ratings. They work well by measuring prediction errors but not that good in ranking metrics (e.g. precision, etc) as shown in our previous work [14]. It is because users may not rate items multiple times in different contextual situations. As a result, it is easy to introduce biases to the DCM models, which further results in the overfitting problem.

Contexts were also incorporated into the MF-based algorithms. Karatzoglou et al. [4] proposed to use tensor factorization (TF) to integrate contexts. Their approach assumed that contextual variables are independent of other dimensions and contexts can be directly considered as the additional ones in the multi-dimensional rating space, in addition to the traditional user and item dimensions. But the computation cost in TF is prohibitive increasing exponentially as the number of contextual variables increases. Context-aware matrix factorization (CAMF) [2] was then developed by modeling contextual dependencies with the user or item dimensions. But CAMF was built based on traditional MF [5], where both users and items are represented by factor weights in a matrix. There are also other approaches, such as those based on factorization machines [8]. They work better than DCM but the issue in those MF-based algorithms is that it is difficult to extract patterns from the latent factors to interpret the contextual effects.

3. SLIM RECOMMENDER

Sparse linear method (SLIM) is an approach designed for top-N recommendations. It improves upon the traditional item-based K-nearest neighbor (ItemKNN) collaborative filtering by learning, directly from the data, a sparse matrix of aggregation coefficients that are analogous to the traditional item-item similarities [6].

Assume that there are M users, N items, and let us denote the associated 2-dimensional rating matrix by R. We use u_i to denote user i and t_j to denote the item j. An entry, $R_{i,j}$, in matrix R represents u_i's rating on t_j. A row vector in R representing u_i's ratings over all items is denoted by $R_{i,:}$, and $R_{:,j}$ denotes a column vector in Matrix R representing ratings on item t_j from all users.

In SLIM, the ranking score for user u_i on item t_j is represented by $\widehat{S}_{i,j}$, which is calculated by a sparse aggregation of the ratings on the other items that have been rated by u_i. We denote this approach as SLIM-I, since it assigns a N by N non-negative matrix W to represent the aggregation coefficients between each two items. Accordingly, $\widehat{S}_{i,j}$ can be estimated by Equation 1.

$$\widehat{S}_{i,j} = R_{i,:}W_{:,j} = \sum_{\substack{h=1 \\ h \neq j}}^{N} R_{i,h}W_{h,j}, \text{where } diag(W) = 0 \quad (1)$$

An example of how the SLIM-I approach works is shown in Figure 1. To estimate the ranking score of u_2 on item t_1, SLIM extracts u_2's ratings on the other items, and aggregates the ranking score by multiplying of those ratings by the corresponding coefficients between the item t_1 and t_h (i.e. t_h belongs to one of the other items u_i has rated) in matrix W. The estimated ranking score will be used to rank the items to finally provide top-N recommendations. Similarly, a SLIM-U approach can be easily derived, where $\widehat{S}_{i,j}$ is calculated by a sparse aggregation of ratings on this specific item t_j but were given by other users, where W is a M by M non-negative matrix representing the coefficients between every two users.

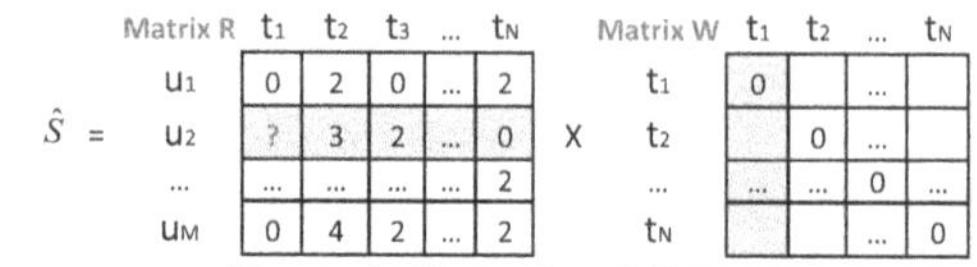

Figure 1: Example of SLIM-I

Traditional matrix factorization techniques, such as those proposed by Koren et al. [5], usually represent users and items by a set of weights on individual latent factors, and both the number of latent factors and training iterations are required to tune the model and find the optimal solution. In contrast to those approaches, the sizes of matrices R and W are fixed and there is only a single matrix, W, required to be learned in SLIM-I and SLIM-U. W is also easy to be interpreted, where the coefficients between each two items are analogous to item-item similarities.

4. CURRENT STATE OF THE RESEARCH

In this section, we mainly introduce our current work on how to build CSLIM approaches based on contextual rating deviations.

4.1 Deviation-Based CSLIM

Analogously to context-aware matrix factorization techniques [2], we propose to incorporate context into the SLIM approach for top-N recommendations by modeling contextual rating deviations. We refer to this as the Deviation-Based *Contextual SLIM (CSLIM)* approach [15]. In the following, we use *contextual factor* to refer to the contextual variables such as "Time", "Location", and "Companion". The term *contextual condition* refers to a specific value in a contextual factor. For example, "weekend" and "weekday" are two contextual conditions for the "Time" contextual factor.

Assume there are F contextual factors and L contextual conditions in total in a context-aware data set, in addition to the M users and N items. The primary task in the CSLIM approach is to estimate the ranking score $\widehat{S}_{i,j,c}$ for user u_i on item t_j in contexts c. We use a binary vector, c = <$c_1, c_2, ..., c_L$>, to denote the contextual situation. For example, assume all contextual conditions with L=4 can be represent by {Time=*weekend*, Time=*weekday*, Location=*school*, Location=*home*}. Then, the vector c = <1, 0, 1, 0> indicates that the current contextual situation is {Time=*weekend*, Location=*school*}.

In CARS, users' preferences may vary from context to context for same item. Therefore, it is necessary to make predictions based on rating profiles in the same context c. Recall that the estimated ranking score matrix $\widehat{S}$ in SLIM-I is derived based upon the idea in ItemKNN – aggregation of users' ratings on other items. As a result, it is possible to estimate the ranking score $\widehat{S}_{i,j,c}$ by an aggregation of u_i' ratings on other items in the same contexts c. However, a context-aware data set, with multiple ratings for each item, is usually very sparse – it is not guaranteed that a user has rated other items in the same context c. In this case, we estimate u_i's rating on an item t_j in context c (i.e. $\widehat{R}_{i,j,c}$) based on the user's non-contextual rating on this item (i.e. $R_{i,j}$, ratings without considering contexts) and the aggregated contextual rating deviations (CRD, i.e., the rating deviations in different contextual conditions). Accordingly, we can build different CSLIM models based on how to estimate the CRD.

In this section, we present how CSLIM-I models can be built based on how to estimate the CRD. Accordingly, similar ways can be applied to SLIM-U in order to build CSLIM-U models. First, we estimate contextual ratings (i.e. $\widehat{R}_{i,j,c}$) based on the non contextual rating $R_{i,j}$ and aggregated CRD. Specifically, we model CRD as the contextual rating deviations on items. In other words, we assume there is a rating deviation for each <item, context condition> pair. Thus, $\widehat{R}_{i,j,c}$ can be estimated as follows:

$$\widehat{R}_{i,j,c} = R_{i,j} + \sum_{l=1}^{L} D_{j,l} c_l \quad (2)$$

where R is the 2D non-contextual rating matrix. Typically, users may provide non-contextual ratings in addition to the ratings for an item in given contexts. But it is not necessary that both non-contextual ratings and contextual ratings are assigned to a same <user, item> entry. The average rating of each user on each item rated within multiple contexts can be added to the rating matrix R if there is no knowledge about the non-contextual ratings.

We build a $N \times L$ CRD matrix D where each row represents an item, and each column represents an individual contextual condition as shown in Figure 2. Thus, $D_{j,:}$ is a row in D representing CRD for the item t_j in L different contextual conditions.

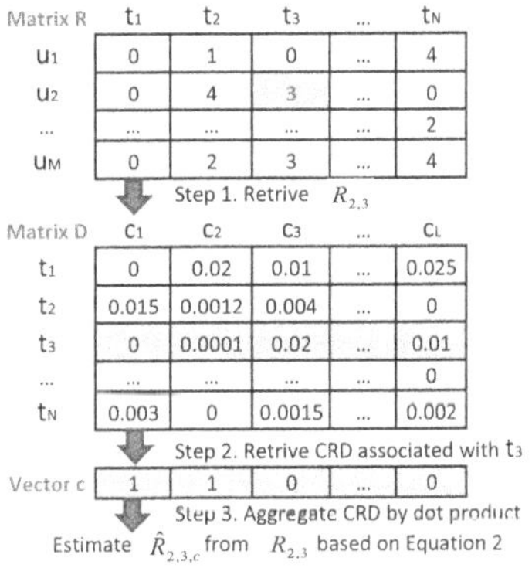

Figure 2: Example: Estimation of Contextual Rating

We can then use the SLIM-I approach to estimate the ranking score $\widehat{S}_{i,j,c}$ for user u_i on item t_j in contexts c. This is described in Equation 3, where t_h belongs to the set of items for which user u_i has provided non-contextual ratings (i.e. $R_{i,h} > 0$). The ranking score is estimated by an aggregation of user's ratings on other items in the same context c. We call this approach CSLIM-I-CI because the CRD are assumed for each <item, context condition> pair, and D is built as a CI matrix (i.e. columns and rows represent contexts and items respectively).

$$\widehat{S}_{i,j,c} = \sum_{\substack{h=1 \\ h \neq j}}^{N} \widehat{R}_{i,h,c} W_{h,j} = \sum_{\substack{h=1 \\ h \neq j}}^{N} (R_{i,h} + \sum_{l=1}^{L} D_{h,l} c_l) W_{h,j} \quad (3)$$

It is important to note that we set $h \neq j$ to avoid the model learning from u_i's non-contextual rating on t_j. Generally, the CSLIM-I-CI model will learn the parameters in D and W based on each entry of known contextual ratings $R_{i,j,c}$ in the training set, and make predictions only relying on three matrices: non-contextual rating matrix R, CRD matrix D, and the aggregation coefficient matrix W. Using squared error as the optimization criteria, the loss function with regularization terms can be described in Equation 4, which can be solved by stochastic gradient descent (SGD) approach. ∂ and β parameters are the learning rates. Both ℓ_F terms (e.g. $\|W\|_F^2$) and ℓ_1 terms (e.g. $\|W\|_1$) are included, where the ℓ_1 regularization term is usually applied for sparse models.

$$\underset{D,W}{Minimize} \ \frac{1}{2} \left\| R_{i,j,c} - \widehat{S}_{i,j,c} \right\|_F^2 + \frac{\beta_1}{2} \|D\|_F^2 + \frac{\beta_2}{2} \|W\|_F^2 + \partial_1 \|D\|_1 + \partial_2 \|W\|_1 \quad (4)$$

In CSLIM-I-CI, D is modeled as a CI matrix, where the deviation is computed for each <item, context condition> pair. The deviations can also be considered for users – we assume there is a rating deviation for each <user, context condition> pair, where D results in a CU matrix (i.e. columns denote contexts and rows represent users). The latter model is called CSLIM-I-CU. In addition to these two approaches, the rating deviations can also simply be viewed as the deviations only associated with each contextual condition rather than as being paired with users or items. In this case, the CRD can be represented by a L-length vector d instead of a matrix D. We call this approach CSLIM-I-C. Note that the only difference among those three CSLIM-I models is the matrix D, while the matrix W is still the same – a $N \times N$ non-negative matrix of item-item coefficients.

Also, contexts can also be introduced to the SLIM-U models. In this case, W is a $M \times M$ matrix representing user-user coefficients. The matrix D can be built using a similar approach as introduced in the CSLIM-I models. In other words, we can build three CSLIM-U models: CSLIM-U-CI, CSLIM-U-CU, CSLIM-U-C.

In a summary, CSLIM-I and CSLIM-U models utilize the intuitions behind ItemKNN and UserKNN, respectively, with the CRD matrix computed in one of three ways: CRD associated to each individual contextual condition, CRD associated with each <item, contextual condition> pair, or CRD associated with each <user, contextual condition> pair, which results in six CSLIM models.

The complexity of CSLIM models is associated with the number of users or items and the number of contextual conditions. For large-scale recommendations, contexts can be selected in advance based on contextual relevance [7], and feature selection can also be applied to reduce the number of user or item dimensions in computation process, which was explored in the original SLIM algorithm [6]. The process of this feature selection is necessary and important, especially when it comes to large scale of data sets which result in increased computational cost to learn the large matrix W or D. In CSLIM approaches, there are only two matrices to be learned – the CRD matrix D and coefficient matrix W, and those two matrices can be easily used for explanation, where D interprets how the rating is deviated from non-contextual rating when user is under different contextual conditions, and W measures the coefficients between each two items which are analogous to item-item similarities in NBCF.

4.2 Experimental Evaluations

We have successfully evaluated the deviation-based CSLIM algorithms over five context-aware data sets [1], where CSLIM approaches are demonstrated as more promising and effective context-aware recommenders which provide substantial improvements in the top-N recommendation task, compared with the state-of-the-art CARS algorithms, including TF [4], CAMF (i.e. CAMF-CI, CAMF-CU, CAMF-C) [2] and context-aware splitting approaches (CASA) using biased MF as the recommender (i.e. item splitting, user splitting and UI splitting) [14]. Due to limited space, we do not present experimental results here, please refer to our preliminary work on the deviation-based CSLIM algorithms [15].

[1]Context-aware Dataset Repository, http://tiny.cc/contextdata

5. ONGOING WORK & CHALLENGES

Recall that the deviation matrix D in the CSLIM algorithms estimates the contextual rating deviations from a non-contextual rating one. Actually, the non-contextual rating can be considered as a special contextual rating, where the contextual conditions are all EMPTY. Thus, the deviations in D can be viewed as the ones deviated from EMPTY contexts.

In addition to the CSLIM models, a general CSLIM (GCSLIM) approach can be built, where the contextual deviations could be the ones deviated from any contexts other than the EMPTY contexts. In this case, the matrix D is expected to be a CC matrix, where the rows and columns represent the L contextual conditions, and each entry in D represents the rating deviation from a context to another.

Table 1: Example of Ratings within Different Contexts

Contexts	$R_{u,i,c}$	Companion			Time	
		Kids	Family	Partner	Weekday	Weekend
c-1	?	1	0	0	1	0
c-2	5	0	0	1	0	1
c-3	2	0	0	0	0	0

We can build two GCSLIM models: GCSLIM-I-CC and GCSLIM-U-CC. Take the GCSLIM-I-CC model for example, it is derived from the CSLIM-I model, but user's contextual rating on the items in c-1 (Equation 2) can be estimated by user's rating on the items within other contexts. As shown in Table 1, we have no knowledge about $R_{u,i,c\text{-}1}$, but we know the $R_{u,i,c\text{-}2}$ and $R_{u,i,c\text{-}3}$. In c-3, all values are 0s which represent the EMPTY contexts. Previous C-SLIM models only estimate the contextual rating deviations from c-3 to c-1, but in GCSLIM models, the D is in shape of a CC matrix and it is able to estimate the $R_{u,i,c\text{-}1}$ from any contextual ratings, such as $R_{u,i,c\text{-}2}$; namely, $R_{u,i,c\text{-}1} = R_{u,i,c\text{-}2} + D$ (Kids, Partner) + D (Weekday, Weekend). Namely, multiple contextual ratings can be used to train the matrix D in the GCSLIM-I-CC model instead of using non-contextual ratings only in the CSLIM models.

Similarly, the CC matrix can be paired with either users or items. But it would be expensive to assign a CC matrix to each user or item. A possible solution is to assign a CC matrix to each group of users or items, where users or items can be put into different groups by clustering techniques. Due to that a user may give multiple ratings on an item within different contexts, using all contextual ratings for training may leave a challenge on computational efficiency. In our future work, we'd like to develop strategies to select limited contextual ratings for training, for example, we can simply use the contextual rating where its contexts are the most similar ones to the target contexts. For example, in the table above, c-3 is more similar to c-1 than c-2, because there are more same bits in the binary contextual vector.

Currently, those models introduced above are named as *Deviation-Based CSLIM* approaches. Apparently, the contextual ratings can be derived by contextual similarity other than CRDs. Take the example shown in Table 1, $R_{u,i,c\text{-}1}$ can be estimated by $R_{u,i,c\text{-}2} \times$ Sim (Kids, Partner) $\times$ Sim (Weekday, Weekend). In other words, D can be replaced by a contextual similarity matrix Sim which measures the similarity between each two contextual conditions. We name those approaches as *Similarity-Based CSLIM* and we will explore them in future.

Beyond those deviation-based and similarity-based CSLIM approaches, contexts may also be directly incorporated into the coefficient matrix W instead of additionally creating the CRD matrix, which could be a new series of contextual SLIM algorithms. The underlying idea behind is to infer the users' contextual rating in contexts c by users' contextual ratings in other contexts (including ratings placed in the EMPTY contexts) multiplying by the coefficients of different contextual conditions. In other words, those models can be directly derived from the original SLIM-I models, where the CRD matrix is not required and there is only one matrix W (size: L $\times$ L) which measures coefficients between every two contextual conditions. Those models can be named as *CSLIM-C*. Also, the coefficient matrix W can be assigned to each user or item too. To reduce the learning complexity, we can assign a W to each group of users or items.

6. CONCLUSIONS

In this paper, we introduce and discuss how to incorporate contexts into the SLIM models to build CSLIM algorithms. More specifically, we mainly introduce our current state of research on building deviation-based CSLIM approaches and our ongoing work on a more general CSLIM model, as well as the similarity-based C-SLIM algorithms. In addition, CSLIM-C could be a new series of CSLIM approaches which incorporate contexts to the coefficient matrix W. Our current experimental results on deviation-based C-SLIM demonstrate that CSLIM algorithms are promising and provide substantial improvement over the state-of-the-art CARS algorithms. Furthermore, the matrices D and W in CSLIM are easier for explanations to further interpret the contextual effects. We will continue to work on CSLIM models and explore the proposed new CSLIM approaches in our future work.

Acknowledgement

Special thanks to Prof. Bamshad Mobasher and Prof. Robin Burke for their support, guidance and valuable feedbacks.

7. REFERENCES

[1] G. Adomavicius, B. Mobasher, F. Ricci, and A. Tuzhilin. Context-aware recommender systems. *AI Magazine*, 32(3):67–80, 2011.

[2] L. Baltrunas, B. Ludwig, and F. Ricci. Matrix factorization techniques for context aware recommendation. In *ACM Conference on Recommender Systems*, pages 301–304. ACM, 2011.

[3] P. G. Campos, F. Díez, and I. Cantador. Time-aware recommender systems: a comprehensive survey and analysis of existing evaluation protocols. *User Modeling and User-Adapted Interaction*, 24(1-2):67–119, 2014.

[4] A. Karatzoglou, X. Amatriain, L. Baltrunas, and N. Oliver. Multiverse recommendation: n-dimensional tensor factorization for context-aware collaborative filtering. In *ACM RecSys*, pages 79–86, 2010.

[5] Y. Koren, R. Bell, and C. Volinsky. Matrix factorization techniques for recommender systems. *IEEE Computer*, 42(8):30–37, 2009.

[6] X. Ning and G. Karypis. Slim: Sparse linear methods for top-n recommender systems. In *IEEE ICDM*, pages 497–506. IEEE, 2011.

[7] A. Odic, M. Tkalcic, J. F. Tasic, and A. Košir. Relevant context in a movie recommender system: Users' opinion vs. statistical detection. *ACM RecSys Workshop on Context-Aware Recommender Systems*, 2012.

[8] S. Rendle, Z. Gantner, C. Freudenthaler, and L. Schmidt-Thieme. Fast context-aware recommendations with factorization machines. In *Proceedings of the ACM SIGIR conference on Research and development in Information Retrieval*, pages 635–644. ACM, 2011.

[9] Y. Zheng, R. Burke, and B. Mobasher. Differential context relaxation for context-aware travel recommendation. In *13th International Conference on Electronic Commerce and Web Technologies*, pages 88–99, 2012.

[10] Y. Zheng, R. Burke, and B. Mobasher. Optimal feature selection for context-aware recommendation using differential relaxation. In *ACM RecSys' 12, Proceedings of the 4th International Workshop on Context-Aware Recommender Systems*. ACM, 2012.

[11] Y. Zheng, R. Burke, and B. Mobasher. Differential context modeling in collaborative filtering. In *Proceedings of School of Computing Research Symposium*. DePaul University, Chicago IL, USA, 2013.

[12] Y. Zheng, R. Burke, and B. Mobasher. Recommendation with differential context weighting. In *User Modeling, Adaptation, and Personalization*, pages 152–164. Springer, 2013.

[13] Y. Zheng, R. Burke, and B. Mobasher. The role of emotions in context-aware recommendation. In *ACM RecSys Workshop on Human Decision Making in Recommender Systems*. ACM, 2013.

[14] Y. Zheng, R. Burke, and B. Mobasher. Splitting approaches for context-aware recommendation: An empirical study. In *ACM Symposium On Applied Computing*, pages 274–279, 2014.

[15] Y. Zheng, B. Mobasher, and R. Burke. Cslim: Contextual slim recommendation algorithms. In *Proceedings of the 8th ACM Conference on Recommender Systems*. ACM, 2014.

Author Index

www.ingramcontent.com/pod-product-compliance
Ingram Content Group UK Ltd.
Pitfield, Milton Keynes, MK11 3LW, UK
UKHW051413290926
15471UKWH00009B/1574

9 781450 333726